Magill's
Cinema
Annual
1 9 9 5

Magill's Cinema Annual 1 9 9 5

14th Edition
A Survey of the Films of 1994

Shawn Brennan, Editor

James M. Craddock, Kelly M. Cross, Beth A. Fhaner,
Julia C. Furtaw, Christopher P. Scanlon, and Terri
Kessler Schell, Contributing Editors

Christine Tomassini and Devra M. Sladics, Associate Editors

Michelle Banks, Assistant Editor

A VideoHound® Reference

Gale Research

An ITP Information/Reference Group Company

I(T)P
Changing the Way the World Learns

NEW YORK • LONDON • BONN • BOSTON • DETROIT
MADRID • MELBOURNE • MEXICO CITY • PARIS
SINGAPORE • TOKYO • TORONTO • WASHINGTON
ALBANY NY • BELMONT CA • CINCINNATI OH

Shawn Brennan, *Editor*

James M. Craddock, Kelly M. Cross, Beth A. Fhaner, Julia C. Furtaw, Christopher P. Scanlon,
and Terri Kessler Schell, *Contributing Editors*
Christine Tomassini and Devra M. Sladics, *Associate Editors*
Michelle Banks, *Assistant Editor*

Mary Beth Trimper, *Production Director*
Shanna Heilveil, *Production Assistant*

Cynthia Baldwin, *Product Design Manager*
Michelle S. DiMercurio, *Art Director*

James G. Lesniak, *Editorial Technical Services Manager*
Roger M. Valade III, *Editorial Technical Services Specialist*

Victoria B. Cariappa, *Research Manager*
Andrew Guy Malonis, *Research Specialist*
Mary Beth McElmeel and Norma Sawaya, *Research Associates*
Julia C. Daniel and Michelle Lee, *Research Assistants*

Benita L. Spight, *Manager, Data Entry Services*
Gwendolyn S. Tucker, *Data Entry Coordinator*
Frances L. Monroe and Maleka Imrana, *Data Entry Associates*

∞™ The paper used in this publication meets the minimum requirements of American National Standard for Information Sciences—Permanence Paper for Printed Library Materials, ANSI Z39.48-1984

Table of Contents

Preface

Magill's Cinema Annual 1995 is a noteworthy addition to the VideoHound series of entertainment industry reference products published by Gale Research Inc. The fourteenth annual volume in a series that developed from the 21-volume core set, *Magill's Survey of Cinema*, the *Annual* was formerly published by Salem Press. Gale's first volume, as with the previous Salem volumes, contains essay-reviews of significant domestic and foreign films released in the United States during the preceeding year. But in order to better serve our readers, we've made some significant changes and enhancements—modifications that ensure *Magill's* will more completely cover the exciting and unpredictable film industry.

The new *Magill's* editorial staff at Gale, comprising the VideoHound team and a host of *Magill's* contributors, is confident that regular users—students, academia, entertainment industry professionals, librarians and film buffs—will find these enhancements a welcome change, and hopes to win some new fans of this already popular work. These new features include:

- A 50% increase in film coverage from the previous volume

- More essay-length reviews of significant films released during the year

- Photographs which accompany the reviews and illustrate the obituaries and Life Achievement Award sections

- Trivia and "fun facts" about the reviewed movies, their stars, and crew

- Quotes and dialogue "soundbites" from reviewed movies, or from stars and crew about the film

- More complete awards and nominations listings, including the American Academy Awards, British Academy of Film and Television Arts, Cannes Film Festival, Chicago Film Festival, Golden Globe, New York Critics Awards, and others (see the User's Guide for more information on awards coverage)

- Box office grosses, including year-end and other significant totals

- Critics' and publicity taglines featured in film reviews and advertisements

- A new cumulative title index which serves as a one-stop source for access to all the films covered in the *Magill's Survey of Cinema* series

- An attractive new page design and cover, plus an expanded trim size

In addition to these enhancements, Gale's *Magill's Cinema Annual 1995* continues to feature:

- An annual list of awards bestowed upon the year's films by ten international associations, from the Academy of Motion Picture Arts and Sciences to the Cannes International Film Festival and the British Academy Awards.

- An essay reviewing the career and accomplishments of the recipient of the American Film Institute's Life Achievement Award presented each year to Hollywood luminaries. Actor/director Jack Nicholson is the 1994 award recipient profiled in this volume.

- An obituaries section profiling major contributors to the film industry who died in 1994

- An annotated list of selected film books published in 1994

- Nine indexes: Title (now cumulative), Director, Screenwriter, Cinematographer, Editor, Art Director, Music, Performer, and Subject

Compilation Methods

A variety of entertainment industry publications, including trade magazines and newspapers, as well as online sources, are checked on a daily and weekly basis to select significant films for review in *Magill's Cinema Annual*. Reviews are written by the *Magill's* editorial staff and other contributing reviewers, including film scholars and university faculty.

Magill's Cinema Annual: A VideoHound Reference

Magill's Cinema Annual, now part of the VideoHound family of movie and entertainment reference products, was acquired in 1995 from Salem Press Inc., an honored and highly respected publisher serving the library market. The *Magill's Survey of Cinema* series, now supplemented by the *Annual*, was honored with the Reference Book of the Year Award in Fine Arts by the American Library Association.

Gale Research, Inc., an award-winning publisher of reference products, is confident that it will uphold the Salem standard of quality that *Magill's* users have come to expect and welcomes this opportunity to introduce *Magill's* users to Gale's popular VideoHound product line, which includes *VideoHound's Golden Movie Retriever*, *VideoHound Multimedia*, and the *Video Sourcebook*. Other Gale film-related products include the *St. James Dictionary of Films and Filmmakers* and the *Contemporary Theatre, Film, and Television* series.

Electronic Formats Available

Data from the *Magill's* series is also available in the following alternate formats:

Knight Ridder (formerly Dialog): Includes 3,300 entries from the *Magill's* core series as well as the *Annual*, plus 27,000 brief reviews not contained in the print series. These brief reviews offer credits information and a capsule description.

Prodigy: Includes 3,300 reviews from the core series, nearly 7,000 brief entries, and approximately 1,500 full-length reviews.

Acknowlegments

Kenneth T. Burles, Dawn Dawson, and Mark Rehn, Salem Press, are thanked for their graciousness, cooperation and counsel (and years of work in creating the original *Magill's* series). Thank you, Terri Dieckoff, Saztec Computer Services Corp., for your electronic processing assistance, and Judy Hartman, General Graphics Services, for your help in making this book a reality. Michelle DiMercurio, Gale Research, is most appreciated for her design efforts. We thank Gale's Roger Valade for his technical assistance. The *VideoHound/Video Sourcebook* staffs are thanked for their contributions to this project, particularly Michelle Banks, Jim Craddock, Kelly Cross, Beth Fhaner, Chris Scanlon, Devra Sladics, and Chris Tomassini, for their patience, interest, hard work, and goodwill, as well as Marty Connors, Julia Furtaw, and Terri Schell for their guidance and direction.

We most appreciate the following people for their assistance in obtaining photographs: Margarita Medina, Columbia Pictures; Erica Potter, First Look Pictures; Bob Cosenza, the Kobal Collection; Robyn Worthington, Miramax Films; Robin Zlatin, New Line/Fine Line Features; Stephanie Layton-Campbell, Orion Pictures; Larry McAlister, Paramount Pictures; and Nancy Cushing-Jones, Universal Pictures.

Introduction

The editorial transition that resulted in the enhanced *Magill's Cinema Annual* came on the heels of a particularly intriguing year in cinema. Several of the industry's most notable trends—the return to *film noir*, the celebration of pop culture, the fascination with life outside of the mainstream, and the Academy's reluctance to recognize films outside that mainstream—were simultaneously revealed to American audiences in one big, black-humored, bloody package—Quentin Tarantino's tour-de-force, *Pulp Fiction*. Joined by *Romeo Is Bleeding*, *The Last Seduction*, and *Red Rock West* as part of the growing revival of *film noir*, *Pulp Fiction* was unique in that it both nodded to the past with its classic *noir* elements, while incorporating hip, pop culture references. Tarantino took his love affair with pop culture several steps further in another over-the-top-pop screenplay which served as a basis for Oliver Stone's in-your-face media slam/homage mockumentary, *Natural Born Killers*, which, like the year's $300 million hit, *Forrest Gump*, blurred the boundaries between fact, fiction, and fantasy.

Only truth proved stranger than *Pulp Fiction* in 1994, as witnessed by the year's many films which were based on true stories: *Heavenly Creatures*, *Immortal Beloved*, *The Madness of King George*, *Queen Margot*, *Princess Caraboo*, *Dr. Bethune*, *Cobb*, *Mrs. Parker and the Vicious Circle*, *Tom & Viv*, *Wyatt Earp*, *Andre*, *Backbeat*, *It Could Happen to You*, *Quiz Show*, and *Ed Wood*.

This latter film was among several 1994 releases that led mainstream audiences to cross over to what might be considered alternative films, including the camp-cuddling, cross-dressing *The Adventures of Priscilla, Queen of the Desert* and the extremely low-budget, highly acclaimed *Clerks*. Hip soundtracks from *Clerks*, *Pulp Fiction*, *Natural Born Killers*, and *Reality Bites* helped position these films to the MTV generation of moviegoers, an audience segment that has become so important that, since 1992, MTV has presented its own movie awards as an alternative to the Academy Awards.

Reality did indeed bite in 1994 when it came to a real-life drama too poignantly, painfully real for the aging, out-of-touch Academy to relate to. The acclaimed documentary *Hoop Dreams* was unceremoniously snubbed by the Academy for Best Picture or Best Documentary, earning only a nomination for Best Film Editing. The film was in good company this year with Krzysztof Kieslowski's *Red*, which the Academy declared ineligible for Best Foreign Film because it failed to meet the requirement that two out of three among director, producer and writer be natives of the nominating country; and John Dahl's *The Last Seduction*, whose star Linda Fiorentino was disqualified from a potential Oscar nomination as Best Actress because the film first ran on the HBO cable television network. Film critic Roger Ebert called the Academy's *Hoop Dreams* snub a "a miscarriage," and told *USA Weekend*, "I'm ashamed of having anything to do with the movie business today." As William Gates, one of *Hoop Dreams*' NBA hopefuls, noted of the film, "African Americans say, 'I can relate to that.' White people say, 'This can't really be happening.' It's definitely not *Forrest Gump*."

Real life is no box of chocolates when it is outside of Hollywood's idea of the true American experience. The special effects-created pseudo-reality of *Forrest Gump* waxed nostalgic for the liberal baby-boomer generation even as it served up a slice of American pie for the family values-embracing conservative right, all the while offering an omni-politically correct agenda which touched upon such hot sociopolitical issues as AIDS, sexual abuse, single parenthood, war, drugs, and the rights of the physically and mentally challenged.

Gump won over the Academy and audiences, stockpiling Oscars for Best Picture, Best Director (Zemeckis), Best Film Editing, Best Visual Effects, Best Adapted Screenplay (Roth), and a back-to-back Best Actor Oscar for Tom Hanks after his 1993 win for *Philadelphia*. Number one at the box office for five weeks, *Gump* was the movie industry's fifth highest-grossing film and a record-breaker for Parmount Pictures.

However, as 1994's box office records showed, a film does not have to be acknowledged by the Academy to gain widespread appeal. The simple-minded splendor of *Forrest Gump* led a pack of varyingly successful, audience-pleasing films in which ignorance was bliss, including *Dumb and Dumber*, *Ace Ventura: Pet Detective*, *Cabin Boy*, *Airheads*, *The Mask*, *P.C.U.*, *Trapped in Paradise*, and *Naked Gun 33⅓: The Final Insult*. While social critics labeled this media-inspired celebration of idiocy "the dumbing of America," box offices and stars smartly cleaned up, most notably rubber-faced comedian Jim Carrey, who became Hollywood's $20 million man after his back-to-back successes.

Hollywood banked hard on an old standby, the sports movie, to reach popular audiences in 1994. Basketball fans disillusioned by the gritty real-life drama of *Hoop Dreams* were entertained by lighter fare with *Above the Rim*, *The Air Up There*, and *Blue Chips*. If basketball wasn't your game, plenty of choice existed in the sports genre, including *Little Giants* (football), *D2: The Mighty Ducks* (hockey), and a mitt-full of films about the national pastime, including *Angels in the Outfield*, *Little Big League*, *Major League II*, *Cobb*, and *The Scout*, which attempted to placate fan fever during the major league strike that precluded the 1994 World Series.

Off the field, competition among Hollywood stars for the most big screen appearances in 1994 was led by the ubiquitous Tommy Lee Jones and new contenders Nicolas Cage and Eric Stoltz, who each racked up five appearances, followed by Lara Flynn Boyle, Bridget Fonda, Juliette Lewis, Stephen Rea, Tim Robbins, and Bruce Willis, each with four appearances. Other busy actors for the year included Jim Carrey, Hugh Grant, Dennis Hopper, Samuel L. Jackson, Harvey Keitel, Christopher Lloyd, Gary Oldman, Winona Ryder, Susan Sarandon, Madeleine Stowe, Tracey Ullman, and Dianne Wiest, each with three appearances.

The movie industry also saw the death of some legends and well-loved stars in 1994, some of whom made their last film appearances during the year: Hollywood luminary Burt Lancaster; grand dame of theater and film Jessica Tandy, who starred in *Camilla* and *Nobody's Fool*; Don Ameche, who appeared in *Corrina, Corrina*; Raul Julia, who starred in *Street Fighter*; and John Candy, who died while filming *Wagons East!* See the Obituaries section in the back of this book for profiles of these and other major contributors to the film industry who died in 1994.

As the curtain descends upon the year of the film centennial, the *Magill's* staff looks forward to preparing the 1996 *Annual*, for which additional changes and enhancements are planned. We invite your comments. Please direct all questions and comments to:

Editor, *Magill's Cinema Annual*
Gale Research Inc.
835 Penobscot Bldg.
Detroit, MI 48226-4094
Phone: (313) 961-2242
Toll-free: 800-347-GALE
Fax: (313) 961-6812

Contributing Reviewers

Michael Adams
Fairleigh Dickinson University

JoAnn Balingit
Freelance Reviewer

Mary E. Belles
Freelance Reviewer

Michael Betzold
Freelance Reviewer

David L. Boxerbaum
Freelance Reviewer

Cynthia K. Breckenridge
Freelance Reviewer

Beverley Bare Buehrer
Freelance Reviewer

Reni Celeste
Freelance Reviewer

Robert F. Chicatelli
Freelance Reviewer

Paul B. Cohen
Freelance Reviewer

Jarred Cooper
Freelance Reviewer

Jonathan David
Freelance Reviewer

Bill Delaney
Freelance Reviewer

Tom W. Ferguson
Freelance Reviewer

Michael L. Forstrom
Freelance Reviewer

Rick Garman
Freelance Reviewer

Sandra G. Garrett
Freelance Reviewer

Sidney Gottlieb
Sacred Heart University

D. Douglas Graham
University of Maryland

Roberta F. Green
Virginia Polytechnic Institute and State University

Diane Hatch-Avis
Freelance Reviewer

Glenn Hopp
Howard Payne

Nicholas Kirgo
Freelance Reviewer

Patricia Kowal
Freelance Reviewer

Jim Kline
Freelance Reviewer

Leon Lewis
Appalachian State University

Alexandra M. Mather
Freelance Reviewer

John J. Michalczyk
Freelance Reviewer

Paul Mittelbach
Freelance Reviewer

Lisa Paddock
Freelance Reviewer

Francis Poole
Freelance Reviewer

Carl Rollyson
Baruch College, The City University of New York

Brenda Scott Royce
Freelance Reviewer

Gaylyn Studlar
University of Michigan

Kirby Tepper
Freelance Reviewer

Terry Theodore
University of North Carolina at Wilmington

James M. Welsh
Salisbury State University

Philip C. Williams
Freelance Reviewer

User's Guide

Alphabetization

Film titles and reviews are arranged on a word-by-word-basis, including articles and prepositions. English leading articles (A, An, The) are ignored as well as foreign leading articles (El, Il, La, Las, Le, Les, Los). Other considerations:

- Acronyms appear alphabetically as if regular words. For example, C.H.U.D. is alphabetized as "CHUD."

- Common abbreviations in titles file as if they are spelled out, so *Mr. Write* will be found as if it was spelled *"Mister Write."*

- Proper names in titles are alphabetized beginning with the individual's first name, for instance, *Ed Wood* will be found under "E."

- Titles with numbers, for instance *8 Seconds,* are alphabetized as if the number was spelled out under the appropriate letter, in this case, "Eight." When numeric titles gather in close proximity to each other, the titles will be arranged in a low to high numeric sequence.

Special Sections

List of Awards. An annual list of awards bestowed upon the year's films by ten international associations: Academy of Motion Picture Arts and Sciences, British Academy Awards, Directors Guild of America Award, Golden Globe Awards, Golden Palm Awards (Cannes International Film Festival), Los Angeles Film Critics Awards, National Board of Review Awards, National Society of Film Critics Awards, New York Film Critics Awards, and the Writers Guild Awards.

Life Achievement Award. An essay reviewing the career and accomplishments of the recipient of the American Film Institute's Life Achievement Award presented each year to Hollywood luminaries. Actor/director Jack Nicholson is the 1994 award recipient profiled in this volume.

Obituaries. An obituaries section profiling major contributors to the film industry who died in 1994.

Selected Film Books of 1994. An annotated list of selected film books published in 1994.

Indexes

Film titles and artists are arranged into nine indexes, allowing the reader to effectively approach a film from any one of several directions, including not only its credits but its subject matter.

Title Index. A cumulative alphabetical list of nearly 4,250 films covered in the fourteen volumes of the *Magill's Cinema Annual,* including nearly 500 films covered in this volume. Films reviewed in past volumes are cited with a roman numeral indicating the volume number in which the film was originally reviewed; films reviewed in this volume are cited with the film title in bold with a bolded arabic number indicating the page number on which the review begins. Original and alternate titles are cross-referenced to the American release title in the Title Index. Titles of retrospective films are followed by the year, in brackets, of their original release. Also indexed are those films discussed at some length in the special sections.

Director, Screenwriter, Cinematographer, Editor, Music, Art Director, and *Performer Indexes* are arranged according to artists appearing in this volume, followed by a list of the films on which they worked and the titles of the special sections (such as "Life Achievement Award" or "Obituaries") in which they are mentioned at length.

Subject Index. Films may be categorized under several of the categories arranged alphabetically in this section.

Sample Review

Each *Magill's* review contains up to sixteen items of information. A fictionalized composite sample review containing all the elements of information which may be included in a full-length review follows the outline below. The circled number preceding each element in the sample review on page XV designates an item of information that is explained in the outline on the next page.

(1) Title: Film title as it was released in the United States.

(2) Foreign or alternate title(s): The film's original title or titles as released outside the United States, or alternate film title or titles. Foreign and alternate titles also appear in the Title Index to facilitate user access.

(3) Taglines: Up to ten publicity or critical taglines for the film from advertisements or reviews.

(4) Box office information: Year-end or other box office domestic revenues for the film.

(5) Film review or abstract: A one-paragraph abstract or 750-1500-word signed review of the film, including brief plot summary, and for full-length reviews, an analytic overview of the film and its critical reception.

(6) Principal characters: Up to 25 listings of the film's principal characters and the names of the actors who play them in the film. The names of actors who play themselves are cited twice (as character and actor).

(7) Country of origin: The film's country or countries of origin if other than the United States.

(8) Release date: The year of the film's first general release.

(9) Production information: This section typically includes the name(s) of the film's producer(s), production company, and distributor, director(s), screenwriter(s), author(s) or creator(s) and the novel, play, short story, television show, motion picture, or other work, or character(s), that the film was based upon; cinematographer(s) (if the film is animated, this will be replaced with Animation or Animation Direction); editor(s); art director(s), production designer(s), set decorator(s) or set designer(s); music composer(s); and other credits such as visual effects, sound, casting, costume design, and song(s) and songwriter(s).

(10) MPAA rating: The film's rating by the Motion Picture Association of America. If there is no rating given, the line will read, "no listing."

(11) Running time: The film's running time in minutes.

(12) Reviewer byline: The name of the reviewer who wrote the full-length review. A complete list of this volume's contributors appears in the "Contributing Reviewers" section which follows the Introduction.

(13) Reviews: A list of up to 25 brief citations of major newspaper and journal reviews of the film, including publication title, date of review, and page number.

(14) Awards information: Awards won by the film, followed by category and name of winning cast or crew member. Listings of the film's nominations follow the wins on a separate line for each award. Awards are arranged alphabetically. Information is listed for films which won or were nominated for the following awards: American Academy Awards, Australian Film Institute, Berlin Film Festival, Blockbuster Entertainment Awards, British Academy of Film and Television Arts, Canadian Genie, Cannes Film Festival, Chicago Film Festival, Directors Guild of America, Edgar Allan Poe Awards, French Cesar, Golden Globe, Independent Spirit, Los Angeles Film Critics Association Awards, Montreal Film Festival, MTV Movie Awards, National Board of Review Awards, National Society of Film Critics Awards, New York Critics Awards, Sundance Film Festival, Toronto-City Awards, Writers Guild of America, and others.

(15) Film quotes: Memorable dialogue directly from the film, attributed to the character who spoke it, or comment from cast or crew members or reviewers about the film.

(16) Film trivia: Interesting tidbits about the film, its cast, or production crew.

① The Gump Diaries (Los Diarios del Gump)

③ "Love means never having to say you're stupid."
—Movie tagline

"This was a really good movie. I liked it." —Joe
Critic, *Daily News*

④ **Box Office Gross:** $10 million
(December 15, 1994)

⑤ In writer/director Robert Zemeckis' *Back to the Future* trilogy (1985, 1989, 1990), Marty McFly (Michael J. Fox) and his scientist sidekick Doc Brown (Christopher Lloyd) journey backward and forward in time, attempting to smooth over some rough spots in their personal histories in order to remain true to their individual destinies. Throughout their time-travel adventures, Doc Brown insists that neither he nor Marty influence any major historical events, believing that to do so would result in catastrophic changes in humankind's ultimate destiny. By the end of the trilogy, however, Doc Brown has revised his thinking and tells Marty that, "Your future hasn't been written yet. No one's has. Your future is whatever you make it. So make it a good one."

In *Forrest Gump*, Zemeckis once again explores the theme of personal destiny and how an individual's life affects and is affected by his historical time period. This time, however, Zemeckis and screenwriter Eric Roth chronicle the life of a character who does nothing but meddle in the historical events of his time without even trying to do so. By the film's conclusion, however, it has become apparent that Zemeckis' main concern is something more than merely having fun with four decades of American history. In the process of re-creating significant moments in time, he has captured on celluloid something eternal and timeless—the soul of humanity personified by a nondescript simpleton from the deep South.

The film begins following the flight of a seemingly insignificant feather as it floats down from the sky and brushes against various objects and people before finally coming to rest at the feet of Forrest Gump (Tom Hanks). Forrest, who is sitting on a bus-stop bench, reaches down and picks up the feather, smooths it out, then opens his traveling case and carefully places the feather between the pages of his favorite book, *Curious George.*

In this simple but hauntingly beautiful opening scene, the filmmakers illustrate the film's principal concern: Is life a series of random events over which a person has no control, or is there an underlying order to things that leads to the fulfillment of an individual's destiny? The rest of the film is a humorous and moving attempt to prove that, underlying the random, chaotic events that make up a person's life, there exists a benign and simple order.

Forrest sits on the bench throughout most of the film, talking about various events of his life to others who happen to sit down next to him. It does not take long, however, for the audience to realize that Forrest's seemingly random

The action shifts to the mid-1950's with Forrest as a young boy (Michael Humphreys) being fitted with leg braces to correct a curvature in his spine. The action shifts to the mid-1950's to a in his spine. When the first U.S. Ping-Pong team to This of movie magic has not accomplished by special effects or computer-altered images, by something much more impressive and harder to achieve.

⑫ *—John Byline*

⑮
"The state of existence may be likened unto a receptacle containing cocoa-based confections, in that one may never predict that which one may receive." —Forrest Gump, from *The Gump Diaries*

AWARDS AND NOMINATIONS

⑭ **Academy Awards 1994:** Best Film, Best Actor (Hanks), Best Special Effects, Best Cinematography
Nominations: Best Actress (Fields), Best Screenplay, Best Director (Zameckis)
Golden Globe Awards 1994: Best Film,
Nominations: Best Actor (Hanks), Best Supporting Actress (Wright), Best Music, Best Special Effects

chatter to a parade of strangers has a perfect chronological order to it. He tells his first story after looking down at the feet of his first bench partner and observing, "Mama always said that you can tell a lot about a person by the shoes they wear." Then, in a voice-over narration, Forrest begins the story of his life, first by telling about the first pair of shoes he can remember wearing.

The action shifts to the mid-1950's with Forrest as a young boy (Michael Humphreys) being fitted with leg braces to correct a curvature in his spine. Despite this traumatic handicap, Forrest remains unaffected, thanks to his mother (Sally Field) who reminds him on more than one occasion that he is no different from anyone else. Although this and most of Mrs. Gump's other words of advice are in the form of hackneyed cliches, Forrest whose intelligence quotient is below normal, sincerely believes every one of them, namely because he instinctively knows they are sincere expressions of his mother's love and fierce devotion.

⑯
Hanks was the first actor since Spencer Tracy to win back-to-back Oscars for Best Actor. Hanks received the award in 1993 for his performance in *Philadelphia.* Tracy won Oscars in 1937 for *Captains Courageous* and in 1938 for *Boys Town.*

CREDITS

⑥ **Jim Carroll:** Leonardo DiCaprio
Swifty: Bruno Kirby
Jim's Mother: Lorraine Bracco
Mickey: Mark Wahlberg

⑦ **Origin:** United Kingdom
⑧ **Released:** 1993
Production: Liz Heller, John Bard Manulis for New Line Cinema; released by Island Pictures
⑨ **Direction:** Scott Kalvert
Author: Bryan Goluboff; based on the novel by Jim Carroll
Cinematographer: David Phillips
Editing: Dana Congdon
Production design: Christopher Nowak
Set decoration: Harriet Zucker
Sound: William Sarokin
Costume design: David C. Robinson
Music: Graeme Revell
⑩ **MPAA rating:** R
⑪ **Running time:** 102 minutes

REVIEWS

⑬ *Entertainment Weekly.* July 15, 1994, p. 42.
The Hollywood Reporter. June 29, 1994, p. 7.
Los Angeles Times. July 6, 1994, p. F1.

Magill's Cinema Annual
1995

Á la Mode (Fausto)(In Fashion)

"There's nothing wrong with life that a few alterations won't fix." —Movie tagline

"...a warm, funny and inspired coming-of-age comedy." —*Los Angeles Times*

"A modern fairy tale." —*San Francisco Chronicle*

"Delicious! A charming delight." —Jeanne Wolf, *Jeanne Wolf's Hollywood*

"The perfect date-night ticket." —Bob Healy, *Satellite News Network*

"Delirious." —*Seattle Point Intelligencer*

 Box Office Gross: $211,790 (September 9, 1994)

Florence Darel and Ken Higelin star in Remy Duchmin's *Á la Mode.* © Buena Vista Pictures Distribution, Inc.

When a seventeen-year-old orphan, Fausto (Ken Higelin), is apprenticed to a kindly Parisian tailor, Mietek (Jean Yanne), Fausto's creativity surfaces in some wildly imaginative costumes. He is transfixed by lovely mechanic Tonie (Darel) and decides what he really wants (besides the girl) is to design women's fashions. Very frothy coming-of-age tale, anchored by Yanne's veteran charm. Based on the novel *Fausto* by Richard Morgiève. Directorial debut of Rémy Duchemin. Higelin's half brother Parisian pop star Arthur H. makes an appearance as an awestruck celebrity.

REVIEWS

Atlanta Constitution. August 26, 1994, p.P10.
Boston Globe. August 31, 1994, p.30.
Chicago Tribune. August 19, 1994, P.7H.
Entertainment Weekly. February 3, 1995, p.65.
Los Angeles Times. August 12, 1994, p.F10.
The New York Times. August 12, 1994, p.C3.
People Weekly. XLII, August 29, 1994, p.21.
The Washington Post. August 27, 1994, p.B3.

CREDITS

Mietek: Jean Yanne
Fausto: Ken Higelin
Raymond: François Hautesserre
Tonie: Florence Darel
Lucien: Maurice Benichou

Origin: France
Released: 1994
Production: Joël Foulon and Daniel Daujon for Lili Productions, BBD Productions, and France 2 Cinema; released by Miramax Films
Direction: Rémy Duchemin
Screenplay: Richard Morgiève and Rémy Duchemin; based on the novel *Fausto*, by Morgieve
Cinematography: Yves Lafaye

Editing: Mayline Marthieux
Production design: Fouillet et Wieber
Art direction: Gilber Druart
Production management: Christine De Jekel
Sound: Michel Kharat
Costume design: Philippe Guillotel: Annie Perier
Music: Denis Barbier
MPAA rating: R
Running time: 87 minutes

> "Their stomachs must announce proudly, 'I am dressed by Mr. Breslauer!'"—Mietek Breslauer in Á la Mode

Above the Rim

"Eye-popping basketball action. Puts the NBA to shame." —Paul Wunder, *WBAI Radio*

Box Office Gross: $16,036,534 (February 1995)

 A high school basketball star (Duane Martin) is torn between the bad influence of a local gangster (Tupac Shakur) and the helpful support of his school's security guard (Leon), who was once a local star player himself, during a competitive playground tournament. Energetic basketball sequences and strong performances lose impact amid formidable melodrama and the usual obscenities. Film debut for director Pollack.

REVIEWS

Atlanta Constitution. March 23, 1994, p.E8.
Boston Globe. March 23, 1994, p.69.
Chicago Tribune. March 23, 1994, Sec. 1 p.18.
Chicago Tribune. March 25, 1994, p.7C.
Entertainment Weekly. April 8, 1994, p.39.
Entertainment Weekly. September 30, 1994, p.70.
Los Angeles Times. March 23, 1994, p.F6.
The New York Times. March 23, 1994, p.C17.
The New York Times. October 7, 1994, p.D18.
People Weekly. XLI, April 4, 1994. p.17.
Rolling Stone. April 21, 1994, p.93.
Variety. CCCLIV, March 21, 1994, p.57.
The Washington Post. March 23, 1994, p.B2.

CREDITS

Kyle-Lee: Duane Martin
Shep: Leon
Birdie: Tupac Shakur
Rollins: David Bailey
Mailika: Tonya Pinkins
Bugaloo: Marlon Wayans
Flip: Bernie Mac
Monroe: Byron Minns

Released: 1994
Production: Jeff Pollack and Benny Medina; released by New Line Cinema
Direction: Jeff Pollack
Screenplay: Barry Michael Cooper and Jeff Pollack; based on a story by Pollack and Benny Medina
Cinematography: Tom Priestley, Jr.
Editing: Michael Ripps and James Mitchell
Production design: Ina Mayhew
Set decoration: Paul Weathered
Casting: Marie E. Nelson: Ellyn Long Marshall
Sound: Michael Barosky
Costume design: Karen Perry
Stunt coordination: Jeff Ward
Music: Marcus Miller
MPAA rating: R
Running time: 93 minutes

AWARDS AND NOMINATIONS

MTV Awards Nomination 1995: Best Song ("Regulate")

Ace Ventura: Pet Detective

"A riot from start to finish." —Rita Kempley, *The Washington Post*

"Kids will love it and so will adults." —Barry Caine, *The Oakland Tribune*

"...the most unexpected giggle fits." —Chris Williams, *Los Angeles Times*

 Box Office Gross: $72,208,397 (July 4, 1994)

Ace Ventura: Pet Detective answers the question why films such as *Aladdin* (1992) are known as "animated cartoons." For *Ace Ventura* is live-action cartoon, and it succeeds only on those terms.

Expectations that a film with live actors will be something more than a cartoon can only ruin the considerable though sporadic pleasures of *Ace Ventura*. From the first glimpse of actor Jim Carrey's rubbery face, from the first over-enunciated words which issue from his mouth, it is clear that Carrey plays Ace as a cartoon figure. Carrey's Ace is more animated than the most hyperkinetic cartoon characters. His clothing—striped pants and Hawaiian shirts—is cartoonish. His lanky, India-rubber body, his elastic face, his high-powered-salesman vocal delivery, in fact, everything about him is more animated than human. Carrey has taken over-the-top acting to a new level of ridiculousness.

Motion pictures with main characters this overdrawn tend to be derivative of comic-book or cartoon superheroes such as Batman or Superman. The character of Ace Ventura—an up-and-coming pet detective who uses his strange instincts to hone in on lost animals—had a more complicated pedigree. Writer Jack Bernstein conceived the idea. Former stand-up comic Tom Shadyac was hired to direct. In his directorial debut, Shadyac wanted Carrey, a zany comic who had been on television's *In Living Color* for over seven years, for the part. Then the three improvised the rest. The result is more evidence, if any is needed, that television has taken over Hollywood. Nearly everyone involved with this film had worked in television. Like the television commercial pitchman Ernest who made the jump into motion pictures Carrey plays Ace so broadly that it is a long way into the film before the irritation factor subsides. Carrey wants Ace to be broadly cartoonish, and there is no concession to the subtler possibilities that cinema offers. His contorted face fills the big screen; his always-at-top-volume words boom through the

 "I made this movie for only one reason: I'm just sick of the honorable profession of pet detection being ignored."—Jim Carrey on *Ace Ventura: Pet Detective*

large speakers; he is a bull in a china shop. Carrey is funny in exactly the same way that Daffy Duck and Fred Flintstone are funny. Human beings, however, are not supposed to act this way. Human beings learn rules of conversation: They do not speak every word in capital letters. Ace Ventura is outrageous because he does not follow those rules—or too many others.

Unfortunately, the plot follows too many hackneyed rules while exploding others. The story line—someone has stolen Snowflake, the Miami Dolphins' aquatic mascot just before the Super Bowl—ends up dragging down the comedy with the sheer weight of its own banality. When the culprit turns out to be a grudge-carrying scapegoat of an earlier Super Bowl loss, any edge to the story turns to mush. When the thief turns out to be someone else entirely, the story falls off the cliff into absurdity—which is perhaps where it should have been all along. The late-in-the-film satire of *The Crying Game* (1992) is wicked; more wickedness earlier on would have been welcome.

The task of finding Snowflake falls to Melissa Robinson (Courteney Cox), who turns in desperation to Ace. Ace first targets a wealthy industrialist (Udo Kier), but extensive skulking shows this line of investigation to be a dead end. When Dolphin star quarterback Dan Marino (making his acting debut playing himself) also disappears, and a club official plunges to a mysterious death, Ace finally starts sniffing the right tracks. They turn out to belong to a disgruntled former placekicker whose errant kick that lost a previous Super Bowl for the Dolphins has turned him into a scapegoat seeking revenge. Yet the culprit is not at all who he seems, and neither is the icy police lieutenant (Sean Young) who is ostensibly competing with Ace to solve the case.

Although Shadyac and company strive for outrageousness, and Carrey certainly does his part, too much of the action is far too pedestrian. It is a gamble to attempt to sustain an antic, frantic pace and mood for an entire film, and Bernstein and Shadyac do not even give it a game try. Perhaps this is another legacy of television, where it is relatively simple to sustain an antic pace between the frequent commercial breaks. In feature films, however, this is no easy matter. Carrey looks up to the task—he does not seem to have an "off" button—but no one else does.

The rest of the cast has the usual problems that come from playing around a tornado: Most would have been better off allowing themselves to be sucked into the Ventura vortex. Raynor Scheine comes closest to trumping Ace, but his role as an underground high-tech animal-rights extremist is all too brief. Cox, as the woman who by dictate of the wooden plot must become slightly smitten with Ace, somehow manages to turn in a believable dramatic performance—which contributes very little to a film that is supposed to be a cartoon. Cox comes off too genuine, an effect which only heightens the discrepancy between the hyper Ace and the listlessness of the rest of the proceedings. Sean Young is simply miscast, though that is part of the film's ultimate dirty little joke. Although there have been worse performances by jocks in film, Dan Marino obviously is more comfortable with charging 250-pound linemen than

CREDITS

Ace Ventura: Jim Carrey
Melissa: Courteney Cox
Einhorn: Sean Young
Emilio: Tone Löc
Dan Marino: Dan Marino
Riddle: Noble Willingham
Podacter: Troy Evans
Woodstock: Raynor Scheine
Camp: Udo Kier

Released: 1994
Production: James G. Robinson for Morgan Creek; released by Warner Bros.
Direction: Tom Shadyac
Screenplay: Jack Bernstein, Tom Shadyac, and Jim Carrey; based on a story by Bernstein
Cinematography: Julio Macat
Editing: Don Zimmerman
Production design: William Elliott
Art direction: Alan E. Muraoka
Set design: Rich Fojo
Set decoration: Scott Jacobson
Casting: Mary Jo Slater
Sound: Russell C. Fager
Costume design: Bobbie Read
Animal coordination: Cathy Morrison
Stunt coordination: Artie Malesci
Music: Ira Newborn
MPAA rating: PG-13
Running time: 93 minutes

AWARDS AND NOMINATIONS

Blockbuster Entertainment Awards 1995: Male Newcomer, Video (Carrey); Comedy Actor, Video (Carrey)
MTV Movie Awards Nomination 1995: Best Comedic Performance (Jim Carrey)

he is with motion-picture cameras. Tone Löc, a rap singer, is also featured. Not only will he appeal to a younger crowd but he can act as well as sing. The white-bread film could use a little more of the soul Löc puts into the song that plays when the credits roll.

It is no surprise, and no indictment, that much of the film's humor seems aimed at adolescent boys, many of whom are fans of Dan Marino and fond of jokes about genitalia. It is faint, but deserved, praise to observe that there is less reliance on grossness, obscenity, and homophobic humor in *Ace Ventura* than in many comparable undertakings.

What is puzzling is that, for a film about a pet detective, there is so little fun with animals. One great scene near the beginning is promising: Ace insists to his landlord that he has no pets, even invites the man in to make an inspection; when the man leaves, however, animals of every description emerge from every conceivable hiding place. Yet that is the only really good sequence involving animals, though Ace's pets appear on his shoulder or person from time to time.

It is not too hard to find the reason for this film's considerable commercial success: Carrey. He has created a unique comic character: L'il Abner meets Sam Spade meets Elvis in overdrive. Should there be a sequel, one hopes that a writer and director can be found who are at least half as lunatic as the star.

—*Michael Betzold*

REVIEWS

The Hollywood Reporter. January 31, 1994, p. 6.
Los Angeles Times. February 4, 1994, p. F6.
The New York Times. February 5, 1994, p. 12.
The New Yorker. March 14, 1994, p. 28.
Premiere. February 1994, p. 20.
Variety. February 1, 1994, p. 10.

Acting on Impulse

A horror film star (Linda Fiorentino) becomes a murder suspect when her producer (Patrick Bachau) is found dead in her trailer. She then flees, assumes a new name, becomes romantically involved with a salesman (C. Thomas Howell) attending a convention, and is stalked by a fan. Made for cable television.

REVIEWS

Chicago Tribune. July 9, 1993, Sec. 5 p. 3.
Los Angeles Times. July 10, 1993, p. F15.
TV Guide. XLII, January 15, 1994, p.36.
USA Today. July 9, 1993, p. D3.
Variety. CCCLI, June 28, 1993, p.25.

CREDITS

Susan Gittes: Linda Fiorentino
Paul Stevens: C. Thomas Howell
Cathy Thomas: Nancy Allen
Gail Black: Judith Hoag
Dave Byers: Adam Ant
Yoram Sussman: Patrick Bachau
Detective Stubbs: Isaac Hayes
Brunop: Paul Bartel
Leroy: Don Most
John: Miles O'Keeffe

Released: 1993
Production: David Peters for Spectacor Films
Direction: Sam Irvin
Screenplay: Mark Pittman and Alan Moskowitz; based on a story by Sol Weingarten
Cinematography: Dean Lent
Editing: James Mitchell and Neil Grieve
Production design: Gary Randall
Casting: Gale Salus
Sound: Giovanni Di Simoni
Costume design: Jill Ohanneson
Music: Dan Licht
MPAA rating: no listing
Running time: 92 minutes

The Adventures of Priscilla, Queen of the Desert

"Finally, a comedy that will change the way you think, the way you feel, and most importantly...the way you dress." —Movie tagline

"*Priscilla* subtly shifts from high camp to quiet dignity." —Clifford Terry, *Chicago Tribune*

"Roaringly comic!" —Peter Travers, *Rolling Stone*

 Box Office Gross: $10,277,915 (January 2, 1995)

With the energy and momentum of a Broadway musical, *The Adventures of Priscilla, Queen of the Desert* spins a tale of an aging transsexual entertainer and two drag queens who cross the Australian outback in a dilapidated bus. Along the way, they learn about themselves and resolve their internecine differences with wit, flair, some hilarious musical numbers, and a lot of eye-popping costumes. Priscilla captures its audience in a giddy riot of color and humanity. It has rightfully garnered wide critical praise for its director/writer, Stephan Elliott, and its star, Terence Stamp.

Bernadette (Terence Stamp), Mitzi (Hugo Weaving), and Felicia (Guy Pearce) are performers in a Sydney drag club, dressing in outlandish costumes and lip-syncing to everything from opera to pop music. Bernadette is the only transsexual among the trio, having changed sexes long ago: the other two still alternate their drag names with their real ones (Mitzi is also Tick; Felicia is also Adam). The film's producer, Al Clark, says that "the basic comic premise of the movie is three people, who may as well be martians, standing in the middle of this enormous country—where, in fact, they are martians."

The plot is simple, dealing only with the journey across the outback to a far-away resort (where the trio has a performing engagement). This film follows the classic structure known in literature as "the night sea journey," whereby protagonists embark on a journey that challenges their perceptions of themselves and their world, changing them forever. The underlying premise of this theme is that the only way for true change to take place within an individual is for the individual to abandon the status quo and leave the "old life" behind. This plot device is arguably the oldest and most dependable basic plot in drama: examples of this structure are Homer's *Odyssey*, William Shakespeare's *A Midsummer Night's Dream*, Voltaire's *Candide*, or *The Wizard of Oz*. *Priscilla, Queen of The Desert* wisely uses the simplicity

 "There are two things I don't like about you...your face. So how about shutting both of 'em."— *Priscilla's* Mitzi to Felicia

of the plot to great advantage; the plot's lack of intricacy makes room for much character development.

The producers and writer/director Stephan Elliott, however, are not trying to compare themselves to great drama. *Priscilla* is an accessible and engaging piece of entertainment in the tradition of another Australian hit film, *Strictly Ballroom* (1993). The film is also a cousin to *La Cage aux Folles* (1978), for obvious reasons: It is about individuality, fatherhood, feathers, and high heels.

Wisely, Elliott and his cast recognize that this script should be played for laughs. There are some wonderful moments: Bernadette explains her husband's death by saying, "he went to peroxide his hair again and choked on the fumes"; the trio performs a Supremes-style number in the middle of the desert for a tribe of aborigines, one of whom joins them in drag; there is another sequence where all three enter a small-town pub in outlandish drag, only to win over the patrons by showing them how to do cucumber facials, or by out-drinking the drunken locals. One of the funniest moments in the film comes at the very end of the final credits—it is an extremely funny surprise which reminds the audience that the *raison d'etre* of the film is to make people laugh; this hilarious moment is probably missed by numerous people who have not heard that they should sit through the entire final credit sequence. It is exemplary of the indefatigability of director/writer Elliott: He keeps the laughs coming, all the way through the last second.

Arguably the most consistent laugh-getter in the film is the Oscar-winning costume design by Lizzy Gardiner and Tim Chappel. Their costumes set the cinematic mood: They are funny, ingenious, and wildly colorful. Gardiner and Chappel's ingenuity comes from their ability to push standard drag styles into increasingly outlandish new territory. For example, when the three drag queens perform the Supreme-style number, Gardiner and Chappel have put them in 1960's-style bell bottoms and big hair but with a twist: the bell bottoms stretch out around the feet, so that the shoes are built into the bell-bottoms and are invisible to the eye—creating a bigger-than-life quality to the costume. This bigger-than-life quality is also seen in an eye-popping trio of costumes for the scene in the small-town bar: Felicia/Adam wears a monstrous wig made entirely of pink and blue telephone cord, with a dress to match, and Tick/Mitzi wears a dress made of beach slippers, with earrings to match. In one sequence, there is even a costume which is a replica of the famous Sydney opera house. The film's final musical sequence is built around a series of indescribable costumes which accelerate in their inventiveness as the number progresses, leaving the observer to assume that the designers' imaginations are limitless.

It is of no consequence that the elaborate costumes worn by these three indigent characters appear too expensive; the director wisely shows them making costumes at all times, so that it seems possible that the trio would be able to create such amazing costumes out of sheer ingenuity and will. Furthermore, that ingenuity and conviction is echoed in the performances.

Australian actors Guy Pearce (as Felicia/Adam) and Hugo Weaving (as Mitzi/Tick) both deliver rip-roaring performances which are funny and poignant. Pearce's childlike quality is appropriately annoying, as his character tries (in the early parts of the film) to annoy Bernadette for the sheer

CREDITS

Bernadette: Terence Stamp
Tick (Mitzi): Hugo Weaving
Adam (Felicia): Guy Pearce
Bob: Bill Hunter
Marion: Sarah Chadwick
Benji: Mark Holmes
Cynthia: Julia Cortez
Frank: Ken Radley
Aboriginal man: Alan Dargin
Shirley: June Marie Bennett
Logowoman: Rebel Russell
Priest: Al Clark
Adam's mother: Margaret Pomeranz

Released: 1994
Origin: Australia
Production: Al Clark and Michael Hamlyn for Polygram Filmed Entertainment, in association with the Australian Film Finance Corporation and Latent Image/Specific Films; released by Gramercy Pictures
Direction: Stephan Elliott
Screenplay: Stephan Elliott
Cinematography: Brian J. Breheny
Editing: Sue Blainey
Production design: Owen Paterson
Art direction: Colin Gibson
Sound: Gunter Sics
Makeup: Cassie Hanlon
Costume design: Lizzy Gardiner: Tim Chappel
Choreography: Mark White
Stunt coordination: Robert Simper
Executive producer: Rebel Penfold-Russell
Production management: Sue Seeary
Music: Guy Gross
MPAA rating: R
Running time: 102 minutes

AWARDS AND NOMINATIONS

Academy Awards 1995: Best Costume Design
Australian Film Institute Awards 1994: Best Costume Design
Nominations: Best Film, Best Director (Elliott), Best Actor (Stamp), Best Actor (Weaving), Best Screenplay, Best Cinematography
Golden Globe Awards 1995: Best Film—Musical/Comedy, Best Actor—Musical/Comedy (Stamp)
Priscilla also won the audience award for most popular film at the Cannes, San Francisco, and Seattle film festivals.

pleasure of it. Pearce is a skillful performer who easily conveys the varying moods of his fun-loving character, while capturing the inner pain of a young man who has never truly felt accepted and has, perhaps, covered his anguish in an excess of booze and make-believe. From sitting atop the moving bus singing an operatic aria (with a huge train of gold lamé flowing from his headdress), to being the catalyst for a frightening brawl in a small town, Pearce is astonishing in his ability to keep his character hilarious and pathetic at the same time.

Similarly, in a less showy role, Hugo Weaving is funny and poignant as he creates a character full of ambiguity and worry. Weaving's character catalyzes the plot, and the mystery shrouding his past, followed by his concern about how to deal with it, are perfectly underscored by his nuanced performance. He is particularly delightful in the drag sequences; his gangly frame and goofy expression make him a homely but lovable drag queen.

It is Terence Stamp's wonderful performance as the transsexual, Bernadette, however, that has helped to catapult this film into international prominence. Stamp is an internationally recognizable actor whose credits include *Billy Budd* (1962), both *Superman* (1978) and *Superman II* (1980), *Wall Street* (1987), and other appearances in films by Federico Fellini, Pier Paolo Pasolini, and Peter Brook. Stamp has received much attention in the press for undertaking a role so radically different from his image. Similar to the attention given William Hurt for his Oscar-winning role in *Kiss of the Spider Woman* (1985), or Tom Hanks for his Oscar-winning performance in *Philadelphia* (1993), much has been made, in the American press, of Stamp's heterosexuality, and of what a radical departure this role is for him. It is a curious piece of current American culture that requires that heterosexuals are seen as being "brave" for portraying homosexuals or transsexuals.

Regardless of his motivation, Stamp is wonderful as the gentle, world-weary Bernadette. He looks something like a masculine version of Olympia Dukakis in *Tales of the City* (1994), as he adopts his resigned expression for yet another of Felicia/Adam's attempts at verbal assault. Consistently coming back with withering ripostes to Felicia's childish attacks, Stamp's Bernadette is the true "queen" of the desert:

a regal woman who quietly rules everything around her out of sheer will and perseverance. Stamp delivers one knockout line after another with dead-on acuity; one of the audience's apparent favorites is his denunciation of one of the emblematic rock groups of the disco era, as he erupts with a definitive "No more f*****g Abba!" It is a classic moment, which has already begun to become one of those expressions to which cult films seem to give birth.

Stamp is sweet and lovable, tough and funny, and though his assaying of this role surprised many, it is no surprise he was nominated for an Oscar.

One of the most beautiful scenes in the film, and there are many, happens early in the adventure, when the trio stops their bus and steps outside to survey the road ahead. Director Elliott pulls his camera up and back to take in the desolate panorama of the outback as the three drag queens realize what is ahead of them. Underscored by Guy Gross'

haunting music, Elliott shows the audience, in that moment, what his film is made of: a wonderful "fish-out-of-water" story told through a visual lens that knows when to stand back and let the scenery tell the story. When the scenery is as wondrous as the Australian outback and Terence Stamp in drag, it is not surprising that critical raves and bountiful box-office receipts should follow.

—*Kirby Tepper*

REVIEWS

Entertainment Weekly. September 9, 1994, p. 62.
The Hollywood Reporter. May 9, 1994, p. 163.
Los Angeles Times. August 10, 1994. p. F1.
The New York Times. August 10, 1994, p. B1.
Variety. May 9-15, 1994, p. 76.

The Advocate

"a provocative and fascinating film!" —*Sneak Previews*

"clever" —*The Washington Post*

"Sexy" —*The Chicago Reader*

"absorbing!" —*Los Angeles Daily News*"

Box Office Gross: $581,762 (October 30, 1994)

Set in a medieval French village, this quirky murder mystery stars Colin Firth as attorney Richard Courtois, whose talents are put to the test defending a mysterious alleged murderer. His first client is a pig accused of murdering a child and is owned by beautiful gypsy Samira (Annabi). There's religion and superstition, there's power struggles, there's ignorance versus knowledge—all very modern indeed. Miramax cut several seconds from a barnyard sex romp between Courtois and a servant-prostitute (Sophie Dix in her film debut).

REVIEWS

Boston Globe. September 2, 1994, p.88.
Chicago Tribune. September 2, 1994, p.7D.
Chicago Tribune. September 4, 1994, Sec.13, p 20.
Christian Science Monitor. August 26, 1994, p.10.
Entertainment Weekly. April 14, 1995, p.72.
Los Angeles Times. August 24, 1994, p.F8.
Los Angeles Times. September 12, 1994, p.F3.
The New York Times. August 24, 1994, p.C11.
The New York Times. CXLIV, April 21, 1995, p.B9.
The New York Times. April 21, 1995, p.D18.
The Wall Street Journal. September 8, 1994, p.A16.
The Washington Post. September 2, 1994, p.D1.
The Washington Post. September 2, 1994, p.WW38.

CREDITS

Richard Courtois: Colin Firth
Samira: Amina Annabi
Mathieu: Jim Carter
Pincheon: Donald Pleasence
Albertus: Ian Holm
The Seigneur: Nicol Williamson
Maria: Sophie Dix
Filette: Lysette Anthony
Magistrate: Michael Gough

Released: 1994
Origin: France and Great Britain
Production: David Thompson for Ciby 2000 and BBC Films, with the participation of British Screen Finance and the assistance of the European Co. Production Fund; released by Miramax Films
Direction: Leslie Megahey
Screenplay: Leslie Megahey
Cinematography: John Hooper
Editing: Isabelle Dedieu
Production design: Bruce Macadie
Sound: Daniel Brisseau
Costume design: Anna Buruma
Music: Alexandre Desplat
MPAA rating: R
Running time: 101 minutes

"Don't grow old and tired in a place like this."—*The Advocate*'s Pincheon

Aelita

This 1924 Soviet silent science-fiction film centers on an Earth inventor (Nikolai Tseretelli) who murders his wife in a fit of jealousy. He then takes off for Mars, where he meets the queen of the Martians, Aelita (Yulia Solntseva), who is intrigued by human behavior.

REVIEWS

The Nation. CCLIV, March 9, 1992, p.311.
Video Magazine. XVI, August 1992, p.45

CREDITS

Aelita: Yulia Solntseva
Soldier: Nikolai Batalov
Police informant: Igor Illinski
Inventor: Nikolai Tseretelli

No character identified: Vera Orlova
No character identified: Pavel Pol
No character identified: Konstantin Eggert
No character identified: Yuri Zavadski
No character identified: Valentina Kuindzi
No character identified: N. Tretyakova

Released: 1924
Origin: USSR
Direction: Jakov Protazanov
Screenplay: Fedor Ozep and Aleksey Fajko; based on the play by Alexei Tolstoy
Cinematography: Yuri Zheliabovsky and Emil Schoenemann
Art direction: Isaak Rabinovitch, Vikto Simov and Sergei Kozlovski
Costume design: Aleksandra Ekster
MPAA rating: no listing
Running time: 85 minutes

Africa the Serengeti

Set in the Serengeti of East Africa, this ambitious IMAX documentary centers on the annual migration of the wildebeest and their age-old fight for survival against the harsh forces of nature.

REVIEWS

Boston Globe. October 29, 1994, p.25.
Los Angeles Times. June 10, 1994, p.F10.

CREDITS

Narrator: James Earl Jones

Released: 1994
Production: Paul Novros and George Casey for Serengeti Partners, in collaboration with the Houston Museum of Natural Science
Direction: George Casey
Screenplay: George Casey and Mose Richards
Cinematography: Andrew Kitzanuk
Editing: Tim Huntley
Music: Hans Zimmer
MPAA rating: no listing
Running time: 40 minutes

Age Isn't Everything (Life in the Food Chain)

A Jewish business executive (Jonathan Silverman) suffers from a mysterious illness that causes him to age more rapidly than normal, in this satire set in the 1960's. He abruptly becomes an old man while keeping his youthful exterior. He looks the same, but walks slowly and talks with a thick Yiddish accent. A clumsy comedy with an inexplicable ending. Directorial debut of Douglas Katz.

CREDITS

Seymour: Jonathan Silverman
Max: Paul Sorvino
Rita: Rita Moreno
Grandpa Irving: Robert Prosky

Released: 1991
Production: Joan Fishman for Katzfilms
Direction: Douglas Katz
Screenplay: Douglas Katz
Cinematography: Mike Spillar
Editing: Dorian Harris
Casting: Deborah Brown
Music: Glen Roven
MPAA rating: no listing
Running time: 89 minutes

REVIEWS

Variety. CCCXLVIII, August 10, 1992, p.56.

Aileen Wuornos: The Selling of a Serial Killer

Centering on Aileen Wuornos, said to be America's first female serial killer, this documentary examines the media hype surrounding Wuornos' sensational case. Prostitute Wuornos admitted to the murder of seven men in Florida between 1989 and 1990, pleaded no contest, and was sentenced to death. Director Broomfield not only interviews Wuornos, but her lawyer, her lesbian lover who elicited her confession, and the woman who adopted Wuornos after her sentencing.

CREDITS

Aileen Wuornos: Aileen Wuornos
Tyria Moore: Tyria Moore
Arlene Pralle: Arlene Pralle
Steven Glazer: Steven Glazer

Released: 1994
Production: Rieta Oord; released by Strand Releasing
Direction: Nick Broomfield
Cinematography: Barry Ackroyd
Editing: Richard M. Lewis and Rick Vick
Music: David Bergeaud
MPAA rating: no listing
Running time: 101 minutes

REVIEWS

The Advocate. February 22, 1994, p.75.
Atlanta Journal and Atlanta Constitution. July 1, 1994, p.P6.
Boston Globe. May 6, 1994, p.86.
Chicago Tribune. March 25, 1994, p.7G.
Entertainment Weekly. March 24, 1995, p.75.
Los Angeles Times. March 31, 1994, p.F11.
Los Angeles Magazine. XXXIX, April 1994, p.107.
New York. XXVII, February 7, 1994, p.65.
The New York Times. February 4, 1994, p.C15.
Newsweek. CXXIII, March 7, 1994, p.66.
Playboy. XLI, April 1994, p.17.
Rolling Stone. March 10, 1994, p.60.

The Air Up There

"Jimmy Dolan went to Africa to recruit a new player. What he found was a whole new ball game." —Movie tagline

"Lots of fun!" —Jeffrey Lyons, *Sneak Previews, CNBC*

"Highly entertaining!" —*American Radio Network*

 Box Office Gross: $21,011,318 (February 1995)

This entrant into the derby of sports films about has-been coaches and ragtag teams received tepid reviews upon its initial release. And while it is true that *The Air Up There* is filled with by-the-numbers sequences, it is still engaging. Interesting locations, charming performances, and Paul M. Glaser's well-paced direction add up to a pleasant hour-and-a-half of untaxing entertainment.

CREDITS

Jimmy Dolan: Kevin Bacon
Saleh: Charles Gitonga Maina
Sister Susan: Yolanda Vasquez
Urudu: Winston Ntshona
Nyaga: Mabutho "Kid" Sithole
Ray Fox: Sean McCann
Father O'Hara: Dennis Patrick
Mifundo: Ilo Mutomobo
Halawi: Nigel Miguel

Released: 1994
Production: Ted Field, Rosalie Swedlin, and Robert W. Cort for Hollywood Pictures and Interscope Communications/PolyGram Filmed Entertainment, in association with Nomura Babcock and Brown and Longview Entertainment; released by Buena Vista Pictures
Direction: Paul M. Glaser
Screenplay: Max Apple
Cinematography: Dick Pope
Editing: Michael E. Polakow
Production design: Roger Hall
Art direction: Leigh Ridley: Hans van der Zanden
Set decoration: Karen Mary Brookes
Casting: Mali Finn: Donn Finn
Costume design: Hope Hanafin
Basketball technical adviser: Bob McAdoo
Music: David Newman
MPAA rating: PG
Running time: 106 minutes

Jimmy Dolan (Kevin Bacon) is the assistant coach of a basketball team at St. Joseph's college. His mentor and the head coach, Ray Fox (Sean McCann), ready to retire and announce his replacement, would like nothing better than to turn over the winning team to Jimmy, but Jimmy's inability to bring in good recruits, combined with an irresponsible nature, may lock him out of the head coach position.

Enter Saleh (Charles Gitonga Maina), a six-foot-ten-inch African player who Jimmy spots playing in the background of a videotape from the St. Joseph's mission among the Winabi tribe of Africa. Jimmy impulsively goes to Africa to bring Saleh to St. Joseph's, and (surprise) he learns something about himself during his journey. Jimmy has to jump through a number of hoops to convince Saleh's tribal chief father (Winston Ntshona) that it would be all right for Saleh to play basketball for "nuba" (the NBA).

Along the way, Jimmy saves the foundering Winabi village and undergoes the rigorous (and surprisingly bloody) ritual to become a Winabi. It is in this area of the plot that many critics correctly called foul, because it seems a bit too convenient, self-congratulatory, and even racist to think that the salvation of an entire African village rests in the hands of a self-absorbed, white, American basketball coach. The film is reminiscent of the amiable *Cool Runnings* (1993) in that its washed-up, Caucasian hero helps a group of black athletes and himself to triumph and self-discovery. (And both films were loosely based on true stories.) But this film, though filled with charming moments, is less successful in hiding the exploitation of the third-world characters by the first-world hero.

For example, in the final game sequence where the Winabi tribe is pitted against the Mingori townspeople's team, the celebration of western culture over African culture is a bit extreme. Cheerleaders with pom-poms, pennant flags, referee uniforms, and incessant "high-fiving" take the culture-clash idea too far. Moreover, the characters seem to overlook that Jimmy's arrival catalyzes much of the trouble for the Winabi, given that he came there to steal away the heir to the Winabi chieftain's throne, thereby raising the stakes in the Winabi's battle against the neighboring Mingori.

If one is willing to overlook the specious triumph of the stereotypical "ugly American," then there are elements to enjoy. Kevin Bacon turns in a fine performance as Jimmy, moving from shallow smoothie to thoughtful leader with believability and charm. His first scene, where he outfoxes an egotistical recruit with a dazzling basketball play, is one of his best. And Bacon's early shallowness serves his transformation well, so that when he quietly tells Saleh (at the film's climax) that Saleh's happiness is more important than recruiting him for St. Joseph's, it is quite affecting.

Maina is a comfortable screen presence as the affable Saleh, and the venerable African actor Winston Ntshona makes the most of his role as the skeptical chieftain. Yolanda Vasquez gets the film's best lines as the irate missionary who thinks Jimmy is a "sports pimp" who is "going a mile-a-minute to nowhere." And Sean McCann is wise and warm as Coach Fox.

Glaser's direction is excellent in the area of building tension, especially in the well-shot game sequence (aided by basketball adviser Bob McAdoo), and a sequence where Jimmy is chased by a warthog. Glaser uses a sweeping circular shot several times to great effect, particularly in Jimmy's arrival in the village of Winabi. Where one might find fault with Glaser is in his inability to play against the tackiness of much of Max Apple's script. In particular, Apple rests too heavily on scatological humor, and a few gags related to the "Winabi trots" are a few too many.

This film contains elements found in many films, from *Cool Runnings* to *The Mighty Ducks* (1992) to *Hoosiers* (1986), to *The Scout* (reviewed in this volume) and many more. It is admittedly a derivative and at times shallow film. But nowhere is it written that "derivative and shallow" means "not entertaining."

—*Kirby Tepper*

REVIEWS

Atlanta Constitution. January 7, 1994, p. P3.
Boston Globe. January 7, 1994, p. 71.
Chicago Tribune. January 7, 1994, p.7I.
Christian Science Monitor. January 11, 1994, p. 15.
Entertainment Weekly. January 21, 1994, p. 36.
Entertainment Weekly. June 10, 1994, p. 71.
The Hollywood Reporter. January 3, 1994, p. 12.
Los Angeles Times. January 7, 1994, p. F4.
The New York Times. January 7, 1994, p. B12.
The New York Times. June 10, 1994, p. D16.
People Weekly. XLI, January 10, 1994, p. 18.
Sports Illustrated. LXXX, January 10, 1994, p. 12.
USA Today. January 7, 1994, p. D8.
Variety. January 5, 1994, p. 12.
Variety. CCCLIII, January 10, 1994, p. 58.
The Washington Post. January 7, 1994, p. B1.
The Washington Post. January 7, 1994, p. WW34.

Airheads

"Fraser and Buscemi are deadpan delights. Sandler is red-hot." —*Rolling Stone*

"Few comedies have offered such escape and genuine laughs." —*The New York Post*

"You're about to be taken hostage by this year's maddest rock group." —*The Washington Post*

 Box Office Gross: $4,939,559 (August 21, 1994)

Since the time of the Baby Boomers, adolescents have grown up dreaming of being rock-and-roll stars. They have grasped the myth so firmly that thousands of teens have created hundreds of garage bands. Decades later, things have not changed. Teens still dream of being the next Elvis, John Lennon, Billy Idol, Van Halen, or Red Hot Chili Pepper. Motion pictures validate this notion. Just ask Bill and Ted whose "bogus" and "excellent" adventures revolved around the godship of guitar players. In *Airheads*, Chazz Darby (Brendan Fraser) and his friends Pip (Adam Sandler) and Rex (Steve Buscemi) together form the logically impossible Lone Rangers band—how they can be "lone" and still plural is questioned by disc jockey Ian the Shark (Joe Mantegna).

The Lone Rangers have played the usual small clubs and competed in battles of the bands only to watch as bands that they feel are worse than they have gone on to record contracts and fame—the elusive brass rings that are always just out of their reach. Chazz, the band's leader, has

 Screenwriter Rich Wilkes tried to sneak into Capitol Records while doing research for *Airheads* and was tackled and thrown out by security.

tried everything, including sneaking into Palatine Records, where he succeeds in talking with producer Jimmie Wing (Judd Nelson) only to find Wing cannot accept unsolicited demo tapes. On the brink of despair, Chazz, Pip, and Rex sneak into a radio station using plastic Uzi squirt guns filled with red pepper sauce and demand that their demo be played.

The radio station of choice is Rebel Rock's KPPX with its Hawaiian-shirted DJ Ian the Shark. Unfortunately, once they get their chance, the three are foiled by technology: The Lone Rangers have only brought a 1/4" reel-to-reel tape and the station no longer has a working playback machine. After the tape catches fire, their only hope is to find Chazz's hostile girlfriend, Kayla (Amy Locane), who has a cassette of the demo in her car.

Meanwhile, the police have surrounded the station, as well as have hundreds of rock 'n' roll fans who want to be a part of the action. Now the boys start making crazy demands—football helmets filled with cottage cheese and naked pictures of Bea Arthur—so that they will be able to plead insanity. They also make a not-so-crazy demand, how-

"When a band visited the set, one of the members pulled Steve [Buscemi] aside and said 'Hey man, how're you doing? You're the guy from Metallica, right?'"— *Airheads* director Michael Lehmann (*Premiere*, June 1994)

ever, a record contract. Seeing the incredible media exposure the band is basking in because of their caper, Jimmie Wing is now interested in signing them without hearing their music. Yet Chazz has integrity and demands that the band be heard. So a new demand follows. While Jimmie and sleazy station manager Milo (Michael McKean), who is acting as the boys' agent, argue over contract specifics, the Lone Rangers have their three minutes and thirty-one seconds of glory playing live before the crowd gathered outside the radio station.

Of course, the band is a hit. Their first video, called "Live in Prison," is made while they serve their few months sentence and will be followed by a tour when their album goes triple platinum and the boys are paroled. The rock-and-roll myth has once again been retold.

Although the film has promise, it does not deliver. It undertakes to comment on the desire for rock-and-roll fame and how the media can make heroes out of criminals, but then chickens out. What viewers want is more anarchy, more biting satire, more danger, more of an edge. They would probably settle simply for more humor. What they are given instead is a docile comedy that offers sincerity instead of spirit and characterizations instead of plot. Even that last element might have worked if the characters were better written and not such stiff symbols who are often hard to decipher. The viewer will wonder whether Chazz, Pip, and Rex are rock renegades or idiots, whether they are dangerous or merely stupid, and finally whether desperation for so shallow a goal justifies their actions.

First time scriptwriter Rich Wilkes owes much to films like *Dog Day Afternoon* (1975), *The King of Comedy* (1983), and the ultimate spoof of the rock-and-roll life, *This is Spinal Tap* (1984). Unlike these, however, Wilkes' script is too mild mannered and lacks force and intensity.

Director Michael Lehmann has shown in the past that he is capable of biting humor as he demonstrated in his debut film, *Heathers* (1989). That auspicious beginning was followed, however, by the likes of the blandly absurd *Meet the Applegates* (1991) and the disastrous *Hudson Hawk* (1991). *Airheads* does little to restore Lehmann's career.

The one thing that does carry this film is the appealing performances turned in by actors who had little to work with in the script. Probably the best is given by Joe Mantegna as the jaded, unflappable disc jockey Ian the Shark. Fraser's Chazz, however, is a bit too heartfelt, and when combined with Sandler's Pip, who is a bit too slow and insipidly sweet, they cancel out any suggestion of danger from Buscemi's Rex. Speaking of danger, Amy Locane's Kayla is a dead ringer for television's Christina Applegate, the dumb blond who stars on TV's *Married with Children*, but with a real mean streak.

CREDITS

Chazz: Brendan Fraser
Rex: Steve Buscemi
Pip: Adam Sandler
Ian: Joe Mantegna
Wilson: Chris Farley
Milo: Michael McKean
Kayla: Amy Locane
Jimmie Wing: Judd Nelson
O'Malley: Ernie Hudson
Suzzi: Nina Siemaszko
Marcus: Reginald E. Cathey
Carter: David Arquette
Doug Beech: Michael Richards
Chris Moore: Harold Ramis

Released: 1994
Production: Robert Simonds and Mark Burg for Island World; released by Twentieth Century-Fox
Direction: Michael Lehmann
Screenplay: Rich Wilkes
Cinematography: John Schwartzman
Editing: Stephen Semel
Production design: David Nichols
Art direction: Edward McAvoy
Set decoration: Jan Bergstrom: Jerie Kelter
Set design: Larry Hubbs: Robert Fechtman
Casting: Billy Hopkins: Suzanne Smith
Sound: Douglas Axtell: Russell C. Fager
Costume design: Bridget Kelly
Music: Carter Burwell
MPAA rating: PG-13
Running time: 91 minutes

Most of the rest of the cast has stereotyped characters with little to do. Michael McKean's station manager is typically sleazy, as is Nelson's opportunistic recording executive. Ernie Hudson's and Chris Farley's police officers are far too stupid to be funny or even threatening, and Michael Richards seems to be in the film just to provide his trademark physical comedy.

The film does boast several cameo performances: A call to the station from MTV's cartoon characters Beavis and Butt-Head, an appearance by MTV's Kurt Loder as himself, music provided by metal bands White Zombie and Galactic Cowboys, and Motorhead's Lemmy, who according to Pip is God, plays a rocker, as does China Kantner and radio's "Stuttering John" Melendez from *The Howard Stern Show*. In the end, however, even the cameos can not save *Airheads*. The film is too nice to be cut from irreverent cult cloth and yet too dumb and aimless to be mainstream material.

—*Beverley Bare Buehrer*

REVIEWS

Chicago Tribune. August 5, 1994, p. F7.
Entertainment Weekly. August 19, 1994, p. 42.
The Hollywood Reporter. August 1, 1994, p. 9.
Los Angeles Times. August 5, 1994, p. F8.
The New York Times. August 5, 1994, p. B12.
USA Today. August 5, 1994, p. 4D.
Variety. August 1, 1994, p. 15.
The Village Voice. August 9, 1994, p. 50.

Les Amants du Pont Neuf

Set in Paris, this drama centers on two homeless people, Alex (Denis Lavant) and Michele (Juliette Binoche), who meet and fall in love at the Pont Neuf, a bridge that has been closed for repairs and has become a haven for street people.

REVIEWS

New Statesman and Society. V, September 11, 1992, p. 34.

CREDITS

Michele: Juliette Binoche
Alex: Denis Lavant
Hans: Klaus-Michael Gruber

Origin: France
Released: 1992
Production: Christian Fechner; released by Films Christian Fechner-Films A2
Direction: Leos Carax
Screenplay: Leos Carax
Cinematography: Jean-Yves Escoffier
Editing: Nelly Quettier
Production design: Michael Vandestien
MPAA rating: no listing
Running time: 125 minutes

Amelia Lopes O'Neill

A young virgin, Amelia (Laura del Sol), is seduced by a doctor, Fernando (Franco Nero), with whom she becomes obsessed. While Fernando tries to convince Amelia that he does not love her, he falls in love with Amelia's invalid sister, Anna (Laura Benson).

CREDITS

Amelia: Laura del Sol
Fernando: Franco Nero
Anna: Laura Benson
Igor: Sergio Hernandez
Ginette: Valerie Mairesse
Lawyer: Jaime Vadell
Fernando's wife: Claudia di Girolamo
Journalist: Roberto Navarrete

Origin: Chile, Spain, Switzerland, and France
Released: 1991
Production: Patrick Sandrin for Arion Productions, Ariane Films, and Thelma Film AG
Direction: Valeria Sarmiento
Screenplay: Valeria Sarmiento and Raul Ruiz
Cinematography: Jean Penzer
Editing: Rodolfo Wedeles
Production design: Juan Carlos Castillo
Music: Jorge Arriagada
MPAA rating: no listing
Running time: 95 minutes

American Cyborg: Steel Warrior

"The Ultimate Science Fiction Battle of the New Year." —Movie tagline

"*The Terminator* meets *The Last of the Mohicans*." —*The Hollywood Reporter*

Box Office Gross: $369,648 (January 9, 1994)

Set in the future, seventeen years after a nuclear holocaust, this sci fi thriller centers on one of the last human survivors, Mary (Nicole Hansen), and her attempt to protect her unborn fetus from the evil cyborgs who have taken over. She is helped by handsome Austin (Joe Lara), who they later discover is really a cyborg himself. Most of the movie was shot in a deserted factory complex in Tel Aviv.

REVIEWS

Chicago Tribune. January 13, 1994, Sec. 5 p. 3.
Entertainment Weekly. April 29, 1994, p. 82.
Los Angeles Times. Jan 10, 1994, p. F4.
Variety. CCCLIII, January 17, 1994, p. 105.
The Washington Post. January 10, 1994, p. B2.

"They must have screwed up when they made me."—*American Cyborg*'s Austin

CREDITS

Austin: Joe Lara
Mary: Nicole Hansen
Cyborg: John Ryan
Akmir: Yoseph Shiloa
Leech: Uri Gavriel
Carp: Helen Lesnick
Arlene: Andrea Litt
Dr. Buckley: Jack Widerker

Released: 1994
Production: Mati Raz for Yoram Globus, Christopher Pearce, and Global Pictures; released by Cannon Pictures
Direction: Boaz Davidson
Screenplay: Brent Friedman, Bill Crounse, and Don Peqingnot; based on a story by Boaz Davidson and Christopher Pearce
Cinematography: Avi Karpick
Editing: Alain Jakubowicz
Production design: Kuly Sander
Casting: Nancy Lara-Hansch, Alecia C. Dixon and Shaul Dishy
Sound: Eli Yarkoni
Stunt coordination: Clay Boss
Music: Blake Leyh
MPAA rating: R
Running time: 94 minutes

...And God Spoke

"The World Was Created In Six Days. It Was Beautiful. But It Was Way Over Budget!" —Movie tagline

"A hilarious 'mockumentary' in the tradition of *This is Spinal Tap*." —Kevin Thomas, *Los Angeles Times*

"Playful, good-natured and often disarmingly funny." —Ralph Novak, *People*

Two B-filmmakers (Michael Riley and Stephen Rappaport) attempt to film a low-budget Biblical epic, in this mock documentary. Since they have no budget, they settle with Soupy Sales as Noah, Lou "The Incredible Hulk" Ferrigno as Cain, and Eve Plumb (Jan from *The Brady Bunch*) as Noah's wife. Directorial debut of Arthur Borman. The Borman brothers are better known in Michigan as kin to the Detroit-based Farmer Jack's grocery store chain clan.

REVIEWS

Atlanta Constitution. November 7, 1994, p. C10.
Boston Globe. January 13, 1995, p. 76.
Entertainment Weekly. January 20, 1995, p. 60.
Los Angeles Magazine. XXXIX, September 1994, p. 139.
Los Angeles Times. September 23, 1994, p. F15.
People Weekly. XLII, October 17, 1994, p. 22.

"We've got an eight-billion-person target audience!"—*...And God Spoke*'s Clive Walton and Marvin Handleman on the biblical epic they're planning

CREDITS

Clive Walton: Michael Riley
Marvin Handleman: Stephen Rappaport
Moses: Soupy Sales
Cain: Lou Ferrigno
Mrs. Noah: Eve Plumb
God: R. C. Bates
Claudia: Anna B. Choi
Abel: Andy Dick
Noah: Fred Kaz
Chip Greenfield: Daniel Tisman

Released: 1994
Production: Mark Borman and Richard Raddon for Brookwood Entertainment; released by Life Entertainment
Direction: Arthur Borman
Screenplay: Gregory S. Malins and Michael Curtis; based on a story by Arthur Borman and Mark Borman
Cinematography: Lee Daniel
Editing: Wendey Stanzler
Production design: Joseph B. Tintfass
Art direction: Jamie Foley
Casting: Maryclaire Sweeters
Costume design: Zelda Hacker
Music: John Massari
MPAA rating: R
Running time: 80 minutes

And Life Goes On (Zebdegi Edame Darad)

In this fictionalized documentary, a filmmaker (Farhad Kheradmand) and his young son (Pooya Pievar) travel to earthquake-ravaged northern Iran in 1990, seeking to discover the fate of several actors living in the area and interviewing passersby on the way.

REVIEWS

Film Comment. XXVIII, Nov-Dec 1992, p. 70.

CREDITS

Father: Farhad Kheradmand
Son: Pooya Pievar

Origin: Iran
Released: 1992
Production: Ali-Reza Zarrin for the Iranian Institute for Intellectual Development of Children and Youth
Direction: Abbas Kiarostami
Screenplay: Abbas Kiarostami
Cinematography: Homayun Piever
Editing: Changiz Sayyad and Abbas Kiarostami
MPAA rating: no listing
Running time: 91 minutes

Andre

"The greatest adventure is finding your way home." —Movie tagline

"A 'must-see' film for all ages." —Bonnie Churchill, *National News Syndicate*

"A worthy successor to *Free Willy*." —Kevin Thomas, *Los Angeles Times*

"An excellent film for everyone. Go see it!" —Gary Franklin, *KCOP-TV*

"This is what family entertainment is all about." —Diane Garrett, *L.A. Parent Magazine*

Box Office Gross: $16,789,544 (December 4, 1994)

Paramount Pictures' summer release *Andre* is first a family film and, second, a "based on a true-life" story. Many viewers and reviewers found it irresistible and considered it a reworking of the previous season's *Free Willy* (1993), without the propaganda and the contrivance. Certainly, those particular elements do define the differences between the two films; it simply depends which side of the fence a viewer falls on as to which type is preferable.

While 1993's *Free Willy* was "inspired" by a real marine mammal and a particular interest group's perspective on its plight, the filmmakers chose to follow established dramatic rules to bring the action toward it's Hollywood-style climactic conclusion. Andre is much more a "slice of life" nar-

rative, episodic and halting in its plot line. It does have very clearly drawn, believable characters and what little action there is evolves realistically out of the small-town setting and dynamics.

An orphaned baby seal is rescued by a lackadaisical harbor master, Harry Whitney (Keith Carradine), who has a gift for communicating with animals but not his two older children. His youngest daughter, Toni (Tina Majorino), shares Harry's comfort with creatures. She is less at ease among her own peers and develops a deep bond with Andre,

Tina Majorino as Toni Whitney, a little girl adopted by a seal in the true story, *Andre*. © 1994 Paramount Pictures. All rights reserved.

as the seal comes to be called. As Harry begins to pay more and more attention to Andre, his wife (Chelsea Field) and the rest of the townsfolk begin to lose their patience, and the family is reported for keeping a wild animal captive. Before Andre can be removed, he proves his loyalty to the family, and ultimately, Harry is able to turn his fascination with animals into a career in itself.

The successes of the *Andre* production all stem from the nicely shaded nuance of the world created in the film, where good character's have shortcomings and the antagonists are not all stereotypical movie villains. This is in fact where most children's pictures (including *Free Willy*) break down, with their one-dimensional villains. The world of *Andre* is a romantic and nostalgic one, told with the standard romantic screen device: voice-over narration. Set in the 1960's, where most dramas still played within smaller dimensions, there is a certain amount of validity to this approach.

Andre was shot on location in Vancouver, rather than in Maine, where the story takes place. A Pacific sea lion was the stand-in for the harbor seal.

"We relate to animals in a very special way because they are so honest. They simply are who they are. And sometimes their devotion can be quite remarkable."—actor Keith Carradine on *Andre*

While *Andre*'s characters seem quite real, no one really changes as a result of the escalating sequence of events. There is no true character development, in the sense that someone is tested and has to act in a new way to bring about what they want or need. Things fall into place, coming from external sources, like Harry's new job. While his lackadaisical nature is responsible for most of the conflict that exists, there is never any clear sense of his understanding of it. The inevitable scene, in which the child is put in jeopardy, is one of the few sequences that actually engages the viewer in some sort of cause-and-effect relationship of events and is almost a relief despite its rather sudden eruption.

Cute and truthful as the little individual moments are, *Andre* fails by being illustrative instead of dramatic. While it gets good marks for suggesting the disruption that a hammy, exotic stranger can cause to an already tenuous interfamily relationship, there is no follow through. The overall result in this translation of a charming anecdotal book into a feature film is awkward. It seems as forced into that structure as the voice-over narration is tacked onto the opening shot.

Andre deserves credit for showing the disruptive realities that such an odd addition to a town and a family makes but it sticks to *real life* to the point of failing to explore these issues. While this film loosely shows the merit in choosing to study natures creatures rather than hold to the man view of them as the enemy, competition, or convenient scapegoat, this sort of lesson is one that society has moved a few degree's past.

Reviewers, for the most part, embraced this film as delightful family entertainment—more so than *Free Willy*. For the attention span of very young children, *Andre* is a conscientiously safe bet. For those older folks longing for a romantic glow to validate the simplicity of their memories, it offers some pleasant escapism. For those in-between these ages, however, expectations should remain "realistic."

—*Mary E. Belles*

CREDITS

Harry Whitney: Keith Carradine
Toni Whitney: Tina Majorino
Thalice Whitney: Chelsea Field
Paula Whitney: Aidan Pendleton
Steve Whitney: Shane Meier
Billy Baker: Keith Szarabajka
Mark Baker: Joshua Jackson
Andre the Seal: Tory the Sea Lion

Released: 1994
Production: Annette Handley and Adam Shapiro for Kushner-Locke; released by Paramount Pictures
Direction: George Miller
Screenplay: Dana Baratta; based on the novel *A Seal Called Andre*, by Harry Goodridge and Lew Dietz
Cinematography: Thomas Burstyn
Editing: Harry Hitner and Patrick Kennedy
Production design: William Elliott
Art direction: Sheila Haley
Set decoration: Barry Kemp
Casting: Annette Benson: Lindsay Walker
Sound: Michael McGee
Costume design: Maya Mani
Animal coordination: Bruce McMillan
Stunt coordination: Danny Virtue
Music: Spencer Proffer
Score: Bruce Rowland
MPAA rating: PG
Running time: 94 minutes

REVIEWS

Daily Variety. August 12, 1994, p. 8.
The Hollywood Reporter. August 12-14, 1994, p. 10.
Los Angeles Times. CC, August 17, 1994, p. F1.
The New York Times. CXLIII, August 17, 1994, p. B1.
San Francisco Chronicle. CLXXXIII, August 17, 1994, p. F1.
The Washington Post. August 17, 1994, p. B1.

Angels in the Outfield

"God's favorite game." —Movie tagline
"Enormously entertaining." —*New York Post*
"A flat-out wonderful movie." —Gene Shalit, *The Today Show*

 Box Office Gross: $50,226,141 (November 13, 1994)

In 1993, the Disney studios released *Homeward Bound: The Incredible Journey*, a remake of an earlier Disney film about two dogs and a cat traipsing across the wilderness in search of their masters. Although both versions told basically the same story, the way in which each approached the

CREDITS

George Knox: Danny Glover
Mel Clark: Tony Danza
Maggie Nelson: Brenda Fricker
Al the Angel: Christopher Lloyd
Hank Murphy: Ben Johnson
Ranch Wilder: Jay O. Sanders
Roger: Joseph Gordon-Levitt
J. P.: Milton Davis, Jr.
David Montagne: Taylor Negron
Roger's father: Dermot Mulroney

Released: 1994
Production: Irby Smith, Joe Roth, and Roger Birnbaum for Walt Disney Pictures, in association with Caravan Pictures; released by Buena Vista Pictures
Direction: William Dear
Screenplay: Dorothy Kingsley, George Wells, and Holly Goldberg Sloan; based on the motion picture *Angels in the Outfield* (1951)
Cinematography: Matthew F. Leonetti
Editing: Bruce Green
Production design: Dennis Washington
Art direction: Thomas T. Targownik
Set decoration: John Anderson
Production management: Richard H. Prince
Casting: Pam Dixon Mickelson
Visual effects supervision: Giedra Rackauskas
Sound: Willie Burton
Costume design: Rosanna Norton
Music: Randy Edelman
MPAA rating: PG
Running time: 103 minutes

subject was radically different. The original—released in 1963—was closer in spirit to the Disney studios' nature films produced during the 1950's and 1960's. It was even narrated by Rex Allen, who supplied the narration to dozens of Disney nature documentaries. The remake, on the other hand, was more in the comical spirit of the *Look Who's Talking* series (1989, 1990, 1993). *Homeward Bound* featured well-known celebrities who supplied wise-cracking dialogue for the animal stars. The original version enjoyed a modest commercial success, while the remake went on to become one of the studio's surprise hits of the year.

Encouraged by the success of *Homeward Bound*, Walt Disney Pictures took a similar approach to *Angels in the Outfield*. Based on a 1951 fantasy sports film, it combines elements from the older version with such later successful baseball films as *Major League* (1989), *A League of Their Own* (1992), and *Rookie of the Year* (1993). It also takes advantage of the country's fascination with angels in the early 1990's. This time, however, the attempt to update a modestly successful cinematic gem from an earlier era with trendy elements from the 1990's results in a film that has no unique spirit of its own.

The story is told from the point of view of eleven-year-old Roger (Joseph Gordon-Levitt), who lives in a temporary foster home with his caretaker, Maggie Nelson (Brenda Fricker), and two other children. Roger's best friend is J. P. (Milton Davis, Jr.), one of the other boys with whom he lives. The two share a common love for baseball, their favorite team being the California Angels, despite the fact that the team has had a losing streak for quite some time and is in last place.

When Roger's irresponsible father (Dermot Mulroney) pays him a rare visit, Roger is excited, hoping that maybe this time his father will make an effort to heal the rift that tore the family apart following the sudden death of his mother. Roger learns, however, that his father has only come to say that he is moving out of state to look for a job and will not be able to visit him again for some time. Roger, obviously crushed, asks his father, "When can we be a family again?" His father answers sarcastically, "When the Angels win the pennant." Shortly after his father leaves, Roger begins praying for such a miracle to occur.

On an outing with several other orphans, Roger and J. P. attend an Angels game, cringing along with the others in attendance as the team stumbles around the field. When a rival batter hits the ball deep into the outfield, however, Roger watches stunned as an angel—complete with wings, white gown, and halo-swoops down and lifts the fielder in time for him to catch the ball. Later, when the Angels are up to bat, Roger sees another angel guide the swing of the batter, resulting in a shattered bat and a home run. After this miracle occurs, an angel appears to Roger and introduces himself as Al (Christopher Lloyd). Al tells Roger that he and his angel helpers have come to answer Roger's prayer. Roger is ecstatic and tells J.P. that his prayers have been answered. J.P., however, is confused since the angels only appear to Roger.

"Keep your nose clean and your heart open. The angels are on, sonny."—Al the Angel, *Angels in the Outfield*

After the game, which the Angels win, Roger wins a chance to have his picture taken with the team's belligerent manager, George Knox (Danny Glover). During the photo session, Roger tells Knox about the angels. Quite naturally, Knox thinks the boy is crazy. Yet after Knox reviews a videotape of the game, watching the outfielder soar into the sky to catch the ball, he decides to ask Roger for more details. Knox visits Roger on the pretext of delivering the photos. Because he is so desperate for his team to win, Knox asks Roger to attend another baseball game as his personal guest, believing the boy might bring the team good luck.

The result is another visit from the angels and another win for the team. After that, Roger becomes the team's unofficial mascot, attending every home game, eventually providing Knox with advice on which players to use according to the angels he sees hovering around key teammates. At first, Knox is reluctant to accept Roger's advice, especially when Roger keeps suggesting players who have performed terribly in the past. When Roger's suggestions result in spectacular performances by these players, however, Knox begins to pay closer attention, eventually coming to believe in angels himself.

With his team on a winning streak at last, the usually aggressive, loudmouthed Knox becomes a much more diplomatic and supportive manager. He also begins to make more of an interest in Roger and J. P., visiting them at Maggie's, taking them to special events, even volunteering to coach their sandlot baseball team.

Angels in the Outfield was filmed at Oakland Coliseum, home to the Oakland A's. Anaheim Stadium, where the California Angels actually play, was unavailable because of the Los Angeles Rams football season. The film's technical advisor, retired Oakland A's all-star third baseman Carney Lansford, spent two weeks teaching the cast to be believable baseball players.

During a crucial game, a sports announcer with a grudge against Knox, Ranch Wilder (Jay O. Sanders), overhears Knox and J. P. talking about angels. When he leaks the story to the press, Knox is ordered by the team's owner (Ben Johnson) to make a formal announcement denouncing his belief in angels. During the press conference, Knox instead makes a passionate speech in favor of believing in spiritual helpers, saying, "Why is it okay to believe in God, but not in angels? I thought they were on the same team." Knox inspires his teammates, the team owner, and the fans as well.

During the final game for the league pennant, Al the head angel tells Roger that the team must win without any supernatural assistance. With everyone believing the power of divine intervention, the Angels go on to win the pennant. In the end, the radically transformed Knox adopts Roger and J. P., while the angels fly off and play a celestial ball game among the stars.

There have been numerous baseball fantasy films in the past, such as *It Happens Every Spring* (1949), in which a scientist becomes a winning pitcher after he invents a substance that causes baseballs to avoid wooden bats; *Damn Yankees* (1958), in which the devil answers a baseball fan's wish for a winning team; and *Field of Dreams* (1989), in which a farmer is visited by famous deceased ballplayers after a celestial voice convinces him to turn his cornfield into a baseball diamond. All these films boast far-fetched premises. Yet, because the fantastical elements are so well integrated into the story lines of each, and supported by boldly distinctive characters, these films had a logical believability about them and were all critical and commercial successes.

With *Angels in the Outfield*, however, the supernatural elements are used primarily as an excuse for the filmmakers to indulge in flashy special effects. Although there is much talk throughout the film about the need to believe in the supernatural, all of it is superficial and unconvincing since it is delivered by shallow, poorly conceived characters. In other words, the film fails because it puts forth a premise that it tries to exploit rather than develop with any real conviction.

The film's failure is even more dramatic when compared with the original version. In the original, the story is told from the point of view of the manager, played to perfection by Paul Douglas. Douglas is far more convincing than Glover as a cynical, loudmouthed manager, namely because his character is shown to be much more unrepentantly nasty at first. Glover is not given the chance to project a cynical demeanor before he is called upon to transform into an angelic foster dad.

Also in the original, it is the manager who develops a friendly relationship with the angels, all of whom remain invisible to him and to the audience as well. As in *Field of Dreams*, the angels in the original version are all former baseball players. Therefore, the relationship that develops between the head angel and the manager is a playfully antagonistic one infused with great depth and intimacy. In the remake, the head angel and his celestial companions act more like life-size Tinker Bells zooming mischievously about with much flash but with only a superficial empathy for the characters they are influencing.

The remake's primary flaw is that, even when it is dealing with characters who act harsh and unsympathetic, it attempts to maintain an artificially upbeat tone. The result is characters whose actions lack any emotional conviction. A good example of this is the character of the team owner played by Ben Johnson. In the beginning, he is depicted as a good-natured country-boy type, an obvious caricature of country-western star Gene Autry, the original owner of the California Angels. Near the end of the film, the team owner suddenly turns nasty and threatens to fire manager Knox if he does not stop talking about angels. Yet moments after Knox gives his speech to the press praising the power of belief, the team owner suddenly turns into an impassioned supporter and is first to condemn those who do not believe in divine intervention. The effect of all this flip-flopping of

attitudes is that ultimately the audience fails to believe in any of the characters, much less in angels.

Although the film is obviously attempting to exploit the fascination with angels evidenced in the early 1990's, it remains an essentially harmless, lighthearted children's entertainment. Because it preaches rather than involves, however, its worth as a children's film is diminished. For, as every child knows, with the right amount of emotional conviction, a person is capable of believing in anything.

—*Jim Kline*

REVIEWS

The Hollywood Reporter. July 11, 1994, p. 6.
Los Angeles Times. July 15, 1994, p. F7.
The New York Times. July 15, 1994, p. B2.
Variety. July 11, 1994, p. 10.

Angie

"A heartwarming, heartbreaking, fabulous film."
—Pam Thompson, *KABC-TV*
"Geena Davis is wonderfully funny." —*Toronto Star*
"Geena Davis gives a sexy, scrappy performance."
—*Rolling Stone*

 Box Office Gross: $9,153,575 (April 3, 1994)

Rare is the comedy that can evoke tears without being preachy or overly sentimental. *Terms of Endearment* (1983) and *Tootsie* (1982), for example, examined family relationships and women's issues, respectively; the fact that the films were funny made the tears even more poignant. Although *Angie* is not in the same league with these two classic films; it too depicts self-discovery with great humor and humanity. *Angie* is an amusing and warm film that has received well-deserved critical acceptance. It has style, wit, pathos, and wonderful performances.

Angie Scacciapensieri (Geena Davis) is an independent and upbeat young woman from Bensonhurst, Brooklyn's Italian neighborhood. She is best described later in the film by

 "You're carrying around some foreign guy's number, you're pregnant, you're not married...you're going to end up on Oprah."—Tina to Angie, from *Angie*

another character: "I've never met a woman like you....I've met Teamsters like you, but...." She is funny, loving, and tough-talking, and in great film tradition, she wants more out of her life. She has a nice boyfriend, Vinnie (James Gandolfini), a neighborhood plumber whose big ambition is to expand his business and buy a house; a terrific best friend, Tina (Aïda Turturro); and a caring father (Philip Bosco), who lives nearby with his neurotic wife, Kathy (Jenny O'Hara).

For years, Angie has wondered why her mother ran off and left her (and her father) when she was very young. Davis is quite adept at showing a young woman with a tough exterior, who hides her confusion and pain resulting from this early traumatic experience. Brief flashbacks point up how important the memory of her mother is to Angie. Little Angie, crying, is held by her lovely young mother for a brief moment; that memory, combined with the memory of her mother dancing in the snow (danced by ballerina Susan Jaffe), is virtually all she has to connect her to that part of her childhood. Her mother was replaced by her father's second wife, Kathy, an Irish-American who has tried desperately for many years to befriend Angie, to no avail. Kathy's attempts to learn how to cook Italian food and her well-intentioned but frightening concoctions are hilarious. One example is "little pizzas" made with English muffins and ketchup.

Once all the characters are established, it is revealed that Angie is pregnant. Her pregnancy proves to be a revelation: Angie realizes that she does not want to be stuck in the same dysfunctional life as her friend Tina, who is married to a crude and cruel man (Michael Rispoli), merely doing what is expected of her. Longing for more, Angie goes uptown to a museum, where she meets an offbeat Irishman named Noel (Stephen Rea), a relationship that will help her change her life. She gives birth to her baby and goes on an odyssey of self-discovery, leading to a new understanding of her mother and of herself.

Todd Graff's script is amusingly on target. The characters are straight out of Brooklyn, as are some of the actors, and their comic repartee hits home. Tina tells Angie, "You're carrying around some foreign guy's number, you're pregnant, you're not married...you're going to end up on Oprah." Not only does she emphasize that Angie is in trouble but she also foreshadows the drama ahead. In another example, Noel, after he and Angie meet at the Metropolitan Museum of Art, tries to impress her by pro-

Madonna was first cast as Angie, but was bounced when the filming of *Dangerous Game* conflicted.

voking a fight with one of the guards, telling him, "The guards at the Whitney could kick your ass."

Graff shows a highly developed sensibility to two important themes of this film: Women's issues and Brooklyn. He has elaborated on these subjects before, in *Used People* (1992), which attracted three of the most prominent actresses of the day: Kathy Bates, Jessica Tandy, and Shirley MacLaine. *Angie*, however, is far more successful. Where *Used People* appeared merely to "cover the bases" to show it had its heart in the right place, *Angie* is simpler and truer. Perhaps it is because it is adapted from the book by Avra Wing, *Angie, I Says*. Where *Used People* seemed to idle as its characters complained about their lives and about one another, *Angie* moves forward as the characters' personalities cause them to take actions that further the plot.

For example, blue-collar Vinnie is baffled by Angie's reaction to his telling her that he bought a house without consulting her. A wonderful scene ensues in which Angie tells him she can not marry him. In other words, his actions precipitate more than just dialogue. Angie takes action that drives the plot forward. It is, incidentally, a wonderfully played scene. Gandolfini is superb in that he never crosses the line into stereotype, yet he remains an identifiable archetype of Italian-American Brooklyn. Angie clearly cares for him, and her halting speech and inability to look him in the eye is heartbreaking.

In another example, after the birth of Angie's baby, Angie moves in with her father and stepmother. Kathy, having told her that a baby is "a miracle from God," desperately wants to be a part of Angie and the baby's life. Angie, meanwhile, is having a hard time bonding with her child. Upon waking up and hearing the baby cry in the middle of the night, Angie goes into the baby's room and finds Kathy offering her breast to the baby. This unexpected and profound scene sends Angie on a search for her real mother.

Geena Davis, as usual, is superb. Her accent sounds flawless. Her leggy, off-center beauty is intact. So is her ability to make an audience laugh and cry. She is hilarious when she is in the gynecologist's office, as she tries to make conversation with the extremely short doctor by saying, "I think it's great that you don't have to stoop down or nothin'." Her first voice-over, in heavy Brooklyn accent, tells it all, describing herself as a child: "I was eleven. I looked like a forty-year-old with a drinking problem." As Angie, Davis is called upon to be funny, tender, quirky, pregnant, waif-like, womanly, serene, uneducated yet intelligent, and angry. All of this she does with her perfect Brooklyn accent. She is reminiscent of the actresses of the 1940's, such as Jean Arthur or Katharine Hepburn, who were able to be funny and heartbreaking at the same time. Davis is a rarity: a beautiful character actress.

CREDITS

Angie Scacciapensieri: Geena Davis
Noel Riordan: Stephen Rea
Vinnie: James Gandolfini
Tina: Aïda Turturro
Frank: Philip Bosco
Kathy: Jenny O'Hara
Jerry: Michael Rispoli
Joanne: Betty Miller

Released: 1994
Production: Larry Brezner and Patrick McCormick for Hollywood Pictures, in association with Caravan Pictures; released by Buena Vista Pictures
Direction: Martha Coolidge
Screenplay: Todd Graff; based on the novel *Angie, I Says*, by Avra Wing
Cinematography: Johnny E. Jensen
Editing: Steven Cohen
Production design: Mel Bourne
Art direction: Gae S. Buckley
Set decoration: Etta Leff and Leslie Bloom
Casting: Juliet Taylor
Sound: Ed Novick
Sound design: Leslie Shatz
Costume design: Jane Robinson
Music: Jerry Goldsmith
MPAA rating: R
Running time: 107 minutes

Mention must be made of the many fine contributors to this film: the strong hand of director Martha Coolidge, the dizzy and painful performance of Jenny O'Hara, the offbeat Stephen Rea, and the absolutely believable and lovable Aïda Turturro as best friend Tina.

The spirit of this film is best captured in its rambunctious and hilarious birth scene, superbly directed by Coolidge. So much is going on that it is hard to follow all the action. The scene appears spontaneous, but it is so intricate that it must have been rehearsed, giving it the momentum and theatricality of a stage play. In order to calm her down, the nurses get Angie to sing the song "One," from *A Chorus Line.* Coolidge received special dispensation to change the lyrics for this scene: Angie, in the throes of labor, angrily sings, "One, singular sensation, every [expletive] move she makes...." This scene is the entire film in microcosm: a mixture of humanity and profundity ushered in with true wit.

—*Kirby Tepper*

REVIEWS

Entertainment Weekly. March 11, 1994, p. 38.
The Hollywood Reporter. February 28, 1994, p. 73.
Los Angeles Times. March 4, 1994, p. F1.
The New York Times. March 4, 1994, p. B1.
Variety. February 28, 1994, p. 7.

Anima Mundi

This nature documentary features a series of close-ups of animal life, underscored by music by Philip Glass, glorifying the beauty of nature.

REVIEWS

Booklist. XC, January 1, 1994, p. 838.
The New York Times. May 7, 1993, p. C12.
The Washington Post. April 17, 1993, p. C2.
The Washington Post. April 16, 1993, p. WW40.

CREDITS

Released: 1993
Production: Lawrence Taub; released by Tara Releasing
Direction: Godfrey Reggio
Cinematography: Graham Berry
Editing: Miroslav Janek
Music: Philip Glass
MPAA rating: no listing
Running time: 28 minutes

Anna Karamazova

This avant-garde drama set in the Soviet Union centers on a woman released in the 1940's from a Stalinist labor camp and the difficulties she experiences trying to fit into the new Soviet society. Directorial debut of Rustam Khamdamov.

CREDITS

Woman: Jeanne Moreau
Natasha: Natasha Eble
Young man: Victor Sibilyov
Silent film star: Elena Solovei
Rich man: Yuri Solomine
His wife: Natalia Fateeva

No character identified: Olya Nosova

Origin: France and USSR
Released: 1991
Production: Serge Silberman for Mosfilm/Victoria Film Productions/Parimedia- Mosmedia
Direction: Rustam Khamdamov
Screenplay: Rustam Khamdamov
Cinematography: Yuri Klimenko
Editing: Irina Brozkovskaya
Production design: Vladimir Murzine
Production management: Gennadi Kovalenko
Music: Alexander Vustin
MPAA rating: no listing
Running time: 113 minutes

Apex

"Trapped in a future they didn't create. Fighting an enemy they cannot stop." —Movie tagline
"A cut above most time-travel cyborg thrillers." —*Seattle Times*

When a scientist (Richard Keats) time travels from 2073 to 1973 to retrieve a faulty robot probe called A.P.E.X. (Advanced Prototype Extermination Unit), he inadvertently spreads a virus that alters the future. When he returns to his own time, he finds the world at war with an army of robots that were created to fight the virus and instead have gone on a killing rampage. Though the budget is limited, the special effects are still impressive.

CREDITS

Nicholas Sinclair: Richard Keats
Shepherd: Mitchell Cox
Natasha Sinclair: Lisa Ann Russell
Taylor: Marcus Aurelius
Rashad: Adam Lawson
Dr. Elgin: David Jean Thomas
Desert Rat: Brian Richard Peck
Mishima: Anna B. Choi
Johnson: Kristin Norton
Rebel: Kristin Norton
Gunney: Jay Irwin

1973 Father: Robert Tossberg
1973 Mother: Kathy Lambert
Joey: Kareem H. Captan

Released: 1994
Production: Talaat Captan for Green Communications, Inc.; released by Republic Pictures
Direction: Phillip J. Roth
Screenplay: Phillip J. Roth and Ronald Schmidt; based on a story by Roth and Gian Carlo Scandiuzzi
Cinematography: Mark W. Gray
Editing: Daniel Lawrence
Casting: Elizabeth Weintraub
Special visual effects: Ultra Matrix
Sound: Bill Reinhardt
Robot suits and special makeup effects: Altered Anatomy FX
Music: Jim Goodwin
MPAA rating: R
Running time: 103 minutes

"Time is a strange thing. No matter what happens, no matter what you do, things change, and they can never be quite the same."— Nicholas Sinclair, *Apex*

Archangel

This low-budget black-and-white comedy-drama, set in a Russian village during World War I, focuses on three people who form a quirky romantic triangle: Canadian lieutenant John Boles (Kyle McCulloch), Russian nurse Veronkha (Kathy Marykuca), and Belgian aviator Philbin (Ari Cohen).

Origin: Canada
Released: 1991
Production: Greg Klymkiw; released by Zeitgeist Films Ltd.
Direction: Guy Maddin
Screenplay: Guy Maddin and George Toles
Cinematography: Guy Maddin
Editing: Guy Maddin
Production design: Jeff Solylo and Guy Maddin
MPAA rating: no listing
Running time: 90 minutes

CREDITS

Lieutenant John Boles: Kyle McCulloch
Veronkha: Kathy Marykuca
Philbin: Ari Cohen
Danchuk: Sarah Neville
Jannings: Michael Gottli
Geza: David Falkenberg

Art Deco Detective

In this satire of *noir* detective thrillers, an aging Los Angeles detective, Art Decowitz (John Dennis Johnston), gets caught up in international espionage and terrorism.

Released: 1994
Production: Philippe Mora and Bruce Critchley for Experimental Pictures; released by Trident Releasing, Inc.
Direction: Philippe Mora
Screenplay: Philippe Mora
Cinematography: Walter Bal
Editing: Janet Wilcox-Morton
Production design: Pamela Krause Mora
Sound: Kermit Samples
Costume design: Sarah Hackett
Music: Allan Zavod
MPAA rating: no listing
Running time: 102 minutes

REVIEWS

Variety. CCCLVI, September 19, 1994, p. 77.

CREDITS

Arthur Decowitz: John Dennis Johnston
Hyena: Stephen McHattie
Jim Wexler: Brion James
Detective Guy Lean: Joe Santos
Julie Hudson: Rena Riffel
Meg Hudson: Rena Riffel
Irina Bordat: Sonia Cole
Lana Torrido: Max John-James
Peter Wood: Mel Smith

Atlantis

Shot entirely underwater, this wordless documentary captures some spectacular and rare fish. The beautiful cinematography is complemented by Eric Serra's symphonic score.

REVIEWS

Atlanta Constitution. July 22, 1994, p. P7
Atlanta Constitution. September 9, 1994, p. P7.
Chicago Tribune. November 4, 1994, p. 7K.
The Washington Post. May 20, 1994, p. C7.
The Washington Post. May 20, 1994, p. WW53.

CREDITS

Origin: France
Released: 1993
Production: Claude Besson for Les Films du Loup, Gaumont, Cecchi Gori Group, and Tiger CA; released by Milestone Films
Direction: Luc Besson
Cinematography: Christian Petron
Music: Eric Serra
MPAA rating: no listing
Running time: 75 minutes

Aventure Malgache (Madagascar Landing)

This French-language dramatic short film directed by Alfred Hitchcock for the British Ministry of Information during World War II stars the Moliere Players, a French acting troupe, and centers on a French Resistance agent who is betrayed and condemned to five years of hard labor. In French with English subtitles. Also known as *Alfred Hitchcock's Bon Voyage & Aventure Malagache*.

REVIEWS

Atlanta Constitution. December 3, 1993, p. P6.
Los Angeles Times. April 26, 1994, p. F1.
The Washington Post. July 23, 1993, p. C7.
The Washington Post. July 23, 1993, p. WW46.

CREDITS

Origin: France and Great Britain
Released: 1944
Production: British Ministry of Information; released by Milestone Films
Direction: Alfred Hitchcock
Cinematography: Gunther Krampf
Art direction: Charles Gilbert
MPAA rating: no listing
Running time: 31 minutes

Baby's Day Out

"The kids will love it." —*People Weekly*

"...blissfully funny..." —*The Philadelphia Inquirer*

"an absolutely perfect child's-eye view of the fantasies that they might have." —Gene Siskel, *Siskel & Ebert*

"Hilarious, adorable summer fun! A genuine joy!" —Barry ZeVan, *Channel America*

 Box Office: $16,562,572 (September 25, 1994)

This family comedy by producer/screenwriter John Hughes centers on a precocious nine-month-old baby who is kidnapped from his wealthy parents by a trio of inept crooks. As the film opens, the audience is introduced to cute little Baby Bink (Adam Robert Worton and Jacob Joseph Worton), whose favorite book tells of another baby, Boo, who goes on wonderful adventures in the city. Boo travels by bus and taxi to a department store, the park, the zoo, and even a construction site with his mother. It is a simple story told in primary colors and a Dick-and-Jane text, which Baby Bink wants his loving nanny, Gilbertine (Cynthia Nixon), to read to him over and over and over again.

Bink has a nanny because his parents, Laraine (Lara Flynn Boyle) and Bennington (Matthew Glave) Cotwell, are very wealthy. Unfortunately, they are caught up in their social positions and lineage to the point where the most important goal in Laraine's life is to have her baby's photo in the newspaper's society pages. Laraine gets her wish—but not exactly as she wanted: The photographers she hires kidnap Bink and hold him for $5 million ransom. She now finds her son's photo in the paper, but on the front page as news.

While police and FBI agents search and the Cotwells fret, Bink finds himself in the hands of three desperate criminals: ringleader Eddie (Joe Mantegna) and his henchmen Norby (Joe Pantoliano) and Veeko (Brian Haley). Luckily for Bink, this trio is not very adept at their task. When Norby puts Bink down for a nap, it is Norby who falls asleep. Bink, who can crawl, follows a pigeon out onto the building's roof, kicking off a comic chain of events. When the kidnappers realize what has happened, they chase after Bink, going from one adventure to another.

The film was shot on location in and around Chicago, and features such landmarks as the original Marshall Fields Department Store, the vacant Ovaltine Factory in Villa Park, the Lincoln Park Zoo and Grant Park in downtown Chicago. One entire month of shooting took place at Jones Armory where a construction site was erected for a stunt. It was one of the biggest sets ever built. The technological team developed eleven mechanical dolls as stand-ins for the twins.

For Bink, these adventures perfectly echo Baby Boo's adventures in his favorite book. He sees a big, blue bus like the one Boo rides in and Bink does the same. Bink sees a department store like the one in his book, so Bink goes in too. Meanwhile, in hot pursuit, are his bungling kidnappers desperate to catch up with their multimillion-dollar meal ticket. When Bink falls asleep in the arms of a gorilla at the zoo, the kidnappers try to sneak him away only to have the protective ape strike back. In fact, each of Bink's adventures serves to provide ingenious ways to wreak havoc on various parts of the trio's anatomy—the groin area being a special favorite.

Yet while the incompetent kidnappers are always in danger, Bink seems to have a guardian angel guiding his every step, right up to the last one in which, like Boo, he visits an Old Soldiers Home. Back at the Cotwells', FBI agent Grissom (Fred Dalton Thompson) tells of a number of places where a baby has been seen throughout town. It is then that Gilbertine realizes that Bink is reenacting his favorite nursery story. Guessing what his next stop will be, the nanny guides the family and police to the retirement home where Bink is being serenaded by its residents.

Although Bink is now safely back with his family, the criminals are still on the loose. Unfortunately for them, however, Baby Bink manages to communicate that his "Boo book" is under the "tick tock" they are driving by on the expressway. By pointing out the building with the clock where the trio lives—and where his book has been left—Bink manages to get the crooks captured.

Producer/screenwriter John Hughes had previously scored a major hit with 1990's *Home Alone* starring Macaulay Culkin, another film that featured a youngster in peril at the hands of bogeymen. While Culkin's character was old enough to realize he could be in trouble by being left alone and was also creative enough to find ways to fend for and defend himself, Baby Bink is too young to discern any of these facts. He is blissfully ignorant of the hazards and threats around him. He is innocence personified and contagiously happy.

Therefore, the filmmakers have seen to it that no harm will befall him—and the audience knows it. While one may catch one's breath at the special effects that seem to place the baby in precarious positions, one always knows he will be safe. The filmmakers even go so far as to find inventive ways for the baby to acquire food and have his monogrammed diaper changed. Consequently, the one thing that might have killed the comedy in *Baby's Day Out*—fear for the baby's safety and well-being—is so well anticipated that audiences can relax and enjoy the adventure.

Yet while as one character says in the film, "Someone somewhere watches over the babies," the same is not true for Bink's kidnappers. For them, "babies are more dangerous than [they] thought." Thus *Baby's Day Out* bears resemblance to both O. Henry's short story "The Ransom of Red Chief" and a live-action Road Runner cartoon. Neither the Road Runner nor Baby Bink can speak, but while the bird is crafty in avoiding his nemesis, Bink is protected by his innocence. Audiences do not hate the coyote and yet they laugh at the penalties he pays for his pursuit. The same is true for Eddie and his gang. Like a good cartoon, *Baby's Day Out* manages to be both funny and cruel at the same time.

 "They slept a lot. If they yawned, 150 people would have to wait for someone to nap, which I guess isn't that unusual in the movie business."—*Baby's Day Out* producer John Hughes about the Worton twins (*Entertainment Weekly*, May 27, 1994)

Part of the credit for this belongs to Joe Pantoliano, Brian Haley, and especially Joe Mantegna, who manage to be likable despite the fact that, they have kidnapped an innocent baby. Evil and malice are not their motives, money is. Mantegna had proved himself to be a very able dramatic actor in such films as *Bugsy* (1991) and *The Godfather, Part III* (1990). With *Baby's Day Out*, he has shown himself to be skillful at comedy as well.

Besides the successful trio of villains on the screen, however, there was also a trio of talent behind it: the editors, the visual special effects, and the mechanical special effects. Because of the choreography, editing, and special effects, it looks as though the baby is really in danger. These realistic effects are achieved with camera placement, blue screens, and puppet babies. These are the components that bring what might have been an animated feature successfully to life. Using George Lucas' ILM company, *Baby's Day Out* incorporated effects such as split screens, blue and green screens with computer imaging, and an enormous 421-foot-by-55-foot photograph of the Chicago cityscape against which to film Baby Bink's adventures.

Where audiences might cringe to see a baby crawling across a busy city street, oblivious to the traffic above him, here it is all made more palatable by the use of believable mechanical puppets created by Academy Award-winning special-effects makeup artist and creature creator Rick Baker, who had previously contributed to such films as *An American Werewolf in London* (1981) and *Harry and the Hendersons* (1987). Baker made casts of the actual babies, then created eleven lifelike dolls, each with a specific movement: crawling, sitting, kicking and arm waving, head gestures and intricate hand motions. These dolls were then manipulated by puppeteers using radio controls and cables. While some times the dolls may be a bit more noticeable than others (as when a viewer might say "how did they do that!"), on the whole, they are seamlessly inserted in the story.

Baby's Day Out is not a great film, but it is fun summer family fare. Should it prove profitable at the box office, there is already a built-in sequel potential: When Bink is safely back in his nursery at the end of the film, he pulls a new book down from the shelves, *Baby's Trip to China*.

—*Beverley Bare Buehrer*

CREDITS

Eddie: Joe Mantegna
Laraine: Lara Flynn Boyle
Norby: Joe Pantoliano
Veeko: Brian Haley
Gilbertine: Cynthia Nixon
FBI agent Grissom: Fred Dalton Thompson
Bennington: Matthew Glave
Mr. Andrews: John Neville
Baby Bink: Adam Robert Worton
Baby Bink: Jacob Joseph Worton
Sally: Brigid Duffy
FBI agent: Guy Hadley
Old-timer: Eddie Bracken

Released: 1994
Production: John Hughes and Richard Vane; released by Twentieth Century-Fox
Direction: Patrick Read Johnson
Screenplay: John Hughes
Cinematography: Thomas E. Ackerman
Editing: David Rawlins
Production design: Doug Kraner
Art direction: Joseph Lucky
Set decoration: Beth Rubino
Casting: Janet Hirshenson and Jane Jenkins
Visual effects supervision: Michael Fink
Mechanical effects designer: Rick Baker
Sound: Ronald Judkins
Costume design: Lisa Jensen
Music: Bruce Broughton
MPAA rating: PG
Running time: 98 minutes

REVIEWS

Chicago Tribune. July 1, 1994, p. 7L.
The Hollywood Reporter. June 20, 1994, p. 10.
Los Angeles Times. July 1, 1994, p. F6.
The New York Times. July 1, 1994, p. 86.
USA Today. July 1, 1994, p. 7D.
Variety. June 20, 1994, p. 4.
The Village Voice. July 12, 1994, p. 48.

Babyfever

Set primarily at a baby shower, this comedy-drama centers on the issues of pregnancy, motherhood, careers, and romantic relationships from the diverse points of view of the various women present. Director Jaglom captures the essence of the stories without disturbing their flow. Foyt, Jaglom's wife and co-screenwriter, makes her acting debut.

REVIEWS

Boston Globe. May 6, 1994, p. 88.
Chicago Tribune. May 6, 1994, p. 7D.
Chicago Tribune. May 8, 1994, Sec. 13 p. 28.
Entertainment Weekly. June 3, 1994, p. 40.
Los Angeles Times. April 13, 1994, p. F10.
National Review. XLVI, June 13, 1994, p. 71.
The New York Times. May 4, 1994, p. C16.
Playboy. XLI, July 1994, p. 22.
Variety. CCCLIV, April 18, 1994, p. 63.
The Wall Street Journal. May 5, 1994, p. A12.
The Washington Post. June 6, 1994, p. D7.

CREDITS

Gena: Victoria Foyt
James: Matt Salinger
Roz: Dinah Lenney
Anthony: Eric Roberts
Rosie: Frances Fisher
Milly: Elaine Kagan
Mark: Zack Norman

Released: 1994
Production: Judith Wolinsky for Jagtoria; released by Rainbow Film Co.
Direction: Henry Jaglom
Screenplay: Henry Jaglom and Victoria Foyt
Cinematography: Hanania Baer
Editing: Henry Jaglom
Sound: Sunny Meyer
MPAA rating: R
Running time: 110 minutes

Backbeat

"5 guys 4 legends 3 lovers 2 friends 1 band"
—*Movie tagline*

"You won't just cheer, you'll 'Twist & Shout'!"
—*ABC-TV*

"Lively, galvanizing and unexpectedly well-made"
—Janet Maslin, *The New York Times*

"...sure-fire entertainment, stunning for its candor and emotionally explosive. Stephen Dorff is brilliant..." —*Entertainment Weekly*

"...audaciously entertaining...a thrilling spectacle that rocks the house...defiant, raucous, erotic. "
—Peter Travers, *Rolling Stone*

"has a compulsive energy, a raw and joyous explosiveness, it's a rousingly seductive rock-the-house whirlwind." —*Chicago Tribune*

 Box Office Gross: $2,375,666 (January 12, 1994)

The early days of the phenomenally successful rock group the Beatles are beautifully depicted in this outstanding and entertaining film. *Backbeat* is the story of the rock group's growing pains, set during the exciting period of their early club performances and recording career. It takes a most interesting perspective in that it focuses on the intense relationship between John Lennon (Ian Hart) and Stu Sutcliffe (Stephen Dorff), the "lost Beatle." Superbly written, directed, and acted, the film boasts a showstopping performance by Hart as the young and passionate Lennon.

The Beatles were arguably the most influential voice in pop music in history. They certainly were the most widely celebrated, and the mythology surrounding them has only been matched by Elvis Presley. From their working-class roots, their phenomenal appearance on the Ed Sullivan television show in 1964, their breakup, and the 1980 assassination of John Lennon, their legend is familiar to virtually everyone in the world. Lesser-known facts in Beatle lore are that Pete Best was the original drummer and that the group originally had Sutcliffe as a fifth member. Sutcliffe was a mediocre bass player, but an intense and promising painter. His tragic life and his turbulent relationship with

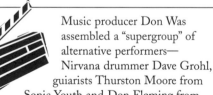

Music producer Don Was assembled a "supergroup" of alternative performers—Nirvana drummer Dave Grohl, guiarists Thurston Moore from Sonic Youth and Don Fleming from Gumball, Greg Dulli from The Afghan Whigs, who did the Lennon Vocals, and Dave Pirner from Soul Asylum, who did the McCartney vocals—to record the classic rock tunes the Beatles performed in Hamburg.

John Lennon and with Astrid Kirchherr (Sheryl Lee) provide a dramatic backdrop to the Beatles' early story.

It is the early 1960's, and Lennon and his best friend Sutcliffe have been performing in a garage band with their friends Paul McCartney (Gary Bakewell), George Harrison (Chris O'Neill), and Pete Best (Scot Williams). As the film opens, the young men are seen losing a fight with some local stevedores in Liverpool. It is a fitting opening, foreshadowing the literal and metaphorical brawls to come while reinforcing the close relationships they share. They take their beating with good humor, particularly Lennon, who says to the bloodied Sutcliffe, "You'll get better.... I'll always be ugly."

The band has been hired to perform at a low-class strip joint in Hamburg, Germany. The group's single-minded drive to succeed is evident early: They lie about their ages in order to be able to play in the strip club, and they boldly stride on stage the first night in their gray suits and black ties, pretending to ignore the indifference of the audience. Director Iain Softley and his actors wonderfully capture the electricity of the early Beatles. Their passionate performances of "Good Golly, Miss Molly," "Long Tall Sally," and other early rock tunes help the audience to understand what it must have been like to witness the birth of a cultural phenomenon.

The band proves itself on the first night, and the members' progression from scared eighteen-year-olds to seasoned musicians is part of the fun: A wonderful montage intercuts quick shots of lazy strippers with performances by the kinetic young band members as they appear progressively more comfortable on stage. Eventually, the audiences grow, and the story deepens.

Problems arise between the highly professional McCartney and Sutcliffe, who insists on wearing sunglasses on stage and is virtually motionless as he plays. "He just stands there," complains McCartney; but Lennon defends his friend with the fierceness of a guard dog. Further complications arise when Sutcliffe becomes enamored with Astrid Kirchherr, a beautiful photographer and a leading figure among artists and intellectuals in Hamburg. Sutcliffe eventually begins a relationship with Astrid, sparking the jealousy of Lennon and provoking the anger of the other Beatles as he shows less and less interest in the band.

Simultaneously, the Beatles begin to emerge as leaders of the crowded Hamburg club scene: Scouts from record

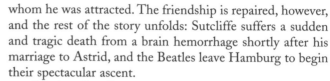

CREDITS

John Lennon: Ian Hart
Stuart Sutcliffe: Stephen Dorff
Astrid Kirchherr: Sheryl Lee
Paul McCartney: Gary Bakewell
George Harrison: Chris O'Neill
Pete Best: Scot Williams
Klaus Voormann: Kai Wiesinger
Cynthia Powell: Jennifer Ehle

Origin: Great Britain
Released: 1994
Production: Finola Dwyer and Stephen Woolley for Polygram Filmed Entertainment and Scala Productions, in association with Channel Four Films and Forthcoming; released by Gramercy Pictures
Direction: Iain Softley
Screenplay: Iain Softley, Michael Thomas, and Stephen Ward
Cinematography: Ian Wilson
Editing: Martin Walsh
Production design: Joseph Bennett
Art direction: Michael Carlin and Joseph Plagge
Casting: John Hubbard, Ros Hubbard and Dianne Crittenden and Vicky Hinrichs
Sound: Chris Munro
Costume design: Sheena Napier
Music supervision: Bob Last
Music: Don Was
MPAA rating: R
Running time: 100 minutes

companies come to see them, the crowds increase, and a record deal emerges. Lennon only becomes more intense as the heat gets turned up on his band; he is depicted as a fierce and highly driven individual. When John tells Stu that "we're gonna be big...too big for Hamburg...too big for Liverpool," Stu responds "too big for our own bloody good." As the brilliance of the band is recognized, the relationship between Stu and Astrid grows deeper; they decide to marry, and Stu decides to leave the Beatles, live with Astrid, and attend art school in Hamburg.

"We're gonna be big...too big for Hamburg...too big for Liverpool...."
"...too big for our own bloody good."—Stuart Sutcliffe responding to John Lennon in *Backbeat*

Lennon is furious over Stu's defection and is quite rude to Astrid, presumably because her relationship with Stu is threatening to the band. "You're the angriest person I've ever met," says Astrid. "I'm not angry, sister, I'm desperate," says Lennon. "You're jealous of me," she responds. The audience later discovers Lennon's repressed infatuation with Astrid: His anger appears to come from his desperation at becoming famous and at the loss of his best friend to a woman to whom he was attracted. The friendship is repaired, however, and the rest of the story unfolds: Sutcliffe suffers a sudden and tragic death from a brain hemorrhage shortly after his marriage to Astrid, and the Beatles leave Hamburg to begin their spectacular ascent.

Stephen Dorff captures Sutcliffe's brooding nature and cool demeanor perfectly. His understated performance is the linchpin of the film: Sutcliffe's detachment was the very essence of rock 'n' roll and the very center of the lives of these young people who were trying to forge a new rock-and-roll artistry. Dorff spent time with the real Astrid Kirchherr, who was still living in Hamburg in order to learn about the true character of the man she loved. He also captures the tortured artistic essence in several scenes that show Sutcliffe's painting style, as he hurls paint on the canvas, fervently thrashing out a painting that seems to express the boiling feelings inside.

For many, the film's most pyrotechnic performance comes from Ian Hart as John Lennon. Ironically, Hart has already starred in another film as John Lennon, called *The Hours and Times* (1992). In interviews, Hart has said that he believes he looks nothing like Lennon. Yet in fact, he has so captured the essence of John Lennon's early years that he appears to look exactly like him. His thick Liverpudlian accent and his single-minded push toward fame bring another dimension to the mellow, peace-loving John Lennon of later years. Hart is achingly touching in his scenes where he defends Stuart from the rest of the Beatles and when he tells Astrid that he was in love with her but stepped aside rather than be a rival to his best friend. The sheer bravado and energy he brings to the concert segments of the film are infectious and exciting. It is a fully realized performance that has already won for him much recognition.

Technical elements of the film are excellent. Don Was created the sound track for the film. Re-creating the early sound of the most famous rock group in history is no easy task, but Was puts together a band of wonderful musicians and singers for the sound track that capture the raw intensity of the early group perfectly. Their versions of some of the greatest early rock 'n' roll songs are infectious. Was additionally created original music for the sound track that perfectly underscores the action. Particularly touching is music under a scene where Astrid's lover Klaus (Kai Wiesinger) discovers that Astrid and Stu are lovers. Was's tender music is a great example of how underscoring can help define the mood of a scene.

Visual elements are similarly excellent. The settings by Joseph Bennett and cinematography by Ian Wilson provide a dark and moody setting for the bittersweet story. Wilson uses backlighting and shadows to great effect, building tension and creating a somber, overcast mood. Sheena Napier provides the film with detailed period costumes, also reflecting the somber mood of the film with dark colors. The working-class clothes of the young band vividly contrast with the outlandish outfits of the strippers in the early scenes; Napier also provides much sparkle in a costume ball segment.

Iain Softley, in his directorial debut, has orchestrated his group of designers, actors, and musicians with finesse and dignity. He uses quick-cutting montages to great effect, such as the aforementioned "stripper montage" and another one in which Astrid takes publicity pictures of the band. He is as adept at working with his cinematographer at creating moody visual images as he is in directing his actors in emotionally charged scenes.

Stu's death scene is a visual poem: Light streams in from a window onto a dark studio, filtering light onto Stu's painting as an overhead camera watches Astrid holding Stu's lifeless body. Another wonderful image is of Astrid watching the Beatles among an audience full of screaming fans. Amid young girls crying and screaming, amid young men clapping their hands, Astrid smiles and disappears into the crowd as the camera pulls farther and farther back to reveal the huge crowd of gyrating young fans.

Astrid Kirchherr was credited with influencing much of the visual style of the early Beatles. Sutcliffe was similarly credited and is thought to have provided the group's name. Metaphorically speaking, however, they disappeared into the crowded world of fans and became footnotes to an incredible history. This film pays homage to Kirchherr and Sutcliffe while doing justice to the extraordinary memory of the Beatles in the process.

—Kirby Tepper

REVIEWS

Entertainment Weekly. April 15, 1994, p. 38.
The Hollywood Reporter. January 24, 1994, p. 10.
Los Angeles Times. April 15, 1994, p. F1.
The New York Times. April 15, 1994, p. B3.
Variety. January 25, 1994, p. 2.

Bad Girls

"It was a dangerous time to be a woman. And a good time to have friends." —Movie tagline

Box Office: $15,179,126 (July 4, 1994)

When the "civilizing" influence of religion comes to Echo City, Colorado, this 1890's Wild West town must clean up its act. The first to go are the local prostitutes, especially after Cody Zamora (Madeleine Stowe) shoots and kills the Colonel (Will MacMillan) while he is beating up one of the saloon girls, Anita Crown (Mary Stuart Masterson). As Cody is about to be hung, however, Anita enlists the aid of two other ladies of the evening, Eileen Spenser (Andie MacDowell) and Lilly Laronette (Drew Barrymore), and, at the last minute, the three of them rescue Cody from the noose's fatal grip.

Unfortunately, the four former prostitutes must find a way to survive in a man's world. Anita, whose husband died of cholera, still has his homesteader's claim to 640 acres in the Oregon Territory. So the women decide to do what Anita and her husband were going to do: go to Oregon and start a sawmill. For capital to get started, Cody volunteers the $12,000 she has salted away in a bank in Agua Dulce, Texas, where these former harlots head first.

As Cody is closing her account at the bank, it is robbed by a former acquaintance, Kid Jarrett (James Russo). He is camped across the Mexican border, making the occasional raid into U.S. territory, and this time he takes Cody's $12,000 with him. Much to their dismay, Cody and her pals are suspected of being the Kid's accomplices. Now they are caught between the Pinkerton detectives who have been hired by the Colonel's widow to find her husband's killer and a Texas posse out looking for them and the Kid's gang. To make matters worse, Eileen has been captured by the town sheriff.

When Cody calls on the Kid at his hideout in order to get her money back, she learns that the gang is about to rob a military train for gold and a Gatling gun. Her mission fails when she is instead beaten and whipped by the ruthlessly sadistic Kid, who is still angry at Cody for running out on him in the middle of the night years ago.

Cody is found unconscious by Josh McCoy (Dermot Mulroney), a prospector the women have met along the way. Meanwhile, back in town, Lilly and Anita have broken

> "We sold our bodies. Why can't we sell wood?"—*Bad Girls*

Eileen out of jail. Now they regroup at the ranch of William Tucker (James LeGros), the green young rancher who was deputized at the last minute to guard Eileen and instead fell in love with her.

Since the four women still need Cody's cash, they plan to rob the Kid's gang after the gang robs the military train. The women also discover that Josh is not really a prospector but another victim of the Jarett family. It seems that the Kid's father, Frank (Robert Loggia), jumped the McCoy family claim and, like son like father, whipped Josh's mother and killed his father.

Most of *Bad Girls'* Aqua Dulce sequences were shot at the Alamo Village set constructed in 1957 for the production of John Wayne's *The Alamo*. Before shooting, the cast spent three weeks at a "cowboy camp" learning to ride, mount, dismount, tumble, rope, draw a gun, ride while shooting, and chew tobacco.

During the tumult of the post-robbery robbery, Lilly is captured by the Kid and Frank is captured by Cody. An exchange of prisoners is arranged but Josh's desire for revenge and Frank's taunting result in Josh's shooting the older man. A final shoot-out at the Kid's hideout sees Lilly released, Cody regaining her money, and the women riding off to find their freedom and independence.

To say that the Western is an all-American genre, one of the few sources of purely American myth, would be an understatement. To say that it has been the exclusive purview of men would be simplistic. There have been several instances where women have co-opted the genre: 1954's kinky *Johnny Guitar* starring Joan Crawford comes to mind, as does the later and better-made *The Ballad of Little Jo* (1993). Yet on the whole, this has remained male territory, where men are men and women are women (except in *The Ballad of Little Jo*, of course).

In most respects, is *Bad Girls* a traditional male Western. It has everything an old-fashioned Western has: gunfights, runaway buckboards, campfires, jail breaks, ambushes, bank robberies, rape scenes, showdowns, riding off into the sunset, and even a corny love interest. Nevertheless, where in traditional Westerns it is the women who stop the action to provide a bland love story, here it is a man's job. Where traditionally the women are just background ornaments for the heroic men, here the women are the heroes. These females do not quiver in corners waiting to be rescued while the men duke it out—they rescue each other. These women can do everything a man can do, including shooting guns and throwing knives and riding a horse—without sitting sidesaddle.

Yet, when all is said and done, this revisionism merely camouflages what is otherwise cliche. Its story really is nothing special. It is very derivative: The opening seems to pay homage to Clint Eastwood's *Unforgiven* (1992); the Gatling gun sequence is swiped from Sam Peckinpah's *The Wild Bunch* (1969); the graveyard scene is flatly similar to one in John Ford's 1949 *She Wore a Yellow Ribbon*; the final shoot-out brings the OK Corral to mind; and if the town of Agua Dulce looks familiar, it is because the picture was filmed at Alamo Village, a frontier film set constructed in 1957 for John Wayne's production of *The Alamo* (1960).

In short, the only innovation in this Western is that here the girls get to do what the boys usually do. Yet maybe it is about time that women filmgoers get a chance to feel the vicarious excitement of participating in this most American of icons. After all, despite Sigourney Weaver's turn as Ripley in *Alien* (1979) and its sequels, most action films of the early 1990's still clung tenaciously to convention, such as Sylvester Stallone's 1993 *Cliffhanger*, where the hero and villain fight it out while the heroine (Jeannine Turner) cowers in corners instead of doing anything to

CREDITS

Cody Zamora: Madeleine Stowe
Anita Crown: Mary Stuart Masterson
Eileen Spenser: Andie MacDowell
Lilly Laronette: Drew Barrymore
Kid Jarrett: James Russo
William Tucker: James LeGros
Frank Jarrett: Robert Loggia
Josh McCoy: Dermot Mulroney
Detective Graves: Jim Beaver
Detective O'Brady: Nick Chinlund
Ned: Neil Summers
Roberto: Daniel O'Haco
Rico: Richard E. Reyes
Colonel Clayborne: Will MacMillan

Released: 1994
Production: Albert S. Ruddy, Andre E. Morgan, and Charles Finch; released by Twentieth Century-Fox
Direction: Jonathan Kaplan
Screenplay: Ken Friedman and Yolande Finch; based on a story by Albert S. Ruddy, Charles Finch, and Gray Frederickson
Cinematography: Ralf Bode
Editing: Jane Kurson
Production design: Guy Barnes
Art direction: M. Nord Haggerty
Set decoration: Michael Taylor
Casting: Mike Fenton, Julie Ashton and Julie Selzer
Sound: Jose Antonio Garcia
Costume design: Susie DeSanto
Stunt coordination: Walter Scott
Music: Jerry Goldsmith
MPAA rating: R
Running time: 100 minutes

improve the odds. One would have hoped that filmmakers by the end of the twentieth century would have excised that type of scene from their cinematic vocabulary, but evidently not. Therefore, despite a trite story and some often laughable dialogue, *Bad Girls* is still worth seeing.

Director Jonathan Kaplan is no amateur when it comes to films with strong women. His *Heart Like a Wheel* (1983) had Bonnie Bedelia changing spark plugs and racing cars with the best of the men and his *The Accused* (1988) showed a powerfully talented Jodie Foster and a feisty Kelly McGillis fighting for a rape victim's rights. Unfortunately, in *Bad Girls*, Kaplan's writers lacked the creativity and originality needed to make this a true revisionist Western.

This is not to take anything from the actresses. Stowe's steeliness, MacDowell's intelligence, Barrymore's dangerousness, and even Masterson's passion make for an attractive cast. Although Jerry Goldsmith's music seems as tiredly

clichéd as the plot, Ralf Bode's cinematography takes advantage of the rugged and spectacular landscape, which is drenched in golden earth tones.

In short, despite *Bad Girls'* lack of originality, there is something appealing about a B picture in which women can actually stand tall in the proverbial saddle.

—*Beverley Bare Buehrer*

REVIEWS

Chicago Tribune. April 22, 1994, p. 7C.
The Hollywood Reporter. April 22-24, 1994, p. 8.
Los Angeles Times. April 22, 1994, p. F1.
The New York Times. April 22, 1994, p. B10.
USA Today. April 22, 1994, p. 4D.
Variety. April 22, 1994, p. 2.

Barcelona

"The sexy new comedy from the director of *Metropolitan*." —Movie tagline

"Funny and charming—two thumbs up!"—*Siskel & Ebert*

"Superb! Sophisticated, absorbing and very funny." —Jeffrey Lyons, *Sneak Previews*

"This movie is a gem." —Steven Rea, *Philadelphia Enquirer*

"Reason to rejoice...a wise, robust, dazzlingly idiosyncratic romantic comedy." —Guy Flatley, *Cosmopolitan*

"A remarkable find... An exuberant bite of fresh comic thinking." —Peter Travers, *Rolling Stone*

"Brilliant... Whit Stillman has achieved the kind of growth we always hope for in a major artist." —Donald Lyons, *Film Comment*

"Sheer pleasure!" —Jay Carr, *Boston Globe*

"Whit Stillman's wry, funny follow-up to *Metropolitan*." —Janet Maslin, *The New York Times*

 Box Office Gross: $7,193,673 (October 30, 1994)

The dominant trend in American filmmaking has often been identified with director Alfred Hitchcock, who believed that motion pictures, like children, should be

seen and not heard. Most Hollywood filmmakers consider dialogue a necessary evil because talking is part of normal human behavior; nevertheless, they abhor what they call "talking heads" or any other dialogue conspicuously contrived to convey information to the audience.

A notable exception is Woody Allen. Typically, his characters—and particularly the over-psychoanalyzed nebbishes played by Allen himself—overexplain everything, including their compulsions, phobias, fantasies, and inhibitions. The success of *Barcelona* suggests that Allen's influ-

Taylor Nichols, Tushka Bergen, Chris Eigeman, and Mira Sorvino in *Barcelona*. Photo: Bob Marshak © 1994 Castle Rock Entertainment.

ence over the years may have been more pervasive than suspected and that there might be an incipient countermovement from the action-oriented film to the type of film rooted in stage drama.

Whit Stillman, author and director of *Barcelona*, has gone Woody Allen one better by creating not one but two neurotic protagonists. This innovation seems more viable than a single nonstop talker such as Allen because it is more dramatic and provides more variety.

Barcelona is a story of sibling rivalry. Although Ted Boynton (Taylor Nichols) and Fred Boynton (Chris Eigeman) are only cousins, they grew up together and have a stronger love-hate relationship than most brothers. Fred, a U.S. Navy lieutenant junior grade, appears on Ted's doorstep with his luggage, characteristically taking it for granted that he is welcome to move in. Fred is an "advance man" responsible for smoothing the way for the pending goodwill visit of the U.S. Sixth Fleet.

> In *Barcelona*, Chris Eigeman actually wears Tom Cruise's uniform from *A Few Good Men*. (*Entertainment Weekly*, May 27, 1994)

Ted is the narrator and viewpoint character. He is a sales representative for Chicago-based IHSMOCO (the Illinois High-Speed Motor Corp.)

CREDITS

Ted Boynton: Taylor Nichols
Fred Boynton: Chris Eigeman
Montserrat: Tushka Bergen
Marta: Mira Sorvino
Ramón: Pep Munne
Aurora: Nuria Badia
Greta: Hellena Schmied
Frank: Francis Creighton
Dickie: Thomas Gibson
Consul: Jack Gilpin

Released: 1994
Production: Whit Stillman for Castle Rock Entertainment and Westerly Films; released by Fine Line Features
Direction: Whit Stillman
Screenplay: Whit Stillman
Cinematography: John Thomas
Editing: Christopher Tellefsen
Production design: José María Botines
Production management: Fernando Marquerie
Casting: Billy Hopkins and Simone Reynolds
Sound: Licio Oliveira
Costume design: Edi Giguere
Music: Mark Suozzo
MPAA rating: PG-13
Running time: 101 minutes

but wonders whether he really wants a career in sales; at the same time he is afraid that he might get fired. The story is nominally about him, but Chris Eigeman is such a charismatic young actor that he steals the show. Eigeman's performance resembles that of the young Michael Keaton in his film debut as the zany Billy Blazejowski in *Night Shift* (1982). Oddly enough, Nichols bears a strong resemblance to Henry Winkler, who played the uptight Charles Lumley and was upstaged by Keaton all the way.

The contrast between the two principals in *Barcelona*, as in *Night Shift*, is what gives the film its piquancy. Both Ted and Fred are "worrywarts," but Ted is an introverted conformist while Fred is an extroverted nonconformist. It is not until tragedy touches their young lives for the first time that they understand their real kinship beneath their superficial differences. They trade in their imaginary problems for real problems.

The time is established as "the last decade of the Cold War." Many Spaniards harbor socialist sympathies never extinguished under the police state of Generalissimo Franco. Many resent Americans and the North Atlantic Treaty Organization (NATO). At the American Consulate, Fred is advised to wear civilian clothes but refuses to comply. He is proud of his new uniform and feels personally responsible for correcting the false conceptions Barcelonans have of America's culture and foreign policy. In his outspokenness he is reminiscent of Holly Martins (Joseph Cotten) in *The Third Man* (1949), and the audience senses that sooner or later Fred, like Martins, is going to stumble into serious trouble.

Barcelona is Whit Stillman's second production. His first was a low-budget film about preppies entitled *Metropolitan* (1990). It won the best first feature award from the New York Film Critics' Circle and was nominated for an Academy Award in the original screenplay category, making Stillman a filmmaker to watch. He lived in Barcelona for some years and loves the city. As the title of his new film suggests, it is as much about Barcelona itself as about the characters whose stories are only ephemeral incidents in the history of a city older than Rome.

Not the least photogenic feature of Barcelona is its beautiful women, who, according to their candid admissions in various conversational settings, have become, practically overnight, even more sexually liberated than their American

AWARDS AND NOMINATIONS

Independent Spirit Awards 1994:   Best Cinematography

counterparts. Stillman's talented cinematographer John Thomas displays some of these young beauties naked in bed with the two American heroes, who hardly seem to appreciate their good luck but go right on complaining about their personal problems. The naked women are bathed in the same glow that is lavished upon some of Barcelona's famous landmarks. Through Thomas' lens, all of Barcelona acquires a golden patina, suggestive of Spain's history of exploration and plunder motivated by lust for gold.

"I think it's well known that anti-Americanism has its roots in sexual impotence, at least in Europe."—Fred, from *Barcelona*

All the young women speak English well because—when they have their clothes on—they work as hostesses and translators at the Barcelona Trade Fair. They listen to Fred and Ted with interest, partly because they are always seeking to improve their English and partly because their limited understanding of the American vernacular makes them suspect there is deeper significance to the juvenile bickering and neurotic self-revelations than is actually the case.

The fact that all the attractive young women can speak English makes it easy for Stillman to avoid subtitles and pidgin English. It seems so natural for the Spaniards to be communicating in charmingly accented English that no one in the audience questions it. Those bit players in the film who presumably do not know English do not speak at all, and this too seems natural because Americans expect some Spaniards at least to be brooding and inscrutable.

Montserrat, played by Tushka Bergen, is the most striking-looking woman in the film, not only because she is a blonde in a country where brunettes predominate but also because of her flawless features. Both Ted and Fred fall in love with her, which naturally makes them hate each other all the more. They learn to their chagrin that even though Montserrat is willing to go to bed with any man who attracts her, she is still living with Ramón (Pep Munne), a handsome, womanizing journalist who is deliberately fomenting anti-American hostility with his incendiary political articles.

Ramón sincerely believes that the Americans themselves were responsible for the bombing of the American Library and a local USO. Like many Spaniards, he still remembers the *USS Maine*, which the Americans were accused of blowing up in Havana harbor in 1898 in order to have an excuse to start a war that cost Spain most of its empire. In beautiful, brooding Barcelona with its wedding-cake buildings perched on fairy-tale hilltops there is a sense of lurking danger. The brash, outspoken Fred Boynton, who is flaunting his uniform all over the city, becomes one of the

victims of Ramón's agitation. From out of nowhere two men on a motorcycle pull abreast of Fred's taxi. One produces a heavy-caliber automatic and fires at point-blank range. The camera dissolves on a close-up of shattered safety glass.

This sudden transition from comedy to tragedy is one of the most daring aspects of Stillman's film. Fred is hospitalized under intensive care. It is here that Ted realizes how much he actually loves his cousin and how childish their long-term rivalry has been. Ted spends his days and nights at Fred's bedside, praying for his recovery. This is probably the first time in his life he has thought about anybody besides himself.

Fred's brush with death and Ted's brush with bereavement make both young men grow up quickly and realize what things are important in life and what things are not. The story ends with Fred married to Montserrat and Ted married to a less ravishing young Spanish woman who is temperamentally a better match. They are all back in the prosaic United States, preparing to dive headfirst into the consumer culture that so many Europeans despise and envy. The marriages symbolize a synthesis of cultures—American knowing how to get things done and European knowing how to live—as a solution to international discord.

Barcelona received mostly enthusiastic critical response as well as impressive box-office receipts. *Variety* noted that the film "possesses a strong authorial voice and an appealing intelligence" in spite of the "no-name cast and director's limited profile." By mid-August of 1994, *Barcelona* had leapfrogged from the art houses to the suburban multiplexes and was being featured on marquees alongside such 1994 blockbusters as *The Lion King*, *The Client*, *Forrest Gump*, and *Clear and Present Danger* (all reviewed in this volume).

Nothing succeeds like success in Hollywood, and the success of Stillman's film may herald a flurry of brand-new old-fashioned films crackling with witty dialogue among beautiful people in exotic settings, reminiscent of the black-and-white classics starring Katharine Hepburn, Bette Davis, Cary Grant, and Jimmy Stewart.

—*Bill Delaney*

REVIEWS

Entertainment Weekly. August 12, 1994, p. 39.
The Hollywood Reporter. June 13, 1994, p. 6.
Los Angeles Times. August 5, 1994, p. F1.
The New York Times. July 29, 1994, p. B2.
Variety. June 13, 1994, p. 18.

The Beans of Egypt, Maine (Forbidden Choices)

"Provocative filmmaking, beautifully acted and directed." —Paul Wunder, *WBAI Radio*

"Lusty...dramatic and funny." —Jeff Craig, *Sixty Second Preview*

This drama centers on a young woman, Earlene Pomerleau (Martha Plimpton), living in rural Maine, and her fascination with her lower-class neighbors, the rowdy Bean clan, which includes vicious drunk patriarch Reuben (Rutger Hauer), his long-suffering companion and mother of nine, Roberta (Kelly Lynch), and the brutish young Beal (Patrick McGaw). Based on Carolyn Chute's novel of the same name. Directorial debut of Jennifer Warren. Released on video as *Forbidden Choices*.

REVIEWS

Boston Globe. September 12, 1994, p. 38.
Boston Globe. February 3, 1995, p. 51.
Los Angeles Times. Nov 23, 1994, p. F6.
The New York Times. November 23, 1994, p. C13.
Time. CXLIV, December 5, 1994, p. 92.
Variety. CCCLV, May 30, 1994, p. 51.
The Washington Post. December 2, 1994, p. F7.
The Washington Post. December 8, 1994, p. D7.

AWARDS AND NOMINATIONS

Independent Spirit Awards Nominations
1995: Best Supporting Actress (Lynch), Best Cinematography

CREDITS

Earlene Pomerleau: Martha Plimpton
Roberta: Kelly Lynch
Reuben Bean: Rutger Hauer
Beal Bean: Patrick McGaw
Mr. Pomerleau: Richard Sanders

Released: 1994
Production: Rosilyn Heller for Live Entertainment and American Playhouse Theatrical Films; released by I.R.S. Media
Direction: Jennifer Warren
Screenplay: Bill Phillips; based on the novel by Carolyn Chute
Cinematography: Stevan Larner
Editing: Paul Dixon
Production design: Rondi Tucker
Casting: Donald Paul Pemrick, Judi Rothfield and Katie Ryan
Sound: Mark Weingarten
Costume design: Candace Clements
Music: Peter Manning Robinson
MPAA rating: R
Running time: 97 minutes

Begotten

"The result is a thing of beauty where realistic images are turned upside down by the grotesque and flowers are trampled by the darkening clouds of a nightmare." —*Film Threat*

"Nobody will get through *Begotten* without being marked. One of the 10 best of the year." —Richard Corliss, *Time*

This violent avant-garde drama depicts God killing himself and Mother Earth giving birth to a man who is then tortured and mutilated. 🎞️

REVIEWS

Christian Science Monitor.February 16, 1995, p. 13.
Time. CXXXVII, May 13, 1991. p. 70.
Variety. CCCXLIII, June 17, 1991. p. 67.

CREDITS

God killing himself: Brian Salzberg
Mother Earth: Donna Dempsey
Son of Earth (Flesh on Bone): Stephen Charles Barry

Released: 1991
Production: E. Elias Merhige for Theater of Material
Direction: E. Elias Merhige
Screenplay: E. Elias Merhige
Cinematography: E. Elias Merhige
Production design: Harry Duggins
Art direction: Harry Duggins
Film effects: E. Elias Merhige
Sound: William Markle Associates
Sounds composition: Evan Albam
Costume design: Celia Bryant and Harry Duggins
Special effects: Harry Duggins
MPAA rating: no listing
Running time: 78 minutes

Being Human

"From the dawn of time man has struggled for just four things: Food. Safety. Someone to love. And a pair of shoes that fit." —Movie tagline

"Delightful! It radiates a rare glow of humor and warmth, fired by a wonderful Robin Williams performance. —Bob Campbell, *Newhouse News Service*

Box Office Gross: $1,487,020 (May 30, 1994)

While combining the talents of numerous household-name performers and filmmakers, involving shoots on three different continents, and spanning five thousand years of human love and loss, *Being Human* nevertheless remains a surprisingly small, frustratingly gentle film. The production notes report that Scottish director Bill Forsyth, who also directed *Gregory's Girl* (1981), *Local Hero* (1983), and *Housekeeping* (1987), set out to make a film about "man's need to find his place in the world." Unfortunately, the result is a film that seems largely lost itself.

Being Human is structured around five characters all named Hector (each of whom is played by Robin Williams). The earliest Hector, a meek Bronze Age primitive, watches as his family is captured by Nordic-looking raiders. Try as he might, rescue is beyond him. The Roman Hector is a slave whose master, Lucinnius (John Turturro), is driven to suicide by his creditors. The post-Crusades, Middle Ages Hector lives a life reminiscent of such literary wanderers as Odysseus and Chaucer's Canterbury pilgrims, as the film captures Hector traveling home, being tempted by distractions, and encountering characters, most notably Beatrice (Anna Galiena), along the way. Next a selfish, cowardly, conquistador-style Hector is marooned on the coast of Africa and proclaims himself a survivor at whatever cost. Finally there is the 1990's Hector, a divorced father and ex-convict, struggling to reach his children, Betsy (Helen Miller) and Tom (Charles Miller). Each Hector deals with the pain of being human—and with an odd assortment of chickens, shoes, slavery, families, and loss.

Perhaps the biggest disappointment of the film is the structure itself. Obviously episodic, the film becomes mired in the repetitions within the five vignettes revolving more or less around love, loss, and family. Soon the few variations and many similarities among the scenes take center stage, reducing audience members to comparing and contrasting the scenes' technical features, such as Williams' evolving hairdo and attire. Uniting this sleepy structure is a voice-over narration that not only drives home the obvious, but also piles on the platitudes.

For the shot of a medieval skirmish, a Scottish historical battle re-enactment society stood in to bring authenticity to the fighting scene.

Fortune-cookie-style, the narrator (Theresa Russell) intones, "Sometimes one day can change everything. Sometimes years change nothing." Later, "This is a story of a story." At another point, "What's in the story? A man on a beach all washed up." Finally, " 'Well,' the story said to itself, 'I must be a love story.' " Director Forsyth describes this project as trying to show that "the beginning and the end of it is that human beings are the same, whether they're wearing animal skins or three-piece suits. It's about the human predicament." Succinct, perhaps even true, yet a story about sameness—let alone five thousand years of sameness—has little to say and even fewer places to go. Therefore, it is not its fault that *Being Human* slowly chases its tail, trots a beaten path, and falls into a deep sleep.

Certainly the film is a disappointment for Bill Forsyth fans, who over the years have searched art-film houses and video stores for his films. Through such sleeper hits as *Gregory's Girl* and *Local Hero*, Forsyth carved a niche for himself, garnered a following, and won such prizes as the British Academy of Film and Television Arts Award for Best Director. Even in *Being Human*, he offers a clear, nonpyrotechnic alternative to the box-office competition—television remakes, runaway buses, and risque romances. Yet a film as sleepy as *Being Human* makes the audience's choice to attend action films more understandable.

The shortcomings of the film, however, cannot obscure its several strengths. The film is often lovely to look at, as cinematographer Michael Coulter, who has worked with Forsyth several times before, captures the beauty of the Scottish coast (caveman Hector), the Scottish Highlands (medieval Hector), and the Moroccan coast (conquistador Hector). Each setting appears completely untouched by the twentieth century, and each provides an isolated backdrop for the period action.

Further, the performances of several of the actors are entertaining, even if some fall short of inspired. In the medieval section of the film, Hector must decide whether to continue his journey home or stay with Beatrice. As the film calls for Beatrice to speak a language foreign to Hector, actress Anna Galiena is left to act without meaningful communication. This she does ably, with her remarkable smile and body language. Perhaps best known for her role in *The Hairdresser's Husband* (1992), Galiena warms the screen by her presence and leaves audience members questioning Hector's wisdom.

Furthermore, John Turturro's Roman businessman/slave master achieves a fine-tuned idiocy, as he sacrifices chickens, searching for a good omen, and as he manages to accomplish the requisite suicide in an unplanned slip and fall. Also exceptionally fine is Helen Miller's Betsy, who speaks believably with wisdom beyond her years. She consoles the 1990's Hector, guiding his return to love and to life. In a practical vein, she prescribes chicken (instead of steak) and recycled paper products (over first-run bleached ones). Spiritually, she tells her erstwhile father to relax and to enjoy having his children around him, as life gets no better than that. Young, calm, with a steady gaze, Miller makes a fine mouthpiece. *Being Human* also marks her (and her brother Charles') screen debut.

CREDITS

Hector: Robin Williams
Lucinnius: John Turturro
Beatrice: Anna Galiena
Priest: Vincent D'Onofrio
Dom Paulo: Hector Elizondo
Anna: Lorraine Bracco
Janet: Lindsay Crouse
Deirdre: Kelly Hunter
Betsy: Helen Miller
Tom: Charles Miller
Boris: William H. Macy
Thalia: Grace Mahlaba
Storyteller: Theresa Russell
Girl child: Maudie Johnson
Boy child: Max Johnson

Released: 1994
Production: Robert F. Colesberry and David Puttnam for Enigma, in association with Fujisankei Communications Group, British Sky Broadcasting, and Natwest Ventures; released by Warner Bros.
Direction: Bill Forsyth
Screenplay: Bill Forsyth
Cinematography: Michael Coulter
Editing: Michael Ellis
Production design: Norman Garwood
Art direction: Keith Pain
Casting: Susie Figgis and Sharon Howard Field
Sound: Louis Kramer
Costume design: Sandy Powell
Music: Michael Gibbs
MPAA rating: PG-13
Running time: 125 minutes

The film also is the result of key teamwork. Great effort was put into researching the Bronze Age segment of the film. Researcher Gina Todd consulted experts and researched the materials available in the British Museum library. Among the results of the inquiry was goat-skin apparel, decorated with authentic geometric prints. Costume designer Sandy Powell worked on costumes that would dress down Robin Williams in each scene, completing his transformation into Everyman. "Because he's playing the ordinary man," said Powell in the production notes, "his costumes had to blend in with everyone." While the costumes may indeed have been appropriate, often even authentic, at times their blandness made the film even more soporific.

"It's like five separate movies all sheltered under one overarching concept. And the thread is me, the human thread of who and what we are." —Robin Williams on *Being Human*

Filmed prior to (but released after) Robin Williams' hit *Mrs. Doubtfire* (1993), *Being Human* presents what most Williams fans will find to be a largely subdued Robin Williams. While in both *Being Human* and *Mrs. Doubtfire* Williams tries repeatedly to gain a home, to win and keep his family, it is a very different Robin Williams who plays Hector. Creating what Howie Movshovitz of the *Denver Post* called "a poster child for unmitigated woe," Williams faces each segment's disappointments with a repetitious look of despondency. For example, for their reunion weekend, 1990's Hector and his children attend a small carnival. The disappointment each character feels while isolated on the small, seedy ride, circling endlessly, is virtually palpable, and the forlorn expression on Williams' face is familiar by this point in the film. After all, it is the same expression he wore as he watched his family be captured by Vikings and the same one he wore as he left Beatrice. Perhaps best known for his over-the-top characters, such as the genie in *Aladdin* (1992), Williams is an odd choice to play a character who is relentlessly discouraged. He is mired here.

Unfortunately, the film unifies its segments even further with recurring motifs. Trinkets figure largely: As the raiders take Hector's family, they leave him a necklace ornamented with chicken feet. As a slave, Hector wears a similar pendant, and as medieval Hector, he wears a relic he purchased in Jerusalem—a cup from the Last Supper. Ironically, the least redeemable of the Hectors, the conquistador, wears a cross, and by the twentieth century, Hector wears a tie.

Shoes also repeat. Hector the Roman slave steals his master's sandals as he escapes, a free man. Beatrice (in the medieval segment) steals the shoes from a dead child to bring to her son, wearing them home herself. Conquistador Hector takes boots from one of his soon-to-be-abandoned friends. The twentieth century Hector borrows the shoes of his former wife's new husband, finding them as inhospitable as conquistador Hector finds his purloined boots. While maintaining a certain unity, these recurring motifs tend to squelch surprise and interest.

Also in Bill Forsyth's tale, religion has improved little from the Bronze Age, where the raiders consult a pile of rocks for guidance. In the next segment, in Ouija-board style, Lucinnius consults a diviner who augurs the rise and fall of his commercial future. In the Middle Ages, Hector travels with a corrupt, perhaps even bogus, priest (Vincent D'Onofrio), who preaches against fornication even as he negotiates for it. The shipwrecked explorers hang two slaves, using a cross as a gallows, and the priest in the party begins visibly to rot as the vignette develops. By the twentieth century, a New Age, television call-in fortune teller guides the needy flock, once again, five thousand years later, turning to "holy" rocks for guidance.

For all its beauty, *Being Human* is finally a very disappointing film. Bill Forsyth and Robin Williams fans may want to pass on seeing *Being Human*, instead waiting and watching for the next work by either of these gifted artists.

—*Roberta F. Green*

REVIEWS

Atlanta Constitution. May 6, 1994, p. P4.
Boston Globe. May 6, 1994, p. 88.
Chicago Tribune. May 6, 1994, Tempo, p. 4.
Denver Post. May 6, 1994, p. 6.
Entertainment Weekly. May 20, 1994, p. 42.
The Hollywood Reporter. May 5, 1994, p. 8.
Los Angeles Times. May 6, 1994, p. F4.
The New York Times. May 6, 1994, p. B3.
Variety. May 5, 1994, p. 2.
The Washington Post. May 6, 1994, p. B7.

Belle Epoque

"...spirited ode to life, love and free will." —Bruce Williamson, *Playboy*

"One of the brightest and most delightful films of the year so far." —Jeffrey Lyons, *Sneak Previews*

"A hot-blooded human comedy." —Janet Maslin, *The New York Times*

"Sexy...comedy with the wisdom and detached compassion of Jean Renoir, to whom *Belle Epoque* could stand as an homage..." —*Los Angeles Times*

Box Office Gross: $5,908,732 (August 14, 1994)

Fernando Trueba, in his heartfelt acceptance speech for *Belle Epoque*'s Academy Award for Best Foreign-Language Film, quipped that he "would like to believe in God so that I could thank him, but I just believe in Billy Wilder. So, thank you, Billy Wilder." The line was no idle expression of hero worship: In *Belle Epoque*, the Spanish writer-director masters the lessons of the great seriocomic directors he reveres—Wilder, Jean Renoir, Ernst Lubitsch, Preston Sturges, and Howard Hawks—to spin his own wry, bucolic, ultimately poignant fable about a young man who discovers the importance of reveling in youth's fleeting pleasures, but also learns that the ability to choose among those pleasures, and to devote oneself to them, is the true measure of maturity.

In paying homage to his predecessors, Trueba also manages the welcome trick of bringing a worthy but moribund genre, the sex farce, back to its full glory without ever succumbing to mere pastiche. Like the film's young cook protagonist, Trueba has a natural talent for blending ingredients, and those of his idols are of the highest quality: From the classic Renoir of *Une Partie de Campagene* (1946, *A Day in the Country*) and *La Regle du Jeu* (1939, *The Rules of the Game*), Trueba stirs together the dappled sunlight of the countryside, the bemused gaze at the whirl of human sexual passions, and the sense of impending tragedy of which the characters are blissfully unaware; from the Wilder of *The Apartment* (1960), the Lubitsch of *Ninotchka* (1939), and the Sturges of *Hail the Conquering Hero* (1944), he mixes in the fundamentally decent protagonist who cannot tell if his or her newly awakened passion means freedom or corruption; from Hawks' entire oeuvre he adds an essential dose of strong-willed, independent female characters; and from

Belle Epoque's Maholo was inspired by director Trueba's father-in-law.

Shakespeare's *Henry the Fourth* (1596-1597), he steals a pinch of Falstaff and Prince Hal. Yet the recipe, the vision, remain firmly Trueba's. Like another of his spiritual mentors, the late French singer-songwriter Georges Brassens, Trueba uses his sly wit and wistful appreciation of the fires of youth to transform what is essentially a folk tale—in this case a crude one about a traveler and four farmer's daughters—into a multilayered work of art that bears his distinctive imprint.

The film begins with the image of a suitcase lying in the middle of a deserted country road. It appears to indicate a traveler irrevocably lost in the wilderness, but palm trees lining the road hint that Eden may not be too far away. The traveler is Fernando (Jorge Sanz), a young army deserter wandering the countryside in the chaotic aftermath of the 1931 rebellion against the Spanish monarchy. The opening scene itself plays like a tragicomic parable out of Brassens: Fernando is captured by a squabbling pair of military officers—a father and his son-in-law who—instead of taking Fernando to jail, begin a political argument about whether to release him. The son-in-law then shoots the father-in-law in defense of the monarchy and kills himself out of remorse.

Fernando finds refuge on the country estate of Don Manolo (Fernando Fernán Gómez), an aging, artistically blocked painter impressed by the agnostic Fernando's seemingly paradoxical religious expertise and sincere search for faith, as well as by his crack cooking skills. Manolo takes him in and confesses to his new drinking buddy that the three frustrations in his life have been, first, not "being born among heathens. Second, because of my feet, I wasn't called up for the army—so I couldn't desert. And third, it so happens that I can only get it up with my wife. So I can't cheat. You see the paradox. As I couldn't rebel against the church or the army or matrimony...here I am a rebel, an infidel, and a libertine by nature, living life like a scared old bourgeois." Fernando listens carefully to the old man's lessons, not knowing that within hours Manolo's idyllic estate will provide him the opportunity to live out the rebellious youth Manolo never had.

That opportunity arrives the next morning in the form of Manolo's four daughters. The scene in which Fernando, about to leave Manolo's, sees these four gorgeous, gossamer creatures alight from the train from Madrid is one of the most delicious ever filed. In an instant, Fernando's wandering has ceased; he has seen the promised land. Each daughter, however, for a different reason, gives Fernando a glance that betrays her needs—which range from sex to mourning to love. Fernando, as he will discover is as much the object of desire as the pursuer, and the games begin.

Fernando stays on at the estate as cook, and his good fortune rapidly turns to confusion as he becomes more and more embroiled in each of the daughters' lives. Rocío (Maribel Verdú) flirts shamelessly with him in order to make her stuffy hometown fiancé, Juanito (Gabino Diego), jealous enough to cut the apron strings that bind him to his royalist mother (Chus Lampreave). Violeta (Ariadna Gil), the tomboy of the sisters, seduces Fernando while they are both in drag at the town's masked ball, then confuses him by rejecting his proposal of marriage. Clara (Miriam Díaz-Aroca), the oldest, uses Fernando to come to terms with the recent death of her husband and her fears of becoming an old maid. Finally, Luz (Penélope Cruz), the youngest, must overcome her own jealousy and her sisters' self-centeredness in order to express her

"[I] would like to believe in God so that I could thank him, but I just believe in Billy Wilder. So, thank you, Billy Wilder."—Fernando Trueba, in his acceptance speech after winning an Academy Award for *Belle Epoque* for Best Foreign-Language Film

innocent love for Fernando. How Fernando comes to comprehend and accept his and Luz's feelings for each other amid the whirl of competing passions is the core of the film.

Winding their way through the farce, however, are two more melancholy motifs: the doomed Falstaff-Hal friendship between Don Manolo and Fernando, and the fate of the fragile Spanish democratic spring of 1931. Both motifs cast the shadow of the film's first murderous scene. In the case of Don Manolo and Fernando, Don Manolo repeatedly reminds Fernando that if he gains a son-in-law, he will lose a friend. Although Fernando dismisses the suggestion, his choice of Luz will indeed result in Don Manolo's once again being left alone with his memories, like Falstaff. It is hardly parricide, to be sure, but it is another small death for Manolo, nevertheless. The backdrop of Spanish history is more tragic. In only five years, Spain would plunge into the civil war foreshadowed at the outset of the film, and this dramatic irony accentuates the preciousness of this idyll at Don Manolo's, this chance for each character to break old boundaries and find love and acceptance.

Trueba knows that the real villain in sex farces and romantic comedies is the passage of time, the loss of youth. In the more tragic film farces such as Hal Ashby's *Shampoo* (1975) and Renoir's *La Regle du Jeu*, time runs out: the protagonist finds love too late, or cannot surmount unspoken social rules and taboos. In Trueba's sunny world, however, everything works out. Rocío gets a liberated Juanito, Clara gets confirmation she is not an old maid, Violeta gets respect for her independence, and Fernando and Luz get each other. Even Don Manolo gets the once-a-year return of his touring opera-singer wife (Mary Carmen Ramírez)—although with her lover-manager (Michel Galabru) in tow—which provides the third-act catalyst to resolve the sexual snarl.

Still, the scenes from *Belle Epoque* that endure are those that contrast the sunny discoveries of love, sex, friendship, and freedom with the relentless passage of time. In the most moving of them, Don Manolo drives his carriage, drawn by his faithful horse, Lucero, through the night with surrogate

CREDITS

Fernando: Jorge Sanz
Manolo: Fernando Fernán Gómez
Rocío: Maribel Verdú
Violeta: Ariadna Gil
Clara: Miriam Díaz-Aroca
Luz: Penélope Cruz
Juanito: Gabino Diego
Doña Asun: Chus Lampreave
Amalia: Mary Carmen Ramírez
Danglard: Michel Galabru
Don Luis: Agustín González

Origin: Spain
Released: 1993
Production: Fernando Trueba for Lola Films, Animatografo, and French, with the cooperation of Sogepaq and Eurimages; released by Sony Pictures Classics
Direction: Fernando Trueba
Screenplay: Rafael Azcona; based on a story by Azcona, José Luis García Sanchez, and Fernando Trueba
Cinematography: José Luis Alcaine
Editing: Carmen Frías
Art direction: Juan Botella
Sound: Georges Prat
Costume design: Lala Huete
Music: Antoine Duhamel
MPAA rating: R
Running time: 108 minutes

AWARDS AND NOMINATIONS

Academy Awards 1993: Best Foreign Language Film
Goya Awards: Best Picture, Best Direction (Fernando Trueba), Best Actress (Ariadna Gil), Best Supporting Actor (Fernando Fernán Gómez), Best Supporting Actress (Chus Lampreave), Original Screenplay (Rafael Azcona), Cinematography (José Luis Alcaine), Art Direction (Juan Botella), and Editing (Carmen Frías)

son Fernando at his side. Manolo waxes poetic and quotes Thomas Mann: " 'O charming organic beauty, not composed of painting or stone, but of living, uncorruptible matter. Look at the shoulders and hips, and the flowery bosoms on both sides of the chest, and the ribs, aligned in pairs, and the navel in the belly's softness, and the dark sex between the thighs. Let me feel your pores exhaling, and touch your down, a human image of water and albumen, destined to the anatomy of the tomb, and let me die with my lips pressed to yours!.....' Such youth!" It is a lament for the youth Manolo never had himself, but which he has, as an old man, been able to confer upon his daughters and his future son-in-law. The film's final image is of Manolo, having taught his loved ones the lessons he could and having bid them all farewell, riding off with Lucero into the night.

Not only has Trueba learned the lessons of his elders but he has also created a paean to the passing down of life's lessons from generation to generation. *Belle Epoque* is a whispered admonition to seize the day, and the title refers to this "beautiful time" in Fernando's life. It also marks the arrival on the international scene of a major and prodigiously talented filmmaker.

—*Paul Mittelbach*

REVIEWS

The Christian Science Monitor. February 25, 1994, p. 12.
Entertainment Weekly. April 15, 1994, p. 41.
The Hollywood Reporter. January 20, 1994, p. 14.
Los Angeles Times. March 2, 1994, p. F3.
The New Republic. CCX, February 21, 1994, p. 28.
The New York Times. February 25, 1994, p. B4.
Time. CXLIII, March 21, 1994, p. 71.
The Wall Street Journal. February 24, 1994, p. A16.

Between the Teeth

David Byrne, former member of the defunct rock band Talking Heads, performs with his band 10 Car Pileup as well as co-directs this concert film.

CREDITS

David Byrne: David Byrne
Bobby Allende: Bobby Allende
Jonathan Best: Jonathan Best
Angel Fernandez: Angel Fernandez
Ite Jerez: Ite Jerez
Lewis Kahn: Lewis Kahn
George Porter, Jr.: George Porter, Jr.
Hector Rosado: Hector Rosado

Steve Sacks: Steve Sacks
Oscar Salas: Oscar Salas

Released: 1994
Production: Joel D. Hinman for Scorched Earth Productions; released by Todo Mundo Ltd.
Direction: David Byrne and David Wild
Cinematography: Roger Tonry
Editing: David Wild and Lou Angelo
Sound: Randy Ezratty
Music: 10 Car Pileup
MPAA rating: no listing
Running Time: 70 minutes

Beverly Hills Cop III

"Eddie Murphy's Axel Foley has never been funnier."—Jim Ferguson, *KMSB-TV*

"Hilarious! A wild, funny action-comedy."
—Bill Diehl, *ABC Radio Network*

 Box Office Gross: $42,570,665 (October 9, 1994)

Eddie Murphy as Detroit Police Detective Axel Foley and Bronson Pinchot as Serge in *Beverly Hills Cop III*. Copyright © 1994 Paramount Pictures. All rights reserved.

I n the opening sequence of *Beverly Hills Cop III*, Detroit detective inspector Todd (played by former Detroit homicide inspector Gil Hill) dies after taking two or three of the several thousand bullets fired during a chop-shop raid. Todd expires largely because police detective Axel Foley (Eddie Murphy) ignores Todd's advice to call in a SWAT team before descending on the crime site. Unfortunately, this is but one instance among many when Murphy's wise-cracking cop character loses audience sympathy. This scene is also indicative of the many problems plaguing the film: The extreme violence and nonsensical plot overshadow what little humor exists.

A little over a decade earlier, star Eddie Murphy burst out of television's *Saturday Night Live* and into theaters with *48 Hrs.* (1982), a classic film among action/adventure fans, tempered by wit, selective verisimilitude, and interesting characters. Some would nominate Murphy's redneck bar scene from *48 Hrs.* as one of the funniest scenes ever filmed. This mating of Murphy's hip humor and the police beat was too appealing to let slide, so *Beverly Hills Cop* (1984) introduced detective Axel Foley and a format that tilted heavily toward comedy without losing sight of key realities within the police milieu. Its sequel, *Beverly Hills Cop II* (1987), however, got silly, more violent, and much less funny.

The release of *Beverly Hills Cop III* after a seven-year interval undoubtedly found many fans of Murphy and the genre hoping for a return to glory and a recapturing of the proper comedic and dramatic sensibilities. Instead, despite a screenwriting credit to Steven E. de Souza, who also shared credit for *48 Hrs.*, *Beverly Hills Cop III* is one of the most wrongheaded cop stories ever put before a camera. All but the most rabid Murphy fans will emerge gasping for a believable story or at least a little gratuitous humor. John Landis had previously directed Murphy in two successful comedies, *Coming to America*

 Former Detroit homicide detective Gilbert Hill returns as Inspector Todd, Axel's boss. Celebrity cameos include George Lucas as a vacationer Axel cuts in front of in line at Wonder World and John Singleton as a fireman.

(1988) and *Trading Places* (1983). He also directed the amusing *National Lampoon's Animal House* (1978) and *Three Amigos* (1986), so he clearly understands the concept of making an audience laugh. Yet something somewhere went very wrong.

The film begins promisingly enough: Inside the chop shop are three corpulent car thieves pantomiming a Supremes tune that blares from the shop's boom box. Then strangers arrive, and what follows makes the St. Valentine's Day Massacre look like an ice cream social. No prisoners taken. Uzis ooze lead everywhere. Among the many casualties, the man in the paint booth sinks to his death with his finger on the trigger spraying red paint over everything.

Into the fracas jump Axel Foley's crack team, who choose this moment to raid the small-time thieves, who are inside dying at the hands of the mysterious strangers. Todd, dropping back to the scene to see how his charges are doing, is shot point-blank by chief bad guy Ellis DeWald (Timothy Carhart). The fact that DeWald, as it will turn out, is essentially a white-collar criminal well respected in the highest business circles some two thousand miles to the west in Los Angeles does not exactly jibe with his hands-on leadership of an untidy blood bath in Detroit. Yet that is the least of the purposeless inattention to reality this script will indulge.

As it turns out, DeWald and his cohorts are executives of a Disney-like amusement park called WonderWorld, where they are manufacturing counterfeit money in the bowels of a ride that is closed for remodeling. The park's founder, beloved Uncle Dave, is played by Alan Young, best known as the star of the classic television show *Mr. Ed*. Kind Uncle Dave has no idea that his Gestapo-like security force is cranking out funny money on stolen Treasury paper, using what looks like a photocopying machine turning out what look like one-dollar denominations. In this ultraviolent outing, even lovable Uncle Dave gets shot in cold blood before the script winds down, although he does survive.

"You gotta refrigerator! Not even J. Edgar Hoover had a refrigerator! Maybe some rollers and a dryer, though."—Axel Foley (*Beverly Hills Cop III*)

Thus it is that Todd's dying words—imploring Foley to get DeWald and friends—lead Axel to chase the bad guys out of Detroit, while eluding approximately 2,000 more rounds fired from the vehicle he pursues, and return once again to Los Angeles. Once there, Axel leaps from car to car

of an aerial ride called the Spider, goes one-on-one-hundred with DeWald's security force, disguises himself as a humorous theme-park character, and engages in yet another shoot-out—the gory aftermath of which is punctuated by comedic music.

Of Axel's old buddies in the Los Angeles Police Department (L.A.P.D.), only Billy Rosewood (Judge Reinhold) remains on duty. Rosewood has become a techno dweeb with a permit to carry a concealed weapon. Jon Flint (Hector Elizondo) is a new character, a cop who is near retirement and yearning for a job with WonderWorld security. The script forces the very competent Elizondo to believe in his future employers' innocence even after the popcorn girl in the lobby has figured out that they are the devil incarnate.

Reprising his role from *Beverly Hills Cop* is Bronson Pinchot, whose portrayal of Serge, the gay art-gallery denizen, was a showstopper the first time around. This time he is Serge, proprietor of a weapons boutique, and is still funny. Whether he is still funny several minutes after the last drop is milked from the character is probably a matter of personal taste. The unedited, unending visit with Serge looked and sounded like the flag of desperation being run up the producer's mast.

All in all, *Beverly Hills Cop III* will prove a disappointment. Its weak script, pointless violence, and strained humor relegate it to the bin of formulaic Hollywood sequels. Most disappointing of all is Murphy, who down plays his character to excess and lacks his now-expected comic repartee. At least Serge's big scene is unambiguously a time to be funny. Axel Foley just stands there watching Serge do his thing.

—*Tom W. Ferguson*

CREDITS

Axel Foley: Eddie Murphy
Billy Rosewood: Judge Reinhold
Jon Flint: Hector Elizondo
Ellis DeWald: Timothy Carhart
Steve Fulbright: Stephen McHattie
Janice: Theresa Randle
Orrin Sanderson: John Saxon
Uncle Dave Thornton: Alan Young
Serge: Bronson Pinchot
Minister: Al Green
Ticket booth girl: Tracy Lindsey
Todd: Gil Hill

Released: 1994
Production: Mace Neufeld and Robert Rehme, in association with Eddie Murphy Productions; released by Paramount Pictures
Direction: John Landis
Screenplay: Steven E. de Souza; based on characters created by Danilo Bach and Daniel Petrie, Jr.
Cinematography: Mac Ahlberg
Editing: Dale Beldin
Production design: Michael Seymour
Art direction: Thomas P. Wilkins
Set decoration: Marvin March
Casting: Jackie Burch
Special effects coordination: Jon G. Belyeu
Sound: Joseph Geisinger
Costume design: Catherine Adair
Music: Nile Rodgers
MPAA rating: R
Running time: 109 minutes

REVIEWS

Atlanta Constitution. May 25, 1994, p. C10.
Boston Globe. May 25, 1994, p. 69.
Christian Science Monitor. December 29, 1994, p. 10.
Ebony. June, 1994, p. 100.
Entertainment Weekly. June 3, 1994, p. 34.
Entertainment Weekly. November 11, 1994, p. 89.
The Hollywood Reporter. May 25, 1994, p. 10.
Los Angeles Times, May 25, 1994, p. F1.
New York. XXVII, June 6, 1994, p. 53.
The New York Times. May 25, 1994, p. C16.
People Weekly. XLI, June 6, 1994, p. 16.
Rolling Stone. June 30, 1994, p. 81.
Time. CXLIII, June 6, 1994, p. 66.
TV Guide. XLII, November 19, 1994, p. 49.
Variety. May 25, 1994, p. 2.
Variety. CCCLV, May 30, 1994, p. 42.
The Washington Post. May 25, 1994, p. C12.
The Washington Post. May 26, 1994, p. D7.

Bhaji on the Beach

"A must see. A superintelligent comedy—for rude girls everywhere." —Amy Taubin, *The Village Voice*

"Sheer entertainment—a spicy feminine brew." —Judy Stone, *San Francisco Chronicle*

"An effervescent vision of sisterhood." —Heather Mackey, San Francisco Weekly

"Boldly irreverent and hilariously disapproving!" —B. Ruby Rich, *Elle*

"Vibrant, bustling and energetic. A colorful cross-section of attitudes." —Janet Maslin, *The New York Times*

 Box Office Gross: $594,933 (August 21, 1994)

Bhaji on the Beach is a delightful film by first-time director Gurinder Chadha. Chadha and screenwriter Meera Syal have created a story that is charming, tender, funny, and moralistic without being didactic. "Bhaji" refers to something that started out Indian and changed its identity. For example, "Bhajia" is a traditional Indian food that has changed into a variation called "Bhaji" as it is served in Great Britain and the United States. *Bhaji on the Beach* is about a life-changing day for several British-Indian women. It is about cultural identity, about the female identity in a male-dominated world, and about the clash of old and new culture.

Director Chadha is a former documentary filmmaker who has been greatly influenced by films of the British social realism school.

 Director and co-storywriter Gurinder Chadra received financing for *Bhaji on the Beach* at Barclay's in London, where her father had been rejected from a job thirty years earlier. The film was produced by the "Film on Four" series, which also produced *My Beautiful Laundrette*, *The Crying Game*, and *Four Weddings and a Funeral*.

Her film poses important questions about the validity of traditional culture and the validity of traditional male and female roles. Without being overly polemic or political, Chadha and writer Syal have made an entertaining film that asks the questions without bludgeoning the audience with simplistic answers.

Asha (Lalita Ahmed) is a rather traditional woman who owns a video and newspaper store. Her nephew Ranjit (Jimmi Harkishin) is separated from his beautiful wife, Ginder (Kim Vithana), with whom he has a young son. One of the film's central conflicts is that Ginder has left Ranjit, taking their son with her. This goes against tradition, and the fact that Ginder is not obeying her husband's wishes to return home is humiliating to Ranjit and his family.

Ginder's friend Simi (Shaheen Khan) has arranged a day-trip to the beach to see "The Illumination Festival," a parade of lighted floats and cars. She convinces Ginder to bring her son and accompany her on the day-trip, along with several other women: Hashida (Sarita Khajuria), a pre-med student who has just discovered that she is pregnant by a black man, Oliver (Mo Sesay); Ladhu and Madhu (Nisha Nayar and Renu Kochar), two teenage, boy-crazy sisters; Asha; and two other older women, Bina (Surendra Kochar) and Pushpa (Zohra Segal). Pushpa is particularly crotchety and tradition-bound, causing much friction when she discovers that young Hashida is pregnant—by a man of another race, no less.

Writer Syal and director Chadha add one more character to the clever mixed bag of day-trippers: an Indian woman named Rekha (Souad Faress), who lives in Bombay and is visiting England. Rekha is one of the smaller roles in the ensemble, but her presence is essential to the audience's understanding of Chadha's theme. Although Rekha is the only woman in the group still living in India, she dresses in a garishly modern way and is quite untraditional in her thinking. She is a wonderful contrast to the expatriate Pushpa and Asha, who maintain Indian traditions although they no longer live in India.

Indeed, Asha is already quite worried about the encroaching British culture. The film begins with the first of several hilarious "visions" seen by Asha, where she begs the God Rama to help her cope with the changes going on around her. Apparently, these visions are a reference to similar histrionic sequences employed in the Bombay cinema (termed "Bollywood" by many in the Indian cinema community). Overblown fantasy sequences are frequently used in these films, and here director Chadha uses them for a multilayered effect: They no only are funny parodies of "Bollywood" films but also illuminate the character of Asha and underscore the thematic exploration of the loss of traditional culture. These sequences are also reminiscent of Tevye's dream sequence in the musical, *Fiddler on the Roof*.

Initially, the women are no more than fellow passengers. There is a noticeable rift between Asha and Ginder, simply because Ginder has chosen to separate from Asha's nephew. The women board a rickety bus, and leader/driver Simi cheerfully chirps that they should have a "female fun time" as she steers the bus on to the highway. While the women begin their trip, Ranjit and his two brothers (Tanveer Ghani and Akbar Kurtha) set out to find Ginder, bring her home, and restore peace to their humiliated family. Meanwhile, Oliver, the man by whom Hashida has become pregnant, sets out on his motorcycle to find Hashida and patch up the argument they had about her pregnancy.

The men, however, appear confused by the independent actions of "their" women. Ranjit is the stereotypical male found in any culture who feels that he has a right to dictate his wife's actions. Oliver is emblematic of the more progressive thinker who realizes that he must instead cooperate with the woman he loves.

"Have a female fun time!"—tour organizer Simi, from *Bhaji on the Beach*

The themes of adaptation and change are played out on the levels of male/female relations, racism, and culture. When Oliver's friend tells him that "all this infusion only causes confusion," the young black man is expressing what is apparently a fairly universal fear: that "mixing" with other races results in the loss of traditional cultural values.

CREDITS

Ginder: Kim Vithana
Ranjit: Jimmi Harkishin
Hashida: Sarita Khajuria
Oliver: Mo Sesay
Asha: Lalita Ahmed
Simi: Shaheen Khan
Pushpa: Zohra Segal
Ladhu: Nisha Nayar
Madhu: Renu Kochar
Bina: Surendra Kochar
Rekha: Souad Faress
Ambrose Waddington: Pecter Cellier
No character identified: Tanveer Ghani
No character identified: Akbar Kurtha

Origin: Great Britain
Released: 1993
Production: Nadine Marsh-Edwards for Umbi Films and Film Four International; released by First Look Pictures
Direction: Gurinder Chadha
Screenplay: Meera Syal
Cinematography: John Kenway
Editing: Oral Ottley
Production design: Derek Brown
Sound: Ronald Bailey
Costume design: Annie Symons
Music: John Altman, Craig Pruess and Kuljit Bhamra
MPAA rating: no listing
Running time: 100 minutes

The culture of India had rarely been depicted in Western cinema. Although *My Beautiful Launderette* (1985) was actually about the culture clash among British Pakistanis, the Pakistani and Indian communities were still lumped together in the minds of many Westerners. Another film exploring the clash of Indian and Western culture was the romantic *Mississippi Masala* (1992), starring Denzel Washington. Though the Indian cinema was hugely popular, there was little crossover with Western cinema.

Consequently, each of the women is a unique and refreshing presence on film. Kim Vithana as Ginder is stunningly beautiful and delivers a subtle performance as a young woman who vacillates between strength and uncertainty. Vithana's luminous beauty and natural acting ability are among the strongest assets of this film. The elderly Pushpa is played hilariously by Zohra Segal, who manages to make the old woman funny without being so ridiculous that loses audience sympathy. The fact that the character is lovable in spite of her racism and narrow mindedness is due to Segal's ability to ground her character in truth, making a comic "villain" who is a real person. Asha, the aunt who has visions, is a difficult role because of the constant need to look worried, but Lalita Ahmed's subtle performance is never passive and overindulgent. All the other characters are similarly realistic and engaging.

The males all deliver fine performances as well. Yet the film's showstopping performance goes to actor Peter Cellier as the aging thespian, Ambrose Waddington, who becomes smitten with the uptight Asha. Ambrose meets Asha on the beach and offers to show her the sights of the dilapidated beachside town, saying "it would be an honor to escort a lady around this fallen woman I call home." From his dapper seersucker suit to his straw hat, he looks like he stepped off the stage of a British music hall. Cellier is hilarious and touching, delivering amusing lines, such as "I'm on the short list to play the Widow Twanky in the Christmas pantomime," with the skill of an expert vaudevillian.

His, too, is a fully realized performance, which is thematically integrated into the film as well: He tells Asha, "We [British] are not like you. You've kept hold of your traditions." The irony of this man, a veritable icon of British culture, telling Asha that she is more virtuous than he because she has supposedly kept her culture sends Asha over the edge—into another vision. She says, "I went to college. My life was not meant to be like this. Duty, honor, sacrifice...what about me?" Her questions about the validity of her life lead her and the other women to new understanding of Ginder and Hashida's more modern ways.

Ultimately, the women are bound together on the most basic level: as women. Revelations about Ranjit's treatment of Ginder unite the women in a way that transcends culture and stereotypical values. Thus, the audience comes to realize that for all the world's struggles with racism, xenophobia, and cultural diversity, all people regardless of race are united by a common desire for love and respect.

This simple film points out that all women are united by their struggle for respect and fair treatment. It is indeed a painful truth that mutual respect, kindness, and tolerance are not intrinsic to most cultures. *Bhaji on the Beach* has universal appeal because of its humorous and gentle depiction of the struggle of individuals to overcome their personal prejudices and foibles in the context of an ever-changing world.

—Kirby Tepper

REVIEWS

The Hollywood Reporter. October 14, 1993, p. 5.
Los Angeles Times. June 22, 1994, p. F1.
The New York Times. March 19, 1994, p. 12.
Variety. October 7, 1993, p. 7.

Bitter Moon

"One of the great all-time trashy sex films"
—Glamour

"A cruise full of eroticism...a carnal hoot fest."
—Peter Rainer, *Los Angeles Times*

"wickedly funny." —Peter Travers, *Rolling Stone*

"a gleefully masochistic love story." —Janet Maslin, *The New York Times*

"The Polanski film we've all been waiting for."
—Entertainment Weekly

"Perversely comic...*The Love Boat* meets *Last Tango in Paris*." *—Newsday*

"The most powerful film about sensuality and passion since *Last Tango in Paris*." —Rod Lurie, *Los Angeles Magazine*

 Box Office Gross: $1,811,767 (July 17, 1994)

On a Mediterranean cruise ship, Nigel (Hugh Grant) and Fiona (Kristin Scott-Thomas), an English couple married seven years, meet Mimi (Emmanuelle Seigner) and Oscar (Peter Coyote), a French-American couple. Fiona first encounters Mimi in the ladies' room, suffering from a bout of seasickness, and Nigel helps Fiona guide Mimi to the deck for fresh air. Nigel later observes a very sexy woman dancing by herself in the bar, and when she comes to the counter for a drink, he recognizes her as Mimi. Obviously interested in her, he tries to make conversation, but she ridicules his boring English formality. Embarrassed, he retreats. Soon, however, he is accosted by Oscar, a wheelchair-bound raconteur, who invites Nigel to his cabin to hear about his life with Mimi.

Although Mimi is attractive, why should Nigel accept Oscar's invitation? Oscar knows how to spin a story, but Nigel is revolted by his sexual revelations and his cynicism concerning love. Nigel expresses his disgust, yet he keeps returning for more of Oscar's story. One soon sees that Oscar is playing a game with Nigel: His story is riveting pre-

Emmanuelle Seigner as Mimi and Hugh Grant as Nigel in *Bitter Moon*.

CREDITS

Oscar: Peter Coyote
Mimi: Emmanuelle Seigner
Nigel: Hugh Grant
Fiona: Kristin Scott-Thomas
Mr. Singh: Victor Banerjee
Amrita: Sophie Patel
Steward: Patrick Albenque
Bridge player: Smilja Mihailovitch
Bridge player: Leo Eckmann
Dado: Luca Vellani

Origin: France and Great Britain
Released: 1992
Production: Roman Polanski for R.P. Productions and Timothy Burrill Productions, in association with Les Films Alain Sarde and Canal Plus
Production: Released by Fine Line Features
Direction: Roman Polanski
Screenplay: Roman Polanski, Gérard Brach, and John Brownjohn; based on the novel *Lunes de Fiel*, by Pascal Bruckner
Cinematography: Tonino Delli Colli
Editing: Herve de Luze
Production design: Willy Holt and Gerard Viard
Casting: Bonnie Timmerman and Mary Selway-Francoise Menidrey
Sound: Daniel Brisseau
Costume design: Jackie Budin
Music: Vangelis
MPAA rating: R
Running time: 139 minutes

cisely because it is so intimate and prurient. Oscar's a brand of pornography excites Nigel precisely because it is in bad taste and because Nigel has never allowed himself to eavesdrop on someone else's life—it is not something a gentleman would do.

Fiona becomes increasingly irritated by Nigel's obsession with Oscar and Mimi. It is obvious to Fiona that Nigel lusts after Mimi, and she is not fooled for a minute by his protests that he is merely placating the plaintive Oscar, who needs a sympathetic ear. It also becomes apparent at a shipboard meal that Nigel and Fiona's marriage has become a bit stale. They tell Mr. Singh (Victor Banerjee) they are on their way to India, the land of spiritual fulfillment. Mr. Singh laughs, for he regards his homeland as hardly the setting for spiritual renewal; it is intolerably noisy and the last place where the self can be reborn. His response underscores the unreality of Nigel and

> "We were inseparable by day and insatiable by night. We just lived on love and stale croissants."—Oscar on his initial relationship with wife Mimi in *Bitter Moon*

Fiona's trip. It is a kind of dream journey, meant to jog them out of their normal selves.

Oscar has done what Nigel can only imagine doing. Oscar has lived in Paris, pursuing his dream of becoming a great writer in the tradition of Ernest Hemingway and other American expatriates. He is completely self-absorbed, involving himself with women as a projection of his literary power and sometimes seducing women because he has failed as a writer. Ironically, none of his novels has been published.

Oscar lives with an intensity that leaves the low-throttle Nigel gasping with wonder and revulsion. Nigel learns that Oscar first saw Mimi on a bus and was smitten with her beauty. Oscar let the moment pass, however, without saying anything to her. Thereafter, Oscar haunted that bus hoping to meet Mimi again. Instead, he discovered her working in a restaurant. Their meeting was as accidental as Nigel's with Mimi. The difference is that Oscar did not try to make small talk; he immediately told Mimi he was looking for her and asked her for a date. This kind of detail is what binds Nigel to Oscar, even when Oscar taunts Nigel with his English timidity and sense of propriety. Oscar is, in fact, Nigel's alter ego.

Midway through his story Oscar comes to the point: He knows Nigel is interested in Mimi. Oscar raises no objection to Nigel's bedding Mimi, but he exacts a price: Nigel must hear Oscar's story to the end before acting on his sexual impulses. Nigel is given the opportunity to do just that when Fiona succumbs to a monumental case of seasickness and is knocked out by several Dramamine tablets.

Until this point, Mimi has kept to herself. Now she asks Nigel to come to her cabin. Thinking he is about to consummate his desire, Nigel enters her unlocked compartment and grasps a hand. It turns out to be Oscar's, however, who laughs as Mimi flees the room. Yet even this humiliation does not deter Nigel, who realizes he must sit through the denouement of Oscar's story in order to enjoy Mimi.

Oscar narrates the way his relationship with Mimi went through various stages from the rapture of their early days to a middle period, where they could only excite each other by engaging in various sexual games and sadomasochistic practices, to a final period when a bored Oscar humiliated Mimi, who continued to love him. No cruelty was great enough to drive her away. So he resorted to the ruse of embarking on a trip with her, only to abandon her on the airplane minutes before take off. Free to indulge himself, he abandoned all pretense of writing and wallowed in the women he was able to pick up. One drunken night, having said good-bye to one of two young women, he walked right into the path of a passing car, which knocked him down and broke his femur.

Oscar was surprised to get a hospital visit from Mimi, who had begun to look as cynical as he. She had returned for revenge, knocking him out of his hospital bed and causing the injury that left him paralyzed in a wheelchair. The rest of his life, as he relates it to Nigel, has been a torment provoked by his wretched treatment of Mimi. She is cruel to him and yet, in her own way, cares for him. The couple, however, has reached a dead end—not only in their relationship but in their ability to respond to life. In other words, pursuing lives so different from Nigel and Fiona, Oscar and Mimi have also gone stale.

Bitter Moon's themes emerge gradually in the revelations of human character. Nigel is a stereotype of the stiff Englishman, but it is futile to deny such types exist. Fiona shares Nigel's manners, but there is an undercurrent of passion in her that links her to Mimi—an undercurrent that suddenly erupts in the dance she performs with Mimi during the New Year's Eve party near the end of the film.

Peter Coyote is superb as the hard-boiled writer, cynical and sentimental, the very essence of a degenerated Hemingwayesque tradition. In the flashbacks of Oscar's narrated story, he appears with soft hair combed to the side, falling on his face. Camera angles capture his profile and his softer features. In this early period, Oscar can still appear as a hero to himself and others, especially to Mimi and perhaps to Nigel, although he does not admit it. Aboard ship, however, Oscar is shot head-on with projecting parts of his face—such as his nose—making him seem harder and more brutal. With his hair combed back, looking slightly wet and greasy, he presents a visage squeezed of its tenderness and sensitivity. He is a hollow shell of a man, subsisting in the shadows. He is rarely shot in natural light, for he is a creature of the bowels of the ship, a narrator of the lover's baser instincts.

Bitter Moon is a subtle, disturbing film about how love is lost when it is pursued to the exclusion of everything else. Lovers can kill their love; they can so enclose themselves in each other—as Mimi and Oscar did, who often did not leave their Paris apartment for days—that love turns into hatred and even self-loathing. By itself, the story seems schematic and its moral trite, yet the high quality of the performances, the skill of the direction—especially in the alternation of interior and exterior shots—and the cinematography and makeup combine to make the film a fascinating and upsetting experience.

—*Carl Rollyson*

REVIEWS

Entertainment Weekly. March 25, 1994, p. 36.
Film Comment. January, 1994, p. 12.
The Hollywood Reporter. September 15, 1993, p. 5.
Interview. February, 1994, p. 72.
Los Angeles Times. March 18, 1994, p. F1.
New Statesman and Society. October 2, 1992, p. 36.
New Woman. March, 1994, p. 32.
The New York Times. March 18, 1994, p. B9.
Playboy. March, 1994, p. 17.
Rolling Stone. February 24, 1994, p. 62.
Sight and Sound. October, 1992, p. 53.
Sight and Sound. June, 1993, p. 72.
Spectator. October 3, 1994, p. 38.
Times Literary Supplement. October 9, 1992, p. 19.
Variety. September 1, 1992, p. 10.
Vogue. February, 1994, p. 116.

Bix (1990)

This Italian-made biography tracks the short but illustrious career of jazz musician Leon "Bix" Beiderbecke (Bryant Weeks), who died at age twenty-eight in 1931. Story unfolds in flashbacks, through friend Joe Venuti's memories of the dissipated genius and the music he created with Hoagy Carmichael, Pee Wee Russell, Paul Whiteman, and others.

REVIEWS

Los Angeles Times. May 30, 1994, p. F6.
The Washington Post. June 16, 1994, p. C7.

CREDITS

Leon "Bix" Beiderbecke: Bryant Weeks
Joe Venuti: Emile Levisetti
Aggie Beiderbecke: Julia Ewing
Burnie Beiderbecke: Mark Collver
Hoagy Carmichael: Romano Luccio Orzari
Don Murray: Matthew Buzzel
Bismark: Ray Edelstein
Frankie Trumbauer: Mark James Sovel
Marie-Louise: Barbara Wilder

Lisa: Sally Groth
Pee Wee: Michael T. Henderson

Origin: Italy
Released: 1990
Production: Antonio Avati
Direction: Pupi Avati
Screenplay: Pupi Avati, Antonio Avati, and Lino Patruno
Cinematography: Pasquale Rachini
Editing: Amedeo Salfa
Production design: Carlo Simi
Costume design: Graziella Virgili and Carla Seinera Bertonik
Music: Bob Wilber
MPAA rating: no listing
Running time: 111 minutes

Two films about jazz musician Leon "Bix" Beiderbecke were released in the United States in 1994.

Bix (1991)

Innovative jazz musician Bix Beiderbecke is the subject of this documentary. Incorporating rare musical recordings and interviews with such famous personages as Hoagy Carmichael and Louis Armstrong, this documentary pays homage to the great musician whose illustrious career was short-lived, as he died at age twenty-eight in 1931.

REVIEWS

Variety.CCCXLIII, May 13, 1991, p. 105.

CREDITS

Narrator: Richard Basehart

Released: 1991
Production: Brigitte Berman
Direction: Brigitte Berman
Editing: Brigitte Berman
Project consultation: Richard Williams
MPAA rating: no listing
Running time: 117 minutes

Black Beauty

 Box Office Gross: $4,581,486 (September 25, 1994)

Black Beauty, based on the classic 1877 children's novel by Anna Sewell, is the episodic tale of the life of a good-natured horse that passes from owner to owner in late nineteenth century England. Although nominally a children's film, *Black Beauty*'s bleak story line and serious social themes may deter its target audience.

The film opens with the birth of Black Beauty to kindly Farmer Grey (Sean Bean) and depicts him growing up happy alongside his loving mother in the idyllic countryside. When he is about four years old, Black Beauty is sold to Squire Gordon (Peter Davison) of Birtwick Park, a kind man with an ailing wife and three children. It is here that Black Beauty befriends two other horses—Ginger, a feisty chestnut mare, and Merrylegs, an aptly named dapple-gray pony. The scenes of the three frolicking in the fields together, unfettered, are by far the cheeriest of the film. Then reality sets in: Black Beauty is broken to the bit and bridle and must learn to pull his own weight—literally. He at first rebels but soon learns that it can be a pleasant thing to serve a good master. Squire Gordon's head man, John Manly (Jim Carter), is kind, intelligent, and dedicated to the care of the horses under his charge.

One dark and stormy night, Black Beauty proves his worth when he saves John Manly's life: As he pulls Manly and Squire Gordon in a carriage, the bridge gives way in a flash flood. Manly—who had been trying to coax Black Beauty across what the horse could sense was an unsafe bridge—falls in the water when the bridge gives way. He would have been swept away were it not for Black Beauty's firm grip on his bit while Manly struggled to hang onto the horse's reins. Unfortunately, once back on the estate, Manly, who was slightly injured, is rushed indoors while Black Beauty is left in the inexperienced hands of Manly's assistant, young Joe Green (Andrew Knott). Joe, in a misguided

1994's *Black Beauty* is the fifth movie version of Anna Sewell's classic.

attempt to help, gives the steaming, sweaty horse cold water to drink and decides against covering him with his customary blanket. By morning, Black Beauty has taken deathly ill. Wracked with guilt, Joe spends every waking moment caring for the sick horse and, in nursing Black Beauty back to health, forms a lifelong attachment to him. Later, however, when Squire Gordon's wife becomes so ill that the entire family is forced to relocate to a warmer climate, Black Beauty finds himself sold to a new owner once again.

Black Beauty then finds himself on the elegant estate of the aristocratic Earl of Wexmire (Peter Cook). It is here that Black Beauty begins to learn that not all human masters are as kind and considerate as Squire Gordon and Farmer Grey. The earl's wife, the Countess of Wexmire (Eleanor Bron), insists on the use of the check-rein when she rides—a method of keeping the horse's head high by tightening the rein. Although it was considered very stylish in its day, the method was very uncomfortable for the horse. Yet Black Beauty endures every indignity, until one night when the earl's driver, Reuben Smith (Alun Armstrong), takes off on Black Beauty, dead drunk. The horse suffers a dreadful fall and permanently injures his knees. Although it is determined that Black Beauty was not at fault for the accident, his injured knees force the earl to sell him. Thus begins Black Beauty's agonizing decline as he is sold from one harsh master to the next, considered fit only to pull carts and to perform other menial labor.

Black Beauty does find himself at one point with a kind, if poor, man: Jerry Barker (David Thewlis), a London cabdriver who is reminiscent of Bob Cratchit in Charles Dickens' *A Christmas Carol* (1843), right down to his devoted wife and children. This position is short-lived, however, when Jerry is struck down with bronchitis after being forced to wait hours in the dead of winter for a fare. Black Beauty is again sold.

When all seems lost and Black Beauty has become a broken-down shadow of his former self, he finds himself once more up for sale at a horse show. While there, he spots the now-adult Joe Green looking over the horses and whinnies until he gains Joe's attention. Joe does not at first recognize the once-beautiful horse but, at Black Beauty's insistence, gives him a second glance. Realizing who the horse is, Joe buys him and returns him to the country, where Black Beauty is allowed to live out his remaining years in peaceful content.

The film, *Black Beauty*, like the novel, is narrated from start to finish by the horse himself—in the film, this narration is provided by the voice of Alan Cumming. Black Beauty functions as an equine David Copperfield, as he grows to adulthood observing and learning from the vagaries of human nature. Via the film, the viewer is transported to late nineteenth century England and experiences a now-vanished way of life, a time before the invention of the automobile when people were dependent on horses for transportation.

The modern viewer is made aware of the care required to maintain a horse, of the limitations of the animals when hauling cargo or working long hours, and of the damage that can be caused by mere thoughtlessness and ignorance. Author Sewell was indeed an "animal-rights activist before her time," as was noted by one reviewer. Yet *Black Beauty* is more than simply a running commentary on humankind's inhumanity to animals; the story also indirectly points out "man's inhumanity to man." Nineteenth century England was a class-based society in which the wealthy few ruled over the poverty-stricken many, where the working class barely eked

"We don't get to choose the people in our lives. For us, it's all chance."
—from *Black Beauty*

out a living for themselves and hence could scarcely do better by their horses. As bleak as its subject matter is, the film shows that good masters did exist and that kindness, as well as cruelty, exists in every class.

The film, in fact, alleviates several of the atrocities recounted in the book. In the novel, a stable fire not only threatens Black Beauty's life but kills two other horses as well. In the film, however, all the horses make it out safely. In the book, when drunk Reuben Smith rides Black Beauty at night and is thrown, he is killed by the fall. In the film, he survives.

Furthermore, the film adds moments of levity where none existed in the novel. The Countess of Wexmire is depicted as a cold-hearted society matron, more interested in appearances than in the welfare of the living creatures (animal as well as human) that work under her. When one male underling remarks, in reference to her carriage, "My lady craves a new coat of paint," and another answers, "Your lady needs a lot more than a new coat of paint," the filmmakers have added an observation not to be found in the original. When the countess paints Black Beauty's portrait inside her mansion, forcing the horse and groom to stand still for what must have been hours on end, Black Beauty, at a particularly well-timed moment, relieves himself on the floor. Later in the film, as a nasty groom walks through a stable, each horse in turn kicks out, narrowly missing him. When he pauses to taunt them, saying, "Ay, you missed me, you stupid beasts," the last horse lands him a good kick in the behind—yet another scene that does not appear in the book.

Despite these alterations, *Black Beauty* remains a bleak tale, relieved only by the beautiful cinematography and music and by the performances of the animal actors. In the film, Black Beauty is portrayed by a six-year-old American quarter horse named Justin, trained by chief horse trainer Rex Peterson. Ginger is played by a Russian Thoroughbred named Rat, and a Shetland/Welsh cross named Legs plays Merrylegs. The picture was filmed in Southern England, and director/screenwriter Caroline Thompson noted amusingly in the film's production notes that "the weather was far tougher to deal with than horses and child actors!"

The human actors play basically cameo roles, as the animal actors take center stage throughout the film. This fact notwithstanding, the film attracted the talents of some of England's finest actors: Sean Bean as Farmer Grey; David Thewlis, the award-winning star of *Naked* (1993), as Jerry Barker; character actor Jim Carter as John Manly; Peter Davison, who starred as veterinarian Tristan Farnon in James Herriot's *All Creatures Great and Small* on British television, as Squire Gordon; Andrew Knott, who costarred in

CREDITS

Farmer Grey: Sean Bean
Jerry Barker: David Thewlis
John Manly: Jim Carter
Squire Gordon: Peter Davison
Reuben Smith: Alun Armstrong
Mr. York: John McEnery
Countess of Wexmire: Eleanor Bron
Earl of Wexmire: Peter Cook
Joe Green: Andrew Knott
Black Beauty: Alan Cumming (voice)

Released: 1994
Production: Robert Shapiro and Peter Macgregor-Scott; released by Warner Bros.
Direction: Caroline Thompson
Screenplay: Caroline Thompson; based on the novel by Anna Sewell
Cinematography: Alex Thomson
Editing: Claire Simpson
Production design: John Box
Art direction: Les Tomkins and Kevin Phipps
Set decoration: Eddie Fowlie
Casting: Mary Selway
Sound: Simon Kaye
Costume design: Jenny Beavan
Horse training: Rex Peterson
Music: Danny Elfman
MPAA rating: G
Running time: 85 minutes

Agnieszka Holland's *The Secret Garden* (1993), as young Joe Green; and Peter Cook, the noted British comedian perhaps best known to American audiences for his role in *The Princess Bride* (1987), as the Earl of Wexmire.

Screenwriter Caroline Thompson makes her directorial debut with *Black Beauty*. She had previously adapted two other children's classics to the big screen, *Homeward Bound: The Incredible Journey* (1993) and *The Secret Garden*. Unfortunately, *Black Beauty* lacks the comic appeal of *Homeward Bound* and the magic of *The Secret Garden*. Although *Black Beauty* is a fine adaptation of a classic story, its subject matter will probably prove too grim for the young audiences that it will attract.

—*Cynthia K. Breckenridge*

REVIEWS

Entertainment Weekly. August 12, 1994, p. 38.
The Hollywood Reporter. July 25, 1994, p. 5.
Los Angeles Times. July 29, 1994, p. F1.
The New York Times. July 29, 1994, p. B12.
Variety. July 25, 1994, p. 4.

Black Harvest

Old world and new world clash in this documentary filmed in Papua New Guinea: A mixed-race businessman, Joe Leahy, develops a cooperative coffee-growing business with the Ganiga tribe just as coffee prices drop and the Ganiga declare war on a neighboring tribe. Sequel to *First Contact* (1983) and *Joe Leahy's Neighbors* (1989).

REVIEWS

Booklist. LXXXIX, Feb 1, 1993, p. 994.
Los Angeles Times. February 21, 1994, p. F5.

CREDITS

Joe Leahy: Joe Leahy
Popina: Popina

Origin: Australia
Released: 1992
Production: Bob Connolly and Robin Anderson, in association with the Australian Broadcasting Corporation, Channel Four Television, La Sept, and the Institute of PNG Studies
Direction: Bob Connolly and Robin Anderson
Cinematography: Bob Connolly
Editing: Ray Thomas, Bob Connolly and Robin Anderson
MPAA rating: no listing
Running time: 90 minutes

Black Lizard

A celebrated jewel thief, the Black Lizard (female impersonator Akihiro Maruyama), kidnaps a jeweler's daughter (Kikko Matsuoka) in order to gain possession of a priceless diamond, only to fall in love with the detective (Isao Kimura) investigating the case, in this campy Japanese comedy. Mishima, who wrote the original drama and the screenplay, has a cameo as an embalmed corpse. In Japanese with English subtitles.

REVIEWS

Entertainment Weekly. May 29, 1992, p. 70.

CREDITS

Black Lizard: Akihiro Maruyama
Detective Akechi: Isao Kimura
Jeweler: Junya Usami
Sanaye: Kikko Matsuoka
Human statue: Yukio Mishima

Origin: Japan
Released: 1968
Production: Released by Cinevista
Direction: Kinji Fukasaku
Screenplay: Masashige Narusawa; based on the novel by Edogawa Rampo
Cinematography: Hiroshi Dowaki
Production design: Kyohei Morita
Music: Isao Tomita
MPAA rating: no listing
Running time: 86 minutes

Blank Check

"If you loved *Home Alone*, you'll love *Blank Check*."—*The Movie Minute*

 Box Office Gross: $30,568,658 (August 14, 1994)

In this comic fantasy, Preston Waters (Brian Bonsall) is an eleven-year-old boy who is handed a blank check by a big-time criminal, Quigley (Miguel Ferrer), when Quigley's car runs over Preston's bike. The fun begins when Preston cashes the check—for a million dollars and goes on a spending spree under an assumed name. And where are his parents? Apparently they don't have a problem with a shadowy benefactor taking him under his wing. This rip-off of *Home Alone* attempts to throw in a morality check of an ending, but this probably won't fool the kids either. Parents may want to make sure their own checkbooks haven't been nabbed after this one. Star Brian Bonsall made his acting debut as Andrew on TV's *Family Ties*.

REVIEWS

Atlanta Constitution. February 11, 1994, p. P3.
Boston Globe. February 11, 1994, p. 46.
Chicago Tribune. February 11, 1994, p. 7M.
Entertainment Weekly. July 15, 1994, p. 74.
Entertainment Weekly. March 4, 1994, p. 48.
Los Angeles Times. February 11, 1994, p. F8.
The New York Times. February 11, 1994, p. C12.
Variety. CCCLIV, February 14, 1994, p. 41.
The Washington Post. February 12, 1994, p. G12.

 "You know the Golden Rule. He who has the gold makes the rules."—Fred Waters from *Blank Check*

CREDITS

Preston Waters: Brian Bonsall
Shay Stanley: Karen Duffy
Quigley: Miguel Ferrer
Fred Waters: James Rebhorn
Juice: Tone Löc
Sandra Waters: Jayne Atkinson
Henry: Rick Ducommun
Yvonne: Debbie Allen
Damian Waters: Chris Demetral
Ralph Waters: Michael Faustino
Butch: Alex Zuckerman
Biderman: Michael Lerner

Released: 1994
Production: Craig Baumgarten and Gary Adelson for Walt Disney Pictures; released by Buena Vista Pictures
Direction: Rupert Wainwright
Screenplay: Blake Snyder and Colby Carr
Cinematography: Bill Pope
Editing: Hubert de La Bouillerie and Jill Savitt
Production design: Nelson Coates
Art direction: Burton Rencher
Set decoration: Cecilia Rodarte
Casting: Reuben Cannon and Associates
Sound: David Kirschner
Costume design: Deborah Everton
Stunt coordination: Patrick Romano
Music: Nicholas Pike
MPAA rating: PG
Running time: 93 minutes

Blankman

"Coming to Save Your Butt."—Movie tagline

"A heartfelt comedy that's falling down funny."
—*Kansas City Star*

"...devilishly funny satire of the superhero genre."
—*The Hollywood Reporter*

"...it's a showcase for the chameleonic Wayans and his from-the-hip humor."—*Variety*

 Box Office Gross: $7,422,076 (September 18, 1994)

D amon Wayans stars as mild-mannered inventor Darryl Walker, who metamorphoses into the would-be superhero Blankman in order to fight inner-city crime, in this comedy-adventure. Garbed in his underwear and a cape made from his grandmother's bathrobe, life is simple until a nosy reporter (Givens) finds out about him. Silly one-joke premise is carried a little too far. Gifted comedian Wayans tries, but can't make this guy fly. Director Mike Binder is a stand-up comedian, best known for writing *Coupe de Ville*.

Damon Wayans and David Alan Grier as Blank Man and Other Guy.
© 1994 Columbia Pictures Industries, Inc. All rights reserved.

Mr. Stone: Jason Alexander
Sammy the Blade: Nicky Corello

Released: 1994
Production: Eric L. Gold and C. O. Erickson for Wife 'N' Kids; released by Columbia Pictures
Direction: Mike Binder
Screenplay: Damon Wayans and J. F. Lawton; based on a story by Wayans
Cinematography: Tom Sigel
Editing: Adam Weiss
Production design: James Spencer
Art direction: Keith Burns
Set design: Stephanie J. Gordon
Set decoration: Michael C. Claypool
Casting: Lucy Boulting
Sound: Simon Kaye and Jonathan Bates
Costume design: Michelle Cole
Music: Miles Goodman
MPAA rating: PG-13
Running time: 92 minutes

REVIEWS

Atlanta Constitution. August 22, 1994, p. B5.
Boston Globe. August 20, 1994, p. 27.
Chicago Tribune. August 19, 1994, Sec. 1 p. 24.
Entertainment Weekly. February 3, 1995, p. 64.
Entertainment Weekly. September 9, 1994, p. 64.
Los Angeles Times. August 22, 1994, p. F3.
The New York Times. August 20, 1994, p. A13.
People Weekly. XLII, September 5, 1994, p. 18.
Rolling Stone. September 8, 1994, p. 87.
Variety. CCCLVI, August 22, 1994, p. 55.
The Washington Post. August 20, 1994, p. B2.
The Washington Post. August 25, 1994, p. C7.

CREDITS

Darryl Walker: Damon Wayans
Kevin Walker: David Alan Grier
Kimberly Jonz: Robin Givens
Mayor Marvin Harris: Christopher Lawford
Grandma Walker: Lynne Thigpen
Michael "The Suit" Minelli: Jon Polito

"You're a virgin!"
"No!... I'm a gentleman."—Kevin Walker and brother Darryl from *Blankman*

Blast 'em

An amusing documentary, *Blast 'em* centers on the ambush-style photography and aggression employed by the paparazzi in order to capture photos of such celebrities as Sean Penn, Robert De Niro, Matt Dillon, Madonna, Marla Maples, Jack Nicholson, and Sigourney Weaver. Features the antics of aggressive photographer Victor Malafronte.

CREDITS

Victor Malafronte: Victor Malafronte
Sally Kirkland: Sally Kirkland

Origin: Canada
Released: 1992
Production: Anders Palm for Silent Fiction Films; released by Cinema Esperanca International
Direction: Joseph Blasioli
Screenplay: Joseph Blasioli
Cinematography: Robert Garrard
Editing: Joseph Blasioli
Editing: Egidio Coccimiglio
Sound: Antonio Arroyo, Ivan and Marty Casparian
Music: Yuri Gorbachow
MPAA rating: no listing
Running time: 100 minutes

Blink

"Illusion. Deception. Murder. Things are not what they seem."—Movie tagline

"A suspenseful, provocative, romantic thriller."
—Bruce Williamson, *Playboy*

"An erotic mystery packed with scary surprises that will keep you gasping and guessing."—Jeanne Wolf, *Jeanne Wolf's Hollywood*

"Michael Apted has delivered the year's first thriller and it's a knockout."—Bill Diehl, *ABC Radio Network*

"*Blink* has hit written all over it. It's intense, terrifying and erotic."—Liz Smith

 Box Office Gross: $16,656,958 (April 17, 1994)

The time-tested plot device of a disabled woman in jeopardy is used effectively in *Blink*. Just the year before, in 1993, Marlee Matlin starred in a similar scenario in *Hear No Evil*. Yet the classic film of this type is probably the 1967 film *Wait Until Dark* with Audrey Hepburn. *Blink* carries the proverbial torch for this subset of the psychological thriller pictures and does it with style and intelligence—even if it is more "psychological" than "thriller."

Madeleine Stowe as Emma Brody being stalked by a hallucination in *Blink*. Photo: Joyce Rudolph © 1994 New Line Cinema Corp. All rights reserved.

Madeleine Stowe stars as Emma Brody, a woman who was blinded as a child in a vicious attack by her alcoholic mother. Emma was subsequently reared in the darkness of not only her physical state but a psychological one as well. Now in her twenties and working as a fiddler in a New-Age-bluegrass-grunge-Irish-folk band (played by real-life band The Drovers), she gets the opportunity of her young lifetime: Another young woman has died and donated her corneas so

CREDITS

Emma Brody: Madeleine Stowe
Detective John Hallstrom: Aidan Quinn
Thomas Ridgely: James Remar
Dr. Ryan Pierce: Peter Friedman
Lieutenant Mitchell: Bruce A. Young
Candice: Laurie Metcalf

Released: 1994
Production: David Blocker; released by New Line Cinema
Direction: Michael Apted
Screenplay: Dana Stevens
Cinematography: Dante Spinotti
Editing: Rick Shaine
Production design: Dan Bishop
Art direction: Jefferson Sage
Set decoration: Dianna Freas
Casting: Linda Lowy
Digital effects supervision: Art Durinski
Sound: Chris Newman
Costume design: Susan Lyall
Music: Brad Fiedel
MPAA rating: R
Running time: 106 minutes

that a sightless person can see. Emma jumps hesitantly at the chance and within a few days has regained her sight.

Her biggest obstacles, however, lie ahead. Even though the transplants worked, Emma has only partial vision. Most things are blurry at best, she is extremely sensitive to light, and most frighteningly she sometimes sees things after she has seen them. Called "retroactive vision" in the film, it is best described by saying that her eyes see a figure or an object but her brain does not process the image until later. The result is something like a hallucination only these are things that were really seen by her at one point.

This phenomenon leads to the primary conflict in the film. Late at night, after consuming most of a bottle of cheap wine, Emma is awakened by a noise outside her door. She gets up to check but cannot quite make out the features of the shadowy figure making his way down the stairs past her door. It is not until the next day that she "sees" the man on the stairs from the previous night—the same night that her neighbor was brutally raped and murdered.

The images Stowe's character sees in *Blink* after her vision is restored were created by rotating special lenses and filters in front of the camera and by digital computer. Stowe learned fiddle for her place as the fictional member of the real-life Irish-American band, The Drovers.

Enter John Hallstrom played by Aidan Quinn, the police officer assigned to the case and frustrated by the fact that his only witness was blind up until six weeks prior to the murder. Sparks fly between these two strong-willed people, and it probably comes as no surprise that a major romance is simmering under their gritty exteriors of nonchalance.

Stowe is remarkable as the determined Emma. Her character is not a one-note hysteric, pursued by the relentless bad guy. Stowe does a marvelous job showing both the strong, sarcastic side and the frightened, lonely side of Emma's very complex life. Quick-witted, intelligent, and sexy are not adjectives that are usually assigned to the heroines in the typical "disabled-woman-in-peril" film. It was a bold choice by all involved and adds to the depth of this film.

Unfortunately, the same cannot be said of Detective Hallstrom. Although Quinn performs solidly as usual, his role is not as interesting or well defined as Emma's. This is the same character that has been seen in virtually every thriller ever made: the tough grizzled cop with a soft side that wants to surface but needs the attention of a loving woman. It has been done before and it has been done better. Yet this in no way diminishes *Blink*. It simply makes it obvious that it could have been an even better film if as many chances had been taken with John as with Emma.

Stowe and Quinn work well together, and it is their slightly lustful bantering and sparring that move the film along to its inevitable bloody ending. Their on-screen chemistry justifies the romance angle. It is interesting to note that the more satisfying of the two major love-making scenes in this film focuses on the characters' passion instead of their naked bodies. In fact, their second tryst, which probably earned the film its R rating, seems almost gratuitous and oddly out of place.

Most of the screen time is devoted to Stowe and Quinn and so the supporting cast, although talented, goes mostly unnoticed. Peter Friedman as Emma's smitten doctor is solid but unremarkable. Likewise James Remar as John's equally gritty partner at the police station. One bright note is Laurie Metcalf as Emma's best friend, Candice. Metcalf is probably best known for her role as Jackie Harris on the television series *Roseanne*, but she seems to specialize as an underutilized talent in films as well. From John Hughes's *Uncle Buck* (1989) to Oliver Stone's *JFK* (1991), Metcalf has always delivered strong performances in small parts.

Award-winning film and documentary director Michael Apted has delivered a fine film with help from Dana Stevens' script. They took an old premise and breathed new life into it to create a solid psychological drama. Yet it is in its aspirations to be a "thriller" that the film stumbles. There are few tense moments in *Blink*, the most effective being a frightening chase in an elevated train racing down the Chicago rails. Emma is running madly from a killer who, because of her "retroactive vision," may or may not be there and along the way runs into the ghosts from her tortured past. This is the one scene that creates any substantial suspense. The rest of the film dwells more on the psychological aspects of everything from serial killers to child abuse. The result is people thinking about being afraid rather than actually being afraid.

Perhaps this is the difficulty created by writing Emma as such a strong woman—she never really gets the chance to be truly scared. Therefore, the audience never gets pulled into her fear either. Everything is a bit too logical in *Blink*. Even the serial killer is not merely a random killer who chooses his victims by hair color or occupation. No, he has to have a deep-seated (and convoluted) psychological motive for whom he kills. Although this plot device is interesting and different, it does not make for the kind of chills and thrills that these types of films should have.

A chilling device that does work is the photography, hence special mention should be made of Dante Spinotti, the director of photography, and Art Durinski, the computer

> "Couldn't you have said something she wanted to hear? Anything? Couldn't you have lied?"
> "I did lie."—Thomas Ridgely to Detective John Hallstrom in *Blink*

effects specialist. Spinotti's dizzying camera work allows the audience to see, or not see, through Emma's eyes. Great special effects and lens tricks create a claustrophobic and intentionally confusing atmosphere.

Blink tries to do something a little different with the thriller genre. It tries to give the audience more than just cardboard characters and standard cheap thrills. On this level it succeeds. Yet it sacrifices one of the primary tenets of the very genre upon which it wants to improve: A scary film should be scary.

—*Rick Garman*

REVIEWS

Entertainment Weekly. January 28, 1994, p. 36.
The Hollywood Reporter. January 17, 1994, p. 9.
Los Angeles Times. January 26, 1994, p. F4.
The New York Times. January 26, 1994, p. B1.
Variety. January 17, 1994, p. 9.

Blood in Blood Out

"Epic Storytelling."—*Chicago Tribune*

Beginning in the 1970's, this drama centers on three Hispanic youths growing up in East Los Angeles—Paco (Benjamin Bratt), Cruz (Jesse Borrego), and Miklo (Damian Chapa)—and the diverse paths their lives take: one a drug-addicted artist, one a narc, and one a prison regular. Written by acclaimed poet Baca, the film touches on issues such as poverty, racism, and drugs as they pertain to Hispanic life. Unfortunately, the extreme violence overwhelms the rest of the plot. Based on a story by Ross Thomas.

REVIEWS

Los Angeles Times. February 6, 1993, p. F2.
The New York Times. January 14, 1994, p. D16.
Variety. CCCXLIX, January 25, 1993, p. 133.

CREDITS

Miklo: Damian Chapa
Cruz: Jesse Borrego
Paco: Benjamin Bratt
Montana: Enrique Castillo
Magic Mike: Victor Rivers
Bonafide: Delroy Lindo
Red Ryder: Tom Towles
Popeye: Carlos Carrasco
Wallace: Teddy Wilson
Chuey: Raymond Cruz
Frankie: Valente Rodriguez
Big Al: Lanny Flaherty

Released: 1993
Production: Taylor Hackford and Jerry Gershwin for Hollywood Pictures, in association with Touchwood Pacific Partners I; released by Buena Vista Pictures
Direction: Taylor Hackford
Screenplay: Jimmy Santiago Baca, Jeremy Iacone, and Floyd Mutrux; based on a story by Ross Thomas
Cinematography: Gabriel Beristain
Editing: Fredric Steinkamp and Karl F. Steinkamp
Production design: Bruno Rubeo
Art direction: Marek Dobrowolski
Set decoration: Cecilia Rodarte
Casting: Richard Pagano and Sharon Bialy
Sound: Edward Tise
Costume design: Shay Cunliffe
Stunt coordination: Gary Davis
Music: Bill Conti
MPAA rating: R
Running time: 174 minutes

Blown Away

"5...4...3...2...1 Time's up"—Movie tagline

"Devastating thrill-a-minute, stop your heart thriller, easily one of the year's best."—Jeffery Lyons, *Sneak Previews*

 Box Office Gross: $30,059,999 (October 2, 1994)

Jeff Bridges stars in this action thriller as Jimmy Dove, an expert on the Boston bomb squad with a secret past that is about to explode into his life again. It seems that in his youth, Jimmy lived in Ireland, was named Liam, became good friends with Ryan Gaerity (Tommy Lee Jones), and was recruited to Ryan's cause of terrorism. Liam studied the art of bomb making under Ryan and even fell in love with Ryan's sister. When Liam realized that Ryan's terrorist activities would kill the innocent as well as the "guilty," however, he set off a bomb early. Although this action saved many lives in the marketplace, Ryan's sister was killed. For this, Ryan vows revenge from a jail cell in Ireland.

Now Ryan has escaped, and like Liam before him, he has come to America. When he sees Liam, now Jimmy Dove, on television performing the heroic acts of a bomb squad defuser, Ryan decides on a course of action: He plants a series of ingenious bombs that threaten the lives of Jimmy's comrades on the force, his relatives, and even his new wife, Kate (Suzy Amis), and daughter (Stephi Lineburg).

The final explosion in *Blown Away* was more than even the special effects coordinator expected—windows were blown out in nearby buildings.

CREDITS

Jimmy Dove: Jeff Bridges
Ryan Gaerity: Tommy Lee Jones
Max O'Bannon: Lloyd Bridges
Anthony Franklin: Forest Whitaker
Kate: Suzy Amis
Lizzy: Stephi Lineburg
Captain Roarke: John Finn
Rita: Caitlin Clarke
Cortez: Chris De Oni
Bama: Loyd Catlett
Blanket: Ruben Santiago-Hudson
Nancy: Lucinda Weist
Kevin: Brendan Burns
Connie: Patricia A. Heine

Released: 1994
Production: John Watson, Richard Lewis, and Pen Densham for Trilogy Entertainment Group; released by Metro-Goldwyn-Mayer
Direction: Stephen Hopkins
Screenplay: Joe Batteer and John Rice; based on a story by Rice, Batteer, and M. Jay Roach
Cinematography: Peter Levy
Editing: Timothy Wellburn
Production design: John Graysmark
Art direction: Steve Cooper and Lawrence A. Hubbs
Set decoration: Peg Cummings
Casting: Mike Fenton and Allison Cowitt
Special effects coordination: Clay Pinney
Technical advice: Lieutenant Bob Molloy and Herb Williams
Sound: Thomas Causey
Costume design: Joe I. Tompkins
Music: Alan Silvestri
MPAA rating: R
Running time: 121 minutes

Helping Jimmy to find Boston's latest bomber are the newest member of the force—the cocky Anthony Franklin (Forest Whitaker—and a wizened old man from the old country, Max O'Bannon (Lloyd Bridges—who is also Jimmy's uncle. Both men now become targets. Thus Jimmy and Ryan are pitted against each other in a battle of wits—Jimmy racing against the clock to save his family and friends from Ryan's demented genius, all the while hiding his true identity.

For a film that is critically dependent on suspense, there is surprisingly very little. The story, which is overly complicated and foggy, seems like nothing more than the thinnest of backgrounds against which to set explosion after explosion after explosion. Soon, one can almost set one's watch by the intervals between bombs, exploded or unexploded.

Predictable and unfocused, the film fails to create any kind of dramatic tension. Worse, it fails to involve the viewer. One does not really care about the characters, whose motivation is sketchy at best. Nor does one care about where the next bomb will be or who might be hurt or even whether the bombs go off at all. Hence, what was touted as a white-knuckle roller-coaster ride never quite gets up to speed.

In the end the viewer is left with more questions than answers. Why is Ryan so antisocial? What pushed him over the edge? How does he make bombs out of virtually nothing? Where did he learn all this? Why did he create such an

AWARDS AND NOMINATIONS

MTV Movie Awards 1995: Best Action Sequence, Best Villain (Jones)

elaborate bomb on his hideout ship? How could Ryan find Jimmy so easily when Interpol failed to? And last but not least, how does Jimmy know the car bomb is in the brakes?

Usually in a suspense film, there is a character with whom the audience can identify and thus experience vicariously the thrills and chills. In *Blown Away*, however, the characters are thin, perplexing, or implausible. None seem capable of being our conduit into the action. They posture, they perform unbelievable heroics, and they have only the foggiest motivation and little believability.

When one considers the cast, this is incredible. Here are some of Hollywood's best actors: Tommy Lee Jones, who practically blew Harrison Ford out of the picture in 1993's *The Fugitive*; Jeff Bridges, who carried the underexposed gem *Fearless* (1993); Forest Whitaker, who won acclaim for

his small but pivotal role in *The Crying Game* (1992); and Suzy Amis, who turned in a bravura performance in the captivating *The Ballad of Little Jo* (1993). These are no second-string actors. It is a shame that such a talented cast would be given so little to work with.

In short, *Blown Away* relies too heavily on expensive special effects to the detriment of plot and characterization. *Blown Away* is so overblown that it sabotages itself from within. Even Jimmy Dove would be unable to defuse this bomb.

—Beverley Bare Buehrer

REVIEWS

Chicago Tribune. July 1, 1994, p. 7C.
Entertainment Weekly. July 8, 1994, p. 37.
The Hollywood Reporter. June 24-26, 1994, p. 13.
Los Angeles Times. July 1, 1994, p. F1.
The New York Times. July 1, 1994, p. B2.
USA Today. July 1, 1994, p. 7D.
Variety. June 24, 1994, p. 2.

Blue

"Perhaps not since Andy Warhol's *Sleep* and *Empire State* has there been a film quite like Derek Jarman's *Blue*."—Todd McCarthy, *Variety*

This aptly-named film features nothing but a constant blue screen, accompanied by music and commentary by filmmaker Derek Jarman and three friends on his life and eventual death from AIDS (acquired immune deficiency syndrome) February 19, 1994. Jarman ponders the associations with the color blue (sky, ocean, blindness, heaven, eternity) and his own physical problems, alternately expressed with vagueness and contempt.

REVIEWS

Atlanta Constitution. March 18, 1994, p. P1.
Boston Globe. January 23, 1994, p. B36.
Boston Globe. February 4, 1994, p. 53.
Chicago Tribune. February 11, 1994, p. 7C.
Chicago Tribune. February 20, 1994, Sec. 13 p. 8.
The Christian Century. CXI, March 16, 1994, p. 267.
The Christian Century. CXII, March 15, 1995, p. 283.
Entertainment Weekly. August 26, 1994, p. 121.
Maclean's. CVII, January 17, 1994, p. 61.
The Nation. CCLVII, October 4, 1993, p. 364.
National Catholic Reporter. XXX, January 7, 1994, p. 17.
The New Leader. LXXVII, April 11, 1994, p. 20.
New Statesman and Society. VI, September 10, 1993, p. 35.
The New Yorker. LXIX, December 13, 1993, p. 122.
People Weekly. XLI, January 24, 1994, p. 19.
Time. CXLII, December 6, 1993, p. 90.
Vogue. CLXXXIII, December 1993, p. 128.
The Wall Street Journal. January 20, 1994, p. A12.
The Washington Post. March 4, 1994, p. C7.
The Washington Post. March 4, 1994, p. WW44.

CREDITS

John Quentin: John Quentin (voice)
Nigel Terry: Nigel Terry (voice)
Derek Jarman: Derek Jarman (voice)
Tilda Swinton: Tilda Swinton (voice)

Origin: Great Britain
Released: 1993
Production: James Mackay and Takashi Asai for Channel Four, in association with Arts Council of Great Britain, Opal, BBC Radio 3, and Baselisk Communications/Uplink
Direction: Derek Jarman
Screenplay: Derek Jarman
Sound design: Marvin Black
Music: Simon Fisher Turner
MPAA rating: no listing
Running time: 76 minutes

"If I lose half my sight, will my vision be halved?"—Derek Jarman, from *Blue*

Blue Chips

"Nolte is terrific...the action is breathtaking."
—Joel Siegel, *Good Morning America*

"Exhilarating.... Exciting.... Altogether authentic."—Michael Medved, *New York Post*

Box Office Gross: $22,243,270 (April 10, 1994)

Films about sports have been a staple of the American cinema from *Knute Rockne, All American* (1940), where Ronald Reagan got "one for the Gipper," to Robert Aldrich's irreverent *The Longest Yard* (1974), to Ron Shelton's clever and sexy *Bull Durham* (1988). Shelton serves up some colorful characters and considerable well-photographed sports action in *Blue Chips*. This time, he wrote the screenplay and executive-produced, leaving the directing chores to William Friedkin. In spite of some critical acceptance, however, this is one of Shelton's weaker endeavors. *Bull Durham* was great fun: A humorous look at baseball, which boasted a terrific performance by Susan Sarandon and launched the career of Tim Robbins. Unfortunately *Blue Chips* is short on story and long on one-dimensional characters.

The film takes a look at the increasingly competitive world of college basketball, which has come under fire in recent years because of ethical violations, such as paying the student athletes and allowing them to play without passing their classes. *Blue Chips* has a strong moral compass, taking a stand against the lack of ethics in college sports, and that is commendable. Yet its rather simplistic story gives way to a preachy polemic about the devils who are corrupting the All-American world of college basketball. Unfortunately, its drama falls flat even while its basketball action crackles with excitement.

Coach Pete Bell (Nick Nolte), the ornery, disheveled basketball coach at fictional Western University, needs to win: His team has been losing all season, and he has barely recovered from a failed marriage and a scandal in which he was accused of fixing a game. As the film opens, he is nearly frantic as he delivers a loud harangue to his inept team before their final game of the season. "You're the dumbest team I ever coached!" he screams, and then he throws a water bottle against the wall as the team watches passively. They have seen this before. With the end of the season comes the beginning of the search for new players to recruit.

"We need horses," says Nolte. "We've got horses; what we need are thoroughbreds," says the school's athletic director (played by basketball legend Bob Cousy).

Bell finds three amazing possible recruits: Butch (Anfernee "Penny" Hardaway), Ricky (Matt Nover), and Neon (Shaquille O'Neal, the real-life basketball sensation who plays for the Orlando Magic). With these three men Bell sees his redemption: They can turn his losing team into a winner. In order to ensure that these athletes will come to Western, Bell is tempted by the slimy chairman of the alumni association (J. T. Walsh) to pay off the players with money, houses, and cars. Though it is completely against the ethically rigid Bell's moral fiber, his desire to win is so great that he accepts the Faustian deal.

The rest of the plot deals with a perfunctorily written conflict between Bell and his former wife (Mary McDonnell) over his desperate need to win. There is also a secondary subplot revolving around a sharp newspaper reporter (Ed O'Neill) who believes Bell to be unethical and sets out to prove that this time he has in fact paid his athletes. Before the reporter can uncover the ethical violations, however, Bell realizes the error of his ways and makes amends, learning the time-tested lesson that playing is more important than winning. It is an inevitable conclusion in a film with few surprises.

Despite the film's pedestrian plot, *Blue Chips* has its merits. Most notable is the performance of Nick Nolte as the frenzied and passionate Bell. Nolte is known for being one of the most talented and committed of contemporary film stars, and his reputation is well deserved. His preparation for this film included two weeks closely watching Indiana University basketball coach Bobby Knight, studying motivational techniques used by coaches, and gaining technical insight from the film's technical adviser, Pete Newell. As a result, Nolte is completely believable as a coach: A scene in which Bell holds a practice session with his players, teaching them how to "lock off" someone they are guarding, feels as if there were a hidden camera taping a real practice session. It is a performance based in reality, but still full of heightened drama: His initial speech to the team, as he bellows with his gravelly voice, is ferocious in its rage and frightening in its velocity. When he comes home to an empty apartment with no furniture except a television set surrounded by the videotapes of his basketball games, the audience completely sympathizes with this unkempt and driven man.

Friedkin has made much of this thin material. For example, when Bell goes on his recruiting trip, he embarks

"If he bends the rules, what's he gonna become?"
"A millionaire?"—Lavada McCrae to Pete Bell in *Blue Chips*

on an almost mythological quest: He climbs hills and marches through the Louisiana swamp to find himself in a little village where all the townspeople gather to watch Neon (O'Neal) play. The setting underscores the mythological feeling: Heavenly shafts of light radiate on a wide-eyed audience that watches as Neon plays his game, and the first camera shots of O'Neal illuminate the wonder and excitement that Bell feels upon finding this athletic giant. Friedkin imbues these scenes with a sense of drama. Furthermore, the players are filmed so that their heads are "cut off" from the top of the picture, making them look taller and more imposing; when O'Neal slams the ball into the basket there is an amplified thud.

Much attention has been paid in this film to re-creating the exciting atmosphere of college basketball. In fact, the games were played by teams created from the best col-

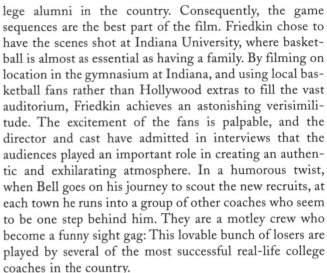

lege alumni in the country. Consequently, the game sequences are the best part of the film. Friedkin chose to have the scenes shot at Indiana University, where basketball is almost as essential as having a family. By filming on location in the gymnasium at Indiana, and using local basketball fans rather than Hollywood extras to fill the vast auditorium, Friedkin achieves an astonishing verisimilitude. The excitement of the fans is palpable, and the director and cast have admitted in interviews that the audiences played an important role in creating an authentic and exhilarating atmosphere. In a humorous twist, when Bell goes on his journey to scout the new recruits, at each town he runs into a group of other coaches who seem to be one step behind him. They are a motley crew who become a funny sight gag: This lovable bunch of losers are played by several of the most successful real-life college coaches in the country.

This concern with verisimilitude, however, points up a problem with many contemporary films: Excessive attention to a film's technical aspects can lead to neglect in such areas as originality, creativity, and structure. *Blue Chips'* story and characters certainly appear less well planned than the basketball sequences. For example, Jenny, played by Mary McDonnell, is a one-dimensional character whose *raison d'etre* is simply to highlight Bell's workaholism by standing in contrast to it. She is calm, well-ordered, and yet knows her way around a basketball court—in short, she is perfect. McDonnell, an accomplished actress and two-time Academy Award nominee, is reduced to playing another helpless ex-wife-who-just-doesn't-understand-what-drives-her-man. Other than a few limp scenes in which Jenny has mild conflict with Bell, her character is superfluous to the plot.

Shelton nevertheless has a wonderful way with dialogue that helps to keep things moving. One funny example is an exchange between the greedy mother of one of the recruits (Alfre Woodard) and Bell. She tells Bell that her son has been offered money to attend other schools, to which he responds, "If he bends the rules, what's he gonna become?" She looks at him quizzically and says, "A millionaire?"

When all is said and done, *Blue Chips* is made for the sports fan: Shaquille O'Neal makes a relaxed and charming film debut, and the basketball sequences and cameo appearances are entertaining. 🎞️

—Kirby Tepper

CREDITS

Pete Bell: Nick Nolte
Jenny: Mary McDonnell
Happy: J. T. Walsh
Ed: Ed O'Neill
Lavada McRae: Alfre Woodard
Vic: Bob Cousy
Neon: Shaquille O'Neal
Butch: Anfernee (Penny) Hardaway
Ricky: Matt Nover
Father Dawkins: Louis Gossett, Jr.
Slick: Cylk Cozart
Tony: Anthony C. Hall
Jack: Kevin Benton
Freddie: Bill Cross
Mel: Marques Johnson
Marty: Robert Wuhl

Released: 1994
Production: Michele Rappaport; released by Paramount Pictures
Direction: William Friedkin
Screenplay: Ron Shelton
Cinematography: Tom Priestley, Jr.
Editing: Robert K. Lambert and David Rosenbloom
Production design: James Bissell
Art direction: Ed Verreaux and William Arnold
Set design: John H. M. Berger and Lauren Polizzi
Set decoration: Thomas L. Roysden
Casting: Louis Di Giaimo
Sound: Kirk Francis
Costume design: Bernie Pollack
Basketball coordination: Rob Ryder
Music: Nile Rodgers, Jeff Beck and Jed Leiber
MPAA rating: PG-13
Running time: 108 minutes

REVIEWS

Entertainment Weekly. March 4, 1994, p. 42.
The Hollywood Reporter. February 16, 1994, p. 5.
Los Angeles Times. February 18, 1994, p. F6.
The New York Times. February 18, 1994, p. B4.
Variety. February 16, 1994, p. 2.

Blue Ice

Michael Caine stars as Harry Anders, a former spy who is recruited by the U.S. ambassador's beautiful wife, Stacy Mansdorf (Sean Young), to locate her former boyfriend (Todd Boyce).

REVIEWS

Chicago Tribune. July 25, 1993, Sec. 11 p. 3.
Variety. CCCXLIX, November 2, 1992. p. 88.

CREDITS

Harry Anders: Michael Caine
Stacy Mansdorf: Sean Young
Sir Hector: Ian Holm
Osgood: Alun Armstrong
George: Sam Kelly
Stevens: Jack Shepherd
Kyle: Todd Boyce
Buddy: Bobby Short
Sam Garcia: Bob Hoskins

Origin: Great Britain
Released: 1992
Production: Martin Bregman and Michael Caine for Guild Film Distribution and M & M Productions, Inc., in association with HBO Pictures
Direction: Russell Mulcahy
Screenplay: Ron Hutchinson; based on a character created by Ted Allbeury
Cinematography: Denis Crossan
Editing: Seth Flaum
Production design: Grant Hicks
Art direction: Lawrence Williams
Casting: Joyce Nettles
Sound: Terry Elms and Dave Weathers
Costume design: Les Lansdown
Stunt coordination: Alan Stuart
Music: Michael Kamen
MPAA rating: no listing
Running time: 104 minutes

The Blue Kite

"Of all the remarkable films to come out of China over the past few years, *The Blue Kite* could well be the most authentic, accessible, and finally, the most powerful. Daring politically...quietly shattering emotionally, it tells the truth in a compelling, human way." —Kenneth Turan, *The Los Angeles Times*

"The most amazing act of political courage and defiance I have ever seen in the cinema." —Andrew Sarris, *New York Observer*

"Two thumbs up! A courageous and fascinating portrait." —*Siskel & Ebert*

"A triumph... Harrowing... Moving... Gorgeous" —Vincent Canby, *The New York Times*

 Box Office Gross: $243,973 (July 4, 1994)

The plot of director Tian Zhuangshuang's tender drama, *The Blue Kite*, is made even more poignant by the knowledge that it was banned in its country of origin, China. *The Blue Kite* is a very political film that doubles as a compelling family drama: The destruction of a young boy's family occurs against the backdrop of political upheaval. Focusing on the changes in China in the 1950's and 1960's, this film portrays a government run by a cruel and fickle Communist Party. It is an emotionally taxing but fascinating look into a world that few Americans have seen.

The film is composed of three parts, each part named for one of the three men who help rear a young boy named Tietou (represented at three ages by three different actors). The first part begins in 1953. Librarian Lin Shaolong (Pu Quanxin) and Chen Shujuan (Lu Liping) are about to marry. They are planning to move into a small apartment in a courtyard near Dry Well Lane, so named because there is a well that has no water. Immediately, the intrusion of the state into the lives of these people is apparent: The first thing they do before the ceremony begins is bow to a huge picture of Chairman Mao on the wall. Then they entertain the celebrants with a song extolling the virtues of the Communist state.

Shujuan's relative indifference to political tradition is evident, however, when she initially refuses to wear a red kerchief over her head, as per custom, on her wedding night.

 The film was banned by the Chinese government, who wanted to sue the Dutch company that had acquired world rights.

At her husband's insistence, however, she agreeably complies with his wish. The kerchief becomes a symbol both for her attempts at independence from politics as well as of the blood that will be shed by so many members of her family.

Several years pass, and Shaolong and Shujuan have a son named Tietou. Their life is simple but pleasant: Tietou plays in the courtyard with the neighborhood children. Tietou's life appears to be the life of any other child: He plays with toys, gets into mischief, and particularly loves a blue kite, which his father flies for him. When the kite tears, Shaolong builds another for his young son. The recurring image of the torn blue kite becomes an important thematic symbol in the film.

This idyllic life changes, however, when Mao launches the Rectification Movement in 1957. The Rectification Movement urged people to offer constructive criticism about the party. Subsequently, however, the party reversed itself, arresting people who accepted the invitation to criticize. The movement and its quixotic reversal tragically affect Tietou's family and friends. His father, Shaolong, is wrongly branded as a "rightist" when Shaolong's coworker, Li Guodong (Li Xuejian), wrongly names Shaolong as an attacker of the party. Shaolong is sent to a labor camp, where he dies days before his release.

Part two of the film begins as Mao's Great Leap Forward is initiated. During this period, the country engaged in state-sponsored programs to promote Communism, some of which would be difficult to understand in American society. For example, part two of the film opens with a burst of color and noise, as Tietou's street is filled with crowds of people bearing drums, noisemakers, and banners all designed to scare sparrows from landing on the ground and eating all the grain.

Shujuan marries Guodong, the man indirectly responsible for her husband's imprisonment and death. Guodong's guilt drives him to treat Tietou and Shujuan with love and care; but he dies as well, a victim of overwork due in part to China's agricultural shortages. Part three of the film involves Shujuan's marriage of convenience to prosperous Wu Leisheng. He, too, becomes another victim of upheaval, as the country goes through its Cultural Revolution in 1966.

It is at first difficult for an American audience to empathize with the characters because of the chasm between 1990's American traditions and the culture of China thirty years previous. It is difficult to know whether

CREDITS

Chen Shujuan: Lu Liping
Uncle Li: Li Xuejian
Lin Shaolong: Pu Quanxin
Lao Wu: Guo Baochang
Tietou (as a child): Zhang Wenyao
Tietou (as an adolescent): Chen Xiaoman
Shusheng: Zhong Ping
Shuyan: Chu Quanzhong

Origin: China
Released: 1993
Production: Longwick Film, Fortissimo Film Sales, and Beijing Film Studio; released by Kino International
Direction: Tian Zhuangzhuang
Screenplay: Xiao Mao
Cinematography: Hou Yong
Editing: Qian Lengleng
Art direction: Zhang Xiande
Costume design: Don Juying
Music: Yoshihide Otomo
MPAA rating: no listing
Running time: 138 minutes

the blue kite's shape, for example, has any specific traditional meaning in Chinese culture. Other evidence of the cultural gap for American audiences occurs around the dinner table at the home of Shujuan's mother, brothers, and sisters. They talk of the People's Liberation Army, of the Great Leap Forward, of communal dining and of the Neighborhood Committee.

The American audience unaware of Chinese history might be distracted by trying to figure out exactly what these terms mean. The twists and reversals of the Communist Party were difficult enough to follow for the people who lived through it: Americans may find this film a bit confusing without prior knowledge that the Chinese Communist Party went through several reversals, branding people revolutionaries one year and counterrevolutionaries the next.

Regardless of the culture gap, however, this is an unquestionably affecting film, on all levels. The story, performances, and script are superb. Tian Zhuangzhuang is a wonderful director who creates magnificent visual images out of the most prosaic of material. For example, Tian uses the simple colors of the costumes to great visual advantage.

Throughout the film, the predominant colors of the clothes are red and blue. In part one, the characters are mostly seen in shades of blue. Part two begins with a burst of red—with red banners and kerchiefs everywhere. The red seems to represent the Communist Party's Great Leap Forward, while the blue seems to represent the gentle past (which also may be symbolized by the blue kite of the film's title). Shujuan is dressed in both red and blue throughout the film, seemingly underscoring her place in the middle of the party changes.

It is unclear, however, whether those colors were dictated by the director's artistry, Chinese traditional style, or historical accuracy. Whatever the case, the film's somber colors play an important role in the effect this film has on its audience. The splashes of red amid the other subdued colors become a metaphor for the party's intrusive and mercurial changes.

Light also plays an important role: Guodong (Shujuan's second husband) lights a lantern on New Year's Eve for Tietou, and the destruction of the lantern becomes a symbol for Guodong's death. Another example of the use of light is when Shujuan's brother, Shusheng (Zhong Ping), begins to lose his eyesight—blinding light fills the windows. It appears that his loss of sight coincides with his disenchantment with the party, as if he has lost the idealistic vision he may have had at one time. Similarly, another sister remains a strong revolutionary—the glasses she wears may be a metaphor for the adjustments she makes to the party in terms of her own vision of her future and the party's future.

The performances are tender and highly realistic. Lu Liping as Shujuan is particularly affecting. She maintains a nobility and dignity throughout, the archetype of the noble woman who accepts great sorrow with equanimity. As the film moves forward, her progression from carefree bride to tormented widow is sad without being maudlin, and painful without being melodramatic.

AWARDS AND NOMINATIONS

Tokyo Film Festival: Grand Prix

The young actors portraying Tietou at various stages in his childhood are similarly realistic and touching. Zhang Wenyao, who plays Tietou as a toddler, is so believable in his relentless pursuit of play that it appears as if director Tian were simply following a little boy with a camera, documentary-style. Chen Xiaoman provides an intelligent and wise performance as the adolescent Tietou; his world-weariness is heartbreaking.

Director Tian Zhuangzhuang is one of China's most controversial filmmakers. He was born to Communist parents: His father was the first chief of the Beijing Film Studio and later became vice head of the Ministry of Culture's Film Bureau; Tian's mother was a major star who took charge of the Children's Film Studio and still holds that position. The film was deemed inappropriate by Chinese censors, who intended to prosecute its producers for presenting it in an international film festival competition. Nevertheless, it won accolades at Cannes and the Grand Prix at the Tokyo Film Festival. The film remains unreleased in mainland China.

The images of blue kites that appear several times throughout the film seem to represent both the tragedy and the beauty of Tietou's life. Accompanied by the offscreen singing of a child's nursery rhyme about a crow who is about to fly away, the kite continues to be repaired or replaced by someone in Tietou's life. Eventually, he is able to repair a kite for his little stepniece, indicating that the cycle will continue. The irony and tragedy of the film is that a playful child can be caught up in, and destroyed by, the social and political upheaval of the adult world—much like a kite that is blown by a wind and gets caught in a tree. This film is an ironically beautiful reminder of that sad fact.

—*Kirby Tepper*

REVIEWS

The Hollywood Reporter. June 1, 1994, p. 16.
Los Angeles Times. June 1, 1994, p. F3.
The New York Times. October 2, 1993, p. 13.

Blue Sky

"a wonderful posthumous triumph."—Caryn James, *The New York Times*

"a flashy and fleshy performance by Jessica Lange"—Bruce Williamson, *Playboy*

"fierce, brave, sexually charged"—Owen Gleiberman, *Entertainment Weekly*

"A side of Tommy Lee Jones you have never seen before"—Jeffrey Lyons, *Sneak Previews*

"[Lange] smolders, storms, rages... Acting with every muscle in her body."—David Kehr, *New York Daily News*

"Jones alone makes *Blue Sky* worth watching."
—Kevin McManus, *The Washington Post*

 Box Office Gross: $2,359,375 (October 30, 1994)

Tommy Lee Jones and Jessica Lange as Hank and Carly Marshall in *Blue Sky*. © 1994 Orion Pictures. All rights reserved.

B*lue Sky* was the last film directed by the Academy Award-winning British director Tony Richardson before he died of AIDS on November 14, 1991. In her "Foreword" to her father's autobiography *The Long-Distance Runner*, published in 1993, Natasha Richardson wrote that this was one of her father's "very best" films, and the reviews tended to support that opinion. The film was shelved for three years because Orion Pictures went bankrupt, but Caryn James of *The New York Times* described the film as "a wonderful posthumous triumph."

The screenplay is loosely based upon the childhood memories of screenwriter Rama Stagner, especially memories of her parents' marital and personal problems in 1962, when her father was stationed in Anniston, Alabama. "Blue Sky" is a military code word for a program to measure nuclear contamination resulting from nuclear testing. Hank Marshall (Tommy Lee Jones) is a military scientist, who comes to believe that the radiation released by nuclear tests is dangerous and argues for underground testing. None of his military superiors take his warnings seriously, however, and only one Atomic Energy Commission scientist seems willing to listen to Hank. Because Hank is a man of integrity who is willing to question authority, his military career is not very secure. As a scientist, Hank seeks truth; the military is only interested in short-term results.

Hank has another liability in the form of his neurotic wife, Carly (Jessica Lange), who constantly embarrasses him with her flirtatious behavior. She lives in a world of self-deluded fantasy. She thinks that she could have been a film star, and she emulates Brigitte Bardot one moment and Marilyn Monroe the next. She sunbathes topless on the beaches of Hawaii, where she and her husband are first stationed, and indulges in exposing herself to the military helicopters that fly overhead. She is not only an exhibitionist but also an adulteress and possibly a nymphomaniac. She appears to be mentally disturbed.

Blue Sky was the last film for director Tony Richardson, who died of AIDS in 1991. Release date of the film, made in 1991, was delayed to 1994 due to Orion's financial problems.

Hank is amazingly tolerant of her unstable behavior because he loves her. Her daughters, Becky (Anna Klemp) and Alex (Amy Locane), are distressed by her frequent temper tantrums. When Hank is called away from his base in Alabama to measure radiation at a nuclear testing site in Nevada, Carly remains behind, playing the tease and ultimately having sex with the base commander Vince Johnson (Powers Boothe), but they are not discreet, and they are discovered in flagrante delicto by Carly's oldest daughter and her seducer's son. The daughter forces her mother to call Nevada and confess her indiscretion to her husband. He returns and confronts the base commander, not about the adultery, but about the commander's stonewalling stance on atomic policy. Hank loses his temper and is put in the stockade. The commander then misleads Carly and persuades her to sign papers that will put her husband in the base hospital, where he is drugged senseless. She thinks signing the papers will get him released from the stockade, but she does not understand the political motive until she sees what the military doctors have done to him.

Carly goes through her husband's briefcase and reads the "Blue Sky" documents. At the site of one test two cowboys were "cooked" when they inadvertently rode too close to the testing ground, but they were not warned that they had been seriously exposed to radiation. Carly, whose natural instinct is to dramatize events, drives to Nevada to locate these cowhands, explain what has happened to them, and to ask them to testify, but they refuse. Even though their faces are blistering from radiation poisoning, they believe in their government and are uncooperative.

Carly learns from them that another test is scheduled, so she steals a horse and rides onto the testing ground herself, shortly before the device is to be triggered, and gets noticed by the press who are in the bunker as observers. In this way she gets the attention of the military and manages to negotiate her husband's release and discharge. An officer from Nevada is sent to Alabama to secure Hank's release and to relieve the corrupt base commander of his duties. Carly returns home from Nevada with her daughters and finds Hank waiting for her, willing to forgive her

CREDITS

Carly Marshall: Jessica Lange
Hank Marshall: Tommy Lee Jones
Vince Johnson: Powers Boothe
Vera Johnson: Carrie Snodgress
Alex Marshall: Amy Locane
Glenn Johnson: Chris O'Donnell
Ray Stevens: Mitchell Ryan
Colonel Mike Anwalt: Dale Dye
Ned Owens: Tim Scott
Lydia: Annie Ross
Becky Marshall: Anna Klemp

Released: 1994
Production: Robert H. Solo; released by Orion Pictures
Direction: Tony Richardson
Screenplay: Rama Laurie Stagner, Arlene Sarner, and Jerry Leichtling; based on a story by Stagner
Cinematography: Steve Yaconelli
Editing: Robert K. Lambert
Production design: Timian Alsaker
Art direction: Gary John Constable
Set decoration: Leslie Rollins
Casting: Lynn Stalmaster
Sound: Jacob Goldstein, Susumu Tokunow
Costume design: Jane Robinson
Music: Jack Nitzsche
MPAA rating: PG-13
Running time: 101 minutes

AWARDS AND NOMINATIONS

Academy Awards 1994: Best Actress (Lange)
Golden Globe Awards 1995: Best Actress—Drama (Lange)
Los Angeles Critics Awards 1994: Best Actress (Lange)
Screen Actors Guild Awards Nomination 1994: Best Actress (Lange)

indiscretions. The next day, they drive off the base and out of the service.

The screenplay by Rama Laurie Stagner, Arlene Sarner, and Jerry Leichtling branches in two directions, the personal and the political. *Blue Sky*, described as a love story, is a domestic melodrama, but Hank is obviously caught in a larger political drama involving atomic secrets. This larger context concerns terrible decisions made by the United States government and the military to develop programs of nuclear testing without regard for ordinary citizens, who might be contaminated as a consequence. The film became timely since a Congressional investigation into such matters was underway in 1994 after the film was released; but records still classified as "Top Secret" stored at Los Alamos were still protected under the veil of national security, while allegations were being made that the military made use of human guinea pigs to calculate the effects of radiation.

"Blue Sky" is the name of a government project in the film to study the effects of radiation, particularly from open-air nuclear tests, which the military wants to continue, as well as underground testing, which also releases radiation. "Blue Sky" suggests the invisibility of nuclear radiation, which cannot be seen, felt, or tasted but has life-threatening long-range consequences. Hank Marshall is a strong proponent of underground testing, but he seems to be coming around to the position that all such testing is dangerous. His commanding officers are oblivious to the dangers and, through their ignorance, unconcerned about the human consequences. They consider only the pragmatic, short-term goals of the nuclear testing program and consider Hank merely as a bothersome obstructionist.

Hank, wonderfully represented by Tommy Lee Jones, has the patience of a saint. He describes love to his daughters as "the exchange of energy over time," but they cannot understand his detached tolerance. "He's blind and she's crazy," the older daughter remarks, but the viewer can understand what holds this combustible marriage together, and that is the main accomplishment of the film. Some reviewers complained that the conclusion was too pat, too forced. Even so, the ending of the political plot is not exactly "happy," since nuclear victims of reckless testing and experimentation are still being discovered.

Jessica Lange was justly praised for her "fierce, brave, sexually charged performance," that, in the words of *Entertainment Weekly*'s Owen Gleiberman, "flirts with craziness without quite crossing into it." The film's reception might have been influenced by the tendency of some critics to pay a final tribute to Tony Richardson, who turned British drama around during the 1950's before

demonstrating his talents as a filmmaker. Both *Variety* and *Newsweek*, however, praised the film in similar terms. Todd McCarthy found the film very like "a solid melodrama from the 1950s" in which "a small number of characters define themselves in terms of their interaction within well-proscribed physical and social limits." David Ansen wrote that *Blue Sky* felt "like a Hollywood film from another era" because of "its belief that character can drive a movie; that there is nothing more fascinating than the complexities of the human heart." Ansen would agree with McCarthy that the picture "feels like a throwback, but in a refreshing way."

This film is also a "throwback" in another way because of its political message. Nuclear fear was a common component of motion pictures during the Cold War, so it is surprising to see a film with a nuclear message after the collapse of Communism and the fall of the "Iron Curtain" during the late 1980's, yet the film is a potent reminder that people still live with the consequence of nuclear politics. People tend to forget that the nuclear issue remains.

Blue Sky may be considered flawed in the way it rushes to its melodramatic conclusion, but it is a better and a more important film than many of Tony Richardson's later works, such as *The Border* (1982), starring Jack Nicholson, which was even more seriously flawed. During a career that spanned over forty years, Tony Richardson made a number of groundbreaking films, including *Look Back in Anger* (1959), *The Entertainer* (1960), *A Taste of Honey* (1961), *The Loneliness of the Long Distance Runner* (1962), and *Tom Jones* (1963), which won Oscars but which Richardson considered to be "incomplete and botched in much of its execution." In fact, his later Henry Fielding adaptation, *Joseph Andrews* (1977) was a better made film, but one that tended to be ignored because it was not so cute in its execution as *Tom Jones*. *The Hotel New Hampshire* (1984) was another splendid adaptation that failed to receive its critical due. *Blue Sky* provides a dignified closure to Richardson's distinguished career as a filmmaker. Sympathetic reviewers understandably tended to evaluate this posthumous picture in the context of Richardson's lifetime achievements. Even so, the picture is strong enough to stand on its own merits.

Jessica Lange won the Academy, Los Angeles Critics, and Golden Globe Awards for Best Actress for her performance as Carly; but Tommy Lee Jones, Powers Boothe, and Carrie Snodgress (as the base commander's betrayed wife) all turned in performances that were worthy of Academy Award nominations. Despite strong and favorable reviews, Orion Pictures did not give the film a strong promotional campaign, however, and allowed it to be buried in

"You always look so stylish. Women like you are the reason that men like women in the first place."—Vera Johnson to Carly Marshall in *Blue Sky*

the usual avalanche of fall releases; unfortunately, the film had all but disappeared from sight within a month of its release and was not given wide distribution or much of a chance at the box office. It became one of the most outrageously neglected intelligent films of 1994.

—James M. Welsh

REVIEWS

Entertainment Weekly. No 242, September 30, 1994, p. 38.
The Hollywood Reporter. September 18, 1994, p. 5.
Los Angeles Times. September 16, 1994, p. F6.
The New York Times. September 16, 1994, p. B6.
Newsweek. September 26, 1994, p. 64.
USA Today. September 16, 1994, p. 5D.
Variety. September 12-18, 1994, p. 41.
Washington Post. September 16, 1994, p. F7.
Washington Post Weekend. September 16, 1994, p. 49.

Body Melt

A mad doctor (Ian Smith) invents a vitamin pill that causes human bodies to melt, in this horror film. Directorial debut of Philip Brophy.

CREDITS

Detective Sam Phillips: Gerard Kennedy
Johnno: Andrew Daddo
Dr. Carrera: Ian Smith
Pud: Vince Gil
Shaan: Regina Gaigalas
Gino: Maurie Annese
Sal: Nick Polites
Paul Matthews: William McInnes
Brian Rand: Brett Climo
Thompson Noble: Adrian Wright
Cheryl Rand: Lisa McCune
Kate: Suzi Dougherty
Angelica Noble: Jillian Murray

Origin: Australia
Released: 1993
Production: Rod Bishop and Daniel Scharf for Dumb Films and Body Melt, in association with the Australian Film Commission, Film Victoria
Direction: Philip Brophy
Screenplay: Philip Brophy and Rod Bishop
Cinematography: Ray Argall
Editing: Bill Murphy
Production design: Maria Kozic
Casting: Greg Apps
Sound: Gary Wilkins
Special effects makeup: Bob McCarron
Costume design: Anna Borghesi
Music: Philip Brophy
MPAA rating: no listing
Running time: 84 minutes

Body Snatchers

"The Invasion Continues."—Movie tagline

"One of the few films in several years that has scared me. It works brilliantly. Thumbs up! A good horror movie!"—Roger Ebert, *Chicago Sun Times/Siskel & Ebert*

"Ferrara's camera is tireless, stalking each new victim with baleful delight."—John Powers, *New York Magazine*

"The film's ghoulish transformation scenes are both beautiful and repellent."—Kenneth Turan, *Los Angeles Times*

"...shockingly vivid special effects, this new *Body Snatchers* is the most graphic of all."—Peter Travers, *Rolling Stone*

Box Office Gross: $379,598 (February 27, 1994)

In this remake of the classic science-fiction horror story, Gabrielle Anwar stars as the teenage daughter of an Army scientist, who discovers that alien pods are taking over the human population. The pods have something to do with a mysterious toxic spill. This remake takes advantage of the advances of special effects, especially in Anwar's bathtub scene, but has few spine-tingling scenes. This is the third screen version of the novel *The Body Snatchers* by Jack Finney; the first two were entitled *Invasion of the Body Snatchers* (1956 and 1978).

REVIEWS

Atlanta Constitution. February 25, 1994, p. P6.
Boston Globe. February 25, 1994, p. 48.
Boston Globe. February 27, 1994, p. A7.
Chicago Tribune. February 25, 1994, p. 7C.
Entertainment Weekly. February 11, 1994, p. 36.
Entertainment Weekly. July 15, 1994, p. 73.
Los Angeles Times. February 4, 1994, p. F1.
New York. XXVII, February 21, 1994 p. 48.
The New York Times. February 4, 1994, p. C6.
The New York Times. July 8, 1994, p. D15.
People Weekly. XLI, February 28, 1994, p. 18.
Rolling Stone. November 11, 1993, p. 79.
Time. CXLIII, February 14, 1994, p. 68.
Variety. CCCLI, May 3, 1993, p. 39.
The Washington Post. February 18, 1994, p. G7.

CREDITS

Marti Malone: Gabrielle Anwar
Steve Malone: Terry Kinney
Tim Young: Billy Wirth
Carol Malone: Meg Tilly
Dr. Collins: Forest Whitaker
Jenn Platt: Christine Elise
General Platt: R. Lee Ermey
Andy Malone: Reilly Murphy
Pete: G. Elvis Phillips
Mrs. Platt: Kathleen Doyle

Released: 1994
Production: Robert H. Solo; released by Warner Bros.
Direction: Abel Ferrara
Screenplay: Stuart Gordon, Dennis Paoli, and Nicholas St. John; based on a story by Raymond Cistheri and Larry Cohen and on *The Body Snatchers*, by Jack Finney
Cinematography: Bojan Bazelli
Editing: Anthony Redman
Production design: Peter Jamison
Art direction: John Huke
Set decoration: Linda Spheeris
Casting: Ferne Cassel
Special effects supervision: Phil Cory
Sound: Michael Barosky
Special makeup effects: Thomas R. Burman and Bari Dreiband-Burman
Costume design: Margaret Mohr
Stunt coordination: Phil Neilson
Music: Joe Delia
MPAA rating: R
Running time: 87 minutes

"They're out there. They get you when you sleep."—a hysterical soldier warning of the body snatchers, from *Body Snatchers*

Bon Voyage

Directed by Alfred Hitchcock, this short propaganda film was commissioned by the British Ministry of Information during World War II in order to encourage French Resistance fighters. The drama centers on an RAF pilot (John Blythe) who escapes from Nazi-occupied France only to discover that the heroic Polish soldier who "helped" him was really a Gestapo agent intent on identifying Resistance fighters.

REVIEWS

Atlanta Constitution. December 3, 1993, p. P6.
Entertainment Weekly. June 3, 1994 p. 64(1).
Los Angeles Times. April 26, 1994, p. F1.
The Washington Post. July 23, 1993, p. C7.
The Washington Post. July 23, 1993, p. WW46.

CREDITS

John Dougall: John Blythe

Origin: France and Great Britain
Released: 1944
Production: British Ministry of Information; released by Milestone Films
Direction: Alfred Hitchcock
Screenplay: J. O. C. Orton; based on an original idea by Arthur Calder-Marshall
Cinematography: Gunther Krampf
Production design: Charles Gilbert
MPAA rating: no listing
Running time: 26 minutes

Brainscan

"Wanna Play? I Dare You."—Movie tagline
"An Interactive Trip to Hell."—Movie tagline
"A virtual-reality-charged suspense thriller."
—Michael Rechtschaffen, *The Hollywood Reporter*

 Box Office Gross: $3,051,000 (May 1, 1994)

A teenage boy, Michael (Edward Furlong), lives a real-life nightmare when he plays what he believes is a virtual-reality computer game only to find out that the murders he imagines to have committed really occurred. Smith plays the Trickster , who is the virtual reality tour guide from hell and Langella is the local cop hot on the trail. Horror fans will be disappointed by the lack of violence and special effects fans will not notice anything new. The ending is left wide open, so expect a sequel.

"Real, unreal, what's the difference, so long as you don't get caught?"—The Trickster, from *Brainscan*

CREDITS

Michael: Edward Furlong
Detective Hayden: Frank Langella
Trickster: T. Ryder Smith
Kimberly: Amy Hargreaves
Kyle: Jamie Marsh
Martin: Victor Ertmanis
Dr. Fromberg: David Hemblen

Released: 1994
Production: Michel Roy; released by Triumph Releasing
Direction: John Flynn
Screenplay: Andrew Kevin Walker; based on a story by Brian Owens
Cinematography: Francois Protat
Editing: Jay Cassidy
Production design: Paola Ridolfi
Visual effects and character design: Rene Daalder
Sound: Don Cohen
Makeup effects: Steve Johnson
Costume design: Gaudeline Sauriol
Stunt coordination: Dave McKeown
Music: George S. Clinton
MPAA rating: R
Running time: 95 minutes

The Branches of the Tree

Celebrated Indian filmmaker Satyajit Ray wrote and directed this drama that centers on the Majunda family headed by the elderly Ananda (Ajit Banerjee). When Ananda suffers a heart attack on his seventieth birthday, the family members, including his four sons, gather and reveal the skeletons in their closets.

REVIEWS

The New Republic. , May 11, 1992, p. 30.

CREDITS

Ananda Majunda: Ajit Banerjee
Probodh: Maradan Banerjee
Uma: Lily Charraborty
Proshanto: Soumitra Chatterjee
Probir: Deepankar De
Tapati: Mamata Shankar
Protap: Ranjit Mallik

Origin: India
Released: 1992
Production: Toscan du Plantier and Gerard Depardieu for Erato, DD Productions, Soprofilms, and Satyajit Ray Productions
Direction: Satyajit Ray
Screenplay: Satyajit Ray
Cinematography: Barun Raha
Editing: Dulal Dutt
Music: Satyajit Ray
MPAA rating: no listing
Running time: 120 minutes

Bread and Salt

This documentary revolves around the 1991 trip to Moscow undertaken by two friends—a Russian native, Irina Muravyova, and an American Sovietologist and translator, Richard Lourie. The two visit and interview numerous people, discovering the despair and poverty rampant in the Soviet Union just prior to its breakup. The title refers to the Russian proverb "Eat bread and salt and always tell the truth."

REVIEWS

Boston Globe. October 1, 1993, p. 53.
Los Angeles Times. July 9, 1993, p. F8.

CREDITS

Irina Muravyova: Irina Muravyova
Richard Lourie: Richard Lourie

Released: 1993
Production: Irina Muravyova and Richard Lourie for MML, in association with Program Bravo, Russian Central Television, and Company Ostankino; released by World Artists
Direction: Jeanne Collachia
Screenplay: Irina Muravyova and Richard Lourie
Cinematography: Charles Domokos and Gerard Hooper
Editing: Jeanne Collachia
Sound: Robert Silverthorne
Music: Dick Hamilton
MPAA rating: no listing
Running time: 94 minutes

The Bride with White Hair

Tragedy threatens to separate two star-crossed lovers (Leslie Cheung and Brigitte Lin) forever in this period martial-arts fantasy.

REVIEWS

Los Angeles Times. February 4, 1994, p. F13.

CREDITS

Zhou Yihang: Leslie Cheung
Lian Nichang: Brigitte Lin
Ji Wu Shang (Siamese male twin): Ng Chun-Yu
Ji Wu Shang (Siamese female twin): Lui Sau-Ling

Released: 1994
Origin: Hong Kong
Production: Ronnie Yu and Clifton Ko for Eastern Films; released by Rim Films
Direction: Ronnie Yu
Screenplay: David Wu, Jason Lam, Tang Pik-Yin, and Ronnie Yu
Cinematography: Peter Bao
Editing: David Wu
Production design: Eddie Ma
Art direction: Eddie Ma
Sound: Ng Jae-Do
Costume design: Cheung Sun-Yiu
Music: Richard Yu
MPAA rating: no listing
Running time: 88 minutes

The Browning Version

"The greatest lessons in life are the ones learned by heart."—Movie tagline

"One of Albert Finney's greatest performances.... Sweeping, lavish and beautiful."—Jeffrey Lyons, *Sneak Previews*

"Finney is amazing."—Peter Rainier, *Los Angeles Times*

 Box Office Gross: $401,067 (December 18, 1994)

Albert Finney stars as an aging professor whose forced retirement from his long-time position at a boys' school also forces him to realize that he failed both as a teacher and as husband to his much younger wife (Greta Scacchi), who is driven to an affair with visiting American science teacher Modine. Remake of the Terrence Rattigan play, previously filmed in 1951.

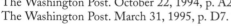
REVIEWS

Atlanta Constitution. February 10, 1995, p. P8.
Boston Globe. September 10, 1994, p. 72.
Boston Globe. October 14, 1994, p. 63.
Chicago Tribune. October 12, 1994, Sec. 5 p. 5.
Christian Science Monitor. October 14, 1994, p. 12.
Entertainment Weekly. October 21, 1994, p. 46.
Los Angeles Magazine. XXXIX, November 1994, p. 139.
Los Angeles Times. October 12, 1994, p. F3.
The New Republic. CCXI, October 31, 1994, p. 38.
The New York Times. October 12, 1994, p. C17.
The New Yorker. LXX, October 31, 1994, p. 106.
People Weekly. XLII, October 31, 1994, p. 19.
The Washington Post. October 14, 1994, p. WW48.
The Washington Post. October 17, 1994, p. B4.
The Washington Post. October 22, 1994, p. A2.
The Washington Post. March 31, 1995, p. D7.

CREDITS

Andrew Crocker-Harris: Albert Finney
Laura Crocker-Harris: Greta Scacchi
Frank Hunter: Matthew Modine
Tom Gilbert: Julian Sands
Dr. Frobisher: Michael Gambon
Taplow: Ben Silverston
Diana: Maryam D'Abo
David Fletcher: David Lever

Released: 1994
Origin: Great Britain
Production: Ridley Scott and Mimi Polk; released by Paramount Pictures
Direction: Mike Figgis
Screenplay: Ronald Harwood; based on the play by Terence Rattigan
Cinematography: Jean-Francois Robin
Editing: Herve Schneid
Production design: John Beard
Casting: Susie Figgis
Sound: Chris Munro
Costume design: Fotini Dimou
Music: Mark Isham
MPAA rating: R
Running time: 97 minutes

Building Bombs

The gross mismanagement of the Savannah River nuclear weapons facility in South Carolina is the subject of this eye-opening documentary. The plant was partially shut down in 1988 because of safety concerns.

REVIEWS

Atlanta Constitution. August 10, 1993, p. E10.
Los Angeles Times. March 19, 1993, p. F4.
Los Angeles Times. August 10, 1993, p. F12.
USA Today. August 10, 1993, p. D3.

AWARDS AND NOMINATIONS

Academy Awards Nomination: Best Feature (Documentary)

CREDITS

Narrator: Jane Alexander

Released: 1991
Production: Mark Mori and Susan Robinson; released by Tapestry International
Direction: Mark Mori and Susan Robinson
Screenplay: Mark Mori, Susan Robinson, and William Suchy
Cinematography: Larry Robertson
Editing: Philip Obrecht
Music: Steve Hulse
MPAA rating: no listing
Running time: 54 minutes

Bullets Over Broadway

"Side-splitting comedy!"—*The New York Times*

"gorgeous and inventively bright!"—Jack Mathews, *New York Newsday*

"A bright, energetic comedy."—Janet Maslin, *New York Times*

"Dazzling fun"—Peter Travers, *Rolling Stone*

"Delicious! Farcical perfection"—David Ansen, *Newsweek*

"A howling good time. Guaranteed!"—*USA Today*

 Box Office Gross: $8,605,614 (January 2, 1995)

Although Woody Allen is an American filmmaker of the highest rank, it has been the drama of his private life that has garnered attention during 1993-1994. Since his bitter split from Mia Farrow, and the child custody suit in which he was involved, Allen has made two movies: *Manhattan Murder Mystery* (1993) and *Bullets Over Broadway*, the latter written with a new collaborator,

Douglas McGrath. Primarily zany comedies, the two films signal Allen's return to his comic roots.

Set during the Prohibition era, *Bullets Over Broadway* brings together the unlikely worlds of the theater and the mafia. Young, intense playwright David Shayne (John Cusack) brings his new work to agent/producer Julian Marx (Jack Warden). Although Marx admires it, he fears it will not find enough backing to mount a Broadway production. In the meantime, mobster Nick Valenti (Joe Viterelli) orders his reliable henchmen Cheech (Chazz Palminteri) to murder a number of opponents, in the first of the motion picture's darker moments.

Valenti's girlfriend Olive (Jennifer Tilly) is providing the gangster with more problems. A highly strung girl with dreams of stardom, she demands that Valenti provide an opportunity for her on the stage. A night club conversation between Marx and Valenti leads to the latter's proposal that he back Shayne's play as long as Olive gets the lead part.

Playwright Shayne's reaction is to reject the proposal, but faced with no other way of seeing his work produced, he allows himself to be swayed—especially if veteran stage star Helen Sinclair (Dianne Wiest) can be persuaded to join the project. Needing a hit herself, and intrigued by the handsome if naive young writer, Sinclair signs on. Naturally, she will take the lead role, and opening rehearsals are scheduled.

Olive is very unhappy at having to play a supporting role, and at the opening read through, she is screechingly dismissive of Cheech's presence; he has been assigned by Valenti to look after her. The cast is introduced on stage, and it includes the bulky English actor Warner Purcell (Jim Broadbent)—who is apparently going on a diet—and Eden Brent (Tracey Ullman), a woman who laughs at her own jokes in a shrill voice.

Offstage, Helen Sinclair begins to manipulate David Shayne. Attracted to him sexually, and desirous to effect changes in her role, she has soon enthralled the writer. Shayne's live-in girlfriend Ellen (Mary-Louise Parker) sees the changes in him but can do little.

Rehearsals bring joys and disasters to the playwright. He is tormented by Olive's complete inability to perform and is anguished by objections to various scenes and lines voiced by the cast. Bodyguard Cheech is at first bored by the play, but in time, he finds himself drawn into making suggestions about lines and motivations. Shayne is infuriated by Cheech's comments, but the cast makes him see that they make good sense.

CREDITS

David Shayne: John Cusack
Helen Sinclair: Dianne Wiest
Cheech: Chazz Palminteri
Olive Neal: Jennifer Tilly
Nick Valenti: Joe Viterelli
Sheldon Flender: Rob Reiner
Ellen: Mary-Louise Parker
Julian Marx: Jack Warden
Sid Loomis: Harvey Fierstein
Warner Purcell: Jim Broadbent
Eden Brent: Tracey Ullman
Rocco: Tony Sirico
Venus: Annie-Joe Edwards

Released: 1994
Production: Robert Greenhut for Sweetland Films and Jean Doumanian; released by Miramax Films
Direction: Woody Allen
Screenplay: Woody Allen and Douglas McGrath
Cinematography: Carlo Di Palma
Editing: Susan E. Morse
Production design: Santo Loquasto
Art direction: Tom Warren
Set decoration: Susan Bode and Amy Marshall
Casting: Juliet Taylor
Sound: Frank Graziadei
Costume design: Jeffrey Kurland
MPAA rating: R
Running time: 99 minutes

As the play moves toward opening night, Warner Purcell not only gains weight rapidly but also begins an affair with Olive. Threatened by the menacing Cheech, the English thespian backs off. Shayne is more and more ensnared by Helen Sinclair, and less in control of his play, allowing much of the work to be rewritten by Cheech—to the undoubted benefit of the production. At least he is aware of the irony.

On the trip back from their Boston premier Shayne declares his love for Helen Sinclair. He proclaims that he must tell his girlfriend, as he can no longer suppress his feelings. Upon returning to New York, however, Shayne initially denies his affair with Helen to Ellen. When he does confess, Ellen in turn reveals that she is sleeping with their friend, the pseudo-intellectual Sheldon Flender (Rob Reiner).

The biggest problem for the play remains Olive, although the production enjoys favorable reviews and positive audience reception. Cheech is so incensed by her talentless rendition of her lines that, after producer Marx refuses to fire her (fearing death in reprisal from Valenti), the henchman takes her to his favorite killing spot (a jetty), where he murders her. Although her replacement succeeds admirably, Shayne is horrified when Cheech reveals that he killed the girl.

When Olive's murder becomes widely known, Nick Valenti becomes increasingly suspicious of Cheech. Finally, as the film moves to its climax, Nick orders Cheech's death while Shayne's play "God of Our Fathers" plays to packed houses. It is during a performance that Cheech is eliminated. Playwright Shayne feels unable to take any pride in a play that seems no longer his own, and ignoring a grand party to celebrate the production's success, he beseeches Ellen to come back with him to Philadelphia. Forsaking Flender, she agrees, and the two walk off in the moonlight.

AWARDS AND NOMINATIONS

Academy Awards 1994: Best Supporting Actress (Wiest)
Nominations: Best Supporting Actor (Palminteri), Best Supporting Actress (Tilly), Best Director (Allen), Best Original Screenplay Best Art Direction/Set Direction, Best Costume Design
Chicago Critics Awards 1994: Best Supporting Actress (Wiest)
Golden Globe Awards 1995: Best Supporting Actress (Wiest)
Independent Spirit Awards 1994: Best Supporting Actress (Wiest), Best Supporting Actor (Palminteri)
Nominations: Best Film, Best Screenplay (Allen, McGrath)
Los Angeles Critics Awards 1994: Best Supporting Actress (Wiest)
National Society of Critics Awards 1994: Best Supporting Actress (Wiest)
New York Critics Awards 1994: Best Supporting Actress (Wiest)

Bullets Over Broadway has been welcomed by critics as a breezy film tinged with irony. Janet Maslin in *The New York Times* saluted the motion picture's "bright energetic comedy," while Anthony Lane called it a "nicely structured piece of silliness." Gene Siskel and Roger Ebert singled out Chazz Palminteri for special mention; they both felt he stole the film.

One of the strongest elements of *Bullets Over Broadway* is the exemplary production and costume design. Woody Allen traditionally uses the same technical crew time and again, and his technicians and artists have excelled themselves in this film. The 1920's in all its colors and drabness are rendered wonderfully well by designer Santo Loquasto. The art deco of Valenti's posh house, the brownstones of Manhattan, the rich woods and fine tapestries of Helen Sinclair's home, and the opulence of the Broadway theater are pleasures in themselves. In fine support to the visual look are Jeffrey Kurland's period costumes, which are particularly prominent on the women. Tilly's Olive sports a new garish outfit each day, while Helen Sinclair adorns herself with lavish furs and long dresses of the finest material.

Mention should also be made of director of photography Carlo Di Palma's work. Another long-time Allen collaborator, he chooses more conventional camerawork here over the sometimes eye-spinning photography of Allen's last two motion pictures.

One of Allen's greatest abilities is his direction of actors. He is known to be a filmmaker who allows flexibility and improvisation, and performers usually shine in his projects. Casting director Juliet Taylor has done a fine job for *Bullets Over Broadway*, and several performances stand out in Allen's cast. Dianne Wiest, who has appeared in a number of Allen films, clearly revels in her role here. Reminiscent of the character Norma Desmond from *Sunset Boulevard* (1950), Wiest's Helen Sinclair is overpowering, scheming, magnetic, and funny—especially when she repeatedly silences star-struck David Shayne with her "Don't speak! Don't speak!" In constrast, Jennifer Tilly as Olive is so petulant and insufferable that her presence on screen becomes an irritant, whereas Tracy Ullman and Jim Broadbent make the

"You don't write like people talk."—mobster bodyguard Cheech to playwright David Shayne, in *Bullets Over Broadway*

most of their time on camera. The talented Mary-Louise Parker is underused, and John Cusack as David Shayne is sincere without being intriguing.

While *Bullets Over Broadway* has its share of Allen one-liners, its most interesting component is the re-creation of mounting a Broadway play in the Prohibition era. Theater was seen as an art form, certainly, but the commercial pressures on the production seem no less intense than today. Other interesting components of the film are the themes of the importance of art and what makes an artist. These themes are pondered by both the characters in the film and by the film itself. Shayne's acceptance of his limited abilities as an artist is a good choice by Allen and his partner McGrath, but his reunion with Ellen in the final scene is not believable. There seems little reason for Ellen to go back to David; indeed their relationship when together is never presented as being successful or fulfilling.

It is Cheech's elevation as an artist as he contributes to Shayne's play that forms the most pleasing surprise here. The irony is piquant as the rough bodyguard grows into the role of artist, while a self-conscious Shayne is finally able to resign his pretensions to mastering the theatrical art form.

Bullets Over Broadway represents a welcome continuation of the renewed comic direction Woody Allen took in the early 1990's. It is amusing, nicely ironic, and visually pleasing. It is also the first of Allen's films to be included in the New York Film Festival. Whether viewed as a silly comedy or a funny film with some intersting themes, *Bullets Over Broadway* is a well made production.

—*Paul B. Cohen*

REVIEWS

Daily Variety. September 6, 1994, p. 4.
Entertainment Weekly. October 21, 1994, p. 42.
The Hollywood Reporter. September 6, 1994, p. 10.
Los Angeles Times. October 21, 1994, p. F1.
The New York Times. September 30, 1994, p. B1.

Buried on Sunday

A small Canadian fishing village gets up in arms, literally as well as figuratively, when Ottawa government officials make impossible demands, in this quirky satire.

REVIEWS

Atlanta Constitution. May 19, 1995, p. P7.
Boston Globe. May 19, 1995, p. 63.
Chicago Tribune. May 19, 1995, p. 7M.
Entertainment Weekly. May 5, 1995, p. 46.
Los Angeles Times. April 21, 1995, p. F12.
Maclean's. CVI, April 26, 1993, p. 46.
Maclean's. CVIII, May 15, 1995, p. 73.
The New Republic. CCXII, May 8, 1995, p. 27.
New York Magazine. XXVIII, May 1, 1995, p. 64.
The New York Times. March 21, 1995, p. C15.
The New York Times. CXLIV, April 21, 1995, p. B11.
The New Yorker. LXXI, May 8, 1995, p. 92.
People Weekly. XLIII, May 22, 1995, p. 18.
Playboy. XLII, June 1995, p. 17.
Rolling Stone. May 18, 1995, p. 97.
Time. CXLV, May 8, 1995, p. 88.
The Washington Post. May 19, 1995, p. D1.
The Washington Post. May 19, 1995, p. WW57.

CREDITS

Dexter Lexcanon: Maury Chaykin
Augustus Knickle: Paul Gross
Noel Desnoyers: Denise Virieux
Nelson Stidwell: Henry Czerny
Russian prisoner: Tommy Sexton

Released: 1992
Origin: Canada
Production: Suzanne Colvin and Bill Fleming for Salter Street Films; released by Alliance Releasing
Direction: Paul Donovan
Screenplay: Paul Donovan and Bill Fleming
Cinematography: Les Krizsan
Editing: Stephan Fanfara
Production design: Harold Thrasher
Casting: John Buchan
Sound: Allan Scarth
Music: Marty Simon
MPAA rating: no listing
Running time: 90 minutes

Burnt by the Sun

"Four stars. Highest rating."—Jami Bernard, *New York Daily News*
"Mikhalkov's film is emotionally overpowering."
—Andrew Sarris, *The New York Observer*

Burnt by the Sun tells the story of one day in the life of a Russian family during the Stalin years. As their seemingly idyllic life slowly unfolds, layers of the happy family's not-so-happy history come to light. The resulting revelations have tragic consequences, and by the end of the day, the family is irrevocably undone.

Winner of the Oscar for Best Foreign-Language Film and the Cannes Grand Jury Prize, *Burnt by the Sun* has also enjoyed a huge success in Russia. The director Nikita Mikhalkov, who also co-wrote the film with Rustam Ibraguimbekov, has created an emotionally charged tribute to the Russian family during the dark days of Stalin. A self-proclaimed monarchist, who traces his family lineage back to Tsar Nicholas I, Mikhalkov says, "Our film is dedicated to the victims, to all those who were burnt by the 'betraying sun' of the revolution."

As the film opens, that sun innocuously shines down on fields of ripe summer wheat spanning the vast Russian horizon for as far as the eye can see, forming an illusory buffer from the outside world. The day is viewed through the innocent eyes of a six-year-old girl, who witnesses all and understands nothing. This is the nostalgically lyrical stage Mikhalkov has set for the betrayal of Kotov and his trusting and unsuspecting family.

The film's bucolic setting is dotted with a backdrop of the Soviet reality. Whether it be in the form of a small parade, local war games, or an inpromptu disaster preparedness practice by the town's civil defense group, Stalin's presence is ubiquitous.

In the quiet rural village, on a balmy summer day in 1936, Stalin intrudes in the person of his messenger, Dimitri (Oleg Mechikov). When we are first introduced to Dimitri, he is playing Russian roulette with a loaded gun. After the gun goes off without a shot, Dimitri phones someone and tells them he will "do it." What he will "do" is the mystery of the film.

In the privacy of the family's sweat lodge, we meet

CREDITS

Dimitri (Mitia): Oleg Menchikov
Maroussia: Ingeborga Dapkounaite
Sergueï Kotov: Nikita Mikhalkov
Nadia: Nadia Mikhalkov

Origin: Russia
Released: 1993
Production: Nikita Mikhalkov and Michel Seydoux; released by Sony Classic Pictures
Direction: Nikita Mikhalkov
Screenplay: Nikita Mikhalkov and Roustam Ibraguimbekov
Cinematography: Vilen Kaluta
Editing: Enzo Meniconi
Art direction: Vladimir Aronin and Alexandre Samuelkine
Costume design: Natalia Ivanova
Sound: Jane Umansky
Makeup: Larissa Avdiouchko
Music: Edouard Artemiev
MPAA rating: R
Running time: 152 minutes

Sergueï Kotov (played by the director, Nikita Mikhalkov), his young wife Maroussia (Ingeborga Dapkounaite), and his endearing six-year-old daughter Nadia (Nadia Mikhalkov, the director's real-life daughter). The wheat fields have been invaded by a tank division out to play war games, and the peasants rush to protect their fields from certain destruction. They call Kotov to stop them.

During the ensuing scene between Kotov and the tank division officer, we learn that this big yet gentle grey-haired man is a famous war hero of the revolution. He saves the day, convincing the commanding officer to stop the games, and he returns to his adoring family to enjoy his "one day off."

Back at their rambling old house, we meet the family: the two "grandmothers," as little Nadia calls them; the silly aunt and uncle; Kirik, a buffoon who has been with the family for years; and Mokhova, the hypochondriacal maid. It is a holiday, the sixth anniversary of the manufacturing of Stalin's airships and balloons, and the family is in high spirits. They laugh and pull pranks on one another, and it is obvious that Kotov rules the house, but does so with humor and love.

Director Milhakov succeeds in disarming the viewer with his amusing and tender story of Kotov and his comical

"All the governments since 1917 have been illegitimate, because they have achieved power by means of blood and violence.... Repentance is a duty for all those who have lived in this era and who are still alive today. Without repentance there would be no peace or rest in Russia.... Our film is dedicated to the victims, to all those who were burnt by the 'betraying sun' of the revolution."—*Burnt by the Sun* director Nikita Mikhalkov

AWARDS AND NOMINATIONS

Academy Awards 1994: Best Foreign Language Film
Cannes Film Festival Awards 1994: Grand Jury Prize

family, lulling the viewer into a false sense of security. But when a small parade of Soviet Youth marches by the house, they leave in their wake a strange man posing comically as a blind man. It is really Dimitri of the opening scene, a long lost friend of the family.

Dimitri, or Mitia as the family touchingly calls him, is charming, funny, and handsome, and yet there is a malevolence about him that belies that charm. His character surfaces in a scene when the family go bathing at the riverside. Kotov is removing his shoes and next to his foot is a broken bottle. Mitia sees the glass and coolly watches Kotov remove his shoes with a certain malicious pleasure, almost hoping Kotov will slice his foot open. When he doesn't, Mitia simply turns away, losing interest in the game. But when little Nadia, also barefoot, goes running by, he shouts to her as if to warn her of the glass. But when she stops, he hesitates, then tells her "never mind." After that, each time Mitia reaches for the little girl the viewer can't help but wince.

As the family reminisces it becomes clear that the house does not belong to Kotov. It is Maroussia's family home, where she grew up with her father, who was a music master before the revolution and has since died.

As a young man, Mitia studied piano under Maroussia's father and later become her suitor. Ten years ago, he left without a word, even to his fiancee. With Mitia's homecoming, the family, remembering their aristocratic past, nostalgically shares memories of life before the revolution, when everyone spoke French and "life had more quality." Under Mitia's manipulative influence, they seem to return to those happier days, even if only for an afternoon. At one point he plays a raucous piano piece and leads them into a wild can-can with everyone dancing and laughing—everyone, that is, except Kotov. Kotov, the hero of the revolution, hasn't the same longing for the life before 1917.

In one of the most memorable scenes in the film, Kotov takes his daughter in a row boat on the river to drift downstream. They adore each other, and it is heartwarming to watch as he tenderly instructs the young Nadia to "work hard, respect your parents, and love your fatherland." Softly taking her little foot in his hands, he promises her that her feet will never be rough and hard as his, because the Soviet dream is coming true for her generation. You can see Kotov's absolute faith in that dream as he holds his daughter and, leaning his leathery cheek against her fresh young face, they both look toward the new world that her papa has won for her. From our perspective in the not-so-bright future, it is heartbreaking to watch Kotov's big blue eyes shining as innocently as his daughter's, as he promises her that together they will drift into their future and into their happiness.

But they have left their door open to Mitia and tragedy follows him in, as he artfully manipulates the family into trusting and loving him. The only one who isn't fooled is Kotov, who knows more than he is saying.

Finally, after dinner, Mitia reveals what they all have been afraid to ask. Why did he leave them ten years before without a word? In the form of a fairy tale to Nadia, Mitia tells his story.

As the secrets of Mitia's past and Kotov's future are revealed, Kotov and his family's happy lives are destroyed by the ensuing revelations and accusations.

In *Burnt by the Sun*, director Milhalkov brings to the screen a dance of the seven veils, each scene revealing more of the mystery. But he is also very clever, successfully seducing the viewer down the primrose path of speculation, then forcing the viewer to double back and retrace its steps. But at last, in the final scene all the veils are dropped, and Kotov and Mitia are seen as they really are.

Oleg Mechikov's charmingly sinister portrayal of Mitia is mesmerizing. He brings to life a personality so complex that it isn't until the very end of the film that we can grasp just who he really is. The horror of that reality turns out to be even too much for Mitia to bear.

Credit also goes to Ingeborga Dapkounaite in her role as Maroussia. She plays the fragile and loving young wife with an emotional power that is wonderful to watch.

Cinematographer Vilen Kaluta, has created a visual delight. Professionally and delicately filmed, Kaluta has successfully reproduced a period in Russian history with a warmth and graceful beauty one doesn't usually associate with the Stalinist era.

If the film has any flaws, it would be the heavy-handed symbolism throughout. The film is dedicated to "those burnt by the sun of the revolution." As a preamble to the dedication, the song, "Burnt by the Sun" emerges first as it is played in a band shell in the snow and then is sung over and over again.

Another symbol of this "burning" is fireballs. Fireballs are described in the very first scene in a newspaper story as unwelcome guests that have hurt some of the nation's workers. With this prediction, fireballs roam through various rooms of the house unobserved as Mitia weaves his web.

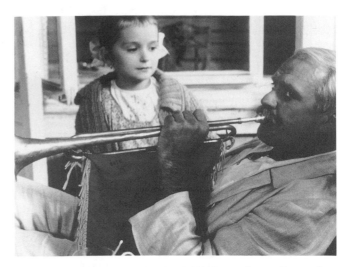

Nadia Mikhalkov as Nadia and Nikita Mikhalkov as Sergueï Petrovitch Kotov in *Burnt by the Sun*. © 1995 Sony Pictures Entertainment Inc. All rights reserved.

At the end of the film, in case the viewer is left with the image of Stalin's pervasively evil presence as a red banner with his giant portait looms hugely over the countryside, carried by a hot air balloon. The camera hugs the image forever.

The symbolism, although sometimes too overt, never hinders the power and appeal of the film. *Burnt by the Sun* has something for everyone: comedy, romance, mystery, and tragedy, all beautifully filmed amid the splendor of the Russian countryside. Although an unlikely setting for a political film, *Burnt by the Sun* is most definitely political. It dramatically brings to life how private lives are arbitrarily torn apart by bloody shifts in power, in this instance the Bolshevik revolution and Stalin's rise to power.

According to Milhalkov, "...all the governments since 1917 have been illegitimate, because they have achieved power by means of blood and violence."

His opinions about government, current and past, are well-known in Russia, and some feel that he himself has political ambitions. But when he was asked if he will run for President in 1996, he neither denied nor confirmed his intentions, saying simply, "Man proposes but God disposes." In the end, Milhalkov, the genius behind *Burnt by the Sun*, remains as elusive and mysterious as a character in one of his own films.

—*Diane Hatch-Avis*

REVIEWS

Los Angeles Times. April 21, 1995, p. F12.
The Village Voice. April 25, 1995, p.47.

Cabin Boy

"Fun!"—*The Washington Post*

"Hilarious"—*WGN-AN, Chicago*

"A magnificently goofy comedy."—*Boston Globe*

 Box Office Gross: $3,469,493 (February 13, 1994)

An insufferable rich kid, Nathanial Mayweather (Chris Elliott), embarks on a fantastic adventure when he mistakenly boards a ship whose bawdy crew force him to be their cabin boy as they sail toward "Hell's Bucket." Surprisingly produced by Tim Burton, even diehard fans will be diappointed. Elliot's real dad plays his dad on screen also, and longtime friend David Letterman appears as the nasty "Old Salt," but uses the alias Earl Hofert in the final credits.

REVIEWS

Atlanta Constitution. January 11, 1994, p. B7.
Boston Globe. January 8, 1994, p. 51.
Chicago Tribune. January 10, 1994, Sec. 5 p. 3.
Entertainment Weekly. January 21, 1994, p. 36.
Entertainment Weekly. July 22, 1994, p. 59.
Los Angeles Times. January 7, 1994, p. F6.
The New York Times. January 7, 1994, p. C12.
People Weekly.XLI, January 24, 1994, p. 17.
Variety. CCCLIII, January 10, 1994, p. 58.
The Washington Post. January 8, 1994, p. G2.

"Man, oh, man, do I hate them fancy lads."—Earl Hofert, from *Cabin Boy*

CREDITS

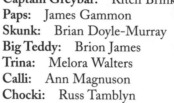

Nathanial Mayweather: Chris Elliott
Captain Greybar: Ritch Brinkley
Paps: James Gammon
Skunk: Brian Doyle-Murray
Big Teddy: Brion James
Trina: Melora Walters
Calli: Ann Magnuson
Chocki: Russ Tamblyn
Figurehead: Ricki Lake

Released: 1994
Production: Tim Burton and Denise Di Novi for Touchstone Pictures; released by Buena Vista Pictures
Direction: Adam Resnick
Screenplay: Adam Resnick; based on a story by Chris Elliott and Resnick
Cinematography: Steve Yaconelli
Editing: Jon Poll
Production design: Steven Legler
Art direction: Nanci B. Roberts and Daniel A. Lomino
Set design: Stephen Alesch
Set decoration: Roberta J. Holinko
Casting: Rik Pagano, Sharon Bialy and Debi Manwiller
Visual effects supervision: Michael Lessa
Sound: Edward Tise
Costume design: Colleen Atwood
Music: Steve Bartek
MPAA rating: PG-13
Running time: 80 minutes

The Cabinet of Dr. Ramirez

A pretentious silent drama based on the 1919 film *The Cabinet of Dr. Caligari*, this film stars Mikhail Baryshnikov, Joan Cusack, Peter Gallagher, and Ron Vawter. Directorial debut of controversial opera and theater director Peter Sellars.

REVIEWS

The New York Times. April 14, 1993, p. C15.
USA Today. April 14, 1993, p. D3.
The Wall Street Journal. April 12, 1993, p. A8.

CREDITS

Cesar: Mikhail Baryshnikov
Cathy: Joan Cusack
Matt: Peter Gallagher
Ramirez: Ron Vawter
Sue: Kate Valk
Bruce: Gregory Wallace
No character identified: Werner Klemperer

Origin: USA and Germany
Released: 1991
Production: Rainer Mockert and Eberhard Scheele, in association with Canal Plus Productions, Mod Films, Paladin Films, Thirteen/WNET, BBC, and WDR; released by Mediascope
Direction: Peter Sellars
Screenplay: Peter Sellars; in collaboration with Mikhail Baryshnikov, Joan Cusack, Peter Gallagher, and Ron Vawter, and loosely inspired by the film *The Cabinet of Dr. Caligari* (1919), directed by Robert Wiene and written by Carl Mayer and Hans Janowitz
Cinematography: David Watkin
Editing: Robert Estrin
Production design: George Tsypin
Art direction: John Magolin
Set decoration: Gretchen Rau
Casting: Diane J. Malecki
Sound: Milan Bor
Costume design: Dunya Ramicova
Stunt coordination: Pete Bucossi
Music: John Adams
MPAA rating: no listing
Running time: 111 minutes

Cage/Cunningham

This documentary pays homage to the forty-five-year-long collaboration of composer John Cage and choreographer Merce Cunningham, through archival and recent footage as well as interviews with the two subjects and with some of the dancers and artists with whom they have worked.

REVIEWS

Los Angeles Times. November 19, 1994, p. F24.
The New Yorker. LXVII, December 16, 1991, p. 8.
Variety. CCCXLV, December 2, 1991, p. 89.

CREDITS

John Cage: John Cage
Merce Cunningham: Merce Cunningham
Jasper Johns: Jasper Johns

Nam June Paik: Nam June Paik
Robert Rauschenberg: Robert Rauschenberg

Released: 1991
Production: Cunningham Dance Foundation, Inc., in association with La Sept; released by Cunningham Dance Foundation, Inc.
Direction: Elliot Caplan
Screenplay: David Vaughan
Cinematography: Elliot Caplan
Editing: Elliot Caplan
Sound: Elliot Caplan
Choreography: Merce Cunningham
Music: John Cage
MPAA rating: no listing
Running time: 95 minutes

Calendar

"Finely constructed and beautifully acted...Its game of detective is quite enticing."—Stephen Holden, *The New York Times*

"Edgy...wryly funny...one of those films that deepens with each viewing. A more original director than Egoyan is hard to find."—Lloyd Sachs, *Chicago Sun-Times*

"A haunting hit.... Among Egoyan's finest works."—Chuck Stephens, *San Francisco Bay Guardian*

A Canadian photographer (Atom Egoyan) travels to his homeland, Armenia, to take pictures of historic churches for a calendar. His wife (Arsinee Khanjian) accompanies him in order to serve as a translator only to fall in love with their driver (Ashot Adamian) and decide to remain in Armenia while her husband returns to Canada. Was once made for German television as an opening for *Exotica* (reviewed in this volume). Uses a combination of 8mm video, photographs and 16mm film.

REVIEWS

Atlanta Constitution. March 4, 1994, p. P4.
Boston Globe. May 13, 1994, p. 40.
Chicago Tribune. August 19, 1994, p. 7M.
The New York Times. March 11, 1994, p. C14.
The Washington Post. May 27, 1994, p. D7.

CREDITS

Translator: Arsinee Khanjian
Driver: Ashot Adamian
Photographer: Atom Egoyan

Origin: Canada, Germany, and Armenia
Released: 1993
Production: Atom Egoyan and Doris Hepp for Armenian National Cinema/ZDF and Ego Film Arts; released by Zeitgeist Films
Direction: Atom Egoyan
Screenplay: Atom Egoyan
Cinematography: Norayr Kasper
Editing: Atom Egoyan
Sound: Yuri Hakobian and Ross Redfern
Sound design: Steven Munro
MPAA rating: no listing
Running time: 70 minutes

Camilla

"Two women are about to share the adventure of a lifetime in a comedy that proves friendship is ageless."—Movie tagline

"A warm, funny road movie featuring a terrific standout performance by Jessica Tandy."—Brendan Kelly, *Weekly Variety*

"*Camilla* has considerable charm."—*Los Angeles Times*

"One of Jessica Tandy's finest roles."—Sharon Sontag, *Calgary Sun*

 Box Office Gross: $167,599 (December 18, 1994)

Jessica Tandy brings grace and illuminates the big screen for one of the last times in her career in *Camilla*. The radiant actress was considered by many to be one of the great actresses of her time and will be sorely missed by both the film and stage communities. Her career has spanned decades, but it wasn't until her Oscar winning performance in *Driving Miss Daisy* (1989) that the consummate actress became a film "star." She then went on to work in other films such as *Fried Green Tomatoes* (1991) with Kathy Bates, *Nobody's Fool* (reviewed in this volume) with Paul Newman, and *Camilla* with Bridget Fonda, which was her last starring role on the screen. It was always inspiring to see an actress gain popularity in her seventies in a medium that is notoriously "age-conscious." Her skill and artistry demolished these barriers and she soared to new heights right up to the end.

Camilla is the story of a rather quirky, elderly lady, played by Tandy, who befriends a much younger woman named Freda (Fonda). The screenplay, written by Paul Quarrington, is based on an original story by Ali Jennings and directed by Deepa Mehta. It chronicles the lives of two women at different stages in their lives who embark on a road trip which ultimately becomes a journey of self-discovery. The thin plot may be weak in spots but the film is not without its merits. It may not contain any monumental, earth shattering events but it does tell a story. The audience does get a look inside the psyches of the main characters and will find that they are indeed worth watching.

The film opens with a shot of the ocean's waves with a violin in the background. Then comes a voice-over by Fonda asking the question: "Have you ever heard Brahms'

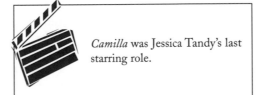

Camilla was Jessica Tandy's last starring role.

Violin Concerto?" as the camera shows us a figure on the beach playing the violin. It is the first suggestion to the audience that music will play an integral part in the film. The camera then cuts to a moving shot along the water heading into the city of Toronto, where Freda is revealed practicing on her guitar. It has the effect of showing two different musical styles and eras about to converge upon one another. This moving shot in the opening scene has been used in many films. However, the juxtaposition of the old and the new which this shot accomplishes in *Camilla* justifies its use.

It is then disclosed that Freda and her husband Vince (Elias Koteas) are about to embark on a vacation to Georgia. At first glance they appear to be an attractive young couple, very much in love with each other. However, upon closer examination, there seem to be some underlying problems between them. When Vince attempts to make love on the beach Freda rejects him on the grounds that "she doesn't want to get pregnant." This scene reveals that they are at odds with one another on certain issues. Eventually Freda meets Camilla (Tandy) who lives next door. Upon entering Camilla's house, Freda sees an old poster of the great Camilla ("named for one of the great whores of all times") appearing in concert at the Wintergarden. Camilla bursts out "Yes, I stepped on to the stage—there was absolute silence. I took a deep breath, placed my bow on the strings and abandoned myself to the music." Except for the violin, it was hard not to imagine Tandy saying this line describing her portrayal of Blanche du Bois in *A Streetcar Named Desire* on Broadway many years ago. It was one of those moments when the actress and the character co-exist at the same moment in time. It was also a revealing scene about the former concert violinist of world renown, reveling in the past glories and days gone by. This particular scene would have been more believable, however, if the director had given Camilla and Freda a little more time to get to know one another. As it is it comes across as a theatrical moment, written into the script rather than a normal progression in the conversation. It is too abrupt, which makes it seem artificial. This awkwardness in the script can be compared to a musical where the character simply breaks into song because it is written that way. The script does not flow naturally, and this is a recurring problem throughout the film. The fault lies within the screenplay and with the director. The actors attempt to make the transitions as seamless as possible, and because of their expertise it becomes less noticeable and distracting.

When Freda's husband, Vince, decides to cut short the vacation to pursue a job offer, he insists that Freda come with him, patronizingly pointing out that her music is only a hobby. She decides to stay on in Georgia alone and, with Camilla as her guide, embarks on a journey of self-realization. As in *Fried Green Tomatoes*, Tandy once again gets to play the mentor of a confused soul. It is interesting to note that Fonda chose to give a surprisingly monochromatic performance. It's as if she knew better than to try to compete with Tandy, so instead she downplayed everything. Although the

 "It's wonderful working with my husband. I wouldn't do it if I didn't think so. There's a kind of rapport and a sort of short-hand between us...."—Jessica Tandy, on working with her husband, Hume Cronyn, in *Camilla*

actress is innately appealing, this approach made the character seem dull and lifeless. In contrast to Fonda, Vincent Lopez, who plays her husband, gives a charming, natural and totally believable characterization. He is very much in love, but is honestly confused about what is wrong. Fortunately for him Freda's excursion offers him the opportunity to examine himself and investigate his responsibility in the marriage problems. Lopez appears to be an instinctual actor and in *Camilla* his instincts were right on target.

In a battered old jeep, Freda and Camilla (with violin in hand) take off to Toronto. Typically, as it is with most "road pictures," the two encounter various trials and tribulations along the way. The jeep ends up in the bottom of a river and they are forced to hitchhike. Somehow, seeing Jessica Tandy hitchhiking seems slightly implausible but, fortunately, the director minimizes any cute devices. The pair naturally bond with each other and end up playing music together, fishing together, and they even go skinny dipping. Encountering a stranger in a coffee shop reading a book on Gandhi, Camilla announces, "Gandhi likes enemas. One of Gandhi's little quirks. Liked to give them to his close friends." Lines such as these seem tailor-made for someone like Ruth Gordon. But the twinkle in Tandy's eye made them forgivable and palatable. Her understated humor can enhance even the crudest of lines.

Camilla's sentimental journey back to the Wintergarden leads to a reunion with the love of her life, Ewald, played by Hume Cronyn (Tandy's real-life husband). The couple have appeared together throughout their respective careers and were certainly one of the brightest spots in Ron Howard's *Cocoon* (1985). The two add a class and grace to all of their endeavors and are two of the reasons to see *Camilla*. There is a lovely moment when Camilla climbs into Ewald's

CREDITS

Camilla Cara:	Jessica Tandy
Freda Lopez:	Bridget Fonda
Vincent Lopez:	Elias Koteas
Harold Cara:	Maury Chaykin
Hunt Weller:	Graham Green
Ewald:	Hume Cronyn
No character identified:	Ranjit Chowdhry
No character identified:	George Harris
No character identified:	Sandi Ross
No character identified:	Gery Quigley
No character identified:	Atom Egoyan
No character identified:	Devyani Saltzman
No character identified:	Camille Spence
No character identified:	Martha Cronyn
No character identified:	Sheilanne Lindsay
No character identified:	Don McKellar

Origin: Canada and Great Britain
Released: 1994
Production: Christina Jennings and Simon Relph for Shaftesbury Films/Skreba, with the participation of Telefilm Canada, Ontario Film Development Corporation, Foundation Fund to Underwrite New Drama for Pay Television, Norstar, and British Screen. Released by Miramax Films
Direction: Deepa Mehta
Screenplay: Paul Quarrington; based on an original story by Ali Jennings
Cinematography: Guy Dufaux
Editing: Barry Farrell
Production Design: Sandra Kybartas
Sound: Bruce Nyznik
Costume design: Milena Canonero and Elisabetta Beraldo
Music: Daniel Lanois and Stephen Endelman
MPAA rating: PG-13
Running time: 90 minutes

bed after many decades apart. As he extols on her beauty, Camilla becomes like a young, bashful bride. Tandy takes on an indefinable incandescence, while Cronyn becomes the knight in shining armor. Instead of watching an elderly couple about to make love, they become Romeo and Juliet. Theirs was truly a great real life love story.

The closer the two get to Toronto, the more honest they become with each other. It turns out that Camilla's auspicious debut at the Wintergarden those many years ago was fraught with nerves and jitters and costly mistakes. Camilla finally reveals her human frailties and bursts the bubble of fantasy. Upon learning of these events. Freda still views her as "amazing" and cherishes their friendship. This gives Camilla some new confidence to make some decisions about her choices from this point forward. Freda also comes to terms with her own inadequacies and is able to start anew.

Whatever luster or poignance *Camilla* possesses cannot be credited to the screenwriter or director. If Deepa Mehta had chosen anyone other than Jessica Tandy to play the title role the film would have very little redeeming value. The pacing was slow at times and the script, played by a lesser actress, would have resonated with syrupy sentimentality. This major pitfall was avoided due to the eloquent talents of the star. To watch this film without her would not have been desirable.

In viewing *Camilla* it becomes evident what a great loss that Jessica Tandy's passing is to film and theatre. Fortunately she has left behind a body of work that will remind audiences of her lasting beauty and accomplishments. In an era where movies have such few great leading ladies, Tandy's absence leaves a bigger void.

The movie's final shot shows Camilla on a beach with violin in hand while her lover, Ewald, applauds. He moves to tenderly kiss his wife's hand. It is the last moment in the film and, in retrospect, is Cronyn's final farewell to his wife on screen. It is a touching tribute to this great lady and leaves the audience with a haunting reminder of the loss of greatness. It also leaves a sense of gratitude for the many great moments this skilled artist has given to people throughout her career.

—*Robert F. Chicatelli*

REVIEWS

Atlanta Constitution. March 13, 1995, p. B6.
Boston Globe. March 24, 1995, p. 62.
Chicago Tribune. March 24, 1995, Sec. 1 p. 30.
Los Angeles Times. Decemebr 16, 1994, p. F10.
Maclean's. CVII, November 28, 1994, p. 86.
The New York Times. December 16, 1994, p. C16.
People Weekly. XLIII, January 23, 1995, p. 17.
The Washington Post. March 25, 1995, p. D6.

Camp Nowhere

"This summer. Kids rule."—Movie tagline

"Funny."—*The New York Times*

"Sheer high spirits... Fulfills every summer camp veteran's dream"—*Los Angeles Times*

 Box Office Gross: $10,438,786 (December 11, 1994)

When a group of kids are pressed into attending summer camp by their parents, they decide to band together to create their own and hire a loopy former drama teacher (Christopher Lloyd) to help. What follows is a summer camp in the Hollywood tradition with lots of junk food, video games, and of course, no rules.

REVIEWS

Atlanta Constitution. August 29, 1994, p. D9.
Boston Globe. August 27, 1994, p. 27.
Chicago Tribune. August 26, 1994, Sec. 1 p. 28.
Entertainment Weekly. March 24, 1995, p. 74.
Los Angeles Times. August 26, 1994, p. F18.
The New York Times. August 26, 1994, p. C3.
People Weekly. XLII, September 12, 1994. p. 19.
TV Guide. April 1, 1995, p. 39.
Variety. CCCLVI, August 29, 1994, p. 42.
The Washington Post. August 27, 1994, p. B3.
The Washington Post. September 1, 1994, p. D7.

 "Just because you're smart it doesn't mean you can't be stupid. It's your constitutional right"—*Camp Nowhere*'s Dennis Van Welker, to "Mud"

CREDITS

Morris "Mud" Himmel: Jonathan Jackson
Dennis Van Welker: Christopher Lloyd
Zack Dell: Andrew Keegan
Trish Prescott: Marne Patterson
Gaby Nowicki: Melody Kay
Norris Prescott: Ray Baker
Rachel Prescott: Kate Mulgrew
Dr. Celeste Dunbar: Wendy Makkena
Donald Himmel: Peter Scolari
Nancy Himmel: Romy Walthall
Karl Dell: Peter Onorati
T. R. Polk: M. Emmet Walsh
Lieutenant Eliot Hendricks: Tom Wilson
Feln: Burgess Meredith

Released: 1994
Production: Michael Peyser for Hollywood Pictures; released by Buena Vista Pictures
Direction: Jonathan Prince
Screenplay: Andrew Kurtzman and Eliot Wald
Cinematography: Sandi Sissel
Editing: Jon Poll
Production design: Rusty Smith
Art direction: Keith Neely
Set decoration: James I. Samson
Casting: Amy Lippens
Sound: David Kelson
Costume design: Sherry Thompson
Music: David Lawrence
MPAA rating: PG
Running time: 96 minutes

Il Capitano

B ased on a true story, this shocking drama centers on two young criminals who murder a couple and their son in northern Sweden.

CREDITS

No character identified: Maria Heiskanen
No character identified: Antii Reini
No character identified: Berto Marklund
No character identified: Antii Vierikko
No character identified: Harri Malenius
No character identified: Marjut Dahlstrom
No character identified: Eva Stellby
No character identified: Matti Dahlberg
No character identified: Christina Pramback

Origin: Sweden
Released: 1991
Production: Goran Setterberg and Jan Troell for Sandrews, Pan Film AB, Four Seasons Venture Capital, Film Teknik, Bold Productions, and Svenska Filminstitutet
Direction: Jan Troell
Screenplay: Per Olov Enquist, Jan Troell, and Goran Setterberg
Cinematography: Jan Troell
Editing: Jan Troell
Production design: Stig Limer
Sound: Eddie Axberg
Costume design: Gunnel Blomberg
Music: Lars Akerlund and Sebastian Oberg
MPAA rating: no listing
Running time: 110 minutes

A Captive in the Land

I n this combination psychological drama and adventure tale, an American (Sam Waterston) parachutes to the rescue of a crashed Soviet plane in the Arctic Circle, where he finds one survivor (Alexander Potapov), who is unable to walk. The two then struggle together to cross the icy region and return to civilization, forging a tentative friendship in the process. Based on a novel by James Aldridge.

REVIEWS

Christian Science Monitor. January 22, 1993, p. 11.
The New York Times. January 15, 1993, p. C6.
Variety. CCCXLIII, May 13, 1991, p. 104.

CREDITS

Royce: Sam Waterston
Averyanov: Alexander Potapov

Origin: USA and USSR
Released: 1991
Production: Malcolm Stuart and John Berry for Gorky Film Studios and Soviet American Films; released by Gloria Productions
Direction: John Berry
Screenplay: Lee Gold; based on the novel by James Aldridge
Cinematography: Pierre William Glenn
Editing: George Klotz
Production design: Yurih Konstantinov
Art direction: Jacques Voizot
Special effects: Philippe Alleton
Sound: Henri Roux and Jean-Michel Chauvet
Costume design: Eugenia Chervonskaya
Music: Bill Conti
MPAA rating: no listing
Running time: 96 minutes

Car 54, Where Are You?

"The most arresting officers in police history are back."—Movie tagline

Box Office Gross: $1,177,211 (February 13, 1994)

I n this witless film adaptation of the popular 1960's television series, David Johansen stars as goofy Brooklyn cop Gunther Toody and John C. McGinley is his more sober partner, Francis Muldoon. The two suffer numerous problems when they are assigned to protect a key witness (Jeremy Piven) from a Mafia boss (Daniel Baldwin). The film was held up at Orion for three years.

REVIEWS

Atlanta Constitution. February 1, 1994, p. D5.
Boston Globe. January 29, 1994, p. 30.
Chicago Tribune. January 30, 1994, Sec. 5 p. 7.
Entertainment Weekly. February 11, 1994, p. 38.
Entertainment Weekly. July 8, 1994, p. 62.
People Weekly. XLI, February 14, 1994, p. 14.
Variety. CCCLIII, January 31, 1994, p. 66.
The Washington Post. January 29, 1994, p. G2.

"*Car 54* should have a short patrol of theaters before being towed away to the vacant lot of '10 worst lists.'"—Brian Lowery, *Daily Variety*

CREDITS

Gunther Toody: David Johansen
Francis Muldoon: John C. McGinley
Velma Velour: Fran Drescher
Captain Dave Anderson: Nipsey Russell
Lucille Toody: Rosie O'Donnell
Don Motti: Daniel Baldwin
Herbert Hortz: Jeremy Piven
Carlo: Bobby Collins
Nicco: Louis Di Bianco
Leo Schnauzer: Al Lewis

Released: 1994
Production: Robert H. Solo; released by Orion Pictures
Direction: Bill Fishman
Screenplay: Erik Tarloff, Ebbe Roe Smith, Peter McCarthy, and Peter Crabbe; based on a story by Tarloff and on the 1960's television series created and produced by Nat Hiken
Cinematography: Rodney Charters
Editing: Alan Balsam and Earl Watson
Production design: Catherine Hardwicke
Art direction: Gregory P. Keen
Set decoration: Anthony Greco
Casting: Eliza Simons
Sound: Peter Shewchuk
Costume design: Margaret M. Mohr
Music: Pray for Rain and Bernie Worrell
MPAA rating: PG-13
Running time: 89 minutes

La Carne (The Flesh)

This nasty sex comedy centers on a divorced nightclub pianist, Paolo (Sergio Castellitto), who has a torrid affair with a sexy woman, Francesca (Francesca Dellera), then kills her and eats her.

CREDITS

Paolo: Sergio Castellitto
Francesca: Francesca Dellera
Nicola: Philippe Leotard
Aldo: Farid Chopel
Giovanna: Petra Reinhardt

Origin: Italy
Released: 1991
Production: Giuseppe Auriemma; released by MMD
Direction: Marco Ferreri
Screenplay: Marco Ferreri, Liliana Betti, Paolo Costella, and Massimo Bucchi
Cinematography: Ennio Guarnieri
Editing: Ruggero Mastroianni
Production design: Sergio Canevari
Sound: Jean-Pierre Ruh
Costume design: Nicoletta Ercole
MPAA rating: no listing
Running time: 90 minutes

Caro Diario (Dear Diary)

"Funny...captivating, delightfully offbeat. One of the hight points of this year's New York Film Festival. A charming comedy."—Janet Maslin, *The New York Times*

"Magnificent and hilarious...a heroic tale, told with a child's wide-eyed wonder."—Mary Corliss, *Film Comment*

"Intimate and funny! People will lose their hearts to *Caro Diario*."—Georgia Brown, *The Village Voice*

 Box Office Gross: $365,673 (December 4, 1994)

Italian director/screenwriter Nanni Moretti stars as himself in this comedy, which is divided into three sections. Moretti first takes the viewer on a motorcycle tour of Rome in "On My Vespa," then he and a friend (Renato Carpentieri) tour several idyllic island communities in "Islands," and finally Moretti leads the viewer through the prolonged diagnosis and treatment of a peculiar medical condition of his in "Doctors." Throughout, Moretti displays his trademark oddball antics and offbeat sense of humor. Italian with English subtitles, this film is Moretti's first U.S. release.

REVIEWS

Atlanta Constitution. December 9, 1994, p. P4.
Boston Globe. April 7, 1995, p. 90.
The Christian Century. CXI, September 21, 1994, p. 844.
The Nation. CCLIX, October 17, 1994, p. 434.
New York. XXVII, October 10, 1994, p. 73.
Time. CXLIV, October 24, 1994, p. 77.
The Washington Post. October 21, 1994, p. C7.
The Washington Post. October 21, 1994, p. WW48.

CREDITS

Nanni Moretti: Nanni Moretti
Gerardo: Renato Carpentieri
Jennifer Beals: Jennifer Beals
Film critic: Carlo Mazzacurati
Mayor of Stromboli: Antonio Neiwiller
Lucio: Moni Ovadia
Prince of dermatologists: Mario Schiano

Origin: Italy
Released: 1994
Production: Nanni Moretti, Nella Banfi, and Angelo Barbagallo for Sacher Film, Banfilm, La Sept Cinema, and Studio Canal Plus, in association with RAI Uno and Canal Plus; released by Fine Line Features
Direction: Nanni Moretti
Screenplay: Nanni Moretti
Cinematography: Giuseppe Lanci
Editing: Mirco Garrone
Production design: Marta Maffucci
Costume design: Maria Rita Barbera
Music: Nicola Piovani
MPAA rating: no listing
Running time: 96 minutes

AWARDS AND NOMINATIONS

Cannes Film Festival 1994: Best Director (Moretti).

The Cement Garden

Box Office Gross: $135,339 (March 6, 1994)

Four children find themselves orphaned in an isolated house when both their parents die in close succession. After burying their mother in a cement coffin in the basement to hide her death from the authorities, the children indulge their weird, Freudian fantasies: Fifteen-year-old Jack (Andrew Robertson) and sixteen-year-old Julie (Charlotte Gainsbourg) grapple with their burgeoning sexuality and incestuous feelings, and six-year-old Tom (Ned Birkin) dresses in girls' clothing.

REVIEWS

Atlanta Constitution. May 6, 1994, p. P4.
Boston Globe. May 6, 1994, p. 87.
Chicago Tribune. March 4, 1994, p. 7J.
Film Quarterly. XLVIII, Fall 1994, p. 32.
Los Angeles Times. February 24, 1994, p. F4.
Maclean's. CVII, July 1, 1994, p. 61.
The New York Times. February 11, 1994, p. C24.
Playboy. XLI, February 1994, p. 22.
The Washington Post. April 1, 1994, p. D6.

AWARDS AND NOMINATIONS

Berlin International Film Festival: Best Direction (Birkin)

CREDITS

Jack: Andrew Robertson
Julie: Charlotte Gainsbourg
Sue: Alice Coulhtard
Tom: Ned Birkin
Mother: Sinead Cusack
Father: Hanns Zischler
Derek: Jochen Horst
William: Gareth Brown

Origin: Germany, Great Britain, and France
Released: 1993
Production: Bee Gilbert and Ene Vanaveski for Neue Constantin, Laurentic Ltd., and Torii; released by October Films
Direction: Andrew Birkin
Screenplay: Andrew Birkin; based on the novel by Ian McEwan
Cinematography: Stephen Blackman
Editing: Toby Tremlett
Production design: Bernd Lepel
Art direction: Amanda Grenville
Sound: Guillaume Sciama
Costume design: Bernd Lepel
Music: Edward Shearmur
MPAA rating: no listing
Running time: 105 minutes

Century

"At the dawn of a new century, she gave him the courage to challenge the future."—Movie tagline

Set in turn-of-the-century England, this drama centers on an ambitious and outspoken young doctor, Paul Reisner (Clive Owen), who butts heads with his powerful mentor, Professor Mandry (Charles Dance), at a London research hospital.

REVIEWS

Atlanta Constitution. April 21, 1995, p. P3.
Boston Globe. March 17, 1995, p. 87.
Los Angeles Times. December 9, 1994, p. F8.
Variety. CCCLII, September 20, 1993, p. 29.
The Washington Post. March 31, 1995, p. D7.

CREDITS

Professor Mandry: Charles Dance
Paul Reisner: Clive Owen
Clara: Miranda Richardson
Mr. Reisner: Robert Stephens
Mrs. Whitweather: Joan Hickson
Felix: Neil Stuke
Miriam: Lena Heady
Theo: Graham Loughridge
James: Carlton Chance

Origin: Great Britain
Released: 1993
Production: Therese Pickard for I. R. S. Media, in association with ITC Entertainment Group, and BBC Films, in association with Beambright; released by I. R. S. Releasing
Direction: Stephen Poliakoff
Screenplay: Stephen Poliakoff
Cinematography: Witold Stok
Editing: Michael Parkinson
Production design: Michael Pickwoad
Art direction: Henry Harris
Casting: Joyce Gallie
Sound: Hugh Strain
Costume design: Anushia Nieradzik and Daphne Dare
Medical advice: Dr. Ghislaine Lawrence
Music: Michael Gibbs
MPAA rating: no listing
Running time: 112 minutes

Chantilly Lace

This comedy-drama centers on three social gatherings of a group of women friends, who discuss such familiar topics as relationships and careers. The film is notable for its excellent cast, which includes JoBeth Williams, Ally Sheedy, and Martha Plimpton.

REVIEWS

Chicago Tribune. July 16, 1993, Sec. 5 p. 1.
Los Angeles Times. July 17, 1993, p. F12.
The New York Times. July 18, 1993, Sec. 2 p. 25.
Premiere. VI, August 1993, p. 103.
USA Today. July 13, 1993, p. D10.
USA Today. July 16, 1993, p. D3.
USA Today. August 11, 1994, p. D3.
The Wall Street Journal. July 19, 1993, p. A8.

CREDITS

Rheza: Lindsay Crouse
Val: Jill Eikenberry
Anne: Martha Plimpton
Elizabeth: Ally Sheedy
Maggie: Talia Shire
Hanna: Helen Slater
Natalie: JoBeth Williams

Released: 1993
Production: Linda Yellen and Rosanne Ehrlich; released by Showtime
Direction: Linda Yellen
Screenplay: Linda Yellen and Rosanne Ehrlich
Cinematography: Paul Cameron
Editing: Christopher Cooke
Production design: Arnold Skolnick and Suzanne Columbia
Set decoration: Janet Swain
Casting: Risa Bramon Garcia and Heidi Levitt
Sound: Frank Stettner
Costume design: Sharon Lynch
Music: Patrick Seymour
MPAA rating: no listing
Running time: 102 minutes

The Chase

"A high-speed romance."—Movie tagline

"It's fast, it's wild, and it's funny."—Jim Ferguson, *KMSB-TV*

"...[a] rollicking piece of movie road kill."—Peter Rainer, *Chicago Times*

"...detonates laughs."—Steven Holden, *The New York Times*

 Box Office Gross: $7,879,500 (April 24, 1994)

C harlie Sheen stars as an escaped prisoner who kidnaps a young heiress (Kristy Swanson) from a convenience store and heads for the Mexican border in her red BMW. A high-speed chase ensues during which the two are pursued by not only the police but also the television news media, in this lightweight social satire. Skewers the media hype that surrounds crime, taking on news programs that offer immediate coverage and reality based shows with unnerving glee. Even though the story is set in Southern California, the film was shot in Houston and many of the car chases were done on a new highway in Houston that was not yet opened to the public. In order to make the Houston highways look as if they were from California, production designer Sherman Williams brought specially made fiberglass palm trees and road signs. Members of the rock group Red Hot Chili Peppers have cameos.

CREDITS

Jack Hammond: Charlie Sheen
Natalie Voss: Kristy Swanson
Officer Dobbs: Henry Rollins
Officer Figus: Josh Mostel
Chief Boyle: Wayne Grace
Byron Wilder: Rocky Carroll
Liam Segal: Miles Dougal
Dalton Voss: Ray Wise
Ari Josephson: Marshall Bell

Released: 1994
Production: Brad Wyman and Cassian Elwes for Capitol Films; released by Twentieth Century-Fox
Direction: Adam Rifkin
Screenplay: Adam Rifkin
Cinematography: Alan Jones
Editing: Peter Schink
Production design: Sherman Williams
Art direction: Jack Cloud
Set decoration: Craig Loper
Casting: Jakki Fink
Sound: Tim Himes
Costume design: Yvette Correa
Stunt coordination: Buddy Joe Hooker
Music: Richard Gibbs
Music supervision: Tarquin Gotch
MPAA rating: PG-13
Running time: 88 minutes

REVIEWS

Atlanta Constitution. March 4, 1994, p. P3.
Boston Globe. March 4, 1994, p. 54.
Chicago Tribune. March 4, 1994, p. 7B.
Entertainment Weekly. July 29, 1994, p. 60.
Entertainment Weekly. March 18, 1994, p. 77.
Los Angeles Times. March 4, 1994, p. F14.
The New York Times. March 4, 1994, p. C14.
TV Guide. XLII, August 6, 1994, p. 31.
Variety. CCCLIV, March 7, 1994, p. 60.
The Washington Post. March 4, 1994, p. C9.

"The media sensationalizes these chases in an almost bloodthirsty fashion; they are turned into entertainment with each station jockeying for the best coverage."—*The Chase* director Adam Rifkin

Chasers

"a rip-roaring comic adventure."—Kevin Thomas,
Los Angeles Times

 Box Office Gross: $1,590,191 (May 30, 1994)

Two Navy men (Tom Berenger and William McNamara) get more than they bargained for when they are assigned to transport a beautiful and feisty prisoner (Erika Eleniak) back to their base, in this comic adventure. Toni, however, is out to escape her jail sentence for going AWOL. Considering how dumb her jailers are, this shouldn't be too difficult. Considered to be a carbon copy of *The Last Detail* (1973).

REVIEWS

People Weekly. XLI, May 9, 1994, p. 19.
TV Guide. XLII, August 13, 1994, p. 36.
Variety. CCCLV, May 2, 1994, p. 90.

 "I'm gonna be your worst nightmare."—Rock Reilly, from *Chasers*

CREDITS

Rock Reilly: Tom Berenger
Toni Johnson: Erika Eleniak
Eddie Devane: William McNamara
Howard Finster: Crispin Glover
Rory Blanes: Matthew Glave
Vance Dooly: Grand L. Bush
Salesman Stig: Dean Stockwell
Flo: Bitty Schram
Sergeant Vince Banger: Gary Busey
Master Chief Bogg: Seymour Cassel
Duane: Frederic Forrest
Katie: Marilu Henner
Doggie: Dennis Hopper

Released: 1994
Production: James G. Robinson for Morgan Creek; released by Warner Bros.
Direction: Dennis Hopper
Screenplay: Joe Batteer, John Rice, and Dan Gilroy; based on a story by Batteer and Rice
Cinematography: Ueli Steiger
Editing: Christian A. Wagner
Production design: Robert Pearson
Art direction: Natalie Wilson
Set decoration: Kate Sullivan
Casting: Mary Jo Slater
Sound: Roger Pietschmann
Costume design: Michael Boyd
Music: Dwight Yoakam and Pete Anderson
MPAA rating: R
Running time: 101 minutes

Chicken Hawk: Men Who Love Boys

This controversial documentary centers on the North American Man-Boy Love Association (NAMBLA), balancing interviews with the group's members with those of its hostile detractors. The film met with 200 anti-NAMBLA protesters when it opened at the New York Underground Film Festival in the spring of 1994.

Direction: Adi Sideman
Cinematography: Nadav Harel
Editing: Nadav Harel
Music: Cesar Franck and Maurice Ravel
MPAA rating: no listing
Running time: 58 minutes

REVIEWS

The Advocate. August 23, 1994, p. 118.
Los Angeles Times. August 19, 1994, p. F22.
Los Angeles Times. August 14, 1994, p. CAL25.
The New York Times. July 8, 1994, p. C8.
Variety. CCCLV, June 20, 1994, p. 43.

CREDITS

Narrator: Barbara Adler
Narrator: Mimi Turner

Released: 1994
Production: Adi Sideman for Side Man; released by Stranger Than Fiction Films

"When we do a film, we feel like there's a line in the sand. Companies like Miramax and New Line have taken the term 'independent' and ruined it by using it as a marketing device so we're ready to take it back. A film like *Chicken Hawk* attracked us because as a small company we don't have the ad money to fully promote a film from scratch—so we have to ride that NAMBLA wave."—Todd Phillips, Stranger Than Fiction kingpin and organizer of the New York Underground Film Festival, Spring 1994 (*Film Threat*, October 1994)

Children of Nature

An old man (Gisli Halldorsson) meets up with his childhood sweetheart (Sigridur Hagalin) in a nursing home, and the two decide to run away together to their home village by the coast. Crossing the rugged landscape of Iceland and pursued by the police, the two are helped by an angel (Bruno Ganz). The film earned Iceland's first Academy Award nomination.

REVIEWS

Chicago Tribune. October 25, 1993, Sec. 5 p. 5.
The Washington Post. March 14, 1994, p. D3.

AWARDS AND NOMINATIONS

Academy Awards Nomination 1992: Best Foreign Language Film

CREDITS

Old man: Gisli Halldorsson
Old woman: Sigridur Hagalin
Angel: Bruno Ganz

Origin: Iceland
Released: 1991
Production: Fridrik Thor Fridriksson for Icelandic Film Corporation
Direction: Fridrik Thor Fridriksson
Screenplay: Einar Mar Gudmundsson and Fridrik Thor Fridriksson
Cinematography: Ari Kristinsson
Production design: Geir Ottar Geirsson
Music: Hilmar Orn Hilmarsson
MPAA rating: no listing
Running time: 85 minutes

China Moon

"Heated Thriller."—Joan Juliet Buck, *Vogue*

"A Sexy Mystery."—Jeff Craig, *Sixty Second Preview*

"*China Moon* is one of those labyrinthine police procedurals where you're constantly trying to out-think the plot, and you can't."—Roger Ebert, *Chicago Sun-Times*

 Box Office Gross: $2,971,071 (April 10, 1994)

This thriller centers on a lonely homicide detective, Kyle Bodine (Ed Harris), whose romantic involvement with a beautiful married woman, Rachel Munro (Madeleine Stowe), leads to his becoming an accessory to the murder of her abusive husband (Charles Dance). Kyle's problems escalate when his rookie partner (Del Toro) turns out to be smarter than anyone thinks. The film was a victim of Orion's bankruptcy phase and was shelved for a couple of years before being released. Filmed on location in Florida.

Ed Harris as homicide detective Kyle Bodine and Madeleine Stowe as Rachel Munro in *China Moon*. © 1993 Orion Pictures. All rights reserved.

CREDITS

Kyle Bodine: Ed Harris
Rachel Munro: Madeleine Stowe
Lamar Dickey: Benicio Del Toro
Rupert Munro: Charles Dance
Adele: Patricia Healy
Fraker: Tim Powell
Pinola: Robb Edward Morris

Released: 1994
Production: Barrie M. Osborne for Tig; released by Orion Pictures
Direction: John Bailey
Screenplay: Roy Carlson
Cinematography: Willy Kurant

Editing: Carol Littleton and Jill Savitt
Production design: Conrad E. Angone
Art direction: Robert W. Henderson
Set decoration: Don K. Ivey
Casting: Elizabeth Leustig
Special effects coordination: Lawrence J. Cavanaugh
Sound: Jim Webb
Costume design: Elizabeth McBride
Music: George Fenton
MPAA rating: R
Running time: 99 minutes

 "My grandmother used to say that when the moon is like a big old plate of china, strange things happen."—Kyle Bodine, from *China Moon*

China, My Sorrow

Set in 1960's China, this drama centers on an adolescent boy (Guo Liang Yi) who is sent to a rehabilitation camp for life where he is ritually humiliated, all because he tried to impress a pretty girl by playing a love song on his record player. There he befriends another enemy of the revolution and a Buddhist monk who help him maintain his familial traditions and identity. Tragi-comic look at how freedom's spirit survived the Cultural Revolution. In Mandarina and Shanghaiese with English subtitles.

REVIEWS

Chicago Tribune. October 22, 1993, p. 7D(36).
Christian Science Monitor. February 5, 1993.

CREDITS

Four Eyes: Guo Liang Yi
Monk: Tieu Quan Nghieu
Camp boss: Vuong Han Lai
Bei Mao: Chi-Vy Sam
Artist: Truong Loi

Origin: China
Released: 1989
Production: Released by Milestone
Direction: Dai Sijie
Screenplay: Dai Sijie and Shan Yuan Zhu
Cinematography: Jean Michel Humeau
Editing: Chantal Delattre
Music: Chen Qi Gang
MPAA rating: no listing
Running time: 86 minutes

Ciao, Professore! (Io Speriamo Che Me Lo Cavo) (Me, Let's Hope I Make It)

"One of this year's high points!"—*New York Observer*
"Rambunctious comedy! Bursting with life!"
— *Los Angeles Times*
"Refreshing vitality!"— *The Orange County Register*
"A fine heart-warming picture! Deftly directed by Lina Wertmuller."— Paul Wunder, *WBAI Radio*
"If you liked the kid in *Cinema Paradiso*, you'll love these youngsters!"—*The Orange County Register*
"Unforgettable! It will steal your heart! Wildly funny and very moving."— Jeannie Wolf, *Jeannie Wolf's Hollywood*

 Box Office Gross: $1,082,009 (October 23, 1994)

The word "cute" is generally used as a compliment but often carries a simple or light-hearted or even fluffy connotation. Cute, though, is a very fitting description of *Ciao, Professore!*, connotations included. Those familiar with director Lina Wertmuller will quickly realize that *Ciao,*

Professore! is a radical departure from her earlier tough, serious films. But different doesn't necessarily mean bad. Ms. Wertmuller takes a potentially boring, age-old story, injects sharp, comedic dialogue, delivered mostly by children, and creates a comical, sometimes touching film. The cute children theme may be reminiscent of Francois Truffaut's *Small Change* (1976).

Professore Sperelli is accidently sent to the poor, crime-ravaged town of Corzano in Southern Italy instead of the affluent town of Corsano in the North from where he comes. The moment he arrives, he is seen as a stranger in a strange land. Sperelli is taken aback by everything he sees; the degenerating buildings, the mounds of trash in the streets, the young boys wearing earrings and especially the children at work and not in school. An eight-year-old boy working in an ice cream shop explains that he must work, just to get by. Such is the plight of most of the child laborers the teacher encounters. All seem mature beyond their years with their understanding of money and survival, and especially with their language, which rivals that of a truck driver. But that is exactly what makes this film so humorous—innocent-looking third-graders, complete with missing teeth, acting, sounding and even thinking like world-weary adults.

It doesn't take long for Sperelli to see where the problem is. The school is decrepit, the principal, ingrained with the criminal ways of Corzano, has no interest in making a difference, and the janitor is so corrupt he sells chalk and toilet paper (by the square!) to the children. And thanks to his mafia connections, he has more authority than the principal herself. At first Sperelli is disgusted and requests a transfer. But after talking with a boy's mother who treats him like a messiah, and for lack of knowing any better, he decides that he can make a difference and stays.

On his first day in class, only three of fifteen students are present. With these three as his guides, he combs the streets and literally drags the children, kicking and screaming, from their jobs off to the classroom. Many of them are still wearing their work clothes, and one girl who works at a fruit stand still has a rope of garlic around her neck.

Once in the classroom, the teaching begins. But the children are not the only ones who learn something. As this very familiar story goes, the educated adult learns a thing or two from the children who have a very different perspective

> "You stole a van; you smacked a nun against a wall. A few weeks more, and you'd learn how to live."—Raffaele to Professor Sperelli in *Ciao, Professore!*

of life and living than he does. While discussing prehistoric man, the most intelligent student naively describes characteristics of the caveman and his environment that not coincidentally resemble conditions of Corzano and its inhabitants. Sperelli quickly learns with what he is dealing.

In a scene that delivers one of the underlying messages of the film, the most rebellious of the students talks back and shows utter contempt towards the teacher. Sperelli, in a moment of rage, slaps the boy and is immediately sorry and shocked at what he has done. He rushes to the principal's office, explains what has transpired and insists that she take disciplinary action against him. The principal says that that was the best thing he has done since he's been there and that now the children will respect him. He can't believe what he is hearing and argues that violence doesn't earn respect, only fear. He returns to his class and delivers this all-important lesson, but the children, all too familiar with violence and fear, don't quite get the message.

Their mutual education continues, and Wertmuller wisely shows most of the learning taking place outside of the classroom. The children have already adapted to life on the streets, but its the teacher who must learn about a lifestyle that he may not be familiar with, but one that exists more often than he may care to recognize. Near the end of the film, Raffaele, the rebellious one, pleads with Sperelli to help his mother who is deathly ill. When the hospital refuses to send an ambulance, Sperelli responds by stealing a truck. Once at the hospital, a nun casually takes her time treating the woman who is writhing in pain. Sperelli shoves the nun against a wall and orders her to take care of the woman immediately. This scene represents a graduation in the teacher's own education; he has learned that when in Corzano, do as the Corzanos do.

CREDITS

Marco Sperelli: Paolo Villaggio
Raffaele: Ciro Esposito
Nicola: Mario Blanco
Vincenzio: Adriano Pantaleo
Ludovico: Paolo Bonacelli
Peppiniello: Pier Francesco Borruto
Esterina: Esterina Carloni
Principal: Isa Danieli
Custodian: Gigio Morra
Cardboard dealer: Sergio Solli
Giustino: Marco Troncone

Origin: Italy
Released: 1994
Production: Ciro Ippolito, Mario Cecchi Gori, and Vittorio Cecchi Gori; released by Miramax Films
Direction: Lina Wertmuller
Screenplay: Lina Wertmuller, Leo Benvenuti, Piero De Bernardi, AlessandroBencivenni, and Domenico Saverni; based on the book *Io Speriamo Che Me Lo Cavo*, by Marcello D'Orta
Cinematography: Gianni Tafani
Editing: Pierluigi Leonardi
Production design: Enrico Job
Costume design: Gino Persico
Music: D'Angio Greco
MPAA rating: R
Running time: 91 minutes

Paolo Viallagio as third-grade teacher Marco Sperelli in *Ciao, Professore!*

Young Raffaele's observation, "You stole a van; you smacked a nun against a wall. A few weeks more, and you'd learn how to live," neatly wraps up this theme.

The film is nearly carried by the young actors and actresses, many of whom have no prior experience. They seem completely natural in their roles and effortlessly portray these charismatic urchins. Paolo Villaggio, a veteran of Italian cinema, upholds his end of the film and effectively portrays the uptight teacher who learns more than he teaches. *Ciao, Professore!* would be an excellent teaching aid for teachers, parents and children, with its lessons about survival, hardship, perseverance, respect, adaptation, and the benefits of learning on many levels, although the film's salty language is enough to send parents scrambling for the VCR's stop button.

—*Christopher P. Scanlon*

REVIEWS

Atlanta Constitution. August 5, 1994, p. P12.
Boston Globe, July 29, 1994, p. 52.
Chicago Tribune. July 29, 1994, p. 7K.
Chicago Tribune. July 31, 1994, Sec. 13 p. 9.
Christian Science Monitor. February 2, 1995, p. 10.
Los Angeles Times. July 22, 1994, p. F12.
National Review. XLVI, August 1, 1994, p. 63.
The New York Times. July 10, 1994, Sec. 2 p. 14.
The New York Times. July 15, 1994, p. C17.
The New York Times. January 6, 1995, p. D15.
The Washington Post. July 29, 1994, p. D6.
The Washington Post. February 3, 1995, p. D6.

City Slickers II: The Legend of Curly's Gold

"The funniest movie of the year!"—Rod Lurie, *Los Angeles Magazine*

"*City Slickers II* is fall-off-your-horse funny."
—*WWOR-TV*

"Best comedy of the year.... A marvelous comedy romp."—Marilyn Beck, *Tribune Media Services*

"Pure enjoyment!...a gleefully galloping ride from one surprise treat to another!"—David Sheehan, *KCBS Los Angeles*

"A comic adventure that hits the trail at full gallop and a saddlebag full of laughs"—*ABC Radio Network*

"The best sequel since *The Godfather*."—Patty Spitler, *Wish-TV Indianapolis*

 Box Office Gross: $43,446,080 (October 2, 1994)

City Slickers II: The Legend of Curly's Gold is about both discovering the child within and making money. Although, the film itself is about a trio of New York yuppie-types who head West to find a lost treasure, the filmmakers search for the kind of box-office treasure earned by its predecessor, *City Slickers* (1991). The search for gold this time around has indeed been successful as well, with audiences returning to see the further adventures of Mitch (Billy Crystal) and Phil (Daniel Stern) as they brave more stampedes and snakebites while discovering "the one important thing in life" in the process.

Besides buried treasure, this film is also about brotherhood, both literal and figurative. There are two brother relationships in the film. Jack Palance returns in this sequel, this time playing the twin brother, Duke, of the character that won for him an Academy Award in the first film. As if one brother was not enough, Billy Crystal's character gets a brother this time around as well: Jon Lovitz appears as Glen, Mitch's freeloading younger sibling.

Oddly enough, the film itself has a kind of kid-brother quality in that it is not quite as mature or sophisticated as its predecessor. There are more sophomoric sex references, more shallow attempts at male bonding, and an underlying homophobia that make this film to some extent more irritating than *City Slickers*. Yet the film is fun nevertheless. In spite of its often sappy messages about friendship and its now-familiar jokes about cactus needles in the posterior or cellular phones on horseback, this is an entertaining and highly diverting film.

In the original film, three thirty-something New Yorkers went out West "to find their smiles" at a dude ranch, which took its pampered guests on a grueling cattle drive. While on the cattle drive, the three men met the grizzly trail boss, Curly (Palance), who taught Billy Crystal's character, Mitch, that there is more to life than just roping cattle. At the end of that film, Curly died and Mitch helped birth a calf, probably representing the birth of his new spirit.

As the sequel opens, Mitch is having nightmares and visions of Curly that are intruding on his idyllic life with his wife, Barbara (Patricia Wettig). Unfortunately, Wettig's considerable talents are wasted once again. It is Mitch's fortieth birthday, and not only do visions of Curly intrude on his happiness but so does his slovenly brother, Glen. Meanwhile, Mitch has been promoted at the a radio station and has been able to hire his hapless best friend, Phil. Although Phil is lousy at the job, Mitch is such a nice guy that he will not fire him.

Mitch is also too nice to say no to his luckless brother when Glen asks to join Mitch and Phil on a business trip to Las Vegas. Through a combination of events, Mitch and Phil decide that Curly

> When Crystal wanted to make a sequel to *City Slickers*, Bruno Kirby objected. After arguments on the set of the original, Kirby's character Ed was replaced by Lovitz's new character, Mitch's brother. (*Entertainment Weekly*, May 27, 1994)

may be alive and, as luck would have it, may have inadvertently left Mitch with a map to buried treasure, which is near Las Vegas. So the three men ditch the business trip and strike out in search of fortune. It is unfortunate that all this exposition appears to be particularly labored.

CREDITS

Mitch Robbins: Billy Crystal
Phil Berquist: Daniel Stern
Glen Robbins: Jon Lovitz
Duke Washburn: Jack Palance
Barbara Robbins: Patricia Wettig
Bud: Pruitt Taylor Vince
Matt: Bill McKinney
Holly Robbins: Lindsay Crystal
Clay Stone: Noble Willingham
Ira Shalowitz: David Paymer
Barry Shalowitz: Josh Mostel
Talk-show host: Bob Balaban

Released: 1994
Production: Billy Crystal for Castle Rock Entertainment and Face; released by Columbia Pictures
Direction: Paul Weiland
Screenplay: Billy Crystal, Lowell Ganz, and Babaloo Mandel; based on characters created by Ganz and Mandel
Cinematography: Adrian Biddle
Editing: William Anderson
Production design: Stephen J. Lineweaver
Art direction: Philip Toolin
Set design: Richard McKenzie and Nancy Patton
Set decoration: Clay A. Griffith
Casting: Naomi Yoelin and Amy Gerber
Sound: Jeff Wexler, Don Coufal and Gary Holland
Costume design: Llandys Williams
Boss wrangler: Jack Lilley
Music: Marc Shaiman
MPAA rating: PG-13
Running time: 116 minutes

As if getting Mitch and Phil back in the saddle again was not tricky enough, the filmmakers go for broke in signing on the enormously popular Jack Palance: His character was unmistakably dead at the end of the last film. Their contrivance to get actor Palance back by casting him as Curly's identical twin is straight out of a daytime television drama. In order to win viewer sympathy, writers Billy Crystal, Lowell Ganz, and Babaloo Mandel create a weepy story of Duke's lonely life as a merchant marine. His search for the gold is apparently a search for retirement money: When he despairs of finding it, sad music and stiff-upper-lip acting from Palance add to the unctuousness of the character. Only if audiences are willing to overcome the laboriousness of the exposition and the shallowness of the film's central event can they enjoy the rest of the film.

Crystal, Stern, and Lovitz work beautifully together, reminiscent of the comic trio in the classic *The Wizard of Oz* (1939): Crystal as the Scarecrow, Stern as the Tin Man, and Lovitz as the Cowardly Lion. There is a charming scene in which their characters decide to huddle together for warmth one night on the trail, getting their legs tangled and trying hard to pretend they are not embarrassed by the situation.

There is a playfulness combined with a strong sentimentality that affects much of the trio's action. This is visually captured in one wonderful brief sequence of the silhouettes of the three men doing the "happy dance"—an allusion to the classic film *The Treasure of the Sierra Madre* (1948). Their strikingly different silhouettes and their comic dances form a whimsical image, representing the sense of playfulness that permeates this film.

Particularly amusing is a scene in which the hapless Phil thinks he has been bitten in the rear by a rattlesnake and insists that one of the others suck out the poison. This scene is played for all it is worth by the three comedians—it is truly hilarious to watch Crystal go through his facial contortions as his character realizes he has to do this to save his friend. This sequence should prove memorable to audiences.

Director Paul Weiland works well with his actors and writers, allowing the comics to do what they do best. There is no fancy editing or cutaways that detract from the fun of the three comics—one mark of a good director. Weiland also manages to capture some vivid images of the beautiful Utah locations where the film was shot.

The film's story calls for a stampede and a runaway carriage, among other sequences, and this allows Weiland to have some fun with modern film technology. A large portion of the dangerous action sequences appear to have been filmed in front of a "blue screen." This is a process where the actors are filmed in front of a blue screen, then their images are inserted into action footage that would otherwise be impossible to shoot.

For example, in one sequence, Crystal appears to be running to the very edge of a cliff. It is reminiscent of the initial sequence of *Cliffhanger* (1993), in which Sylvester Stallone was seen on top of a sheer cliff. The difference, however, is in the sophistication of the technology: Somehow, in *Cliffhanger*, it seemed as if Stallone was actually on the cliff. In *City Slickers* II, it is evident that Crystal's image has been inserted into the shot.

> "I can't believe you two are from the same gene pool."
> "He's from the shallow end."—
> Phil Berquist to Mitch Robbins about his brother Glen, from *City Slickers II: The Legend of Curly's Gold*

Furthermore, the stampede scene is similar to the way in which actors used to be filmed on horses: Crystal and company are riding their horses in the foreground, with film of the stampede appearing out of perspective behind them. The only reason to mention the disparity between these action sequences and their more sophisticated cinematic cousins is to point out how much "reality" an audience expects in order to suspend disbelief willingly.

Audiences by the early 1990's were accustomed to extraordinarily real action sequences in films such as *Cliffhanger* and *Speed* (reviewed in this volume). Although it is ludicrous to compare this light comedy to those action films, it is interesting to note how the expectations of sophisticated filmgoers could detract from this film. Nevertheless, it is evident that the stars do their own riding, adding a wonderfully realistic touch.

In the central role of Mitch, Billy Crystal is less charming than usual, despite an early sequence where he jogs with the cow that he birthed in the first film. Lovitz was also much criticized in his role as Mitch's annoying brother.

The film also contains another melodic and rousing score by Marc Shaiman, which helps keep the action going and tenderly points the way when audiences' hearts should be tugged. Shaiman is one of the new masters of film music, being the brains behind the music of *Sleepless in Seattle* (1993), *Misery* (1990), and other excellent film scores.

All in all, this is a funny and entertaining film, which, unlike most sequels, does not disappoint. It may not be a brilliant film, but the creators of *City Slickers II: The Legend of Curly's Gold* should be proud that they went after treasure and had fun along the way.

—*Kirby Tepper*

REVIEWS

Entertainment Weekly. June 10, 1994, p. 44.
The Hollywood Reporter. June 2, 1994, p. 7.
Los Angeles Times. June 10, 1994, p. F1.
The New York Times. June 10, 1994, p. B3.
Variety. June 3, 1994, p. 2.

City Zero

A n engineer (Leonid Filatov) finds himself trapped in a small Russian town, in this award-winning surrealistic drama.

REVIEWS

The New Republic. CCIV, April 8, 1991, p. 26.

AWARDS AND NOMINATIONS

Chicago International Film Festival: Grand Prize

CREDITS

Alexei Varakin: Leonid Filatov
No character identified: Oleg Basilashvili
No character identified: Vladimir Menshov
No character identified: Armen Djigarkhanian
No character identified: Yevgeny Yevstigenev
No character identified: Elena Arjanik

Origin: USSR
Released: 1991
Production: Released by International Film Exchange
Direction: Karen Shaknazarov
Screenplay: Karen Shaknazarov and Alexander Borodyansky
Cinematography: Nikolai Nemolyayev
Production design: Lyudmila Kusakova
Music: Edward Artemiev
MPAA rating: no listing
Running time: 84 minutes

Clean Slate

"It's a day he'll never forget. Until tomorrow."
—Movie tagline
"A truly unforgettable comedy."—Movie tagline
"Outrageously funny"—Paul Wunder, *WBAI Radio*
"Dana Carvey is hysterically funny and Valeria Golino is hysterically sexy, in this wild comic ride full of unexpected twists that keep you guessing while you're laughing."—Jeanne Wolf, *Jeanne Wolf's Hollywood*
"A wonderful, winning movie surprise"
—*WCBS-TV*
"Carvey makes *Clean* sparkle."—Michael Medved, *New York Post*

 Box Office Gross: $7,334,943 (June 19, 1994)

B y the 1990's, big-budget Hollywood films became increasingly high-concept, relying on a simple and clever plot device and often little else. In *Kindergarten Cop* (1990), for example, tough-guy Arnold Schwarzenegger

portrayed a police officer who went undercover as a kindergarten teacher. Sylvester Stallone teamed with Estelle Getty of television's *Golden Girls* as a hard-boiled cop whose mother joins him in capturing criminals in *Stop! Or My Mom Will Shoot* (1992). Now Dana Carvey is given the high-concept treatment in *Clean Slate*, a comedy about a private investigator who suffers amnesia every time he falls asleep. Thus he solves a crime by discovering ingenious ways to remind himself who he is every day.

It is an entertaining and well-executed concept, similar to *Groundhog Day* (1993), with Bill Murray, in which Murray's character wakes up every day only to discover that it is the same day as the day before. In effect, *Groundhog Day* is the opposite of *Clean Slate*: In the former, the main character is the only one who remembers, and in the latter, the main character is the only one who forgets. Comparisons between the two films are inevitable. *Clean Slate* is amusing and fun, but in general it lacks some of the warmth and humanity of *Groundhog Day*.

Maurice Pogue (Carvey) is a private investigator who lives and works in his ramshackle office with his dog, Baby (Barkley). As the film opens, Pogue wakes up only to discover that he remembers absolutely nothing. Not even knowing his name, he (and the audience) begin to discover pieces of information that lead him to discover who he is. Each day, Pogue adds bits of information to a small tape recorder before he falls asleep and suffers amnesia once again. The tape recorder becomes his savior: He leaves it by his bedside at night, with a note attached telling him to turn it on upon awakening. As more days pass, he adds whatever new information he has gathered and is slowly able to put together enough information to discover who he is and why people are trying to kill him.

The early segments where Pogue wakes up completely unaware of the prior day's events are amusing. His meeting with a beautiful woman named Sarah (Valeria Golino), who bursts into his office/apartment begging for protection, is comic, particularly when he does not remember that they have been sexually intimate. Eventually Pogue discovers, among other things, that he is quite a ladies' man and is involved in a steamy affair with yet another woman, who happens to be his best friend's girlfriend. He also discovers that he is a key witness in an important criminal trial, the only witness who can identify a dangerous mob boss (Michael Gambon).

> Barkley, a Jack Russell Terrier, has been seen on TV's *Full House* and makes his film debut as Carvey's sidekick in *Clean Slate*.

CREDITS

Pogue: Dana Carvey
Sarah: Valeria Golino
Dolby: James Earl Jones
Rosenheim: Kevin Pollak
Cornell: Michael Gambon
Dr. Doover: Michael Murphy
Paula: Jayne Brook
Hendrix: Vyto Ruginis
Judy: Olivia D'Abo
Baby: Barkley

Released: 1994
Production: Richard D. Zanuck and Lili Fini Zanuck; released by Metro-Goldwyn- Mayer
Direction: Mick Jackson
Screenplay: Robert King
Cinematography: Andrew Dunn
Editing: Priscilla Nedd-Friendly
Production design: Norman Reynolds
Art direction: William Hiney
Set decoration: Anne Kuljian
Casting: Mindy Marin
Sound: Willie Burton
Costume design: Ruth Myers
Music: Alan Silvestri
MPAA rating: PG-13
Running time: 107 minutes

The audience discovers information along with Pogue. In fact, the first section is the best, as Pogue pieces his identity together, interacting with close friends he has forgotten and who have no idea that he has amnesia. His friends include Dolby (James Earl Jones), a wheelchair-bound district attorney; Dr. Doover (Michael Murphy), Pogue's rather smarmy personal physician; Rosenheim (Kevin Pollak), his jealous best friend; and his strange dog, Baby. The most colorful of these characters is arguably the dog, because the filmmakers have created a wonderful "character" for him: Baby wears a patch on one eye and suffers from a depth-perception problem. One of the funniest moments in the film occurs when Baby growls at the villains who are attacking Pogue, lunges at them, and accidentally jumps into a closet. It is safe to say that the dog steals the show.

This is not to disparage the human performers, however. James Earl Jones appears to be enjoying himself playing the gruff and garrulous Dolby, apparently named to reflect Jones' famous booming voice. Kevin Pollak turns in another polished performance as Rosenheim, Pogue's best friend who has asked Pogue to find the man sleeping with his fiancée—unaware that it is Pogue himself. Pollak's increasingly desperate characterization is fun as he begs Pogue to help him. This young actor (and former stand-up comic) has been building a steady and respected career with performances in comedies such as *Grumpy Old Men* (1993) and dramas such as *A Few Good Men* (1992). Pollak wisely does not overplay his character's desperation; if he went too far it would take away from the fun of Pogue's fear of being discovered.

Michael Murphy is a perfect choice for the friendly but sinister Dr. Doover. Murphy, like Pollak, is known for his versatility, having appeared in everything from Robert Altman's version of *The Caine Mutiny Court-Martial* (1988) to the farcical *What's Up, Doc?* (1972). Finally, highly respected British theater actor Michael Gambon is appropriately evil as Cornell. He maintains his dignity through a rather sophomoric recurring joke about his character's missing thumb. His befuddled stare when Pogue hands him a rent check one morning—thinking that he is the landlord—is priceless. It is wise to have actors of such high caliber as these—they play their roles as if it were a serious drama, allowing the comedy to come from the ridiculous situations.

These situations are what drive the film, giving Carvey an assortment of comic moments as his character tries to figure out who he is. For example, when Rosenheim's fiancée (Olivia D'Abo) appears at Pogue's house, scantily clad and bearing sex toys, he goes along with her with a "if-you-can't-beat-'em-join-'em" approach that is funny because it seems so pragmatic. He is equally pragmatic when, early in the film, he is taken into custody by two policemen who brusquely drag him to the station for what turns out to be a surprise birthday party in Pogue's honor. He finds himself in the middle of a crowd of police officers, all of whom seem to love him and know him well. Their perfectly starched uniforms contrast with his rumpled street clothes; their adoration contrasts with his inability to remember who they are. The situation is even more ridiculous when they clamor for him to make a speech, and he reluctantly obliges, offering a hilarious speech that is part Lewis Carroll and part Rod McKuen (in other words, it makes no sense but it makes everybody cry).

There are several such moments in this film where Carvey is given a chance to be extremely funny. Audiences particularly enjoy a scene in which he is chased onto the stage and mistaken for an eminent archaeologist: Once again he gives a speech that is as earnest as it is absurd. Oddly enough, however, Carvey's performance is rather tepid throughout the rest of the film, perhaps because of the inherent passivity of the character. It is hard to say whether Carvey's apparent lack of energy results from the requirement that his character constantly be a "clean slate," from the fact or that Carvey himself is simply a bit shocked that this big-budget film has been created all around him.

Dana Carvey has the potential to become a contemporary version of Jerry Lewis—he can play a vulnerable, agile, and silly Everyman who bumbles his way into solving the crime or getting the girl. His sweetness is reminiscent of Lewis' performance in *Cinderfella* (1960) and his confusion recalls the character Lewis played in *The Patsy* (1964). Similar to Lewis, he is a funny-looking little guy who seems irresistible to luscious women. Valeria Golino is adorable as the love interest, Sarah. Unfortunately, however, she is not as strong an actor as some of the other supporting players. Yet her mixture of innocence and sex appeal make her a good match for Carvey's earnest silliness.

Director Mick Jackson creates just the right atmosphere. His camera angles are unusual: At times, his camera looks at the actors as if from the ground, and he shoots very close up. This is perhaps intended to render the audience a bit off-balance so that audience members empathize with the confused leading man. He also includes some fun symbolism in the form of a mural painter who changes his painting every day because of offhand comments made by Pogue, a blind man who helps Pogue, and the dog with the perception problem. Thus Jackson echoes thematic elements rather than belaboring the themes of personal perception and reality by the use of dialogue.

Yet these themes remain only undercurrents. Although the director and performers are capable of providing a higher-quality, more textured comedy, they instead opt to forget further exploration of these themes in favor of relying on the one-joke central premise. This talented director and these talented actors, not to mention the audience, deserve more than just a concept.

—*Kirby Tepper*

REVIEWS

Entertainment Weekly. May 20, 1994, p. 45.
The Hollywood Reporter. May 6-8, 1994, p. 8.
Los Angeles Times. May 6, 1994, p. F4.
The New York Times. May 6, 1994, p. B2.
Variety. May 6, 1994, p. 2.

Clear and Present Danger

"Truth needs a soldier."—Movie tagline

"Ford is perfect. Another triumph in his illustrious career"—Jeff Craig, *Sixty Second Preview*

"Harrison Ford is riveting"—Susan Granger, *CRN Radio Network*

"the best and certainly the most intelligent action picture of the summer"—Harper Barnes, *St. Louis Post-Dispatch*

"Since *The Empire Strikes Back* in 1980, Harrison Ford has been the equivalent of a Good Housekeeping seal for the adventure genre, his presence guaranteeing an enviable level of professionalism, excitement and involvement."
—Kenneth Turan, *Los Angeles Times*

 Box Office Gross: $122,758,219 (January 2, 1995)

C*lear and Present Danger* is a study of the abuse of power at the highest levels of government. It describes what happens when a U.S. chief executive, assisted by elements within the intelligence community, attempts unilaterally to launch an illegal military venture in a foreign land. While many films have dealt competently with similar subject matter, few have done so with such chilling authenticity. In a genre characterized by potboilers, *Clear and Present Danger* is a fine effort that delivers its cautionary message with intelligence and panache.

Harrison Ford as Jack Ryan in *Clear and Present Danger*. © 1994 Paramount Pictures. All rights reserved.

The film is based on the novel *Clear and Present Danger* by Tom Clancy. The book, published in 1989, quickly climbed to number one on *The New York Times* best-seller list. By 1994 it had sold more than 6 million copies. The film is the third adaptation of a Clancy novel to feature as its main character Doctor Jack Ryan.

At the opening of *Clear and Present Danger*, the Coast Guard pursues a large pleasure craft through choppy seas off South Florida. When they board the vessel, they find only two Colombians and blood everywhere. It turns out that the craft is registered to a close friend and supporter of U.S. president Edward Bennett (Donald Moffat). The Colombians have assassinated the president's friend and all others on board. Ultimately it is revealed that this individual had close ties to the drug cartels and that his murder was a result of that association.

When President Bennett hears the news, he demands an immediate response. The assassination is evidence that the cartels assume they may act with impunity within U.S. borders. This, in the president's view, represents "a clear and present danger" to the security of the United States. The punitive measures suggested by national security adviser, James Cutter (Harris Yulin) are nodded at by the president himself. Thus a small but extremely efficient commando strike force, headed by a mysterious former Central Intelligence Agency (CIA) operative known only as Mr. Clark (Willem Dafoe), is dispatched to the Colombian jungles. Their target is the drug lord responsible for the death of the president's friend.

As these events transpire, Jack Ryan (Harrison Ford) is promoted to deputy director of intelligence for the CIA when his close friend and superior, Admiral James Greer (James Earl Jones), is suddenly afflicted with pancreatic cancer. He knows nothing at first about the commandos or their intended target.

As the plot unfolds, Ryan uncovers conspiracy puzzle pieces and slowly puts them together. This proves a difficult and dangerous process. He travels to Bogotá with a team of investigators, where rooftop snipers blast away. Back home in Washington, he is threatened by members of his own organization and is drawn deeper into the web of conspiracy. In such a Byzantine atmosphere where enemies are friends, and friends are enemies, Ryan has only his conscience to guide him.

Ryan finds himself torn between his loyalty to the president and his desire to act properly. With no one to turn to, he seeks the counsel of the now-dying Admiral Greer. In what must surely be the film's most poignant moment, Greer lying in his hospital bed tells Ryan that his true loyalty is to his "boss," that is to the people of the United States. Although this kind of scene tends to be didactic and hopelessly corny, under Phillip Noyce's skillful direction, Jones and Ford make it believable. In the end, the viewer will approve of Ryan's decision to do the right thing, to expose the conspiracy and all players therein.

Here, of course, lies the film's central problem, an ethical one for the viewer. With gang warfare and crack babies as regular items on the network news, it is difficult to have much sympathy for drug dealers. Yet at the time the film was made, America was waging and losing a legal war on narcotics. How does one answer such a challenge without compromising the moral character of the United States? This is the question at the heart of *Clear and Present Danger*.

Clear and Present Danger is the third film to be adapted from Tom Clancy's bestsellers featuring the Jack Ryan character, following *The Hunt for Red October*, which starred Alec Baldwin, and *Patriot Games*, also with Ford. The film was shot inside the actual CIA head-quarters.

Ryan answers it by busting the conspiracy and just about everyone connected with it. When word of the mission inevitably leaks out, it is instantly aborted, leaving the strike force to fend for itself against overwhelming odds. Ryan, without authorization, travels to Latin America on a personal rescue mission. Once in Colombia, he confronts Ernesto Escobedo (Miguel Sandoval), the man behind the assassination of the president's friend and the ultimate target of the conspiracy. Ryan provides convincing evidence that Escobedo's most trusted aide, Felix Cortez (Joaquim de Almeida), has betrayed him. Cortez has been working to undermine his boss all along, and it is through secretly tape-recorded conversations between Cortez and Escobedo's competitors that Ryan learns of the connection between the drug lord and the conspiracy. Following this sequence are ten minutes of cinema slaughter in which Escobedo and Cortez are killed, and Ryan and the ragtag remnants of the strike force exit via helicopter.

Ryan returns to Washington ready to finish off the conspiracy. He sleuths his way through classified computer files, hoping to uncover the hard evidence he will need to hang the guilty parties. He finds it among the records of Robert Ritter (Henry Czerny), who is linked in the conspiracy with National Security Adviser Cutter.

Ritter's office is next door, and as Ryan attempts to retrieve the damning information, Ritter is busy deleting computer files. This little contest, one of the most interesting sequences in the film, ends as Ryan and Ritter confront each other face to face. Ritter has eliminated most of the evidence. He hints that the conspiracy goes all the way up to the top and that Ryan, in attempting to crush it, is way out of his league. "The world is gray," he says, justifying the actions of the conspiracy. Yet Ryan goes away unconvinced. Even the president does not dissuade him from revealing what he knows to a congressional subcommittee.

Clear and Present Danger has been favorably reviewed by critics across the country. Harper Barnes of the *St. Louis Post-Dispatch* called it "the best and certainly the most intelligent action picture of the summer." Barnes drew parallels between the film and the Reagan administration's covert support of the Nicaraguan Contras. Certainly the film does have historical precedents, most of them probably unknown to the public.

CREDITS

Jack Ryan: Harrison Ford
Clark: Willem Dafoe
Cathy Ryan: Anne Archer
Admiral James Greer: James Earl Jones
Felix Cortez: Joaquim de Almeida
Robert Ritter: Henry Czerny
James Cutter: Harris Yulin
President Bennett: Donald Moffat
Ernesto Escobedo: Miguel Sandoval
Ramirez: Benjamin Bratt
Chavez: Raymond Cruz

Released: 1994
Production: Mace Neufeld and Robert Rehme; released by Paramount Pictures
Direction: Phillip Noyce
Screenplay: Donald Stewart, Steven Zaillian, and John Milius; based on the novel by Tom Clancy
Cinematography: Donald M. McAlpine
Editing: Neil Travis
Production design: Terence Marsh
Art direction: William Cruse
Set decoration: Mickey S. Michaels and Jay R. Hart
Set design: Dawn Snyder
Casting: Mindy Marin
Special effects supervision: Joe Lombardi and Paul Lombardi
Visual effects supervision: Robert Grasmere
Sound: Arthur Rochester
Costume design: Bernie Pollack
Stunt coordination: Dick Ziker
Music supervision: Tim Sexton
Music: James Horner
MPAA rating: PG-13
Running time: 141 minutes

AWARDS AND NOMINATIONS

Academy Awards Nomination 1994: Best Sound
MTV Movie Awards Nomination 1995: Best Action Sequence

Harrison Ford's performance in *Clear and Present Danger* is certainly up to the high standard expected of him by film audiences, but it is the exemplary work of the supporting cast that brings this film to life. New York stage actor Joaquim de Almeida as the scheming Felix Cortez is totally villainous. Cortez is charming, but it is a cold-blooded charm, and beneath the polished exterior beats the heart of a reptile.

"Want to know about politics in Washington? Four words: watch your back, Jack."—Admiral James Greer to Jack Ryan in *Clear and Present Danger*

Willem Dafoe as CIA field operative Mr. Clark comes across as a hard-bitten professional, a dedicated and dangerous man. Clark lives in his own world where morality and decency are indefinitely suspended in order that the "mission" may be carried out efficiently. Clark's loyalty is to his men. He has no apparent ideology and no particular allegiance to the government he serves. He is, in short, the ideal mercenary. Dafoe is quite good in this kind of role and in *Clear and Present Danger* he carries it off particularly well. He is a film veteran and has appeared in such diverse productions as *Mississippi Burning* (1988) and *The Last Temptation of Christ* (1988).

James Earl Jones competently portrays the ailing Admiral Greer, while Donald Moffat and Harris Yulin also do well by their roles. Yet it is Henry Czerny that gives the film its best performance. Czerny, winner of the Canadian Genie award for Best Actor in a miniseries for *The Boys of St. Vincent* (1994), is downright nasty as CIA deputy director of operations Robert Ritter. A dedicated cynic, he finds Ryan's Boy Scout morality insufferable. In Ritter, one sees one's worst suspicions about the CIA and the whole U.S. intelligence apparatus confirmed in flesh and blood. Such a role might well become cliché in less competent hands, but Czerny pulls it off. One may not like Robert Ritter, but one believes in him.

Clear and Present Danger is an excellent piece of filmmaking but it is also much more than that. In a world in which U.S. foreign policy is no longer governed by the anticipated response of cold war adversaries, the frightening premise of the film might well take place in real life. For people living in a free society it is potentially a dangerous time.

—D. Douglas Graham

REVIEWS

Entertainment Weekly. August 12, 1994, p. 36.
The Hollywood Reporter. August 1, 1994, p. 9.
Los Angeles Times. August 3, 1994, p. F1.
The New York Times. August 3, 1994, p. B1.
Variety. August 1, 1994, p. 2.

Clerks

"A Hilarious Look at Over-the-Counter Culture."—Movie tagline

"A wonderful comedy! The funniest movie of the year."—John Anderson, *New York Newsday*

"One of the Top Ten films of the year."—*Time*

"Screamingly funny!"—*Rolling Stone*

"...a wonderfully screwy send-up of down-low Americana...a comedic breath of fresh/stale air."
—Duane Byrege, *The Hollywood Reporter*

"...appealingly minimalist and amusingly deadpan."—Todd McCarthy, *Variety*

 Box Office Gross: $2,370,943 (January 2, 1995)

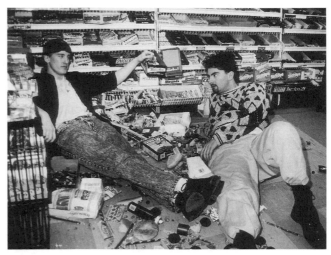

Jeff Anderson as Randal and Brian O'Halloran as Dante in *Clerks*. © 1994 Miramax Films. All rights reserved.

Twenty-three-year-old Kevin Smith's debut film, *Clerks*, is dedicated to John Cassavetes, Jim Jarmusch, and Spike Lee, independent directors who bucked the Hollywood system and sensibility. If, however, its black-and-white cinematography, miniscule $27,575 budget, and "real life" protagonists played by non-professional actors are indeed reminiscent of those directors' early work—Cassavetes's *Shadows* (1961), Jarmusch's *Stranger than Paradise* (1984), and Lee's *She's Gotta Have It* (1986), Smith's style of slightly exaggerated comedy is, in fact, more akin to that of the early Woody Allen. Director-writer Smith and co-producer/co-editor Scott Mosier have crafted a hilarious series of sketches around one employee's nightmarish day at a Quick Stop convenience store in Leonardo, New Jersey. Like some early Allen films—*Take the Money and Run* (1969) and *Bananas* (1971)—the film's comic structure appears loose and episodic, but does, in fact, provide an opportunity for its beleaguered protagonist to undergo a moral transformation. Based on Smith's own four years of employment at the same Quick Stop, *Clerks* is also a pungent, ribald slice of life at an American institution often seen, but rarely examined, in American films.

Clerks spans exactly one day in the life of Dante Hicks (Kevin O'Halloran), the film's twenty-two-year-old convenience-store everyman, forced to come in on his day off because his boss has run off to Vermont. "I'm not even supposed to be here," is Dante's muttered refrain as the day goes haywire. The director's Allenesque sense of humor is imme-

> The budget of *Clerks* was $27,500, the lowest at the 1994 Sundance Film Festival. It was filmed at the Quick Stop Groceries store in Leonardo, New Jersey where writer/director Kevin Smith worked. It initially earned an NC-17 rating because of its explicit language, but was given an R rating after an appeal and some editing.

diately evident in the montage of sight gags that show Dante wearily opening the store: the storefront gate will not open; a sign on the cash register reads, "If you plan to shoplift, let us know, thank you"; and Dante makes up for the store's lack of newspapers by taking the entire stack from the vending machine out front. Smith also uses a series of intellectual-sounding intertitles ("Vilification," "Syntax," "Purgation," "Denouement," similar to those Allen used in *Hannah and Her Sisters* (1986), which break the film into segments and contrast with the film's grungy, mind-numbing setting.

Dante makes clear, despite the intelligence evinced in his sense of humor and in his innovative ways of making the store run smoothly, that he is drifting. His main priority is essentially leisure. He moans about a hockey game that he has to play in the afternoon at which he will not do well because of lack of sleep. Like the typical Allen protagonists of *Annie Hall* (1977) and *Manhattan* (1979), Dante has a sense of humor tinged with superiority that masks an abundant lack of self-esteem, direction, and moral fiber, which only becomes apparent to him as the story progresses, when he runs out of quips and must face the consequences of his actions.

The fast-paced absurdity of Dante's day at the Quick Stop, however, hardly leaves room for self-examination. Dante's girlfriend, Veronica (Marilyn Ghigliotti), is intro-

CREDITS

Dante Hicks: Brian O'Halloran
Randal: Jeff Anderson
Veronica: Marilyn Ghigliotti
Caitlin: Lisa Spoonauer
Jay: Jason Mewes
Silent Bob: Kevin Smith

Released: 1994
Production: Scott Mosier and Kevin Smith for View Askew; released by Miramax Pictures
Direction: Kevin Smith
Screenplay: Kevin Smith
Cinematography: David Klein
Editing: Kevin Smith
Editing: Scott Mosier
Music: Scott Angley
MPAA rating: R
Running time: 89 minutes

duced when she uses a fire extinguisher to rescue Dante from a cigarette-throwing horde of customers led by a Chewels Gum sales representative. When she admonishes Dante that he needs to return to school to escape this kind of life, however, the self-centered Dante is hardly appreciative; in fact, he becomes upset when she reveals in passing that she has fellated thirty-seven different men in her life. Veronica points out his hypocritical stance, that she did not get upset when Dante told her how many girls he had slept with, but Dante argues that sleeping with somebody is one thing, oral sex is something else again. Veronica leaves in a huff, and this gives Dante the opportunity to waste even more of his day obsessing about his lost high-school love, Caitlin (Lisa Spoonauer), with whom he has been back in touch. Although Caitlin cheated on him eight times ("eight-and-a-half"— she had sex with Dante in a dark room at a party and called him Brad), Dante is certain that they will reunite, putting meaning back into his empty life— until he reads in the local newspaper about Caitlin's impending nuptials.

Dante's buddy and alter-ego, Randal (Jeff Anderson), arrives late to open the video store attached to the Quick Stop and becomes the catalyst for Dante to change his life. "That's what high school is about," says Randal, ever the dime-store philosopher, advising him about Caitlin, "Algebra, bad lunch, and infidelity." At first, Dante and Randal pass the time commenting on bizarre customers— the man who always looks for the perfect carton of eggs, another who asks whether the toilet tissue in the bathroom is "rough or cottony"—and wasting their formidable brains

AWARDS AND NOMINATIONS

Cannes Film Festival Awards 1994: International Critics Week Prize
Independent Spirit Awards Nominations 1995: Best First Feature, Debut Performance (Anderson), First Screenplay
Sundance Film Festival 1994: Filmmaker's Trophy

on weighing the comparative merits of *The Empire Strikes Back* (1980) and *Return of the Jedi* (1983). While Dante adheres to his code, "Title Dictates Behavior," which he feels constrains him to be polite to customers and loiterers, Randal soon reveals that he has no compunction about spitting a mouthful of water in a customer's face because the customer has objected to his language. "Who cares?" says Randal. "Everybody who comes in here is way too uptight." He advises Dante to follow his example. Randal also does not subscribe to Dante's theory of behavior and tells him that it is merely symptomatic of what "seems to be the latent motif in your life—ever backing down." A conciliatory Veronica arrives with lasagna for Dante, who at this point all but ignores her.

Dante puts Randal's advice to the test when Caitlin appears, having caught a train from college in Ohio because she realized Dante would see the announcement of her impending marriage. "I hopped the train because I knew you'd be a wreck," she says. She explains that her mother placed the announcement and that even though she is, indeed, seeing the architecture student pictured in the paper, she is now choosing Dante. Dante agrees to leave the store to "get naked" and get back together. "What happened to 'title dictates behavior'?" asks Randal. "Let's say this is my way of spitting water at life," says Dante. Ultimately, however, Caitlin's own bizarre behavior stymies their reconciliation, and Dante learns from one of the bums who loiters outside the store the simple lesson that he should appreciate the one thing he has going for him and has been taking for granted—Veronica. "There're many fine looking women in the world," says the bum, "but not all of them bring you lasagna. Most of 'em just cheat on you." Realizing he has made a mistake Dante runs off, *Manhattan*-style, to reconcile with Veronica. Randal has a convenience-store epiphany of his own: "We look down on [the customers] because we're so advanced," he later says to Dante, "Well, if we're so advanced, what are we doing working here?" Quick Stop, however, is not a dead end at all but rather a place of higher learning. Perhaps, contrary to Dante's refrain, "I'm not even supposed to be here," this is exactly where he is supposed to be, at least for the moment.

"If we're so advanced, what are we doing working here?"—*Clerks'* Randal

Literally shot in the front and edited in the back of the Quick Stop where Smith worked, *Clerks* proves the adage that writers should write about what they know. Smith's familiarity with every inch of the Quick Stop and every idiosyncrasy of its employees and customers makes the film and its characters instantly recognizable and sympathetic to anyone who has spent even a few moments in a convenience store. It also gives *Clerks* an impressive lived-in visual feel and plenty of material for comedic bits with products and strange customers. Although amateurish cutting, worn sight gags (Dante drinking out of a large cookie jar), and the overused shot of a character's feet swinging out of a car door and hitting the sidewalk all mark the pre-Quick Stop scenes of *Clerks* as those of a first feature, the film quickly recovers, and once the film enters the world of the Quick Stop, it is on solid ground. Only when the story takes the characters out of the convenience store setting (the opening, a brief scene outside a funeral home) does Smith's natural visual sense fail him.

Smith's dialogue and the amiable, often hilarious performances he elicits from his cast also go a long way to make up for shortcomings in the story. Several offscreen incidents in the film—Randal's knocking over the casket at the funeral of one of Dante's former girlfriends; Caitlin's becoming catatonic because she has sex with a corpse she thinks is Dante in the darkened Quick Stop bathroom, repeating with a twist what she did in high school—are not so much tasteless as ridiculous and break the believability Smith has so carefully established through setting and character. Yet even these scenes are saved by some of Smith's funniest dialogue. En route to and from the ill-fated funeral, Anderson's hilarious deadpan readings of Randal's monologues on sex overshadow the silliness of the action, and Dante's explanation to a police officer that Caitlin was having sex with a dead man because she thought it was him incites the query, "What kind of convenience store do you run here?" which has become the film's advertising catchphrase.

Clerks, in spite of gaffes typical of an overeager first-time director working on a limited budget, is a classic example of how an overlooked corner of the culture, deeply experienced and well-observed, can be more than adequate grist for an artist's mill. With its abundant humor skillfully masking a moral point, *Clerks* arrives as the freshest, funniest, least pretentious, and most sympathetic portrait of the so-called "Generation X" yet put on film.

—*Paul Mittelbach*

REVIEWS

Film Comment. XXX, May-June, 1994, p.9.
The Hollywood Reporter. January 28, 1994, p. 24.
Los Angeles Times. October 19, 1994, p. F1.
The New York Times. March 25, 1994, p. B1.
The New York Times. CXLIV, October 16, 1994, p. H20(N).
The New York Times. CXLIV, October 19, 1994, p. B4(N).
Newsweek. CXXIV, October 31, 19914, p. 68.
Rolling Stone. DCXCIV, November 3, 1994, p. 104.
Variety. January 27, 1994, p. 10.

The Client

"Pulse-pounding entertainment ...and the smartest thriller since *The Fugitive*.—Bob Campbell, *Newhouse Newspapers*

"A thriller with three winning performances and a fast, no-nonsense pace."—Janet Maslin, *New York Times*

"The most successful movie yet from a John Grisham novel."—Richard Schickel, *Time*

"A high-voltage charge of suspense, action and humor! Sarandon is spellbinding. Jones is electrifying. It keeps you riveted."—Peter Travers, *Rolling Stone*

"A film of hammering suspense that keeps you riveted in its spell. Susan Sarandon is unforgettable."—Rex Reed, *New York Observer*

 Box Office Gross: $92,089,139 (November 27, 1994)

The *Client* is based on the best-selling book by Mississippi novelist John Grisham, two of whose other books preceded *The Client* onto the screen—*The Firm* (1993) and *The Pelican Brief* (1993). *The Client*, released in the summer of 1994, had been awaited with much anticipation since October 1992, when Arnon Milchan's Regency Enterprises bought the film rights for more than $2 million—a price believed to be one of the highest ever paid—before the book even appeared in stores.

The Client stars Susan Sarandon, Tommy Lee Jones, and newcomer Brad Renfro. It is the story of young Mark Sway (Renfro), an eleven-year-old boy who lives outside of Memphis in a trailer park with his working-class single mother, Dianne Sway (Mary-Louise Parker), and his eight-year-old brother, Ricky (David Speck).

The opening scene is by far the most powerful sequence in the film. While Mark and Ricky are surreptitiously smoking in the woods, a man drives to a secluded spot just beyond where the boys are hiding. He attaches a hose to his exhaust pipe and reenters his car. Streetwise Mark realizes the man is attempting suicide and, in an innocent act of compassion, tries to prevent it. The man catches him removing the hose and drags Mark into the car, insisting that the boy die with him.

In the car, the man, who is alternately crying and threatening Mark, tells him he is Romey Clifford (Walter Olkewicz), the lawyer for Barry "The Blade" Muldano (Anthony LaPaglia). The Blade killed a Louisiana senator and told Romey where he buried him, and now every police officer in New Orleans is looking for the body. The Mafia need to silence Romey for good, so cowardly Romey has decided to save the Mafia the trouble. Before he dies, however, he wants to tell someone the awful secret that has become his death sentence. That someone is Mark.

Mark escapes and, grabbing his sobbing brother, jumps off a small cliff and hides. Romey, now quite drunk and full of pills, grabs his gun and takes his own life. The experience sends Ricky into a coma. At the charity hospital where they take Ricky, the police take fingerprints from Mark's soda can to determine whether the boy was in the car with Romey before his death.

When the word gets out that the prominent New Orleans attorney has committed suicide, high-profile federal prosecutor "the Reverend" Roy Foltrigg (Jones) flies from Louisiana with his entourage to determine just what the boy knows. Foltrigg needs to find the senator's body in order to convict Muldano and win his bid for the governor's office.

A frightened Mark decides he needs a lawyer. In a run-down law building, he finds Reggie Love (Sarandon), who matches Mark's toughness with unflinching candor. When she hears that Mark is going up against the famous Foltrigg, she takes his case for a dollar. That night at the hospital where he and his mother are keeping watch over Ricky, Mark encounters the sinister Paul Gronke (Kim Coates), sent by the Mafia, who threatens to kill him and his family if he utters a word to anyone.

In court, Love tries to prevent federal agents from forcing Mark to talk until she can get him and his family into a witness protection program. Before she can do this, however, Mark is removed to jail for his own protection. Mark feigns illness and is sent to the hospital, where he slips away. Unfortunately, he is followed—then chased—by Gronke through the hospital's corridors, autopsy room, and finally the morgue, in a wonderful tension-packed chase scene that only a child could carry off.

Mark calls Love, who slips away from the police to meet him. Mark wants to make certain that the corpse really is where Romey said it was before he will talk, so the two go to New Orleans to find the body. On the riverfront, the two come to Romey's boathouse, where Mark sneaks in through an open gable

Brad Renfro, who makes his acting debut in *The Client*, was chosen for the role of Mark Sway after director Joel Schumacher's crew had seen close to 5,000 applicants.

window, just as the Mafia arrive in a boat to move the body. In a departure from the novel, director Joel Schumacher trades credibility for suspense as Love and the boy outsmart the Mafia and frighten the thugs away.

The Client is more faithful to the original novel than either *The Pelican Brief* or *The Firm* were, and Schumacher's excellent directing maintains the intense pace of Grisham's successful page-turner novel. Schumacher, whose credits include *Flatliners* (1990), *Dying Young* (1991), and *Falling Down* (1993), and turns hospital corridors into dank, shadowy halls that promise trouble. In another scene, the Mafia thug and the private investigator meet in a dark café whose oppressive, decaying atmosphere sets the scene for their evil intentions. Thus, Schumacher

> "I feel very comfortable letting Joel Schumacher make the movie."— John Grisham, author of *The Client*

and director of photography Tony Pierce-Roberts have created an ambience that is powerfully eerie and unwholesome, in stark contrast to Mark's youthful innocence.

Furthermore, Pierce-Roberts, director of photography on *Howard's End* (1992), *A Room with a View* (1986), and *The Remains of the Day* (1993), has very effectively filmed many of the scenes from the child's perspective. As the film opens, Mark's mother moves erratically in and out of the screen, with the camera filming her at waist level, her voice ubiquitous as she rushes to leave for work. In another scene, where Mark is hiding from the police and the Mafia in the hospital, this lower camera angle allows the viewer to feel the vulnerability of the child.

The screenplay, a collaboration by Akiva Goldsman and Robert Getchell, has some high points, such as the courtroom scene where Judge Harry Roosevelt (Ossie Davis) presides like an emperor in his throne room. With a word, Roosevelt brings the slick Foltrigg and his gaggle of lawyers down to mortal size. The dialogue in this scene is some of the best in the film. Love and Foltrigg parry and thrust in sizzling repartee; the dialogue is at its best when adversarial. The movement of the narrative gets bogged down, however, when the action is held up to give the viewer character background. In one clumsy effort, Mark blurts out the story of his alcoholic father to explain his distrust of Love, who had a drinking problem. It is a little too pat to be convincing.

Unfortunately, Barry "The Blade" Muldano's weaselly character is more cartoonish than villainous, and his fellow thugs wear their moles and tattoos like the bad guy's proverbial black hat. The Mafia characters are sleazy at best and buffoonish at worst. It is easy to imagine an eleven-year-old outsmarting these villains.

Yet despite the lack of characterization, the actors give some notable performances—credit goes to casting director Mali Finn. Brad Renfro was discovered by a police officer in Knoxville, Tennessee, where auditions for the part of Mark Sway were held. Renfro was chosen out of fifteen hundred boys, and he is a natural. Renfro is convincing and at the same time endearing in an entirely unsentimental way.

Susan Sarandon plays Reggie Love, the battling maternal figure protecting young Mark. Sarandon is excellent in the part, showing a wary maternalism toward Mark at first

CREDITS

Reggie Love: Susan Sarandon
Roy Foltrigg: Tommy Lee Jones
Dianne Sway: Mary-Louise Parker
Barry Muldano: Anthony LaPaglia
Clint Von Hooser: Anthony Edwards
Harry Roosevelt: Ossie Davis
Mark Sway: Brad Renfro
Ricky Sway: David Speck
McThune: J. T. Walsh
Sergeant Hardy: Will Patton
Thomas Fink: Bradley Whitford
Trumann: Anthony Heald
Paul Gronke: Kim Coates
Romey: Walter Olkewicz

Released: 1994
Production: Arnon Milchan and Steven Reuther, in association with Regency Enterprises and Alcor Films; released by Warner Bros.
Direction: Joel Schumacher
Screenplay: Akiva Goldsman and Robert Getchell; based on the novel by John Grisham
Cinematography: Tony Pierce-Roberts
Editing: Robert Brown
Production design: Bruno Rubeo
Art direction: P. Michael Johnston
Set design: Marco Rubeo and Kevin Cross
Set decoration: Anne D. McCulley
Casting: Mali Finn
Sound: Petur Hliddal
Costume design: Ingrid Ferrin
Music: Howard Shore
MPAA rating: PG-13
Running time: 124 minutes

AWARDS AND NOMINATIONS

Academy Awards Nomination 1994:   Best Actress (Sarandon)
British Academy Awards 1995:   Best Actress (Sarandon)
Screen Actors Guild Awards 1994:
Nomination: Best Actress (Sarandon)

and totally surrendering to him in the end. Her encounters with Foltrigg fill the screen as both Sarandon and Jones plays off each other with perfect timing and intelligent dialogue.

Jones is mesmerizing. He plays the publicity-loving, tyrannical power-seeker with ease, berating his minions with sinister yet sugary charm. The viewer has to enjoy his arrogance, it is so blatant, his self-centeredness so total. In contrast, Love swings between being intimidated by Foltrigg and being stoutly protective of her client. When these opponents lock horns the energy bounces off the screen.

Mary-Louise Parker plays Dianne Sway who, at the start of the film, is barely treading water and, after her youngest child goes into a coma and her world falls apart, begins to drown. This family, no stranger to suffering, now is suffering from the American judicial system, the very system that is intended to work for them. Parker's treatment of a woman struggling to keep her family together after an abusive marriage, custody battles, and poverty brings a certain class sensibility to the film without proselytizing or impeding the flow of the action. She says it all with her bent posture and the look of unbelieving despair on her pale face.

Another wonderful performance was found in the sadistic policeman, Sergeant Hardy (Will Patton), who promises Mark a seat in a child-size electric chair if he refuses to talk. His surreptitious asides to the boy give the first clue that the Mafia are not the only bad guys in the film.

Howard Shore's score moves with the force of a freight train, successfully hurtling the action forward. His credits include two critically acclaimed films, *The Silence of the Lambs* (1991) and *Philadelphia* (1993).

The Client is technically and professionally executed, with star performances by its actors and direction that captures the spirit of the novel. Yet because the characters are so inherently good or evil, the outcome of the plot becomes obvious, spoiling the effect of the exciting editing and diminishing the overall tension. It becomes absorbing yet shallow. Nevertheless, Grisham's writing and Schumacher's direction combine in a way that sweeps the viewer into the action, making the lack of characterization and the unbelievable plot twists secondary considerations. The primary function of *The Client* is to entertain, and that it does.

—*Diane Hatch-Avis*

REVIEWS

Entertainment Weekly. July 29, 1994, p. 42.
The Hollywood Reporter. June 8, 1994, p. 6.
Los Angeles Times. July 20, 1994, p. F1.
The New York Times. July 20, 1994, p. B1.
Newsweek. CXXIV, July 25, 1994, p. 53.
Variety. June 8, 1994, p. 4.

Clifford

"A comedy with a lot of laughs. And a ten-year-old terror."—Movie tagline

 Box Office Gross: $7,294,579 (May 15, 1994)

Martin Short plays spoiled, precocious ten-year-old, Clifford, who has been foisted temporarily on his bachelor uncle Martin (Charles Grodin). Clifford is obsessed with going to Dinosaurworld—a dinosaur theme park—and poor Uncle Martin soon discovers that Clifford will stop at nothing to get his way. Martin Short's double in the film was twelve-year-old Ryan Moon. In order to pull off the premise of a forty-two-year-old actor playing a ten-year-old child, the filmmakers had co-stars stand on six-inch apple boxes and very tall teenagers were cast as extras. The sets were built slightly larger and a combination of miniatures, models, and full scale sets were also used. Filmmakers constructed Dinosaurworld amusement park using six separate stages, including one to store the huge "Larry the Scary Rex." *Clifford*, made a couple of years ago, was shelved when Orion went bankrupt.

Martin Short as a 10-year-old genius in *Clifford*. © 1994 Orion Pictures. All rights reserved.

REVIEWS

Boston Globe. April 1, 1994, p. 52.
Chicago Tribune. April 1, 1994, p. 7C.
Entertainment Weekly. April 15, 1994, p. 70.
Entertainment Weekly. October 28, 1994, p. 98.
Entertainment Weekly. November 25, 1994, p. 101.
Los Angeles Times. April 1, 1994, p. F4.
The New York Times. April 1, 1994, p. C8.
People Weekly. XLI, April 11, 1994, p. 19.
USA Today. April 4, 1994, p. D3.
Variety. CCCLIV, April 4, 1994, p. 35.
The Washington Post. April 1, 1994, p. D6.
The Washington Post. April 7, 1994, p. C7.

CREDITS

Clifford: Martin Short
Martin Daniels: Charles Grodin
Sarah Davis: Mary Steenburgen
Gerald Ellis: Dabney Coleman
Parker Davis: G. D. Spradlin
Annabelle Davis: Anne Jeffreys

Julien Daniels: Richard Kind
Theodora Daniels: Jennifer Savidge
Roger: Ben Savage

Released: 1994
Production: Larry Brezner and Pieter Jan Brugge for Morra, Brezner, Steinberg, and Tenenbaum Entertainment, Inc.; released by Orion Pictures
Direction: Paul Flaherty
Screenplay: Jay Dee Rock and Bobby Von Hayes
Cinematography: John A. Alonzo
Editing: Pembroke Herring and Timothy Board
Production design: Russell Christian
Art direction: Bernie Cutler
Set decoration: Catherine Mann
Casting: Lynn Stalmaster
Sound: Larry Kemp and Lon Bender
Costume design: Robert de Mora
Stunt coordination: George "Bud" Davis
Music: Richard Gibbs
MPAA rating: PG
Running time: 90 minutes

 "I get a kick out of Clifford as an equal opportunity avenge artist—but it's not random nastiness."—*Clifford* director Paul Flaherty

A Climate for Killing (A Row of Crows)

When Yuma, Arizona, sheriff's captain Kyle Ship (John Beck) is called in on a murder investigation, he must also contend with an efficiency expert (Steven Bauer) who has been sent from Phoenix. Police are baffled when a woman murdered 16 years earlier shows up murdered again.

REVIEWS

Variety. CCCXLIII, June 17, 1991, p. 68.

CREDITS

Kyle: John Beck
Paul: Steven Bauer
Grace: Katharine Ross
Click: Phil Brock
Elise: Mia Sara

Released: 1991
Production: Carol Kottenbrook for Propaganda Films
Direction: J. S. Cardone
Screenplay: J. S. Cardone
Cinematography: Michael Cardone
Editing: Tom Meshelski
Production design: William Maynard
Set decoration: Charlie Doane
Sound: Jan Brodin
Costume design: Kelly White
Music: Robert Folk
MPAA rating: no listing
Running time: 103 minutes

Cobb

"Everyone hated this baseball legend
—And he loved it."—Movie tagline

"One of the year's best. Tommy Lee Jones gives a landmark performance, with bruising intensity and raucous wit. The *Raging Bull* of baseball movies."—Peter Travers, *Rolling Stone*

"Superb. Mesmerizing. Tommy Lee Jones gives the performance of his career—a riveting Oscar-caliber performance. One of the year's best, most profound films."—Jeffery Lyons, *Sneak Previews*

"A powerful, compelling portrait. Ron Shelton's screenplay and direction have intensity, vision and imagination."—Susan Granger, *CRN/American Movie Classics*

 Box Office Gross: $267,106 (January 2, 1995)

Ty Cobb is considered by many baseball historians to have been the greatest player of all time, with Babe Ruth his only serious rival to this title. Cobb, who played for the Detroit Tigers and Philadelphia Athletics from 1905 through 1928, compiled the highest batting average in the history of major-league baseball to date and long held the record for most runs scored, most hits, and most stolen bases. Nicknamed "the Georgia Peach," Cobb represents far more than statistics in baseball history. He played with such ruthless intensity that not only opposing players but his own teammates hated him. Off the field, he abused wives and the public at large and was a virulent racist. A man of many contradictions, Cobb is a compelling subject for a screen biography, and writer-director Ron Shelton makes *Cobb* a powerful meditation upon the nature of heroism.

Many reviewers expressed surprise that so few baseball scenes are presented in *Cobb*. Apparently, Shelton was much more interested in the essence of the man than in his athletic accomplishments. As such, he depicts Cobb (Tommy Lee Jones) as an enigma. In Shelton's method, clearly influenced by Orson Welles' *Citizen Kane* (1941), the film opens with newsreel footage about Cobb's baseball accomplishments to establish the official, public, superficial view of the man upon which Shelton will elaborate, filling in the blanks implied by the newsreel.

> Tommy Lee Jones reportedly broke his ankle during the production of *Cobb* but continued playing the role without taking any time off.

This technique is apt since this is how Cobb spent the last year of his life. Seriously ill with several ailments, the seventy-three-year-old decides in 1960 to write his autobiography and hires the prominent magazine writer Al Stump (Robert Wuhl) to ghostwrite it. The young sportswriter worships the legend of Cobb but knows little about the man. All this changes upon Stump's arrival at Cobb's mountain lodge near Lake Tahoe. A black servant (Lou Myers) flees the vile employer whose abuse he can no longer abide. Then, the bedridden Cobb fires gunshots randomly into doors, walls, and ceilings while giving orders about buying and selling stocks to another employee (William Utay).

Stump must learn to hold his ego in check while bowing to the massive will of the baseball legend, who insists Stump compose a sanitized version of his life and who forces the writer at gunpoint to drive to Reno, Nevada, during a fierce snowstorm. In the course of this trip, which continues cross-country to a banquet at the National Baseball Hall of Fame in Cooperstown, N.Y., and south to Cobb's hometown of Royston, Ga., Cobb reveals some truths about his life but denies Stump the right to publish them. Stump, however, cooperates with Cobb while secretly writing his own version of the life of the Georgia Peach.

Stump published the official version of Cobb's career as *My Life in Baseball* (1961). Following Cobb's death in 1961, however, he wrote "Ty Cobb's Wild Ten-Month Fight to Live" for *True* magazine. The events depicted in this legendary, award-winning article form the basis of the film. Stump did not publish his life of the baseball legend, *Cobb: A Biography*, until 1994. Stump's Cobb beat his first wife, assaulted a handless heckler, conspired with fellow baseball legend Tris Speaker to fix a game, and pistol-whipped to death a man who tried to rob him.

This Cobb is also haunted by the death, during his rookie year with the Detroit Tigers, of his beloved father (J. Kenneth Campbell), an educator and politician who was shot to death accidentally by his wife (Rhoda Griffis), who thought he was a burglar. Professor Cobb had suspected his wife of adultery, and, while he was supposed to be out of town, sneaked back to their house to catch her in the act. This is the first account Cobb gives Stump of his father's death. Later, he admits he perjured himself by testifying for his mother, whose lover actually shot her husband deliberately. The way Shelton arranges these conflicting accounts near the beginning and end of his film emphasizes the difficulty of ever knowing the complete truth about any historical figure.

During their trip east and south, Stump witnesses Cobb's psychopathological behavior firsthand as Cobb takes the stage at Harrah's Club in Reno to deliver a diatribe against blacks and Jews, knocks Stump unconscious, and attempts to rape the writer's date (Lolita Davidovich). When impotence prevents the latter, he pays the woman $1,000 to tell others how great it was to have sex with "the great Ty Cobb." When not firing his gun, Cobb ridicules Stump about his

"The desire for glory is not a sin."—Ty Cobb, in *Cobb*

impending divorce. Yet there is another side to Cobb. Stump discovers in Cooperstown that Cobb gives money to former baseball players, such as Mickey Cochrane (Stephen Mendillo), who are unable to support themselves. Cobb leaves much of his $12.1 million estate, earned through early investments in such companies as Coca-Cola and General Motors, to charity, including the establishment of the Cobb Memorial Hospital in his hometown.

Cobb invites comparison with Martin Scorsese's portrait of boxer Jake La Motta in *Raging Bull* (1980). While Scorsese's film is much more visually striking than Shelton's, its concern with its protagonist seems much more interior and personal. Scorsese's La Motta is just as crude, violent, and impulsive as Shelton's Cobb, but La Motta is only a moderately famous athlete, not an icon. The boxer seems to be begging to be understood; the baseball player refuses to be either type or archetype. Cobb constantly insists that Sigmund Freud's theories of human behavior cannot possibly explain him. His father's murder did not taint his character since it was already tainted. He is just naturally vicious and perverse.

The larger question posed by Shelton—a former minor-league baseball player who has written and directed one great sports film, *Bull Durham* (1988), and a less effective one, *White Men Can't Jump* (1992)—is whether a hero's personal life can offset his accomplishments and whether the public needs to know all the sordid details. The answers are that a hero, whether athlete, artist, or politician, cannot be appreciated—not necessarily the same as being understood—without these details and that towering figures such as Cobb demand such appreciation.

This Ty Cobb is as much a creation of Tommy Lee Jones as of Shelton. This great character actor excels in parts in which he conveys the joy of acting, as in *Under Siege* (1992) and *The Client* (reviewed in this volume), and it is Jones' pleasure in portraying Cobb that helps keep *Cobb* from toppling over into the downbeat. Jones actually presents three versions of Cobb: the violent monster, the comic caricature of a man aware that he is performing a role he has assigned himself, and the sensitive man who appreciates William Shakespeare and violinist Fritz Kreisler.

The latter is most apparent during a showing of newsreel highlights of Cobb's career, the same that opens the film, during a Hall of Fame banquet as Cobb imagines that many of his most prominent sins are being displayed and is mortified. Whether he feels guilt or remorse is not clear; his embarrassment is. Prior to the newsreel, several of Cobb's fellow Hall of Famers file by his table to shake his hand. After the banquet, they refuse to allow him into their private party, and Cochrane, not too proud to take Cobb's money, shoves

CREDITS

Ty Cobb: Tommy Lee Jones
Al Stump: Robert Wuhl
Ramona: Lolita Davidovich
Mickey Cochrane: Stephen Mendillo
Rogers Hornsby: Tommy Bush
Willie: Lou Myers
Jameson: William Utay
Professor Cobb: J. Kenneth Campbell
Ty's mother: Rhoda Griffis
Young Ty: Tyler Logan Cobb
Process server: Bradley Whitford
Ray: Ned Bellamy
Jimmy: Scott Burkholder
Mud: Allan Malamud
Bill: Bill Caplan
Louis Prima: Eloy Casados
Keely Smith: Paula Rudy
Opposing pitcher: Roger Clemens
Hall of Fame master of ceremonies: Ernie Harwell

Released: 1994
Production: David Lester, in association with Regency Enterprises and Alcor Films; released by Warner Bros.
Direction: Ron Shelton
Screenplay: Ron Shelton; based on the book *Cobb: A Biography*, by Al Stump
Cinematography: Russell Boyd
Editing: Paul Seydor and Kimberly Ray
Production design: Armin Ganz and Scott T. Ritenour
Art direction: Troy Sizemore and Charles Butcher
Set decoration: Claire Jenora Bowin
Casting: Victoria Thomas
Special effects supervision: Jim Fredburg
Sound: Kirk Francis
Makeup: Ve Neill
Costume design: Ruth E. Carter
Baseball coordination: Rob Ryder
Music: Elliot Goldenthal
MPAA rating: R
Running time: 128 minutes

him out of the room. Shelton's point here, as elsewhere in *Cobb*, is that no one can be completely unsympathetic.

Cobb is not without numerous weaknesses. The actor portraying Al Stump should be Jones' equal since the characters are battling for the legend's sordid soul. Unfortunately, Wuhl is a likable but bland supporting comic actor so far out of his depth here as to produce cringes of embarrassment. The vile treatment of the Davidovich character is also unnecessarily embarrassing, especially from a writer-director who has created one of the greatest women's roles in film with Susan Sarandon's Annie Savoy in *Bull Durham*. The mixing of shots of the real Cobb and Jones' Cobb in the newsreels is a bad idea since the two men little resemble each other. Elliot Goldenthal has composed effective scores, as with his lushly romantic music to accompany the excesses of the protagonists in *Interview with the Vampire* (reviewed in this volume), but here his music is too obvious and constantly intrudes upon the drama. Despite such defects, *Cobb* is an enthralling drama and handles its ambivalent attitude toward its hero better than any sports film since *Downhill Racer* (1969).

—*Michael Adams*

REVIEWS

The Christian Science Monitor. LXXXVII, December 2, 1994, p. 14.
Daily Variety. November 28, 1994, p. 2.
Entertainment Weekly. December 2, 1994, p. 44.
The Hollywood Reporter. November 28, 1994, p. 6.
Interview. XXIV, December, 1994, p. 48.
Los Angeles Times. December 2, 1994, p. F1.
The New York Times. December 2, 1994, p. B1.
The New Yorker. LXX, December 5, 1994, p. 130.
Newsweek. CXXIV, December 12, 1994, p. 72.
People Weekly. XLII, December 12, 1994, p. 21.
Rolling Stone. December 15, 1994, p. 104.
Time. CXLIV, December 5, 1994, p. 92.
The Village Voice.XXXIX, December 6, 1994, p. 53.
The Wall Street Journal. December 1, 1994, p. A16.

Cold Moon (Lune Froide)

Two dissolute friends, Simon (Jean-Francois Stevenin) and Dede (Patrick Bouchitey), roam a French coastal town at night, getting drunk and picking up women. Feature-film directorial debut of Patrick Bouchitey.

CREDITS

Simon: Jean-Francois Stevenin
Dede: Patrick Bouchitey
Gerard: Jean-Pierre Bisson
Nadine: Laura Favali
Aunt Suzanne: Marie Mergey
Whore: Sylvana de Faria
Blonde: Consuelo de Haviland
Mermaid: Karin Nuris
Denis: Alain Le Floch
Priest: Jacky Berroyer

Origin: France
Released: 1991

Production: Luc Besson and Andree Martinez for Les Films du Dauphin-Studio Lavabo, with the participation of Studio Canal Plus and Canal Plus; released by Gaumont
Direction: Patrick Bouchitey
Screenplay: Patrick Bouchitey and Jacky Berroyer; based on the short stories "Copulating Mermaid of Venice" and "Trouble with the Battery," by Charles Bukowski
Cinematography: Jean-Jacques Bouhon
Editing: Florence Bon
Production design: Frank Lagache and Jean-Marc Pacaud
Production management: Jerome Chalou
Sound: Guillaume Sciama
Costume design: Carine Sarfati
Music: Didier Lockwood and Jimi Hendrix
MPAA rating: no listing
Running time: 92 minutes

Colonel Chabert (Le Colonel Chabert)

"Everything's fair in love and war."—Movie tagline
"A riveting film."—*New York Newsday*
"...a quietly intense...thoughtful debut of famed cinematographer Yves Angelo."—Janet Maslin, *The New York Times*
"[a] small gem of a film."—*The New Republic*

Box Office Gross: $238,158 (January 2, 1995)

In a career spanning more than seventy films, Gérard Depardieu has long been considered France's foremost actor. Though his first English-language film resulted in a huge hit—*Green Card* (1990)—Depardieu has not "gone Hollywood." He continues to produce the bulk of his work in his native France. His increasing fame on American shores has, however, added to the commercial viability of his French films, many of which, such as *Le Colonel Chabert*, would not otherwise have generated much attention beyond the art-house circuit.

Depardieu, who aspires to one day portray Honoré de Balzac himself, here enacts the title character in the master storyteller's 1832 novella, *Le Colonel Chabert*. The film opens on the corpse-covered battlefield at Eylau, in the aftermath of a bloody battle that claimed 53,000 French, Russian, and Prussian casualties. In preparation for burial, the nameless, faceless dead are stripped of their uniforms, weapons, and valuables. This harrowing sequence sets a somber mood, which is maintained throughout most of the piece.

The story is picked up ten years later, as a shabbily dressed man (Depardieu) visits the offices of attorney Derville (Fabrice Luchini) in Paris. The man claims to be Colonel Chabert, a cavalry hero believed to have been killed in the Battle of Eylau. He has returned to prove his identity and reclaim his fortune from his wife, Countess Ferraud (Fanny Ardant). Believing Chabert dead, his wife married the ambitious Count Ferraud (André Dussollier) and used Chabert's fortune to finance her new husband's political career.

Derville's interest mounts as Chabert recounts his experiences over the past ten years. Severely wounded in battle, he was thrown into a mass burial pit, not dead but cataleptic. He was rescued and spent years in a succession of hospitals and madhouses, slowly regaining his health and memory. His wife does not respond to his letters. Chabert has come to Derville because all the other lawyers think him an insane imposter. Derville is not convinced, at first, of his client's identity, but he is excited and intrigued by the tale. He accepts the case despite the fact that he also represents Countess Ferraud, and despite Chabert's indigence. Derville gives Chabert a weekly stipend to support himself until his case is settled.

Evidence is collected that supports Chabert's claim, and Derville brings his clients together to attempt an amicable settlement. He proposes that Chabert give up his rights to his wife in exchange for 400,000 francs and the annulment of his death. Chabert, though he still loves his wife, agrees to this arrangement. The countess, however, refuses to acknowledge Chabert's identity and rejects the settlement amount. Derville tries to manipulate the countess, alluding to problems in her marriage that would make a quick, quiet settlement desirable. Count Ferraud covets an appointment to the Peers of France, but

> Director Yves Angelo was once a classical pianist and chose the chamber music for this film, which was recorded several months before filming. It was made primarily to accompany the film rather than to be released as a soundtrack. Gérard Depardieu's daughter Julie appears in a minor role as a maid.

his ascension is impeded by his wife's Napoleonic background. It is two years after Napoleon's final defeat, and society shuns those whose fortunes were amassed under Napoleon. Ferraud has been counseled to excise the countess from his life and enter into a more politically acceptable union with a baroness. Derville implies that the count would welcome the legal escape from his marriage that Chabert's resurrection would provide.

Desperate to hold on to her marriage, the countess lures Chabert to her country home to try to coerce him to sign a statement renouncing his claim. She offers him recompense of one thousand francs per month. Chabert refuses to sign the agreement and leaves, disgusted with her machinations. His experience has left Chabert with a contempt for humanity, and he decides to live out his days as a pauper rather than be part of the material world.

The film's initial mystery—whether Chabert is who he claims to be—brings to mind an earlier Depardieu film, *Le Retour de Martin Guerre (1983; The Return of Martin Guerre)*, in which the question of Guerre's identity is left uncertain until the denouement. In *Colonel Chabert* the viewer is assured fairly early on that the claimant is indeed Chabert. The remainder of the drama concerns the disposition of money. Money is the glue that bonds the characters together and threatens to tear them apart.

Le Colonel Chabert marks the directorial debut of acclaimed cinematographer Yves Angelo, whose credits include *Tous Les Matins du Monde* (1991), *Un Coeur en Hiver* (1992), and *Germinal* (1993). His visual expertise served him well in staging *Le Colonel Chabert*. Together with cinematographer Bernard Lutic, he has delivered arresting imagery, particularly in the opening battlefield sequence. Patrick Bordier's exquisite production design and costumes by Franca Squarciapino enhance the period flavor.

Angelo also drew upon his musical background—he trained as a classical pianist prior to becoming a filmmaker—in scoring *Colonel Chabert*. Works by Mozart, Beethoven, Schumann, and Schubert, recorded specifically for the film by some of Europe's most accomplished musicians, complement the visual images without being intrusive. Angelo selected the pieces months before filming began, searching for music to echo the characters' emotions for each particular scene. As a result of this kind of meticulous attention to every aspect of the production, *Le Colonel Chabert* is a technically superior film. Its only drawback lies in the choice of source material.

Reviewing an earlier film version of *Le Colonel Chabert* in 1947, *The New York Times*' Bosley Crowther wrote, "It is mostly a lot of talking with lawyers about signing things and

CREDITS

Chabert: Gérard Depardieu
Countess Ferraud: Fanny Ardant
Derville: Fabrice Luchini
Count Ferraud: André Dussollier
Boucard: Daniel Prevost
Huré: Olivier Saladin
Godeschal: Maxime Leroux
Desroches: Eric Elmosnino
Simonnin: Guillaume Romain
Boutin: Patrick Bordier
Chamblin: Claude Rich

Origin: France
Released: 1994
Production: Jean-Louis Livi for Film Par Film; released by October Films
Direction: Yves Angelo
Screenplay: Jean Cosmos and Yves Angelo; based on the novel by Honoré de Balzac
Cinematography: Bernard Lutic
Editing: Thierry Derocles
Production design: Patrick Bordier
Art direction: Bernard Vezat
Sound: Pierre Gamet
Costume design: Franca Squarciapino
MPAA rating: no listing
Running time: 110 minutes

precious little action of a revealing or absorbing sort." The updated story, adapted by Jean Cosmos and Angelo, is still brimming with legalese. Lengthy discourses on financial matters and societal pressures tend to distance the viewer. *The Hollywood Reporter* found that the characters "function more as legal abstractions than as flesh and blood."

Angelo's intent was to "express the profound complexity of the interior journey of all individuals," but the camera is not always adept at illuminating the psyche. This is a character-driven piece, and the characters are complex and often contradictory. Each is capable of good and evil, greed and compassion, and vacillations thereof. The action is cerebral, rather than physical, so the characters' intentions and motivations are conveyed by covert gestures, glances, and expressions, which are often inscrutable to the viewer. Non-French-speaking viewers are further handicapped, as these subtleties are easily missed while reading subtitles.

Depardieu and Ardant, last seen together in *La Femme d'Acote* (1981; *The Woman Next Door*), give restrained performances as the once-married couple. Depardieu effectively communicates his character's spite and outrage in earlier sequences, and his despondency and resignation in the end. The middle ground is murkier, as epitomized by his reaction after a hostile confrontation with the countess—seeing his reflection in a mirror, he smiles cryptically. The countess' anguish is evident, but contemporary audiences are unlikely to sympathize with the societal pressures of post-Napoleonic France that torment her.

Both these accomplished stars are eclipsed by Luchini, in a spirited performance as the wily Derville. The role of Derville was much smaller in the novel, and Angelo's deci-

> "The dead are wrong to reappear."—*Colonel Chabert*

sion to expand the part was a wise one. Luchini is the best of the trio at conveying the subtle shadings of his character.

One can almost see the wheels churning in Derville's brain as he listens to Chabert's plea, his eyes flashing with anticipation of the game. Derville is the master puppeteer, calculating which strings to pull and how to manipulate the players. Yet with all his cunning, Derville is not without compassion. Chabert's renunciation is his defeat, and it is deeply felt.

Media response to *Le Colonel Chabert* was chiefly positive. The performers and production values were consistently praised, while some reviewers found that the overall production had a distanced feel due to the ambiguity of key moments. *Variety* lauded its technical excellence and predicted "a critical and commercial hit on the arthouse circuit." *The New Republic* called it a "small gem of a film." A notable detractor was *The Hollywood Reporter*, who judged, "The stiff screenplay adaptation is a drawback and will cause this handsomely mounted production to receive only tepid word-of-mouth." Angelo's direction was universally and justifiably praised. If Depardieu ever gets his wish to play Balzac, he could do no better than to have Angelo at the helm.

—*Brenda Scott Royce*

REVIEWS

Daily Variety. September 13, 1994, p. 17.
The Hollywood Reporter. September 13, 1994, p. 63.
Los Angeles Times. December 23, 1994, p. F10.
The New Republic. December 26, 1994, p. 26.
The New York Times. December 23, 1994, p. B6.
The Village Voice. December 27, 1994, p. 74.

Color Adjustment

This provocative documentary centers on the evolving images of African Americans presented on television, beginning with the demeaning stereotypes seen in *Amos 'n' Andy* and continuing through the decades, offering commentary on such landmark programs as Nat (King) Cole's variety show, Diahann Carroll's series *Julia*, the successful miniseries *Roots*, and 1990's *The Cosby Show*.

REVIEWS

Journal of American History. LXXX, December 1993, p. 1193.

CREDITS

Narrator: Ruby Dee
Diahann Carroll: Diahann Carroll
Tim Reid: Tim Reid
Esther Rolle: Esther Rolle
Dr. Henry Louis Gates, Jr.: Dr. Henry Louis Gates, Jr.

Released: 1992
Production: Marlon T. Riggs and Vivian Kleiman
Direction: Marlon T. Riggs
Screenplay: Marlon T. Riggs
Cinematography: Rick Butler
Editing: Deborah Hoffmann
Music: Mary Watkins
MPAA rating: no listing
Running time: 86 minutes

Color of Night

"In the heat of desire love can turn to deception. Nothing is what it seems when day turns to night."—Movie tagline

 Box Office Gross: $19,660,050 (December 18, 1994)

This big-budget erotic thriller casts Bruce Willis as a troubled psychologist who finds himself embroiled in a murder mystery when he takes over his friend's group therapy session. The film received some pre-release publicity for its promise of steamy sex scenes, including full-frontal nudity from Willis and a lesbian encounter between Jane March and Lesley Ann Warren. In order to avoid an NC-17 rating, these scenes were cut from the final release.

Psychologist Bill Capa (Bruce Willis) abandons his Manhattan practice after witnessing a patient (Kathleen Wilhoite) commit suicide by jumping out of his office window. The guilt over possibly prompting her action, combined with the trauma of seeing the woman's shattered body in a widening pool of blood, leave him unable to see the color red.

Sexually explicit scenes cut from the theatrical release of *Color of Night* are included in home video and laserdisc versions.

Although he knows he can not run away from the problems in his head, Capa flies to Los Angeles to visit his long-time friend, Dr. Bob Moore (Scott Bakula), also a psychologist. The years since they interned together at Penn State have apparently been kinder to Dr. Moore than to Capa. Moore drives a Mercedes, lives in a sumptuous hill-top home with ultra-tight security, and has authored a best-selling book on psychotherapy.

Moore coerces Capa to sit in on his Monday night group therapy session. The group is comprised of five patients: nymphomaniac Sondra (Lesley Ann Warren), obsessive-compulsive Clark (Brad Dourif), guilt-ridden widower Buck (Lance Henriksen), masochistic artist Casey (Kevin J. O'Connor) and a sexually confused teen named Richie. Capa watches as the five misfits verbally, and sometimes physically, attack one another. He refuses to open up about his recent troubles. Moore later admits that he had a special reason for having Capa sit in on the therapy session: He has been receiving death threats and believes that the culprit is one of the five patients in his Monday night group.

Before the next Monday night group can convene, Moore is brutally murdered—stabbed thirty-plus times and impaled on a shattered glass door in his office. Detective

Martinez (Rubén Blades) wants Capa to break the news to the group so that he can gauge their reactions. The patients persuade Capa to take over the group, despite his assertions that he is crazier than any of them. Capa takes over for his dead friend in more ways than one. He continues to stay in Moore's house, uses his office, and drives his Mercedes.

While driving the Mercedes, Capa is rear-ended by a beautiful young woman named Rose (Jane March). Though he knows neither her last name nor her telephone number, Capa is captivated by the mysterious woman. They soon forget about the bumped fender and start a steamy affair. She appears then disappears from his life without warning, leaving the doctor utterly befuddled.

"It was a little confusing having to do a whole film without a gun in my hand."—Bruce Willis on *Color of Night*

Coincidentally, as Capa has found Rose, the Monday night group members each talk about a perfect new woman in their lives, never suspecting that they (and their previous doctor, Bob Moore) have each been charmed by the same woman. When several attempts are made on his life, and another member of the group is murdered, Capa investigates the backgrounds of the group members. When he finds a photograph of Rose in Moore's office, Capa begins to piece together the various bits of information.

Suspecting that the murders are somehow connected to Richie and his over-protective brother Dale (Andrew Lowery), Capa visits the widow of Richie's former therapist. An anguished Mrs. Niedelmeyer (Shirley Knight) reveals that her husband had molested young Richie, and the boy subsequently killed himself. She mentions that Richie was survived by his brother, Dale and sister, Rose.

Capa realizes that Rose and Richie are the same person and arrives at Dale's shop just in time to rescue her from the nail gun-wielding killer: her brother Dale. Rose reveals to Capa that she had been forced, by Dale, to assume Richie's identity after his death, and her own personality eventually faded. When she started to resurface to dally with the members of the group, Dale's secret was threatened, and he killed anyone who came close to realizing that Richie and Rose are the same person.

Color of Night is director Richard Rush's first film in fourteen years, his last was the critically acclaimed *The Stunt Man* (1980). He clashed with the production company, Cinergi, over the final cut and has publicly announced that the final film is not in keeping with his vision. Rush's cut, six minutes longer and inclusive of the steamy sex scenes snipped from the theatrical release, is on the video release. *The New Yorker* previewed the director's cut and found that the characters' behavior makes more sense and the performances of Willis and March are more effective.

Color of Night was trounced by the press. The *Los Angeles Times* called it "a disappointment in almost every respect...overloaded with [plot] twists both preposterous

CREDITS

Capa: Bruce Willis
Rose: Jane March
Martinez: Rubén Blades
Sondra: Lesley Ann Warren
Bob Moore: Scott Bakula
Clark: Brad Dourif
Buck: Lance Henriksen
Casey: Kevin J. O'Connor
Dale: Andrew Lowery
Anderson: Eriq La Salle
Ashland: Jeff Corey
Michelle: Kathleen Wilhoite
Edith Niedelmeyer: Shirley Knight
Medical examiner: John T. Bower
Bouncer: Avi Korein
Cop #1:   Steven R. Barnett
Receptionist: Roberta Storm

Released: 1994
Production: David Matalon and Buzz Feitshans for Andrew G. Vanja, Cinergi Productions, and Hollywood Pictures; released by Buena Vista Pictures
Direction: Richard Rush
Screenplay: Matthew Chapman and Billy Ray; based on a story by Billy Ray
Cinematography: Dietrich Lohmann
Editing: Jack Hofstra
Production design: James L. Schoppe
Art direction: Jack Morrisey
Set decoration: Cynthia McCormac
Casting: Wendy Kurtzman
Special effects coordination: Terry King
Makeup: Michele Burke
Costume design: Jacki Arthur
Music: Dominic Frontiere
Song: Jud J. Friedman, Lauren Christy and Dominic Frontiere; "The Color of the Night"
MPAA rating: R
Running time: 123 minutes

AWARDS AND NOMINATIONS

Golden Globe Awards Nomination 1995: Best Song ("The Color of Night")

and obvious." Some reviewers, however, found merit in the film's unintended high-comedy aspect. *The New York Times* opined that Rush "hasn't come close to making a good movie out of *Color of Night*. But he does succeed...in creating something memorably bizarre." "This one-star movie is, in truth, actually five-star trash," wrote the *USA Today* reviewer. *The New Yorker* judged the film "terrifically enjoyable if you're willing to overlook a few yawning gaps in continuity and if you're not troubled by abrupt shifts of mood."

Even after the murder mystery is resolved *Color of Night* leaves viewers mystified. How and why Capa seems to inherit Moore's house and car, the absence of any other friends or relatives of the dead doctor, and why these five patients are the sole suspects are only some of the questions left lingering after the final credits roll. Capa's inability to see red serves no plot purpose and is only cinematically interesting in one scene, when he realizes that the gray glop that he has been slipping in is blood. A couple of gratuitous car chases, like the acrobatic sex scenes, appear to take place only to give the audience a break from the convoluted plot twists.

The standout performance among the diverse cast is Rubén Blades as a sarcastic cop who says exactly what is on his mind, without regard to political correctness. His brief appearances punctuate the piece with much needed comic relief. The group therapy members interact like an improvisational comedy troupe. Of the patients, Brad Dourif as the persnickety Clark, and Lesley Ann Warren as the giggly, oversexed Sondra are the most compelling to watch. Lance Henriksen and Kevin J. O'Connor endow their characters with interesting quirks.

Surrounded by these over-the-top performances, the serious demeanor of Bruce Willis seems out of place. Without guns or wisecracks to support him (as in his most successful and best remembered film, 1988's *Die Hard*), his performance is flat and colorless. Better suited to action than introspection, Willis is saddled with an inscrutable character who does not gain audience sympathy even after shedding tears over his lost patient.

Jane March is more likely to be remembered for her uninhibited nude scenes than her acting skill, though she does an able job of portraying two distinct, disturbed characters. Perceptive viewers guess the truth before Capa does, but the transformation is nevertheless intriguing.

Color of Night is stylishly lensed by cinematographer Dietrich Lohmann with some inventive camera angles, particularly in the opening suicide sequence when the dead body is viewed from underneath a sheet of glass, as pools of blood ooze forth. Production designer James L. Schoppe put great effort into decorating the characters' homes in ways befitting their individual personalities, from the suicide victim's garishly colorful apartment to Clark's stark, sterile home. The film is adorned throughout with Gothic set pieces and architecture containing carved heads or gargoyles, which the camera zooms in on repetitively as if to make a point.

Many reviewers have noted the Hitchcockian elements of *Color of Night*, and indeed there are parallels to many Hitchcock films. The most notable parallel is to *Vertigo* (1958), in which a tale of murder and dual-identity hinges upon the hero's (Jimmy Stewart) trauma-induced fear of heights. Had Hitchcock and Stewart made *Color of Night*, the result may have been more watchable, but the general consensus is that they would have known better.

—*Brenda Scott Royce*

REVIEWS

The Hollywood Reporter. August 19, 1994, p. 5.
Los Angeles Times. August 19, 1994, p. F1.
The New York Times. August 19, 1994, p. B2.
The New Yorker. September 5, 1994, p. 107.
People Weekly. September 5, 1994, p. 16.
USA Today. August 19, 1994, p. 10D.
Variety. August 22, 1994, p. 55.

Combination Platter

"Refreshingly candid...funny, involving...serves up many things not on the usual menu."—Janet Maslin, *The New York Times*

"As winning as it is original!"—Manohla Dargis, *The Village Voice*

"A treat!"—Jay Carr, *Boston Globe*

"Genuine...with humor and poignancy."—Kevin Thomas, *Los Angeles Times*

Combination Platter is just that: a combination of ingredients such as drama, suspense, comedy and romance. It takes seriously its use of the American-Chinese restaurant as a metaphor for the melting of cultures in America. It deals with the unique (to Americans) problem of difference between Cantonese and Mandarin speakers, and the difference between Americans and Chinese. It also concerns itself with examining some of the motivations behind arranged marriages where Americans marry aliens in order to help

First-time director Tony Chan made *Combination Platter* operating on a $250,000 budget, using his parents' restaurant after-hours as a set.

them obtain a green card. And finally, it sweetly depicts the awkwardness of romance between two shy people.

Robert (Jeff Lau) is a recent immigrant who is in search of a wife to get a green card. Helped by his friend Andy (Kenneth Lu), he is searching for a woman who is willing to undergo the risks involved in such a marriage. He works as a waiter at the Szechuan Inn, a Chinese restaurant owned by Mr. Lee (Thomas K. Hsiung), and he sends much of his money back to his parents in Hong Kong.

The restaurant's employees include Sam (Lester "Chi-Man" Chan), Benny (Colin Mitchell), and several Chinese waiters and dishwashers, all of whom are struggling with life as an immigrant in the United States. Gambling addict Sam is in increasing financial difficulty, and young Caucasian Benny is learning what it is like to be the minority. The themes of immigration and racism are subtly explored through these and other characters, with the problem of languages (and the racism language can cause) being a particular target. For example, Sam flashes a friendly smile and a laugh at two regular customers who tell bad jokes, but little do they know that he is cursing them in Chinese. For his part, Benny tells Robert how uncomfortable he is when the waiters get together and speak Chinese, knowing that he doesn't understand. When Benny notices Sam stealing a tip and notifies Robert, Robert tells Mr. Lee that it was he and not Benny who saw Sam steal the tip— no one would believe Benny because he is not Chinese.

Racism is also pointed out among the regular customers: One of them wears a T-shirt that says, "Welcome to America...now learn English." The language barrier between Cantonese and Mandarin speakers is interestingly explored in a tentative scene between Robert and one of the dishwashers: their difficulty in communicating due to language will, for many Americans, be an unusual glimpse into the diversity among Asian people.

Robert's attempts to marry an American cause him to enter into a relationship with a sweet Caucasian woman, Claire (Colleen O'Brien). Their strained discussions (" don't know why they call it moo-goo-gai pan...." says Claire) and

CREDITS

Robert: Jeff Lau
Claire: Colleen O'Brien
Sam: Lester (Chit-Man) Chan
Benny: Colin Mitchell
Andy: Kenneth Lu
Mr. Lee: Thomas K. Hsiung
Noriko: Eleonara Kihlberg
James: James DuMont

Released: 1993
Production: Judy Moy and Tony Chan Ulla Zwicker for Bluehorse Film; released by Arrow Releasing
Direction: Tony Chan
Screenplay: Edwin Baker and Tony Chan
Cinematography: Yoshifumi Hosoya
Editing: Tony Chan
Editing: James Y. Kwei
Art direction: Pat Summa
Casting: Amanda Ma
Sound: Bob Taz
Music: Brian Tibbs
MPAA rating: no listing
Running time: 84 minutes

AWARDS AND NOMINATIONS

Sundance Film Festival 1993: Best Screenplay
Independent Spirit Awards Nominations 1994: Best First Feature, Best Supporting Actor (Chung), Best Screenplay

their overly polite dates are almost sad. These appear to be two lonely people who cannot communicate—and language is not their only barrier. When Robert reveals that he is seeing Claire in order to marry someone, her hurt is obvious and painful. O'Brien is so real that she is nearly heartbreaking.

Jeff Lau is excellent as Robert. He is so real that it is hard to tell whether or not Lau is an actor or a "real person" being filmed for camera. Lau's ability to traverse two languages and struggle in several dialects is impressive. In his scene with O'Brien in which he asks if she will marry him, he appears to find the situation as painful as she does.

The action progresses simply. Director Tony Chan has created a "slice-of-life" film which takes some of the themes of *The Wedding Banquet* (1993) and *Green Card* (1990) and mixes them into a low-key but effective story. Without creating obvious plot points which seem to propel the plot to an inevitable conclusion, Robert's actions toward finding a wife combine with an Immigration and Naturalization Service raid on Mr. Lee's restaurant to build toward quite an interesting climax. The INS raid in particular provides a great deal of excitement, as the camera gamely follows Robert in his frantic attempts to find a hiding place in the restaurant basement. Chan handles the tender scenes between Claire and Robert with aplomb, and films the action in and around the restaurant with a documentary-style realism that is fascinating.

This is a small film which earned Mr. Chan a good deal of notoriety when it was first entered in the 1993 Sundance Film Festival. Mr. Chan, at twenty-three, was the youngest entrant into the director category. This is a most promising feature debut.

—*Kirby Tepper*

REVIEWS

Daily Variety. February 10, 1993. p. 12
Los Angeles Times. February 16, 1994. p. F3
The New York Times. March 27, 1993. p. 12
Atlanta Constitution. April 8, 1994, p. P6.
Chicago Tribune. February 4, 1994, p. 7M.
Los Angeles Times. January 13, 1994, p. F5.
Los Angeles Times. February 16, 1994, p. F3.
Variety. CCCL, February 8, 1993, p. 76.
The Washington Post. January 21, 1994, p. G6.

The Comedian Harmoniest: Six Life Stories

A German singing group of the 1920's and 1930's, the Comedian Harmonists, is the focus of this documentary, which incorporates interviews with the surviving members in the 1970's and vintage photographs. The talented sextet worked together for some eight years, until the Nazis forced them to disband because three of the members were Jewish.

CREDITS

Robert Biberti: Robert Biberti
Harry Frommerman: Harry Frommerman
Roman Cycowski: Roman Cycowski
Erich Collin: Erich Collin

Ari Leshnikoff: Ari Leshnikoff
Erwin Bootz: Erwin Bootz

Origin: Germany
Released: 1976
Production: Dieter Meichsner
Direction: Eberhard Fechner
Screenplay: Eberhard Fechner
Cinematography: Rainer Schaeffer
Editing: Brigitte Kirsche
Sound: Dieter Schulz and Hans Dietel
MPAA rating: no listing
Running time: 191 minutes

Common Bonds (Chaindance)

An initially unwilling prisoner (Michael Ironside) is drafted by a welfare worker (Rae Dawn Chong) into an experimental reform program, in which he is handcuffed to the wheelchair of a cerebral palsy victim (Brad Dourif). Although the two men start off hating each other, they eventually form a strong friendship.

Released: 1991
Production: Richard Davis for Festival Films and R & R Motion Pictures, Inc.
Direction: Allan A. Goldstein
Screenplay: Alan Aylward and Michael Ironside
Cinematography: Tobis Schliessler
Editing: Allan Lee
Music: Graeme Coleman
MPAA rating: no listing
Running time: 108 minutes

CREDITS

J. T. Blake: Michael Ironside
Eileen: Rae Dawn Chong
Johnny Reynolds: Brad Dourif
No character identified: Bruce Glover
No character identified: Ken Pogue

Complex World

A nightclub singer, Morris Brock (Stanley Matis), joins a group of inept political terrorists who have been hired by the club owner's presidential-candidate father, Senator Robert Burgess (Bob Owczarek), to blow the club up, in this low-budget farce.

REVIEWS

Variety. CCCXLI, November 26, 1990, p. 14.

CREDITS

Morris Brock: Stanley Matis
Jeff Burgess: Dan Welch
Senator Robert Burgess: Bob Owczarek
Gilda: Margot Dionne
Boris Lee: Captain Lou Albano
Malcolm: Daniel Von Bargen
Harpo: Allen Oliver
Alex the Janitor: Joe Klimek
Klem: Jay Charbonneau
Waiter: Ernesto Luna
Miriam: Dorothy Gallagher
Larry Newman: David P. B. Stevens
Mayor: Rich Lupo

Released: 1989
Production: Geoff Adams, Rich Lupo, and Denis Maloney; released by Hemdale Releasing Corporation
Direction: James Wolpaw
Screenplay: James Wolpaw
Cinematography: Denis Maloney
Editing: Steven Gentile
Music: Steven Snyder
MPAA rating: R
Running time: 82 minutes

Cops and Robbersons

"*Cops and Robbersons* is constantly amusing! Chevy Chase returns to doing what he does best! Jack Palance has great fun with his role!"—*Sneak Previews*

"This is a funny movie! It's hysterical...a lot of laughs."—Larry King, CNN

"He's Chevy Chase, we're not, and that makes us laugh. Few images in the movies are funnier than the sight of Chevy Chase, swinging Tarzan-style smack into a cinderblock wall."—*Philadelphia Inquirer*

 Box Office Gross: $11,354,170 (July 10, 1994)

C hevy Chase stars as a dim-witted suburban family man, Norman Robberson, whose dream comes true when his house becomes the command post for a police stakeout. A television detective-drama addict, Norman decides to play "cops and robbers" to the dismay of crusty cop Jack Stone (Jack Palance) and associate Tony Moore (David Barry Gray), who move in with the Robbersons in order to keep an eye on their neighbor, Osborn (Robert Davi), a suspected mobster.

REVIEWS

Atlanta Constitution. April 15, 1994, p. P8.
Boston Globe. April 15, 1994, p. 94.
Chicago Tribune. April 15, 1994, p. 7M.
Christian Science Monitor. April 22, 1994, p. 12.
Entertainment Weekly. April 22, 1994, p. 38.
Entertainment Weekly. November 11, 1994, p. 89.
Los Angeles Times. April 15, 1994, p. F8.
The New York Times. April 15, 1994, p. C23.
The New York Times. May 1, 1994, Sec. 2 p. 26.
People Weekly. XLI, April 25, 1994, p. 17.
TV Guide. XLII, November 19, 1994, p. 49.
USA Today. April 15, 1994, p. D4.
Variety. CCCLIV, April 18, 1994, p. 63.
The Washington Post. April 15, 1994, p. D6.
The Washington Post. April 21, 1994, p. C7.

CREDITS

Norman Robberson: Chevy Chase
Jake Stone: Jack Palance
Helen Robberson: Dianne Wiest
Osborn: Robert Davi
Tony Moore: David Barry Gray
Kevin Robberson: Jason James Richter
Cindy Robberson: Fay Masterson
Billy Robberson: Miko Hughes
Fred Lutz: Richard Romanus

Released: 1994
Production: Ned Tanen, Nancy Graham Tanen, and Ronald L. Schwary for Channel; released by TriStar Pictures
Direction: Michael Ritchie
Screenplay: Bernie Somers
Cinematography: Gerry Fisher
Editing: Stephen A. Rotter
Editing: William S. Scharf
Production design: Stephen J. Lineweaver
Art direction: Philip Toolin
Set decoration: Gary P. Fettis
Casting: Rick Pagano, Sharon Bialy and Debi Manwiller
Sound: Kim H. Ornitz
Costume design: Wayne Finkelman
Music: William Ross
MPAA rating: PG
Running time: 95 minutes

 "I learned this from an old Rastafarian friend in college."
"Where was he from?"
"Oh, Rastafaria."
"I never been there."—Jake Stone and Norman Robberson in *Cops and Robbersons*

Corrina, Corrina

"a tenderly crafted original...a deft romantic comedy-drama."—*The Hollywood Reporter*

"Whoopi Goldberg is wonderful. Ray Liotta is excellent. The stars make you cry and care."—Joel Siegel, *Good Morning America*

"A wonderful movie."—Jeffery Lyons, *Sneak Previews*

"Whoopi is excellent."—Bruce Williamson, *Playboy*

 Box Office Gross: $20,137,840 (December 4, 1994)

Academy Award winning actress Whoopi Goldberg is always worth watching, whether in hits (*Ghost*, 1990; *Sister Act*, 1992) or misses (*Burglar*, 1987; *Made in America*, 1993). She turns in another fine performance in *Corrina, Corrina*, her third turn as a domestic worker (*Clara's Heart*, 1988, and *The Long Walk Home*, 1990).

Since the death of her mother, seven-year-old Molly Singer (Tina Majorino) has refused to speak. Her father Manny (Ray Liotta), a jingle writer, is also having a hard time coping with the loss of his wife. His work is slipping—his inability to write a catchy tune to promote "Mr. Potato Head" may jeopardize his job. Into their lives comes Corrina Washington (Whoopi Goldberg), whom Manny hires as a housekeeper/nanny. With a college degree in musicology and aspirations of writing album liner notes, Corrina is highly over-qualified for the job. Her submissions to music magazines, however, are summarily rejected, so she must make her living cleaning other people's homes.

Atheist Manny does not like Corrina teaching Molly about heaven, but this and other obstacles quickly melt away. Despite warnings from her over-protective sister, Jevina (Jenifer Lewis), Corrina becomes attached to the Singers. With patience and compassion, she draws Molly out of her shell. Soon, the little girl is talking and smiling again. Next, Corrina helps Manny compose a snappy Jell-O jingle. Through her counsel, both father and daughter learn how to deal with and express their grief.

Enjoying a happy home life once again, Molly hopes for a more permanent arrangement. She tries to play matchmaker for her father and Corrina, whose husband "went out for cigarettes and never came back." This fact and a televised report from the Surgeon General convince Molly that

no good can come from cigarettes, so she filches all the cigarettes in the house, to ensure that neither her father nor her surrogate mother ever leave her.

A romantic relationship slowly develops between Manny and Corrina, to Molly's unabashed glee. Though Molly sees nothing unusual in the prospect of her father courting the maid, others do. She is taunted at school for drawing a family picture featuring her black maid. Manny's friends try to pair him with a snobbish divorcee, while Corrina's sister encourages her to date "one of her own kind." Further interference comes from a gossipy, bigoted neighbor, and Manny's mother (Erica Yohn), who worries about Corrina's influence on Molly when the girl starts talking jive and singing gospel songs.

Their biggest obstacle, however, lies in Molly's extended absence from school. After a horrible first day back, Corrina decides Molly is not ready to return to school and lets the girl spend her days helping her clean rich people's houses. After the floors are scrubbed and the silver is polished, Molly sings in an all-black gospel choir with Corrina's nieces and nephews. When he learns of this deception, Manny fires Corrina and forcibly drags Molly, kicking and screaming, out of her house.

The death of Manny's father (Don Ameche, in his last film performance) causes him to examine his life and faith and leads him back to Corrina's doorstep. He wants her in his life again but not as his employee. They kiss in front of her house, not caring who sees them or what people think. A closing scene in which Molly teaches her Jewish grandmother to sing "This Little Light of Mine," illustrates how Corrina's influence has pervaded the family.

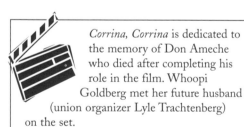

Corrina, Corrina is dedicated to the memory of Don Ameche who died after completing his role in the film. Whoopi Goldberg met her future husband (union organizer Lyle Trachtenberg) on the set.

Corrina, Corrina is producer/director/writer Jessie Nelson's first feature film. Nelson based the title character in this semi-autobiographical film on the seventy-year-old housekeeper who helped to rear her after her mother died.

The critical reception of *Corrina, Corrina* was mixed. In a glowing review, *The Hollywood Reporter* called it a "tenderly crafted original" and a "deft romantic comedy-drama." At the other end of the spectrum, *People Weekly* likened the film to a "montage of bad memories," describing it as a "lame mismatch comedy-cum-antismoking commercial." Most critics cited first-rate performances by the three leads as the film's saving grace and the ambiguity in the relationship between Corrina and Manny as its downfall.

The plot, which was described as "schmaltzy" by *Variety*, was criticized for tugging too hard at the heartstrings and glossing over the issue of racial prejudice. The few brief scenes to depict the bias faced by Manny and Corrina seem very mild compared to the opposition an interracial couple in 1950's suburbia would actually encounter. More compelling are the innocent explorations of their racial disparity made by Molly and her new black playmates. In one exchange, Molly wonders if her friend

"If you cast a really gorgeous, hunky model-type woman in this role, who wouldn't want to kiss her? If you cast me, it's really a love story."—Whoopi Goldberg on her role in *Corrina, Corrina* (*Entertainment Weekly*, May 27, 1994)

tastes like chocolate and the friend gamely allows her to take a lick to find out. The kids also fight over racial slurs, then admit that they do not know what the words mean.

Corrina, Corrina is also hampered by uneven pacing and a lack of definable genre. Conflicts are resolved too quickly and patly, and the film wavers between comedy and drama without committing itself either way. Though the film was promoted as a romance, the love story is its weakest element. There is palpable familial love between the three lead characters but no special spark between Manny and Corrina. They share a bond borne out of mutual concern for Molly, which grows into something more. That "something," however, seems more like camaraderie than passion. Their screen kisses seem forced and awkward.

Careful attention was paid to period detail in *Corrina, Corrina*, which is set in the 1950's. Costumes and hairstyles are true to the era, while also reflecting each character's individual style. The nostalgic feel is enhanced by television program snippets (including *Queen for a Day*, *Zorro* and *The Nat King Cole Show*), and vintage recordings by such artists as Sarah Vaughan, Billie Holiday, Duke Ellington, and Louis Armstrong. Clever period touches, from hula hoops to car hops, add to the authentic 1950's flavor.

Hailed as "an acting natural" by *Variety*, Majorino received high praise for her performance. The youngster, who also starred in *When a Man Loves a Woman* and *Andre* (both reviewed in this volume), more than holds her own in the company of seasoned professionals. Concern for Molly's plight is what pulls the viewer into the story, and Majorino believably expresses the complex emotions required of her pivotal role.

CREDITS

Corrina Washington: Whoopi Goldberg
Manny Singer: Ray Liotta
Molly Singer: Tina Majorino
Grandpa Harry: Don Ameche
Jenny Davis: Wendy Crewson
Sid: Larry Miller
Grandma Eva: Erica Yohn
Jevina: Jenifer Lewis
Jonesy: Joan Cusack
Frank: Harold Sylvester
Anthony T. Williams: Steven Williams
Wilma: Patrika Darbo
Shirl: Lucy Webb
Howard: Courtland Mead
Lewis: Asher Metchik
Percy: Curtis Williams
Brent Witherspoon: Brent Spiner

Released: 1994
Production: Jessie Nelson, Paula Mazur, and Steve Tisch for New Line Productions; released by New Line Cinema
Direction: Jessie Nelson
Screenplay: Jessie Nelson
Cinematography: Bruce Surtees
Editing: Lee Percy
Art direction: Dina Lipton
Production design: Jeannine Claudia Oppewall
Set design: Louisa Bonnie
Costume design: Francine Jamison-Tanchuck
Music: Bonnie Greenberg
Score: Rick Cox
Casting: Mary Gail Artz and Barbara Cohen
Makeup: Mike Germain
Hair styling: Candy Walker
Song: Mitchell Parish, Bo Chatman, J. Mayo Williams, Big Joe Tuner (performer) and "Corrina, Corrina"
MPAA rating: PG
Running time: 115 minutes

Whoopi Goldberg as Corrina and Tina Majorino as Molly in *Corrina, Corrina*. Photo: S. Hanover © 1994 New Line Productions, Inc. All rights reserved.

Whoopi Goldberg plays Corrina with warmth and dignity, her comedic timing adding welcome touches of humor. She has been criticized for donning a maid's costume too often, but Corrina is not a stereotypical servant. Goldberg had a hand in the development of her character, insisting that Corrina have a college degree and loftier aspirations than keeping house. Goldberg's Corrina is a strong, willful, and admirable character.

Liotta, better known for action/adventure roles (*Goodfellas*, 1990; *Unlawful Entry*, 1992), is charming as the sensitive, well-meaning Dad. Standouts among the supporting cast include Joan Cusack as a psycho-maid, and scene-stealing Curtis Armstrong as Corrina's jolly nephew. Patrika Darbo provides some comic relief in an all-too-brief segment. Larry Miller's comedic talents are wasted in his role as Manny's boss, and in a bigger waste, the performance of Brent Spiner, Goldberg's costar from television's *Star Trek:*

The Next Generation, must have remained on the cutting room floor, his role reduced to that of an extra with a character name. In his last film performance, Don Ameche has little screen time, but his mere presence enriches the film.

—*Brenda Scott Royce*

REVIEWS

Boston Globe. August 19, 1994, p. 47.
Entertainment Weekly. August 19, 1994, p. 38.
Hollywood Reporter. July 29, 1994, p. 10.
Los Angeles Times. August 12, 1994, p. F1.
The New York Times. August 12, 1994, p. B2.
People Weekly. August 15, 1994, p. 15.
Variety. August 1, 1994.

The Cowboy Way

"How the east was won."—Movie tagline
"...wildly funny, edge-of-your-seat romp!"—*ABC Radio Network*

 Box Office Gross: $19,636,765 (July 7, 1994)

Out of the West they rode, bone-tired and hell-bent for leather, hard-living cowboys with a hard-luck job to do. Surrounded by enemies, they walk tall through a lonely, godforsaken wilderness that some call Hell and some just call—New York City.... And if they can survive the traffic, they just might take New Yorkers for the ride of their lives," says the production notes for *The Cowboy Way*. From the sound of this, perhaps the film was doomed from the beginning.

Pepper Lewis (Woody Harrelson) and Sonny Gilstrap (Kiefer Sutherland), erstwhile best friends and one-time rodeo champions, travel from New Mexico to New York City in search of their friend Nacho (Joaquin Martinez) and his daughter, Teresa (Cara Buono). Nacho had been making payments to sweat-shop operator Stark (Dylan McDermott), who had arranged to have Nacho's daughter, Teresa, smuggled in from Cuba on one of his boats of illegal immigrants—labor for his sweat shop.

After preparing for his role in *The Cowboy Way*, Kiefer Sutherland became so good at roping that he competed in a real rodeo.

Once Teresa lands in this country, however, she falls prey to Stark's greed and lechery. This beauty in the hands of this beast proves too much for Nacho, which creates a big-city problem that is ripe for some big-country heroes.

Unfortunately, the character development of Pepper and Sonny is reminiscent of the children's comic characters Goofus and Gallant. That is, Pepper is always making mistakes: arriving late, saying the wrong thing, making a mess. For example, throughout the film he hoards his entire fortune (eight dollars) while he tries to write short checks to everyone he meets, from the desk clerk at the Waldorf-Astoria to the pawnbroker who has Sonny's guns. He is irrepressible—and needs a keeper. Enter Sonny. As the opening credits demonstrate, Sonny has spent his life getting Pepper out of scrapes, and while even as youngsters Pepper was the better cowboy, he would start fights that Sonny would have to step in and finish.

Indeed, Pepper causes fistfights wherever he goes, and Sonny must either calm the participants or fight the fights. Early in the film, Pepper wants to participate in a gambling pool among bronc riders to see whose time is the best on the bucking bronco, winner take all. No one wants to let Pepper participate, as he already owes money to almost everyone present. As the discussion turns to violence, Sonny appears, convinces the cowboys to let Pepper participate, and even puts in Pepper's share of

CREDITS

Pepper: Woody Harrelson
Sonny: Kiefer Sutherland
Nacho: Joaquin Martinez
Officer Sam Shaw: Ernie Hudson
Stark :   Dylan McDermott
Teresa: Cara Buono
Chango: Luis Guzman
Margarette: Marg Helgenberger

Released: 1994
Production: Brian Grazer for Imagine Entertainment;
released by Universal Pictures
Direction: Gregg Champion
Screenplay: Bill Wittliff; based on a story by Wittliff and
Rob Thompson
Cinematography: Dean Semler
Editing: Michael Tronick
Production design: John Jay Moore
Art direction: William Barclay
Set decoration: Leslie Pope
Casting: Billy Hopkins, Suzanne Smith and Kerry
Barden
Sound: Tom Brandau
Costume design: Aude Bronson-Howard
Stunt coordination: Conrad E. Palmisano
Music supervision: Danny Bramson
Music: David Newman
MPAA rating: PG-13
Running time: 102 minutes

Kiefer Sutherland and Woody Harrelson as Sonny and Pepper, modern-day rodeo cowboys in New York in *The Cowboy Way*. © 1994 Universal City Studios Inc. All rights reserved.

the money. Pepper responds by spitting chewing tobacco on one of the men's boots. This is just one scene; the film is filled with others exactly like it.

Hardly breaking new ground, *The Cowboy Way* is reminiscent in many ways of other films that lift primitives or waifs and place them in the big city. Indeed, reviews of this film compared it to at least a half dozen other productions to which it bears striking resemblance: *Coogan's Bluff* (1968), *Midnight Cowboy* (1969), *48 Hrs.* (1982), *"Crocodile" Dundee* (1986), and television's *McCloud*. As do the protagonists in each of these earlier films, Pepper and Sonny learn quickly that the only way to make it in New York is their way—the cowboy way. This entails a variety of barroom brawls, a mountain of broken glass, and endless bathroom humor, such as when Pepper tells Chango, played by Luis Guzman, that his face looks like "a hat full of assholes."

Reviewers were also quick to point to inaccuracies in the film's use of Manhattan. For example, Caryn James of *The New York Times* chides the filmmakers for plotting a circuitous route for the cowboys so that their trip from the Upper East Side to Brooklyn could include a trip past the Statue of Liberty, a noteworthy sight—but in the opposite

direction. Stephen Hunter, reviewing the film for the *Baltimore Sun*, lamented the inaccurate details surrounding the pawning of handguns: "This in New York City, which has strenuously controlled legal access to handguns since 1916!"

The supporting characters in *The Cowboy Way* are also devoid of any depth or complexity. For example, mounted police officer Sam Shaw (Ernie Hudson) is totally wasted in the film, lampooning himself yet falling quite flat. His version of "the cowboy way" is to ride his horse into a series of buildings, such as the police station and a nightclub. While he does look out of place, the humor goes little further than the visual incongruity.

One character, however, breaks new ground for himself, although his character is clearly overblown. That is, Dylan McDermott's Stark menaces with glee. In one telling scene, Stark's oily charm rises to the surface as he attempts to win Teresa's trust. He tells her of the dangers of the city and of the sweatshop. All the while, the audience has also seen the violence of which he is capable, killing both his partners and his enemies. When the film begins, he looks nervous, perhaps even a little embarrassed, when he is caught in his misdeeds. By the film's end, however, he has learned his own method for solving problems—he kills everyone who gets in his way. Certainly the thug Lothario is not a new character. What is surprising here is that McDermott is much better known for his straight-arrow characters in such films as *Steel Magnolias* (1989) and *In the Line of Fire* (1993), in which he plays Clint Eastwood's sympathetic and short-lived partner. For a performance against type, McDermott's Stark is interesting viewing.

Plot-wise, the film promises more than it delivers. For example, when the film begins, Sonny is barely speaking to Pepper, giving him what Pepper calls "the Eskimo treatment." While it would be easy to imagine several reasons to be angry with this irrepressible half-wit, the film makes a big secret of the real reason Pepper failed to show up when the two cowboys had a chance to ride in—and a good chance to win—the national championship. When the reason is revealed late in the film, it is remarkably mundane, a fizzle rather than a pop. Also, throughout the film Pepper proves irresistible to women—and to many men. He attends a swinging New York penthouse party and is wooed by everyone in sight. The relationship between much of what occurs there and the rest of the film remains a mystery. Late in the film, however, the loose ends are tied up; once again the effect is dulled, a smile rather than a laugh.

"The cowboy way is still alive and well—even in New York."—Woody Harrelson, on *The Cowboy Way*

While the film itself is a disappointment, the process of producing it seems to have been more fun. Director Gregg Champion staged a rodeo in order to get the footage he needed of his stars in action. Held in Sante Fe, the event included dozens of real broncobusters, animal wranglers, animals, ropers—and rodeo fans. Woody Harrelson and Kiefer Sutherland spent months perfecting their lassoing skills for the rodeo scenes.

While they were prepared for the rodeo sequences, the New York segments proved more of a challenge. "The first time we rode the horses on the street," Harrelson is quoted as saying in the production notes, "everybody told me, 'If it's too hard to handle, just grab onto the horn and hold on tight to the horse.' And these horses were jumping horses. They're bred for competition and they're really fast. But I said, no big deal, I'm tough. Then, as soon as they said action, these horses fly. My hat flies off and I'm just hanging on. It was the scariest thing I'd ever experienced. It was pretty heart-thumpin'."

The Cowboy Way also involved a little production magic. Late in the film the cowboys chase Stark, who is escaping on a subway train. For two weekends, the filmmakers shot on the Manhattan Bridge, 100 feet above the East River. To make the shot possible, production designer John Jay Moore placed a quarter-mile platform over the subway tracks for better safety and traction for the horses. "If you look at the bridge, you'll see that there's nothing but railroad ties with spaces in between, which makes it hard enough for a person, let alone a horse," said Moore in the production notes. "We put the platform down over the bridge surface, added a special rubber matting to keep the horses from slipping and then painted the platform to camouflage it into the structure of the bridge."

The Cowboy Way was written by Bill Wittliff, who also created screenplays for television's *Lonesome Dove* and such films as *The Black Stallion* (1979) and *Barbarosa* (1982). Despite a screenplay by the man widely credited with revitalizing the modern Western and two young, handsome box-office stars, this cowboy tale provides much more dust than light or joy.

—*Roberta F. Green*

REVIEWS

Baltimore Sun. Maryland Live section, June 3-9, 1994, p. 11.
Chicago Tribune. June 3, 1994, Tempo Section, p. 4.
Entertainment Weekly. June 10, 1994, p. 44.
The Hollywood Reporter. May 31, 1994, p. 57.
Los Angeles Times. June 3, 1994, p. F1.
The New York Times. June 3, 1994, p. B 87.
Rolling Stone. June 30, 1994, p. 81.
Time. June 13, 1994, p. 74.
Variety. May 31, 1994, p. 10.
The Washington Post. June 3, 1994, Weekend Section, p. 44.

Cronos

"An ancient device. A modern discovery. A terrifying tale of the eternal."—Movie tagline

"Great macabre gusto...exotic...very stylish and sophisticated."—Janet Maslin, *The New York Times*

"A remarkable blend of fun, fright and moral fervor."—Peter Travers, *Rolling Stone*

"Creepy, funny & dazzlingly original."—Rex Reed, *The New York Observer*

Hailed as the standard-bearer of the current renaissance in Mexican cinema and winner of the Grand Prize at the 1993 Cannes Film Festival's Critics Week, Guillermo del Toro's *Cronos* is a darkly comic look at death, vanity, and the monstrous pursuit of eternal life.

As the film opens, a fourteenth century alchemist (Mario Ivan Martinez) is forging an ornate device, about the size and shape of a Fabergé Egg and made of 24-carat gold. Encased within it are both the cogs of an intricate machine and an insect that appears to be the revolting spawn of leech and scorpion. The object is called the Cronos Device, and it offers its user freedom from death, at a very heavy price.

The action then moves forward in time some six centuries, where the alchemist, still barely alive, has been crushed by the rubble of a crumbling building. Having been trapped for days without his beloved device, the alchemist finally dies. Police locate the dead man's house, finding a grisly tableau of corpses and containers of human blood. Also at the house is the book containing the alchemist's schematic for the Cronos Device and instructions on how to use it. The device itself has disappeared, and the remaining contents of the house are auctioned off.

The story then moves to present-day Mexico City. An aging antique dealer, Jesús Gris (Federico Luppi), and his orphaned granddaughter, Aurora (Tamara Shanath), stumble upon the device hidden in a newly acquired statuette. As they playfully examine the strangely beautiful item, Jesús trips a mechanism that sets it in motion. Gold-plated, gleaming claws emerge from it as its motor whirs, grasping Jesús' hand. A stinger then protrudes and strikes deep into his flesh. He pulls the machine from his bloody hand, horrified but fascinated. Later that night, as his wife, Mercedes (Margarita Isabel), and Aurora sleep, Jesús awakens with a feverish thirst. He feels an insatiable need for the Cronos Device to pierce him again. Aurora finds him lying on the stairs in an orgasmic swoon, the device attached to his chest.

The next morning Jesús awakens feeling spry and chipper. He senses himself as somehow younger and more vital. Mercedes laughs at his enthusiasm. At the shop, he is confronted by Angel De le Guardia (Ron Perlman), a sadistic henchman working for his demented, dying, and very rich uncle, Dieter (Claudio Brook). Dieter has been tipped off that Jesús is in possession of the Cronos Device, which the mad uncle has sought ever since obtaining the alchemist's notebook. Jesús, however, refuses to give him the device. Thus ensues the battle that takes up much of the rest of film's narrative.

Jesús slowly begins to develop an intense lust for human blood, though he obtains it not through violence but rather through random encounters—a man with a bloody nose leaves a trail of blood in a public bathroom, for example. Although Jesús is disturbed by this hunger, he is compelled to continue to use the device.

CREDITS

Jesús Gris: Federico Luppi
Angel De la Guardia: Ron Perlman
Dieter De la Guardia: Claudio Brook
Mercedes Gris: Margarita Isabel
Aurora Gris: Tamara Shanath
Alchemist: Mario Ivan Martinez
Manuelito: Farnesio de Bernal

Origin: Mexico
Released: 1993
Production: Bertha Navarro and Arthur Gorson for Producciones Iguana, in association with Ventana Films; released by October Films
Direction: Guillermo del Toro
Screenplay: Guillermo del Toro
Cinematography: Guillermo Navarro
Editing: Raul Davalos
Production design: Tolita Figueroa
Art direction: Brigitte Broch
Sound: Fernando Camara
Special effects: Laurencio Cordero
Costume design: Genoveva Petitpierre
Music: Javier Alvarez
MPAA rating: no listing
Running time: 92 minutes

AWARDS AND NOMINATIONS

Cannes Film Festival: Best Picture—Critics Week

Cronos won nine Ariels (the Mexican equivalent of an Academy Award), including Best Picture and Best Direction.

Angel, when not contemplating the nose job he will buy when he inherits his uncle's money, continues to hound Jesús, eventually, and against his uncle's wishes, killing him. This leads to a hysterical scene at the funeral home where Jesús is interred, featuring a brilliant comic turn by Farnesio de Bernal as the embalmer. Of course, in Gothic tradition, Jesús rises from his coffin, horribly disfigured but still alive. The Cronos Device allows him to shed, in the most grotesque fashion, his now-dead skin.

Aurora touchingly comforts and shepherds her disfigured grandfather through his attempts at obtaining the alchemist's notebook from Dieter, which he believes can provide him a way out of his vampirish purgatory. In fact, it is Aurora who deals the death blow to Dieter as he attempts to kill Jesús (again) and grab the device. The story's pivotal moment comes when Jesús has to choose between killing Aurora to satisfy his need for blood or destroying the Cronos Device and himself along with it. Happily, sweetly, he chooses the latter.

The budget for *Cronos* was only $2 million, but was the second-highest budgeted film in the history of Mexican cinema.

Upon release in the United States, *Cronos* garnered raves in both the *The New York Times* and *Los Angeles Times*. In addition to the Cannes award, *Cronos* also won nine Ariels (the Mexican equivalent of an Academy Award), including Best Picture and Best Direction.

The twenty-nine-year-old del Toro, who has claimed to be "genre-impaired" and incapable of working outside the Horror/Gothic mode, has, in his directorial debut, created a charming film that manages to be ghoulish, tender, and comic all at once. The relationship between Aurora and Jesús, in particular, has a touching sweetness that counterbalances the explicit gore in which the director obviously delights.

Made for the paltry sum of $2 million, and financed by everything from government agencies to the director's own credit cards, *Cronos* looks better than many an American film made at ten times the cost. The production design by Tolita Figueroa and cinematography by Guillermo Navarro are nothing short of stunning, with a keen eye for period and detail—after all, the film spans roughly six hundred years. The score by Javier Alvarez is a sumptuous blend of orchestral tango and twentieth century modernity.

Federico Luppi, one of Latin America's biggest stars, brings just the right blend of simplicity, decency, and childish vanity to the role of Jesús Gris. It is a sad and heroic performance. Ron Perlman, best known for his starring role in the television series *Beauty and the Beast*, is alternately funny and overly cartoonish as the hulking henchman of Uncle Dieter. His performance is marred by genre-film bad-guy clichés. Claudio Brook, one of Luis Buñuel's favorite actors after the director emigrated to Mexico from Spain, is similarly and perhaps intentionally cartoonish as Dieter, but he does project an aura of menace as a man holding tenaciously to the last moments of a cruel and pitiless life. Margarita Isabel, also well known to Latin American audiences, is lovely as the bemused and wistful Mercedes Gris. She and Luppi convincingly convey, unsentimentally, an intimacy born of many years as man and wife.

As Aurora Gris, Tamara Shanath brings a naturalism to her role that is both refreshing and necessary. Her character embodies an almost magical and unconditional love for her grandfather, even as his body decays and he grows more and more physically hideous. Aurora functions as a nearly wordless Greek chorus in this Gothic morality play and Shanath lets her remain a child, not, as in so many films made in the United States, a child-actress.

While slightly too old to be hailed as a wunderkind, Guillermo del Toro has made a strikingly mature debut, both as a director and writer. The subject matter encompasses everything from vampirism to Catholic and biblical symbology, and does so both effortlessly and entertainingly. Del Toro is obviously happily in love with films and filmmaking and is as concerned with human relationships as he is with special effects, letting neither one suffer in his first labor, *Cronos*.

—*Nicholas Kirgo*

REVIEWS

The Hollywood Reporter. March 30, 1994, p. 7.
Los Angeles Times. April 22, 1994, p. F1.
The New York Times. March 24, 1994, p. B3.

Crooklyn

"Two Thumbs up!"—*Siskel & Ebert*

"The smart choice is Spike Lee's hilarious *Crooklyn*."—Peter Travers, *Family Life*

"...filled with evocative fragments of family life and street life."—Julie Salamon, *Wall Street Journal*

"A touching and generous family portrait, a film that exposes new aspects of this director's talent." —Janet Maslin, *The New York Times*

"It's the one to see."—Joel Seigel, *Good Morning America*

 Box Office Gross: $13,000,370 (July 4, 1994)

It is difficult to be lukewarm about Spike Lee, and the release of one of his films predictably sends critics and audiences to one of two corners. Some complain that he is a bright but ultimately annoying and sophomoric artist, characterized by sizzle and shuck more than sincerity and seriousness. Others proclaim that he is at the forefront of a revitalized modern cinema, making vitally engaging, provocative, dramatic, and visually interesting films that in particular offer a much-needed assertion of the African American presence in contemporary America. Little agreement but much useful debate is generated by these two critical camps. Lee's films are, in the very least, an important part of the national dialogue—and sometimes the national screaming match—on such topics as interracial sex, radical political activism, black economic entrepreneurialism, and the rights to ethnic images and history.

After a series of powerful films, including *Do the Right Thing* (1989), *Jungle Fever* (1991), and *Malcolm X* (1992), that are characteristically inflammatory and high-strung and have established him as an angry provocateur of a filmmaker, his most recent release, *Crooklyn*, is an unexpected change of pace. Cowritten with his sister, Joie Susannah Lee, and brother Cinque Lee, the film is a nostalgic re-creation of the Brooklyn neighborhood in which they grew up during the early 1970's. The publicity campaign for *Crooklyn* insistently positions it as a "moving comedy-drama," aimed at family audiences.

Lee runs the risk, however, of falling into a trap that he has outspokenly warned other young black filmmakers to beware: that of losing one's edge and becoming part of a Disney-type establishment producing successful feel-good

 "[It's]...the same story again and again—the hip-hop, drug, gangsta rap, urban, inner-city movie. I don't think that's the totality of the African American experience and I really think that audiences are starting to want more than these movies can give them."—*Crooklyn* writer/director/producer Spike Lee

fantasies. Yet Lee's intention was evidently to avoid another common trap, that of, as he says, "telling the same story again and again—the hip-hop, drug, gangsta rap, urban, inner-city movie. I don't think that's the totality of the African American experience and I really think that audiences are starting to want more than these movies can give them."

Crooklyn is loosely structured and episodic, focusing on the African American Carmichael family. They live in a neighborhood and household with a never-ending abundance of cares and joys, trivial and series crises. Carolyn (Alfre Woodard), the mother, struggles to keep the family together—she is a patient and also heroically determined comforter, disciplinarian, organizer, and breadwinner. Yet much of the comedy and the pathos of the film derives from her losing battle against the centrifugal, entropic, disorderly energy and desires of her housemates. The five kids live in a summer-vacation frenzy of yelling, playing, teasing, arguing, watching television, and eating junk food.

The characters of the three youngest boys, Wendell (Sharif Rashed), Nate (Christopher Knowings), and Joseph (Tse-Mach Washington), are never really fully developed in the course of the film, but they help add a kind of critical mass to the confusion of the house. Clinton (Carlton Williams), the oldest, is more carefully delineated, and his adolescent awkwardness, eyeglasses, and passion for the New York Knicks make him not only a stand-in for the director but also the focal point of one of the crucial experiences and epiphanies of the film. Clinton chooses to go to a Knicks game rather than to his father's concert recital. This an illustration that, for better or worse, he is truly his father's son, willful, independent, and selfish.

Clinton's relationship to the Knicks is ironically connected to his feelings for his mother as well as his father. It is a championship year for the Knicks, but this triumph, which Clinton shares, occurs in the same season as an unfathomable tragedy, the death of his mother. Here and elsewhere, Lee subtly but effectively shows that some of life's most dramatic moments involve collisions of simultaneous emotions, in this case exhilaration and grief.

In some ways, the biggest child in the family is Woody (Delroy Lindo), Carolyn's husband, whose ability to provide for the family is undercut by his commitment to his music, which is commercially unsuccessful. Lee does not mask Woody's many inadequacies, but he presents him affectionately as a loving father and a figure of quiet strength and idealism. He is a constant reminder to his children that there is

CREDITS

Carolyn Carmichael: Alfre Woodard
Woody Carmichael: Delroy Lindo
Tony Eyes: David Patrick Kelly
Troy: Zelda Harris
Clinton: Carlton Williams
Wendell: Sharif Rashed
Joseph: Tse-Mach Washington
Nate: Christopher Knowings
Tommy La La: José Zuniga
Vic: Isaiah Washington
Jessica: Ivelka Reyes
Snuffy: Spike Lee
Right Hand Man: N. Jeremi Duru
Aunt Song: Frances Foster
Clem: Norman Matlock
Viola: Patriece Nelson
Aunt Maxine: Joie Susannah Lee
Uncle Brown: Vondie Curtis-Hall
Minnie: Tiasha Reyes

Released: 1994
Production: Spike Lee for 40 Acres and a Mule Filmworks, in association with Child Hoods Productions; released by Universal Pictures
Direction: Spike Lee
Screenplay: Joie Susannah Lee, Cinque Lee, and Spike Lee; based on a story by Joie Susannah Lee
Cinematography: Arthur Jafa
Editing: Barry Alexander Brown
Production design: Wynn Thomas
Art direction: Chris Shriver
Set decoration: Ted Glass
Casting: Robi Reed
Sound: Rolf Pardula
Sound design: Skip Lievsey
Costume Design: Ruth E. Carter
Music: Terence Blanchard
MPAA rating: PG-13
Running time: 132 minutes

more to life than good manners, balancing a checkbook, and getting up on time.

The fact that Woody fills the house with warmly shimmering candlelight is ultimately more memorable than the fact that the electricity for the lights was turned off in the first place because of his fiscal ineptness. Carolyn is often exasperated by Woody, angry that in the family menu she is the black-eyed peas and he is the ice cream. Yet despite temporary separations they remain together: Unresolvable differences do not necessarily destroy a relationship, and Lee takes great pains to stress that despite the stereotypes and statistics, this family stays fundamentally intact.

Crooklyn takes off in many directions, following these characters on their daily rounds. If the film has any unity it is as a coming-of-age story about the only girl in the family, Troy (Zelda Harris). Lee knows a good thing when he sees it and capitalizes fully on the tried-and-true tradition of charming his audience with children. Troy is more than cute and endearing, however; she is a sensitive and occasionally troubled observer of a world that is filled with more than fun and games. One wonders to what extent Lee consciously fashions the Carmichaels as an answer or complement to the Huxtable family of television's enormously popular *Cosby Show*, which rarely went beyond comic cuteness. In one of the early scenes in the film, Troy leaves her bed late at night and pees on the floor. This is one of several bows to the current convention that kids' films must contain some gross-out scenes, but it is also an indication that Troy is overwhelmed by what is happening around her.

This is not surprising, because the world in which Troy grows up is in many respects tense and weird. Their next-door neighbor is a maladjusted, incessantly complaining white musician, Tony Eyes (David Patrick Kelly), whose paranoia turns out to be justified: He is indeed tormented by the neighborhood kids and punched out by Vic (Isaiah Washington), a macho Vietnam War veteran. Troy also has nightmares about Snuffy, a glue-sniffer played by Spike Lee, and Right Hand Man (N. Jeremi Duru), an amputee, both of whom represent the comic horror of street life. Wherever she goes, Troy witnesses disturbing sights: Even the nearby candy store is a bizarre place of potato chips, Popsicles, and a transvestite (RuPaul) more than suggestively bumping and grinding in the aisle.

Despite all this, one of the ironies of the film is Lee's insistence that true weirdness is found not in the city streets but in the conventional heartland of the South. Troy spends a few weeks visiting Aunt Song (Frances Foster), who in true American archetypal aunt fashion—like Aunt Polly in *Huckleberry Finn* (1885)—tries to civilize her with a vengeance, redoing her hip hairstyle and in general stifling her with smug and smarmy advice about manners, morals, and religion. All the scenes set in this household are slightly distorted, shot through an anamorphic lens to squeeze everything unnaturally. Lee gets no points for subtlety here, but the audience is brought closer to Troy's perspective and is constantly reminded of how uncomfortable she is in this alien world.

Troy cannot wait to return to the city, even though she returns to confront tremendous pressures. Her bratty brothers are the least of her worries: Mostly she faces the task of learning everything she can quickly from her mother, coping with her mother's death, and then standing in for her after she is gone. The last part of the film is elliptical, and here Lee does get points for subtlety. Much more effectively than the obvious compression of space in the previous section of the film, the compression of time here creates an interesting dream-like mood, in which Troy's shock, anger, and disorientation are part of a rapid and almost magical process of growth and transformation. Even at age ten, she emerges as the new woman of the house, strong enough to beat up her nemesis, Snuffy, with a broom handle, and tender and patient enough to comb her young brother's hair before sending him outside to the street to play and grow up. A soul train runs on television and also through the family, especially from Carolyn to Troy, and the film ends confirming the deep message of one of the many songs that echo constantly in the background: "ooh child, things are gonna get easier."

The early critical reviews, at least in mainstream newspapers and magazines, tended to agree that *Crooklyn* is a disappointingly lightweight film, superficial, sentimental, and self-indulgent. It is difficult to disagree completely with these judgments. *Crooklyn* is not particularly ambitious, profound, or analytically probing, and unlike Lee's previous works, which are problem-and issue-oriented, this film seems curiously evasive. The problems are there—drug addiction, unemployment, racial conflict, the disintegrating family, media numbness and exploitation, and so on—but they are not named as such and tend to recede fleetingly into the background.

Overall, the film tends to substitute a facile evocation of weirdness for a more sustained attempt to comprehend its origin and effect. The plot line is often disconcertingly fragmented, at times even pointless. Although the acting is consistently good, the depth of the characters is intimated rather than fully developed, and Lee relies heavily on easily achieved bits of humor, tension, and sadness. *Crooklyn* does not stand up well alongside other, similar films. It does not have the wit and visual imagination of Woody Allen's equally self-indulgent, personal, sentimental, and semiautobiographical stories of growing up in Brooklyn. It can not match Jim Jarmusch's films as sustained studies of city weirdness. Finally, it lacks the consistent power and insightfulness of such commonly acknowledged classic films of childhood, adolescence, or coming-of-age as *Les Quatre Cents Coups* (1959; *The 400 Blows*), *Stand by Me* (1986), and *Boyz N the Hood* (1991).

Dwelling on what the film does not have, though, may blind one to what it does have. Each of the above critical terms used to denigrate *Crooklyn* can, from a slightly different perspective, give some insight into the real strengths of the film. To call it a nice little film, rather than a profound, big picture, need not be a criticism or a backhanded compliment. To emphasize its superficiality may call attention to the way it strives to capture the concrete surfaces rather than the abstract depths, the color and texture of real life, as it is lived and as it is remembered by children and grown children. Other films are arguments and essays: This film is a series of pictures and dramatized feelings. To note that it is sentimental and embodies a fantasy of a character growing through adversity to conquer death and deprivation immediately places it in the company of many of the classic and most popular American myths and films.

At the very end of the film, after all the credits, Lee inserts one of his familiar logos and credos: "By any means necessary." It is important to recognize that the "means" that he chooses in *Crooklyn* is not the same as that of his other films. *Malcolm X* was born out of the serious and fiery *The Autobiography of Malcolm X* (1965) and evolved into a triumph of mythologizing and merchandising. *Crooklyn*, however, comes at least in part out of lesser stuff, *The Partridge Family* and *Soul Train*, two television shows watched avidly by the Carmichael kids. Lee takes this unexpected conjunction and turns it into a lighthearted, uplifting story that modern generations of Carmichael kids—and their parents—may find entertaining.

—*Sidney Gottlieb*

REVIEWS

Entertainment Weekly. May 13, 1994, p. 36.
The Hollywood Reporter. May 9, 1994, p. 6.
Los Angeles Times. May 13, 1994, p. F1.
The New York Times. May 13, 1994, p. B1.
The New Yorker. LXX, May 23, 1994, p. 95.
Time. CXXIII, May 23, 1994, p. 60.
Variety. May 9, 1994, p. 2.

The Crow

"In a world without justice one man was chosen to protect the innocent."—Movie tagline

"...the best movie of its kind since the original *Batman.*"—*Chicago Tribune*

"A triumph! Brandon Lee is a vivid presence."
—Bruce Williamson, *Playboy*

"dazzling and fiercely hypnotic"—Peter Travers, *Rolling Stone*

"A futuristic dreamscape right out of *Blade Runner* and *Batman.*"—Owen Gleiberman, *Entertainment Weekly*

 Box Office Gross: $50,627,490 (September 25, 1994)

People once believed that when someone dies, a crow carries their soul to the land of the dead. But, sometimes, something so bad happens that a terrible sadness is carried within and the soul can't rest. And...sometimes...just sometimes...the crow can bring that soul back to set the wrong things right." It is difficult to listen to the prologue opening *The Crow* and not be chilled by the ominous significance. The star of the motion picture, rising action/adventure star and martial-arts expert Brandon Lee (1965-1993), was killed while filming it. The tragedy occurred about one week before filming ended and while his fiancée, Eliza Hutton, was flying out to be with him. They were to be married in Ensenada, Mexico, immediately after Lee finished the film.

Lee was making the motion picture in Wilmington, North Carolina, at Carolco Studios on Stage Number 4. The date was March 30, 1993. The shooting schedule for that evening consisted of nine shots and filming began close to 8:00 p.m. Lee was not needed until later, so he came onto the set close to midnight. Lee's character, killed by hoodlums at the beginning of the film, returns from the dead seeking vengeance on his killers. The filming that night, ironically, was to be his character's death scene. Lee was to come into his attic apartment with a bag of groceries and see four thugs violating his sweetheart. Before he could stop them, one of the punks was supposed to shoot him at close range. Unknown either to Lee, the "killer," the director, or the prop person, the real gun used—a silver .44 magnum—had a bullet tip lodged sideways in the barrel, left from several weeks before. The barrel was not checked when it was loaded with a blank shell, which then discharged the object. It entered just below Lee's navel, lodging in his spine. His vital organs were severely damaged, and he lost a lot of blood. Lee died later that day while in the intensive-care unit.

All the film footage taken during the shooting was destroyed, and the killing scene was later reworked, using doubles and specialized technology. This choice by the filmmakers showed their respect for Lee and his family by not sensationalizing his death and holding it up for public viewing and respect for their film, which could attract viewers on its own merits—on Lee's acting ability and not on his death.

For Brandon Lee, son of legendary martial-arts master and international film star Bruce Lee (1941-1973), his acting career was just taking off at the time of his death. Prior to *The Crow*, Lee had appeared in a pair of *Kung Fu* television films with David Carradine, starred in

> Brandon Lee, son of action star Bruce Lee, was accidentally shot and killed while filming *The Crow.* The unfinished motion picture would have been shelved except for the direct intervention of Lee's fiancée, Eliza Hutton, and his mother, Linda Lee Cadwell. *The Crow* is dedicated: "To Brandon and Eliza."

two feature films in Hong Kong, made his American screen debut in *Showdown in Little Tokyo* (1991), with Dolph Lundgren, and starred in *Rapid Fire* (1992). Lee appeared well on his way to wearing the martial-arts mantle of his illustrious father. He saw *The Crow* as a turning point in his career. The actor was enthusiastic about the role and had already signed an agreement to make two sequels if the film was successful.

The Crow is set in the inner-city slums of Detroit, in some bleak, future time. It is Devil's Night, the evening preceding Halloween, when violence and murder stalk the streets. The camera races over the city rooftops as the prologue is spoken and swoops down to two victims lying on the street below. The Detroit police are investigating the

CREDITS

Eric Draven: Brandon Lee
Albrecht: Ernie Hudson
Top Dollar: Michael Wincott
T-Bird: David Patrick Kelly
Skank: Angel David
Sarah: Rochelle Davis
Myca: Bai Ling
Tin Tin: Lawrence Mason
Funboy: Michael Massee
Shelly: Sofia Shinas
Darla: Anna Thomson
Grange: Tony Todd
Gideon: Jon Polito

Released: 1994
Production: Edward R. Pressman and Jeff Most for Entertainment Media Investment Corporation; released by Miramax/Dimension Films
Direction: Alex Proyas
Screenplay: David J. Schow and John Shirley; based on the comic book series and comic strip by James O'Barr
Cinematography: Dariusz Wolski
Editing: Dov Hoenig and Scott Smith
Production design: Alex McDowell
Art direction: Simon Murton
Set design: William Barcley
Set decoration: Marthe Pineau
Casting: Billy Hopkins and Suzanne Smith
Visual effects supervision: Andrew Mason
Sound: Buddy Alper
Special makeup effects: Lance Anderson
Costume Design: Arianne Phillips
Stunt coordination: Jeff Imada
Music: Graeme Revell
MPAA rating: R
Running time: 100 minutes

crime. One victim is Eric Draven (Brandon Lee), a promising rock guitarist, who was stabbed, shot twice, and fell six stories to his death. The other is his fiancée, Shelly Webster (Sofia Shinas), who was brutally raped and stabbed. They were to be married the next day. Hours later, Shelly dies in the hospital. Two sympathetic characters are introduced— Sarah (Rochelle Davis), an abandoned, skateboarding street child who had been befriended by Shelly, and Albrecht (Ernie Hudson), an honest street cop, later demoted because he investigated the crime too closely.

Cut to one year later, again on Devil's Night. Eric Draven crawls out of his grave, screaming, with a crow on hand to guide and assist him. The bird lends significance to the hero's name—Eric D-raven. He rips off his clothes, wanders half-naked to his abandoned loft apartment, and discovers his pet cat, Gabriel, waiting. While there, he begins experiencing flashbacks that occur regularly throughout the film. The audience eventually learns that Shelly and Eric had been fighting an eviction notice by an unscrupulous slumlord. Four thugs—T-Bird (David Patrick Kelly), Skank (Angel David), Tin Tin (Lawrence Mason), and Funboy (Michael Massee)—were sent to intimidate and silence the lovers. Somehow, the hoodlums veer out of control and proceed to molest Shelly and kill Eric. The newly aroused "Lazarus" swears vengeance for the crimes, dons black clothes, applies white clown makeup, and goes out, seeking the killers with the crow as his guide. One character dubs Eric "The Mime From Hell." Eric, possessed of supernatural powers, cannot be stopped by ordinary means.

The middle section of *The Crow* is spent with Eric tracking down each of the four killers and murdering them in imaginatively grim fashion. All the confrontational scenes are violent and showcase Lee's martial-arts abilities. During this same period, five other characters are introduced—the sleazy pawnshop owner, Gideon (Jon Polito); Sarah's drug-addict mother, Darla (Anna Thomson); the film's primary villain, Top Dollar (Michael Wincott); his sadistic sister, Myca (Bai Ling); and his ruthless lieutenant, Grange (Tony Todd).

The final section of *The Crow* deals with Eric's discovery that Top Dollar is responsible not only for the murders of Draven and his girlfriend but for all the violence plaguing Detroit. On three separate occasions, the avenger gives the evildoer an opportunity to walk away from harm, but the charming and corrupt chieftain, who snacks on eyeballs for-

AWARDS AND NOMINATIONS

MTV Movie Awards 1994: Best Song ("Big Empty")
Nominations: Best Film, Best Male Performance (Lee)

mer lovers, refuses. The final showdown, played out on a church rooftop, surrounded by spires and gargoyles, costs him his life. The motion picture closes with Eric saying farewell to Albrecht, and Sarah receiving Shelly's engagement ring. The final sequence shows Eric being reunited with his dead sweetheart in the graveyard.

The Crow is a fascinating film to watch. The motion picture is taken from a comic-book series by writer/artist James O'Barr, who created the character in the early 1980's from a personal tragedy. Screenwriter David J. Schow and John Shirley adapted and rearranged the material for the screen. The book's dark Gothic quality is captured by production designer Alex McDowell, who creates wonderful atmospherics of death and decay, eerily reminiscent of *Batman* (1989) and *Blade Runner* (1982), but on a much smaller budget. The use of the crow, introduced at the opening and appearing continuously to the end, serves to unify the artistic, visual, psychological, and symbolic elements. The film, like O'Barr's original creation, was heavily inspired by American horror writer and poet Edgar Allan Poe. In one sequence, Draven even quotes from Poe's "The Raven," in case anyone misses the connection.

Credit should also go to Australian director Alex Proyas, better known for his American television commercials and rock videos. He, too, captures O'Barr's original vision, shows flashes of originality, introduces an interesting visual style, coaxes strongly etched performances from his cast, and sustains interest to the finale. Cinematographer Dariusz Wolski should also be mentioned for his collaborative contributions in creating a well-executed mythical world. Finally, Graeme Revell's haunting music score, complemented by fourteen rock songs, adds much to the film's overall effect. Within several weeks of release, the sound-track album quickly rose to number one on the music charts.

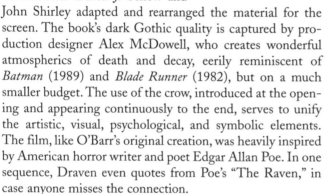

"People once believed that when someone dies, a crow carries their soul to the land of the dead. But, sometimes, something so bad happens that a terrible sadness is carried within and the soul can't rest. And...sometimes...just sometimes...the crow can bring that soul back to set the wrong things right."—Prologue from *The Crow*

The Crow, however, suffers from a number of critical weaknesses. First, and foremost, is the clunky plot, which is poorly written and suffers from continuity problem. There is no room for subtleties or interesting subplots. The film could have used more imaginative dialogue; the few witty one-liners given to Albrecht and Top Dollar begged for much more. All the actors playing villains give over-the-top performances as if in competition to win the most-scuzzy contest. The motion picture, sadly, failed to sustain a strong anticrime or antidrug message and glorifies violence for its own sake. Also, there is a slick superficial feel to the film that robs it of much-needed poignancy.

Even so, what makes *The Crow* work as an interesting, if flawed, film is Lee himself. The actor poured all his energies into it. He shed fifteen pounds for the role, modeled his character's look after rock singer Chris Robinson, and invested Eric with a gaunt, daunting cinematic aura. An avenging angel, clad in black with mime makeup, heightened by teardrops and black lips, Lee exuded sweetness, lithe grace, and mesmerizing intensity. Like other teen idols who die young such as James Dean and River Phoenix—Lee will be missed as much for his presence as well as his future promise.

—Terry Theodore

REVIEWS

Entertainment Weekly. May 13, 1994, p. 40.
The Hollywood Reporter. April 29-May 11, 1994, p. 6.
Los Angeles Times. May 11, 1994, p. F1.
The New York Times. May 11, 1994, p. B3.
Newsweek. CXXIII, May 16, 1994, p. 66.
People Weekly. XLI, May 16, 1994, p. 27.
Variety. April 29, 1994, p. 2.

Daddy and the Muscle Academy

This documentary celebrates the artistry of the late Tom of Finland, whose paintings of macho men wearing uniforms, leather, and other "masculine" attire served as inspiration to gay men.

REVIEWS

Atlanta Constitution. August 13, 1993, p. B7.
Boston Globe. March 12, 1993, p. 39.
Vogue. CLXXXII, December 1992, p. 104.

CREDITS

Origin: Finland
Released: 1992
Production: Kari Paljakka and Alvaro Pardo for Filmitakomo, supported by AVEK/the Finnish Film Foundation/Tom of Finland Foundation/YLE TV 2; released by Zeitgeist Films
Direction: Ilppo Pohjola
Screenplay: Ilppo Pohjola
Cinematography: Kjell Lagerroos
Editing: Jorma Hori
Sound: Pekka Karjalainen and Kauko Lindfors
Music: Elliot Sharp
MPAA rating: no listing
Running time: 55 minutes

Dangerous Game

"Brilliant!"—Paul Wunder, *WBAI Radio*

"It's a movie about the moviemaking process, and if Ferrara understands something about that, he knows at least as much about enacting solitude, emptiness, and rage."—J. Hoberman, *The Village Voice*

"Abel Ferrara is well known for having nerve to spare, and for stopping at nothing when it comes to putting his raw corrosive visions on screen." —Janet Maslin, *The New York Times*

Centering on filmmakers and filmmaking, this drama revolves around sadistic director Eddie Israel (Harvey Keitel) and the stars of the picture he is filming— Francis Burns (James Russo) and Sarah Jennings (Madonna)—whose off-screen lives parallel their on-screen ones. The stars find the on-camera violence spilling over into their tangled private lives while Eddie finds his personal traumas intruding into the fictional material. Madonna holds her own in her least showy role to date. Ferrera, director Abel's wife, sympathetically plays Eddie's betrayed and confused wife. Formerly known as *Snake Eyes*, the film is the first production by Madonna's own production company, Maverick.

REVIEWS

Boston Globe. March 11, 1994, p. 66.
Entertainment Weekly. December 3, 1993, p. 46.
Los Angeles Times. March 18, 1994, p. F10.
New Statesman & Society. VII, June 3, 1994, p. 40.
The New York Times. June 10, 1994, p. D16.
People Weekly. XL, November 29, 1993, p. 14.
Rolling Stone. December 9, 1993, p. 78.

CREDITS

Eddie Israel: Harvey Keitel
Sarah Jennings: Madonna
Francis Burns: James Russo
Madlyn Israel: Nancy Ferrara
Tommy: Reilly Murphy

Released: 1993
Production: Mary Kane for Mario and Vittorio Cecchi Gori, in association with Maverick Productions; released by Metro-Goldwyn-Mayer
Direction: Abel Ferrara
Screenplay: Nicholas St. John
Cinematography: Ken Kelsch
Editing: Anthony Redman
Production design: Alex Tavoularis
Sound: Greg Sheldon
Costume design: Marlene Stewart
Music: Joe Delia
MPAA rating: R
Running time: 107 minutes

> "*Dangerous Game* is a 'Bad Director' to Mr. Ferrara's previous *Bad Lieutenant*, with Harvey Keitel again personifying the filmmaker's darkest, most mischievous thought about the human condition."— Janet Maslin, *The New York Times*

The Dark Wind

Set on an Arizona reservation, this mystery centers on a murder investigation led by Navajo police officer Jim Chee (Lou Diamond Phillips). This is the first of Tony Hillerman's popular Native American mysteries coming to the screen. The name comes from the Navajo belief that a "dark wind" enters a man's soul when he does evil.

REVIEWS

Variety. CCCXLV, November 25, 1991, p. 41.

CREDITS

Officer Jim Chee: Lou Diamond Phillips
Lieutenant Joe Leaphorn: Fred Ward
Albert (Cowboy) Dashee: Gary Farmer
Jake West: John Karlen
Mr. Archer: Lance Baker
Larry: Gary Basaraba
Edna Nezzie: Arlene Bowman
Gail Pauling: Jane Loranger
Taylor: James Koots
Lomatewa: Neil Kayquoptewa
Ben Gaines: Blake Clark

Released: 1991
Production: Patrick Markey for Dark Wind Productions and Northfork Motion Picture Company; released by New Line Cinema
Direction: Errol Morris
Screenplay: Eric Bergren, Neal Jimenez, and Mark Horowitz; based on the novel by Tony Hillerman
Cinematography: Stefan Czapsky
Editing: Freeman Davies
Production design: Ted Bafaloukos
Art direction: John Reinhart
Set decoration: Corey Kaplan
Casting: Ellen Chenoweth
Sound: David Brownlow
Special sound effects: Randy Thom
Costume design: Eugenie Bafaloukos
Stunt coordination: Dan Bradley
Music: Michel Colombier
MPAA rating: no listing
Running time: 109 minutes

Deadfall

Featuring multiple cameo appearances, this mediocre *film noir* thriller centers on a con artist (Michael Biehn) whose relationship with his uncle, his dead father's identical twin brother (both roles played by James Coburn), incurs the jealousy of his uncle's partner (Nicolas Cage). Writer/director/producer Christopher Coppola is filmmaker Francis Coppola's nephew, and the film features a cameo appearance by Talia Shire, Christopher Coppola's aunt.

REVIEWS

Los Angeles Times. February 28, 1994, p. F8.

CREDITS

Joe Donan: Michael Biehn
Mike Donan: James Coburn
Eddie: Nicolas Cage
Diane: Sarah Trigger
Lou Donan: James Coburn

Released: 1994
Production: Christopher Coppola; released by Trimark Pictures
Direction: Christopher Coppola
Screenplay: Christopher Coppola
Cinematography: Maryse Alberti
Production design: Clare Scarpulla
Art direction: Paul Holt
Set design: Bruce Hill
Set decoration: Lisa Monti
Music: Jim Fox
MPAA rating: R
Running time: 98 minutes

Death and the Maiden

"Tonight, mercy will be buried with the past."
—Movie tagline
"Two thumbs up!"—*Siskel & Ebert*
"Unbelievably powerful"—*Sneak Previews*
"...electrifying."—*Rolling Stone*

Box Office Gross: $200,383 (January 2, 1995)

Ariel Dorfman's play about the nature of truth and justice is given an excellent film adaptation by renowned director Roman Polanski. It is a suspenseful psychological drama, well-acted by stars Sigourney Weaver, Ben Kingsley, and Stuart Wilson. Dorfman turned his play into a screenplay with the help of Rafael Yglesias without losing any of the play's inherent intensity. *Death and the Maiden* was first presented in the United States on Broadway, starring Glenn Close, Gene Hackman, and Richard Dreyfuss.

Death and the Maiden takes place in a "South American country" (probably Chile or Argentina) where a new democratic regime has recently come to power and is about to investigate the past abuses of power by the previous regime, a military dictatorship. Gerardo (Stuart Wilson) is an attorney whose political star is on the rise, having just been appointed by the president to head the investigation of those who were formerly in power. His wife, Paulina (Sigourney Weaver), is a victim of the former regime, having been incarcerated and tortured as a political prisoner.

All the film's action takes place in one night. The setting is Paulina and Gerardo's isolated beach house. Polanski and writers Dorfman and Yglesias provide much information, filling the screen with expectation and tension from the moment the credits roll: Paulina is seen setting a romantic dinner while a thunderstorm pelts the beach house with rain. Then the power goes out. It is clear from the outset that something is wrong with Paulina—she appears nervous and angry when her husband is late for dinner. When Gerardo arrives, it is discovered that his car had a flat tire, and he was driven home by a passerby, Dr. Roberto Miranda

(Ben Kingsley). Paulina, in the bedroom as Gerardo and Miranda arrive, hears Miranda's voice and is convinced that Miranda is the doctor who raped and tortured her many years ago. She never knew what he looked like, but she remembers the sound of his voice, a few idiomatic phrases he was in the habit of using, and the fact that he obsessively listened to Franz Schubert's classical piece entitled *Death and the Maiden*.

The rest of the film centers on Paulina's capture and mock trial of the mild-mannered Dr. Miranda, who insists he is not the man she thinks he is. Paulina ties Miranda to a chair, tapes his mouth shut, pistol-whips him, and threatens to kill him if he does not confess on videotape. Gerardo, dumbfounded, is caught in the middle between assisting his troubled wife and trying to figure out whether Miranda is indeed the man Paulina says he is or simply an innocent bystander. Gerardo becomes the eyes and the ears of the audience, who become the "jury," trying to assess the evidence and uncover the truth of the situation.

The filmmakers maintain a harrowing pitch as the night rolls on to the climax and resolution. Along the way, it becomes truly difficult for the audience, as well as Gerardo, to discern whether Paulina is crazy or Dr. Miranda is a liar. Evidence mounts that supports both theories. Ultimately, the film becomes a treatise about just how fragile the scales of justice are. Paulina and Miranda find themselves on opposite ends of the scales of justice, balanced by attorney Gerardo in the middle. The film raises interesting questions,

Sigourney Weaver as Paulina Escobar and Ben Kingsley as Dr. Alberto Miranda in *Death and the Maiden*. Photo: Francois Duhamel © 1994 Fine Line Features. All rights reserved.

such as whether revenge is justified or whether victims should take the law into their own hands.

The film also raises thoughts about how an individual's past can haunt and destroy a life. Polanski is clearly fascinated with this theme. After all, he fled the United States in the early 1970's after being found guilty of having sex with a minor. Ever since, Polanski's films can be viewed through the prism of this lens: Is he fascinated by the past because of his own demons, or is his interest merely academic? Clearly, films such as his *Bitter Moon* (reviewed in this volume), about the destruction of a man's life told in a series of flashbacks, indicate that Polanski has more than a passing interest in the past-present connection.

Either way, Polanski has long been considered a master of psychological suspense. In classics such as *Rosemary's Baby* (1968) and *Chinatown* (1974), and in such other films as *Repulsion* (1965), *The Tenant* (1976), and *Frantic* (1988), Polanski has provided audiences with films of eerie intensity, which he also does here. From the claustrophobic feeling of the beach house, to the potent scenes where Paulina threatens to rape Miranda with a broom handle, to the desperate final scene where Paulina nearly pushes Miranda over a cliff, Polanski causes the audience to feel as uncomfortable as the characters in the story. Polanski's genius is not in making the audience uncomfortable but in making them empathize with the characters while they are being taken on the psychological roller coaster provided by Dorfman's story.

CREDITS

Paulina Escobar: Sigourney Weaver
Dr. Roberto Miranda: Ben Kingsley
Gerardo Escobar: Stuart Wilson

Origin: USA, France, and Great Britain
Released: 1994
Production: Thom Mount and Josh Kramer, in association with Capitol Films and Mount/Kramer, in association with Channel 4 Films and Flach Films, with the participation of Canal Plus; released by Fine Line Features
Direction: Roman Polanski
Screenplay: Rafael Yglesias and Ariel Dorfman; based on the play by Dorfman
Cinematography: Tonino Delli Colli
Editing: Hervé De Luze
Production design: Pierre Guffroy
Art direction: Claude Moesching
Casting: Mary Selway and Patsy Pollock
Sound: Daniel Brisseau
Costume design: Milena Canonero
Music: Wojciech Kilar
MPAA rating: R
Running time: 103 minutes

AWARDS AND NOMINATIONS

Independent Spirit Awards Nomination 1995:
Best Director (Polanski)

Metaphorically, the film is about shedding light on the past. Consequently, much of the mysterious mood comes from the beautiful lighting by cinematographer Tonino Delli Colli. Because the story requires that the power is out in the beach house, and that there are no other sources of light nearby on the isolated cliff, Delli Colli's work was cut out for him. His use of candles and other soft lighting add to the suspense without sacrificing realism. A lighthouse in the distance, visible from the porch, and a huge full moon are utilized to great effect by Polanski and Delli Colli. The lighthouse may be symbolic of the beacon of truth, which shines far away from these troubled characters, but shines nevertheless. The moon provides an unearthly glow as it peeks from behind the thunderclouds.

Being a former resident of Chile and political prisoner, Ariel Dorfman knows this territory well. The dramatic event—Paulina's "arrest" and mock trial of Miranda—is embedded in an excellent dramatic structure. The action takes place in and around the beach house, all in one night. Dorfman further draws in his audience by observing the unities of time, place, and action. The sheer relentlessness of the film requires attention and emotional participation from the audience.

Of course, a small film such as this is driven by the performances. There are only three characters, and each actor splendidly contributes to the suspense. In the film's central role, Weaver is characteristically forceful and compelling. From *Aliens* (1986) to *Gorillas in the Mist* (1988), Weaver has given performances that utilize her own personal strength. It is important for the audience to believe that Paulina is as potentially dangerous as the man she thinks is her torturer. Weaver's intensity helps raise the question of whether her character is going too far. When Miranda pleads with Gerardo to not "just stand there," Weaver spits out the response "he's the law; that's all they do" with such venom as to make her character momentarily unsympathetic. She also occasionally indulges in some exaggerated histrionics to show her character's anxiety, such as in a monologue where Paulina describes how the doctor repeatedly raped her. Weaver's attempts at showing her character's fear and vulnerability are overplayed, however, making Paulina seem temporarily disingenuous. Nevertheless, it is a fine performance.

Where Weaver's histrionics can occasionally appear one-dimensional, Ben Kingsley delivers yet another under-

> "Don't just stand there."
> "He's the law; that's all they do."—Paulina Escobar responding to Dr. Roberto Miranda as he pleads with Gerardo Escobar in *Death and the Maiden*

stated and complex performance. With blood dripping down his face, begging to use the restroom, Miranda seems to be a gentle fool fearing for his life. Yet when the doctor brags about having power over his patients, saying "I could hurt them if I wanted to," he seems every bit the cold-blooded torturer.

Stuart Wilson rounds out the cast as Gerardo. In many ways, this is a more difficult role than the other two because of the very nature of the character: Stuck between two opposing forces, he is required to react more than anything else. Yet Wilson, an accomplished British actor, beautifully defines his character. A simple but evocative aspect of his character is provided by costumer Milena Canonero: Gerardo remains in his terry-cloth bathrobe throughout the film. His inability to think about getting dressed is indicative both of his indecisiveness and of the urgency of the situation. Wilson's open-mouthed expression at Paulina's account of the rapes, his bleary-eyed, testy attempts to assist Miranda in writing a confession that will please Paulina, and his desperate pleas for Paulina to allow the wheels of justice to turn on their own beautifully underscore his character's thematic place as the "jury." To put it another way, Wilson clearly defines his character's indecisiveness.

Death and the Maiden has momentum, suspense, a haunting score, fine performances, an excellent script, and strong direction. It is one of those films that audiences will discuss long after the film is over. Indeed, at the time of the film's release, high-profile trials, such as the O. J. Simpson and Rodney King cases, caused Americans to question their own justice system. That this film, about the nature of political and personal justice in a South American country, can have resonance for Americans is a testament to its brilliance.

—Kirby Tepper

REVIEWS

Daily Variety. December 9, 1994, p. 2.
Enteratinment Weekly. February 3, 1995, p. 32.
The Hollywood Reporter. December 9-11, 1994, p. 10.
Los Angeles Times. December 23, 1994, p. F16.
The New York Times. December 23, 1994, p. B3.

Death Wish V: The Face of Death

"No judge. No jury. No appeals. No deals."
—Movie tagline

 Box Office Gross: $1,677,262 (May 22, 1994)

Charles Bronson returns as vigilante Paul Kersey, who takes the law into his own hands in particularly gruesome fashion to avenge the murder of his fashion designer girlfriend (Lesley-Anne Down). Sequel to *Death Wish* (1974), *Death Wish II* (1982), *Death Wish III* (1985), and *Death Wish IV: The Crackdown* (1987).

REVIEWS

Entertainment Weekly. June 10, 1994, p. 70.
Los Angeles Times. January 17, 1994, p. F3.
The New York Times. January 17, 1994, p. C18.
Variety. CCCLIII, January 17, 1994, p. 105.
The Washington Post. January 15, 1994, p. G5.
The Washington Post. September 23, 1994, p. F7.

CREDITS

Paul Kersey: Charles Bronson
Olivia Regent: Lesley-Anne Down
Tommy O'Shay: Michael Parks
Tony Hoyle: Saul Rubinek
Lieutenant Mickey King: Kenneth Welsh
Chelsea Regent: Erica Lancaster

Released: 1994
Production: Damian Lee for Menahem Golan, Ami Artzi, and 21st Century Film Corporation; released by Trimark Pictures
Direction: Allan A. Goldstein
Screenplay: Allan A. Goldstein; based on characters created by Brian Garfield
Cinematography: Curtis Petersen
Editing: Patrick Rand
Production design: Csaba A. Kertesz
Casting: Kathy A. Smith and Anne Tait
Sound: Valentin Pricop
Music: Terry Plumeri
MPAA rating: R
Running time: 95 minutes

Desire (Salt on Our Skin)

Spanning three decades, this romantic drama centers on two lovers, George (Greta Scacchi) and Gavin (Vincent D'Onofrio), who are constantly drawn together yet never marry.

CREDITS

George: Greta Scacchi
Gavin: Vincent D'Onofrio
No character identified: Anais Jenneret
No character identified: Petra Berndt
No character identified: Claudine Auger
No character identified: Rolf Illig
No character identified: Laszlo I. Kish
No character identified: Shirley Henderson
No character identified: Hanns Zischler
No character identified: Barbara Jones

Origin: Germany, France, and Canada
Released: 1993
Production: Bernd Eichinger and Martin Moszkowicz for Constantin Film, in association with Torii Productions/Telescene Film Group, Inc./RTL and Canal Plus
Direction: Andrew Birkin
Screenplay: Andrew Birkin and Bee Gilbert; based on the novel *Les Vaisseaux du Coeur*, by Benoite Groult
Cinematography: Dietrich Lohmann
Editing: Dagmar Hirtz
Production design: Jean-Baptiste Tard and Robert Laing
Sound: Patrick Rousseau
Costume design: Catherine Leterrier
Music: Klaus Doldinger
MPAA rating: no listing
Running time: 110 minutes

Desperate Remedies

Box Office Gross: $56,788 (August 7, 1994)

Set in nineteenth century New Zeland, this period drama centers on a beautiful woman, Dorothea (Jennifer Ward-Lealand), who runs a dress shop with her lover, Anne (Lisa Chappell). When Dorothea tries to arrange a romance with her pregnant drug-addict sister, Rose (Kiri Mills), and a handsome sailor, Lawrence (Kevin Smith), Dorothea and Lawrence fall in love instead.

REVIEWS

The Advocate. May 3, 1994, p. 76.
Boston Globe. June 17, 1994, p. 77.
Los Angeles Times. July 20, 1994, p. F6.
The New York Times. May 23, 1994, p. C14.
Opera News. LVIII, May 1994, p. 58.
Variety. CCCLI, June 7, 1993, p. 42.

CREDITS

Dorothea Brook: Jennifer Ward-Lealand
Lawrence Hayes: Kevin Smith
Anne Cooper: Lisa Chappell
Fraser: Clifford Curtis
William Poyser: Michael Hurst
Rose: Kiri Mills

Origin: New Zealand
Released: 1993
Production: James Wallace; released by Miramax Films
Direction: Stewart Main and Peter Wells
Screenplay: Stewart Main and Peter Wells
Cinematography: Leon Narbey
Editing: David Coulson
Production design: Michael Kane
Art direction: Shane Redford
Costume design: Glenis Foster
Music: Peter Scholes
MPAA rating: no listing
Running time: 98 minutes

Destiny in Space

This IMAX documentary features breathtaking film footage shot on several space shuttle missions, combined with computer-generated images and narration by Leonard Nimoy.

REVIEWS

Chicago Tribune. July 17, 1994, Sec. 13 p. 12.
The Washington Post. July 1, 1994, p. WW48.
The Washington Post. June 22, 1994, p. D12.

CREDITS

Narrator: Leonard Nimoy

Origin: USA and Canada
Released: 1994
Production: Graeme Ferguson for the Smithsonian Institution's National Air and Space Museum and the Lockheed Corporation, in cooperation with the National Aeronautics and Space Administration; released by the IMAX Corporation
Direction: James Neihouse
Screenplay: Toni Meyers
Cinematography: James Neihouse and David Douglas
Editing: Toni Meyers
Sound: Peter Thillaye
Astronaut training management: James Neihouse
Music: Maribeth Solomon and Micky Erbe
MPAA rating: no listing
Running time: 40 minutes

Dialogues with Madwomen

Filmmaker Allie Light showcases seven mentally ill women from diverse backgrounds in this insightful and encouraging documentary.

CREDITS

Released: 1994
Production: Allie Light and Irving Saraf
Direction: Allie Light
Cinematography: Irving Saraf
Editing: Allie Light and Irving Saraf
Music: Rachel Bagby and Larry Seymour
MPAA rating: no listing
Running time: 90 minutes

REVIEWS

Atlanta Constitution. June 15, 1994, p. E11.
Atlanta Constitution. June 17, 1994, p. P5.
Boston Globe. June 17, 1994, p. 78.
Chicago Tribune. June 3, 1994, p. 7J.
Los Angeles Times. May 26, 1994, p. F4.
The Progressive. LVIII, February 1994, p. 12.
The Washington Post. July 15, 1994, p. B6.

Disclosure

"Sensational! A taut thriller that builds to a powerful climax."—Bob Diehl, *ABC Radio Network*

"A big-star crowd-pleaser with a big table-turning finale."—Mike Clark, *USA Today*

"The hot button, date movie of the year."—Peter Travers, *Rolling Stone*

"It's so much fun! You will be cheering. Michael Douglas is terrific."—Joel Siegel, *Good Morning America, ABC-TV*

 Box Office Gross: $51,674,942 (January 2, 1995

Based on Michael Crichton's best-selling, sensationalistic novel about a male victim of sexual harassment, *Disclosure* certainly offered a crack production team. Director Barry Levinson surely needed a successful picture to re-establish his bankability after *Jimmy Hollywood* (reviewed in this volume) and the infantile *Toys* (1992), both of which failed at the box office, offset the earlier successes of *Bugsy* (1991) and *Rain Man* (1988). Screenwriter Paul Attanasio, who had worked with Levinson on the innovative NBC television series *Homicide: Life on the Street*, also wrote the screenplay for *Quiz Show* (reviewed in this volume), which was well regarded in 1994 despite its liberties with the facts of that scandal. Although Todd McCarthy of *Variety* found

Crichton's novel "potentially risible," Attanasio managed to craft it into a plausible narrative.

Tom Sanders (Michael Douglas) is a forty-one-year-old high-tech yuppie engineer in charge of operations for a Seattle firm, Digital Communications Technology, about to be acquired by a New York publishing conglomerate, Conley-White. Sanders expects to be promoted to vice president and expects to make a fortune as a result of the merger. Tom's wife, Susan (Caroline Goodall), a lawyer, demands help getting the kids their breakfast on the eventful Monday the story begins. Hence, Tom is late for work and finds the company rife with rumors.

His one-time friend, Philip Blackburn (Dylan Baker), DigiCom's chief legal counsel, gives Tom the disappointing news that the new vice president for Advanced Operations and Planning will be a female hotshot from the Marketing Division, Meredith Johnson (Demi Moore), who had once been Tom's live-in lover before he got married. At the end of the workday, Meredith invites Tom to her office. He thinks this is an after-hours briefing, but he soon discovers that she apparently wants to resume their affair. In the novel, Meredith's secretary, Betsy Ross, thoughtfully provided Meredith with wine and condoms. Less interested in safe sex, however, the filmmakers have dispensed with the condoms.

After some foreplay and heavy breathing, Tom, though most certainly aroused, thinks of his wife and family and refuses penetration. In the novel, he later remembers that Meredith coughed during the foreplay, signaling to him subconsciously that she was not exactly swept away with passion but putting on an act. This is not explained in the film, but a

CREDITS

Tom Sanders: Michael Douglas
Meredith Johnson: Demi Moore
Bob Garvin: Donald Sutherland
Susan Hendler: Caroline Goodall
Philip Blackburn: Dylan Baker
Catherine Alvarez: Roma Maffia
Marc Lewyn: Dennis Miller
Ben Heller: Allan Rich
Don Cherry: Nicholas Sadler
Stephanie Kaplan: Rosemary Forsyth
Mary Anne Hunter: Suzie Plakson
Cindy Chang: Jacqueline Kim
John Conley, Jr.: Joe Urla

Released: 1994
Production: Barry Levinson and Michael Crichton for Baltimore Pictures/Constant c; released by Warner Bros.
Direction: Barry Levinson
Screenplay: Paul Attanasio; based on the novel by Michael Crichton
Cinematography: Anthony Pierce-Roberts
Editing: Stu Linder
Production design: Neil Spisak
Art direction: Richard Yanez-Toyon and Charles William Breen
Set decoration: Garrett Lewis
Casting: Ellen Chenoweth
Special visual effects: Industrial Light and Magic
Visual effects supervision: Eric Brevig
Sound: Steve Cantamessa
Costume design: Gloria Gresham
Music: Ennio Morricone
MPAA rating: R
Running time: 127 minutes

cough can be heard on the sound track, if purists are listening. Angry, embarrassed, and humiliated, Tom returns home with four deep scratches on his chest from the tussle, which became more violent after he rejected Meredith. He does not tell his wife about the incident that evening, although he obviously feels guilty about what has happened. His rejection of Meredith, after all, was tardy in this laptop seduction.

On Tuesday, he is late again for work because Meredith had left a misleading message with his wife concerning an important meeting. Much to his surprise, he discovers that Meredith has accused him of sexual harassment. As a result, Blackburn advises Tom that he will be transferred to another division of the company in Austin, Tex. Tom has heard rumors, however, that that division is to

> "You just lie back and let me be the boss."—Meredith Johnson from *Disclosure*

Blockbuster Entertainment Awards
1995: Drama—Actress, Theatrical (Moore)
MTV Movie Awards Nominations 1995:
Most Desirable Female (Moore); Best Villain (Moore)

be sold or closed. The transfer would be a dead-end move for him and cause him to lose a fortune in stock options because of the forthcoming merger.

Tom decides to fight back and file a countercharge of sexual harassment against Meredith. He contacts a tough-minded woman lawyer to represent him, Catherine Alvarez (Roma Maffia). In the novel, Tom explained to his wife what happened and sent her and the children out of town to Phoenix while he rode out the storm. In the film version, however, his wife stays in Seattle and attends the legal mediations on the case, a good opportunity to intensify the personal drama.

The mediation works to his advantage. When Meredith began making advances that Monday evening, Tom had just placed a call on his cellular telephone and the whole event was taped on the recording device of the person he called, as he later discovers. Although this is not admissible legal evidence, Tom's lawyer speculates significantly about the embarrassment that this tape would cause if it somehow got turned over to the media. This could endanger the merger, and Bob Garvin (Donald Sutherland), the founding president of DigiCom, decides to drop charges against Tom.

Nevertheless, the battle is not over yet, for there is a conspiracy afoot by Meredith, Blackburn, and Garvin. They plan to discredit Tom at a forthcoming meeting with Conley-White in such a way that he will seem to be incompetent and then fire him on that basis. The film dramatizes Tom's struggle for survival as he attempts to prepare himself for the final showdown.

At this point, the film turns into a techno-thriller. There are quality-control problems on the production line in Malaysia caused by Meredith, who has compromised the manufacturing process by making deals with the Malaysian government. Tom knows the units produced are not functioning properly, but he does not know why. The plant manager in Malaysia is in cahoots with Meredith, but fortunately Tom knows another man he can trust in Malaysia. From him, Tom gets the evidence he needs.

Meanwhile, Tom has been getting mysterious advice from odd E-mail correspondence signed "A Friend," urging him to "solve the problem" and advising him where to look for answers. This turns out to be part of the corporate espionage plot. Stephanie Kaplan (Rosemary Forsyth), an older and even more devious woman than Meredith, feeds Tom these anonymous E-mail tips because she intends to torpedo Meredith. Her son, Jonathan, works for a chemistry professor named Arthur A. Friend and has access to his professor's computer. Stephanie ends up being the new vice president in charge of Advanced Planning. With her in place, Tom is safe.

DigiCom has developed a state-of-the-art CD-ROM system, which Tom enters to search the files and research "the problem." This plot device is very cine-matic because it provides a wonderful excuse for high-tech visual effects (created by Industrial Light and Magic) that are fully and expertly exploited in the film. In both the novel and the film, Tom is locked out of the system. In the novel, he found a colleague's entry card, which did the trick for him. In the film, he breaks into a Conley-White hotel suite, where the technology has been set up for demonstration purposes. To have him breaking into the hotel room in the film makes for some tense moments as he is floating through cyberspace examining the "files," for at any time the Conley-White people could return to the room. Will he get out in time?

> The DigiCom office buildings in *Disclosure* were built on the Warner Bros. studio lot from scratch. Filming then moved to Seattle and director Levinson shot scenes in Pike Place Market, The Four Seasons Olympia Hotel, Pioneer Square, J&M Cafe, the Conservatory in Volunteer Park, and on Bainbridge Island. *Disclosure* marks the motion picture debut of comedian Dennis Miller.

The film's casting is peerless, though Demi Moore's vamp tramp is a one-dimensional cardboard cutout. As the wife Susan, Caroline Goodall plays a woman conflicted between sympathy and betrayal. She played Emilie Schindler in *Schindler's List* (1993), and her nondescript looks are a nice counterpoint to Demi Moore's sleek seductiveness. Roma Maffia convincingly plays the no-nonsense lawyer who has seen it all, a perfect advocate for Tom. Donald Sutherland plays Bob Garvin as a good-humored, devious villain, a double-dealer not to be trusted.

Michael Douglas is again ahead of the curve of trend-setting films. He was there dramatizing the awful complications of marital infidelity in *Fatal Attraction* in 1987, and he was there again dramatizing a crazed vigilante's response to urban crime in *Falling Down* in 1993. He has embraced controversial projects and has an instinctive awareness of issues that upset contemporary Americans. So does Michael Crichton, whose *Rising Sun* (1993) was as controversial in its own right as *Falling Down*. Both the actor and the novelist-producer know how to exploit the national psyche and to generate public interest in their work.

Despite the publicity, *Disclosure* is not so much about attempted rape or sexual harassment as it is about corporate intrigue and corruption; the seduction, in short, is merely a red herring, just as the murder of a call girl was a red herring in *Rising Sun*, which was also about corporate espionage and double-dealing. Tom Sanders is being framed in *Disclosure* and manipulated out of a power position by a deceptive femme fatale, a corporate whore who has slept her way to the top.

Tom fights back to save his reputation, his marriage, and his job. Sexual harassment, like rape, is not about sexual gratification; it is about power, and, as Tom asks reasonably at one point, "When did I have the power?" Meredith is his boss; he is her subordinate. Meredith is a classic femme fatale who uses her body to manipulate men to get what she wants. Her archetype can be traced back through fifty years of film history to the spiderwoman figure of *film noir*. She is a classic motion-picture villain, and the audience is gratified to see her get her comeuppance.

Some reviewers called the sexual harassment issue "silly" and criticized alleged holes in the plot. Lacking the fully developed context of the novel, the film may seem less than perfectly plotted, though in most respects it follows the novel's general design faithfully. Yet it is patently unfair to dismiss the plot as "silly." According to a report broadcast on National Public Radio, nine percent of the 12,000 sexual harassment cases on record for 1993 were filed by men. Moreover, *People Weekly* reported that, according to the federal government's Equal Employment Opportunity Commission, of 14,400 harassment cases filed in 1994, "roughly ten percent were brought by men—against both males and females."

So the role-reversal male victimization is happening in the workplace, and, as usual, Crichton is ahead of the curve in fabricating his plot dilemma. In an afterword to the novel, Crichton stated that the "episode related here is based on a true story." That being the case, life itself may be "silly," but the story is not. It is merely art imitating all-too-human nature. 🎞️

—*James M. Welsh*

REVIEWS

Baltimore Sun. December 9, 1994, Sec. E, p. 1.
Baltimore Sun. Maryland Live, December 9, 1994, p. 16.
Entertainment Weekly. December 16, 1994, p. 42.
The Hollywood Reporter. December 5, 1994, p. 8.
Los Angeles Times. December 9, 1994, p. F1.
The New York Times. December 9, 1994, p. B1.
The New Yorker. December 19, 1994, p. 107.
Newsweek. December 19, 1994, p. 63.
People Weekly. December 19, 1994, p. 21.
Time. December 19, 1994, p. 75.
USA Today. December 9, 1994, D1
Variety. December 5, 1994, p. 4.
The Washington Post. December 9, 1994, D1
The Washington Post Weekend. December 9, 1994, p. 55.
The Washington Times. December 9, 1994, C16.

Do or Die

"This may be the last game they'll ever play."
—Movie tagline

Two crack CIA operatives (Dona Speir and Roberta Vasquez) are hunted down by hitmen hired by an international gangster (Pat Morita), in this variation on *The Most Dangerous Game* (1932).

REVIEWS

Variety. CCCXLIII, June 17, 1991, p. 66.

CREDITS

Kaneshiro: Pat Morita
Richard Estaban: Erik Estrada
Donna Hamilton: Dona Speir
Nicole Justin: Roberta Vasquez
Bruce Christian: Bruce Penhall
Lucas: William Bumiller
Shane Abilene: Michael Shane
Atlanta Lee: Stephanie Schick
Silk: Caroline Liu
No character identified: Richard Cansino
No character identified: Chu Chu Malave
No character identified: Ava Cadell
No character identified: Skip Ward
No character identified: James Lew
No character identified: Eric Chen

Released: 1991
Production: Arlene Sidaris; released by Malibu Bay Films
Direction: Andy Sidaris
Screenplay: Andy Sidaris
Cinematography: Mark Morris
Editing: Michael Haight
Production design: Cherie Day Ledwith
Special effects: Eddie Surkin
Sound: Mike Hall and Ken Segal
Costume design: Merrie Lawson
Music: Richard Lyons
MPAA rating: R
Running time: 97 minutes

Docteur Petiot (Dr. Petiot)

This grisly tale centers on a French doctor (Michel Serrault) during World War II who murdered Jews whom he was pretending to help escape to Argentina, stole their belongings, and burned their bodies in his furnace.

REVIEWS

Atlanta Constitution. August 26, 1994, p. P3.
Playboy. XXXIX, May 1992, p. 22.
Premiere. IV, April 1991, p. 24.

CREDITS

Dr. Petiot: Michel Serrault
Drezner: Pierre Romans
Nathan Guzik: Zbigniew Horoks
Georgette Petiot: Berangere Bonvoisin
Celestin Nivelon: Andre Chaumeau
Madame Guzik: Aurore Prieto
Louis Rossignol: Maxime Coillion
Forestier: Andre Julien
Collard: Nini Crepon

Madame Kern: Nita Klein
Cecile Drezner: Martine Mongermont
Vampire: Jean Lio

Origin: France
Released: 1990
Production: Michel Serrault, Alain Sarde, and Philippe Chapelier-Dehesdin for M. S. Productions, Sara Films, and Cine 5, in association with Canal Plus; released by Aries Film Releasing
Direction: Christian de Chalonge

Screenplay: Dominique Garnier and Christian de Chalonge
Cinematography: Patrick Blossier
Editing: Anita Fernandez
Production design: Yves Brover
Production management: Francois Menny
Sound: Marie-Jeanne Wyckmans
Costume design: Corinne Jorry
Music: Michel Portal
MPAA rating: no listing
Running time: 102 minutes

Dr. Bethune

This biographical drama set in the 1930's centers on Canadian legend Dr. Norman Bethune (Donald Sutherland), who not only traveled to Spain where he fought for the Loyalists during the Spanish Civil War but also joined Mao Tse-tung in China as chief medical officer. Despite his many achievements, the film concentrates on his downside as he was also an alcoholic and a womanizer. Sutherland's performance shows the intensity and vision of a complicated man. He previously played the part in 1977's *Bethune*.

REVIEWS

Los Angeles Times. March 9, 1994, p. F6.
The New Republic. CCIX, August 2, 1993, p. 32.
Playboy. XL, September 1993, p. 18.

CREDITS

Dr. Norman Bethune: Donald Sutherland
Frances Penny Bethune: Helen Mirren
Mrs. Dowd: Helen Shaver
Chester Rice: Colm Feore
Mr. Tung: James Pax
Alan Coleman: Ronald Pickup
Dr. Chian: Guo Da
Marie-France Coudaire: Anouk Aimee

Origin: Canada
Released: 1993
Production: Nicolas Clermont and Pieter Kroonenberg for Filmline International, with the participation of Telefilm Canada, in association with China Film; released by Tara Releasing
Direction: Phillip Borsos
Screenplay: Ted Allan
Cinematography: Raoul Coutard and Mike Molloy
Editing: Yves Langlois and Angelo Corrao
Music: Alan Reeves
MPAA rating: no listing
Running time: 115 minutes

Double Dragon

"Evil has just met its match!"—Movie tagline
"A double blast of fun...an entertaining high energy mix."—*The New York Post*

 Box Office Gross: $2,431,309 (November 20, 1994)

Two teenage brothers—Jimmy Lee (Mark Dacascos) and Billy Lee (Scott Wolf—in a post-apocalyptic Los Angeles (it was actually filmed in Cleveland) battle the evil Koga Shuko (Robert Patrick), who seeks half of a magic medallion that is in their possession, in this action/adventure based on a popular video game. Directorial debut of James Yukich.

REVIEWS

Atlanta Constitution. November 4, 1994, p. P4.
Boston Globe. November 4, 1994, p. 50.
Chicago Tribune. November 4, 1994, p. 7M.
Entertainment Weekly. April 14, 1995, p. 72.
Los Angeles Times. November 4, 1994, p. F13.
The New York Times. November 4, 1994, p. C19.
The New York Times. November 13, 1994, Sec. 2 p. 28.
The New York Times. CXLIV, May 5, 1995, p. D17.
USA Today. November 4, 1994, p. D4.
The Washington Post. November 7, 1994, p. D3.

CREDITS

Koga Shuko: Robert Patrick
Jimmy Lee: Mark Dacascos
Billy Lee: Scott Wolf
Linda Lash: Kristina Malandro Wagner
Satori Imada: Julia Nickson
Marian Delario: Alyssa Milano

Released: 1994
Production: Sunil R. Shah, Ash R. Shah, Alan Schechter, Jane Hamsher, and Don Murphy for Imperial Entertainment, Scanbox, and Greenleaf; released by Gramercy Pictures
Direction: James Yukich
Screenplay: Michael Davis and Peter Gould; based on a story by Paul Dini and Neal Shusterman
Cinematography: Gary Kibbe
Editing: Florent Retz
Production design: Mayne Berke
Art direction: Maya Shimoguchi
Set decoration: Kristan Andrews
Casting: Harriet Greenspan and Annette Benson
Special effects: Joseph Lombardi and Paul Lombardi
Sound: Patrick Hanson
Costume design: Fiona Spence
Stunt coordination: Jeff Imada
Music: Jay Ferguson
MPAA rating: PG-13
Running time: 95 minutes

 "I just want total domination of one American city. Is that too much to ask?"—*Double Dragon*'s Koga Shuko

Dream Lover

Box Office Gross: $210,652 (May 30, 1994)

One of screenwriter Nicholas Kazan's most celebrated pieces of dialogue occurs in *Reversal of Fortune* (1990), the film based on the Claus von Bülow trial. Defense attorney Alan Dershowitz has just concluded a cryptic and perhaps incriminating conversation with his client, von Bülow, the bizarre socialite accused of trying to murder his wife. von Bülow, played by Jeremy Irons, is getting into his chauffeur-driven car. "You're a very strange man, Claus," Dershowitz says as a parting shot. Replies von Bülow, hinting at depths of depravity inconceivable to Dershowitz, "You have no idea."

This exchange sums up both Kazan's view of the strangeness of the damaged human heart and Kazan's methods, as a screenwriter, of keeping that strangeness tantalizingly mysterious and ultimately unknowable. Each of Kazan's previous screenplays—*Frances* (1982), *At Close Range* (1986), *Patty Hearst* (1988), and *Reversal of Fortune*—has at its core strange, damaged characters and the twisted relationships they form, between mother and daughter, father and son, a captive and her kidnappers, a potentially murderous husband and a potentially suicidal wife. Yet each screenplay also uses devices that distance the audience from the true horror of these relationships by showing the characters' own unawareness of that horror.

In *Frances*, the glamour of Hollywood conceals from Frances Farmer her pathological struggle with her mother. The desire of the characters played by Sean and Chris Penn to be close to their father in *At Close Range* blinds them to his criminal madness. Telling Patty Hearst's story entirely from her point of view merely accentuates the mystery of how she gave herself over to her captors' cause. Finally, Sunny von Bülow's blackly comical narration from a coma in *Reversal of Fortune* coyly refuses to tell whether she or her husband is responsible for her condition—and intimates that she does not care. Thus Kazan's screenplays provide more questions than answers, dealing in labyrinths of guilt and responsibility. Kazan makes it impossible for the audience to fathom completely the damage at the hearts of his characters because the characters cannot fathom it themselves—they merely act out the damage, with tragic results. His characters are engaged in dances of death.

In *Dream Lover*, his directorial debut, Kazan makes this theme of the dance of death, of the impossibility of one damaged individual's truly knowing another, the center of his *film noir* plot. A man whose cool, stylish demeanor and milieu conceal his violent impulses even from himself falls in love with a beautiful woman and discovers—too late—both that she is not who she seems to be and that he is not the docile man he thought he was. Unfortunately, this time out, Kazan takes his tendency to make his characters unknowable too far. Whereas Kazan's making real-life characters such as Frances Farmer, Patty Hearst, and Claus and Sunny von Bülow inscrutable allows the audience to ponder the complexity of their real tragedies and to see their loneliness, his making fictional characters inscrutable diminishes them to the point where it feels like cheating.

In *Dream Lover*, Kazan's two main characters are so oversimplified that they become cardboard pawns at the mercy of a complex *film noir* plot. Oddly, Kazan dispenses with his usually acute understanding of the psychology of damaged characters and gives his characters here so little substance that the film's plot ultimately comes to seem as manipulative as the film's femme fatale antagonist. Kazan seems shackled, like so many other contemporary filmmakers, by the outdated conventions of the *noir* genre.

Ray Reardon (James Spader) is a thirtyish, recently divorced architect whose days seem to have the quality of waking dreams. Ray spends most of his time in upscale offices, in galleries, and at tony wedding receptions where white, glass, aluminum, blond wood, and fancy suits dominate. Ray's sleep, however, is filled with nightmares of seedy carnivals inhabited by clowns and sideshow hags. Even Ray's dreams seem shallow caricatures of scary dreams that betray Ray's fear that the thin, stylish veneer of his waking life conceals a grotesque freak show.

In the film's first waking scene, Ray ceases to contest his unfaithful former wife's divorce settlement, apparently because he wants to be a nice guy. In the following scene, however, Kazan begins to question Ray's values: Ray refuses to lend his "best" friend Norman (Larry Miller) $10,000, ostensibly because "it isn't my job to rescue you from yourself." Kazan implies, by contrasting Norman's annoying pushiness and penchant for sweating with Ray's expansive office, that in fact Ray refuses Norman

Nicholas Kazan got the idea for *Dream Lover*, his directorial debut, from his girlfriend's strange behavior.

because Norman is simply not as attractive as the former wife to whom he has just given half his estate. In addition to Ray's obsession with appearances, Kazan provides one other salient detail: When Ray found out that his wife was having an affair, he slapped her. Unfortunately, this dichotomy in Ray's personality, between the shallow obsession with appearances and a "violent" undercurrent, remains largely undeveloped. Thus his transition from yuppie to violent, desperate man seems mechanistic, fated.

Ray then meets the mysterious and alluring Lena (Mädchen Amick), who seems the embodiment of everything he wants: Her body and face are beautiful; her remarks are suggestive; her smile is feral. Ray does business in Japan; Lena speaks Chinese. Ray becomes instantly obsessed with her, and within a few dreamlike scenes, they have made love, gotten married, and had a child. Lena reveals, however, that she was severely abused by her parents: "My mother used to hit me a lot.... My father watched."

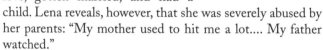

"Doesn't life seem sometimes...like this very strange dream?"—Lena, from *Dream Lover*

Ray, however, feels blessed that "the most beautiful creature on Earth" has chosen him and vows to take care of her. Kazan effectively uses extreme close-ups and disorienting jumps in time and place during this sequence to convey the dreamlike nature of how Ray experiences life and his

two-year whirlwind romance with Lena. Yet this device is ultimately the film's fatal flaw: By deliberately collapsing the early part of their relationship into a dreamlike fugue, Kazan omits scenes in which Ray and Lena would presumably have to have gotten to know each other. When Lena's deceptions crop up later on, it seems odd that Ray would not have caught on earlier. His obsession with her appearance as the sole explanation for his blindness seems more imposed by Kazan than deriving from a full-bodied character.

Doubts about Lena's identity now begin to surface—fellow restaurant diners recognize her as someone else from Texas, and Ray catches her in a lie about the college she claims to have attended. The mounting discrepancies in Lena's past finally send Ray on a trip to Texas to ferret out his wife's true identity. He finds her parents, and, far from being abusive, they seem merely boring and banal. They welcome Ray, who brings them home to force a confrontation. Lena admits to Ray that she invented herself and was "afraid if you knew the real me I would lose you." Says Ray, "No matter who you were, no matter who you are, no matter who you will be, I will always love you."

What Ray cannot know is that Lena is a sociopath— perhaps not abused the way she described, but the victim of some type of damage early on. Ray begins to find evidence that she is having an affair—hotel bills, telephone conversations cut short when he enters the room, a "friend" of Lena's showing up in his office as a temporary secretary. When Ray becomes violent and Lena has him committed to an institution, the final deception is revealed: Lena picked Ray years ago as a potentially rich husband and played her part as "dream lover" to the hilt. She then coaxed out the violent, jealous instincts she knew lurked beneath Ray's need to look good and to be in control so she could inherit his estate.

The notion that Lena has maneuvered Ray into both marriage and an insane asylum—that in this dance of death she has led every step of the way—is a big conceit to swallow, and it sinks the film. Kazan's excuse that, in Lena's words, "doesn't life seem sometimes...like this very strange dream?" by this time looks more like an excuse to keep the incredible plot in motion than a governing aesthetic. By contrast, the dreamscape in David Lynch's *Twin Peaks: Fire Walk with Me* (1992) is revealed to be the world as seen through the mind of a desperate, sexually abused teenager acting out psychotically; the seemingly mad dreamscape in fact has a tragic, moral center. In *Dream Lover*, the dreamscape is revealed to be the result of one woman's expert psychological manipulation of one man's neuroses and insecurities, more a function of plot than of real tragedy.

So little information is given about each character's life beneath the surface that both Ray and Lena seem paper-thin

CREDITS

Ray Reardon: James Spader
Lena Reardon: Mädchen Amick
Elaine: Bess Armstrong
Larry: Fredric Lehne
Norman: Larry Miller
Martha: Kathleen York
Cheryl: Blair Tefkin
Billy: Scott Coffey
Judge: Clyde Kusatsu
Buddy: William Shockley

Released: 1994
Production: Sigurjon Sighvatsson, Wallis Nicita, and Lauren Lloyd for Polygram Filmed Entertainment and Propaganda Films, in association with Nicita/Lloyd Productions and Edward R. Pressman; released by Gramercy Pictures
Direction: Nicholas Kazan
Screenplay: Nicholas Kazan
Cinematography: Jean-Yves Escoffier
Editing: Jill Savitt and Susan Crutcher
Production design: Richard Hoover
Art direction: Bruce Hill
Set decoration: Brian Kasch
Casting: Johanna Ray
Sound: David Brownlow and Mary Jo Devenney
Costume design: Barbara Tfank
Music: Christopher Young
MPAA rating: R
Running time: 103 minutes

by film's end—Ray an object example of the unexamined life gone wrong, and Lena merely a catalyst for Ray's transformation. The film's final twist—Ray's outwitting Lena as his true, violent nature comes to the surface—seems predetermined, rather than emerging from believable characters. Kazan has simply not provided enough information about his characters to begin with to allow him to withhold even more as required by the intricate plotting of the mystery genre.

In his previous films, Kazan, by refusing to settle for simple, pop psychological explanations for his characters' actions, created a body of work that underlined the impossibility of understanding an individual in his or her full complexity, yet ennobled the search of flawed protagonists—Frances Farmer, Patty Hearst, Alan Dershowitz—for the truth. In *Dream Lover*, Kazan attempts to infuse the *noir* genre with that sensibility: It may simply be a genre that cannot take the weight.

—*Paul Mittelbach*

REVIEWS

The Hollywood Reporter. April 11, 1994, p. 49.
Los Angeles Times. May 6, 1994, p. F8.
The New York Times. May 6, 1994, p. B13.
Rolling Stone. June 2, 1994, p. 78.
Variety. CCCLIV, April 11, 1994, p. 7.
Vogue. CLXXXIV, May, 1994, p. 153.
The Wall Street Journal. May 19, 1994, p. A12.

Dream of Light (El Sol del Membrillo)

Real-life Spanish painter Antonio Lopez Garcia stars in this fictional documentary that focuses on the creative process. As the artist paints a quince tree in his backyard, friends and admirers drop by to visit, thus providing snippets of information about the artist and his life.

REVIEWS

Boston Globe. July 7, 1994, p. 55.
Film Quarterly. XLVI, Spring 1993, p. 41.

AWARDS AND NOMINATIONS

Cannes Film Festival Awards 1992:   Jury Prize

CREDITS

No character identified:	Antonio Lopez Garcia
No character identified:	Maria Moreno
No character identified:	Enrique Gran
No character identified:	Jose Carrtero
No character identified:	Maria Lopez Garcia
No character identified:	Carmen Lopez Garcia
No character identified:	Elisa Ruiz
No character identified:	Amalia Avia
No character identified:	Lucio Munoz
No character identified:	Esperanza Parada
No character identified:	Julio Lopez Fernandez
No character identified:	Janusz Pietrziak
No character identified:	Marek Domagala
No character identified:	Grzegorz Ponikwia
No character identified:	Fan Xiao Ming
No character identified:	Yan Sheng Dong

Origin: Spain
Released: 1992
Production: Maria Moreno, with the participation of Euskal Media and Igeldo Zine Produkzioak
Direction: Victor Erice
Screenplay: Victor Erice and Antonio Lopez Garcia
Cinematography: Javier Aguirresarobe, Angel Luis Fernandez and Jose Luis Lopez Linares
Editing: Juan Ignacio San Mateo
Music: Pascal Gaigne
MPAA rating: no listing
Running time: 139 minutes

DROP Squad

"No struggle, no progress."—Movie tagline

Members of an African American vigilante-style group—the Deprogramming and Restoration of Pride (DROP) Squad—target a young black advertising executive, Bruford Jamison, Jr. (Eriq LaSalle), to try to persuade him to see the error of his ways. Because the group feels that Jamison creates ad campaigns that are demeaning to blacks, they kidnap him and attempt to brainwash him, even resorting to violence when they believe it to be necessary. Based on the short story "The Deprogrammer" by David Taylor.

REVIEWS

Atlanta Constitution. October 28, 1994, p. P3.
Atlanta Constitution. January 27, 1995, p. P8.
Chicago Tribune. October 28, 1994, p. 7M.
Entertainment Weekly. April 7, 1995, p. 104.
Los Angeles Times. October 28, 1994, p. F6.
The New York Times. October 28, 1994, p. C19.
Variety. XXXLVI, October 24, 1994, p. 67.
The Washington Post. October 28, 1994, p. F7.
The Washington Post. April 14, 1995, p. D6.

 "Sometimes when you get over the wall, you gotta throw a rope back—not help them build it higher."—*DROP Squad*

CREDITS

Bruford Jamison, Jr.: Eriq LaSalle
Rocky Seavers: Vondie Curtis-Hall
Garvey: Ving Rhames
June Vanderpool: Kasi Lemmons
XB: Leonard Thomas
Stokely: Eric A. Payne
Mali: Vanessa Williams
Trevor: Michael Ralph
Huey: Billy Williams
Lenora Jamison: Nicole Powell
Berl (Flip) Mangum: Afemo Omilami
Spike Lee: Spike Lee
Dwania Ali: Crystal Fox

Released: 1994
Production: Shelby Stone and Butch Robinson for Spike Lee and 40 Acres and a Mule Filmworks; released by Gramercy Pictures
Direction: David Johnson
Screenplay: David Johnson and Butch Robinson; based on a story by David Taylor
Cinematography: Ken Kelsch
Editing: Kevin Lee
Production design: Ina Mayhew
Art direction: Paul Weathered
Set decoration: Judy Rhee
Production management: Buddy Enright
Casting: Jaki Brown-Carmen
Sound: Matthew Price
Costume design: Darlene Jackson
Music: Mike Bearden
MPAA rating: R
Running time: 86 minutes

Drop Zone

"Something Dangerous is in the Air."—Movie tagline

"...a chute-to-thrill adventure."—Ron Brewington, *American Urban Radio Network*

"If you liked the adrenaline rush of *Speed,* see what a free fall from a plane traveling at 200 miles an hour does for ya!"—Lisa Schwarzbaum, *Entertainment Weekly*

Box Office Gross: $23,058,218 (January 2, 1995)

Director John Badham, who was at the helm of *Saturday Night Fever* (1977) and *WarGames* (1983), directs this thriller about skydiving. It is intended to be a fast-paced and exciting view into the rough-and-tumble world of skydiving. Admittedly, the skydiving sequences, directed primarily by second-unit director and co-producer D.J. Caruso, are truly thrilling. Unfortunately, a predictable plot, flat dialogue, and stereotyped characters render this film earthbound.

Yet, *Drop Zone* appears to have a *raison d'etre* that transcends plot and dialogue. This film clearly is a labor of love for its dedicated creative team, which has an admirable reverence for its subject. The story was coauthored by Guy Manos, a skydiving world-record holder and world champion. Two of the film's stars, Gary Busey and Michael Jeter, are amateur sky divers, and in interviews, director Badham and star Wesley Snipes have said that during filming they developed a love for the sport as well.

Wesley Snipes and Malcolm-Jamal Warner as U.S. marshalls Pete and Terry Nessip in *Drop Zone.* © 1994 Paramount Pictures. All rights reserved.

As the film opens, U.S. marshal Pete Nessip (Snipes) and his brother (Malcolm-Jamal Warner), also a U.S. marshal, are escorting a convicted computer hacker named Earl Leedy (Jeter), when their airplane is taken over by a team of daredevil sky divers who kidnap Leedy, kill Pete's brother, nearly blow up the plane, and escape via parachute. Eventually it is discovered that the skydiving team, led by the sinister Ty Moncrief (Busey), is working with computer wizard Leedy on a plot to enter U.S. government computers and identify all undercover Drug Enforcement Administration operatives.

At first, it appears as if Pete is at fault for his brother's death, and he is put on suspension from the U.S. Marshal Service. He insists, however, that his brother's death was not his fault, and somehow he correctly concludes that Leedy is alive and well and working in conjunction with his brother's killers.

It is standard in action films for the hero to be "fighting the system," and this film is no exception. Pete goes on a mission of his own to avenge his brother's death, prove who the real culprits are, and bring them to justice. This is not unlike the basis of another Snipes vehicle, *Boiling Point* (1993), in which his law-enforcement, good-guy character goes on an obsessive manhunt for the murderer of his buddy and partner. Perhaps it is time for this character type— the renegade cop who is taking the law into his own hands—to be put to rest for awhile.

Then again, perhaps it is expecting too much of an action film to break the mold in every aspect of its production. After all, this film does stray from convention in its use of the world of skydiving as a backdrop for the rest of the story. Pete decides that the only way to capture the band of sky divers is to integrate himself into the relatively small society of sky divers. It may appear illogical to the audience when Pete says, of the criminals, "I'm not going to catch them down here," as justification for his learning skydiving. Yet, when a film promises to deliver action, logic sometimes takes a backseat to thrills and chills.

Pete joins up with attractive female sky diver Jessie (Yancy Butler), who has reasons of her own for wanting to capture the gang of evil sky divers. That no romance appears to develop between Pete and Jessie is one of the film's strong points, in that it reinforces the idea that men and women are capable of having strong friendships as well as romantic relationships. Further, their platonic friendship proves to be a respite from the many clichés the story has to offer.

In order to find Moncrief's gang, Jessie and Pete travel to a skydiving show in Washington, D.C., forming a team with fellow daredevils Selkirk (Corin Nemec) and Swoop (Kyle Secor). Swoop actually proves to be a perplexing and moderately irritating character; he is legendary in the community of sky divers, inciting thunderous shouts of "Swoop! Swoop! Swoop!" from large crowds of people at the skydiving show. As played by Secor, he looks a bit like a regular guy from the suburbs who considers himself to be "zany," rather than the reckless hellion revered by the other characters. His primary identifying characteristic is that he refuses to speak to people unless he has shared a skydiving adventure with them. When he finally acknowledges Pete, the moment appears to be intended as a significant one for Pete, but for the audience it is merely another inevitable plot point.

The elaborate stunt work demanded by the film's aerial sequences required the hiring of a large team of professional skydivers. The leader of the team was the co-author of script, Guy Manos, who is a sky-diving world champion.

Eventually Pete, Jessie, and their team enter the skydiving contest over Washington, D.C., and discover the villainous plot to take over the Drug Enforcement Administration computers. Not surprisingly, the good guys prevail. Interestingly, the film's climax does not occur in the sky, but in an office building. This is surprising given the brilliant direction and choreography used in the skydiving scenes.

Director Badham and second-unit director D.J. Caruso have fashioned some remarkable scenes in the sky, and these scenes are what give the film its excitement. For example, there is an adrenaline-pumping scene in which Selkirk's parachute does not open, and Swoop must save him. Another exciting scene is one in which Moncrief performs the reckless murder of one of his henchmen—by causing him to be caught in an electrical tower during a routine jump. Another scene displays a group of virtuoso sky divers performing an intricate series of formations in the sky; with their red, white, and blue uniforms and dance-like movements, they resemble formations of dancers from the old Busby Berkeley films. Clever editing by Frank Morriss and fine photography by Roy Wagner make it hard to discern whether these stunts were actually filmed in the air with stunt actors, or were done against a "blue screen" with the real actors. It is this kind of technical expertise that virtually defines American filmmaking—and, in particular, American action-filmmaking.

Badham also excels in the film's early hijacking sequence, in which the villains blow open a hole in a flying passenger jet. The ensuing chaos and pandemonium are reminiscent of the superb air-crash sequence in Peter Weir's *Fearless* (1993). People are blown to the back of the plane, along with falling luggage, oxygen masks, and personal belongings; screams and cries fill the air; and the plot presses forward as the gang of thieves captures Leedy, kills Pete's brother, and escapes. It is a riveting and taut episode, which demonstrates Badham's prowess with the visual aspects of film as a medium.

It is difficult to report that Badham demonstrates less prowess with the dialogue sequences in *Drop Zone*. When Jessie first meets Pete, she says, "You're either a cop or a sky diver, and you don't look like any sky diver I've ever seen." With this rather trite introduction to her character, it becomes hard for Yancy Butler to infuse Jessie with anything more than a two-dimensional, tough-as-nails characterization reminiscent of those found in one-hour television cop dramas. Badham also allows some questionable clowning from Snipes—press materials indicate that Snipes would spontaneously add humor to spice up the proceedings. Rather than add the irony similar to that which audiences found in *Terminator II: Judgment Day* (1991) when Arnold Schwarzenegger said, "Hasta la vista, baby," however, Snipes confines his humor to smirks and mugging, which do not

CREDITS

Pete Nessip: Wesley Snipes
Ty Moncrief: Gary Busey
Jessie Crossman: Yancy Butler
Earl Leedy: Michael Jeter
Selkirk: Corin Nemec
Swoop: Kyle Secor
Jagger: Luca Bercovici
Terry Nessip: Malcolm-Jamal Warner
Bobby: Rex Linn
Winona: Grace Zabriskie
Deputy Dog: Robert LaSardo
Torski: Sam Hennings
Kara: Claire Stansfield
Deuce: Mickey Jones
Tom McCracken: Andy Romano

Released: 1994
Production: D. J. Caruso, Wallis Nicita, and Lauren Lloyd; released by Paramount Pictures
Direction: John Badham
Screenplay: Peter Barsocchini and John Bishop; based on a story by Tony Griffin, Guy Manos, and Barsocchini
Cinematography: Roy H. Wagner
Editing: Frank Morriss
Production design: Joe Alves
Casting: Carol Lewis
Sound: Russell Williams II
Costume design: Mary Vogt
Skydiving supervision: Guy Manos
Aerial stunt coordination: B. J. Worth
Music: Hans Zimmer
MPAA rating: R
Running time: 101 minutes

provide any ironic commentary. He unfortunately appears as if he is trying to be funny, rather than being himself.

Snipes is a gifted and charismatic actor, who has proven himself in numerous films where the material was not as impressive as he was: *Boiling Point (1993)*, *Demolition Man* (1993), and *Passenger 57* (1992) are all examples of less-than-brilliant material enlivened by Snipes's screen presence. He throws himself into this role with gusto, having learned to sky dive prior to the production, and providing a character whose anguish at the loss of his brother is replaced by determination to set the record straight.

Gary Busey is a characteristically reckless good ol' boy—and an evil one at that. Busey always appears to be comfortable on the screen, and transmits that feeling to his audience. He is believable and fun to watch. Even in the face of the aforementioned trite dialogue, Busey seems to have a good time. Early in the film, in a scene with Michael Jeter as Leedy, Moncrief tells him, "you're mine now," to indicate that Leedy owes him his life. A cliché such as this can only be delivered by an assured actor, and Busey is the man to do it.

"You're either a cop or a sky diver, and you don't look like any sky diver I've ever seen."—Jessie upon meeting Pete, in *Drop Zone*

Also assured and winning is Michael Jeter as the nerdy Earl Leedy. Jeter is remembered for his Emmy-winning performances on television's *Evening Shade*, starring Burt Reynolds. Jeter, a Tony Award winner as well, for the Broadway musical *Grand Hotel*, is as unusual and likable as ever.

All in all, *Drop Zone* is a diverting but sometimes trite film with interesting action sequences. If it misses in its attempt to become a film with the momentum of *Speed* (reviewed in this volume), or even *Terminal Velocity* (reviewed in this volume), it should at least be acknowledged for having great respect for its subject.

—*Kirby Tepper*

REVIEWS

Daily Variety. December 9, 1994, p. 8.
Entertainment Weekly. December 16, 1994, p. 46.
The Hollywood Reporter. December 9-11, 1994, p. 10.
Los Angeles Times. December 9, 1994, p. F6.
The New York Times. December 9, 1994, p. B4.

D2: The Mighty Ducks

"The Mighty Ducks are back!"—Movie tagline

"Duck power triumphs again."—*American Movie Classics*

"Twice as many laughs as the original."—Jeffery Lyons, *Sneak Previews*

 Box Office Gross: $45.6 million (February 1995)

In the initial film *The Mighty Ducks* (1992), hockey coach Gordon Bombay (Emilio Estevez) transformed a clumsy crew of prepubescents into a lucky team that won a championship. The surprising box-office success of that film has helped spawn a series of similar high-grossing, "feel-good" sports films in which, to quote Time magazine's Richard Corliss, "nice guys always finish first." Corliss refers to such films as a whole new genre, which includes such imminent releases as *Major League II, Angels in the Outfield, Little Big League* (all reviewed in this volume), and Steven Spielberg's *Little Heroes.*

D2: The Mighty Ducks picks up where the original story left off. As the film opens, a knee injury has sidelined Bombay's professional hockey career, forcing him to sharpen skates at a local shop owned by the grandfatherly Jan (Jan Rubes). Bombay longs to be back on the ice and is bitter about the cheap shot that ended his career. Unknown to Bombay, Jan has arranged for Don Tibbles (Michael Tucker) to visit the shop. Tibbles is senior vice president of Hendrix, Inc., a marketing corporation eager to sponsor Team USA at the Junior Goodwill Games, and Tibbles wants Bombay to coach.

Seizing the challenge, Bombay resurrects his lucky wooden duck call and begins rounding up the old "Ducks." These include teammates Charlie (Joshua Jackson), Averman (Matt Doherty), Jesse (Brandon Adams), Connie (Marguerite Moreau), Goldberg (Shaun Weiss), Banks (Vincent A. Larusso), Guy (Garette Ratliff Henson) and Fulton (Elden Ryan Ratliff).

Bombay then sets out to add some depth to his team. He finds Luis (Mike Vitar), the fastest Cuban skater in Miami, whose only weakness is his inability to stop. Texas cowboy Dwayne (Ty O'Neal) is an excellent puck handler but cannot avoid the temptation to show off. Champion goalie Julie (Colombe Jacobsen) hails

Before filming *D2: The Mighty Ducks*, all actors had to go through an eight-week hockey camp to get in shape. To achieve the authentic look of an international championship game, over 24,000 extras filled the arena. Filming of *D2* inaugurated the brand new Anaheim Arena (The Pond).

from Maine and can stop anything slower than a rifle bullet. Korean-American Ken Wu (Justin Wong) is an Olympic figure skater, whose graceful leaps and twists enable him to float past baffled defenders. Finally, Portman (Aaron Lohr) becomes the team's strongman, whose lack of hockey talent is more than compensated for by his goonlike mentality and willingness to fight.

Coaching this chaotic group is no picnic for Bombay, especially when Tibbles begins adding his two cents at the training sessions. Enticing Bombay into the back seat of a limousine, Tibbles fast-talks the coach into signing a lucrative endorsement contract. To further complicate matters, the children are not allowed to compete unless they also continue their schooling under tutor Michele (Kathryn Erbe), who is suspicious of the corrupting influence of the Hendrix sponsorship. Her fears are soon borne out, as the children find their pictures on the front of Wheaties cereal boxes and their old Mighty Ducks uniforms discarded in favor of new ones bearing the Hendrix logo.

The Junior Goodwill Games open in Los Angeles, with Bombay's Team USA facing a weak team from Trinidad. After winning easily, however, Team USA finds itself taunted by the heavily favored Team Iceland. Its coach—the malevolent Wolf (Carsten Norgaard)—promises that Team USA will be defeated.

Encouraged by Team USA's easy victory over Trinidad, Tibbles beguiles Coach Bombay into accepting an expensive Malibu condo rather than stay with the team, who are housed in a common dormitory. In blatant contrast to Tibbles' assurances that dorm life will be good for the kids, loud music and dorm pranks add up to a lack of sleep for the now leaderless team. Furthermore, as the boys cruise the streets of Los Angeles, they are shocked to spot Coach Bombay out on a date with Marria (Maria Ellingsen), the beautiful trainer from Team Iceland.

Despite their lack of sleep, the Ducks manage to trounce Team Italy, after which Tibbles arranges a cocktail party at Coach Bombay's Malibu condo. Numerous sports real-life stars are invited, treating the film audience to cameo appearances by Kareem Abdul-Jabbar, Cam Neely, Chris Chelios, Luc Robitaille, Greg Louganis, and Kristi Yamaguchi.

The following day, the Ducks face the dreaded Team Iceland. Portman is thrown out of the match in the early stages and the Ducks are demolished in a lopsided game. As Wolf taunts Coach Bombay, Hendrix—unwilling to be associated with a loser—threatens to withdraw its sponsorship. The Ducks blame Bombay for their loss, citing his association with Marria, the enemy trainer. Bombay counters by calling a night practice, which results in exhausting everyone on the team, so that they are unable to pay

"This ia a metaphor for America. We wanted to make America the symbol for the Ducks and vice-versa, so we included the entire spectrum of races and ethnicities all playing on one team with one purpose in mind. After a few problems they unite."—Steven Brill, producer of *D2: The Mighty Ducks*

CREDITS

Gordon Bombay: Emilio Estevez
Michele Mackay: Kathryn Erbe
Tibbles: Michael Tucker
Jan: Jan Rube
Wolf: Carsten Norgaard
Marria: Maria Ellingsen
Luis: Mike Vitar
Guy: Garette Ratliff Henson
Connie: Marguerite Moreau
Charlie: Joshua Jackson
Fulton: Elden Ryan Ratliff
Goldberg: Shaun Weiss
Averman: Matt Doherty
Banks: Vincent A. Larusso
Julie: Colombe Jacobsen
Portman: Aaron Lohr
Russ: Kenan Thompson
Ken: Justin Wong
Jesse: Brandon Adams
Dwayne: Ty O'Neal

Released: 1994
Production: Jordan Kerner and Jon Avnet for Walt Disney Pictures; released by Buena Vista Pictures
Direction: Sam Weisman
Screenplay: Steven Brill; based on characters created by Brill
Cinematography: Mark Irwin
Editing: Eric Sears and John F. Link
Production design: Gary Frutkoff
Art direction: Dawn Snyder
Set decoration: Kathryn Peters
Casting: Judy Taylor and Lynda Gordon
Sound: David Kelson
Costume design: Grania Preston
Hockey technical advise: Jack White
Music: J. A. C. Redford
MPAA rating: PG
Running time: 107 minutes

attention in Michele's classroom the next day. Against Bombay's orders, Michele cancels the next practice.

The Ducks then encounter a ghetto gang, who offer to teach them some street tactics to counter the dirty maneuvers of Team Iceland. Meanwhile, Jan arrives from Minneapolis and lectures Bombay on the importance of being a man. As Bombay struggles with this message and his pride, he misses the opening of the match with Team Germany, and the Ducks are threatened with a forfeit. Michele saves the day by agreeing to step in as coach at the last minute, although she knows nothing about the sport. With some adroit teamwork and a few lucky breaks, the Ducks manage to defeat Germany by a single goal as Bombay arrives late to the stadium.

The news arrives that Team Russia has defeated Team Iceland, forcing a rematch between Iceland and Team USA When an injury leaves the Ducks a player short, they recruit Russ Tyler (Kenan Thompson), one of the streetwise kids from the gang who taught the Ducks how to fight. Russ has developed a "knucklepuck" shot that travels erratically, like a knuckleball pitch in baseball. As practice ends and the rematch looms, hockey star Wayne Gretzky makes a cameo appearance. Wolf challenges Coach Bombay to a one-on-one duel on the ice and wins only by slashing Bombay with a cheap shot across his injured knee.

The big game arrives and Team Iceland skates to an early four-goal lead, as three Ducks find their way to the penalty box. After a brief pep talk by Coach Bombay, the team discards its Hendrix uniforms in favor of the old Ducks uniforms and manages to tie the game in the final seconds. An overtime shoot-out has Julie substituting for goalie Goldberg. She stops the final blistering shot and saves the gold medal for Team USA.

Director Sam Weisman makes his feature-film directorial debut with *D2: The Mighty Ducks*, after a distinguished career as a director and executive producer of several television series. He received an Emmy Award nomination as director of *Brooklyn Bridge*, the CBS Television comedy/drama. He has also acted in such television series as *Mary Hartman, Mary Hartman* and starred in the NBC miniseries *Studs Lonigan*.

All the actors in *D2: The Mighty Ducks*, including Emilio Estevez, underwent a rigorous eight-week hockey camp, coached by thirty-year veteran hockey player and coach Jack White. For filming of the Junior Goodwill Games, more than 24,000 extras were hired to fill the stadium.

D2: The Mighty Ducks failed to receive much critical attention, probably because it is a sequel with a cookie-cutter plot. With its outlandish story line, contrived cameo appearances, and stereotyped villains, this mediocre action comedy is strictly for the kiddies.

—Philip C. Williams and Sandra G. Garrett

REVIEWS

The Hollywood Reporter. March 25, 1994, p. 10.
Los Angeles Times. March 25, 1994, p. F10.
The New York Times. March 25, 1994, p. B3.
The New York Times. April 17, 1994, Section 2, p. H25.
Variety. March 25, 1994, p. 8.
Time. April 11, 1994, p. 68.

Dumb and Dumber

"If they each had half a brain, they'd still only have half a brain."—Movie tagline

"For Lloyd and Harry, everyday is a no-brainer."—Movie tagline

"I laughed till I stopped!"—Sonya Smithya, *Sneaky Previews* (Movie tagline)

"One of the year's 10 best."—*San Francisco Chronicle*

"Obnoxiously triumphant."—*Newhouse News Syndicate*

"makes you laugh out loud for almost its entire running time"—Richard Schickel, *Time*

 Box Office Gross: $125 million (February 1995)

Some films can be said to be brilliant because of their spectacular visual images, such as *2001: A Space Odyssey* (1968). Others are brilliant because of their crackling dialogue, such as Preston Sturges' *The Lady Eve* (1941) or Woody Allen's *Manhattan* (1979). Some films are notable for their brilliant dramatization of history—such as *Schindler's List* (1993)—or their epic storytelling—such as *The Godfather* series (1972, 1974, 1990). Two common attributes of these films are artistic excellence and an understanding of the film's audience.

Dumb and Dumber may not have achieved artistic excellence, but it can be argued that it knows its audience. While *Dumb and Dumber* is not even a blip on the radar screen of what passes for artistic achievement, its inanity has touched so many people—box-office grosses were staggeringly high—that it cannot be ignored. This film is not for everyone, however; many people who consider themselves to be "mature" or "sophisticated" will hate it. This is a film for those who like slapstick, gross-out, silly humor.

Jim Carrey splashed onto the screen at a time when American culture seemed to devalue what has been termed "liberal-elitist" humor. Robert Altman's *Ready to Wear* (reviewed in this volume) failed at the box office, and Woody Allen's wonderful *Bullets Over Broadway* (reviewed in this volume) did not make the financial killing that *Dumb and Dumber* did. Carrey's outlandish, visceral, and irritating foolishness tapped a nerve in America. It is as if Americans wished to see someone, who was more hapless than they, succeed. In Carrey's previous box-office hits, such as *The Mask* (reviewed in this volume) and *Ace Ventura: Pet Detective* (reviewed in this volume), he played variations on his obnoxious good guy who stumbles into success. Ultimately, these films appear to be wish fulfillment: a lack of education, average physical appearance, and bad manners entitle the protagonists to enjoy unearned financial success and beautiful women.

Ultimately, it makes no difference where Carrey's films fit into the continuum of popular culture. Some would say that if people are entertained, then the films have just as valid a place as the works of Shakespeare. Amazingly, audiences have found this film highly entertaining. Much of *Dumb and Dumber* is indeed funny. Some of it has the innocence of the Jerry Lewis films in which Lewis' bizarre clown continued to fall "up," Carrey is not, however, as innocent or benign as Lewis.

In *Dumb and Dumber*, Carrey plays Lloyd Christmas, a narcissistic goon whose optimism has him believing good fortune is just around the corner. As the film begins, he and his partner, Harry (Jeff Daniels), are working to save enough money to open a worm store called "I Got Worms." Harry owns a van, which is decorated to look exactly like a shaggy dog, from which he gives doggie haircuts. Lloyd is a chauffeur.

The film's plot is set into motion when Lloyd drives a beautiful socialite, Mary (Lauren Holly), to the airport, falling in love with her along the way. He follows Mary into the terminal, weeping because she is leaving him (after knowing him a few minutes), and tries to help out when it appears that Mary has left a briefcase in the terminal. Actually, Mary is leaving the briefcase in a specific place for an important reason: The case is full of ransom money to pay off her husband's kidnappers. Lloyd's misguided attempt to save his ladylove is the centerpiece of the film. He eventually convinces Harry to go on a cross-country odyssey to Aspen to find Mary and return her briefcase.

Meanwhile, the kidnapper, Nicholas (Charles Rocket), sets his hit men on Lloyd's trail when it is discovered that

Lloyd has the briefcase. Eventually, Lloyd and Harry arrive in Aspen only to bumble their way into discovering the kidnappers and saving the day.

The writers (Peter Farrelly, Bennett Yellin, and Bobby Farrelly) utilize the classic "road picture" framework. This film is a stupid white male version of *Thelma and Louise* (1991)—with the gross humor of *Porky's* (1981). The "road" idea serves the film well, in that it sets up an important goal (to find Mary) with high expectations (Lloyd's dream sequence of Mary's reaction to him is a hoot), with many chances for adventure along the way. Although it would be ludicrous to expect these characters to learn something along the way, as most characters in a "road" picture seem to do, Harry and Lloyd have changed just the slightest bit by the film's end. Of course, true to the film's goofy nature, Harry and Lloyd's stupidity remains intact in the film's final sequence—perhaps the wittiest in the film. Without giving away the film's ending, suffice it to say that for a moment it looks as if Lloyd has finally achieved one of his life goals, only to be so completely foolish and obtuse as not to recognize that paradise has dropped in his lap.

The performances are splendid, although, as mentioned before, many audiences may find the characterizations simplistic and silly. It is important to remember that the world of *Dumb and Dumber* is a silly and simplistic one, and that performances should match. Jim Carrey's humor is either brilliant or irritating, depending upon the viewer. Carrey's lack of inhibition can be wonderful, as when he runs into the airline terminal to deliver the briefcase to Mary, holding up his card and shouting, "Don't worry, I'm a limo driver!" as if he were saying, "Don't worry, I'm a cop" in the most important high-speed chase ever seen. Then he runs through the tunnel to the airplane, falling out the other side when the camera reveals that the plane has already taken off.

At times, Carrey's putty face and bizarre behavior recall Jerry Lewis. In *Cinderfella* (1960) and *The Patsy* (1964), among others, Lewis had a similar witlessness that somehow made him come out on top. While Carrey's characterization has the same borderline-crazy quality that made Lewis famous, there are moments when the artistry of Carrey's humor is reduced to sophomoric foolishness. Where Lewis' characters were benign, Carrey's are lethal and downright mean at times.

CREDITS

Lloyd Christmas: Jim Carrey
Harry Dunne: Jeff Daniels
Mary Swanson: Lauren Holly
Helen Swanson: Teri Garr
J.P. Shay: Karen Duffy
Joe Mentalino: Mike Starr
Nicholas Andre: Charles Rocket
Beth Jordan: Victoria Rowell
Sea Bass: Cam Neely
Detective Dale: Felton Perry

Released: 1994
Production: Charles B. Wessler, Brad Krevoy, and Steve Stabler for Motion Picture Corporation of America; released by New Line Cinema
Direction: Peter Farrelly
Screenplay: Peter Farrelly, Bennett Yellin, and Bobby Farrelly
Cinematography: Mark Irwin
Editing: Christopher Greenbury
Production design: Sidney J. Bartholomew, Jr.
Art direction: Arlan Jay Vetter
Set decoration: Bradford Johnson
Casting: Rick Montgomery and Dan Parada
Sound: Jonathan Stein
Costume design: Mary Zophres
Music: Todd Rundgren
MPAA rating: PG-13
Running time: 106 minutes

AWARDS AND NOMINATIONS

MTV Movie Awards 1995: Best Kiss (Carrey/Holly), Best Comedic Performance (Carrey)
Nomination: Best On-Screen Duo (Carrey/Daniels)

At one point, he gets mad at Harry for going out with Mary: Lloyd gleefully retaliates by pouring a bottle of laxatives into Harry's drink, setting off perhaps one of the most truly obnoxious scenes in the film. Another example is when the hit men kill Harry's beloved canary: Lloyd sells it to the blind neighbor boy, hoping he will not notice it is dead. For some audiences, these moments will dampen their enjoyment of Carrey's over-the-top yet lovable silliness. He is hilarious and charming when getting drunk in a bar to overcome his sorrow when Mary stands him up for a date. He is very funny in the opening scene with Mary, looking longingly into her eyes through the car's rearview mirror, assuming that she feels the same way.

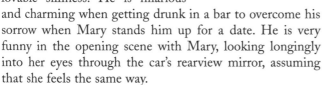

"When the cameras roll we just get the glassy, 'I-just-ate-lead-paint-for-breakfast' look. We don't gear up for it, we gear down."—Jim Carrey, on working with Jeff Daniels in *Dumb and Dumber*

Jeff Daniels, one of America's more accomplished actors, has finally achieved well-deserved public recognition for his work in this film. He has starred in many successful plays and films, such as Broadway's *Fifth of July*, *Terms of Endearment* (1983), and *The Purple Rose of Cairo* (1985). Daniels is a fine actor who attacks this material gleefully. For some, however, it will be disturbing to see someone of his caliber performing some of the most sophomoric antics in recent cinema: Throwing mustard-covered hot dogs into the back of his doggie van, sitting on a commode trying to overcome the effects of too many laxatives, or getting his tongue stuck on the frozen handlebar of a ski lift.

One of the funnier of these moments is when Harry is meeting a beautiful woman (Victoria Rowell) at a gas station and tries to keep her from noticing that his shoes have caught fire. Daniel's understated attempts to get her to finish her sentence so that he can douse his feet in water are hilarious and emblematic of his wonderful ability to be funny and real at the same time. Many will wish that an actor of his caliber would not have to stoop to gross-out humor to achieve great heights of celebrity.

While *Dumb and Dumber* may not be for those who like their comedy verbally clever and thematically important, it has excellent production design, the courage of its moronic convictions, a lively sound track, and dynamic—if occasionally irritating—central performances. Audiences who enjoy goofy slapstick that barely passes a high-school level will adore this film. Everyone else would do best to stay home and let Jim Carrey's huge audience have a great time.

—*Kirby Tepper*

REVIEWS

Daily Variety. December 16, 1994, p. 2.
The Hollywood Reporter. December 15, 1994, p. 10.
Entertainment Weekly. January 13, 1995, p. 34.
Los Angeles Times. December 16, 1994, p. F1.
The New York Times. December 16, 1994, p. B12.

Dust Devil: The Final Cut

A spirit—the Dust Devil (Robert Burke)—murders and mutilates people across Africa, as a police officer (Zakes Mokae) tries to solve the horrible crimes. A woman on the run and her abusive husband find themselves in the path of the deadly supernatural being, who kills human beings in order to steal their souls and increase his other worldly powers.

REVIEWS

Variety. CCCL, April 19, 1993, p. 45.

CREDITS

Dust Devil: Robert Burke
Wendy: Chelsea Field
Ben: Zakes Mokae
Joe: John Matshikiza
Mark: Rufus Swart
Cornelius: William Hootkins
Dr. Leidzinger: Marianne Sagebrecht

Origin: Great Britain and USA
Released: 1993
Production: Joanne Sellar for Palace and Film Four International, in association with Miramax Film Corporation and British Screen; released by Miramax
Direction: Richard Stanley
Screenplay: Richard Stanley
Cinematography: Steven Chivers
Editing: Derek Trigg and Paul Carlin
Production design: Joseph Bennett
Art direction: Graeme Orwin and Michael Carlin
Special effects: Rick Creswell
Sound editing: Richard Rhys-Davies
Special makeup effects supervision: Little John
Costume design: Michele Clapton
Stunt coordination: Roly Jansen
Music: Simon Boswell
MPAA rating: no listing
Running time: 108 minutes

The East is Red (Swordsman III)

In this period Hong Kong action fantasy, Asia the Invincible (Brigitte Lin), a supernatural warrior-demon, returns from the dead and seeks vengeance on imposters masquerading as Asia, inevitably crossing swords with Naval Officer Koo (Yu Rong-guang) in an epic battle. Sequel to *Swordsman II*.

REVIEWS

Los Angeles Times. May 20, 1994, p. F6.
Variety. CCCLI, July 12, 1993, p. 55.

CREDITS

Asia the Invincible: Brigitte Lin
Snow: Joey Wong
Naval Officer Koo: Yu Rong-guang
No character identified: Jean Wang

Origin: Hong Kong
Released: 1993
Production: Tsui Hark for Film Workshop; released by Golden Princess/Rim Film Distributors, Inc.
Direction: Ching Siu-tung and Raymond Lee
Screenplay: Tsui Hark, Roy Szeto, and Carbon Cheung
Cinematographer: Lau Moon-tong
Editing: Chiang Chuen-tak
Art direction: Eddie Ma
Costume design: William Chang and Mark Chiu
Martial arts direction: Ching Siu-tung
Music: Wu Wai-lap
MPAA rating: no listing
Running time: 103 minutes

Eat Drink Man Woman

"An appetizingly sexy new comedy from the director of *The Wedding Banquet*."—Movie tagline

"A delicious stew of food and sex."—Edward Guthmann, *San Francisco Chronicle*

"The most delectable food-related hit this side of *Like Water for Chocolate!*"—Janet Maslin, *The New York Times*

"Superb, wonderful and compelling! A movie that will stay with you a long time."—Jeffrey Lyons, *Sneak Previews*

 Box Office Gross: $7,028,797 (January 2, 1995)

Ang Lee's *The Wedding Banquet* was one of the surprise hit films in the United States in 1993. According to *Variety*, it was the year's most profitable film, based on a ratio of cost to box-office receipts. *The Wedding Banquet* centers on the life of a Taiwanese immigrant in Greenwich Village, who is living with his Caucasian male lover. Because his traditional parents expect him to marry, he weds a young Taiwanese woman and unexpectedly finds himself in love with members of two sexes at once. *Eat Drink Man Woman* offers a delightful variation on the generational, sexual, and cultural conflicts of Lee's previous film.

Chu (Sihung Lung), master chef at a large Taipei restaurant, enjoys preparing lavish Sunday dinners for his three unmarried daughters. The sisters, who still live with their father, unwillingly tolerate this painstaking and often painful ceremony despite their preoccupation with matters seemingly more important than food and family. The eldest, Jia-Jen (Kuei-Mei Yang), is a spinster teacher supposedly not interested in men since being spurned by her college lover. The youngest, Jia-Ning (Yu-Wen Wang), is a university student in the process of stealing her best friend's boyfriend, Guo Lun (Chao-Jung Chen). The middle sister is the proudly independent Jia-Chien (Chien-Lien Wu), an ambitious airline executive, who conducts a casual affair with Raymond (Lester Chen), a gallery owner. Seemingly more sophisticated and Westernized than her sisters, Jia-Chien's secret passion is traditional Taiwanese cooking, and while she would prefer being a chef like her father, women chefs are not taken seriously in her country.

All four members of the family, including the seemingly placid, long-widowed Chu, feel unfulfilled and undergo often-dramatic changes as the film progresses. Jia-Ning becomes pregnant. Jia-Jen, despite herself, is drawn to Ming-Dao (Chin-Cheng Lu), an exhibitionistic volleyball coach. Jia-Chien is offered a promotion to a post in Amsterdam and is attracted to Li Kai (Winston Chao), a married airline executive. She is divided about both matters: In one sense, she wants to leave her often tiresome family, and in another, they are an integral part of her life. Complicating the Li Kai problem is that he is the one who supposedly abandoned her older sister years earlier.

Chu, wearied by his country's declining respect for traditional recipes, attempts to make up for his daughters' indifference to his food by preparing school lunches for Shan-Shan (Yu-Chien Tang), the daughter of his divorced neighbor Jin-Rong (Sylvia Chang), Jia-Jen's best friend from college days. Madame Liang (Ah-Leh Gua), Jin-Rong's ostentatious mother, returns from living in the United States and seems interested in Chu. He apparently considers changing his life because of the growing possibil-

CREDITS

Mr. Chu: Sihung Lung
Jia-Chien: Chien-Lien Wu
Jia-Jen: Kuei-Mei Yang
Jia-Ning: Yu-Wen Wang
Jin-Rong: Sylvia Chang
Madame Liang: Ah-Leh Gua
Li Kai: Winston Chao
Raymond: Lester Chen
Ming-Dao: Chin-Cheng Lu
Guo Lun: Chao-Jung Chen
Old Wen: Jui Wang
Shan-Shan: Yu-Chien Tang

Origin: Taiwan
Released: 1994
Production: Li-Kong Hsu for Central Motion Picture Corporation, in association with Ang Lee Productions and Good Machine; released by the Samuel Goldwyn Company
Direction: Ang Lee
Screenplay: Ang Lee, Hui-Ling Wang, and James Schamus
Cinematographer: Jong Lin
Editing: Tim Squyres
Art direction: Fu-Hsiung Lee
Set decoration: Hsi-Chien Lee
Sound: Tom Paul
Music: Mader
MPAA rating: no listing
Running time: 123 minutes

AWARDS AND NOMINATIONS

Academy Awards Nomination 1994: Best Foreign Language Film
Golden Globe Awards Nomination 1995: Best Foreign Language Film
Independent Spirit Awards Nominations 1995: Best Film, Best Director (Lee), Best Actress (Wu), Best Actor (Lung), Best Screenplay, Best Cinematography
National Board of Review Awards 1994: Best Foreign Film

ity of losing his daughters and his increasing awareness of mortality brought on by the illness and death of his closest friend, Old Wen (Jui Wang), a fellow chef.

Jia-Chien is shocked to learn that Li Kai barely remembers Jia-Jen, that his college romance was with Jin-Rong, and that her sister has created this myth as an excuse for her timidity with the opposite sex. After Jia-Jen's students torment her with anonymous love notes she thinks are from Ming-Dao, she sheds her reserve, blossoms from mousy to glamorous, and pursues the coach. When Jia-Chien finds that Raymond is too casual about their relationship and that Li Kai promises more of the same, she is reconciled to moving to Amsterdam, but only after preparing a sumptuous meal for her father. The biggest surprise comes from Chu, who decides to marry not the vulgar Madame Liang but her daughter.

As with *The Wedding Banquet*, Lee comments on the differences between generations. The daughters resent the Sunday meals with their father as his attempt to indoctrinate them into accepting the old ways, while he simply uses the food as a way of communicating the love he can express no other way. Ironically, he is as little hidebound as they, and they are at first shocked by his decision to marry someone of their generation. Children often have more difficulty accepting change in their parents than vice versa. The cultural conflict comes not in contrasts between countries, as in *The Wedding Banquet*, but in understanding and appreciating traditional attitudes and ceremonies within a family. The film's sexual commentary comes through dramatizing the Chu sisters' feelings about sex: Jia-Jen's fear, Jia-Chien's worldly cynicism, and Jia-Ning's romantic openness.

The title of *Eat Drink Man Woman* comes from Old Wen's observation that these four words describe the essence of life. While Lee tries to show how food and romance intermingle, the film is only one of several recent foreign films to do so, the most notable being Juzo Itami's *Tampopo* (1986), Gabriel Axel's *Babette's Feast* (1987), and Alfonso Arau's *Como Agua Para Chocolate* (1992; *Like Water for Chocolate*). *Eat Drink Man Woman* is less stylistically striking than these three films, Lee's aims are quieter, and despite what the reviews and publicity about the film indicate, food is not as central to either its plot or themes as it might have been.

Approximately one hundred recipes prepared by three master chefs and numerous assistants are on display in *Eat Drink Man Woman*, but after the opening sequence of Chu preparing a meal for his daughters, food drifts into the background, with one notable exception. An irony of Chu's status as a master chef is that he has lost his sense of taste, a metaphor for his declining interest in life as a whole. When Jia-Chien cooks for him, as much a demonstration of her admiration and affection as of her culinary skills, his taste miraculously returns. As in *The Wedding Banquet*, Lee shows how love—and, to a lesser degree, ritual—can restore order to life.

Food is important in *Eat Drink Man Woman* only as one of several components Lee and coscreenwriters Hui-Ling Wang and James Schamus show to be integral to happy lives, the others including love, respect, loyalty, and tolerance. Jia-Chien never confronts Jia-Jen with her discovery of her sister's lie about Li Kai because she understands the older woman's need to protect herself from emotional wounds. Similarly, Jia-Chien rejects Raymond and Li Kai because of their emotional shortcomings.

As a director, Lee displays surer technical skill and a more distinctive visual style than in *The Wedding Banquet*, perhaps partly as much a result of having a larger budget with which to work. Aided by the work of cinematographer Jong Lin, the film seems much larger than its intimate subject because of the way Lee weaves the striking landscape of Taipei into his narrative. His talent for comic timing ranges from the subtle, as with Shan-Shan's joy at selling Chu's lunches to her classmates, to the slapstick, as Madame Liang collapses at the news of her daughter's betrothal. Lee also enjoys toying with his audience's expectations. During the preparation of the opening meal, Lee shows Chu killing and gutting a la⎵ ⎵ followed by grabbing a chicken from a

pen in his yard. While the audience is worried about having to witness more bloodshed, Chu reenters his kitchen and passes several beautiful large bullfrogs also bound for slaughter, as the director pokes fun both at viewers' squeamishness and at the cultural differences between East and West.

Despite such weaknesses as the underwritten parts of Jia-Ning and Jin-Rong, *Eat Drink Man Woman* is an entertainingly joyful celebration of life's vicissitudes. It is held together finally by the uniformly excellent performances, especially the vivacious Chien-Lien Wu, who can display confidence and confusion simultaneously; Ah-Leh Gua, whose dignified mother in *The Wedding Banquet* is worlds away from the hilariously horrid Madame Liang; and Sihung Lung, memorable as the father in *The Wedding Banquet*, who convincingly portrays the turmoil beneath Chu's dignified surface.

—*Michael Adams*

REVIEWS

Atlanta Constitution. January 27, 1995, p. P8.
Boston Globe. August 19, 1994, p. 49.
Entertainment Weekly. August 12, 1994, p. 40.
The Hollywood Reporter. May 17, 1994, p. 7.
Interview. September, 1994, p. 68.
Los Angeles Times. August 3, 1994, p. F1.
Mademoiselle. C, September, 1994, p. 104.
New Woman. XXIV, September, 1994, 40.
The New York Times. August 3, 1994, p. B3.
Newsweek. CXXIV, August 22, 1994, p. 62.
People Weekly. XLII, August 29, 1994, p. 20.
Playboy. XLI, September, 1994, p. 24.
Time. CXLIV, August 15, 1994, p. 61.
Us. September, 1994, p. 36.
Variety. May 16, 1994, p. 17.

Ed Wood

"One of the year's ten best!"—*Entertainment Weekly, New York Daily News, Los Angeles Times*

"One of the year's funniest! Two big thumbs up!" —*Siskel & Ebert*

"Outrageously entertaining. Depp is terrific!" —Peter Travers, *Rolling Stone*

"One of the best films of the year"—Joel Siegel, *Good Morning America*

 Box Office Gross: $5.7 million (February 1995)

Director Tim Burton leads viewers through a strange chapter of Hollywood's past in *Ed Wood*, a film about the man who many consider to be the worst film director of all time. Edward D. Wood, Jr., was one of the many low-budget B-movie directors of the 1950's thriving on the emergence of the double feature, which created a market for these hasty, bizarre, low-tech companions to the feature film. What distinguished Wood was his ceaseless optimism in the face of repeated failure, the conviction with which he clung to his delusions of grandeur, and his habit of wearing angora sweaters and female clothing. These traits combined to make him a cult hero, an emblem for the ambition, bad taste, and quirkiness of the American spirit—a spirit which is captured vividly in the B cinema of the 1950's and to which this film pays homage.

Ed Wood pursued his cinematic vision almost single handedly. He pulled together financing against great adversity, hastily wrote the scripts, and gathered his devoted, motley crew of players: his girlfriend, Dolores (Sarah Jessica Parker); Tor Johnson (George "The Animal" Steele), a bald, hulking, heavyweight wrestler; Bunny Breckinridge (Bill Murray), an aging homosexual who dreams of a sex change; Chriswell (Jeffrey Jones), a charlatan psychic; Vampira (Lisa Marie), the horror-movie television hostess; and most important, an aged and tired Bela Lugosi (Martin Landau), years after his stardom, addicted to morphine, discarded by Hollywood, penniless, and alone.

Much of the film focuses on the tender and symbiotic friendship that emerged between Ed Wood and Bela Lugosi. At moments they seem like two falling torpedoes grasping at each other for support. Wood uses Lugosi's past fame to sell his bad films, and Lugosi uses Wood's films to support his morphine addiction and his desire to appear once more on film. Beyond this mutual need, however, Wood also idolizes Lugosi, having been raised on Hollywood horror. On the first day of shooting, Wood lectures his actors on not overreacting when Lugosi walks through the door, urging them to treat him as if he were one of them. When Lugosi makes his entrance it is not the actors but Ed Wood who loses control and rushes to his side in adoration. Throughout the film Wood is shown pampering Lugosi's bitter temper and unleashed egotism. Some of the most moving scenes involve Lugosi's final days, when he would call "Eddie" in the middle of the night begging for help in a tired, trembling, voice—and Eddie would come.

Bela Lugosi came to prominence in the title role of *Dracula* (1931) and starred in horror films throughout the 1930's and 1940's, but gradually lost popularity in the 1950's; he was not well-suited for the science fiction atomic-age horror genre of that era. When he first meets Ed Wood, he expresses his preference for the traditional monsters, who had a poetry to them, and he relates a theory that equates horror with blood, tying them both to childbirth, which is both repelling and impressive. Martin Landau portrays the aged Lugosi with impeccable realism, capturing an astounding likeness in form, spirit, and style. He expresses the fatigue, vanity, and pathos of a star who has come to his end, exalting into tragic what threatens to be merely pathetic.

The drama of the film revolves around the mishaps and follies of filming Ed Wood's three best-known works. Wood's first film, *Glen or Glenda?* (1953), concerns the life of a transvestite who must reveal his identity to his girlfriend. Wood was passionate about this film and convinced a third-rate producer with a specialty in exploitation films that he was the one to write and direct it, because of his own passion for cross-dressing. *Glen or Glenda?* is one of the first films to deal candidly with this theme and to educate viewers about the distinctions between transexuals and transvestites. The film also served as an occasion for Wood to reveal his own clandestine transvestitism to his girlfriend Dolores, who plays the role of the girlfriend. Dolores never completely recovers and eventually leaves him in disgust. The film is received so badly that the production company vows that they will never make another one of his films.

This misfortune does not deter Wood or even introduce an instant of self-doubt. He is, however, forced to produce *Bride of the Monster* (1955) on his own. Finding financing proves to be rather difficult and the filming is at one point

"Where's my pink sweater? I can never seem to find my clothes anymore."—*Ed Wood*'s Dolores to boyfriend Ed Wood about her angora sweater (which he has taken)

halted. The film is resumed when Wood makes a financial deal, but the budget is far from sufficient. One memorable scene finds the cast stealing a rubber octopus from a Hollywood studio and dragging it to a man-made pond on the outskirts of Hollywood. Upon learning that they forgot to steal the motor, Wood still manages to keep his optimism and instructs the now fragile and exhausted Lugosi to climb into the pond and throw the octopus about to simulate a struggle with the inert prop. What follows is a ridiculously bad rendition of an octopus attack, lit by the headlights of the crew's cars, to which Wood responds with absolute delight and total satisfaction.

Plan 9 from Outer Space (1959) is financed by a church, after Wood convinces the reverend (G. D. Spradlin) that the film will bring in enough funds for the church to produce their own series of films on the apostles. The reverend agrees, but the cast must first be baptized and the words "grave robbers" removed from the title. Bela Lugosi has died by this point, but will appear as the star of the film nevertheless. A tiny roll of footage Ed Wood shot of the actor before he died still exists. A chiropractor, whose forehead resembles Lugosi's, struts about holding a cape up to his eyes for the remainder of the film.

Amazingly Ed Wood always believed wholeheartedly in his greatness. At one point in the filming of *Plan 9 From Outer Space*, he quarrels with the reverend over the content of the film and rushes out in a fury. He goes to the legendary Musso and Frank's bar in full drag and encounters Orson Welles (Vincent D'Onofrio). They discuss their problems over a drink, and Wood discovers that they have the same problems. He jumps from this premise to the conclusion that he, like Welles, must struggle against all obstacles to see his artistic visions materialized. He returns to the set with his delusions refueled.

Johnny Depp, who has starred in a number of films as the misunderstood, introspective outcast, including Tim Burton's *Edward Scissorhands* (1990) and *What's Eating Gilbert Grape?* (1993) is excellent as Ed Wood. He breaks from the sluggishness of his previous characters to portray Wood as a man of ceaseless energy, zest, and perkiness.

Shot entirely in black and white, the film mimics the amateur style and techniques of an original Ed Wood creation, while at the same time striving for visual excellence. Cinematographer Stefan Czapsky describes his dilemma as trying to "create a look that combined the best with the worst." While Burton insisted on realism in the re-creation of shots from Ed Wood's films, the film itself is more expressionistic in nature, with exaggerated angles and the use of low lighting to give the characters a ghoulish and sinister appearance. The credits appear in classic 1950's typefaces, and the music score by Howard Shore re-creates the

CREDITS

Ed Wood: Johnny Depp
Bela Lugosi: Martin Landau
Dolores Fuller: Sarah Jessica Parker
Kathy O'Hara: Patricia Arquette
Vampira: Lisa Marie
Criswell: Jeffrey Jones
Bunny Breckinridge: Bill Murray
Reverend Lemon: G. D. Spradlin
Orson Welles: Vincent D'Onofrio
Tor Johnson: George "The Animal" Steele
George Weiss: Mike Starr
Paul Marco: Max Casella
Conrad Brooks: Brent Hinkley
Loretta King: Juliet Landau
Ed Reynolds: Clive Rosengren

Released: 1994
Production: Denise Di Novi and Tim Burton for Touchstone Pictures; released by Buena Vista Pictures
Direction: Tim Burton
Screenplay: Scott Alexander and Larry Karaszewski; based on the book *Nightmare of Ecstacy: The Life and Art of Edward D. Wood, Jr.*, by Rudolph Grey
Cinematographer: Stefan Czapsky
Editing: Chris Lebenzon
Production design: Tom Duffield
Art direction: Okowita
Set design: Chris Nushawg and Bruce Hill
Set decoration: Cricket Rowland
Casting: Victoria Thomas
Visual consulting: Richard Hoover
Sound: Edward Tise
Costume design: Colleen Atwood
Music: Howard Shore
MPAA rating: R
Running time: 124 minutes

AWARDS AND NOMINATIONS

Academy Awards 1994:   Best Supporting Actor (Landau), Best Makeup
Chicago Critics Awards 1994:   Best Supporting Actor (Landau), Best Cinematography
Golden Globe Awards 1995:   Best Supporting Actor (Landau)
Nominations: Best Film—Musical/Comedy, Best Actor—Musical/Comedy (Depp)
Los Angeles Critics Awards 1994:   Best Supporting Actor (Landau), Best Cinematography, Best Original Score
National Society of Critics Awards 1994:   Best Supporting Actor (Landau), Best Cinematography
New York Critics Awards 1994:   Best Supporting Actor (Landau), Best Cinematography
Screen Actors Guild Awards 1994:   Best Supporting Actor (Landau)

funky mood of the era, lapsing into a melancholic Tchaikovsky during shots of Lugosi.

The overall mood of the film is neither 1950's nor 1990's, but rather a unique meeting ground. It is a contemporary interpretation to attribute a cult-value to Ed Wood's films and to aggrandize their low-tech strangeness. Therefore, the film does not provide a realistic rendition of Ed Wood, but rather presents a mood and perspective which is attained only in the light of the present.

The cinematographer's attempt to combine the best with the worst is mirrored throughout the film. First, one of Hollywood's best directors makes a film that reconstructs the style of Hollywood's worst. Second, a high-budget film depicts a low-budget film. Third, successful, first-rate actors mimick failed third-rate actors.

The most striking dichotomy, though, exists within the life of Ed Wood himself. On the one hand, he is tirelessly devoted to filmmaking and will suffer any humiliation and compromise to get his films made, and on the other, he devotes virtually no energy to the artistic execution and quality of his works. Ed Wood filmed an average of twenty-five shots in one day, zipping from one to the next, always satisfied with the first take, even if the cardboard tombstones were knocked over and the string from which the toy flying saucer was suspended was clearly visible. Ultimately, his greatest concern was that he loved films and was making them.

Director Tim Burton has demonstrated a preference for American gothic in such other films as *Edward Scissorhands*, *Nightmare Before Christmas* (1993), *Batman* (1989), and *Batman Returns* (1992). What Burton portrays in this film is the broken Hollywood of *Sunset Boulevard* (1950), or *What Ever Happened to Baby Jane?* (1962). It is an America where the glamorous is peeled back to reveal the strangeness and garishness of even the most commonplace images. Accustomed to a Hollywood that reveals its better side, big budgets, beautiful stars, and success stories, it is compelling to look behind the curtain and find a cast that resembles the players in a traditional traveling show, led by a man scrambling to make a buck and to keep the wheels rolling on their caravan. Homage is paid here to filmmaking at its purest and at its worst.

—*Reni Celeste*

REVIEWS

Chicago Sun-Times. October 7, 1994, p. 41.
Chicago Tribune. October 7, 1994, p. 7c.
Daily Variety. September 7, 1994, p. 2.
Entertainment Weekly. September 30, 1994, p. 36.
The Hollywood Reporter. September 23-25, 1994, p. 10.
Los Angeles Times. September 28, 1994, p. F1.
The New York Times. September 23, 1994, p. B7.
Time. October 10, 1994.

8 Seconds

"Hang on for the ride of your life."—Movie tagline
"Scores as a bull-busting *Rocky*."—Bruce Williamson, *Playboy*

 Box Office Gross: $19,570, 825. (July 31, 1994)

Luke Perry abandons his pompadoured cool-guy image from television's *Beverly Hills 90210* to play a simple country boy in this outstanding biography of real-life rodeo legend Lane Frost. From Perry's charming central performance to John Avildsen's excellent direction, this is a thoroughly entertaining and touching film.

Director Avildsen seems to be a natural for this material, given his past successes with such films as the first *Rocky* (1976) and *The Karate Kid* trilogy (1984, 1986, 1989). Like those films, *8 Seconds* is about a young hero and his rise to the top of his particular sport (and his struggles once he gets there).

In particular, his taut storytelling (combined with the excellent screenplay by Monte Merrick) moves quickly through Lane's brief life, beginning from the first moments when he realized he wanted to be a champion bull rider to his tragic death in the rodeo ring at twenty-five years of age. In between, Avildsen keeps the action moving, using superimposed dates (e.g., "Texas, 1987") to pinpoint chronological changes for the audience.

The story really begins when twenty-year-old Lane goes with his rodeo traveling buddies Tuff (Stephen Baldwin) and Cody (Red Mitchell) to start up the ladder of bull riding stardom. Avildsen and company capture the boyish playfulness of the trio as they travel around the west, staying in fleabag motels and getting into barroom brawls. In fact, Avildsen draws parallels between the stereotypical "wild west" of cowboy movies and modern-day rodeo life: A scene in a bar where the trio gets in a fight for no apparent reason has the momentum and gusto of a saloon brawl in a John Wayne movie. Similarly, the constant movement of the trio across the west is done with the same adventurous spirit as the movement of the pioneers across the prairies in *How the West Was Won* (1962) or *The Big Sky* (1952).

Soon, Lane meets lovely Kellie Kyle (Cynthia Geary) and eventually marries her. Several scenes of the couple as they tentatively fall in love are beautifully performed. In particular, the scene of their first date—at a fast-food joint—is very real, with Lane grandly holding forth about his future plans, only interrupting himself to see if she is enjoying her hamburger.

"8 seconds" refers to the time a bull rider must stay on the bull in order to win.

One of Avildsen's best techniques is his use of depth in his camera shots. For example, a scene in which Lane is angrily pitching hay while talking to Kellie is shot so that Lane is in the foreground in silhou-ette and Kellie is lit in the background through the barn door. This juxtaposition of foreground and background is emblematic of the depth of the film as a whole.

As the story progresses, Avildsen and writer Merrick show the parallel difficulties of maintaining a marriage and facing the intense pressures of rodeo super-stardom. Infidelities, injuries, triumphs, arguments and reconcili-ations are deftly portrayed, and each character has fully realized motiva-tions. The scenes are brief but effec-tive, and the filmmakers neither rush their story nor let it drag. Bill Conti's stirring Aaron Copland-esque score helps to keep the pace: New scenes and new time periods are heralded with rousing western themes which echo the excitement, spirit, and sense of upheaval in the characters' lives.

Luke Perry is nothing short of wonderful. He captures Lane's well-bred country charm perfectly, definitely worthy of Tuff's lament that Lane's fans act like "he hung the moon." Perry does a dead-on Oklahoma accent, and looks every bit the bull riding champion as he sits astride the bulls and yells "Okay, boys!" before the gate is opened for each bull ride. He seems so involved in his role that his *Beverly Hills 90210* image is swept clean away, and in its place is a wiry country-boy who made good. Perry's depiction of Lane's desire to win the affec-tion of his loving but demanding father brings further depth to the characterization.

All the other actors contribute to the success of the film. Stephen Baldwin is raunchy, funny, and lovable as a young man whose feelings for Lane grow from resentment to adoration. Cynthia Geary, from television's *Northern Exposure*, brings grace and strength to her role as Kellie, and Carrie Snodgress and James Rebhorn are loving, stoic parents straight out of the old west.

Real-life footage of Lane Frost (during the final credits) puts a wonderful cap on this wonderful tribute to a young man's life. Bravo.

—*Kirby Tepper*

CREDITS

Lane Frost: Luke Perry
Kellie Frost: Cynthia Geary
Tuff Hedeman: Stephen Baldwin
Clyde Frost: James Rebhorn
Elsie Frost: Carrie Snodgress
Cody Lambert: Red Mitchell
Carolyn Kyle: Ronnie Claire Edwards
Martin Hudson: Linden Ashby
Lane (as an adolescent): Dustin Mayfield
Lane (as a child): Cameron Finley

Released: 1994
Production: Michael Shamberg for Jersey Films; released by New Line Cinema
Direction: John G. Avildsen
Screenplay: Monte Merrick
Cinematographer: Victor Hammer
Editing: J. Douglas Seelig
Production design: William J. Cassidy
Art direction: John Frick
Set decoration: Jenny C. Patrick
Casting: Caro Jones
Sound: Michael Scott Goldbaum
Costume design: Deena Appel
Stunt coordination: Mike McGaughy
Music: Bill Conti
MPAA rating: PG-13
Running time: 104 minutes

REVIEWS

Entertainment Weekly. March 3, 1994, p. 45
The Hollywood Reporter. February 14, 1994, p. 8
Los Angeles Times. February 25, 1994, p. F8
The New York Times. February 25, 1994, P. B5
Variety. February 14, 1994, p.2

The Elementary School (Obecna Skola)

This Czech comedy set in the 1940's centers on two mischievous ten- year-old boys, Eda (Vaclav Jakoubek) and Tonda (Radoslav Budac). They come to revere their strict new teacher, Igor Hnizdo (Jan Triska), an inveterate womanizer and self-proclaimed war hero. Directorial debut of Jan Sverak.

REVIEWS

Chicago. XLI, October 1992, p. 22.

CREDITS

Igor Hnizdo: Jan Triska
Soucek: Zdenek Sverak
Mrs. Soucek: Libuse Safrankova
Schoolmaster: Rudolf Hrusinsky
Miss Maxova: Daniela Kolarova
Eda: Vaclav Jakoubek
Tonda: Radoslav Budac
Tram driver's wife: Irena Pavlaskova
Tram driver: Oudrej Vetchy
Pliha: Boleslav Polivka
Fakir: Petr Cepek
Doctor: Jiri Menzel
School inspector: Karel Kachyna

Origin: Czechoslovakia
Released: 1992
Production: Jaromir Lukas for Barrandov Film Studios, Creative Production Group Vydra, and Dudova; released by Filmexport Prague
Direction: Jan Sverak
Screenplay: Zdenek Sverak
Cinematographer: F. A. Brabec
Editing: Alois Fisarek
Production design: Vladimir Labsky and Gabriela Kubenova
Sound: Jiri Kriz
Costume design: Jan Kropacek
Music: Jiri Svoboda
MPAA rating: no listing
Running time: 100 minutes

AWARDS AND NOMINATIONS

Academy Awards Nomination 1991: Foreign-Language Film

The Endless Summer II

"The journey continues..."—Movie tagline

"Dazzling...awesome...breathtaking."—Susan Wloszcyna, *USA Today*

"What a way to get stoked!"—Roger Ebert, *Chicago Sun-Times*

Box Office Gross: $2,071,091 (July 24, 1994)

A sequel to Bruce Brown's 1966 documentary, this film charts the course of champion surfers Patrick O'Connell and Robert (Wingnut) Weaver as they travel the far points of the globe, finding exotic locales in which to try to catch the perfect wave. Breathtaking scenery and spectacular sequences highlight this look at a unique subculture. This semi-documentary film is a sequel to *The Endless Summer* (1966) which ignited the surfing craze in Southern California and earned over $30 million. Also known as *Bruce Brown's Endless Summer II.*

REVIEWS

Atlanta Constitution. June 3, 1994, p. A3.
Atlanta Constitution. June 3, 1994, p. P3.
Boston Globe. June 3, 1994, p. 85.
Chicago Tribune. June 3, 1994, p. 7F.
Entertainment Weekly. June 17, 1994, p. 36.
Entertainment Weekly. December 23, 1994, p. 81.
Los Angeles Times. May 29, 1994, p. CAL7.
Los Angeles Times. June 3, 1994, p. F12.
The New York Times. June 3, 1994, p. C12.
People Weekly. XLI, June 13, 1994, p. 18.
TV Guide. XLII, December 31, 1994, p. 39.
USA Today. June 3, 1994, p. D1.
Variety. CCCLV, June 6, 1994, p. 44.
The Washington Post. June 3, 1994, p. C7.
The Washington Post. June 3, 1994, p. WW44.
The Washington Post. June 9, 1994, p. C7.

CREDITS

Narrator: Bruce Brown
Patrick O'Connell: Patrick O'Connell
Robert (Wingnut) Weaver: Robert (Wingnut) W

Released: 1994
Production: Ron Moler and Roger Riddell; released by New Line Cinema
Direction: Bruce Brown
Screenplay: Bruce Brown and Dana Brown
Cinematographer: Mike Hoover
Editing: Bruce Brown and Dana Brown
Sound: Beverly Johnson
Executive music production: Joel Sill and Lonnie Sill
Music: Gary Hoey and Phil Marshall
MPAA rating: PG
Running time: 107 minutes

Europa

An idealistic young American, Leopold Kessler (Jean-Marc Barr), working as a railroad conductor in 1945 Germany, becomes unwittingly involved with a group of terrorists, in this thriller.

REVIEWS

Film Comment. XXVII, July-August 1991, p. 68.

CREDITS

Leopold Kessler: Jean-Marc Barr
Katharina Hartmann: Barbara Sukowa
Lawrence Hartmann: Udo Kier
Uncle Kessler: Ernst-Hugo Jaregard
Pater: Erik Mork
Max: Jorgen Reenberg
Colonel Harris: Eddie Constantine
Jew: Lars von Trier
Narrator: Max von Sydow

Origin: Denmark, France, and Germany
Released: 1991
Production: Peter Aalbeck Jensen and Bo Christensen for Nordisk Film and TV, Gunnar Obel, Gerard Mital, PCC, and WMG; released by Pathe-Nordisk
Direction: Lars von Trier
Screenplay: Lars von Trier and Niels Vorsel
Cinematographer: Henning Bendtsen, Edward Klosinky, and Jean-Paul Meurisse
Editing: Herve Schneid
Production design: Henning Bahs
Special effects: Dansk Special Effekt Service
Front-projection effects: Paul Witz
Sound: Per Streit Jensen
Special makeup effects: Morten Jacobsen
Costume design: Mann Rasmussen
Music: Joakim Holbek
MPAA rating: no listing
Running time: 114 minutes

Even Cowgirls Get the Blues

"From the beloved novel that charmed a generation comes a magical new film from the director of *Drugstore Cowboy* and *My Own Private Idaho*."
—Movie Tagline

"The hippest, most astounding and enjoyable, yes, the most utterly outrageous time-capsule of a hybrid western you're ever likely to see on the screen"—B. Ruby Rich, *Elle*

"A hip...psychedelic road movie"—*The Hollywood Reporter*

  Box Office Gross: $1,635,591 (June 12, 1994)

Novelist Tom Robbins is a master of the elaborately humorous digression. All of his novels are filled with quirky, seemingly irrelevant musings about life's myriad wonders. Everything from the rectal temperature of a bumblebee (110.8 degrees Fahrenheit) to the true cause of natural disasters ("Earth is God's pinball machine") can be found between the covers of one of his novels. In fact, Robbins' books are not so much novels as they are comic almanacs filled with funny facts, hilarious anecdotes, and outrageous observations. Plot and characters are secondary to the playful meanderings and off-the-wall metaphors, such as "The moon was narrow and pale, like a paring snipped from a snowman's toenail."

Uma Thurman as Sissy Hankshaw and Angie Dickinson as Miss Adrian in *Even Cowgirls Get the Blues*. Photo: Abigayle Tarsches © 1993 Fine Line Features. All rights reserved.

Because Robbins' main appeal as a novelist is his offbeat comic style rather than his story lines and characters, his books would seem a poor choice for cinematic adaptation. Although filmmakers in the past have succeeded in adapting difficult novels to the screen—a good example is David Cronenberg's superb reworking of William Burroughs' plotless Beat-era classic *Naked Lunch* (1991)—such achievements are extremely rare.

When it was announced that Gus Van Sant had been signed to adapt and direct Robbins' most famous novel, *Even Cowgirls Get the Blues* (1976), the general consensus was that if anyone could capture the essence of Robbins on celluloid, Van Sant could. The two artists have much in common, most notably their love for the offbeat and the eccentric, and the stylistic playfulness that each brings to his artistic medium. For example, Van Sant's previous films, *My Own Private Idaho* (1991), was a skillful interweaving of Shakespeare, gay porn, stream-of-consciousness dream imagery, gritty realism, and still-life poses. Van Sant successfully used these disparate styles to explore the tragic/comic world of a young narcoleptic male prostitute whose passion for cross-country hitchhiking and obsession with reestablishing a sense of family takes him on a picaresque journey of self-discovery. Since the main character of *Even Cowgirls Get the Blues* is also a hitchhiking outcast who ends up involved in a homosexual relationship, Van Sant seemed destined to do justice to Robbins' picaresque hodgepodge of a novel. Ultimately, however, it turns out that the traits that distinguish Van Sant's work from Robbins' are more profoundly dissimilar than the ones they have in common.

The film is narrated by Robbins himself, a casting choice that at first seems inspired but actually is a perfect example of everything that is wrong with the film. It turns out that Robbins' flat, nasal voice is distracting, his narration is amateurish and unemotional, and the material he reads is too uncomplimentary to the screen images. In other words, Robbins sounds as if he is unfamiliar with the material, as if he were reading it off-the-cuff. His narration fails to capture the whimsically playful essence inherent in his own work.

This amateurish, unrehearsed feeling permeates every aspect of the film. It is an artistic approach that is consistent with Van Sant's previous works, a primarily cinema verité approach that complements the earlier films' more realistic settings and serious subject matter. Nevertheless, it is totally inappropriate for the highly stylized, comically exaggerated tall-tale subject matter of *Even Cowgirls Get the Blues*.

The picaresque story chronicles the adventures of Sissy Hankshaw (Uma Thurman) who, because she is born with a pair of huge thumbs, is destined to become a master hitchhiker. On one of her frequent cross-country hitchhiking excursions, Sissy befriends the Countess (John Hurt), an eccentric, cross-dressing millionaire who has made his fortune by developing and promoting a line of feminine hygiene products. The Countess ends up hiring Sissy as a model for his products, eventually sending her on a modeling assignment to his posh health resort, the Rubber Rose Ranch, located in the rustic Pacific Northwest.

Upon arriving at the ranch, Sissy encounters the resort's glamorous manager Miss Adrian (Angie Dickinson), who gives her a warm welcome followed by a stern warning to steer clear of the ranch's cowgirl assistants, especially their rebellious leader, Bonanza Jellybean (Rain Phoenix). Apparently, Bonanza and her cowgirl cohorts have been disrupting Miss Adian's health and beauty seminars and discouraging guests from using the chemically harsh beauty products developed by the Countess.

While waiting for her modeling assignment, Sissy becomes involved with Bonanza, ultimately preferring the down-to-earth cowgirl life-style to the Countess' crassly commercial approach to life. The two women become fast friends and, eventually, lovers. When the tension between Miss Adrian and the cowgirls finally results in a full-scale

Upon receiving a cold reception at both the Venice and Toronto Film Festivals, the U.S. release of *Even Cowgirls Get the Blues* was delayed more than six months so that Van Sant could edit the film further.

ranch riot, all the guests vacate the resort, leaving the cowgirls in full command.

During the melee, Sissy runs off, finally taking refuge with the Chink (Noriyuki "Pat" Morita), an old philosophizing hermit who lives in the mountains overlooking the ranch. After enduring his loony lectures about achieving oneness with the universe, Sissy decides to return to the Countess' East Coast estate. Shortly after she arrives, Sissy gets into a heated argument with the Countess when he begins berating the cowgirls for taking over his ranch. Sissy hits the Countess with one of her huge thumbs, after which he suffers a concussion and sinks into a coma.

Horrified, Sissy believes her thumbs have become lethal weapons and decides to have them amputated. Returning to her rural Virginia hometown, Sissy asks her old family doctor (Buck Henry) to reconstruct her thumbs. After the doctor performs the operation on just one of her thumbs, however Sissy decides to return to the Rubber Rose Ranch and help the cowgirls defend the resort from being invaded by Federal agents.

Sissy finds the cowgirls in fine spirits despite the huge gathering of armed troops outside the ranch. The troops have been called out not just to reclaim the resort but also to rescue a flock of whooping cranes that have migrated to a lake inside the ranch grounds and are being held hostage by the cowgirls. Sissy discovers that the cowgirls have been feeding the cranes peyote to keep them from flying off. When the supply of peyote is depleted, the cranes finally depart. Bonanza rides off to tell the troops about the cranes and is gunned down. In the end, the ranch remains in the hands of the cowgirls with Sissy as the new ranch forewoman.

When reduced to its basic linear sequence of events, the film's story line has a loopy but logical forward progression. As stated previously, however, the main appeal of a Tom Robbins story is not founded in its plotline but in its playfully digressive meanderings. Unfortunately, Van Sant has eliminated most of the digressive material in order to simplify the plot. This might be a dramatically sound approach but the result in this instance is the elimination of the essence of Tom Robbins from the film. What is even more damaging is Van Sant's decision to have the actors speak Robbins' overly ornate dialogue while having them maintain an off-the-cuff naturalness to their delivery and mannerisms. Van Sant used a similar approach in *My Own Private Idaho* when his rough street hustlers suddenly began spouting dialogue from William Shakespeare's *Henry the Fourth* (1597-1598). In the earlier film, these scenes were the least successful but fortunately were offset by the film's other more effective stylistic approaches. In *Even Cowgirls Get the Blues*, however, the clash between the disparate styles is unrelenting.

CREDITS

Sissy Hankshaw: Uma Thurman
The Countess: John Hurt
Bonanza Jellybean: Rain Phoenix
The Chink: Noriyuki "Pat" Morita
Delores Del Ruby: Lorraine Bracco
Julian: Keanu Reeves
Miss Adrian: Angie Dickinson
Marie Barth: Sean Young
Howard Barth: Crispin Glover

Released: 1994
Production: Laurie Parker; released by Fine Line Features
Direction: Gus Van Sant
Screenplay: Gus Van Sant; based on the novel by Tom Robbins
Cinematographer: John Campbell and Eric Alan Edwards
Editing: Gus Van Sant and Curtiss Clayton
Production design: Missy Stewart
Art direction: Dan Self
Costume Design: Beatrix Aruna Pasztor
Music: k. d. lang and Ben Mink
MPAA rating: R
Running time: 97 minutes

Not even the presence of an all-star cast can make up for Van Sant's wrongheaded handling of the material. Everyone does have the right look, most especially Uma Thurman as a lanky, leather-clad Sissy standing impressively in the middle of the road performing ballet-like movements as she flags down every motorist in sight; Rain Phoenix as the diminutive but feisty cowgirl par excellence Bonanza Jellybean; and Angie Dickinson as the fussily elegant Miss Adrian. Unfortunately, no one in the cast is able to breathe any life into their paper-thin characters, nor can anyone handle the artificially ornate dialogue. Many well-known personalities make cameo appearances throughout the film—Roseanne Arnold as a fortune-telling Gypsy, Ken Kesey as Sissy's father, William Burroughs as a street person, Keanu Reeves as a tearful suitor, and Crispin Glover as a decadent party reveler, among others. Yet, as with the other more substantial parts, the cameos fail to bring any life to this quirky film.

The critical reaction to the film was unanimously negative. Some criticized the film's failure to recapture the era in which it is set—the 1970's and its inability to develop any of the myriad themes touched upon in the novel—the women's movement, Eastern mysticism, environmentalism, hallucinogenic drugs, the sexual revolution, the joys of hitchhiking, and the significance of the single-cell amoeba. Most agreed that Van Sant's attempt to combine realism with picaresque exaggeration was the wrong approach to take. Yet

"I think it's somewhat of an encapsulation of a small minature sixties world wherein there's a miniature cultural and aesthetic revolution in the face of conformity."—director Gus Van Sant on *Even Cowgirls Get the Blues*

not every aspect of the film was condemned. The original music score by k. d. lang and Ben Mink was correctly singled out as the film's most outstanding attribute.

The film was in trouble before it was officially released. It had originally been scheduled to premiere in the fall of 1993; however, after disastrous showings at the Venice and Toronto film festivals, release was held up for six months so Van Sant could reedit the film. When it was finally released the following spring, it failed to find an audience and quickly disappeared from theaters.

Aside from *Even Cowgirls Get the Blues*, Van Sant has proven to be an innovative and resourceful filmmaker, leaving little doubt that he will recover from the failure of this effort and go on to create more accomplished works. What is more difficult to predict is whether anyone else will attempt to adapt another Tom Robbins novel to the screen.

—*Jim Kline*

REVIEWS

Entertainment Weekly. May 20, 1994, p. 42.
The Hollywood Reporter. September 13, 1993, p. 7.
Los Angeles Times. May 20, 1994, p. F2.
The New York Times. May 20, 1994, p. B10.
Newsweek. May 30, 1994, p. 64.
Rolling Stone. May 19, 1994, p. 107.
Variety. September 8, 1993, p. 4.

The Events Leading Up to My Death

This Canadian comedy centers on a dysfunctional suburban family—stoic Dad (Peter MacNeill), flirtatious Mom (Rosemary Radcliffe), and daughters Lindsay (Linda Kash) and Katie (Karen Hines)—that gathers to celebrate the twenty-first birthday of son Angus (John Allore).

CREDITS

Angus: John Allore
Dad: Peter MacNeill
Mom: Rosemary Radcliffe
Lindsay: Linda Kash
Katie: Karen Hines
Julia: Maria Del Mar
Rita: Mary Margaret O'Hara

Origin: Canada
Released: 1991
Production: Bill Robertson; released by Flat Rock Films
Direction: Bill Robertson
Screenplay: Bill Robertson
Cinematographer: Derek Underschultz
Editing: Bill Robertson
Editing: David Ostry
Sound: Peter Clements
Music: Mary Margaret O'Hara and Bill Robertson
MPAA rating: no listing
Running time: 89 minutes

AWARDS AND NOMINATIONS

Vancouver International Film Festival Awards:
Best Screenplay

Every Breath

In this thriller, a failed actor (Judd Nelson) has a steamy affair with Lauren, (Joanna Pacula), a married woman. Lauren's husband (Patrick Bauchau) is impotent and is into kinky sex games and voyeurism.

REVIEWS

Variety. CCCLI, June 21, 1993, p. 43.

CREDITS

Jimmy: Judd Nelson
Lauren: Joanna Pacula
Richard: Patrick Bauchau
Bob: Willy Garson
Mimi: Rebecca Arthur
Hal: John Pyper Ferguson
Kris: Cynthia Brimball
Kim: Kathleen Beaton

Released: 1993
Production: Brad Krevoy and Steve Stabler; released by Motion Picture Corporation of America
Direction: Steve Bing
Screenplay: Andrew Fleming, Steve Bing, and Judd Nelson
Cinematographer: Chris Taylor
Editing: Eric Beason
Production design: Stuart Blatt
Art direction: Carey Meyer
Set decoration: David A. Konoff
Casting: Ed Mitchell and Robyn Ray
Sound: Peter V. Meiselmann
Music: Nils Lofgren
MPAA rating: R
Running time: 85 minutes

Exchange Lifeguards (Wet and Wild Summer)

An American land developer, Mike McCain (Elliott Gould), sends his son, Bobby (Christopher Atkins), to Australia to pose as a lifeguard and check out a surfing beach that his father would like to purchase and turn into an expensive resort, in this comedy.

CREDITS

Bobby McCain: Christopher Atkins
Mike McCain: Elliott Gould
Mick: Julian McMahon
Julie Thomas: Rebecca Cross
Richard Grey: Christopher Pate
Cheryl: Vanessa Steele
Tishi: Peter Gow
Donna: Amanda Newman-Phillips
Max: Mark Hembrow

Origin: Australia
Released: 1993
Production: Phil Avalon for Avalon Films, with the participation of the Australian Film Finance Corporation; released by Beyond Films
Direction: Maurice Murphy
Screenplay: Phil Avalon
Cinematographer: Martin McGrath
Editing: Alan Trott
Production design: Richard Hobbs
Sound: Bob Clayton
Costume design: Jenny Campbell
Stunt coordination: Richard Bone
Music: John Capek
MPAA rating: no listing
Running time: 93 minutes

The Execution Protocol

Set at the Potosi Correctional Center in Missouri, this thought-provoking documentary focuses on the issue of capital punishment in the United States. Interviews are provided from three convicted murderers, one of whose death sentence was stayed only hours before his scheduled execution, as well as the prison warden and the inventor of the lethal injection machine Fred Leuchter.

REVIEWS

Christian Science Monitor. May 7, 1993, p. 15.
The New York Times. April 28, 1993, p. C13.

CREDITS

Bill Armontrout: Bill Armontrout
Dr. Pedro Cayabyab: Dr. Pedro Cayabyab
Paul Delo: Paul Delo
Don Roper: Don Roper
Gary Sutterfield: Gary Sutterfield
Gary Tune: Gary Tune
Joe Amrine: Joe Amrine
A. J. Bannister: A. J. Bannister
Doyle Williams: Doyle Williams

Released: 1993
Production: Mitch Wood and Stephen Trombley; released by First Run Features
Direction: Stephen Trombley
Cinematographer: Paul Gibson
Editing: Peter Miller
Music: Robert Lockhart
MPAA rating: no listing
Running time: 90 minutes

Exit to Eden

"To crack this case, these two cops will have to flash more than their badges."—Movie tagline

"Marvelously funny and enticingly erotic."—Paul Wunder, *WBAI Radio, New York*

"A titillating, provocative comedy."—Susan Granger, *CRN/American Movie Classics*

Box Office Gross: $6,813,570 (December 18, 1994)

Exit to Eden, the film adaptation of Anne Rice's erotic novel set on an island where people are encouraged to live out their sexual fantasies, ends up missing the boat to the island completely. This whips-and-chains comedy struggles to achieve both meaning and content (mixing cops and robbers and romance) and seems strangely indecisive in its approach, which alternates between soft-core pornography and romantic comedy, but fails miserably at both.

CREDITS

Lisa Emerson: Dana Delany
Elliot Slater: Paul Mercurio
Sheila Kingston: Rosie O'Donnell
Fred Lavery: Dan Aykroyd
Dr. Martin Halifax: Hector Elizondo
Omar: Stuart Wilson
Nina Blackstone: Iman
Tommy Miller: Sean O'Bryan
Diana: Stephanie Niznik

Released: 1994
Production: Alexandra Rose and Garry Marshall for Alex Rose/Henderson; released by Savoy Pictures
Direction: Garry Marshall
Screenplay: Deborah Amelon and Bob Brunner; based on the novel by Anne Rice
Cinematographer: Theo Van de Sande
Editing: David Finfer
Production design: Peter Jamison
Art direction: Margie McShirley
Set decoration: Linda Spheeris
Casting: Valorie Massalas
Sound: Jim Webb
Costume design: Ellen Mirojnick
Music: Patrick Doyle
MPAA rating: R
Running time: 113 minutes

The film centers upon an island, named Eden, that caters to people's sexual fantasies. This island resort is run by Mistress Lisa (Dana Delaney), the head dominatrix on Eden. Back on the mainland two diamond smugglers, Nina and Omar (Iman and Stuart Wilson), are photographed in the act smuggling diamonds through customs by photographer Elliott Slater, played by Paul Mercurio of *Strictly Ballroom* (1992) fame. To recover these incriminating pictures, Nina and Omar follow Elliott to Eden, where he hopes to work out his own submission/dominance fantasies.

Anne Rice's novel concerns the romance between Elliott and Lisa on the fantasy island. The screenplay complicates this relationship, which is developed over two years in the book but reduced to a few weeks in the film, by factoring in the jewel thieves and two LAPD detectives, Sheila and Fred (Rosie O'Donnell and Dan Aykroyd) who follow Omar and Nina to the island. Fred pretends to be a maintenance man, while Sheila is undercover, so to speak, as a guest. They spend as much time fighting off sexual advances as they do trying to locate Elliott, Nina, and Omar. The addition of this comedy duo really changes the direction and focus of the movie.

Delany and O'Donnell represent the two themes of the movie, which are at cross-purposes. Lisa takes herself too seriously, while O'Donnell's Sheila tries entirely too hard and fails too often in her attempts at wisecracking comedy. The polarization between these two characters makes the film less believable and removes the story from its source. The film offers a few laughs, but most of the comedy feels forced and unnatural. Just when one seems to be getting the hang of the film, a kinky romantic turn whips the plot in another direction.

Delaney and Mercurio fall in love and elope to New Orleans. As they attempt to solidify their love there, they are chased by the bad guys and the cops towards a lackluster climax at an antebellum mansion. The film ends entirely too neatly, and its contrived happy ending simply does not wash.

The attempts to give Mistress Lisa depth and meaning really fall short of their intended goal. The film attempts to explain her dominatrix lifestyle through flashbacks to both her father after her mother's death, and her college days, when she changed her victim status to that of a dominatrix.

"You're gonna see body parts the size of your garage."—*Exit to Eden* director Garry Marshall

The script attempts to do the same with flashbacks to Elliott's life. The opening scene shows him being spanked by the family housekeeper and enjoying it, thus sparking his eventual, albeit reluctant, interest in the world of submission and dominance.

Director Garry Marshall, best known for *Pretty Woman* (1990), which set a precedence for an odd sexual spin, should have avoided this project altogether. When screenwriters Deborah Amelon and Bob Brunner added the characters played by Akroyd and O'Donnell, they were presumably attempting to make a comedy out of a book about sadomasochistic fantasies, and in the process changed the original narrators of the book from Elliott and Mistress Lisa to O'Donnell's character in the movie. They failed to make the plot and invented subplot mesh into one coherent film. The film ends up lacking in both comedic strength and sex appeal, though the action is far more laughable than erotic.

Unless viewers have a derrière fetish, the supposedly sexiest scene in the film will not convey much sex appeal. Holiday-makers romping in various stages of undress do nothing to spark any real adventuresome sexuality. Even when the people who run the island attempt to create sexual fantasies for their guests (for example the secretary dominating the boss), they fall short of creating much interest. All that remains is a peculiar soft-porn romance disguised as a generally unfunny comedy.

—*Alexandra M. Mather and James M. Welsh*

REVIEWS

The Detroit Free Press. October 14, 1994, E14.
Entertainment Weekly. October 28, 1994, p. 70.
Los Angeles Times. October 14, 1994, F12.
New York Magazine. October 31, 1994, pp. 96-98.
The New York Times. October 14, 1994, B13.
People Weekly. October 31, 1994, p. 19.
The Toronto Globe and Mail. 15 Oct. 1994, C2.
Variety. October 14, 1994, p. 2.
The Village Voice. October 25, 1994, p. 57.

Exotica

"Two enthusiastic thumbs up! One of the freshest and most original films we've seen in a long time."—*Siskel & Ebert*

"Dazzling! Eroticism and secrecy haunt this film. Nothing is what it seems."—Caryn James, *The New York Times*

"A Gripping, Psychological Puzzle."—Renee Rodriquez, *Miami Herald*

"A Lush, Psychological Thriller."—Howard Feinstein, *New York Post*

"An Astonishing, Extraordinary Film."—John Anderson, *New York Newsday*

"A haunting and sensuous film! The best film of the winter!"—J. Hoberman, *Village Voice*

 Box Office Gross: $2,975,575 (December 18, 1994)

Exotica is a refreshingly unique, creative, intriguing and almost perfectly executed parable about the clash between appearances and purposes. By all rights, it ought to propel Canadian filmmaker Atom Egoyan into the front ranks of young directors.

It ought to, but probably won't, because it is too delicate and subtle to be lionized by the critics and audiences that made *Pulp Fiction* (reviewed in this volume) the height of hip mid-1990s filmmaking. Egoyan clearly doesn't care whether he is hip. He breaks all the rules, old and new. Though *Exotica* is about the effects of a violent society, there is scarcely any violence in it. Though *Exotica* appears to be about sleazy sex, there is no sex in it. Its characters don't indulge in profanity for its own sake, they don't swagger or grandstand. They are all too disappointingly human.

The dictionary defines "exotica" as "things excitingly different and unusual." There are at least two aspects of this film that are rare and remarkable. First, its characters don't talk in movie dialogue, but in real voices; they aren't histrionic, but act like ordinary people. Second, nothing is quite what it seems in *Exotica*—it's a meditation on the clash between surface appearance and deeper meaning, between form and function.

The primary setting for the film is a Toronto strip club. Francis (Bruce Greenwood) goes there regularly for one purpose: to pay extra for the tantalizing Christina (Mia Kirshner) to do a table-dance for him. This is a setting and story line that, if recounted without further explanation, is guaranteed to win writer-director Egoyan enmity from some quarters. But Egoyan has disdain for superficialists, and in fact the entire film is a prank on people who jump to conclusions.

One assumption Egoyan unmasks is that the sex industry peddles and delivers sex, when in fact its main commodity is solace. It is a poor and addictive substitute for real understanding and affection, but desperate customers pay for it. Strip clubs sell only the appearance of sexual availability. Touching the performers is strictly prohibited. Men who go there to watch often are trying to quench a deeper, unspoken need.

The plot line for *Exotica*, involving Francis' job of auditing the records of pet shop owner Thomas grew out of *Exotica* director Atom Egoyan's own experience with being audited.

If one buys that premise, then one may understand what Francis is doing at the strip club, which looks like a tropical jungle but is more uptight than steamy. It's the only way he seems to know of to get out of the mental mess he's in. It's important to note that Egoyan isn't praising his characters and their actions, just depicting them.

Egoyan also teases moralists with scenes of Francis repeatedly dropping off a young baby-sitter and thanking her warmly. It's natural to think there's something immoral going on between the two. But later Egoyan reveals that the baby-sitting is also a kind of mutual charade that is part of Francis's self-therapy.

All the characters, in fact, have hidden, loftier reasons for engaging in actions that appear to be immoral or degrading.

They are driven by their sense of obligation to themselves and others to engage in and repeat behavior that seems senseless but has its own inner logic.

Christina displays a cool detachment while doing a hot routine in a schoolgirl outfit. Her dance is purposeful and ritualistic but not jaded. It is innocence lifting up a skirt.

Kirshner, who shows tremendous promise, is masterful at conveying a likeable, sensible person behind the exotic performer. In other films, such a character would be scripted as having a few screws loose, but Christina is straightforward and matter-of-fact. Like the other characters, she is an ordinary person caught in an extraordinary situation. Just why she's doing what she's doing is part of the puzzle.

Eric (Elias Koteas), the macho announcer at the strip club who tries to put patrons in the mood to buy, clearly is agitated by Christina's performance. He spies on her while she dances for Francis. He is enraged, but is it merely with jealousy? All we know at first, through flashbacks, is that Eric and Christina first met on a walk through fields, which turns out to be a search for a missing child.

Other characters are equally puzzling. Thomas (Don McKellar), a timid-looking pet shop proprietor, has strange liaisons and unlikely criminal ties. Zoé (Arsineé Khanjian), the owner of the strip club, is carrying on a family tradition and using an unlikely method to start a new one while carrying on a lesbian relationship with Christina. Tracey (Sarah Polley), the baby-sitter, is learning about the uncomfortable relationship between her father and her employer.

Many of the characters, one eventually realizes, are in various kinds of trances. Christina is in a trance when she dances, Francis when he watches her, Eric when he announces, Thomas the pet shop owner when he goes to a concert looking to pick up a date. Eventually, the characters become enmeshed in a tangle of love, blackmail and murderous intent. And they are redeemed only when all assumptions are exploded.

Watching the film is like working a jigsaw puzzle. One keeps picking up the same pieces, finding new ones, trying out combinations until the scenes gradually take larger shape and begin to make sense. It's demanding and often frustrating work. Egoyan doesn't let the picture emerge easily, and there's plenty of opportunity for mistaken interpre-

CREDITS

Francis: Bruce Greenwood
Christina: Mia Kirshner
Thomas: Don McKellar
Zoé: Arsineé Khanjian
Eric: Elias Koteas
Tracey: Sarah Polley
Harold: Victor Garber
Customs officer: Calvin Green

Origin: Canada
Released: 1994
Production: Atom Egoyan and Camelia Frieberg for Alliance Communications Corporation and Ego Film Arts, with the participation of Telefilm Canada and the Ontario Film Development Corporation; released by Miramax Films
Direction: Atom Egoyan
Screenplay: Atom Egoyan
Cinematographer: Paul Sarossy
Editing: Susan Shipton
Production design: Linda del Rosario and Richard Paris
Sound: Ross Redfern
Costume design: Linda Muir
Music: Mychael Danna
MPAA rating: R
Running time: 104 minutes

AWARDS AND NOMINATIONS

Golden Palm Awards 1994: International Critics' Prize

tations. Don't judge people and their actions until you know them completely, he seems to be saying. And even the final picture has plenty of gaps—like real life.

Other directors have attempted this sort of story, where a web between characters gradually emerges. Robert Altman comes to mind in films such as *Nashville* (1975) and *Short Cuts* (1993), but his characters are always talky and outgoing. Except for their circumstances, Egoyan's characters are utterly unremarkable and rather quiet. Their dialogue is disarmingly ordinary. They don't engage in movie actions, and they don't talk movie talk. Surprisingly, this makes them both more appealing and more unsettling.

Egoyan is masterful at creating a mood and getting all his actors to conform to it. The acting is so good that one never thinks one is watching anyone other than real people. Greenwood's portrayal of Francis is eerie and disarming. Koteas as Eric always appears to be on the brink of erupting, but that behavior is a mask for his real motivations. Kirshner blends titillation, innocence and honesty in a compelling performance. As the pet shop owner, McKellar brings incredible restraint and authenticity to what starts out as a minor role and grows into a crucial one. Polley is perfect in her part as a kind-hearted teenager learning things about life she'd rather not know.

Clearly, *Exotica* isn't everyone's cup of tea. It isn't meant to be. Some will find it unbearably dull; others frustrating. Many will miss the point. Critics were sharply divided on it, and to no one's surprise, it didn't become a box-office hit.

It is risky business to construct a film story around events that are never depicted. The violence that has set the main characters into their ritualized motion is alluded to late in the film and never shown. Egoyan's tack is the exact opposite of filmmakers who try to shock with graphic depictions of brutality and profanity. Egoyan keeps the turmoil that lurks beneath our civilized society quiet and hidden.

That's why *Exotica* is unsettling, because it is closer to the truth. Random violence does erupt in the most ordinary settings while the rest of life goes on seemingly undisturbed. The violence carries with it an air of unreality and everyone shares a sense that it couldn't really be happening. That only adds to its power over us.

Egoyan's characters are gentle people trying to construct and reconstruct their lives, struggling imperfectly to make sense out of a nonsensical society. When violence happens to people like them, they aren't necessarily good at handling it or processing it, especially in the middle of a placid society. So their healing can take on exotic forms.

With exhilarating acuity, *Exotica* debunks the rumors and assumptions that societal prejudices feed on. In a disarming way, it explodes preconceptions. At its heart it is full of genuine humanity.

The flaws in *Exotica* are that the story is somewhat contrived and forced; some of the connections between characters are strained; some characters are not as well developed as they could be; and the film could be tighter and more suspenseful. But these flaws only show what a short distance Egoyan has to go to bridge the gap between virtuosity and a masterpiece. Egoyan is in total control of a very unique approach to moviemaking. His style—though harkening on occasion to that master of deception and irony, Buñuel—is fresh and uncomprising.

Exotica is not a masterpiece, but it is masterful. It is excitingly different and unusual. It holds many marvels for those with the patience to stick with it.

Egoyan's vision has the scope and depth to transcend cult film status. He has the talent and integrity to be one of those rare directors who force the business of film to conform to his artistic vision, rather than the other way around.

—*Michael Betzold*

REVIEWS

The Detroit Free Press. March 29, 1995, p. 4C.
Entertainment Weekly. March 24, 1995, p. 46.
Los Angeles Times. March 3, 1995, p. F10.
New York Magazine. March 13, 1995, p. 63.
The New York Times. Sept. 24, 1994, p. 13.
Variety. May 16-22, 1994, p. 40.
The Wall Street Journal. March 16, 1995, p. 20.

Extramuros

Two nuns, Sor Ana (Carmen Maura) and Sor Angele (Mercedes Sampietro), who are involved in an illicit love affair, fake a miracle, then suffer the consequences, in this drama set during the Spanish Inquisition.

Origin: Spain
Released: 1991
Production: Antonio Martin; released by Frameline
Direction: Miguel Picazo
Screenplay: Miguel Picazo; based on a novel by Jesus Fernandez Santos
Cinematographer: Teo Escamilla
Editing: Jose Luis Matesanz
Music: Jose Nieto
MPAA rating: no listing
Running time: 118 minutes

CREDITS

Sor Ana: Carmen Maura
Sor Angele: Mercedes Sampietro
Prioress: Aurora Bautista
Duchess: Assumpta Serna
Doctor: Antonio Ferrandis

Father

Max von Sydow stars as a man accused of being a Nazi war criminal whose devoted daughter (Carol Drinkwater), a restaurateur, maintains his innocence.

Released: 1992
Production: Paul Douglas Barron; released by Northern Arts Entertainment
Direction: John Power
Screenplay: Tony Cavanaugh and Graham Hartley
Cinematographer: Dan Burstall
Editing: Kerry Regan
Music: Peter Best
MPAA rating: no listing
Running time: 100 minutes

REVIEWS

Library Journal. CXV, May 1, 1990, p. 128.

CREDITS

Joe Mueller: Max von Sydow
Anne Winton: Carol Drinkwater
Bobby Winton: Steve Jacobs
Iya Zetnick: Julia Blake

AWARDS AND NOMINATIONS

Australian Film Institute 1990: Best Actor (von Sydow), Best Actress (Blake)

The Favor

"Two Women. Three Men. One Secret."
—Movie tagline

 Box Office Gross: $2,975,575 (May 15, 1994)

Sweet, but difficult to swallow, *The Favor* is a light romantic farce that achieved only a brief theatrical run. The comedy sat on the shelf for several years while Orion Pictures went through bankruptcy proceedings, and the film's period of dormancy did not do it any favors. The film's biggest problem is simply its implausible central premise, hinted at in its title. Harley Jane Kozak plays Kathy, a Portland wife and mother of two young daughters who is going through a midlife crisis. After ten years of marriage, Kathy has taken to fantasizing about her high school sweetheart, Tom Andrews (Ken Wahl), because of her upcoming fifteenth high school class reunion back in Ohio. Although Kathy has not seen Tom since high school, she knows that he now lives in Denver. When she finds out that her best friend, Emily (Elizabeth McGovern), is heading to Denver on a business trip, Kathy, in desperation, asks Emily to do her a favor: Knowing that Emily is single and has had extensive sexual experience, Kathy asks her if she will look Tom up while she is in town, sleep with him, and report back to her.

Not surprisingly, the plan backfires. Despite her initial understandable reluctance, Emily does indeed find Tom, and she not only sleeps with him but also raves to Kathy about his sexual prowess. Rather than quell Kathy's smoldering passion, Emily's experience fans the flames. Kathy's ensuing jealousy throws the two friends and their respective partners' lives into comic turmoil. Once viewers swallow this ridiculous premise, they can enjoy the rest of the film, as one amusing misunderstanding leads to the next. The first casualty is Peter (Bill Pullman), Kathy's mild-mannered and loving math professor husband. Bewildered by his wife's sudden erratic behavior and her unexplained breakup with Emily—and egged on by his obnoxious best friend, Joe (Larry Miller)—Peter begins to suspect that Kathy is seeing another man.

Meanwhile, Emily reveals to Kathy that she is pregnant—by her youthful artist protege and lover, Elliott (Brad Pitt), with whom she just broke up. Kathy, in a misguided effort to help, takes it upon herself to tell Elliott. Jealous

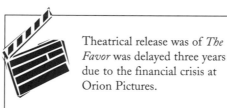

Theatrical release was of *The Favor* was delayed three years due to the financial crisis at Orion Pictures.

Peter, with sidekick Joe in tow, follows Kathy to Elliott's studio and thus suspects that Elliott may be the other man. When Emily discovers what Kathy has done, in a fit of anger, she says that the baby is really Tom's. This new development gives Kathy an excuse to fly to Denver to see Tom, which she happens to do in a sexy red dress and heels—just like in her dreams.

Coincidentally, Elliott is also flying to Denver for an art exhibit, and the two end up on the same plane. Peter, with the help of Joe, finds out and decides to follow the two to Denver to break up what he believes is a romantic tryst. Emily, too, arrives in Denver for Elliott's art show. Thus the story builds to the climax when all five principals—Kathy, Emily, Peter, Elliott, and Tom—converge on Tom's cabin in the Colorado wilderness.

Kathy's fantasizing is perhaps the most innovative and amusing aspect of *The Favor* and must surely account for the film's R rating in an otherwise G story. Reminiscent of the opening scenes of *Romancing the Stone* (1984), *The Favor* begins with Harley Jane Kozak in a red leather minidress strutting down a dark street populated only with men in suits who all turn to ogle her as she passes. She sees a handsome teenage football player, and the two start to make passionate love in a dark corridor when a little girl's voice drags the woman back to reality: It is morning in her middle-class suburban home, and her two young daughters want her to get up. Although she tries to close her eyes and pick up where she left off, the demands of family prevent her. Another standout fantasy sequence takes place after Sunday services as the family leaves church. Kathy sees Peter stumble on the stairs leading out of the building, and the ensuing sequence depicts her as a mourning widow at a cemetery. As with the film's opening fantasy, the sequence starts realistically enough. It is only as the action becomes more and more surreal—as Tom comes striding across the field to whisk the grieving Kathy away in a scene out of a romance novel—that the viewer realizes that Kathy has been fantasizing the entire sequence.

Both Kozak and McGovern are believable and likable in their central roles as best friends. Kozak has been seen in such hit films as *When Harry Met Sally* (1989), *Parenthood* (1989), and *Arachnophobia* (1990). She also costarred in *The Taking of Beverly Hills* (1991), *Necessary Roughness* (1991), and *All I Want for Christmas* (1991). McGovern's film debut in the Academy Award-winning *Ordinary People* (1980) launched her on a notable career that has included such films as

Ragtime (1981), *Racing with the Moon* (1984), *The Handmaid's Tale* (1990), and *King of the Hill* (1993). It is refreshing to see, as several critics noted, a friendship between women so realistically and positively portrayed in a film, as well as a sex comedy with a feminine outlook.

Yet it is the men in *The Favor* who really stand out. Bill Pullman plays Peter as a kind man who is completely baffled by his wife's erratic behavior. His amusing little musical interludes on the harmonica lend to his very realistic portrayal. Pullman made his film debut in *Ruthless People* (1986) and has had starring roles in such hit films as *Sommersby* (1993) and *Sleepless in Seattle* (1993). Kathy and Peter's very comfortable marriage is depicted realistically in various small scenes, such as one in which the two are going to bed. Each halfheartedly initiates lovemaking, thinking the other one wants to do it. When they realize that neither one is really interested, they make a date to do so later in the week, when they are both free. Their fatigue and mutual familiarity are touching.

Larry Miller as Peter's amusingly obnoxious buddy, Joe, plays a key role in the ensuing mayhem. Miller was perhaps best known as the obsequious boutique manager in *Pretty Woman* (1990). Joe's lewd, worldly insights into Peter's marital problems goad Peter into rash action, pre-

"You came back with a plastic shark, I came back with crabs."— Emily, to her friend Kathy, in *The Favor*

cipitating the climactic scene at Tom's cabin. Joe delights in playing the little devil who whispers his absurd suspicions into Peter's ear.

The other two supporting players, Ken Wahl and Brad Pitt, contribute winning performances as well. Wahl makes Tom everything that Kathy dreamed he would be—strong, masculine, and outdoorsy down to the fashionable stubble on his face. Yet his character holds a few surprises: He sports a mean streak at the end that catches Kathy, and the viewer, off guard. Wahl had previously costarred with Kozak in *The Taking of Beverly Hills*. Pitt also surprises. He proves to be an adorable Elliott, Emily's considerably younger but surprisingly sensitive lover. Pitt debuted in the hit film *Thelma and Louise* (1991) and continued to find success with roles in such films as *A River Runs Through It* (1992) and *Kalifornia* (1993). In the end, Elliott, in his twenties, proves to be the most mature of this otherwise thirty-something group.

Director Donald Petrie had more success with a later film, *Grumpy Old Men* (1993), that was actually released before *The Favor*. Starring three veteran actors—Jack Lemmon, Walter Matthau, and Ann-Margret—*Grumpy Old Men* had the star power that was noticeably lacking in *The Favor*. His feature-film debut, *Mystic Pizza* (1988), also a romantic comedy, launched the career of superstar Julia Roberts in a film that, like *The Favor*, centered on women, friendship, and romantic relationships.

Screenwriters Josann McGibbon and Sara Parriott had previously worked together on *Worth Winning* (1989), starring Mark Harmon, and on the story for *Three Men and a Little Lady* (1990), starring Tom Selleck, Ted Danson, and Steve Guttenberg. According to the film's press kit, the two women, best friends as well as collaborators, based *The*

CREDITS

Kathy: Harley Jane Kozak
Emily: Elizabeth McGovern
Peter: Bill Pullman
Elliott: Brad Pitt
Tom Andrews: Ken Wahl
Joe Dubin: Larry Miller

Released: 1994
Production: Lauren Shuler-Donner for Nelson Entertainment; released by Orion Pictures
Direction: Donald Petrie
Screenplay: Sara Parriott and Josann McGibbon
Cinematographer: Tim Suhrstedt
Editing: Harry Keramidas
Production design: David Chapman
Art direction: Mark Haack
Set decoration: Clay A. Griffith
Casting: Bonnie Timmerman
Sound: Stephan Von Hase
Costume design: Carol Oditz
Music: Thomas Newman
MPAA rating: R
Running time: 97 minutes

Bill Pullman and Harley Jane Kozak as Peter and Kathy Whiting in *The Favor*. © 1994 Orion Pictures. All rights reserved.

Favor on real-life experience. Apparently, Parriott planned to attend her own high school reunion in Ohio, and McGibbon, married with kids, asked her to look up her old boyfriend. McGibbon had been dreaming about him and hoped that her friend's visit would put her imagination to rest. They then proceeded to brainstorm about what would happen if Parriott actually slept with him and enjoyed it.

Despite an adequate script and good performances, however, the film proved to have limited commercial appeal, perhaps because it is primarily a woman's film and confusion regarding its protagonist. Although Kathy, the happily married wife and mother, is obviously the central character, her best friend Emily—a dissatisfied single career woman whose

biological clock is ticking—perhaps spoke more to the average woman of the 1990's, which was the film's intended audience.

—*Cynthia K. Breckenridge*

REVIEWS

The Hollywood Reporter. April 29-May 1, 1994, p. 7.
Los Angeles Times. April 29, 1994, p. F11.
The New York Times. April 29, 1994, p. B9.
Variety. April 28, 1994, p. 4.

Fear of a Black Hat

"Big laughs, two thumbs up."—*Siskel & Ebert*
"A lewd, laugh-out-loud spoof of rap music that compares favorably to *This Is Spinal Tap*."—Bruce Williamson, *Playboy*

 Box Office Gross: $189,531 (July 10, 1994)

Rap music has become to America in the 1990's what rock and roll was to America in the 1950's and 1960's: It is music of a younger generation, which, in general, scares older people. Back in the days of Elvis Presley's pelvic gyrations on television's *The Ed Sullivan Show*, many Americans saw rock as the beginning of the end of society as we know it. Yet this phenomenon has happened before: Back in the 1920's, dances such as the Charleston or the Black Bottom were scandalous and drew similar fearful responses.

What makes rap so potent and frightening to many is its roots: Rap music is the music of the ghetto, the African American ghetto specifically, and much of the music expresses the angst of young African American men. It also reflects the violence that had become so commonplace in urban black America. Complicating matters were the numerous arrests of several prominent rap performers for serious crimes: Snoop Doggy Dogg was accused of allegedly participating in a murder, and Tupac Shakur faced less serious but still severe charges for

other crimes. Rap music has also been criticized for its victimization of women and use of profanity. This music has also been the center of a Supreme Court case that tested the limits of free speech.

Into this cultural context comes *Fear of a Black Hat*, which is very simply a mock documentary focusing on a fictitious rap group called N.W.H. ("Niggaz With Hats"). As such, it calls to mind the highly successful parody of a rock documentary directed by Rob Reiner, *This is Spinal Tap* (1984). In fact, the film even has the look and flavor of *This is Spinal Tap*. Director/star Rusty Cundieff admitted in the press materials that he wanted to be "the black Rob Reiner." Whereas *This is Spinal Tap* was able to skewer the world of heavy-metal music in a way that was hilarious to anyone who watched, regardless of their knowledge of the music, however, *Fear of a Black Hat* will appeal primarily to those who are well versed in rap music.

The premise of *Fear of a Black Hat* is that sociologist Nina Blackburn (Kasi Lemmons) is doing a video study of rap music. She follows the group N.W.H. from its humble beginnings, when they are still unknown. She tells the group members that she is intrigued by their politics, expressing interest in their album called *Kill Whitey*. Her camera captures the group's discovery of a gimmick that brings them notoriety: During a frustrating preconcert discussion, they discover that they do not have hats to wear for the concert. Their manager, Guy (Howie Gold), a cretinous white man who talks about the group's "rich emotional tapestry," makes hats for them out of

"The butt is like society, and we see that as expansion..."
—*Fear of a Black Hat*'s rapper Ice Cold inanely justifying the song "Booty Juice"

newspaper. This leads to a progressive series of hats, which eventually become so outlandish that they look like something out of Dr. Seuss.

The group is led by street-philosopher Ice Cold (Rusty Cundieff). His inflated philosophizing and his rationalizations for the references to violence and degrading images of women in the group's music is hilarious. For example, when justifying their hit song "Booty Juice," which is a takeoff on a real MTV video celebrating women with big rear ends, Ice waxes philosophic: "The butt is like society, and we see that as expansion..." His explanation about the importance of the group's name, Niggaz With Hats, is impossible to follow, which is the whole point: He says something about how slaves had no hats, and how they would get back to the plantation every night and be too tired to make hats. His illogical meanderings actually point up a basic truth—the group's name is just a name, just a gimmick.

Rusty Cundieff is right on the mark as Ice Cold: steely, serious, and overly impressed with himself, exactly like any other music or film star whose inanities go unchallenged by people afraid to admit that the Emperor is wearing no clothes. What makes *Fear of a Black Hat* resonate beyond mere parody is the gray area between truth and

CREDITS

Tasty Taste: Larry B. Scott
Tone Def: Mark Christopher Lawrence
Ice Cold: Rusty Cundieff
Nina Blackburn: Kasi Lemmons
Guy Friesch: Howie Gold
Marty Rabinow: Barry Heins
Jike Singelton: Eric Laneuville
Vanilla Sherbet: Devin Kamienny
Kurt Loder: Kurt Loder

Released: 1994
Production: Darin Scott for ITC Entertainment Group; released by the Samuel Goldwyn Company
Direction: Rusty Cundieff
Screenplay: Rusty Cundieff
Cinematographer: John Demps, Jr.
Editing: Karen Horn
Production design: Stuart Blatt
Set decoration: Penny Barrett
Casting: Jaki Brown and Kimberly Hardin
Special effects: Kevin McCarthy
Sound: Oliver L. Moss
Makeup: Stacye Branche
Costume design: Rita McGhee
Music supervision: Larry Robinson
MPAA rating: R
Running time: 86 minutes

absurdity in which Ice Cold operates. Did society create the monstrous images of women and violence depicted in this music or are they purely intrinsic to the artist? Is the artist mirroring society, or is it mirroring him?

The other performers also hit their targets perfectly. Larry B. Scott plays the role of Tasty Taste, a dour character who politely shows documentarian Nina around his new home, complete with shooting range. He shows her his arsenal of weapons in a scene that not only satirizes the role of guns in society but also parodies a scene in *This is Spinal Tap*. Where Christopher Guest shows his collection of guitars, Tasty proudly displays his guns: "Now, these guns are good for beginners," says Tasty. "You just spray the area."

Mark Christopher Lawrence is Tone Def, the spiritually aware disc jockey of the group. Tone Def is on a constant search for spirituality, as evidenced by his intense understanding of the ludicrous ideology of yet a new manager: While Tasty and Ice are baffled as to what the man is saying, Tone reverentially responds, "yeah, 'cause when you take that bus, you get there." It is a perfect lampoon of the non-sequitur-style responses that have become a part of 1990's society.

Another target for satire and parody is represented by Vanilla Sherbet (Devin Kamienny), a takeoff on white rappers, specifically Vanilla Ice. Vanilla Ice was challenged when he claimed to have been reared in the "'hood," when he really grew up in a middle-class neighborhood. It has been argued that white rappers merely appropriate the African American experience as their own because it is "hip."

In a similar vein, the film targets exploitative record company executives and managers, who are portrayed as sycophantic jerks: At one point, the group ends up with a black manager who compares them to Malcolm X; elsewhere, a white executive from "Jack 'Em Records" informs them that they do not plan to release the new album, saying, "Yo, homeys, it's not the def chill fresh thing to do."

Many of the song titles and character names are unprintable; all are extremely funny and sharp-witted. Names of other rappers include Parsley, Sage—a takeoff on the group Salt-n-Pepa—Ice Tray, Ice Water, Ice Coffee, Ice Box, and Ice Berg. No stone is left unturned. As all the above examples show, the script, also by Cundieff, is funny and insightful without being didactic. Cundieff understands the difference between satire and parody and uses both to great advantage.

The only place where *Fear of a Black Hat* starts to lose ground is when it gets too involved in the linear story of the rise and fall of the group, and the conflict that arises when Tasty Taste falls for a groupie who plants the seed of jealousy that destroys the group. The scenes where the group breaks up and then meets again are not shot in as interesting a fashion as the rest of the film—they are awkwardly blocked, with the actors in unnatural positions in the room, which are obviously meant for the camera. The documentary gets lost in this process. At first it is quite realistic, with the group asking Nina to turn off the camera á la Madonna's documentary *Truth or Dare* (1991) when situations warrant. Yet later, once this convention has been established, they cease to even acknowledge the camera, and the film begins to resemble a conventional drama.

Fear of a Black Hat is ultimately an entertaining satire of the recording industry in general. The cult of personality that drives much of the music industry in America is deftly skewered here, and deservedly so. That the film has the depth to raise questions about the role society plays in the creation of the personalities that dominate rap music is to its credit.

—*Kirby Tepper*

REVIEWS

Entertainment Weekly. June 3, 1994, p. 39.
The Hollywood Reporter. June 3-5, 1994, p. 18.
Los Angeles Times. June 3, 1994, p. F4.
The New York Times. June 3, 1994, p. B7.
Variety. February 5, 1993, p. 14.

Finzan

When the abusive husband of a tribal African woman, Nanyuma (Diarrah Sanogo), dies, she is promised by the village chief (Balla Moussa Keita) to her crazy brother-in-law (Oumar Namory Keita). Nanyuma runs away rather than be forced into another oppressive marriage, in this drama that focuses on the oppression of women in traditional African society. Her rebellion leads a group of local women to support her, threatening the structure of male privilege in the village. The story also involves Fili, a young city girl, who is sent to the village by her conservative father for a ritual circumcision which she tries to resist. In Bambara with English subtitles.

CREDITS

Nanyuma: Diarrah Sanogo
Bala: Oumar Namory Keita
Village chief: Balla Moussa Keita

Origin: Africa
Released: 1990
Production: Kora Films, VDF, and National Center for Film Production of Mali; released by California Newsreel
Direction: Cheick Oumar Sissoko
Screenplay: Cheick Oumar Sissoko
Cinematographer: Cheick Hamala Keita
Editing: Ouaba Motandi
Sound: Ibrahim Khalil Thera
MPAA rating: no listing
Running time: 107 minutes

Fiorile

"Sweeping and sensuous. A delicious romantic flavor...enhanced with a dash of magic realism."
—Stephen Holden, *The New York Times*

"Magnificent...A lush, romantic, old-fashioned epic that stirs the soul and thrills the senses."
—Michael Medved, *Sneak Previews*

"Lovely! The brothers' most enjoyable work in a decade. Harks back to the glory days of *Night of the Shooting Stars*."—John Powers, *New York Magazine*

"The Tavianis are in top form!"—Vincent Canby, *The New York Times*

Box Office Gross: $325,886 (April 10, 1994)

The pastoral beauty of Tuscany is the extraordinary backdrop for this historical tale about the tragic effects of greed. The Taviani brothers, who made the critically acclaimed *La Notte di San Lorenzo* (1982; *The Night of the Shooting Stars*, 1983) are the directors of *Fiorile*, a bucolic romance that spans several generations of the Benedetti family. Unfortunately, although the film aspires to charm and enchant, it falls short of its mark. In trying to spin a story that spans four or five generations, the filmmakers relinquish some of the texture that a story of this scope demands.

Luigi Benedetti (Lino Capolicchio) tells his two young children the family legend as he drives them and his French wife (Constanze Engelbrecht) from Paris to Tuscany to meet his father

"You came from far away to sow the seeds of a great plant...but the roots have gotten tangled...and have destroyed the vase." Massimo in *Fiorile*

for the first time. The scene then shifts to the eighteenth century, where his ancestor Corrado Benedetti (Claudio Bigagli) steals a cache of gold coins from the occupying French forces of Napoleon's army. Little does Corrado know, however, that in stealing the gold, he is responsible for the military execution of the soldier entrusted to watch over the treasure, Jean (Michael Vartan). Jean, unbeknownst to Corrado, was in love with Corrado's sister, Elisabetta (Galatea Ranzi). When Jean is killed, Elisabetta, pregnant with Jean's baby, goes mad and vows revenge—and the Benedetti curse is begun.

The scene shifts to 1903, and Elisabetta's descendant, Alessandro Benedetti (again played by Claudio Bigagli), is running for a seat in Parliament. He is manipulative and cunning, and, fearing that someone will discover how the Benedetti family got their vast fortune, he arranges for the removal to Argentina of the beloved, Elio (Giovanni

Guidelli), of his sister Elisa (Galatea Ranzi again.) Elisa, like her ancestor, is pregnant and goes mad. She kills her brothers in revenge, yet another episode in the family legacy of madness and greed.

Tragedy is played out once again through the World War II-era story of Massimo (Michael Vartan again), Elisa's grandson, who feels the emotional weight of his family's curse. His fate is to lose his beloved in the Resistance movement, punished by Mussolini's Blackshirts. He is the father of Luigi. The story comes full circle as Luigi finishes the tale just as he and his young family arrive at his father's home, the home in which the Benedettis have lived for two centuries, where sadness and sorrow have been handed down through the generations.

As melodramatic as the story is, it is a good dramatization, with much literary license, of the transmission of family problems through the ages. On one level, it succeeds in showing generational emotional destruction. Massimo talks of that "cursed gold" that his ancestor stole. He also becomes unable to speak whenever he thinks too hard about the family curse. Furthermore, he keeps a mannequin dressed as Jean (the Napoleonic hero who was the first victim in the family cycle) near his bedside in order to give him strength.

On the level of entertainment, however, the film is surprisingly flat for such a rich story. The problem appears to be that the film, paradoxically, loses steam because it is an epic: Its story becomes top-heavy with tragic characters just when it should soar with interesting new character and plot developments. The historical sweep of *War and Peace* (1956), *Indochine* (1992), and numerous other sagas is echoed in its vast story line. Yet that is precisely why there is a problem: There is too much story to cover—each of the several generations of the tragic victims of Corrado's greed get short shrift before the film moves on to the next story.

For example, when Elisa meets secretly with Elio, both unaware that Elio will be sent away by the evil Alessandro, it is difficult for the audience to be caught up in their romance: The audience has met them only seconds before they profess their undying love for each other. (The rather corny American translation does not help: "I'm like your dog; I hate being far from you," says Elisa.) The "stories" of the Benedetti family legend might truly feel tragic to the audience if only one had a chance to get to know the characters in each section of the film and identify with them before moving on to the next part of the story. As it is, the film is quite episodic, reminiscent more of the obscure Shirley MacLaine film *Sept Fois Femme* (1967; *Woman Times Seven*)—where MacLaine played seven roles—than of the combination of *Gone with the Wind* (1939), *The Princess Bride* (1987), and *Como Agua Para Chocolate* (1992; *Like Water for Chocolate*, 1993) that it aspires to be.

To dismiss the film would be a mistake, however, because it does possess a rare beauty and innocence. The gorgeous hills, meadows, and farmhouses of Tuscany are well represented, particularly in the early scenes in which Jean and Elisabetta meet their tragic fate. When Elisabetta discovers that Jean has been executed because of her brother's theft, she goes mad and runs out into the meadow, followed by her mother and Corrado: The camera stays close enough to the action to capture the anguish they are all feeling, but far enough away to keep the beautiful scenery of Tuscany as a serene backdrop to the calamitous scene. By keeping the camera distant and including the panoramic vis-tas, the Taviani brothers maintain visually the storybook quality they seek.

In fact, they use the camera in a most creative way when moving from one part of the story to the next: As Elisabetta and her family struggle in the meadow, the camera pulls up and back and then slowly sweeps over to the nearby road, returning the audience to the present day and to Luigi's car. This technique proves to be one of the most useful in the film. When Luigi begins the story, his daughter looks out the window of the car to the countryside and imagines Jean while Luigi describes him. Then, all of a sudden, Jean and the other soldiers appear. This seamlessness unites the stories very well.

The Taviani brothers and their cinematographer, Giuseppe Lanci, have re-created the beauty of Tuscany in such a way as to recall the paintings of Caravaggio and other masters of light and genre. From the beautiful food on the banquet table at Alessandro's feast to the piercing shafts of light entering the attic and shining on the mannequin that Massimo uses to keep alive the memory of Jean, this is a film of earthy beauty.

Unfortunately, there are no outstanding performances, perhaps because no single character is on-screen for very long. One possible exception is the gentle Duilio (Pier Paolo Capponi), the father of Corrado and Elisabetta, who prophesizes that "this gold will only bring misfortune to the thief." Little does he realize that the thief is his son and the misfortune will plaque his descendants. His weary earthiness is a wonderful foundation to the film.

There is much use of the word "legend" in the film's English translation. Luigi specifically tells his children that he is relating the family legend, and with his manner he brings a sense of mystery much as did the grandfather in *The Princess Bride* when he told the story to his young grandson. Yet for all its references to a "legend" and a "family curse" and "all those old family stories," the film prepares the audience for a much more mysterious tale than they get. Taken individually, each story is rather earthbound in that each deals with the drama of unrequited love and death and of individual fears about the discovery of the generations-old thievery of Corrado, concerns that appear quite contemporary rather than mysterious and fable-like. The music contributes in this way, also: Whenever the scene shifts, there is a haunting theme reminiscent of Kurt Weill's music. Yet underscoring of scenes, which might direct the audiences feelings and heighten the drama, is curiously missing throughout much of the film.

Early in the film, after Jean's execution, a friend of his delivers a letter to Elisabetta in which Jean tells her that he has nicknamed her "Fiorile," after the month of May in the French revolutionary calendar. He writes that he had wished to "talk to you about my love of freedom." At the end of "Fiorile"—which is Italian for "wild flower"—Luigi's father, Massimo (Renato Carpentieri), speaks to

CREDITS

Corrado: Claudio Bigagli
Elisabetta: Galatea Ranzi
Jean: Michael Vartan
Old Massimo: Renato Carpentieri
Alessandro: Claudio Bigagli
Elisa: Galatea Ranzi
Massimo: Michael Vartan
Luigi: Lino Capolicchio
Juliette: Constanze Engelbrecht
Gina: Athina Cenci
Chiara: Chiara Caselli
Elio: Giovanni Guidelli
Livia: Norma Martelli
Duilio: Pier Paolo Capponi
Dragons Marshall: Laurent Shilling

Origin: Italy, France, and Germany
Released: 1993
Production: Grazia Volpi, Jean-Claude Cecile, Luggi Waldleitner, and Karl Spiehs; released by Fine Line Features
Direction: Paolo Taviani and Vittorio Taviani
Screenplay: Sandro Petraglia, Paolo Taviani, and Vittorio Taviani
Cinematographer: Giuseppe Lanci
Editing: Roberto Perpignani
Art direction: Gianni Sbarra
Set design: Luca Gobbi
Sound: Danilo Moroni: Bruno Pupparo
Costume design: Lina Nerli Taviani
Music: Nicola Piovani
MPAA rating: PG-13
Running time: 116 minutes

the mannequin that represents Jean: "You came from far away to sow the seeds of a great plant...but the roots have gotten tangled...and have destroyed the vase." It appears that all of this refers to Jean's role as a soldier in the French Revolutionary movement into Tuscany. Yet the symbolism is unclear. Had the Benedetti family story told in this film been more clearly a metaphor for historical events, it might have been as involving and resonant as it wishes to be. Then again, this film may not appeal to an American audience which will not understand its histori-

cal context, any more than *Gone with the Wind* would an Italian audience.

—*Kirby Tepper*

REVIEWS

The Hollywood Reporter. May 17, 1993, p. 6.
Los Angeles Times. February 16, 1994, p. F4.
The New York Times. October 14, 1993, p. B4.
Variety. March 25, 1993, p. 21.

The Fire This Time

This hard-hitting documentary examines the underlying historical and social problems that set off the 1992 Los Angeles riots following the verdicts in the Rodney King trial.

REVIEWS

Los Angeles Times. April 29, 1994, p. F13.
Variety. CCCLIV, February 7, 1994, p. 39.

CREDITS

Narrator: Brooke Adams
Dr. Betty Shabazz: Dr. Betty Shabazz
Andrew Young: Andrew Young
Dr. Ernest Smith: Dr. Ernest Smith
Bobby Lavender: Bobby Lavender
Michael Zinzun: Michael Zinzun
Donald Freed: Donald Freed

Released: 1994
Production: Randy Holland for Blacktop Films
Direction: Randy Holland
Screenplay: Randy Holland
Cinematography: Jurg Walther, David May and Sal Paradise
Editing: Barbara Kaplan
Sound: Jurg Walther, David May, Diane Hall and Tark Abdul Wahid
Music: James Verboort
MPAA rating: no listing
Running time: 90 minutes

Fires of Kuwait

Narrated by Rip Torn, this IMAX documentary centers on the more than 600 oil-well fires started by the retreating Iraqi troops after Operation Desert Storm and the international crew of firefighters who risked their lives to put them out.

REVIEWS

Playboy. XLII, April 1995, p. 30.

AWARDS AND NOMINATIONS

Academy Awards Nomination: Best Documentary

CREDITS

Narrator: Rip Torn

Released: 1993
Production: Sally Dundas for Black Sun Films Ltd.; released by IMAX Corporation
Direction: David Douglas
Screenplay: David Douglas
Cinematographer: David Douglas
Editing: Barbara Kerr
Postproduction management: Lorne Orleans
Supervising sound editing: Peter Thillaye
Music: Michael Brook
MPAA rating: no listing
Running time: 36 minutes

Flesh Gordon Meets the Cosmic Cheerleaders

"Flesh is back!"—Movie tagline
"An out-and-out outrageous comedy"—*Video Business*

This bawdy sex comedy is a feeble sequel to *Flesh Gordon* (1974), which parodied the classic Buster Crabbe serials. Emperor Wang (Hunt) threatens the Universe with his powerful Impotence ray. Flesh (Murdocco), along with Dale (Kelly) and Dr. Flexi Jerkoff (Travis), do battle with a belt of farting asteroids and other weirdos. Director Ziehm delivers this one on a shoestring of under $1 million, even improving technically on the original. The sex scenes, however, are watered down in an effort to gain a wider audience.

Released: 1991
Production: Maurice Smith; released by Filmvest International
Direction: Howard Ziehm
Screenplay: Doug Frisby and Howard Ziehm
Cinematographer: Danny Nowak
Production design: Robert Kalafut
Special effects: Jim Towler and Bob Maine
Music: Paul Zaza
MPAA rating: NC-17
Running time: 94 minutes

CREDITS

Flesh Gordon: Vince Murdocco
Dale Ardor: Robyn Kelly
Robunda Hooters: Morgan Fox
Evil Presence: Bill Hunt
Master Bator: Bruce Scott
Dr. Flexi Jerkoff: Tony Travis

The Flintstones

"Yabba-dabba do-it!"—Movie tagline

"rock-solid entertainment...a brontosaurus-sized hit"—Michael Medved, *New York Post*

"funny and inventive with lots of surprises and dazzling special effects"—Jeffrey Lyons, *Sneak Previews*

 Box Office Gross: $130.6 million (February 1995)

Anyone who was six years old when *The Flintstones* debuted as a television cartoon had turned forty by the summer of 1994, when *The Flintstones* emerged as a feature-length film with living, breathing cavepersons. *The Flintstones*, based on the popular 1960's animated television series, was evidently a labor of love on the part of its creators. John Goodman, who portrays Fred Flintstone, recalls that as a child his Cub Scout meetings meant missing one episode a month of Hanna-Barbera's animated sitcom. Comedian Rosie O'Donnell knew the words to the Bedrock 'n' roll classic "The Twitch" years before being cast as Betty Rubble, wife of Fred's buddy and neighbor Barney Rubble. Brian Levant, a serious collector of Flintstones memorabilia, actively sought the screenwriting assignment for several years before learning that he was wanted, instead, to direct.

The series' creators, Bill Hanna and Joseph Barbera, were to television animation what Walt Disney was to the big screen. Popular Hanna-Barbera characters included such favorites as Huckleberry Hound and Quick Draw McGraw. What made *The Flintstones* so unusual was that with its debut on September 30, 1960, it became the first prime time animated series, the first animated situation comedy, and the first program-length cartoon. The satirical working-class adventures of Fred and Wilma Flintstone and Barney and Betty Rubble ran for six years and 166 episodes before going into an endless loop of reruns.

Except for its prehistoric setting and the "rocky" texture of its gags, the television show was an unabashed reworking of another working-class situation comedy, *The Honeymooners*. Both series centered on two married couples. The working-class husbands were buddies who

John Goodman and Rick Moranis as Fred Flintstone and Barney Rubble in *The Flintstones*. © 1994 Universal City Studios Inc. and Amblin Entertainment, Inc. All rights reserved.

proudly endured a drab work life so as to afford the pleasures of bowling night, lodge meetings, the cockamamy schemes of the lead buddy, and turbulent but loving relationships with their housebound wives who, nevertheless, possessed a decidedly firmer grip on reality.

 In *The Flintstones*, Wilma's original voice, Jean VanderPyl, has a cameo and Harvey Korman (the voice of "the Great Gazoo" in the animated series) voices in as the dictaphone.

 "I stole just about everything from Gleason... *Flintstones* was always borrowed from *The Honeymooners* so I might as well borrow big if we're going to do the live version."—John Goodman on his role as Fred in *The Flintstones*

The full-length, feature-film version of *The Flintstones* is a live-action cartoon featuring the inimitable John Goodman in the lead role of Fred Flintstone. Goodman tackles his assignment with enough gusto to make the viewer wish a Flintstones film were a good idea. Good-hearted, good-natured, susceptible to temptation and flattery, morose over his own transgressions, truly happiest when making good on his errors, Goodman navigates his cheerily beefy countenance through this middle-class morality play as well as anyone possibly could. Producer Steven Spielberg was absolutely correct when he reportedly told colleagues that only Goodman should be allowed to assay Fred's role. Furthermore, the principal supporting players are flawless. Elizabeth Taylor's 50-karat cameo as Fred's razor-tongued mother-in-law, Pearl Slaghoople, borders on ingenious. Casting, however, is not what makes *The Flintstones* sink like a ton of quarry stone.

The film's basic problem is its sitcom-sized story that has been stretched to fill an hour and a half. The script was jackhammered together by an army of writers—first in the best Hollywood tradition of passing drafts from one person to another, and finally in the best sitcom tradition of a gaggle of gagsters gathering at the roundtable. So instead of being fully translated to the big screen, in the end *The Flintstones* remains a television commodity.

In the film, good-guy Barney (Rick Moranis) sees Fred struggling with a job promotion exam at the Slate & Co. quarry. Barney secretly switches his test answers with Fred's. Fred therefore wins promotion to the executive suite, where he becomes unwittingly involved in an embezzlement scheme by an evil Paleolithic yuppie named Cliff Vandercave (Kyle MacLachlan). Fred succumbs, meanwhile, to the pleasures of the big paycheck. He takes to dining at Cavern on the Green,

CREDITS

Fred Flintstone: John Goodman
Wilma Flintstone: Elizabeth Perkins
Barney Rubble: Rick Moranis
Betty Rubble: Rosie O'Donnell
Cliff Vandercave: Kyle MacLachlan
Miss Stone: Halle Berry
Pearl Slaghoople: Elizabeth Taylor
Mr. Slate: Dann Florek
Hoagie: Richard Moll
Joe Rockhead: Irwin "88" Keyes
Grizzled man: Jonathan Winters
Dictabird: Harvey Korman

Released: 1994
Production: Bruce Cohen for Steven Spielrock and Hanna-Barbera/Amblin Entertainment; released by Universal Pictures
Direction: Brian Levant
Screenplay: Tom S. Parker, Jim Jennewein, and Steven E. de Souza; based on the animated series by Hanna-Barbera Productions, Inc.
Cinematographer: Dean Cundey
Editing: Kent Beyda
Production design: William Sandell
Art direction: Jim Teegarden, Nancy Patton and Christopher Burian-Mohr
Set design: Paul Sonski, Elizabeth Lapp and Erin Kemp
Set decoration: Rosemary Brandenburg
Casting: Nancy Nayor
Visual effects supervision: Mark Dippe
Special visual effects: Industrial Light and Magic
Sound: Charles Wilborn
Costume design: Rosanna Norton
Animatronic creatures: Jim Henson's Creature Shop
Music: David Newman
MPAA rating: PG
Running time: 92 minutes

AWARDS AND NOMINATIONS

MTV Awards Nomination 1995:   Most Desirable Female (Berry)

where the BC-52s perform "The Twitch", and ignores the misfortunes of his old pal and neighbor, Barney. When most of his former fellow quarry grunts get laid off because of Vandercave's chicanery, Fred has been set up to take the blame. Needless to say, harmony is restored in the Bedrock universe—and between Barney and Fred—before the closing credits roll.

If that string of events were the only attraction, few viewers would be around at the end. The actors go as far as possible toward sustaining interest, however. Moranis' Barney is as good-natured as his cartoon counterpart. Elizabeth Perkins is indomitably alive as Fred's wife, Wilma, and her interaction with O'Donnell's Betty Rubble—O'Donnell captures Betty's giggle dead-solid perfect—makes for a comfortable female buddy bit. MacLachlan applies all possible gloss to his cardboard part as Vandercave, and Halle Berry does well as the femme fatale secretary and Vandercave cohort who diverts Fred from the dirty business at hand.

Besides the casting, the other attraction of this film is the nonstop array of real-time and computer-animated special effects. Fred works the quarry high atop his dino-crane, zips around Bedrock in his foot- powered vehicle, and is greeted at the door of his home by his affectionate pet Dino. Another key character is the Dictabird that sits on Fred's desk after his promotion at Slate & Co., courtesy the mechanical and puppeteering wizardry of Jim Henson's Creature Shop and the suitably insouciant voice of Harvey Korman.

With its interesting special effects, all-star cast, and sitcom-type plot, *The Flintstones* ought to do record business in the videotape phase. It makes for superb television, provided the set is big enough to do justice to the Bedrock pan shots and to the sounds emanating from the Cavern on the Green.

—Tom W. Ferguson

REVIEWS

Entertainment Weekly. May 27, 1994, p. 64.
The Hollywood Reporter. May 18, 1994, p. 11.
Los Angeles Times. May 27, 1994, p. F1.
New York. May 30, 1994, p. 58.
The New York Times. May 27, 1994, p. B1.
Newsweek. May 30, 1994, p. 64.
Premiere. May, 1994, p. 62.
Time. May 30, 1994, p. 58.
Variety. May 17, 1994, p. 4.

Floundering

"A post-riot comedy."—Movie tagline

"Delightfully warped."—Ella Taylor, *The Atlantic Monthly*

"A seriously subversive social comedy."—Bruce Williamson, *Playboy*

An unemployed Los Angeles man, John Boyz (James Le Gros), who obsesses over the Los Angeles riots and the state of modern society, also grapples with more immediate problems: The Internal Revenue Service has frozen his assets, his unemployment benefits have run out, his drug-addict brother needs professional help, and his girlfriend (Lisa Zane) is having an affair with another man, in this social satire. Directorial debut of Peter McCarthy.

REVIEWS

Entertainment Weekly. May 19, 1995, p. 68.
Playboy. XLI, December 1994, p. 32.
Variety. CCCLIII, January 24, 1994, p. 65.

CREDITS

John Boyz: James Le Gros
JC: John Cusack
Jimmy: Ethan Hawke
Jessica: Lisa Zane
Ned: Steve Buscemi
Commander K: Sy Richardson
Gun clerk: Billy Bob Thornton
Unemployment clerk: Kim Wayans
Elle: Maritza Rivera
Chief Merryl Fence: Nelson Lyon

No character identified: Nina Siemaszko
No character identified: Jeremy Piven
No character identified: Ted Raimi
No character identified: Alex Cox
No character identified: Brian Wimmer
No character identified: Biff Yaeger
No character identified: Jo Harvey Allen
No character identified: Viggo Mortensen
No character identified: Exene Cervenka

Released: 1994
Production: Peter McCarthy for Front Films, Inc.; released by Strand Releasing
Direction: Peter McCarthy
Screenplay: Peter McCarthy
Cinematographer: Denis Maloney
Editing: Dody Dorn and Peter McCarthy
Production design: Cecilia Montiel
Set decoration: Lisa Monti
Casting: Jeanne McCarthy
Sound: Aletha Rodgers
Costume design: Keron Wheeler
Music: Pray for Rain
MPAA rating: no listing
Running time: 97 minutes

Fly by Night

Three African Americans—Rich (Jeffrey Sams), I (Ron Brice), and Kayam (Darryl "Chill" Mitchell)—form a rap group, in this documentary-like look at the contemporary New York City music scene. When they're propelled to the top, forces both personal and professional work to tear them apart.

REVIEWS

Boston Globe. April 22, 1994, p. 38.
Rolling Stone. May 5, 1994, p. 49.
Variety. CCCL, February 8, 1993, p. 76.

CREDITS

Rich: Jeffrey Sams
I: Ron Brice
Kayam: Darryl (Chill) Mitchell
Naji: Todd Graff
Rickey Tick: Leo Burmester
Rock: Soulfood
Jed Lyte: Larry Gilliard
Lihad: Omar Carter
Denise: Maura Tierney
Sam: Yul Vazquez
Akusa: MC Lyte
Maurice: Christopher Michael Gerrard
Charlotte: Ebony Jo-Ann

Released: 1993
Production: Calvin Skaggs; released by Lumiere Productions
Direction: Steve Gomer
Screenplay: Todd Graff
Cinematographer: Larry Banks
Editing: Norman Gay
Production design: Ruth Ammon
Art direction: Llewellyn Harrison
Set decoration: Nancy Friedman
Casting: Pat Golden: John McCabe
Sound: Fred Rosenberg
Costume design: Alexander White
Music: Sidney Mills, Dwayne Sumal and Kris Parker
MPAA rating: R
Running time: 100 minutes

Forbidden Quest

Box Office Gross: $7,955 (January 16, 1994)

Intertwining fact and fiction, filmmaker Peter Delpeut tells the story of a fictional 1905 expedition to the South Pole through interviews with the only survivor, J. C. Sullivan (Joseph O'Conor), and actual archival footage of early polar expeditions.

REVIEWS

The New York Times. January 5, 1994, p. C15.

CREDITS

J. C. Sullivan: Joseph O'Conor
Interviewer: Roy Ward

Origin: The Netherlands
Released: 1993
Production: Suzanne Van Voorst for Ariel Film; released by Zeitgeist Films
Direction: Peter Delpeut
Screenplay: Peter Delpeut
Cinematographer: Stef Tijdink
Editing: Menno Boerema
Music: Loek Dikker
MPAA rating: no listing
Running time: 75 minutes

Foreign Student

"The people are different. The food is strange. The customs are unusual. Welcome to America."
—Movie tagline

 Box Office Gross: $95,595 (August 7, 1994)

French foreign-exchange student Philippe Le Clerc (Marco Hofschneider) attends a prestigious white Southern University in the 1950's only to experience racial prejudice firsthand when he falls in love with the African American housekeeper, April (Robin Givens), of his English professor. Dutton and Battle are notable in their roles as blues musicians Howlin' Wolf and Sonny Boy Williamson. Directorial debut for Eva Sereny. Based on the novel *The Foreign Student* by Philippe Labro.

REVIEWS

Atlanta Constitution. August 5, 1994, p. P10.
Boston Globe. July 29, 1994, p. 52.
Chicago Tribune. July 29, 1994, p. 7F.
Entertainment Weekly. December 23, 1994, p. 80.
Los Angeles Times. July 29, 1994, p. F10.
The New York Times. July 29, 1994, p. C10.
The New York Times. January 6, 1995, p. D15.
People Weekly. XLII, August 29, 1994, p. 19.
Rolling Stone. September 8, 1994, p. 87.
TV Guide. XLII. December 31, 1994, p. 39.
USA Today. July 29, 1994, p. D7.
The Washington Post. July 29, 1994, p. D6.

 "I'm not a redneck! I'm not a Southern gentleman! I am French!"—Philippe shouting at the locals who are chasing him, in *Foreign Student*

CREDITS

Philippe Le Clerc: Marco Hofschneider
April: Robin Givens
Cal Cate: Rick Johnson
Sue Ann: Charlotte Ross
Zach Gilmore: Edward Herrmann
Rex Jennings: Jack Coleman
Howlin' Wolf: Charles S. Dutton
Sonny Boy Williamson: Hinton Battle
Coach Ballard: Anthony Herrera

Origin: France
Released: 1994
Production: Tarak Ben Ammar and Mark Lombardo for Silvio Berlusconi Communications, Carthago Films, Libra U.K., and Holland Coordinator, in association with Featherstone Prods.; released by Gramercy Pictures
Direction: Eva Sereny
Screenplay: Menno Meyjes; based on the novel *The Foreign Student*, by Philippe Labro
Cinematographer: Franco Di Giacomo
Editing: Peter Hollywood
Production design: Howard Cummings
Art direction: Jeffrey McDonald
Set decoration: Jeanette Scott
Sound: Brit Warner
Costume design: Carol Ramsey
Music: Jean-Claude Petit
MPAA rating: R
Running time: 96 minutes

Forever

This weak mystery-romance involves a music video director, Ted Dickson (Keith Coogan), and long-gone matinee idols, such as Mabel Normand (Dianc Ladd), Mary Pickford (Ashley Hester), and Mary Miles Mintner (Sean Young), with whom he communes via an old film that he discovers in his home. It seems that the home was the scene of the murder of film director William Desmond Taylor (Steve Railsback) some seventy years earlier.

REVIEWS

Variety. CCCXLVII, May 18, 1992, p. 47.

CREDITS

Angelica: Sally Kirkland
Mary Miles Minter: Sean Young
Ted Dickson: Keith Coogan
Mabel Normand: Diane Ladd
Wallace Reid: Terence Knox
Billy Baldwin: Nicholas Guest
Charlotte: Renee Taylor
William Desmond Taylor: Steve Railsback
Mary Pickford: Ashley Hester

Released: 1992
Production: Jackelyn Giroux; released by Triax Entertainment Group/DDM Film
Direction: Thomas Palmer, Jr.
Screenplay: Jackelyn Giroux and Thomas Palmer, Jr.
Cinematographer: Gary Graver
Editing: Jeffrey Fallick
Set decoration: Stacie Burton
Sound design: Leslie Chew
Costume design: Linda Susan Howell
Music: RH Factor
MPAA rating: no listing
Running time: 87 minutes

Forrest Gump

"A miracle!....A skyrocketing swirl of imagination, humor and heartstopping emotion...fantastic comedy-drama. The journey leaves you dizzy and fulfilled."—Bob Campbell, *Newhouse News Service*

"A miraculous movie that will revive your faith in the human race. Put it at the top of your must-see list."—Rex Reed, *New York Observer*

"Ingenious! A fascinating fable filled with hopeful feelings and an exhilarating sense of life. An acting triumph for Tom Hanks."—David Sheehan, *CBS-TV*

"Flawless. A classic movie that will be around forever."—Jimmy Carter, *TNN Country News*

"This is not only the best movie of the year, it's one of the most amazing and meaningful films ever made."—Mike McKay, *WBTV (CBS)*

"Tom Hanks is unforgettable.... Forrest is everything we admire in the American character—honest, brave, loyal. The effects dazzle.... Powerful."—Peter Travers, *Rolling Stone*

 Box Office Gross: $298,535,927 (January 2, 1995)

Tom Hanks as Forrest Gump and Gary Sinise as Lieutenant Dan Taylor in *Forrest Gump*. © 1994 Paramount Pictures. All rights reserved.

In writer/director Robert Zemeckis' *Back to the Future* trilogy (1985, 1989, 1990), young Marty McFly (Michael J. Fox) and his scientist sidekick Doc Brown (Christopher Lloyd) journey backward and forward in time, attempting to smooth over some rough spots in their personal histories in order to remain true to their individual destinies. Throughout their time-travel adventures, Doc Brown insists that neither he nor Marty influence any major historical events, believing that to do so would result in catastrophic changes in humankind's ultimate destiny. By the end of the trilogy, however, Doc Brown has revised his thinking and tells Marty that, "Your future hasn't been written yet. No one's has. Your future is whatever you make it. So make it a good one."

In *Forrest Gump*, Zemeckis once again explores the theme of personal destiny and how an individual's life affects and is affected by his historical time period. This time, however, Zemeckis and screen writer Eric Roth chronicle the life of a character who does nothing but meddle in the his-

Forrest Gump is the movie industry's fifth highest-grossing film and was #1 at the box office five (non-consecutive) weeks. It is Paramount Pictures' biggest film and the first in the studio's history to achieve $100 and $200 million domestic grosses.

torical events of his time without even trying to do so. By the film's conclusion, however, it has become apparent that Zemeckis' main concern is something more than merely having fun with four decades of American history. In the process of re-creating significant moments in time, he has captured on celluloid something eternal and timeless—the soul of humanity personified by a nondescript simpleton from the deep South.

The film begins following the flight of a seemingly insignificant feather as it floats down from the sky and brushes against various objects and people before finally coming to rest at the feet of Forrest Gump (Tom Hanks). Forrest, who is sitting on a bus-stop bench, reaches down and picks up the feather, smooths it out, then opens his traveling case and carefully places the feather between the pages of his favorite book, *Curious George*.

In this simple but hauntingly beautiful opening scene, the filmmakers illustrate the film's principal concern: Is life a series of random events over which a person has no control, or is there an underlying order to things that leads to the fulfillment of an individual's destiny? The rest of the film is a humorous and moving attempt to prove that, underlying the random, chaotic events that make up a person's life, there exists a benign and simple order.

Forrest sits on the bench throughout most of the film, talking about various events of his life to others who happen to sit down next to him. It does not take long, however, for the audience to realize that Forrest's seemingly random chatter to a parade of strangers has a perfect chronological order to it. He tells his first story after looking down at the feet of his first bench partner and observing, "Mama always said that you can tell a lot about a person by the shoes they wear." Then, in a voice-over narration, Forrest begins the story of his life, first by telling about the first pair of shoes he can remember wearing.

The action shifts to the mid-1950's with Forrest as a young boy (Michael Humphreys) being fitted with leg braces to correct a curvature in his spine. Despite this traumatic handicap, Forrest remains unaffected, thanks to his mother (Sally Field) who reminds him on more than one occasion that he is no different from anyone else. Although this and most of Mrs. Gump's other words of advice are in the form of hackneyed clichés, Forrest whose intelligence quotient is below normal, sincerely believes every one of them, namely because he instinctively knows they are sincere expressions of his mother's love and fierce devotion.

Mrs. Gump runs a boardinghouse in the small Southern town of Greenbow, Alabama. Shortly after Forrest

CREDITS

Forrest Gump: Tom Hanks
Jenny Curran: Robin Wright
Lieutenant Dan Taylor: Gary Sinise
Bubba Blue: Mykelti Williamson
Mrs. Gump: Sally Field
Forrest (as a child):   Michael Humphreys
Jenny (as a child):   Hanna Hall

Released: 1994
Production: Wendy Finerman, Steve Tisch, and Steve Starkey; released by Paramount Pictures
Direction: Robert Zemeckis
Screenplay: Eric Roth; based on the novel by Winston Groom
Cinematographer: Don Burgess
Editing: Arthur Schmidt
Production design: Rick Carter
Art direction: Leslie McDonald and Jim Teegarden
Set design: Erin Kemp, James C. Feng, Elizabeth Lapp and Lauren E. Polizzi
Set decoration: Nancy Haigh
Casting: Ellen Lewis
Visual effects supervision: Ken Ralston
Special visual effects: Industrial Light and Magic
Sound: William B. Kaplan
Costume design: Joanna Johnston
Music: Alan Silvestri
MPAA rating: PG-13
Running time: 142 minutes

receives his leg braces, he strikes up a friendship with one of the boarders, a young singer- guitarist whose song about a hound dog starts Forrest shimmying and clacking around the young man's room. Later, Forrest sees the singer on television mimicking his movements while an audience of swooning teenagers screams its approval. Forrest says the musician eventually became known as "The King" and met a sad fate.

This early scene of Forrest inadvertently impacting a significant moment in popular culture is the first of many, all of them presented in the same humorously low-key manner. Also throughout, Forrest mentions the fate of some of the people he has met, pointing out that many of these acquaintances met violent or messy deaths for no apparent reason. These offhand comments, many illustrated with archival footage of political figures and other historical personages being gunned down by madmen, subtly illustrate the film's underlying theme of the random and the destined.

Forrest goes on to tell about how he met young Jenny (Hanna Hall) on the bus to school. Although the other kids shun him because of his leg braces and simpleton ways, Jenny immediately accepts him. Soon, they develop a loving friendship, one that will grow and endure over the next four decades despite the radically different paths their lives take.

Jenny's life is presented as the antithesis of Forrest's. Raised and sexually abused by an alcoholic father, she grows into a beautiful but troubled woman (Robin Wright). During the rest of the film, Jenny's directionless meanderings through life are contrasted with Forrest's amazing triumphs.

Like Mrs. Gump, Jenny gives Forrest advice on how to live his life. The most significant advice she gives him is her own personal credo— whenever there is trouble, run away. Forrest embraces this seemingly nebulous bit of information and ends up becoming a star running back for his high school football team. Later, he earns a football scholarship, then makes the American all-star team. As part of the team, he is invited to the White House to meet President Kennedy. Most people would consider a meeting with the president a significant moment in their life. For Forrest, the best part of the event is the food.

After he graduates from college, Forrest enlists in the Army where he meets two people who have a much more influential impact on his life than any mere president: Bubba (Mykelti Williamson), a fellow Alabaman with a burning desire to become a shrimp-boat captain; and Lieutenant Dan (Gary Sinise), who believes his destiny is to die with dignity in battle just like the rest of the male members of his family. After the threesome ends up in the jungles of Vietnam, however, it is Bubba who dies in battle, with Lieutenant Dan losing his legs and eventually becoming a bitter alcoholic. As for Forrest, he takes Jenny's advice and runs away during a horrendous enemy attack, but then runs back into the melee to rescue Bubba. Instead, he rescues his platoon. For his actions, he is awarded the medal of honor

AWARDS AND NOMINATIONS

Academy Awards 1994: Best Picture, Best Actor (Hanks), Best Director (Zemeckis), Best Film Editing, Best Visual Effects, Best Adapted Screenplay (Roth)
Nominations: Best Supporting Actor (Sinise), Best Supporting Actress (Thurman), Best Sound, Sound Effects Editing, Best Art Direction/Set Direction, Best Cinematography, Best Makeup, Best Original Score
Blockbuster Entertainment Awards 1995: Movie—Theatrical, Actor—Theatrical (Hanks)
Chicago Critics Awards 1994: Best Actor (Hanks)
Directors Guild of America Awards 1994: Best Director (Zemeckis)
Nomination: Outstanding Achievement in Motion Pictures (Zemeckis)
Golden Globe Awards 1995: Best Film—Drama, Best Actor—Drama (Hanks), Best Director (Zemeckis)
Nominations: Best Supporting Actress (Wright), Best Supporting Actor (Sinise), Best Screenplay, Best Original Score
MTV Movie Awards Nominations 1995: Best Film, Best Male Performance (Hanks), Breakthrough Performance (Williamson)
National Board of Review Awards 1994: Best Film, Best Actor (Hanks), Best Supporting Actor (Sinise)
Producers Guild Awards Nomination: Golden Laurel (Finerman, Tisch, Starkey)
Screen Actors Guild Awards 1994: Best Actor (Hanks)
Nominations: Best Supporting Actor (Sinise), Best Supporting Actress (Field), Best Supporting Actress (Wright)
Writers Guild Awards 1994: Best Adapted Screenplay

and again journeys to the White House to accept his award from President Johnson.

While in Washington, D.C., Forrest inadvertently becomes a guest speaker at a massive antiwar rally hosted by Abbie Hoffman and other radicals of the time. Jenny suddenly appears out of the crowd and the two enjoy a brief reunion, Jenny relating some of her experiences as free-spirited hippie.

When Forrest returns to active duty, he takes up Ping-Pong as a hobby, eventually becoming so skilled at the game that he becomes part of the first U.S. Ping-Pong team to play in China. For his efforts, he is invited to appear on television's *Dick Cavett Show*. Cavett's other guest is John Lennon who, after hearing Forrest describe China as a place where the citizens have no possessions and no religion too, is inspired to write his most famous song, "Imagine."

Forrest's Ping-Pong-playing fame also gets him invited to the White House again. This time, he meets President Nixon who, upon learning about Forrest's modest hotel accommodations, puts him up in the posh Hotel Watergate. Naturally, it is Forrest who notices something suspicious going on in one of the

"Life is like a box of chocolates. You never know what you're gonna get."—*Forrest Gump*

other rooms and calls the desk clerk to complain. The follow-up scene is Nixon resigning from office.

After his discharge from the Army, Forrest decides to honor his friend Bubba's dying request and attempts to make a living as a shrimp-boat captain. Everyone thinks he is stupid for even considering such an endeavor. Nevertheless, Forrest merely repeats one of his mama's hackneyed sayings, "Stupid is as stupid does," and presses on. When the rest of the shrimp-boat fleet is destroyed during a hurricane, Forrest makes a killing, eventually founding the Bubba-Gump Shrimp Corporation with help from an amazed Lieutenant Dan. More important to Forrest than the fortune is Lieutenant Dan's belated thanks for saving his life in Vietnam.

Multimillionaire Forrest returns to his home in Greenbow to live out his days as the town's grass cutter. While puttering around his estate one day, he looks up and finds Jenny has returned home. Jenny's path through life has been much rougher than Forrest's. Yet Forrest's love for her has remained undiminished over the decades, and he asks her to marry him. She refuses his proposal and eventually runs off again, but not before declaring her love for him with a night of gentle lovemaking.

Forrest is so traumatized by Jenny's latest parting that he impulsively begins running. He runs across town, then across the state, then across the country. As he runs, he attracts a cultlike following along with a swarm of media coverage, everyone finding profound meaning in his tireless, single-minded jogging feat.

After three years of nonstop running, Forrest suddenly stops and goes home, having finally recovered from the trauma of Jenny's sudden departure. The two are reunited once again when Forrest receives a letter from Jenny asking him to come visit. Jenny is now a waitress, living in a small apartment in Savannah, Georgia. She is also the mother of a three-year-old boy, whom she has named Forrest, after his father.

Forrest hardly has time to adjust to the news that he is a father when Jenny tells him that she is dying and wants him to care for their son. She also asks Forrest to marry her. Jenny spends her final days watching her childlike husband rain affection on their young son. When she dies, Forrest buries her under the giant oak in which the two played together as children. Standing over her grave, Forrest answers the question that the filmmakers raised with the floating feather at the film's beginning: "I don't know if we each have a destiny or if we're floating accidental-like on the breeze.... Maybe both are happening at the same time."

With *Forrest Gump*, Zemeckis has done something he had never quite managed to achieve before in his long, successful career as a writer/director: He has made a film overflowing with heartfelt sentiment. Even more significant, Zemeckis has given the viewer a fully realized, three-dimensional character to embrace.

Nearly all of Zemeckis' previous films have been dominated by his hyperkinetic directorial style, cartoonish story lines, and overreliance on special effects. *Forrest Gump* does contain some dazzling effects, especially in the scenes in which Forrest meets with historical figures. In these scenes, archival footage was blended with computer-altered images, resulting in an uncanny interweaving of fact and fiction, allowing Forrest to meet and make small talk with famous figures from recent history. Other films have attempted similar effects—most notably *Citizen Kane* (1941) in its opening newsreel scene, and various moments from Woody Allen's *Zelig* (1983). With *Forrest Gump*, however, the effect reaches a new level of artistic sophistication.

As dazzling as these effects are, for once Zemeckis manages to keep them from overpowering the story. His pacing is also less frenetic, matching the film's ambling, picaresque story line and Forrest's charmingly folksy narration. In fact, if the film has a major flaw it is that Zemeckis has slowed the pace too much. He and screenwriter Roth have also tried to cover too much ground, presenting not only Forrest's adventures but also Jenny's in an attempt to chronicle four decades from the perspective of both a wide-eyed innocent and a world-weary cynic.

Overall, the film's shortcomings are minor, especially when compared to its chief attribute: Tom Hanks. Although the acting by all the principals is top notch, Hanks's brilliant portrayal outshines the rest. Hanks also surpasses the performances of others who have attempted to capture the mannered speech inflections, child-like body movements, and blank-face expressions of mentally challenged characters, such as Dustin Hoffman's Raymond Babbitt from *Rain Man* (1988) and Peter Seller's Chauncey Gardiner from *Being There* (1979). Hanks achieves this by refusing to let his character's mental handicap become his dominant trait, instead emphasizing Forrest's sincere, gentle nature as well as Forrest's subtle reactions to the people and events of his life.

By the film's conclusion, Tom Hanks the actor has disappeared from the screen, replaced by a slow-talking simpleton from the South with the amusing name of Forrest Gump. This bit of movie magic has not been accomplished by special effects or computer-altered images, but by something much more impressive and harder to achieve—an instinctive understanding of the human condition, and the ability to convey this timeless, enduring insight to others.

—*Jim Kline*

REVIEWS

Entertainment Weekly. July 15, 1994, p. 42.
The Hollywood Reporter. June 29, 1994, p. 7.
Los Angeles Times. July 6, 1994, p. F1.
The New York Times. July 6, 1994, p. B1.
The New Yorker. July 15, 1994, p. 76.
Newsweek. July 11, 1994, p. 50.
Time. July 11, 1994, p. 58.
Variety. June 23, 1994, p. 2.

Four Weddings and a Funeral

"a magical romantic comedy"—Peter Travers, *Rolling Stone*

 Box Office Gross: $52,700,832 (September 5, 1994)

Four Weddings and a Funeral, despite the sound of finality in its title, proves that romantic comedy is alive and well. With a picaresque format and a sense of life's more ludicrous moments, the film tells the tale of one young Brit's search for happiness—and true love.

The film begins with an introduction of the romantically hapless Charles (Hugh Grant), a good-looking if rumpled chap who seems to have little of importance to do other

CREDITS

Charles: Hugh Grant
Carrie: Andie MacDowell
Fiona: Kristin Scott Thomas
Gareth: Simon Callow
Tom: James Fleet
Matthew: John Hannah
Scarlett: Charlotte Coleman
David: David Bower
Hamish: Corin Redgrave
Father Gerald: Rowan Atkinson
Henrietta: Anna Chancellor
Bernard: David Haig
Lydia: Sophie Thompson

Origin: Great Britain
Released: 1994
Production: Duncan Kenworthy for Polygram Filmed Entertainment, Channel Four Films, and Working Title; released by Gramercy Pictures
Direction: Mike Newell
Screenplay: Richard Curtis
Cinematographer: Michael Coulter
Editing: Jon Gregory
Production design: Maggie Gray
Set decoration: Anna Pinnock
Casting: Michelle Guish and David Rubin
Sound: David Stephenson
Costume design: Lindy Hemming
Music: Richard Rodney Bennett
MPAA rating: R
Running time: 118 minutes

AWARDS AND NOMINATIONS

Academy Awards Nominations 1994: Best Picture, Best Original Screenplay
British Academy Awards 1995: Best Film, Best Actor (Grant), Best Director (Newell), Best Supporting Actress (Scott Thomas)
Chicago Critics Awards 1994: Most Promising Actor (Grant)
Directors Guild Awards Nomination 1994: Best Director (Newell)
Golden Globe Awards 1995: Best Actor—Musical/Comedy (Grant)
Nominations: Best Film—Musical/Comedy, Best Screenplay, Best Actress—Musical/Comedy (MacDowell)
MTV Movie Awards Nomination 1995: Breakthrough Performance (Grant)
Writers Guild Awards 1994: Best Original Screenplay

than attend his friends' weddings. Accompanied by his punked-out roommate, Scarlett (Charlotte Coleman), Charles is off to another wedding, late as usual. With four-letter words flying, he and Scarlett race to the lovely country wedding of one of Charles' many very rich friends. Unfortunately, after they arrive, best man Charles cannot find the couple's wedding rings, and his friends must bail him out, as usual, with some last- minute resourcefulness.

The reception proves more hopeful when Charles meets Carrie (Andie MacDowell), an American whose sophisticated appearance and Vogue connections render her an interesting counterpoint to Charles. As one friend bluntly states, "She's out of your league." Despite Charles' bumbling machinations, his visit to the inn where she is staying results in their sleeping together. Charles is smitten, but shocked to learn the next morning that she is engaged to the seventh richest man in Scotland and has no intention of pursuing a relationship with him. Carrie is off to America, and Charles, as usual, has nowhere to go until his next wedding invitation.

Three months later, his friends Bernard (David Haig) and Lydia (Sophie Thompson) are marrying, in the wake of their drunken discovery of each other's charms at the preceding nuptial festivities. Rather than driving over sidewalks and endangering London schoolchildren, Charles and Scarlett run to this wedding, just around the corner. Late once again, Charles arrives in better shape than Scarlett, whose half-fastened bridesmaid's dress displays her undies for all to see. Charles has a miserable time at the reception, where he is wedged in at a table with four of his former girlfriends, who begin to dissect his miserable, "serially-monogamous" character.

He is doubly miserable because Carrie has appeared, looking blissful, on the arm of her very wealthy and very much older fiancé, Hamish (Corin Redgrave). In the ultimate, nightmarish humiliation, Charles gets trapped in the bridal couple's room. He finally and awkwardly escapes the spectacle of the wedding couple's passion and runs into Carrie, sans fiancé. An innocent nightcap leads to a repeat of their first sexual encounter.

Nevertheless, a month later Charles receives yet another invitation: to Carrie's wedding. Looking like a British beach bum, a disheartened Charles encounters Carrie in town. Acting diffident, Charles agrees to help her shop for her wedding dress. Lunch leads to confessions of the soul (and sexual experience). As a result, Charles begins to feel even more inadequate; in spite of this, he cannot help but declare his love to this woman who, he says, has "ruthlessly" slept with him. Carrie kisses his cheek tenderly, but walks away.

In spite of his bruised feelings, Charles goes to Scotland to attend Carrie and Hamish's grand wedding at the latter's ancestral estate. Charles is distraught. His friend Fiona (Kristin Scott Thomas) is equally distraught because she finally has gathered the courage to tell Charles that she loves him. All issues of love are set aside, however, when their mutual friend, Gareth (Simon Callow), suddenly collapses and dies of a heart attack in the midst of a Scottish reel.

Gareth's funeral brings all the ironies of love into focus for the characters, especially Charles. Although he moved in an upper-class circle, Gareth's funeral is in the overly-industrialized, working-class neighborhood of his parents. His gay lover, Matthew (John Hannah), attempts to explain not why he loved a man but why he loved a man many others thought "fat" and "terribly rude." Charles has no explanation, either, as to why he loves the elusive Carrie, but he is relieved and hopeful when she arrives, alone, to mourn Gareth. Even though they talk, their relationship is unresolved, and a frustrated and saddened Charles decides time is running out. As he tells his shy friend Tom (James Fleet), he must get married.

Months later, Charles is once again awakening for a wedding his own. With his dozens of alarm clocks set an hour early by his loyal and realistic friends to ensure his punctuality, Charles is off to get married, but not to Carrie. He is marrying "duck-face," his obsessively committed former girlfriend Henrietta (Anna Chancellor). Charles arrives at the church on time, but so does Carrie, who announces that she has separated from her husband. Despite his best efforts to stall the wedding, the ceremony begins. When he turns to his smirking bride, however, he is panicked. Following tradition, the priest asks if anyone

objects to the marriage. Charles' all-knowing younger brother, David (David Bower), speaks up, in the only language he, as a deaf-mute, knows: In sign language, he declares that Charles loves someone else. The bride reacts to the news like a prizefighter to the bell. When next Charles is seen, he is back at his apartment, nursing a black eye. Carrie, however, is at the door.

Four Weddings and a Funeral is a very funny film with an unusually sophisticated sense of timing. In spite of the condensations, the coincidences, and the gaps in character construction as well as time, this most unlikely of hits is on its way to becoming a box-office smash. Its popularity speaks to the spontaneous, lively charm of director Mike Newell's film. Yet its success may also result from the hunger of audiences to see intelligently scripted films dealing with the adventure of human emotions and relationships. Richard Curtis' screenplay at once demonstrates why he was awarded the Writer's Guild of Great Britain Award for Top British Comedy Writer of 1993.

Like *Enchanted April* (1992), another film directed by Newell, *Four Weddings and a Funeral* depends on its clever screenplay and the talents of its ensemble of talented actors to convey a heightened, comedic sense of life as it is lived, in this case, in posh circles. Of particular appeal is the film's ability to convey the characters' utter familiarity with one another as friends, enemies, and lovers. In this respect, reviewers concentrated on only one noticeable flaw with the film: the enigmatic role of Carrie, and relative newcomer Andie MacDowell's inability to infuse life and logic into the perplexing character. By contrast, Hugh Grant was acknowledged as ably leading a cast whose polish of finely honed comic nuance extended even into the smallest roles, from blathering priest to an aristocratic but senile (and hostile) wedding guest.

Four Weddings and a Funeral proves that life's dramatic moments can be forged into a charming romantic comedy. This achievement is especially impressive in an era when Hollywood demonstrated an increasing reliance on dehumanized and depressing film fare.

—*Gaylyn Studlar*

"In the words of David Cassidy, while he was still with The Partridge Family, I think I love you."—Charles to Carrie, in *Four Weddings and a Funeral*

REVIEWS

Entertainment Weekly. March 25, 1994, p. 38.
The Hollywood Reporter. January 20, 1994, p. 13.
Los Angeles Times. March 9, 1994, p. F1.
The New York Times. March 9, 1994, p. B1.
Variety. January 20, 1994, p. 19.

Frauds

When a yuppie couple (Hugo Weaving and Josephine Byrnes) file a fraudulent insurance claim, a weirdo investigator (Phil Collins) traps them in his gigantic fun house, where they fight a battle of wits, in this black comedy.

REVIEWS

Variety. CCCLI, June 7, 1993, p. 39.

CREDITS

Roland Copping: Phil Collins
Jonathan: Hugo Weaving
Beth: Josephine Byrnes
Michael Allen: Peter Mochrie
Margaret: Helen O'Connor
Young Roland: Mitchell McMahon
Young Matthew: Andrew McMahon
Mother: Rebel Russell
Detective Simms: Nicholas Hammond

Origin: Australia
Released: 1993
Production: Andrena Finlay and Stuart Quin for Live Entertainment, J & M Entertainment, and Latent Image
Direction: Stephan Elliott
Screenplay: Stephan Elliott
Cinematographer: Geoff Burton
Editing: Frans Vandenburg
Production design: Brian Thomson
Costume design: Fiona Spence
Music: Guy Gross
MPAA rating: no listing
Running time: 94 minutes

Freedom On My Mind

"A superb profile in civil rights courage."
—Hal Hinson, *Washington Post*

Centering on the Mississippi Voter Registration Project of the early 1960's, this award-winning documentary uses recent interviews of participants in the movement and archival footage to depict the courageous struggle of African Americans to fight racism in American society as well as the Democratic Party.

REVIEWS

Atlanta Constitution. July 22, 1994, p. P7.
Boston Globe. January 27, 1995, p. 53.
Chicago Tribune. October 28, 1994, p. 7Q.
Christian Science Monitor. June 24, 1994, p. 12.
Los Angeles Times. September 29, 1994, p. F1.
The New Republic. CCX, June 27, 1994, p. 27.
The New York Times. June 19, 1994, Sec. 2 p. 13.
The New York Times. June 22, 1994, p. C13.
The New York Times. July 6, 1994, p. B3.
Variety. CCCLIV, February 14, 1994, p. 39.
The Washington Post. August 12, 1994, p. F7.
The Washington Post. August 12, 1994, p. WW38.

CREDITS

Narrator: Ronnie Washington
Bob Moses: Bob Moses
Endesha Ida Mae Holland: Endesha Ida Mae Holland
L. C. Dorsey: L. C. Dorsey
Marshall Ganz: Marshall Ganz
Curtis Hayes: Curtis Hayes

Released: 1994
Production: Connie Field and Marilyn Mulford for Clarity Film Productions; released by Tara Releasing
Direction: Connie Field and Marilyn Mulford
Screenplay: Michael Chandler
Cinematography: Michael Chinn, Steve Devita and Vicente Franco
Editing: Michael Chandler
Sound: Don Thomas, Larry Loewinger and Curtis Choy
Music: Mary Watkins
MPAA rating: no listing
Running time: 105 minutes

AWARDS AND NOMINATIONS

Academy Awards Nomination 1994: Best Documentary Feature
Sundance Film Festival Awards 1994: Grand Jury Prize: Best Documentary

Freeze-Die-Come to Life

Set in a small Russian mining town, this semiautobiographical film centers on the struggle for survival of a mischievous young man, Valerka (Pavel Nazarov), amid extreme hardship and poverty. Beautifully filmed images, fine acting, touching, but never overly sentimental story. The picture is the first feature film of Kanevski, who spent eight years in a labor camp before Glasnost. The title comes from a children's game of tag. In Russian with English subtitles.

CREDITS

Valerka: Pavel Nazarov
Galiya: Dinara Drukarova
Valerka's mother: Yelena Popova
Vitya: Vyacheslav Bambushek

Origin: Russia
Released: 1990
Production: Vitaly Kanevski and Valentna Tarasova for Lenfilm Studios; released by International Film Exchange Ltd.
Direction: Vitaly Kanevski
Screenplay: Vitaly Kanevski
Cinematographer: Vladimir Brylyakov
Editing: Galina Kornilova
Art direction: Yuri Pashigorev
Costume design: Tatyana Kochergina and Natalya Milliant
Music: Sergei Banevich
MPAA rating: no listing
Running time: 105 minutes

AWARDS AND NOMINATIONS

Cannes Film Festival Awards 1992: Camera d'Or (Kanevski)

Fresh

"In a world where criminals make the rules, someone new is out to beat them at their own game."—Movie tagline

"Powerful and riveting."—*Rolling Stone*

"Two thumbs up."—*Siskel & Ebert*

Box Office Gross: $8,086,684 (November 13, 1994)

Fresh is a stark morality play told from the point of view of an inner-city child already deeply entrenched in the amoral world of drug dealers, gangs, and violence. It marks the directorial debut of screenwriter (*The Rookie*, 1990) Boaz Yakim and was co-produced by Quentin Tarantino's associate Lawrence Bender (*Resevoir Dogs*, 1992, and *Pulp Fiction*, reviewed in this volume).

As the film opens, twelve-year-old Fresh (Sean Nelson) is seen going about what, for him, is a routine day—selling crack for a local dealer, hiding the wad of cash he has made from his efforts, and worrying about getting to school on time. Although he has several friends his own age, much of his time is spent in the company of adults, most of whom are in the drug business. Fresh lives with his sainted Aunt Frances (Cheryl Freeman) and eleven cousins. His mother is long since gone and his father Sam (Samuel

Fresh marks the directorial debut of Boaz Yakim.

L. Jackson) is an unemployed, alcoholic chess hustler. Their meetings are in the park, where Sam does his business, and consist of father-son chess matches. Sam offers stern instruction in the game and, as best he can given his demoralized condition, in life.

Fresh has other mentors, notably Esteban (Giancarlo Esposito), a family man who deals heroin, and Corky (Ron Brice), whose business is crack. Both of them see Fresh—hyper-responsible and unafraid to ask these much-feared men for a raise in pay when he thinks he deserves it—as their eventual successor.

Fresh is pulled by the various and opposing influences in his life. He wants to please his aunt and do well in school but, lacking a moral compass, clearly sees the drug money he is stockpiling as the only ticket out of the projects.

Two events change what seems to be the inevitable course of his life. First, his older sister Nicole (N'Bushe Wright) has succumbed to heroin addiction and has become the property of a pimp and pusher named Jake (Jean LaMarre). Nicole, whose beauty has been her only recognized attribute, is also being sought by Esteban. Seeing her being used by these two men torments Fresh, and he begins to ponder ways of freeing her. Secondly, his sweetheart at school, Hilary (Afi McClendon), is killed by a stray bullet fired by a psychotic crack runner, Red (Anthony Thomas), who is employed by Jake. From that moment, Fresh is on an ineluctable mission of revenge.

Using his own precocious intellect and strategy culled from his father's chess tutorials, Fresh manages to have Esteban jailed for murder, Red and Jake killed, and he and his sister moved out of the projects under a witness protection program. All of these events are orchestrated by the simple, duplicitous words of a twelve-year-old boy. Much of the second half of the film is taken up with the execution of these clever and dangerous manipulations, and though the film becomes less and less character-driven and turns more suspenseful, the tragic nature of Fresh's struggle is not lost. Though his goal of complete revenge is achieved, it has been obtained at a heavy cost. What was left of his already shattered innocence is lost. It is almost a relief when, at the film's conclusion, the stoic little boy finally breaks down and cries.

Winner of the 1994 Sundance Film Festival Filmmakers Trophy Award, *Fresh* distinguishes itself from the glut of inner-city, gang related films by telling its story from the perspective of a child. Screenwriter Yakim has not,

Sean Nelson as Fresh and Samuel L. Jackson as Sam in *Fresh*. © 1994 Buena Vista Pictures Distribution, Inc. All rights reserved.

however, avoided presenting the cliched images that prevade even the most sensitive of these films—black males as pimps, pushers, and disappeared fathers; black women as saints, junkies, or whores.

The film is graced by several finely nuanced performances, showing that Yakim is a gifted director of actors. Samuel L. Jackson, who already established himself as a brilliant character actor in such films as *Do the Right Thing* (1989) and *Goodfellas* (1990), delivers the perfect mix of anger, disappointment, shame, and resignation as Fresh's washed up, deadbeat dad.

As Fresh, big-screen newcomer Sean Nelson is convincing, conveying intelligence and a carefully cultivated emotional distance from the tumult and decay of his environment. It is, in its quiet way, a genuinely heartbreaking performance.

Also heartbreaking is N'Bushe Wright as Nicole. Seen in a starring role in *Zebrahead* (1992) her extraordinary per-

> "The only reason you ain't the man, you too goddamned little. When you get bigger, you be the man."—Corky to Fresh, in *Fresh*

formance in *Fresh* should, by all rights, bring her more widespread recognition. Her brief monologue detailing her self-hate and descent into heroin addiction is saved from bathos by her restrained delivery.

Such restraint is sometimes lacking in Giancarlo Esposito's portrayal of Esteban. Esposito, seen to great affect in *Malcolm X* (1992) and *Bob Roberts* (1992), fairly oozes menace as the heroin kingpin but, at times, crosses the line into caricature. Still, his intensity brings needed energy to the role. This quality of caricature is shared by most of the drug men in the film. Certain characters (particularly Corky and Esteban) who, early in the film, had been portrayed with shades of gray (Esteban the family man, Corky the business entrepreneur) have by film's end become entirely evil.

Unfortunately, much of the blame for this can be placed on the uneven script by Yakim. While parts of the film resonate with unusual insight (for example, the way in which

CREDITS

Fresh: Sean Nelson
Esteban: Giancarlo Esposito
Sam: Samuel L. Jackson
Nicole: N'Bushe Wright
Corky: Ron Brice
Jake: Jean LaMarre
Chuckie: Luis Lantigua
Chillie: Yul Vasquez
Aunt Frances: Cheryl Freeman
Red: Anthony Thomas
Smokey: Charles Malik Whitfield
Hilary: Afi McClendon

Released: 1994
Production: Lawrence Bender and Randy Ostrow for Lumiere; released by Miramax Films
Direction: Boaz Yakim
Screenplay: Boaz Yakim
Cinematographer: Adam Holender
Editing: Dorian Harris
Executive producer: Lila Cazes
Co-producer: Chrisann Verges
Associate producer: JoAnn Fregalette Jansen
Production design: Dan Leigh
Art direction: None listed
Sound: Michael Barosky
Costume design: Ellen Lutter
Music: Stewart Copeland
Casting: Douglas Aibel
MPAA rating: R
Running time: 113 minutes

AWARDS AND NOMINATIONS

Independent Spirit Awards 1995: Debut Performance (Nelson)
Nomination: Best Supporting Actor (Esposito)
Sundance Film Festival Awards 1994:
Filmmakers Trophy, Special Jury Prize (Nelson)

Fresh carries out his revenge shows the writer's real ingenuity), the dialogue and staging can just as frequently degenerate into stock urban drama formula, with all its familiar villains and evils. Though Yakim's colleagues in this production, from director of photography Adam Holender—known for *Midnight Cowboy* (1969) and *Sea of Love* (1989)—to co-producer Randy Ostrow—*State of Grace* (1990)—are seasoned professionals, *Fresh*, at times, looks and feels amateurish.

A film full of promise and affecting performances, *Fresh* is a decidedly mixed effort, although certainly yielding rewards for the viewer. The performances of Sean Nelson and N'Bushe Wright are reason enough to see this film and, though flawed, there is value to this child's-eye-view of the decaying urban nightmare.

—*Nicholas Kirgo*

REVIEWS

The Hollywood Reporter. January 26, 1994, p. 14.
Los Angeles Times. August 31, 1994, p. F1.
The New York Times. August 24, 1994, p. B4.
Variety. February 2, 1994, p. 4.

Frosh: Nine Months in a Freshman Dorm

An entertaining and uplifting look at college life in the early 1990's, this documentary centers on a group of freshmen at Stanford University, tracking them through their first year at school. This study of college life reveals that freshman are introduced to more than academic stress as they embark on a journey of self-discovery. The film explores racial, academic, political, and gender issues common to all college campuses. It is a two-part program, including "Freshman (Dis)Orientation" and "Making a Home."

CREDITS

Released: 1994
Production: Daniel Geller and Dayna Goldfine
Direction: Daniel Geller and Dayna Goldfine
Cinematography: Daniel Geller and Dayna Goldfine
Editing: Daniel Geller, Dayna Goldfine and Deborah Hoffman
MPAA rating: no listing
Running time: 93 minutes

REVIEWS

Boston Globe. September 7, 1994, p. 76.
Los Angeles Times. April 28, 1994, p. F2.
The New York Times. October 5, 1994, p. C18.
Variety. CCCLIII, January 17, 1994, p. 106.
The Washington Post. September 23, 1994, p. F7.

The Garden

This avant-garde film by Derek Jarman is composed of a series of mystifying images that incorporate religious and homoerotic themes. He examines the role of the Church in the persecution of homosexuality by recreating the story of the Passion and replacing the figure of Christ in some sequences with two male lovers, who are arrested, humiliated, and tortured.

CREDITS

No character identified: Tilda Swinton
No character identified: Johnny Mills
No character identified: Philip MacDonald
No character identified: Roger Cook
No character identified: Kevin Collins
No character identified: Pete Lee-Wilson
No character identified: Spencer Lee
No character identified: Jody Graber
No character identified: Michael Gough (voice)
No character identified: Stephen McBride (voice)

Origin: Great Britain
Released: 1990
Production: James MacKay for Channel Four Television and British Screen, in association with ZDF, Uplink, Sohbi Corporation, and Space Shower Television; released by Basilisk
Direction: Derek Jarman
Screenplay: Derek Jarman
Cinematography: Christopher Hughes and Derek Jarman
Editing: Peter Cartwright
Production design: Derek Brown and Christopher Hobbs
Music: Simon Fisher Turner
MPAA rating: no listing
Running time: 90 minutes

The Getaway

"A dangerous deal. A double cross. And the ultimate set-up is yet to come."—Movie tagline

"It's escapist fun with non-stop action that never lets up!"—Pia Lindstrom, *WNBC-TV*

Box Office Gross: $15,513,510 (March 20, 1994)

The decision to remake the action-adventure film *The Getaway* (1972) is a curious one. It certainly was not one of director Sam Peckinpah's best artistic achievements, although it did garner impressive box-office receipts, rendering it a commercial success. Perhaps the most notable thing about the original film was the on- screen pairing of tough-guy leading man Steve McQueen with former model Ali MacGraw, casting which led to an off-screen romance.

This latest version of *The Getaway* comes from director Roger Donaldson, best known for the Kevin Costner thriller *No Way Out* (1987), and stars another off-screen couple, this time the husband and wife pair of Alec Baldwin and Kim Basinger.

The Getaway is a remake of the 1972 Sam Peckinpah film starring Steve McQueen and Ali MacGraw, which led to a real-life romance between the two. This remake features real-life husband and wife, Alec Baldwin and Kim Basinger.

Although the two can generate sexual intensity, the film itself fails to blaze new cinematic ground, presenting a near scene-by-scene copy of the original, including screenwriter Walter Hill's romanticized ending, as well as the thrilling garbage-truck scene. While the film does not attempt a fresh interpretation of Jim Thompson's gritty novel, *The Getaway* does succeed in updating and thereby strengthening the female lead character of Carol McCoy. Kim Basinger presents an interesting blend of toughness and vulnerability, along with dazzling beauty, all of which combine to make her Carol more of a partner in crime to Baldwin's Doc rather than a mere arm piece. One believes this Doc could not fully exist without Carol. Baldwin and Basinger bring a sexual

"Hell of a way to make a living, Doc."
"Well, you should have married a dentist."—Carol McCoy to Doc McCoy in *The Getaway*

chemistry to the screen that is fun to watch, and like Susan Sarandon's character in *Thelma and Louise* (1991), Carol proves that women can be great drivers.

Peckinpah softened the characters of Doc and Carol McCoy considerably from the original Thompson story, one that offered much promise as a complex—and bleak—examination of dangerous love. Thompson gave his readers two star-crossed lovers who end up miserable in some hellish Mexican village, forced to spend the rest of their lives in constant mistrust and suspicion of each other. Of the twenty-eight novels he wrote, several of Thompson's other works have found their way to the screen in such films as Stephen Frears's *The Grifters* (1990) and James Foley's *After Dark, My Sweet* (1990); however, no screenwriter to date has been able to capture fully Thompson's desolate world view.

Peckinpah's *The Getaway* opens with an unforgettable montage sequence: shots of Doc McCoy, master safecracker, incarcerated, doing time and struggling against the claustrophobia of prison life, intercut with fleeting memories of his wife, Carol. The sequence brilliantly employed the repetitiveness of an automated shuttle loom, the sound drilling through the silence, slowly driving Doc to desperation, willing to do whatever it took to win his freedom—even sending his wife to make a deal with a sleazy businessman named Jack Benyon (played in the new version by the master of lowlife himself, James Woods). This is in extreme contrast to Donaldson's right-wing politicized beginning of glorified sexy gunplay and the visual articulation not of paying for one's crime but rather of being double-crossed by one's peers, of choosing one's friends badly, so to speak. Doc reads more like a poor victim of circumstance than a ruthless criminal.

Once out of prison, Doc and Carol agree to repay Benyon by setting up one last heist, this time suspensefully executed at the dog races. Things inevitably go wrong and the McCoys must hit the road with the stolen loot, but not before their double-crossing accomplice, Rudy (Michael Madsen), is hot on their trail. Further complications evolve when Doc discovers that Carol has had sex with Benyon in order to secure his release from prison, which triggers a lengthy bout of mutual suspicion and distrust. Rudy, meanwhile, kidnaps a veterinarian (James Stephens) and his whorish wife (Jennifer Tilly in the film's most offensive role) who quickly decides to enslave herself to the killer. Director Donaldson keeps up a relentless pace with high-speed car chases and Peckinpah-style slow-motion shoot-outs as the

CREDITS

Doc McCoy: Alec Baldwin
Carol McCoy: Kim Basinger
Rudy Travis: Michael Madsen
Jack Benyon: James Woods
Jim Deer Jackson: David Morse
Fran Carvey: Jennifer Tilly
Harold Carvey: James Stephens
Slim: Richard Farnsworth
Frank Hansen: Philip Hoffman
Gollie: Burton Gilliam
Gun shop salesman: Royce D. Applegate
Mendoza: Daniel Villareal

Released: 1994
Production: David Foster, Lawrence Turman, and John Alan Simon for Largo Entertainment, in association with JVC Entertainment; released by Universal Pictures.
Direction: Roger Donaldson
Screenplay: Walter Hill and Amy Holden Jones; based on the novel by Jim Thompson
Cinematography: Peter Menzies, Jr.
Editing: Conrad Buff
Production design: Joseph Nemec III
Art direction: Dan Olexiewicz
Set design: Wm. Law III
Set decoration: R. W. "Inke" Intlekofer
Casting: Michael Fenton and Allison Cowitt
Sound: Richard Bryce Goodman
Stunt coordination: Glenn R. Wilder
Music supervision: Danny Bramson
Music: Mark Isham
MPAA rating: R
Running time: 115 minutes

AWARDS AND NOMINATIONS

MTV Movie Awards Nomination 1994: Most Desirable Female (Basinger)

couple make their way to the Mexican border.

It was Alec Baldwin who actively pursued the remake of *The Getaway*. Kim Basinger reportedly professed reluctance to become involved in the project, perhaps fearing the same kind of thrashing at the hands of the critics as Ali MacGraw received for her performance in the Peckinpah film. The painfully shy Basinger had only recently undergone public humiliation, as well as personal financial bankruptcy, following an adverse court decision in her case involving the producers of *Boxing Helena* (1993). The producers accused Basinger of failing to honor a verbal agreement to play the female lead in the film and, much to the surprise of people in the film industry, the jury agreed to award the producers more than $8 million in damages.

It is Basinger, however, and not Baldwin, who actually fares better in Donaldson's *The Getaway*. Whenever an actor participates in a remake of a film, he or she invites comparison to the actor who originated the role. It is not necessarily just, but it is unfortunately part of the risk involved. If the original character interpretation was weak and the actor forgettable, the second actor might stand a chance of making the role his or her own. Such is the case with Basinger. Her strength and innate ability to survive under very difficult situations come shining through in her interpretation of the character of Carol McCoy. (Admittedly, it did not take a quantum leap in acting ability to outpace the stilted Ali MacGraw.) For Alec Baldwin, however, attempting to eclipse the enigmatic Steve McQueen proves no easy feat. McQueen, along with a mere handful of other talented actors from the 1960's and early 1970's, transcended the role of mere "actor" into the realm of "movie star." He possessed an on-screen charisma and an inner complexity that was often masked by a minimalist acting style, not unlike current screen icon Clint Eastwood. McQueen could convey a range of emotions with a single movement—as though there were a million different, conflicting thoughts racing through his mind at any given moment. The talented actor was a rare breed of male who could combine machismo with vulnerability.

While *The Getaway* was far from his best work, Steve McQueen nevertheless was able to mesmerize the viewing audience with his on-screen persona. While Alec Baldwin is a gifted performer, he proves no match for McQueen's Doc McCoy. Baldwin's fashion-model good looks work to his disadvantage here. Maybe it is the slick, stylized hair, but he is almost too handsome here to be believable as a cold-blooded killer, which is surprising given his ability to transform himself into the psychopathic Junior in the compelling *Miami Blues* (1990). It is disappointing that Baldwin could not find a way to make the role of Doc McCoy his own. The actor's other past critical successes include a memorable turn as the young Jimmy Swaggart in the story of 1950's rocker Jerry Lee Lewis, *Great Balls of Fire!* (1989); Michelle Pfeiffer's hitman-husband in Jonathan Demme's *Married to the Mob* (1988); and the slick station manager in Eric Bogosian's *Talk Radio* (1988). In addition, the actor received a Tony nomination as Best Actor for his work in the Broadway revival of *A Streetcar Named Desire*.

While the filmmakers have succeeded in delivering yet another well-oiled action-adventure film replete with steamy sex, exploitative violence, and happy endings, it is disappointing that they have missed the opportunity to imbue *The Getaway* with any moral or psychological depth. Once again, Hollywood seems content to offer little more than cheap thrills and a good ride. What a waste of talent.

—*Patricia Kowal*

REVIEWS

Entertainment Weekly. February 11, 1994, p. 34.
The Hollywood Reporter. February 10, 1994, p. 10.
Los Angeles Times. February 11, 1994, p. F1.
New York. XXVII, February 21, 1994, p. 48.
The New York Times. CXLIII, February 11, 1994, p. B1.
The New Yorker. LXX, February 21, 1994, p. 110.
Rolling Stone. February 24, 1994, p. 62.
Variety. February 10, 1994, p. 4.

Getting Even With Dad

"Timmy's not getting mad he's...*Getting Even with Dad.*"—Movie tagline

"Funny and sweet...it will win your heart."
—*Satellite News Network*

 Box Office Gross: $18,111,932 (August 28, 1994)

One of Hollywood's most time-tested genres is the heartwarming family comedy. The line of child stars who have taken their turn at the genre includes, among others, Jackie Coogan, Shirley Temple, Mickey Rooney, Freddie Bartholomew, and Margaret O'Brien. Popular successes have resulted more often than critical successes, however. After all, the quality family film requires that sentiment not wither into sentimentality, or at least not for very long, a balance that has proved elusive for filmmakers. Though film history features a number of noteworthy performances of children in supporting roles, a child protagonist must be more than merely cute for the film to remain memorable. These requirements point up both the strengths and the weaknesses of *Getting Even with Dad*.

Macaulay Culkin plays Tim, an eleven-year-old who is abruptly dropped off at the apartment of his estranged father, Ray (Ted Danson), apartment by his Aunt Kitty (Kathleen Wilhoite). For Ray, his son's arrival is inopportune: Ray has been deep in plans for a robbery that would enable him to buy the bakery where he works. He refuses to answer the telephone out of fear that his girlfriend, who has started giving him houseplants, may call. Ray's explanation, heard over a shot of the neglected plant, speaks volumes

"When a woman gives you something you have to water, feed, or take for walks, it's time to dump her."—Carl speaking to Ray about Nadine in *Getting Even with Dad*

about his personality: "When a woman gives you something you have to water, feed, or take for walks, it's time to dump her." With the help of his dim-witted fellow ex-convicts, Bobby (Saul Rubinek) and Carl (Gailard Sartain), Ray plans to steal a valuable coin collection when security guards transfer it for appraisal. These unimpressive crooks have, surprisingly, worked out a clever ploy of waylaying the guards as they pass through some construction equipment. While the thieves escape with the coins, a wail of sirens announces the police arriving too late.

Stranded at home during his father's caper, Tim listens to news reports of the robbery, observes the newspaper cuttings around the apartment describing the value of the coins, and puts two and two together. Tim then videotapes Ray and his partners unloading the loot and overhears the crooks argue on the roof about where to hide the coins until they can meet with their fence. Tired of being shuffled from one surrogate parent to another, Tim works out a plan of his own. He rehides the stolen coins, mails to a friend the incriminating videotape, and then calls his dad and friends into the kitchen for a talk.

Tim decides to blackmail himself into his father's life. He tells Ray that if Ray spends a week taking him to ball games and amusement parks, he will then disclose the location of the coins. Although Ray registers a fatherly admiration for Tim's ingenuity, Bobby and Carl are outraged at being outsmarted by a boy. A montage of shots shows the three men searching the apartment but, of course, failing to find the money. Tim smugly tells them that his plan really protects their larger interests since, he assures them, in time they would make a foolish mistake and get themselves caught.

As Tim predicts, the police have been running computer checks on released convicts whose prior arrests indicate a possibility for involvement in a plan such as the coin theft. Ray's picture appears in the printout, and an officer is sent to observe his actions. As the week of enforced father-son closeness begins, Bobby and Carl tag along to see whether Tim tells Ray the location of the coins, and Theresa (Glenne Headly), the policewoman assigned to Ray, follows the four of them from a distance.

The remainder of the film is the most predictable. Visits to an aquarium, a miniature-golf course, and a skating rink forge a bond between Tim and Ray. Meanwhile, Bobby and Carl spend their time tracking down the false leads in a treasure map that Tim has surreptitiously drawn and then hidden for them to find. The film divides its attention between scenes of Ray and Tim that focus on their deepening relationship and those of Bobby and Carl that focus on their slapstick pursuit of the stolen loot.

Over dessert at an ice-cream parlor, Tim mentions the possibility of Ray's returning the coins. Later, while shooting baskets with his father, Tim listens to Ray expound on the art of picking up girls and applies Ray's teachings when, retrieving the stray basketball, he meets the police woman, Theresa, and asks her to dine with them. Theresa, who is unhappy in her work and unappreciated by her lieutenant (Hector

CREDITS

Timmy: Macaulay Culkin
Ray: Ted Danson
Theresa: Glenne Headly
Bobby: Saul Rubinek
Carl: Gailard Sartain
Alex: Sam McMurray
Lieutenant Romayko: Hector Elizondo
Kitty: Kathleen Wilhoite
Wayne: Dann Florek

Released: 1994
Production: Katie Jacobs and Pierce Gardner; released by Metro-Goldwyn-Mayer
Direction: Howard Deutch
Screenplay: Tom S. Parker and Jim Jennewein
Cinematography: Tim Suhrstedt
Editing: Richard Halsey
Production design: Virginia L. Randolph
Art decoration: Clayton R. Hartley
Set decoration: Barbara Munch
Casting: Richard Pagano, Sharon Bialy and Debi Manwiller
Sound: Bill Phillips and John Phillips
Costume design: Rudy Dillon
Music: Miles Goodman
MPAA rating: PG
Running time: 110 minutes

AWARDS AND NOMINATIONS

Film Advisory Award of Excellence

Elizondo), like Tim, longs for someone to take her seriously. As the three grow closer, Ray eventually confronts the dilemma of whether to choose the fortune or a future with his son. Tim surrenders the key to the locker in which he has stored the coins, which—he had hid in the last place his father would have looked—stuck in the dried-out mulch encasing Ray's dying houseplant. His fate is now in his father's hands.

This growing emphasis on slapstick and sentimentality ushers some implausibilities into the developing story and replaces the cleverness of the early scenes. The pratfalls involving the red herring of Tim's false treasure map result in the already flat characters of Bobby and Carl shrinking to cartoon dimensions. This running joke is reminiscent of Culkin's first hit, *Home Alone* (1990), in which he played a boy who fended off two criminals until help arrived. The slapstick in *Getting Even with Dad*, however, is less inventive. One joke simply shows the many different ways that Carl can spill food on his neckties. The love story also fits somewhat awkwardly into the film. Theresa develops feelings for Ray before she even meets him, simply by observing the father-son outings in the line of duty. Reviewers faulted the film strongly for these lapses without, however, pointing out that the first third of the film adapts the genre of the family film with greater originality.

In its early, less predictable scenes, the film establishes characters and unfolds its premise economically. The scriptwriters make especially good use of Tim's camcorder to develop plot and character. For example, Tim annoys his Aunt Kitty's new husband (Dann Florek) by taping him while he drives, thus provoking the couple to leave him with Ray. Tim records the thieves' return from the robbery and uses the tape as leverage in his effort to spend time with his father. After he films Ray on ice skates, Tim later notices when playing the tape that Theresa was observing them at the rink. From this, he deduces her job as a policewoman, a plot point that permits him to shield his father and to set up Bobby and Carl to take the blame for the robbery. The camcorder, in depicting Tim's shrewdness, becomes a useful shorthand device for the filmmakers. When Tim, therefore, is shown as someone who is smart enough to outwit the masterminds of the clever coin heist, the film acquires energy and freshness. With the introduction of the treasure map, however, Tim becomes one of the many screen children who too effortlessly outmaneuver adults, and the film reveals the flatness that so many reviewers criticized.

As a result, the performances are more effective in the first third of the film, where the script is the strongest. Ted Danson conveys in the running banter Ray has with Tim the growing affection the father feels for his son. Macaulay Culkin outsmarts and negotiates with the crooks in a straightforward, understated manner. His nonchalance in these scenes diverts from the audacity of his offer to Ray, but it also calls attention to the thinness of the later scenes that rely heavily on wholesome reaction shots of Culkin. The design and packaging of the film suggest that Culkin's box-office popularity was influential in shaping the project. Unfortunately, the personality of the star does not completely carry the film. *Getting Even with Dad* shows in its better scenes that a good script can enliven a timeworn film genre, but that predictability sets in when cuteness and sentimentality are all that a film offers.

—Glenn Hopp

REVIEWS

Entertainment Weekly. July 8, 1994, p. 38.
The Hollywood Reporter. June 10-12, 1994, p. 6.
Los Angeles Times. June 17, 1994, p. F12.
The New York Times. June 17, 1994, p. B6.
The New Yorker. July 11, 1994, p. 94.
Time. June 27, 1994, p. 71.
USA Today. June 17, 1994, p. 5D.
Variety. June 10, 1994, p. 4.

A Gift From Heaven

A mother (Sharon Farrell) lives with her two grown children, Charlie (David Steen) and Messy (Gigi Rice), in rural North Carolina. The arrival of naive Cousin Anna (Sarah Trigger) triggers a series of emotional and sexual revelations among the family members.

REVIEWS

Boston Globe. September 14, 1994, p. 78.
Variety. CCCLV, June 13, 1994, p. 60.

CREDITS

Ma Samuals: Sharon Farrell
Messy Samuals: Gigi Rice
Charlie Samuals: David Steen
Cousin Anna: Sarah Trigger
Hesley: Gene Lythgow
No character identified: Mark Ruffalo
No character identified: Nicholas Worth
No character identified: Molly McClure

Released: 1994
Production: Laurent Hatchwell for Hatchwell-Lucarelli Productions; released by Hills Communications
Direction: Jack Lucarelli
Screenplay: David Steen
Cinematography: Steve Yaconelli
Editing: Steve Mirkovich
Production design: Robert Varney
Casting: Jeannie Wilson
Sound: Joe Kenworthy
Costume design: Laura Slakey
Music: Jean-Noel Chaleat
MPAA rating: no listing
Running time: 102 minutes

Glamazon: A Different Kind of Girl

This documentary centers on the very colorful Barbara LeMay, nee Sammy Hoover, a sixty-two-year-old transvestite and former carnival dancer.

REVIEWS

Variety. CCCLI, July 12, 1993, p. 54.

CREDITS

Barbara LeMay: Barbara LeMay

Released: 1994
Production: Maria Demopoulos
Direction: Rico Martinez
Screenplay: Rico Martinez
Cinematography: David Morrison
Editing: Jim Makiej
Production design: Kevin Adams
Music: Kristen McCord
MPAA rating: no listing
Running time: 83 minutes

Go Fish

"The girl is out there."—Movie tagline

"Four stars! A Sexy, Free-Wheeling and Bracing Tale of Love!"—Gene Seymour, *New York Newsday*

"Real Comic Verve! *Go Fish* looks at love between women with a wit that's long overdue."—Janet Maslin, *The New York Times*

"A jaunty, low-budget tomgirl of a film that's something new.... In its way, *Go Fish* does for lesbian culture what Spike Lee's *She's Gotta Have it* did for black culture back in 1986: opens the doors and invites the entire neighborhood in for some fun."—Lisa Schwarzbaum, *Entertainment Weekly*

 Box Office Gross: $2,439,346 (September 18, 1994)

The diversity of the lesbian community is given a wonderful showing in this delightful directorial debut by screenwriter/director Rose Troche. Troche displays a caustic wit and a loving objectivity about the lesbian community, creating a number of familiar and not-so-familiar characters, all of whom are interestingly portrayed in this quirky romance. Its "odd couple" storyline and its clever humor make it a fascinating and entertaining glimpse into lesbian culture.

The story, written by Troche with one of the film's stars (Guinevere Turner), is simple but cleverly told. Kia (T. Wendy McMillan), an African-American college professor, plots to find a girlfriend for her quirky roommate, Max (Turner). Kia, having found happiness with her lover, Evy (Migdalia Melendez), is quite opinionated about how everyone else should or can find happiness, hence her interest in finding a mate for Max. She eventually sets Max up with Ely (V.S. Brodie), a shy ex-student of Kia's who is finding difficulty ending a long-term relationship.

The difference between Max and Ely is apparent from the beginning: Max is vivacious and hip, Ely is quiet and decidedly reserved; Max is short and cute, Ely is tall and somewhat "nerdy"; and finally, Ely is older than Max. Their friends gossip about them when they aren't around in a series of delightful scenes which re-define "girl talk." Troche makes an interesting visual image out of the chatty friends. Many of the scenes where they discuss their (and Max's) relationships are arranged so that the women are lying down, their exchanges being photographed by an overhead camera. The resulting image of the talking heads becomes a visual icon to which Troche returns, and by which she seems to be making a comment about the interconnectedness of women in general and lesbians in particular.

Their connections to each other because of their sexual identity is explored in several different ways. In the first scene, Kia is seen teaching her class about women and lesbians, listing "lesbians and lesbian wanna-be's" such as Roseanne or Madonna. The emphasis on the importance of being lesbian is also shown in a revealing scene in which promiscuous Daria (Anastasia Sharp) undergoes a surrealistic interrogation by her friends for the possible transgression of having slept with a man. With the scene, Troche and company are able to evoke the political nature of being a lesbian in the nineties while poking fun at the rigidity practiced by some. It is interesting that some of these characters, who are oppressed by the lack of freedom afforded them by their families, are just as oppressive to one of their own when she even considers sleeping with a man. That Daria is portrayed as being ultimately unfazed by their grilling is in keeping with the good-natured tone of the film: the lessons are learned without too emotional a price.

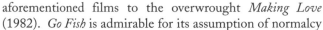

"The girl you're going to meet doesn't look like anyone you know."—*Go Fish*

Go Fish never strays into the over-emotional sensibility shared by many other films about being gay which have "made it" in the mainstream. *Claire of the Moon* (1992) and *Desert Hearts* (1985) were earlier lesbian-themed films which succumbed to the drama of "coming out" in their depiction of lesbian characters. The central plot of many gay films, in fact, has had to do with "coming out," from the

aforementioned films to the overwrought *Making Love* (1982). *Go Fish* is admirable for its assumption of normalcy and personal comfort among its lead characters.

Troche and Turner have, with the help of the wonderful cinematography of Ann T. Rossetti, created a strong sense of realism which causes the ear and eye to perk up at the slightest lack of believability. In other words, they have done their jobs very well: the realistic dialogue ("I think Ely has a severe case of hippie-itis"), the grainy black-and-white camerawork, and the simple two-shots and less-than perfect camera angles make for a wonderful sense of reality.

The actors are particularly realistic and interesting, with Turner and Brodie leading the pack with unique and touching performances. Brodie is especially endearing as a mousy woman who is smitten enough with her new love that she gets a radical new haircut to try and please her. Brodie negotiates the "kookiness" of her character with grace and ease, providing a decidedly non-stereotypical performance.

All of the participants in this film deserve credit for the creation of an off-beat comedy that is interesting enough for the mainstream even while it celebrates its quirkiness.

—*Kirby Tepper*

CREDITS

Ely: V. S. Brodie
Max: Guinevere Turner
Kia: T. Wendy McMillan
Evy: Migdalia Melendez
Daria: Anastasia Sharp

Released: 1994
Production: Rose Troche and Guinevere Turner for Islet and Can I Watch Pictures/KVPI; released by the Samuel Goldwyn Company
Direction: Rose Troche
Screenplay: Rose Troche and Guinevere Turner
Cinematography: Ann T. Rossetti
Editing: Rose Troche
Sound: Missy Cohen
Music: Brendan Dolan, Jennifer Sharpe and Scott Aldrich
MPAA rating: no listing
Running time: 85 minutes

AWARDS AND NOMINATIONS

Independent Spirit Awards Nomination 1995: Best Supporting Actress (Brodie)

REVIEWS

Daily Variety. January 25, 1994. p. 9
Los Angeles Times. July 1, 1994. p. F12
The New York Times. June 10, 1994. p. B9
The Advocate. June 14, 1994, p. 93.
Atlanta Journal and Atlanta Constitution. July 1, 1994, p. P6.
Boston Globe. July 1, 1994, p. 48.
Chicago. XLIII, July 1994, p. 12.
Chicago Tribune. January 25, 1994, Sec. 1 p. 18.
Chicago Tribune. July 1, 1994, p. 7M.
Entertainment Weekly. June 17, 1994, p. 34.
Los Angeles Times. July 1, 1994, p. F12.
The Nation. CCLIX, July 25, 1994, p. 137.
New Statesman & Society. VII, July 15, 1994, p. 32.
The New York Times. June 10, 1994, p. C6.
Newsweek. CXXIII, June 27, 1994, p. 53.
People Weekly. XLI, June 13, 1994, p. 18.
Playboy. XLI, July 1994, p. 22.
Rolling Stone. June 30, 1994, p. 82.
Vogue. CLXXXIV, June 1994, p. 91.
The Washington Post. July 2, 1994, p. D1.

Golden Gate

"Some loves are impossible. But they are loves just the same."—Movie tagline
"A Tale of Mystery, Intrigue and Revenge!"
—*The Houston Post*

 Box Office Gross: $258,040 (January 30, 1994)

This drama set in 1950's San Francisco centers on an eager-beaver FBI agent, Kevin Walker (Matt Dillon), who is assigned to track down suspected Communists in Chinatown. In his misguided zeal, he unjustly implicates an innocent man (Tzi Ma)—who later jumps to his death—only to fall in love with the man's daughter (Joan Chen), who is crusading to vindicate her father. *Golden Gate*'s screenplay was written by Tony award-winning writer David Henry Hwang (*M. Butterfly*).

REVIEWS

Atlanta Constitution. January 28, 1994, p. P8.
Boston Globe. January 28, 1994, p. 50.
Chicago Tribune. January 28, 1994, p. 7C.
Christian Science Monitor. April 13, 1994, p. 15.
Entertainment Weekly. October 7, 1994, p. 84.
The New York Times. January 28, 1994, p. C10.
People Weekly. XLI, February 7, 1994, p. 23.
The Wall Street Journal. January 27, 1994, p. A12.
The Washington Post. January 28, 1994, p. C7.

CREDITS

Kevin Walker: Matt Dillon
Marilyn Song: Joan Chen
Ron Pirelli: Bruno Kirby
Cynthia: Teri Polo
Chen Jung Song: Tzi Ma
Bradley Ichiyasu: Stan Egi
FBI chief: Jack Shearer
Byrd: Peter Murnik
Meisner: George Guidall

Released: 1994
Production: Michael Brandman, in association with American Playhouse Theatrical Films; released by the Samuel Goldwyn Company
Direction: John Madden
Screenplay: David Henry Hwang
Cinematography: Bobby Bukowski
Editing: Sean Barton
Production design: Andrew Jackness
Art direction: Edward Rubin
Casting: Risa Bramon Garcia, Juel Bestrop and Mary Vernieu
Sound: Andy Wiskes
Costume design: Ingrid Ferrin
Music: Elliot Goldenthal
MPAA rating: R
Running time: 90 minutes

 "Damn, I hate due process."—Ron Pirelli, from *Golden Gate*

Good Evening, Mr. Wallenberg

This drama focuses on the heroism of Raoul Wallenberg (Stellan Skarsgard), a Swede who saved thousands of Hungarian Jews from the Nazis during World War II. Using phony documents he first had small groups of Jews smuggled to safety, but when he learns that 65,000 Jews in the Budapest ghetto are to be killed, he uses a bluff to prevent their deaths. He was later taken by the Soviet Army and his fate has never been determined. In Swedish, German, and Hungarian with English subtitles.

REVIEWS

The New York Times. May 6, 1994, p. D17.

CREDITS

Raoul Wallenberg: Stellan Skarsgard
Rabbi in Stockholm: Erland Josephson
Marja: Katharina Thalbach

Origin: Sweden
Released: 1993
Production: Katinka Farago
Direction: Kjell Grede
Screenplay: Kjell Grede
Cinematography: Esa Vuorinen
Editing: Darek Hodor
MPAA rating: no listing
Running time: 115 minutes

A Good Man in Africa

"Deep in the heart of Africa the British practice bizarre rituals. They call it diplomacy."
—Movie tagline

 Box Office Gross: $2,295,371 (October 2, 1994)

A *Good Man in Africa* is a parody of British life and diplomacy in post-colonial West Africa. It focuses on the life of a cynical, fairly ignoble and bumbling mid-level diplomat, Morgan Leafy (Colin Friels), following the arrival of a new High Commissioner (John Lithgow) and his wife Chloe (Diana Rigg) and daughter Priscilla (Sarah-Jane Fenton).

Ironically, the film was shot in South Africa in mid-1993, a period of terrible unrest and tension prior to the country's first democratic elections involving black South Africans. Regrettably, however, it presents few realities of contemporary African life; most of the film occurs either indoors or at night. Nor does the film pander to European and American audiences, at least not to the thirst for the exotic. It is neither sentimental nor documentary, and there are few shots of beautiful landscapes, wild animals, or exotic people. It is not *Out of Africa* (1985) or *Herdsmen of the Sun* (1988) and is unique in this regard for a European or American production shot in Africa.

Early in the film, Morgan meets with the people who come to have some decisive influence in his life, the new High Commissioner and his family, leading presidential candidate Sam Adekunle (Louis Gossett, Jr.), and the well-known and respected Dr. Murray (Sean Connery). Commissioner Fanshawe comes to Kinjanja (the fictitious name of this nation) to supervise relations with Kinjanjan political and business leadership. The country is preparing for presidential elections, and oil reserves have been discovered off the coast. Morgan becomes the liaison between the Commissioner and professor Adekunle. Morgan first meets Adekunle and his British-born wife, Celia (Joanne Whalley-Kilmer), at a dinner party. Morgan and Celia flirt, and she promises to arrange a private meeting for him with her husband.

Morgan is drawn into a crooked deal involving Adekunle. Morgan arranges for Adekunle to visit London, and he winds up dining and sleeping with Celia while Adekunle is away. Adekunle learns of their affair and uses this knowledge to coerce Morgan into helping him bribe Dr. Murray. Dr. Murray holds veto power on the city council and is expected to block Adekunle's plans to make a lot of money in a large construction project. Morgan tries to bribe Dr. Murray but fails.

One of the objects of the story is Morgan's maturation through his contact with Dr. Murray. Dr. Murray is hard-working, honest, forthright, stubborn, even ill-tempered, presumably compassionate and selfless: he is the good man in Africa. He also provides Morgan with several moral lessons before his unfortunate death in an automobile accident. He even tells Morgan to quit work as a diplomat. As the doctor lies dying, Morgan promises him that he will expose Adekunle and try to live a more virtuous life.

The film pokes fun at British cultural and racial prejudices. Director Bruce Beresford has called the film a naturalistic comedy based on observations of British life in Africa; the film's author (William Boyd) was born in Africa, and Beresford lived for two years in Nigeria. On one level, the film is merely a comedy of manners. The film, however, goes deeper than that, and it certainly benefits from the perception, or notoriety, of the British as insensitive to other cultures, unable or unwilling to learn foreign languages or understand and appreciate foreign cultures. According to Beresford the film is about cultural conflict and lack of understanding, and the comedy is meant to derive from these realities.

CREDITS

Morgan Leafy: Colin Friels
Dr. Alex Murray: Sean Connery
Arthur Fanshawe: John Lithgow
Chloe Fanshawe: Diana Rigg
Priscilla Fanshawe: Sarah-Jane Fenton
Sam Adekunle: Louis Gossett, Jr.
Celia Adekunle: Joanne Whalley-Kilmer
Hazel: Jackie Mofokeng
Friday: Maynard Eziashi
Kojo: Themba Ndaba
Dalmire: Jeremy Crutchley
Jones: Russel Savadier
Innocence: Lillian Dube
Peter: Peter Thage

Released: 1994
Production: John Fiedler and Mark Tarlov for Southern Sun and Polar Entertainment, in association with Capitol Films; released by Gramercy Pictures
Direction: Bruce Beresford
Screenplay: William Boyd; based on the novel by Boyd
Cinematography: Andrezj Bartkowiak
Editing: Jim Clark
Production design: Herbert Pinter
Production management: Genevieve Hofmeyr
Art direction: Graeme Orwin
Set decoration: Vic Botha
Costume design: Rosemary Burrows
Casting: Billy Hopkins and Susie Figgis
Music: John du Prez
MPAA rating: R
Running time: 95 minutes

Morgan has supposedly spent a few years in Kinjanja, yet he speaks only a few words of French, knows nothing of the local language, and apparently little of the local culture. He is exasperated to have to speak a few words of French to communicate to his servant Friday (Maynard Eziashi). There are also no signs that Commissioner Fanshawe or his family speak any French or know much about the place and culture to which they have been assigned. Presumably some of the diplomat's contact would take place in French.

The diplomats' lack of understanding and disrespect for Kinjanjan culture is illustrated by the death of one of the Commissioner's servants. One night, a maid (Lillian Dube) is struck dead by lightening just outside the house. Some Kinjanjans fear the God of thunder and lightening and, according to custom, the victim must undergo ritual purification before the body may be touched. Before the body may be moved and buried, the family must be notified, money must be collected, and a ritual must be performed by a special figure.

Morgan and Fanshawe are unaware of the these beliefs and rituals, and Fanshawe is exasperated by the idea of a corpse decomposing outside the house and horrified by the idea that it should coincide with an upcoming visit by a member of the royal family. He is unwilling to accept the Kinjanjan's needs and tells Morgan to get rid of it. Some of the events surrounding the corpse are among the most outrageous in the film. First Morgan steals it. The staff responds by refusing to work until it is returned. When Fanshawe complains of this turn of events, the audience learns that Morgan has hidden the body in his icebox. On Christmas night, drunk and dressed as Santa Claus, Morgan distracts the other servants with a small explosion in order to return the corpse unnoticed.

The film comes to an abrupt and surprising conclusion. Adekunle wins the election (as expected), and, during a celebration at the Commissioner's house, a mob of Kinjanjan protesters swarm outside the iron gates and threaten the celebration party. Too little of the election and business dealings are known for the audience to anticipate this crisis—people are apparently angry at the secret oil deal Adekunle has made with the British. Morgan volunteers to disguise himself as Fanshawe and lure the mob away from the party. He is joined by Fanshawe's wife, who is excited by Morgan's sudden courage. Their getaway turns into a crazy chase with Morgan and Chloe crawling in the woods, at one point, to avoid the gunfire of their pursuers. They eventually come upon the accident involving Dr. Murray.

Critics have focused on the troubling aspects of this film. Michael Wilmington of the *Chicago Tribune* suggests the characters are inconsistent in their styles: "The actresses are almost all treated as sex-comedy foils. Connery gives monumental, heroic readings. Gossett satirizes statesmanship. Lithgow—looking and acting a bit like John Cleese—does arch high comedy. And Friels, the Australian star... whips up a twitching nervous stew." Janet Maslin of *The*

New York Times claims the film fails to keep the comic context of the novel by leaving out some caustic narration (by Morgan) and considers the film insulting.

What is wrong with this film? The film does lack consistency. It mixes different comic forms, switching back and forth between satire, parody, and farce. This means changes in tempo and mood. There are also too many stereotypes of Africans. They are shown as servile, or obedient, fanatic or strange in their beliefs, corrupt, savage, and perhaps dependent on the generosity and technology of more industrial nations—Dr. Murray, a Scot, is the only doctor seen in the film, and long lines of black Kinjanjans regularly sit outside his door waiting to see him. All the British have black Kinjanjans assist and serve them at work and at home. Morgan has an office assistant, house servant, and driver; the High Commissioner has an all-Kinjanjan staff. To a certain extent this must be expected—they are, after all, in Africa. The film, however, definitely suffers from the lack of stronger, more admirable, black characters. Adekunle, the only strong black character, is portrayed as ambitious, greedy, and corrupt.

Morgan is also clumsy, furtive, and duplicitous in his affairs with women, but worst with his Kinjanjan lover Hazel (Jackie Mofokeng), with whom he has a second apartment. He visits her at night in their apartment, and he either does not want to make his relationship with her public or is afraid to make it public. She complains that they never go out, he promises her they will.

There is no question that this film tries to be funny, and has its moments, but it also tries to sell Dr. Murray's goodness and Morgan's moral development. Morgan resists sleeping with Priscilla when he fears he has venereal disease; he resists Chloe's advances during their flight; he promises Murray he will expose Adekunle; and in the final scene he pays for the ritual he had found so bewildering. The audience is left to believe that he would have done these things differently had he not been influenced by Dr. Murray.

The film ultimately suffers from a loose or scattered plot, inconsistent comic performances (or shifts in comic forms), and poor judgment. The film may have achieved a more consistent mood and comic spirit had it not also tried to develop Murray's moral character, but since it did, it could have benefitted by a strong, admirable black character.

—*Michael L. Forstrom*

REVIEWS

Chicago Tribune. September 9, 1994, II, p.4.
The Hollywood Reporter. August 15, 1994, p. 8.
Los Angeles Times. September 9, 1994, p. F8.
Minneapolis Star and Tribune. September 9, 1994, p. E1.
The New York Times. September 9, 1994, p. B4.
Variety. August 15, 1994, p. 7.

Grand Isle

In the setting of the Grand Isle, a nineteenth century Louisiana woman (Kelly McGillis) decides to leave her husband (Jon DeVries) and two children in order to pursue a career as an artist, in this drama based on *The Awakening*, by Kate Chopin. Her attempt to liberate herself from the strictures of society lead her to tragedy.

REVIEWS

Variety. CCCXLIV, September 23, 1991, p. 78.

CREDITS

Edna Pontellier: Kelly McGillis
Leonce Pontellier: Jon DeVries
Robert LeBrun: Adrian Pasdar
Mademoiselle Reisz: Ellen Burstyn
Adele Ratignolle: Glenne Headly
Alcee Arobin: Julian Sands
Victor LeBrun: Anthony DeSando

Released: 1991
Production: Kelly McGillis and Carolyn Pfeiffer; released by Turner Pictures
Direction: Mary Lambert
Screenplay: Hesper Anderson; based on the novel The Awakening, by Kate Chopin
Cinematography: Toyomichi Kurita
Editing: Tom Finan
Production design: Michelle Minch
Art direction: Marcus Kuhn
Set decoration: Molly Flanegin
Casting: Fern Champion
Sound: Rudy Lara
Costume design: Martin Pakledinaz
Music: Elliot Goldenthal
MPAA rating: no listing
Running time: 87 minutes

A Great Day In Harlem

"Four Stars. Charming."—Gene Santoro, *New York Daily News*

It's the summer of 1958: the hula-hoop craze sweeps the nation, Russia has just launched the first sputnik into space, Eisenhower is president, and *Esquire* magazine is printing a cover story on the Golden Age of Jazz.

That was the temporal backdrop the day that Art Kane took a group picture of the world's greatest jazz musicians for *Esquire*. The musicians had been notified either by special invitation or by word of mouth to meet in front of an old brownstone on 126th Street in Harlem, New York City. Everyone was surprised to see so many jazz legends show up for the photo session, with as many as 57 jazz greats immortalized for the first and what would turn out to be the last time in one photograph.

Although no one is sure of the exact date of that summer day in 1958, it was an historical day in the jazz world and the documentary, *A Great Day in Harlem*, does it honor. Mixing interviews with the surviving musicians and others who were there with numerous stills and home movies taken that day, the film brings to the screen a reverent and nostalgic vignette of a special moment in time. Between reminiscences are black-and-white outtakes of original performances by musicians, most of whom are now deceased. The clips spotlight the unique and fantastic talents of well-known musicians as well as lesser-known greats.

The film chronicles an event that for some was a reunion, while for others was an unforgettable first meeting. Whatever the circumstances, the assembly pretty much ignored the photographer assigned by *Esquire* magazine to photograph them. With such luminaries as Thelonius Monk, Count Basie, Dizzy Gillespie, Coleman Hawkins, Lester Young, Roy Eldridge, Pee Wee Russell, Gene Krupa, Art Blakey, Bud Freeman, Willie "The Lion" Smith, Jimmy Rushing, Mary Lou Williams, Jerry Mulligan, Sahib Shahab, Marian McPartland, Hank Jones, Johnny Griffin, Maxine Sullivan, Rex Steward, Dicky Wells, Luckey Roberts, Zutty Singleton, Joe Thomas, Chubby Jackson, and Charles Mingus (to name only a few) all in one place, the photographer was lucky they noticed him at all.

Piano players embraced other piano players, drummers flocked together, horn players high-fived other horn players, and, although it wasn't arranged that way, that's the way the photo captures them, proving that, as one musician in the film put it, "Water seeks its own level."

Luckily, for the filmmakers, Mike Lipskin, a stride pianist, also took stills of the event, and bassist Milt Hinton and his wife Mona recorded it in color on their 8-millimeter camera. The Hinton's home movie reminds you of one big family reunion. Everyone seems to know everyone, and they probably did, if only by reputation. It was truly a meeting of the "lions" and no one was more aware of that than the musicians themselves.

"The picture was a fluke. It's crazy and serendipitous that so many people that played so big a part in jazz history were together in one place at one time."—*A Great Day In Harlem* producer Jean Bach.

Narrated by Quincy Jones, the film includes some funny and touching interviews with Art Kane and Dizzy Gillespie (both recently deceased), Art Blakey, Sonny Rollins, Marian McPartland, and others.

The photo session was to be at 10:00 A.M., and with most jazz musicians getting to bed at about 4:00 A.M., the musicians themselves were surprised at the turnout. One musician is remembered to have said that he "wasn't aware there were two ten o'clocks in the same day."

Another interviewee remarked that jazz musicians loved to gossip about one another, and this proved true in a number of the interviews. One musician looking at the photo remarked which of his peers had "put on a little weight." Sonny Rollins, only 27 at the time, speaks about his memories of Coleman Hawkins and Lester Young. Remembering the unique talents of porkpie-hatted Young, Rollins says, "It was like he was from another planet."

Thelonius Monk was remembered by some as a quiet genius, by others as a clever self-promoter. Bud Freeman, saxophonist, predicted that in a hundred years Pee Wee Russell would be recognized as greater than Benny Goodman. Mary Lou Williams is praised for her knowledge and her status as the first woman to write band arrangements. Maxine Sullivan is lauded for her incredible memory, knowing the verses to more than 200 songs. But it's not just the "lions" who are remembered. Vic Dickerson, Henry "Red" Allen, and Stuff Smith are some of the lesser-known musicians whose performances are showcased and whose talents are generously recognized by their better-known peers.

The common denominator of each interview was the sincere awe each musician expressed when speaking about their colleagues' unique and incredible talent. Joking stopped when they spoke about what they learned from one, what another contributed to jazz, or how still another never got the recognition that he or she deserved.

The famous photo of that occasion has been made into posters, postcards, and other memorabilia, representing the only photograph of its kind to group so many jazz legends in one photo. The film goes on to explain the process that gave birth to the event. Robert Benton, who went on to become an award-winning film director (*Kramer vs. Kramer* 1979; *Places in the Heart*, 1984; and *Nobody's Fool*, reviewed in this volume), was the art director at *Esquire* who suggested doing a cover story on jazz. *Esquire* hired Art Kane, a famous photographer who was a freelance art director at the time, to do the cover. The idea for the group photo was his brainchild, and Kane was responsible for putting out the word for the photo session that spread like wildfire through the jazz community.

"The picture was a fluke," said producer Jean Bach, in an interview with Peter Watrous for *The New York Times*. "It's crazy and serendipitous that so many people that played

CREDITS

Narrator: Quincy Jones
Art Kane: Art Kane
Dizzy Gillespie: Dizzy Gillespie
Sonny Rollins: Sonny Rollins
Art Farmer: Art Farmer
Marian McPartland: Marian McPartland
Mona Hinton: Mona Hinton
Robert Benton: Robert Benton
Horace Silver: Horace Silver
Art Blakey: Art Blakey

Released: 1994
Production: Jean Bach for Flo-Bert Ltd. and the New York Foundation for the Arts; released by Castle Hill Productions
Direction: no listing
Screenplay: Jean Bach, Susan Peehl, and Matthew Seig
Cinematography: Steve Petropoulos
Editing: Susan Peehl
Music consulting: Johnny Mandel
MPAA rating: no listing
Running time: 60 minutes

AWARDS AND NOMINATIONS

Academy Awards Nomination 1994: Best Documentary

so big a part in jazz history were together in one place at one time." Bach, veteran producer of radio and TV, began working on the documentary by placing an advertisement in the *Amsterdam News*. It was slow going though, and after four years of sporadic interviews, she finally tracked down and interviewed the last survivors of that day.

That the photo came together at all is one of the miracles of the moment. It was Art Kane's first job as a professional photographer, and the assistant he chose was even more of a rookie, at one time loading the film backwards in Kane's camera.

But before Art Kane could even take that historical photograph, he had to get the musicians' attention. With all the mayhem that occurred when the musicians got together, the purpose of the gathering was becoming irrelevant to the meeting itself. Long after the photographer lost control of the group, ineffectually using a rolled up newspaper for a megaphone to be heard over the din of the crowd, some of the musicians started to get tired of standing. Count Basie, for one, took a seat on the curb, to the delight of about ten of the neighborhood boys, who joined him there. Other children were beginning to hang out of adjacent windows to see what all the noise was about.

Luckily for the photographer, Rex Stewart had brought his trumpet. And when he decided enough was enough, Stewart blew his horn. That did the trick. After 120 exposures, Art Kane finally got his famous picture of the jazz greats, spilling down the steps and onto the sidewalk in front of an old brownstone between Fifth and Madison Avenues in Harlem. The rest is history.

The free-form interweaving of the interviews, the still photos and home-movie films, and the musical performances all come together to bring alive an era and the individuals who made it happen. What becomes clear in *A Great Day in Harlem* is that jazz is not simply a static music form, but rather an evolving form growing out of the unique and individual expression of its innovators.

The film is directed to the jazz afficionado, aptly having its world premiere at the Playboy Jazz Festival. With its anecdotal and "then and now" footage, it is truly a film for the serious lover of jazz. Yet, as its nomination for an Oscar in the division of Best Documentary show, the film also has popular appeal.

A Great Day in Harlem is a small film, only sixty minutes long, and perhaps a little thin in its substance, but in that short time, Jean Bach brings to life a community of artists who are now gone, but whose music is still fresh and alive. The film would perhaps have attained more substance if the interviews had been more hard-hitting and less reverent, but the result is still captivating. As it is, for the jazz novice, the film is a delightful introduction to jazz and the personalities who made it; for the serious jazz lover, it is a loving tribute to the men and women who, according to one musician, "lived hard and surrendered themselves to their art."

It's just too bad that the musicians didn't bring their instruments along—that would have been some jam session!

—*Diane Hatch-Avis*

REVIEWS

Entertainment Weekly. March 10, 1995, P. 48.
The Hollywood Reporter. September 28, 1994, p. 6.
The New York Times. February 12, 1995, p. 13; February 17, 1995, p. C12.
The New Yorker January 23, 1995, p.95.
The Observer. April 23, 1995, Arts p. 7.
Variety, February 17, 1995, p. 48.
The Village Voice. October 25, 1994, p. 82.

Greedy

"Where there's a will...there's a relative."
—Movie tagline

"*Greedy* is riotously funny!"—Jeffrey Lyons, *Sneak Previews*

 Box Office Gross: $12,384,725 (April 3, 1994)

According to the production notes, director Jonathan Lynn describes his film as asking the question, "How far will you humiliate yourself to get your hands on twenty-five million dollars?" Therefore, continues Lynn, it is a motion picture for "anyone who's ever wanted more money or isn't too fond of their relatives." The production notes take the inquiry from there, asking what viewers would sacrifice for $25 million. "Loyalty? Honesty? Self-respect?" After all, *Greedy* has sacrificed them all.

Joe McTeague (Kirk Douglas) is a self-made millionaire. An orphan, McTeague started a scrap-metal business, which, over the years and thanks to his wheeling and dealing, has earned for him a fortune valued at $25 million. While McTeague has no children of his own, he has his older brother's grandchildren—Joe McTeague's great-nieces and great-nephews—eagerly anticipating his demise and their inheritances. Carl (Ed Begley, Jr.) and his wife, Nora (Mary Ellen Trainor), court Uncle Joe by naming all their children after him: Joseph (Adam Hendershott), Jonas (Eric Lloyd), and the soon-to-be-born Josiah. Patti (Colleen Camp) and Ed (Bob Balaban) also flatter Uncle Joe with namesakes: Jolene (Kirsten Dunst) and Joette (Lisa Bradley). The greediest McTeague of all, Frank (Phil Hartman), a lawyer, and his alcoholic wife, Tina (Siobhan Fallon) specialize in private investigation to unearth unsavory details to discredit the other heirs. Womanizing Glen (Jere Burns) and his estranged wife, Muriel (Joyce Hyser), pretend they still have a happy marriage, fearing otherwise to lose out on the inheritance. In other words, all these unhappy people gather to consider how they can get their Great-Uncle Joe to die and leave the money to them. As the film begins, the newest disappointment is that Uncle Joe has invited a young, attractive "nurse," Molly (Olivia d'Abo), into the house to care for him, whom the greedy relatives see as a threat to their money.

Into this unhappy group also comes Daniel Jr. (Michael J. Fox), son of Daniel Sr. (Francis X. McCarthy), who left the McTeague family years ago over an argument concerning the politics of eating grapes. Daniel Jr. (a.k.a. Danny) is now a luckless professional bowler who at least had the good fortune to meet girlfriend Robin (Nancy Travis). Initially Danny is honest and unmoved by the prospect of a huge inheritance. It is not long, however, before he too is submitting to Uncle Joe's humiliating tests of "love" and "loyalty." Finally, *Greedy* becomes a film about who gets what and why.

Several of the characters in this film are great fun to watch. For instance, Kirk Douglas, veteran of seventy-one feature films, has a real twinkle in his eye as he plays this monstrous Uncle Joe, putting his relatives through various humiliating tests. The script gives Douglas great range, asking him to play a viral patriarch, a doddering old man, and a prankster not unlike the title character in the French comedy *Tatie Danielle* (1991). In an early scene, the relatives have come to celebrate Uncle Joe's birthday. With the group assembled around the table, each niece and nephew tries to reveal the most amazingly incriminating detail about the others. Douglas plays them off one another, surgically extracting information from each. Certainly his Uncle Joe is no fool. Later in the film, when Danny and Uncle Joe sit talking in the scrap yard's office, the older man forgets himself momentarily, loses twenty years, and thinks he is elsewhere. It appears that Uncle Joe's mind is beginning to fail him; he has lapses. Not only does Douglas play the scene believably but it is also heartrending to watch him work to regain himself. Yet by film's end, Douglas' Uncle Joe evolves again, believably—and as a great surprise.

Also interesting, sympathetic, and well-played are Robin and Molly, the two women—actually the two characters of either gender—in the film who are faithful, honest, and level-

 "Her tongue is practically in his wallet."—Frank describing a kiss between Molly Richardson and Uncle Joe, in *Greedy*

headed. Travis plays Robin, a successful television sportscaster, with great style. While Robin is clearly intended to be Danny's conscience, Travis is able to play her so as to avoid becoming preachy. For example, early in the film, Danny asks his Uncle Joe if he can borrow $300,000 to buy into a bowling alley on Long Island. Uncle Joe agrees on one condition: Danny must swear allegiance to him and renounce his father, the ne'er-do-well dreamer. Danny leaves the house immediately, angrily. Only days later, however, Danny does a Jimmy Durante impersonation that Uncle Joe used to love, humiliating himself in the process. Robin is honest with Danny; she tells him that he is going too far, that he is degrading himself for money. She asks him to leave with her. While Danny can resist her logic and her charm, audience members will no doubt judge how far gone Danny is by his ability to do just that. Travis' Robin is strong and successful, yet loving and generous. She is kind, but she refuses to stay around to watch Danny deceive himself.

D'Abo's Molly is also strong and honest. While Molly gets caught up in the greed momentarily, she is able to pull back before she makes the Faustian bargain. That is, the characters accept it as a given that if Molly sleeps with Uncle Joe, he will leave the $25 million to her. Pushed to the limit, Molly herself accepts the notion, and dressed in a crocheted bikini and spider-web-patterned "cover-up," she sets out to seduce Uncle Joe. While Joe quickly acquiesces, Molly pulls back at the last minute, In making Molly believable both as vamp and as self-respecting woman, d'Abo creates a character that far exceeds the bounds of the many brainless lines and scanty costumes given her. While she could be seen as a seductress, a spi-

der, drawing in the poor old man, d'Abo's Molly is actually quite a likable character.

The rest of the characters, however, are too broadly drawn. Each is repulsive, self-serving, and completely lacking in self-respect. While some of the gags are funny, it soon becomes apparent that these characters' lives have been totally dedicated to—and therefore, totally wasted by—the search for money. For example, Carl and Nora are the parents of two children and are expecting a third. Instead of building a life and a home for those children, they spend their weekends trying to ingratiate themselves with Uncle Joe. In one scene, Joseph admits that his father paid him to come to Uncle Joe's and will pay him an extra $20 if he kisses Uncle Joe hello. Also, Frank's son, Dennis (Sean Babb), is allowed to sit at the adult's table for the birthday party until he begins to make odd noises and his father tells him to stop. When Dennis answers, "Make me," Frank's response is remarkably unpleasant. He yanks his son from his seat and angrily, violently, pushes, pulls, carries him to the children's table. Although potentially humorous, these scenes go too far. These one-sided characters, arguably creatures of satire, are ugly, unkind, and unforgiving. It is a grim little comedy that showcases them.

While Michael J. Fox's nudity received much press, his more remarkable feat is his bowling. For his role, Fox practiced with Hall of Famer Johnny Petraglia, and after eight weeks of practice, Fox could bowl a solid 190. Said Fox in the production notes, "I prepared for my role as a soldier in *Casualties of War* by spending weeks in a kind of boot camp, humping heavy equipment through the boonies and doing military training. All in all, bowling is a much more enjoyable way to do research."

The filmmakers of *Greedy* have among them many successful comedies: Director Lynn—*My Cousin Vinny* (1992); producer Brian Grazer—*Parenthood* (1989), *Kindergarten Cop* (1990), *My Girl* (1991), *Housesitter* (1992); and writers Lowell Ganz and Babaloo Mandel—*Parenthood* (1989), *City Slickers* (1991), and *A League of Their Own* (1992), to name a few. Even with this combined talent, *Greedy* received at best mixed reviews and remains a film with little heart, few laughs, and only a handful of good performances.

—*Roberta F. Green*

CREDITS

Daniel McTeague, Jr.:   Michael J. Fox
Uncle Joe McTeague: Kirk Douglas
Robin Hunter: Nancy Travis
Molly Richardson: Olivia d'Abo
Frank: Phil Hartman
Carl: Ed Begley, Jr.
Nora: Mary Ellen Trainor
Joseph: Adam Hendershott
Jonas: Eric Lloyd
Patti: Colleen Camp
Ed: Bob Balaban
Jolene: Kirsten Dunst
Joette: Lisa Bradley
Tina: Siobhan Fallon
Glen: Jere Burns
Muriel: Joyce Hyser
Daniel McTeague, Sr.:   Francis X. McCarthy
Dennis: Sean Babb
Douglas: Jonathan Lynn
TV director: Lowell Ganz

Released: 1994
Production: Brian Grazer; released by Imagine Entertainment
Direction: Jonathan Lynn
Screenplay: Lowell Ganz and Babaloo Mandel
Cinematography: Gabriel Beristain
Editing: Tony Lombardo
Production design: Victoria Paul
Art direction: Dan Webster
Set decoration: Anne H. Ahrens
Casting: Karen Rea
Sound: Robert Anderson, Jr.
Costume design: Shay Cunliffe
Music: Randy Edelman
MPAA rating: PG-13
Running time: 113 minutes

REVIEWS

Atlanta Journal/Constitution. March 4, 1994, p. P4.
Baltimore Sun. March 4-10, 1994, Maryland Live Section, p. 18.
Boston Globe. March 4, 1994, p. 53.
Chicago Tribune. March 4, 1994, p. H.
The Hollywood Reporter. February 28, 1994, p. 10.
Los Angeles Times. March 4, 1994, p. F4.
The New York Times. March 4, 1994, p. B9.
Variety. February 28, 1994, p. 4.
The Washington Post. March 4, 1994, Weekend Section, p. 44.

Grief

"They gave at the office."—Movie tagline

"Witty and warm."—Dave Kehr, *The New York Times*

"Funny and unexpected."—Manohla Dargis, *The Village Voice*

"Hilarious...hip...moving as it is funny."—B. Ruby Rich, *Elle*

 Box Office Gross: $137,958 (June 5, 1994)

M ark (Craig Chester) is having bad time. When the audience first meets him, Mark is standing on the roof of his office building, considering a jump. His longtime lover, Kevin, died of AIDS recently, the television show on which he is a story editor is about to undergo major changes, and the straight man on whom he has a crush is having a secret affair with another member of the office staff. As the anniversary of Kevin's death approaches, Mark is forced to face his feelings of grief and loss while those around him suffer their own slings and eros.

Grief was reportedly made for only $40,000 and shot in ten days. It was an official film festival selection at the Sundance, Toronto, and Berlin film festivals.

CREDITS

Mark: Craig Chester
Jo: Jackie Beat
Leslie: Illeana Douglas
Bill: Alexis Arquette
Jeremy: Carlton Wilborn
Paula: Lucy Gutteridge
Love Judge: Mickey Cottrell

Released: 1994
Production: Ruth Charny and Yoram Mandel; released by Strand Releasing
Direction: Richard Glatzer
Screenplay: Richard Glatzer
Cinematography: David Dechant
Editing: Robin Katz and William W. Williams
Production design: Don Diers
Set decoration: David Carpender
Costume design: Laser N. Rosenberg
Music: Tom Judson
MPAA rating: no listing
Running time: 87 minutes

In this slight and moderately hip independent film, the life behind the scenes of a soap opera is more interesting and more dramatic than the life on screen. It is a sort of gay but surprisingly (for an independent) tame knock-off of *Soapdish* (1991). The film itself is less interesting than real life, however, possibly due to the limitations of the film-making budget, the relative lack of ingenuity in its direction, and the tepid performances of its lead actors.

That is not to say the film is bad; it is just not as interesting as it promises to be. For instance, the casting of one of the lead roles to huge drag queen Jackie Beat should be more interesting than it is. Somehow Beat's performance as Jo, the motherly producer of "The Love Judge," is almost too genuine, as if her sweetness takes the fun out of the casting of a drag queen in the role. When John Waters cast drag queen Divine as the suburban mom in *Hairspray* (1988), he was able to make a commentary on the stereotypical stage-mother by the overstylization of the character. Beat's casting does not serve a similar purpose. It would have been fun to see a bit more mining of Beat's comic potential.

But there are some funny moments nonetheless, mostly when the gargantuan Beat sits on her puny sofa next to another character. Beat's character, Jo, is obsessed with the certainty that someone is having sex on her sofa when she is out of the office, and this too offers some funny, if off-color, moments. The other funny moments come from the bizarre scripts of the fictional television show, "The Love Judge." A sort of combination of television's *Divorce Court*, *People's Court* and circus sideshow, "The Love Judge" themes deal with the sexuality of lepers, "circus lesbians," transsexuality, and others with a comic frankness that Oprah and Geraldo could never dare. Occasionally, these scenes lapse into simple bad taste (the discussion of the "leper" episode is particularly odious), but in general are harmless, sophomoric fun.

For conservative audiences, this film might be considered far too raunchy, with its drag queen lead character, its frank and (appropriately) unapologetic depiction of homosexual characters, and its recurring joke about the evidence of sexual activity on Jo's sofa. But the good-natured camaraderie of the ensemble cast undercuts any sense of subversity in the story's content.

Director/author Richard Glatzer further dilutes the satirical possibilities through rather static direction. Most often, the actors are filmed in "two-shots," sitting across the desk from each other. When Glatzer veers from this course, the results are more interesting, as in a scene where Mark and Bill (Alexis Arquette) share an intimate moment beneath the desk. Several scenes on the rooftop of the building are potentially interesting, but again Glatzer's static camera doesn't allow the actors much freedom to move around. When his colleagues think that Mark may have jumped off the roof, they all run into frame in a tight group, clearly looking like they hit a "mark," their concern for Mark's welfare being diluted by the concerns about fitting into the camera frame. The lack of activity is further augmented by simplistic lighting and by the lack of any physical action by the actors.

The exception is Ileana Douglas as Leslie, the office secretary. Douglas is bright, vivacious, and funny, making the most of her role through the use of inventive physical behavior which counteracts the stagnant nature of the camera shots. Alexis Arquette and Carlton Wilborn provide

solid support, while Craig Chester is a bit one-note and glum as the grief-stricken Mark.

This film won much attention in its release at some Gay and Lesbian Film Festivals. It is hard to know why, except that it is good-natured fun and well-intended.

—*Kirby Tepper*

REVIEWS

The New York Times. June 7, 1994. p. B9
Los Angeles Times. April 1, 1994. p. F6
The Hollywood Reporter. April 4, 1994. p. 12
Chicago Tribune. July 15, 1994, p. 7K.
Los Angeles Times. April 1, 1994, p. F6.
The New York Times. June 3, 1994, p. C6.

Guarding Tess

"Cage and MacLaine are the odd couple of the nineties."—*Flicks*

"Hilarious! The year's first big movie surprise."
—*Rolling Stone*

"*Guarding Tess* is funny, feisty and full of life!"
—*KCBS-TV*

 Box Office Gross: $27,001,774 (July 4, 1994)

At the time of the film's release, more former presidents and former First Ladies were alive than ever before, and "all of them are entitled to protection for the rest of their lives," said Hugh Wilson, director and cowriter of *Guarding Tess*, according to the film's production notes. "At this very moment there could be a whole contingent of Secret Service people sitting around Lady Bird Johnson's house or driving down Rodeo Drive with Nancy Reagan. The agent in the front seat would have a sawed-off shotgun between his knees." Wilson became fascinated with Secret Service methodology and with the relationships that develop between the protected persons and their protectors. Out of this fascination arose *Guarding Tess*.

As the film begins, Secret Service agent Doug Chesnic

(Nicolas Cage) is leaving his current post—a sleepy Ohio town—happily exchanging final barbs with those who will remain on duty. Chesnic travels to the airport, catches a jet to Washington, D.C., and hurries to Secret Service headquarters for his new assignment. Reporting on his years of service to his former charge, former First Lady Tess Carlisle (Shirley MacLaine), Agent Chesnic is respectful and gracious—until he is notified that Mrs. Carlisle has spoken to the president and requested (demanded?) that Agent Chesnic return to his post with her. It seems that since Agent Chesnic had served in the Carlisle White House, Mrs. Carlisle has a certain affinity for him and wants him to continue to head the detail that protects her. Agent Chesnic's pleas aside, he finds himself right back in Ohio at the side of the impossible Mrs. Carlisle.

Most of the film chronicles not only a battle of wills but also the difficulties and rewards of guarding a national treasure who also happens to be a major pain in the neck. In the course of the film, and in the course of the day-to-day disappointments and the life-threatening misadventures the two encounter together, Agent Chesnic and Mrs. Carlisle's relationship grows into one of mutual respect and admiration.

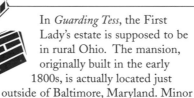
In *Guarding Tess*, the First Lady's estate is supposed to be in rural Ohio. The mansion, originally built in the early 1800s, is actually located just outside of Baltimore, Maryland. Minor alterations were made to it for the film.

The characters Tess Carlisle and Doug Chesnic are by far the most entertaining and valuable part of the film. Each is drawn carefully and in great detail and is expertly presented by the performers. For example, Tess Carlisle initially seems merely impossible. Yet a series of scenes that catch her in private moments draws a more complex picture. At one point in the film, Mrs. Carlisle receives a letter from her son, Barry (Edward Albert). She is visibly pleased, particularly when she learns that he will come to visit her soon. When he does arrive, however, he asks to use her name as an endorsement for his current business project (much to her chagrin). Much of Mrs. Carlisle's life becomes a series of disappointments: The current president fails to attend the dedication of the last wing of the Carlisle Library (built in memory of her husband); her daughter never writes or calls; and her health is deteriorating. Hence, she spends most of her time alone with scrapbooks and videotapes.

"At this very moment, there could be a whole contingent of Secret Service people driving down Rodeo Drive with Nancy Reagan. The agent in the front seat would have a sawed-off shotgun between his knees."—*Guarding Tess* director and co-writer Hugh Wilson

Shirley MacLaine prevents Tess from becoming maudlin by conveying her love of pranks and misadventures. When the former First Lady goes grocery shopping, she enjoys using the Secret Service agents to check prices and to chase down false alarms. MacLaine, who has starred in more than forty motion pictures and who received the Best Actress Oscar for *Terms of Endearment* (1983), captures Tess's sadness, humor, and beauty.

Doug Chesnic's character is equally finely drawn. The audience will quickly recognize that Agent Chesnic yearns for fast-track Secret Service duty. When he travels to

Washington for reassignment, he requests duty guarding the president. When persons unknown attempt to assassinate the current president, Agent Chesnic and his fellow agents in Ohio watch enviously as the more high-profile presidential agents face real danger by responding to deadly threats. Yet, even from his post in Middle America, Agent Chesnic performs dutifully and by the book. He enforces the ban on smoking in the house and on guns in Mrs. Carlisle's private quarters. When going for a drive, he insists that Mrs. Carlisle sit in the back seat, opposite the driver's side, so that she is visible to both persons in the front seat—otherwise the vehicle and its occupants will not move.

Agent Chesnic is dedicated to his charge, and his acts of loyalty produce not only the most touching scenes in the film but also some of the funniest. For example, Mrs. Carlisle decides she wants to attend the opera, yet once she does so, she dozes off, snoring slightly. Noting the adverse reactions of those around her, Agent Chesnic attempts to pull her chair farther back into the box and out of view of the gossipers. During his attempt to move the chair to protect her, however, Agent Chesnic manages to startle Mrs. Carlisle (who emits an audible gasp) and to dislodge her hairpiece, which subsequently slides down to her chin, creating a makeshift beard. Although rather slapstick in execution, the scene provides a series of laughs while further demonstrating Agent Chesnic's urge to protect Mrs. Carlisle and his inability to do anything quite right.

While Nicolas Cage usually plays colorful misfits—the romantic punk rocker in *Valley Girl* (1983), a tormented, disfigured Vietnam veteran in *Birdy* (1984), a romantic, child-snatching ex-con in *Raising Arizona* (1987), a carefree, careless romantic hoodlum in *Wild at Heart* (1990), and a hapless good guy in the *noir*ish *Red Rock West* (reviewed in this volume) among others—here he brings passion and respectability to a much tamer role. In the process, he demonstrates a range not clearly visible in his earlier work.

Several of the strongest scenes in the film involve only Mrs. Carlisle and Agent Chesnic. After one particularly horrendous disagreement, Mrs. Carlisle asks for the agents to be pulled from duty at her house. Agent Chesnic, however, refuses to leave his post, stationing himself outside the

CREDITS

Tess Carlisle: Shirley MacLaine
Doug Chesnic: Nicolas Cage
Earl: Austin Pendleton
Barry Carlisle: Edward Albert
President's voice: Hugh Wilson

Released: 1994
Production: Ned Tanen and Nancy Graham Tanen for Channel; released by TriStar Pictures
Direction: Hugh Wilson
Screenplay: Hugh Wilson and Peter Torokvei
Cinematography: Brian J. Reynolds
Editing: Sidney Levin
Production design: Peter Larkin
Art direction: Charley Beal
Set decoration: Leslie Rollins
Casting: Aleta Chappelle
Sound: James Sabat
Costume design: Ann Roth and Sue Gandy
Music: Michael Convertino
MPAA rating: PG-13
Running time: 98 minutes

AWARDS AND NOMINATIONS

Golden Globe Awards Nomination 1995: Best Actress-Musical/Comedy (MacLaine)

main gate. Inside, Mrs. Carlisle watches videotapes of her life in the White House, including tapes of her husband's funeral after his death from a massive heart attack. In one of the tapes, Mrs. Carlisle sees Agent Chesnic among those in attendance at President Carlisle's funeral. In what is a masterful depiction of grief, Nicolas Cage's Agent Chesnic simply bows his head and covers his eyes. Greatly moved, Mrs. Carlisle strikes a truce, and the two begin to forge the friendship that structures the second half of the film.

Director/cowriter Wilson comes to this project with extensive television credits: He wrote, directed, and produced *WKRP in Cincinnati*, *Frank's Place*, and *The Famous Teddy Z*. In addition, he wrote and directed the feature film *Rustler's Rhapsody* (1985). Peter Torokvei, who co-wrote *Guarding Tess*, rose from Second City television and was hired by Wilson originally to work on the new *WKRP in Cincinnati*. His feature-film-writing experiences include *Real Genius* (1985) and *Back to School* (1986). Producers Ned Tanen and Nancy Graham Tanen's Channel Productions has a "unique, long-term production deal with Sony Pictures Entertainment, providing films for TriStar and Columbia," according to the production notes. Says Nancy Graham Tanen of the current production, "The humor of this film comes from rich, complex character. "Producer Ned Tanen adds that" the relationship is between two people you really do care about and have a good time with. It's unique."

While the screenplay places the Carlisle estate in Ohio, the film was actually photographed in Baltimore, Maryland. The house itself, built in the early 1800's, is in the Second Federal style and, in 1869, was named Laboroere, for the owner's wife. Production designer Peter Larkin modified the house for *Guarding Tess*, adding wings and porticos, and old-fashioned glass-fronted cabinets in the kitchen. "The house was altered to suggest the presidency without really being part of it," commented Larkin, according to the production notes. The film's opera, *Mozart's Abduction from the Seraglio*, was staged in the Maryland Theater, built in the early 1900's. Only a few minor changes were made to the interior of the theater, but the lobby underwent major refurbishment, with the walls repaneled and the floor recarpeted. The Maryland winter, on the other hand, proved more of a problem for the production designers, who "upholstered [the muddy outdoor locations] with plywood painted green or brown and covered with earth and green-painted hay."

Guarding Tess is alternately heartwarming and harrowing. While the film received mixed reviews, many critics agreed that its two leads—Shirley MacLaine and Nicolas Cage—spice up an otherwise ordinary Hollywood recipe.

—*Roberta F. Green*

REVIEWS

Atlanta Journal/Constitution. March 11, 1994, p. P3.
Baltimore Sun. March 11-17, 1994, Maryland Live Section, p. 4.
Chicago Tribune. March 11-17, 1994, Take 2 Section, p. A.
Entertainment Weekly. March 18, 1994, p. 74.
The Hollywood Reporter. March 7, 1994, p. 10.
Los Angeles Times. March 11, 1994, p. F9.
The New York Times. March 11, 1994, p. B4.
Variety. March 7, 1994, p. 26.
The Washington Post. March 11, 1994, p. 42.

Guelwaar

When a local Senegalese activist, Guelwaar (Thierno Ndiaye), dies, his Catholic family and friends prepare for an elaborate funeral only to discover that his body has been mistakenly buried in a Muslim cemetery. Filmmaker Sembene turns his camera to his native land to explore political opportunism, class differences, and religious conflict. The story is simply told and gracefully directed, capturing the plain truths of the human heart. In Wolof and French with English subtitles.

REVIEWS

Atlanta Constitution. July 29, 1994, p. P12.
Boston Globe. January 14, 1994, p. 77.
Chicago Tribune. April 22, 1994, p. 7J.
National Catholic Reporter. XIX, May 21, 1993, p. 13.
National Catholic Reporter. XXIX, October 8, 1993, p. 15.
The New Republic. CCIX, September 6, 1993, p. 30.
The Washington Post. February 4, 1994, p. C6.

CREDITS

Gora: Omar Seck
Nogoy Marie Thioune: Mame Ndoumbe Diop
Pierre Henri Thioune (Guelwaar): Thierno Ndiaye
Barthelemy: Ndiawar Diop
Aloys: Moustapha Diop
Sophie: Marie-Augustine Diatta
Gor Mag: Samba Wane
Father Leon: Joseph Sane
Alfred: Coly Mbaye
Veronique: Isseu Niang
No character identified: Myriam Niang

Origin: Senegal
Released: 1993
Production: Ousmane Sembene and Jacques Perrin; released by New Yorker Films
Direction: Ousmane Sembene
Screenplay: Ousmane Sembene
Cinematography: Dominique Gentil
Editing: Marie-Aimee Debril
Music: Baaba Maal
MPAA rating: no listing
Running time: 115 minutes

Gunmen

"An ex-cop and a team of mercenaries are on a mission to take down the world's most powerful drug lord. It's justice at point blank!"
—Movie tagline

"The heaviest concentration of rapid-fire action since *New Jack City!*"—Mike Price, *Ft. Worth Star-Telegram*

 Box Office Gross: $3,400,308 (March 27, 1994)

Mario Van Peebles and Christopher Lambert star as a drug-enforcement agent and a small-time smuggler who team up and head for South America to search for a stolen boatload of cash. Unfortunately, they are pursued by a killer (Denis Leary) hired by a ruthless drug kingpin (Patrick Stewart).

REVIEWS

Atlanta Constitution. February 4, 1994, p. P3.
Boston Globe. February 4, 1994, p. 54.
Los Angeles Times. February 4, 1994, p. F6.
The New York Times. February 4, 1994, p. C8.
People Weekly. XLI, January 31, 1994, p. 15.
Playboy. XLI, February 1994, p. 24.
USA Today. February 9, 1994, p. D8.
Variety. CCCLIV, February 7, 1994, p. 41.
The Washington Post. February 4, 1994, p. C6.

CREDITS

Dani Servigo: Christopher Lambert
Cole Parker: Mario Van Peebles
Armor O'Malley: Denis Leary
Loomis: Patrick Stewart
Izzy: Kadeem Hardison
Bennett: Sally Kirkland
Chief Chavez: Richard Sarafian
Rance: Robert Harper
Maria: Brenda Bakke

Released: 1994
Production: Laurence Mark, John Davis, and John Flock for Davis Entertainment Company; released by Dimension Films
Direction: Deran Sarafian
Screenplay: Stephen Sommers
Cinematography: Hiro Narita
Editing: Bonnie Koehler
Production design: Michael Seymour
Art direction: Hector Romero, Jr.
Set decoration: Ian Whitaker and Enrique Estevez
Casting: Terry Liebling
Special effects: Jesus "Chucho" Duran
Sound: Fernando Camara
Costume design: Betsy Heimann
Music: John Debney
MPAA rating: R
Running time: 90 minutes

Hans Christian Andersen's Thumbelina

"Exciting! Parents will be cheering, girls will be in heaven, and boys will be rewarded with exciting derring-do. It casts a lovely spell."—Peter Travers, *Family Life*

"A beautiful movie. What a delight!"—Jeffrey Lyons, *Sneak Previews/Lyons Den Radio*

"Children and parents will love this film. Wonderful songs from Barry Manilow, Jack Feldman and Bruce Sussman."—*Film Advisory Board*

 Box Office Gross: $11,371,080 (June 26, 1994)

T he world is full of fearsome things, but if you follow your heart and believe in your dreams, you can achieve the impossible. These are simple, timeworn but important messages, and *Hans Christian Andersen's Thumbelina* delivers them to a young audience with gentle and inventive aplomb.

This Don Bluth production adapts the fairy tale of the miniature girl born from a flower to a lonely woman who always wished for a daughter. When Thumbelina becomes lonely for people her own size, her mother tells her, "Don't ever wish to be anything but what you are."

Soon, Thumbelina finds there are other beings of her stature—the fairies who help paint the leaves that turn summer to autumn. She falls in love with Prince Cornelius, the son of the fairy king and queen.

The film takes many liberties with the original fairy tale, which emphasized Thumbelina's difficulties in dealing with an adult-sized world. Here, it is not so much Thumbelina's size that causes her trouble, but a raft of villains from the smaller realms of the animal kingdom.

Thumbelina (voice by Jodi Benson, who did the lead for Disney's *The Little Mermaid*, 1991) first is abducted by the Spanish songstress Mrs. Delores Toad (voice of the singer Charo) who wants to include the tiny sprite in her family musical group. One of the toad sons wants to marry Thumbelina, so she flees.

Next, she falls into the clutches of Berkeley Beetle. Voiced by Gilbert Gottfried, the spats-wearing, sweet-talking, sinister Berkeley is the film's most original and interesting character. In a heavy New York accent, he repeatedly calls Thumbelina "toots," to which Thumbelina repeatedly replies, "I'm not your toots."

CREDITS

Thumbelina: Jodi Benson (voice)
Prince Cornelius: Gary Imhoff (voice)
Ms. Fieldmouse: Carol Channing (voice)
Mrs. Toad: Charo (voice)
Jacquimo: Gino Conforti (voice)
Mother: Barbara Cook (voice)
Baby Bug: Kendall Cunningham (voice)
Queen Tabitha: June Foray (voice)
King Colbert: Kenneth Mars (voice)
Gnatty: Tawny Sunshine Glover (voice)
Mr. Beetle: Gilbert Gottfried (voice)
Mr. Mole: John Hurt (voice)

Released: 1994
Production: Don Bluth, Gary Goldman, and John Pomeroy; released by Warner Bros.
Direction: Don Bluth and Gary Goldman
Screenplay: Don Bluth; based on the story by Hans Christian Andersen
Editing: Thomas V. Moss
Supervising directing animation: John Pomeroy
Directing animation: John Hill, Richard Bazley, Jean Morel, Len Simon, Piet Derycker and Dave Kupczyk
Special effects supervising animation: Tom Hush
Production design: Rowland Wilson
Art direction: Barry Atkinson
Casting: Judy Taylor and Lynda Gordon
Sound: John K. Carr
Music: William Ross and Barry Manilow
Original songs: Barry Manilow, Jack Feldman and Bruce Sussman
MPAA rating: G
Running time: 86 minutes

In a hilarious production number, Berkeley Beetle takes Thumbelina to the Beetle Ball where she is dolled up in a beetle costume. When it falls off to reveal her human form, she is musically reviled because she lacks feelers, wings and a shell, and Berkeley is disgusted with her ugliness.

 *Thumbelina*'s score was recorded in Dublin at Ringsend Road Studios by the Irish Film Orchestra, a collection of 66 musicians and a choir.

As winter falls, Thumbelina is saved from freezing by Miss Fieldmouse (Carol Channing), who introduces her to the dour and greedy Mr. Mole (John Hurt). Given a financial incentive to arrange a match, Mrs. Fieldmouse urges Thumbelina to abandon her heart and wed a man who can take care of her. Channing's big number, "Marry the Mole" has some great lyrics. "Just think of all the ways you can decorate a hole," she croons to Thumbelina.

While Thumbelina is enduring all these adventures, Prince Cornelius (Gary Imhoff) is buzzing around on his steed, a dive- bombing bumble bee, looking for her. A swallow named Jacquimo (Gino Conforti), who also serves as the film's narrator, comes to her aid and reminds her to follow her heart. Eventually, of course, Thumbelina finds her true love and spring arrives.

None of this breaks new ground, but Bluth populates the film with plenty of interesting little bugs, birds and tiny critters and paints the scenes with care. Younger children especially will love the many delicate and endearing touches.

Barry Manilow's inventive songs carry the film along nicely and provide much of the humor and pathos. "Let Me Be Your Wings" is one of Manilow's most precious love songs ever.

At eighty-six minutes, the film seems overlong, and too many scenes feel like filler. Tighter editing would have better held the attention span of a preschool audience, which is probably the film's strongest market. Older children might find much of the film a little tame.

But even if the storyline goes on a few too many side roads, the message, the animation and the music keep *Thumbelina* on track. It's true and heartfelt and keeps just the right mix of wonder and wit. That's no small feat.

—Michael Betzold

REVIEWS

Atlanta Constitution. March 30, 1994, p. E8.
Boston Globe. March 30, 1994, p. 73.
Boston Globe. March 31, 1994, p. 62.
Chicago Tribune. April 1, 1994, p. 7B.
Christian Science Monitor. April 8, 1994, p. 17.
Los Angeles Times. March 30, 1994, p. F5.
The New York Times. March 30, 1994, p. C19.
The New York Times. April 17, 1994, Sec. 2 p. 25.
USA Today. March 30. 1994, p. D8.
Variety. March 28, 1994, p. 69.
The Wall Street Journal. March 31, 1994, p. A12.
The Washington Post. March 30, 1994, p. B10.
The Washington Post. March 31, 1994, p. C7.
The Washington Post. August 26, 1994, p. D7.

"Don't ever wish to be anything but what you are."—Thumbelina's mother to her daughter in *Thumbelina*.

Hard Hunted

A team of female secret agents (Dona Speir and Roberta Vasquez) on vacation in Arizona stumble upon a plot to gain possession of an atomic bomb part that was stolen from a Chinese laboratory. The film also stars Gregory Peck's son Tony Peck. It is the U.S. feature-film debut of Roger Moore's son, R. J. Moore.

REVIEWS

Entertainment Weekly. April 9, 1993, p. 60.
Variety. CCCXLVIII, September 21, 1992, p. 87.

CREDITS

Donna Hamilton: Dona Speir
Nicole Justin: Roberta Vasquez
Bruce Christian: Bruce Penhall
Kane: R. J. Moore
Lucas: Tony Peck

Edy Stark: Cynthia Brimhall
Raven: Al Leong
Pico: Rodrigo Obregon
Shane Abeline: Michael J. Shane

Released: 1992
Production: Arlene Sidaris; released by Malibu Bay Films
Direction: Andy Sidaris
Screenplay: Andy Sidaris
Cinematography: Mark Morris
Editing: Craig Stewart
Production design: Cher Ledwith
Art direction: William Pryor
Special effects: Eddie Surkin
Sound: Mike Hall
Costume design: Miye Matsumoto
Stunt coordination: Christian Drew Sidaris
Music: Richard Lyons
MPAA rating: R
Running time: 97 minutes

The Harvest

"They stole one of his kidneys...and told him he would survive with only one.... Now, they want that one, too."—Movie tagline

"A tense, tough thriller that keeps you on your toes and guessing."—Bill Hoffman, *The New York Post*

A screenwriter (Miguel Ferrer) travels to Mexico to do research for his new script only to have a kidney stolen by a black-market organ ring. Then the perpetrators decide to come after the second one in this thriller. Directorial debut of David Marconi.

REVIEWS

Chicago Tribune. Mar 2, 1995, Sec. 5 p. 9C.
Variety. CCCXLIX, January 18, 1993, p. 78.

CREDITS

Charlie Pope: Miguel Ferrer
Natalie Caldwell: Leilani Sarelle Ferrer
Bob Lakin: Harvey Fierstein
Noel Guzman: Anthony John Denison
Steve Mobley: Joseph Timothy Thomerson
Hank: Matt Clark
Detective Topo: Henry Silva

Released: 1992
Production: Jason Clark and Morgan Mason for Curb Musifilm/Mike Curb and Lester Korn, in association with Ron Stone Productions and RCA/Columbia Tristar Home Video; released by Arrow Releasing
Direction: David Marconi
Screenplay: David Marconi
Cinematography: Emmanuel Lubezki
Editing: Hubert C. de La Bouillerie and Carlos Puente
Production design: J. Rae Fox
Set decoration: Graciela Torres
Casting: Rick Montgomery and Dan Parada
Visual consulting: Alex Tavoularis
Sound: Alex Silvi and Salvador De La Fuente
Costume design: Ileane Meltzer
Music: Dave Allen and Rick Boston
MPAA rating: R
Running time: 97 minutes

The Hawk

"The first person you want to trust. The last person you want to suspect."
—Movie tagline

"...a gratifying psychological thriller...."
—Kevin Thomas, *Los Angeles Times*

An English housewife, Anne Marsh (Helen Mirren), begins to suspect that her husband, Stephen (George Costigan), may be a grisly serial murderer who has been terrorizing the area.

REVIEWS

Boston Globe. March 23, 1994, p. 69.
Los Angeles Times. May 13, 1994, p. F6.
Maclean's. CVII, March 7, 1994, p. 58.
The New York Times. December 10, 1993, p. C21.

CREDITS

Anne Marsh: Helen Mirren
Stephen Marsh: George Costigan
Mrs. Marsh: Rosemary Leach
Ken Marsh: Owen Teale
Norma: Melanie Hill
Chief Inspector Daybury: Clive Russell

Origin: Great Britain
Released: 1992
Production: Ann Wingate and Eileen Quinn for BBC Films and Initial; released by Castle Hill Productions, Inc.
Direction: David Hayman
Screenplay: Peter Ransley; based on his novel
Cinematography: Andrew Dunn
Editing: Justin Krish
Production design: David Myerscough-Jones
Art direction: Charmian Adams
Casting: Leo Davis
Sound: Kant Pan
Costume design: Pam Tait
Music: Nick Bicat
MPAA rating: R
Running time: 86 minutes

Heavenly Creatures

"The true story of the mystery writer who committed murder herself."—Movie tagline

"Not all angels are innocent"—Movie tagline

"An extraordinary friendship. A shared fantasy. A lethal imagination. These are the clues to the year's most diabolical mystery."—Movie tagline

"One of the year's 10 best!"—*Los Angeles Times, New York Post, Time*

"Two thumbs up!"—*Siskel & Ebert*

"A spellbinder! A wildly hypnotic thriller!"—Peter Travers, *Rolling Stone*

"Chilling!"—Janet Maslin, *The New York Times*

"A thrilling film!"—Richard Corliss, *Time*

"A dazzler! It's impossible to take your eyes off it...innocent yet erotic."—Owen Gleiberman, *Entertainment Weekly*

Box Office Gross: $1,362,356 (January 2, 1995)

Sarah Peirse as Honora Parker, Melanie Lynskey as Paulina Parker, and Kate Winslet as Juliet Hulme in *Heavenly Creatures*. Copyright © Miramax Films.

New Zealand filmmaker Peter Jackson's *Heavenly Creatures* is a film hampered by its own audacious imagination. Based on a well-known New Zealand murder case, *Heavenly Creatures* tells the story of two Christchurch teenagers, Pauline Parker (Melanie Lynskey) and Juliet Hulme (Kate Winslet), who became lovers and clubbed Pauline's mother, Honora (Sarah Peirse), to death in 1954. The case gained renewed notoriety in 1994 when the mystery writer, Anne Perry, revealed that she was, in fact, Juliet Hulme.

Jackson attempts to depict the inner workings of these girls' disturbed minds by using both voiceover narration from Pauline's actual diary and elaborate morphing and animation effects that show the girls' shared fantasy world. This world consists of an imaginary kingdom of living statues and gorgeous landscapes they call the Fourth World, or Borovnia, in which they reign as supreme beings—"heavenly creatures." In attempting to visualize this world, Jackson goes further than any film to date—save, perhaps, the television drama *Sybil* (1976)—in trying to capture the inner experience of profoundly damaged human beings undergoing a psychotic break.

Based on a true story of events that happened in Christchurch, New Zealand in 1954. The real Pauline and Juliet served only brief sentences for their crimes and were released on the promise that they would never associate with each other again. Juliet was recently revealed to be a successful mystery writer using the pseudonym Anne Perry.

Yet Jackson's focus on imagining this inner life comes at the expense of making the girls comprehensible. By relying almost entirely on Pauline's point of view, Jackson, unlike the makers of *Sybil*, neglects to show the family dynamics that made the girls needy and lonely enough to turn to obsessive fantasy and violence. Although Jackson hints at an atmosphere of repression and hypocrisy in both families, what he shows hardly adds up to psychosis and murder. In the end, the girls' madness is brilliantly visualized, but remains woefully underexplained.

The film begins with newsreel footage of a seemingly serene 1950's Christchurch, then cuts jarringly to a violent forward tracking shot of the two blood-spattered girls screaming that "Mummy's been terribly hurt." What makes this opening sequence visually unique is that Jackson intercuts the posthomicidal horror with slow-motion black-and-white images of what appear to be memories of happier times for Pauline and Juliet. In fact, these images turn out to be pure fantasy—the dying throes of their dreams of an idyllic future together.

The film then proceeds in flashback from the girls' first encounter at school two years earlier. Jackson's cameraman, Alun Bollinger, uses drifting pans and slow zooms in these opening sequences to reflect Pauline's aimless yearning for something out of the ordinary; when she finally discovers

CREDITS

Pauline Parker: Melanie Lynskey
Juliet Hulme: Kate Winslet
Honora Parker: Sarah Peirse
Hilda Hulme: Diana Kent
Henry Hulme: Clive Merrison
Herbert Rieper: Simon O'Connor

Origin: New Zealand
Released: 1994
Production: Jim Booth for Wing Nut Films and Fontana Film Productions, in association with the New Zealand Film Commission; released by Miramax Films
Direction: Peter Jackson
Screenplay: Peter Jackson and Frances Walsh
Cinematography: Alun Bollinger
Editing: James Selkirk
Production design: Grant Major
Art direction: Jill Cormack
Digital effects: George Port
Casting: John Hubbard, Ros Hubbard and Liz Mullane
Sound: Michael Hedges
Prosthetic effects: Richard Taylor
Costume design: Ngila Dickson
Music: Peter Dasent
MPAA rating: R
Running time: 99 minutes

Winslet's Juliet brilliantly talking back to a teacher, the camera settles on Juliet and her milky white skin as something virtually miraculous.

Juliet, as portrayed by Winslet and lit by the filmmakers, possesses an icy, budding, almost contemptuous eroticism, and one of the visual themes of the film is how Pauline comes to draw her only sustenance and warmth from the forbiddingly beautiful Juliet. For Pauline, the only time she feels truly alive is when she is with Juliet; Juliet, pale and prone to illness, is shown as more and more flushed and excited when in Pauline's presence. Jackson uses extreme close-ups to punctuate their first meeting and to emphasize their fascination with each other, and these obsessive, fetishistic close-ups recur throughout the film.

What follows is the kind of intense adolescent bonding common to lonely, creative children who have no one else to whom to turn. Juliet shares with Pauline her idolatry of Mario Lanza and her legs, with their symptoms of osteomyelitis, and from these beginnings the girls create their shared, hermetically sealed fantasy world: Juliet's illness and Pauline's alienation are romanticized; their cult-like worship of celebrities (Lanza, Orson Welles) is elevated to quasi-religious status; and all others are excluded with contempt.

Feeling omnipotent, yet sad that no one can appreciate their "genius," the girls romp through the countryside in their

AWARDS AND NOMINATIONS

Academy Awards Nomination 1994: Best Original Screenplay
Venice Film Festival Awards 1994: Silver Lion
Toronto Film Festival Awards 1994: Metromedia's Critic's Choice

knickers, perform candlelit rituals with offerings to "St. Mario" and to Welles, and make vows to enter the Fourth World. "It's better than Heaven," says Juliet. Here, too, the camera settles on Juliet as the object of Pauline's desire: Her complexion grows ruddier in the glow from their private altar.

The film's narrative spine is the series of emotional events that force the girls even further into their isolated psychotic universe. Juliet's therapist mother, Hilda (Diana Kent), beautiful, icy, and distant, is having a barely concealed affair in which Juliet's father, Henry (Clive Merrison), an aloof college dean, seems to acquiesce, perhaps even participate. Until now, Juliet has adopted her mother's cool selfishness and contemptuous attitude as a veneer for her longings for affection. When her parents tell her she will not be accompanying them on a trip out of the country and imply that their marriage is crumbling, Juliet's barely contained neediness and the fiction that her family is normal explode. Juliet runs out of the house in operatic hysterics with Pauline in hot pursuit, visions of Borovnia dancing in their heads.

As for the Parkers, Pauline becomes painfully aware that Honora Parker became pregnant with her at seventeen out of wedlock, and her parents' hateful reaction when they discover she is sleeping with their boarder reinforces her unspoken suspicion that she was an unwanted child. Soon, the girls' emotions are sublimated entirely into their private cult, and it becomes inevitable that they will lash out at anyone who tries to break them up.

Visually, Jackson makes vivid the girls' descent into this delusional, dependent world. When Pauline follows the hysterical Juliet over the hills, Jackson morphs the real landscape into a Borovnia of giant butterflies, snow-white horses, and flower-carpeted gardens. The effect is that of a self-induced acid hallucination, and Jackson shows how it soothes them, allows them to believe in something. At each step toward their private cul-de-sac, Jackson demonstrates how the fantasies they use as balm for their psychic wounds are leading them irrevocably to a break with reality.

At the visual center of each grandiose fantasy is Juliet: Her blood spatters the pure white paper on her school desk as she shows the first signs of tuberculosis, another "romantic" disease; her face reddens with strain as she play acts her Borovnian character Deborah giving birth; and she lies in almost erotic stillness in the tuberculosis sanitarium as Pauline rushes to her with violent urgency. Even when seduced by John, the family boarder, Pauline fantasizes about Juliet.

In a complex sequence, Jackson intercuts John panting over Pauline with Pauline's fantasy of finding Juliet in an idyllic Borovnia and then hacking one of the golem-like male stone figures in two. This act reflects her feelings of being literally split in two by having sex with John, as well as her hatred of anything that is not Juliet. Jackson then cuts back to Pauline's look of horror as John asks if he has hurt her. For Pauline, John, who says he loves her, is no longer real; her fantasy of bringing Juliet from iciness to warmth is.

Jackson reinforces this visual motif in a scene in which Pauline and Juliet bathe together in the warm orange glow of candlelight. Previously, Jackson had used similar lighting to show Pauline's unwrapping the cellophane around her new diary on Christmas Day. Here, Juliet's porcelain skin is now infused with Christmas Day warmth, and, in the visual scheme of things, Juliet takes the place of Christmas, of love, of the diary. Jackson also begins to accentuate the ugly brackish green hues of Pauline's household, which seem to contrast more and more vividly with the colors of the fantasy world. As the "reality" of these drab colors sinks in, Pauline's hatred of her mother grows commensurately: "How I loathed mother," she writes.

Honora Parker's threat to prohibit Pauline from seeing Juliet and Dr. Hulme's decision to send Juliet to school in South Africa drive the girls further into their delusions and seal Pauline's mother's fate. As Pauline and Juliet plan an imaginary departure for Hollywood, Pauline writes that she must get rid of her mother as an "obstacle."

The story reaches a visual crescendo in a brilliantly choreographed sequence in which Pauline envisions her drab living room expanding to accommodate the thunderous waltzing of the Borovnian stone figures and the swooning cadences of Mario Lanza, singing live. When Pauline and Juliet return to the house and consummate their relationship sexually, their union is complete, and their dream must be preserved at all costs—including the death of Pauline's mother. Jackson continues the visual theme of Juliet representing warmth for Pauline right through to the end: As Pauline chillingly writes of being "excited" on the morning of the murder, Mrs. Hulme remarks on Juliet's rare rosy cheeks.

In the final scenes, Jackson ties all his visual motifs together. The sickening bluish-green of Pauline's family kitchen as they all prepare breakfast is at its most pronounced, and Jackson lingers on each detail of the morning to reflect the girls' obsessive tunnel vision, the dreamlike aspect of their madness. In the final murder sequence, in which the girls take Honora Parker out to tea, Honora's drab blue and green outfit evokes pity from them as tearoom clocks tick in the mortal world.

> "Next time I write in this diary, Mother will be dead. How odd—yet how pleasing."—from Pauline Parker's diary before killing her mother in *Heavenly Creatures*

The final, almost soundless walk in the woods before the girls beat Honora's head in with rocks has a rapt, churchlike quality to it, as if the girls were making their final, blissful descent into Borovnia. When the bloody mess of the murder is once again intercut with the black-and-white footage of the imaginary boat departing for "Hollywood," it becomes clear how far into their secret world the girls have gone.

In spite of Jackson's visual prowess, the girls' psyches remain a mystery. Had Jackson chosen to use either Juliet's or a third-person omniscient point of view for even small portions of the film, *Heavenly Creatures* might have provided enough information on the neuroses in each family to explain the girls' ghastly pain. As it is, with only Pauline's purple prose about Borovnia and her clinically distant descriptions of her family to go on, the film simply becomes a visual poem to their psychosis. Many neglected creative children form this type of bond with a friend, but not all of them kill their parents. How were these girls different? Jackson gives only the barest hints.

The depiction of the girls' fantasy world does, indeed, break new ground. For once, the new morphing technology—the computer-generated transformation of one face or landscape into another—is used to a psychological end rather than purely for fantasy effects, and Jackson tries to harness it to the fullest to express the inner workings of their minds. To admit that *Heavenly Creatures* represents an advance over the average television docudrama, however, is not to say that it is entirely successful. Without showing the wellsprings of Pauline and Juliet's shadow world, the director does *Heavenly Creatures*, and the case it is based on, a disservice. Jackson reveals himself as a magisterial visual stylist, and a mediocre psychologist.

—*Paul Mittelbach*

REVIEWS

The Christian Science Monitor. November 29, 1994, p. 14.
Daily Variety. September 12, 1994, p. 16.
Entertainment Weekly. November 25, 1994, p. 48.
The Hollywood Reporter. October 14-16, 1994, p. p. 7.
Los Angeles Times. November 23, 1994, p. F1.
The New York Times. November 13, 1994, p. H15.
The New York Times. November 16, 1994, p. B3.
The New Yorker. LXX, November 21, 1994, p. 131.
Rolling Stone. DCXCIV, November 3, 1994, p. 104.
Time. CXLIV, November 21, 1994, p. 110.
The Wall Street Journal. December 8, 1994, p. A14(W).

Helas Pour Moi

"Beautiful, terse, perplexing, allusive as it is elusive."—Kevin Thomas, *Los Angeles Times*

"Only a genius or a madman—or some divinely ordained combination of the two—could have dreamed up a movie experience as revelatory, perplexing, and masterly as *Helas Pour Moi.*"—Hal Hinson, *Washington Post*

In the fable "The Emperor's New Clothes," sycophantic throngs of people celebrate the emperor's supposed new suit, each afraid to admit the truth. Only one little boy dared to say that the emperor had no clothes on at all. While it would be inaccurate to say that there is "nothing there" in Jean-Luc Godard's film *Helas Pour Moi*, the fable of the emperor's clothes still resonates: This is an impenetrably artistic and abstract film, the type of film some audiences take pride in appreciating because it shows how "deep" they are. Many audiences, however, will find themselves more like the little boy in the fable, asking themselves just why this rather overblown film appears to have any appeal at all.

Gerard Depardieu stars as Simon Donnadieu, a man whose body is apparently taken over by God. His wife, Rachel (Laurence Masliah), has been greatly affected by the experience, as have the other residents of a beautiful village in Switzerland. A mysterious man named Abraham Klimt (Bernard Verley) arrives on the scene; he is a publisher interested in preserving the story of Rachel and Simon.

The story is derived from the Greek myth of Alcmene, in which Zeus assumes the form of Alcmene's husband, Amphitryon, in order to experience human physical love.

CREDITS

Simon Donnadieu: Gerard Depardieu
Rachel Donnadieu: Laurence Masliah
Abraham Klimt: Bernard Verley
Max Mercure: Jean-Louis Loca

Origin: France and Switzerland
Released: 1994
Production: Ruth Waldburger for Vega Film AG and Les Films Alain Sarde; released by Cinema Parallel
Direction: Jean-Luc Godard
Screenplay: Jean-Luc Godard
Cinematography: Caroline Champtier
Editing: Jean-Luc Godard
MPAA rating: no listing
Running time: 101 minutes

The story line is not made clear until the last half hour or so: Rather, Godard's characters and script provide an impressionistic series of images that eventually accumulate into a cogent plot. The film is a lofty exercise in the discovery of truth, and even though only the most sophisticated audiences will even remotely understand what is going on, Godard's effort is admirable.

The film begins with a series of images of the stodgy Klimt arriving in town, walking on country roads, and taking in the sights of the village and its odd inhabitants. A voice-over narration sets the thematic tone: Klimt's voice talks about being a young boy and hearing about how to discover the truth behind a story. "We don't know how to light the fire or say the prayer, but we know the exact place where the mystery occurred," and that should be enough. At that moment he seems to be saying that all that is needed to uncover truth is to know where it occurred. Then he says, "We don't know how to light the fire, tell the prayer, or the place in the forest. But we know how to tell the story." As Klimt's voice says these words, one sees a protracted image of different villagers standing near a lake in various positions, standing completely still—as if ready to begin telling the story.

Numerous beautiful and perplexing vignettes follow: of Klimt trying to ascertain where Rachel and Simon live; of young couples arguing in the breezy warmth of an outdoor cafe; of literature students who beg their teacher for answers to impossible questions about the nature of romance. That these vignettes are perplexing seems to be a part of Godard's overall plan: Rather than relate the story in linear fashion, he allows it to unfold by bits and pieces until it makes sense. Godard's intention appears to be to tease the audience with the elements of a story, forcing them to find the truth of the story themselves. It is a noble intention—but also very difficult. He reinforces his ideas with much dialogue about the nature of truth: "Events are that which happen. That which has a story exists because it is being told." Further, "Our age is in search of a lost question, weary of all the right answers," and, "What makes a house stand and the roof strong is the truth."

These proverb-like quotations, reminiscent of the Christian Bible, are perfectly in keeping with what is evidently a cinematic investigation into the painful journey a person's soul undergoes in its search for meaning. Abraham Klimt, the publisher, perhaps symbolizes the rabbis who wrote the Old Testament: In the Old Testament, it is Abraham who makes the early covenants with God. Rachel (in this film) is the wife of Simon; she is visited by, and physically intimate with, God (in the form of her husband). In the Bible, it is Rachel who eventually gives birth to children blessed by God and promised by God to be brought into the promised land.

These images, combined with other images and bits of dialogue, form Godard's theme about the need for retelling of essential, perhaps Biblical truths in order to cleanse spiritually a spiritually laissez-faire world. The image of the young villagers who are discontented with their lives and unsure about the meaning of Romanticism; a statement that "erudition is not the acquisition of knowledge;" images of couples sitting in the sidewalk cafe, not looking at each other; and the statement uttered by Depardieu that "I am in all of you...I had a son who died for you...Last night I sought refuge in Simon, because he is weak." these images combine to represent Godard's depiction of the struggle for the search for spiritual truth in a complicated world.

 "We don't know how to light the fire or say the prayer, but we know the exact place where the mystery occurred."—Abraham Klimt in *Helas Pour Moi*

Godard even manages to have a little fun with the exchange of ideas on the subject of truth. At various points, off-camera voices discuss that "the scene needs to be redone" and make other subtle references to the fact that this is a film. One piece of dialogue is particularly revealing: "Cinema language is imperfect," says an off-camera voice of the ability of cinema to discover truth.

To comment on the performances in this film would be superfluous, since the actors are subordinate to the theme and ideas. Depardieu is an obvious choice for the role of God, given his almost mythical international persona created by such films as *Le Retour de Martin Guerre* (1983; *The Return of Martin Guerre*) and *Le Dernier Metro* (1980; *The Last Metro*), among others. Comparing Depardieu to other actors who have played God in films can be amusing: the most notable comparison is with George Burns in *Oh, God!* (1977) Depardieu is a terrific choice. When Simon wades into the lake, many in the audience fully expect him to walk on the water. Not many actors can command that kind of response from an audience. Although the other actors are serviceable, the ensemble nature of the film and the craft of its director render them background players to the theme and settings.

In fact, the settings are a character unto themselves: lush, bucolic, and typical of many of the French films that find their way to America, reinforcing the notion of the pastoral beauty of Europe (in this case, Switzerland). Luxuriant vegetation, quiet lakes, beautiful rolling hills— these images are de rigueur in foreign films, from *Manon des Sources* (1986; *Manon of the Spring*) to *Babette's Feast* (1987) to countless others.

The bulk of American audiences have tended to shun foreign films, ostensibly because subtitles are a hindrance. Perhaps it is also because many of the foreign films that are distributed in the United States are so abstract in theme and content: *Léolo* (1992), *Jesus de Montreal* (1989; *Jesus of Montreal*), the films of Francois Truffaut, Pedro Almodovar, Godard, and many others. Although a film such as *Helas Pour Moi* has great value as a conversation piece, the fact that it is impenetrably hard to follow will severely limit its appeal.

—*Kirby Tepper*

REVIEWS

Los Angeles Times. June 30, 1994, p. F7.
The New York Times. March 21, 1994, p. B5.

Herdsmen of the Sun

This short documentary by director Werner Herzog centers on the rich traditions of the otherwise impoverished Wodaabe tribe of the Sahara Desert.

REVIEWS

Variety. CCCXLIII, May 13, 1991, p. 109.

CREDITS

Narrator: Werner Herzog

Origin: Germany
Released: 1991
Production: Patrick Sandrin; released by Interama, Inc.
Direction: Werner Herzog
Cinematography: Thomas Weber
Editing: Rainer Standke
MPAA rating: no listing
Running time: 52 minutes

Hidden Hawaii

The natural beauty of the Hawaiian islands is the focus of this IMAX documentary that ventures into remote locations to capture some impressively rich images.

CREDITS

Kammy Hunt: Kammy Hunt
Richard Grigg: Richard Grigg
Steve Perlman: Steve Perlman

Released: 1994
Production: Richard W. James and Andrew Gellis for Destination Cinema; released by IMAX
Direction: Robert Hillmann
Screenplay: Olivia Crawford
Cinematography: David Douglas
Editing: Vivien Hillgrove
Sound design: Randy Thom
Music: Mark Isham
MPAA rating: no listing
Running time: 35 minutes

High Lonesome: The Story of Bluegrass Music

This intelligent documentary traces the evolution of American bluegrass music. Centering on the "father of bluegrass," Bill Monroe, the film combines interviews with archival and concert film footage to trace the genre from its roots in Depression-era America to its continued popularity in the 1990's, with artists such as Alison Krauss.

REVIEWS

Boston Globe. February 18, 1994, p. 42.
Los Angeles Times. June 8, 1994, p. F3.
The New York Times. April 29, 1994, p. C8.
Newsweek. CXXIII, May 16, 1994, p. 67.
The Washington Post. April 8, 1994, p. C1.

CREDITS

Bill Monroe: Bill Monroe
Ralph Stanley: Ralph Stanley
Mac Wiseman: Mac Wiseman
Jimmy Martin: Jimmy Martin
Earl Scruggs: Earl Scruggs
Jim McReynolds: Jim McReynolds
Jesse McReynolds: Jesse McReynolds
Alison Krauss: Alison Krauss

Released: 1994
Production: Rachel Liebling and Andrew Serwer for Northside Films; released by Tara Releasing
Direction: Rachel Liebling
Screenplay: Rachel Liebling
Cinematography: Buddy Squires and Allen Moore
Editing: Toby Shimin
MPAA rating: no listing
Running time: 95 minutes

Highway Patrolman

Set in Mexico, this dark satire centers on an idealistic young highway patrolman, Pedro (Roberto Sosa), who grows increasingly frustrated by the legal and ethical realities of the profession. One tragedy after another drives him further into his own world of defeat. Finally the death of a close friend pummels him into a one-man war against the drug trade. Roberto Sosa won the Best Actor Award at the San Sebastian Film Festival for his portrayal of Pedro. Alex Cox also directed *Repo Man* (1984), *Sid and Nancy* (1986), and *Straight to Hell* (1987), as well as music videos for The Pogues, Joe Strummer, Debbie Harry, and Iggy Pop.

REVIEWS

Atlanta Constitution. June 17, 1994, p. P3.
Boston Globe. September 23, 1993, p. 62.
Boston Globe. February 25, 1994, p. 50.
Chicago Tribune. March 18, 1994, p. 7K.
Los Angeles Times. February 4, 1994, p. F2.
The New York Times. November 17, 1993, p. C26.

AWARDS AND NOMINATIONS

San Sebastian Film Festival Awards Best Actor (Sosa)

CREDITS

Pedro: Roberto Sosa
Aníbal: Bruno Bichir
Maribel: Vanessa Bauche
Griselda: Zaide Silvia Gutierrez
Sergeant Barreras: Pedro Armendariz, Jr.
Abuela: Malena Doria

Origin: Mexico
Released: 1991
Production: Lorenzo O'Brien; released by Together Brothers/Ultra Film and First Look Pictures
Direction: Alex Cox
Screenplay: Lorenzo O'Brien
Cinematography: Miguel Garzón
Editing: Carlos Puente
Production design: Cecilia Montiel
Art direction: Bryce Perrin and Homero Espinoza
Set decoration: Brigitte Broch
Sound: Roberto Munoz
Costume design: Manuela Loaeza
Music: Zander Schloss
MPAA rating: no listing
Running time: 104 minutes

> "...it's ironic that I portray a prostitute. Most of the roles I've played in theater are either Snow White or Cinderella."—Vanessa Bauche on her character in *Highway Patrolman*

Hit the Dutchman

This drama centers on the life and death of Prohibition gangster Dutch Schultz (Bruce Nozick), starting with his exit from prison at age twenty-four when he is taken under the wing of mob chief Legs Diamond (Will Kempe).

CREDITS

Dutch Schultz: Bruce Nozick
Joey Noey: Eddie Bowz
Legs Diamond: Will Kempe
Emma Fleggenheimer: Sally Kirkland
Bo Weinberg: Matt Servitto
Vincent Coll: Christopher Bradley
Peter Coll: Jeff Griggs
Frances Ireland: Jennifer Miller
Frances: Abigail Lenz
Thomas E. Dewey: Jack Conley
Helen Fleggenheimer: Jennifer Pusheck
No character identified: Leonard Donato
No character identified: Rick Giolito
No character identified: Menahem Golan

Origin: USA and Russia
Released: 1992
Production: Menahem Golan for Power Pictures-Start Corporation; released by 21st Century Film Corporation
Direction: Menahem Golan
Screenplay: Joseph Goldman; based on a story by Alex Simon
Cinematography: Nicholas Von Sternberg
Editing: Bob Ducsay
Production design: Clark Hunter
Casting: Abigail R. McGrath
Sound: Alexander Gruzdev
Costume design: Natasha Landau
Music: Terry Plumeri
MPAA rating: no listing
Running time: 118 minutes

Hoop Dreams

"The countdown has begun to the most extraordinary true story of the year!"—Movie tagline

"One of the great moviegoing experiences of my lifetime.... Extraordinarily moving...recording moments of deep human emotion.... One of the best films about American life I have ever seen"
—Roger Ebert, *Chicago Sun-Times*

"One of the best movies of the year."—Peter Travers, *Rolling Stone*

"The best movie of 1994."—*Siskel & Ebert*

"Four stars. An intimate and compelling close-up of a classic American Dream."—*Playboy*

"Four stars. An astonishing experience!"
—*New York Post*

 Box Office Gross: $1,988,076 (January 2, 1995)

No American film of the 1980's or 1990's better displays the patience and persistence of its filmmakers, and the possibilities of capturing the fullness of life on film, than *Hoop Dreams*. The final film was culled from more than 250 hours of footage shot by the documentary filmmaking team of Steve James, Frederick Marx, and Peter Gilbert between 1987 and 1991. *Hoop Dreams* chronicles four-and-a-half years in the lives of two Chicago teenagers, William Gates and Arthur Agee, who aspire to basketball stardom. The filmmakers allow the narratives of their subjects' lives to emerge naturally from what they observe, rather than from any arbitrary notions they have. Their dedication to this documentary technique jibes with what turns out to be the film's theme: the integrity of the boys' search for their own identities when almost all the people around them—family, coaches, recruiters—seem to have placed their own self-serving bets on how the boys' stories will play out.

By the end of the film, the filmmakers have dispensed entirely with the traditional winner-loser distinctions, which are part and parcel of sports films and of sports thinking, and come down on the side of the boys' emotional development: for James,

Hoop Dreams was originally planned to be a half-hour documentary about street basketball, shot on video rather than film and taking only five or six days to shoot, but became a seven-year collaboration between Peter Gilbert, Steve James and Frederick Marx. The film, ranked among the year's top 10 by more than 110 critics, was snubbed by the Academy Awards in the Best Documentary and Best Picture categories. Critic Roger Ebert called this lapse "a miscarriage," and told *USA Weekend*, "I'm ashamed of having anything to do with the movie business today."

Marx, and Gilbert, this is not a game, this is life, and if the brass ring still matters to William and Arthur after four-and-a-half years, it is the journey to reach it that has taught them about themselves. Through sheer tenacity, the filmmakers have created a one-of-a-kind work that shows the amazing capacity of human beings to write, over time, their own stories, in defiance of the expectations set by family, society—even filmmakers. As well, in their extreme commitment to showing William's and Arthur's stories unfold over time without imposing their own narrative expectations, the filmmakers put *Hoop Dreams* in the small, distinguished category of intimate documentary epics, along with Michael Apted's ongoing *7 Up* series (1963-1992).

The film begins in early 1987, as William and Arthur, both fourteen and African American, watch the NBA All-Star game on television in their families' apartments in Cabrini Green, one of Chicago's best-known and most dangerous public housing projects. The filmmakers make clear that "hoop dreams" of escape from the inner city are what sustain them: "Right now," says William, smooth and collected, "all I think about is playing in the NBA." Arthur, smaller and goofier but with a winning smile, watches his hero, Isaiah Thomas, and tells the filmmakers how one day he will buy his mother a house and a big Cadillac for himself. The scenes establish from the start how much is at stake for both boys and their families, how in the world of Cabrini Green, basketball stardom is the equivalent of the holy grail.

Soon, both Arthur and William are recruited from the playground by Earl Smith, a freelance scout whose motives later come into question, and given a chance to go to St. Joseph—the suburban high school renowned for the best preparatory basketball program in the state, for its tough coach, Gene Pingatore, and for being the alma mater of Arthur's hero, Isaiah Thomas. If the film's opening scenes represent a kind of intimate portrait of the boys, the film's second section quickly becomes a teeming fresco of families, coaches, schools, crowds, neighborhoods, and the impersonal forces of poverty and money, all bent on reshaping William and Arthur and often menacing their dreams.

The boys begin making the daily three-hour round trip by bus from Cabrini Green to St. Joseph's, and interviewer-director James's ability to coax from Arthur and William their aspirations and apprehensions is remarkable. "Are you scared?" James asks Arthur on his first bus ride. "Yes, I am," says Arthur. "I've never been to a school way out before. There'll be new races, new kids." That Arthur thinks of the suburbs as "way out" is as telling an indicator of his psychogeography as anything in the film, and foreshadows the boys' movement into the world beyond Cabrini Green.

The filmmakers vividly contrast life in the projects with the clean-cut Catholic school's rigorous religious curriculum, the concrete courts of Cabrini Green with the polished wooden courts of St. Joseph's. The boys are surprised by the clean hallways, and Arthur notes the most fundamental difference: they have never been around so many white people. Even in this early section of the film, the filmmakers find moments that show that the boys' conceptions of themselves do not necessarily match everyone else's. Just after capturing the delight on Arthur's face when Isaiah Thomas visits a team practice, the filmmakers also catch Pingatore coldly explaining that he sees the playground in Arthur, but not the confidence.

Both boys, the filmmakers show viewers early in the film, are burdened not only by their own dreams and by those of coaches, recruiters, and school officials, but also by those of their families. Curtis Gates, William's older brother, working at a $6-an-hour security guard job, speaks wistfully of his having been named "Player of the Decade" at a junior college, only to falter when he transferred to a four-

CREDITS

William Gates: William Gates
Arthur Agee: Arthur Agee
Steve James: Steve James
Emma Gates: Emma Gates
Sheila Agee: Sheila Agee
Arthur "Bo" Agee: Arthur "Bo" Agee
Gene Pingatore: Gene Pingatore
Curtis Gates: Curtis Gates
Earl Smith: Earl Smith
Isaiah Thomas: Isaiah Thomas

Released: 1994
Production: Frederick Marx, Steve James, and Peter Gilbert for Kartemquin Films and KTCA-TV; released by Fine Line Features
Direction: Steve James
Cinematography: Peter Gilbert
Editing: Frederick Marx, Steve James and Bill Haugse
Executive producer: Gordon Quinn and Catherine Allan
Sound: Adam Singer and Tom Yore
Music: Ben Sidran
Creative consultation: Gordon Quinn
MPAA rating: PG-13
Running time: 169 minutes

AWARDS AND NOMINATIONS

Academy Awards Nomination 1994: Best Film Editing
Chicago Film Critics Awards 1994: Best Film
Los Angeles Film Critics Awards 1994: Best Feature (Documentary)
MTV Awards 1995: Best New Filmmaker (James)
National Board of Review Awards 1994: Best Feature (Documentary)
National Society of Film Critics Awards 1994: Best Feature (Documentary)
New York Film Critics Awards 1994: Best Feature (Documentary)
Sundance Film Festival Awards 1994: Audience Award

year institution. His constant presence at William's games is a poignant reminder that Curtis feels he has as much at stake in William's success as William does. Bo, Arthur's father, also claims, without elaborating, that he could have made it at the professional level. He does not want Arthur to face the bad things that he went through, he wants him to have only the good things in life. The filmmakers make it clear that the hopes William's family and Arthur's father have for them come primarily from their own needs, rather than from a real desire to have the boys succeed on their own terms. Only Arthur's mother, Sheila, the unexpected heroine of the film, seems exempt from everyone else's tendency to see William's and Arthur's stories as belonging to everyone but William and Arthur.

The academic pressures get to both boys, and this is where the filmmakers' editorial decision to tell the story of not just one but two boys reaps rewards James and company could not have envisioned. During their sophomore year, while William brings up his grades and excels on the varsity squad on full scholarship, Arthur is kicked out of St. Joseph's mid-year because his family cannot pay the tuition. It is this development, with all it says about the Darwinian nature of competitive sports and about the insensitivity and favoritism of school officials (William's family also has financial problems, but Pingatore clearly does not want to lose his star player) that sets up the film's biggest real-life twist. In short order, viewers discover that Arthur's father has left the family, is on crack, and is doing time for burglary and assault. The die seems cast: William will be the lucky, pampered All-Star, Arthur the unfortunate kid swallowed by the ghetto. While Arthur works the summer between junior and senior year at Pizza Hut, William spends it at the elite Nike basketball camp. Even Arthur's new coach at Marshall High in Chicago, Luther Bedford, seems to echo the audience's worst expectations that Arthur will simply wind up—the usual refrain—"on the street."

That the film defies all traditional narrative expectations for a big game, a rousing finale, or a lesson about the lethal qualities of poverty is a tribute to the spirit of both William and Arthur and to the tenacity of the filmmakers in sticking with the story. In the third and climactic section of the film, which consists of the boys' senior year in high school, the film seems to find a kind of equilibrium between William and Arthur and the big world around them: they seem to have learned lessons from the burdens of everyone else's expectations and are now effectively dumping them, making their moves downcourt. For Arthur, being set loose from the confines of St. Joseph turns out to have been a blessing. The pressure is off, and he leads Marshall to play-offs that they have not made since 1960. Although the filmmakers show that Arthur's mind is still young at age eighteen—the way he describes his science report on butterflies is childlike—and indicate he may have intellectual obstacles to overcome in junior college, Arthur seems to have rejected his father's example in favor of his mother's strength and integrity. When Sheila Agee, who has been battling just to keep electricity in their apartment and food on the table, finds out she has passed her nurse's training program with flying colors and breaks down sobbing, it is the most moving scene in the film and, unexpectedly, its climax. She has performed in the clinch, and so, the film indicates, will Arthur.

As for William, the epiphanies come as he begins to forge his own identity—by the film's end, he has a girlfriend and a one-year-old daughter—and realizes that that identity may or may not involve basketball, a big admission. As the receptacle of all of his family's expectations, William has fallen easily into the same role with Coach Pingatore, but he finally begins to express his dissatisfaction even as he prepares to go to Marquette on a basketball scholarship. Resenting the label of "the next Isaiah Thomas" that Pingatore and others have pinned on him, William tries to build his own identity: "When I leave, they'll say, 'You're the next William Gates.'" Later he reveals that his brother should not be living his dream through William. At the end of the film he spouts off against Pingatore's abusive coaching style and speaks for all kids who have had to play a role for someone else. For William, articulating that life does not equal basketball is a start.

The film's mid-section contains minor flaws. The filmmakers miss several crucial events in William's and Arthur's lives—namely the pregnancy of William's girl-

"African Americans say, 'I can relate to that.' White people say, 'This can't really be happening.' It's definitely not *Forrest Gump*." William Gates on *Hoop Dreams'* appeal to African Americans (*USA Weekend*, March 24, 1995)

friend and Arthur's reactions to his father's arrest and drug addiction—and the precarious circumstances of both families at this juncture demand responses from both boys as to how they are feeling. Aside from these odd gaps, however, the filmmakers' demonstrate amazing stamina. Their constant ability, in both the interviewing and the editing processes, to locate the critical moments where the boys' dreams clash with the convulsive pressures of the real world keeps the audience rooting for William and Arthur, and not just as athletes but as young men going for the brass ring of self-definition. A freelance college basketball scout calls the recruiting process a meat market, an indication of what William and Arthur are up against. In the end, the story is about both boys' struggle to avoid becoming meat, to avoid becoming commodities (either for the profit of coaches, talent scouts, or universities), or to meet the unfulfilled needs of family and friends. It is also, the filmmakers seem to caution viewers, about people's need to impose, as Joan Didion writes, "a narrative line upon disparate images," often to the detriment of those to whom the narrative in fact belongs. *Hoop Dreams* shows that, as in the best documentaries, if people look long enough at the messiness of life, if people allow themselves to feel the textures, emotions, and pressures that other people feel, then preconceptions are lost. Life is seen in a new way.

—*Paul Mittelbach*

REVIEWS

Christian Science Monitor. LXXXVI, October 14, 1994, p. 12.
The Entertainment Weekly. November 11, 1994, p. 46.
The Hollywood Reporter. October 19, 1994, p. 46.
Los Angeles Times. October 19, 1994, p. F1.
The New York Times. CXLIV, October 7, 1994, p. B1(N).
The New York Times. CXLIV, October 9, 1994, p. H1(N).
The New York Times. CXLIV, October 9, 1994, p. H26(N).
The New York Times. CXLIV, October 16, 1994, p. H13(N).
The New York Times. CXLIV, October 16, 1994, p. H28(N).
The New Yorker. LXX, October 17, 1994, p. 113.
Newsweek. CXXIV, October 17, 1994, p. 81.
Time. CXLIV, October 24, 1994, p. 76.
Variety. CCCLIV, February 14, 1994, p. 39.

Hors la Vie (Out of Life)

A French freelance photographer (Hippolyte Girardot), who is covering the ongoing civil war in Lebanon, is taken hostage in Beirut, in this drama.

REVIEWS

Variety. CCCXLIII, May 13, 1991, p. 107.

CREDITS

Patrick: Hippolyte Girardot
Walid: Rafic Ali Ahmad
Omar: Hussein Sbetty
Ali (Philippe): Habib Hammoud
Moustapha: Magdi Machmouchi
Ahmed (Frankenstein): Hassan Farhat
De Niro: Hamzah Nasrullah
Khaled's mother: Nidal El Achkar
No character identified: Hassan Zbib
No character identified: Nabila Zeitoun
No character identified: Sami Hawat
No character identified: Sabrina Leurquin
No character identified: Roger Assaf

Origin: France, Italy, and Belgium
Released: 1991

Production: Jacques Perrin, Mario Gallo, and Benoit Lamy for Galatee Films, Films A2, Filmalpha Roma, and Lamy Films Bruxelles, with the participation of Canal Plus and Raidue; released by Bac Films
Direction: Maroun Bagdadi
Screenplay: Maroun Bagdadi, Didier Decoin, and Elias Khoury; based on the book by Roger Auque and Patrick Forestier
Cinematography: Patrick Blossier
Editing: Luc Barnier
Production design: Dan Weil
Production management: Catherine Pierrat
Sound: Guillaume Sciama, Chantal Quaglio and Dominique Hennequin
Costume design: Magali Guidasci and Frederique Santerre
Music: Nicola Piovani
MPAA rating: no listing
Running time: 97 minutes

AWARDS AND NOMINATIONS

Cannes Film Festival 1992: Jury Prize (tie)

The House of the Spirits

"In a time of passion, an extraordinary family controlled the fate of a nation. From the highly acclaimed novel comes the year's most provocative love story."—Movie tagline

"Sensational! One of the year's best movies!"
—Jim Ferguson, *Fox-TV*

"Amazing! A 10! A powerful love story with a stellar cast and amazing performances!"
—Gary Franklin, *WCOP-TV, Los Angeles*

 Box Office Gross: $6,214,128 (June 5, 1994)

The House of the Spirits is based upon the novel by Isabel Allende, niece of assassinated Chilean president Salvador Allende. His socialist regime, like the "People's Front" regime portrayed in the film, was overthrown by a bloody military coup; but unlike the fictitious regime, Allende's government never attained a popular electoral majority.

Notwithstanding Isabel Allende's family roots, the screenplay downplays this theme of South American political chaos, relegating it to the capacity of backdrop upon which to spotlight the more intricate issues of familial love, masculine violence, and supernatural wonders. As if to emphasize these broader themes, Allende insisted that Danish-born Bille August be the only person allowed to adapt her novel to the screen. August is best known for his direction of Ingmar Bergman's autobiographical love story *Den Goda Viljan* (1992; *The Best Intentions)* and Best Foreign Film Oscar-winner *Pelle Erobreren* (1988; *Pelle the Conqueror)*, which also won the Golden Globe, the Palme d'Or at the Cannes Film Festival, and Sweden's Golden Ram.

Continuing its international scope, *The House of the Spirits* was produced by Bernd Eichinger's German production company, Neue Constantin, and boasts a cast headed by Oscar winners and former nominees from Great Britain and the United States, including Jeremy Irons, Vanessa Redgrave, Meryl Streep, Glenn Close, and Winona Ryder. These are joined by former Miss Venezuela Maria Conchita Alonso and European veteran stars such as Armin Mueller-Stahl and Antonio Banderas.

Spanning three generations, the film focuses on the family of patriarch Esteban Trueba (Jeremy Irons), whose skill in rebuilding the estate Tres Marias into an agricultural success is counterbalanced by the macho brutality of his management methods. Early scenes depict his heavy-handed treatment of women, including his casual rape of a peasant girl and his dispassionate, businesslike decision to marry Clara (Meryl Streep) based upon her childbearing capabilities. He ignores her parents' warnings that she has been mentally unbalanced and has refused to utter a word since the death of her sister.

In fact, Clara is truly psychic and even tells the stuttering Esteban that she knows he has come to propose to her. After the wedding she becomes the Trueba matriarch and continues to exercise her spiritual powers—once to levitate a tray of honeymoon champagne, once to sense the very moment in which her first child, a daughter, is conceived. During the pregnancy, Clara bonds with Esteban's sister, Ferula (Glenn Close), and "sees" the distant death of her own parents, Severo (Armin Mueller-Stahl) and Nivea (Vanessa Redgrave) in a train accident. Meanwhile, Esteban is confronted by the young woman he raped. Esteban appears unmoved by the fact that she has given birth to a boy—Segundo—whom she claims is Esteban's illegitimate son.

As time passes, Clara gives birth to her own daughter, Blanca, who, throughout her childhood, remains ignorant of the existence of her half-brother. Jealous of Clara's close relationship with Ferula, Esteban banishes Ferula from the estate. She curses him as she leaves, predicting that he will live a guilty life and die a lonely death. Clara is devastated by the loss of her companion.

As Blanca (Winona Ryder) matures, she rejects Satigny (Jan Niklas), the Swiss nobleman her father has chosen, in favor of her secret lover, the revolutionary Pedro (Antonio Banderas). Pedro's union-organizing activities result in his being publicly flogged and later shot by Esteban, who believes he has killed Pedro. Clara, however, senses that Pedro is still alive and counsels Blanca—now pregnant with Pedro's daughter—to remain steadfast. This decision causes Esteban to turn his wrath upon Clara and Blanca. Clara responds by vowing never to speak to him again as long as she lives, a vow she keeps despite her continuing love for him. Esteban seeks solace with Transito (Maria Conchita Alonso), a savvy, compassionate prostitute, who is well-connected in political circles.

 "It was very important that we made him unsympathetic all the way through. But that wasn't hard for me. I never find that hard."
—Jeremy Irons on his character, Esteban Trueba, in *The House of the Spirits* (*Entertainment Weekly*, August 27, 1993)

As the years pass, Esteban becomes entrenched as a conservative politician, but is surprised when his powerful machine is unseated by a grassroots movement led by, among others, the fearless Pedro. Pedro and Blanca are reunited at a political celebration, and he finally meets his school-aged daughter under the guise of being Blanca's "friend." Meanwhile, Esteban participates in a military coup that successfully unseats the popular government, but is shocked when the new military leaders, including his illegitimate son, Segundo (Joaquin Martinez), curtail his political power and arrest Blanca for consorting with Pedro, their enemy.

Plagued by guilt and inspired by Clara's selfless love, Esteban finds it within himself to muster the remnants of his political influence—including his relationship with Transito—to arrange Pedro's escape, Blanca's release, and the young family's eventual reunification in Canada. On his

CREDITS

Esteban Trueba: Jeremy Irons
Clara: Meryl Streep
Ferula: Glenn Close
Blanca: Winona Ryder
Pedro: Antonio Banderas
Transito: Maria Conchita Alonso
Esteban Garcia: Vincent Gallo
Satigny: Jan Niklas
Segundo: Joaquin Martinez
Pancha: Sarita Choudhury
Rosa: Teri Polo
Nana: Miriam Colon
Severo: Armin Mueller-Stahl
Nivea: Vanessa Redgrave

Origin: Germany, Denmark, Portugal, and USA
Released: 1993
Production: Bernd Eichinger for Neue Constantin, in association with Spring Creek; released by Miramax Films
Direction: Bille August
Screenplay: Bille August; based on the novel by Isabel Allende
Cinematography: Jorgen Persson
Editing: Janus Billeskov Jansen
Production design: Anna Asp
Art direction: Augusto Mayer
Set decoration: Soren Gam
Casting: Billy Hopkins and Suzanne Smith
Sound: Niels Arild Nielsen
Makeup: Horst Stadlinger
Costume design: Barbara Baum
Music: Hans Zimmer
MPAA rating: R
Running time: 138 minutes

deathbed, Esteban is visited by the ghost of Clara, whose loving presence counteracts the power of Ferula's curse.

Given the degree of character development spanning several decades, it is hard to fault the actors for their somewhat strained performances. Irons, for example, must portray Esteban as a young man in his early twenties, as a middle-aged politician, and as an elderly patriarch, all with a rather unnatural attempt at a South American accent. The youthful Ryder must appear old enough to have a school-aged daughter, while Streep must portray a woman half her age. Close does not quite reassure the viewer that Ferula will not rise suddenly from near death, as did Close's character in *Fatal Attraction* (1987). By way of contrast, Vanessa Redgrave appears flawless in her brief, uncomplicated appearance as Clara's mother, Nivea. Though not often mentioned in the same critical breath as the other all-star performers, Joaquin Martinez's performance as the bitter Segundo is gripping and memorable.

Throughout the motion picture, August avoids the temptation to use modern special effects or even plaster makeup to re-create the appearance of ghosts. Instead, characters whose deaths have been shown simply reappear on screen as they appeared in life, though their physical movements seem more deliberate. Streep's portrayal as Clara's ghost is particularly effective.

Despite the South American setting, photography director Jorgen Persson chose Portugal and Denmark as the respective sites for his barren landscapes and urban settings. Cathartic moments are portrayed not with the clichéd use of close-ups on actors' faces, but from distances that permit the viewer to gauge the importance of dramatic events by comparing the simultaneous reactions of more than one actor.

Production designer Anna Asp, who has worked with Ingmar Bergman on several occasions, designed Tres Marias, the Trueba family estate. Hans Zimmer, who is best known for his musical scoring of such films as *Rain Man* (1988), *Driving Miss Daisy* (1989), *Thelma and Louise* (1991), and *Backdraft* (1991), has successfully integrated advanced computer effects with traditional orchestral performances.

Critical reception to *The House of the Spirits* was mixed. Those deprecating the film generally maintained that the novel's characters were forced into hackneyed roles due to the compression of four decades of plot into just over two hours. For example, *Newsweek*'s David Ansen, while praising the film's sumptuous production, complained that it declined into inauthenticity and unfolded like "the longest trailer ever made." Similarly, while lauding the film's visual splendor, *People*'s Joanne Kaufman complained that Isabel Allende's epic novel had been sapped of its juice, with the film retaining only a "hacienda-high pile of pulp."

Those praising the film, including *The New York Times'*

Janet Maslin and *Time*'s Richard Schickel, believed that the whole in this case was greater than the sum of its parts and that the film worked despite its daunting objectives. Schickel credited August—"a man of apparently dauntless conviction"—and fine performances by Street, Irons, Close, and Ryder.

—*Philip C. Williams and Sandra G. Garrett*

REVIEWS

Entertainment Weekly. April 8, 1994, p. 38.
The Hollywood Reporter. December 27, 1993, p. 6.
Los Angeles Times. April 1, 1994, p. F1.
Maclean's. CIV, April 11, 1994, p. 69.
New York. April 11, 1994, p. 56.
The New York Times. April 1, 1994, p. B1.
Newsweek. April 11, 1994, p. 74.
People. April 11, 1994, p. 20.
Rolling Stone. March 10, 1994, p. 60.
Time. CXLIII, April 18, 1994, p. 73.
Variety. December 27, 1993, p. 2.

House Party III

"The best *House Party* yet!"—Movie tagline
"This bachelor party's gonna bring down the house!"—Movie tagline

 Box Office Gross: $19,223,609 (April 17, 1994)

In this uninspired sequel, Kid (Christopher Reid) gets engaged to sweetheart Veda (Angela Means), and his best friend and business partner, Play (Christopher Martin), plans the bachelor party. Kid runs into typical problems including meeting his disapproving in-laws dealing with his lifelong friend Play who feels threatened by the impending nuptials, and feeling pre-wedding jitters himself. Sequel to *House Party* (1990) and *House Party II* (1991).

REVIEWS

Atlanta Constitution. January 13, 1994, p. D9.
Boston Globe. January 13, 1994, p. 54.
Chicago Tribune. January 13, 1994, Sec. 1 p. 32.
Entertainment Weekly. January 28, 1994, p. 38.
Los Angeles Times. January 14, 1994, p. F8.
The New York Times. January 13, 1994, p. C17.
People Weekly. XLI, January 31, 1994, p. 17.
USA Today. January 14, 1994, p. D8.
Variety. CCCLIII, January 17, 1994, p. 104.
The Washington Post. January 12, 1994, p. D4.

CREDITS

Kid: Christopher Reid
Play: Christopher Martin
Stinky: David Edwards
Veda: Angela Means
Sydney: Tisha Campbell
Aunt Lucy: Betty Lester
Uncle Vester: Bernie Mac
Showboat: Michael Colyar
Johnny Booze: Chris Tucker
Janelle: Khandi Alexander

Released: 1994
Production: Carl Craig, in association with Doug McHenry and George Jackson; released by New Line Cinema
Direction: Eric Meza
Screenplay: Takashi Bufford; based on a story by David Toney and Bufford and on characters created by Reginald Hudlin
Cinematography: Anghel Decca
Editing: Tom Walls
Production design: Simon Dobbin
Set decoration: M. Claypool
Casting: Robi Reed, Tony Lee and Andrea Leed
Sound: Darryl Linkow
Makeup: Judy Murdock
Costume design: Mel Grayson
Music supervision: Dawn Soler
Music: David Allen Jones
MPAA rating: R
Running time: 93 minutes

The Hudsucker Proxy

"The Coen brothers score again with their stylish lunacy."—Raj Bahadur, *Westwood One Scene Magazine*

"You'll be wowed! A madcap romp that will tickle your funny bone and knock your eyes out. A dazzler! Triumphantly fresh and witty."
—Peter Travers, *Rolling Stone*

"A hit. Devilishly funny. Energetic, effervescent, exhilarating."—Bob Campbell, *Gannett News Service*

"Funny! Clever, triumphant, immensely entertaining. A comedic tour de force!"—Paul Wunder, *WBAI Radio*

"Outrageously funny and fascinating!"—Jeffrey Lyons, *Sneak Previews/Lyons Den Radio*

"Brilliantly salutes '40s filmmaking...It's a visual extravaganza."—*Los Angeles Times*

"A high-flying comedy! Fast and funny. Do yourself a favor...see *The Hudsucker Proxy!*"
—Pia Lindstrom, *WNBC-TV*

 **Box Office Gross:** $2,803,504 (May 30, 1994)

T he Coen brothers' fifth film is an almost unclassifiable hybrid. On the one hand, it is a hyperkinetic parody of the Frank Capra populist comedies of the 1930's and 1940's—*Mr. Deeds Goes to Town* (1936), *Mr. Smith Goes to Washington* (1939), *Meet John Doe* (1941)—that pitted individual idealists against corrupt institutions. On the other, it is a visually stunning industrial fantasy celebrating the victory of colorful 1960's toy design—the Wham-O Hula Hoop and Frisbee—over the gray corporate conformism of the 1950's.

The film, originally conceived by the Coens during the 1980's, has a Capra-era heroine helping the Hula Hoop inventor conquer an evil Eisenhower-era corporation. The idea may well have been intended as a gentle metaphor for how 1960's-era idealism might help a kind of 1990's Zen-Wham-O ethic emerge from 1980's-era corporate greed—the 1930's and 1950's standing in for the 1960's and 1980's, respectively. Unfortunately, this or any other reading of *The Hudsucker Proxy* has been buried under the

 Charles Durning's 45-story leap as Waring Hudsucker in *The Hudsucker Proxy* was accomplished by hanging the actor in mid-air with 1/8-inch-thick steel cables attached to a body cast under his suit. In true life, the fall would have lasted seven seconds, but the movie fall lasted half a minute, giving Durning time to improvise and wave pedestrians out of the way of his fall.

Coen brothers' usual avalanche of in-jokes and film-buff allusions, now abetted by mega-producer Joel Silver of the *Lethal Weapon* (1987, 1989, 1992) and *Die Hard* (1988, 1990) films. Like their previous films, including *Raising Arizona* (1987) and *Barton Fink* (1991), *The Hudsucker Proxy* is an exhaustive and exhausting pastiche of parodies of, homages to, and clichés from other films, delivered at the rapid-fire pace of a Tex Avery cartoon.

The film visually or in dialogue alludes to *Mr. Deeds Goes to Town*, *Mr. Smith Goes to Washington*, *Meet John Doe*, *It's a Wonderful Life* (1946), *Brazil* (1985), *The Apartment* (1960), Preston Sturges' *Christmas in July* (1940), Charlie Chaplin's *Modern Times* (1936), the children's film *The Red Balloon* (1956), and the Gumby and Pokey Claymation television shows, and those are just for starters. This compulsive and ceaseless inventiveness crowds out not only any possibility for interpretation but also any possibility for real emotion or identification with any character. *The Hudsucker Proxy* is finally a maddeningly overstuffed and self-conscious pastiche that becomes all imitation, all parody—a virtual art-house *Airplane!* (1980), but without the eagerness to get a laugh that made the latter so ingratiating.

The film opens with an *It's a Wonderful Life*-like prologue from which it flashes back. Norville Barnes (Tim Robbins) is perched on a ledge high atop the Hudsucker Industries building in New York City on New Year's Eve, 1958, ready, as the narrator says, to "jelly up the sidewalk," in a scene that calls up *Meet John Doe*. Even the narrator, as in *It's a Wonderful Life*, is a kind of guardian angel, in this case Moses (William Cobbs), the keeper of the giant Hudsucker building clock, which reads "The Future Is Now" and is about to toll midnight (in *It's a Wonderful Life* it was Christmas Eve). The scene has a dreamlike quality to it, accentuated by its being shot without sound and by Micheal J. McAlister's stunning scale model of an imaginary mid-twentieth-century New York City skyline, spookily combining in one shot the great skyscrapers of the era of mass capital formation.

The story of Barnes's rise to the top begins with his arrival in New York at the bottom. A rube fresh out of the Muncie School of Business Administration and ready to conquer the world, Barnes is armed only with his design for a Hula Hoop—a circle drawn in pencil on a worn piece of paper. This sketch produces bewilderment when Barnes explains that the invention is "You know—for kids." Robbins plays the role like a starstruck nine-year-old who ultimately goes through a difficult puberty but emerges as a nice young man, and it works. The performance is reminiscent of Tom Hanks's in *Big* (1988). One of *The Hudsucker Proxy*'s most enjoyable set pieces is Barnes becoming glassy-eyed as he watches a board like those in railroad stations that flip destinations, except this one is feverishly flipping New York City employment opportunities.

"You know, for the kids."— Norville Barnes, describing his invention in *The Hudsucker Proxy*

Just as Barnes begins his nightmarish mailroom job in the basement of Hudsucker Industries (shades now of *Brazil*, *1985*), the founder of the company, Waring Hudsucker (Charles Durning, looking remarkably like the Edward Arnold villain character in the Capra films), leaps from the top-floor boardroom to the sidewalk below. Since Hudsucker's will stipulates that his controlling shares in the company be offered to the public as common stock January 1, company henchman Sidney J. Mussburger (Paul Newman) plots to devalue the shares by hiring "a puppet, a proxy, a pawn" as company president, thereby enabling the board members to buy back the shares and retain a controlling interest.

Barnes, like Mr. Smith and John Doe of the Capra films, is picked as the patsy, and the company, predictably, begins its downhill slide. Amy Archer (Jennifer Jason Leigh), however, a Pulitzer Prize-winning reporter, smells a rat and goes undercover as Barnes's secretary to try to prove him a fraud. Equally predictably, she ends up falling in love with Barnes instead, just as Barnes's Hula Hoop becomes successful and foils Mussburger's nefarious plans.

Leigh and the Coen brothers make Archer a Barbara Stanwyck, Rosalind Russell, Katharine Hepburn, and Jean Arthur character rolled into one, and it is here, where the film's 1930's and 1950's styles collide, that the film begins to go seriously awry. Leigh, one of the most gifted actresses working in Hollywood at the time, gives a performance of untold virtuosity—the college try of all time—and it is all pastiche. The Coen brothers refuse to give the character any inner life, and Leigh becomes practically unwatchable, a sort of puppet possessed by screwball comedy. When they do allow Archer to feel bad about her deception of Norville, Leigh is too good an actress not to show a world of emotion behind her eyes, and then she is forced to come up with one of the Coen brothers' self-consciously corny lines like, "Ah, he's the bunk" and "And that's just potato, Smitty. And here comes the gravy." Watching Leigh, in spite of her remarkable talents, becomes a peculiarly grating exercise. By the time Archer becomes Barnes's secretary, the film should be in high comedic gear, but the filmmakers make it impossible to care. They keep insisting on the pastiche, turning on the style.

This is unfortunate, because the film's pleasures are considerable. *The Hudsucker Proxy* remains the closest that motion pictures have yet come to visualizing the emblematic American sociological works of the 1950's, *The Lonely Crowd* (1950) and *Organization Man* (1956), and that is no small accomplishment. The ways the film creates that look are marvels of photography, art direction, special effects, costuming, and, most of all, casting. From the model of New York to the brilliant monochromatic cinematography by Roger Deakins, which evokes perfectly the corporate style of the late 1940's and early 1950's, to the impeccable choices of actors with 1930's and 1950's "looks," the Coen brothers successfully evoke this bygone era. Paul Newman, in a rare

CREDITS

Norville Barnes: Tim Robbins
Amy Archer: Jennifer Jason Leigh
Sidney J. Mussburger: Paul Newman
Waring Hudsucker: Charles Durning
Chief: John Mahoney
Buzz: Jim True
Moses: William Cobbs
Smitty: Bruce Campbell
Lou: Joe Grifasi
Benny: John Seitz
Beatnik Barman: Steve Buscemi
Vic Tenetta: Peter Gallagher

Released: 1994
Production: Ethan Coen, in association with Polygram Filmed Entertainment, Silver Pictures, and Working Title Films; released by Warner Bros.
Direction: Joel Coen
Screenplay: Ethan Coen, Joel Coen, and Sam Raimi
Cinematography: Roger Deakins
Editing: Thom Noble
Production design: Dennis Gassner
Art direction: Leslie McDonald
Set design: Gina Cranham, Tony Fanning and Richard Yanez
Set decoration: Nancy Haigh
Casting: Donna Isaacson and John Lyons
Visual effects supervision: Micheal J. McAlister
Sound: Allan Byer
Costume design: Richard Hornung
Music: Carter Burwell
MPAA rating: PG
Running time: 111 minutes

funny performance, shows off his comedy chops as the scheming Sidney J. Mussburger. When he reacts to Barnes's diagram of the Hula Hoop, Newman invests his response— "Huh. Hm. Hmm"—with a dawning Machiavellian glee that steals the show. Yet even these assets do not make a satisfying film.

At the end, the Coen brothers seem to be saying that a bright, new, goofy era epitomized by Hula Hoops and beatniks emerged from the sterile conformism of the 1950's. On the other hand, perhaps the film is merely intended as a simple paean to childlike inventiveness. Yet there is nothing simple about the Coen brothers' inventiveness, and it crowds out the fable. *The Hudsucker Proxy* is ultimately strictly about style, style as seen through the infinitely subtle sensibilities of the Coen brothers. Their film is the cinematic equivalent not of the streamlined Hula Hoop they celebrate but of the oppressive, Brobdingnagian, out-of-control industrialism the film claims to deplore. One waits for the day when the Coens can let up on their oppressive style and find material to match their prodigious talents.

—Paul Mittelbach

REVIEWS

The Christian Science Monitor. LXXXVI, March 15, 1994, p. 13.
Entertainment Weekly. March 11, 1994, p. 36.
The Hollywood Reporter. January 31, 1994, p. 6.
Los Angeles Times. March 11, 1994, p. F1.
The Nation. CCLVIII, March 21, 1994, p. 390.
The New York Times. CXLIII, March 11, 1994, p. B1.
Newsweek. CXXIII, March 14, 1994, p. 72.
Time. CXLIII, March 14, 1994, p. 103.
Variety. CCCLIII, January 31, 1994, p. 4.
The Wall Street Journal. March 10, 1994, p. A16.

Hyenas (Hyenes)

A woman, Linguere Ramatou (Ami Diakhate), who was betrayed by her lover, Dramaan Drameh (Mansour Diouf), and fled her small African village thirty years earlier, returns to seek revenge on the man who wronged her. Now a very wealthy woman, she offers to end the village's poverty—provided the villagers forsake Dramaan.

CREDITS

Dramaan Drameh: Mansour Diouf
Linguere Ramatou: Ami Diakhate
Mayor: Mahouredia Gueye
Teacher: Issa Ramagelissa Samb
Toko: Kaoru Egushi
Gaana: Djibril Diop Mambety
Amazon: Hanny Tchelley
Head of Protocol: Omar Ba

Origin: Senegal, Switzerland, and France
Released: 1992
Production: Pierre-Alain Meier and Alain Rozanes for Thelma Film and ADR Productions
Direction: Djibril Diop Mambety
Screenplay: Djibril Diop Mambety; based on the play *The Visit of the Old Woman*, by Friedrich Durrenmatt
Cinematography: Matthias Kalin
Editing: Loredana Cristelli
Sound: Maguette Salla
Costume design: Oumou Sy
Music: Wasis Diop
MPAA rating: no listing
Running time: 110 minute

I Am My Own Woman

This weakly dramatized combination of documentary and docudrama set in Germany centers on Charlotte von Mahlsdorf, a homosexual and transvestite born Lothar Berfelde in 1928. The film traces his life and career from an abusive childhood, through the Nazi and Communist regimes, to his rise as a leading figure of the German gay movement. Mahlsdorf appears in the film periodically to comment on the actors playing him in his younger years.

REVIEWS

The Advocate. November 16, 1993, p. 88.
Boston Globe. April 15, 1994, p. 94.
Los Angeles Times. June 17, 1994, p. F16.
The New York Times. April 29, 1994, p. C15.

AWARDS AND NOMINATIONS

Rotterdam Film Festival: International Film Critics Prize

CREDITS

Charlotte von Mahlsdorf: Lothar Berfelde
Charlotte von Mahlsdorf (as the middle-aged Charlotte): Ichgola Androgyn
Charlotte von Mahlsdorf (as the teen-aged Lothar): Jens Taschner

Origin: Germany
Released: 1994
Production: Rosa von Praunheim Filmproduktion, Scala Z Film GmbH, and Rene Perraudin; released by Cinevista
Direction: Rosa von Praunheim
Screenplay: Rosa von Praunheim and Valentin Passoni
Cinematography: Lorenz Haarman
Editing: Mike Shephard
Production design: Peter Kothe
Costume design: Joachim Voeltzke
Music: Joachim Litty and Cello Familie
MPAA rating: no listing
Running time: 91 minutes

I Don't Want to Talk About It (De Eso No Se Habla)

"Superb! A poignant, often funny fable...the film's images seize the memory."—Richard Corliss, *Time*

"A stately, haunting fable!"—Janet Maslin, *The New York Times*

"Illuminating! An engrossing story that builds to a stunning, utterly surprising climax."—*Los Angeles Times*

"Four stars! One of 1994's very best!"—Larry Worth, *New York Post*

"...plays like a dream, a luxuriant excursion into magic realism....gorgeous to look at."—*Boston Globe*

Box Office Gross: $212,835 (November 27, 1994)

I Don't Want to Talk About It (*De Eso No Se Habla*) is the sixth feature film release that Spanish filmmaker María Luisa Bemberg both wrote and directed. American audiences became aware of her in 1984 for her critically acclaimed *Camila*, which was her first film to be released in America. *Camila* received an Academy Award nomination for Best Foreign Language Film, marking an auspicious

debut. This was followed by *Miss Mary* in 1986 starring the luminous Julie Christie and, five years later with *Yo, La Peor De Godas* (*I, the Worst of All*) based on an essay by Nobel Prize winner Octavio Paz. These films established Bemberg as a distinctive force in cinema and also as the first successful woman director in Argentina. A late starter, she began her career as a filmmaker at the age of fifty-six. Since *I Don't Want to Talk About It* had already been given a Special Jury Prize Award for Best Actress and Best Screenplay by the La Habana (Cuba) Film Festival, expectations for the film were exceedingly high when it arrived in the United States.

The film, which is based on a story by Julio Llinàs, is certainly an intriguing one. Set in an isolated town in Latin America in the 1930's, it tells the tale of Leonor (Luisina Brando), a wealthy widow who refuses to accept the fact that her daughter, Charlotte (Alejandra Podesta), was born a dwarf. Her denial becomes an obsession and, in the opening, she is shown methodically destroying all books, figurines, and statues that have anything remotely to do with gnomes, dwarfs, or little people. She even goes to the extent of burning a copy of *Snow White*. She forbids anyone in the town to mention Charlotte's stature in order to protect her daughter from feeling different. She believes that if her daughter's dwarfism is completely ignored then it will not be true. Her main objective is to hide the truth from Charlotte at all costs and ultimately from herself.

Leonor's agenda seems to work quite well. Charlotte appears to be a well adjusted adolescent content in living her life and practicing the piano. All seems to be going well until Ludovico D'Andrea (Marcello Mastroianni) arrives in the town. A somewhat mysterious stranger, he manages to befriend simultaneously both Leonor and Charlotte and charms everyone with his wit, style, and romantic stories of mysterious, distant places. It is all done quite innocently. All of this tranquility, however, comes to an abrupt end when Ludovico discovers (to his own horror and disbelief) that his feelings have changed and that he now finds himself in love with Charlotte. He flees the town hoping to run from the consequences of his feelings, but his passion for Charlotte lures him back. He consequently asks for her hand in mar-

CREDITS

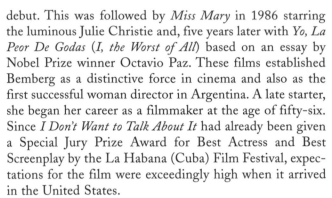

Ludovico D'Andrea: Marcello Mastroianni
Leonor: Luisina Brando
Charlotte: Alejandra Podesta
Madama: Betiana Blum
Padre Aurelio: Roberto Carnaghi

Origin: Argentina
Released: 1993
Production: Oscar Kramer; released by Sony Pictures Classics
Direction: María Luisa Bemberg
Screenplay: María Luisa Bemberg and Jorge Goldenberg; based on a short story by Julio Llinàs
Cinematography: Felix Monti
Editing: Juan Carlos Macias
Art direction: Jorge Sarudiansky
Costume design: Graciela Galàn
Sound: Carlos Abbate
Music: Nicola Piovani
MPAA rating: PG-13
Running time: 102 minutes

AWARDS AND NOMINATIONS

La Habana (Cuba) Film Festival Awards
1992: Special Jury Prize—Best Actress, Best Screenplay

riage. When she accepts, he is both thrilled and bewildered as is everyone in the town. Their unique wedding affirms their love, and they appear destined for happiness or so it appears.

In depicting this story on the screen, the director chooses a very simplistic style to tell this complicated story. From the moment the film begins, each scene keeps giving the audience more information about these people and what is going on in their lives. There is no emphasis on the fact that one of the main characters is a dwarf. "I never would have dared write a story about a dwarf. I would have been much too afraid of being disrespectful," said the director. In making *De Eso No Se Habla*, it was as if she wanted the audience to suspend all judgement about the specifics and to view it in a larger context. Charlotte just happens to be a dwarf, but it could be anyone who is different from the norm or at least perceived to be different. In many ways, Bemberg approached the subject matter as if it were an allegory. Children's voices and laughter are heard over the credits almost requesting the viewers to acquire the innocence of children as they watch the story unfold. The use of a narrator also adds to the "once upon a time" mood of the piece. These devices are used to avoid any sense of exploitation or elements implying the grotesque. A delicate line is drawn from the beginning, and it is never crossed due to the innate sensitivity of the filmmaker.

Luisina Brando works for the third time with director Bemberg, following her award-winning leading roles as the heroine in *Senora De Nadie* (*Nobody's Wife*, 1982) and the sexy Perla in *Miss Mary*. Aside from her film career, Brando has worked on numerous stage and television productions in Argentina. In this film, she plays the part of Leonor, Charlotte's mother. It was a wise casting choice by Bemberg. The actress gives a compelling and sympathetic performance of the wealthy widow. She is also beautiful, which makes Leonor's pain about giving birth to a deformed child more poignant. Her face in close-ups reveals the guilt and suffering that this woman experiences on a daily basis. She reflects a shame and a fear that there was some underlying ugliness inside of her that caused this terrible thing to happen. Her only means of coping with the tragic event is complete denial. It is as if she wants to erase the facts and make it go away. Brando's depth as an actress enables her to convey all of this by a simple look or gesture. Her eyes are indeed a window to the soul of this somewhat tortured woman. The underlying torment is smoldering underneath the passionate actress' multifaceted portrayal. She has the sensuality and womanliness of another one of Marcello Mastroianni's costars, Sophia Loren. Brando radiates every nuance of a mother's primal instinct to shield her child from harm. Her determination is impenetrable and her strength, indominatable.

"This tale is dedicated to all people who have the courage to be different in order to be themselves"— María Luisa Bemberg's dedication for *I Don't Want to Talk About It*

"I choose Marcello when the character is man in all his contradictions. In Marcello I have the right actor to express something ineffable," said Federico Fellini in an interview. This quote certainly capsulizes the indefinable quality of Mastroianni, the legendary star of some 150 films. In a career that spans more than thirty years, this versatile actor has tackled every conceivable role from a sexy journalist in Fellini's renowned *La Dolce Vita* (1960) to a pregnant man in Jacques Demy's *A Slightly Pregnant Man* (1973). His willingness to expose himself emotionally, his humor, wit, charm, and comedic talents are all evident in *I Don't Want to Talk About It*. His Ludovico has all the contradictions and frustrations of a real human being trying to make sense out of a nonsensical world. He wears the somewhat wearied, wandering world-traveller with grace and style. He escapes into his darker nature in the confines of the local brothel. He continually gives glimpses of the complexity of his character, much the same as Brando does with her Leonor. Mastroianni's talents are particularly evident in a scene that takes place in Leonor's parlor, where he is entertaining guests. He sings and weaves a spell over Charlotte and charms everyone in the room and also in the audience. He is truly a deft and remarkable performer.

Certainly, this film deals with a delicate subject. Not only is Ludovico much older than Charlotte, but she is also a dwarf. It is necessary to view this piece as an allegory that demonstrates that true love knows no boundaries or limitations. The controversial theme is never exploited due to Bemberg's integrity both as a director and as a human being. There is a meticulous sensitivity to the nature of the subject matter and also to the feelings of Alejandra Podesta, who plays Charlotte. According to the director, it was an extremely difficult role to cast until she discovered Podesta. The girl had never acted before. Perhaps there was a special quality that Bemberg saw in the young girl that led her to make this risky casting decision. Unfortunately, that quality did not come across on film. The girl certainly has some charm, but she is never able to convey the luminosity or radiance that would make Ludovico propose marriage. It is essential for the audience to understand what about this girl is so enticing as to justify such a bold decision by Ludovico. It is never conveyed. Beauty certainly is in the eye of the beholder, but the chemistry between this unlikely pair never surfaces. The role of Charlotte requires a solid performance by an accomplished actress. Podesta does not have the necessary skills and unfortunately the impact of the film is weakened because of this inappropriate casting.

This film did not have wide commercial appeal, but it certainly has merit. It is a revelation in subtlety, which so many American films seem to lack. It is never condescending to the viewers and asks that it be watched with an open mind and an open heart. As a filmmaker, Bemberg's main goal is to tell the story faithfully and simply. She uses the images on the screen to reveal the inner lives of the characters and to convey the message. Although she lacks the vitality of a Fellini, she prompts comparisons to the legendary director's style. There are vibrant images thrust out at the viewers that are revealing and, at times, startling. A memorable example of this is the pivotal scene when Ludovico realizes his feelings for Charlotte have changed. Charlotte is riding atop a beautiful white stallion (a gift from Ludovico) circling the barn in slow motion. The scene has an ethereal quality to it. The camera moves to Ludovico, who has been secretly watching this dreamlike vision from atop a ladder. Viewers see Ludovico's face go from paternal interest to confusion to realization that he is now in love with this child/woman and finally to disgust and horror as he descends the ladder. The camera then returns to the vision of this small being majestically riding atop a magnificent animal. This dreamlike sequence seems to suggest that Charlotte is rising above all the limitations that being a dwarf could ever impose on her.

The film's individuality places it in somewhat of a special category and may not appeal to everyone. It does, however offer the moviegoer the opportunity to challenge their own belief systems about beauty and normalcy. What may appear grotesque to some may represent beauty to others. Are people liberated in some areas and find themselves shocked and appalled by others? Certainly, these issues can be confronted in *I Don't Want to Talk About It*. Perhaps, the film will expand the parameters of acceptance for all who go to see it. If that be the case, then María Luisa Bemberg has done everyone an enormous service.

—*Robert F. Chicatelli*

REVIEWS

The Hollywood Reporter. September 30, 1994 - October 2, 1994, p. 11.
Los Angeles Times. October 14, 1994, p. F8.
The New York Times. October 3, 1994, p. B4.

I Like It Like That

"Two thumbs up!"—*Siskel & Ebert*
"Ms. Martin's terrifically buoyant debut feature is as scrappy and alluring as its heroine."—*The New York Times*
"It reverberates with the passions and intensities of life."—*New York Daily News*
"A gritty Cinderella story that moves easily from comedy to romance to unblinking reality without compromising its integrity."—*Los Angeles Times*
"A fresh inner-city love story from first time director Darnell Martin, who brings an entire neighborhood alive."—*Chicago Tribune*

 Box Office Gross: $1,760,527 (December 4, 1994)

I Like It Like That is the kind of film that the trade describes as a "sleeper." It has the ingredients of a hit and received favorable reviews but came and went so quickly that the public was hardly aware of its existence. The powerful critics Gene Siskel and Roger Ebert gave the film "two thumbs up" on their weekly television program, and *The New York Times* said that "Ms. Martin's terrifically buoyant debut feature [as author and director] is as scrappy and alluring as its heroine."

Darnell Martin received considerable media attention as the first African American woman to direct a motion picture for a major studio. She does a creditable job working with unknown actors on a limited budget and shooting most of her scenes on the streets of New York. Nevertheless, *I Like It Like That* was quickly crowded off the screens by the many better-publicized productions clamoring for attention in a market made increasingly lucrative by cable television, VCR, and the growing international demand for American films.

Lauren Veléz, the scrappy, alluring star, plays Lisette Linares, a Latino housewife of African ancestry, who lives in a noisy, congested ghetto in the Bronx with her handsome, supermacho husband and their three small children. The whole story has to do with Lisette's liberation from domestic slavery. She breaks with the Latino tradition of male domination and female subservience by going out and getting a job. She does this when her husband is sent to the Bronx House of Detention for stealing merchandise out of a store during a looting riot, which was triggered by a power blackout.

Chino Linares (Jon Sedas) naturally resents his wife's liberation and the haughty attitude she assumes at home. Like many American males, he is shocked to find that his wife can earn a great deal more than he can. She is aggressive, resourceful, and talented. She also has the moral support and practical advice of her amusing transvestite brother, Alexis (Jesse Borrego), who knows more about how to be a well-dressed, sexy woman than most women. Alexis turns

CREDITS

Lisette Linares: Lauren Veléz
Chino Linares: Jon Seda
L'il Chino Linares: Tomas Melly
Minnie Linares: Desiree Casado
Pee Wee Linares: Isaiah Garcia
Alexis: Jesse Borrego
Magdalena Soto: Lisa Vidal
Stephen Price: Griffin Dunne
Rosaria Linares: Rita Moreno

Released: 1994
Production: Ann Carli and Lane Janger for Think Again; released by Columbia Pictures
Direction: Darnell Martin
Screenplay: Darnell Martin
Cinematography: Alexander Gruszynski
Editing: Peter C. Frank
Executive producer: Wendy Finerman
Production design: Scott Chambliss
Art direction: Teresa Carriker-Thayer
Set decoration: Susie Goulder
Casting: Meg Simon
Sound: Rosa Howell-Thornhill
Costume design: Sandra Hernandez
Music: Sergio George
MPAA rating: R
Running time: 95 minutes

AWARDS AND NOMINATIONS

Independent Spirit Awards Nominations
1995: Best Actor (Seda), Best Actress (Veléz), Best Cinematography, Best First Feature

self-discipline and hard work are not really needed by either women or men in order to escape from urban ghettos. Unfortunately, this attitude is already far too prevalent and hardly needs reinforcement.

Chino, who lost his job when he went to jail, is forced to take an even lower-paying job as a security guard when he gets out. His dark mood is further deepened because he must do much of the feeding and diapering at home. Since Lisette has become the main breadwinner, she expects Chino, her mother-in-law, and Alexis to take care of all the household chores. She often works late and comes home when she feels like it. On one occasion, her boss gives her a ride to her Bronx tenement in his expensive sports car, creating the impression in the close-knit Latino community that she is having an affair with the wealthy gringo.

Lisette's neighbors' suspicions are not entirely unfounded. Lisette has traditional Latino ideas about marital fidelity but succumbs to a combination of internal and external pressures, including jealousy, curiosity, and a desire to hold on to her job. She discovers that Chino has been having an extramarital affair with Magdalena Soto (Lisa Vidal), and her wounded feelings make her more susceptible to the ongoing sexual overtures of Price, who takes it for granted that his female subordinates represent a sort of harem and that they should feel flattered by his attentions. Lisette finally gives in to him in order to spite her husband. She quickly repents what she has done but has already confessed her sin to Chino during one of the loud, recriminative arguments, which the whole neighborhood enjoys as if they were installments of a soap opera. Chino has felt free to indulge in extramarital affairs but cannot understand how a Latina wife and mother could possibly do the same thing. He not only feels outraged but also senses that his own freedom is being threatened by his arguments in favor of marital fidelity.

out to be a sort of fairy godmother in this Cinderella story. The seemingly gratuitous inclusion of a transvestite may be intended to symbolize the reversal of gender roles which is becoming more and more common in modern society.

Lisette makes the short but psychologically intergalactic journey to lower Manhattan and quickly finds a job as an assistant to an oversexed white yuppie male, who has a high-salaried job promoting Latino musicians for a major record company. Her boss, Stephen Price (Griffin Dunn), quickly becomes dependent on Lisette's taste and promotional judgement because he has little understanding of what personalities, styles, and music appeal to the Latino market.

Perhaps the weakest aspect of *I Like It Like That* is its Cinderella motif. That a young woman with no education and no business experience could walk so easily into a prestigious job in a Manhattan executive suite is difficult to believe. Her magical metamorphosis may solve the financial problems of one exceptionally gifted individual but does not offer any practical example for the average housebound, culturally conditioned Latina to emulate. It suggests that education,

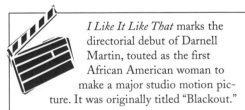

I Like It Like That marks the directorial debut of Darnell Martin, touted as the first African American woman to make a major studio motion picture. It was originally titled "Blackout."

Lisette's and Chino's mutual infidelity leads to a serious marital rift. This is exactly the opportunity for which the sensual, promiscuous Magdalena has been waiting. She drives another wedge between the Linares by claiming that Chino is the father of the infant she recently bore out of wedlock. She persuades her prosperous father to give Chino a managerial job in his grocery store and gradually draws the gullible, resentful Chino deeper into the web of her own extended family. It seems only a matter of time before Chino will sue for divorce and marry Magdalena, although he has only her word that the baby is actually his.

Like many other American women, Lisette is faced with a choice between career and family. She is caught in one of the worst social dilemmas of modern times. There is no easy solution, especially since she already has three children. Most American career women face the choice before having children.

The plot reflects the influence of such films as *Kramer vs. Kramer* (1979) and *Strictly Business* (1991). In *Kramer vs. Kramer*, both the husband and wife are forced to grow as a result of powerful twentieth-century economic and social pressures that they only vaguely understand. Both become better persons as a result. Ted Kramer (Dustin Hoffman) learns to assume his fair share of parental responsibilities, while Joanna Kramer (Meryl Streep) learns that she needs more to fulfill herself than domesticity and motherhood.

Chino has the same kind of problems with his obstreperous son L'il Chino (Tomas Melly) that Ted Kramer had with his precocious son Billy. Through his problems with his son, Chino is made to realize that he has not been setting a good example because he has been gone so much of the time, either at work, or carrying on an affair with Magdalena, or hanging out with his irresponsible buddies, letting Lisette carry the whole burden of discipline. Like Ted Kramer, he realizes that he has been trying to be a husband and father without relinquishing any of his freedom. When he is forced to take a firm hand with his son, both father and son benefit visibly.

In the musical-drama *Strictly Business*, the African American hero Waymon Tinsdale III (Joseph C. Phillips) finds that he has become an "Oreo," losing his roots through immersion in the white-dominated world of big business, and he is forced to make a hard choice between success and identity. Lisette is faced with a similar choice and learns, in time, that worldly success without true love and spiritual integrity is a bad bargain.

I Like It Like That establishes a problem that it does not solve. Is it possible for men and women to grow as individuals and still remain united by the bonds of traditional marriage? If husbands and wives do not stay together, what will happen to the children? What will happen to civilization? In the end, Lisette comes back to her family. She and Chino agree to share parental responsibilities equitably, but she is sleeping on the couch in the living room and refusing to share their bed.

The story's ending is ambiguous. Their relationship will never be the same, but they are still tied by memories and mutual love for their children. They may work out some new kind of relationship which would be a healthier one if such a new man-woman relationship is really possible. The ending recalls Henrik Ibsen's famous and highly influential play *A*

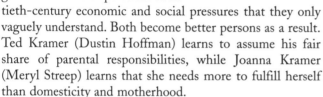

"I got the face and I got the body and I got your man."—Magdalena Soto from *I Like It Like That*

Doll's House (1879) in which Nora suggests to her husband Torvald that they might be able to start over again if "the most wonderful thing of all" were to happen. Torvald echoes those words with a question mark in his voice as Nora exits and the door shuts behind her. Ibsen did not clarify what that most wonderful thing of all might be—probably because he did not know what it was himself—and so far the modern world has not discovered it.

The ambiguous ending of *I Like It Like That* has a modern sensibility. It reflects the changes that are taking place in the Latino community as a result of exposure to the dominant Anglo culture. The problem is only emerging; it is far from being resolved. No doubt a synthesis will evolve representing a compromise between male machismo and the feminine urge for greater freedom and independence. Whatever the outcome, it will be related to the problems being ironed out by men and women of many different ethnic backgrounds in America, Europe, and elsewhere in this changing world.

Originally titled "Blackout", the title *I Like It Like That* does not do anything to help promote the film. It seems to have been derived from *As You Like It* (1599), William Shakespeare's comedy about a resourceful, adventurous woman who has a problem with gender identification. *I Like It Like That* might have done better at the box office with a title that suggested the film is about Latinos and features the latest Latino music. At any rate, it certainly would have done better with more advertising and sales promotion. It is ironic that a film dealing with big-time sales promotion would do so little to promote itself.

The production may have more success on videotape than it experienced on the big screens. It features two soundtrack albums from Columbia Records and Sony Discos. The albums represent the latest, hottest Latin American music and many popular performers who should have been given more camera attention. Lauren Veléz herself does not sing or dance in the film, nor do any of the other principals. The musical aspect of the film is limited to cameo appearances of Latino entertainers represented by Lisette's employer. Opportunities for big musical street scenes reminiscent of the film version of *West Side Story* (1961) are ignored, probably because of the same budget limitations that hampered promotion.

—*Bill Delaney*

REVIEWS

Daily Variety. May 20, 1994, p. 2.
Entertainment Weekly. October 21, 1994, p. 47.
The Hollywood Reporter. May 23, 1994, p. 6.
Los Angeles Times. October 14, 1994, p. F4.
The New York Times. October 14, 1994, p. 4.

I Love Trouble

"A thriller that charms and delights with wit, style and suspense!"—Bill Diehl, *ABC Radio Network*
"Nolte and Roberts are double fun in *Trouble*."
—*USA Today*

 Box Office Gross: $30,750,432 (October 9, 1994)

I Love Trouble is a romantic thriller by the successful writing team of Nancy Meyers and Charles Shyer, writers whose credits include *Baby Boom* (1987), *Irreconcilable Differences* (1984) and, in collaboration with Harvey Miller, *Private Benjamin* (1980). This film, like some of their previous films, is a comic look at people balancing relationships with high-powered careers, but more important it is a tribute to the romantic films of the 1930's and 1940's. *I Love Trouble* is a sexy, lighthearted escape from reality, where murder is just a news story and emotions are saved for the bedroom. It stars Nick Nolte and Julia Roberts as rival reporters investigating the same front-page story. Peter Brackett (Nolte) is a womanizing ace reporter turned best-selling author who, in a departure from his celebrity status at *The Chicago Chronicle*, is back on the newsbeat. Covering a train derailment, Brackett meets Sabrina Peterson (Roberts) in a scene that is beautifully choreographed. The camera focuses on her legs first. Peterson walks along the tracks, coolly detached from the mayhem of the disaster. As smoke and sparks from burning steel light her entrance, the camera pans upward. She catches Brackett's admiring gaze and sparks fly.

Peterson is a cub reporter for the less affluent competitor paper, *The Chicago Globe*. After Brackett patronizes Peterson at the derailment, she becomes preoccupied with showing up the arrogant Brackett and works through the night looking for more leads on the story. Finally, she stumbles upon the alcoholic past of the man who last repaired the car's couplings.

The next day, after giving a television interview about his book, Brackett finds that Peterson's paper has scooped him. There is a wonderful shot of him coming out of the studio, where a wall of television monitors are running his interview. Spying Peterson's article, he groans in humiliation as myriad images of Brackett smugly laugh in unison behind him.

> Nolte and Roberts performed many of their own stunts in *I Love Trouble*. Nolte actually wrote all the articles his character writes in the film and Roberts studied with magician Ricky Jay to learn sleight of hand, a secret skill of her character, Sabrina.

The rivalry is now in full swing, as each reporter gets banner headlines and their faces are plastered on newspaper trucks all over town. Then Brackett discovers a video taken by a father seeing off his wife and son at the train. In it, he sees an unknown man tinkering with the couplings. He realizes that they have been following the wrong story, and he suspects that the train has been sabotaged.

Meanwhile, Peterson has a lead. She gets a phone call from a boy who found something at the derailment that he thinks might be important. They plan an assignation at the abandoned bank building in which the boy lives. When she gets there, however, she finds him dead, with the letters "LD" scrawled on his outstretched hand. Now both reporters are on the same trail, and they meet in a deserted building. It is a setup, and there follows a chase that sends them up and down the elevator shaft in one of the most thrilling scenes in the film.

After this attempt on their lives, the two reporters decide to team up. The trail leads the two through the Wisconsin countryside in search of Dr. Beekman, the father of one of the train-wreck victims, only to find a burned house. After researching, they find that the home was burned a week before the train wreck and no one survived the fire. The owner, the late Dr. Beekman, was a researcher at Chess Chemical Corporation and inventor of the genetically engineered hormone LDF.

Brackett and Peterson contact Sam Smotherman (Saul Rubinek), a senator's aide from Wisconsin, to ask him about LDF. Smotherman tells them that the discovery is worth millions to Chess Chemical and, more specifically, to Wilson Chess (Dan Butler), who runs Chess Chemical. It appears that Smotherman knows Chess from Yale, where they both went to college. Later Brackett and Peterson discover that Chess and a fellow student, Ernesto Vargas, had been expelled from Yale, because they were caught in an act of arson against a professor.

The next day at Chess Chemical, the reporters accidentally meet Chess, who, in a panic, phones Ernesto to tell him the two were at the plant. After another close call with a gunman, the two reporters board a plane for Las Vegas to uncover the dead researcher's colleague, hoping to find clues as to what the gunmen are looking for. When they arrive, they notice they are being followed and duck into a wedding chapel. They don tuxedo and veil to disguise themselves and, in the process, are inadvertently declared "man and wife."

That night, they share the honeymoon suite, complete with a heart-shaped bed. Peterson has a little too much champagne and tells Brackett how much she has enjoyed working on the story with him. No sooner has she admitted, this she sees that he has betrayed her—he has gotten hold of a security card from Chess Corporation and never told her. So the next day on the plane back to Chicago, they discuss their annulment and seal it with a kiss.

Back at Chess, Brackett is about to use the security card to get into the research lab. Unbeknown to Brackett, however, Peterson has gotten herself a job as a tour guide at the company in order to get her own security card. When she sees Brackett, she has him thrown out.

"If you knew what I knew and I knew what you knew, maybe we could live through this story."—Peter Brackett from *I Love Trouble*

Upset, Brackett calls the aide, Smotherman, to tell him that Peterson is undercover at Chess and he has given up on the story. He boards a plane to return to Chicago, then tries to call Smotherman again. The operator at the state capitol gives him the extension number before transferring him. That same number has recurred throughout the investigation. Brackett, realizing that Peterson is in danger, rushes to the aid of his old rival and new bride.

Meyers and Shyer intentionally made these two characters alike in one thing—they are both amoral. As Brackett sifts through Peterson's luggage, Peterson picks Brackett's pocket. Despite their antics—or perhaps because of them—the characters remain likable.

Peterson's pickpocketing and finger-snapping cockiness add a nice edge to Julia Roberts' innate softness and add dimension to Peterson's underdeveloped character. Although Brackett's character is also shallow, it is as recognizable as an old friend—or perhaps an old stereotype. Both Roberts' and Nolte's talented acting and their relationship with the camera allow them to reveal their characters' thoughts with a glance, which helps to give their characters depth and keep the viewer's attention glued to the screen. The film also boasts some outstanding talent in Marsha Mason, Olympia Dukakis, and Robert Loggia, but their parts are so small that the viewer is left wanting more.

Meyers and Shyer have written this film with an eye to the films of another era—a more innocent time, a time when a female reporter would blush at a sexual innuendo, when a sex scene meant a kiss, and when the dog in a film would cock his head right on cue. *I Love Trouble* is a 1990's cross between *His Girl Friday* (1940) and *The Thin Man* (1934). The writers even make allusions to the former film when Peterson tells Brackett that she is not "his girl Friday." Meyers and Shyer leave another allusion in the credits, where James Rebhorn's part is listed as "The Thin Man." One is also reminded of Alfred Hitchcock's *The 39 Steps* (1935), as both films portray an uneasy alliance between the protagonists that is based on their mutual survival. In *I Love Trouble*, however, the suspense scenes lack the tension of a Hitchcock film.

The film is set in what is supposed to be the early 1990's, but in the filmmakers' effort to retain the look of the Golden Age of Hollywood, the Chicago street scenes are sterile enough to have been done in a studio. In the film's "present," the streets of Chicago are immaculate, without a trace of urban squalor, and the pedestrians are all beautiful people dressed in designer togs. The reporters themselves are dressed more like television anchors than newswriters, and although Roberts looks gorgeous, the viewer is left with a problem of credibility.

The appeal of this film lies primarily in the nostalgical-

CREDITS

Peter Brackett: Nick Nolte
Sabrina Peterson: Julia Roberts
Sam Smotherman: Saul Rubinek
Matt Greenfield: Robert Loggia
The Thin Man: James Rebhorn
Kim: Kelly Rutherford
Jeannie: Olympia Dukakis
Senator Gayle Robbins: Marsha Mason
Wilson Chess: Dan Butler
Justice of the peace: Eugene Levy
Rick Medwick: Charles Martin Smith
Kenny Bacon: Paul Gleason
Evans: Jane Adams
Virginia Hervey: Lisa Lu
Lindy: Nora Dunn

Released: 1994
Production: Nancy Meyers for Touchstone Pictures, in association with Caravan Pictures; released by Buena Vista Pictures
Direction: Charles Shyer
Screenplay: Nancy Meyers and Charles Shyer
Cinematography: John Lindley
Editing: Paul Hirsch, Walter Murch and Adam Bernardi
Production design: Dean Tavoularis
Art direction: Alex Tavoularis
Set decoration: Gary Fettis
Casting: Bonnie Timmermann
Sound: Richard Bryce Goodman
Costume design: Susan Becker
Stunt coordination: Jack Gill
Music: David Newman
MPAA rating: PG
Running time: 123 minutes

ly romantic relationship between the reporters and the chemistry between the actors. Peterson and Brackett play tricks and outwit each other in scenes that are as charming as an old Spencer Tracy/Katharine Hepburn film. Yet, although Peterson's health-conscious jabs at Brackett and his "real men eat mayonnaise" retorts are beguiling, they lack the wit of the films the writers are imitating.

In an effort to keep the film modern, the writers have Peterson inform Brackett that she is a streetwise, competitive woman of the 1990's, and one is almost convinced. Yet Brackett's response confirms the viewer's belief that he is a man transported through time, full- length trench coat and all—straight out of 1940. This is the major flaw of the film. The anachronisms that pervade the film create an unreality that diminishes the tension of the thriller. Nothing bad can happen to the characters, because they are not quite believable in the first place.

The film is enriched by the musical score of David Newman, whose most recent work was the score for *The Flintstones* (reviewed in this volume), and the stylized cam-

era work of John Lindley, whose credits include *Field of Dreams* (1989) and *Sleeping with the Enemy* (1991).

I Love Trouble is a glamorous, beautifully filmed motion picture, with just enough thrills to make it a thriller. It is a sexy, carefree break from the real world—as playful as a summer romance. Yet this romance is from a summer long past.

—*Diane Hatch-Avis*

REVIEWS

Chicago Tribune. June 26, 1994, Sec. 2, p. 3.
Entertainment Weekly. July 8, 1994, p. 34.
The Hollywood Reporter. June 27, 1994, p. 6.
Los Angeles Times. June 29, 1994, p. F1.
The New York Times. June 29, 1994, p. B1.
Newsweek. July 4, 1994, p. 71.
Time. July 4, 1994, p. 73.
Variety. June 27, 1994, p. 2.

I Only Want You to Love Me

A young married man, Peter (Vitus Zeplichal), falls prey to modern-day consumerism when he continues to spend beyond his means in a misguided effort to buy his wife's affection with gifts.

REVIEWS

The Advocate. April 19, 1994, p. 74.
Boston Globe. July 29, 1994, p. 52.
Christian Science Monitor. April 15, 1994, p. 12.
Los Angeles Times. June 2, 1994, p. F5.
The New York Times. April 15, 1994, p. C10.

CREDITS

Peter: Vitus Zeplichal
Erika: Elke Aberle
Mother: Ernie Mangold
Father: Alexander Allerson
Grandmother: Johanna Hofer

Origin: Germany
Released: 1976
Production: Peter Marthesheimer for Bavaria Atelier GmbH and Westdeutscher Rundfunk (WDR); released by Leisure Time Features
Direction: Rainer Werner Fassbinder
Screenplay: Rainer Werner Fassbinder; based on the book *Life Sentence*, by Klaus Antes and Christine Erhardt
Cinematography: Michael Ballhaus
Editing: Liesgret Schmitt-Klink
Production design: Kurt Raab
Music: Peer Raben
MPAA rating: no listing
Running time: 104 minutes

I'll Do Anything

"From the creator of *Terms of Endearment* and *Broadcast News*"—Movie tagline

"*I'll Do Anything* is a lovely, wayward comedy in high Jim Brooks style, with all his pinwheeling wit and edgy ruminations."—Richard Corliss, *Time*

"...wickedly funny and surprisingly touching."
—*Newsweek*

"Pure joy! Funny and witty, warm and real. You should do anything to see *I'll Do Anything*."
—*NBC-TV*

"Two thumbs up!"—*Siskel & Ebert*

 Box Office Gross: $10,163,951 (February 27, 1994)

The comedy *I'll Do Anything* opens in 1980 Los Angeles, where Matt Hobbs (Nick Nolte), an up-and-coming actor, has just lost in his bid for an Emmy Award. As a sort of consolation prize, he agrees to wed his girlfriend, Beth (Tracey Ullman). Unfortunately, Matt's career goes into a slump, and by the late 1980's, Beth has moved to Georgia, taking with her their young daughter, Jeannie (Whittni Wright).

Matt's career continues to slip until he makes contact with Cathy Breslow (Joely Richardson), a development script reader at Popcorn Pictures. She just happens to know about a casting call at the studio and invites Matt to show up. While Matt fails to get the part from the studio's producer, Burke Adler (Albert Brooks), he does, however, find employment as Burke's temporary chauffeur. This job not only keeps him in touch with possible acting jobs at the studio but also allows him to become better acquainted and fall in love with Cathy.

Then one day Beth calls Matt to tell him he must take six-year-old Jeannie for a three-week visit. When he arrives in Georgia to pick her up, however, he finds that Beth is about to be taken to prison because her boyfriend was "financially imaginative with a pension fund." Jeannie is coming to live with Matt, and Matt does not have a clue how to handle this new situation. In fact, Jeannie proves to be a nightmare for Matt. She is undisciplined and throws tantrums to get her way, even to the point of slapping herself during an argument with her father to win sympathy from those around her.

I'll Do Anything was originally filmed as a musical.

Matt gets some advice from the understanding Nan Mulhanney (Julie Kavner), a movie pollster who reports to the neurotic Burke on how his films fair with preview audiences. Incredibly, Nan also is in love with the producer even though they are complete opposites. Burke is insincere, self-centered, and artificial, while Nan is down-to-earth and honest. She is even "forced" to tell the truth because of a combination of drugs and vitamins she is taking that act as a truth serum.

When Cathy is given the opportunity to develop her dream script (a remake of Frank Capra's 1936 classic *Mr. Deeds Goes to Town*), she wants Matt to play Longfellow Deeds. Matt takes Jeannie with him to the studio, and while he does a screen test, she lands a job on a television sitcom from only one reading. Although Matt fails to get the part (mostly because of Cathy's betrayal of him under pressure from her peers), he now finds himself with a new role: learning to be a father at the same time he is mentoring his daughter on how to be an actress. Her success will become his success.

I'll Do Anything was supposed to have been Columbia's big Christmas picture for 1993, but its release was delayed for two months. The problem was that the film originally was a musical. With songs by Prince, Carole King, and Sinead O'Connor and a dance number choreographed by Twyla Tharp, and in an uncanny reflection of the film's own plot, the film fared terribly with preview audiences. Consequently, director/writer James L. Brooks had to rethink his project. The result is probably Hollywood's first non-musical musical. With the disastrous walkout of most of the preview audience, Brooks decided to junk the music (with the exception of one Carole King song delivered by Whittni Wright) and reshoot scenes in order to make the film comprehensible with the tunes missing.

To Brooks's credit, if one did not know the film was originally a musical, one might never guess it. The resulting picture is not only coherent but touching, gently satirical, and intelligent. If there is any residual effect of the missing music it might be that the story seems just a little too flat in spots. One surmises that emotional highs and lows, as is usual for musicals, might have been presented in the now-missing songs, and even Brooks's sharp dialogue and reshot scenes could not compensate for the passions edited out with the music. This is not to say that the unassuming comedy that is left is less than enjoyable to watch.

It is still a finely crafted piece of work with solid scenes, clever dialogue, compassionate characters, and terrific ensemble acting.

Although some elements of the plot are fairly predictable (Will Jeannie be able to cry sitcom tears on demand?), and some scenes are slower than others (watching Matt turn into the caring father), when the film focuses on the world of Hollywood and the offices of Popcorn Pictures, Brooks's keen insight into the insecurity of actors and the arrogance of those in power zeroes in with a cynicism that balances the parts that are sometimes too sentimental. Those characteristics that made Brooks' 1983 *Terms of Endearment* and 1987 *Broadcast News* award winners and that won for him thirty-two Emmy Award nominations for his television shows such as *The Simpsons*, *The Mary Tyler Moore Show*, and *Taxi* also shine through in this film: intelligent plots, sharp dialogue, and complicated yet attractive characters.

"I'm here for the same reason that 86 percent of older women loved *Beauty and the Beast*."—Nan Mulhanney in *I'll Do Anything*.

CREDITS

Matt Hobbs: Nick Nolte
Jeannie Hobbs: Whittni Wright
Burke Adler: Albert Brooks
Nan Mulhanney: Julie Kavner
Cathy Breslow: Joely Richardson
Beth Hobbs: Tracey Ullman
Male D Person: Jeb Brown
Female D Person: Joely Fisher
John Earl McAlpine: Ian McKellen
Assistant director: Joseph Malone
Audience research captain: Harry Shearer
Makeup: Rosie O'Donnell
Ground Zero hero: Woody Harrelson

Released: 1994
Production: James L. Brooks and Polly Platt for Gracie Films; released by Columbia Pictures
Direction: James L. Brooks
Screenplay: James L. Brooks
Cinematography: Michael Ballhaus
Editing: Richard Marks
Production design: Stephen J. Lineweaver
Art direction: Bill Brzeski
Set decoration: Cheryl Carasik
Casting: Paula Herold
Sound: David M. Kelson
Costume design: Marlene Stewart
Music: Hans Zimmer
MPAA rating: PG-13
Running time: 115 minutes

In *I'll Do Anything*, the characters and those gifted actors who bring them to life are what really shine. Nick Nolte's Matt is apprehensive in his dealings with his acting jobs and his daughter while also being earnest and forceful when he has to defend his craft and his decisions. Joely Richardson's Cathy is both idealistic about her standards and ambitious about her professional goals, but at the same time, when challenged, she cowardly betrays a man she says she loves. In other words, Brooks's characters are complex and human while never becoming unnatural or illogical.

Nick Nolte once again proves that he is more than merely a solid character actor. When his Matt is rejected for the role he had counted on, the audience feels his rejection. Nolte can create very likable characters, and to his credit, even after being voted *People Weekly*'s "Sexiest Man of the Year," one can understand how, in the film, Popcorn studio executives reject him because they fear he is not sexy enough.

Whittni Wright's Jeannie is temperamental and manipulative, difficult and scheming (in other words, a natural actress). Incredibly, she was only five years old when shooting the film and delivering this solid performance.

In this film, however, even the peripheral actors are standouts. Julie Kavner's Nan and Albert Brooks's gravelly-voiced Burke play off each other to great effect. In the small role as Beth, Tracey Ullman once again shows that she is a chameleon who never plays the same character twice. When Beth delivers her good-bye admonitions to Jeannie, she positively steals the scene.

Nick Nolte as Matt and Whittni Wright as Jeannie in *I'll Do Anything*. Copyright © 1994 Columbia Pictures Industries Inc. All Rights Reserved. Courtesy of Columbia Pictures.

As an insider's view of Hollywood, *I'll Do Anything* may not be as hard-hitting or shrewd as Robert Altman's *The Player* (1992), but as a compassionate comedy about people struggling to make the right decisions in their lives, it is eminently watchable.

—*Beverley Bare Buehrer*

REVIEWS

Chicago Tribune. February 4, 1994, p. 7A.
Entertainment Weekly. February 4, 1994, p. 36.
The Hollywood Reporter. January 31, 1994, p. 6.
Los Angeles Times. February 4, 1994, p. F1.
The New York Times. February 4, 1994, p. B1.
Newsweek. February 7, 1994, p. 61.
Time. January 31, 1994, p. 103.
USA Today. February 4, 1994, p. D1.
Variety. January 31, 1994, p. 2.
The Village Voice. February 8, 1994, p. 53.

Imaginary Crimes

"Magnificent! An amazing story. Don't miss this heartwarming and inspiring movie."—Ron Brewington, *American Urban Radio Networks*

"Emotionally luminous, poignant, richly textured. Handsomely and involvingly acted."—Jay Carr, *Boston Globe*

"Harvey Keitel is astounding. *Imaginary Crimes* will capture your heart. Don't miss it."—Jules Peimer, *WNWK Radio*

"Fairuza Balk's performance is absolutely stunning."—Jeff Craig, *Sixty Second Preview*

"A classic. Excellent performances and brilliant direction."—Paul Wunder, *WBAI Radio*

"Harvey Keitel is richly rewarding. *Imaginary Crimes* has a big heart."—Rex Reed, *New York Observer*

Box Office Gross: $70,701 (October 30, 1994)

Watching *Imaginary Crimes* is like sitting next to someone as they leaf through their old photo albums and tell you the stories behind the images. In this case, that someone is Sonya Weiler (Fairuza Balk), whose world-weary voice-over connects scenes from her troubled past. She is in the process of trying to make sense of that past, jettison the pain, and, finally unburdened, move on. The memories that tear Sonya apart most involve her father, Ray (Harvey Keitel). She is torn because he was capable of actions that elicited feelings of

both tender love and gnawing despair in her. Sonya remembers that her father used to make regular trips to the corner store (usually for booze), and how honored and grown-up she felt when he asked her to come along one icy winter night. She recalls his vitality and unlimited optimism, his advice to always "buck the wind" when life gets stormy, and the exuberant duet they sang of "Don't Fence Me In" on the way home that night. She also has warm memories of Ray taking care of her when she was ill. Lovely memories like these are inseparably intertwined in her mind with others far less pleasant.

As far back as Sonya can remember, life was dominated by her father's powerful presence and roaring ambition to find a way to get rich or, more to the point, get rich quickly. He was always coming home to their basement apartment and announcing that he had found the invention or venture which ensured that their millions, and his wife, Valery's (Kelly Lynch) dream house, were "only a technicality away." Whether it was a metal detector called "Finders Keepers" ("...so simple to use, even a child can strike it rich!") or a process to restore the nap to old serge suits, Ray always described the endeavor to potential investors as the chance of a lifetime, one that comes along "once in a blue moon." None of them ever panned out. Whether Ray was conning other people, himself, or both, the fact was that his schemes only succeeded in adding to the family's economic instability and creating an emotionally insecure atmosphere that worsened with the bursting of each bubble.

Valery tried to be hopeful and cheerful when she would hear Ray's newest plans, but it became increasingly hard to be optimistic when her hopes had been dashed countless times before by other "foolproof" plans. She tried to keep her worries at bay by concentrating hard on games of solitaire and trips to the movies. One night at the movies Valery won some plates in a raffle, and Sonya remembers looking up at Valery's beaming face as her mother revelled in this small but welcome and needed injection of delight into her life. The only time that Valery seemed at ease was when she, Sonya and little Greta (Elisabeth Moss) vacationed in her native Canada. Ironically, it is during one of these vacations that Valery learns that she has cancer, and when she dies, Ray finds himself ill- prepared to assume the role of sole, hands-on parent to his two shaken little girls.

"I wonder if it's possible that the wish to love can be stronger than the need to hate." Sonya in *Imaginary Crimes*

For "The Three Little Weilers," as Ray merrily calls his family, life begins to revolve around his irresponsible pursuits in an even more focused way. His daughters often find themselves deflecting phone calls and visits from the landlord, investors and creditors who demand to see him. Sonya is forced to attend a rich girl's party so that Ray can stop by and lure in investors. It is during this time that the adolescent Sonya begins to try to make sense of her family's past and present by writing stories for English class, and her nurturing teacher (Vincent D'Onofrio) encourages her to continue her studies in college to become a writer. At long last, Sonya has something self-affirming to counter the devastation of Ray's critical barbs about the books she likes to read, the way she takes care of Greta, and even her desire to go to college. Turning the negatives from her past into something positive and successful seems to be a liberating experience for Sonya.

When Ray wants to skip town with his daughters and head for Reno, Sonya grabs Greta, gets out of Ray's car, and refuses to go with him. When she springs from the car, it is as if Sonya has found the strength to finally get off of a harrowing roller coaster ride she has been trapped on for years. Ray goes on to Reno, but returns to beg a judge to reunite his daughters after Greta is taken away by Social Services. He joins his daughters at Sonya's graduation from prep school, after which he is carted off to prison. One winter, years after his parole, Ray goes up into the mountains, and is found dead by a hunter the following spring.

Anyone viewing *Imaginary Crimes* will sympathize with Sonya's confusion and heartache as she tries to make peace with the memory of her complex father. She tries to see him for what he was, but what he seems to have been changes with each remembrance. Sonya wants to remember the loving, tender moments, but she wonders if "a con man was capable of real love." She feels guilty about the rage she feels towards him because she wonders if he was actually incapable of being the trustworthy, reliable father she wishes he had been. "Now," she says near the end of the film, "I wonder if it's possible that the wish to love can be stronger than the need to hate." One gets the feeling that, in the end, she will embrace her father's memory, and, in forgiving him, free herself.

Imaginary Crimes was made on a small budget by Hollywood's standards (under $10 million) and took in approximately $1 million in limited release. Reviews were predominately positive, with specific praise going to Keitel and Balk in this well-cast film. Director Anthony Drazan, whose *Zebrahead* (1992) won the Filmmakers Trophy at the Sundance Film Festival, continues to show promise. The attention to detail in set decoration and costume design is also noteworthy, as is John J. Campbell's cinematography. *Imaginary Crimes* is based on the 1982 novel by Sheila Ballantyne, which in turn was based on the difficult early years of the author's life. "I wrote it as a kind of expiation," she has said, "a way to come to terms with my own past." In her book, the negative side of Ray's personality is even more distasteful. There were other

CREDITS

Ray Weiler: Harvey Keitel
Sonya: Fairuza Balk
Valery: Kelly Lynch
Mr. Webster: Vincent D'Onofrio
Abigale Tate: Diane Baker
Jarvis: Chris Penn
Margaret: Amber Benson
Greta: Elisabeth Moss
Eddie: Seymour Cassel
Ginny Rucklehaus: Annette O'Toole

Released: 1994
Production: James G. Robinson for Morgan Creek; released by Warner Bros.
Direction: Anthony Drazan
Screenplay: Kristine Johnson and Davia Nelson; based on the book by Sheila Ballantyne
Cinematography: John J. Campbell
Editing: Elizabeth Kling
Production design: Joseph T. Garrity
Art direction: Pat Tagliaferro
Set decoration: Dena Roth
Casting: Deborah Aquila and Jane Shannon
Sound: Mark Ulano
Costume design: Susan Lyall
Music: Stephen Endelman
MPAA rating: PG
Running time: 104 minutes

changes made in the adaptation process that make Ray, and even Sonya, more palatable, and some omissions of important material have been made at the expense of clarity. Still, what has made it to the screen in this poignant little gem has a profound and memorable glow.

—*David L. Boxerbaum*

REVIEWS

Atlanta Constitution. October 28, 1994, p. P5.
Boston Globe. September 9, 1994, p. 49.
Boston Globe. October 14, 1994, p. 62.
Chicago Tribune. October 28, 1994, p. 7O.
The Christian Science Monitor. October 21, 1994, p. 11.
Entertainment Weekly. October 28, 1994, p. 74.
Entertainment Weekly. March 24, 1995, p. 74.
Los Angeles Times. October 14, 1994, p. F12.
The New York Times. October 14, 1994, p. C16.
The New York Times. April 7, 1995, CXLIV, p. B18.
People Weekly. November 7, 1994, p.19.
TV Guide. XLIII, April 15, 1995, p. 36.
Variety. CCCLVI, September 12, 1994, p. 42.
The Washington Post. October 28, 1994, p. F6.
The Washington Post. November 3, 1994, p. D7.

Immortal Beloved

"The genius behind the music. The madness behind the man. The untold love story of Ludwig van Beethoven."—Movie tagline

"Mr. Oldman is never farfetched and he captures Beethoven....his performance combines bitterness and eccentricity with the deep romanticism that can be heard in the music."—Janet Maslin, *The New York Times*

"Lively, lusty and full of love for the subject."
—Stephen Farber, *Movieline*

"Wildly romantic evocation of the world's most romantic composer. It's not high-brow, but it's serious fun."—James Verniere, *The Boston Herald*

"An excellent film with a fascinating tale to tell."
—Leonard Maltin, *Entertainment Tonight*

 **Box Office Gross:** $582,875 (January 2, 1995)

Gary Oldman performing as Beethoven in *Immortal Beloved.* Copyright © 1994 Paramount Pictures. All Rights Reserved.

Film biographies of famous people are rarely completely satisfying, especially when the subjects are artists or intellectuals. Such screen treatments of real lives have traditionally been sentimentalized, bowdlerized, and superficial. Writer-director Bernard Rose's portrait of the great Romantic composer Ludwig van Beethoven (1770-1827) attempts to provide impressions of the great man's life and career without slavish regard for the facts and succeeds surprisingly well as an intelligent entertainment.

Immortal Beloved opens with the death of Beethoven (Gary Oldman) in Vienna and the discovery by his secretary, Anton Felix Schindler (Jeroen Krabbé), of a letter leaving his estate to someone identified only as his "immortal beloved." Schindler's attempt to discover the woman's identity evokes the structure of Orson Welles' *Citizen Kane* (1941), wherein the mysterious "Rosebud," Charles Foster Kane's dying word, played a similar role. All Schindler knows for certain, after an interview with hotelier Nanette Streicher (Miriam Margolyes), is that Beethoven went berserk after a rendezvous with a veiled woman in a Karlsbad, Germany, hotel.

CREDITS

Ludwig van Beethoven: Gary Oldman
Anton Felix Schindler: Jeroen Krabbé
Anna Marie Erdödy: Isabella Rossellini
Johanna Reiss van Beethoven: Johanna Ter Steege
Julia Guicciardi: Valeria Golino
Karl van Beethoven: Marco Hofschneider
Karl van Beethoven (as a child): Matthew North
Casper Anton Carl van Beethoven: Christopher Fulford
Nikolaus Johann van Beethoven: Gerard Horan
Nanette Streicher: Miriam Margolyes
Clemens Metternich: Barry Humphries
Therese Obermayer: Alexandra Pigg
Franz Josef Guicciardi: Luigi Diberti
Jakob Hotscevar: Michael Culkin
Karl Holz: Donal Gibson

Origin: Great Britain
Released: 1994
Production: Bruce Davey for Icon; released by Columbia Pictures
Direction: Bernard Rose
Screenplay: Bernard Rose
Cinematography: Peter Suschitzky
Editing: Dan Rae
Production design: Jiri Hlupy
Art direction: John Myhre and Olga Rosenfelderova
Casting: Marion Dougherty
Sound: Peter Glossop
Sound design and supervision: Nigel Holland
Costume design: Maurizio Millenotti
Music direction: Sir Georg Solti
Music supervision: John Stronach
MPAA rating: R
Running time: 123 minutes

Looking at Beethoven's life in flashback, Rose focuses on two of several women with whom the composer had affairs: young Julia Guicciardi (Valeria Golino), an Italian countess, and the widow Anna Marie Erdödy (Isabella Rossellini), a Hungarian countess. That neither is particularly interesting is a major flaw in Rose's interpretation of Beethoven's love life. There should be at least a modicum of balance among Rose's three candidates for Beethoven's immortal beloved. Yet the third candidate is an unlikely choice.

Rose presents several scenes of Beethoven's strongly denouncing the character and morals of Johanna Reiss (Johanna Ter Steege) both before and after she marries his brother, Casper (Christopher Fulford). Ludwig sees Johanna

Immortal Beloved was shot mostly around Prague. The music was provided by the London Symphony Orchestra conducted by George Solti.

as a sluttish peasant unworthy of his beloved brother, and his harangues contribute to Casper's early death. How could such a woman be Beethoven's secret passion? Rose lays out his case slowly and carefully, presenting the evidence as Schindler finds it, jumping back and forth between periods of the composer's life.

Half of *Immortal Beloved* is devoted to Beethoven's war with his sister-in-law over the custody of her son, Karl (Matthew North), and Beethoven's effort to make him into a piano virtuoso. Beethoven wins his custody case by convincing the court that Johanna is an unsuitable mother. He has less luck with Karl's musical education; the boy is clearly a mediocre pianist. Beethoven's refusal to accept the truth drives Karl to attempt suicide.

Immortal Beloved succeeds in part by avoiding the clichés of its genre. It is neither an overheated melodrama like Ken Russell's *The Music Lovers* (1971), *Mahler* (1974), or *Lisztomania* (1975), nor a pretentious spectacle like *Amadeus* (1984), from Peter Shaffer's play about Wolfgang Amadeus Mozart, nor a reverential bore like *A Song to Remember* (1945), with Cornel Wilde blandly impersonating Frédéric Chopin. Rose does not sentimentalize Beethoven as either a tortured artist or a noble soul, nor does he try to understand his subject by reducing him to a psychological case study.

Realizing the limitations of the medium, Rose also does not try to explain the composer's genius. He avoids the trap Richard Attenborough fell into with *Chaplin* (1992) in emphasizing the lack of domestic bliss at the expense of the artist's work. Rose's Beethoven is a highly complex man who created beautiful music despite a chaotic personality. Rose merges the man and the work by underscoring the sensuality of the music considered dangerously erotic in its time and by showing how it is a natural outgrowth of the composer's romantic spirit.

Rose has been criticized by Beethoven experts for identifying Johanna as the immortal beloved. Sieghard Brandenburg, editor of a forthcoming edition of Beethoven correspondence, claims she was in prison during the time Rose has her meeting the composer in Karlsbad. Biographer Maynard Solomon says the immortal beloved was Antonie Brentano, the wife of one of Beethoven's friends and supporters. Antonie, with whom Ludwig had a seemingly platonic relationship and who is not even mentioned in the film, is the candidate put forth by most Beethoven authorities. Rose goes even further by claiming that Karl was the composer's son: Johanna is pregnant when she marries Casper. Such speculation may irritate the purists, but it adds flavor to Rose's romantic mystery and poignance to the failure of Ludwig's relationship with the boy.

Rose has also been criticized by the Beethoven establishment for having the composer's legendary deafness occur earlier than it apparently did and for making him completely deaf. Such changes can be defended as artistic license to underscore Beethoven's isolation as both musician and man. One of the most moving scenes is his pathetic effort to conduct an orchestra that he cannot hear: Anna Marie steps in to rescue him from a laughing audience. As his music becomes the art he can create but not enjoy, Beethoven's uniqueness and courage stand out.

Immortal Beloved represents a major leap forward in Rose's skills as writer and director. His first film, *Paperhouse* (1988), was an original but finally unsatisfying look at the pain of sensitive, imaginative children, and his second, *Candyman* (1992), despite some visual flourishes, was a gruesome horror film. *Immortal Beloved* is better written and paced than the earlier films, which meander at times. It is consistently striking visually. The shot of Beethoven resting his head on a piano while playing the "Moonlight Sonata" and seeming to caress his music with his flesh, intellect, and spirit is exceptionally moving.

While Valeria Golino makes her silly Julia too inconsequential and Isabella Rossellini plays Anna Marie as too proud, almost cold, Johanna Ter Steege conveys Johanna's mixed feelings about the composer with great skill. Ter Steege, who played Vincent van Gogh's mistress in Robert Altman's *Vincent and Theo* (1990), has a pale beauty recalling the depictions of peasant women in Flemish paintings. She can look both coarse and ethereal, transforming herself seemingly effortlessly. When Johanna is so transported by the beauty of Beethoven's Ninth Symphony that she cannot keep herself from forgiving him, Ter Steege glows with passion and compassion. Although Jeroen Krabbé lends his usual dependable support as the secretary and Matthew North effectively conveys the confusion of the young Karl, Marco Hofschneider plays the adult Karl as a lightweight nonentity.

With all its virtues, *Immortal Beloved* could not have succeeded without the right actor playing Beethoven. At first, Gary Oldman seems an odd choice because he looks nothing like the composer. In most of his previous roles, Oldman epitomized the modern alienated hipster or punk. It is at first difficult to accept the screen incarnation of Sid Vicious, from *Sid and Nancy* (1986), as a nineteenth century German sophisticate, but Oldman and Rose uncover the

> "It is the power of music to carry one into the mental state of the composer. The listener has no choice. It is like hypnotism."
> —Beethoven in *Immortal Beloved*

pain and anger inside the composer. Rose blames the deafness on childhood beatings by Beethoven's father.

Despite Oldman's inclination to seize upon his character's perversities, his Beethoven is as tender as he is vindictive. Oldman is even convincing in one of the most demanding parts of such musical roles: He actually seems to be playing the piano pieces performed on the sound track by Emmanuel Ax and Murray Perahia. Because of Oldman's astonishing range and his ability to reveal the humanity inside monsters, as he did in *Bram Stoker's Dracula* (1992), there does not seem to be any limits to this magnificent actor's skills.

Rose and Oldman are aided in their achievement, of course, by the beauty of Beethoven's music, as conducted by Sir Georg Solti. All the elements of *Immortal Beloved* come together at the end when, during the first performance of the Ninth Symphony, the composer remembers, while the "Ode to Joy" is playing, escaping as a boy from his brutal father by running into the woods and throwing himself into a pond. As Beethoven gazes skyward to drink in the stars, Rose switches perspectives to show the boy surrounded by the reflection of the stars in the water. Although this merger of heaven, earth, and art is hokey, it is nevertheless effective, like *Immortal Beloved* itself.

—Michael Adams

REVIEWS

Boston Globe. January 6, 1995, p. 53.
The Christian Science Monitor. LXXXVII, December 16, 1994, p. 11.
Daily Variety. December 12, 1994, p. 13.
Entertainment Weekly. January 20, 1995, p. 34.
The Hollywood Reporter. December 12, 1994, p. 15.
Los Angeles Times. December 16, 1994, p. F6.
New York. XXVIII, January 9, 1995, p. 48.
The New York Times. December 16, 1994, p. B1.
People Weekly. XLIII, January 16, 1995, p. 19.
Rolling Stone. January 26, 1995, p. 66.
San Francisco Chronicle. December 16, 1994, p. C3.
USA Today. December 16, 1994, p. D5.
The Village Voice. XXXIX, December 20, 1994, p. 65.
The Wall Street Journal. December 29, 1994, p. A8.
The Washington Post. January 6, 1995, p. WW37.

The Importance of Being Earnest

This version of Oscar Wilde's classic comedy of manners sets the action in 1990's England and stars an all-African American cast. The plot revolves around two women who believe they can only love a man named Earnest, and two men who each have assumed that name.

REVIEWS

Variety. CCCXLV, November 4, 1991, p. 61.

CREDITS

Algernon: Wren T. Brown
Jack: Daryl Roach
Gwendolyn: Chris Calloway
Cecily: Lanei Chapman
Lady Bracknell: Ann Weldon
Dr. Chausible: Brock Peters
Miss Prism: C. C. H. Pounder
Lane: Obba Babatunde
Merriman: Barbara Isaacs
Butler: Sylvester Hayes

Released: 1991
Production: Nancy Carter Crow for Eclectic Concepts/Paco Global
Direction: Kurt Baker
Screenplay: Kurt Baker and Peter Andrews; based on the play by Oscar Wilde
Cinematography: Mark Angell and Joseph Wilmond Calloway
Editing: Tracey Alexander
Art design: Lennie Barin
Set design: Toni Singman
Sound: Romeo Williams
Music: Roger Hamilton Spotts
MPAA rating: no listing
Running time: 123 minutes

In Custody (Hifazaat)

"Rich and Enticing [Mr. Merchant] shows himself to be a passionate, accomplished director."
—Caryn James, *The New York Times*

A small-town professor in India, Deven (Om Puri), embarks on a much-anticipated in-depth interview with the greatest living Urdu poet, Nur (Shashi Kapoor), only to encounter an overweight has-been surrounded by greedy "admirers" and a shrewish wife, in this comic drama. The film is the directorial debut of distinguished producer Ismail Merchant. It is the winner of the Best Picture award from the National Film Award of India. Shashi Kapoor, who plays the aging poet in the film, appeared thirty years ago in another Merchant Ivory production *Shakespeare Wallah*. The poems recited are by Faiz Ahmed Faiz. The filming of Nur's house was shot at Gauhar Mahal at Bhopal Lake, the palace of female ruler of Bhopal, Nawab Khudesia Begum. Other palaces of the Begums were used for other locations, including one still belonging to a direct descendent of the Begums.

REVIEWS

Atlanta Constitution. August 19, 1994, p. P7.
Boston Globe. July 1, 1994, p. 48.
Chicago Tribune. August 19, 1994, p. 7L.
Entertainment Weekly. April 14, 1995, p. 72.
Los Angeles Magazine. XXXIX, May 1994, p. 167.
Los Angeles Times. May 4, 1994, p. F4.
The New York Times. April 15, 1994, p. C6.
Playboy. XLI, May 1994, p. 20.
TV Guide. XLIII, April 1, 1995, p. 39.
USA Today. May 3, 1994, p. D4.
The Wall Street Journal. April 14, 1994, p. A12.
The Washington Post. April 30, 1994, p. G2.

CREDITS

Nur: Shashi Kapoor
Deven: Om Puri
Imtiaz Begum: Shabana Azmi
Sarla: Neena Gupta
Safiya Begum: Sushma Seth
Siddiqui: Ajay Sahni
Murad: Tinnu Anand
Jain: Prayag Raj

Origin: Great Britain
Released: 1993
Production: Wahid Chowhan for Merchant Ivory Productions, in association with Channel 4 Films; released by Sony Pictures Classics
Direction: Ismail Merchant
Screenplay: Anita Desai and Shahrukh Husain; based on the novel by Desai
Cinematography: Larry Pizer
Editing: Roberto Silvi
Production design: Suresh Sawant
Sound: Mike Shoring and John Hayward
Costume design: Lovleen Bains
Music: Zakir Hussain and Ustad Sultan Khan
MPAA rating: PG
Running time: 123 minutes

AWARDS AND NOMINATIONS

National Film Award of India: Best Picture

In the Army Now

"America, sleep tight. The safety of the free world is in his hands."—Movie tagline

Box Office Gross: $28,881,266 (January 2, 1995)

Whatever one wishes to say about slacker comedian Pauly Shore, he certainly deserves credit for knowing his niche and sticking to it. That could be the explanation for the success of this comedian who is the idol of many young people due to his MTV show, comedy club appearances and recent film successes. For some, he is hilarious. For others, he is irritating. Everyone can agree that he knows his audience and gives them what they want: silly jokes and a simple story where the

"I'm gonna be all over your butt." "Is that a promise?"—Bones Conway 's response to a female drill sergeant's threat.

CREDITS

Bones Conway: Pauly Shore
Jack Kaufman: Andy Dick
Christine Jones: Lori Petty
Fred Ostroff: David Alan Grier
Sergeant Stern: Esai Morales
Sergeant Ladd: Lynn Whitfield
Sergeant Williams: Art LaFleur
Gabriella: Fabiana Udenio

Released: 1994
Production: Michael Rotenberg for Hollywood Pictures; released by Buena Vista Pictures
Direction: Daniel Petrie, Jr.
Screenplay: Ken Kaufman, Stu Krieger, Fax Bahr, Adam Small, and Daniel Petrie, Jr.; based on a story by Steve Zacharias, Jeff Buhai, and Robbie Fox
Cinematography: William Wages
Editing: O. Nicholas Brown
Production design: Craig Stearns
Art direction: Randy Moore
Set design: Thomas Reta
Set decoration: Ellen Totleben
Casting: Mary Jo Slater and Steve Brooksbank
Sound: Mark Hopkins McNabb
Costume design: Michael T. Boyd
Music: Robert Folk
MPAA rating: PG
Running time: 91 minutes

laziest guy always wins. Beginning with *Encino Man* (1992) Shore has discovered success in the movies. *In the Army Now* begins a series of films in which Pauly takes on hallowed American institutions: in this film it is the Army, in *Son-in-law* (1993) it is the American family, and in *Jury Duty* (1995) it is the American justice system. Each time his egocentric, oafish character ends up saving the very system he mocks.

Following a well-worn path, *In the Army Now* is a retread of the familiar plot found in *No Time for Sergeants* (1958), *Stripes* (1981), *Private Benjamin* (1980), and others. It is the story of Bones (Shore) and his hapless sidekick Jack (Andy Dick), who, dreaming of opening their own electronics store, discover that the Army Reserves will pay them to learn a trade and be available for the unlikely event of a war. They enter boot camp and are immediately horrified to discover that their long, rocker-dude hairstyles will be shaved. This sequence is a lot of fun, perhaps because the haircuts actually happen right before the audience's eyes. Eventually, the guys end up in the water purification unit of the Reserves, thinking that it will be easy. After a tough boot camp, they are called to active duty in Africa, and after several mishaps in the middle of the desert, end up saving the day for the American Army.

It is hard to say whether Shore is effective in his foray into territory covered so well by predecessors Goldie Hawn and Bill Murray. People that like Shore will think it is funny when he jumps up and down in his underwear on leopard sheets, or when he and Jack have an impossibly difficult time putting up a tent. The whole idea of his shiftless character seems to be to laugh at it, and Shore is admittedly funny when he says, "fortunately, I'm too shallow to be bummed out for long." But unfortunately, Shore's funny lines and clever moments are few and far between. Interestingly, as in his other films, Shore has several ham-fisted jokes about how his character is not gay. These, combined with his put-downs of the Arab characters, are in keeping with his character but are beneath even Shore's brand of humor.

There are some bright spots for those who are annoyed by Shore's limp attempts at imitating the spontaneity of Robin Williams. One such bright spot is David Alan Grier (of TV's *In Living Color*), who brings class and character to his role of Fred Ostroff, the most fearful Army private in history. Grier is very funny in his screaming fits about scorpions, and in his opening explanation about why he is in the Reserves (he says, "be all that you can be...on the weekends").

Lori Petty, who stars in 1995's *Tank Girl*, brings spunk and sexuality to her role as a tough-talking private who is inexplicably attracted to Shore. Lynn Whitfield is terrific as a mean drill sergeant. Andy Dick makes a respectable sidekick: he is sort of a mixture of Ichabod Crane and Bud Abbott, and his frustration with Shore's antics provide kinship to those in the audience unmoved by Shore's witlessness. A nice attempt to make the characters similar to the characters from *The Wizard of Oz* (1939) is one of the few subtle touches. The occasional funny line, such as the commanding officer breathlessly asking into the radio, "so, you are the reservists from Glendale, California, right?" spice up the proceedings.

One of the funniest aspects of this film is the number of writers in the screenplay credits: It is written by Ken Kaufman & Stu Kreiger & Daniel Petrie, Jr. and Fox Bahr & Adam Small. It is hard to tell why so many writing teams had to wrestle with this material. It is not exactly brain surgery: take one part *Private Benjamin*, one part *Encino Man*, and the film is written.

Some will love it and some will hate it. In general, this film hits its mark. Unfortunately, its mark is low.

—*Kirby Tepper*

REVIEWS

Atlanta Constitution. August 12, 1994, p. P4.
Boston Globe. August 12, 1994, p. 51.
Chicago Tribune. August 12, 1994, p. 7B.
Chicago Tribune. August 12, 1994, p. 7D.
Entertainment Weekly. August 19, 1994, p. 42.
Entertainment Weekly. February 17, 1995, p. 68.
Los Angeles Times. August 12, 1994, p. F6.
The New York Times. August 12, 1994, p. C6.
The New York Times. August 21, 1994, Sec. 2 p. 22.
People Weekly. XLII, August 22, 1994, p. 16.
USA Today. August 12, 1994, p. D4.
Variety. CCCLVI, August 15, 1994, p. 43.
The Washington Post. August 12, 1994, p. F7.
The Washington Post. August 12, 1994, p. WW37.
The Washington Post. August 18, 1994, p. D7.

Inevitable Grace

A psychiatrist (Stephanie Knights) abuses the doctor-patient relationship when she enters into an affair with the abusive husband (Maxwell Caulfield) of a patient (Jennifer Nicholson). Directorial debut of Alex Canawati.

REVIEWS

Variety. CCCLIV, February 21, 1994, p. 42.

CREDITS

Adam Cestare: Maxwell Caulfield
Lisa Kelner: Stephanie Knights
Veronica: Jennifer Nicholson
Dr. Marcia Stevens: Tippi Hedren
Simone: Sylvia B. Suarez
Philip: John Pearson
Britt: Samantha Eggar

Released: 1994
Production: Christian Capobianco; released by Silverstar Pictures
Direction: Alex Canawati
Screenplay: Alex Canawati
Cinematography: Christian Sebaldt
Editing: Grace Valenti
Production design: Marc Rizzo
Art direction: Christina Shellen
Set decoration: Allison McVann
Sound: Sean Sullivan
Costume design: Alison Edmond
Music: Christopher Whiffen
MPAA rating: no listing
Running time: 103 minutes

The Inkwell

"1976. It was the summer when they finally found out what life was all about. It all happened at *The Inkwell*."—Movie tagline

"Summer's never been so much fun!"—Movie tagline

"Two thumbs up!"—*Siskel & Ebert*

"Big laughs."—*Chicago Sun-Times*

"*The Inkwell* is a warm, sensitive and moving coming of age film."—Paul Wunder, *WBAI Radio*

 Box Office Gross: $8,873,000 (August 14, 1994)

Coming-of-age for the American adolescent has normally been an unsettling, complex undertaking: Serious issues of personal identity, relationships, and sexuality all scream to be resolved. A few films, such as *Breaking Away* (1979), *Summer of '42* (1971), and *Diner* (1982), have captured the pain the progress of the teenager confronting these soul-searching issues. Matty Rich's *The Inkwell* attempts to depict this rite of passage for an extremely sensitive African American teenager during the mid-1970's.

Set in 1976, *The Inkwell* opens in a small, tranquil town in upstate New York with the Tate family's preparations for a two-week summer vacation on Martha's Vineyard. Teenage Drew (Larenz Tate) reluctantly accompanies his former Black Panther father, Kenny (Joe Morton), and his concerned mother, Brenda (Suzzanne Douglas), for what he fears will be two weeks of boredom at his relatives' home.

Once the Tates arrive, trouble brews among the family members. Representing the "nouveau riche," Spencer Phillips (Glynn Turman) and his wife, Frances (Vanessa Bell Calloway), live an economic level or two above the Tates, a fact which Spencer dwells on to an irritating degree. Tension fills every scene, every conversation.

While the adult brothers-in-law fight it out with words and then fists, their sons try to take advantage of the party-time atmosphere to enjoy themselves. Always moving in the fast lane, Junior Phillips (Duane Martin) serves as mentor for his naïve, conservative cousin. For his part, Drew discovers the joy—and sorrow—of romance when he develops an interest in the pert, standoffish Lauren Kelly (Jada Pinkett)—who will eventually reject him.

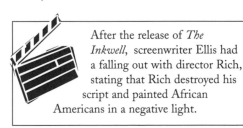
After the release of *The Inkwell*, screenwriter Ellis had a falling out with director Rich, stating that Rich destroyed his script and painted African Americans in a negative light.

Visits to local psychiatrist Dr. Wade (Phyllis Yvonne Stickney), a friend of Spencer and Frances, help Drew learn more about himself. When Lauren brushes him aside, he metaphorically lands in the arms of Heather Lee (Adrienne-Joi Johnson), to whom he has revealed the infidelity of her husband, Harold (Morris Chestnut). Following a tête-à-tête with his father and this sexual initiation rite, Drew returns home a fulfilled young man.

The Inkwell's primary focus is the psychological and sexual rite of passage of an awkward teenager who feels ill at ease with himself and his family. One can readily identify with the sensitive Drew, a sympathetic adolescent who means well. Although his family fears he may have pyromaniac tendencies following a fire in the garage, Drew appears to be a normal, misunderstood youth struggling to find out who he is in a seemingly hostile, ever-changing society.

Within Drew's immediate family, relations are strained. Father and son find themselves worlds apart, especially as Kenny fails to understand Drew's teenage angst. Drew's only comfort is in his black doll "Iago," named for the Shakespearean character in *Othello*. His father, as to be expected, finds this foolish and tries to prevent him from taking it on vacation. Only after a father-son discussion on sex does the relationship improve. The same can be said of Drew's parents' relationship, which also suffers in its evolution. A confrontation initiated by Brenda results in a clearing of the air and a discovery of the real love that exists between her and Kenny. Furthermore, once on vacation, Brenda finds her mother abrupt and condescending. There is both a psychological and an economic barrier that separates the two. A glimmer of hope for reconciliation appears as the mother finally admits to Brenda that she does love her.

At the core of the film is Drew's quest for romantic love. Naïve and uninitiated, he discovers Lauren Kelly, noted by her peers for her aloof temperament. Although Junior and his cohorts deem her unconquerable, Drew makes some progress with her. He succeeds in dating Lauren, although she maintains absolute control. Lauren discusses her fragmented family relationships and wonders with whom Drew will go when his parents are split by divorce. They agree on a second date for the Fourth of July festivities, but Drew is completely distraught when he finds Lauren making love to another young man.

Drew accidentally discovers that Heather's husband, Harold, is cheating on her. Sympathetic because of his

CREDITS

Drew Tate: Larenz Tate
Kenny Tate: Joe Morton
Brenda Tate: Suzzanne Douglas
Spencer Phillips: Glynn Turman
Frances Phillips: Vanessa Bell Calloway
Heather Lee: Adrienne-Joi Johnson
Harold Lee: Morris Chestnut
Lauren Kelly: Jada Pinkett
Junior Phillips: Duane Martin
Dr. Wade: Phyllis Yvonne Stickney

Released: 1994
Production: Irving Azoff and Guy Riedel for Touchstone Pictures, released by Buena Vista Pictures
Direction: Matty Rich
Screenplay: Tom Ricostronza and Paris Qualles
Cinematography: John L. Demps, Jr.
Editing: Quinnie Martin, Jr.
Production design: Lester Cohen
Art direction: Daniel Talpers
Set decoration: Karen Wiesel
Casting: Chemin Sylvia Bernard
Sound: Robert L. Warner
Costume design: Ceci
Music: Terence Blanchard
MPAA rating: R
Running time: 112 minutes

recent experience, Drew helps Heather. Both burned by rejection, Heather and Drew turn to each other, a slight twist in a conventional plot.

In the end, Drew experiences only ephemeral love in his vacation world. Yet he returns to his everyday life not only satisfied with his first sexual encounter but also comforted by the knowledge that there is a solid basis of love in his parents' relationship. The lessons Drew learns on vacation put him that much farther on the road to adulthood.

One obvious weakness to the script, however, is the belief that a first sexual experience marks the central and unique rite of passage for a teenager. The initial sexual encounter with the older Heather marks this transition for Drew. There are, however, many other complex and fundamental concerns for a teenager that dominate his or her evolution, primarily concerning self-identity and relationships.

Another level of discourse can be found in the sociopolitical structure of the characters. Situated just a few years after the tumultuous political science of the late 1960's and early 1970's, *The Inkwell* provides a diverse range of African

"[Rich] said my script wasn't black enough. I think it wasn't stereotypically black enough."—novelist Trey Ellis speaking about *The Inkwell* director Matty Rich (*Entertainment Weekly*, April 29, 1994)

American experiences. The Tates are a middle-class family from upstate New York. Kenny's past is linked to the struggles of the Black Panther party, and he still carries some of the political fire inside him.

This is in total opposition to the Phillips family. Spencer's struggles are more economic. He is now at the top, part of the "nouveau riche" in African American society. Symbolic for him is "the inkwell," the black area of Martha's Vineyard, which shows that blacks can find a place among the affluent in American society. Dr. Wade, however, reinforces the characters' African roots. Her dress as well as the artifacts surrounding her invite Drew to become reacquainted with his heritage. She is able to wear down Drew's resistance and allow him to discover in part his own identity, perhaps outwardly represented by his new hairstyle.

The Inkwell is director Matty Rich's second feature. His first, the autobiographical *Straight Out of Brooklyn* (1991), drew on traumatic personal experiences about death and won the Sundance Film Festival Jury Award. For the script, Rich depends heavily on the work of writers Tom Ricostronza and Paris Qualles. Qualles's television credits include *China Beach*, *Quantum Leap*, and *The Trials of Rosie O'Neill*.

The acting in *The Inkwell* appears natural and convincing for the most part, the burden of which is primarily carried by Larenz Tate as Drew. With experiences in television—*The Twilight Zone*, *The Royal Family*, and *Clippers*—Tate brings a sensitivity to the awkwardness of an American teenager confronting the ambiguous transition to adulthood. Joe Morton as Drew's father appears sympathetic despite some of his sharp and brusque tendencies. Morton's work in classical theater, in plays such as *Oedipus Rex*, *Two Gentlemen of Verona*, and *The Tempest*, gives him the depth and range of the serious character portrayal in *The Inkwell*.

Other performances, by Suzzanne Douglas as Brenda and Phyllis Yvonne Stickney as Dr. Wade, are notable for their strength and sensitivity. Two of the male roles-Spencer, played by Glynn Turman, and Junior, played by Duane Martin—however, come across as forced and at times strident. Painting the character of Spencer as the villain creates strong polarity for the narrative, but detracts from the naturalness of the drama.

The Inkwell did not receive warm critical praise at its release. In general, it was considered too predictable and at times stereotypical in its depiction of the "nouveau riche" and the Black Panthers. The conclusion offers no open-ended nuances as it neatly wraps up and resolves many of the interwoven tensions. The central story, however, dealing with the coming-of-age problems, offers fresh insight into the African American milieu. Marked by pain and humor, the film also reveals the unsettled feelings any adolescent must pass through before arriving at the threshold of adulthood.

—*John J. Michalczyk*

REVIEWS

Entertainment Weekly. May 6, 1994, p. 47.
The Hollywood Reporter. January 27, 1994, p. 10.
Los Angeles Times. April 22, 1994, p. F6.
The New York Times. April 22, 1994, p. B4.
Variety. January 28, 1994, p. 22.

The Inland Sea

Mourning the encroachment of Western culture and technology upon Japanese society, celebrated Japan scholar Donald Richie focuses his documentary on an isolated area of Japan that yet maintains its traditional way of life.

REVIEWS

Booklist. XC, December 1, 1993, p. 704.
Variety. CCCXLVI, February 10, 1992, p. 83.

AWARDS AND NOMINATIONS

Hawaii International Film Festival Awards: Best documentary

CREDITS

Narrator: Donald Richie

Released: 1992
Production: Brian Cotnoir and Lucille Carra for Travelfilm Company, in association with the Japan Foundation and the Hoso Bunka Foundation
Direction: Lucille Carra
Screenplay: Donald Richie; based on his book
Cinematography: Hiro Narita
Editing: Brian Cotnoir
Sound: Tom Hartig
Music: Toru Takemitsu
MPAA rating: no listing
Running time: 57 minutes

Intersection

"Make every move as if it were your last."
—Movie tagline

"Gere...suave and sexy."—Michael Medved, *New York Post*

 Box Office Gross: $20,704,401 (March 27, 1994)

Inspired by the French novel and film entitled *Les Choses de la Vie* (1970), *Intersection* stars Richard Gere as a middle-aged man, Vincent Eastman, caught at a crossroads: Should he leave his estranged wife, Sally (Sharon Stone), and his adoring daughter, Meaghan (Jenny Morrison), or should he end his relationship with his loving girlfriend, Olivia (Lolita Davidovich)? *Intersection* is about the struggle to make difficult decisions and about the consequences of those decisions. It is a respectable but rather slow-paced romance reminiscent of such films as *Back Street* (1932; 1941; 1961) or *The Stolen Hours* (1963), seen through a more philosophical lens.

CREDITS

Vincent Eastman: Richard Gere
Sally Eastman: Sharon Stone
Olivia Marshak: Lolita Davidovich
Neal: Martin Landau
Richard Quarry: David Selby
Meaghan Eastman: Jenny Morrison

Released: 1994
Production: Bud Yorkin and Mark Rydell, in association with Frederic Golchan; released by Paramount Pictures
Direction: Mark Rydell
Screenplay: David Rayfiel and Marshall Brickman; based on the novel by Paul Guimard and on the screenplay by Guimard, Jean-Loup Dabadie, and Claude Sautet
Cinematography: Vilmos Zsigmond
Editing: Mark Warner
Production design: Harold Michelson
Art direction: Yvonne Hurst
Set design: Marco Rubeo
Set decoration: Dominique Fauquet-Lemaitre
Casting: Lynn Stalmaster and Stuart Aikins
Sound: Eric Batut
Costume design: Ellen Mirojnick
Music: James Newton Howard
MPAA rating: R
Running time: 98 minutes

Vincent and his wife, Sally, are a married couple who are also partners in a highly successful architectural firm in the Pacific Northwest. They have a beautiful and loving daughter, Meaghan, and a materially rich but emotionally bankrupt life. As the story unfolds, the audience discovers that Vincent has moved out of his home to live with his girlfriend, magazine columnist Olivia Marshak, making an occasional return home to get clothing or his car. He has designed a house, as yet unbuilt, where he plans to live with Olivia, while continuing a polite business relationship with Sally.

Vincent is ambivalent about leaving his daughter, however, and has occasional longings for Sally and doubts about Olivia. This ambivalence causes him to be in a constant inner tug-of-war about what he wants from his life. The film begins with a car accident, and the story unfolds through a series of flashbacks that illustrate Vincent's steps leading him literally to this crossroads of his life (hence the literal and symbolic "Intersection" of the title).

David Rayfiel, who cowrote the screenplay for *The Firm* (1993), wrote this screenplay with Marshall Brickman, cowriter, with Woody Allen, of such films as *Annie Hall* (1977), *Manhattan* (1979), and *Sleeper* (1973). They have woven together a series of flashbacks that bring the audience "along the road" with Vincent, trying to understand the path of his life. The film goes from one flashback to another, emphasizing that one apparently insignificant episode in a person's life can have serious consequences later. The flashbacks are in Vincent's memory as he drives toward his fate, and one memory leads to another like a Chinese box that has another smaller box inside it. His reminiscences are triggered by inconsequential things—a word or a photograph—but each memory is of consequence. For example, as Vincent is preparing to go to a dinner honoring a museum he has designed, he flashes back to a scene with Olivia where she discusses how she is always being invited to dinners as the unwanted or unattached female. This becomes a scene of significance because it teaches the audience how Olivia views herself, and foreshadows her arrival at the museum dinner, where she confronts Sally for the first time and sets up the immediate series of events that lead to Vincent's accident.

Rayfiel, Brickman, and director Mark Rydell employ much symbolism and symbolic language to underscore their themes. About architect Vincent's lack of commitment, Olivia tells him, "You'd think with all those bridges you build, you guys wouldn't be afraid to burn one once in a while." Martin Landau, as Sally and Vincent's partner, tells Vincent that his indecision about Sally and Olivia is "Bad design. You're supposed to have everything under one roof." Besides its verbiage, the film has ample visual and thematic symbolism as well. For example, the car in which Vincent has his accident is a symbol of Vincent's path toward an unknown fate. The car and the accident are also foreshadowed early in the film during a conflict between Olivia and Vincent about where he parks his car.

Other symbols underscore the events and themes of the film. In a flashback to the first date between Olivia and Vincent, she discovers he is married. This scene takes place on his sailboat, inside the cabin: The claustrophobic space and the rolling waves underneath appear to underscore the unsteady and secretive start of their relationship. The most overtly sentimental symbolism comes toward the end of the film when Vincent is about to make his decision about whether to stay with Olivia. He sees a little girl, about six years old, with the same sweet smile and the same vividly red hair as Olivia; the little girl is with an older man with long gray hair, much like actor Gere's own. The little girl offers him a sweet roll, and it is evident through the close-ups on Gere and the little girl that everything will change for Vincent at this moment. The lack of subtlety brings a heavy-handedness to the moment.

"We weren't a family. We were a corporation with a kid."—Vincent Eastman in *Intersection*

Symbolism can be a delicate thing: Sometimes an obvious symbol or image overstates the filmmaker's case, as it does here. Discovering symbolic images in film can be enjoyable and can illuminate the thematic content of the film: In *Close Encounters of the Third Kind* (1977), Steven Spielberg used a young, wide-eyed boy to underscore the wonder of the adults at discovering alien beings and to prefigure the aliens themselves (all of whom had a similar childlike gaze). In *Intersection*, however, the little red-haired girl is so precious and the moment is so clearly meant to have huge meaning that it only appears insincere.

In the end, much of *Intersection* is best enjoyed for what it is: a love triangle reminiscent of those in old films of the 1940's or 1950's, which involved beautiful people agonizing over love. In that spirit, there is much to offer: The locales are lush and romantic, the performers are talented and beautiful, and the story is appropriately emotional, if a little slow-moving. Rydell, Rayfiel, and Brickman do not hesitate to be sentimental. For example, after a climactic encounter, Vincent writes a letter to Olivia, saying, "It's not going to work. Try someone else. Someone with no history." This is woven in with lilting music and countless close-ups of the stoic Vincent.

Rydell chooses to use many tight close-ups, a technique which effectively keeps the audience involved in the inner life of the characters even while very little is occurring in the story. In the aforementioned scene where Vincent meets the little girl, Rydell has had him go into a phone booth immediately after the girl and her grandfather drive away and keeps a tight close-up on Gere, who delivers what is apparently meant to be his big emotional speech of the film. Yet the speech is delivered over the phone, to Olivia's answering machine. Gere appears uncomfortable during the long speech, having nothing to react to because he is talking into a phone, not to mention that a camera is very close to his face. Gere tends to opt for doing very little in the guise of "being real," and while he is an able actor and a strong screen presence, an extreme close-up on a long speech such as the one described here highlights his lack of believability during the most climactic moment of the film.

Rydell has been quite successful directing films with good women's roles, having directed Oscar-nominated performances from Katharine Hepburn in *On Golden Pond* (1981), Bette Midler in *The Rose* (1979) and *For the Boys* (1991), Sissy Spacek in *The River* (1984), and Marsha Mason in *Cinderella Liberty* (1973). This time he has two wonderful actresses to work with and elicits excellent performances from them.

Stone is icily beautiful as always, and in *Intersection* she gets a chance to show her acting ability more than in her past femme fatale roles in *Basic Instinct* (1992) and *Sliver* (1993). This time, she plays a sexually repressed, unhappy woman trying to put on a good appearance at all costs. She is outstanding in her scenes of stony reserve, which depict her chilly present-day relationship with Vincent. She contrasts it beautifully with a scene as a younger woman in flashback: She is childlike and giddy, while showing signs of the cold and angry woman she is to become. She brings nuance, range, and beauty to her role, and this should establish her as a capable dramatic actress.

Similarly, Lolita Davidovich has received much praise for her role as the warm, offbeat Olivia. Davidovich has been in films for quite a while without having a breakthrough role: She starred as Blaze Starr in *Blaze* (1989) with Paul Newman, but the film generated little box-office interest, and she did not find the recognition she deserves. She has received some attention for her performance in *Intersection* and deservedly so: She is captivating.

Though not for everyone, *Intersection* will surely appeal to Richard Gere or Sharon Stone fans. It is also the kind of film that Hollywood rarely makes any longer; its sentimentality and lack of action will most definitely be considered assets among those people who enjoy a handsomely made, well-acted romance. 🎞️

—*Kirby Tepper*

REVIEWS

Entertainment Weekly. February 4, 1994, p. 38.
The Hollywood Reporter. January 21-23, 1994, p. 10.
Los Angeles Times. January 21, 1994, p. F1.
The New York Times. January 21, 1994, p. B9.
Variety. January 21, 1994, p. 4.

Interview with the Vampire

"The most eagerly anticipated movie of the season."—David Ansen, *Newsweek*

"Hypnotic, scary, sexy, perversely funny and haunting. An audacious Tom Cruise performance."—Peter Travers, *Rolling Stone*

"Powerful. One of the best films of the year."
—Caryn James, *The New York Times*

"Sensational entertainment! Thrilling, moving, horrifying and humorous. *Vampire* belongs at the top of your must-see list."—Paul Wunder, *WBAI Radio*

Box Office Gross: $100,689,360 (January 2, 1995)

Anne Rice, author of the best-selling 1976 novel, *Interview with the Vampire*, waited seventeen years to see the film version take shape. Producer Stephen Woolley began working closely with director Neil Jordan in 1982, and their partnership resulted in the release of six films, including *The Company of Wolves* (1984), *High Spirits* (1988), and *The Crying Game* (1992). In 1992, when the pair was in the United States receiving critics' praise and festival prizes for *The Crying Game*, media mogul David Geffen offered Jordan the chance to direct *Interview with the Vampire*. Woolley agreed to collaborate, and Jordan quickly wrote a script based closely on the book.

The first major hurdle to clear was casting. Daniel Day-Lewis was the team's first choice for the starring role of the vampire Lestat. When he proved unavailable, a short list of possible actors for the part quickly narrowed to Tom Cruise. Cruise was invited to meetings to discuss the film, and his enthusiasm and charm quickly broke down any barriers or reservations the producers had. Anne Rice, however, was outspoken in her criticism of the casting of Cruise, and for a time there was negative press coverage of the production. Other gossip during filming included rumors that Cruise wore elevator shoes so he would appear as tall as his costar Brad Pitt.

For the other leads, Pitt was chosen to play Louis, Kirsten Dunst as Claudia, and River Phoenix as the interviewer. The tragic death of Phoenix from a drug overdose result-

ed in another casting call to find a replacement. Following the testing of several well-known actors, Christian Slater agreed to take the part. He generously refused to accept payment for his work in the film. Instead, he donated his fee to various charities. Before shooting finally began, cast and crew had to sign secrecy forms, swearing not to talk about the production to outsiders.

Interview with the Vampire is the story of a group of vampires who spend their immortality in a diabolical pursuit to satisfy their hunger for blood. This thirst for other people's blood carries them along on a journey that covers two hundred years, from the late eighteenth century to the late twentieth century, and from a Louisiana plantation to New Orleans, Paris, and San Francisco. Louis, a vampire with a burning desire to tell his story, visits the interviewer, Malloy, one rainy night in a seedy office in downtown San Francisco. The interviewer, at first skeptical of his guest, turns on his tape recorder and asks a few questions that lead Louis to recount his bizarre tale.

As Louis describes his life as a wealthy plantation owner in eighteenth century Louisiana, the narrative goes back in time to that rural bayou country. Despondent and suicidal over the death of his young wife, Louis spends his time drinking and carousing aimlessly. Inconsolable, he is stalked and finally approached one evening at an outdoor celebration by Lestat, a lone, itinerant vampire who desires companionship on his nightly rounds of debauchery and bloodletting. When Louis lets down his guard, Lestat swoops him up in his arms and drinks his blood. Now under Lestat's spell, Louis is offered eternal youth and immortality. This Faustian pact is sealed when a weakened Louis drinks Lestat's blood.

Soon, Lestat and Louis are living off the land, literally, biting and draining the blood from nearly anything that has two or four legs. When Lestat gets desperate, he even drinks the blood of rats. Dressed like courtly fops, they tour the bayous at night, picking up and then ravishing prostitutes and young virgins. At grand plantation balls and parties, they zero in on wealthy old widows, draining them of blood and stealing their jewels. The fun for Lestat is spoiled, however, because Louis is revolted by murder and the drinking of human blood. They bicker incessantly over vampire nature, and Lestat pushes and prods Louis to

> The filming of *Interview with the Vampire* required a waterfront city to be built on the Orleans Parish levee at Jackson Barracks, home to the Louisiana National Guard. The Pointe du Lac family mansion scenes were filmed at the famous Oak Alley Plantation, near Vacherie, Louisiana. The company also filmed in the Pere Antoine Alley in New Orleans. It required 4 1/2 hours to apply make-up and affix the special prosthetics and wigs that turn Lestat into the mire-covered demon.

CREDITS

Lestat: Tom Cruise
Louis: Brad Pitt
Armand: Antonio Banderas
Santiago: Stephen Rea
Malloy: Christian Slater
Claudia: Kirsten Dunst
Madeleine: Domiziana Giordano
Yvette: Thandie Newton
New Orleans whore: Indra Ove
Mortal woman on stage: Laure Marsac

Released: 1994
Production: David Geffen and Stephen Woolley for Geffen Pictures; released by Warner Bros.
Direction: Neil Jordan
Screenplay: Anne Rice; based on her novel
Cinematography: Philippe Rousselot
Editing: Mick Audsley
Production design: Dante Ferretti
Art direction: Malcolm Middleton, Alan Tomkins, Jim Tocci and Jean-Michel Hugon
Set design: Stella Furner and Munroe Kelly
Set decoration: Francesca Lo Schiavo
Casting: Juliet Taylor and Susie Figgis
Visual effects supervision: Rob Legato
Sound: Clive Winter
Makeup: Michele Burke
Vampire makeup and effects: Stan Winston
Costume design: Sandy Powell
Music: Elliot Goldenthal
MPAA rating: R
Running time: 120 minutes

AWARDS AND NOMINATIONS

Academy Awards Nominations 1994: Best Score, Best Art Direction/Set Direction
Chicago Film Critics Awards 1994: Most Promising Performance (Dunst)
Golden Globe Awards Nominations 1995: Best Score, Best Supporting Actress (Dunst)
MTV Movie Awards 1995: Best Male Performance (Pitt), Breakthrough Performance (Dunst), Most Desirable Male (Pitt) *Nominations:* Best Film, Most Desirable Male (Slater & Cruise), Best Villain (Cruise), Best On-Screen Duo (Pitt/Cruise)

relax and enjoy his new life-in-death.

After Louis clumsily bungles an attempt at drinking the blood of one of his maidservants, the two vampires are driven from the plantation by the enraged and fearful blacks who live on his land. Lestat and Louis make their way to New Orleans, where they settle into a nocturnal routine, attacking and murdering two or three unsuspecting prostitutes each night. After a time, Lestat and Louis meet and befriend Claudia, a lovely young girl who has been orphaned in the red-light district. They turn her into a child-vampire whose own blood lust rivals that of Lestat. Tired of Lestat's reckless and savage blood-sucking orgies, Louis attempts to rid himself of Lestat. He and Claudia flee to Europe, finally settling in Paris. There, Louis encounters and becomes ensnared by Armand (Antonio Banderas), a four-hundred-year-old vampire who heads a sort of vampire aristocracy. All the vampires live together in a cavernous underground tomb. These beehive-like catacombs are both prison and refuge for the Paris vampires. Armand and his associate, Santiago (Stephen Rea), introduce Louis to their bloodthirsty culture.

The Paris vampires perform perverse and horrific rituals on the stage of an enormous theater, which resembles a decaying opera house. Victims are sacrificed before an audience of black-clad cultists and devotees who enthusiastically applaud the blood lust. Armand imprisons Louis and Claudia in a prison tower for violating certain vampire taboos. When Louis finally escapes, he tries to destroy all the vampires in their underground lair. In a hellish fury, he sets fire to the vampires while they sleep. Back in San Francisco, Louis pauses in his story as sunrise approaches. The interviewer, amazed and excited by what he has heard, takes the audiotapes and heads home. The film ends with the interviewer driving across the Golden Gate Bridge and about to be confronted by a rejuvenated Lestat, who is on the prowl for another victim.

Interview with the Vampire was one of the year's most eagerly awaited releases. Not only is this a bold attempt at making a major film in the fantasy-thriller genre but also it revisits a popular horror-film subject, vampires. It also casts two of the biggest box-office stars in contemporary films, Tom Cruise and Brad Pitt. As a vampire film, however, *Interview with the Vampire* veers away from the familiar trappings of vampire lore found in earlier Dracula films. There seems to be a kind of rarified vampirism working here, without the comforting continuity provided by such Bram Stoker elements as crosses, garlic, wooden stakes, and empty mirrors. The vampires in this film neither have animal familiars such as wolves nor assume the forms of bats or other creatures. Only the custom-fit coffins connect the vampires in *Interview with the Vampire* with their predecessors.

"Oh, what I wouldn't give for a drop of good old-fashioned Creole blood."
"Yankees are not to your taste?"
"Their democratic flavor doesn't suit my palate."—Lestat and Louis in *Interview with the Vampire*

Interview with the Vampire really does not play with the vampire genre much at all, which may be a result of the novel on which it is based rather than any plan by director Jordan to be conservative with the use of the more melodramatic trappings of vampirism. Louis and Lestat do not glide across the floor or float through open windows like fog as Count Dracula did in Francis Ford Coppola's *Bram Stoker's Dracula* (1992). They do not seem in need of supernatural powers. Still, they manage to avoid raising the suspicions of police even while blatantly committing murder. Even the people around them are unaware of their deadly habit. It is as if the vampires occupy a realm where they are immune to the consequences of their actions. This is in contrast to the typical Dracula film where dedicated vampire hunters track them to their coffins and destroy them.

The primary themes in this film are the sexual nature of the conquest and the homoerotic relationship between Louis and Lestat. One would care more about these two, however, if there was time to get to know their victims first. Instead, the people they kill are throwaways, easily gotten, quickly consumed, and disposed of. Thus, there is no way to accurately gauge the monstrousness of the evil they do. While Louis seems to be more sensitive than Lestat, and even shows guilt at times, he does not let the audience share

his sorrow, and much of the emotional focus is lost. The film does not develop the kind of human drama necessary to offset the scenes of physical violence.

Interview With the Vampire was an ambitious project, from the elaborate sets built on seven soundstages at Pinewood Studios outside London, to the huge waterfront city constructed on the Orleans Parish levee in New Orleans. It is a film of rich imagery and elaborately staged sequences, such as the burning of New Orleans. Tom Cruise gives an energetic performance, but never really makes Lestat interesting as a villain or a vampire. Brad Pitt, while good at pouting and looking depressed, does not adequately define the character of Louis. Ultimately, the story lacks the good old stuff of vampire legend, and the thrill of a righteous chase to find and kill the unholy demons.

—Francis Poole

REVIEWS

Daily Variety. November 7, 1994, p. 2.
Entertainment Weekly. November 18, 1994, p. 74.
The Hollywood Reporter. November 7, 1994, p. 5.
Los Angeles Times. November 11, 1994, p. F1.
The New York Times. November 11, 1994, p. B1.

I.Q.

"With Einstein as Cupid what could possibly go wrong?"—Movie tagline

"Think love."—Movie tagline

"Wonderful comic performances from both Meg Ryan and Tim Robbins."—Janet Maslin, *The New York Times*

"A fun, warm-hearted romantic comedy. Matthau is wonderful as Einstein."—Roger Ebert, *Chicago Sun-Times*

 Box Office Gross: $13,039,461 (January 2, 1995)

I.Q., the latest offering from Australian director Fred Schepisi, is a warm, good-natured, and very funny romantic comedy filled with witty exchanges about fate, relativity, the nature of accidents, the concepts of time and of synchronicity, and of course, love. At the core of its premise is the issue of self-esteem and self-acceptance. While the film

falters toward the end, it is a laudable effort: a film whose goal it is to make one laugh at how hard some people are on themselves. It is smart and clever, perhaps too smart for its own box-office good.

Set in 1955 at Princeton University, *I.Q.* revolves around Catherine Boyd (Meg Ryan), a beautiful, brainy, but neurotic mathematics graduate student who just happens to be the niece of renowned physicist, Albert Einstein (Walter Matthau). Catherine is engaged to be married to the staid and often condescending behavioral psychology professor, James Morland (Stephen Fry), but theirs is more of an intellectual attraction, rather than a mad, passionate affair. Catherine's heart is in serious deep freeze; as her uncle points out, she seems destined to think only with her head. This saddens lovable Uncle Albert who, along with his band of roving geniuses (Lou Jacobi, Gene Saks, and Joseph Maher), soon falls upon a golden opportunity to play Cupid.

Confronted with car problems, Catherine and James stop at the nearest repair shop. In an instant, the auto mechanic with a fondness for comets, Ed Walters (Tim

Robbins), falls head over heels in love with Catherine—an experience in which he glimpsed his future in such rapid succession that Ed later describes it as "like death, only in a good way." Catherine, too, feels something unexpected happen, but she quickly dismisses it. Despite the emotional stirrings, Catherine would never allow herself to fall in love with someone whom she does not consider at least her intellectual equal. Upon meeting Ed when he attempts to return Catherine's mislaid watch, Einstein and his friends hatch a scheme to give fate a helping hand by maneuvering to get Catherine and Ed together.

"Don't let your brain get in the way of your heart."—Albert Einstein from *I.Q.*

Attempting to pass the auto mechanic off as a kind of latent genius, Einstein arranges for Ed to deliver a paper on cold fusion, which causes a stir both within the physics community and within Catherine's heart—until Catherine discovers what she thinks is the truth. Ultimately, what she learns, however, is to let go and accept the gifts that fate has given her: her intellect, a car mechanic, and a comet named after her father. "Do you know why a comet's tail always points away from the sun?" Ed asks Catherine. "Yes!" she says excitedly. "Me, too," he replies.

Director Schepisi, who displayed a flair for romantic comedy with *Roxanne* (1987)—the retelling of the story of Cyrano de Bergerac, written by and starring Steve Martin—displays a deftness with comedy, cutting in and out of scenes with near-perfect timing. His precision was apparent even in his earlier, socially-conscious films, *The Devil's Playground* (1976), which won six Australian Film Awards, and the more widely known *The Chant of Jimmy Blacksmith* (1978), a harrowing indictment of racism and the first Australian film ever accepted in competition at the Cannes Film Festival. Schepisi's other works include *A Cry in the Dark* (1988), *The Russia House* (1990), and *Six Degrees of Separation* (1993).

As penned by former television writers Andy Breckman (*Saturday Night Live* and *Late Night with David Letterman*) and Michael Leeson (*Taxi*, *The Cosby Show*, and *The Mary Tyler Moore Show*), the character of Albert Einstein functions as a kind of "traveling angel," an individual who acts as a catalyst for change among a film's protagonists. Actor Bill Murray has made a career out of portraying such a character in such films as *Meatballs* (1979), *Stripes* (1981), and *What About Bob?* (1991). Other examples of traveling angels include the main characters in *Mary Poppins* (1964), *Ferris Bueller's Day Off* (1986), and *Good Morning, Vietnam* (1987). It is the job of traveling angels to bring fun to the world, to show the other characters how both to have a good time and to learn to listen to what their hearts tell them to do.

Walter Matthau plays Einstein with such grand simplicity, a twinkle in his eye and a longing in his heart. There is little that can compare to the sight of the seventy-four-year-old Matthau, replete with a gray wig, riding on the back of a motorcycle, yelling "Yahoo!", or simply walking down the street eating an ice-cream cone. Other memorable Matthau roles include Mr. Wilson in *Dennis the Menace* (1993), Max in *Grumpy Old Men* (1993), and of course, the slovenly Oscar Madison in both the Broadway play and the film version of *The Odd Couple* (1968)—which was directed by his *I.Q.* costar Gene Saks.

The performances in *I.Q.* are consistently of the caliber that audiences have come to expect from actors Robbins, Ryan, and Matthau. The chemistry is excellent between Robbins, best known for his work in *Bull Durham* (1988), Robert Altman's *The Player* (1992), and *The Shawshank Redemption* (reviewed in this volume), and perky Ryan, who finally graduated into leading-lady status with Rob Reiner's *When Harry Met Sally* (1989),

CREDITS

Ed Walters: Tim Robbins
Catherine Boyd: Meg Ryan
Albert Einstein: Walter Matthau
Kurt Godel: Lou Jacobi
Boris Podolsky: Gene Saks
Nathan Liebknecht: Joseph Maher
James Morland: Stephen Fry
Louis Bamberger: Charles Durning
Bob Rosetti: Tony Shalhoub
Frank: Frank Whaley

Released: 1994
Production: Carol Baum and Fred Schepisi for Sandollar; released by Paramount Pictures
Direction: Fred Schepisi
Screenplay: Andy Breckman and Michael Leeson; based on a story by Breckman
Cinematography: Ian Baker
Editing: Jill Bilcock
Production design: Stuart Wurtzel
Art direction: Wray Steven Graham
Set decoration: Gretchen Rau
Casting: David Rubin
Sound: Danny Michael
Costume design: Ruth Myers
Music: Jerry Goldsmith
MPAA rating: PG
Running time: 95 minutes

opposite Tom Hanks in Nora Ephron's surprise box-office hit, *Sleepless in Seattle* (1993), and as the alcoholic wife and mother in *When a Man Loves a Woman* (reviewed in this volume).

As in previous roles, Robbins appears as the quintessential Everyman. With his lanky frame and rubbery face, Robbins imbues Ed with a naïveté and romantic longing for the intellectually insecure Catherine that is so heart-wrenching that it is reminiscent of a puppy in a pet-store window. Dressed fetchingly in 1950's apparel, Ryan brings an accessible glamour to the role of Catherine that prompted some critics to compare her to the late Grace Kelly. Ryan is perfectly suited for distracted dreaminess, even if she does occasionally fall into an inadvertent impersonation of actress Diane Keaton in *Annie Hall* (1977); she is attractive in a nonthreatening, old-fashioned way. Men find her appealing, and women relate to that lovelorn woman longing to meet Mr. Right—a character that has become Ryan's specialty. The only disappointment in the acting arises from the predictability of the performances; no one does anything surprising, no one takes any risks, no one ventures too far from his or her successful on-screen persona.

I.Q. is solid entertainment for most of its ninety-five minutes of running time, falling short only in its attempts at plot resolution. Perhaps it is because in real life romance is never so easily resolved, preferring instead to be free-flowing and ever-changing. For a writer, romantic comedy is perhaps one of the toughest film genres to master. It is, by its very nature, a contrary one; love and comedy do not necessarily mix well. While love wants to intensify the feelings, to pull the audience closer to the characters, comedy wants to pull back and make light of everything and everybody. It is a very tenuous tightrope that the writer must tread. When it is done well and the

> Filming of *I.Q.* took place in many places that Einstein actually frequented. Matthau, as Einstein, sits in seat 11 in Princeton University's Palmer Hall, the same seat Einstein always sat in for lectures. Einstein's house in *I.Q.* is next door to Einstein's actual house on Mercer Street.

audience responds, a good romantic comedy can translate into sizable box-office receipts. If the audience, or film critics, fails to connect with the story, however, it can mean either lackluster box-office performance or worse, certain death for the film.

The failure of *I.Q.* to ignite the box office was puzzling. It offered romance, appealing and talented actors, smart writing, snappy direction. So what went wrong? Why did audiences fail to embrace *I.Q.* in the way they did Meg Ryan's previous romantic comedies? Perhaps it is telling that in a year that saw audiences flocking to the simplistic comedy *Dumb and Dumber* (reviewed in this volume), a film filled with slapstick and bathroom humor, viewers stayed away from brainier fare such as *I.Q.*, as well as the less successful and, admittedly, poorly executed, *Speechless* (reviewed in this volume). Whatever the reason, one can only hope that *I.Q.* gets a second chance to find the audience it deserves among video viewers. Reviews for the film were decidedly mixed.

—*Patricia Kowal*

REVIEWS

Daily Variety. December 19, 1994, p. 4.
Entertainment Weekly. December 23, 1994, p. 47.
The Hollywood Reporter. December 19, 1994, p. 6.
Los Angeles Times. December 23, 1994, CXIV, p. F12.
The New York Times. December 23, 1994, CXLIV, p. B3.
The New Yorker. LXX, December 26, 1994/January 2, 1995, p. 142.
San Francisco Chronicle. December 23, 1994, CCXCIII, p. D1.
The Washington Post. December 23, 1994, Weekend, p. 37.

Iron Will

"It's not a question of age. Or strength. Or ability. It's a matter of will."—Movie tagline

"Two solid hours of excitement!"—*The New York Post*

"A sweet and upbeat adventure!"—*The Associated Press*

"A wild adventure!"—*ABC-TV, Los Angeles*

 Box Office Gross: $20,577,430 (April 3, 1994)

In 1971, Bing Crosby and Mort Briskin's production company commissioned John Michael Hayes, whose screenplay for *Rear Window* (1954) was nominated for an Academy Award, to write the true story of a young American musher who competed in a 1917 dogsled race from Winnipeg to Como Park, St. Paul, Minnesota. The resultant screenplay was entitled *Hartman*, but it was not until 1988, when producer Robert Schwartz discovered the material, that the story actually had a chance to come to the screen. Twelve weeks of virtual nonstop subzero shooting produced the action-adventure film Iron Will, a Disney adventure that will give each member of the family something to root for.

As the film opens, Will Stoneman (Mackenzie Astin) is racing along on his dogsled, trying to beat the train into town. Soon it is evident that Will is young, determined, talented—and careless. He barely misses getting run over by an Army truck (it is 1917, and war is at hand). He arrives late with the mail in spite of the breakneck speed at which he travels. Yet he and his dogs make a strong team, full of heart and dreams. Will lives on a farm with his mother Maggie (Penelope Windust), father Jack (John Terry), and farmhand Ned Dodd (August Schellenberg), and in many ways it is a perfect existence. The family members are fond of one another, and although poor, they are happy. They work and play together. For example, father and son race their sleds toward home, and while Will's team is young, responsive, and fast, Jack Stoneman's team is older, wiser, and led by a champion dog, Gus (Beau).

The next year Will is to go to college, and while the money has not yet appeared, the family is hopeful something will come up. Soon, however, everything begins to change. Jack Stoneman dies when his sled slides off course, sinking him beneath the weight of the sled in an icy river. Only his dogs are saved, and then only at the last moment. His furniture business is beyond rescue, and soon it appears even the family farm will be lost, to say nothing of what the changes will mean to Will's college career. With the begrudging approval of Maggie Stoneman, Will enters a 522-mile dogsled race with a $10,000 grand prize—enough money to save the farm and to pay for college. With Ned's help, Will trains for the race. Yet even with all of Ned's guidance, the race will take every ounce of Will's strength, courage, and determination.

Mackenzie Astin, son of actress Patty Duke and actor/director/writer John Astin, has a certain earnest quality that contributes to his believability as Will Stoneman. Astin, portrays a young man who is able to mourn his father and nuzzle his dogs while keeping the audience with him. "Mackenzie has an honest sense about him, a sort of midwestern American look," said producer Schwartz in the production notes. "It's a cross between having real guts inside but also a tenderness, which is especially important when you have to do dialogue with your dog." Through the process of the film, Will grows from a boy to a man, beginning with trusting his parents, then trusting his dogs, then his own instincts.

While the ordeal of the race supports the idea of change in Will, other small details help, also. For example, Jack Stoneman's lead dog, Gus, is a one-man dog who responds only to a simple tune Jack whistled to signal time to go. When Will enters the race, Ned encourages him to take Gus as his lead dog, although Will fears that Gus will not respond to him. Because Will is unable to whistle the command tune in such a manner as to encourage Gus to respond, Ned gives him a homemade whistle to play the necessary tune. After a few days of the grueling race, Will discovers he has lost the whistle. His pleas to Gus to go, to run, are of no avail. Will has already grown more mature, however, and has seen enough to make him wiser. He has saved the life of another competitor; he has withstood the taunts and attacks of the less-than-civil mushers. This time, when Will whistles for Gus, Gus responds. As Ned once told him, when Gus respects Will, he will respond to the whistle. It is a small clue to a large change, but it works.

The relationship between the boy and his dogs is key to the film in terms of theme, and hence the majority of the

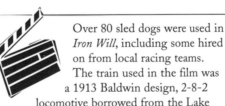

Over 80 sled dogs were used in *Iron Will*, including some hired on from local racing teams. The train used in the film was a 1913 Baldwin design, 2-8-2 locomotive borrowed from the Lake Superior Museum of Transportation in Duluth.

screen time focuses on just that. Because much of the screenplay required close-ups of Will operating the sled, it was necessary for Astin to learn to handle the dogs and the sled. By all accounts, Astin was a natural, quickly learning the sport and building a good relationship with the dogs. All of this is evident on screen. As in any dog film, *Iron Will* banks on its shots of attractive dogs. Early in the film, during Will's training, he spends the night with the dogs in the barn. By morning he is snuggled among his blue-eyed Alaskan huskies—a very successful dog shot. Also, in the production notes, director Charles Haid comments on Beau's ability to react visibly to the activities around him. Therefore, Haid decided to film each of Beau's reactions, many of which make it into the final version of the film. Alert and attractive, Beau carries his role as Gus well, such as when Will collapses and Gus must take control of the team and encourage them over the finish line. Clearly the dogs are also stars of the film.

The production notes also chronicle the hazards of

"Don't let fear stand in the way of your dreams."—Jack Stoneman to son Will in *Iron Will*

filming in frigid climes—the wilds of Minnesota and Wisconsin. The first day of shooting, the temperature hit -35 degrees Fahrenheit, and all the equipment froze: tailgates on trucks, cables, cameras. Much of the crew was then put in charge of temperature control, and the production was able to limp along. Purportedly the only cast members not to mind the cold were the eighty sled dogs recruited for the film. Consisting of Siberian and Alaskan huskies and malamutes, twenty of the dogs were animal actors brought from California, while the rest were recruited from local racing teams. The local sled dogs became frustrated with the hurry-up-and-wait of film production, preferring to run thirty miles a day rather than two hundred feet and stop. Humane Society personnel monitored the production and gave it an "A-1" rating for its treatment of the dogs.

Beyond the boy racer and his dogs, much of the rest of the film gets lost. Two minor characters, however, do have an impact on what Will is able to accomplish and learn. Ned teaches Will a respect for nature and the importance of determination. Tying the film to Native American lore, Ned becomes a spiritual and surrogate father to Will. Also important is Harry Kingsley (Kevin Spacey), a newspaper reporter who makes it possible for Will to enter the race (he supplies the missing $20). Kingsley also undergoes a change, a passage from ennui to enthusiasm, from jaded cynic to enthusiast. He learns to believe in something again, and the audience takes part of its cues from him. Where Kingsley was once motivated by simply getting a cover story on the race, he finally comes to care for Will and see his determination as a life force. On the morning of the last day of the race, Kingsley has to help the worn-out young racer to stand, to ease through muscles that refuse to work. In doing so, he comes to understand what it means to fight beyond pain and never give up.

Other minor characters make less of an impact. The chief villain, Borg Guillarson (George Gerdes), tries to discourage Will from racing and later works to put him out of the race any way he can. The bald-headed Gerdes was cited by reviewers as everything from "a cross between *Ben Hur's* Messala and Mr. Clean" to "a stump-fingered Norwegian maniac who appears to have wandered in from some Strindberg drama about howling angst in the bitter wilderness." He plays his villain's role broadly, yet he conveys true menace when necessary: waving a large knife, cheating at every possible opportunity, even attempting to kill other racers' dogs. It is a one-note performance, but then perhaps that is all that is needed.

Also underdone are Will's friends at home. Becky (Paige Litfin) seems sweet on Will and takes a real interest in his well-being. Not only does Becky give Will a fur hat

CREDITS

Will Stoneman: Mackenzie Astin
Harry Kingsley: Kevin Spacey
J. P. Harper: David Ogden Stiers
Ned Dodd: August Schellenberg
Angus McTeague: Brian Cox
Jack Stoneman: John Terry
Maggie Stoneman: Penelope Windust
Becky: Paige Litfin
Borg Guillarson: George Gerdes
Gus: Beau
Becky: Paige Litfin

Released: 1994
Production: Patrick Palmer and Robert Schwartz for Walt Disney Pictures; released by Buena Vista Pictures
Direction: Charles Haid
Screenplay: John Michael Hayes, Djordje Milievi and Jeff Arch
Cinematography: William Wages
Editing: Andrew Doerfer
Production design: Stephen Storer
Art direction: Nathan Haas
Set decoration: Hilton Rosemarin
Casting: Jennifer Shull
Sound: Richard Lightstone
Costume design: Betty Madden
Music: Joel McNeely
MPAA rating: PG
Running time: 109 minutes

that he takes with him on the trek but she also tries to help Will put his father's death in perspective. It is a throwaway role that could have brought a new dimension to the film had it been developed. Further, while Disney seems to have carved a niche for itself in the dead-parent genre—everything from *Bambi* (1942) to last season's *A Far off Place* (1993)—the relationship between the father and son might have proved fertile ground to explore. Clearly Will is forced to grow up more quickly with his father gone, and Ned supplies advice from an arena otherwise not clearly available. Yet it is possible that young viewers could profit more by learning how to grow up with their parents still in place, arguably as challenging as facing the world alone.

Iron Will is an adventure film filled with amazing stunts and attractive dogs. While the film received mixed reviews, it is exciting, enjoyable family entertainment in a season filled with more adult fare.

—Roberta F. Green

REVIEWS

Atlanta Journal/Constitution. January 14, 1994, p. 3.
Baltimore Sun. January 14-20, 1994, Maryland Live, p. 17.
Boston Globe. January 14, 1994, p. 76.
The Hollywood Reporter. January 11, 1994, p. 12.
Los Angeles Times. January 14, 1994, p. F1.
The New York Times. January 14, 1994, p. B4.
Variety. January 10, 1994, p. 14.
The Washington Post. January 14, 1994, Weekend section, p. 45

It Could Happen to You

"Two big thumbs up with terrific comedy performances by Nicolas Cage, Rosie Perez and Bridget Fonda."—*Siskel & Ebert*

"Sweetly amusing...with winning simplicity."
—Caryn James, *The New York Times*

"Four stars. Bridget Fonda and Nicolas Cage are this generation's Hepburn and Tracy. Funny and quirky! Who says they don't make movies like they used to?"—*Mademoiselle*

"The movie delivers more of the old-style pleasures of moviegoing than any other picture in a long while. A delicious fairy-book romance."
—*The Washington Post*

"*It Could Happen to You* should happen to everyone. It's this year's *Sleepless in Seattle*."—*Good Morning America*

"A charming comedy. Cage and Fonda generate a sunny, easygoing chemistry tht can't fail to win a smile.... The warmhearted spirit of Frank Capra hovers over the entire project. Cage displays an unmistakable resemblance to Capra's favorite star, Jimmy Stewart."—*The New York Post*

Box Office Gross: $37,791,414 (December 4, 1994)

It Could Happen to You is a sweet, simplistic fairy tale about people getting what they deserve. Here, the good are rewarded and the bad are punished. The film, originally titled "Cop Tips Waitress $2 Million", focuses on the story of two honest, hard-working but poor individuals, Charlie Lang (Nicolas Cage) and Yvonne Biasi (Bridget Fonda), and the success, happiness, and support that comes their way despite the greed, pettiness, and cruelty of the world around them. Charlie is a good man and cop, Yvonne a compassionate but unlucky woman and waitress. In a single day, they meet, Charlie wins the New York State lottery, and their lives are changed forever.

The film progresses swiftly from short, introductory scenes with various principal and secondary characters to longer scenes focusing on the principal characters. First, one sees Charlie and his partner, Bo Williams (Wendell Pierce), on a beat somewhere in Manhattan. Next, Charlie's wife, Muriel (Rosie Perez),

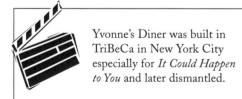

Yvonne's Diner was built in TriBeCa in New York City especially for *It Could Happen to You* and later dismantled.

a hairdresser in Queens, complains to a customer that she needs more money, that she is unhappy with her husband's modest income and life. Then, Yvonne tries to explain at a courthouse hearing why she is thousands of dollars in debt on one of her credit cards. These first images acquaint the viewer with the characters' financial difficulties and unhappiness, especially Muriel's ambition and Yvonne's poverty and failed marriage. These scenes help illustrate why lotteries exist and why people buy lottery tickets.

The story takes off when Charlie and Bo stop for lunch at a run-down coffee shop, where they are served by Yvonne. When Charlie discovers that he lacks money for a tip, he half-seriously offers to split his lottery winnings with her and promises to return the next day with her share or a decent tip.

That night, Charlie and Muriel do indeed win four million dollars in the lottery. This extraordinary event turns everything upside down. The rest of the film shows how the money affects their lives, the lives of those around them, the media (specifically tabloid newspapers), the tabloid-reading public, and the community.

Charlie is thrilled at his luck. There is no question his mind that he will honor his promise to Yvonne until Muriel puts her foot down. She is furious enough as it is when she learns they must share the award with a nine-member bowling team from upstate New York. Charlie dreads telling Muriel of his promise, anticipating the inevitable conflict it will provoke.

Charlie returns to the coffee shop the next day, still undecided about what to do. He witnesses Yvonne's victimization by her boss, sees her kindness to customers, and listens to the story of her bankruptcy. Charlie finally tells her that she may choose between her share of the winnings or a tip. She flippantly claims her share, is incredulous when he tells her that it is two million dollars, and then is positively jubilant. Fonda is delightful as the shocked and joyous Yvonne. Her face gradually lights up, then radiates, and she screams and dashes around the shop hugging and kissing customers and scooping out dollops of ice cream.

The money illustrates the natures of the characters. Although Charlie enjoys his work and stays with the police force, his bravery during a robbery results in his being wounded in action and he is forced to take a leave of absence. After winning the lottery, Charlie makes numerous gifts: He gives money to beggars, gives Bo season tickets to the Knicks' home games, makes a donation to the police department's widow fund, and, with Yvonne, gives out subway tokens to fellow New Yorkers and rents Yankee Stadium for the neighborhood kids. Yvonne buys and renovates the coffee shop at which she worked and establishes a table in Charlie's name for anyone who needs a free meal.

Muriel, however, embodies selfishness, greed, and poor taste. She promotes herself to the press at the award ceremony, goes on a shopping spree, has their apartment rebuilt and redecorated, commissions a garish portrait of herself, courts the friendship of a dubious financier (Seymour Cassel), has her breasts enlarged, files for divorce from Charlie, claims all the lottery winnings for herself—even Yvonne's share—and lies in court.

Yvonne's estranged husband, Eddie (Stanley Tucci), an actor, is, according to Yvonne, a liar and a lowlife. Because of Eddie, Yvonne had to file bankruptcy and could not even afford a divorce. Although they have been separated for some time, he calls her following the announcement of her winnings. He lies, tells her he has been out of town and does not know about the money, even congratulates her. She, however, resists his efforts.

While attending a party with Muriel on a ferry along

> "A promise is a promise."—Charlie Lang in *It Could Happen to You*

the East River given for the winners, Charlie spots Yvonne arriving by taxi. He leaves the ferry and is separated from his wife by the ferry's departure. Charlie and Yvonne have dinner, talk about their marriages, dance, and agree to meet the following afternoon. Charlie feels guilty and wonders how he will explain his disappearance from the dinner party. Ironically, he finds Muriel having the time of her life in the company of the financier, so preoccupied that she was unaware of his absence. Since Muriel passed the evening with another man and did not miss him, Charlie no longer feels guilty about having passed the evening with Yvonne.

Charlie and Yvonne meet several times before another twist of fate brings them to adjoining rooms at the Plaza Hotel: Charlie has been kicked out of the apartment by Muriel who wants a divorce, and Yvonne has fled from Eddie after he stations himself in her apartment, demanding money. They spend the night together. Their romance, here and throughout, has the nervous awkwardness and gentleness of a young love.

The film climaxes at Muriel and Charlie's divorce proceedings. Muriel's greed makes the proceedings and trial ugly and ridiculous. Although Charlie concedes their share (two million dollars) Muriel demands and wins everything, including the money Charlie gave Yvonne. Throughout, the tabloids cover much of the story, the award ceremony, Charlie's decoration, one of Charlie and Yvonne's dates, the apparent rendezvous, and the trial.

Yvonne stands up for Charlie in court, but she is horrified and humiliated by the rhetoric of the trial, its nastiness and falsehoods. She flees at the conclusion, with Charlie in hot pursuit. Nevertheless, love and justice do prevail. A reporter stalks them dressed as a beggar and his exclusive of their generosity toward him wins for them the support of New York: letters and money come pouring in, enabling them to remain in the city, and Yvonne to keep her coffee shop.

As for their two-faced spouses, Muriel marries her financier, who swindles her out of her money and disappears, forcing her to return to her wretched life in Queens. Eddie gets nothing from Yvonne and ends up driving a cab.

Unfortunately, the characters in the two marriages are so one-sided and ill-suited that the relationships seem implausible, even absurd. One must wonder how Charlie and Muriel, not to mention Yvonne and Eddie, came together and married. The brief summaries Charlie and Yvonne give of their personal lives are uninspired, though one learns that Charlie and Muriel were high school sweethearts. The circumstances and the tension created by the differences between these mismatched spouses succeed, however, in making their stories, and the film, both silly and charming.

John Lyons deserves special mention for the casting of

CREDITS

Charlie Lang: Nicolas Cage
Yvonne Biasi: Bridget Fonda
Muriel Lang: Rosie Perez
Bo Williams: Wendell Pierce
Angel: Isaac Hayes
Eddie Biasi: Stanley Tucci
Jack Gross: Seymour Cassel

Released: 1994
Production: Mike Lobell for Adelson/Baumgarten and Lobell/Bergman; released by TriStar Pictures
Direction: Andrew Bergman
Screenplay: Jane Anderson
Cinematography: Caleb Deschanel
Editing: Barry Malkin
Production design: Bill Groom
Art direction: Dennis Bradford
Set decoration: George DeTitta, Jr.
Casting: John Lyons
Sound: Paul P. Soucek
Costume design: Julie Weiss
Music: Carter Burwell
MPAA rating: PG
Running time: 101 minutes

this film: Cage and Fonda are excellent. Cage conveys feelings of casualness, modesty, and generosity, Fonda of strength, honesty, and vulnerability. Perez's performance as the irascible wife, a caricature of ambition, greed, and poor taste, is both amusing and successful. All in all, *It Could Happen to You* is a light and charming romantic comedy, with fine performances by its three principals.

—*Michael Forstrom*

REVIEWS

Chicago Tribune. July 29, 1994, sec. 2, p. 5.
Entertainment Weekly. July 29, 1994, p. 40.
The Hollywood Reporter. July 15-17, 1994, p. 9.
Los Angeles Times. July 29, 1994, p. F1.
Newsweek. August 1, 1994, p. 56.
The New York Times. July 29, 1994, p. B2.
The New Yorker. August 1, 1994, pp. 74-76.
USA Today. July 29, 1994, p. 7D.
Variety. July 15, 1994, p. 2.
The Washington Post. July 29, 1994, p. 36.

It's Pat

"A comedy that proves love is a many gendered thing."—Movie tagline

"A delightfully silly comedy...."—*The Register*

Box Office Gross: $31,370 (August 28, 1994)

Julia Sweeney brings her androgynous character, Pat, from television's *Saturday Night Live*, to the big screen in this lame comedy. Co-stars David Foley from TV's *The Kids in the Hall*. Camille Paglia, author of *Sexual Personae* makes a cameo as herself as she comments on the social significance of Pat's androgyny. A cameo by Harvey Keitel wound up on the cutting room floor. Music by Mark Mothersbaugh, formerly of the new wave group, Devo. Hooray for androgyny, indeed.

REVIEWS

Los Angeles Times. February 3, 1995, p. F6.
Variety. CCCLVI, August 29, 1994, p.43.

Julia Sweeney had to wear a 30-pound latex suit to create the androgynous illusion of Pat. The suit was equipped with a system of water-cooling circulation tubing to keep Sweeney's body temperature down while filming in the summer weather.

CREDITS

Pat: Julia Sweeney
Chris: David Foley
Kyle: Charles Rocket
Kathy: Kathy Griffin
Stacy: Julie Hayden
Doctor: Timothy Stack
Nurse: Mary Scheer
Mrs. Riley: Beverly Leech
Postal supervisor: Larry Hankin
Tippy: Kathy Najimy
Arlene Sorken: Arlene Sorken
Camille Paglia: Camille Paglia
Station manager: Tim Meadows

Released: 1994
Production: Charles B. Wessler for Touchstone Pictures; released by Buena Vista Pictures
Direction: Adam Bernstein
Screenplay: Jim Emerson, Stephen Hibbert, and Julia Sweeney; based on characters created by Sweeney
Cinematography: Jeffrey Jur
Editing: Norman D. Hollyn
Production design: Michelle Minch
Art direction: Mark Worthington
Set decoration: Beth De Sort
Casting: Carol Lewis
Sound: Russell Williams II
Costume design: Tom Bronson
Music: Mark Mothersbaugh
MPAA rating: PG-13
Running time: 77 minutes

"Who am I? What am I? Where do I come from? As I remember it I started life down the road most traveled."—Pat's opening monologue from *It's Pat*

Ivan and Abraham

The friendship between two boys—one a Jew, Abraham (Roma Alexandrovitch), and the other a Christian, Ivan (Sacha Iakovlev)—in 1930's Poland is the focus of this drama. First fiction feature film by documentarian Yolande Zauberman.

REVIEWS

Boston Globe. May 20, 1994, p. 52.
Los Angeles Times. October 13, 1994, p. F8.
The New York Times. March 23, 1994, p. C17.
Variety. CCCLVI, August 29, 1994, p. 43.
The Washington Post. July 22, 1994, p. C7.

CREDITS

Abraham: Roma Alexandrovitch
Ivan: Sacha Iakovlev
Aaron: Vladimir Machkov
Rachel: Maria Lipkina
Reyzele: Helene Lapiower
Mardoche: Alexandre Kaliaguine
Nachman: Rolan Bykov
Prince: Oleg Iankovski
Stepan: Daniel Olbrychski

Origin: France
Released: 1994
Production: Rene Cleitman and Jean-Luc Ormieres; released by New Yorker Films
Direction: Yolande Zauberman
Screenplay: Yolande Zauberman
Cinematography: Jean-Marc Fabre
Editing: Yann Dedet
Production design: Alexandre Sagoskin
Costume design: Marina Kaishauri
Music: Ghedalia Tazartes
MPAA rating: no listing
Running time: 105 minutes

Jason's Lyric

"Love is courage."—Movie tagline

"Sizzling hot with an explosive soundtrack!"
—Charla Krupp, *Glamour*

"A classic and powerful romance with wonderful performances."—Paul Wunder, *WBAI Radio*

 Box Office Gross: $20,546,658 (January 2, 1995)

*J*ason's Lyric is an example of "edu-tainment," a term coined by the production team of Doug McHenry and George Jackson. Their previous work, most notably the film *New Jack City* (1991), helped to create and popularize the genre of black gangster films that explore modern urban environments. McHenry and Jackson later co-directed the popular black comedy *House Party II* (1991). *Jason's Lyric*, which contrasts the struggles of young lovers amid the setting of urban gangs, is McHenry's first motion picture as a solo director.

The opening shots show Jason Alexander (Allen Payne) looking thoughtfully out of a bus window. Jason is trying to put to rest the ghosts of his past. As the bus leaves Houston, Texas, Jason reflects on his childhood and recent past in the Houston's Wards district, the tough neighborhood in which Jason and his brother Joshua (Bokeem Woodbine) grew up. The remainder of the film presents in flashback Jason's coming of age and his difficult decisions concerning his loyalty to Joshua and to his new girlfriend Lyric (Jada Pinkett).

Some of the most pleasant and most painful memories of Jason's past concern his father Maddog (Forest Whitaker), who taught Jason and Joshua about magic. Playing with his young sons in a field of flowers, Maddog instructs the boys to wait for the rainmaker, and he points to the airplane about to pass over and spray water on the flowers. In their bedroom before falling asleep, the boys talk about Maddog. Joshua thinks their father is nothing but a drunk, but Jason can see that Maddog was physically and emotionally broken as the result of his experiences in Vietnam. Both boys' fears for their mother, Gloria (Suzzanne Douglas), are realized one night when Maddog arrives at their house drunk, and he begins to hit Gloria. The sounds of their argument wake the boys, and Joshua takes a gun to the living room to confront Maddog. A gunshot leads to a quick fade out.

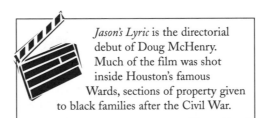

Jason's Lyric is the directorial debut of Doug McHenry. Much of the film was shot inside Houston's famous Wards, sections of property given to black families after the Civil War.

The next portion of the film shows the boys as young adults, trying to create a life for themselves. Jason drives to prison to pick up Joshua as he is released. They meet with some friends and begin to celebrate. When Joshua and Jason finally arrive home, Joshua is too drunk to appreciate the surprise party that Gloria has arranged for him. A subsequent conversation between the brothers during a one-on-one basketball game establishes that Jason wants to make the most of his job at an appliance store and that Joshua has become hardened and bittered by his years in prison. When Jason next arrives at work, he is encouraged by the possibility of a transfer to Dallas to become an assistant manager. Joshua's decline also continues. The film implies a parallel between Maddog's ruinous tour of Vietnam and Joshua's years in prison. Joshua steals money from Gloria's cash register at work and is rescued from bars by his concerned brother. Jason regretfully refuses the job in Dallas in the hope of solidifying his family. This brother plot takes some of its elements from John Steinbeck's *East of Eden* (1952) and Eugene O'Neill's 1920 play *Beyond The Horizon* and places them in an urban black setting.

Jason's own life gains additional purpose when he meets Lyric at the appliance store. They talk at a restaurant, and Jason later offers her a rose as he walks her home. On a railroad trestle dwarfed by the distant Houston skyline, Jason and Lyric talk about their hopes and dreams. Their romance develops after Jason seeks Gloria's advice on how to find a special place to dine with Lyric. Acting on his mother's advice, Jason briefly overcomes the unromantic squalor of inner-city Houston by surprising Lyric at her bus stop, blindfolding her, and driving her to the colorfully muralled foyer of a bus station, where he arranges a table for their privacy and serves her a picnic dinner. Jason and Lyric desire to escape together and plan to meet later at a bayou.

Just as Jason and Lyric's dinner signals a new closeness in their relationship, an argumentative Sunday lunch foreshadows Joshua's growing difficulties. Joshua has planned the Sunday meal for Gloria after she returns home from church, but she knows that much of his money comes from selling drugs. While Jason looks on helplessly, Gloria overturns the table and shouts that she will not eat food bought with drug money. Angered, Joshua becomes more deeply involved with a city gang. He steals cars with his gang friends and listens to their plans to rob a bank. Lyric's half-brother Alonzo (Treach) is the bullying leader of this gang.

The plot moves to the climax of the bank robbery. Jason hears about the gang's plans from Lyric, who has overheard Alonzo's instructions to his gangsters on their front porch. Jason tries to talk Joshua out of involving himself in the robbery, but Joshua's indecisiveness only makes him arrive late at the bank, botching the robbery. Later, Alonzo and the gang members bind Joshua and beat him for spoiling their plans. Joshua tells the gang that Jason and Lyric are to blame for his failure to arrive on time. When Joshua staggers home bloodied from the gang's revenges, Jason goes in search of Alonzo and arrives late in meeting Lyric at the bayou. She waits with suitcase in hand, quoting John Donne's poem "The Bait" (1633): "Come live with me, and be my love,/And we will

> "Booze is like garlic—it keeps the ghosts away."—Joshua from *Jason's Lyric*

some new pleasures prove/Of golden sands, and crystal brooks/With silken lines, and silver hooks." The reality of the gang violence, however, has dispelled most of Jason's romantic dreams. He tells Lyric about the night of Maddog's death, admitting that it was he and not Joshua who pulled the trigger. She now sees the source of Jason's recurrent nightmares. Both return to their urban worlds. At the restaurant where she works, Lyric's girlfriend comforts her by telling Lyric that she had found some quiet "in a world of thunder."

The script by Bobby Smith, Jr., attempts to combine the savagery of urban gang life with some tender lyrical vignettes. Although the film proved to be relatively successful—grossing over $20 million against modest production costs of $7 million—reviewers usually faulted the film for mixing its elements of realism and romanticism a bit clumsily. The first love scene of Jason and Lyric, for example, takes place in a field of flowers with a song playing loudly on the soundtrack. The director of photography, Francis Kenny, has said that these scenes are "shot like a poem." The graphic nature of the sex, however, jeopardizes the subtlety of the scene's poetry. The rhapsodic moments of the film, like Jason and Lyric's picnic lunch at the bus station, become the visual equivalents of Lyric's fondness for quoting love poetry, but the lushness risks being overblown. Even in a theater of the film's intended audience of young people, the sound of suppressed laughter accompanies some of these romantic interludes.

The concluding scenes of the motion picture illustrate another scripting problem faulted by critics. The withheld secret of the identity of Maddog's killer and the string of retaliations in which Joshua shoots Lyric in a final stand-off with Jason rely more on surprising plot twists than on the climate of urban realism that strengthens the better portions of the film. In returning in its last scene to the shot of the bus leaving Houston, the filmmakers show a wider shot of Jason than the establishing shot that opened the film. Lyric now appears at his side, somehow having recovered from her injuries, and she and Jason ride out of town to begin a new life. The arbitrariness of the forced happy ending defeats much of the honesty of the preceding moments of realism.

Nevertheless, the acting in the film is effective. Allen Payne conveys Jason's sensitivity quite well, and Jada Pinkett makes Lyric's desire to escape her sad life believable. Bokeem Woodbine makes Joshua a menacing gang thug, and Suzanne Douglas presents well the hopes and frustrations Gloria sees in her sons. In the small part of Maddog, Forest Whitaker brings out both his character's vulnerability and anger at the world.

Jason's Lyric balances the struggle of inner-city life with

CREDITS

Jason Alexander: Allen Payne
Lyric Greer: Jada Pinkett
Maddog: Forest Whitaker
Joshua Alexander: Bokeem Woodbine
Gloria Alexander: Suzanne Douglas
Alonzo: Treach
Rat: Eddie Griffin
Ron: Lahmard Tate
Marti: Lisa Carson
Elmo: Clarence Whitmore
Teddy: Asheamu Earl Randle
Fast Freddy: Rushion McDonald
Ms. Murphy: Bebe Drake
Leroy: Kenneth Randle
Street Preacher: Wayne DeHart
Jason (11 years old): Sean Hutchinson
Joshua (8 years old): Burleigh Moore

Released: 1994
Production: Doug McHenry and George Jackson for Propaganda Films; released by Gramercy Pictures
Direction: Doug McHenry
Screenplay: Bobby Smith, Jr.
Cinematography: Francis Kenny
Editing: Andrew Mondshein
Production design: Simon Dobbin
Art direction: David Lazan
Set decoration: Tessa Posnansky
Casting: Jaki Brown-Karman and Kimberly Hardin
Sound: David Yaffe
Costume design: Craig Anthony
Music supervision: Adam Kidron
Music: Afrika and Matt Noble
MPAA rating: R
Running time: 119 minutes

the dreams of romance and a better existence. It recalls John Singleton's second film, *Poetic Justice* (1993), and in spite of its stylistic excesses, *Jason's Lyric* has greater success than Singleton's film in placing a believable love story against the backdrop of urban gang violence. Though marred by some contrivances in plotting, the film also presents a promising directorial debut for Doug McHenry.

—Glenn Hopp

REVIEWS

Daily Variety. September 20, 1994, p. 12.
Entertainment Weekly. October 7, 1994, p. 54.
The Hollywood Reporter. September, 27, 1994, p. 6.
Los Angeles Times. September 28, 1994, p. F6.
The New York Times. September 28, 1994, p. B2.
The New Yorker. October 10, 1994, p. 32.

Jimmy Hollywood

"One thing stands between Jimmy and stardom. Reality."—Movie tagline
"They took a shot at stardom and it shot back."—Movie tagline

 **Box Office Gross:** $3,730,888 (May 1, 1994)

Jimmy Hollywood is a comic drama about dreams among the ruins. It is a highly personal look at the Hollywood myth and the people who still dare to believe in it.

Jimmy Alto (Joe Pesci) is an aluminum-siding salesman from New Jersey who has come to Hollywood to be a motion-picture star. As the film opens, Jimmy marches down the Hollywood Boulevard Walk of Fame, eyes closed, chanting the names of the stars who are immortalized in concrete. When he misses one he is upset that his buddy, the simple-minded but resourceful William (Christian Slater), has neglected to count the stars he has correctly named up to that point. For some reason this is terribly important to Jimmy—almost a superstition. Perhaps if he correctly names them all he will become a star also.

Jimmy hangs out most days with William, one of the lost souls from the boulevard. William can run a camcorder, a digital labeling machine, almost anything electronic, but his own mental mechanics are on the fritz. The friendship between Jimmy and William is touching: Jimmy likes William because he lets him talk and listens to his ideas; William depends on Jimmy to explain things.

Tired of waiting for his big break to stardom, Jimmy takes out an ad on a bus-stop bench, hoping the right per-

Joe Pesci as Jimmy Alto and Christian Slater as William in *Jimmy Hollywood*. Copyright © 1994 Paramount Pictures. All rights reserved.

son will drive by and see it. The ad includes a photo of himself with the epithet "Actor Extraordinaire" and his phone number, 213-02-Actor. The only attention it seems to garner, however, is a drive-by heckler who shouts at Jimmy that the bus-bench photo looks better than he does, and a graffiti artist who retouches the ad with his own artwork.

In the film, writer-director-producer Barry Levinson succeeds in contrasting the Hollywood of the 1990's—seedy, full of graffiti and drug traffic—with the Hollywood of Jimmy's dreams, which Jimmy keeps alive by watching the classic documentary *Hollywood and the Stars* on his Sony Watchman. An amusing scene recurs throughout the film. Jimmy and William wile away the hours lying out by the pool of Jimmy's shabby apartment building. Jimmy tells his girlfriend, Lorraine (Victoria Abril), he is getting some color to

Many of Jimmy's fascinations about Hollywood are taken from director Barry Levinson's personal experiences. He came to Hollywood in 1970, lived with two friends in a studio on Hollywood Boulevard and worked in a deli, as Jimmy does in *Jimmy Hollywood*.

try out for a part that calls for someone tan. As they sun, the phone rings and Jimmy always asks William if that is his phone ringing. William always says no, but the viewer suspects otherwise. This suspicion is confirmed when the answering machine clicks on one day and the viewer overhears a message for Jimmy, telling him he did not, after all, get a part in a film he had read for and thought he had finally won.

Jimmy is upset when Lorraine is held up at an automatic teller machine. He is livid when his radio is stolen from his car. When the police tell him there is nothing they can do, Jimmy becomes so angry he decides to do something about it himself. As a result, he and William stake out the area with a camcorder. Not only do they record the thief in the act of vandalizing another car but they capture him and toss him on the steps of the police station with a note signed S.O.S. The police think a terrorist vigilante organization is at work headed by a secretive leader called Jericho. The media give the story full play.

All of a sudden Jimmy has found a starring role as Jericho of the S.O.S. The public likes what he is doing and he thrives on the adulation, although the level-headed Lorraine warns him that he will get in trouble with the police if he does not stop. Yet stop he cannot, as the audience and airplay have become too important to him.

Things become tense as Jimmy continues to pursue

"I gave a hell of a reading for that part, but I think they felt I was a little too strong for Andy Griffith."—Jimmy describing a reading for *Matlock* in *Jimmy Hollywood*

criminals and the police start to close in on him and William. After Jimmy goes public about Jericho, the two prepare to leave town for awhile. Jimmy starts rehearsing his farewell speech for the final taping at the Hollywood Bowl. Unfortunately, the police are onto them, and they find themselves trapped in an old abandoned theater, surrounded by police, the media, and mobs of fans.

The police let Lorraine inside the theater to try to persuade Jimmy to give himself up, but he refuses. Instead, he persuades William to leave with her. Finally, after rehearsing the scene over and over, Jimmy comes out, pistol blasting. Lorraine, however, has had the foresight to tell the police that the gun is loaded with blanks. Jimmy is apprehended and given six months in prison and 800 hours of community service.

In an amusing coda, Jimmy, upon his release, becomes the adviser to director Barry Levinson on a film about his adventure, starring Harrison Ford as Jimmy. Lorraine is the hairdresser for the film and William is a cameraman. The film concludes with Jimmy giving Ford advice on how best to play the role of Jimmy.

Jimmy Hollywood is a departure in setting, style, and budget for director Levinson, whose other films include *Good Morning, Vietnam* (1987), *Rain Man* (1988)—for which he won an Academy Award for Best Direction—and *Bugsy* (1991). According to reviewers Anthony Lane of *The New Yorker* and David Ansen of *Newsweek*, *Jimmy Hollywood* is reminiscent of Levinson's *Diner* (1982) and *Tin Men* (1987) days. According to Ansen, "The director of *Rain Man* and *Good Morning, Vietnam* is back in the small, low-budget, personal mode of *Diner* and *Tin Men*." Said Lane, "This is the Levinson of *Diner* and *Tin Men*, the connoisseur of rough edges and loose tongues."

Director of photography Peter Sova has worked with Levinson on *Diner*, *Tin Men*, and *Good Morning, Vietnam*. They filmed on location in Hollywood and the vicinity, often utilizing steadicams and multicamera setups to follow Jimmy and William as they wander the streets. As a result, the filmmakers achieved a backdrop of authentic local residents, street people, and tourists. Levinson also worked daily with editor Jay Rabinowitz utilizing a digital editing system installed in a bus that accompanied the production unit. This allowed them to edit and evaluate the work in progress during breaks in shooting. The sound track for the film is also notable featuring the original music of Robbie Robertson and including an eclectic mix of contemporary and world music's leading talents. The role of Jimmy suits Pesci well. He plays the cocky, complaining pest with a natural flair, yet makes the audience want him to succeed in spite of everything. Slater is particularly winsome as William, who, with his slow-moving sweetness and simple-

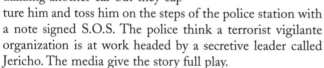

CREDITS

Jimmy Alto: Joe Pesci
William: Christian Slater
Lorraine: Victoria Abril
Detective: Jason Beghe
Detective: John Cothran, Jr.

Released: 1994
Production: Mark Johnson and Barry Levinson for Baltimore Pictures; released by Paramount Pictures
Direction: Barry Levinson
Screenplay: Barry Levinson
Cinematography: Peter Sova
Editing: Jay Rabinowitz
Production design: Linda De Scenna
Set decoration: Ric McElvin
Casting: Louis Di Giaimo
Sound: Steve Cantamessa
Costume design: Kirsten Everberg
Music: Robbie Robertson
MPAA rating: R
Running time: 109 minutes

minded philosophy of life, is a perfect foil for the hyperactive Jimmy. In her first starring role in an American film, Spanish actress Abril is also enjoyable in her role as Jimmy's girlfriend, Lorraine. Abril is reminiscent of a Spanish Goldie Hawn in a wacky, wonderful scene where she is being held up at an ATM and frustrates the robber so much with her nervous arguing that he flees in disgust.

Although Ralph Novak, of *People* magazine called *Jimmy Hollywood* an "unfocused, self-important comedy," David Ansen of *Newsweek* said, "Both a character study of a colorful failure and an elegy on the rotted dream of Hollywood glory, Levinson's atmospheric movie both fascinates and frustrates.... It may not be Hollywood's idea of a socko entertainment, but, unlike many a hit, it follows you home." Anthony Lane, in *The New Yorker*, said, "*Jimmy Hollywood* tells an old story, but the telling of it feels new-

minted, bright with surprises—the images seem to break free of the script and lead the way."

—*Sandra G. Garrett and Philip C. Williams*

REVIEWS

Entertainment Weekly. April 8, 1994, p. 34.
The Hollywood Reporter. March 25-27, 1994, p. 10.
Los Angeles Times. March 30, 1994, p. F1.
Maclean's. CVII, April 4, 1994, p. 59.
The New York Times. February 3, 1994, p. B1.
The New York Times. March 30, 1994, p. B3.
The New Yorker. April 4, 1994, p. 97.
Newsweek. April 11, 1994, p. 74.
People. March 28, 1994, p. 18.
Variety. March 25, 1994, p. 4.

Jit

An ambitious young man, UK (Dominic Makuvachuma), goes to the city to find a job only to fall in love with a beautiful young woman, Sofi (Sibongile Nene). Complicating matters are Sofi's gangster boyfriend, the sizable bride price being asked by her father, and a pesky ancestral spirit, Jukwa (Winnie Ndemera), who disapproves of Sofi and insists that UK send his earnings back home to his parents instead. *Jit* is the first all-Zimbabwean feature film. The title refers to the local music, which is a blend of traditional African rhythms and reggae-pop.

REVIEWS

Chicago Tribune. December 17, 1993, p. 7J(34).
Christian Science Monitor. November 10, 1994, p. 12.
Entertainment Weekly. October 21, 1994, p. 74.
The New York Times. March 20, 1993, p. A16.
The New York Times. November 4, 1994, p. D19.
The Washington Post. September 4, 1993, p. F6.

CREDITS

UK: Dominic Makuvachuma
Sofi: Sibongile Nene
Johnson: Farai Sevenzo
Jukwa: Winnie Ndemera
Oliver: Oliver Mtukudzi
Chamba: Lawrence Simbarashe

Origin: Zimbabwe
Released: 1993
Production: Rory Kilalea; released by Northern Arts Entertainment
Direction: Michael Raeburn
Screenplay: Michael Raeburn
Cinematography: Joao (Funcho) Costa
Editing: Justin Krish
MPAA rating: no listing
Running time: 98 minutes

Jo-Jo at the Gate of Lions

This drama centers on a disturbed young woman, Jo-Jo (Lorie Marino), who hears voices, obsesses about nuclear war, and is harassed by her sleazy employer. Feature-film directorial debut of Britta Sjogren.

REVIEWS

Variety. CCCXLVI, February 3, 1992, p. 81.

CREDITS

Jo-Jo: Lorie Marino
Jon: Chris Shearer
Luke: David Schultz

Released: 1992
Production: Britta Sjogren for Nana Films
Direction: Britta Sjogren
Screenplay: Britta Sjogren
Cinematography: Greg Watkins
Editing: Britta Sjogren
Production design: Adam Braff
Sound: Rory Kelly
Music: Jonathan Sampson
MPAA rating: no listing
Running time: 103 minutes

The Judas Project

"The ultimate encounter."—Movie tagline
"An inspiring film."—Jeff Craig, *60 Second Prevoew*
"...moving and highly entertaining...."—*Morning Star*

 Box Office Gross: $253,030 (October 2, 1994)

A contemporary retelling of the story of Jesus Christ, this drama stars John O'Banion as Jesse, the Jesus figure who preaches love and faith.

REVIEWS

Variety. CCCL, March 22, 1993, p. 52.

CREDITS

Jesse: John O'Banion
Jude: Ramy Zada
Cunningham: Richard Herd
Ponerous: Jeff Corey
Jackson: Gerald Gordon

Released: 1992
Production: James Nelson and Ervin Melton for the Judas Project Limited Partnership; released by RS Entertainment
Direction: James H. Barden
Screenplay: James H. Barden
Cinematography: Bryan England
Editing: Noreen Zepp-Linden
Production design: Philip Dean Foreman
Visual effects: Richard Edlund
Music: James H. Barden
MPAA rating: PG-13
Running time: 97 minutes

The Jungle Book

"See the Legend Come to Life!"—Movie tagline

"The Best Family Movie of the Season!"
—*American Movie Classics*

"Breathtaking."—*New York Newsday*

"A howling, growling, hissing good time."
—David Hunter, *The Hollywood Reporter*

"An encyclopedia of wonders, from the dazzling scenery, cinematography, costumes and sets, to the animals."—Brian Lowry, *Daily Variety*

 Box Office Gross: $22,078,837 (January 2, 1995)

While *The Jungle Book* is clearly intended as family fun, it touches upon the incendiary issues of racism, exploitation, and western colonialism. These elements form the subtext to the story of Mowgli, a feral child who suddenly finds himself among "civilized" men and women who treat him with varying degrees of civility and contempt.

The Disney people rarely tackle such discomforting material, and in this case they do so with kid gloves. Nevertheless, by the end of *The Jungle Book* even the child audience at whom this movie is mostly targeted must ask itself the question: who's the most civilized, the British overlords of India with their immaculate white uniforms and Victorian virtues, or the illiterate native boy who lives by the simple code of the forest?

Mowgli overcomes persecution, imprisonment, expulsion, and exploitation at the hands of the sociopathic Captain Boone (Cary Elwes) and his greedy companions. He triumphs against adversaries who, despite cultivated trappings, are truly savage. In the end it is Mowgli, not the Brits, who emerges as genuinely civilized. In *The Jungle Book*, the heroes do not wear white.

As the story opens, a very young Mowgli is accidentally dispatched to the forest following an attack by a tiger. He is adopted by a wolf pack, makes friends with many of the other animals, and becomes familiar with the mysterious ways of the jungle.

One day, Mowgli stumbles upon an ancient city. Hidden amid the rubble is a treasure protected by series of lethal booby traps, a troop of territorial monkeys, and a fiercesome cobra roughly the size of the Loch Ness Monster. Mowgli tousles with the snake and makes off with

a jewel-encrusted dagger. It is at this point that his troubles really begin.

While strolling down a river, he happens upon a beautiful English school girl. Mowgli recognizes her at once as Kitty Brydon (Lena Headey), a childhood friend with whom he has been smitten since the age of five. Mowgli steals into the fortress where Kitty and her father Major Brydon (Sam Neill) reside. There he is captured by Boone but released when Kitty tells her father who Mowgli really is.

Kitty and a buffoonish scientist named Doctor Plumford (John Cleese) then instruct Mowgli in the various arts of western civilization. In a few short weeks, Mowgli transcends savagery. He learns to speak, read and write in English. He is also schooled in music, history and philosophy. This transformation is the film's most serious weakness. With mind-numbing speed, Mowgli the wolf boy begins to look and act as though he has just graduated from Cambridge.

Captain Boone, meanwhile, begins to make his plans against Mowgli. He resents the attention Kitty gives the jungle boy—who is, after all, a mere savage—and a native to boot. Boone has his own plans for Kitty and for the jewel-encrusted dagger he found on Mowgli. Boone goes for the jugular at a coming-out party in which Mowgli is to be introduced to British society. He deliberately embarrasses Mowgli, then sends him packing back into the forest.

Boone and his avaricious pals follow Mowgli into the woods, hoping he will lead them to the lost city. Along the

Twenty-nine animal trainers are credited for their work on *The Jungle Book*

way, Boone kidnaps Kitty and nearly kills her father. To save the Brydons, Mowgli leads Boone and party to the city where the colossal cobra and other perils await them. In time-honored Disney style, Mowgli triumphs and the bad guys get what's coming to them.

The Jungle Book has been extremely well-received by critics. *Entertainment Weekly* praised the film's "canny casting," and compared it favorably to earlier movies based on the same material. *The Hollywood Reporter*, meanwhile, was even more lavish with its praise, describing *The Jungle Book* as "a howling, hissing, growling good time."

The Jungle Book was directed by relative newcomer Stephen Sommers, who is best known for his work in screenwriting. His experience shows up in the dialog which is often cute, and sometimes downright clever. Performances are exemplary. Lee is a near-perfect fit as Mowgli, while Neill and Headey competently mimic the British upper classes. Cleese's twit bit is as amusing as ever, while Elwes as lead rotter is the consummate villain. All of the actors do a

CREDITS

Mowgli: Jason Scott Lee
Boone: Cary Elwes
Kitty: Lena Headey
Brydon: Sam Neill
Dr. Plumford: John Cleese
Wilkins: Jason Flemyng
Buldeo: Sefan Kalipha
Harley: Ron Donachie

Released: 1994
Production: Edward S. Feldman and Raju Patel for Walt Disney Pictures and Sharad Patel; released by Buena Vista Pictures
Direction: Stephen Sommers
Screenplay: Stephen Sommers, Ronald Yanover, and Mark D. Geldman; based on a story by Yanover and Geldman, and on characters from *The Jungle Book*, by Rudyard Kipling
Cinematography: Juan Ruiz-Anchia
Editing: Bob Ducsay
Production design: Allan Cameron
Set decoration: Crispian Sallis
Casting: Celestia Fox
Visual effects supervision: Peter Montgomery
Sound: Joseph Geisinger
Costume design: John Mollo
Animal Training: Steve Martin
Stunt coordination: Gerry Crampton, David Ellis and Tim Davidson
Music: Basil Poledouris
MPAA rating: PG
Running time: 108 minutes

fine job in *The Jungle Book*. Even Mowgli's animal chums perform well.

Does *The Jungle Book*, with its subtle references to racism and British colonialism represent a major departure for the Disney Studios? These days even school kids have a pretty good idea what the British and the other colonial powers did to India, Africa and southeast Asia. With or without kid gloves, it is far better to handle such material honestly then to avoid it altogether.

—*D. Douglas Graham*

REVIEWS

Atlanta Journal and Atlanta Constitution. December 23, 1994, p. P12.
Boston Globe. December 23, 1994, p. 53.
Chicago Tribune. December 25, 1994, Sec. 5 p. 5.
Christian Science Monitor. December 23, 1994, p. 10.
Daily Variety. December 19, 1994, p. 12.
Entertainment Weekly, January 13, 1995, p. 36.
Entertainment Weekly. May 12, 1995, p. 71.
The Hollywood Reporter, December 19, 1994, p.8.
Los Angeles Times, December 23, 1994, p. F8.
The New York Times. December 23, 1994, p. C5.
The New York Times, December 23, 1994, p. B4.
The New York Times. January 8, 1995, Sec. 2 p. 23.
Newsweek. MMCXXV, January 16, 1995, p. 66.
People Weekly. XXXIV, July 30, 1990, p. 21.
Premiere. IV, December 1990, p. 40.
The Wall Street Journal. January 5, 1995, p. A12.
The Washington Post. December 23, 1994, p. WW37.
The Washington Post. December 25, 1994, p. G11.
The Washington Post. December 29, 1994, p. C7.

Junior

"Nothing is inconceivable."—Movie tagline

"Go ahead, surrender to it. It won't make you a better person, but it might...make you a happier one."—Richard Schickel, *Time*

Box Office Gross: $30,808,210 (January 2, 1995)

Arnold Schwarzenneger as expectant father Dr. Alex Hesse, Emma Thompson as Dr. Diana Reddin, and Danny Devito as Dr. Larry Arbogast, in *Junior*. Copyright © by Universal City Studios, Inc. Courtesy of MCA Publishing Rights, a Division of MCA Inc. All Rights Reserved.

In the idiom of Hollywood deal-making, *Junior* illustrates a "high-concept" property. Arnold Schwarzenegger cast against type as playing a research scientist who experiments on himself with a drug that allows him to become pregnant and carry the child to term is the comic premise on which the entire film depends. As director Ivan Reitman, however, points out, "Even the most high-concept comedy should ultimately be grounded in the reality of being human. What makes us laugh is not so much what happens to people as what happens between them." His words describe a useful way of approaching his film. If the idea that became the film *Junior* sold because of its ready-made premise, it succeeds because of its humanity.

As the film opens, Dr. Alexander Hesse (Arnold Schwarzenegger) and his associate, gynecologist Larry Arbogast (Danny DeVito), try to get the Food and Drug Administration to approve financing for Expectane, their new drug to prevent miscarriages. The government, however, rejects their request, which leads their rescarch administrator, Noah Banes (Frank Langella), to cut off the money provided by their university. Before they can even gather their equipment, Banes turns over their spacious lab to Dr. Diana Reddin (Emma Thompson), a cryogenics expert who kindly offers to share the lab with Alex and Larry.

Thompson aptly referred to her character as "the kind of girl who was always more fascinated by algebra than boys.... She's really kind of masculine in comparison to Alex." Diana's clumsiness in moving her equipment into the research facility results in her losing her balance and toppling onto her cryogenics freezer, which rolls down a loading ramp, crashes through the lab door, and flattens a surprised Alex. This scene is a great example of "meeting cute," a phrase from the old studio era of Hollywood that describes the unconventional ways future lovers often encountered each other in romantic comedies. This first meeting in which Diana apologetically thanks Alex for stopping her

> The set decorator and art team for *Junior* did extensive research on genetic and fertility labs, modeling their own Lufkin Laboratory after labs at USC, UCLA, and UC Berkeley, complete with authentic lab equipment like cryogenic freezers.

runaway freezer of frozen ova dramatizes the basis for Alex and Diana's eventual romance. Their biology will loosen their restraints. The lovers-to-be are thus fittingly brought together by the tools of their trade—test tubes and freezers, eggs and sperm.

Both plot and comedy develop quickly once egg and sperm unite. It is fitting that Larry secretly chooses an ovum labeled "Junior" from Diana's supply of frozen eggs when he has talked Alex into using Expectane on himself to prove the success of the drug. "Junior" is Diana's own ovum, which Larry implants in Alex, fertilizes through a catheter, and safeguards with daily doses of Expectane. Alex participates reluctantly. He and Larry make an odd couple even under normal circumstances. Physical opposites, their temperaments also contrast. Fast-talking and manipulative, Larry sees the hidden pregnancy as a desperate last resort to save years of research. Introverted and easily intimidated, Alex hesitantly agrees. As his pregnancy progresses, however, Alex begins to wake and stretch emotionally. After a banquet at which he gets to know Diana better and feels attracted to her, he informs Larry that he intends to carry the fetus to term.

Though the comedy of the middle scenes mostly follows a predictable path—Alex admiring his softening skin, crusty Noah Banes remarking on Alex's radiance, Kodak commercials making Alex tear up—Schwarzenegger captures Alex's softer side convincingly. Alex is part of the

CREDITS

Dr. Alexander Hesse: Arnold Schwarzenegger
Dr. Larry Arbogast: Danny DeVito
Dr. Diana Reddin: Emma Thompson
Noah Banes: Frank Langella
Angela: Pamela Reed
Naomi: Judy Collins
Dr. Ned Sneller: James Eckhouse
Louise: Aida Turturro

Released: 1994
Production: Ivan Reitman for Northern Lights; released by Universal Pictures
Direction: Ivan Reitman
Screenplay: Kevin Wade and Chris Conrad
Cinematography: Adam Greenberg
Editing: Sheldon Kahn and Wendy Greene Bricmont
Production design: Stephen Lineweaver
Art direction: Gary Wissner
Set decoration: Clay A. Griffith
Set design: Barry Chusid and Dawn Snyder
Casting: Michael Chinich and Alan Berger
Sound: Gene Steven Cantamessa
Prosthetics makeup: Matthew W. Mungle
Costume design: Albert Wolsky
Technical consulting: Dr. Richard Buyalos
Music: James Newton Howard
MPAA rating: PG-13
Running time: 110 minutes

AWARDS AND NOMINATIONS

Academy Awards Nomination 1994: Best Original Song ("Look What Love Has Done")
Golden Globe Awards Nominations 1994: Best Actor—Musical/Comedy (Schwarzenegger), Best Actress—Musical/Comedy (Thompson), Best Original Song ("Look What Love Has Done")

American screen tradition of lovable but shy romantic heroes. Alex even hides behind round horn-rims like Harold Lloyd's boy-next-door characters in his silent comedies from the 1920's.

Cary Grant's character in Howard Hawks' classic screwball comedy *Bringing up Baby* (1938), a more likely influence on *Junior*, is another inhibited scientist with the same Clark Kent glasses, who learns to leave the laboratory and participate in life and love more fully. Like Grant, Schwarzenegger engages the audience by undergoing a series of unexpected and uncharacteristic comic ordeals. Being cast against type is not that rare for a well-known performer in Hollywood, but being able to bring off the challenge in light comedy is. Schwarzenegger's screen finesse goes far toward offsetting the predictability of the plot. The greatest appeal of the film is his performance.

The film's ties to the tradition of screwball comedy do not end with Schwarzenegger's character. Larry and Alex's

"Does my body disgust you?"— Arnold Schwarzenegger as the pregnant Dr. Alex Hesse in *Junior*

efforts to keep the pregnancy concealed recall some of the improbabilities of screwball comedies of the 1930's. For example, when Alex's pregnancy begins to show, he and Larry concoct a wild story to keep others from getting suspicious. Alex tells Diana that he suffers from *Glandensprung* disease, a little-known hereditary condition in Austria that makes men gain weight and become very emotional. Although Diana seems to accept this story, Noah Banes becomes more suspicious of Alex's size and odd behavior. In the last weeks of the pregnancy, Larry takes Alex, outfitted now in drag, to a maternity spa. Larry then heads for another meeting with pharmaceutical representatives to tout the success of Expectane, while Alex nears his delivery date and Banes grows more suspicious. The conclusion of the film involves a race to the lab to deliver Alex and Diana's baby without Banes finding out.

The production design of the film is calculated to represent visually the changing emotions of Alex. Early scenes emphasize the research lab, overstocked with computers, test tubes, technical contraptions, and metallic shelves. Though some humor develops in this setting—such as Diana's comic entrance atop the cryogenic freezer—the implication is that this is the lifeless home from which Alex has been evicted by Noah Banes. When Alex becomes more humanized by his pregnancy, however, Larry hides him at his home, where the medical equipment is confined to the bedroom.

Key scenes occur between Alex and Larry's pregnant former wife, Angela (Pamela Reed), in the kitchen, where they swap stories about their cravings, and between Alex and Diana in the living room, where for the first time they kiss. The change of setting from lab to home accords well with Alex's new feelings. Production designer Stephen Lineweaver explains that "our colors and environments early in the film are very monochromatic, almost sterile, to represent Alex's contained and closed life. But as he begins to 'blossom' with the pregnancy, the palette of the film changes to serene, warm and inviting colors."

The film's critical reception on the whole was favorable. Reviewers usually qualified their praise of the film by noting that its premise resulted in some predictable moments but that the performances and style generally redeemed the formulaic elements. Richard Schickel's comment in *Time* represents the tone of other reviewers: "Go ahead, surrender to it. It won't make you a better person, but it might, very briefly, make you a happier one."

The phrase "high-concept" can connote both good and bad things about a film. Just as it implies a desire to give the audience what it wants, it also suggests the avoidance of risk. *Junior* develops all the permutations of its surefire premise, but its efforts to go further and introduce touches of reality and humanity give the film its deepest comic appeal.

—Glenn Hopp

REVIEWS

Daily Variety. November 17, 1994, p. 2.
Entertainment Weekly. November 18, 1994, p. 16.
Entertainment Weekly. November 25, 1994, p. 46.
The Hollywood Reporter. November 17, 1994, p. 5.
Los Angeles Times. November 23, 1994, p. F1.
The New York Times. November 23, 1994, p. B1.
The New Yorker. December 12, 1994, p. 37.
Premiere. December, 1994, p. 76.
Time. November 28, 1994, p. 80.
USA Today. November 23-24, 1994, p. 1D.

Just Like a Woman

"I fell head-over-heels for a cross-dresser."
—Movie tagline

Box Office Gross: $71,880 (August 21, 1994)

A closet transvestite, Gerald (Adrian Pasdar), is thrown out of his home by his unsuspecting wife, who believes he is having an affair—because she found feminine lingerie in their bedroom. Gerald then has an affair with his new landlady, Monica (Julie Walters), who encourages him in his unusual predilection. A subplot involves Gerald attempting to foil his boss' underhanded deal with Japanese investors.

REVIEWS

The Advocate. July 26, 1994, p. 76.
Boston Globe. September 30, 1994, p. 65.
Los Angeles Times. July 22, 1994, p. F8.
The New Republic. CCXI, August 22, 1994, p. 34.
The New York Times. July 22, 1994, p. C12.
People Weekly. XLII, August 1, 1994, p. 15.
Playboy. XLI, August 1994, p. 17.
The Washington Post. August 12, 1994, p. F7.

"But all I have is evening wear."—
Gerald about his girlish wardrobe
in *Just Like a Woman*

CREDITS

Monica: Julie Walters
Gerald (Geraldine): Adrian Pasdar
Miles Millichamp: Paul Freeman
Louisa: Susan Wooldridge
C.J.: Gordon Kennedy

Origin: Great Britain
Released: 1994
Production: Nick Evans for Rank Film Distributors and LWT, in association with British Screen and Zenith; released by the Samuel Goldwyn Company
Direction: Christopher Monger
Screenplay: Nick Evans; based on the book *Geraldine*, by Monica Jay
Cinematography: Alan Hume
Editing: Nicolas Gaster
Production design: John Box
Art direction: Michael White
Set decoration: Peter Howitt
Costume Design: Suzy Peters
Music: Michael Storey
MPAA rating: no listing
Running time: 102 minutes

Kamikaze Hearts

A pornographic filmmaker, Tigr (Tigr Mennett), falls in love with her leading lady, an uninhibited exhibitionist, Mitch (Sharon Mitchell), in this study of sexual power and the effects of pornography.

REVIEWS

New Statesman & Society. III, July 27, 1990, p. 38.

CREDITS

Tigr: Tigr Mennett
Mitch: Sharon Mitchell
Gerald Greystone: Jerry Abrahms

Released: 1986
Production: Heinz Legler, Sharon Henessey, and Bob Rivkin
Direction: Juliet Bashore
Screenplay: Juliet Bashore and Tigr Mennett
Cinematography: David Golia
Editing: John Koop
Art direction: Hans Fuss
Set design: Hans Fuss
Sound: Leslie Schatz
Costume design: Hans Fuss
MPAA rating: no listing
Running time: 85 minutes

Kika

"Naughty, outrageously ribald!"—Rene Rodriguez, *Miami Herald*

"Outrageous!"—Bruce Williamson, *Playboy*

"A sexy farce! A joy to watch!"—Rick Marin, *Mademoiselle*

 Box Office Gross: $2,012,971 (August 28, 1994)

Few filmmakers have inspired both controversy and adoration to the same degree as Spanish filmmaker Pedro Almodóvar. Although Almodóvar's work is not yet as universally beloved as that of such film giants as Alfred Hitchcock, Federico Fellini, and Jean Cocteau, he has nevertheless continued to inspire devotion in legions of fans. His films, including *La Ley del Deseo* (1987; *The Law of Desire*), *Mujeres al Borde de un Ataque de Nervios* (1988; *Women on the Verge of a Nervous Breakdown*), and *Atame* (1990; *Tie Me Up! Tie Me Down!*), have become controversial cult favorites.

Now Almodóvar adds *Kika* to his oeuvre. He has described it in interviews as "my most complex film." *Kika* is a mixture of genres: It is comedy, drama, soft-core pornography, and satire. Like *Tie Me Up! Tie Me Down!*, *Kika* has

caused some to react with disgust at its treatment of women. *Tie Me Up! Tie Me Down!* concerned itself with a female star who is kidnapped and held hostage by a crazy but sexy man; eventually she succumbs and falls in love with him. That film created considerable controversy in that it appeared to perpetuate the fallacy that women like to be brutalized by men. It can also be argued, however, that Almodóvar's intention was to satirize the objectification of women that dominated much of European and American culture.

Kika shares this theme of the degradation of women with *Tie Me Up! Tie Me Down!* Yet a mosaic of other themes reflect typical Almodóvar concerns: communication, love, the nature of truth, and the destructive power of television. The film is the story of Kika (Verónica Forqué), an offbeat makeup artist who is in love with Ramon (Alex Casanovas), a photographer. She is also having an affair with his American stepfather, mysterious writer Nicholas (Peter Coyote). Nicholas is a brooding, strange man who has returned to Spain to reclaim his half of Ramon's mother's fortune. She had died a violent death in an apparent suicide several years before.

Other main characters include Juana (Rossy de Palma), housekeeper to Ramon and Kika, and Andrea Scarface (Victoria Abril), a former psychologist who now hosts a popular reality-based television show. The plot is driven by a central event: Juana's brother Pablo (Santiago Lajusticia) escapes from prison and violently rapes Kika. This event serves as the catalyst for a bloody finale, where the true nature of Ramon's mother's death is discovered and Kika's life irrevocably changes.

Truth has been absent from the lives of Kika and Ramon. Kika has hidden her relationship with Nicholas, and Ramon has hidden some important secrets from her. In addition, Ramon is unaware of the true causes of his mother's death. Moreover, Kika's best friend, Amparo (Anabel Alonso), has been concealing the fact that she, too, is having an affair with Nicholas. Into this web of lies comes Andrea Scarface, whose television show, *Today's Worst*, depicts despicable crimes in gory detail. Kika is unaware that Andrea is a friend of Nicholas and a former lover of Ramon.

"A rape is one thing, but this is taking all day."—Kika, as she defends herself against a rapist in *Kika*

Ironically, Andrea's television show is "reality-based": Almodóvar does a wicked and horrific parody of these shows, which had inundated prime-time television in the United States and were gaining popularity in Europe by the early 1990's. With the inclusion of this "reality" show in the middle of all the deceit occurring in Kika's life, Almodóvar satirizes the cultural trend toward telling the "truth" only when it is sensational and grotesque, and even then only in public. Truth between individuals is nonexistent in Kika's world, and Almodóvar underscores the fact by making Kika a makeup artist, a perfect symbol for cover-up and deception.

Kika is an extraordinary film in that it is wildly funny

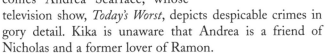

CREDITS

Kika: Verónica Forqué
Nicholas: Peter Coyote
Andrea Scarface: Victoria Abril
Ramon: Alex Casanovas
Juana: Rossy de Palma
Amparo: Anabel Alonso
Pablo: Santiago Lajusticia

Origin: Spain
Released: 1994
Production: Augustín Almodóvar; released by October Films
Direction: Pedro Almodóvar
Screenplay: Pedro Almodóvar
Cinematography: Alfredo Mayo
Editing: José Salcedo
Production design: Javier Fernandez and Alain Bainee
Costume design: Jose Maria Cossio, Gianni Versace and Jean Paul Gaultier
MPAA rating: no listing
Running time: 115 minutes

and truly grotesque at the same time. Kika's rape is appalling on two levels. First, she is completely helpless against the former boxer, as are the people around her—even the police have trouble stopping him. Yet, it is also a very comic scene: Forqué is astounding in her ability to retain the horror of the scene all the while playing it like a farce. She beats her attacker on the chest as he is on top of her; she goads him, saying "a rape is one thing, but this is taking all day."

Forqué is a wonderful actress; she plays Kika as a red-haired cartoon character whose nonstop chatter is as charming as it is annoying. Forqué is an actress of stunning range: Her tearful shock at the way she is treated by Ramon after the rape is devastating. She is a campy and typical Almodóvar character. Her satirical theatricality is also reminiscent of the style of camp/cult favorite John Waters. In fact, Waters' *Serial Mom* (1994) is a thematic and stylistic cousin to *Kika*, in that it deals with mayhem and murder with a merry twinkle and a wicked sense of irony. One of the characters in *Kika* even turns out to be a serial killer.

Of course, *Kika* is a much more thoughtful and complex film than *Serial Mom*. The intrusiveness of Andrea Scarface, who insists on "covering" the rape on her television program, is reminiscent of the media freak show that propels the latter part of *Serial Mom*. Yet in *Kika*, Almodóvar's genius takes him one step further, because his characters are not oblivious to their pain. They are not two-dimensional characters: The writing is so close to real, and the characterizations are so grounded in reality, that much of the film is as tragic as it is comic. Audience members leave wondering why they were laughing, perhaps leading them to look at the nature of truth in their world and in their mass media from a different perspective.

Almodóvar has populated the film with references to his other films. For example, Kika wears huge earrings similar to the ones in Almodóvar's *Tacones Leganos* (1991; *High Heels*); a female television star is in peril, like in *Tie Me Up! Tie Me Down!* and *Women on the Verge of a Nervous Breakdown*; and several of the stars have appeared in his other films. This is a film to be seen in context of Almodóvar's oeuvre to be appreciated; much of it is more understandable and palatable in light of the rest of his work.

Stylistically, *Kika* is one of Almodóvar's best. The settings, by Javier Fernandez and Alain Bainee, are wondrous. They have created a modern apartment for Kika and Ramon that perfectly reflects Kika's kookiness. Huge fake flowers hang on the wall. A large marble eye sits on the bar. Lampstands are curvy, colors are penetrating, and bizarre combinations of shapes and textures fill the screen. The expensive kitschy design adds to the fun of the film and wonderfully highlights its offbeat nature.

Similarly, the costumes are terrific: Jose Maria Cossio and world-famous designers Gianni Versace and Jean Paul Gaultier add to the whimsical depravity of the film. In particular, the costumes for the outlandish Andrea are a hoot. She hosts her program in an indescribably bizarre series of getups that combine glamour with gore. Yet the film's most amazing creation is Andrea's high-tech jumpsuit-with-helmet: The helmet actually has a working video camera, the suit has working lights built into the breasts, and the sleeves have control panels. The outfit becomes a character unto itself as Andrea desperately pushes her way into crime scenes with her camera moving, Medusa-like, on her head.

The acting is uniformly excellent. The character played by the intense Victoria Abril, star of *Tie Me Up! Tie Me Down!*, is the antithesis to the breezy Kika. Abril provides a kind of seductive detachment that is reminiscent of Sonia Braga in *Kiss of the Spider Woman* (1985). Peter Coyote has made a career out of playing dissolute intellectuals. He is appropriately sleazy, talking about how killing is probably as easy as "cutting your toenails." His voice has been dubbed (presumably because his Spanish is not up to par), so audiences who know him will miss the mixture of gravel and cream that is his voice. Finally, the exotic and peculiar Rossy de Palma is pathetically amusing as the lesbian maid in love

with Kika. Her deadpan expression is perfectly suited to the strange things she says and does, such as telling Kika, "I want to be a prison matron," or telling her brother to "tie me up and punch me."

Almodóvar has created a good script that weaves together several disparate elements in an intriguing and entertaining way. He is particularly successful at creating tension in the climax of the film. It is uncertain who will end up alive and who dead. A strange curve in the film's very last frames is only understandable on reflection. Almodóvar, though, is a filmmaker to reflect on afterward. His films in general (and *Kika* in particular) are the kind that inspire interesting discussion for a long time. No matter how much money they make, not many filmmakers can claim that they are able to be truly entertaining and truly thought-provoking. Almodóvar is truly one of a kind.

—*Kirby Tepper*

REVIEWS

The Hollywood Reporter. May 3, 1994, p. 6.
Los Angeles Times. May 6, 1994, p. F6.
The New York Times. May 6, 1994, p. B1.
Entertainment Weekly. May 27, 1994, p. 66.

Killer Instinct (Mad Dog Coll)

This drama centers on the Coll brothers, Vincent (Christopher Bradley) and Peter (Jeff Griggs), who ran liquor in Prohibition New York City for Dutch Schultz (Bruce Novick) until creative differences turned them against him.

REVIEWS

Publishers Weekly. CCXXXIX, June 15, 1992, p. 97.

CREDITS

Vincent Coll: Christopher Bradley
Peter Coll: Jeff Griggs
Dutch Schultz: Bruce Novick
No character identified: Rachel York

Origin: USA and Russia
Released: 1992
Production: Menahem Golan for Power Pictures-Start Corporation; released by 21st Century Film Corporation
Direction: Greydon Clark and Ken Stein
Screenplay: Neil Ruttenberg and Ken Stein
Cinematography: Janusz Kaminski
Editing: Patrick Rand
Production design: Clark Hunter
Casting: Abigail R. McGrath
Music: Terry Plumeri
MPAA rating: no listing
Running time: 98 minutes

The Killing Floor

An African American working-class man, Frank Custer (Damien Leake), battles racism and job layoffs through union membership at the meat-packing plant where he works, in World War I-era Chicago.

Released: 1984
Production: Elsa Rassbach for Public Forum Productions-American Playhouse
Direction: Bill Duke
Screenplay: Leslie Lee; based on a story by Elsa Rassbach and adapted by Ron Milner
Cinematography: Bill Birch
Editing: John Carter
Music: Elizabeth Swados
MPAA rating: PG
Running time: 118 minutes

REVIEWS

The Nation. CCLIV, March 30, 1992, p. 427.

CREDITS

Frank Custer: Damien Leake
Bill Bremer: Clarence Felder
Heavy Williams: Moses Gunn
Thomas Joshua: Ernest Rayford
Mattie Custer: Alfre Woodard
Harry: Dennis Farina

Killing Zoe

"From the creators of *Pulp Fiction* and *True Romance.*"—Movie tagline
"A seductive roller-coaster ride through the mountains of madness."—*Entertainment Today*
"A fiesta of high-octane, badass attitude."—J. Hoberman, *Premiere*
"Hold on for a summer jolt."—Pia Lindstrom, *WNBC-TV*
"A brilliantly filmed, spellbinding thriller."—Paul Wunder, WBAI Radio

 Box Office Gross: $469,489 (October 9, 1994)

In the neo-nihilist school of filmmaking, where shocking violence is a symbol for the meaninglessness of life, *Killing Zoe* is a jejune yet stylistically interesting addition.

Writer/director Roger Avary, co-writer with Quentin Tarantino on *True Romance* (1993) and *Pulp Fiction* (reviewed in this volume) (and former co-worker at the same video store), has in his directorial debut created a sort of "bad-boy" fantasy. When his friend and producer Lawrence Bender found a bank where they could film for free, Avary decided to write about a bank robbery gone wrong.

Zed (Eric Stoltz) is a safecracker who comes to Paris at the behest of his childhood friend, Eric, to help in a Bastille Day bank robbery. Zed arrives in Paris with what appears to be major jet lag, but the taxi driver taking Zed from the airport to his hotel has just the ticket. He hooks Zed up with a prostitute named Zoe, played by the unlikely and angelic Julie Delpy. It seems Zed, the "bad-boy," always sleeps with pros. "Sometimes you just need the honesty and security of a whore," he concedes, but this time it's different. In this fantasy, Zed finds a pure romantic love with Zoe, whose saving grace is that she's really an art student who simply needs the money.

But idyllic bliss doesn't come that easily, at least not in this film. It is disrupted by the arrival of Zed's friend Eric, whose entrance changes the whole mood of the film from Zed's hip chill to Eric's anarchic energy, of the "for tomorrow we may die" variety. Eric pushes past Zed and unceremoniously shoves a buck-naked Zoe into the hotel hallway to fend for herself. Zed's inaction while Eric manhandles Zoe is a key to his character. He is unable to act on his own, naively drifting along with the tide, wherever it may lead him.

His friend, Eric, played by Jean-Hugues Anglade, hasn't seen Zed for eleven years and as they catch up during a night out with the boys that turns into a phantasmagoric drug orgy, Eric tells Zed in an offhand way that he has AIDS "from the needle." Indeed, all of the band of merry men seem to be junkies except for Zed, who, as the night wears on, slowly becomes a little skeptical about the group.

In preparation for *Killing Zoe*, director Roger Avary had his cast read *Beowulf*, in an attempt to bring to the film the abandon and wildness of a Viking marauder.

Eric has choreographed a spree in underground Paris that ends in a cellar nightclub where jazz musicians play Dixieland and the drugs are ubiquitous. The filming takes the viewer on a dizzying journey, with camera tricks that even include animation, where blue animated musical notes seem to flow from the instruments. Eric wants his old friend to enjoy himself so much that he pins him to the wall and forces a giant red pill into his mouth that finally makes Zed sick.

Needless to say, the following day the group is a little worse for the wear as they prepare for the heist. Their preparation actually amounts to very little. The gist of the master plan is "We go in, we take what we want, we leave."

But the heist itself changes the rhythm of the film from spinningly groggy to dynamically jolting, with energy and excitement to spare.

As in all great plans of mice and men, and this group is closer to the Mickey Mouse variety, the plans go awry. The first wrench in the works is when Eric notices Zoe. She works at the bank and recognizes both Eric and Zed. The second blunder is the noisy killing of a hostage that tips-off the police to the ongoing robbery.

While the unaware Zed is punctiliously working on the safe in the basement, Eric and his gang go berserk upstairs. Although each of the gang members is interesting in themselves, we aren't given enough insight into any of them to build any compassion for their plight. In fact the viewer, also a little groggy from the night before, may have difficulty remembering who is who, which makes their deaths of very little concern.

In one fit of rage where Eric takes out more than a few of the bank customers and workers, and the rest of the gang act in more or less melodramatic and absurd ways, the bank floor turns into a veritable bloody Slip-n-Slide.

Meanwhile, Zed labors away on his safe, and upon opening it, finds a guard inside. Zed, ignorant of the carnage taking place upstairs, sees this as an almost insurmountable obstacle, but Eric, always the man of action, throws dynamite into the safe and quickly eliminates this hindrance. Here we have the cataclysmic change in Zed, as it finally dawns on him that his friend Eric is not quite the professional that he had thought he was.

After Eric takes a moment to shoot up heroin, he returns meaner than ever and twice as impatient. The police don't seem to want to give them a get-away plane and this infuriates him, with obvious consequences to the hostages.

At this juncture, Zoe unfortunately gets in Eric's way and when he turns to kill her, Zed finally comes to life and steps in to stop Eric. As the gendarmes storm the bank, and all hope of salvaging the heist is lost, Eric attacks Zed with a knife, telling him that he no longer belongs in their club of dwindling members. Eric cuts Zed and is poised to finish him off when the police storm in and riddle Eric with machine gun fire.

As they push their way through the carnage, Zoe tells the police that the bloodied Zed is a customer and hastens him out of the bank and into her car. A bloodier but hopefully wiser Zed is whisked away from blame and responsibility as Zoe promises to show Zed "the real Paris." From

CREDITS

Zed: Eric Stoltz
Zoe: Julie Delpy
Eric: Jean-Hugues Anglade
Oliver: Gary Kemp
Ricardo: Bruce Ramsay
Jean: Kario Salem
Francois: Tai Thai
Claude: Salvator Xuereb
Bank manager: Gian Carlo Scandiuzzi
Martina: Cecilia Peck

Released: 1994
Production: Samuel Hadida for Davis Film; released by October Films
Direction: Roger Avary
Screenplay: Roger Avary
Cinematography: Tom Richmond
Editing: Kathryn Himoff
Production design: David Wasco
Art direction: Charles Collum
Set design: Michael Armani
Set decoration: Sandy Reynolds-Wasco
Casting: Rick Montgomery and Dan Parada
Sound: Giovanni Di Simone
Costume design: Mary Claire Hannan
Music: Tomandandy
MPAA rating: R
Running time: 96 minutes

the look on Zed's face, the viewer wonders if he can handle much more of Paris, but Zoe's cherubic smile assures us that he is now in good hands.

Director Avary affords the viewer a thrill a minute as this "bloodier than thou" ending degenerates into a theater of the absurd. In preparation for the film, Avary had his cast read *Beowulf,* in an attempt to bring to the film the abandon and wildness of a Viking marauder. In the film itself there is an allusion to the Viking film genre, along with posters in Eric's apartment, bringing to the fantasy a sense of Nordic mythology.

"Before we do a job, we live life! It's better that way. O.K.?"—Eric to Zed in *Killing Zoe.*

Killing Zoe has all the adrenaline-injected elements necessary to sweep a young man into its fantasy and adventure, bringing our hero through his bad-boy phase unscathed and a little wiser: a sort of Treasure Island for the nineties.

The superficial aspect extends itself to the characters as well as the plot. The absence of characterization in *Killing Zoe* is a very real flaw. The only characters that are actually filled out are Eric and Zed, with an ineffectual stab at Zoe's character.

Eric is indeed the most interesting character in the film, bouncing around the screen in an almost disorienting way, filling the vacuum of characterization. Jean-Hugues Anglade soaks the screen with his well-placed energy, and captivates the viewer with his sheer power and fury.

"'Zoe' means 'life' in Latin," says Avary. "The title can interpreted as *Killing Life* and that is what this character of Eric is doing. Jean-Hugues captured the very essence of Eric's nihilism." Anglade does indeed make it believeable that the force of Eric's madness could gather such strength that others would follow him unwittingly into his own bizarre death dance. As Director Avary puts it, "The movie is made up of two descents into Eric's brain—one of them is the night out in the nightclub, the other one is the bank. Even though it's being told from Zed's point of view, the whole film is literally played out inside the brain of this insane man, who is Eric. As Eric starts losing control mentally, control in the bank begins to slip."

Eric Stoltz, as Zed, plays the world-weary young man who needs a major psychopath to wake him out of his ennui, and a brush with death to awaken his sensibilities. Stoltz's "good guy/bad boy" act is captivating and endearing, though at times his hipness balances on the edge of boring.

Julie Delpy is a fine actress who is virtually unused in this film, but perhaps that goes with the fantasy. For the most part, female characters do not play a significant role at all in the film.

Despite the film's boyish fantasies, Avary's debut shows a self-assured talent whose range hasn't begun to be probed. He speaks to an audience so dulled by violence that blood and gore have taken on almost comedic insinuations; it is an audience looking for a spokesperson.

Director Avary, twenty-seven, wants to be that spokesperson, "For the most part, I wanted to write an extreme example of what my generation is about—people who are living for the moment. I know there are optimists out there, those who are trying to make things better, but it's the momentum of a diseased culture that is difficult to stop. At the same time, the film is still kind of a comedy. You really have to look at the craziness for its comic value."

The film's fantasy aspect, though obviously entertaining in a sort of "Hardy Boy" gone bad way, turns against its own genre. The nihilism is simply a ploy for decadent adventure, and instead of making any meaningful statement, the excesses of violence are simply unrestrained "fun." It's just a shame that *Killing Zoe* couldn't have said more and romped less.

—*Diane Hatch-Avis*

REVIEWS

Atlanta Constitution. October 14, 1994, p. P14.
Boston Globe. November 25, 1994, p. A7.
Chicago Tribune. September 9, 1994, p. 7B.
Chicago Tribune. September 9, 1994, p. 7F.
Christian Science Monitor. September 2, 1994, p. 11.
Entertainment Today. September 2-8, 1994, p. 14.
Entertainment Weekly. September 16, 1994, p. 92.
Entertainment Weekly. January 27, 1995, p. 56.
The Hollywood Reporter. August 19-21, 1994, p. 5.
Interview. September 1994, p. 130.
Los Angeles Reader, August 26, 1994, p. 32.
Los Angeles Times. August 26, 1994, p. F4.
Los Angeles Weekly. August 26-September 1, 1994, p. 36.
The New Republic. CCXI, September 12, 1994, p. 27.
The New York Times. August 19, 1994, p. C3.
The New Yorker. LXX, August 22, 1994, p. 113.
Playboy. XLI, October 1994, p. 21.
Rolling Stone. September 8, 1994, p. 87.
USA Today. August 19, 1994, p. D10.
The Village Voice. August 23, 1994, p. 49.
Variety. CCCLIII, January 24, 1994, p. 64.
The Washington Post. September 9, 1994, p. D7.
The Washington Post. September 9, 1994, p. WW43.

L.627

L.627, a French film by director Bertrand Tavernier, is titled after Article L.627 of the Public Health Code, which "prosecutes all offenses related to the possession, trade, and consumption of narcotics." It is a film about the squalid underworld of Paris, where squatters live in filth and human waste, and junkies live for their next shot. It is also a film about Lulu (Didier Bezace), a cop in the Narcotics Squad. *L.627* shows viewers who Lulu is, opening like a flower, slowly blooming in its own season to reveal the man within.

The film is written by director Tavernier in collaboration with Michel Alexandre, a police detective. *L.627* exposes the immense poverty of the emigre community and the resultant crime and heroin use in the areas of Paris that the tourist does not see. Alexandre has brought the experiences of his fifteen years as a policeman to bear witness to this darker side of the city of lights.

L.627 is titled after Article L.627 of the Public Health Code, which "prosecutes all offenses related to the possession, trade, and consumption of narcotics."

Tavernier, known in the U.S. for *Round Midnight* (1986), has brought to the screen an unflinching look at the bowels of Paris and the men and women whose job it is to prevent street crime there. Tavernier reveals his hero slowly, each scene drops another veil to bring viewers closer to understanding what drives Lulu toward the underworld of Parisian life.

The film is seen through Lulu's eyes: first on a stakeout, then—after his demotion to a desk job—when he is transferred to a newly formed drug squad, again working the streets that he loves.

At first Lulu is just another member of the squad, but slowly viewers come to learn more and more about the man. Although he has been working for the department for more than fifteen years, Lulu is as impassioned as any rookie, working days and nights to gather information on where and when deals will transpire. Lulu has established a small network of people he calls his "cousins," who are police informers, and he courts them even during his off hours. He has developed such a relationship with them, that when they are in trouble they call Lulu, and he never fails them.

In contrast, his chief, Dodo (Jean-Paul Comant), is all jokes and pranks; but in his work he is impulsive and racist, wanting only to fill his quota of arrests. If they are dealers, users, or even "cousins," he does not really care. One feels that he has stopped fighting the streets and is only seeking self-aggrandizement. Although his fatigue and frustration are felt throughout the squad, there are those who continue the fight with energy.

Lulu has had an effect on those few. He befriends Antoine (Philippe Torreton) and Marie (Charlotte Kady). Antoine, in the beginning, is as lazy and indifferent as his boss, Dodo, but Lulu's influence upon him has roused him from his lethargy. He joins Lulu one evening after work to meet a cousin who lives in a condemned squatter's building. Antoine is horrified at the stench and filth in which these people live, but Lulu is accustomed to the squalor and greets his friend warmly.

Tavernier eloquently depicts the depth of urban poverty in this scene, which is as shocking as it is honest. This scene and another, which deals with a large gathering of dealers and junkies—the former doing business, the latter withering under the influence—are effectively political. Tavernier achieves this not through any use of dialog or plot but simply through the visual revelation of the horrors inherent in the life on the streets. He captures the realism by filming unseen from inside a van, while about forty extras mingled among the pushers, pimps, and junkies. The effect is staggeringly realistic.

Lulu, viewers learn, is driven in great part by his sympathy for the addicts, whom he sees as the victims. His first priority is to catch the big dealers who keep the drug machine going and who, through their greed, kill addicts by cutting the heroin to make it go farther. Yet despite the stakeouts and the street busts, Lulu wants to dig deeper than his comrades, delving into the underworld of street life, and his cousins are the key to entering that world.

One of his cousins is Cécile (Lara Guirao), a young prostitute and former secretary who got hooked on heroin. She is attracted to Lulu, and although he is attracted to her, he remains simply a dear friend who is concerned about her. She is HIV-positive, and Lulu tries again and again to get her to stop the life. In one scene, she has been arrested, and calling Lulu, she begs him to keep her out of the tank where the other arrests spend the night. He brings her to his police trailer and spends the night with her on the couch. In the morning, Lulu leaves her back on the street and gives her some money. Lulu's frustration with the girl is almost as painful to watch as her indifference to anything but her next high.

After he leaves her, he and Marie form a team to visit one of Lulu's cousins. Marie, at first seems to be like the other members of the drug squad, but soon viewers realize that she has driving ambition and energy. She is fearless on stakeouts and does not hesitate to cuff her own arrests. Kady's performance in this film is remarkable in its naturalness. She plays the fiesty Marie so believably that it is hard to remember that she is acting.

At the hotel, the cousin tips them off to some dealers in the room downstairs. They bust them, and one is a dealer who they have been unsuccessfully trying to catch in the subways.

Although Lulu strongly supports his cousins and acts as a catalyst to his peers, his private life is not predictable. Almost as an aside, viewers are introduced to Lulu's wife and infant daughter. It is clear that he must surely neglect them, since he is always "on the street" even in his off hours. His wife Kathy, (Cécile García-Fogel), wants to leave the city but knows that it is Lulu's life and that his love for his work is greater than his love for her. He has a

> "We don't have money, we don't have means. We've got our bare hands and have to make do."— Lulu in *L.627*

distance from his wife and family that he does not have with his cousins. She is understanding to a fault, yet her sadness at not really connecting with Lulu is evident in every scene in which she appears.

In another touching scene, Lulu is in the hospital, and a nurse is scolding him for not coming to see her. Viewers discover it is his mother. She is quite ill, and Lulu is torn, dividing his time between his private life and his professional life. His work, although a crusade, is also an escape from his private life.

Tavernier has succeeded in making a compelling film about a policeman's day-to-day life without the use of plot. He does this using two tools: documentary realism and an unwavering focus on one point of view. The former he achieves with quickly paced mood changes—from the comic rapport between the members of the squad to the tension and chaotic frenzy of a drug bust, from a tender moment with Lulu's family to a shocking glimpse of the lives of the very poor. Always, it is through the eyes of the hero, and always it is powerfully emotional.

Through these and other contrasts, viewers come to know Lulu's life, his dreams, his utter frustration with police bureaucracy, and his underlying love for his work. Tavernier has dealt with the subject of people who define their lives through their work before: *The Judge and the Assassin* (1973), *A Week's Vacation* (1980), and *Round Midnight*. In *L.627*, he has used the routines of interrogation, paperwork, drug busts, and the general interplay among the investigators as the surrounding ambience that determines the quality of Lulu's life. The director seems to say that Lulu's life, had he been an accountant, would be just as influenced by the strictures of his work-a-day routine as it is as an investigator.

L.627 is at times a film within a film. Lulu, it is learned, had gone to film school when he was young and incorporates these skills into his work by making surveillance tapes during stakeouts, so that he can memorize the faces of the dealers.

In his spare time, he also videotapes weddings to make extra cash. In the film, he pores over the tape of a wedding, editing it with the same passion that he has on a drug bust. He tells his wife, "I have the impression that filming helps me understand things better." He even suggests that he film his wife. The implication that Lulu is a voyeur is impossible to overlook, as well as the suggestion that the filmmaker is a voyeur, and, ultimately, the film viewers are voyeurs. The documentary realism of the film makes viewers feel like they are looking through a keyhole, but there are no judgments made. Problems are revealed, but the film intentionally offers no solutions.

This is a very political film about the indifference of the rest of society to what happens to the drug addicts and

CREDITS

Lucien (Lulu) Marguet: Didier Bezace
Dodo: Jean-Paul Comart
Marie: Charlotte Kady
Manuel: Jean-Roger Milo
Vincent: Nils Tavernier
Antoine: Philippe Torreton
Cécile: Lara Guirao
Kathy: Cécile García-Fogel
Adore: Claude Brosset

Origin: France
Released: 1992
Production: Frédéric Bourbouon for Little Bear Films and Les Films Alain Sarde; released by Kino International
Direction: Bertrand Tavernier
Screenplay: Bertrand Tavernier and Michel Alexandre
Cinematography: Alain Choquart
Editing: Ariane Boeglin
Set decoration: Guy-Claude Francois
Costume design: Jacqueline Moreau
Music: Philippe Sarde
Production management: Christine Raspillere
Sound: Michel Desrois
MPAA rating: no listing
Running time: 145 minutes

the lack of support to the men and women who are fighting this war on drugs.

The film is at once comic, intense, shocking, and ultimately frustrating. Didier Bezace is excellent as Lulu. He underplays his role in such a way that the viewer is drawn in closer and closer to unravel the mystery of the man's drives, dreams, and ambitions. The hero is a good man, and one comes to understand his crusade in the end. Viewers feel the frustrations of his position, working in a milieu where, when one dealer is removed, there are a hundred waiting to take his place.

The film is 145 minutes long, and although it is successful in its intentions, it is too long. Yet despite the length and the lack of plot, the viewer is riveted to the screen. The episodes, although short, are captivating. Viewers want to look deeper and deeper still into the inferno. More important, one wants to know more and more about Lulu. The film delivers on both counts.

—*Diane Hatch-Avis*

REVIEWS

Los Angeles Times. September 30, 1994, p. F10.
The New York Times. July 15, 1994, p. C14.
The Sunday Times (London). December 27. 1992, p. 4.8.
The Village Voice. July 19, 1994, p. 47.
Variety. September 10, 1992, p. 16.

Ladybird, Ladybird

"One of the best films of the year!"—Roger Ebert, *Chicago Sun-Times*
"An utterly absorbing film."—Janet Maslin, *The New York Times*

This intense true-life story of a woman whose children were taken away from her has won international acclaim for its director, Ken Loach, and its star, Crissy Rock. Loach is known in filmmaking circles for his realistic and powerful films about the British working class. *Cathy Come Home* (1966), which was made for television, *Raining Stones* (reviewed in this volume), and *Riff-Raff* (1991) have garnered him attention as a director who looks at social issues and personal drama with an uncompromising eye. *Ladybird, Ladybird* is similarly uncompromising—in fact, portions of it are painful to watch, as the audience witnesses the story of an emotionally and physically abused wife and mother who becomes increasingly abused by the social welfare system set up to protect her and her children. It is the dramatization, by Rona Munro, of the life of a real woman who was forced to give up her children for adoption in the name of protecting them.

Maggie (Crissy Rock) is a working-class woman in Liverpool, England. The audience is introduced to her in a scene in a bar, where she meets Jorge (Vladimir Vega), a Paraguayan political refugee. Jorge befriends her, takes her home, and hears her incredible story:

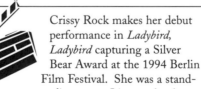
Crissy Rock makes her debut performance in *Ladybird, Ladybird* capturing a Silver Bear Award at the 1994 Berlin Film Festival. She was a stand-up comedienne at a Liverpool pub before she went to the open-call auditions on a whim.

Four children, by four different fathers, have been taken from her by the British child-protection services because of the danger posed by her violent common-law husband, Simon (Ray Winstone), and by her own volatile temper. Through flashbacks, the audience sees the frightening world in which Maggie's children are reared: When she is the slightest bit late for dinner, Simon sadistically beats her in front of the petrified children. Maggie eventually and reluctantly tells Jorge the tragic story of how her children were lost to adoption. Through flashback, the audience sees her lock her children in a room at a boardinghouse, hoping to protect them from the other dangerous children in the building. While she is at work, a fire in the locked room injures her son Sean (Jason Stracey).

Her account of these sad events is juxtaposed with scenes of her struggling with a desire to open up to Jorge at the same time that she wants to run away because she is so used to being with abusive men. She tells him, "You'll go in the end, so you might as well go, and make it easier for both of us."

Maggie and Jorge do get married, however, and have a child. Just when it seems that Maggie has finally found a good man and can begin to forget the past, a knock on the door begins another frightening chain of events: A social worker comes to assess Maggie and Jorge's ability to take care of the child. The child is taken away. Incredibly, yet another child, her sixth, is taken from them nearly a year later. The system cannot accept that Maggie has found a

CREDITS

Maggie Conlan: Crissy Rock
Jorge Arellano: Vladimir Vega
Simon: Ray Winstone
Mairead: Sandie Lavelle
Adrian: Mauricio Venegas
Jill: Clare Perkins
Sean: Jason Stracey
Mickey: Luke Brown
Serena: Lily Farrell

Origin: Great Britain
Released: 1994
Production: Sally Hibbin for Parallax Pictures and Film Four International; released by the Samuel Goldwyn Company
Direction: Ken Loach
Screenplay: Rona Munro
Cinematography: Barry Ackroyd
Editing: Jonathan Morris
Production design: Martin Johnson
Art direction: Fergus Clegg
Sound: Ray Beckett
Music: George Fenton
MPAA rating: no listing
Running time: 102 minutes

AWARDS AND NOMINATIONS

Berlin Film Festival Awards 1994: Best Actress (Rock), Fipresci Prize (Loach), Ecumenical Prize (Loach)
Chicago International Film Festival Awards: Best Actress (Rock)

man who is not abusive. It also cannot accept that her own volatile temper has abated. Ironically, the intransigence of the social system ignites Maggie's temper, making her behave like a wild animal when the authorities are attempting to remove her children, further proving to them that she is a dangerous person.

This is an intimate film with a bravura performance by Crissy Rock as Maggie. Rock was discovered by director Loach at a casting call for the film. She has stated in interviews that she auditioned for the film on a whim, never expecting anything to come from it. Until then, she was a stand-up comic in Liverpool—a woman with a husband and family, working in a pub to make ends meet.

Her astonishing realism and depth have made her an overnight sensation, and rightfully so. In one of the film's early scenes, Maggie tries to see her son in the hospital after being notified that he was burned in the boarding-house fire. She runs into the emergency room and frantically tries to push her way in to see him, breathlessly screaming for her son and nearly overpowering the nurses who hold her at bay. This depiction of a mother afraid for her child is so vivid and real that it is as if one is watching a documentary where the subjects do not know they are being filmed.

"You'll go in the end, so you might as well go, and make it easier for both of us."—Maggie to Jorge in *Ladybird, Ladybird*.

Rock achieves an unrelenting emotional pitch throughout the film. Her volcanic anger is so real that the audience will not be able to tell where Maggie's anger leaves off and Rock's anger begins. Rock keeps Maggie's anger just under the surface at all times, so that even when she is at rest, it appears that she could erupt at any time. For example, there is a tense scene where Maggie tries to impress several social workers with baked cookies and a fresh smile. She tries to impress upon them what a genteel lady she is—so that they will not take away yet another child. Her anger clearly builds, however; the audience is held in suspense wondering if and when she is going to throw the cookies in the face of one of the social workers. Yet Rock never seems to wail or moan in the name of acting. She appears to identify with Maggie's pain and brings this portrayal to a dramatic pitch achieved by few actresses.

Vladimir Vega, as Jorge, offers sharp contrast to Rock's minefield of emotion. Vega's Jorge is patient and gentle, offering kindness and compassion where all Maggie has seen is abuse and cruelty. Jorge is a refugee from Paraguay, a man critical of government. He says of his homeland, "I don't want to miss it, I don't want to love it, because I have no hope left. But you have to love something, or you are empty." Jorge gently coos these words, as if they are music. Eventually, Maggie learns about trust and love from Jorge. It is Vega's understated and unusually gentle portrayal that makes it believable. Jorge's quiet voice and unthreatening countenance make it clear that he is able to handle Maggie's wild ups and downs. While it is less showy, Vega's role is as essential as Rock's in telling the story of how two people can find happiness even under the worst of circumstances.

Loach and screenwriter Munro have carefully researched the story of the real-life Maggie and Jorge—their names were changed for the film—including much factual detail in their story. Although Loach and Munro have admitted to simplifying the real-life story, they insist that they have retained only factual information for their film.

Loach has an extraordinary ability to make a dramatization look like a documentary. The film is not glossy, the lighting is not arty—light is not used to set up beautiful visual images or to underscore thematic elements—and there are no special visual effects. Instead, he focuses on the characters' relentless pain through extended close-ups. One of his simplest and most eloquent visual statements comes in the scene where Jorge and Maggie make love for the first time. Loach focuses on the movement of their hands, allowing the sensuality to be expressed through the meeting of their hands. He also allows his camera longer shots without cutting away. This is particularly effective, though difficult to endure, in the scene where Maggie is beaten by her husband.

Loach's gift for verisimilitude extends to his use of dialogue. He allows the speakers to fumble and interrupt one another, much like American filmmakers Woody Allen and Robert Altman have done in their films. Loach achieved the spontaneous feel of the dialogue through improvisation. He also employed another technique—which Allen used in *The Purple Rose of Cairo* (1985)—of keeping the outcome of the film's plot from the actors. He "fed" them their scenes without telling them how the film would end, generating an urgency and spontaneity that is palpable. One scene in particular, in which Simon and Maggie take the kids and try to escape the authorities, is frightening because it is impossible to tell what is going to happen next: Will they end up in a crash? Will Simon beat Maggie again? It can only be assumed that the subsequent scenes were unknown to the actors, and

that lack of expectation fueled their own internal anxiety, which transmits to the screen.

Ladybird, Ladybird achieved great critical notoriety, but like most films without a big star, it did not reach a wide audience in the United States. This is a shame because it is not only an intense personal drama but also a severe indictment of a well-meaning but misguided welfare system. *Ladybird, Ladybird* exposes the flaws in the British social services, inspires its audience through its heroine's story, and inspires other filmmakers to greater artistic heights. Few directors and actors can claim that they make a true contribution to their art. Loach, Rock, Munro, and their collaborators deserve all the accolades they receive.

—*Kirby Tepper*

REVIEWS

Daily Variety. February 22, 1994, p. 13.
The Hollywood Reporter. February 23, 1994, p. 12.
The Hollywood Reporter. October 7-9, 1994, p. 12.
Los Angeles Times. December 30, 1994, p. F1.
The New York Times. October 7, 1994, p. B4.

Lassie

"Best friends are forever."—Movie tagline
"A solid family hit if there ever was one."
—David Sheehan, *KCBS-TV*
"An exciting and intriguing film for all ages...."
Elayne Blythe, *Film Advisory Board*
"First class family entertainment that will produce thrills, tears and a warm satisfied glow for moviegoers of all ages."—Michael Medved, *Sneak Previews/The New York Post*

 Box Office Gross: $9,936,939 (November 13, 1994)

Since the 1940's, in books, films, and television, Lassie has symbolized loyalty and courage. Indeed, Lassie has been the subject of nine feature films, more than six hundred television episodes, a short story, and a novel. The collie who appears in the title role in 1994's feature film *Lassie* is a direct descendant (eight generations later) of the original Lassie who starred in *Lassie, Come Home* (1943). While the filmmakers have updated the story slightly, the essence of

the original—love, compassion, daring rescues—remains unchanged. As Richard Leiby of *The Washington Post* has commented, "If Lassie can't save us from our cynical, naysaying selves, nothing can."

The story begins when the Turner family travels from Baltimore to the Shenandoah Valley of Virginia to escape the problems of big-city life and to make a fresh start. As the father of two young children, Steve Turner (Jon Tenney), a widower, worries especially about his son, Matt (Thomas Guiry), who each day grows more introverted. Steve's new wife, Laura (Helen Slater), worries about leaving her job at a bank in Baltimore and about the distance between her and the children, particularly Matt. Matt worries about giving up the concrete of the city, a surface integral to good skateboarding, and his friends. He is angry, dislocated, disenfranchised: He is a teenager. Daughter Jennifer (Brittany Boyd) watches hour after hour of *Lassie* on television—at least until her brother forces her to watch MTV instead.

Once on the road, as the family travels through the night to reach their destination, they come upon a wreck of a tractor trailer. One of the passengers in that demolished trailer, a collie survives the wreck and, as fate would have it, joins the Turners on their trip. While the family begrudg-

CREDITS

Matt Turner: Thomas Guiry
Laura Turner: Helen Slater
Steve Turner: Jon Tenney
Jennifer Turner: Brittany Boyd
Sam Garland: Frederic Forrest
Len Collins: Richard Farnsworth
April: Michelle Williams
Jim Garland: Charlie Hofheimer
Josh Garland: Clayton Barclay Jones

Released: 1994
Production: Lorne Michaels for Broadway Pictures; released by Paramount Pictures
Direction: Daniel Petrie
Screenplay: Matthew Jacobs, Gary Ross, and Elizabeth Anderson; based on the character created by Eric Knight
Cinematography: Kenneth MacMillan
Editing: Steve Mirkovich
Production design: Paul Peters
Casting: Gretchen Rennell
Sound: Stacy Brownrigg
Costume design: Ingrid Price
Lassie's owner/trainer: Robert Weatherwax
Music: Basil Poledouris
MPAA rating: PG
Running time: 92 minutes

Thomas Guiry as Matt Turner in *Lassie*. Copyright © 1994 Paramount Pictures. All Rights Reserved.

ingly allows the dog—named Lassie by Jennifer—to join them, it is not long before Lassie manages to bring the family together happily. In many ways, *Lassie* becomes a film about seeing clearly, about recognizing the value of what one sees every day and yet ignores, about seeing the natural world with renewed interest and respect.

Another piece of the puzzle falls into place when the Turners reach their destination and are greeted by Len Collins (Richard Farnsworth), father of Steve Turner's deceased wife, and Matt and Jennifer's grandfather. Collins has provided the house in which the little family will live: the old Collins home. The character Len Collins provides an anchor for a family set adrift by modern problems. Actor Farnsworth has often played endearing, grandfatherly roles, such as Matthew in television's *Anne of Green Gables*. He adds the same stability and dignity to life in the country in *Lassie*. In a small but important scene, Len Collins, father of the first Mrs. Turner, warms to the second Mrs. Turner, asking her to dance at the country fair. It is a small moment pressed in among other scenes

> Since the first of the Lassies, trained by Rudd Weatherwax in 1943, careful breeding has kept the same markings in descendants. The dog in 1994's *Lassie* is the eighth-generation descendant of the original Lassie. She is also trained by a Weatherwax descendant, Robert, Rudd's son.

more central to the action. Yet that one kind gesture emphasizes the extent of the healing that this family has experienced. All are welcome; all are family.

When a story has been retold as often as the Lassie story, few surprises remain. In fact, even this Lassie's appearance is remarkably similar to the Lassies of yesteryear: white blaze running the length of the face, a full white collar of fur and four white feet. The production notes explain that the strong resemblance is due to careful breeding, and while more than one puppy in each litter is trained to be Lassie, only one is selected finally to fill the slot.

As have earlier Lassies, the current Lassie is called upon to help a young boy with his problems, to encourage him to see his world more imaginatively, and to save the boy (and his home and family) from ruin, danger, even death. One of the film's early scenes shows Lassie stealing Matt's earphones to his portable cassette player. Lassie runs out of Matt's room, out of the Turners' house, and runs until reaching the local swimming hole. Predictably, Matt's response turns from anger to amazement that Lassie knew of the swimming hole (audience members may wonder at that, too). While the scene presents few surprises, it provides a respite from the emotional turmoil. It allows the audience to see Matt as other than a headstrong, headband- and earring-wearing, skateboard-toting, MTV-watching, self-centered problem child. This scene, then, serves as Lassie's first official "rescue," arguably saving Matt from his pessimism and self-destructive ennui.

Lassie also manages to point out Matt's deceased mother's journal, tucked away in the closet in his room. Through this record of his mother's hopes and adventures, Matt is able to maintain touch with his mother and finally to reach out to Laura, his new mother. While some of the scenes of the children rediscovering their dead mother are a bit heavy-handed (such as Matt's discovery of a heart carved in a tree in the yard or Jennifer's discovery of Beatle 45 r.p.m. records), these scenes serve as part of the weave of the film, part of the message that it is possible for past and present to coexist, for everything finally to come together. It is possible to change and to grow while remaining true to the past.

> "Like the first Lassie film, *Lassie Come Home, Lassie* is a story of the bond between a boy and his dog."—*Lassie* director Daniel Petrie

As might be expected, however, not everything works out for the Turners in the country. For example, Steve's contracting job, the job that brought them to the country, falls through almost immediately upon their arrival. Although Steve finds a position working odd jobs, he is desperate to return to the city and to regular work. Matt and Len Collins have a better idea, however: raising sheep. Cinematically, the choice is a good one, as it allows the film to focus on green meadows filled with white sheep, with a white farmhouse perched nearby. It allows for close-ups of lambs, nursing from handheld bottles. It allows for action sequences in which Lassie herds the flock expertly.

Thematically, the choice to begin raising sheep also opens the door to several exciting plot twists, including the introduction of the evil that the Turners and Lassie will have to battle. Driven by the love of power and by pure greed, Sam Garland (Frederic Forrest), the Turners' neighbor and the richest man in the area, employs a series of dirty tricks and dangerous threats to discourage the Turners from competing with him in the sheep business. While Garland and his two ill-bred sons, Jim (Charlie Hofheimer) and Josh (Clayton Barclay Jones), are rather two-dimensional characters, they do manage to threaten with a certain menacing swagger. Unfortunately, although the Garlands are merely greedy and unkind, they also carry firearms, which makes them even more of a force with which to reckon.

An example of the Garland-style petty tyranny is a scene in which the Garland boys and April (Michelle Williams), the cutest girl in the junior high school class, come upon Matt swimming in the swimming hole. The group of young people get to talk, and soon the issue becomes whether Matt can do a back flip. He contends he can but does not want to; the Garland boys maintain that Matt is unable to do one. The disagreement reaches an advanced level in large part because each side is playing it out for April's benefit. When Matt succeeds in doing a back flip, the Garlands back down, April takes renewed interest in Matt, and the audience is certainly relieved. Because Matt is a teenager who just moved to a new town, much of the film deals with being an outsider, learning to belong, and learning what really matters between friends. While such matters have not necessarily been part of the traditional Lassie films, these scenes add a certain sting to what otherwise could become a very sweet film.

Beyond its heartwarming story, Lassie is also beautiful to look at. Filmed largely in Tazewell County, Virginia, the film offers unspoiled countryside, green hills, and, as it progresses, autumn leaves. Samson Falls in Hinton, Virginia, was the site for the river action. Wet suits, helmets, and lifelines helped ensure that director Daniel Petrie could get the shots he needed without placing his cast and crew into significant danger.

Perhaps Petrie sums up *Lassie* best when he says, "The charm, sweetness, commitment, intelligence, wanting to please, wistfulness—those qualities make the story work on a level that wouldn't be possible without Lassie. She has a wonderfully expressive nature that is most endearing." This is clearly a film the whole family should make a point of seeing.

—*Roberta F. Green*

REVIEWS

Boston Phoenix. July 29, 1994, p. 6.
Entertainment Weekly. August 5, 1994, p. 60.
The Hollywood Reporter. July 21, 1994, p. 5.
Los Angeles Times. July 22, 1994, p. F13.
The New York Times. July 22, 1994, p. B1.
Newsweek. August 29, 1994, p. 56.
Variety. July 21, 1994, p. 2.
The Washington Post. July 22, 1994, p. C1.

The Last Seduction

"Everyone has a dark side, she had nothing else."
—Movie tagline

"Sex. Greed. Power. Murder."—Movie tagline

"*The Last Seduction* leaves you begging for more."
—John Anderson, *New York Newsday*

"Fiorentino is ferociously good."—Richard Schickel, *Time*

"The holy grail for lovers of *film noir*."—Rod Lurie, *Los Angeles Magazine*

"The year's most provocative thriller"—*Newsday*

"A smart tough thriller."—Gene Siskel

Box Office Gross: $2,510,252 (January 2, 1995)

Crime pays in *The Last Seduction*, a darkly comic *film noir* about greed, manipulation, and deception. The latest in a tradition characterized by movie landmarks such as director Billy Wilder's *Double Indemnity* (1944), this is the one to which all future efforts in the genre must aspire. It is well done in all respects.

The story centers on the wicked works of Bridget Gregory (Linda Fiorentino), a frustrated New York City insurance executive who longs for the life only money can buy. Bridget runs her little office with an iron hand, verbally brutalizing her staff of male telephone solicitors as she clutches the wad of bonus money she uses to spur them on. She is cunning, sexy, and extremely intelligent, and she freely uses all of these attributes to her best advantage.

Her husband Clay (Bill Pullman) is a medical doctor who makes ends meet by transacting an illegal pharmaceutical business at home. The Gregorys are burdened with huge debts, which keep them poor despite two incomes. They live in a shabby apartment in a lower-rent district of Manhattan. Bridget pines for an uptown address and uses her feminine wiles to get Clay to attempt an incredibly dangerous drug deal. Clay, who is as amoral as his spouse but not nearly as bright, goes along with the crazy plan.

Clay leaves home one day with an attaché case full of medical-grade cocaine. He meets two hoods in a grimy, dockside neighborhood, where, after a hair-raising transaction, he is left considerably richer. Clay literally runs back to the apartment, but as he showers to clean the grime from his body, Bridget steals the cash.

Bridget hastily leaves Manhattan, heading for Chicago. Along the way she stops for gas in the tiny Upstate town of Beston, a city not far from Buffalo, New York. Something about the place suits her compulsive nature, and she decides to stay for a few hours. She wanders into a neighborhood bar, where her cocky attitude leaves the Bestonians cold. After offending nearly everyone, including the bartender, she is approached by the innocent Mike Swale (Peter Berg) who is intrigued by her big-city grittiness. Mike has recently returned from Buffalo, where, it is implied, things did not go well for him.

As Mike persists, Bridget rebukes him sarcastically, telling him to go find some nice little cowgirl and produce "little cow babies." Mike is immediately transfixed, and Bridget, sensing that she has snared an eager fish, elects to reel him in. What follows is the first of several steamy sex scenes, in which Mike is willingly employed as a boy toy. Bridget and Mike couple intensely but lovelessly, as Bridget will have it no other way. Mike, with his small-town upbringing, is perplexed and repulsed by her emotional indifference but remains, nevertheless, a semi-permanent fixture in Bridget's bed.

Bridget grows to hate Beston, but at the advice of her lawyer, Frank Griffith (J. T. Walsh), she decides to establish tentative roots. Clay misses his money, says Griffith, and will cheerfully break bones and teeth to get it back. Bridget, therefore, changes her name to Wendy and takes a job in a local insurance company. She rents a house in the suburbs, where the kids, the dogs, and the friendly neighbors greatly annoy her.

Anxious to spend the money, Bridget contacts Clay hoping to work out a deal. Clay has anticipated this and has his hired gun, Harlan (Bill Nunn), camped in the apartment with his telephone monitoring equipment. When Bridget's whereabouts are finally discovered, Harlan is sent to Beston to retrieve the stolen money. He confronts Bridget, who in turn employs an utterly ludicrous ruse to coldly dispatch him.

Clay remains a problem, however, and Bridget decides that since he is apparently unwilling to negotiate, he too must go.

At this point, Mike's status as occasional boy toy is upgraded to full-time dupe. Bridget devises a brilliant scheme embroiling him in Clay's murder as she orchestrates events from a distance. Several painful plot twists are employed to allow her to pull it all off, a few of which seem contrived. Some of the audience may be overwhelmed by

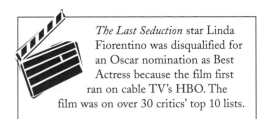

The Last Seduction star Linda Fiorentino was disqualified for an Oscar nomination as Best Actress because the film first ran on cable TV's HBO. The film was on over 30 critics' top 10 lists.

the razzle-dazzle of Bridget's carefully executed deviousness, but thanks to John Dahl's skillful direction, the film does not suffer badly, and the story thunders on.

Mike is sent to New York to murder Clay. To get him to do it, Bridget sets up a completely fictitious scenario involving insurance fraud. Mike believes that he is after somebody else, an utterly despicable person, who, as Bridget says, completely deserves what he is about to get.

Mike breaks into Clay's Manhattan apartment. He rousts his intended victim out of bed, but squeamish about the idea of killing him in cold blood, merely ties him up. Clay uses his borrowed time to reveal his actual identity and convince Mike that he has been the victim of another of Bridget's scams. Bridget arrives on cue and in a series of highly improbable events, Clay is killed, and Mike is arrested. Viewers who want to see Bridget get her comeuppance will be gravely disappointed.

This is a film about amorality in which the bad guys win. It is not for everybody, and certainly not for those who go to films about theft, murder, and deception, hoping to see justice done. There are no good guys in *The Last Seduction*. This is a

> "A woman loses 50 percent of her authority when people find out who she's sleeping with."—Bridget from *The Last Seduction*

film in which bad people attempt, with varying degrees of success, to victimize one another, and the worst of the bunch ultimately triumphs. Clay is every bit as nasty as his wife but not skillful enough in the various arts of duplicity to effectively compete with her. Mike is not intrinsically evil but is criminally foolish. He allows himself to be drawn into Bridget's web and offers only feeble protests as she eats him. He is not motivated by love but by self-destructive obsession. To Mike, Bridget is a drug.

Bridget herself as prime mover emerges immediately as baddest of the bad. She exults in every wicked act and never looks back. She is completely cavalier in her approach to men, to all men. They are fodder, plain and simple. Worse than that, they are willing fodder: weak, foolish, malleable, volunteers all, well deserving of the punishment she gives them. Furthermore, Bridget has absolutely no compunction about using her considerable physical charm to get exactly what she wants.

Nearly everywhere it has shown, *The Last Seduction* has met with rave reviews. Rod Lurie of the *Los Angeles Times* called it "the Holy Grail for lovers of modern *film noir*," while *Paper Magazine* described headliner Linda Fiorentino's character of Bridget Gregory as "a work of art." Critics have unanimously acclaimed Fiorentino's performance—she won both Independent Spirit and New York Film Critics Circle Awards for best actress for her performance—and this is completely justified. She is smashing. Never before has evil been depicted as cleverly, as subtly, or with such cunning humor. Bridget uses her wit and wits at the same time, dropping lines as she takes heads. The result is emotional confusion and like the men she destroys, the viewer simultaneously loves and loathes her.

While Fiorentino definitely steals the show, she is assisted by a superb cast. Bill Pullman is splendid as the oafish Clay Gregory, a man who puts his foot in it every time he takes a step. By marrying Bridget, Clay has sold his soul cheaply. The irony is, he knows it, and he spends much of the film chuckling over his stupidity as he applies the boot to his own backside. Peter Berg does extremely well by the character of Mike Swale, a corrupted innocent who would like to be less innocent. Bill Nunn as gumshoe Harlan is appropriately cool and businesslike, while J. T. Walsh as Frank Griffith is delightfully sardonic.

Linda Fiorentino made her film debut as the lead performer in *Vision Quest* (1985), a film directed by Harold

CREDITS

Bridget Gregory: Linda Fiorentino
Mike Swale: Peter Berg
Clay Gregory: Bill Pullman
Frank Griffith: J. T. Walsh
Harlan: Bill Nunn
Bob Trotter: Herb Mitchell
Chris: Brien Varady
Shep: Dean Morris
Stacy: Donna Wilson

Released: 1994
Production: Jonathan Shestack and William Christopher Gorog (executive producer) for ITC Entertainment Group; released by October Films
Direction: John Dahl
Screenplay: Steve Barancik
Cinematography: Jeffrey Jur
Editing: Eric L. Beason
Production design: Linda Pearl
Art direction: Dina Lipton
Set decoration: Katherine Lucas
Sound: Mark Deren
Costume design: Terry Dresbach
Music supervision: Karyn Rachtman
Music: Joseph Vitarelli
MPAA rating: R
Running time: 110 minutes

AWARDS AND NOMINATIONS

Independent Spirit Awards 1995: Best Actress (Fiorentino)
New York Film Critics Circle Awards 1994: Best Actress (Fiorentino)

Becker. She went on to play the Soho sculptress in Martin Scorsese's off-the-wall black comedy *After Hours* (1985). Other film credits include; *The Moderns* (1988), *Queens Logic* (1991), and *Acting on Impulse* (1993).

Bill Pullman began his career in film with the 1986 comedy *Ruthless People*. He worked with Kevin Costner in *Wyatt Earp* (1994), and has played memorable roles in many other films such as *Malice* (1993), *Sleepless in Seattle* (1993) and 1995's *While You Were Sleeping*. Peter Berg first appeared on the television series *21 Jump Street*. His film credits include, *Crooked Hearts* (1991) and *Fire in the Sky* (1993). Bill Nunn is best known for his work with controversial director Spike Lee, and J. T. Walsh is a film and stage veteran with many character parts to his credit. Walsh also worked with director John Dahl on *Red Rock West* (reviewed in this volume).

The Last Seduction is an in-your-face confrontation with the meaner side of the real world. This is pure *film noir,* and more. In an age when winning is everything and "greed is good," John Dahl's film is a polished mirror, accurately reflecting what some people are and what others could be when the opportunity for material gain is sufficiently attractive.

—*D. Douglas Graham*

REVIEWS

Daily Variety. February 24, 1994, p. 14.
The Hollywood Reporter. October 24, 1994, p. 8.
Los Angeles Times. October 26, 1994, p. F1.
The New York Times. October 26, 1994, p. B2.

Latcho Drom (Safe Journey) (Bonne Route)

"Some of the most glorious music to be heard on this planet"—Dave Kehr, *New York Daily News*

Box Office Gross: $471,831 (November 20,1994)

There is a Hungarian proverb which says, "If you give a Hungarian a glass of water and some Gypsy music he will become completely drunk." Prepare yourself for a binge. *Latcho Drom* is a musical journey tracing the culture of the Rom or "Gypsy" people from their original home in India, through Egypt, Turkey, Romania, Hungary, Slovakia, France, and ending in Spain. There is not a word of dialogue in the film, yet volumes are spoken through the exotic whirling and mutating rhythms that crescendo into ecstatic climaxes. The frenetic cadences alternate with painfully beautiful ballads of deep melancholy.

In this hypnotically beautiful film, director Tony Gatlif, himself of Romany heritage, allows us a glimpse into the Gypsy life style through their music and dance. According to Gatlif, "The search for singers, dancers and musicians for the film took me through a dozen countries, from Rajasthan to Spain. I became captivated by the Gypsy men and women of India, stirred by the Gypsy violins of Romania, fascinated by Caita, a Spanish Gypsy singer. And I thought, what a pity people can't see and hear all this on the screen! And that is when I decided that *Latcho Drom* wouldn't be

filmed in video, or in 16 mm, but in 35 mm with stereophonic sound." The result is entrancing.

Our first glimpse is of a family of Gypsies in Rajasthan crossing the barren, sun-baked earth on their long trek to meet up with their clan. As their ox cart plods along, with sleeping children slung across donkeys and women pulling goats, a young boy sings a song of longing for home. "I will burn my horoscope that's sent me so far from my family," he sings to the beat of their tramping feet.

When they reach the campsite, a small girl dances barefoot in the dirt to the rhythm of a metalworker's hammer on hot iron. The tempo now quickens, as a young woman performs a seductive whirling dervish of a dance alone in the late afternoon sun.

By evening the whole camp is seated around a tree, set on its trunk and hung from its branches ablaze with the dancing flames of offertory candles. Songs that seem to be enchanted emerge from the group, captivating you in their transforming rhythms until you can feel your very soul ebb and flow with the beat of the music. You have just reached your first stop on the film's magical journey.

Gatlif, born in Algiers of French nationality and Gypsy descent, has explored the Gypsy life through film before. In 1982 he directed *Corre Gitano*, but he is better known for his films *Pleure Pas My Love* (1988) and *Gaspard and Robinson* (1990). Says Gatlif, "When I first became interested in movies in the seventies, I didn't think I would ever make films about my past or my people.... Later on I became interested in myself because people I met...asked me...'Who are you?... Where do you come from?'...and I didn't know what to answer. I asked my grandfather...he told me. . . my great-grandfather came from Andalusia on a donkey. In 1980 I went to Spain. It was a very emotional experience. Throughout Andalusia I searched the tombstones for the name of my family. Without any luck, of course, because they had to change names many times to protect themselves. Even I don't have the same name as my brother.

Latcho Drom is neither a documentary nor a fiction film. It's a musical that tells the story of the historic odyssey of the Gypsies from India to Egypt. The Roms need to be respected, even if it's a little bit. They suffer from being perpetually rejected by others."

"It takes a strong love of life to resist five centuries of persecution and sorrow."—*Latcho Drom* director, Tony Gatlif.

This persecution is evident in *Latcho Drom*, where Gypsies are pulling their wagons by hand through the snowy roads of Romania, being run off French meadows where they have stopped to put up camp, and being driven from empty buildings in deserted Spanish villages. Yet they rise above their suffering through their music and dance.

An interesting transition takes place as the film moves from the Gypsies of India, with their finery and jewelry, to the west, where the clothing of the Gypsies hints at the poverty of the wearers. That poverty is nowhere more dramatically displayed than in the scene in Eastern Europe where Gypsies, on their way to immigrate to Germany, are camping in trees to avoid the bitter cold and wet of the snow beneath them. It is painful to hear them sing a hopeful song about their new lives in Germany knowing that the stereotypes of Gypsies as kidnappers and chicken thieves are still prevalent, even in our modern times.

As Gatlif tells it, "Some Gypsy friends from Paris and I wanted to buy three thousand chickens with my author's royalties, put them in two semi-trailers and set them loose at dawn on the Champs-Elysees, handing out flyers saying:

'The Gypsies give you back your chickens!'...It was with all these thoughts in mind I started planning a film, *Latcho Drom*, with the Gypsy *joie de vivre*, even if some of the songs are about persecution. It takes a strong love of life to resist five centuries of persecution and sorrow."

Gatlif succeeds in capturing the Gypsy in this moment of their history without preaching or glorifying. In fact, some scenes, although staged for the performances, are still heart-renderingly real. In Slovakia, an old woman sitting under a tree in the snow, sings a woeful lament. The music is traditional, but the lyrics are her own. Her name is Marichka and her song is about Auschwitz. At the end of the ballad the camera pans to her forearm and the number tattooed there.

In another scene on a train in Hungary, a little girl sings a song that sounds deceptively gay. But the subtitles disclose the song's true meaning. The child sings of the disgust and hatred people feel for them and wonders why "the whole world hates us." The lyrical beauty of the song coupled with the innocence of the child breaks your heart.

But not all the songs in *Latcho Drom* are so tragic. In fact, most of the music is quite merry—from the joyful strains of a band of Hungarian gypsies as they improvise on spoons and jugs, to a stirring Spanish flamenco, the music is infectious.

In one segment of the film, thousands gather at the annual meeting of the Gypsies in Les Saintes Maries, France, to honor the patron saint of the Rom people, Saint Sara. There is a scene in which a group of musicians gather in her crypt to play in her honor. In another scene, her statue is carried to the sea in a colorful procession by a throng of Gypsy worshippers that include Gypsy guards on horseback, in medieval costumes. The event, where musicians from all over the world meet and play, showcases some of the best music in the film.

Gatlif spent eighteen months on the road, searching for the best and most representative music to be found. The skill of the musicians that he has documented and their genius for improvisation is at times almost incredible. In Romania, a man plays a melody on a loose violin string between his thumb and forefinger, creating a poignant yet exotically eerie song that is a musical record of their freedom from the tyrant Ceausescu, while nearby a boy sits in rapt attention, watching and learning.

CREDITS

Origin: France
Released: 1993
Production: Michèle Ray; released by Shadow Distribution
Direction: Tony Gatlif
Screenplay: Tony Gatlif
Cinematography: Eric Guichard
Editing: Nicole D. V. Berckmans
Production design: Denis Mercier
Sound: Nicolas Naegelen
Musical advise: Alain Weber
MPAA rating: no listing
Running time: 103 minutes

AWARDS AND NOMINATIONS

Cannes Film Festival Awards 1993: Prix Gervais

The film has many scenes of children learning the instruments and songs that are the repositories of the Gypsies' unwritten history. The songs themselves are hauntingly similiar in their shifting movements and hypnotic rhythms and yet each is strongly influenced by the music of the country in which they live It is a testament to the Rom people that they can endure such immense poverty and persecution and yet somehow still preserve a culture sent adrift from its homeland more than a thousand years ago.

Latcho Drom, winner of the Prix Gervais at Cannes, 1993, is a compendium of Gypsy music recorded, as Gatlif explains, "as a living memory" for his people, perhaps the first of its kind. The only flaw in the film is a lack of sufficient subtitles in some of the songs and the total lack of subtitles to identify locales. The latter may spring from an intentional Gypsy disregard for borders, but this breach distracts and confuses the viewer, who is straining to place the scene.

Despite this flaw, Gatlif has been able to tell his story without one word. The medium of music and dance is far more effective than any conventional documentary would have been. The film is powerful and, if at times the scenes appear to be too posed, the performances are so genuine and guileless that they more than compensate for this weakness.

Much credit goes to cinematographer Eric Guichard for his brilliant filming in settings that must have been difficult. He has teased beauty and nobility out of the ashes of old campfires and the loneliness of forsaken back roads.

Soundman Nicolas Naegelen brings even the subtlest nuances of the music alive with pristine clarity, from the tinkle of an ankle bracelet to the whine of a single violin string.

The film ends in a scene where a woman and small boy sit by a campfire on a plateau overlooking the urban squalor in the distance. The woman is Spanish Gypsy singer La Caita, and she sings a hauntingly tortured song written by director Tony Gatlif. Caita's heart-wrenching wailing is a veritable shaking of Gypsy fists against centuries of persecution. The scene seems to hint at the inevitable disintegration of the vagabond culture of the Gypsies as they are forced to settle in urban areas. But the spirit of the song defies that future.

Gatlif made this film in the expectation that in thirty years the culture of the traveling Gypsy would be gone. Should that be the case, it would be our loss. After all, what would our world be like without Gypsies to remind us of what freedom is and at what price it comes?

—*Diane Hatch-Avis*

REVIEWS

The Hollywood Reporter. November 8, 1994, p. 10.
L.A. Village View, November 4-10, 1994, p.15.
Los Angeles Times, October 31, 1994, p. 2.
The Village Voice, July 26, 1994, p. 47.

The Legend of Wolf Mountain

When three children—Kerrie Haynes (Nicole Lund), Casey James (Matthew Lewis), and John Page (Jonathan Best)—are kidnapped by two escaped convicts (Robert Z'Dar and David Shark) and taken to nearby Wolf Mountain National Park, they must not only outsmart the villains and escape but also survive in the wilderness.

REVIEWS

Variety. CCCXLIX, December 14, 1992, p. 45.

CREDITS

Ranger Haynes: Bo Hopkins
Jensen: Mickey Rooney
Jocko Painter: Robert Z'Dar
Dewayne Bixby: David Shark
Simcoe: Don Shanks
Kerrie Haynes: Nicole Lund
Maggie Haynes: Natalie Lund

John Page: Jonathan Best
Casey James: Matthew Lewis
Sheriff Page: Frank Magner

Released: 1992
Production: Bryce Fillmore for Majestic Entertainment, in association with Wolf Mountain Productions; released by Hemdale
Direction: Craig Clyde
Screenplay: Craig Clyde and James Hennessy
Cinematography: Gary Eckert
Editing: Michael Amundsen
Production design: Michael Klint
Casting: Billy DaMota
Sound: Michael McDonough
Music: Jon McCallum
MPAA rating: PG
Running time: 91 minutes

Legends

Documentarian Ilana Bar-Din interviews members of a Las Vegas celebrity look-alike stage show—Jonathon Von Brana who plays Elvis Presley, Susan Griffiths who plays Marilyn Monroe, and Monica Maris who plays Judy Garland—just as its members are suffering creative differences with the show's producer, John Stuart, as well as personal problems.

CREDITS

John Stuart: John Stuart
Jonathon Von Brana: Jonathon Von Brana
Monica Maris: Monica Maris
Susan Griffiths: Susan Griffiths

Released: 1991
Production: Ilana Bar-Din, Claes Thulin, and Sarah Jackson; released by Crosswinds Productions
Direction: Ilana Bar-Din
Cinematography: Claes Thulin
Editing: Kate Amend
MPAA rating: no listing
Running time: 55 minutes

Legends of the Fall

"Two thumbs up. A star-making performance by Brad Pitt."—*Siskel & Ebert*

"One of the best pictures of this year or any year."—Alan Silverman, *Voice of America*

"Live the legend, heartbeat by heartbeat."
—Bonnie Churchill, *National News Syndicate*

"The kind of rich, old-fashioned family saga seldom seen nowadays."—Bruce Williamson, *Playboy*

"Quite simply, epic!"—Steven Rea, *The Philadelphia Inquirer*

 Box Office Gross: $66 million (June 18, 1995)

The idea of an American film with the range and sweep of a substantial nineteenth century novel that chronicles the process of change across several generations of a tempestuous family is particularly engaging in an era of lowered expectations, narrowing vistas, and a diminishing sense of human possibility. With *Legends of The Fall*, Edward Zwick—the director of *Glory* (1989), an inspiring film about a regiment of black soldiers in the Civil War, and the creator of the Emmy Award-winning television series *thirtysomething*—has attempted to convey something of the epic grandeur of such films as *Doctor Zhivago* (1965) or *Gone with the Wind* (1939). The film is set in the first decades of twentieth century America, when the country was emerging on the world stage as a major power.

Legends of the Fall utilizes many of the most distinctive elements of the classic cinematic epic, including the continuous interpolation of panoramic vistas; a lush, swelling orchestral score; references to great historical events, including a tableau of men in battle; and most crucially for this genre, a family engulfed in emotional turmoil precipitated by the demands of a stern-but caring father whose three sons are all in love with the same woman. Although Zwick has captured some of the dynamic appeal of the traditional "big" picture, he has been unable to avoid some of its most conspicuous pitfalls.

The film is based on a novella by Jim Harrison about a retired army officer rearing his boys in the severe but awesomely beautiful backcountry of the Montana frontier just before

Legend of the Fall's Gordon Tootoosis (One Stab) grew up on the Poundmaker Indian Reserve in Saskatchewan, Canada and was raised in the Plains Cree cultural tradition. He helped Brad Pitt learn his Cree lines and took him to tribal gatherings. Many scenes were shot on the Stoney Indian Reserve outside Calgary, Alberta, Canada.

the outbreak of World War I. Zwick's film tries to connect the family saga to the pressures on the open land stemming from the expansion of big cities and an intrusive government. This linkage is often unclear, and the theme involving the conflict between the ways of the wilderness and the encroachment of greedy speculators and their minions is treated sporadically and with little development beyond its repeated restatement.

In addition, Zwick's presentation of the picturesque terrain is a series of scenic vistas that have little feeling for the specific geography of the setting. Furthermore, James Horner's score is banal and derivative, emphasizing the most obvious emotional mood of a scene. Finally, the plot is convoluted and relatively formless when a taut narrative structure is required to give some shape to the sprawl of historical and familial crises. Nevertheless, a strong cast and a conviction that the material is important keep the film from sinking into excess and absurdity.

Colonel William Ludlow, the family patriarch, is played by Anthony Hopkins with a gusto that is calculated to obliterate any recollection of his decorum in films such as *The Remains of the Day* (1993) or *Howard's End* (1992). At times, especially after Ludlow is devastated by a stroke, Hopkins approaches the bizarre in his skewed gait and snarled speech. Yet he is generally quite convincing in his portrayal of a hardened pioneer who combines Victorian erudition with an appreciation of the ways of the Native Americans whom he fought and grew to respect. He embodies a uniquely new-world fusion of British cultivation and American initiative, which stands for a promise that is never realized—one of the aspects of the "Fall" that the title suggests. His sons, who bear practically no physical resemblance to him or to one another, are drawn initially as types, also a problem with Zwick's characterizations in *Glory*. Canny casting and some very intelligent acting, however, help to overcome the thinness of the screenplay.

As the middle son—Tristan Ludlow, an enigmatic figure at the center of the narrative—Brad Pitt holds the audience's attention whenever he occupies the screen and incites speculation as to his whereabouts when he is absent. His incarnation of a wild young man of the old West, a contemporary version of an American icon, is clearly meant to recall James Dean or the young Marlon Brando—actors whose emotional intensity overcame the limitations of their lesser roles. Because Pitt is so obviously

CREDITS

Tristan: Brad Pitt
Ludlow: Anthony Hopkins
Alfred: Aidan Quinn
Susannah: Julia Ormond
Samuel: Henry Thomas
Isabel Two: Karina Lombard
One Stab: Gordon Tootoosis
Pet: Tantoo Cardinal
Decker: Paul Desmond

Released: 1994
Production: Edward Zwick, Bill Wittliff, and Marshall Herskovitz for Bedford Falls/Pangaea; released by TriStar Pictures
Direction: Edward Zwick
Screenplay: Susan Shilliday and Bill Wittliff; based on the novella by Jim Harrison
Cinematography: John Toll
Editing: Steven Rosenblum
Production design: Lilly Kilvert
Art direction: Rick Roberts and Andrew Precht
Set decoration: Dorree Cooper
Casting: Mary Colquhoun
Sound: Douglas Ganton
Costume design: Deborah Scott
Music: James Horner
MPAA rating: R
Running time: 133 minutes

the subject of various promotions calculated to exploit his rock-star public personality, and because the character of Tristan is conceived in terms akin to a brooding rock rebel including costume, hair styles, and an assertive irreverence, Peter Travers in *Rolling Stone* believes "Pitt carries the picture" while Stanley Kauffmann in *The New Republic* calls the casting "problematic."

Beyond a response conditioned by audience expectations, Pitt's performance is impressive in the manner in which he manages to make Tristan's restless wandering, need for solitude, and sudden rages as plausible as his banter with his brothers, his warmth with his wife, and his ecstasy and serenity in the darkness of the forest. His character is inherently laconic, something like Gary Cooper without the suppressed sexuality, and with little help from the screenplay, he remains true to the demands of almost every scene he is in through gesture and controlled nuance of expression. Since he follows a pattern of departure and (prodigal) return throughout the film, the other main characters are also very important even as they are seen mostly in reaction to Tristan.

Henry Thomas, who is still associated with his role in *E.T.: The Extraterrestrial* (1982) as the alien's young friend

Elliott, gives Tristan's younger brother, Samuel, an air of gentle innocence and idealism. He captures the strong sense of social obligation and unpretentious refinement that a year at Harvard has added to the intellectual direction and principled perspective provided by Colonel Ludlow. Tristan's immediate decision to join the army to keep his brother safe when Samuel enlists is understandable in terms of Tristan's impulsiveness and because of the fragility and cerebral emphasis that Thomas places in the characterization.

The oldest of Colonel Ludlow's sons, Alfred (Aidan Quinn), is the most difficult part to present since it is not grounded in any fundamental traits. Gradually, Alfred begins to develop an identity as Tristan's opposite, a man of the city with a mercantile mentality and mundane political ambitions who is too weak to avoid the temptations of petty compromise. Until the film begins to follow his progress into the corridors of power in Helena, Quinn is forced to exaggerate almost every exchange into a confrontation and to overplay anger, bitterness, and a kind of abject love so that he is often on a precarious edge between composure and a strident near-frenzy.

To give the film an air of gravity, a narrative frame around the action is built by a Native American named One Stab (Gordon Tootoosis), Colonel Ludlow's Cree scout who works on the ranch and who has taught Tristan the lure of the wild and the ways of a warrior culture. In the most engrossing section of the film, One Stab, chanting in his own language, sets Tristan apart by musing on the destiny of the extraordinary individual; then all three brothers are shown in their idyllic youth, lending a degree of plausibility to claims for brotherly love that are asserted but not demonstrated beyond Tristan's attempt to save Samuel on the battlefield of Ypres.

The early scene in which Tristan challenges, or bonds with, a bear—a parallel with Jack Nicholson's encounter in *Wolf* (reviewed in this volume), which was also based on a Harrison book—establishes his spiritual link to the animal world and foreshadows the violent resolution of almost every episode of *Legends of the Fall*. The element of danger in the first part of the film is more exhilarating than threatening, and Colonel Ludlow's comment that to be surrounded by his sons is a source of great happiness reinforces the feeling of an Edenic paradise in spite of its latent irony.

The "Fall" from this rugged mountain garden is partially precipitated by the arrival of Samuel's fianceé

AWARDS AND NOMINATIONS

Academy Awards 1994: Best Cinematography
Nominations: Best Sound, Best Art Direction/Set Direction
Golden Globe Awards Nominations
1995: Best Film—Drama, Best Actor—Drama (Pitt), Best Director (Zwick), Best Score

Susannah (Julia Ormond), who accompanies him when he returns from Harvard. Although Ormond may not carry the picture, she could easily have fractured its tenuous construction by striking a false note at many critical junctures. Instead, with the assured craft of an accomplished London stage actress, she manages to project the charm and intelligence that captivate all three brothers and then darkens her disposition following the disruptions of Samuel's death, Tristan's roaming, and Alfred's disappointing soullessness. *Legends of the Fall* inclines toward the position that women are attractive but extraneous: Colonel Ludlow's wife, Isabel, returns to Boston; Tristan's wife, called Isabel Two, is killed in an absurd accident. Yet when Susannah ends her own life in discouragement, the feeling of loss is palpable due to the radiant images of Ormond in happier times.

> "Some people hear their own inner voices with great clearness and live by what they hear. Such people become crazy. Or they become legends."—One Stab from *Legends of the Fall*

Zwick gives the actors the opportunity to fashion performances that depend for their impact on the actors' own resources since the screenplay, credited to coproducer Bill Wittliff and *thirtysomething* story editor Susan Shilliday, is deficient in providing adequate explanations for much of their behavior. Many individual sequences work well, however, among them the romantic interlude between Tristan and Susannah; a rare light-hearted conversation between Samuel and Tristan in a film that is often very solemn; Samuel's declaration of his humane convictions before he leaves the United States to enlist in Canada; and some of the scenes on Colonel Ludlow's ranch with his other "family" of mixed ethnic backgrounds.

Pitt has observed that he liked the idea of a film about "living and dying and the journey along the way," and the journey or quest for meaning on which Tristan embarks is the operative motif of the film. The film concludes with One Stab's closing commentary about Tristan's adventurous life and his mythic death in a second confrontation with his bear/anima in 1963, an effective ending in which the two figures fuse in a hazy blur of motion. The implication is that he has completed his Odyssean voyage through the known and unknown world and fulfilled his destiny as a hunter, warrior, and exemplary legend.

The social dimension of the film, however, eventually fades away, reducing the epic scope to an individual's life. This is appropriate since Zwick, by calculation or inclination, has basically directed the film toward a target audience of young people on a weekend date for whom questions of history may not yet be important.

—*Leon Lewis*

REVIEWS

Entertainment Weekly. January 10, 1995, p. 34.
The Hollywood Reporter. December 12, 1994, p. 8.
Los Angeles Times. December 23, 1994, p. F1.
The Nation. January 23, 1995, p. 108.
The New Republic. January 2, 1995, p. 26.
The New York Times. December 23, 1994, p. B2.
The New Yorker. January 9, 1995, p. 84.
Rolling Stone. January 26, 1995, p. 65.

Leon the Pig Farmer

"The most acclaimed British comedy of the year"
—Movie tagline

"Hilarious...It's the sprightliest comedy to come from England since *A Fish Called Wanda*."
—*Chicago Tribune*

A young London Jew, Leon Geller (Mark Frankel), discovers—much to his surprise—that his biological father (Brian Glover) is an eccentric Gentile pig farmer, in this British comedy. Rejected by his Jewish father, Leon seeks out his true father and is welcomed with open arms by his new family. Finally the two families meet in a London restaurant and mayhem ensues. In the meantime he dates a woman who dates him merely because of his Jewish ethnicity and kicks him out when she discovers his true heritage.

REVIEWS

Boston Globe. December 17, 1993, p. 98.
Chicago Tribune. February 18, 1994, p. 7L.
Interview. XXIII, October 1993, p. 66.
Los Angeles Times. September 21, 1994, p. F4.
The New York Times. September 10, 1993, p. C8.

CREDITS

Leon Geller: Mark Frankel
Judith Geller: Janet Suzman
Brian Chadwick: Brian Glover
Yvonne Chadwick: Connie Booth
Sidney Geller: David De Keyser
Madeleine: Maryam D'Abo
Lisa: Gina Bellman

Origin: Great Britain
Released: 1994
Production: Vadim Jean and Gary Sinyor for Unapix; released by Cinevista
Direction: Vadim Jean and Gary Sinyor
Screenplay: Gary Sinyor and Michael Normand
Cinematography: Gordon Hickie
Editing: Ewa J. Lind
Production design: Simon Hicks
Music: John Murphy and David Hughes
MPAA rating: no listing
Running time: 102 minutes

AWARDS AND NOMINATIONS

Edinburgh Film Festival Awards: Best First Film
Venice Film Festival Awards: International Critics Prize

Leprechaun II

"This time...luck has nothing to do with it."
—Movie tagline

"Faith and Be Gory, *Leprechaun II* Better Than the First"—*Los Angeles Times*

 Box Office Gross: $2,202,697 (June 12, 1994)

B ritish actor Warwick Davis reprises his role as a vengeful leprechaun, this time determined not only to reclaim his missing gold but also to marry a pretty Los Angeles teenager, Bridget (Shevonne Durkin), much to her horror. Sequel to *Leprechaun* (1993).

REVIEWS

Boston Globe. March 20, 1993, p. 23.
Entertainment Weekly. September 9, 1994, p. 90.
Los Angeles Times. January 11, 1993, p. F3.
Los Angeles Times. April 11, 1994, p. F6.
The New York Times. January 9, 1993, p. A17.
USA Today. January 12, 1993, p. D8.
Variety. CCCLIV, April 18, 1994, p. 63.
The Washington Post. January 9, 1993, p. G3.

CREDITS

Leprechaun: Warwick Davis
Bridget: Shevonne Durkin
Cody: Charlie Heath
Morty: Sandy Baron
Ian: Adam Biesk
William O'Day: James Lancaster
Tourist: Clint Howard
Tourist girlfriend: Kimmy Robertson

Released: 1994
Production: Donald P. Borchers; released by Trimark Pictures
Direction: Rodman Flender
Screenplay: Turi Meyer and Al Septien; based on characters created by Mark Jones
Cinematography: Jane Castle
Editing: Richard Gentner and Christopher Roth
Production design: Anthony Tremblay
Art direction: Claire Kaufman
Visual effects supervision: Paolo Mazzucato
Casting: Linda Francis
Sound: Oliver Moss
Leprechaun makeup: Gabe Z. Bartalos
Costume design: Meta Jardine
Music: Jonathan Elias
MPAA rating: R
Running time: 85 minutes

The Life and Times of Allen Ginsberg

This documentary pays homage to poet Allen Ginsberg through the use of television footage, home movies, interviews, and photographs.

REVIEWS

The Advocate. February 22, 1994, p. 76.
Boston Globe. March 4, 1994, p. 51.
Chicago Tribune. May 27, 1994, p. 7F.
Christian Science Monitor. February 18, 1994, p. 12.
Los Angeles Times. February 17, 1994, p. F3.
The New York Times. February 18, 1994, p. C10.
Rolling Stone. March 10, 1994, p. 60.
Variety. CCCL, April 26, 1993, p. 70.
The Washington Post. February 25, 1994, p. D6.

CREDITS

Allen Ginsberg: Allen Ginsberg
Edith Ginsberg: Edith Ginsberg
Joan Baez: Joan Baez
Amiri Baraka: Amiri Baraka
Ken Kesey: Ken Kesey
Norman Mailer: Norman Mailer

Released: 1994
Production: Released by First Run Features
Direction: Jerry Aronson
Cinematography: Jean De Segonzoc, Roger Carter and Richard Lerner
Editing: Nathaniel Dorsky
Sound: Lori Loeb, Michael Harrison, Erik Houseman and Greg Poschman
Music: Tom Capek
MPAA rating: no listing
Running time: 83 minutes

A Life in the Theater

Jack Lemmon stars as aging actor Robert and Matthew Broderick as newcomer John, two members of a second-rate repertory company who share a dressing room and discuss their dreams and disappointments in this adaptation of a David Mamet play. Feature-film directorial debut of Gregory Mosher.

REVIEWS

Atlanta Constitution. October 8, 1993, p. D9.
Boston Globe. October 8, 1993, p. 53.
The New York Times. October 3, 1993, Sec. 9 p. 3.
The New York Times. October 8, 1993, p. D19.

CREDITS

Robert: Jack Lemmon
John: Matthew Broderick

Released: 1994
Production: Patricia Wolff and Thomas A. Bliss for Beacon Communications and Bay Kinescope, in association with Jalem Productions; released by Turner Pictures
Direction: Gregory Mosher
Screenplay: David Mamet; based on his play
Cinematography: Freddie Francis
Editing: Barbara Tulliver
Production design: David Wasco
Art direction: Charles Collum
Set decoration: Sandy Reynolds-Wasco
Sound: John Pritchett
Costume design: Jane Greenwood
MPAA rating: no listing
Running time: 78 minutes

Life on the Edge

An unfortunate man, Ray Nelson (Jeff Perry), who owes a large sum of money to Las Vegas loan sharks, has a very bad day, during which he is beaten up (twice), loses his house in an earthquake, and discovers that his wife (Jennifer Holmes) is cheating on him. Most of the film takes place at a quirky party in the home of his wife's lover, Roger (Andrew Prine). Feature-film directorial debut of Andrew Yates.

REVIEWS

Variety. CCCXLVII, June 22, 1992, p. 44.

CREDITS

Ray Nelson: Jeff Perry
Karen Nelson: Jennifer Holmes
Joanie Hardy: Greta Blackburn
Roger Hardy: Andrew Prine
Suzi Hughes: Jennifer Edwards
Elliot Goldman: Tom Henschel
Shelli Summers: Denny Dillon

No character identified: Thalmus Rasulala
No character identified: Martine Beswicke
No character identified: Susan Powell
No character identified: Kat Sawyer-Young
No character identified: Liz Sagal
No character identified: Ralph Bruneau
No character identified: Ken Stoddard
No character identified: Michael Tulin
No character identified: Jessie Scott

Released: 1992
Production: Eric Lewald and Andrew Yates for Movers and Shakers; released by Festival Entertainment
Direction: Andrew Yates
Screenplay: Mark Edens
Cinematography: Tom Fraser and Nicholas von Sternberg
Editing: Armen Minasian
Production design: Amy Van Tries
Art direction: Greg P. Oehler
Casting: Jean Sarah Frost
Special visual effects supervision: Barry A. Nolan
Sound: Clifford (Kip) Gynn
Music: Mike Garson
MPAA rating: no listing
Running time: 78 minutes

Lightning Jack

Box Office Gross: $16,796,775 (June 5, 1994)

CREDITS

Lightning Jack Kane: Paul Hogan
Ben Doyle: Cuba Gooding, Jr.
Lana: Beverly D'Angelo
Pilar: Kamala Dawson
Marshal Kurtz: Pat Hingle
Marcus: Richard Riehle
Mr. Doyle: Frank McRae
John T. Coles: Roger Daltrey
Sheriff: L. Q. Jones
Bart: Max Cullen

Origin: Australia
Released: 1994
Production: Paul Hogan, Greg Coote, and Simon Wincer for Lightning Ridge/Village Roadshow; released by Savoy Pictures
Direction: Simon Wincer
Screenplay: Paul Hogan
Cinematography: David Eggby
Editing: O. Nicholas Brown
Production design: Bernard Hides
Art direction: Lisette Thomas and Virginia Bieneman
Set decoration: Lynn Wolverton Parker and Susan Maybury
Casting: Mike Fenton and Julie Ashton
Sound: Bud Alper and Lloyd Carrick
Costume design: Bruce Finlayson
Stunt coordination: Bill Burton
Music: Bruce Rowland
MPAA rating: PG-13
Running time: 93 minutes

Paul Hogan stars as Lightning Jack Kane, a minor outlaw in the Old West who is disappointed by his lack of notoriety. In an effort to boost his career, Lightning Jack attempts a few more robberies and inadvertently ends up with a partner/sidekick, a mute African American man, Ben (Cuba Gooding, Jr.). The two team up, with ludicrous results. The Who's Roger Daltrey also makes an appearance as an outlaw.

REVIEWS

Atlanta Constitution. March 11, 1994, p. P4.
Boston Globe. March 11, 1994, p. 67.
Chicago Tribune. March 11, 1994, p. 7B.
Chicago Tribune. March 24, 1994, Sec. 5 p. 13F.
Entertainment Weekly. March 25, 1994, p. 39.
Entertainment Weekly. July 29, 1994, p. 64.
Los Angeles Times. March 11, 1994, p. F8.
The New York Times. March 11, 1994, p. C8.
People Weekly. XLI, March 21, 1994, p. 22.
TV Guide. XLII, August 6, 1994, p. 31.
USA Today. March 16, 1994, p. D10.
The Washington Post. March 14, 1994, p. D9.
The Washington Post. March 17, 1994, p. D7.

"Lightning Jack is shallow, vain, self-centered, egotistical, superstitious, short sighted, and occasionally stupid, which makes him someone we can all identify with, I think."—Paul Hogan on his character in *Lightning Jack*

Lillian

This dramatic representation of a day in the life of a remarkable woman, Lillian Folley, focuses on her acts of charity toward children and the elderly.

REVIEWS

Variety. CCCL, February 15, 1993, p. 85.
The Washington Post. March 18, 1994, p. D1.

CREDITS

Lillian: Lillian Folley
Nina: Wilhamenia Dickens
Ricky: Ricky Green
Frank: Steve Perez
Maria: Danita Rountree-Green
Joy: Joy Buckner
Niecey: Dynisha Dickens
Red: Stanley Holcomb
Mrs. Evans: Helen Jervey
Charles: John Wise
Karen: Karen Motley
Insurance salesman: Sam Wells

Released: 1993
Production: David D. Williams
Direction: David D. Williams
Screenplay: David D. Williams
Cinematography: Robert Griffith
Editing: David D. Williams
Sound: Jeff Kenton
Costume design: Tracy Styron
Music: H. Shep Williams
MPAA rating: no listing
Running time: 82 minutes

AWARDS AND NOMINATIONS

Chicago International Film Festival
Awards: Special Jury Award for Distinction

The Lion King

"The greatest wonder of all."—Kenneth Turan, *Los Angeles Times*

"No less than perfection...Stunning!"—*New York Daily News*

 Box Office Gross: $300.4 million (January 2, 1995)

Disney's thirty-second full-length animated feature, *The Lion King* followed in the footsteps of such other successful Disney animated musical adventures as *Aladdin* (1992) and *Beauty and the Beast* (1991). As with these two previous films, *The Lion King* boasts superb animation and musical numbers. Lyricist Tim Rice and legendary pop singer and songwriter Elton John teamed up and won both Academy and Golden Globe Awards for best song for *The Lion King*, while Hans Zimmer won a Golden Globe and Oscar for his score.

The film opens with the spectacular large-scale production number "Circle of Life," featuring a Zulu choir on the soundtrack. The herds of zebras, elephants, giraffes, and other animals roaming the African plain are a marvel. Of special note is a scene in which a stream of ants marching the length of a twig is in focus in the foreground then goes fuzzy as a herd of zebras in the background comes into focus—giving the illusion that the images were filmed with a real camera. The animals have gathered to witness the birth of a lion cub, Simba (voice of Jonathan Taylor Thomas), born to king of the beasts Mufasa (voice of James Earl Jones) and his mate, Sarabi (voice of Madge Sinclair).

Next introduced is Mufasa's jealous and evil brother, Scar (voice of Jeremy Irons), who resents Simba's birth and claim to the throne. His vocal number, "Be Prepared," drips with malevolent foreboding. Scar wastes no time trying to exploit Simba's mischievous nature for his own nefarious ends. First, he entices young Simba to venture into a forbidden elephant graveyard, where Simba, accompanied by his best friend, Nala (voice of Niketa Calame), encounters three dangerous, but comically dim-witted, hyenas: Shenzi (voice of Whoopi Goldberg), Banzai (voice of Cheech Marin), and Ed (voice of Jim Cummings). Fortunately, Mufasa comes to their rescue in the nick of time.

The next trap proves deadly as Scar places Simba in the path of a wildebeest stampede that he has orchestrated. Although Mufasa saves Simba, he cannot save himself. Clinging to the edge of a cliff, Mufasa is sent to his death by Scar, who then proceeds to lay the blame on Simba. Scar advises Simba to leave and never return, only to send the hyenas after him. Simba narrowly escapes and miraculously finds refuge in a tropical paradise with two comic creatures—a foul-smelling but sweet-natured warthog, Pumbaa (voice of Ernie Sabella), and a fast-talking, savvy meerkat, Timon (voice of Nathan Lane). With these two friends, Simba matures to adolescence (voice of Matthew Broderick), to the rollicking tune of "Hakuna Matata," which roughly translates as "no worries."

Inevitably, Simba's past comes back to haunt him in the form of the now-adolescent Nala (voice of Moira Kelly), who encounters Simba by accident. Apparently, Simba's former home has gone into decline under Scar's rule, and Nala implores Simba to return and reclaim his birthright. Although Simba initially refuses, a comic encounter with an elderly tribal wiseman, the baboon Rafiki (voice of Robert Guillaume), convinces Simba to return and overthrow his uncle. Simba eventually succeeds in his quest, and the film comes full circle with a reprisal of the opening number, "Circle of Life," this time with the animals celebrating the birth of Simba and Nala's son.

Although *The Lion King*, unlike its Disney predecessors, was not based on a fairy tale or literary classic, its original story line is actually a cross between *Hamlet* and a typical coming-of-age tale. Special emphasis is placed on the loving father-son relationship between Mufasa and Simba. Hence, the scene in which Mufasa is killed is particularly difficult to watch, especially for younger viewers; it is reminiscent of a similar scene in Disney's *Bambi* (1942) in which Bambi's mother dies. *The Lion King* shares yet another theme with *Bambi*: Both films emphasize the natural cycles in nature.

With its rather conventional plot, *The Lion King*'s strengths lie in its musical numbers, its animation, its humor, and the vocal talents of a stellar cast. In addition to the three aforementioned songs are "I Just Can't Wait to Be King," a pop song celebrating Simba's youth, ambitions, and naivete, and the award-winning "Can You Feel the Love Tonight?" a ballad depicting the blossoming love between Simba and Nala that is reminiscent of *Aladdin*'s Academy Award-winning number "A Whole New World."

Although lyricist Rice had worked with Disney before, winning an Academy Award for his lyrics for "A

CREDITS

Mufasa: James Earl Jones (voice)
Simba: Matthew Broderick (voice)
Young Simba: Jonathan Taylor Thomas (voice)
Scar: Jeremy Irons (voice)
Nala: Moira Kelly (voice)
Young Nala: Niketa Calame (voice)
Pumbaa: Ernie Sabella (voice)
Timon: Nathan Lane (voice)
Rafiki: Robert Guillaume (voice)
Zazu: Rowan Atkinson (voice)
Sarabi: Madge Sinclair (voice)
Shenzi: Whoopi Goldberg (voice)
Banzai: Cheech Marin (voice)
Ed: Jim Cummings (voice)

Released: 1994
Production: Don Hahn for Walt Disney Pictures; released by Buena Vista Pictures
Direction: Roger Allers and Rob Minkoff
Screenplay: Irene Mecchi, Jonathan Roberts, and Linda Woolverton
Editing: Tom Finan and John Carnochan
Production design: Chris Sanders
Art direction: Andy Gaskill
Artistic coordination: Randy Fullmer
Music: Hans Zimmer
Songs: Tim Rice (lyrics) and Elton John (music)
MPAA rating: G
Running time: 88 minutes

AWARDS AND NOMINATIONS

Academy Awards 1994: Best Score, Best Song ("Can You Feel the Love Tonight?")
Nominations: Best Song ("Circle of Life" & "Hakuna Matata")
Blockbuster Entertainment Awards 1995: Best Family Movie—Theatrical, Best Soundtrack
Chicago Critics Awards 1994: Best Score
Golden Globe Awards 1995: Best Score, Best Song ("Can You Feel the Love Tonight?"), Best Film—Musical/Comedy
Nominations: Best Song ("Circle of Life")
MTV Movie Awards Nominations 1995: Best Villain (Irons), Best Song ("Can You Feel the Love Tonight?")

Whole New World," the choice of pop star Elton John was a surprising break from the Broadway tradition established by the award-winning team of the late Howard Ashman and Alan Menken in *Aladdin*, *Beauty and the Beast*, and *The Little Mermaid* (1989). John was recommended by Rice to Disney executives after Rice had been recruited for the project in 1991. While John provided the melodies, composer and music supervisor Hans Zimmer is credited with transforming them, per the film's production notes, "into fully realized African-flavored melodies complete with authentic Zulu chanting, extensive choral arrangements and rhythms and instrumentation associated with Africa."

 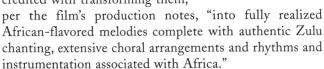

"Look inside yourself, Simba. You are more than what you have become. You must take your place in the circle of life."—Mufasa to Simba in *The Lion King*

The Lion King's animation lives up to Disney's fine tradition. Key personnel traveled to Africa to view the real-life settings in order to better commit the African landscape to film. According to art director Andy Gaskill, "We wanted to give the art direction the same sense of grand sweep and epic scale that David Lean put into *Lawrence of Arabia*" (1962). Thus, Africa itself becomes a key character—one witnesses the vastness of the savannah, the beauty of sunrises and sunsets, rain, drought, dust, wind, jungles, deserts—epic landscapes rendered in visually rich detail. Besides requiring two directors, the film employed more than six hundred animators, artists, and technicians, as well as the use of computer-generated imagery.

In order to animate realistically the many creatures that appear in *The Lion King*, the studio recruited the assistance of wildlife experts, sent animators to various zoos, and brought lions and other animals into the studio for the animators to observe up close. The final confrontation between Simba and Scar is an awe-inspiring duel portrayed in slow motion in which the two engage in mortal combat, realistically raised on their hind legs and drawn against a red and gold backdrop of flame and flying embers. The animators also worked closely with the actors supplying the voices for the principal animal characters, in order to imbue them with aspects of the actors' personalities.

The two-and-a-half-minute stampede, featuring the visually stunning image of thousands of wildebeests pouring over a hilltop into a gorge below, would have been too laborious an undertaking to draw by hand— yet it still took more than two years to complete using computer- generated imagery. This sequence recalls another film, a documentary released about the same time as *The Lion King* that centered on the annual migration of the wildebeest: *Africa the Serengeti* (reviewed in this volume). This IMAX film was narrated by James Earl Jones, who provided the voice of Mufasa in *The Lion King*, and featured music by Hans Zimmer, who composed *The Lion King*'s score.

Juxtaposed with the masterfully regal bass tones of James Earl Jones as Mufasa, Jeremy Irons' intonations convey a delightfully wicked Scar, Mufasa's evil brother. Not only was this the first time Irons had provided his voice for an animated film but it was also the first film in which he was called upon to sing. Both classically trained and award-winning actors, Jones and Irons lend the weight and authority needed to establish their characters as the film's polar opposites of good and evil.

Jonathan Taylor Thomas, who stars on the hit television series *Home Improvement*, has a slightly husky voice that aptly conveys Simba's youth through the use of contemporary slang. As the adult Simba, Matthew Broderick is appealing, conveying Simba's newfound maturity but still lacking the ringing bass authoritative tones of his father, Mufasa.

Comic relief comes from Simba's buddies Timon and Pumbaa, Mufasa's majordomo Zazu, and the three hyenas. Nathan Lane and Ernie Sabella, who provided the voices for Timon and Pumbaa, were offstage friends who had worked together previously in a Broadway revival of the musical *Guys and Dolls*. Whether teaching young Simba survival techniques, such as the proper way to eat grubs ("Oo, the little cream-filled kind!") or imparting words of wisdom ("Home is where your rump rests"), these two characters enliven every scene in which they appear. Especially amusing is a scene in which the two break spontaneously into a rendition of the song "The Lion Sleeps Tonight" and another in which Timon dresses in a hula skirt and performs a frenzied version of the "Hawaiian War Chant."

British wit Rowan Atkinson provides the voice of Mufasa's right-hand bird, Zazu. Just as Robin Williams poked fun at Disney occasionally in his portrayal of the Genie in *Aladdin*, so does Zazu in a scene opposite Scar. Following Scar's rise to power, Zazu, who has been singing plaintive prison tunes from his small cage in Scar's lair, is ordered to sing something cheerier. Zazu starts in on "It's a Small World," the chipper little tune that is piped at tourists as they tour the exhibit of the same name at Disneyland. Scar responds with a comically desperate, "No, anything but that."

Finally, Scar, too, has his comic sidekicks, in the form of the three hyenas Shenzi, Banzai, and Ed. As portrayed by the vocal talents of Whoopi Goldberg, Cheech Marin, and Jim Cummings, the three help relieve the tension generated by the evil Scar. Throughout, Goldberg and Marin trade barbs—such as Shenzi's comic reference to their being stuck "dangling at the bottom of the food chain"—as Cummings consistently responds with a truly loony laugh. The trio make for a multiethnic, wickedly malevolent Three Stooges.

Although *The Lion King's* story line is not as compelling as that of previous Disney outings, the film certainly lives up to Disney's standard of excellence in the field of family-oriented motion pictures.

—*Cynthia K. Breckenridge*

REVIEWS

The Hollywood Reporter. June 13, 1994, p. 6.
Los Angeles Times. June 12, 1994, Calendar section, p. 4.
Variety. June 13, 1994, p. 4.
Los Angeles Times. June 15, 1994, p. F1.

Little Big League

"The Minnesota Twins have a new owner."
—Movie tagline

"Delightful!"—*Sneak Previews*

"Score this one funny, touching and inspiring."
—*ABC Radio Network*

"...well crafted and immensely engaging."
—*Houston Post*

"A pennant-winning comedy!"—*Jeanne Wolf's Hollywood*

"An enticing fantasy."—*Chicago Tribune*

Many baseball films have preposterous plots, but few take their fantasies as seriously as *Little Big League*. This is thegently told story of a twelve-year-old baseball fanatic who inherits the Minnesota Twins when his grandfather dies, and then names himself manager. The film is sincere but flamboyant. The typical boyhood fantasy is to play on a major league team, not to manage one. But young Billy Heywood (Luke Edwards), aptly tutored by his grandfather (Jason Robards), is a baseball whiz-kid who knows everything from who made the fielding blunder that lost the 1924 World Series (it was Freddie Lindstrom) to whether to bunt with your number three hitter up in the eighth inning of a tie game (Billy wouldn't).

Few kids will identify with Billy's encyclopedic knowledge of the game. This film is geared more toward adults who want to brood about baseball's lost virtues. It takes a boy to remind today's major league players, as Billy does, that the game is supposed to be fun and that they are lucky to be playing it for a living.

Billy is what baseball fans call a throwback. He is a nostalgic icon of the game's golden days. Billy even knows

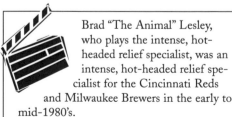

Brad "The Animal" Lesley, who plays the intense, hot-headed relief specialist, was an intense, hot-headed relief specialist for the Cincinnati Reds and Milwaukee Brewers in the early to mid-1980's.

how to pull off a bizarre double steal last performed by Ty Cobb and a teammate, and he almost wins the big game by using a fancy hidden-ball trick, another lost art. These are clever sequences that will delight baseball fans, but probably will fail to excite anyone else.

An irony seemingly lost on the filmmakers is that Billy, so tuned in to baseball tradition, must manage a team that plays in a domed stadium with artificial turf.

Adults spoil the fun in fantasies by injecting too much morality and retribution. *Little Big League*'s theme is the loss of innocence, and so Billy must discover that managing a big-league team isn't all fun. He gets a swelled head. He gets ground down by the business of modern baseball and forgets to have fun.

Billy's Twins don't win the World Series or even finish in first place. Talk about diminished expectations: The climactic battle in the film is against the hapless Seattle Mariners for a wild-card playoff spot, another slap at baseball tradition. In a reversal of almost every baseball movie ever made, the hero's bid to win the big game falls short.

The film's realism is unstinting. It includes some of the most authentic baseball action sequences ever filmed, which mix actors with real professional players such as Ken Griffey Jr., Randy Johnson and Mickey Tettleton. Most of the plays are crisp and compelling. But in a movie pinned to an absurd fantasy, the overabundant realism is depressing. At two hours, the film is too long and often flat. It is filled with annoying moral lessons for Billy. In a particularly morose scene, Billy even has to release his favorite boyhood hero because the former star no longer can cut the mustard.

Director and co-author Andrew Scheinman keeps deflating balloons, as if the audience needs constant reminders that life isn't a homer that wins the World

Series. Maybe *Little Big League* is the strongest evidence yet for baseball's demise. The game is supposed to be about improbable hope, but in this film it is about dashed expectations.

As Billy, Luke Edwards has to carry a heavy load. He is good at conveying the boyish agony of situations where he has to be strong beyond his years, as when he goes to the mound to remove a hothead pitcher. He is believable but lacks the emotional range and depth needed to make him and his plight compelling.

"We have trouble differentiating it from *Rookie of the Year* or *Major League*."—*Little Big League* director Andrew Scheinman. (*Entertainment Weekly*, May 27, 1994)

Even more low-key and colorless is Timothy Busfield as nice-guy star player Lou Collins. He looks and speaks like an accountant and it's hard to believe he's a ballplayer. In a predictable plot line, Collins woos Billy's widowed mother (Ashley Crow). Since both are scripted as absolute saints who never say the wrong thing, they are well-matched for one of the most mundane and underplayed romances in screen history.

Most fictional baseball teams are stocked with wacky and profane characters, but not the Twins of *Little Big League*. Once Billy fires the caustic manager and chastises the hothead pitcher, he has only to battle the apathy and greed of the modern player. Everyone on the team turns out to be a regular guy. Jonathan Silverman is fine as an overly intellectual relief pitcher, but the rest of the players are unremarkable and forgettable.

A prime example of the film's stubborn refusal to inject any tension into the plot comes when Collins, on his way to the plate for the biggest at-bat of the Twins' season, tells Billy he's asked Billy's mom to marry him. Billy says he'll approve the match if Collins hits a game-winning homer, then instantly rescinds the demand.

While sensitivity is fine, this is a sports film, and it could use a little testosterone. *Little Big League* is like one of those three-hour-plus games that are the scourge of the modern major leagues. The dwindling number of baseball fanatics will appreciate its authenticity and its fine points of baseball trivia and strategy. Most others in the stands will want more action and more heroics.

—*Michael Betzold*

CREDITS

Billy Heywood: Luke Edwards
Lou Collins: Timothy Busfield
Mac Macnally: John Ashton
Jenny Heywood: Ashley Crow
Arthur Goslin: Kevin Dunn
Thomas Heywood: Jason Robards
Chuck Lobert: Billy L. Sullivan
Joey Smith: Miles Feulner
Jim Bowers: Jonathan Silverman
George O'Farrell: Dennis Farina
Spencer Hamilton: Wolfgang Bodison
Jerry Johnson: Duane Davis

Released: 1994
Production: Mike Lobell for Castle Rock Entertainment; released by Columbia Pictures
Direction: Andrew Scheinman
Screenplay: Gregory K. Pincus and Adam Scheinman; based on a story by Pincus
Cinematography: Donald E. Thorin
Editing: Michael Jablow
Production design: Jeffrey Howard
Set decoration: Ethel Robin Richards
Casting: Mary Gail Artz and Barbara Cohen
Sound: Bob Eber
Costume design: Erica Edell Phillips
Music: Stanley Clarke
MPAA rating: PG
Running time: 119 minutes

REVIEWS

Entertainment Weekly. July 15, 1994, p. 46.
The Hollywood Reporter. June 20, 1994, p. 12.
Los Angeles Times. July 29, 1994, p. F5.
The New York Times. June 29, 1994, p. C21.
People Weekly. July 4, 1994, p. 14.
Playboy. August 1994, p. 17.
TV Guide. November 12, 1994, p. 50.
Variety. June 20, 1994, p. 42.

Little Buddha

"From the creator of *The Last Emperor* comes a magical journey to a place where the past and present meet."—Movie tagline

"A richly entertaining, visually stunning masterpiece. Bernardo Bertolucci surpasses himself."
—Paul Wunder, *WBAI Radio*

"Exhilarating! Ravishingly beautiful! Filled with amazing sights and dazzling discoveries."—Bob Campbell, *Newhouse News Service*

"Dazzling...mesmerizing...a gorgeous spectacle."
—*The New York Times*

"A triumph!"—*Time*

 Box Office Gross: $4,784,770 (September 11, 1994)

Keanu Reeves in *Little Buddha*. Copyright © Miramax Films.

In Bernardo Bertolucci's drama *Little Buddha*, some Tibetan monks in Seattle believe they have sighted the reincarnation of their revered Lama Dorje. Supposedly, vision of him appeared one day in front of a Seattle home occupied by Dean Conrad (Chris Isaak), an architect, his schoolteacher wife, Lisa (Bridget Fonda), and their young son, Jesse (Alex Wiesendanger). Lama Norbu (Ying Ruocheng) comes all the way from the remote monastery in the kingdom of Bhutan to investigate. The funny thing is, his fellow monks tell him, Lama Dorje appeared wearing jeans. The monks actually laugh about it, even though they take the possibility of reincarnation seriously. Their warm and very human responses are only one of the light touches that make *Little Buddha* a charming film.

The monks introduce themselves to Lisa Conrad and explain the nature of their search. She is intrigued but wary, not knowing exactly how to react to these cheerful religious zealots. They are patient and realize it will take her time to grasp the significance of their quest. They believe, they finally tell her, that her son, Jesse, may be a reincarnation of Lama Dorje. Dean Conrad arrives home perplexed to find Tibetan monks in his living room. Although he is in no mood for visitors, having learned that his business partner has gone bankrupt, his wife coaxes him to listen to the monks. When they leave, they present Jesse with a children's book about the adventures of Siddhartha and the story of how he became the Buddha.

In order to film *Little Buddha*, Bertolucci secured permission to use locations in Nepal by presenting the King of Nepal, a film enthusiast, with a copy of *The Last Emperor*.

Jesse becomes interested in the story. His mother reads him parts of it, and then the film segues to one of several episodes dramatizing Siddhartha's life, his upbringing in a royal court, and his father's extraordinary efforts to protect his son, hiding from him the knowledge of evil, old age, and suffering. Yet a restless Siddhartha yearns to travel beyond his city's walls, where he discovers—in spite of his father's elaborate precautions—lives of misery and scenes of death. He then begins his own journey of enlightenment, learning about the nature of the world, secluding himself for several years among ascetics who deny themselves the pleasures of the flesh, and finally emerging as a full participant in the world, realizing he must find a middle way between self-sacrifice and self-fulfillment.

Essentially Siddhartha's story is of a boy's growing up, of his struggle to mature and come to terms with the world. Jesse identifies with the story on this level, and soon his parents are dropping him off at the Tibetan temple for lessons with the monks. Neither parent takes the religion seriously, but they

CREDITS

Prince Siddhartha: Keanu Reeves
Dean Conrad: Chris Isaak
Lisa Conrad: Bridget Fonda
Jesse Conrad: Alex Wiesendanger
Lama Norbu: Ying Ruocheng
Raju: Raju Lal
Gita: Greishma Makar Singh
Lama Dorje: Tsultim Gyelsen Geshe
Kenpo Tenzin: Sogyal Rinpoche

Released: 1994
Production: Jeremy Thomas; released by Miramax Films
Direction: Bernardo Bertolucci
Screenplay: Mark Peploe and Rudy Wurlitzer; based on a story by Bernardo Bertolucci
Cinematography: Vittorio Storaro
Editing: Pietro Scalia
Production design: James Acheson
Sound: Ivan Sharrock
Costume design: James Acheson
Music: Ryuichi Sakamoto
MPAA rating: PG
Running time: 123 minutes

are gratified by the monks' interest in their son and recognize his affection for them. Nevertheless, Dean balks when he realizes that Lama Norbu wants to take Jesse to Bhutan, where it can be definitively determined whether Jesse is the reincarnation of Lama Dorje. Perhaps because the monks have treated Jesse as someone very special, he begins to consider seriously the possibility that he is a "Little Buddha." Dean, however, decides to break off contact with the monks.

Dean changes his mind about Bhutan when his business partner commits suicide. Suddenly, Dean's whole world is shattered, and he needs to get away and rethink the rest of his life. Lisa is reluctant at first to let him and Jesse go, because it is the middle of the school term and the trip to Bhutan is an experience that she would like to share with her family. The urgency in Dean's manner, however, reconciles her to the trip.

The film are the scenes in the Tibetan monastery are outstanding. Bhutan is rarely accessible to tourists, and it had never appeared in a feature film. The inside of the temple, the beauty of its surroundings, the sense of a life removed from reality and yet devoted to understanding the fundamentals of existence are overpowering. Jesse's wonder at this world is entirely convincing; the camera simply registers the boy's excited and awed reaction to an alien and yet welcoming world.

"It really sensitized me to what I have and what is around me and to suffering...but I'm still an actor, so I haven't put down my joy."—Keanu Reeves on *Little Buddha*

Jesse learns that he is one of three candidates for the reincarnation of Lama Dorje. The other two—Raju (Raju Lal) and Gita (Greishma Makar Singh)—befriend him, even though Gita is scornful of the two boys and calls them impostors. Their different sizes, ages, and sexes are fitting embodiments of the film's message about the universality of the search for Lama Dorje. He represents the life of a religion that can be reborn in any individual, male or female, in any culture.

It is perhaps best not to reveal how the search concludes. Suffice it to say that the end fully justifies Lama Norbu's explanation of reincarnation. Each person, he suggests, is a vessel of life, of life that goes on after the individual dies. He illustrates his point by smashing a pot of tea: The container is no more but the tea it contained remains tea. So life remains life even after a person's body dies.

Although *Little Buddha* is based on an original story by the film's director, Bernardo Bertolucci, his inspiration derives from several documented cases in the United States and elsewhere in which children have been identified as reincarnations of powerful Buddhist spirits. Bertolucci is fascinated with the relationship between the monks and the children, because he sees in the children the pure spirit of life, the proper vessels of the spiritual life the monks seek.

One of Bertolucci's achievements in the film is to capture both the otherness of the Tibetan monks—the sense that they do come from a faraway place and practice a religion that is foreign to the West—and their familiar humanity. The more the camera plays on their faces, the less odd and remote the monks seem. They yearn to establish the continuity of life even as Jesse's own family does in its own terms. In a sense, this is why Jesse's family becomes so responsive to the monks; the monks behave like family and treat Jesse as an extension of themselves.

Besides Seattle and Bhutan, *Little Buddha* also has important scenes in Katmandu and India. The authenticity of the settings and the breathtaking differences among them—the modernistic, all-window Seattle home with its wonderful lofty views of the city contrasts with the crowded, dusty streets of Katmandu, teaming with struggling life—provide a kaleidoscopic view of the world. The well-fed, cherubic Jesse and Raju, his scrawny but scrappy and vibrant counterpart, unite in the possibility that they are both little Buddhas.

For all its charm and integrity, however, *Little Buddha* is also a little too obvious in its message and pious in its presentation of the scenes set in ancient India. It is true that Keanu Reeves does an extraordinarily good job of making Siddhartha into a dynamic figure—the opposite of the cliché portrayed in the staid, fat Buddha figurines. Yet the story itself is presented quite conventionally—as it would be in the picture book the monks present to Jesse. This approach seems a little dull when compared to the wit and deft interactions of the contemporary settings.

Several performances, however, redeem the film's prosaic script. Alex Wiesendanger is the perfect Jesse, with a sharp, intuitive, and responsive grasp of what the monks have to teach him. He gradually grows into the role of their reincarnated teacher and protégé, as he apparently did with his acting role—according to Bertolucci. Ying Ruocheng, one of China's most distinguished actors, was approved for the role of Lama Norbu by the Dalai Lama, who believed that a Chinese playing a Tibetan monk would actually strengthen Tibet's desire for peace with China. Ruocheng gives a subtle performance, expressing both the Lama's dignity and his affability. Finally, it is the film's love of human

character and its extraordinary feeling for place that makes it succeed.

—*Carl Rollyson*

REVIEWS

Entertainment Weekly. June 17, 1994, p. 32.
The Guardian. February 14, 1994, p. 2.
Harper's Bazaar. November 1993, p. 164.
The Hollywood Reporter. December 1, 1993, p. 9.
Los Angeles Times. May 25, 1994, p. F1.
The New York Times. May 25, 1994, p. B1.
Variety. December 1, 1993, p. 24.

Little Giants

"For everyone who's waited to be chosen, and wasn't... Your day has come."—Movie tagline
"The Comic Telling of a Gridiron Miracle."
—Movie tagline
"A comedy worthy of cheers...a well-made film."
—Kevin Thomas, *Los Angeles Times*
"Highly entertaining...smart script, thoughtful casting and nimble direction."—*The Hollywood Reporter*

 Box Office Gross: $19,299,064 (January 2, 1995)

From the animated opening credits to the rousing climactic football game, *Little Giants* is a worthy successor to the genre of "team" films such as *The Bad News Bears* (1976). In this genre of film, usually there is a grizzled, curmudgeonly protagonist—Walter Matthau in *The Bad News Bears* or Tom Hanks in *A League of Their Own* (1992)—who takes a motley crew of losers and turns them into a winning team. The more recent entrants into the genre, such as *Major Payne* (1995), itself a re-make of *The Private War of Major Benson* (1955), have been respectable but predictable.

Little Giants , though, is one of those movies that takes the genre and twists it just enough to make it fresh without

making it unfamiliar. Director Duwayne Dunham has dusted off the old form and polished it up with zest and style, utilizing some fine screen comedians, a whole bunch of excellent child actors, and a lot of wonderfully choreographed physical comedy. Much like Robert Aldrich's *The Longest Yard* (1974), Dunham and company find the humor inherent in the characters and run with it, choreographing funny bits which make the scenes about Pee-Wee football feel quite original and quite entertaining.

Bending a standard element of the genre right from the start, the film has two protagonists—and neither of them is a grizzled curmudgeon. The film begins in the sixties, setting up a rivalry between the O'Shea brothers as they play football. The film cuts to the present day, when Kevin O'Shea (Ed O'Neill), a former Heisman-trophy winning football player, trades on his former notoriety by virtually running their hometown of Urbania from his Chevrolet dealership. His nerdy brother Danny (Rick Moranis), whose wife abandoned him and his daughter Becky (Shawn Waldron), has lived for years in the shadow of his overbearing brother.

Their rivalry returns to the gridiron once again as Becky, shut out of Pee-Wee football because she is a girl (even though her brilliance on the field has earned her the nickname "Ice-Box"), insists that Danny coach her team of ragtag geeks. No sooner does Danny agree to become a Pee-Wee football coach than the upcoming "big-game" (all these films have a "big game") becomes more than a game. Kevin's reputation, Danny's

> "Football is 80 percent mental and 40 percent physical."—a pro-football player talking to the children on the Little Giants team

self-esteem, Becky's femininity and individuality, and the nerdy kids' self-esteem are all on the line.

Young Waldron definitely holds her own against veteran comedians Moranis and O'Neill, making a thoroughly convincing tomboy and a thoroughly promising physical comedienne.

For his part, Moranis, one of the most versatile comedians around, is charming and slightly goofy without being

CREDITS

Danny O'Shea: Rick Moranis
Kevin O'Shea: Ed O'Neill
John Madden: John Madden
Becky O'Shea: Shawna Waldron
Karen O'Shea: Mary Ellen Trainor
Nubie: Mathew McCurley
Patty Floyd: Susanna Thompson
Mike Hammersmith: Brian Haley
Jake Berman: Todd Bosley
Bobby Tasker: Eddie Derham
Tad Simpson: Danny Pritchett
Junior Floyd: Devon Sawa
Rasheed Hanon: Troy Simmons
Johnny Vennaro: Jon Paul Steuer
Marcus: Marcus Toji
Timmy Moore: Christopher Walberg
Rudy Zolteck: Michael Zwiener
Spike Hammersmith: Sam Horrigan

Released: 1994
Production: Arne L. Schmidt for Amblin Entertainment; released by Warner Bros.
Direction: Duwayne Dunham
Screenplay: James Ferguson, Robert Shallcross, Tommy Swerdlow, and Michael Goldberg; based on a story by Ferguson and Shallcross
Cinematography: Janusz Kaminski
Editing: Donn Cambern
Production design: Bill Kenney
Art direction: William Ladd Skinner
Set decoration: Rick T. Gentz
Casting: Janet Hirshenson and Jane Jenkins
Sound: J. Paul Huntsman
Costume design: April Ferry
Music: John Debney
MPAA rating: PG
Running time: 105 minutes

silly. When he takes off in a go-cart to race his brother's Corvette down the streets of Urbania, Moranis recalls the intelligent lunacy of Fred MacMurray in *Son of Flubber* (1963), happily flying around in an old jalopy. His banter with O'Neill is touching and real, in that Moranis creates a character still living with the scars of his brother's football fame.

O'Neill finds the humanity in the fatuous Kevin, having a great time wearing sunglasses and spying on his brother's team, but also sharing sweet moments with his niece "Ice-Box." He is both fathead and good guy, and the audiences ends up rooting for Kevin just as much as Danny. O'Neill is particularly funny in the moments where his character reminds his team of his past victories in a speech that everyone seems to have heard a thousand times before.

Special mention should be made of the casting by Jane Jenkins and Janet Hirshenson: the nerds on Danny's team are all winners. Though they are stereotypes they are perfectly cast and perform with infectious charm. The smaller roles are equally well-cast and performed, especially Elizabeth Anne Smith as the mother of wheezy, skinny Jake (Todd Bosley). Smith is a riot in her two scenes, especially in an hilarious monologue about Jake's countless physical ailments. There is a wonderful sequence with pro-football legends John Madden, Emmit Smith and others which adds to the fun.

From the wonderful music by John Debnay to the stunts by Richard Butler, to Dunham's creative cinematic coverage of some highly unusual football plays (one of them is called "The Annexation of Puerto Rico") *Little Giants* is great fun. This is a film that is sure to entertain everyone willing to take another peek at a familiar story.

—*Kirby Tepper*

REVIEWS

Atlanta Constitution. October 14, 1994, p. P10.
Boston Globe. October 14, 1994, p. 62.
Chicago Tribune. October 14, 1994, p. 7L.
Entertainment Weekly. October 28, 1994, p. 74.
Entertainment Weekly. February 3, 1995, p. 64.
Los Angeles Times. October 14, 1994, p. F6.
The New York Times. October 14, 1994, p. C12.
The New York Times. October 30, 1994, Sec. 2 p. 26.
USA Today. October 14, 1994, p. D4.
Variety. CCCLVI, October 17, 1994, p. 44.
The Washington Post. October 17, 1994, p. B4.
The Washington Post. October 20, 1994, p. D7.

The Little Rascals

"Mischief loves company."—Movie tagline

 Box Office Gross: $51,742,905 (November 27, 1994)

In the 1990s, children aren't rascals anymore. If they misbehave, they are diagnosed as hyperactive, deprived or abused and likely will get therapy. If they roam the streets, they are unsupervised or homeless and likely will get serviced. If they form gangs, they likely will become truly dangerous. Scruffy, unmanageable children just aren't cute anymore. Opportunities for kids to get into the kind of mischief they can get out of are rare nowadays. Thus, remaking "The Little Rascals" episodes for the 1990's presented a dilemma. Rather than completely update the characters and plot, director Penelope Spheeris and her crew retained their look and behavior and gently modernized some of their lines. They get high marks for effort even if they fall short of a complete success.

The new Rascals, based on the crew that was created in the 1920s for Hollywood and persisted through a 1950s television series, are faithful to the originals but seem to live in a time warp. The gang has an anachronistic clubhouse in the midst of a modern city. They have a fishin' hole and a swimmin' hole among the condos. Alfalfa still has his trademark cowlick but the filmmakers can't resist giving it phallic properties. The old theme song still plays in the background along with a few modern tunes. The gang competes in a go-cart race while presumably the rest of their peers are playing Nintendo.

It's largely an agreeable fantasy, this image of children and childhood as it once was, plunked down in a vastly different world. For the most part, Spheeris and four co-writers have fashioned the kind of dialogue and plot that made the original Rascals such a long-running success. Into the mouths of babes are put some jokes and double entendres only adults will get, and thus the film appeals both to grown-ups and tykes.

Some of the updating works well, as when the kids fashion detailed architectural plans for a new clubhouse on an Etch-a-Sketch. Some of it is wretched, as when Reba McEntire asks Alfalfa, "Is that a cowlick, or are you just happy to see me?"

Zachary Mabry as Porky, Kevin Jamal Woods as Stymie, Courtland Mead as Uh-huh, Bug Hill as Alfalfa, Brittany Ashton Holmes as Darla, Travis Tedford as Spanky, Jordon Warkol as Froggy, and Ross Bagley as Buckwheat in *The Little Rascals*. Copyright © by Universal City Studios, Inc. Courtesy of MCA Publishing Rights, a Division of MCA Inc. All rights reserved.

The film works best when its makers simply suspend disbelief and create lines and action most like the original rascally stuff. In this film, casting is crucial, and there are some notable hits and misses. Bug Hall is perfect as Alfalfa, bug-eared and puzzled by pre-adolescent stirrings. Kevin Jamal Woods is so wonderful as the sophisticated Stymie that his part should have been expanded. Jordan Warkol isn't scruffy enough to be Froggy, but he's passable. As Buckwheat, Ross Elliot Bagley has just enough spunk to overcome the directors' penchant for making him too cute.

Unfortunately, that penchant ruins some of the other characters. In key roles, Travis Tedford as Spanky and Brittany Ashton Holmes as Darla are too darling to be effective. In neither case should five-year-olds have been cast in the parts.

Spanky is supposed to be the gang's leader, belligerent enough to make Alfalfa quake. Darla is supposed to be "woman" enough to make Alfalfa melt. But neither is a match for Hall, who was nine years old when playing Alfalfa. Tedford tries hard to be chief rascal but is too adorable and halting in his speech. Holmes is cloying, a little doll who can barely speak her lines. The same cuteness factor diminishes the more minor role of Porky (played by four-year-old Zachary Mabry).

 A local children's dentist had to be on hand because so many baby teeth were lost by the cast over the three months of filming *The Little Rascals*.

"Oh, Darla, we're two hearts with but one beat, two brains with but one thought, two souls with but one...shoe."—Alfalfa to Darla in *The Little Rascals*

Outtakes during the film's closing credit sequence, showing the kids muffing their lines in endearing fashion,

CREDITS

Spanky: Travis Tedford
Alfalfa: Bug Hall
Darla: Brittany Ashton Holmes
Stymie: Kevin Jamal Woods
Porky: Zachary Mabry
Buckwheat: Ross Elliot Bagley
Butch: Sam Saletta
Woim: Blake Jeremy Collins
Waldo: Blake McIver Ewing
Froggy: Jordan Warkol
Uh-Huh: Courtland Mead
Mary Ann: Juliette Brewer
Jane: Heather Karasek
Petey: Petey
Mr. Welling: Mel Brooks
Buckwheat's mom: Whoopi Goldberg
Miss Crabtree: Daryl Hannah
A. J. Ferguson: Reba McEntire

Released: 1994
Production: Michael King and Bill Oakes for King World; released by Universal Pictures
Direction: Penelope Spheeris
Screenplay: Paul Guay, Stephen Mazur, and Penelope Spheeris; based on a story by Spheeris, Robert Wolterstorff, Mike Scott, Guay, and Mazur
Cinematography: Richard Bowen
Editing: Ross Albert
Production design: Larry Fulton
Art direction: Gae Buckley
Set decoration: Linda Spheeris
Casting: Judy Taylor and Lynda Gordon
Sound: Susumu Tokunow
Costume design: Jami Burrows
Stunt coordination: Shane Dixon
Music: William Ross
MPAA rating: PG
Running time: 82 minutes

betray Spheeris' problem. As a director, she should not be doting on her cast. Being cute was never enough to qualify as a Rascal; you also had to be full of mischief.

Unfortunately, Spheeris also feels compelled to insert some feminist moralizing into the battle of the sexes that is the Rascals' constant source of plot tension, in this and many of the old versions. She makes the Rascals see the error of their "womun-hating" ways and ends the film in a very unrascally and unsatisfying image of mass boy-girl pairings. It doesn't ring true; it's like trying to take the sting out of the gang.

Luckily, for the rest of the film, Spheeris does not betray the Rascals' sensibility. There are frogs in pockets, the defiling of a ballet, and delicious come-uppance for the bullies. Had there been more such pranks and less cuteness, this could have been a *Rascals* to take its place among the best of the long series.

Still, it is an entertaining effort and a chance to measure how far we have come from the more innocent and rascally days of long ago.

—*Michael Betzold*

REVIEWS

Atlanta Constitution. August 5, 1994, p. P10.
Boston Globe. August 5, 1994, p. 48.
Chicago Tribune. August 5, 1994, p. 7C.
Christian Science Monitor. August 5, 1994, p. 10.
Entertainment Weekly. August 19, 1994, p. 44.
Entertainment Weekly. February 10, 1995, p. 76.
Hollywood Reporter. August 5, 1994, p. 10.
Los Angeles Times. August 5, 1994, p. F1.
The New York Times. August 5, 1994, p. C21.
The New York Times. August 5, 1994, p. B11.
The New York Times. August 21, 1994, Sec. 2 p. 22.
People Weekly. XLII, August 22, 1994, p. 15.
TV Guide. XLIII, February 18, 1995, p. 34.
USA Today. August 5, 1994, p. D4.
Variety. CCCLVI, August 8, 1994, p. 75.
The Washington Post. August 5, 1994, p. C6.
The Washington Post. August 5, 1994, p. WW38.
The Washington Post. August 11, 1994, p. B7.

Little Secrets

Six women (Cecily Adams, Bettina Devin, Carla Folk, Anne Leyden, Catherine MacNeal, and Lisa Robins) gather on the eve of their ten-year high school class reunion to party and reminisce.

CREDITS

Roxanne: Cecily Adams
Chris: Bettina Devin
Monica: Carla Folk
Jamie: Anne Leyden
Lauren: Catherine MacNeal
Liz: Lisa Robins

Released: 1991
Production: Mark Sobel and Nancylee Myatt; released by Cinecam Film Productions
Direction: Mark Sobel
Screenplay: Nancylee Myatt; based on her play *Slumber Party*
Cinematography: Shane D. Kelly
Editing: Mark Sobel
Sound: Robin Lee
Hairstyling: Kim Frankamp Taylor
Makeup: Debora Wait
Costume design: Candace Walters St. John
Music: Gene Hobson
MPAA rating: no listing
Running time: 96 minutes

A Little Stiff

This winning low-budget black-and-white romantic comedy stars director-producer-screenwriter-editor Caveh Zahedi as himself—a love-struck UCLA film student. The object of his affections is an art student, Erin McKim. Zahedi's filmmaking partner, Greg Watkins, stars as his best friend and confidant.

REVIEWS

The New York Times. September 9, 1994, p. D17.
Variety. CCCXLII, February 11, 1991, p. 111.

CREDITS

Caveh: Caveh Zahedi
Greg: Greg Watkins
Erin: Erin McKim
Patrick: Patrick Park

No character identified: Beat Ammon
No character identified: Arnold Barkus
No character identified: Alison Bradley
No character identified: Leslie Copes
No character identified: Mike McKim
No character identified: David Trauberman

Released: 1991
Production: Greg Watkins and Caveh Zahedi for Just Above The Ground
Direction: Greg Watkins and Caveh Zahedi
Screenplay: Greg Watkins and Caveh Zahedi
Cinematography: Greg Watkins
Editing: Greg Watkins and Caveh Zahedi
Sound: Arnold Barkus
Music: Kath Bloom
MPAA rating: no listing
Running time: 85 minutes

Little Women

"Two enthusiastic thumbs up! This is one of the year's best pictures."—*Siskel & Ebert*

"Four stars. Vivid."—Susan Wloszczyna, *USA Today*

"Alcott's sense, sensibility and sentiment find new life in this handcrafted valentine."—David Ansen, *Newsweek*

"...a snowy picture postcard of youth, innocence, and sisterly devotion."—Jami Bernard, *The New York Times*

Box Office Gross: $20.5 million (January 2, 1995)

Based on the classic 1868 novel by Louisa May Alcott, *Little Women* centers on the coming-of-age of four sisters in Civil War-era Concord, Massachusetts. The novel had been adapted to the big screen before. Perhaps best known was the 1933 version starring Katharine Hepburn. Universally acclaimed and very faithful to Alcott's book, this version won an Academy Award for screenwriters Victor Heerman and Sarah Y. Mason. The film was remade in 1949 with an all-star cast that included June Allyson, Peter Lawford, Margaret O'Brien, and Elizabeth Taylor. Although these two films were tough acts to follow, the 1994 film—directed by Gillian Armstrong—also has its merits.

The film begins at Christmas, and the viewer quickly becomes acquainted with the March family, once one of Concord's finest families but now considerably reduced in circumstances. The mother, Marmee (Susan Sarandon), is a

Christian Bale, Winona Ryder, Trini Alvarado, and Eric Stoltz star in the 1994 version of *Little Women*. Copyright © 1994 Columbia Pictures Industries Inc. All rights reserved. Courtesy of Columbia Pictures.

warm matriarch who heads the household alone while her husband serves as a soldier in the Civil War. Sweet-tempered Meg (Trini Alvarado), at sixteen years old, is the oldest of the four daughters. Tomboy Jo (Winona Ryder) is fifteen and dreams of becoming a writer; she is generally considered to be Alcott's alter ego. Thirteen-year-old Beth (Claire Danes) is the shy and delicate one, and twelve-year-old Amy (Kirsten Dunst) is pretty, spoiled, and self-centered and has some of the best lines.

The opening scenes set the mood and tone of what is to follow. The four girls gather close around their mother, who sits in an armchair in front of the fire, reading a letter from their father. The scene shows the close-knit and loving nature of the March family. Next, the girls give up their much-anticipated Christmas Day breakfast to a poor immigrant family, the Hummels. This scene demonstrates the generosity that is the family's hallmark.

The narrative traces the girls' growing friendship with Laurie (Christian Bale), the teenage boy next door who has recently arrived from Europe to live with his curmudgeonly, wealthy grandfather (John Neville). Laurie and Jo, who are the same age, form a special bond. The girls, despite the customary friction experienced by most siblings, remain very close. They form a literary society called the Pickwick Club and put on original plays written by Jo. Meg slowly falls in love with Laurie's tutor, Mr. Brooke (Eric Stoltz)—much to the dismay of Jo, who wishes that things did not have to change, that they could stay little girls and live together forever.

Tragedy strikes twice when Mr. March is gravely wounded and Marmee must go to Washington, D.C., to attend to him; while she is away, Beth contracts scarlet fever while attending to the Hummel family in Marmee's absence. Although both survive, Beth's bout with illness foreshadows her death near the end of the film.

The narrative then jumps ahead four years. Following Meg's marriage to Mr. Brooke and Laurie's graduation from college, Laurie proposes to Jo—who refuses him. Hurt and angry, Laurie flees to Europe. At the same time, Amy (now played as an adolescent by Samantha Mathis) announces that she is to accompany their cranky, elderly, and wealthy Aunt March (Mary Wickes) to Europe to study art—a trip that Jo had believed was rightfully hers. After all, Jo had toiled as Aunt March's companion for years, hoping to be rewarded with such a trip.

Distraught over Laurie and this latest lost opportunity, Jo moves to New York City to be governess in a boardinghouse and gather experiences for her writing. There, she meets a German immigrant named Friedrich Bhaer (Gabriel Byrne), a shy professor with whom she enjoys a tentative romance.

CREDITS

Jo March: Winona Ryder
Mrs. March: Susan Sarandon
Friedrich Bhaer: Gabriel Byrne
Meg March: Trini Alvarado
Amy March (as an adolescent): Samantha Mathis
Amy March (as a child): Kirsten Dunst
Beth March: Claire Danes
Laurie: Christian Bale
John Brooke: Eric Stoltz
Mr. Laurence: John Neville
Aunt March: Mary Wickes

Released: 1994
Production: Denise DiNovi for DiNovi Pictures; released by Columbia Pictures
Direction: Gillian Armstrong
Screenplay: Robin Swicord; based on the book by Louisa May Alcott
Cinematography: Geoffrey Simpson
Editing: Nicholas Beauman
Production design: Jan Roelfs
Art direction: Richard Hudolin
Set design: Richard St. John Harrison
Set decoration: Jim Erickson
Casting: Carrie Frazier and Shani Ginsberg
Sound: Eric Batut
Sound design: Lee Smith
Costume design: Colleen Atwood
Music: Thomas Newman
MPAA rating: PG
Running time: 118 minutes

Bhaer, however, does not approve of the sensationalistic stories Jo has been selling to the newspapers—stories that pander to popular tastes. He wants her to aspire to something better. Upset and confused, Jo receives word that Beth is dying and hastens home.

The grief over Beth's death inspires Jo to write an autobiographical novel that will bring her the fame she seeks—*Little Women* itself. Beth's death also proves to be the catalyst that brings together Laurie and Amy, who are both still in Europe. When they return home—as husband and wife—Jo is initially taken aback. Yet she accepts this latest blow with the grace becoming her. In the final scene, Professor Bhaer arrives at the March home, bringing word that Jo's book has found a publisher. The two enjoy a romantic exchange under the professor's umbrella in the pouring rain, during which Bhaer proposes and Jo accepts.

1994's *Little Women* is the fifth film version of Louisa May Alcott's novel, including a silent version in 1918, George Cukor's in 1933, Mervyn LeRoy's 1949 remake, and a 1978 TV movie.

AWARDS AND NOMINATIONS

Academy Awards Nominations 1994: Best Actress (Ryder), Best Costume Design, Best Original Score
Chicago Film Critics Awards 1995: Most Promising Actress (Dunst)

Little Women is a fine production of a fine novel. Winona Ryder, in her starring role as Jo, captures equally Jo's tomboyishness and her vulnerability. Her childish gaiety at the beginning of the film, as she swordfights with Laurie in the Laurences' fine mansion or prances behind the scenes of an elegant ball, matures nicely toward the end of the film as her life experiences render her sadder but wiser. Also fine is Christian Bale as the youthful, mischievous Laurie. He and Ryder banter back and forth in their roles as Laurie and Jo like the old friends they are supposed to be. The scene in which Laurie's marriage proposal is refused by Jo is his best. Bale registers a range of emotions from initial adoration to disbelief, comprehension, despair, and finally anger in a matter of minutes.

Susan Sarandon, although definitely in a supporting role, is outstanding as Marmee. Her mild, gentle voice and pretty face belie her inner strength and earthiness. Sarandon's Marmee embodies a pillar of strength and faith as the March girls' beloved mother. Unfortunately, whereas Sarandon is the film's mainstay in its first half, she virtually disappears in its second.

Having Amy be portrayed by two different actors helps to convey the passage of time, as these four young girls mature into the four little women of the title. Kirsten Dunst, who made a striking appearance opposite Tom Cruise and Brad Pitt earlier in the year in *Interview with the Vampire* (reviewed in this volume), is especially charming as young Amy, who infuriates and endears simultaneously. Samantha Mathis has less opportunity to make an impression in her brief role as the grown-up Amy. Trini Alvarado is perfect as gentle, motherly Meg, but Claire Danes is the film's weakest choice in her role as the timid, doomed Beth.

True to Alcott's novel, the male roles are secondary to the female ones. Mr. March is rarely seen or heard from, even after he returns from the war. Laurie's tutor, Mr. Brooke, although portrayed by noted actor Eric Stoltz, has but a few lines. Mr. Laurence, Laurie's grandfather, is granted an even smaller role in the film than he had in the novel. His special friendship with shy, music-loving Beth is downplayed in the film, one of its more notable faults. Of note, however, is character actress Mary Wickes as persnickety old Aunt March. In only a few short scenes, she conveys both the old lady's spitefulness as well as her perverse charm.

Thanks to cinematographer Geoffrey Simpson, the outdoor scenes, many of which take place in the winter, are picture-postcard perfect: beautiful New England winters segueing into equally sumptuous springs and falls. The other locations—the grimy streets and office buildings of New York and the wide avenues and lush gardens of Europe—reflect the experiences of their respective principals, Jo and Amy. Credit also goes to production designer Jan Roelfs for the exquisite interiors.

"Nothing provokes speculation more than the sight of a woman enjoying herself."—Mrs. March from *Little Women*

The one quibble to be made by Alcott purists would be the liberties taken by screenwriter Robin Swicord with the original text. Not only are events transposed at will but themes and even entire scenes have been added as well. Perhaps most jarring are Jo and Professor Bhaer's fireside discussion of the Transcendentalism of Jo's parents and a scene at the boardinghouse in which Jo waxes eloquent about woman's suffrage in a discussion with several male boarders—scenes that were completely fabricated by the filmmakers.

Also in a departure from Alcott's novel, themes of racism and sexism are raised, apparently in order to strengthen the overall impression of the March family as progressive and liberal to a 1990's audience. Marmee delivers several feminist diatribes in the film, and it is hinted that Mr. March's school had to be closed because he accepted a black student. In addition, the connection between fictional Jo March and her real-life creator, Louisa May Alcott, is made manifest in the film by the title given to Jo's much-anticipated first novel *Little Women*. Such a direct connection was never made in Alcott's text.

Despite these minor deviations, Armstrong's *Little Women* was critically acclaimed by reviewers and enjoyed a long run in theaters. Released at Christmastime, the film proved to be a fine holiday family film. Although the 1933 version that starred Katharine Hepburn will remain a classic, and certainly remained truer to Alcott's original text, the 1994 production has its advantages. The casting, Colleen Atwood's costuming, and the production aspects are all outstanding, and the color cinematography and more contemporary style of storytelling will perhaps attract a new and younger generation to what is truly a classic story. 🎞️

—Cynthia K. Breckenridge

REVIEWS

Entertainment Weekly. December 23, 1994, p. 49.
The Hollywood Reporter. December 14, 1994, p. 8.
Los Angeles Times. December 21, 1994, p. F1.
The New York Times. December 21, 1994, p. B1.
Variety. December 14, 1994, p. 4.

Living Proof: HIV and the Pursuit of Happiness

This uplifting documentary centers on a cross section of individuals—men, women, and children—from widely varying backgrounds who have been diagnosed as HIV positive. Through interviews, the film's subjects reveal how they have learned to cope with their condition and how it has helped them to get a new lease on life.

REVIEWS

The Advocate. February 8, 1994, p. 77.
Boston Globe. September 22, 1993, p. 37.
Boston Globe. May 27, 1994, p. 36.
Chicago Tribune. July 29, 1994, p. 7K.
The New York Times. January 28, 1994, p. C8.
Variety. CCCLII, November 1, 1993, p. 43.
The Washington Post. July 2, 1994, p. D1.

CREDITS

Released: 1994
Production: Kermit Cole, Beth Tyler, and Anthony Bennett; released by First Run Features
Direction: Kermit Cole
Screenplay: Jameson Currier
Cinematography: Richard Dallett
Editing: Michael Gersh
Music: James Legg and Mark Suozzo
MPAA rating: no listing
Running time: 72 minutes

Lonely Hearts

A lonely woman, Alma (Beverly D'Angelo), is deceived by the attentions of a handsome man, Frank (Eric Roberts), into investing in a real-estate deal. When she discovers the truth, rather than turn him in, Alma helps him go on to swindle others.

REVIEWS

Variety. CCCXLV, October 14, 1991, p. 246.

CREDITS

Alma: Beverly D'Angelo
Frank: Eric Roberts
Erin: Joanna Cassidy
Annie: Herta Ware
Maria: Bibi Besch

Released: 1991
Production: Andrew Lane and Robert Kenner for Gibraltar Entertainment; released by Live Entertainment
Direction: Andrew Lane
Screenplay: Andrew Lane and R. E. Daniels; based on a story by Daniels
Cinematography: Paul Ryan
Editing: Julian Semilian
Production design: Pamela Woodbridge
Art direction: Carlos Barbosa
Set decoration: Marty Huyette
Casting: Michelle Guillermin
Sound: George Alch
Costume design: Libbie Aroff Lane and Peggy Schnitzer
Music: David McHugh
MPAA rating: R
Running time: 109 minutes

Lost Prophet

A disoriented young man (Jim Burton) wanders the countryside, in this low-budget experimental film that attempts to portray the dream state. Directorial debut of Michael de Avila.

REVIEWS

Variety. CCCXLVII, June 15, 1992, p. 57.

CREDITS

Jim: James Burton
Kym: Zandra Huston
Real estate agent: Drew Monroe
Kid: James Tucker
Kid's brother: Steven Tucker
Park patrolman: Shannon Goldman

Punk No. 1: Larry O'Neil
Punk No. 2: Christian Urich
Punk No. 3: Sophia Ramos
Mick Prophet: Drew Monroe

Released: 1992
Production: Michael de Avila for J-5-1; released by Rockville Pictures
Direction: Michael de Avila
Screenplay: Michael de Avila, Drew Morone, Larry O'Neil, and Shannon Goldman
Cinematography: Michael de Avila
Editing: Michael de Avila
Sound: Chris Cliadakis and Marissa Bennideto
Music: TRF Music Libraries
MPAA rating: no listing
Running time: 72 minutes

The Lost Words

An unemployed New York songwriter, Charles (Michael Kaniecki), has a friend videotape him in the hopes of using the film to win back his girlfriend, Marcie (Zelda Gergel), and to reevaluate his life.

REVIEWS

Chicago Tribune. January 20, 1995, p. 7E.
Los Angeles Times. March 19, 1994, p. F9.
The New York Times. September 21, 1994, p. C18.
Variety. CCCLVI, October 10, 1994, p. 85.

CREDITS

Charles: Michael Kaniecki
Sid: Bob McGrath
Marcie: Zelda Gergel

Released: 1994
Production: Scott Saunders, Katrina Charmatz, and Vanessa Baran for Film Crash and Scopix; released by Headliner
Direction: Scott Saunders
Screenplay: Dan Koeppel, Scott Saunders, and Michael Kaniecki
Cinematography: Mark Kroll and Scott Saunders
Music: Michael Kaniecki and Chris Burke
MPAA rating: no listing
Running time: 85 minutes

Love Affair

"An old-fashioned love story with a wonderful new fashioned style. Pure movie romance."
—David Sheehan, *CDS-TV*

"For glamorous, old-fashioned romance, this is the movie for you!"—Rex Reed, *New York Observer*

"Wonderfully romantic. Warren Beatty and Annette Bening are a dazzling couple."
—Pia Lindstrom, *WNBC-TV*

"A gloriously romantic love story."—Jules Peimer, *WNWK Radio*

 Box Office Gross: $18,266,245 (January 2, 1995)

This lavishly produced film combines the talents of real-life husband and wife Warren Beatty and Annette Bening, the legendary Katharine Hepburn, and a tear-jerker plot which was proven effective twice before—in the original *Love Affair* (1939) starring Charles Boyer and Irene Dunne, and the 1957 remake *An Affair to Remember*, with Cary Grant and Deborah Kerr. Considerable interest in the story was generated by the 1993 romantic comedy *Sleepless in Seattle*, which contained extensive references to *An Affair to Remember*, causing home video rentals of that film to skyrocket. An updated version was inevitable.

 *Love Affair* is Katherine Hepburn's first film since her 1985 Academy Award-winning performance in *On Golden Pond*.

Former pro-football player Mike Gambril (Warren Beatty) is a notorious ladies' man whose engagement to a television talk-show host (Kate Capshaw) has not curtailed his philandering. On a flight to Australia, he meets Terry McKay (Annette Bening), a musician and singer who is engaged to a wealthy investment banker (Pierce Brosnan). Mike's attraction to Terry is immediate, but she is not receptive to his advances.

The plane makes an emergency landing on a South Pacific island, and the passengers are shifted to a cruise ship bound for Tahiti, the nearest place they can board a commercial aircraft. En route, Mike continues his pursuit of Terry, while dodging a tabloid photographer bent on catching him in a compromising position. Mike deftly eludes the photographer, and the other passengers, but is not so adept at charming Terry. Willful

"You know that I've never been faithful to anyone in my life."—Mike warns Terry in *Love Affair*

and self-assured, she is not like the women whose names fill his little black book to overflowing.

The pair take a side trip to a nearby island to visit Mike's Aunt Ginny (Katharine Hepburn), an octogenarian who addresses directly matters of the heart. She gives a discourse on the mating habits of ducks, horses, men, and other animals, and exposes to Terry an unexpected artistic and vulnerable side of Mike. The visit deeply moves Terry and after seeing Mike through his aunt's eyes, she finds herself falling in love. Forgoing an opportunity to return to civilization immediately, the couple spends the remaining two days of the cruise together.

On the flight back to New York, the couple makes a pact to part for three months, then meet atop the Empire State Building on May 8 at 5:02 P.M. to start their lives anew.

Both immediately dump their prospective mates, and Mike Gambril spends the succeeding three months simplifying his life, to the consternation of his business manager, Kip (Garry Shandling). Kip wants his client to endorse products on a home shopping channel, but instead Mike chooses a small-time coaching job in Western Pennsylvania. Terry finds some work as a back-up jingle singer, then takes a more fulfilling job teaching underprivileged children.

Rushing to the appointed rendezvous spot on May 8, Terry is struck by a cab. On the observation deck of the Empire State Building, Mike waits for hours in the rain. Terry learns she will probably never walk and decides not to tell Mike of her accident, because she does not want to be a burden to him. Instead, she lets him believe that she had a change of heart. With the support of her friends, the schoolchildren, and even her former fiance, Terry resolutely gets on with her life.

Months later, Mike and Terry run into each other at a benefit concert. They exchange only a few words, but both are shaken by the encounter. Soon thereafter, Mike appears at Terry's apartment. She is sitting on the sofa, her legs under a blanket. She is still unable to walk, and he is still unaware of her affliction.

Mike gives Terry a shawl that his Aunt Ginny, now deceased, wanted her to have. He then tells her about a painting he had done of her wearing the shawl. He had

Love Affair

CREDITS

Mike Gambril: Warren Beatty
Terry McKay: Annette Bening
Ginny: Katharine Hepburn
Kip DeMay: Garry Shandling
Tina Wilson: Chloe Webb
Ken Allen: Pierce Brosnan
Lynn Weaver: Kate Capshaw
Herb Stillman: Paul Mazursky
Nora Stillman: Brenda Vaccaro
Anthony Rotundo: Glenn Shadix
Robert Crosley: Barry Miller
Sheldon Blumenthal: Harold Ramis
Marissa: Taylor Dane
Martha: Carey Lowell
Ray Charles: Ray Charles

Released: 1994
Production: Warren Beatty for Mulholland; released by Warner Bros.
Direction: Glenn Gordon Caron
Screenplay: Robert Towne and Warren Beatty; based on the motion picture *Love Affair* (1939), screenplay by Delmer Daves and Donald Ogden Stewart, from an original story by Mildred Cram and Leo McCarey
Cinematography: Conrad L. Hall
Editing: Robert C. Jones
Executive producer: Andrew Z. Davis
Production design: Ferdinando Scarfiotti
Art direction: Edward Richardson
Set design: Al Manzer and James Murakami
Set decoration: Dan L. May
Casting: Marion Dougherty
Visual effects supervision: John Richardson
Sound: Jim Tannenbaum
Costume design: Milena Canonero
Music: Ennio Morricone
MPAA rating: PG-13
Running time: 105 minutes

left it at a hotel and later allowed them to give it away to a poor crippled woman. The realization that the woman who coveted the portrait was Terry strikes Mike, and he rushes into the next room. The painting hangs on the wall, as confirmation of his fears. He embraces her and they decide to face the future together.

When measured against the original *Love Affair* (1939) and *An Affair To Remember* (1957), both considered cinema classics, this remake almost invariably drew unfavorable comparisons. The *Los Angeles Times* said the film "never manages to be more than a reasonable facsimile of its progenitor," and *The New York Times* opined, "Warren Beatty isn't quite Cary Grant." Even when the reviewer did not like

the original, the remake fared no better. *Entertainment Weekly* judged, "the trouble with *Love Affair* is that it's a remake of a movie that was lousy to begin with." While the film was not panned, it received very little praise, other than a general consensus of Annette Bening's boundless charms. The assessment of the *New York Magazine* reviewer reflects the tone of the majority of the reviews: "it is not a disaster, but it's not good, either."

Thirteen-time Academy Award winner Warren Beatty is likable in the role of Mike Gambril, but there is very little depth to his performance. As his character's history closely parallels Beatty's real life (notorious womanizer is finally tamed by the love of a good woman), the part was not a stretch for Beatty. His performance seems prefunctory.

Annette Bening invests her role with more soul, making Terry the more compelling of the star-crossed lovers. It is easy to understand why Mike would toss his little black book for her, but harder to comprehend why she would bypass her wealthy, handsome fiance in favor of Mike.

Eighty-seven-year-old Katharine Hepburn looks feeble and ailing, but her ten-minute scene provides the film's most poignant moments. The biggest laughs are scored by Garry Shandling as the glib business manager. As the discarded mates, Pierce Brosnan and Kate Capshaw are given very little to do and thus neither makes much of an impression. Several other talented performers, including Brenda Vacarro, Harold Ramis, and Barry Miller, are wasted in minuscule roles.

The entire film seems bathed in soft focus, which has been attributed to Warren Beatty's desire to keep his age-weathered face in the shadows. This haziness is more appropriate in the second half of the film when fate and tragedy conspire to keep the lovers apart. Earlier indoor scenes, especially those aboard the cruise ship, are dark and murky, contradicting the light and airy mood of the couple's verbal jousting. Two memorable shots enliven Conrad L. Hall's cinematography: reflections of the Empire State Building and Terry's portrait, both at dramatic turning points in the tale.

Though screenwriters Beatty and Robert Towne updated *Love Affair* with some contemporary touches, the film remains unusually chaste for the 1990's. While it is implied that Mike and Terry consummate their relationship on board the ship, the audience only sees them kiss. The film's PG-13 rating is due to one use of profanity which, ironically, is uttered by Katharine Hepburn.

While the basic plot line is the same, this retelling of *Love Affair* does not adhere as closely to the original as *An Affair to Remember* did. Modernizing the story necessitated giving Mike a profession. In the earlier versions, the character was an international playboy, a stereotype which has gone out of vogue. Some of the plot contemporizations make sense, others do not. In the two earlier versions, the lovers meet on a transatlantic cruise. In this day of air travel, it was deemed unlikely that these busy folks would travel at such a leisurely pace, especially since Mike is not a playboy by trade, but a television personality. The plot machinations employed to get the jet-setters to the obligatory cruise ship, however, are cumbersome and contrived.

The remake is most faithful to the original in its closing sequence, in which the dialog was copied almost verbatim. More than half a century after it was first written, this climactic scene still tugs at the heartstrings.

—*Brenda Scott Royce*

REVIEWS

USA Today. October 21, 1994, p. 6D.
Variety. October 10, 1994, p. 84.
The Village Voice. November 1, 1994, p. 56.
The Wall Street Journal. October 20, 1994, p. A24.
Chicago Tribune. October 21, 1994, p. 7A-C.
Entertainment Weekly. October 28, 1994, p. 68.
The Hollywood Reporter. October 10, 1994, p. 5.
Los Angeles Times. October 21, 1994, p. F1.
New York Magazine. November 7, 1994, p. 97.
The New York Times. October 21, 1994, p. B1.
Newsweek. October 24, 1994, p. 76.
People Weekly. October 31, 1994, p. 17.
Time. October 24, 1994, p. 76.

Love After Love (Apres l'amour)

"An endearing and comic sexual roundelay."
—Jay Carr, *Boston Globe*

"Isabelle Huppert is at her most beautiful and poised."—Kevin Thomas, *Los Angeles Times*

A thirty-five-year-old writer, Lola (Isabelle Huppert), suffers writer's block, as well as problems with her live-in lover, David (Bernard Giraudeau).

REVIEWS

Boston Globe. September 17, 1993, p. 53.
Boston Globe. March 11, 1994, p. 66.
Chicago Tribune. October 14, 1994, p. 7M.
Los Angeles Times. July 8, 1994, p. F14.
The New York Times. October 14, 1994, p. C10.
The Washington Post. November 11, 1994, p. D6.

CREDITS

Lola: Isabelle Huppert
David: Bernard Giraudeau
Tom: Hippolyte Girardot
Marianne: Lio
Romain: Yvan Attal
Rachel: Judith Reval

Origin: France
Released: 1994
Production: Robert Benmussa for Alexandre Films, TFI Films, and Prodeve, with the participation of Soficas Sofiarp, Investimage 3, and Canal Plus; released by Rainbow
Direction: Diane Kurys
Screenplay: Diane Kurys and Antoine Lacomblez
Cinematography: Fabio Conversi
Editing: Hervé Schneid
Production design: Tony Egry
Costume design: Mic Cheminal
Music: Yves Simon
MPAA rating: no listing
Running time: 104 minutes

Love and a .45

"A real winner. Don't miss this one!"
—Bob Healy, *Satellite News Network*
"It's the *Citizen Kane* of trailer park trash movies."—Dominic Griffin, *Film Threat*

A fugitive young couple—Watty Watts (Gil Bellows) and Starlene (Renee Zellweger)—flees by car to Mexico, pursued by the police, as well as by Watty's crazed former partner in crime, Billy (Rory Cochrane), and two hit men (Jeffrey Combs and Jace Alexander). Directorial debut of C. M. Talkington. Features music by The Butthole Surfers, The Meat Puppets, Mazzy Star, Johnny Cash, The Jesus and Mary Chain, and The Rev. Horton Heat.

REVIEWS

Atlanta Constitution. March 10, 1995, p. P8.
Entertainment Weekly. March 24, 1995, p. 74.
Los Angeles Times. November 23, 1994, p. F6.
The New York Times. November 23, 1994, p. C14.
Playboy. XLI, December 1994, p. 32.
Variety. CCCLV, June 6, 1994, p. 34.

"My granddaddy told me the only two things you need to get by in this world is never to believe anything anyone says and never point a loaded gun."—Watty Watts in *Love and a .45*

CREDITS

Watty Watts: Gil Bellows
Starlene Cheatham: Renee Zellweger
Billy Mack Black: Rory Cochrane
Dino Bob: Jeffrey Combs
Creepy Cody: Jace Alexander
Ranger X: Michael Bowen
Justice Thurmar: Jack Nance
Thaylene: Anne Wedgeworth
Vergil: Peter Fonda
Stipper: Tammy LeBlanc
Young clerk: Wiley Wiggins

Released: 1994
Production: Darin Scott; released by Trimark Pictures
Direction: C. M. Talkington
Screenplay: C. M. Talkington
Cinematography: Tom Richmond
Editing: Bob Ducsay
Production design: Deborah Pastor
Art direction: D. Montgomery
Set decoration: Marcus Brown
Sound: Bill Fiege
Costume design: Kari Perkins
Music: Tom Verlaine
MPAA rating: R
Running time: 101 minutes

AWARDS AND NOMINATIONS

Independent Spirit Award Nomination
1995:   Debut Performance (Zellweger)

A Low Down Dirty Shame

"Comedy's new name is *Shame*"—Movie tagline
"Funny and entertaining. Explosive action."
—*People Weekly*
"A lowbrow raunchy treat."—*The Hollywood Reporter*
"Humorous and energetic."—Kevin Thomas, *Los Angeles Times*

 Box Office Gross: $27,116,697 (January 2, 1995)

Keenen Ivory Wayans does it all in *A Low Down Dirty Shame*. Wayans not only wrote and directed the film but also stars as Shame, a Los Angeles private detective who was expelled from the police force. The film builds upon certain popular themes: good versus evil, and romance. Shame is pitted against his corrupt former police partner, Rothmiller (Charles S. Dutton), and a gang of Mexican drug dealers led by a man named Mendoza (Andrew Divoff). He is also involved with and must choose between two beautiful women—his conniving former lover, Angela (Salli Richardson), and his young and adoring secretary, Peaches (Jada Pinkett). Predictably, Shame defeats the criminals and chooses Peaches.

As the film opens, Shame is hired by his former colleague, who has moved on to the Drug Enforcement Administration, to track down the missing $20 million from the drug bust that cost Shame his job on the police force. Rothmiller convinces Shame that this is a good opportunity for Shame to clear his name and overcome his ill feelings about the case.

Shame's first task is to find Angela, who left him for Mendoza. When Shame finds her, he discovers that she possesses millions of dollars she stole from Mendoza, and that that is the reason Rothmiller is searching for her. He also learns that not only is Rothmiller involved with Mendoza but the two men have set him and Angela up. Together, they narrowly escape Mendoza's men. Shame then entrusts Angela to Peaches while he tries to find Mendoza. Peaches and Angela argue over Shame, and Angela leaves. Mendoza and Rothermiller kidnap Peaches and arrange a rendezvous with Shame at a shopping mall on the assumption that Shame now has the money they want and is willing to exchange it for Peaches. Shame somehow manages to find Angela again and the money she has stashed at a storage facility.

Wayans did most of his own stunts in *A Low Down Dirty Shame*, including its climax sequence in which he is propelled by a fiery explosion over a fourth-floor railing tied to a bungie cord.

Rothmiller sets Shame up once again, however, at the rendezvous. He goes to the rendezvous with Mendoza and some of Mendoza's men with a Special Weapons and Tactics (SWAT) team to reinforce them. Shame and Peaches prevail, nevertheless, in a frenzy of violence, gun and fistfights, a dog chase, and explosions. Angela kills both Rothmiller and Mendoza, but she is knocked out in a fistfight by the younger and smaller Peaches. The film concludes with Shame and Peaches sitting together on a bench, kissing amid the ruin of the mall and a swarm of police activity.

Many critics found this film unremarkable and shallow, the plot melodramatic and derivative of previous comic action films, and the dialogue loaded with one-liners. The film certainly has many predecessors, but this complaint misses the point—these critics either are disappointed that Wayans did not make a different film or dislike the kind of film Wayans made. This film is intended, primarily, to be entertaining and amusing.

Wayans has claimed to want to create a positive role model and combine different genres—specifically comedy, romance, action, and drama. He is best known for his sketch comedy television series *In Living Color* and, to a lesser extent, his comic first feature, *I'm Gonna Git You Sucka* (1988). Wayans tries to do it all in this film, and therein may be the film's greatest fault.

The film tends to feel sentimental when shifting from comic or action scenes to dramatic ones. The primary reason for this is that Shame's seriousness, specifically his unhappiness and moral integrity, is not convincing, and so these scenes never achieve the weight needed to balance the comic ones. When the film begins, Shame has lost the two things that mattered most to him, his job as a police officer and the woman he loved. Yet the film never establishes the value of Shame's identity as a police officer nor the significance of his lost love.

Shame has brief run-ins with his former police captain (Gregory Sierra), which suggest that they did not get along, that Shame liked to do things his own way and did not respect the old captain. The most effective scene illustrating Shame's greatness comes toward the end of the film when Rothmiller and Shame square off in the shopping mall. Rothmiller tells Shame, and the others present, that there had never been any hope of cutting Shame into the drug deal, of getting him to take drug money. Yet this statement comes too late in the film, and it is not enough.

Furthermore, the two brief encounters between Shame and Angela do not indicate that there was anything more between them than desire and a growing familiarity. When they meet for the first time since her disappearance, in a hotel room where she is hiding, Shame seeks to clarify what happened. Shame has reason to be disappointed, but nothing more. Their relationship was not great enough to be lamented and for Shame to lament the relationship is merely self-pity.

A second reason for the sentimentality of the dramatic scenes is that there are simply too many comic scenes, or a disproportionate number of them versus dramatic ones. The prevailing mood is therefore light and the film lacks suspense.

Finally, it is also the case that some of the action scenes are too far-fetched, making them comic. In the opening scene, Shame retrieves diamonds for a client by breaking up an illegal sale in a hotel. He takes on several men in an

"I went partying with Rodney King and Reginald Denny."—a beaten-up Andre Shame in *A Low Down Dirty Shame*

explosive and violent shoot-out and escapes by leaping through a gigantic glass picture window several stories above ground and falling directly onto an open seat in his getaway car, tearing through the car's roof.

The film calls to mind the James Bond films, the *Shaft* films of the early 1970's and other black comic actioners such as *Beverly Hills Cop* (1984). *A Low Down Dirty Shame* has urban black style, and there is a toughness and playful theatricality to both Wayan's character Shame and Pinkett's character Peaches. Some of the comedy in this film derives from sources rare, or certainly less common, to more white-dominated productions. There are jokes based on racial and homoerotic relations and contemporary pop culture. For example, Shame shows up at Peaches' after getting beat up and tells her he has been partying with Rodney King and Reginald Denny. The same night, Shame stays at Peaches', in her housemate's bed. He awakes the next morning alongside Wayman (Corwin Hawkins), a young cross-dressing black male whom Shame, tired upon waking, mistakes for a woman. After Peaches and Wayman have joked about this incident at the breakfast table, Shame declares that he is going to take a hot shower and pretend he did not wake up in *The Crying Game* (1992).

Wayans is fairly versatile in this film, though he is definitely best when clever and glib. The film is at its best when Shame and Peaches are flirting and when Shame is outsmarting or joking with someone in his duties as a private detective. Wayans is fine in the quiet romantic scenes and surprisingly believable as a tough guy, but he is yet far less capable with the more extreme experiences of pleasure and pain. Jada Pinkett is exciting as Peaches even though her character is more one-dimensional. Peaches is naive, forthright, brash and sexy, and undeniably charming, and her presence keeps the film upbeat in tempo.

—*Michael L. Forstrom*

CREDITS

Shame: Keenen Ivory Wayans
Rothmiller: Charles S. Dutton
Peaches: Jada Pinkett
Angela: Salli Richardson
Mendoza: Andrew Divoff
Wayman: Corwin Hawkins
Captain Nunez: Gregory Sierra

Released: 1994
Production: Joe Roth and Roger Birnbaum for Caravan Pictures; released by Buena Vista Pictures
Direction: Keenen Ivory Wayans
Screenplay: Keenen Ivory Wayans
Cinematography: Matthew F. Leonetti
Editing: John F. Link
Production design: Robb Wilson King
Art direction: Richard L. Johnson
Set decoration: Lance Lombardo
Casting: Robi Reed-Humes
Sound: Willie Burton
Costume design: Francine Jamison-Tanchuck
Stunt coordination: Charles Picerni and Billy Burton
Music: Marcus Miller
MPAA rating: R
Running time: 104 minutes

REVIEWS

Chicago Sun-Times. November 23, 1994, p. 54.
Chicago Tribune. November 23, 1994, p .20.
Entertainment Weekly. December 9, 1994, p. 48.
The Hollywood Reporter. November 23, 1994, p. 5.
Los Angeles Times. November 23, 1994, p. F2.
The New York Times. November 23, 1994, p. B6.

Lumumba: Death of a Prophet

This documentary centers on Patrice Lumumba, a prime minister of the Belgian Congo (later known as Zaire) who worked for African independence, but was eventually imprisoned and executed by his political enemies.

CREDITS

Julianna Lumumba: Julianna Lumumba

Origin: Germany, Switzerland and France
Released: 1992
Production: Raoul Peck and Andreas Honegger
Direction: Raoul Peck
Cinematography: Matthias Kalin and Philippe Ros
Editing: Eva Schlensag, Ailo Auguste and Raoul Peck
MPAA rating: no listing
Running time: 68 minutes

REVIEWS

American Historical Review. XCVIII, October 1993, p. 1156.

Luna Park

When a gang leader, Andrei (Andrei Goutine), who beats up on minorities discovers that his estranged father, Naoum Blumstein (Oleg Borisov), is Jewish, Andrei confronts him only to be won over by the man's humanity and kindness.

CREDITS

Naoum Blumstein: Oleg Borisov
Andrei: Andrei Goutine
Fairground entertainer: Natalia Egorova

Origin: France and Russia
Released: 1992
Production: Erik Weisberg and Marcel Godot
Direction: Pavel Lounguine
Screenplay: Pavel Lounguine
Cinematography: Denis Evstigneev
Production design: Pavel Kaplevitch
Set decoration: Boris Pasternak
Music: Isaac Schwartz
MPAA rating: no listing
Running time: 110 minutes

REVIEWS

Atlanta Constitution. March 14, 1994, p. C7.
Boston Globe. March 18, 1994, p. 69.
Entertainment Weekly. September 30, 1994, p. 71.
New York. XXVII, January 24, 1994, p. 56.
The New York Times. January 21, 1994, p. C6.

Lush Life

"One of the richest and most moving pieces of filmmaking...phenomenal performances."
—*Los Angeles Daily News*

Jeff Goldblum and Forest Whitaker star as Al and Buddy, New York City jazz musicians and best friends, in this drama that highlights the New York music scene. When Buddy is told he has a malignant brain tumor, the two plan a final party and invite the city's best musicians for a big jazz session.

REVIEWS

Los Angeles Times. May 20, 1994, p. F20.

CREDITS

Al Gorky: Jeff Goldblum
Buddy Chester: Forest Whitaker
Janis Oliver: Kathy Baker
Sarah: Tracey Needham
Lucy: Lois Chiles
Beanstrom: Zack Norman
Jack: Don Cheadle
Lester: Alex Desert

Released: 1994
Production: Thom Colwell for Chanticleer Films; released by Showtime
Direction: Michael Elias
Screenplay: Michael Elias
Cinematography: Nancy Schrieber
Editing: Bill Yahraus
Production design: John Jay Moore
Casting: Leslee Dennis
Sound: Peter V. Meiselmann
Costume design: Mary Kay Stolz
Music: Lennie Niehaus
MPAA rating: no listing

The Madness of King George

"His Majesty was all powerful and all knowing. But he wasn't quite all there."—Movie tagline

"Glittering, swift, entertaining and eloquent."
—Caryn James, *The New York Times*

"Four stars. Hugely entertaining, triumphant and funny." Roger Ebert, *Chicago Sun-Times*

"A marvelous movie!"—David Denby, *New York Magazine*

"One of the triumphs of the year!"—Kenneth Turan, *Los Angeles Times*

 Box Office Gross: $91,071 (January 2, 1995)

A growing trend in American films is to air the dirty laundry of prominent historical figures. *The Madness of King George*, which examines the mental instability of a real-life monarch, was released during the same season filmgoers learned about Ty Cobb's abusive, violent personality in *Cobb* (reviewed in this volume), Dorothy Parker's depravity in *Mrs. Parker and the Vicious Circle* (reviewed in this volume), and the tumultuous marriage of poet T. S. Eliot and his insane wife in *Tom & Viv* (reviewed in this volume). A few seasons earlier, Babe Ruth's philandering, hostility, and overindulgence in food and alcohol were exposed in *The Babe* (1992).

If filmmakers are only feeding the general public what it wants, people evidently desire to see their heroes cut down to size: to learn that larger-than-life figures have foibles, that they are mere mortals like the rest of humanity. The ultimate message behind *The Madness of King George* is that George III was just a man who happened to be king; when his faculties began to fail him, his power and position were no safeguard against the indignities he would suffer.

 "I have always been myself even when I was ill. Only now I seem myself. That's the important thing. I have remembered how to seem."—George III in *The Madness of King George*

The story takes place five years after the American colonies won their independence from England, much to the consternation of King George III (Nigel Hawthorne). Also vexing the king is the gradual shift of sovereign power to Parliament. Part of his struggle to keep from becoming a figurehead involves the king's strict enforcement of royal protocol. From the pomp and circumstance surrounding the royal family's attendance at the opening of Parliament, to the edicts against looking at the king, turning one's back on the king, or sitting in the king's presence, George III hopes to keep the commoners sufficiently awed and Parliament in its place.

Inside the walls of Windsor Castle, the gruff, imposing leader brusquely censures his attendants and opposes his minister, but in public he wears a mask of docility, smiling and waving for his subjects, who have affectionately tagged him Farmer George. Shortly after the ceremonial opening of Parliament, the king begins to exhibit symptoms of physical and mental illness. As he has always been eccentric, the king's conduct fails to arouse attention until it becomes alarming. He begins spouting obscenities, rouses his attendants at four in the morning for a dash around the palace grounds, engages in a conversation with a pig, and makes sexual advances toward the Queen's lady-in-waiting, Lady Pembroke (Amanda Donohoe), in the presence of his attendants and his wife, the devoted Queen Charlotte (Helen Mirren).

A contingent of doctors is called in, but their diagnoses are based on secondhand reports, as it is deemed an unthinkable intrusion to perform a physical examination on his royal highness. The blundering practitioners think that the fact that the king's urine has turned blue is of no consequence. The king is subjected to myriad treatments, all to no effect.

The king's state of mind is the source of much speculation, causing his eldest son—the indolent and insolent Prince of Wales (Rupert Everett)—who is next in line for the throne, to plot for his own advancement. The prince has a stormy relationship with his father and is impatient for his eventual accession. He conspires with Charles James Fox (Jim Carter), the leading opponent of Prime Minister Pitt (Julian Wadham), to have the king declared incapacitated. In that event, the prince would be declared regent, wresting effectual control of the government from his father, who would remain king in name only.

The queen and the royal staff try to keep the king's condition a secret, but their efforts are thwarted by the prince, who organizes a royal concert that the king is compelled to attend. The king royally misbehaves, pushing a musician aside to take his place on the keyboard and starting a brawl with the prince. The king's madness thus brought to public attention, the prince has the king removed from the castle and bars the queen from seeing him.

At Lady Pembroke's suggestion, the court summons Dr. Willis (Ian Holm), a former clergyman who has become known for his radical methods of treating psychological disorders. Willis hypothesizes that the king's problem stems from too much compliance—he is never questioned, challenged, or checked. Willis immediately takes the upper hand, refusing to toady to the king. Willis' barbaric disciplinary methods include straitjacketing and gagging the king when he acts "unkingly." Eventually the king's spirit is broken.

In the House of Commons, the prince and his supporters rally for a bill declaring the king unfit, while Pitt tries to reassure the voters of the king's stability. As Parliament assembles on the day the prince is to be declared regent, the king enjoins his courtier Greville (Rupert Graves), Dr. Willis, and Chancellor Thurlow (John Wood) to enact a selection from *King Lear*. The parallels between Shakespeare's mad monarch and himself do not escape the king, and his composure suddenly transforms.

The King's mannerisms revert to those of his pre-madness days. Concomitantly, his attendants observe that the king's urine has regained its yellow hue. The king is rushed to Parliament in time to prove to the masses that he is hale and healthy again. A footnote relates that due to the nature of his symptoms, specifically the discoloration of his urine, it is now surmised that the king's illness was caused by porphyria, a hereditary metabolic disorder that can cause dementia.

Fueled by rave reviews and enthusiastic word of mouth, *The Madness of King George* crossed over from the art-house circuit to become a hit with mainstream audiences. Its appeal can be largely attributed to the extraordinary performance of Nigel Hawthorne, who reprises his award-winning stage role. Hawthorne has been acting for forty-five of his sixty-five years, primarily on the stage and in British television. *The Madness of King George* is his first starring film role. Hawthorne had previously starred in the London and Broadway productions of *Shadowlands* (1993), then watched his role in the film version go to Anthony Hopkins.

Hawthorne expected the same fate to befall him when his long-running vehicle *The Madness of George III* made its way to film, but playwright Alan Bennett, who wrote the screen adaptation, insisted on the involvement of Hawthorne and the play's director Nicholas Hytner as part of his package deal. Hawthorne's casting may have been a gamble, but it paid off handsomely. He dominates every scene, expertly capturing the various stages of the king's decline. Bringing wit, pathos, and intellect to his role, he succeeds in making the king a flesh-and-blood mortal, who inspires audience sympathy and support.

Though the supporting players command less screen time, none is negligible. Helen Mirren's compassionate queen, Rupert Everett's flamboyant Prince of Wales, Rupert Graves' steadfast equerry Greville, Ian Holm's tyrannical Dr. Willis, Amanda Donohoe's fetching Lady Pembroke, and Julian Rhind-Tutt's irreverent Duke of York fill out the perfectly-cast cast of characters.

The dialogue by Bennett—who also appears in a cameo as a member of Parliament—is witty and literate. Director Hytner keeps the action flowing at a lively pace. A Tony Award-winner for his Broadway productions of *Miss Saigon* and *Carousel*, Hytner makes his feature- film directing debut with *The Madness of King George*. Like Hawthorne, he owes his participation in the film to the obstinacy of Bennett. Another recruit from the stage production is costume designer Mark Thompson, who created magnificently

CREDITS

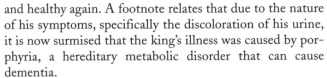

George III: Nigel Hawthorne
Queen Charlotte: Helen Mirren
Dr. Willis: Ian Holm
Prince of Wales: Rupert Everett
Greville: Rupert Graves
Thurlow: John Wood
Lady Pembroke: Amanda Donohoe
Duke of York: Julian Rhind-Tutt
Pitt: Julian Wadham
Fox: Jim Carter

Origin: Great Britain
Released: 1994
Production: Stephen Evans and David Parfitt, in association with Channel Four Films and Close Call Films; released by the Samuel Goldwyn Company
Direction: Nicholas Hytner
Screenplay: Alan Bennett; based on his play *The Madness of George III*
Cinematography: Andrew Dunn
Editing: Tariq Anwar
Production design: Ken Adam
Art direction supervision: Martin Childs
Art direction: John Fenner
Set decoration: Carolyn Scott
Casting: Celestia Fox
Sound: David Crozier
Costume design: Mark Thompson
Music adaptation: George Fenton
MPAA rating: no listing
Running time: 110 minutes

AWARDS AND NOMINATIONS

Academy Awards 1994: Best Art Direction/Set Direction
Nominations: Best Actor (Hawthorne), Best Supporting Actress (Mirren), Best Adapted Screenplay
Cannes Film Festival Awards 1995: Best Actress (Mirren)

ornate garments befitting royalty real or re-created. Elaborate settings, inventive production design, and sumptuous photography—including location scenes filmed at the Arundel and Broughton castles—contribute to a dazzling tableau.

While focusing on an event in one king's reign, the film illuminates a broader issue: the hollowness of noblesse oblige. Restoring the king's sanity is of less urgency to these royals than maintaining propriety. That the king is ranting uncontrollably is a bother; that he behaves this way in public is the tragedy. The king is cured and order is restored when he remembers how to "seem" the king. This peek inside the British crown has the effect of demythologizing royalty and bringing a contemporary relevance to the story.

A delightful balance of farce and tragedy, *The Madness of King George* was originally entitled *The Madness of George III* in its stage incarnation. The distributor, the Samuel Goldwyn Company, insisted on a name change, fearing American audiences would mistake it for a sequel and think they missed parts I and II. As George III suffered periodic relapses of his mala-

dy throughout the remainder of his reign, there could be a basis for sequels—but how off-putting would American audiences find "The Madness of King George III, II"

—*Brenda Scott Royce*

REVIEWS

Daily Variety. December 16, 1994, p. 2.
Entertainment Weekly. January 20, 1995, p. 37.
The Hollywood Reporter. December 16, 1994, p. 8.
Interview. January, 1995, p. 26.
Los Angeles Times. December 28, 1994, p. F1.
The Nation. January 23, 1995, p. 107.
New York. January 2, 1995, p. 66.
The New York Times. December 28, 1994, p. B1.
The New Yorker. January 16, 1995, p. 86.
People Weekly. January 16, 1995, p. 19.
Premiere. February, 1995, p. 25.
USA Today. January 27, 1995, p. 4D.
The Village Voice. January 3, 1995, p. 72.
The Wall Street Journal. December 29, 1994, p. A8.

Major League II

"America's favorite team is back!"—Movie tagline

"*Major League II* steps up to the plate and belts it out of the park!"—Jeffrey Lyons

Box Office Gross: $30,616,359 (July 17, 1994)

The scariest thing about *Major League II* is the threat that it might spawn *Major League III*. In 1989's forgettable hit *Major League*, the hapless Cleveland Indians win their division. In *Major League II*, they win the American League pennant but the film ends without taking them to the World Series. Obviously someone is imagining another sequel where the Indians win it all. Please, stop them.

The original *Major League* was a sometimes spunky, often inane and extremely formulaic sports film in which a team of lovable losers overcomes all odds and wins a championship. In the sequel, the lovable losers have become greedy, arrogant fat cats who care more about their images, wallets and personal fulfillment than about the team, the game or their fans. Of course, these attitudes make them losers again, but they've lost the capacity to be lovable.

Baseball movies have always depended heavily on the ability to evoke audience affection for the national pastime and its heroes. Part of baseball's mystique traded on the Horatio Alger mythology. It was a game not requiring abnormal physiques, a game which nearly every American knew and played and in which anyone could succeed.

Unfortunately, the greed that has overtaken the American game has drowned that mystique in cynicism. The caricatured players of *Major League II* bear modern ballplayers' attitudes and evoke fan anger, not sympathy. One running gag in the film involves a diehard fan (Randy Quaid) who feels betrayed and can't stop hating the Tribe even when they start winning. Unfortunately, the film audience might identify with that lone fan. Any cheering for these characters has to be half-hearted and cynical. The film's premise creates a derisive attitude toward its stars, and that doesn't make for a crowd-pleaser.

With a division championship under their belts, the Indians have become typical modern major leaguers. Rick "Wild Thing" Vaughn (Charlie Sheen) has thrown out his punk-rocker act and become a clean-cut endorsement magnet. Willie Mays Hayes (Omar Epps) cares only about spending money and swinging for the fences. Pedro Cerrano (Dennis Haysbert) has traded voodoo-inspired hostility for meditation and pacifism. None of this is funny.

Most of the rest of the cast indulges in clichéd baseball-movie behavior. Jake Taylor (Tom Berenger) is the aging catcher who helps a new kid take away his job, reluctantly joins the coaching staff and then becomes manager when the crusty old skipper Lou Brown (James Gammon) has a heart attack and watches the playoffs from a hospital bed. Rube Baker (Eric Bruskotter) is the hayseed backstop with an emotional problem (he can't throw the ball back to the pitcher) who rallies the team with his we-all-love-the-game speech. Jack Parkman (David Keith) is the hated prima donna who is traded away to become the team's No. 1 enemy (you have to have a villain who strikes out at the end).

We also have the nefarious owner, Rachel Phelps (Margaret Whitton) and a Japanese import, Isuro Tanaka (Takaaki Ishibashi), who is scripted as a kamikaze—an Asian movie stereotype half-a-century old. Corbin Bernsen is back as the smug, inept third baseman Roger Dorn, and the grating Bob Uecker reprises his role as play-by-play man Harry Doyle.

Of course, the various players who have lost their bearings find their way back to the game and their true selves, in not very ingenious fashion. Vaughn must be redeemed by the former girlfriend he discarded on his way to the top. No surprise there.

"I don't understand Japanese, but he looks like he's having the time of his life."—Dennis Haysbert, who plays Cerrano, in *Major League II*, on actor and Japanese comedy star Takaaki Ishibashi.

The script and the editing of the film seem careless and haphazard, and the actors appear to be going through the motions. Given the material, who can blame them?

David Ward, who created the original characters and returns as director, repeatedly fumbles the few opportunities presented by the cobbled-together script. There are a few funny lines, but far too few to sustain interest.

All those associated with *Major League II* should be sent back to the minors. The film not only epitomizes everything wrong with traditional baseball movies, it adds a modern layer of loathing and cynicism. What's wrong with modern ballplayers and owners isn't funny. Unfortunately, the filmmakers have the same insulting attitude toward their audience as real major league owners and players have toward their fans: They expect us to stop sneering, and start cheering, at the flick of a bat. But there is no heart, no soul and not nearly enough fun to get us through *Major League II*, much less the dreaded possibility of "Major League III."

—*Michael Betzold*

REVIEWS

Boston Globe. March 30, 1994, p. 73.
Chicago Tribune. March 30, 1994, Sec. 5 p. 7.
Entertainment Weekly. April 15, 1994, p. 41.
Hollywood Reporter. March 28, 1994, p. 5.
Los Angeles Times. March 30, 1994, p. F6.
The New York Times. March 30, 1994, p. C16.
The New York Times. May 1, 1994, Sec. 2 p. 26.
People Weekly. XLI, April 18, 1994, p. 18.
TV Guide. XLII, August 6, 1994, p. 31.
USA Today. March 30, 1994, p. D8.
Variety. CCCLIV, March 28, 1994, p. 69.
The Washington Post. March 30, 1994, p. B11.
The Washington Post. April 7, 1994, p. C7.

CREDITS

Rick Vaughn: Charlie Sheen
Jake Taylor: Tom Berenger
Roger Dorn: Corbin Bernsen
Pedro Cerrano: Dennis Haysbert
Lou Brown: James Gammon
Willie Mays Hayes: Omar Epps
Rube Baker: Eric Bruskotter
Harry Doyle: Bob Uecker
Jack Parkman: David Keith
Rachel Phelps: Margaret Whitton
Isuro Tanaka: Takaaki Ishibashi
Flannery: Alison Doody
Nikki Reese: Michelle Burke
Johnny: Randy Quaid
Monte: Skip Griparis

Released: 1994
Production: James G. Robinson and David S. Ward for Morgan Creek; released by Warner Bros.
Direction: David S. Ward
Screenplay: R. J. Stewart; based on a story by Stewart, Tom S. Parker, and Jim Jennewein, and on characters created by David S. Ward
Cinematography: Victor Hammer
Editing: Paul Seydor and Donn Cambern
Production design: Stephen Hendrickson
Art direction: Gary Diamond
Set design: Kyung Chang
Set decoration: Leslie Bloom
Casting: Ferne Cassel
Sound: Robert Anderson, Jr.
Costume design: Bobbie Read
Technical advice: Steve Yeager
Music: Michel Colombier
MPAA rating: PG
Running time: 104 minutes

Making Up! (Abgeschminkt!)

Two young women, Frenzy (Katja Riemann) and Maischa (Nina Kronjager), go on a double date with surprising results, in this comic study of women's issues and the 1990's dating scene. First feature by director and screenwriter Katja von Garnier.

REVIEWS

Boston Globe. November 4, 1994, p. 52.
Chicago Tribune. April 13, 1995, Sec. 5 p. 9D.
The New York Times. September 16, 1994, p. C8.

CREDITS

Frenzy: Katja Riemann
Maischa: Nina Kronjager
Rene: Gideon Burkhard
Susa: Daniela Lunkewitz
Mark: Max Tidof

Origin: Germany
Released: 1994
Production: Ewa Karlstrom for Vela-X/HFF; released by Seventh Art Releasing
Direction: Katja von Garnier
Screenplay: Katja von Garnier, Benjamin Taylor, and Hannes Jaenicke
Cinematography: Torsten Breuer
Editing: Katja von Garnier
Production design: Irene Edenhofer and Nikolai Ritter
Costume design: Birgit Aichele
Music: Peter Wenke and Tillmann Hohn
MPAA rating: no listing
Running time: 55 minutes

A Man in Uniform

"Henry Adler's life was so empty he chose to take another's."—Movie tagline

An aspiring actor (Tom McCamus) cast as a police officer gets caught up in his role when he begins wearing the uniform off the set and passing himself off as a real cop. *A Man in Uniform* was made on a budget of $1.3 million.

REVIEWS

Boston Globe. September 20, 1994, p. 32.
Chicago Tribune. August 5, 1994, p. 7L.
Los Angeles Times. June 24, 1994, p. F16.
The New York Times. August 19, 1994, p. C10.

"Whenever they need a slut to slap around, I seem to get the nod."—Charlie to Henry in *A Man in Uniform*.

CREDITS

Henry Adler: Tom McCamus
Charlie Warner: Brigitte Bako
Frank: Kevin Tighe
Mr. Adler: David Hemblen

Origin: Canada
Released: 1993
Production: Paul Brown for Alliance Communications and Miracle Pictures; released by IRS Releasing
Direction: David Wellington
Screenplay: David Wellington
Cinematography: David Franco
Editing: Susan Shipton
Production design: John Dondertman
Costume design: Beth Pasternak
Music: Ron Sures and The Tragically Hip
MPAA rating: no listing
Running time: 99 minutes

A Man of No Importance

"A sure Oscar contender! Albert Finney's performance is luminous!"—Jeffrey Lyons, *Sneak Previews*

"Comic and tragic. A towering Finney performance."—Lewis Beale, *New York Daily News*

"Albert Finney is at his funny and touching best! A gentle blend of humor and heartbreak."—Peter Travers, *Rolling Stone*

"A cross between *The Dresser* and *My Beautiful Laundrette*"—Peter Keough, *The Boston Phoenix*

"Albert Finney is a guarantee of pleasure! Delicious!"—Jay Carr, *Boston Globe*

 Box Office Gross: $128,408 (January 2, 1995)

A new respect for the Irish cinema has followed release of *My Left Foot* (1989), *The Field* (1990), *Hear My Song* (1991), and *In the Name of the Father* (1993). The respect is well deserved, for these films all contain stirring central performances, superb writing, and sophisticated direction. Into this domain comes *A Man of No Importance*. This film, about the sexual awakening of a middle-aged gay bus conductor, is a touching and entertaining addition to the aforementioned films. It contains a tour-de-force performance by Albert Finney that has earned for him yet another round of critical accolades. It also has a literate and poignant script by Barry Devlin, and sensitive direction by Suri Krishnamma.

Set in the 1960s, the film tells the story of Alfie Byrne (Finney), a bus conductor and community theater director who has repressed his homosexuality all his life. The driver of Alfie's bus, Robbie (Rufus Sewell), is a handsome young man and Alfie's good friend. Robbie is unaware, however, that Alfie is secretly in love with him. Each morning, Alfie enthralls the regular bus riders with readings of Oscar Wilde poetry and plays. In fact, the bus riders are all part of a theater group formed by Alfie, and as the film opens, he is planning to direct them in the little-performed Wilde play *Salomé*.

Alfie casts all of his plays from among the passengers. He discovers the perfect Salomé in a new rider, Adele (Tara Fitzgerald), who, he says, "is like a narcissus flowing in the wind; she is like a silver flower." Adele is hardly a "silver flower," however, telling Alfie "you think more of me than I deserve." He soon learns that the innocence and naïveté he projects onto her are a reflection of his own naïveté, and a

 "The only way to get rid of temptation is to yield to it."—Alfie Byrne quoting Oscar Wilde in *A Man of No Importance*

reaction against his own shame. Alfie has hidden the secret of his homosexuality from everyone, even from the sister (Brenda Fricker) with whom he shares an apartment.

Eventually, events conspire to cause Alfie's "coming out," disrupting the already troubled production of *Salomé*, ending his friendship with Robbie, and forcing a confrontation with his sister. Alfie's repression parallels the sad life of Oscar Wilde, who was imprisoned for having a homosexual relationship, and who died penniless. Yet in this film, the writer and director provide a happier ending, which offers hope for those who do not fit into the mainstream.

A Man of No Importance takes its audience back to a time when a gay male had few role models. Homosexuality in films often centered around a central character's pain. *The Dresser* (1983) also starred Finney, and its central character's homosexuality was central to his pain. Films from *The Boys in the Band* (1970) to *Making Love* (1982) to *Kiss of the Spider Woman* (1985) all dealt with the pain of their male homosexual protagonists. Yet only later did films show "coming out" as having the possibility of being a positive experience, such as in *Boys on the Side* (1995). *A Man of No Importance* should be applauded for not falling prey to the notion that gays are doomed to be pathetic figures.

Devlin's script is entertaining, uplifting, and moving. It is interesting to note the ways in which Alfie's life parallels that of his idol, Oscar Wilde, or the use of *Salomé* to underscore the character of the fallen angel, Adele. A pivotal scene hinges on Adele's inability to say the line, "I was a princess, and thou didst scorn me." The bus serves as a metaphor for life in general, and Alfie symbolizes the artist who leads others down the path of self-discovery via his own personal and artistic journey. Alfie seems to consciously take the role of teacher, telling his enraptured audience of passengers, "We'll amuse ourselves, telling stories from the great river of life." Yet understanding the symbolism is not essential to enjoyment of the film, and it is clear that the viewer need not know anything about Oscar Wilde in order to enjoy the story.

Devlin and director Krishnamma provide a wry sense of humor that adds to the texture of the film. The scenes where Alfie and his motley group of actors rehearse the fanciful *Salomé* are very amusing. Alfie grandly begins the first rehearsal by telling the stage manager, "if you'll illuminate the stage, we'll begin." The stage manager hits the switch, sparks fly, and the lights go out. This does not bode well for the production, to say the least. The ensuing rehearsal sequences all capture Alfie's frustration with working with nonprofessionals. One of the funniest scenes is the first dress

CREDITS

Alfie Byrne: Albert Finney
Lily Byrne: Brenda Fricker
Ivor Carney: Michael Gambon
Adele Rice: Tara Fitzgerald
Robbie Fay: Rufus Sewell
Inspector Carson: Patrick Malahide
Baldy: David Kelly
Father Ignatius Kenny: Mick Lally

Origin: Great Britain
Released: 1994
Production: Jonathan Cavendish for Majestic Films, in association with Newcomm, BBC Films, and Little Bird; released by Sony Pictures Classics
Direction: Suri Krishnamma
Screenplay: Barry Devlin
Cinematography: Ashley Rowe
Editing: David Freeman
Production design: Jamie Leonard
Art direction: Frank Flood
Casting: Michelle Guish
Sound: David Stephenson
Costume design: Phoebe De Gaye
Music: Julian Nott
MPAA rating: R
Running time: 98 minutes

rehearsal, where the dreadful, but hilarious, costumes are submitted to the exasperated Alfie for approval.

A Man of No Importance walks the line between despair and humor with ease. When Alfie's homosexuality is finally exposed, he decides to kill himself by jumping off a bridge. When he jumps into the water, however, it only reaches his ankles. When a passerby stops to see if he needs help, Alfie tries to pretend that it is perfectly normal for him to be standing in the water fully clothed.

Finney is remarkable throughout. From *Tom Jones* (1963), to Hercule Poirot in *Murder on the Orient Express* (1974), to *Scrooge* (1970), Finney is known as one of the best character actors in film. He loses himself once again in one of his multilayered characterizations. This time he paints a portrait of a simple man whose inner defenses are weakening, and whose artistic nature is both an expression of his zest for life and a sublimation of his inner demons. The moment when Alfie retreats to his room, dons flamboyant clothes, and exclaims, "The only way to get rid of temptation is to yield to it" is extraordinary: Finney captures the melodrama and the irony with one look in the

mirror. His scenes with Brenda Fricker blend a strong sense of realism with the more theatrical flourishes that are characteristic of British performers. The scene with Fricker where she refuses the food he prepares because she is horrified "when I think where your hands have been" is especially moving.

The other performances are excellent as well. Michael Gambon, known to American audiences for his starring role in *The Singing Detective*, has taken a small but delightful role as the comically sinister butcher who is angry with Alfie for doing a new play, thus precluding him from portraying the lead in *The Importance of Being Earnest*. Gambon creates a pompous busybody who is certain that Alfie is up to no good. In one very funny scene, he tries to tell Alfie's sister about how the rehearsals have become a place of "excessive drinking, violent behavior, and immoral dancing" as he rests his hand on the snout of a butchered, pig. In another scene, he waits for everyone to leave his shop, then grandly rehearses his lines, ending behind a wall of hanging sausages, which he pretends are curtains so he can take a bow.

Krishnamma, a young director from England, directs his first feature film with style and sophistication. He upholds the balance of whimsy and poignancy found in the script. There are also some beautiful visual images, such as a scene in which Alfie descends the boardinghouse staircase to Adele's room only to find her in the middle of a sexual encounter. The bright light flooding the room from above echoes the religious overtones of Adele's role in *Salomé*. Furthermore, Krishnamma has re-created 1960's Dublin beautifully with the help of production designer Jamie Leonard.

A Man of No Importance is a gem, all the more important a film because of its unassuming nature and its dignified portrait of humanity. Oscar Wilde said that "it is through art, and through art only, that we can realize our perfection; through art and art only that we can shield ourselves from the sordid perils of actual existence." As the film ends, Alfie discovers that the true "art" is in merely being human. While Alfie discovers how he shields himself from actual existence, Albert Finney realizes his "true perfection."

—Kirby Tepper

REVIEWS

Daily Variety. September 13, 1994, p. 17.
The Hollywood Reporter. September 12, 1994, p. 12.
The Hollywood Reporter. December 22, 1994, p. 10.
Los Angeles Times. December 22, 1994, p. F3.
The New York Times. December 22, 1994, p. B4.

Manhattan by Numbers

An unemployed journalist (John Wojda) facing eviction from his New York City apartment embarks on a city-wide odyssey in search of a friend of his who is even more destitute. This is the first American feature film directed by Amir Naderi.

REVIEWS

Atlanta Constitution. January 13, 1995, p. P3.
Los Angeles Times. November 18, 1994, p. F10.
The New York Times. April 2, 1993, p. C34.
The New York Times. November 11, 1994, p. C12.
Variety. CCCL, April 5, 1993, p. 178.
The Washington Post. October 29, 1994, p. D1.

CREDITS

George Murphy: John Wojda
Chuck Lehman: Branislav Tomich
Ruby: Mary Chang Faulk
Floyd: Frank Irwin

Released: 1994
Production: Ramin Niami for Rising Star, Pardis, Inc., and the International Film and Video Center; released by Artistic License
Direction: Amir Naderi
Screenplay: Amir Naderi
Cinematography: James Callanan
Editing: Amir Naderi
Sound: Judy Karp
Music: Gato Barbieri
MPAA rating: no listing
Running time: 88 minutes

Marquis

Based on the writings of the Marquis de Sade, this quirky drama set in 1789 in the Bastille prison centers on a dog named Marquis (voice of Francois Marthouret) and his penis, Colin (voice of Valerie Kling). The two carry on philosophical and sexual discussions as other animal prisoners engage in various forms of sex.

REVIEWS

Boston Globe. February 5, 1993, p. 28.

CREDITS

Marquis: Francois Marthouret (voice)
Colin: Valerie Kling (voice)
Ambert: Michel Robin (voice)
Justine: Isabelle Canet-Wolfe (voice)

Origin: Belgium
Released: 1990
Production: Eric Van Beuren for Y. C. Alligator Film, Constellation Production, and Tchin Tchin Production; released by First Run Features
Direction: Henri Xhonneux
Screenplay: Henri Xhonneux and Roland Topor
Cinematography: Etienne Faudet
Editing: Chantal Hymans
Production design: Roland Topor
Art direction: Pierre-Francois Limbosch
Sound: Joel Rangon and Dominique Hennequin
Costume design: Maryvonne Herzog
Creature design: Roland Topor
Music: Reinhardt Wagner
MPAA rating: no listing
Running time: 83 minutes

Mary Shelley's Frankenstein

"A stirring yarn that sweeps you up."—Rex Reed, *New York Observer*

"They've been making versions of this classic since 1908, but to see this film is to experience the story of Frankenstein for the first time." —*NBC-TV*

"Mr. Branagh's *Frankenstein* means to be a stunner, and delivers, with epic reverberations. This movie comes on like gangbusters."—*The Washington Times*

"Spellbinding storytelling that brilliantly combines the chills and thrills of a horror classic." —*Jeanne Wolf's Hollywood*

 Box Office Gross: $22,006,296 (December 18, 1994)

In the introduction to her novel *Frankenstein* (1818), Mary Shelley said that she wanted to write a story that would speak to the mysterious fear in human nature and awaken the thrill of horror. She said she hoped that her book would curdle the blood and set the reader's heart racing. Kenneth Branagh, whose film versions of William Shakespeare's *Henry V* (1989) and *Much Ado About Nothing* (1993) were praised as successful adaptations, has remade if not redefined one of the icons of the horror film genre. While the most famous monster film is still James Whale's 1931 classic *Frankenstein* starring Boris Karloff, Branagh has chosen to make a more faithful version of Mary Shelley's novel. The title, *Mary Shelley's Frankenstein*, implies that the film will closely follow the book and, for the most part, it does.

The film begins somewhere in the Arctic Sea in 1794 aboard a ship commanded by Captain Walton (Aidan Quinn), which has become ice bound. To compound his problems, from out of the frozen mists comes an exhausted wanderer by the name of Victor Frankenstein (Kenneth Branagh). Captain Walton has him taken on board where, after some needed refreshment, his guest tells his bizarre story. Born in Geneva, Switzerland to a wealthy family, Frankenstein spends his childhood happily at home with a loving mother (Cherie Lunghi) and father (Ian Holm) and adopted sister, Elizabeth (Helena Bonham Carter). Later, when Victor is a young man intent on pursuing all matters relating to the origin of life, his mother dies while giving birth to his brother, William (Charles Wyn-Davies). Victor is overcome with grief at his mother's death and vows to find the key to immortality. Leaving for medical school in Ingolstadt, he promises Elizabeth that they will marry when he returns.

In Ingolstadt, Victor becomes the devoted pupil of Dr. Waldman (John Cleese), whose experiments in the reanimation of dead animal tissue suggest that life can be created and death overcome. While making his rounds on the ward of a charity hospital, Dr. Waldman is attacked and killed by a brutish patient (Robert De Niro). With Waldman now dead, Victor decides to steal his mentor's scientific journals and begin his own experiments in constructing a human being from various body parts. He uses Waldman's brain as well as parts of his murderer's body and assembles a creature in a makeshift laboratory that resembles a large, Gothic warehouse. In a mesmerizing birthing scene complete with energy bolts, smoke, and noise, Victor infuses his creation with life by immersing him in an appliance resembling a huge metallic coffin, which is filled with some sort of amniotic slime. Meanwhile, Elizabeth, who has not heard from Victor in some time, travels to Ingolstadt to find him and persuade him to leave with her. A cholera epidemic is sweeping the city, and Victor catches pneumonia. The creature, by now fully animated, escapes and, assuming cholera has killed him, Victor returns to Geneva with Elizabeth.

The creature, however, does not succumb to the plague. Instead, he manages to elude a mob that has been hounding him and flees to the countryside. There, he stumbles upon the dwelling of a peasant family and seeks shelter in their pig pen. Obviously intelligent, the creature learns to read and gradually increases in self-awareness. At first he is careful to keep out of sight, but one day when the family is away, he approaches their blind grandfather (Richard Briers), who befriends him. This first gesture of kindness and sympathy by another human being is interrupted violently when the family returns unexpectedly and, repelled by the creature's hideous appearance, drives him away. The creature, now filled with hatred and a desire for revenge, makes his way to Geneva to confront Victor.

With cruel and deliberate haste, the creature kills Victor's young brother, William. Justine (Trevyn McDowell), the housekeeper's daughter, is blamed for the crime and despite Victor's frantic protests, she is convicted of murder. A crazed mob seizes Justine and hangs her. Next, the creature requests that Victor create a female partner for him. Victor wishes only to be rid of the torments he suffers

"We save lives every day, but that isn't the whole answer. Sooner or later the best way to cheat death will be to create life."—Dr. Victor Frankenstein from *Mary Shelley's Frankenstein*

CREDITS

Creature: Robert De Niro
Victor Frankenstein: Kenneth Branagh
Henry: Tom Hulce
Elizabeth: Helena Bonham Carter
Walton: Aidan Quinn
Victor's father: Ian Holm
Grandfather: Richard Briers
Professor Waldman: John Cleese
Victor's mother: Cherie Lunghi
Mrs. Moritz: Celia Imrie
Justine: Trevyn McDowell
Professor Krempe: Robert Hardy
William: Charles Wyn-Davies

Released: 1994
Production: Francis Ford Coppola, James V. Hart, and John Veitch for American Zoetrope, in association with Japan Satellite Broadcasting, Inc., and the Indie Prod Company; released by TriStar Pictures
Direction: Kenneth Branagh
Screenplay: Steph Lady and Frank Darabont; based on the novel by Mary Shelley
Cinematography: Roger Pratt
Editing: Andrew Marcus
Production design: Tim Harvey
Art direction: Martin Childs, John Fenner and Desmond Crowe
Casting: Priscilla John
Visual effects supervision: Richard Conway
Sound: Ivan Sharrock
Creature makeup and effects: Daniel Parker
Costume design: James Acheson
Music: Patrick Doyle
MPAA rating: R
Running time: 128 minutes

at the hands of his ill-conceived progeny and in exchange for the creature's promise never to trouble him again, agrees to create a companion being. But instead of keeping his word, Victor decides to escape from Geneva with Elizabeth. The creature pursues them and, seizing Elizabeth on her marriage bed, rips her heart out in front of Victor.

In shock and despair, Victor removes her body to his laboratory. There he creates a woman composed of parts from the bodies of Elizabeth and Justine. When finished, he dresses the woman in a wedding gown and the creature enters the laboratory to claim her. When a struggle ensues between Victor and the creature for possession of the woman, she sets fire to herself and to the house. During the fire, the creature escapes. Victor's grief gives way to rage and despair, and he sets out to track the creature down. Victor follows his trail to the remote Arctic wastes, in hopes of catching and killing

him. There, amid the ice floes and towering bergs, Victor is found by the ship's crew; he is exhausted and near death. After telling his story to Captain Walton, Victor dies. The frozen sea melts, and the ship is freed. Victor's body is placed on a funeral pyre and set adrift on the ice, where the creature at last hovers over his creator and is himself consumed in flames.

If, as the title suggests, Branagh's idea was to produce a film that more closely followed the story line of the novel, he has been partially successful. Here, as in the book, the relationship between Victor Frankenstein and the monster is somewhat more complex than in earlier film versions. In the 1931 *Frankenstein* for example, the monster is rejected and abused by his creator and escapes to terrorize the villagers. In an attempt to exact revenge on his master, he kidnaps Frankenstein and is pursued by the mob until the action reaches a convulsive climax atop a burning windmill. As in the book, Branagh's creature learns to read and to speak. He questions his creator and muses philosophically. The Karloff-inspired monsters only grunted a few monosyllables or shrieked in tormented agony. Their mute confusion made them seem almost innocent and one sympathized with their plight of paternal rejection; they were, however, also terrifying. De Niro's creature is problematic in that he inspires more pity than fear. He seems to be in constant pain and about to cry. When a chance comes for the creature to be really scary, as when he leaps out of the shadows to terrorize Elizabeth, Branagh has him tear open her chest and rip out her still beating heart. This is disgusting but not particularly frightening. Furthermore, the fiendish deed is too reminiscent of one committed by the Indian Magua in Michael Mann's *The Last of the Mohicans* (1993).

Similarities aside, there are also departures in the film from the original story. In the book, Victor refuses to make the creature a female companion even after he has promised he would. This betrayal of his word results in the sworn oath by the creature that he will visit Victor on his wedding night and take revenge. The creature does appear at the appointed hour and, as in the film, kills Elizabeth. Another departure comes at the end of the story. In the film, Frankenstein's body is removed from the ship and placed on the ice, and there it is approached by the creature as it burns on a funeral pyre. In the book, the creature enters the ship following Victor's death and speaks at length to Captain Walton about his own grief and suffering and tells why he hated his creator so much. The creature then leaps overboard onto an ice raft and floats away into the darkness.

AWARDS AND NOMINATIONS

Academy Awards Nomination 1994: Best Makeup

Kenneth Branagh gives a very physical, even acrobatic performance as Victor Frankenstein. In several scenes, he is stripped to his waist as he leaps about, pulling on the ropes, chains, and other rigging of the reanimation apparatus. He sweats and pants during the creature birthing scenes and even wrestles in the amniotic slime with De Niro. For the creation episode, De Niro's face and body are entirely covered with a flexible prosthetic skin. While Karloff's dramatic gestures at times had the stark power of pantomime, De Niro's creature seems sluggish as though weighed down under the heavy make-up and long leathery coat that he wears. His mumbling speech is reminiscent of Marlon Brando's in *The Godfather* (1972). The one real casting surprise is British comedian John Cleese, who turns in a remarkable performance as the intriguing yet sinister Professor Waldman. Helena Bonham Carter, who is known for her work in *A Room With a View* (1986) and Franco Zeffirelli's *Hamlet* (1990), is the beautiful and strong willed Elizabeth. As the creature's macabre love interest, she undergoes one of the most hideous transformations in any horror film yet. Tom Hulce plays Victor's medical school pal Henry as a carefree sort in contrast with Victor's dark, obsessive personality.

Although it works as Saturday matinee fare, *Mary Shelley's Frankenstein* does not quite live up to its title. Director Branagh apparently tried to infuse new life into a classic by attempting to give deeper insight into Victor's obsession with the creation of life and the damning consequences of his actions, especially his abandonment of the creature. The problem is that viewers never begin to understand the nature of the evil he has conjured. Is the creature supposed to represent the physical embodiment of Victor's hubris and his transgression of natural law? As for the romantic theme, the love story between Victor and Elizabeth is never developed enough to become a vital part of the film. Although the elaborate sets and period costumes are rich visually and the violence suitably disturbing, one is finally left with "Kenneth Branagh's Frankenstein," a tale that simply does not do its job of weaving the spell of the novel and thrilling viewers with its horror.

—*Francis Poole*

REVIEWS

Atlanta Constitution. November 4, 1994, p. P3.
Boston Globe. November 4, 1994, p. 45.
Chicago Tribune. November 4, 1994, p. 7B.
Chicago Tribune. November 4, 1994, p. 7C.
The Christian Century. CXII, February 15, 1995, p. 177.
Christian Science Monitor. November 4, 1994, p. 12.
Entertainment Weekly. November 4, 1994, p. 46.
Entertainment Weekly. April 28, 1995, p. 70.
Los Angeles Magazine. XXXIX, December 1994, p. 168.
Los Angeles Times. November 4, 1994, p. F1.
Maclean's. CVII, November 14, 1994, p. 112.
The New Republic. CCXI, November 28, 1994, p. 56.
New Statesman & Society. VII, November 4, 1994, p. 32.
New York. XXVII, November 14, 1994, p. 76.
The New York Times. November 4, 1994, p. C1.
The New York Times. November 13, 1994, Sec. 2 p. 28.
The New York Times. CXLIV, May 5, 1995, p. B8.
The New Yorker. LXX, November 14, 1994, p. 141.
Newsweek. CXXIV, Novemebr 7, 1994, p. 73.
People Weekly. XLII, November 7, 1994, p. 19.
Rolling Stone. December 1, 1994, p. 131.
Time. CXLIV, November 7, 1994, p. 73.
Variety. CCCLVII, October 31, 1994, p. 88.
The Wall Street Journal. November 10, 1994, p. A14.
The Washington Post. November 4, 1994, p. F1.
The Washington Post. November 4, 1994, p. WW43.
The Washington Post. November 10, 1994, p. D7.

The Mask

"From zero to hero." —Movie tagline
"Wildly charismatic...[Jim Carrey is] hotter-than-hot]"—Michael Rechtschaffen, *The Hollywood Reporter*

 Box Office Gross: $118,820,184 (January 2, 1995)

The Mask is another in a line of films whose star is the computer-generated special effects. George Lucas' special-effects empire, Industrial Light and Magic, has used computer technology to extend the cinematic range of representation in such films as *Who Framed Roger Rabbit?* (1988), *Terminator II: Judgment Day* (1991), and *Jurassic Park* (1993). In *The Mask*, they have used their magic to give a man the superhuman capabilities of a cartoon character.

CREDITS

Stanley Ipkiss: Jim Carrey
Tina Carlyle: Cameron Diaz
Charlie Schumacher: Richard Jeni
Lieutenant Kellaway: Peter Riegert
Peggy Brandt: Amy Yasbeck
Dorian Tyrel: Peter Greene
Milo: Max

Released: 1994
Production: Bob Engelman for New Line Productions, in association with Dark Horse Entertainment; released by New Line Cinema
Direction: Charles Russell
Screenplay: Mike Werb; based on a story by Michael Fallon and Mark Verheiden
Cinematography: John R. Leonetti
Editing: Arthur Coburn
Production design: Craig Stearns
Art direction: Randy Moore
Set decoration: Ellen Totleben
Casting: Fern Champion and Mark Paladini
Visual effects consulting: Ken Ralston
Sound: Mark Hopkins McNabb
Special makeup effects: Greg Cannom
Costume designer: Ha Nguyen
Choreography: Jerry Evans
Music: Randy Edelman
MPAA rating: PG-13
Running time: 101 minutes

The film tells the familiar American tale of a timid and unremarkable man turned irresistible hero. Stanley Ipkiss (Jim Carrey) is the Clark Kent of this film, a bank clerk in Edge City—a surreal urban environment under a sky of greens and pinks. Early in the film it is established that Stanley is the epitome of social awkwardness and timidity, a fatally nice guy, a romantic failure, and a lover of Looney Tunes cartoons.

After a particularly dismal evening in which he is humiliated at the entrance of the Coco Bongo—an exclusive nightclub—and subjected to an onslaught of mishaps, his loaner car falls apart on an abandoned bridge. While gazing down despondently from the bridge, he sees what he believes to be a body floating down the river. When he jumps into the water, however, he finds himself clutching a mask.

Stanley discovers later in the privacy of his apartment that this is no ordinary mask. It is a magical ancient mask that when placed on his face transforms him into a green, large-toothed Casanova who wears a bright yellow zoot suit and zooms around charming everyone with his reenactments of popular cultural figures. He can dance, dodge bullets, take on many forms, peel his flattened body off the pavement, pull from his pockets a limitless assortment of objects ranging from the tiny to the enormous, and best of all, he is irresistibly cool and can now attract the interest of the bombshell beauty he desires.

The woman of his desires is Tina Carlyle (Cameron Diaz), a caricature of the desirable woman of a past era: blond, voluptuous, sultry, with high heels and pushed-up breasts. She had entered the bank earlier pretending to be interested in opening an account, while in fact she was casing the bank with a hidden camera in her purse for a robbery that her boyfriend, Dorian Tyrel (Peter Greene), and his gangster friends are plotting. Stanley later discovers that Tina performs at the Coco Bongo and that this is the gangsters' den.

Stanley has an ambivalent attitude toward his new powers and tries unsuccessfully to discard the mask. He

AWARDS AND NOMINATIONS

Academy Awards Nomination 1994: Best Visual Effects
Golden Globe Awards 1995: Best Actor—Musical/Comedy (Carrey)
MTV Movie Awards 1995: Best Comedic Performance (Carrey), Breakthrough Performance (Diaz), Most Desirable Female (Diaz), Best Dance Sequence (Carrey/Diaz)

throws it from the window, but like a boomerang, it returns. His face seems to be drawn uncontrollably into the mask, and he soon finds himself involved in an assortment of illegal activities and sought after by the media and the police. He vandalizes his apartment building to torment the landlady whom he despises, he seeks revenge on the auto shop that is working on his car, and finally he robs the bank where he works just minutes before the gangsters can carry out their robbery.

"You can't make the scene if you don't have the green!"—Stanley Ipkiss from *The Mask*

He then appears in a seemingly limitless stretch limousine at the Coco Bongo and makes the glamorous entrance he would have liked to have made earlier. It is in this next scene, inspired by Tex Avery's cartoon *Red Hot Riding Hood*, that the film reaches its cinematic crescendo. While the Mask watches Tina perform a sizzling number, his eyes pop out of his head, his jaw drops to the table and an enormous tongue rolls across it, his thudding heart jumps from his chest and retreats, and at one point he is even transformed into the howling wolf himself. He takes to the stage and engages Tina in a sultry, superhuman dance that wins her heart.

Jim Carrey, who was a box-office hit earlier this same year in *Ace Ventura: Pet Detective* (reviewed in this volume), proves himself in this role to be a first-class comic actor. He moves from the character of Stanley Ipkiss to that of the Mask with astonishing ease, using his body and gestures to complete and highlight the special-effects efforts. Critics are comparing him to Jerry Lewis, Robin Williams, and even the Three Stooges.

Stanley gradually begins to exhibit signs of rebellion and strength beyond his masked nightlife, but he suffers confusion over his identity and the desire to reveal himself to Tina. Meanwhile, Lieutenant Kellaway (Peter Riegert) has pieced together the evidence and cuts short Stanley's romantic liaison with Tina in a city park. Stanley flees the park only to find the media and a police dragnet awaiting him. At this point, he transforms into an imitation of Desi Arnaz performing "Cuban Pete" and charms the entire crowd into abandoning their roles and joining him in a mad musical number.

He escapes into the arms of Peggy Brandt (Amy Yasbeck), a columnist turned reporter who had once published his letter "good guys finish last" and had earlier sympathized with him. Peggy betrays their friendship by turning him over to the gangsters for a monetary reward, who in turn steal the mask and dump him in the arms of the police.

With Tina's boyfriend, Dorian, now in possession of the mask, Stanley's opportunity for heroism emerges. The mask has the ability to bring to life the innermost desires of the individual who wears it, making Dorian a green demon obsessed with enacting revenge on his former mob leader at the Coco Bongo. Dorian actually responds to his new powers in the same manner that Stanley did, using them to enact revenge on those who have humiliated him. Without the Looney Tunes twist, however, to deem him charming and ultimately harmless, he is now the evil monster. If Stanley can destroy him, Stanley will have progressed, as the film ad promised, "from zero to hero."

Stanley manages to escape from prison by ordering his faithful dog, Milo (Max), to steal the keys of the sleeping guard, and he is just in time to save the day and rescue his damsel in distress at the shakedown at Coco Bongo. He even gets in a few successful punches of his own without the mask. Milo even dons the mask himself for a few brilliant moments of special effects, which transform him from a small, harmless dog into a big-headed, fierce canine.

After his Coco Bongo heroics, Stanley is forgiven for his past deeds and the bad guys are taken away to prison. Tina loves Stanley for who he is, even without the mask, and he tosses it back into the river.

The mask has been praised by critics for Carrey's performance and for its special effects. Besides the impressive work done on computers, special makeup effects by Greg Cannom contributed to the successful transformations. Cannom was also responsible for Robin Williams' new identity in *Mrs. Doubtfire* (1993) and won an Oscar for his work in *Bram Stoker's Dracula* (1993). Production designer Craig Stearns gave the film its patchwork visual appearance, making it reminiscent of several decades simultaneously, from the 1940's to the 1990's. Costume designer Ha Nguyen contributed to the look of the film with her stylized costumes and use of color to emphasize the cartoonish and electrifying presence of Jim Carrey.

Critics were not impressed with the uninteresting, cliché-ridden story. On one hand, *The Mask* is a rather traditional and tired plot dressed up in this year's star and some new technology. On the other hand, it is a film that aspires to bring to the feature film the particular pleasures of the cartoon—and this involves adopting the techniques of the cartoon. These techniques include the use of a simple, mythical plot, which reduces the dynamics of reality into dualities such as good and bad; outrageous occurrences (like the "Cuban Pete" scene); exaggeration of character; the use of intense colors; and most important, the dream-like satisfaction of wish fulfillment, whereby the character achieves in his movements and relationship with the world a freedom from the laws and restrictions of reality.

The success of such a film depends upon the audience's ability to accept the logic of the fantasy. *The Mask* succeeds at this by keeping one leg in reality through the duality of the main character. Stanley represents the "real" world. The masked Stanley represents humanity's desire to create a second self, one which is free from the inhibitions of the first and can go forth correcting mistakes, enacting revenge on oppressors, and fearlessly pursuing objects of desire. Like a cartoon, *The Mask* is a pleasure to watch and thereafter is entirely forgettable.

—*Reni Celeste*

REVIEWS

Chicago Tribune. July 29, 1994, sec. 2 page 4.
Entertainment Weekly. August 5, 1994, p. 38.
The Hollywood Reporter. July 28, 1994, p. 9.
Los Angeles Times. July 28, 1994, p. F1.
The New York Times. July 29, 1994, p. B1.
Newsweek. CXXIV, August 8, 1994, p. 54.
Rolling Stone. August 25, 1994, pp. 95-96.
Time. Vol 144, No. 6, August 8, 1994, pp. 56-8.
USA Today. July 29, 1994, p. D1.
Variety. July 28, 1994, p. 2.
The Washington Post. July 29, 1994, D1,6.

Maverick

"The greatest gambler in the west has met his match."—Movie tagline

"*Lethal Weapon* meets *Butch Cassidy and the Sundance Kid*"—Caryn James, *The New York Times*

"Hilarious! A ten gallon hit."—Pat Collins, WWOR-TV

"Thrills, spills and genuine fun."—Pia Lindstrom, WNBC-TV

 Box Office Gross: $101,619,662 (October 23, 1994)

The Western has been a staple of American films throughout almost the entire twentieth century. The surprising success of *The Great Train Robbery* (1903) proved that Westerns did have box-office appeal. The 1930's saw such film classics as *Cimarron* (1931) and John Ford's

Stagecoach (1939). The latter introduced the audience to the legendary John Wayne, who remained an American hero for decades to come. In the 1940's, Roy Rogers, Alan Ladd, Kirk Douglas, and James Stewart rode into theaters and captured viewers' hearts and imaginations.

The 1950's brought still more Westerns to the screen, such as the unforgettable heartbreaker *Shane* (1953), directed by the giant George Stevens. Clint Eastwood kept the momentum going with his foreboding cowboy image in the spaghetti Westerns of the 1960's.

Television followed the trend with such popular Western series as *Bonanza*, *Gunsmoke*, and *Big Valley*, starring motion-picture queen Barbara Stanwyck. Director Sam Peckinpah showed everyone how violent the Old West could be with his bloody *The Wild Bunch* (1969). Some years later, Paul Newman and Robert Redford showed how charming it could be with the delightful *Butch Cassidy and the Sundance Kid* (1969).

In the 1980's, money, greed, and success dominated everyone's attention and the Western seemed to become obsolete. Then in 1989, along came the miniseries *Lonesome Dove* galloping across the television screens of America and millions of viewers watched. The industry took notice but believed it could be a lark. Kevin Costner persisted against all odds, and the award-winning *Dances with Wolves* burst onto motion-picture screens in 1990. When Clint Eastwood saddled up once again in 1992 in *Unforgiven* and rode off with several Oscars, it was confirmed—Westerns were back, and back big-time.

Coinciding with this Western rebirth was rekindled interest in vintage television series, marked by the success of *The Addams Family* (1991). *The Beverly Hillbillies* (1993), and *The Flintstones* (1994) are further examples of this return to the past. Hence *Maverick* was born, a Western based on the hit television series of the 1950's and 1960's.

The film was directed by Richard Donner, who directed Mel Gibson in the *Lethal Weapon* trilogy (1987, 1989, 1992), and written by William Goldman, who, among his many credits, penned *Butch Cassidy and the Sundance Kid*. It has a trio of bankable

Danny Glover, Gibson's partner from the *Lethal Weapon* series, makes an unbilled cameo in *Maverick*, along with many stars from old TV westerns.

stars: Mel Gibson, Jodie Foster, and James Garner. The creative team also includes four-time Academy Award winner director of photography Vilmos Zsigmond and Oscar nominees production designer Tom Sanders, film editor Stuart Baird, and composer Randy Newman. This assemblage of talent paid off as in its first eleven days of release, *Maverick* earned $41.7 million.

Bret Maverick (Mel Gibson) is a charming con man who is attempting to raise money to win a lucrative, upcoming poker championship. On this journey, Maverick is scammed, beaten, cheated, and nearly killed several times. His dusty ride to the "big game" aboard a riverboat is indeed a perilous one fraught with mishaps and danger.

The film's opening shot shows Maverick atop a horse, with a noose tied snugly around his neck. In a voice-over, Maverick recounts how he got there. It is a pleasant storytelling device that whets the viewer's interest in how

"Being spineless has kept me alive a long time."—Bret Maverick from *Maverick*

Maverick got himself into this present precarious predicament. It also sets the comedic, lighthearted tone that underlies the film.

Mel Gibson is an attractive, likable actor, with a wit and wily charm that he uses to great advantage. The *Lethal Weapon* series was an enormous commercial success, in large part because of Gibson himself, and the actor brings his trademark charisma to the role of Maverick. Unfortunately, he goes too far at times. For example, in a card game in the first part of the film, Gibson mugs and itches and fidgets to the point of distraction. Some of these antics need to be grounded more in a characterization of some sort. It has all been done before in his other films.

In most Westerns, there is usually a love interest for the hero. *Maverick* has Jodie Foster as the beautiful, conniving Annabelle Bransford. An accomplished director and actress, she has won two Academy Awards: one for her stunning portrayal of a rape victim in *The Accused* (1988) and the other for her portrayal of Special Agent Clarice Starling in the 1991 hit thriller, *The Silence of the Lambs*. Although primarily known as a serious actress, Foster manages to be the perfect foil to Gibson's Maverick. She coyly bats her lashes, flirts, and manipulates with the best of the Southern belles in a tongue-in-cheek performance as the cunning femme fatale.

An actress of lesser talent could have appeared a caricature, but not Foster. She fleshes out every inch of Annabelle, reminiscent of the luminosity and comedic talents of Carole Lombard. As she graciously takes Maverick's shirt to be washed, she bats her lashes and sighs, "If I can't touch you, I can at least touch your shirt and dream." This is a truly delightful performance from the actress. It is somewhat of a departure for her and proves she is a versatile and competent star.

Another wise casting choice is James Garner as the wry, questionable lawman, Marshal Zane Cooper, whom Maverick encounters on the journey to the championship poker game. Garner was actually the original Maverick on the television series. Garner then went on to achieve enduring acclaim as an actor for the last four decades in both television and film. His presence in this film provides a welcome nostalgic touch. When the original series was

CREDITS

Bret Maverick: Mel Gibson
Annabelle Bransford: Jodie Foster
Marshal Zane Cooper: James Garner
Joseph: Graham Greene
Commodore: James Coburn
Angel: Alfred Molina
Archduke: Paul L. Smith
Matthew Wicker: Geoffrey Lewis
Johnny: Max Perlich
Beauregard: Clint Black

Released: 1994
Production: Bruce Davey and Richard Donner for Icon, in association with Donner/Shuler-Donner Productions; released by Warner Bros.
Direction: Richard Donner
Screenplay: William Goldman; based on the television show created by Roy Huggins
Cinematography: Vilmos Zsigmond
Editing: Stuart Baird
Production design: Tom Sanders
Art direction: Daniel Dorrance
Set decoration: Lisa Dean
Casting: Marion Dougherty
Sound: Clark King
Costume design: April Ferry
Stunt coordination: Mic Rodgers
Music: Randy Newman
MPAA rating: PG
Running time: 129 minutes

AWARDS AND NOMINATIONS

Academy Awards Nomination 1994: Best Costume Design

created by Roy Huggins, it would poke fun at itself, and fortunately, this sense of humor is maintained throughout the current release, in large part because of Garner's adept skill and craft.

Although *The New York Times* called *Maverick* fast, fun, and full of action, it could also be said to be slow, slick, and sophomoric. Summer films tend to be dominated by escapism, action, big stars, big stunts, and big lines. *Maverick* contains all these elements including an exciting runaway stagecoach sequence—pro form a for most Westerns. What it lacks is a cohesive script that tells a story simply. The screenwriter, William Goldman, relies on too many contrivances in order for Gibson to be zany. Nevertheless, *Maverick* proved to be a crowd pleaser—a light, hip family comedy with winning performances by its three leads.

—*Robert F. Chicatelli*

REVIEWS

Entertainment Weekly. June 3, 1994, p. 36.
The Hollywood Reporter. May 16, 1994, p. 10.
Los Angeles Times. May 20, 1994, p. F.
Variety. May 16, 1994, p. 2.

Me and Veronica

Sensible sister Fanny (Elizabeth McGovern) and ne'er-do-well sister Veronica (Patricia Wettig) reconcile after a five-year feud, with Fanny even offering to take care of Veronica's two children when Veronica is sent to prison for welfare fraud, in this drama. Directorial debut of Don Scardino.

REVIEWS

Boston Globe. September 16, 1993, p. 61.
Boston Globe. January 7, 1994, p. 73.
The New York Times. September 24, 1993, p. C25.
Playboy. XL, September 1993, p. 18.
Variety. CCCXLVIII, September 21, 1992, p. 86.

CREDITS

Fanny: Elizabeth McGovern
Veronica: Patricia Wettig
Michael: Michael O'Keefe
Frankie: John Heard
Boner: Scott Renderer
Red: Will Hare

Released: 1992
Production: Linn-Baker, Max Mayer, Nellie Nugiel, and Leslie Urdang for True One/True Pictures; released by Columbia/TriStar Homevideo
Direction: Don Scardino
Screenplay: Leslie Lyles
Cinematography: Michael Barrow
Editing: Jeffrey Wolf
Music: David Mansfield
Songs: Shawn Colvin
MPAA rating: no listing
Running time: 97 minutes

Memoirs of a Madman

This horror film centers on a homocidal band of escaped mental patients who wreak havoc.

CREDITS

Butch Lee: Brad Bechard
James Bunting: Richard Craven
Leon: Ralph Giordano
Dr. Raji: Ralph Graff
Rose: Jerome Linnemann

Released: 1994
Production: Coyote production; released by Headliner Entertainment Group
Direction: George Baluzy and Mike Baluzy
Screenplay: George Baluzy and Mike Baluzy
Cinematography: Itzik Harel
Editing: George Baluzy and Mike Baluzy
Art direction: David Baluzy
Costume design: Karen Perry
Music: Khris Ganser and Killer Watts
MPAA rating: no listing
Running time: 80 minutes

Metamorphosis: The Alien Factor

When an alien mutation threatens a high-security research center, two teenage girls (Tara Leigh and Dianna Flaherty) looking for their missing father help do battle with the monster.

REVIEWS

Variety. CCCXLIII, May 6, 1991, p. 336.

CREDITS

Sherry Griffen: Tara Leigh
Mitchell: Tony Gigante
Kim Griffen: Dianna Flaherty
Nancy Kane: Katherine Romaine
Dr. Viallini: Marcus Powell
Dr. Elliot Stein: Allen Lewis Rickman
Dr. Michael Foster: George Gerard
Jarrett: Gregory Sullivan

Released: 1991
Production: Ted A. Bohus and Scott Morette for Petrified Films, Inc.; released by International Releasing Corporation
Direction: Glenn Takakjian
Screenplay: Glenn Takakjian; with additional story material by Ted A. Bohus
Cinematography: John A. Corso and Phil Gries
Editing: Janice Keunelian
Production design: John Piano
Visual effects: Dan Taylor
Sound: Steve Rogers and Dorielle Rogers
Makeup and creature effects: R. S. Cole, Paul C. Reilly Jr., Brian Quinn, Patrick Shearn and Ken Walker
Music: John Gray
MPAA rating: R
Running time: 97 minutes

Mi Vida Loca (My Crazy Life)

"Mothers. Warriors. Sisters. Survivors."
—Movie tagline

 Box Office Gross: $3,210,620 (October 30, 1994)

While Steven Spielberg, Sidney Lumet, and Martin Scorsese are directors, Allison Anders is a woman director. In Hollywood, and in the film industry at large, women are still struggling to break through on the creative end of production. Anders, however, has already made her mark, thanks to her well-received debut *Gas Food Lodging* (1992)—although it was in fact her second feature—and *Mi Vida Loca*.

Although not entirely successful, *Mi Vida Loca* is involving, insightful, and poignant. Set in the Los Angeles community of Echo Park—geographically only a few miles from Hollywood, but ethnically and materially in another universe—the film consists of three movements, three interlocking stories concerning the lives of a handful of young Latino men and women.

Utilizing frequent voice-overs as a narrative device, Anders drops the audience into a rarely glimpsed world. The first voice heard is that of Sad Girl (Angel Aviles); her soft voice introduces both the people and the mores of her neighborhood, her "barrio." She reveals that a rift has recently developed between herself and her best friend from childhood, Mousie (Seidy Lopez). The cause of their conflict is the man they share, Ernesto (Jacob Vargas). After Mousie had borne Ernesto's child, and had chosen to spend most of her time with the baby, Ernesto sought attention elsewhere. Soon Sad Girl has also become pregnant by him.

On a windy hillside at night, a confrontation looms between the two former friends; both are armed with a pistol. In an effective twist, however, it is Ernesto, selling drugs on the corner to supplement his income, who is shot dead that night. It later appears that he has spent most of his money on a truck, the possession of which becomes a point of contention following his death. After Ernesto's murder, the two young women begin to rebuild their relationship. The first story closes on this theme: women uniting in the absence of their men.

The film's second section finds a vintage car full of homegirls (including Mousie and Sad Girl) on its way to welcome Giggles (Marlo Marron) following her release from a four-year prison term. Giggles has matured in prison, and, as expected, takes up a position as the homegirls' spiritual leader. They need to take charge of their lives and destinies, Giggles argues, both financially and philosophically, because they cannot rely on their men to be around for long. She is the only character in the film seen even attempting to secure a regular job and establish her independence.

Giggles returns to live at the house of a former homegirl, Rachel (Bertilla Damas); it is Rachel who has been a mother to Giggles' daughter during Giggles' imprisonment. In an unprecedented meeting, Giggles calls together the homegirls to discuss the possible sale of Ernesto's truck. It is agreed that the proceeds will help Ernesto's two widows, as well as Whisper (Nelida Lopez), who was shot in the leg while waiting with Ernesto for his customers.

The ownership of the truck has been a source of tension between the Echo Park gangs and a rival group in River Valley, led by playboy El Duran (Jessie Borrego), and the battle over its ownership is at the heart of the film's last movement. Believing that the truck had been promised to him, El Duran is determined to make it his. Ernesto's timid younger brother Sleepy (Gabriel Gonzalez), however, naturally wishes to keep the truck for himself. Into this final story, Anders also weaves the plaintive longings of Sad Girl's sister, La Blue Eyes (Magali Alvarado), who has fallen in love with a man in prison whom she has never seen. When their correspondence ceases abruptly, she is disconsolate.

At a party in River Valley, La Blue Eyes is introduced to, and dances with, El Duran, who may have been her prison pen pal. The evening ends in violence, however, as El Duran is gunned down in retribution for the sudden disappearance of the truck. Next morning, the truth emerges: The truck was taken for a joy ride—and wrecked—by an Echo Park "vato." El Duran has been killed for something he had no hand in.

In the coda of *Mi Vida Loca*—an incident that throws the film out of balance—a drive-by shooting by a River Valley homegirl kills a young child in Echo Park by mistake, instead of her intended target, Sleepy. The last scene of the film lingers on the child's funeral. It should be poignant, but it is merely somber.

If there is one major problem in *Mi Vida Loca*, it is Anders' unnecessary attempt to place Ernesto's truck center stage, particularly in the latter half of her film. Although Sad Girl refers to it in her opening narrative, it is all but forgotten until it comes into play. When El Duran is shot because of the dispute, his murder seems no less shocking than any random drive-by killing.

 "We girls need new skills 'cause by the time our boys are 21, they're either in prison, disabled or dead."—Giggles from *Mi Vida Loca*

Where Anders notably succeeds is in portraying the bonds among the Echo Park women. Defiant in the fact of shootings and life on welfare, they embody a form of desperate courage, and Anders vividly captures the colors that yet shine in their often gray world.

Performances are generally strong without being showy. Nelida Lopez as Whisper is new to acting and it shows, and Marlo Marron's line delivery is often more ponderous than sincere. Yet Aviles, Seidy Lopez, and Vargas are impressive. The fact that they hail from Latino communities does not guarantee a successful dramatic portrayal. With Anders' empathetic script, however, the actors have a solid foundation, and their committed performances bring veracity to the motion picture.

CREDITS

Sad Girl: Angel Aviles
Mousie: Seidy Lopez
Ernesto: Jacob Vargas
Giggles: Marlo Marron
Whisper: Nelida Lopez
El Duran: Jessie Borrego
La Blue Eyes: Magali Alvarado
Big Sleepy: Julian Reyes
Sleepy: Gabriel Gonzalez
Rachel: Bertilla Damas
Shadow: Art Esquer
Baby Doll: Christina Solis
Gata: Salma Hayek
Joker Bird: Panchito Gomez
Los Lobos: Los Lobos

Released: 1994
Production: Daniel Hassid and Carl-Jan Colpaert for HBO Showcase, in association with Film Four International and Cineville; released by Sony Pictures Classics
Direction: Allison Anders
Screenplay: Allison Anders
Cinematography: Rodrigo Garcia
Editing: Richard Chew, Kathryn Himoff and Tracy Granger
Production design: Jane Stewart
Art direction: Bradley Wisham
Set decoration: Chris Miller
Casting: Betsy Fels
Sound: Mary Jo Devenney
Sound design: Leonard Marcel
Costume design: Susan Bertram
Music supervision: Jellybean Benitez
Music: John Taylor
MPAA rating: R
Running time: 92 minutes

Although Sad Girl and Mousie's relationship undergoes a number of changes during the film, the two women essentially remain the same. They make overtures of reconciliation to each other, but their rapprochement is less a result of personal growth and more a pragmatic acceptance of their widowhood. Theirs is a world in which their man had always provided; now the women have to look to financial matters themselves.

Technically speaking, Rodrigo Garcia's cinematography in *Mi Vida Loca* is fluid, and costume designer Susan Bertram's work has an authentic feel. Los Lobos is featured in the party scene—they are the party band—but allowed little screen time, and are thus somewhat wasted.

Allison Anders directs her script with assurance and an inherent sympathy for her characters without minimizing their dilemmas. Her characters speak in true and strong voices, so much so that *Mi Vida Loca* occasionally comes across as a documentary. Yet the slow-motion depictions of gang initiations and drive-bys remind the audience that Anders is dramatizing the often painful reality of life in the barrio. Her film is not only gritty but also poetic and graceful as it celebrates the strength of friendship.

Critical opinion of *Mi Vida Loca* was mixed, with Anders garnishing significant attention after winning the New York Film Critics Circle Award for *Gas Food Lodging*. The *Los Angeles Times* claimed that despite Anders' good intentions, she stereotypes her characters as too simple to rise above their situations. The *L.A. Weekly*, in contrast, believed that Anders' success in the film lay in its clear-eyed depiction of the Echo Park community and its struggles.

What Anders brings to her projects is sincerity and especially a mark of authenticity. Anders herself reared two children, primarily on welfare, and her understanding of this parenting challenge informs the portrayal of the mothers in *Mi Vida Loca*. In addition, the use of neighborhood locales and a wholehearted depiction of the community ensure that her vision of Echo Park rings true.

Although representative of a disaffected urban life that can be found throughout America, Allison Anders' Echo Park characters are of their place. They cherish their distinctive culture. In *Mi Vida Loca*, Anders has provided a window for the world to observe this culture. It is a culture of love and despair, birth and premature death.

—Paul B. Cohen

REVIEWS

Entertainment Weekly. July 22, 1994, p. 33.
The Hollywood Reporter. July 15-17, 1994, p. 12.
Los Angeles Times. July 22, 1994, p. F4.
The New York Times. July 18, 1994, p. B3.
Variety. May 25, 1993, p. 14.

Milk Money

"You can't get enough of a good thing...But first you have to find it."—Movie tagline

"Melanie Griffith and Ed Harris give us two superb, sweet, smart performances."—Joel Siegel, *Good Morning America*

"The chemistry between Griffith and Harris is just as potent as it was between Julia Roberts and Richard Gere."—Kevin Thomas, *Los Angeles Times*

"A fresh, funny, feel-good film!"—Susan Granger, *CRN Radio Network & American Movie Classics*

"A fun, romantic comedy. A charming fairy tale!" —Jim Ferguson, *Fox-TV*

Box Office Gross: $17,916,031 (January 2, 1995)

Like Julia Roberts' Vivian in *Pretty Woman* (1990), Melanie Griffith's V in *Milk Money* is that cinematic fantasy commonly referred to as the "hooker with a heart of gold." To emphasize this characterization, V (short for Eve) wears a golden, heart-shaped locket, albeit an empty, stolen one. The film is a kind of Cinderella story, in which a lady of the evening is plucked from her tawdry existence and dusted off to reveal prime marriage material.

In *Milk Money*, the aforementioned plucking and dusting is done by a twelve-year-old boy named Frank (Michael Patrick Carter). Driven by curiosity and hormones, Frank and two of his friends (Brian Christopher and Adam LaVorgna) hatch a plan to gather enough money to go to the city and pay a prostitute to strip. After the boys have collected $103.26, they hop on their bicycles and head downtown into unfamiliar territory. Things don't go well from the start. First, Frank propositions a crisply-dressed businesswoman, thinking that she is a hooker. Then the boys are nearly robbed in a dark parking garage. The latter calamity is averted through the intervention of V, a streetwise prostitute who is the embodiment of their lustful fantasies. The boys' money enables them to briefly ogle V's breasts in her seedy, dimly lit hotel room. Afterwards, she drives the boys home.

While it was raining in the city, the boys' suburban neighborhood is bathed in golden sunlight. (*Milk Money*'s idyllic representation of suburbia would make even Norman Rockwell incredulous.) After dropping the boys off, the car

Milk Money's title was nearly changed to "Simply Irresistible."

CREDITS

V: Melanie Griffith
Tom Wheeler: Ed Harris
Frank Wheeler: Michael Patrick Carter
Waltzer: Malcolm McDowell
Betty: Anne Heche
Cash: Casey Siemaszko
Jerry the Pope: Philip Bosco
Kevin Clean: Brian Christopher
Brad: Adam LaVorgna
Mr. Clean: Kevin Scannell
Stacy: Jessica Wesson
Holly: Amanda Sharkey

Released: 1994
Production: Kathleen Kennedy and Frank Marshall; released by Paramount Pictures
Direction: Richard Benjamin
Screenplay: John Mattson
Cinematography: David Watkin
Editing: Jacqueline Cambas
Production design: Paul Sylbert
Set design: Antoinette J. Gordon
Set decoration: Casey Hallenbeck
Casting: Mary Goldberg and Amy Lippens
Sound: Richard Lightstone
Costume design: Theoni V. Aldredge
Music: Michael Convertino
MPAA rating: PG-13
Running time: 108 minutes

V borrowed from her pimp (Casey Siemaszko) breaks down, and she uses Frank's phone to call a tow truck. While in the house, she meets Frank's widowed father (Ed Harris), a rather addled high school science teacher who spends all his free time trying to save a nearby wetlands from encroaching development. Detecting sparks between the two, Frank decides that V would make a terrific wife and mother. He tells his father that she is a math tutor, and, despite her flimsy, revealing outfit, the man believes him. Since Frank tells V that his father knows the truth about her, she is amazed and delighted by his apparent open-mindedness and acceptance. Of course, Frank's lies lead to numerous comic misunderstandings and double entendres.

Melanie Griffith as V and Ed Harris as Tom in *Milk Money*. Copyright © 1994 Paramount Pictures. All rights reserved.

While Frank's father attempts to fix her car, V takes up residence in Frank's tree house, of all places. With the exception of an archly smutty scene in which V's body serves as a visual aid for a class presentation on the female reproductive system, the character assumes a quasi-motherly role in Frank's life, even dressing the part in his late mother's clothes. While V is hurt to learn that Frank's father's open-mindedness was actually ignorance of her profession, the relationship between the three survives and deepens. Their happiness is nearly shattered when V's pimp is murdered by his own boss, Waltzer (Malcolm McDowell), who then goes after her. A car chase and explosion are thrown into the plot as V escapes from Waltzer and is released from all ties to her previous way of life. In the end, V uses money from the dark world she used to inhabit for the betterment of the bright and happy world in which she has found a new home: she buys the wetlands for Frank's father.

What shines in *Milk Money* are the performances of Griffith and Harris. Griffith, who has played this type of role before, comes through with a winning blend of sensitivity and spunk. Harris, in a rare comedic turn, brings an attractive, tender quality to his less fleshed-out character. Michael Patrick Carter is appealing as Frank, and McDowell makes the most of his small, cartoonish role.

The quality of the films Richard Benjamin has directed has varied widely since his 1982 directorial debut, *My Favorite Year*, for which Peter O'Toole received an Oscar nomination for Best Actor. *Milk Money* earned under $18 million in domestic box office receipts and critical reaction was decidedly negative. John Mattson's first feature film script is an uneasy mix of sweetness and vulgarity, sometimes an improbable romantic comedy and at others a rather distasteful coming-of-age film. In the end, *Milk Money* is a mildly entertaining, but ultimately unsatisfying, cinematic hybrid. 🎬

—*David L. Boxerbaum*

REVIEWS

The Christian Science Monitor. March 23, 1995, p. 12.
Entertainment Weekly. September 16, 1994, p. 91.
The Hollywood Reporter. August 22, 1994, p. 7.
Los Angeles Times. August 31, 1994, p. F2.
The New York Times. August 31, 1994, p. B3.
People Weekly. September 12, 1994, p. 19.
Washingtonian. XXX, October 1994, p. 40.
Variety. August 22, 1994, p. 55.

A Million to Juan

"The odds are in his favor."—Movie tagline

 Box Office Gross: $1,163,846 (June 26, 1995)

Loosely based on a short story by Mark Twain, this comedy stars Paul Rodriguez as a Mexican immigrant who is barely scraping by in East Los Angeles when he suddenly finds himself a millionaire for one month. Directorial debut of actor Paul Rodriguez

REVIEWS

Chicago Tribune. September 16, 1994, p. 7L.
Los Angeles Times. May 13, 1994, p. F9.
Variety. CCCLV, May 16, 1994, p. 38.

CREDITS

Juan Lopez: Paul Rodriguez
Olivia Smith: Polly Draper
Jorge: Tony Plana
Mr. Ortiz: Pepe Serna
Alvaro: Bert Rosario
Alejandro Lopez: Jonathan Hernandez
Flaco: Gerardo
Hector Delgado: Victor Rivers
Mr. Angel: Edward James Olmos
Jenkins: Paul Williams

Released: 1994
Production: Steve Paul and Barry Collier for Crystal Sky Communications, in association with Prism Pictures; released by the Samuel Goldwyn Company
Direction: Paul Rodriguez
Screenplay: Francisca Matos and Robert Grasmere; based on a short story by Mark Twain and on characters inspired by Paul Rodriguez
Cinematography: Bruce Johnson
Editing: Michael Ripps
Production design: Mary Patvaldnieks
Casting: Dorothy Koster
Sound: Tony Smyles
Costume design: Jennifer Green
Music: Steven J. Johnson, Jeffrey D. Johnson and Samm Pena
MPAA rating: PG
Running time: 97 minutes

Minotaur

Via a series of flashbacks, this provocative drama follows the meteoric rise and fall of a popular singer of the 1950's called the Minotaur (Michael Faella). Directorial debit of Dan McCormack.

REVIEWS

The New York Times. June 10, 1994, p. C12.

CREDITS

Minotaur: Michael Faella
Mink: Ricky Aiello
Cindy: Holley Chant
Woman: Willo Hausman
Paul: Tom Kurlander
Father: Jack Wallace

Released: 1994
Production: Kris Krengel for RFPL
Direction: Dan McCormack
Screenplay: Dan McCormack
Cinematography: Dan Gillham
Editing: Martin Hunter
Production design: Michael Krantz and Martha Rutan Faye
Art direction: Ann Johnstad White
Set decoration: Mary Gullickson
Sound: David Barr Yaffe and Giovanni Di Simoni
Costume design: Penny Rose
Music: William T. Stromberg
MPAA rating: no listing
Running time: 55 minutes

Miracle on 34th Street

"Discover the miracle."—Movie tagline
"Four stars. This is the new holiday classic America has been waiting for. I loved it!"—Michael Medved, *Sneak Previews*

 Box Office Gross: $17,017,102 (January 2, 1995)

The secret of the success of the 1994 remake of *Miracle on 34th Street* is the same one that made the 1947 original a classic. Both films respect the filmgoer's intelligence while indulging one's child-like need to believe in something irrational or even preposterous. This is no mean feat, and probably harder to achieve in the cynical, disenchanted 1990's than in the hope-filled era following the close of World War II. Few other films of either era speak to children—and the child within every person—without pandering, patronizing, or preaching.

> "This version is a companion to the original, not a continuation. It's almost as if Kriss Kringle has appeared again in modern times."—*Miracle on 34th Street* director John Hughes.

Luckily, the filmmakers who updated the classic for a 1990's audience were not overly concerned about creating a modern, cynical overlay to avoid the appearance of being maudlin or out-of-date. In fact, the new version is even more sentimental than the old and lacks the original's occasional devilish moments. Producer John Hughes and director Les Mayfield left the essence of this delightful tale unchanged. The miracle of *Miracle on 34th Street* is that it is a very wise and knowing tale, that it tweaks the edges of deep spiritual themes without ever being pretentious.

In both versions, everything hinges on the performances of the two central characters: a six-year-old girl who is more grown-up than she wants to be and a gentle old man who truly believes he is Santa Claus. In the original, Natalie Wood charmed and sparkled as the young girl, and the veteran British actor Edmund Gwenn garnered an Oscar for his completely delightful performance as Kriss Kringle. In the 1994 remake, Mara Wilson plays Susan, and veteran British actor, producer, and director Richard

CREDITS

Kriss Kringle: Richard Attenborough
Dorey Walker: Elizabeth Perkins
Bryan Bedford: Dylan McDermott
Susan Walker: Mara Wilson
Judge Harper: Robert Prosky
Ed Collins: J. T. Walsh
Jack Duff: James Remar
Alberta Leonard: Jane Leeves
Shellhammer: Simon Jones
C. F. Cole: William Windom
Tony Falacchi: Jack McGee

Released: 1994
Production: John Hughes for Hughes Entertainment; released by Twentieth Century- Fox
Direction: Les Mayfield
Screenplay: George Seaton and John Hughes; based on a story by Valentine Davies, and on the 1947 motion-picture screenplay by Seaton
Cinematography: Julio Macat
Editing: Raja Gosnell
Production design: Doug Kraner
Art direction: Steve Arnold
Set decoration: Leslie Rollins
Casting: Jane Jenkins and Janet Hirshenson
Visual effects supervision: Gregory L. McMurry
Sound: Ronald Judkins
Costume design: Kathy O'Rear
Music: Bruce Broughton
MPAA rating: PG
Running time: 114 minutes

Attenborough is Kringle. Why Santa is getting typecast as an Englishman is not clear, but the pair are almost as good as the originals, which is high praise indeed.

Miracle on 34th Street centers on a single mother, Dorey Walker (Elizabeth Perkins), and her young yet mature daughter, Susan. Dorey is employed by a department store in New York City. She gets more than she bargained for one holiday season when she hires an elderly gentleman to play Santa Claus—who maintains that he really is the genuine article. A trial ensues to debate the old gentleman's sanity, and handsome attorney Bryan Bedford (Dylan McDermott) accepts Kriss' case. Against all odds, Bryan and Kriss win over not only the court but also the skeptical mother-daughter pair.

Wilson, who debuted in the hit comedy *Mrs. Doubtfire* (1993), manages to be precocious without being cloying in the part of Susan. She masters the nuances of a very complex role with remarkable grace and self-assurance. Playing a child forced to grow up too fast, Wilson

makes the agony of such a child come alive. Though not nearly as playful, smooth, and charming as Wood, Wilson may have a future just as promising. Attenborough plays Kringle as a sweet soul incapable of hurting a fly. He is never sappy, saintly, or sanctimonious, but simply embodies an unfailingly generous human spirit in an increasingly ungenerous world.

Unfortunately, some of the spark and silliness of the original is missing. Too much of the goofiness of the 1947 classic has been cut; this time around, for example, Kringle does not learn how to blow bubble gum from Susan. Compared to the screwball sensibilities of the original, the modern film is somewhat flat. Instead of a delightful farce, it has become a message film, wary of being too frivolous.

Gwenn's Kringle was lovable because he was nice but a little naughty; Attenborough's Kringle does not have a naughty whisker in his beard. In the original, Kringle was an oddball, a character, fighting against attempts to stifle his honesty; in the remake, Kringle is a victim. In the original, Kringle gets in trouble because he can not abide the meddling of a mean-spirited, misanthropic psychiatrist, and stands up to him. In the remake, Kringle is framed by the sinister head of a rival department store, a cut-rate chain, and is helpless to do anything about it.

The other changes are mostly for the worse, too. Susan's mother was played in the original by Maureen O'Hara as a polite, wistful, once-hurt but forgiving single mother. In the remake, Elizabeth Perkins portrays Dorey Walker as a prickly, cold, unreachable career woman who does not merely doubt Kringle but constantly berates him, who does not merely deny her child the comforts of the Santa legend but browbeats her, and who does not merely resist the advances of the attorney who becomes the film's hero but scorns him.

Perkins does not seem to be capable of the nuances necessary for the part, or perhaps she and the filmmakers reject them as old-fashioned; they seem to believe the character can not show any heart and still pass muster as a 1990's woman. Thus another character with gumption and dignity in the original becomes another victim in the remake.

Her suitor, who befriends Susan and saves Kringle, was a bit of a wisecracker as played by John Payne in the original. Dylan McDermott portrays him in the remake, rather stiffly, as yet another victim—an old-fashioned man who has difficulties with the cruel postmodern dating game. McDermott is good-looking but not very compelling, and when he becomes a central character at the end, the film suffers from his bloodless demeanor.

The original film was a comedy about human foibles; this new version is a tragedy about uncaring institutions, capitalist excesses, the loss of childhood, and the hard life of a single mother. The original is funnier, less maudlin, and more spirited; the remake is politically correct, preachy, and formulaic. Yet the story is still solid, and the central performances by Wilson and Attenborough appealing.

Miracle on 34th Street is not really a children's film, but a film for grown-ups who want to indulge their "inner child" at the holiday season. If one can overlook all the victimizing, the film remains at heart a very old-fashioned tale.

—*Michael Betzold*

REVIEWS

Entertainment Weekly. November 18, 1994, p. 76.
The Hollywood Reporter. November 7, 1994, p. 5.
Los Angeles Times. November 18, 1994, p. F1.
The New York Times. November 18, 1994, p. B13.
The New Yorker. December 12, 1994, p. 38.
Time. November 28, 1994, p. 80.
Variety. November 7, 1994, p. 10.

Misplaced

A mother (Elzbieta Czyzewska) and son (John Cameron Mitchell) who immigrate to the United States from Poland in 1981 in search of a better life struggle against poverty, alienation, and loneliness. Feature film directorial debut of Louis Yansen.

REVIEWS

Variety. CCCXXXV, April 26, 1989, p. 26.

CREDITS

Jacek Nowak: John Cameron Mitchell
Halina Nowak: Elzbieta Czyzewska
Zofia: Viveca Lindfors
Bill: Drew Snyder
Ela: Deirdre O'Connell
David: John Christopher Jones
Mrs. Padway: Debralee Scott

Released: 1991
Production: Lisa Zwerling; released by Original Cinema
Direction: Louis Yansen
Screenplay: Louis Yansen and Thomas DeWolfe; based on a story by Yansen
Cinematography: Igor Sunara
Editing: Michael Berenbaum
Production design: Beth Kuhn
Music: Michael Urbaniak
MPAA rating: no listing
Running time: 98 minutes

Mrs. Parker and the Vicious Circle

"At the center of the world's most notorious table...was a woman ahead of her time."
—Movie tagline

"A remarkable new movie."—Roger Ebert, *Chicago Sun Times*

Box Office Gross: $1,137,949 (January 2, 1995)

In New York City in the roaring 1920's, a group of self-proclaimed intellectuals gathered every day at the Algonquin Hotel for lunch. Like junkies needing their daily fix, the members of what would become known as the Round Table seemed to crave the mutual admiration of their cohorts. In retrospect one is hard-pressed to recall the literary accomplishments of the majority of the group, with the exception of perhaps the quickest wit and doubtless, the saddest soul, Mrs. Dorothy Parker. It was Parker herself who later in her life noted that while the members of the famed Round Table gathered at the Algonquin exchanging *bon mots*, their contemporaries, American writers such as Eugene O'Neill, William Faulkner and F. Scott Fitzgerald, were engaged, instead, scouring their souls in order to write what would become some of the most enduringly compelling literature of its time.

While she proved to be somewhat of a master of irony, and sarcasm was her chief stock in trade, Dorothy Parker, for the most part, never allowed herself to journey too far into the depths of self-examination. As a result, her writings, with the exception of some of her short stories and soliloquies, tended to remain fairly superficial, only occasionally showing glimpses of a richer vein; but Parker never struggled to achieve greatness and seemed reluctant to make the kind of intellectual effort at self-exploration that could possibly have assured her longevity and higher acclaim in the literary world. She seemed to prefer, instead, to merely "show off" in front of her colleagues with a sharp observation and a clever turn of a phrase. Glibness, it seemed, was her forte.

Despite her propensity towards verses that glorified death, particularly suicide, Dorothy Parker out-lived most of her Round Table cohorts, dying in 1967 from natural causes at the age of seventy-three—in many ways the final irony, given the degree of contempt Mrs. Parker held for life in general and her own life in particular. In dramatic terms, this proves to be the major challenge faced by director Alan Rudolph and his co-writer, Randy Sue Coburn, in scripting the life of Dorothy Parker. As Owen Gleiberman of *Entertainment Weekly* magazine so succinctly pointed out in his review of *Mrs. Parker and the Vicious Circle:* "How do you get audiences to care about a woman who, in the end, didn't give a damn about herself?"

The film opens in black-and-white with Dorothy Parker (Jennifer Jason Leigh) in Hollywood, working as a screenwriter with the husband for whom she so openly displayed such contempt that she married him twice, Alan Campbell (Peter Gallagher), and with whom she wrote the original *A Star Is Born* in 1937. Parker is queried about her glory days back in New York in the Twenties. "I suppose it was... colorful," she slurs, which triggers a flashback to the start of her career and a switch to color photography. Her first husband, Edwin Pond Parker II (Andrew McCarthy)—the former Dorothy Rothschild once remarked that she married him for "his nice clean name"—has returned home from the war, replete with a nasty morphine habit. Dorothy cautions him, "You don't want to become the town drunk, Eddie. Not in Manhattan." Besides, Eddie proves to be no match for his wife's cultivated and finely honed wit. Not that it matters much, for Dorothy has found her soulmate in fellow *Vanity Fair* editor and drama critic, Robert Benchley (Campbell Scott), a teetotalling wiseguy with a sense of integrity who clearly adores Mrs. Parker, but will not be another in a string of handsome cads who would continually break her heart. Their relationship remained purely platonic throughout the years, yet Parker seemed unable, or at least unwilling, to conceal her longing for the married Benchley. When a partygoer points to Parker and asks, "Would that be Mrs. Benchley?" Alexander Woollcott (Tom McGowan) explains: "Yes, that would be Mrs. Benchley, were it not for the fact that there already is a Mrs. Benchley."

"You don't want to become the town drunk, Eddie. Not in Manhattan."—Dorothy Parker to husband Eddie

When Parker is fired from the magazine for writing one too many negative theater reviews, Benchley quits in supportive protest and the two move into rented office space, typewriters back-to-back, and quips wall-to-wall. The two would later write for fellow Round Table compatriot, Harold Ross (Sam Robards) when he starts up his own magazine. "Since it's about New Yorkers, why not call it *The New Yorker*?" someone so cleverly suggests. *Mrs. Parker* is full of such tedious quips and at times the dialogue strains against its own cleverness. "I'm hungry, aren't you?" "No, I'm Mr. Sherwood." Nearly every imaginable gathering is an occasion for seemingly endless cameos of characters, most of whom are recognizable to only the most well-informed of viewers. Even Keith Carradine, an Alan Rudolph favorite, shows up in a bit of coy casting as Will Rogers. Unfortunately, these scenes do little more than provide a cursory glimpse at Parker's life, and certainly do not offer up true characterizations; the faces that come and go become indistinguishable from the next. The film continues to alternate between the late Twenties/early Thirties and Parker's later years of money-making in Hollywood and later still, back again, this time in near obscurity, in Manhattan. Parker has her heart shredded by Charles MacArthur, surprisingly played to the hilt by that quintessential nice guy, Matthew Broderick, who at one point observes, "You have a passion for unhappiness." Near the end of her life, alone with only her dogs and her alcohol to keep her company—even Robert Benchley managed to die of cirrhosis of the liver—Dorothy Parker is asked to deliver her own epitaph.

CREDITS

Dorothy Parker: Jennifer Jason Leigh
Charles MacArthur: Matthew Broderick
Robert Benchley: Campbell Scott
Alan Campbell: Peter Gallagher
Gertrude Benchley: Jennifer Beals
Eddie Parker: Andrew McCarthy
Horatio Byrd: Wallace Shawn
Jane Grant: Martha Plimpton
Harold Ross: Sam Robards
Edna Ferber: Lili Taylor
Deems Taylor: James LeGros
Paula Hunt: Gwyneth Paltrow
Robert Sherwood: Nick Cassavetes
Will Rogers: Keith Carradine
Alexander Woollcott: Tom McGowan

Released: 1994
Production: Robert Altman, in association with Miramax Films and Odyssey Entertainment Ltd.; released by Fine Line Features
Direction: Alan Rudolph
Screenplay: Alan Rudolph and Randy Sue Coburn
Cinematography: Jan Kiesser
Editing: Suzy Elmiger
Production design: Francois Seguin
Art direction: James Fox
Set decoration: Frances Calder
Sound: Richard Nichol
Costume design: John Hay and Renee April
Music: Mark Isham
MPAA rating: R
Running time: 123 minutes

"What a morbid thing to ask a person!" she responds with glee. "You've just stolen my heart."

Actress Jennifer Jason Leigh, a chameleon who consistently loses herself in the characters she portrays on screen, once again paints a portrait of a woman too terrified to reveal her true self, yet smart enough to know that that would be her only salvation. Leigh uses her voice—some hybrid between Katherine Hepburn and Rosalind Russell that surely evolved from her wickedly funny fast-talking career woman in *The Hudsucker Proxy* (reviewed in this volume)—as almost a shield, keeping most people at bay, barely concealing her contempt. The trouble, however, is it has a tendency to alienate the audience as well as her on-screen victims. At times Leigh's speech is so slurred that it is often difficult to understand her. (Granted, in real life Mrs. Parker's best lines were often muttered under her breath, but when one is trying to paint a portrait on-screen of a woman who was celebrated for her verbal acerbity, it is helpful to be able to hear it.) While Leigh is so good at showing us the tortured soul, there is very little modulation in her performance, which often reads merely as alcoholic haze. Seldom are we privy to the deeper longings of her soul. It is all hinted at and it is easy to fill in the blanks, but after a while, it seems like too much work for so little payback, for in the end, we simply do not care enough to bother.

Writer/director Alan Rudolph has explored the nostalgic milieu of artists and melancholia before, and with far more success, with *The Moderns* (1988), an intoxicating look at life among a community of expatriates in Paris in 1926. This film perhaps works better because it is more dramatic, the scenes build towards a conclusion, and while it is peppered with real-life characters such as Ernest Hemingway and Gertrude Stein providing atmosphere, the focus is on a fictional art forger played by Keith Carradine. The other characters help to evoke a vivid time and place, a quality that, despite the beautiful set design and costumes, seems decidedly missing from *Mrs. Parker*. The cast, furthermore, all seem strangely too young, or perhaps merely too contemporary, giving the impression that they are, indeed, all play-acting, never truly inhabiting their characters. Perhaps this is more the fault of the screenwriters for not clearly delineating the hordes of

AWARDS AND NOMINATIONS

Chicago Film Critics Awards 1994: Best Actress (Leigh)
Golden Globe Awards Nomination 1995: Best Actress—Drama (Leigh)
Independent Spirit Awards Nominations 1995: Best Film, Best Director (Rudolph), Best Actress (Leigh), Best Screenplay, Best Actor (Scott)
National Society of Film Critics Awards 1994: Best Actress (Leigh)

characters that flit across the screen at any given moment.

Mrs. Parker and the Vicious Circle held the potential to be a compelling portrait of a talented writer who chose to shine brightly for a brief moment in time and then quietly slid into near obscurity. But the filmmakers hold the audience at bay, emotionally, and what we are left with is little more than a cursory look at a melancholy alcoholic who is best remembered for her savage wit. Despite a strong performance by actress Jennifer Jason Leigh, *Mrs. Parker and the Vicious Circle* is filled with the same sense of ennui that proved to be the downfall of its subject herself. What it desperately needed was more of the wit that was Dorothy Parker.

—*Patricia Kowal*

REVIEWS

Christian Science Monitor. January 6, 1995, LXXXVII, p. 11.
Entertainment Weekly. December 6, 1994, p. 46.
The Hollywood Reporter. May 16, 1994, p. 6.
Interview. XXIV, December 1994, p. 96.
Los Angeles Times. December 21, 1994, p. F4.
Macleans. CVIII. January 2, 1995, p. 50.
New York Magazine. December 12, 1994, p. 66.
The New York Times. November 23, 1994, p. B3.
Rolling Stone. December 15, 1994, p. 104.
Time. CXLIV, December 12, 1994, p. 90.
Village Voice. December 6, 1994. XXXIX, p. 58.
The Wall Street Journal. December 13, 1994, p. A16.

Mr. Write

"You'll be mad about Paul Reiser in *Mr. Write*!"
Jeanne Wolf, *Jeanne Wolf's Hollywood*

"Paul Reiser exudes a hip, charismatic charm."
—Patrick Stoner, *Flicks*

"Romantic!"—Jeff Craig, *60 Second Preview*

"Charming!"—Kim Williamson, *Venice Magazine*

A shy aspiring playwright (Paul Reiser) lands an acting job in a candy commercial only to fall in love with the boss's daughter (Jessica Tuck), who is engaged to someone else.

REVIEWS

Variety. CCCLV, May 9, 1994, p. 70.

CREDITS

Charlie: Paul Reiser
Nicole: Jessica Tuck
Roger: Doug Davidson
Wylie: Jane Leeves
Mr. Rhett: Calvert De Forest

Shelly: Gigi Rice
Dad: Eddie Barth
Roz: Wendie Jo Sperber
Lawrence: Darryl M. Bell
Billy: Tom Wilson
Dan: Martin Mull
Rollins: Tom David Bailey

Released: 1994
Production: Joan Fishman and Rick Herrington for Leonard Loventhal and Presto; released by Shapiro Glickenhaus Entertainment
Direction: Charlie Loventhal
Screenplay: Howard J. Morris; based on his play
Cinematography: Elliot Davis
Editing: Eric Beason
Production design: Pamela Woodbridge
Set decoration: Marty Iluyette
Casting: Cheryl Bayer
Sound: John Nutt
Costume design: Elsa Ward
Music: Miles Roston
MPAA rating: PG-13
Running time: 90 minutes

Mixed Nuts

"A Comedy on the Edge."—Movie tagline

"*Mixed Nuts* is a delightful romp full of batty characters and unforseen happenings. The cast is inspired, beginning with Steve Martin at the top."—Bob Thomas, *Associated Press*

"There is generosity of spirit at the heart of *Mixed Nuts*, something that shines through every scene. Some of this wild and wacky stuff is undeniably funny."—Wendy Fernane, *San Diego Blade Citizen*

"The movie has a lot of energy."—Jeff Strickler, *Minneapolis Star Tribune*

Box Office Gross: $5,942,599 (January 2, 1995)

M ixed Nuts, like the infamous box-office bombs *Ishtar* (1987) and *The Radioland Murders* (1994), looks great on paper. It has a formidable cast, and an equally formidable group of creative people at the helm. But even the best intentions and talents haven't saved this film from joining *Ishtar* and others in the category of films doomed to be remembered as big bombs.

Beginning with images of a California Christmas, complete with Rollerbladers dashing through crowds of bikini-clad Christmas revelers, Rollerblading snowmen, and more, the film starts out promisingly enough. Taken from the French cult film *Le Père Noël Est une Ordure*, or "Santa Claus is Garbage," it is the story of one Christmas Eve in the pathetic lives the Lifesavers, a group of neurotics trying to maintain a suicide prevention hotline in Venice, California.

Steve Martin plays Philip, a bumbling do-gooder who runs his suicide prevention operation from a Venice flat with the help of prissy Mrs. Munchnik (Madeleine Kahn) and dowdy Katherine (Rita Wilson). Their incompetency in the area of suicide prevention is only surpassed by their incompetency in business, and Lifesavers is about to go under—unless it receives the $5,000 it needs immediately. The greedy landlord Stanley Tannenbaum, interested in the gory details of suicide but disinterested in helping maintain Lifesavers, intends to throw them out as soon as possible.

As Christmas Eve wears on, several other crazy characters from the neighborhood somehow make their way into

Mixed Nuts was originally titled "Life Savers."

CREDITS

Philip: Steve Martin
Mrs. Blanche Munchnik: Madeline Kahn
Mr. Lobel: Robert Klein
Felix: Anthony LaPaglia
Gracie Barzini: Juliette Lewis
Dr. Kinsky: Rob Reiner
Louie: Adam Sandler
Chris: Liev Schreiber
Catherine O'Shaughnessy: Rita Wilson
Stanley Tannenbaum: Garry Shandling

Released: 1994
Production: Paul Junger Witt, Tony Thomas, and Joseph Hartwick; released by TriStar Pictures
Direction: Nora Ephron
Screenplay: Nora Ephron and Delia Ephron; based on the film *Le Père Noël Est une Ordure*
Cinematography: Sven Nykvist
Editing: Robert Reitano
Production design: Bill Groom
Art direction: Dennis Bradford
Set decoration: George DeTitta, Jr.
Casting: Juliet Taylor and Laura Rosenthal
Sound: James Sabat
Costume design: Jeffrey Kurland
Music: George Fenton
MPAA rating: PG-13
Running time: 97 minutes

the Lifesavers office: pregnant airhead Gracie (Juliette Lewis) and her stupid petty-thief boyfriend, Felix (Anthony LaPaglia); frighteningly bad songwriter Louie (*Saturday Night Live*'s Adam Sandler); huge transvestite Chris (Liev Schreiber); and cantankerous dog owner Mr. Lobel (Robert Klein). Like a television situation comedy, each of these characters is given one characteristic, as if characteristics were being rationed by the writers. The characters each do the best with what they can.

It is difficult to identify the central event that propels the incessantly high energy of the actors. Obviously, the urgency of the need for $5,000 is clear, but somehow it does not seem to be the engine driving the rather episodic action. For instance, an extended sequence involving Mrs. Munchnik stuck in an elevator is amusing (especially as played by the indomitable Madeleine Kahn), but it does not have to do with the central dilemma of the main characters, and only serves to divert them from their objectives.

This is the central problem of the film: it is a series of scenes which seem to detour from the central problem, and it serves only to make the audience feel as jumbled and disorderly as the characters. To depict the characters as disorderly is one thing, but to allow the plot to fall into disarray is another—and unfortunately, that is what the usually excellent Nora Ephron and her sister Delia Ephron have done.

Nora Ephron directed the film, and some of the sense of disarray can be found in publicity material in which cast member Juliette Lewis says "Nora doesn't like any dead time." This was apparently the reason that the characters appear to run when they could walk (especially Lewis and LaPaglia) or to overreact to events by running around (as Wilson does occasionally) or become unconscious without a justifiable reason (Kahn, LaPaglia, and Wilson).

"Now Saving 1,423"—Life Savers' suicide prevention tote board

Still, this is a very funny group of people, and many of the gags are funny. Martin and Schreiber do a wonderful tango, and Sandler's ridiculous songs are a stitch. Madeleine Kahn returns to the kind of imperious character she played so beautifully in *What's Up Doc?* (1972), saying, "I am so good at this, and soon I will be high and dry without any outlet for my talents."

The final segment, in which a murder becomes the source of great joy and happiness for all the characters, seems forced. It also seems rather odd that with a dead body lying around, Martin delivers an impassioned speech about the magic of Christmas which causes everyone to applaud and helps to wrap up the story. It doesn't help that the dead character is Jewish and that the revelers are cheering over his body on Christmas Eve.

Seeing brilliant comic performers and writers only talk about magic instead of truly creating it seems a bit of a shame. The good news is that this is only one misstep for these people, who cumulatively have been responsible for some wonderful comedy. Audiences are advised to pretend this film never happened, and to look forward to whatever these talented people try next time.

—Kirby Tepper

REVIEWS

The Hollywood Reporter. December 12, 1994. p. 6.
Los Angeles Times. December 21, 1994. p. F1.
The New York Times. December 21, 1994. p. B3.

Money Man

Eccentric artist J. S. G. Boggs is the focus of this amusing documentary. Boggs draws replicas of U. S. currency as works of art, then "spends" them and receives his change and receipt in order to consider the pieces complete. Needless to say, his efforts have caused him endless trouble with the government.

REVIEWS

The New York Times. January 13, 1993, p. C16.
The Washington Post. January 18, 1993, p. C4.

CREDITS

J. S. G. Boggs: J. S. G. Boggs

Released: 1993
Production: Philip Haas and Belinda Haas; released by Milestone Films
Direction: Philip Haas
Cinematography: Tony Wilson
Editing: Belinda Haas
Music: Philip Johnston
MPAA rating: no listing
Running time: 60 minutes

Monkey Trouble

"What would you do if the pet you wanted most was one of America's most wanted?"
—Movie tagline

"One of those rare children's films to which you can bring your children."—Janet Maslin, *The New York Times*

"A splendid family film, as entertaining as *Free Willy...*"—Roger Ebert, *Chicago Sun-Times*

 Box Office Gross: $16,326,967 (July 24, 1994)

When a little girl, Eva (Thora Birch), wishes she had a pet, her dream comes true in the form of a cute little monkey that she meets in the park and takes home, unbeknownst to her parents. Unfortunately, the monkey is a highly skilled pickpocket belonging to a conniving Gypsy (Harvey Keitel) who follows Eva, trying to retrieve his furry little accomplice.

REVIEWS

Atlanta Constitution. March 21, 1994, p. C7.
Boston Globe. March 18, 1994, p. 73.
Chicago Tribune. March 20, 1994, Sec. 5 p. 3.
Entertainment Weekly. April 1, 1994, p. 38.
Entertainment Weekly. October 14, 1994, p. 70.
Los Angeles Times. March 18, 1994, p. F13.
The New York Times. March 18, 1994, p. C8.
The New York Times. May 1, 1994, Sec. 2 p. 26.
TV Guide. XLII, November 5, 1994, p. 38.
USA Today. March 18, 1994, p. D4.
Variety. CCCLIV, March 21, 1994, p. 57.
The Washington Post. March 18, 1994, p. D7.
The Washington Post. March 24, 1994, p. C7.

CREDITS

Dodger: Finster
Eva: Thora Birch
Azro: Harvey Keitel
Amy: Mimi Rogers
Tom: Christopher McDonald
Peter: Kevin Scannell

Released: 1994
Production: Mimi Polk and Heidi Rufus Isaacs for Ridley Scott/Percy Main, in association with Effe Films and Victor Company of Japan, Ltd.; released by New Line Cinema
Direction: Franco Amurri
Screenplay: Franco Amurri and Stu Krieger
Cinematography: Luciano Tovoli
Editing: Ray Lovejoy and Chris Peppe
Production design: Les Dilley
Art direction: Nathan Crowley
Set decoration: Denise Pizzini
Casting: Karen Rea
Special effects coordination: J. D. Street IV
Sound: Michael Evje and Charles Kelly
Costume design: Eileen Kennedy
Music: Mark Mancina
MPAA rating: PG
Running time: 95 minutes

Mother's Boys

"The Year's Most Terrifying Thriller!"
—Movie tagline

"Three years ago Jude disappeared. Now, she's coming back for her family...whether they like it or not."—Movie tagline

"A Provocative and Erotic Thriller."—*Fox-TV, New York*

"Stylish Suspense!"—*San Francisco Chronicle*

 Box Office Gross: $836,366 (June 26, 1994)

Jamie Lee Curtis gives a fine performance in this moderately suspenseful film about a truly scary mom. The film as a whole is taut and well-directed (by Yves Simoneau), and boasts a competent cast. Somehow, though, it falls a bit flat in its last minutes, losing some of the excellent momentum that it develops until that point. Perhaps that is the reason that this film was not the box office success that its story and central performance may have promised.

With eerie music and impressionistic images of children's faces and frogs swimming

 "You and I are bound together forever."—Jude showing her Caesarean section scar to her oldest son, Kes, in *Mother's Boys*

through rippling water, the film's credits include a voice-over which sets up the plot while it sets the creepy mood. Jude (Jamie Lee Curtis) has apparently discovered that the man she abruptly abandoned three years before (Peter Gallagher) is finally filing for divorce. Their three chil-

dren, brooding Kes (Luke Edwards), amiable Michael (Colin Ward), and little Ben (Joey Zimmerman), having been motherless for three years, are beginning to develop relationships with their father's fiancee, Callie (Joanne Whalley-Kilmer). Jude returns home to reclaim her children and her husband, setting up a fierce competition between herself and Callie.

As determined and as dangerous as was Glenn Close in *Fatal Attraction* (1987) (or Joan Crawford in anything she did), Jude makes it clear from the outset that she will accept nothing less than the return of her family. She tries to seduce the rather wishy-washy Robert, manipulates visitation rights for the children, verbally poisons Kes' view of Callie through a series of calculated lies, and terrorizes Callie by spray-painting "whore" on her car and entrapping her in a dangerous game which leads to the film's climax.

Like other recent violent cinematic villainesses such as Sharon Stone's sexy sociopath in *Basic Instinct* (1992), or Demi Moore's evil seductress in *Disclosure* (reviewed in this volume), Jamie Lee Curtis portrays Jude as an absolute monster with no morals or values at all. She is terrific; as evil as Medea, and as sexy as Cleopatra. Feminists will take note that this portrayal perpetuates the stereotype that ultra-sexy women are absolutely amoral and thoroughly dangerous—but it's still an entertaining performance. Curtis is particularly demonic in the scenes with her oldest son, Kes, whom she virtually seduces in order to win him to her side: she insists that he sit on the edge of her bath and talk to him, then she stands up to show him the scar left over from the Caesarean section in which she gave birth to him, saying "you and I are bound together forever." If this were an old-time melodrama and she were a man, she would twirl her moustache.

Her scenes with Peter Gallagher are erotically charged and almost humorous because she is so predatory that he truly does seem powerless to do anything to stop her. It is a bit hard to believe that Gallagher's character, a dynamic and well-adjusted architect, would have ever been involved with her in the first place, but the always credible Gallagher makes the most of his role.

Joanne Whalley-Kilmer, having herself been an excellent screen temptress in *Scandal* (1989), is less effective in this film due to the built-in foolishness of her character. In the final scenes, she allows herself to be handcuffed by the boys when she is supposedly at home looking after them,

Peter Gallagher as Robert, Joanne Whalley-Kilmer as Callie, and Vanessa Redgrave as Lydia in *Mother's Boys*. Copyright © Miramax Films.

then she tries to take seriously injured Ben on foot to a hospital from their remote countryside home. Finally, she leaves Ben (who is supposedly gushing blood) on the side of the road to jump on top of a precariously balanced car in order to save Kes, not realizing that her weight could send them all over the edge.

It is this sequence, fueled by Callie's ineffectual character, which becomes the downfall of the film. Director Simoneau, having provided a moody intensity up to this point, loses momentum in these final moments. The strange music and the disjointed camera angles, the spooky, jumpy editing, and the ghostly sound effects (which up to this point have made the film a stylish thriller) give way to a by-the-numbers, unsuspenseful climax which uses no significant underscoring, film editing, or sound editing to build to the suspenseful pitch promised by early scenes.

The film's attempts at symbolism (e.g., Kes stabs a frog who his teacher tells him is the type of frog that abandons its young) are an admirable attempt to make this film more than a standard thriller, though they appear a bit obvious and "artsy." But the film works well enough with Curtis' performance to consider itself a respectable addition to the genre of "evil women" movies.

—Kirby Tepper

CREDITS

Jude: Jamie Lee Curtis
Robert: Peter Gallagher
Callie: Joanne Whalley-Kilmer
Lydia: Vanessa Redgrave
Kes: Luke Edwards
Michael: Colin Ward
Ben: Joey Zimmerman

Released: 1994
Production: Jack E. Freedman, Wayne S. Williams, and Patricia Herskovic, in association with CBS Productions; released by Dimension Films
Direction: Yves Simoneau
Screenplay: Barry Schneider and Richard Hawley; based on the novel by Bernard Taylor
Cinematography: Elliot Davis
Editing: Michael Ornstein
CE Art direction: David Bomba
Set decoration: Barbara Cassel
Casting: Francine Maisler
Sound: Clark King
Costume design: Deena Appel and Simon Tuke
Music : George S. Clinton
MPAA rating: R
Running time: 95 minutes

REVIEWS

Daily Variety. March 21, 1994 p.14
The Hollywood Reporter. March 18-20, 1994 p. 8
Los Angeles Times. March 20, 1994 p. F5
The New York Times. March 19, 1994 p.12

Mountain Gorillas

Featuring breathtakingly beautiful cinematography, this IMAX documentary centers on the near-extinct mountain gorillas living in Africa's Rwanda.

REVIEWS

Los Angeles Times. February 26, 1993, p. F4.

CREDITS

Narrator: Rebecca Jenkins

Released: 1993
Production: Sally Dundas for IMAX Corporation Natural History Film Unit and the National Geographic Society
Direction: Adrian Warren
Screenplay: Steve Lucas
Cinematography: Neil Rettig
Editing: Barbara Kerr
Production design: Jordan Craig
Sound: Christopher West
Zoological advice: Craig Sholley
Music: John Wyre
MPAA rating: no listing
Running time: 40 minutes

Munchie

A young boy (Jaime McEnnan) befriends a creature (voice of Dom DeLuise) who grants wishes and protects him against school bullies. Sequel to *Munchies* (1987).

REVIEWS

Variety. CCCXLVII, June 8, 1992, p. 51.

CREDITS

Cathy: Loni Anderson
Munchie: Dom DeLuise (voice)
Elliott: Andrew Stevens
Gage Dobson: Jaime McEnnan
Professor Cruikshank: Arte Johnson
Andrea: Love Hewitt
Ashton: Scott Ferguson
Leon: Mike Simmrin
Mrs. Blaylok: Toni Naples
Miss Laurel: Monique Gabrielle
Principal Thornton: Ace Mask
Mr. Kurtz: Jay Richardson
Undertaker: Angus Scrimm

Released: 1992
Production: Mike Elliott; released by Concorde Pictures
Direction: Jim Wynorski
Screenplay: R. J. Robertson and Jim Wynorski; with additional Munchie dialogue by Vin DiStefano
Cinematography: Don E. Fauntleroy
Editing: Rick Gentner
Production design: Stuart Blatt
Art direction: Carey Meyer
Casting: Andrew Hertz
Sound: Christopher Taylor
Costume design: Lisa Cacavas
Creature design: Gabe Bartalos and Dave Kindlon
Stunt coordination: Patrick Statham
Music: Chuck Cirino
MPAA rating: PG
Running time: 80 minutes

Music for the Movies: Bernard Herrmann

The work of Hollywood film composer Bernard Herrmann, who worked extensively with such directors as Orson Welles, Alfred Hitchcock, and Francois Truffaut, is the focus of this perceptive and entertaining documentary.

REVIEWS

Variety. CCCXLVII, June 22, 1992, p. 43.

CREDITS

Narrator: Philip Bosco
Bernard Herrmann: Bernard Herrmann
Lucille Fletcher: Lucille Fletcher
James G. Stewart: James G. Stewart
Louis Kaufman: Louis Kaufman
Don Cristlieb: Don Cristlieb
David Raskin: David Raskin

Elmer Bernstein: Elmer Bernstein
Paul Hirsch: Paul Hirsch
Christopher Palmer: Christopher Palmer
Royal S. Brown: Royal S. Brown
Norman Corwin: Norman Corwin
Claude Chabrol: Claude Chabrol
Virginia Majewski: Virginia Majewski
Alan Robinson: Alan Robinson
Claudine Bouche: Claudine Bouche
Martin Scorsese: Martin Scorsese

Released: 1992
Production: Margaret Smilow and Roma Baran for Alternate Current, Les Films d'Ici, La Sept, and Channel Four; released by Alternate Current, Inc.
Direction: Joshua Waletzky
Cinematography: Mark Daniels and Jerry Feldman
Editing: Joshua Waletzky
MPAA rating: no listing
Running time: 60 minutes

The Music Tells You

Jazz saxophonist Branford Marsalis, former musical director of television's *The Tonight Show with Jay Leno*, takes center stage in this uninspired documentary.

REVIEWS

Variety. CCCXLVII, June 29, 1992, p. 65.

CREDITS

Branford Marsalis: Branford Marsalis
Robert Hurst: Robert Hurst
Jeff (Tain) Watts: Jeff (Tain) Watts
Sting: Sting
Jerry Garcia: Jerry Garcia
Bruce Hornsby: Bruce Hornsby
Professor David Baker: Professor David Baker

Released: 1992
Production: Frazer Pennebaker for Columbia Records and Pennebaker Associates; released by Pennebaker Associates
Direction: Chris Hegedus and D. A. Pennebaker
Cinematography: Nick Doob, Ronald Gray, Crystal Griffiths, Chris Hegedus and D. A. Pennebaker
Editing: Chris Hegedus, D. A. Pennebaker and Erez Laufer
Sound: Patrick Smith
Music: Branford Marsalis
MPAA rating: no listing
Running time: 60 minutes

Mustang: The Hidden Kingdom

Harrison Ford narrates this documentary that centers on a remote Tibetan village and its devoted Buddhist inhabitants.

REVIEWS

Chicago Tribune. September 9, 1994, Sec. 5 p. 3.

CREDITS

Narrator: Harrison Ford

Released: 1994
Production: Vanessa Schuurbeque Boeye for Intrepid Films Ltd.; released by Discovery Productions
Direction: Tony Miller
Cinematography: Tony Miller
Sound: Glen Marullo
MPAA rating: no listing
Running time: 90 minutes

My Father, the Hero

"Fathers have just one problem with raising daughters. They grow up."—Movie tagline
"Crowd-pleasing entertainment."—*San Francisco Chronicle.*

 Box Office Gross: $25,400,000 (February 1995)

Gérard Depardieu, one of the giants of the cinema world, stars in this English remake of *Mon Pere, Ce Heros* (1991), in which he also starred. Less critically successful than the French original, this film is about a man who faces the fact that his daughter is no longer a little girl.

There is precedent for remaking some classic French comedies: *Three Men and a Baby* (1987) was an English remake whose success spawned a sequel, *Three Men and a Little Lady* (1990); and *La Cage Aux Folles* (1978) which, as of this writing, is being remade by Mike Nichols. Other films have been less successful in the transition to English. For example, *Pure Luck* (1991) was a weak adaptation of *La Chevre* (1982). While not completely unsuccessful in its adaptation to English, *My Father, the Hero* is less successful than it could be.

My Father the Hero is a remake of the French comedy, *Mon Père, Ce Héros* (1991), in which Gérard Depardieu also starred.

While the film has its comic moments, it appears to lack sophistication: it seems more an excuse to show Depardieu in some "zany" situations rather than to mine the comic consequences of a young girl's tall tales about herself and her father. The fun of the film should be to see Depardieu's panic upon seeing his daughter grow into womanhood. Past films such as both versions of *Father of the Bride* (1950, 1991) have depicted every father's nightmare with charm and wit. But here, wittiness gives way to a slapstick tone that doesn't seem appropriate to the film's situation.

Depardieu plays André, a Frenchman divorced from his wife, Megan (Lauren Hutton) and estranged from his daughter, Nicole (Katherine Heigl). In order to repair his relationship with his daughter, the wealthy André takes her to a fabulous resort in the Bahamas. At best, fourteen-year-old Nicole is horrified by everything her father does ("Don't walk around in your underwear in the hotel room, Daddy, it's gross"), and is quite indifferent to him. For his part, André is appalled when he realizes his little girl is growing up fast. When she arrives at the pool dressed in a provocative bathing suit, he tries to cover her with a towel, asking "where is the rest of your bathing suit?" He is positively frantic when he sees her talking to one of the resort's long-haired musicians.

Nicole, setting her sights on a handsome seventeen-year-old, Ben (Dalton James), who works at the hotel, decides to impress Ben by telling him she is sixteen and that André is her boyfriend. Her lie begins to take on a life of its own, as she tells Ben that André has rescued her from a life of drugs and crime, that her mother was a prostitute, and that André has a frightening temper. Some of the lies are fun, particularly in the scene in which her whoppers become really extravagant, intercut with a scene of Depardieu talking on the phone about his sweet little daughter.

"You can't date a musician until all other men are dead."—André to his daughter Nicole in *My Father the Hero*

CREDITS

André: Gérard Depardieu
Nicole: Katherine Heigl
Ben: Dalton James
Megan: Lauren Hutton
Diana: Faith Prince
Mike: Stephen Tobolowsky
Stella: Ann Hearn
Doris: Robyn Peterson
Fred: Frank Renzulli

Released: 1994
Production: Jacques Bar and Jean-Louis Livi for Touchstone Pictures and Cite Films/Film Par Film/D. D. Productions, in association with the Edward S. Feldman Company; released by Buena Vista Pictures
Direction: Steve Miner
Screenplay: Francis Veber and Charlie Peters; based on the film *Mon Père, Ce Héros*, by Gérard Lauzier
Cinematography: Daryn Okada
Editing: Marshall Harvey
Production design: Christopher Nowak
Art direction: Patricia Woodbridge
Set decoration: Don K. Ivey
Casting: Dianne Crittenden
Sound: Joseph Geisinger
Costume design: Vicki Sanchez
Music: David Newman
MPAA rating: PG
Running time: 90 minutes

Where the film seems to derail is in the concept itself: Because of American attitudes (not to mention laws) about such things, the idea that a young girl and an older man together is appalling to several other vacationers (Stephen Toblowsky, Ann Hearn, Robyn Peterson, Frank Renzulli). Through their eyes, it is hard to find Nicole's lie a charming one, especially since in this country people are jailed for having such relationships.

In addition, as played by Ms. Heigl, Nicole is not a particularly winning protagonist. Though it is easy to see why Ben would be physically attracted to her, the fact remains that she is fourteen and grouchy, so it is difficult for the audience to root for this girl's independence or to condone her rather dangerous lie.

Depardieu brings his considerable charm to his role. He is quite winning, especially in his scenes with Ben in which he reluctantly perpetuates Nicole's lie in a vain attempt to help his daughter. He is at his best in a lovely scene which pays homage to Depardieu's success in *Cyrano De Bergerac* (1990), as André gives Nicole the words to woo Ben from below his balcony.

Steve Miner's direction appears especially heavy-handed in the slapstick scenes where Depardieu water-skis, dances, and chases his daughter on the beach. When Miner allows the characters to interact, the film works much better. Production credits are excellent, and the gorgeous Bahamian resort is captured vividly by Miner and cinematographer Daryn Okada.

Depardieu could have done better for his second English-language film; but he could have done much worse than this pleasant comedy.

—*Kirby Tepper*

REVIEWS

Entertainment Weekly. February 18, 1991, p. 95
The Hollywood Reporter, February 4-6, 1994. p. 6.
Los Angeles Times. February 4, 1994, p. F15.
The New York Times. February 4, 1991, p. B7
Variety. February 2, 1994, p. 2.

My Girl II

"Next weekend, fall in love with *My Girl* all over again!"—Movie tagline

 Box Office Gross: $16,571,284 (April 24, 1994)

Austin O' Brien and Anna Chlumsky star in *My Girl II*. Copyright © 1994 Columbia Pictures industries Inc. All Rights Reserved. Courtesy of Columbia Pictures.

My Girl II is a sequel to the 1991 film *My Girl*, starring Macaulay Culkin, which grossed more than $120 million worldwide. The Culkin character, Thomas J. Sennett, was killed off in *My Girl*, which would have made it difficult—though certainly not impossible—for the pale, skinny young actor to appear in a sequel; screenwriters can bring characters back from the dead if there is sufficient financial incentive. At any rate, Culkin, possibly the most popular child actor since Shirley Temple, is conspicuously absent from *My Girl II*, and his presence is sorely missed. Anna Chlumsky becomes the star of the sequel by default. Her new boyfriend, Nick Zsigmond, played by Austin O'Brien—who is already a veteran actor with a leading role in *Last Action Hero* (1993)—is a perfectly competent young actor but lacks the unaccountable charisma of Culkin.

Although top billing in *My Girl II* goes to Dan Aykroyd as small-town Pennsylvania mortician Harry Sultenfuss and Jamie Lee Curtis as his eight-months-pregnant wife, the story is told in such a way that their contributions amount to little more than cameo roles. They are included because, with Culkin absent, the sequel could hardly be called a sequel without them. Their conspicuous absence from the entire middle portion of the sequel deprives the film of the nice balance between adult love and puppy love that made the original so appealing.

Set in 1974, *My Girl II* takes place two years after the incidents documented in *My Girl*. When a junior high school English teacher assigns the class to write a term paper about someone very special whom they have never met, Vada decides to write about her own mother, who died only two weeks after Vada was born. This is the rather flimsy motivation upon which the whole story is based.

Vada has to persuade her father to allow her to go to Los Angeles during the spring break to try to uncover enough information about her mother to complete her composition. Harry is horrified at the thought of sending his thirteen-year-old daughter to Los Angeles all by herself. No

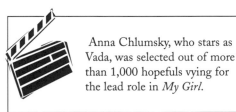

Anna Chlumsky, who stars as Vada, was selected out of more than 1,000 hopefuls vying for the lead role in *My Girl*.

doubt a number of parents in the audience can sympathize with his feelings. The fact that Vada intends to stay with her uncle is not entirely reassuring, since Uncle Phil (Richard Masur) is a fuzzy- haired former-hippie type who is living out of wedlock with his female boss.

Phil's mistress, Rose Zsigmond (Christine Ebersole), owns the foreign-car repair shop where Phil works as a mechanic. It is inevitable that her teenage son, Nick, should be coerced into serving as Vada's guide and companion. The two kids dislike each other at first, but their gradually blossoming friendship is predictably one of the major story threads. The streetwise big-city boy is supposed to advise and protect the innocent small-town girl; however, Vada proves to be more aggressive and enterprising than Nick, leaving Austin O'Brien with a supporting role that does not offer him many opportunities to display his talents.

It turns out that the Los Angeles of the film is the same kind of whitewashed and sanitized metropolis that filmmakers have made of New York City when it has suited their convenience. Woody Allen set a precedent for this kind of instant cinematic gentrification in *Manhattan* (1979), when he showed couples conversing on park benches at midnight with no fear of muggers, rapists, drive-by shooters, or homicidal maniacs. Just as the truth about New York lies somewhere between *Manhattan* and *Escape from New York* (1981), the truth about Los Angeles lies somewhere between *My Girl II* and *Falling Down* (1993).

CREDITS

Harry Sultenfuss: Dan Aykroyd
Shelly Sultenfuss: Jamie Lee Curtis
Vada Sultenfuss: Anna Chlumsky
Nick Zsigmond: Austin O'Brien
Phil Sultenfuss: Richard Masur
Rose Zsigmond: Christine Ebersole
Jeffrey Pommeroy: John David Souther
Maggie Muldovan: Angeline Ball
Alfred Beidermeyer: Aubrey Morris
Dr. Sam Helburn: Gerrit Graham
Stanley Rosenfeld: Ben Stein
Daryl Tanaka: Keone Young
Arthur: Anthony R. Jones
Hilary Mitchell: Jodie Markell
Peter Webb: Richard Beymer

Released: 1994
Production: Brian Grazer for Imagine Films
Entertainment; released by Columbia Pictures
Direction: Howard Zieff
Screenplay: Janet Kovalcik
Cinematography: Paul Elliott
Editing: Wendy Greene Bricmont
Production design: Charles Rosen
Art direction: Diane Yates
Set design: Harold Fuhrman
Set decoration: Mary Olivia McIntosh
Casting: Alan Berger
Sound: John Sutton III
Costume design: Shelley Komarov
Music: Cliff Eidelman
MPAA rating: PG
Running time: 99 minutes

Vada has little to go on in her search for her mother's past. The two young sleuths manage to find a copy of Maggie's yearbook in the storeroom of the printing firm that produced the books for Maggie's high school. They use the yearbook and city phone directories to track down members of Maggie's graduating class. The quest leads them to such visually interesting sights as Grauman's Chinese Theatre, the backlot of a major motion-picture studio, and the La Brea tar pits on Wilshire Boulevard with the statue of the unfortunate mammoth being sucked into the sticky bog.

Since both children are too young to drive, they have to get around by public transportation, mainly on a surprisingly clean and uncrowded #7 Pico-Rimpau bus. They

"I enjoy working with good actors who feed off each other, who are comfortable with improv and who can give a quality to the scene that's far beyond what the original script was written to be...this entire ensemble can give me that, and it makes it a pleasure to come to work every day."—Director Howard Zieff on *My Girl II.*

meet various colorful and totally innocuous characters, including a comical Japanese-American cop (Keone Young), a superannuated poet (Aubrey Morris), and an egocentric film director (Richard Beymer), who all remember Vada's mother as a vivacious teenager but can tell little about her subsequent life except that Maggie was married and divorced before her marriage to Harry Sultenfuss. Vada begins to wonder whether Harry really is her father or whether she might be the daughter of Maggie's first husband, the mysterious and elusive Jeffrey Pommeroy (John David Souther).

Themes involving people searching for lost relatives were very popular in films and on television at the time of the film's release. Two semidocumentary television shows, *In Search of* and *Unsolved Mysteries*, relied heavily on stories about children seeking lost parents, parents seeking lost children, and other relatives attempting to be reunited. *My Girl II's* claim to social significance is in dealing with this important contemporary issue. The young heroine's search for information about her mother in the sprawling megalopolis begins to seem symbolic of the alienated condition of modern man.

Vada has never known what has come to be called an "Ozzie and Harriet" kind of family, consisting of loving parents who have never been married to anyone else and have no emotional attachments except to members of their own family. Children such as Zora (Nia Long) in *Made In America* (1993) are the unhappy products of the liberal attitude about love, sex, and marriage that developed in the Western world during the second half of the twentieth century. *My Girl II* seems to be saying that kids like Vada are experiencing identity crises because traditional marriage bonds are coming undone.

When Vada finally locates her mother's first husband in a picturesque home in Topanga Canyon, he proves to be a kindhearted man who not only can provide abundant information about the girl's mother but actually owns several grainy sixteen-millimeter sound films of Maggie frolicking with friends at the dawn of the 1960's. Pommeroy runs the films on his projector. This is a clever cinematic means of giving the audience a chance to share in Vada's discovery of her mother as she was in her vibrant youth. Pommeroy makes Vada a gift of the films, and she is now ready to go home to Pennsylvania. The viewer understands how this experience of seeming to meet her own mother in person effects a closure in the girl's quest for her personal identity. The home movies will augment Vada's oral presentation of her term paper and guarantee the A-plus she richly deserves.

Joe Leydon, reviewing the film for *Variety*, wrote: "*My*

Girl II is often mildly amusing, and never less than engaging, but it lacks a strong narrative drive." He also commented on the film's "lack of a sense of urgency." The lack of urgency and lack of a strong narrative drive are due to Vada's dubious motivation. It is hard to believe anyone would go all the way across the country to acquire background information for a term paper for a junior high school English class. The fact that she begins to suspect that Harry Sultenfuss is not her true father is a red herring; the whole question is disposed of in less than a minute when she meets Pommeroy.

The love story involving the two adults, Phil and Rose, is disappointing in contrast to that between Harry and Shelly, which served as an effective counterpoint to the juvenile love story in *My Girl*. Dr. Sam Helburn (Gerrit Graham), a wealthy pediatric cardiologist who brings his Jaguar sports coupe to the repair shop, takes an impetuous romantic interest in Rose and keeps returning for unneeded repairs just to have opportunities to woo her. Jealousy forces Phil to overcome his strong resistance to marriage and propose to Rose on the spot. This subplot has a campy, skit-like quality; it is hard to feel good about the prospects of a marriage based on such a shotgun proposal.

The puppy-love plot is hampered by the fact that Vada is not even on a summer vacation but can stay for only five days; the two children have no time to develop a strong relationship. When Nick gives Vada a good-bye kiss at the airport, it hardly represents enough of a bond to justify the title *My Girl II*, although Chlumsky and O'Brien, both good actors, make the best of the moment.

At the very end of the film one learns through Vada's voiceover interior monologue that Nick is coming to visit the Sultenfuss family in the summer. This seems to leave the door open for a "My Girl III" if the public response to *My Girl II* is sufficiently encouraging. The prospects do not look strong.

—*Bill Delaney*

REVIEWS

The Hollywood Reporter. February 11-13, 1994, p. 10.
Los Angeles Times. February 11, 1994, p. F6.
The New York Times. February 11, 1994, p. B12.
Variety. February 11, 1994, p. 4.

My Life's in Turnaround

"Laugh out loud funny."—Thelma Adams, *New York Post*

"A scrappy comedy with lots of charm!"—Janet Maslin, *The New York Times*

"A bouncy, unpredictable ride on the wild side!"—Bruce Williamson, *Playboy*

 Box Office Gross: $158,374 (August 14, 1994)

In this semiautobiographical comedy, screenwriters Eric Schaeffer and Donal Lardner Ward star and make their directorial debut as a New York cab driver and an alcoholic bartender who decide to become filmmakers. Unfortunately, they lack two key ingredients—talent and ambition.

REVIEWS

Entertainment Weekly. May 12, 1995, p. 72.
Mademoiselle. C, July 1994, p. 69.
Playboy. XLI, July 1994, p. 24.
Variety. CCCLI, May 17, 1993, p. 97.

CREDITS

Splick: Eric Schaeffer
Jason: Donal Lardner Ward
Sarah Hershfeld: Lisa Gerstein
Shrink: John Dore
Amanda: Debra Clein
Rachel: Dana Wheeler Nicholson
Beverly: Sheila Jaffe

Released: 1994
Production: Daniel Einfeld for Islet and Third Step, in association with Frontier Productions; released by Arrow Releasing
Direction: Eric Schaeffer and Donal Lardner Ward
Screenplay: Eric Schaeffer and Donal Lardner Ward
Cinematography: Peter Hawkins
Editing: Susan Graef
Music supervision: Susan Cirillo
Music: Reed Hays
MPAA rating: no listing
Running time: 84 minutes

My Sons (Musuko)

An aging father (Rentaro Mikuni), who lives in a rural village, strives to reconcile with his two sons (Ryuzo Tanaka and Masatoshi Nagase), who have moved to Tokyo, in this melodrama.

REVIEWS

Variety. CCCXLVII, July 13, 1992, p. 43.

CREDITS

Akio Asano: Rentaro Mikuni
Tetsuo: Masatoshi Nagase
Seiko Kawashima: Emi Wakui
Tadashi: Ryuzo Tanaka
Toshiko: Miyoko Asada
Reiko: Mieko Harada

Origin: Japan
Released: 1994
Production: Nobuyoshi Otani for Shochiku Company Ltd.
Direction: Yoji Yamada
Screenplay: Yoji Yamada and Yoshitaka Asama; based on the novel by Makoto Shiina
Cinematography: Tetsuo Takaba
Editing: Iwao Ishii
Production design: Mitsuo Degawa
Sound: Takashi Matsumato
Music: Teizo Matsumara
MPAA rating: no listing
Running time: 120 minutes

Naked Gun 33⅓: The Final Insult

"Mostly all new jokes."—Movie tagline

"Two thumbs up!"—*Siskel & Ebert*

"You'll laugh and beg for more."—Jeffrey Lyons, *Sneak Previews*

"Hilarious...scream-out-loud funny!"—Jack Matthews, *New York Newsday*

 Box Office Gross: $50,996,948 (July 24, 1994)

Leslie Nielsen as Lt. Frank Drebin and Priscilla Presley as Jane Spencer-Drebin in *Naked Gun 33⅓*. Copyright © 1994 Paramount Pictures. All rights reserved.

Trying to describe the plot of a *Naked Gun* film is almost irrelevant: Plot is the least of the filmmakers' concerns; it is but the flimsiest of excuses for stringing together a series of sight gags and parodies. In this outing—the third installment based on the short-lived *Police Squad* television show—the perennially obtuse hero, Lieutenant Frank Drebin (Leslie Nielsen), has retired from the force. Now, while his wife, Jane (Priscilla Presley), works as a trial lawyer, Frank stays home watching soap operas, baking muffins, and ironing the laundry while wearing fuzzy pink slippers.

Frank is talked into going back to work, however, when the squad needs him to go undercover to find out more about a terrorist mob's plans. These terrorists consist of Rocco (Fred Ward), the number-one terrorist, who was even responsible for Hurricane Andrew; his nasty mother (Kathleen Freeman); and his stacked, blonde, bombshell of a girlfriend, Tanya (Guess? jeans model Anna Nicole Smith). Eventually Frank earns Rocco's trust, but his joining the terrorist group jeopardizes his marriage to Jane. Yet, when the terrorist's target is discovered—the Academy Awards ceremony—Jane and Frank team up to foil their plans. The result is one of the two best scenes in the film.

The first is the opening sequence in which the filmmakers pay homage to the baby carriage/stairs scene used in both *The Battleship Potemkin* (1925) and *The Untouchables* (1987). Except here not only does a baby carriage roll down the stairs in the middle of a battle but so too do lawnmowers, the president, the pope, terrorists, and even disgruntled postal workers.

This scene is typical of the *Naked Gun* films: Take a famous scene from a classic (or even a not-so-classic) film

 *Naked Gun 33⅓* is the third film based on the television show *Police Squad*, which was cancelled after just six episodes.

 "Like a midget at a urinal, I had to keep on my toes"—Lt. Drebin in *Naked Gun 33⅓: The Final Insult*

and parody it. Also spoofed to humorous effect this time around are *White Heat* (1949), and *The Great Escape* (1963), *Thelma and Louise* (1991), *The Crying Game* (1992). Since lampooning films is one of *Naked Gun*'s fortes, it is only fitting that the climax of this one should take on the Academy Awards ceremony itself.

When Lieutenant Drebin discovers that a bomb has been placed in one of the award envelopes, his disruption of the Academy Awards ceremony causes the other best scene in the film. From ridiculing film titles—which here run the gamut of *Fatal Affair*, *Fatal Proposal*, and *Basic Analysis*—to caricaturing its glitzy guests, including "Weird Al" Yankovic and Vanna White, *Naked Gun 33⅓* takes on the ultimate sacred cow of the film industry. Every year, critics pan the musical numbers at the Oscars. It would be a sure bet, however, that the one performed by Pia Zadora to "This Could Be the Start of Something Big" with the clumsy Drebin taking the part of a backup dancer not only would interest the jaded Hollywood crowd but would live forever in Hollywood history as the most entertaining number ever performed at the ceremony.

Besides its on-target film parodies, the other strong point to a *Naked Gun* film is its many throwaway lines, sight gags, and background shenanigans. In the opening sequence, for example, Drebin is reading a newspaper with the following headline: "Dyslexia for Cure Found." A second viewing of these films is never boring, because there is always some insinuated joke or sly bit of silliness that is missed during the first viewing. This is also true for the credits: Never leave one of these films until the very last credit roles. In this third installment, however, these in-jokes and eagerly anticipated distracting bits of nonsense are scarcer and weaker than in previous offerings. In fact, what there are seem grosser and more mean-spirited. Previous *Naked Gun* films have been more intellectually challenging—if one is allowed to use those two words when discussing a *Naked Gun* film—in the gag department while this one seems to value bathroom humor more.

This might be the fault of director Peter Segal, whose major directing credit before this was television's *The Jackie Thomas Show*. The previous two *Naked Gun* films were both directed by David Zucker, one of the three zany talents behind 1980's *Airplane!* the film that started it all for the ZAZ team (David Zucker, his brother Jerry, and friend Jim Abrahams). Now content to write and produce this latest entry in the *Naked Gun* series, Zucker's touch is missed.

At least the film was able to count on the talents of its previous casts: George Kennedy, O. J. Simpson, Priscilla Presley, and David Zucker's mother, Charlotte, who is in every one of his films and who here plays a nurse at the Karlson Sperm Bank and Fertility Clinic. Yet it is Leslie Nielsen's incredibly deadpan acting amid a sea of stupidity that gives the film its true character. Nielsen's Drebin is the heart of the *Naked Gun* series, and as long as he continues to be the funniest bumbling police officer since Blake Edward's Inspector Clouseau, the *Naked Gun* films will continue to find box-office success with audiences.

—*Beverley Bare Buehrer*

CREDITS

Lieutenant Frank Drebin: Leslie Nielsen
Jane Spencer: Priscilla Presley
Ed Hocken: George Kennedy
Nordberg: O. J. Simpson
Rocco: Fred Ward
Muriel: Kathleen Freeman
Tanya: Anna Nicole Smith
Louise: Ellen Greene
Ted: Ed Williams
Papshmir: Raye Birke
Clayton: Matt Rowe
Defense attorney: Wylie Small
Nurse: Charlotte Zucker
Ann B. Davis: Ann B. Davis
Vanna White: Vanna White
"Weird Al" Yankovic: "Weird Al" Yankovic
Pia Zadora: Pia Zadora

Released: 1994
Production: Robert K. Weiss and David Zucker; released by Paramount Pictures
Direction: Peter Segal
Screenplay: Pat Proft, David Zucker, and Robert LoCash
Cinematography: Robert Stevens
Editing: James R. Symons
Production design: Lawrence G. Paull
Art direction: Bruce Crone
Set decoration: Kathe Klopp
Casting: Pamela Basker
Sound: Hank W. Garfield
Costume design: Mary E. Vogt
Music: Ira Newborn
MPAA rating: PG-13
Running time: 82 minutes

REVIEWS

Chicago Tribune. March 18, 1994, p. 7H.
Entertainment Weekly. April 1, 1994, p. 34.
Los Angeles Times. March 18, 1994, p. F6.
The New York Times. March 18, 1994, p. B5.
USA Today. March 18, 1994, p. 4D.
Variety. March 17, 1994, p. 4.

Naked in New York

"Comic flair! A first film with unusual panache."
—Caryn James, *The New York Times*

"Fresh and engaging! Celebrity spotting is part of the enjoyment."—Bruce Williamson, *Playboy*

Box Office Gross: $1,022,112 (August 7, 1994)

A year after leaving Columbia University's film production program, director Dan Algrant received a phone call from his one-time instructor, Martin Scorsese, who expressed an interest in producing a film for Algrant to direct. The film became *Naked in New York*. Recalls Scorsese, in the film's production notes, "A lot of film students and aspiring filmmakers seem to think it's very easy to get a film made. It isn't. And it's even more difficult to express something that's very personal in film, and beyond difficult to express it in visual terms. Dan's is a very unique and funny story that I thought deserved to be told."

Naked in New York chronicles the life of an aspiring playwright, Jake Briggs (Eric Stoltz), as he tries to have both a successful career and a life—a love life, in particular. Jake lives in Cambridge, Massachusetts, with his college sweetheart, a photographer, Joanne White (Mary-Louise Parker). When Chris (Ralph Macchio), one of Jake's college friends turned actor, convinces Jake to come to New York and helps interest a producer, Carl Fisher (Tony Curtis), in Jake's play, Jake's life becomes more than a little complex.

Over the course of the film, Jake works on pursuing a career and maintaining a relationship that becomes threatened by Joanne's handsome boss, Elliot Price (Timothy Dalton).

As Mr. Algrant's first feature film (although he had directed nearly a dozen short films and won two screenwriting competitions), *Naked in New York* is slick and impressive, yet much of it will remind filmgoers of other New York and art-scene angst films. Much of the film, in fact, is reminiscent of Woody Allen's films, in particular *Annie Hall* (1977). Beyond Stoltz's physical resemblance to Allen—each a red-haired, glasses-wearing worrier—both films chronicle love among the neurotic in New York, relying on voice-over, flashback, and hip pop-culture intellectualism to set the scene and tell the tale. Just as Allen sets the tone of *Annie Hall* with his voice-over citing his reluctance to join a club that would have anyone like him for a mem-

Mary-Louis Parker as Joanne White, Eric Stoltz as Jake Briggs, and Timothy Dalton as Elliot Price in *Naked in New York*. Photo: Bob Marshak © 1993 Fine Line Features. All rights reserved.

ber, Algrant sets the tone of his film by having Jake say, "One of the few things that I know about life, other than that it ends, is that it's a good idea to be with someone during it. Preferably someone you love."

Like many of Woody Allen's films, *Naked in New York* is semiautobiographical. Also, not unlike Allen's segment in *New York Stories* (1989), in which his mother has become so omnipresent as to grow to celestial-orb proportions, directing his life from her heavenly vantage point, Jake's mother, Shirley Briggs (Jill Clayburgh), is also omnipresent, although usually more needy and quirky than pushy. Whereas in *Annie Hall* Woody Allen's meaningful childhood memory is his mother's taking him to the doctor to deal with his fears of the expanding universe, Jake remembers himself as a baby, spinning on a lazy Susan in a Chinese restaurant on the day his parents broke up, which was also the night

> *Naked in New York* is the first feature film directed by Dan Algrant. It was originally conceived as a short film for his studies at Columbia University's film production program.

of the blackout in Manhattan. He further remembers that as a child he calmed his mother by leading her in a chant of "I am the master of my emotions," a statement they both now identify as a joke.

Appearing throughout the film are references to and appearances by pop icons, which is also part of the hip New York film tradition. In *Annie Hall*, Marshall McLuhan stepped from behind a film poster just in time to help Woody Allen flatten a pompous academic. In *Naked in New York*, one of the best and most entertaining sequences centers on Elliot's flying Jake and Joanne to Martha's Vineyard for the weekend. Reluctant to go and nervous on the flight, Jake balks at the music on the tape player. "Why is Patsy Cline playing on the tape? Is that a joke?" (Country-western singer Patsy Cline, who was experiencing a resurgence in popularity, had died in the crash of a private plane nearly thirty years before.) Attending a party brimming with literary superstars, Jake spots his hero William Styron (played by William Styron) and approaches him, telling him that he too is a writer and that he loves Styron's work and had read his novels before they were films. Styron snubs him completely. It is a great scene, even if not a surprisingly original idea. Also appearing in cameos are Richard Price, Quentin Crisp, Arthur Penn, and Eric Bogosian, as well as Whoopi Goldberg, who appears as the talking Mask of Tragedy that hangs above the theater where Jake's play is being performed.

 "One of the few things that I know about life, other than it ends, is that it's a good idea to be with someone during it. Preferably, someone you love."—Jake in *Naked in New York*.

Also entertaining in the film are Tony Curtis and Kathleen Turner, who play their characters broadly and with obvious delight. Carl Fisher (Curtis) is the pleasingly taste- less off-Broadway producer producing Jake's play. He insists on casting soap-opera egomaniac Dana Coles (Turner) in the lead role because, as he so colorfully puts it, "She makes the boat float." Where arguably Stoltz and Parker underplay their roles, although they play them well, clearly Curtis and Turner are over the top in their roles of, as one reviewer has dubbed them, "vulgar pussycat of a producer" and "blithely devouring star."

The film also draws heavily on a tradition of films about the angst of young artists in New York—such as *Slaves of New York* (1989) and "Life Lessons" in *New York Stories*— and arrives in a season of ensemble romantic comedies, such as *Reality Bites* (reviewed in this volume) and *Four Weddings and a Funeral* (reviewed in this volume). As with all such stories, *Naked in New York* has trouble making Jake's life look that bad. Sure, his play is being performed rather badly off-Broadway, but it is being performed. Sure, Jake gets Joanne's answering machine more than Joanne when he calls, but he is surrounded by people who care about him and are interested in his work. Nevertheless, the film is visually and verbally interesting to watch.

Algrant's film is indeed filled with entertaining details, even beyond Angelo Badalamenti's original and pleasing score and the visually interesting production design. For example, the story itself offers quirky surprises. After the performance of Jake's first play, which centered on a psychopathic, homicidal lumberjack, his college drama teacher, Mr. Reid (Roscoe Lee Browne), suggests that he seek help through the health services department. Jake also recalls living across the street from a nut factory that drove squirrels mad from the constant smell of roasting nuts. The film even offers one surprising sexual moment that is well acted and avoids being sensational, where it could have been just the opposite. That was a good judgment call by Algrant.

Naked in New York is not wholly original and is occasionally a bit much (fantasy sequences, self-conscious camera movements), yet it is a slick, self-assured, and entertaining debut film.

—*Roberta F. Green*

CREDITS

Jake Briggs: Eric Stoltz
Joanne White: Mary-Louise Parker
Chris: Ralph Macchio
Shirley Briggs: Jill Clayburgh
Carl Fisher: Tony Curtis
Elliot Price: Timothy Dalton
Helen: Lynne Thigpen
Dana Coles: Kathleen Turner
Mr. Reid: Roscoe Lee Browne
Tragedy Mask: Whoopi Goldberg

Released: 1994
Production: Frederick Zollo; released by Fine Line Features
Direction: Dan Algrant
Screenplay: Dan Algrant and John Warren; based on a story by Algrant
Cinematography: Joey Forsyte
Editing: Bill Pankow
Production design: Kalina Ivanov
Casting: Bonnie Timmermann
Costume design: Julie Weiss
Music supervision: Bonnie Greenberg and Jill Meyers
Music: Angelo Badalamenti
MPAA rating: R
Running time: 91 minutes

REVIEWS

Boston Globe. April 29, 1994, p. 60.
Chicago Tribune. April 29, 1994, p. B.
Entertainment Weekly. April 29, 1994, p. 54.
The Hollywood Reporter. January 25, 1994, p. 10.
Los Angeles Times. April 15, 1994, p. F15.
The New York Times. April 15, 1994, p. B1.

Natural Born Killers

"Brilliant. Hypnotic. Revolutionary."—Owen Gleiberman, *Entertainment Weekly*

"The most radical film any major studio has released since *A Clockwork Orange*...gonzo brilliance"—Stephen Schiff, *The New Yorker*

"Oliver Stone comes roaring in with a commentary on American violence and the media—a big, dazzling, chillingly kaleidoscopic portrait of a whole nation hooked on posing for the camera."—John Powers, *Vogue*

"10. Ruthlessly funny. Packs the visual punch of a neutron bomb."—David E. Williams, *Film Threat*

"Bravura filmmaking."—Corie Brown, *Premiere*

 Box Office Gross: $50,215,954 (January 2, 1995)

Two-time Academy Award winner Oliver Stone roars back onscreen with a vengeance with *Natural Born Killers*, a manic sensory assault on murder, poisoned pop culture, and the media. While there still exists those moments of his trademarked heavy handedness, Stone's audacious filmmaking secures his place as a true American original. The film's message may not be anything particularly new, but more than any other film in recent history, *Natural Born Killers* succeeds in shaking its audience out of its viewing complacency. From practically its first frame, it is clear that this is not your typical Hollywood fare, and it certainly is not any kind of "opiate for the masses."

Mickey (Woody Harrelson) and Mallory (Juliette Lewis) Knox are young, devoted lovers on the lam, a postmodern Bonnie and Clyde for the 1990's. Unlike the characters in previous tortured teen films, such as *Gun Crazy: Deadly is the Female* (1949), *Badlands* (1973), and 1993's *Guncrazy*, there is nothing tormented about this pair. They relish killing, not out of a sense of injustice but merely for the sheer thrill of it. They are a pair of bloodthirsty—victims of both abusive parents and a junk-food culture (admittedly the weakest link in the story, a conceit that negates the power of, as Mickey later tells his viewing audience, "naturally being born bad"). Mickey and Mallory are pure American killers, and Stone floods the screen with images intended as a jumbled reflection of their

 "If I don't kill you, what's there to talk about?"—Mickey Knox from *Natural Born Killers*

inner world of memory and desire. The filmmaker shocked many by depicting Mallory's childhood sexual abuse as a perverted *I Love Lucy* sitcom episode, complete with laugh track and a brilliantly cast Rodney Dangerfield as the lecherous, molesting father. (It is interesting to note that *I Love Lucy* is embraced by generations of television viewers despite Lucy's repeated, wailing pleas to "Don't hit me, Ricky!") Carrying a fifty-pound package of blood-dripping red meat, Mickey appears as Mallory's knight-in-shining-armor, liberating the killer within.

The first half of *Natural Born Killers* depicts Mickey and Mallory's bloodthirsty spree along New Mexico's Route 666, during which fifty-two people are savagely slaughtered. When a character begs for his life to be spared, Mickey viscously reminds him, "Then there'd be nothing to talk about," referring to the growing media hype and the public's increasing fascination with the couple. There is scarcely a character present who does not seek some sort of fame through the Knoxes. The totality of television's tabloid journalism is succinctly represented in the pandering host of *American Maniacs*, Wayne Gale (an inspired Robert Downey, Jr.), an Australian cross between shockmeister Geraldo Riviera and Robin Leach, who will do anything for the highest rates. Actor Tom Sizemore appears as the brutish law enforcement officer, Jack Scagnetti, a published expert on serial killers who seeks even greater fame and a possible new best-seller as the man who eventually captures the the infamous couple. After Mallory seduces and murders a young filling station attendant (Balthazar Getty), and Micky kills a kindly Indian shaman out of sheer reflex (to which Mallory reprimands him with a hilarious, "Bad! Bad, bad, bad, bad, very bad!"), the snake-bitten and delirious couple end up in a drugstore seeking venom antidote. What they get instead is captured.

After their capture, Mickey and Mallory become even bigger stars at their trial. Well-wishers in the crowd outside the courthouse hoist placards reading "Murder Me, Mickey!" and people, fuelled by the media, cannot get enough of "M&M." In prison, under the auspices of the unhinged warden Dwight McCluskey (Tommy Lee Jones), the couple are tortured but, even worse, are separated. McCluskey plots to quietly eliminate them with Scagnetti's help, thus ensuring enduring fame as the man responsible for their deaths. Gale, meanwhile, sets out to capture his highest ratings ever by conducting a live broadcast interview with Mickey following football's Super Bowl. Mickey's survival instincts grant him the power to instigate a full-fledged prison riot that leads to the couple's eventual escape. To the very end, Oliver Stone denies society any measure of redemption.

Whether the viewer chooses to embrace the film or to be repulsed by the violence contained within, there is no denying that Oliver Stone is a man of definite and distinct creative vision. Rather than be complacent with presenting a straight narrative about mass murderers, Stone pushes the story of *Natural Born Killers* into the realm of nearly pure emotion. For a solid two hours, Stone offers a sensational

visceral experience, bombarding the viewer's senses, both visually and aurally, with a psychedelic hodgepodge of non-stop music (an eclectic blend of some seventy-five songs in the score produced by Trent Reznor of the alternative music group Nine Inch Nails), combined with every conceivable cinematic trick employed in both mainstream and avant-garde filmmaking. Stone utilizes slow motion, morphing, rear projection, pixillation, and even animation on five different film stocks, resulting in a continual shift of black and white and blood-drenched color. The images are momentarily raw and grainy, camera askew, violence exploding on-screen, then just as quickly they mutate into moments of eerie tenderness.

The only way the viewer can sit through *Natural Born Killers* is to surrender to it, to allow the barrage of images to wash over and to resist any attempts at instantaneous analysis. Stone takes the sensory-rich, non-narrative 1983 film *Koyaanisqatsi* (Hopi Indian for "life out of balance") one step farther by providing both a story and scathing social commentary. The rapid-fire editing, which took a gruelling eleven months to complete, intensifies the impressionistic feeling, with each two-frame flash well-planned, and builds towards the film's end. The editing keeps the audience at an emotional distance from violence, while almost simultaneously, it allows the viewer to understand and react to the euphoria that the bloodthirsty characters feel when they kill. The violence contained within *Natural Born Killers* has a surreal quality to it, more comic and caricatured than horrific—which is part of Stone's thesis. American pop culture thrives on making mass murderers, who deserve vilification, into pop icons. Simultaneously, the media glorifies the general public's fascination with violence while it also reviles the level of violence presented on television and in films.

Natural Born Killers triggered an onslaught of negative criticism from reviewers who believed that Stone, unlike the more hip Quentin Tarantino (on whose story *Natural Born Killers* is based), bought into the very concepts he sought to satirize and that Stone had far too much fun and embraced the violence far too passionately. While Tarantino seems fully to embrace the insignificance of his characters' lives and escapades, Stone seeks to explore a greater meaning. His films have consistently sought to indict various aspects of American culture, be it the country's involvement in the Vietnam War or the John

CREDITS

Mickey Knox: Woody Harrelson
Mallory Knox: Juliette Lewis
Wayne Gale: Robert Downey, Jr.
Dwight McClusky: Tommy Lee Jones
Jack Scagnetti: Tom Sizemore
Mallory's dad: Rodney Dangerfield
Old Indian: Russell Means
Mallory's mom: Edie McClurg
Gas station attendant: Balthazar Getty
Duncan Homolka: Joe Grifasi
Mabel: O-Lan Jones

Released: 1994
Production: Jane Hamsher, Don Murphy, and Clayton Townsend for Ixtlan/New Regency, in association with J D Productions, and Warner Bros., in association with Regency Enterprises and Alcor Films; released by Warner Bros.
Direction: Oliver Stone
Screenplay: David Veloz, Richard Rutowski, and Oliver Stone; based on a story by Quentin Tarantino
Cinematography: Robert Richardson
Editing: Hank Corwin
Editing: Brian Berdan
Production design: Victor Kempster
Art direction: Alan R. Tomkins and Margery Zweizig
Set design: John Perry Goldsmith and Stella Furner
Set decoration: Merideth Boswell
Animation design: Mike Smith
Casting: Risa Bramon Garcia, Billy Hopkins and Heidi Levitt
Visual effects: Pacific Data Images
Sound: David MacMillan
Costume design: Richard Hornung
Music production: Budd Carr
Soundtrack: Trent Reznor
MPAA rating: R
Running time: 120 minutes

AWARDS AND NOMINATIONS

Golden Globe Awards Nomination 1994: Best Director (Stone)
MTV Movie Awards Nominations 1995: Best Kiss (Harrelson/Lewis), Best On-Screen Duo (Harrelson/Lewis)

Kennedy assassination conspiracy theory. Renown film critics insist that Stone is incapable of satire, that his passion rendered him unable to maintain the kind of detachment necessary, thus negating the film's satiric intent. The American Heritage Dictionary defines satire as "irony, sarcasm or caustic wit used to attack or expose human folly, vice or stupidity," and while Stone may definitely be lacking in irony, his sarcasm, his contempt, and his ridicule of tabloid journalism and American "couch-potato" society seem quite blatant.

— *Patricia Kowal*

REVIEWS

Entertainment Weekly. August 26, 1994, p. 90.
The Hollywood Reporter. August 8, 1994, CCCXXXIII, p. 6.
Los Angeles Times. August 26, 1994, CXIII, p. F1.
Macleans. CVII, August 29, 1994, p. 52.
New York. XXVII, September 5, 1994, p. 46.
The New York Times. August 26, 1994, CXLIII, p. B1.
The New Yorker. LXX, September 5, 1994, p. 106.
Rolling Stone. September 8, 1994, p. 83.
San Francisco Chronicle. August 26, 1994, CXCI, p. C1.
Time. CXLIV, August 29, 1994, p. 66.
Variety. August 8, 1994, CCXLIV, p. 2.
Village Voice. August 26, 1994, XXXIX, p. 41.
The Washington Post. August 26, 1994, p. D1.

Nell

"An extraordinary motion picture about the power of innocence."—Movie tagline

"One of the best pictures of the year!"—David Sheehan, *CBS-TV*

"Jody Foster is brilliant! A sensitive, beautiful film you will long remember."—Jeffrey Lyons, *Sneak Previews/ABC World News Now*

"Jodie Foster gives a fearless, fierce, beautifully attuned performance."—Richard Corliss, *Time*

"A Wonderful Film."—Joel Siegel, *Good Morning America, WABC-TV*

"Two enthusiastic thumbs up!"—*Siskel & Ebert*

Box Office Gross: $12,545,874 (January 2, 1995)

The concept of the "wild child," a person who has been reared in complete isolation from society and culture, is an intriguing one, which raises questions about human experience, language, and the disparities between nature and culture. The complexities of this idea have been explored in such films as Werner Herzog's *The Mystery of Kaspar Hauser* (1975) and François Truffaut's *The Wild Child* (1969). *Nell*, a contemporary rendition of this theme, is in some senses beautifully crafted, but ultimately fails to live up to its predecessors in insight, achieving instead the broad appeal of the sentimental.

Based on the play *Idioglossia* by Mark Handley, *Nell* tells the story of a woman (Jodie Foster) reared by a reclusive mother in rural North Carolina, whose isolation and private language troubles social workers who come to her "aid." The film takes issue more with the question of how modern society responds to Nell, than with how Nell responds to modern society. The assumption that Nell needs society is met with the discovery that perhaps society needs Nell. It also raises the interesting questions of whether the possibility of isolation from society still exists and whether difference can be tolerated in a culture created and sustained by norms.

The film opens with the camera following a dirt bike as it travels farther and farther into nature, first along roads, then trails, then tangled paths through the woods, until it finally arrives at an old, broken house on a lake. The driver unloads groceries and prepares to leave but is startled by a twisted howl of pain and some incomprehensible utterances. He enters the house hesitantly and finds the corpse of an elderly woman laid out on the floor with daisies in her eye sockets, and he flees in horror.

When the authorities come to retrieve the body, the local doctor, Jerome Lovell (Liam Neeson), finds a woman crouched like an animal in a dark corner of the house. To everyone's surprise, the hermit had borne a daughter, Nell, and reared her with no contact from the outside world. This scene illustrates well the horror of what is hidden, unknown, secret, or strange to human experience. The discovery is met with fear, confusion, and an immediate urge to flee, followed later by curiosity.

The doctor informs a psychologist, Paula Olsen (Natasha Richardson), of the situation and takes her to the house to get her opinion. She immediately assumes Nell is suffering from a serious mental disorder and decides to take blood samples, despite Nell's terror, and make arrangements

CREDITS

Nell: Jodie Foster
Jerome Lovell: Liam Neeson
Paula Olsen: Natasha Richardson
Alexander Paley: Richard Libertini
Todd Peterson: Nick Searcy
Mary Peterson: Robin Mullins
Billy Fisher: Jeremy Davies

Released: 1994
Production: Renée Missel and Jodie Foster for Egg Pictures; released by Twentieth Century-Fox
Direction: Michael Apted
Screenplay: William Nicholson and Mark Handley; based on the play *Idioglossia*, by Handley
Cinematography: Dante Spinotti
Editing: Jim Clark
Production design: Jon Hutman
Art direction: Tim Galvin
Set decoration: Samara Hutman
Casting: Linda Lowy
Sound: Chris Newman
Costume design: Susan Lyall
Music: Mark Isham
MPAA rating: PG-13
Running time: 113 minutes

AWARDS AND NOMINATIONS

Academy Awards Nomination 1994: Best Actress (Foster)
Golden Globe Awards Nominations 1994: Best Film—Drama, Best Actress—Drama (Foster), Best Score
MTV Movie Awards Nomination 1995: Best Female Performance (Foster)
Screen Actors Guild Awards 1994: Best Actress (Foster)

guage. The body of the film consists of the gradual discoveries and personal growth of the characters as they begin to pull their resources together in the attempt to break the mysterious code that separates them from the world of Nell.

What they gradually learn is that Nell speaks a private, but rational, language based on the distorted speech patterns of her mother, who had suffered a stroke. She has also inherited her mother's fears and distrust of men. Her mother had apparently been a victim of rape who had recoiled into solitude as a result of unhappiness and dissatisfaction with the world. Another significant discovery occurs when Jerome and Paula coax Nell into leaving her house during the day (she only leaves at night).

Feeling the breeze and the sun, Nell takes off in ecstatic abandon, following the trails and contours of the land that she recalls from her childhood day excursions. Jerome and Paula follow, and Nell introduces them to the burial site where the skeleton of her twin sister lies with flowers in its eyes. This discovery illuminates the many scenes of Nell gazing into the mirror, touching her reflection and uttering the word "May." Nell's relationship with the mirror can be seen both as the attempt to reestablish the lost ideal of perfect union and understanding, and a submersion into the self, the ultimate solitude of narcissism.

The most successful component of the film is the performance of two-time Academy Award winner Jodie Foster, who also coproduced the film— the first for Foster's new production company. Foster achieves a stark simplicity and beauty, and reveals through her body and gestures the most primal forms of expression and communication, reminiscent of dance and the

for her removal. She later begins to share the opinion of psychiatrist Alexander Paley (Richard Libertini) that Nell must be quietly institutionalized for her own protection before the outside world and media discover her.

The response of the social scientists further illustrates the inability of culture to tolerate what exists outside itself. It also sets up the conflict between the sympathetic doctor, Jerome, who begins to explore secretly Nell's world from a distance, and Paula, the psychologist. When Paula arrives with a court order for Nell's removal, she is barred by Jerome who references a law requiring verbal consent from the subject. A judge hears their arguments and rules that there be further study of Nell and that a judgment be made in three months time.

Two-time Academy Award winner Jodie Foster also co-produced *Nell*—the first for Foster's new production company, Egg Pictures.

Jerome and Paula proceed to set up separate posts outside Nell's cabin. Their different approaches establish their conflicting characters. Paula arrives in a well-equipped houseboat and proceeds to plant audiovisual equipment inside Nell's cabin in order to engage in twenty-four-hour surveillance from the comforts of her boat. Jerome sets up a simple one-man tent and approaches Nell directly, trying on her terms to establish trust and learn the rules of her lan-

expressive freedom of childhood. The freedom of Nell contrasts with the restraint and professionalism of Paula, a woman removed from her own authentic experience by submersion in a specialized field that studies the self from a scientific vantage point.

The happy surrogate family is disrupted by the inevitable appearance of the press, which threatens to destroy the fragile truth of Nell by bringing it into the objectifying gaze of the public and media-driven society. When the news helicopter appears above the shack, Jerome succumbs to the pressure of Dr. Paley and institutionalizes Nell. When Nell becomes despondent and catatonic in her new environment, however, Jerome, in desperation, steals her from the hospital and checks into a hotel with her. He has found himself in a seemingly unresolvable conflict: He cannot hide with Nell forever, yet she cannot be returned to her rural privacy and freedom.

 "Everybody who cares for someone has an ulterior motive—even Mother Teresa. She wants to know that her life has been of some use to others."—Dr. Paley in *Nell*

Jerome is a weary man who has fled the city to seek refuge in the country. He sees in Nell a symbol of his own desires for escape and an authentic, simple existence. Nell in this context has become the coveted subject, a symbol of that private realm which resists conformity and is at odds with contemporary culture. At this point in the film, it becomes apparent that there is no escape, nowhere to hide, and the Holiday Inn becomes the last pathetic refuge of subjectivity. Yet rather than indulge in an ending of the sort that occurs in paranoid films such as *Invasion of the Body Snatchers* (1956), where everyone is absorbed and the soul is no match for the greater force of social institutions, *Nell* insists on optimism and lapses into unbelievable melodrama, which must inevitably leave many questions unanswered.

Paula comes to the hotel and expresses her support for Jerome, and they decide to leave the solution to the courts. The scene shifts to the courtroom, where things do not appear to be going well, since Nell has fallen deeper and deeper into silence and resembles in every aspect an emotionally disturbed person. The situation turns around dramatically when Nell stands and makes a last-minute testimony, translated through Jerome, whereby she expresses her knowledge of love, loss, and mortality, and thereby convinces the courts of her mental equality.

The final scene shifts to five years into the future. Paula and Jerome are married and have borne a daughter. They are driving to Nell's house in the woods, where they are met with an assortment of locals who have all come to picnic and celebrate. One sees a silhouette of Nell and the young daughter standing out on the rocks in the lake, their gestures expressing a joy and pleasure with nature. The others watch from the shore and speak of how much they had needed Nell without even knowing it. At this point it is to be believed that the courts made it all right, the media went away, Nell found a niche with the locals, and these two divergent characters married and found happiness. Besides being unbelievable, this ending makes light of all the difficult issues raised by the story.

The script, adapted by William Nicholson from the work of playwright Mark Handley, is the greatest shortcoming of the film. The dialogue resorts too often to clichés to reflect a colloquial simplicity in the rural characters, and as a result it never achieves the kind of complexity the topic deserves. The film adopts an Enlightenment conception of human life, championed by Jean-Jacques Rousseau—the natural state is one of purity, and civilization, or culture, corrupts. The cinematography, done beautifully by Dante Spinotti, also depicts nature as a mystical paradise of twilights, misty dawns, and fresh, sparkling waters. Ultimately, in its effort to maintain an idealistic portrayal of nature and conclude optimistically, the film sacrifices greater ambitions.

—*Reni Celeste*

REVIEWS

Chicago Sun-Times. December 23, 1994, p. 33.
Daily Variety. December 5, 1994, p. 6.
Entertainment Weekly. December 16, 1994, p. 48.
The Hollywood Reporter. December 5, 1994, p. 8.
Los Angeles Times. December 14, 1994, p. F1.
The New York Times. December 14, 1994, p. B1.
Newsweek. December 19, 1994, p. 64.

Nervous Ticks

"For 90 minutes, York Daley's life will be a living hell...and you get to watch!"—Movie tagline

A harried airport luggage handler, York (Bill Pullman), works against the clock so that he can escape to Rio with his married girlfriend, Nancy (Julie Brown), in this frenetic comedy. Among the many delays York encounters, he is taken hostage during a major drug deal and must also deal with Nancy's last-minute decision to murder her husband, Ron (Peter Boyle).

REVIEWS

Variety. CCCXLVI, April 13, 1992, p. 66.

CREDITS

York: Bill Pullman
Nancy: Julie Brown
Ron Rudman: Peter Boyle
Cole: Brent Jennings
Rusty: James Le Gros
Cheshire: Paxton Whitehead

Released: 1992
Production: Arthur Goldblatt for Grandview Avenue Pictures; released by I.R.S. Releasing
Direction: Rocky Lang
Screenplay: David Frankel
Cinematography: Bill Dill
Editing: Carri Coughlin
Production design: Naomi Shohan
Art direction: Dan Whifler
Set decoration: Amy Wells
Sound: Tony Smyles
Music: Jay Ferguson
MPAA rating: R
Running time: 90 minutes

The New Age

"A shopping spree for the morally bankrupt."
—Movie tagline

"Entertaining and comedic. Weller and Davis are outstanding."—Paul Wunder, *WBAI Radio, New York*

"The sexiest, smartest comedy this decade has produced."—Polly Frost, *Harper's Bazaar*

 Box Office Gross: $231,884 (October 16, 1994)

The New Age is writer/director Michael Tolkin's satiric saga of the fall of a chic Los Angeles couple from the ladder of success. Having hit bottom, they spend most of their time trying to manage the expense of maintaining an image, while searching for the next rung of spiritual enlightenment. The film opens with yoga teacher Sarah Friedberg (Rachel Rosenthal) lecturing and pacing. She looks wise and ominous in her glasses and bald head, and speaks a yoga dialect understood by initiates. The scene sets the stage for Tolkin's jabs at so-called New Age religions in this seriocomic yet sympathetic study of New Age materialism, New Age hip health and well-being, and New Age sexual mores. In general, Tolkin points to the most disquieting aspect of postmodern life: truths ring hollow and authenticity must remain questionable. Seduction offers no sensual satisfaction; success means false sense of well-being; and that nice little gift (especially the one offered over the phone) is most likely to become a Trojan horse.

Tolkin manages his satire carefully. His story and characters are smart. Their questions, self-assuredness, and vulnerability are studied with seriousness and compassion, before they are derided. How important are personal wealth and prestige? What is spiritual growth, and how can it be done? Are personal needs fully supported? Are all brain cells and intuition being used? Is it alright to sleep with anybody? Does heaven exist?

CREDITS

Peter Witner: Peter Weller
Katherine Witner: Judy Davis
Jean Levy: Patrick Bauchau
Jeff Witner: Adam West
Sarah Friedberg: Rachel Rosenthal
Dale Deveaux: Samuel L. Jackson
Kevin Bulasky: Corbin Bernsen
Paul Hartmann: Jonathan Hadary
Anna: Patricia Heaton
Sandi Rego: Audra Lindley
Alison Gale: Paula Marshall
Laura: Maureen Mueller
Bettina: Tanya Pohlkotte
Misha: Bruce Ramsay
Mary Netter: Sandra Seacat
Ellen Saltonstall: Susan Traylor

Released: 1994
Production: Nick Wechsler and Keith Addis for Regency Enterprises, Alcor Films, and Ixtlan/Addis-Wechsler; released by Warner Bros.
Direction: Michael Tolkin
Screenplay: Michael Tolkin
Cinematography: John J. Campbell
Editing: Suzanne Fenn
Production design: Robin Standefer
Executive producer: Oliver Stone and Arnon Milchan
Art direction: Kenneth A. Hardy
Set design: Barbara Ann Jaekel
Set decoration: Claire Jenora Bowin
Casting: Deborah Aquila
Sound: Stephen Halpert
Costume design: Richard Shissler
Music: Mark Mothersbaugh
MPAA rating: R
Running time: 112 minutes

Katherine Witner (Judy Davis), a struggling graphic artist, is in her office, angrily destroying computer files because her biggest client has just failed. Consequently, her whole business is also failing. Hence, she goes shopping. Katherine's husband, Peter (Peter Weller), meanwhile, has received a reprimand in the boardroom for his lack of committment to the company, a talent agency. He decides to resign so that he can exercise his true potential. This happens after he goes on a shopping trip. He leaves the office and stops by for a quick rendezvous with his girlfriend, Alison Gale (Paula Marshall).

Katherine and Peter meet at their beautiful, art-filled home in Beverly Hills, share agonizing reports, and make desultory love. Katherine is upset because Peter, she insists, makes love to her unfairly—concealing himself in other personae. They decide to give a party to bolster their confidence.

The party is swank and paid for by credit cards. During the evening, the Witners meet a local guru who tells them that they have blocked energies. Peter flirts doggedly with women, and Katherine tries to ignore his performance. Quite uncharacteristically, she allows herself to be seduced by a handsome cafe owner, whom she has watched. Misha (Bruce Ramsay) tells her what she already knew but hated to know: that her husband is regularly unfaithful.

A sun-drenched morning contrasts with the dark party scenes of the night before. Peter and Katherine discuss their splintered marriage from opposite sides of the pool. Their argument contains all the buzzwords one would expect from a pair of contemporary Californian elite. Peter wants more support, Katherine needs to find herself—needs her own space. They sit close together and declare their love, and weep. Their lack of income, however, seems to upset them the most. Then, Katherine suggests that they live separate lives but share the same house. Peter agrees. The arrangement seems to work, although both have a hard time hiding their jealousy of the other's new partner.

By the time the guru, Jean Levy (Patrick Bauchau) reappears, they are ripe for guidance. He asks them of what they are afraid, and Katherine suggests "real jobs." In answer to what she does best, she jokes, "Shop!" Of their bad situation, Jean declares that they should realize that "in Chinese the word for crisis is the word for opportunity." Katherine and Peter decide to open a store. The very posh store, named Hypocracy (from hypocrite and bureaucracy), is designed with the help of Jean and other spiritualists, who measure intangible vibrations to help place its entrances.

The store does well for about a week. Peter and Katherine continue to endure chaotic emotions for each other and sleep with their new lovers under the same roof. Meanwhile, the bank is about to foreclose on their home. While the store is dying, they learn that their friend Laura (Maureen Mueller) is dying; they are invited to attend her last ceremony, a suicide ritual. It is during this emotional scene that Katherine and Peter are awakened, if only momentarily, to something real: Laura's decision to end her own life, right or wrong, is willful and decisive and thus seems to give her life and suffering some meaning. Their own chronic indecision over much less important details, and their inability to act for themselves or for each other has stagnated their lives. The suicide ceremony is enacted with a background of softspoken people droning chants and ringing triangles. Neither Witner, however, embraces the New Age response to suicide—and Peter seems especially troubled by his inability to place Laura's death into any meaningful context or into a traditionally religious response. Katherine and Peter reunite in a love rekindled by mutual grief and confusion.

Their reunion cannot endure Peter's continued trysts, however. Finally, Katherine stumbles on her husband with Jean Levy's assistant Bettina (Tanya Pohlkotte). This happens while Katherine and Peter are guests at the Lone Pine ranch for a spiritual retreat led by Levy. (Levy's spiritual maxims become more and more ridiculous: "To be born human and not a snake is a tremendous opportunity.") The trouble with Peter is that he is his father's son: egotistical, vain, and unrepentant in his unfaithfulness to Katherine. Jeff Witner (Adam West) is a cold-hearted businessman whose chief enterprise seems to be having affairs with very young and beautiful women. The man's compassion for his son's business dilemma is just about nil: When Peter goes to Dad, finally, for help for Hypocracy, Mr. Witner writes him a worthless check for $10,000.

"Your inner child is running us into bankruptcy! Why don't you get in touch with your inner adult?"—Katherine Witner to newly jobless husband Peter in *The New Age*

The final scenes of Katherine's and Peter's disillusionment reflect the moral and spiritual bankruptcy of America's new age. Attempting to deal with Peter's betrayal and discovering that she has no will to find an answer, Katherine goes reluctantly to Sarah's women-only drumming circle. In the middle of her own cleansing ritual, she bolts away, blurting that she cannot feel anything. Peter, likewise, experiences numbness, much to his surprise, at a group sadomasochistic sex salon he has found. Now, though, with a virtual smorgasbord of sex offered to him, he is unable to respond. Instead, he becomes the wallflower loitering at the hors d'oeuvres table, nibbling half-heartedly while nude women cavort and beckon from a heated pool. Apparently no remedy from the New Age spiritual medicine chest will help repair the Witners or their chronic neurotic ills.

Even suicide does not work for them. As well-planned as theirs at first seems to be, the attempt turns out to be fake. The exquisitely executed ritual is hollow, except that Katherine, who engineers the suicide pact as a final deception for Peter to enjoy, finally gains her freedom. The stylized death scene seems to serve for her as an annullment of their marriage and all other liaisons. Peter goes on to find that what he does best is telemarketing; that is, his greatest talent lies in duping and cheating people out of their hard

earned dollars. These final scenes provide some comedy, black as it is, to temper the realization of just how dark Peter's life has become. Katherine finds success as the proprietor of an upscale eyewear boutique, the metaphor for her newly found insight.

In 1991, Michael Tolkin seemed to appear from nowhere with *The Rapture* (1991), a medium-budget film with a provoking engagement of born-again Christian fundamentalism. The unsettling story contrasts images of modern-life-as-limbo with the protagonist's religious fantasies. Tolkin also wrote the screenplays for Graeme Clifford's *Gleaming the Cube* (1989) and Robert Altman's *The Player* (1992). In his novels and filmscripts, he focuses on the sociological subcultures of Los Angeles: the swingers and born-again Christians in *The Rapture*; the film industry in *The Player*; and the drug underworld in Bill Duke's *Deep Cover* (1992). In *The New Age*, the writer/director studies the cult of materialism—its nihilism, its self-reflexive scrutiny, its giddiness, its desolation—and people's brave, perverse, perhaps even touching attempt to infuse themselves with a healing spirituality. With its clever, compassionate script and brilliant performances, *The New Age* establishes Michael Tolkin as an important new talent in 1990's cinema.

—*JoAnn Balingit*

REVIEWS

Entertainment Weekly. September 30, 1994, p. 38.
Film Comment. XXX, September-October 1994, p. 54.
The Hollywood Reporter. September 6, 1994, p. 10.
Los Angeles Times. September 16, 1994, p. F9.
The New York Times. September 16, 1994, p. B4.
Premiere. September 1994, p. 40.
Premiere. October 1994, p. 68.
Time. CXLIV, September 26, 1994, p. 78.
Variety. CCCLVI, September 5, 1994, p. 53.

New York in Short: The Shvitz and Let's Fall in Love

N *ew York in Short* is composed of two short films: *The Shvitz*, which centers on the history of Jewish steam baths in New York City, and *Let's Fall in Love: A Singles' Weekend at the Concord Hotel*, which focuses on a singles mixer at a resort hotel in the Catskills.

CREDITS

Released: 1994
Production: Jonathan Berman (*The Shvitz*) and Constance Marks (*Let's Fall in Love*)
Direction: Jonathan Berman (*The Shvitz*) and Constance Marks (*Let's Fall in Love*)
Cinematography: Evan Estern (*The Shvitz*), Laurence Salzmann (*The Shvitz*), Ellen Kuras (*The Shvitz*) and Michael Mayers (*Let's Fall in Love*)
Editing: Amanda Zinoman (*The Shvitz*) and Deborah Dickson (*Let's Fall in Love*)
Music: The Klezmatics/Frank London (*The Shvitz*)
MPAA rating: no listing
Running time: 80 minutes

The Next Karate Kid

"Who says the good guy has to be a guy?"
—Movie tagline

"Finally! A movie about a young girl's coming of age...The humor is light and fresh and the message is easy to take."—*The Chicago Sun-Times*

"Hilary Swank does a fine job in a demanding role"—*The Boston Globe*

 Box Office Gross: $8,735,777 (November 20, 1994)

Martial-arts master Miyagi (Noriyuki "Pat" Morita) takes on a new pupil—teenage Julie Pierce (Hilary Swank)—in this sequel to The *Karate Kid* trilogy. Angry and bitter over the death of her parents, Julie blossoms under Miyagi's sage guidance and finds romance with a fellow high school student (Chris Conrad).

Pat Morita, as Mr. Miyagi, trains a new pupil, Hilary Swank as Julie Pierce, in *The Next Karate Kid*. Copyright © 1994 Columbia Pictures Industries Inc. All Rights Reserved. Courtesy of Columbia Pictures.

REVIEWS

Atlanta Constitution. September 13, 1994, p. C5.
Boston Globe. September 10, 1994, p. 71.
Chicago Tribune. September 11, 1994, Sec. 5 p. 7.
Entertainment Weekly. September 30, 1994, p. 39.
Entertainment Weekly. February 10, 1995, p. 78.
Los Angeles Times. September 12, 1994, p. F2.
The New York Times. September 10, 1994, p. A14.
The New York Times. September 18, 1994, Sec. 2 p. 25.
People Weekly. XLII, September 26, 1994, p. 20.
USA Today. September 12, 1994, p. D4.
Variety. CCCLVI, August 22, 1994, p. 56.
The Wall Street Journal. October 5, 1994, p. A14.
The Washington Post. September 10, 1994, p. C3.
The Washington Post. September 15, 1994, p. C1.

 "Grief trapped in heart become big anger"—Mr. Miyagi, in *The Next Karate Kid*

CREDITS

Mr. Miyagi: Noriyuki "Pat" Morita
Julie Pierce: Hilary Swank
Colonel Dugan: Michael Ironside
Louisa: Constance Towers
Eric: Chris Conrad
Abbot Monk: Arsenio Trinidad
Ned: Michael Cavalieri

Released: 1994
Production: Jerry Weintraub; released by Columbia Pictures
Direction: Christopher Cain
Screenplay: Mark Lee
Cinematography: Laszlo Kovacs
Editing: Ronald Roose
Production design: Walter P. Martishius
Set decoration: Tracey A. Doyle
Casting: Joy Todd
Sound: Andy Wiskes
Stunt coordination/martial arts choreography: Pat E. Johnson
Music: Bill Conti
MPAA rating: PG
Running time: 104 minutes

Night and Day

A young French woman, Julie (Guilaine Londez), maintains love affairs with two men, Jack (Thomas Langmann) and Joseph (Francois Negret), until the men's jealousy forces her to choose.

REVIEWS

Chicago Tribune. March 26, 1993, p. 7I(31).
Video Magazine. XVIII, May 1994, p. 64.
The Wall Street Journal. January 7, 1993, p. A12.

CREDITS

Julie: Guilaine Londez
Jack: Thomas Langmann
Joseph: Francois Negret

Origin: France
Released: 1991
Production: Pierre Wallon and Marilyn Watelet; released by International Film Circuit, Inc.
Direction: Chantal Akerman
Screenplay: Chantal Akerman and Pascal Bonitzer
Cinematography: Jean-Claude Neckelbrouck, Pierre Gordower, Bernard Delville and Olivier Dessalles
Editing: Francine Sandberg and Camille Bordes-Resnais
Music: Marc Herouet
MPAA rating: no listing
Running time: 90 minutes

Night of the Demons II

"Celebrate Friday the 13th the old fashioned way...screaming."—Movie tagline

Amelia Kinkade returns as Angela, a demon who haunts an abandoned mansion and terrorizes the students of St. Rita's school, finally battling a feisty nun, Sister Gloria (Jennifer Rhodes). Sequel to the 1988 box office dud, *Night of the Demons*.

REVIEWS

Los Angeles Times. May 13, 1994, p. F13.
Variety. CCCXXXII, September 28 1988, p. 14.

CREDITS

Bibi: Cristi Harris
Perry: Bobby Jacoby
Mouse: Merle Kennedy
Angela: Amelia Kinkade
Father Bob: Rod McCary
Johnny: Johnny Moran

Rick: Rick Peters
Sister Gloria: Jennifer Rhodes
Terri: Christine Taylor
Shirley: Zoe Trilling
Kurt: Ladd York
Z-boy: Darin Heames

Released: 1994
Production: Walter Josten and Jeff Geoffray for Blue Rider Pictures; released by Republic Pictures
Direction: Brian Trenchard-Smith
Screenplay: Joe Augustyn; based on a story by James Penzi and Augustyn
Cinematography: David Lewis
Editing: Daniel Duncan
Production design: Wendy Guidery
Art direction: Darcy Kaye
Set decoration: Mary Gullickson
Casting: Tedra Gabriel
Sound: Bo Harwood
Special makeup effects: Steve Johnson
Costume design: Hollywood Raggs
Stunt coordination: Shane Dixon
Music: Jim Manzie
MPAA rating: R
Running time: 98 minutes

1991: The Year Punk Broke

"Take a trip with Sonic Youth and Nirvana as they stumble through their '91 European club festival tour."—Movie tagline

Punk bands Sonic Youth, Nirvana, Dinosaur Jr., Babes in Toyland, Gumball, and the Ramones are featured in this amateurish documentary.

REVIEWS

Atlanta Constitution. January 7, 1993, p. C9.
Boston Globe. February 26, 1993, p. 34.
Variety. CCCXLIX, December 7, 1992, p. 72.

CREDITS

Sonic Youth: Sonic Youth
Nirvana: Nirvana
Dinosaur Jr.: Dinosaur Jr.
Babes in Toyland: Babes in Toyland
Gumball: Gumball
The Ramones: The Ramones

Released: 1992
Production: Geffen/DGC and Sonic Life/We Got Power; released by Tara Releasing
Direction: Dave Markey
Cinematography: Dave Markey
Editing: Dave Markey
Sonic Youth live sound: Terry Parson
Nirvana live sound: Craig Montgomery
MPAA rating: no listing
Running time: 99 minutes

No Escape

"No guards. No walls. No escape."—Movie tagline

"The year is 2022. In the prison of the future escape is impossible. Survival isn't much easier."—Movie tagline

"Electrifying! A first-rate...fun-filled action feast!"—Jeff Craig, *Sixty Second Preview*

Box Office Gross: $15,322,682 (July 10, 1994)

S et in the year 2022, this science-fiction adventure stars Ray Liotta as a prisoner who has been condemned to a remote island prison, where he escapes the ruthless Outsiders led by Marek (Stuart Wilson) and falls in with the more civilized Insiders led by Father (Lance Henriksen). Adapted from the book *The Penal Colony* by Richard Herley.

REVIEWS

Atlanta Constitution. April 29, 1994, p. P3.
Boston Globe. April 29, 1994, p. 49.
Chicago Tribune. April 29, 1994, p. 7F.
Entertainment Weekly. May 13, 1994, p. 44.
Entertainment Weekly. October 14, 1994, p. 70.
Los Angeles Times. April 29, 1994, p. F9.
The New York Times. April 29, 1994, p. C15.
The New Yorker. LXX, May 9, 1994, p. 97.
People Weekly. XLI, May 2, 1994, p. 18.
USA Today. April 29, 1994, p. D5.
Variety. CCCLV, May 2, 1994, p. 89.
The Washington Post. April 29, 1994, p. C6.
The Washington Post. April 29, 1994, p. WW46.
The Washington Post. May 5, 1994, p. D7.

CREDITS

Robbins: Ray Liotta
Father: Lance Henriksen
Marek: Stuart Wilson
Casey: Kevin Dillon
King: Ian McNeice
Dysart: Jack Shepherd
Warden: Michael Lerner
Hawkins: Ernie Hudson
Stephano: Kevin J. O'Connor

Released: 1994
Production: Gale Anne Hurd, in association with Allied Filmmakers and Pacific Western; released by Savoy Pictures
Direction: Martin Campbell
Screenplay: Michael Gaylin and Joel Gross; based on the novel *The Penal Colony*, by Richard Herley
Cinematography: Phil Meheux
Editing: Terry Rawlings
Production design: Allan Cameron
Art direction: Ian Gracie
Set decoration: Lesley Crawford
Casting: Pam Dixon Mickelson
Sound: Ben Osmo
Costume design: Norma Moriceau
Stunt coordination: Conrad E. Palmisano
Music: Graeme Revell
MPAA rating: R
Running time: 118 minutes

No Fear, No Die (S'en Fout la Mort)

Two friends, Dah (Isaach de Bankole) and Jocelyn (Alex Descas), raise roosters for cockfighting, while Jocelyn falls for the wife (Solveig Dommartin) of their rude boss, Pierre (Jean-Claude Brialy).

REVIEWS

Boston Globe. March 12, 1993, p. 31.
Chicago Tribune. December 17, 1993, p. 7J(34).
Entertainment Weekly. April 22, 1994, p. 68.
The New York Times. April 29, 1994, p. D16.

CREDITS

Dah: Isaach de Bankole
Jocelyn: Alex Descas
Pierre: Jean-Claude Brialy
Toni: Solveig Dommartin

Origin: France and West Germany
Released: 1992
Production: Francis Boespflug and Philippe Carcassonne
Direction: Claire Denis
Screenplay: Jean-Pol Fargeau and Claire Denis
Cinematography: Pascal Marti, Damien Morisot and Agnes Godard
Editing: Dominique Auvray
Music: Abdullah Ibrahim
MPAA rating: no listing
Running time: 97 minutes

Nobody's Fool

"Worn to Perfection"—Movie tagline
"One of the ten best films of 1994."—Janet Maslin, *The New York Times*
"Mr. Newman's performance is the single best of this year"—Caryn James, *The New York Times*
"An irresistible charmer"—Peter Travers, *Rolling Stone*

Box Office Gross: $39,300,000 (June 18, 1994)

Nobody's Fool succeeds primarily as a summation of Paul Newman's career. This subtle, quiet portrait of a ne'er-do-well gives this great actor and motion-picture star—the two are not always inclusive—an opportunity to display most of the skills he has developed as a film actor over the past forty years. Released shortly before Newman's seventieth birthday, the film is a tribute to one of the few stars of his generation whose talents have not dimmed with age.

Based upon a novel by Richard Russo, *Nobody's Fool* is both a character study of Donald Sullivan (Newman), whom most call "Sully," and a portrait of small-town America during an era of limited expectations. Sully is a sixty-year-old con-struction worker in an upstate New York village, who toils for Carl Roebuck (Bruce Willis) when he is not suing Roebuck because of a severe knee injury he received on the job. Because Sully's lawyer, Wirf (Gene Saks), is better at being a drinking-and-gambling companion than at being an advocate, Sully has no chance of collecting any compensation from Carl.

Sully is satisfied renting a room from his former eighth-grade teacher, Beryl Peoples (Jessica Tandy)—the only person to call him Donald. He works occasionally with the assistance of Rub Squeers (Pruitt Taylor Vince), a simple young man who worships Sully. He also flirts, only half seri-ously, with Toby Roebuck (Melanie Griffith), the wife Carl cheats on constantly. Sully spends the rest of his time drink-ing and playing poker in the local tavern with Wirf, Jocko (Jay Patterson), and other friends.

The lazy chaos of Sully's existence begins to change one Thanksgiving when the son he walked out on years earlier comes with his family to visit Sully's former wife, Vera (Elizabeth Wilson). Peter Sullivan (Dylan Walsh) is soon on his own with his eldest son, Will (Alexander Goodwin), after his wife leaves with their youngest for a trial separation. Through Peter's resentment at the father he has rarely seen and Will's tentative affection, Sully begins to discover his neglected sense of responsibility.

CREDITS

Donald (Sully) Sullivan: Paul Newman
Toby Roebuck: Melanie Griffith
Carl Roebuck: Bruce Willis
Beryl Peoples: Jessica Tandy
Rub Squeers: Pruitt Taylor Vince
Peter Sullivan: Dylan Walsh
Wirf: Gene Saks
Clive Peoples, Jr.: Josef Sommer
Judge Flatt: Philip Bosco
Vera: Elizabeth Wilson
Birdy: Margo Martindale
Jocko: Jay Patterson
Will Sullivan: Alexander Goodwin
Wacker Sullivan: Carl John Matusovich
Officer Raymer: Philip Seymour Hoffman
Charlotte: Catherine Dent
Ruby: Angelica Torn

Released: 1994
Production: Scott Rudin and Arlene Donovan, in association with Capella International and Cinehaus; released by Paramount Pictures
Direction: Robert Benton
Screenplay: Robert Benton; based on the novel by Richard Russo
Cinematography: John Bailey
Editing: John Bloom
Production design: David Gropman
Art direction: Dan Davis
Set decoration: Gretchen Rau
Casting: Ellen Chenoweth
Sound: Danny Michael
Costume design: Joseph G. Aulisi
Music: Howard Shore
MPAA rating: R
Running time: 110 minutes

Sully represents the eternally immature American male who follows his whims with little thought for how his actions affect others. The character could easily be either a cliché or an opportunity for a trite, sentimental, unconvincing change in personality, but in the hands of Newman and writer-director Robert Benton, such traps are avoided. Benton has dealt with such a figure before. In his most popular film, *Kramer vs. Kramer* (1979), Benton depicted a selfish husband and father who learned to love after his wife left him and their young son. The changes in Sully, however, are more gradual, subtler, less complete.

"I've got a feeling God's creeping in on me. I've got a feeling this is the year he'll lower the boom."— Miss Beryl in *Nobody's Fool*

AWARDS AND NOMINATIONS

Academy Awards Nominations 1994: Best Actor (Newman), Best Adapted Screenplay
Berlin International Film Festival Awards 1994: Best Actor (Newman)
Golden Globe Awards Nomination 1994: Best Actor (Newman)
National Society of Film Critics Awards 1994: Best Actor (Newman)
New York Film Critics Awards 1994: Best Actor (Newman)
Screen Actors Guild Awards Nomination 1994: Best Actor (Newman)

Sully begins to recognize similarities between himself and Peter. Not only does Peter have a troubled marriage, he also leads a tenuous economic existence, having lost his college teaching position. He wants to work with Sully and Rub when there is barely enough employment available for these two. More important, Sully sees in his grandson, Will, another chance to have a boy look up to him. Sully bonds with Peter by getting his help in drugging Carl's guard dog and stealing his boss' snowblower. Sully and Carl's taking turns stealing the snowblower is about the only action in the somnolent village of North Bath, New York. Sully bonds with his grandson by helping the boy face some of his fears and insecurities, such as having Will return the false leg Sully has won from Wirf in a card game.

Through this developing sense of responsibility, Sully recognizes how much he means to Toby, Beryl, and Rub. He pays more attention to Toby than does her husband and understands much better than Carl how special she is. Sully is also insightful enough to see that she still loves her wayward husband despite his faults. Though he shows it in quiet ways, Sully also cares more for his landlady than her cold banker son (Josef Sommer) does. When Rub becomes jealous of the attention Sully pays to Peter, Sully knows how much their friendship means to them both.

Sully resembles many of Newman's best-known characters. He exudes sexuality like the ambitious Ben Quick of *The Long, Hot Summer* (1958), displays the cockiness of pool hustler Fast Eddie Felson of *The Hustler* (1961), is a more sensitive version of the brutish title character in *Hud* (1963), has the recklessness and insubordination of the title character in *Cool Hand Luke* (1967), is a failure capable of rehabilitation like down-and-out lawyer Frank Galvin in *The Verdict* (1982), and shows some of the world-weariness of the older Eddie Felson in *The Color of Money* (1986). As written and performed, Sully is both a recognizable type and a distinctive individual, a man who understands his flaws yet chooses to indulge them when the mood strikes him. Newman presents him as an unsentimentalized Everyman, capable of change but resistant to it. His Sully is perhaps the best film role for an American actor this age since Burt Lancaster's dandyish small-time criminal in *Atlantic City* (1980).

Many of the other performances are almost as good as Newman's. As in *Pulp Fiction* (reviewed in this volume), Bruce Willis employs a subtlety and strength missing from most of his earlier film work. Willis, who also made an impression with a small role in Benton's *Billy Bathgate* (1991), makes Carl Roebuck a younger version of Sully, guilty of the self- indulgence which Sully is only beginning to regret. Likewise, Melanie Griffith, whose career has been in decline, offers her best performance since *Working Girl* (1988). She gives Toby, with her life of sad disappointment and unfulfilled passion, an intensity that avoids melodramatic cliches. Pruitt Taylor Vince, who has the potential to be a great character actor, also sidesteps the latter in a role that could have been a sentimental wallow. Rub's problem is not so much lack of intelligence as loneliness. The scene in which Rub and Sully make up after a misunderstanding is notable for Vince's restraint and Newman's generosity: Newman is never a screen icon outshining his fellow actors but a performer who recognizes that he is only one part of a larger whole.

While Jessica Tandy, in one of her last roles, provides quiet dignity in the underwritten part of Sully's landlady, Josef Sommer, who has played oily characters like this too many times, is merely unpleasant as her pompous banker son. Furthermore, Dylan Walsh is too bland to make any impression as Sully's grown son.

Benton has said that *Nobody's Fool* was influenced by Howard Hawks's *Only Angels Have Wings* (1939), in which a strong woman, played by Jean Arthur, is the equal of the men around her. Despite the performance of Griffith, whose acting style is a slower version of Arthur's, Toby's role is not that central to the film. Perhaps Benton's biggest debt, as in several of his films, is to Francois Truffaut, for *Nobody's Fool* emphasizes the quiet details of everyday life and the minor tragedies that disrupt the normal flow of events. As Andrew Sarris observed in *Film Comment*, the film is notable for its awareness of the economic instability of small-town American life in the 1990's. Benton's characters simply hope to make it from one day to the next.

Nobody's Fool is at times too quiet and subtle, almost uneventful. It is not the kind of film to sustain any great expectations. Benton's work here, as in most of his films—with the notable exception of *The Late Show* (1977), his masterpiece—is too understated, too civilized—except for a strip-poker scene. *Nobody's Fool* would benefit from the example of Sully's energy.

—*Michael Adams*

REVIEWS

Daily Variety. December 12, 1994, p. 2.
Entertainment Weekly. January 13, 1995, p. 36.
Film Comment. XXXI, January-February, 1995, p. 44.
The Hollywood Reporter. December 12, 1994, p. 13.
Interview. XXV, January, 1995, p. 26.
Los Angeles Times. December 23, 1994, p. F1.
New York. XXVIII, January 16, 1995, p. 56.
The New York Times. December 23, 1994, p. B1.
People Weekly. XLIII, January 9, 1995, p. 18.
Playboy. XLII, February, 1995, p. 20.
Rolling Stone. December 29, 1994, p. 200.
Time. CXLV, January 16, 1995, p. 72.
USA Today. December 23, 1994, p. D1.
The Village Voice. XXXIX, December 27, 1994, p. 68.
The Wall Street Journal. January 10, 1995, p. A18.

North

"Ever wonder what your life would be like with different parents? A boy named North did."
—Movie tagline

"Rob Reiner, Bruce Willis and Elijah Wood deliver a feel-good summer comedy"
—Jim Ferguson, *KMSB-TV*

Box Office Gross: $6,600,252 (August 28, 1994)

North, based on a novel by Alan Zweibel, tells the story of an eleven-year-old boy named North (Elijah Wood) who dreams of replacing his parents (Jason Alexander and Julia Louis-Dreyfus) with new and improved ones. The dream is precipitated by North's frustration and loneliness and illustrates numerous childhood desires and fears. North sees himself as a model child, excelling in academics, sports, and school performances, liked by other children, and admired by other children's parents. Yet he feels unloved by his own parents.

In the opening scene, the camera takes a tour of the multitude of toys filling North's bedroom—a testimony to consumerism. North is portrayed as a young boy who not only needs and desires love and approval but also reflects the values of his culture. When North is upset and wants to be alone, he does not run to the traditional tree house in the woods. He runs instead to a big chair in the furniture department of the local shopping mall. In this chair he can vanish into anonymity—he can appear to be just another bored child waiting for his parents.

It is while sitting in this chair that North meets the narrator of this tale, a sarcastic man (Bruce Willis) dressed as a pink rabbit. The man is taking a break from his job as the Easter bunny. North tells the man his problems and is given some sound advice: You can not choose your parents like a free agent, so you must accept them. North likes the idea of free agency, and when the man leaves, North dozes off. Here the film passes into a dream sequence.

The dream begins with North deciding to find new parents by allowing the adults of the world to make bids for him. When North's opportunistic and precocious friend Winchell (Matthew McCurley), the school newspaper editor, hears about the idea, the wheels start turning. Winchell encourages North to hire a small-time lawyer (Jon Lovitz)

North is based on a book by Alan Zweibel, who was one of the original writers on *Saturday Night Live*. The process of making *North* into a movie began when Zweibel asked eventual co-producer Reiner to write a book jacket quote for the novel.

and appeal to the court system for freedom from his parents. North wins his case—largely because both of North's parents fall into a coma upon learning of his wish to separate from them, and appear in court bound to stretchers and propped upright. The judge (Alan Arkin) awards North a short period of time (his summer break) in which to decide on new parents or to return to his original ones. If he is not in the hands of either when his time expires, he will be placed in an orphanage.

North embarks on a world tour in pursuit of the ideal parents. The first set of parents to be considered are Ma and Pa Tex (Reba McEntire and Dan Aykroyd), who pick North up at the airport in a limousine the length of a diesel truck and live in the "Dallas" mansion. Ma and Pa Tex like everything big: Their motto is "the biggest and the best." North is intimidated by these surroundings, the loudness of the Texans, the roughness of the semirural life, and the overall size of things. Dinner erupts into a country musical.

Ultimately, Ma and Pa Tex are deemed unsuitable by North who discovers that what they seek is a replacement for their beloved son who has recently died. While in their care, he notices that their ranch hand Gabby (Bruce Willis) resembles the man in the bunny suit at the mall. Although Gabby denies this, this character will appear in different forms throughout North's fantasies, like a guardian angel.

North's second stop is with Hawaii's Governor Ho (Keone Young) and his infertile wife (Lauren Tom). The three share the kind of fantasy seen in advertisements of tropical destinations: swimming, snorkeling in clear blue waters, bathing in waterfalls, eating seafood and luscious fruits, being entertained by hula dancers. After accepting them as the ideal parents, North discovers that they intend to use him as a Western public relations symbol for their island in order to boost their fragile self-image.

Next, North is seen in Alaska, living in a frozen version of an American suburb with an Alaskan mom and dad (Kathy Bates and Graham Greene). The igloos are surprisingly up-to-date, with television, garage-door openers, and white picket fences. All is fine until North learns of the morbid custom of sending the elders off to die on a lonely block of ice severed from the mainland. After North accompanies Grandpa (Abe Vigoda) on this journey, he decides Alaska is not for him.

The film then skips through several brief and increasingly ridiculous encounters, perhaps to indicate North's desperation: an Amish community, with Alexander Godunov and Kelly McGillis portraying an Amish couple as they did in *Witness* (1985); China, with a film clip from *The Last Emperor* (1987); central Africa, with North in a rather absurd, primitivistic scenario swinging from trees with his African father and staring at the bare breasts of his African mother; Paris, where North wears a beret and cannot bear finding Jerry Lewis on every channel.

> "A bird in the hand is always greener than the grass under the other guy's bushes...It's a metaphor used mostly by gardeners and landscape people in general."—Joey Fingers from *North*

Director Rob Reiner portrays the dream imagery of the contemporary American child as dominated by clichés and half-digested stereotypes of the world, a body of knowledge composed almost entirely of snips from advertisements, television shows, and blockbuster films. In the classic *The Wizard of Oz* (1939), Dorothy also dreams of a fantastic journey that takes her far from home, but in this journey the characters she meets symbolize relationships she has with people in her waking life. The characters North meets are entirely media-generated images of which he has no tangible experience. In these travel sequences, Reiner also makes fun of how foreign cultures have been affected by or have incorporated American popular culture.

Finally North finds perfection in the Nelsons, a family which resembles the 1950's television dream image: a white, Anglo-Saxon, Donna Reed-like mother (Faith Ford), a *Father Knows Best* dad (John Ritter), and two happy children. Though they love and accept him, North soon realizes that he is not at home and must leave.

When North returns to New York, he discovers that Winchell has led a children's revolution and risen to power and wealth based on North's venture. Winchell reigns from a high-tech penthouse atop Manhattan, and he is set on doing everything in his power to prevent North from ruining his empire. With greased hair and wire-rim eyeglasses, Winchell resembles the familiar film images of German SS officers and corporate bosses. The lawyer, Winchell's sidekick, is portrayed as a submissive pinball-playing child.

North manages to get around Winchell's obstacles and reunite with his parents just before his time expires. He then awakens from his dream and finds that the department store has closed. His angel, the man who works as the Easter bunny, is leaving for the day and gives him a ride home, where he reunites with his parents. They embrace him heartily, having been worried sick by his long absence.

North explores familiar themes in an unfamiliar way. Director Reiner once again focuses on the lives of children and makes use of satire, parody, and fantasy, but in *North* he combines this subject matter and these comic perspectives for the first time. Reiner's earlier *Stand By Me* (1986) was a thoughtful reminiscence on childhood that could be appreciated by both adults and children. *North*, on the other hand, is a film that misses its mark. It is a film about and for younger children, but with jokes and cultural allusions for the adult viewer.

North ultimately fails in its effort to be both humorous and heartwarming. As a comedy it fails because the parodies and inside jokes seem unsuited to the young viewer who might enjoy the story. Most of the jokes are references to media events that predate the experience of the child viewer, and parody and satire are forms of humor better suited to the adult experience. Furthermore, the film fails in its attempt to achieve sentimental drama because its parodic style creates unsympathetic, one-dimensional characters. The moral of *The Wizard of Oz*, "There's no place like home," rings false in *North*.

CREDITS

North: Elijah Wood
Narrator: Bruce Willis
Winchell: Matthew McCurley
Arthur Belt: Jon Lovitz
Judge Buckle: Alan Arkin
North's dad: Jason Alexander
North's mom: Julia Louis-Dreyfus
Ma Tex: Reba McEntire
Pa Tex: Dan Aykroyd
Alaskan mom: Kathy Bates
Alaskan dad: Graham Greene
Grandpa: Abe Vigoda
Amish mom: Kelly McGillis
Amish dad: Alexander Godunov
Donna Nelson: Faith Ford
Ward Nelson: John Ritter
Mrs. Ho: Lauren Tom
Governor Ho: Keone Young

Released: 1994
Production: Rob Reiner and Alan Zweibel for Castle Rock Entertainment, in association with New Line Cinema; released by Columbia Pictures
Direction: Rob Reiner
Screenplay: Alan Zweibel and Andrew Scheinman; based on the novel by Zweibel
Cinematography: Adam Greenberg
Editing: Robert Leighton
Production design: J. Michael Riva
Art direction: David Klassen
Set decoration: Michael Taylor
Casting: Jane Jenkins and Janet Hirshenson
Sound: Bob Eber
Costume design: Gloria Gresham
Music: Marc Shaiman
MPAA rating: PG
Running time: 86 minutes

In *North*, Reiner makes fun of 1990's American popular culture, a media-driven culture in which even the children dream of litigation and the pursuit of personal power. Reiner, however, does not poke fun at any one stereotype—he pokes fun at all of them, or at least he attempts to. *North* is ambitious, but unfortunately, this time out, Reiner's reach exceeds his grasp.

—*Reni Celeste and Michael L. Forstrom*

REVIEWS

Chicago Tribune. July 22, 1994, Sec. 2, p. 4.
Entertainment Weekly. July 29, 1994, p. 44.
The Hollywood Reporter. July 18, 1994, p. 5.
Los Angeles Times. July 22, 1994, p. F1.
The New York Times. July 22, 1994, p. B2.
Newsweek. August 1, 1994, p. 56.
Time. August 1, 1994, p. 58.
USA Today. July 22, 1994, p. 5D.
Variety. July 18, 1994, p. 5.

Nostradamus

"His story is still unfinished five centuries later."
—Movie tagline

 Box Office Gross: $301,274 (November 13, 1994

This historical biography centers on the turbulent life of the celebrated medieval scholar/prophet, starring Tcheky Karyo in the title role. The story of *Nostradamus* takes place in France but was actually filmed in Romania.

REVIEWS

Atlanta Constitution. December 16, 1994, p. P14.
Chicago Tribune. December 9, 1994, p. 7F.
Los Angeles Times. September 16, 1994, p. F8.
The New York Times. November 23, 1994, p. C14.
Entertainment Weekly. March 24, 1995, p. 74.
Variety. CCCXLVI, September 19, 1994, p. 77.

CREDITS

Nostradamus: Tcheky Karyo
Scalinger: F. Murray Abraham
Monk: Rutger Hauer
Catherine De Medici: Amanda Plummer
Marie: Julia Ormond
Anne: Assumpta Serna
King Henry II: Anthony Higgins

Origin: Great Britain and Germany
Released: 1994
Production: Edward Simons and Harold Reichebner for Allied Entertainments and Vereinigte Film Partners; released by Orion Classics
Direction: Roger Christian
Screenplay: Knut Boeser and Piers Ashworth; based on a story by Boeser, Ashworth, and Roger Christian
Cinematography: Denis Crossan
Editing: Alan Strachan
Production design: Peter J. Hampton
Art direction: Christian Nicul
Set decoration: Michael D. Ford
Sound: James Corcoran
Costume design: Ulla Gothe
Music: Barrington Pheloung
MPAA rating: R
Running time: 118 minutes

The Oak

"One of the year's 10 best. A movie of imaginative hysteria.... Blink and you'll miss something outrageous."—J. Hoberman, *Village Voice*

"Wild, fine, irresistible.... It explodes from the screen with the hot energy of something long pent-up."—Jay Carr, *Boston Globe*

"3 1/2 Stars. Witty, utterly original and flawlessly acted."—Joseph Gelmis, *Newsday*

"Fueled with vitriol and a deep, dark wit. A powerful, chaos-filled journey."—Stephen Rea, *Philadelphia Inquirer*

Set in late 1980's Romania, this surrealistic drama centers on the spiritual journey of a young woman, Nela (Maia Morgenstern), whose father has just died. She sets out with her father's ashes in a jar, meeting up with violence, poverty, and eventually companionship in the person of Mitica (Razvan Vasilescu), a radical doctor.

REVIEWS

Atlanta Constitution. August 27, 1993, p. D3.
Boston Globe. July 23, 1993, p. 42.
Chicago Tribune. November 26, 1993, p. 7F(32).
Christian Science Monitor. January 26, 1993, p. 11.
Entertainment Weekly. August 19, 1994, p. 68.
The Nation. CCLVI, February 15, 1993, p. 209.
National Catholic Reporter. XXIX, March 12, 1993, p. 19.
National Review. XLV, March 1, 1993, p. 62.
The New Republic. CCVIII, February 8, 1993, p. 24.
New York. XXVI, February 8, 1993, p. 63.
The New York Times. January 22, 1993, p. C8.
The New Yorker. LXVIII, February 1, 1993, p. 98.
Vogue. CLXXXIII, March 1993, p. 200.
The Wall Street Journal. January 21, 1993, p. A12.
The Washington Post. August 14, 1993, p. D5.

CREDITS

Nela: Maia Morgenstern
Mitica: Razvan Vasilescu
Mayor: Victor Rebengiuc
Country priest: Dorel Visan
Priest's wife: Mariana Mihut
Lawyer: Dan Condurache
Nela's father: Virgil Andriescu
Nela's mother: Leopoldina Balanuta
Butusina: Matei Alexandru
Priest on the train: Gheorghe Visu
Mitica's assistant: Magda Catone
Titi: Ionel Mahailescu

Origin: France and Romania
Released: 1992
Production: Eliane Stutterheim, Sylvain Bursztejn, and Lucian Pintilie; released by MK2 Productions USA
Direction: Lucian Pintilie
Screenplay: Lucian Pintilie; based on the novel *Balanta*, by Ion Baiesu
Cinematography: Doru Mitran
Editing: Victorita Nae
Production design: Calin Papura
MPAA rating: no listing
Running time: 105 minutes

AWARDS AND NOMINATIONS

Felix Award: Best Actress

Oedipus Rex

This retelling of Sophocles' classic tale features puppetry, masks, a dancing double of Oedipus, Japanese narration, and the Saito Kinen Orchestra and Shinyukai Chorus, conducted by Seiji Ozawa.

REVIEWS

Library Journal. CXV, December 1990, p. 179.
The New York Times. March 31, 1993, p. C15.

CREDITS

Oedipus Rex: Philip Langridge
Jocasta: Jessye Norman
Narrator: Kayoko Shiraishi
Creon: Bryn Terfel
Tiresius: Harry Peeters
Shepherd: Robert Swensen
Messenger: Michio Tatara

Origin: USA and Japan
Released: 1993
Production: Peter Gelb and Pat Jaffe
Direction: Julie Taymor
Screenplay: Based on the opera-oratorio by Igor Stravinsky
Production design: George Tsypin
Makeup: Reiko Kruk
Costume design: Emi Wada
Music: Igor Stravinsky
MPAA rating: no listing
Running time: 60 minutes

Oleanna

"One of the most controversial films of our time!"—Movie tagline

"He said it was a lesson. She said it was sexual harassment. Whatever side you take, you're wrong."—Movie tagline

 Box Office Gross: $84,837 (November 20, 1994)

Oleanna is the filmed version of a play written by David Mamet and performed off-Broadway in 1992, where it caused considerable controversy for its apparent depiction of the woman as the villain when she destroys a man's career by charging him with sexual harassment. However, to see Oleanna as merely a dialectic about sexual harassment is to miss its point. It can be seen as a cautionary tale about the dangers of imprecise communication, and also about the natural human drive to fulfill cultural and social stereotypes. Mamet has directed his own screenplay without compro-

mising the controversial nature of the play, and though the two-character piece is not particularly visually involving, it is no less controversial and effective than its stage presentation.

Ever since the initiation of the term "political correctness" at Dartmouth College in the 1980's, many find it difficult to adhere to strict spoken and unspoken codes of verbal conduct which are particularly prevalent at American universities. The term "Oleanna" apparently refers to a Utopian society; perhaps it is used as symbol of the pseudo-Utopian society that "political correctness" is charged with creating.

John (William H. Macy) is a pompous college professor whose tenure is just coming due. He is celebrating his promotion with the purchase of a larger house for his family, and all through the film his conversations are interrupted with discussions about the impending house sale.

Carol (Debra Eisenstadt) is a student of John's, hopelessly confused by his ideas. The essence of what John is trying to teach seems deliberately unclear to the audience as well, and John's byzantine theories about the nature of learning might cause an audience the same anxiety as they cause Carol.

When she comes to John, saying "I don't understand," and "I read your book," as she constantly and hopelessly refers to her notes, she is begging him to help her so that she can avoid getting an "F" in class. She wails, "I have to pass this course," and he responds with a terse, "we must abide by the system we have chosen."

John's arrogant and incomprehensibly difficult attempts to explain himself only cause more trouble. In the second scene, the audience discovers that Carol has brought charges against him for sexual harassment, racism, and a myriad of other crimes for saying things like, "If you'll come back to see me again, you can get an 'A'," or "it is the white man's burden." While it may be clear to the audience that John is only guilty of fatuousness, Carol's perversion of John's words makes sense given her inability to truly grasp his meaning. That he makes no attempt to be sure that she understands him properly is his own fault; that she sees herself as the victim of language is her fault as well.

Eventually, the lack of communication between them worsens, and Carol's power grows as her complaint (which

Oleanna marks the first time David Mamet has directed a screen adaptation of one of his own theatrical works.

"You think I want revenge? I don't want revenge. I want understanding."—Carol to Professor John in *Oleanna*

she describes as the complaint of her "group") causes John to lose his tenure, his job, and his house. She tells him not to call his wife "baby" on the phone, sending him into a rage, and causing him to physically attack her. *Oleanna* is about the shifting power between people who fulfill their cultural roles without wishing to do so, and without attempting to avoid the problems about which they complain.

Mamet's very intellectual play is well-treated in this film version. But his trademark rapid-fire dialogue, with its repetition and half-sentences, is occasionally irritating, and does not seem as intrinsic to the characters as it did in *Glengarry Glen Ross* (1992) or *House of Games* (1987).

Reprising his stage role, William H. Macy creates a character that is severe and cold and quite full of himself. His growing desperation at the loss of his tenure is appropriately pathetic, and his climactic explosion at the film's finale is frightening. As Carol, Debra Eisenstadt's change from whiny co-ed to self-assured control freak seems a bit of a jump, but Eisenstadt's performance on the whole is excellent.

This complicated and sometimes frustrating film is ultimately a thorough examination of the current state of communication in this country. That Mamet doesn't take the obvious route, or that he doesn't provide the audience with an obvious sense of which character is "right," is both testament to his brilliance and explanation for the possibility that not all people will find this film entertaining. But anyone who watches it will be rewarded with a rich examination of a difficult and abstract subject.

—*Kirby Tepper*

CREDITS

John: William H. Macy
Carol: Debra Eisenstadt

Released: 1994
Production: Patricia Wolff and Sarah Green, in association with Channel Four Films and Bay Kinescope; released by the Samuel Goldwyn Company
Direction: David Mamet
Screenplay: David Mamet; based on his play
Cinematography: Andrzej Sekula
Editing: Barbara Tulliver
Production design: David Wasco and Sandy Reynolds Wasco
Set decoration: Kate Conklin
Sound: Peter Kurland, Freddy Potatohead and Ryan Weiss
Costume design: Jane Greenwood
Fight coordination: B. H. Barry
Music: Rebecca Pidgeon
MPAA rating: no listing
Running time: 89 minutes

REVIEWS

The Hollywood Reporter. October 24, 1994. p. 8
Los Angeles Times. November 4, 1994. p. F4
The New York Times. November 4, 1994. p. B2
Variety. November 4, 1994. p. 14

AWARDS AND NOMINATIONS

Independent Spirit Awards Nomination 1995: Best Actor (Macy)

On Deadly Ground

"His battle to save the Alaskan wilderness and protect its people, can only be won *On Deadly Ground*"—Movie tagline

Box Office Gross: $38,572,114 (June 5, 1994)

Actor Steven Seagal's directorial outing, *On Deadly Ground*, opens on the beautiful Alaskan landscape—an area supposedly unspoiled by modern man—then quickly cuts to a very urban-type fire at an Aegis Oil Company oil rig. The fire is out of control as company fire-fighting specialist Forrest Taft (Steven Seagal) arrives on scene. He swaps a slick tasseled suede jacket for an asbestos

CREDITS

Forrest Taft: Steven Seagal
Michael Jennings: Michael Caine
Masu: Joan Chen
MacGruder: John C. McGinley
Stone: R. Lee Ermey
Liles: Shari Shattuck
Hugh Palmer: Richard Hamilton
Silook: Chief Irvin Brink
Homer Carlton: Billy Bob Thorton
Tunrak: Apanguluk Charlie Kairaiuak
Takanapsaluk: Elsie Pistolhead

Released: 1994
Production: Steven Seagal, Julius R. Nasso, and A. Kitman Ho; released by Warner Bros.
Direction: Steven Seagal
Screenplay: Ed Horowitz and Robin U. Russin
Cinematography: Ric Waite
Editing: Robert A. Ferretti
Production design: William Ladd Skinner
Art direction: Lou Montejeno
Set design: Nick Navarro
Set decoration: John Anderson and Ronald R. Reiss
Casting: Pamela Basker
Special effects: Thomas L. Fisher
Sound: Edward Tise
Costume design: Joseph G. Aulisi
Stunt coordination: Glenn Randall
Music: Basil Poledouris
MPAA rating: R
Running time: 101 minutes

one and single-handedly puts out the fire with a case of dynamite. Then, in all his machismo glory, he lights a cigarette on a flaming pipe for good measure. The excitement ends as thousands of gallons of black oil seeps into the ocean, causing a mini-environmental holocaust. Overblown as it is, this opening sequence is mere film foreplay for all the explosive, narcissistic scenes and their eco-conscious wrappings that will soon follow.

The main story line begins when aged oil-rig foreman Hugh Palmer (Richard Hamilton), who has long been blaming a rash of deadly oil explosions on the company's faulty equipment, walks up to Taft and calls him a company "whore." Taft, however, knows the old man

is right; he has traded his ideals for a cushy nine-to-fiver. Later that night, Taft nurses a beer while a group of oil workers harass a drunken Indian. Taft is tired of letting injustice pass, and in typical cooler-than-thou Seagal fashion, Taft saunters up to the workers and calmly suggests they stop. As expected, they do not, and the martial artist cracks bone and tears cartilage until they do, seemingly taking on the whole bar. Unlike a typical Seagal fight, however, compassion is shown when his opponents acknowledge their wrongdoing. Taft is a hero with a conscience.

In stark contrast, his evil employer, Aegis Oil, finds a way to cut benefits to the families of the oil workers who were killed in the explosion. Furthermore, Aegis Oil president Jennings (Michael Caine) is a bottom-line, stop-at-nothing capitalist who is committed to getting a new oil rig—Aegis One—up and running as soon as possible. Otherwise, the leased land will revert back to the Alaskan Indians. When Hugh goes to the Environmental Protection Agency (EPA) with his accusations, the ruthless Jennings sends in his henchman, MacGruder (John C. McGinley), to murder him. A suspicious Taft then goes into the company's top-secret files and discovers all the environmental wrong-doings. In addition to toxic dumping, Jennings knowingly bought defective connectors and is using them to put Aegis One on-line by the deadline.

As expected, Jennings finds out about Taft's snooping. He attempts to contain the problem by sending Taft into a deadly explosives-rigged substation. Taft manages to escape, however, before the blast engulfs the structure. Jennings subsequently announces to a press conference that the rash of explosions were caused by two employee-saboteurs—Hugh and Taft—who were killed in this latest explosion. Meanwhile, Taft is found facedown in the snow by Alaskan Indians and is carefully nursed back to health. During his recovery, he experiences a series of spiritual dreams about humankind's destruction of Mother Earth. Taft becomes convinced he must stop Aegis Oil's assault on the environment. He and the chief's environmental-activist daughter, Masu (Joan Chen), leave the village to stop Aegis One from going on-line.

Soon after, MacGruder and his men arrive in the village and find evidence of Taft's stay there. They kill the chief as punishment and pursue the duo. When Taft proves to be a tough adversary, MacGruder hires some "independent contractors"—trained mercenaries—to track him down. A background check reveals Taft's personal history to be "beyond top secret"—possibly a former Central Intelligence Agency operative. The mercenaries finally find Taft and Masu as they are emptying a mountaintop explosives storage cabin. A horseback chase ensues, with Taft laying explosive traps along the way. Although Taft and Masu manage an escape, there is no question where they are going with all those explosives—to Aegis One.

Weighed down with backpacks of explosives, Taft and Masu forcefully make their way past Jennings' heavily armed workers, and even the Federal Bureau of Investigation (FBI) anti-terrorist units, and find their way into the belly of the rig. They wire the place to blow and systematically kill all the villains but Jennings. They find him last, as he is about to activate the rig. After dumping him in a vat of oil, they escape the structure just before it explodes into a fireball. The film ends on a four-minute Seagal lecture/slide show warning the audience to be good to the environment. Corporate greed and lobby-driven lawmaking are exposed as causes of the planet's slow death.

Though well-intentioned, this end sequence only epitomizes the obvious nature of the whole film. Seagal's attempt to incorporate an environmental theme into an action film is ambitious and respectable, but the script is so muddled with clichés and proselytizing that most of the plot and action are lost. Environmental content aside, there is absolutely nothing new about this picture. It is the typical tale of a lone male taking on greedy big business. Everything is that black and white. The characters are either good or bad, pro- environment or against it. Everyone that works for the company is bad and worthy of death. The Indians, who symbolize Mother Earth, are either drunkards or helpless. The acting, though well played for the most part, is never absorbing or powerful enough to overcome the one-dimensional characterizations.

Similar problems afflict most aspects of the film. Even the scenes of high-decibel pyrotechnics and gunplay are too few and far between to cause any real excitement. The cinematography is fine, but does not invoke any real individual style. The soundtrack, one of the best elements of this film, is still not original enough to carry any real weight.

Maybe if this had been a typical Seagal "beat'em-up, crash'em-up" action film, squeezing in a political message or two would have worked. Here, however, with so little action and so much cliché and preaching, *On Deadly Ground* dredges the bottom of the barrel.

—*Jonathan David*

One Nation Under God

Mixing interviews and archival footage, this insightful documentary centers on the ways in which Christianity and psychiatry have colluded in an attempt to convert gays and lesbians from homosexuality to heterosexuality.

REVIEWS

Atlanta Constitution. June 24, 1994, p. P19.
Chicago Tribune. June 13, 1994, Sec. 5 p. 3.
Los Angeles Times. July 6, 1993, p. F4.
Los Angeles Times. June 14, 1994, p. F8.
The New York Times. June 20, 1994, p. B6.
USA Today. January 12, 1994, p. D1.
USA Today. June 14, 1994, p. D3.
Variety. CCCLI, July 12, 1993, p. 55.
The Washington Post. June 14, 1994, p. C1.

CREDITS

Released: 1993
Production: Teodoro Maniaci and Francine Rzeznik; released by 3 Z/Hourglass Production
Direction: Teodoro Maniaci and Francine Rzeznik
Cinematography: Mark Voelpel and Teodoro Maniaci
Editing: Teodoro Maniaci and Francine Rzeznik
Music: Robert Mitchell
MPAA rating: no listing
Running time: 83 minutes

Only You

"A new comedy designed to delight."
—*The New York Post*

"One of the all-time manic romantic comedies."
—*Glamour*

"An old-fashioned romantic comedy that works."
—*The New York Daily News*

 Box Office Gross: $20,003,957 (December 12, 1994)

As with *Sleepless in Seattle* (1993) or *When Harry Met Sally* (1989), *Only You* is a sweet romance whose *raison d'etre* appears to be to emulate the screwball film romances of the thirties and forties while creating a mar-

CREDITS

Faith Corvatch: Marisa Tomei
Peter Wright: Robert Downey, Jr.
Kate: Bonnie Hunt
Giovanni: Joaquim De Almeida
Larry: Fisher Stevens
False Damon Bradley: Billy Zane
Damon Bradley: Adam LeFevre
Dwayne: John Benjamin Hickey
Leslie: Siobhan Fallon
Fortune-teller: Antonia Rey
Faith's mother: Phyllis Newman

Released: 1994
Production: Norman Jewison, Cary Woods, Robert N. Fried, and Charles Mulvehill for Yorktown Productions Ltd.; released by TriStar Pictures
Direction: Norman Jewison
Screenplay: Diane Drake
Cinematography: Sven Nykvist
Editing: Stephen Rivkin
Production design: Luciana Arrighi
Art direction: Stephano Ortolani, Maria Teresa Barbasso and Gary Kosko
Set decoration: Ian Whittaker, Alessandra Querzola and Diane Stoughton
Casting: Howard Feuer
Sound: Ken Weston
Costume design: Milena Canonero
Music: Rachel Portman
MPAA rating: PG
Running time: 108 minutes

ketable soundtrack. *Only You* is, in a sense, also director Norman Jewison's follow-up to his hugely successful romantic comedy *Moonstruck* (1987). In large part, Jewison and company are successful in creating an atmosphere reminiscent of both the old romantic comedies and the more recent ones. But, while this is by no means a bad film, it is lacking the true wit of *When Harry Met Sally* and the depth of *Moonstruck* (not to mention that its soundtrack is not as wonderful as *Sleepless in Seattle*). However, a charming story, beautifully shot locations, and the witty performances of the leading characters make this an entertaining film that should not be dismissed.

Faith (Marisa Tomei) is a teacher, a woman whose whole life has been guided by the principle of predetermined destiny. She believes that her destiny is to marry a man named Damon Bradley, and when she discovers that her dull fiancee has a friend named Damon Bradley who is on his way to Venice, she jumps on a plane to find him. Her certainty that she must meet him in order to avoid marrying the wrong man is made believable by lovely Marisa Tomei. Tomei has been given a chance to show a rather broad range of late, having won the Oscar for her role as a tough-talking automobile expert in *My Cousin Vinny* (1992), and having played a Cuban refugee in *The Perez Family* (1995). Here she is a winning comic heroine, possessing a mixture of naivete and strength reminiscent of Claudette Colbert in *It Happened One Night* (1934).

 "Did he get down on his knees?" "No, but he turned down his beeper."—Faith describing to her girlfriends her boyfriend's proposal in *Only You*

She is accompanied to Venice by her sister-in-law and best friend (Bonnie Hunt), a pretty but insecure woman unhappy in her marriage to Faith's brother (Fisher Stevens). Bonnie Hunt is a revelation in this simple role, playing the part that Eve Arden would have played in the 1930's. When being romanced by the handsome Giovanni (Joaquim de Almeida) she responds to his seductive talk by asking if he wants a cracker. When arriving at the four-star hotel where they think Damon Bradley is staying she says, "We can't afford this, Kathie Lee Crosby stayed here." Hunt's dry delivery and her doe eyes make a perfect best friend/comic foil, and she all but steals the film.

Stealing the film from Robert Downey Jr. is not an easy thing to do. His effortless physical comedy and his goofy but sexy charm are as effective here as they were in *Chaplin*

(1993) and *Chances Are* (1993). In fact, his character bears a similarity to his role as a reincarnated soul in *Chances Are* (opposite Cybill Shepherd): Downey used his combination of mischievousness and innocence to great effect in that film, and does so again here. He plays a man so smitten with Faith that he allows her to think he is Damon Bradley, and then continues to help her find Damon Bradley once she learns he is just a shoe salesman from New Jersey named Peter.

Norman Jewison knows his way around a romantic comedy, having directed the wonderful *Moonstruck*. He takes the mistaken identities and the beautiful locales and mixes them into a charming paean to those old romantic comedies. From the beauty of Venice by moonlight to the luxury hotels of the seacoast village of Positano, Jewison creates an atmosphere of European romance and beauty similar to films such as *To Catch a Thief* (1953) and *Roman Holiday* (1953). Additionally, Jewison uses the camera in interesting ways, creating shots which artfully use movement as a way to create a flowing pace and maintain visual interest.

After praising the fine performances and the excellent direction, it would seem that this film has no flaws. But it has a few built-in characteristics which keep it from being as fulfilling as many cinematic predecessors. First, Faith's romantic obsession with destiny makes her seem a bit selfish and a bit silly; second, she travels awfully far (and rather irresponsibly) to follow a man she's never met; third, she dumps her fiance by phone, and the audience does not see it happen; and fourth, Peter seems to be a bit cavalier in his manipulation of Faith's attention. More important, however,

is the fact that it seems implausible in the nineties that two people can fall in love at first sight and mean it. But perhaps that's missing the point of a screwball romantic comedy: the characters are just screwball enough to stop being realistic and start being romantic. And there's always that good musical soundtrack...

—*Kirby Tepper*

REVIEWS

Atlanta Constitution. October 7, 1994, p. P14.
Boston Globe. October 7, 1994, p. 56.
Chicago Tribune. October 7, 1994, p. 7J.
Christian Science Monitor. October 7, 1994, p. 12.
Entertainment Weekly. October 7, 1994, p. 52.
Entertainment Weekly. March 17, 1995, p. 99.
Glamour. XCII, November 1994, p. 138.
Los Angeles Times. October 7, 1994, p. F4.
Maclean's. CVII, October 10, 1994, p. 66.
National Review. XLVI, November 7, 1994, p. 76.
The New York Times. October 7, 1994, p. C12.
The New York Times. October 30, 1994, Sec. 2 p. 26.
The New York Times. CXLIV, March 17, 1995, p. D17.
People Weekly. XLII, October 17, 1994, p. 21.
Playboy. XLI, November 1994, p. 16.
Rolling Stone. October 20, 1994, p. 156.
TV Guide. XLIII, March 25, 1995, p. 52.
USA Today. October 7, 1994, p. D10.
Variety. CCCLVI, September 19, 1994, p. 76.
The Washington Post. October 7, 1994, p. B7.
The Washington Post. October 7, 1994, p. WW50.
The Washington Post. October 13, 1994, p. D7.

Over Her Dead Body (Enid Is Sleeping)

Elizabeth Perkins stars as June, a woman who is having an affair with the husband, Harry (Judge Reinhold), of her mean older sister, Enid (Maureen Mueller). When Enid catches them in the act, June accidentally kills her, and she and Harry try to hide Enid's body, in this black comedy.

REVIEWS

Video Review. XII, February 1992, p. 67.

CREDITS

June: Elizabeth Perkins
Harry: Judge Reinhold
Floyd: Jeffrey Jones
Enid: Maureen Mueller
Mavis: Rhea Perlman
Motel manager: Michael J. Pollard

Released: 1990
Production: John A. Davis and Howard Malin for Davis Entertainment Company; released by Vestron Pictures
Direction: Maurice Phillips
Screenplay: A. J. Tipping, James Whaley, and Maurice Phillips
Cinematography: Affonso Beato
Editing: Malcolm Campbell
Production design: Paul Peters
Art direction: Gershon Ginsburg
Casting: Janet Hirshenson and Jane Jenkins
Costume design: Lisa Jensen
Music: Craig Safan
MPAA rating: no listing
Running time: 100 minutes

Over the Hill

Set in the Australian outback, this drama stars Olympia Dukakis as an aging American widow, Alma Harris, whose visit to her daughter, Elizabeth (Sigrid Thornton), in Australia turns into an adventure involving travel and romance.

CREDITS

Alma Harris: Olympia Dukakis
Elizabeth: Sigrid Thornton
Dutch: Derek Fowlds
Maurio: Bill Kerr
Benedict: Steve Bisley
Jan: Andrea Moor
Margaret: Pippa Grandison
Forbes: Martin Jacobs
Nick: Aden Young
Hank: Gerry Connolly
Hank's wife: Jenny Williams
Television reporter: Anne Looby

Origin: Australia
Released: 1992
Production: Robert Caswell and Bernard Terry for Village Roadshow Pictures and Glasshouse Pictures, in association with the Rank Organisation and Australian Film Finance Corporation
Production: Released by Greater Union Distributors
Direction: George Miller
Screenplay: Robert Caswell; based on the book *Alone in the Australian Wilderness*, by Gladys Taylor
Cinematography: David Connell
Editing: Henry Dangar
Production design: Graham (Grace) Walker
Casting: Liz Mullinar
Sound: Gary Wilkins
Music: David McHugh
MPAA rating: no listing
Running time: 99 minutes

Over the Ocean

The Goldfarb family—father Menachem (Arie Muskuna), mother Rosa (Daphna Rechter), ten-year-old son Haim (Uri Alter), and teenage daughter Miri (Mili Avital)—debate whether to stay in war-torn Israel or move on to Canada, in this award-winning Israeli drama set in 1962. The film won nine Israeli Academy Awards.

CREDITS

Menachem Goldfarb: Arie Muskuna
Rosa Goldfarb: Daphna Rechter
Haim Goldfarb: Uri Alter
Morris Greenspan: Moti Giladi
Leizer: Sinai Peter
Miri Goldfarb: Mili Avital
Schultz: Yair Lapid
Gabi: Shai Idelson
Yhiel: Oshik Levi
Rappaport: Yosi Graber

Origin: Israel
Released: 1991

Production: Marek Rozenbaum and Ron Ackerman, in association with the Israel Broadcasting Authority and the Israeli Fund for Quality Films; released by Transfax Productions
Direction: Jacob Goldwasser
Screenplay: Haim Merin
Cinematography: David Gurfinkel
Editing: Anat Lubarski
Production design: Emanuel Amrami
Costume design: Rona Doron
Music: Shlomo Gronich
MPAA rating: no listing
Running time: 88 minutes

AWARDS AND NOMINATIONS

Academy Awards Nomination 1991: Best Foreign Language Film

The Pagemaster

"The *Wizard of Oz* for the '90s."—Garth Biship, *Parent to Parent Magazine*

"Delightful! A magical tale."—Jeffrey Lyons, *Sneak Previews*

"A great ride packed with adventure and fantasy."—Leo Quinones, *Fox Kids Countdown*

"Take the entire family!"—Mike Caccioppoli, *WABC Radio*

"Children's classics come alive."—Elayne Blythe, *Film Advisory Board*

 Box Office Gross: $11,473,414 (January 2, 1995)

The Pagemaster is an adventure fairy tale, mixing live action with animation, about a timid boy named Richard Tyler (Macaulay Culkin) who overcomes his fears by discovering classic literature at his local library. Despite a celebrity cast, the real star of *The Pagemaster* does not occur on-screen but off, in the form of a marketing and merchandising effort of international proportions. There were free tickets in every seventh box of specially marked crackers, activity booklets at the pizza parlor, advertisements on cartons of orange juice and plastic bags, posters at the library and the gas station, and a 24-page insert in the Sunday paper, and this was only the beginning. The network of marketing partners extends beyond the continent and includes companies in Great Britain, Germany, and Sweden.

For half a year before its release, the marketers heralded the simultaneous release of the film and the video game as an industry first, as if to demand that the film and its marketing techniques share the spotlight as equals. In this case, the two are indeed indistinguishable. It is difficult to determine whether the video game was designed around the film, or the film designed in the image of the video game.

The story line, which stresses the virtues of classic literature, was marketed to please the buyers themselves—the parents. As film producer and writer David Kirschner commented in *The Hollywood Reporter*, "The fact that (the film) deals with literature makes it a moral imperative for parents to send their children to see it. They are then that much more willing to buy particular items." The problem is that the film is so focused on selling that little or no interest is

 "Dad, eight percent of all household accidents involve ladders, another three percent involve trees. I'm looking at an eleven percent probability here."—Richard Tyler, refusing to go near the tree house his father has built him, in *The Pagemaster*

taken in developing the two worthwhile themes it is presenting—the pleasure of literature and the fears of childhood.

The story begins by portraying the excessive degree of fear from which the young Richard Tyler suffers. He sleeps in a bedroom rigged with devices to be used in the event of an assortment of imagined disasters, and he rides a bike equipped with every safety feature possible, including a shield. He is an outcast with the children in his neighborhood because he refuses to participate in the ordinary risks and adventures of childhood. His father (Ed Begley, Jr.) is building him a tree house, which he refuses to go near. When challenged, he recites the statistics for accidents in and around the home.

One day, after mustering the courage to leave home on his bike, Richard gets stuck in a terrible storm. He seeks refuge in the library. The librarian (Christopher Lloyd) is disappointed to discover that he has not come to seek books but merely to use the pay phone. The librarian notices Richard's fearfulness and reassures him that if he gets lost on his way to the phone he can always find his way out by the neon exit sign. Richard enters a rotunda and, looking up, finds a wondrous mural depicting characters from classic literature all grouped around a wizard. He slips and falls, and finds himself staring straight up at the mural. To his horror, the mural begins to melt and transform into blobs of cartoon color that engulf him.

At this point, the film becomes an animated dream sequence in which the central figure in the mural, who resembles the librarian, is the Pagemaster (voice of Christopher Lloyd), a wizard who promises Richard that he can leave the library and return home only after he has journeyed through three realms: adventure, horror, and fantasy. As Richard travels through the animated library, an ominous and enchanting wonder, he meets three talking books who represent the three genres and who will accompany him on his journey: Fantasy (voice of Whoopi Goldberg), Adventure (voice of Patrick Stewart), and Horror (voice of Frank Welker). These books are as desperate as he to escape the library, for it is only by being checked out that they find freedom.

The body of the film consists of the adventures the four share as they travel throughout the three realms in pursuit of the exit sign that signifies their freedom. In the land of horror, they come upon Dr. Jekyll (voice of Leonard Nimoy), who drinks the potion that will transform him into his alter

CREDITS

Richard Tyler: Macaulay Culkin
Mr. Dewey (The Pagemaster): Christopher Lloyd
Alan Tyler: Ed Begley, Jr.
Claire Tyler: Mel Harris
Adventure: Patrick Stewart (voice)
Fantasy: Whoopi Goldberg (voice)
Horror: Frank Welker (voice)
Dr. Jekyll (Mr. Hyde): Leonard Nimoy (voice)
Captain Ahab: George Hearn (voice)
Long John Silver: Jim Cummings (voice)

Released: 1994
Production: David Kirschner (animation) and Paul Gertz (animation), and Michael R. Joyce (live action), in association with Turner Pictures, Inc.; released by Twentieth Century-Fox
Direction: Maurice Hunt (animation) and Joe Johnston (live action)
Screenplay: David Casci, David Kirschner, and Ernie Contreras; based on a story by Kirschner and Casci
Cinematography: Alexander Gruszynski
Editing: Kaja Fehr
Supervising animation: Bruce Smith
Animation sequence direction: Glenn Chaika
Animation supervision: Robert Lence (story), Don Morgan (layout), Jim Hickey (background) and Jeffrey Patch (editor)
Production design: Gay Lawrence and Valerio Ventura
Art direction: Pixote
Casting: Amy Kimmelman
Visual effects supervision: Richard T. Sullivan
Sound: Steve Nelson
Music: James Horner
MPAA rating: G
Running time: 75 minutes

ego, Mr. Hyde. In the land of adventure, they sail out to sea and discover Captain Ahab (voice of George Hearn) as he hunts the great white whale, and Long John Silver (voice of Jim Cummings). In the land of fantasy, they ride magic carpets and battle a dragon. Gradually, Richard overcomes his fears as he is challenged to protect his three friends and escape the dangers that present themselves.

After he has traversed the three realms and rescued his friends from the dragon's flames, Richard awakens and the film resumes in live action. He finds himself on the floor under the rotunda with three dusty books at his side. He eagerly checks them out and returns home. In the final scene, his parents arrive home after searching the neighborhood for him and find him asleep inside his tree house with his books.

It is paradoxical that a film which aims to awaken its viewers to the virtues and pleasure of reading classic literature has the underlying goal of sending the viewers not to the library but to the store in search of the game cartridge. The very title, *The Pagemaster*, sounds more like the title of a video game than of a film, and the structure of the film seems designed around the feasibility of arcade action. For example, literature is presented as a tidy grouping of three specific genres: fantasy, horror, and adventure, each with its corresponding universe. The video game boasts a total of 74 levels within these three main stages. In addition, Richard's goal throughout the journey is to find the exit sign and escape from the library. This is the same goal presented in the video game, which offers numerous paths to the neon sign—hardly a concept that teaches the child to enjoy spending time inside the library.

Furthermore, nothing is learned about the various classics that are portrayed in the story. Richard and his friends zoom past the classic characters on their search for the exit, with little insight or acknowledgment. Their appearance is merely an occasion to deliver on the promise to the parents that this film is about literature. The questions that might inspire a child to take an interest in these stories and characters are never explored—questions such as, "How does Dr. Jekyll deal with the problem of evil?" or "Why is Ahab so passionate about the white whale; what does it signify to him?" Instead, the classic characters whiz past like lifeless dummies in a haunted-house ride. The film was in production for 3 1/2 years, and yet has the appearance of being hasty and undeveloped. In fact, it was in production so long that Macaulay Culkin's voice changed, causing some minor complications.

Culkin has become a highly coveted child star since his starring role in the megahit *Home Alone* (1990) and its sequel. Although well-suited for the role, he plays his character half-heartedly. The voice work of Patrick Stewart as Adventure, a peg-legged pirate with a hook for a hand, is the most captivating. Yet the actors in general are working with an uncaptivating screenplay, portraying extraneous characters.

Director of animation Maurice Hunt began his career at Walt Disney, creating visual effects for *The Fox and the Hound* (1981) and *The Black Cauldron* (1985). The best aspect of his work on *The Pagemaster* is the child's-eye view of the library as both a wondrous and a terrifying place. The journeys into the three lands make use of familiar animation techniques, which do not distinguish themselves. Live-action

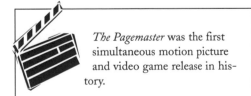

The Pagemaster was the first simultaneous motion picture and video game release in history.

director Joe Johnston, who made his directorial debut with *Honey, I Shrunk the Kids* (1989), succeeds in depicting the tidy landscape and alienation of the suburbs—which could be either completely harmless or terribly treacherous.

The Pagemaster is a film that banked on parents' desires to teach the subtleties of the written word to a generation of children raised on technologically generated media, but it fails to deliver on its promise. Instead, the film is merely representative of the problem.

—*Reni Celeste*

REVIEWS

Chicago Tribune. November 23, 1994, Sec. 1, p. 20.
Chicago Sun-Times. November 23, 1994, p. 41.
Daily Variety. November 21, 1994, p. 2.
The Hollywood Reporter. November 10, 1994, p. 1.
The Hollywood Reporter. November 21, 1994, p. 5.
Los Angeles Times. November 23, 1994, p. F8.
The New York Times. November 23, 1994, p. B7.

The Paint Job

A small-town house painter, Wesley (Will Patton), falls in love with the wife (Bebe Neuwirth) of his demented boss (Robert Pastorelli)—a man who murders drunks who remind him of his father.

REVIEWS

Variety. CCCXLVIII, August 17, 1992, p. 38.

CREDITS

Wesley: Will Patton
Margaret: Bebe Neuwirth
Willie: Robert Pastorelli
Cal: Casey Siemaszko
Tom: Mark Boone, Jr.

Released: 1992
Production: Mark Pollard and Randall Poster; released by Second Son Entertainment Company
Direction: Michael Taav
Screenplay: Michael Taav
Cinematography: Robert Yeoman
Editing: Nancy Richardson
Production design: Mark Friedberg
Art direction: Ginger Tougas
Sound: B. Warner
Costume design: Wendy A. Rolfe
Music: John Wesley Harding
MPAA rating: no listing
Running time: 96 minutes

The Painted Desert

Asian American Sari Hatano (Nobu McCarthy) runs a dilapidated cafe in Nevada, frequented by a friendly gangster, Al (James Gammon), and his cohorts. Several dramas play out in the cafe, involving Sari, Al, and the gangsters, as well as a mysterious Japanese chef (Kayuza Kimura) hired by Sari and Sari's boarder, Barbara (Priscilla Pointer). First American feature film directed by Masato Harada. 🎬

CREDITS

Al: James Gammon
Sari Hatano: Nobu McCarthy
Jiro: Kayuza Kimura
Barbara: Priscilla Pointer
Montana: Don Keith Opper
Franco Vitali: Andreas Katsulas
Latino Scarface: Ron Joseph
Harry: Vincent Schiavelli
Griff: Rudy Diaz
Cosmo: Wayne Pere

Released: 1993
Production: Tikki Goldberg for Kazuyoshi Okuyama, in association with New Dawn Pictures and Skyhawk
Direction: Masato Harada
Screenplay: Masato Harada and Rebecca Ross; based on a story by Harada
Cinematography: David Bridges and Bernard Salzmann
Editing: Rebecca Ross
Production design: Rae Fox
Casting: Miguela Sandoval
Costume design: Eduardo Castro
Music: Masahiro Kawasaki
MPAA rating: no listing
Running time: 106 minutes

REVIEWS

Variety. CCCL, March 22, 1993, p. 53.

The Paper

"A behind-the-lines look at work, marriage, and other forms of combat."—Movie tagline

"Two thumbs up!"—*Siskel & Ebert*

"One of the most entertaining movies to come out of Hollywood in years!"—*US Magazine*

"Don't miss it! I really loved this movie. A terrific cast, well-directed by Ron Howard. You'll have a heck of a good time."—Joel Siegel, *Good Morning America*

 Box Office Gross: $36,745,255 (July 4, 1994)

The world of newspapers has long provided a rich setting for American films. Since the advent of the talkies, the stereotype of the fast-talking journalist, who is part detective, part con artist, part seeker of truth for the republic, has continued to recur in waves over the urban landscape of Hollywood cinema. In the 1930's and 1940's, the intense-

ly driven, wisecracking newspaper reporter was a staple of such films as *Platinum Blonde* (1931), *The Front Page* (1931), *It Happened One Night* (1934), *Front Page Woman* (1935), *Nothing Sacred* (1937), *His Girl Friday* (1940), and *Meet John Doe* (1941). Most of these films emphasized the comic possibilities in the reporter's encounter with the high and the low, the crooked and the innocent.

During the 1950's and 1960's, the reporter's beat seemed supplanted by more interesting arenas such as the corporate boardroom. Yet it resurfaced to grip the public imagination post-Watergate, when the newspaper genre took on a different cast. Reporters acquired the glow of sainthood with *All the President's Men* (1976) and, along the way, lost some of their maniacal, obsessive, and more interestingly human connotations. The newspaper reporter also began to be a slightly anachronistic figure, replaced in the public imagination by the television reporter as a more relevant cultural icon.

With *The Paper*, the newspaper film regains some of its manic fun and relevance. The tabloid-dominated 1990's seemed ripe for a regeneration of the newspaper reporter as sleazoid-hero, and it is no coincidence that a highlight of

CREDITS

Henry Hackett: Michael Keaton
Alicia Clark: Glenn Close
Martha Hackett: Marisa Tomei
Bernie White: Robert Duvall
Dan McDougal: Randy Quaid
Graham Keighley: Jason Robards
Marion Sandusky: Jason Alexander
Paul Bladden: Spalding Gray
Susan: Catherine O'Hara
Janet: Lynne Thigpen
Phil: Jack Kehoe
Carmen: Roma Maffia
Ray Blaisch: Clint Howard
Lou: Geoffrey Owens
Robin: Amelia Campbell
Deanne White: Jill Hennessy
Henry's father: William Prince
Henry's mother: Augusta Dabney
Carl: Bruce Altman
Wilder: Jack McGee

Released: 1994
Production: Brian Grazer and Frederick Zollo for
Imagine Entertainment; released by Universal Pictures
Direction: Ron Howard
Screenplay: David Koepp and Stephen Koepp
Cinematography: John Seale
Editing: Daniel Hanley and Michael Hill
Production design: Todd Hallowell
Art direction: Maher Ahmad
Set decoration: Debra Schutt
Casting: Jane Jenkins and Janet Hirshenson
Sound: Danny Michael
Costume: design Rita Ryack
Music: Randy Newman
MPAA rating: R
Running time: 112 minutes

this Ron Howard-directed comedy-drama should be the hero's theft of a rival newspaper's material while he is interviewing for a job with them. As Henry Hackett (Michael Keaton) later explains to his shocked wife, Martha (Marisa Tomei), he could not stifle the impulse after the *Sentinel*'s representative, Paul Bladden (Spalding Gray), condescendingly called his employer, the SUN, a "cute little newspaper."

"We taint 'em today, make 'em look good tomorrow."—Alicia Clark, in *The Paper*

Such outrageous moments as these make up *The Paper*'s serio-comic story of twenty-four hours in the life of Henry Hackett, the metro editor for a fictional New York

AWARDS AND NOMINATIONS

Academy Awards Nomination 1994: Best Original Song ("Make Up Your Mind")

City tabloid, the "cute little" *New York Sun*. Like Cary Grant's character in Howard Hawks' classic *His Girl Friday*, Henry is married to his job. Although Henry's wife is a reporter too, she is on leave, awaiting the birth of their first child. She is increasingly worried by the prospect that Henry will never be at home to help rear their child. Nevertheless, she allows herself to get sucked into the headline-making vortex that surrounds her husband. In fact, *The Paper* juggles the stories of the Hacketts' personal life and Henry's professional life, as well as touching on the individual trials and tribulations of some of Henry's more colorful colleagues.

Henry's employer is a beleaguered big-city tabloid that goes for the attention-grabbing headlines rather than in-depth analysis. When the senior staff meet, their biggest decision of the day appears to be clearcut: whether to foreground a grisly subway wreck or the racial murder of two white businessmen from out of town. While he handles a workload that keeps him at the paper for most of the day and night, Henry attempts to improve his relationship with his wife. Most crucially, he faces the decision whether to please his wife by accepting a more prestigious nine-to-five job at a rival paper, the upscale *Sentinel*. As Henry's theft during his job interview demonstrates, he makes this decision in an unconventional, half-conscious way because he obviously loves the job he has, in spite of the hours, the deadlines, and the chaos.

As he attempts to juggle work and his personal life, Henry does become keenly aware that no one at his paper seems to have close to a normal life. Alicia Clark (Glenn Close), the managing editor, is a former reporter who got bumped up to "bean counting," that is, keeping the bankruptcy-threatened paper out of the red. She is unhappy in her job and uneasy in her relations with her coworkers, who tend to regard her as the enemy. Alicia has a husband she never sees and a lover who means less to her than the cost of the hotel room where they have their romantic trysts. Grizzled editor-in-chief Bernie White (Robert Duvall) is a consummate professional who also has lived almost solely for his work, but now finds out that he has cancer and no emotional support—his children have long given up on him.

Even though Henry sees how the lives of his coworkers

resonate with his own, he thrives on deadlines and the competition with other papers. An edgy risk-taker, he insists on pursuing a fragile lead that might clear two African American youths jailed for the businessmen's murder, not only that justice might be served but also to scoop the paper's rivals. Only hours before the "type is set," he races against time to prove his hunch and, in the process, utilizes the abilities of everyone around him to secure his story. He ultimately must rely on everything from his pregnant wife's ability to charm a Justice Department official to Alicia's long-untapped core of journalistic integrity.

Henry is abetted in this race against the clock by an unlikely helpmate, a paranoid columnist, Dan McDougal (Randy Quaid), who has taken to sleeping in Henry's office because he fears reprisals for his editorials that target the city's parking commissioner. He has also begun tucking a loaded gun in his pants belt and occasionally using it for crowd control at the office. He and Henry learn that the apparent racial murder that dominates the other papers' headlines was actually a mob hit. They start scouring for the information that will clear the two innocent teenagers of the mob murder and also allow the *Sun* to scoop the competition with an "exclusive." They finally get the necessary official confirmation in an unlikely place: the men's room of a police precinct headquarters. Yet the nail-biting is not over: They have missed the paper's deadline. This situation leads to what may become the film's most infamous scene—a brawl between Alicia and Henry when the latter decides to stop the presses.

The Paper occasionally strains credulity, though not in the outrageousness of its characters' behavioral excesses. The film's snappy delineation of the ambiance of newspaper work as tabloid madness rings true, and it seems no surprise that it was scripted by former newspaper reporter and *Time* magazine senior editor Stephen Koepp and his brother, David Koepp, coscreenwriter on *Jurassic Park* (1993). *The Paper* disappoints only in those moments when it depends on sentimentality instead of energy. The birth of Martha and Henry's baby and Bernie's wistful secret observance of his estranged daughter are two such moments when the script,

Some scenes from *The Paper* were shot inside the newsroom of the *New York Post*.

in combination with director Ron Howard's penchant for close-ups and obvious camera setups, begins to get the best of his outstanding ensemble of actors. In spite of Howard's proven ability to dip successfully into the trough of tears in such films as *Cocoon* (1985), *The Paper* is a film that does markedly better with the sensational than the sentimental.

As to be expected from a picture bursting at the seams with talented actors, including a number who have won or been nominated for Academy Awards, *The Paper's* primary strength is in its ensemble acting, a feature of other Howard-directed films such as *Cocoon* and *Parenthood* (1989). Michael Keaton is ably abetted in the last half of the film by Randy Quaid, who gives what is perhaps the film's best supporting performance in the juicy role of McDougal. It becomes apparent, however, that there are limitations in the script's attempt to juggle the personal stories of some of the major characters. Actors like Close and Duvall are left with little material for creating three-dimensional characters, and the film tends to infuse sentimentality into some roles, as with Bernie's, that seems at odds with its unsentimental look at other characters, especially its women.

The Paper is best at its most frantic, and Michael Keaton captures some of the infectious, I-love-this-stinking-job spirit of classic motion-picture reporters. While, as some critics pointed out, the film is not a serious or realistic portrait of tabloid journalism—a growing phenomenon with important implications—*The Paper* does succeed as entertainment. In this respect, it may prove that it is time, once again, to "start the presses" in Hollywood filmmaking.

—*Gaylyn Studlar*

REVIEWS

Entertainment Weekly. March 18, 1994, p. 72.
The Hollywood Reporter. March 14, 1994, p. 8.
Los Angeles Times. March 18, 1994, p. F1.
The New York Times. March 18, 1994, p. B1.
Variety. March 14, 1994, p. 4.

Paper Hearts

A middle-aged woman, Jenny (Sally Kirkland), deserted by her womanizing husband, Henry (James Brolin), struggles to make ends meet and come to terms with her life as the family gathers for the wedding of her daughter Kat (Renee Estevez). Feature-film directorial debut of Rod McCall.

CREDITS

Jenny: Sally Kirkland
Henry: James Brolin
Samantha: Pamela Gidley
Tom: Kris Kristofferson
Patsy: Laura Johnson
Bill: Michael Moore
Kat: Renee Estevez
Brady: Mickey Cottrell

Released: 1993
Production: Rod McCall and Catherine Wanek; released by King/Moonstone

Direction: Rod McCall
Screenplay: Rod McCall
Cinematography: Barry Markowitz
Editing: Curtis Edge
Production design: Susan Brand
Art direction: Stuart Blatt
Casting: Tom Kahn and Mary Ann Smith
Sound: Jonathan Earl Stein
Costume design: Leslie Daniel Rainer
Music: George S. Clinton
Songs: Kris Kristofferson
MPAA rating: no listing
Running time: 90 minutes

REVIEWS

Variety. CCCL, February 1, 1993, p. 100.

Passages

Set in a German rehabilitation center, this semi-factual drama centers on a group of physically handicapped adolescents coming to terms with their disabilities. Directorial debut of Yilmaz Arslan.

CREDITS

Nina Kunzendorf: Nina Kunzendorf
Dieter Resch: Dieter Resch
Martin Seeger: Martin Seeger
Marco Neumeier: Marco Neumeier
Tarik Senouci: Tarik Senouci
Alexandra Krieger: Alexandra Krieger
Juana Volkers: Juana Volkers
Agnes Steinacker: Agnes Steinacker
Hermine Mischon: Hermine Mischon
Andreas Frank: Andreas Frank
Christian Verhoeven: Christian Verhoeven

Origin: Germany
Released: 1993
Production: Released by O-Film
Direction: Yilmaz Arslan
Screenplay: Yilmaz Arslan
Cinematography: Izzet Akay
Editing: Bettina Bohler
Music: Ralph Graf
MPAA rating: no listing
Running time: 80 minutes

REVIEWS

The New York Times. March 23, 1993, p. C14.

A Passion to Kill

"Beware of the black widow's touch."—Movie tagline

A Los Angeles psychiatrist, Dr. David Lawson (Scott Bakula), initiates an adulterous affair with the beautiful but disturbed wife, Diana (Chelsea Field), of his best friend, Jerry (John Getz). When several people are murdered, Diana becomes the prime suspect.

CREDITS

Dr. David Lawson: Scott Bakula
Diana Chamberlain: Chelsea Field
Beth: Sheila Kelley
Jerry Chamberlain: John Getz
Ted: Rex Smith
Lou: France Nuyen
Morales: Eddie Valez
Martindale: Michael Warren

Released: 1994
Production: Bruce Cohn Curtis for Rysher Entertainment; released by A-Pix Entertainment
Direction: Rick King
Screenplay: William Delligan
Cinematography: Paul Ryan
Editing: David H. Lloyd
Production design: Ivo Cristante
Set decoration: Tim Collohan
Casting: Denise Chamian
Costume design: Barbara Palmer
Music: Robert Sprayberry
MPAA rating: R
Running time: 93 minutes

REVIEWS

Entertainment Weekly. December 23, 1994, p. 80.
Los Angeles Times. October 21, 1994, p. F8.
The New York Times. November 4, 1994, p. C10.
Variety. CCCLVI, October 24, 1994, p. 68.

PCU

"Flunk'em if they can't take a joke."—Movie tagline

 Box Office Gross: $4,318,118 (June 5, 1994)

PCU stands for Port Chester University, dominated by absurd notions of political correctness, but, unfortunately, the filmmakers do not seem to fully grasp what is (or should be) at issue here. It attempts to be a satire, but it fails to define its target: academic folly done in the name of political correctness. The film falls flat as it stumbles over one clumsy caricature after another while it attempts to advance a badly developed, ill-conceived plot that attempts to tell its story by following a preppy from Delaware named Tom Lawrence (Chris Young) through a week of orientation.

In his preppie blazer and necktie, Tom is a misfit and a throwback, but, then, so are the rest of the students, the majority of whom appear to be hippie stereotypes. A few are seen working at their computers on their term papers. Tom, being an awkward klutz, manages to unplug all the computers, causing a riot and an angry chase sequence.

Tom is assigned to an upperclassman named Droz (Jeremy Piven, too old for the role), who lives with other free spirits dedicated to boozing and partying in a converted fraternity house called "The Pit." Droz is sexually interested in Samantha (Sarah Trigger), who has converted to a group of politically correct "Womynists" (led by Viveka Davis) and has forgotten how to have fun. Most of the satire is directed against these feminists and the "Meat is Murder" vegans.

Meanwhile, there is a conspiracy afoot by Conservative preppies to recover their frat house that is now occupied by Droz and his friends. This conspiracy is led by Rand McPherson (David Spade, a regular on *Saturday Night Live*) in cahoots with PCU President Andrea Garcia-Thompson (Jessica Walter), an uptight academic who wants Droz and his crowd expelled. To keep the house, Droz and his friends have to pay $7,000 in damages. To raise the money, they decide to throw a huge party and charge $5.00 a head for admission. Can they get 1,500 partygoers?

They need an attraction, but by coincidence, George Clinton and his Parliament Funkadelic band happens to be passing through and agrees to provide the music. Droz and his friends raise the money needed, but the President then presents them with a list of complaints: "I warned you your attitude was disrupting this campus," she says. "The students have spoken. You're out of here!"

So Droz and his friends conspire to get President Thompson fired by staging a "No Protest" demonstration at the bicentennial celebration that takes place the next day. Droz takes over the microphone and gives an impassioned speech urging students to have a good time. The Trustees are shocked by the demonstration. "Your inability to control the students has convinced us that you are an ineffective President," says the Chairman of the Board of Trustees (Colin Fox). "You're fired, Thompson!" After this contrived climax, Tom, the visiting student goes

"...that's the beauty of college these days, Tommy. You can major in Game Boy if you know how to B.S."—Droz to Tom

back to Delaware, telling Droz and the rest, "I'll see ya in the fall."

The curriculum at Port Chester is said to be political correctness, but PC is not a "curriculum." It is a consequence of our supersensitive times, an attitude, a dogma, and a perversion that replaces thought with feeling and threatens to destroy free speech and academic freedom. The writers reflect this, when President Thompson intervenes to break up the Pit party, accompanied by brown-shirted guards—an academic dictator with her fascist security force.

The learning experience is satirized by Pigman (Jody Racicot), obsessively "researching" his "Caine/ Hackman" thesis by constantly watching videos, while attempting to prove that "no matter what time it is, 24 hours a day, you can find a Gene Hackman or Michael Caine movie playing on TV." In the midst of the film's culminating "Pit Party," he discovers *A Bridge Too Far* (1977), a film that stars both Michael Caine and Gene Hackman together. "This is my thesis, man," he says in jubilation. "This is my closing argument. I don't have to watch television anymore!"

A glance at the cast immediately exposes the inadequacy of this silly little movie. It's a feeble campus comedy, attempting to be an *Animal House* for the 1990s. Jon Favreau does a weak John Belushi imitation portraying a character named Gutter. Its biggest stars are SNL's David Spade and Parliament Funkadelic's George Clinton, famous for such hits as "Maggot Brain" and "Free Your Mind and Your Ass Will Follow."

PCU was the feature film debut for director Hart Bochner. Writers Adam Leff and Zak Penn were classmates at Wesleyan University. Their first original story concept became *The Last Action Hero* (1993), but that concept was developed into a screenplay by more experienced hands, Shane Black and David Arnott, and four other uncredited writers, including William Goldman. Leff and Penn needed help on this one, too.

—*James M. Welsh*

CREDITS

Droz: Jeremy Piven
Tom: Chris Young
Gutter: Jon Favreau
Rand McPherson: David Spade
Samantha: Sarah Trigger
Mersh: Jake Buscy
President Garcia-Thompson: Jessica Walter
George Clinton: George Clinton

Released: 1994
Production: Paul Schiff; released by Twentieth Century-Fox
Direction: Hart Bochner
Screenplay: Adam Leff and Zak Penn
Cinematography: Reynaldo Villalobos
Editing: Nicholas C. Smith
Production design: Steven Jordan
Art direction: David M. Davis
Set decoration: Enrico Campana
Casting: Margery Simkin
Sound: David Lee
Costume design: Mary Zophres
Music: Steve Vai
MPAA rating: PG-13
Running time: 80 minutes

REVIEWS

The Detroit News. April 29, 1994, D2.
Entertainment Weekly. May 13, 1994, p. 42.
The Hollywood Reporter. April 29-May 1, 1994, pp. 7, 14.
Los Angeles Times. April 29, 1994, F8.
The New York Times. April 29, 1994, B10.
People Weekly. May 16, 1994, p. 30.
Variety. April 29, 1994, p. 10.

Peaceful Air of the West

This episodic Italian drama revolves around numerous romantic encounters, the principal one involving a nurse, Veronica (Patrizia Piccinini), who has an affair with a married man, Tobia (Ivano Marescotti).

CREDITS

Cesare Noviti: Fabrizio Bentivoglio
Veronica: Patrizia Piccinini
Tobia: Ivano Marescotti
Irene: Antonella Fattori
Mario: Roberto Accorncro
Clara: Silli Togni
Rosa: Olga Durane
Cesare's friend: Cesare Bocci

Origin: Italy
Released: 1991
Production: Monogatari/PIC Film with SSR-RTSI; released by Pyramide Films
Direction: Silvio Soldini
Screenplay: Silvio Soldini and Roberto Tiraboschi
Cinematography: Luca Bigazzi
Editing: Claudio Cormio
Music: Giovanni Venosta
MPAA rating: no listing
Running time: 100 minutes

The Peyote Road

A 1990 Supreme Court decision concerning Native American use of peyote—a reportedly hallucinogenic substance—during religious ceremonies is the subject of this documentary.

REVIEWS

Booklist. XC, March 15, 1994, p. 1381.
Los Angeles Times. March 4, 1994, p. F15.
School Library Journal. XL, April 1994, p. 87.
The Washington Post. May 20, 1994, p. C7.

CREDITS

Narrator: Peter Coyote

Released: 1994
Production: Gary Rhine, in association with Peacedream Productions, with participation by Eagle Heart Productions and the Native American Religious Freedom Project; released by Kifaru
Direction: Gary Rhine, Fidel Moreno, and Phil Cousineau
Screenplay: Phil Cousineau
Editing: Gary Rhine
Online editing: Dan Hayes
MPAA rating: no listing
Running time: 59 minutes

The Phantom of the Opera

This adaptation of Gaston Leroux's 1911 novel, which stars David Staller in the title role, first opened in 1990 at the Hirschfeld Theater in Miami Beach, Florida. The video version was filmed in 1991 when the play opened in New York City at the 57th Street Playhouse in Manhattan.

REVIEWS

Variety. CCCXXXVII, November 8, 1989, p. 36.

CREDITS

Phantom: David Staller
Christine Daae: Elizabeth Walsh
Carlotta: Beth McVey
Raoul de Chagny: Christopher Rath
Moncharmin: Darin de Paul
Richard: Richard Kinter

Released: 1991
Production: Hirschfeld Productions
Direction: Darwin Knight
Screenplay: Bruce Falstein; based on the 1911 novel by Gaston Leroux
Videotape direction: Angel Hernandez
Choreography: Darwin Knight
Music: Paul Schierhorn and Lawrence Rosen
MPAA rating: no listing
Running time: 93 minutes

The Philadelphia Experiment II

In this science fiction/adventure film, a military time-travel experiment goes wrong, resulting in the Nazis gaining possession of a 1990's stealth bomber and winning World War II. David Herdeg (Brad Johnson) thus finds himself a fugitive living in an alternate present-day United States and must travel back in time to put things right. Sequel to *The Philadelphia Experiment* (1984).

REVIEWS

The New York Times. November 13, 1993, p. A18.
Variety. CCCLIII, November 29, 1993, p. 31.
The Washington Post. March 31, 1994, p. C7.

CREDITS

David Herdeg: Brad Johnson
Jess: Marjean Holden
Dr. William Mailer: Gerrit Graham
Professor Longstreet: James Greene
Logan: Geoffrey Blake
Decker: Cyril O'Reilly
Benjamin Herdeg: John Christian Grass
Friederich Mahler: Gerrit Graham

Released: 1993
Production: Mark Levinson and Doug Curtis; released by Trimark Pictures
Direction: Stephen Cornwell
Screenplay: Kevin Rock and Nick Paine
Cinematography: Ronn Schmidt
Editing: Nina Gilberti
Production design: Armin Ganz
Art direction: Kirk Petruccelli
Casting: Linda Phillips Palo
Special effects: Frank Ceglia
Sound: Ed White and Ken Mantlo
Costume design: Eileen Kennedy
Stunt coordination: Rawn Hutchinson
Music: Gerald Couriet
MPAA rating: PG-13
Running time: 97 minutes

Picture This: The Life and Times of Peter Bogdanovich in Archer City, Texas

Documentarian George Hickenlooper returns the cast and crew of Peter Bogdanovich's *The Last Picture Show* (1971) to Archer City, Texas, where the motion picture was filmed, and focuses on how the turbulent personal lives of those making the film affected the film itself.

REVIEWS

USA Today. CXXIII, March 1995, p. 97.

CREDITS

Larry McMurtry: Larry McMurtry
Peter Bogdanovich: Peter Bogdanovich
Randy Quaid: Randy Quaid
Polly Platt: Polly Platt
Cybill Shepherd: Cybill Shepherd
Timothy Bottoms: Timothy Bottoms

Released: 1991
Production: Timothy Bottoms and Sam Bottoms; released by Kino-Eye American Film and Nelson Entertainment
Direction: George Hickenlooper
Screenplay: George Hickenlooper
Cinematography: Kevin Burget
Editing: Howard Lavick
Sound: Paul Federbush
Music: Stephen Bruton
MPAA rating: no listing
Running time: 62 minutes

A Place in the World

This warmly nostalgic drama centers on a young man, Ernesto (Gaston Batyi), who reminisces about his youth in a small Argentinian village, when his political idealist parents (Federico Luppi and Cecilia Roth) banded together with a like-minded nun (Leonor Benedetto) to fight exploitation of the local shepherds by corrupt landowners.

REVIEWS

Chicago Tribune. November 25, 1994, p. 7M.
Los Angeles Times. February 26, 1993, p. F4.
Los Angeles Times. August 17, 1994, p. F5.
The New York Times. July 1, 1994, p. C3.

CREDITS

Hans: Jose Sacristan
Mario: Federico Luppi
Ana: Cecilia Roth
Nelda: Leonor Benedetto
Ernesto: Gaston Batyi
Andrada: Rodolfo Ranni
Luciana: Lorena Del Rio

Origin: Uruguay and Argentina
Released: 1992
Production: Adolfo Aristarain; released by First Look Pictures Releasing
Direction: Adolfo Aristarain
Screenplay: Adolfo Aristarain and Alberto Lecchi; based on a story by Aristarain and Kathy Saavedra
Cinematography: Ricardo De Angelis
Editing: Eduardo Lopez
Production design: Abel Facello
Costume design: Kathy Saavedra
Music: Camerata Bariloche
MPAA rating: no listing
Running time: 120 minutes

The Plague

This adaptation of Albert Camus's novel *The Plague* (1947) is set in 1990's Buenos Aires and stars William Hurt as Dr. Bernard Rieux, the dedicated physician who tries valiantly to help the city's sick and dying populace. The all-star cast also includes Sandrine Bonnaire, Robert Duvall, Raul Julia, and Victoria Tennant.

CREDITS

Dr. Bernard Rieux: William Hurt
Martine Rambert: Sandrine Bonnaire
Jean Tarrou: Jean-Marc Barr
Joseph Grand: Robert Duvall
Cottard: Raul Julia
Father Paneloux: Lautaro Murua
Alicia Rieux: Victoria Tennant
No character identified: Atilio Veronelli, Francisco Cocuzza and Laura Palmucci

Origin: France and Argentina
Released: 1992
Production: Cyril de Rouvre, Christian Charret, John R. Pepper, and Jonathan Prince for Cyril de Rouvre-the Pepper-Prince Co. Ltd.-Oscar Kramer S.A., in association with Cinemania and with the participation of Canal Plus
Production: Released by Gaumont
Direction: Luis Puenzo
Screenplay: Luis Puenzo; adapted from *The Plague*, by Albert Camus
Cinematography: Felix Monti
Editing: Juan Carlos Macias
Production design: Jorge Sarundiansky and Juan Carlos
Production management: Raul Outeda and Leo Guignier
Sound: Jean-Pierre Ruh
Costume design: Maria Julia Bertotto
MPAA rating: no listing
Running time: 146 minutes

Pontiac Moon

"Original, off-beat and very funny...It's a great ride!"—Bob Healy, *Satellite News Network*

Early in this film, star Ted Danson has an unintentionally funny line. "Being average was never my aspiration," says Washington Bellamy, the over-the-top character created by Danson for this sadly misguided film about a kooky family and a 1949 Pontiac convertible. The irony of that line is difficult to ignore: this film clearly aspires to be something special, but ends up being less-than-average.

Perhaps one of the problems rests in the film's premise. *Pontiac Moon* takes place in 1969 during the first moon landing. It is about a road trip taken by Washington Bellamy (Danson) and his eleven-year-old son Andy (Ryan Todd), the purpose of which is to drive far enough in Bellamy's old Pontiac so as to arrive at the "Spires of the Moon" national park at the same time as the Apollo VII lands on the moon. Concurrently, the agoraphobic Mrs. Bellamy (Mary Steenburgen) leaves home for the first time in seven years, following her husband and son in their supposed grand adventure. The film is about big themes, namely the importance of venturing forth into the unknown and facing your fears. Certainly, this is a worthy idea, but the importance of the central event which drives (no pun intended) the characters is only in the mind of Danson's character, and it is hard for the audience to see the mystical significance of putting several hundred miles on an old Pontiac. It feels more like a ride in an amusement park than the magical journey it purports to be.

"Life is just outside the door."—Washington Bellamy in *Pontiac Moon*

There are some magical moments provided by the camera work of director Peter Medak and cinematographer Thomas Klass, particularly in their filming of the magnificent, sweeping vistas of the west. There is a bit more magic in the theatrical night sky as well as in the film's visually stunning ending where the family rides off in the night, having turned their Pontiac into a boat.

Unfortunately, the actors, working from Finn Taylor and Jeffrey Brown's exaggerated, grandiose script, do not fare as well as the scenery. Ted Danson seems to be having the time of his life playing Bellamy, a combination of Mary Poppins and Mr. Chips. Danson's character says things like, "you can be so careful that you're not alive anymore" or "life is just outside this door." The lack of dimension of the character exacerbates the sappy the dialogue. Danson is apparently so in love with the quirkiness of his handicapped, homily-spouting character that this normally charming actor is actually quite irritating. His affected speech, peppered with the occasional "my dear," and the patronizing tone in his voice make it understandable why he nearly gets pummeled by a redneck (Don Swayze) in a country store.

The normally exquisite Steenburgen also suffers in a role that has little depth and is loosely directed by Medak. The audience first meets Katherine Bellamy when she is cowering in a corner because a neighbor boy comes over to visit her son. Later, when Washington tries to get her to step outside, she nearly has a seizure. So it is particularly hard to believe that this character, whom the audience knows is severely agoraphobic, would go out of the house and drive a car to chase her family across the country. Steenburgen is well-cast, but similar to Danson, does not play against the inherent one-dimensional outlandishness of her character, apparently forcing the humor rather than allowing it to emerge.

Young Ryan Todd fares the best of the leads. Though his character is meant to be the "sane" one of the family, the discrepancy between his normalcy and his parents' cartoon-

CREDITS

Washington Bellamy: Ted Danson
Katherine Bellamy: Mary Steenburgen
Andy Bellamy: Ryan Todd
Ernest Ironplume: Eric Schweig
Lorraine: Cathy Moriarty
Jerome Bellamy: Max Gail

Released: 1994
Production: Robert Schaffel and Youssef Vahabzadeh; released by Paramount Pictures
Direction: Peter Medak
Screenplay: Finn Taylor and Jeffrey Brown; based on a story by Taylor
Cinematography: Thomas Klass
Editing: Anne V. Coates
CE Production design: Jeffrey Beecroft
Art direction: William Ladd Skinner
Set decoration: Robert J. Franco
Casting: Jane Jenkins and Janet Hirshenson
Sound: Kim Ornitz and Ric Waddel
Costume design: Ruth Myers
Music: Randy Edelman
MPAA rating: PG-13
Running time: 107 minutes

like pathology is so vast that Todd appears to be in a different movie than his co-stars.

A serene young Indian man named Ernest Ironplume (Eric Schweig) and Bellamy's cool-guy brother (Max Gail), both pop up at completely illogical places in the story, apparently to teach important lessons to the characters. This specious, all-too-convenient inclusion of these characters is another example of the film's prioritization of style over substance.

On the plus side, there is some fine intercutting of the original Apollo VII landing, the aforementioned beautiful landscape, and the nostalgic, well-designed score by Randy Edelman. The film's biggest plus comes in Cathy Moriarty's performance as a tough waitress. When Steenburgen drives Moriarity home and she points down a deserted road on which sits one lone, dilapidated trailer and says, "mine's the one on the left," the audience knows what this movie could have been.

—*Kirby Tepper*

REVIEWS

Entertainment Weekly. May 12, 1995, p. 72.
The Hollywood Reporter. November 6-9, 1994. p. 10.
Los Angeles Times. November 11, 1994, p. F2.
The New York Times. November 11, 1994, p. C18.
People Weekly. XLII, November 28, 1994, p. 21.
Variety. November 4, 1994. p. 2.
Variety. CCCLVII, November 7, 1994, p. 46.

Primary Motive

Andrew Blumenthal (Judd Nelson)—working for political candidate John Eastham (Frank Converse)—convinces his girlfriend, Darcy Link (Justine Bateman), to go to work for the opposition in order to uncover incriminatory information about the corrupt Chris Poulas (Richard Jordan). Unfortunately, Poulas is able to turn events to his advantage and even manages to seduce Darcy.

REVIEWS

Variety. CCCXLVII, July 20, 1992, p. 64.

CREDITS

Andrew Blumenthal: Judd Nelson
Darcy Link: Justine Bateman
Chris Poulas: Richard Jordan
Wallace Roberts: John Savage
Ken Blumenthal: Malachi Throne
Paul Melton: Joe Grifasi

John Eastham: Frank Converse
Stephanie Poulas: Jennifer Youngs
Helen Poulas: Sally Kirkland

Released: 1992
Production: Thomas Gruenberg, Don Carmody, and Richard Rosenberg for Blossom Pictures; released by Fox Video
Direction: Daniel Adams
Screenplay: William Snowden and Daniel Adams
Cinematography: John Drake
Editing: Jaqueline Carmody
Production design: Dan Yarhi
Casting: Lynn Kressel
Sound: R. Trevor Black
Makeup: Bill Miller-Jones
Costume design: Julie Engelsman
Music: John Cale
MPAA rating: R
Running time: 93 minutes

The Princess and the Goblin

"An enchanting princess, an outrageous goblin, a magical adventure for the entire family."
—Movie tagline

"My children thoroughly enjoyed this animated fairy tale."—Michael Medved, *Sneak Previews*

"*The Princess and the Goblin* is graced with picturebook charm and a sweetly rambunctious spirit."—Bob Campbell, *Newhouse Newspapers*

"The perfect animated feature...thrilling, exciting, magical fun!"—Colleen Hartry, *Parent Film Reviews*

 Box Office Gross: $2,092,033 (July 31, 1994)

This animated adaptation of a nineteenth century novel by George MacDonald centers on a sheltered princess, Irene (voice of Sally Ann Marsh), who teams with a miner's son, Curdie (voice of Peter Murray), to defeat the evil goblins who threaten to overrun her kingdom.

REVIEWS

Atlanta Constitution. June 3, 1994, p. P4.
Boston Globe. June 3, 1994, p. 85.
Chicago Tribune. June 3, 1994, p. 7H.
Los Angeles Times. June 3, 1994, p. F61.
The New York Times. June 3, 1994, p. C15.
School Library Journal. XXXIX, April 1993, p. 72.
The Washington Post. June 6, 1994, p. D7.
The Washington Post. June 9, 1994, p. C7.

CREDITS

Origin: Wales and Hungary
King: Joss Ackland (voice)
Great-Great-Grandmother: Claire Bloom (voice)
Princess Irene: Sally Ann Marsh (voice)
Prince Froglip: Rik Mayall (voice)
Curdie: Peter Murray (voice)
Queen: Peggy Mount (voice)

Released: 1993
Production: Robin Lyons for Siriol Productions and Pannonia Film Company, in association with S4C Wales and NHK Enterprises; released by Hemdale Communications, Inc.
Direction: Jozsef Gemes
Screenplay: Robin Lyons; based on the book by George MacDonald
Editing: Magda Hap
Animation direction: Les Orton
Music: Istvan Lerch
MPAA rating: G
Running time: 82 minutes

Princess Caraboo

"A gentle, charming family comedy, a romp."
—*The New York Times*

"Witty and hilarious...lively and a constant pleasure."—*Los Angeles Times*

"Four stars. The supporting cast is laugh-out-loud hilarious."—*New York Post*

"A splendid surprise."—*Sneak Previews*

 Box Office Gross: $2,974,661 (November 6, 1994)

Whimsical and sweet, this delightful romantic comedy harks back to early nineteenth century England, a time of fascination with sea voyages to exotic and faraway places. A local journalist and the film's protagonist, Gutch (Stephen Rea), provides the opening narration, voicing his own fascination with tropical islands and adventure when he was young, as well as his disappointment with the course his life has since taken. He also adds that this was a time when beggars were harshly dealt with. Enter a mysterious young woman (Phoebe Cates) who appears in a field in rural England, dressed in trousers and a turban, apparently a foreigner who does not speak English.

She is given shelter by a kind-hearted and wealthy local woman—Mrs. Worrall (Wendy Hughes)—who resides on a large estate near Bristol. The young woman manages to communicate that her name is Caraboo. Unfortunately, Mr. Worrall (Jim Broadbent), a blustering, womanizing drunkard, returns home to find what he perceives to be a beggar under his roof and sends her to the assizes. When Mrs. Worrall retrieves her, the young woman conveys, with a few

 *Princess Caraboo* is based on a supposed true story about a Pacific island princess who arrived in England in 1817.

hand gestures and foreign- sounding words, that her father was a king. Those around her surmise that she may have been shipwrecked and enslaved.

Throughout the film, the audience is amused by tales that evolve around this mysterious young woman. Nevertheless, one person stands firm and doggedly refuses to accept any of it—the journalist, Gutch. Intrigued by the mysterious young woman, Gutch investigates all possible leads to her true identity. Gutch is the one who voices the key to Caraboo's success—that she has a certain pride, a certain spirit in her bearing that causes one to doubt that she is a mere beggar. Although Gutch remains firm in his resolve to uncover the truth, he watches amusedly as his "betters" are taken in.

In fact, the magic of this film is based almost entirely on Cates's performance, one that involves virtually no dialogue. Through her facial expressions, hand gestures, colorful idiosyncrasies, and small kindnesses, Cates creates a character for whom all the other characters, as well as the audience, develop a sincere sympathy. Her thick, curved eyebrows, dark complexion, and simple beauty aid in her portrayal. The audience, as well as the characters, want this woman's story to be true. In fact, some of her strongest detractors eventually become her most fervent supporters.

The Worralls, hoping to gain social standing and business favors, do nothing to discourage the idea that the young lady under their roof is royalty. In fact, Mrs. Worrall takes to wearing turbans herself instead of the customary elegant period chapeaus. For his part, Mr. Worrall, seeing the possibility of foreign business deals, tolerates the young woman's presence. Nevertheless, Gutch convinces the couple to allow a pedantic linguist, Professor Wilkinson (John Lithgow), to investigate the young woman's claims. Initially the largest skeptic of them all, Wilkinson interrogates Caraboo relentlessly. Yet the princess has an undeniable charm to which the aging professor is not immune. She wins him over, just as she does everyone else. In fact, Wilkinson is finally evicted from the household, a blubbering, lovesick old man.

Events come to a head when Mrs. Worrall's high-society friends begin to take an interest in Caraboo and kidnap her from the Worralls' home. The princess is to be the guest of honor at an elaborate costume party for the Prince Regent (John Sessions), an effete, pompous young man. The party takes place in an elaborately decorated mansion, the predominant color being red, where all the rather decadent guests are dressed in garish Oriental costume—except Caraboo, who wears a long white gown, much like Cinderella at the ball. Caraboo's quiet yet self-assured manner and beauty charm the prince, so that he, like almost every other man in this film, becomes smitten with her.

Meanwhile, Gutch crashes the party and urges Caraboo to stop the charade. He admits that he loves her yet still maintains that she is a fraud. He is afraid of the consequences should she be found out. Caraboo remains indecipherable—never registering any comprehension of what anyone is saying. Meanwhile, the Worralls, who have been worried that their precious meal ticket into high society may be gone forever, ride to her rescue and wait outside in their carriage all night, until the party dies down. Then Mrs. Worrall, obviously the stronger-willed of the two, enters the

CREDITS

Princess Caraboo: Phoebe Cates
Mr. Worrall: Jim Broadbent
Mrs. Worrall: Wendy Hughes
Frixos: Kevin Kline
Professor Wilkinson: John Lithgow
Gutch: Stephen Rea
Lord Apthorpe: Peter Eyre
Lady Apthorpe: Jacqueline Pearce
Magistrate Haythorne: Roger Lloyd Pack
Reverend Hunt: John Wells
Amon McCarthy: John Lynch
Prince Regent: John Sessions
Betty: Arkie Whiteley

Origin: Great Britain
Released: 1994
Production: Andrew Karsch and Simon Bosanquet for Beacon Communications, Longfellow Pictures, and Artisan Films; released by TriStar Pictures
Direction: Michael Austin
Screenplay: Michael Austin and John Wells
Cinematography: Freddie Francis
Editing: George Akers
Production design: Michael Howells
Art direction: Sam Riley
Set decoration: Sasha Schwertd
Casting: Lucy Boulting
Sound: Peter Glossop
Choreography: Anthony von Laast
Costume design: Tom Rand
Music: Richard Hartley
MPAA rating: PG
Running time: 96 minutes

mansion uninvited, weaves her way among the passed-out partiers, and retrieves the princess.

As the Worralls ride away in their carriage, they are startled when they are stopped by the prince's guards on horseback—reminiscent of the film's opening scene when the guards are shown mercilessly chasing vagrants. Much to the Worralls' relief, however, the prince merely wishes to extend his protection to the princess, and the guards accompany the Worralls and Caraboo to their residence. This action on the part of the Prince Regent marks Princess Caraboo's ultimate victory. Unfortunately, the event also proves to be her undoing.

Shortly after the ball, a well-to-do woman and her daughter, who had been interviewed earlier by Gutch during his investigation, recognize the

"If this girl had really come from the streets but had invented a language and kingdom to make fools of a class she had been taught to fear and obey, I swear I would cherish her forever."—Gutch in *Princess Caraboo*

description of Caraboo in the newspaper as resembling a character in a bedtime story that a former servant of theirs, Mary Baker, was in the habit of telling the little girl. Princess Caraboo, it turns out, is no princess at all. She is, in fact, a simple Irish girl who, homeless and hungry, went from a home for prostitutes to work for an English family. Unable to maintain the charade when confronted by this honest little girl, Caraboo is forced to admit the entire act was a hoax. Looking Mrs. Worrall in the eye, the sometime princess says quite simply, in perfect English, "Very sorry, Mum."

This simple phrase harks back to the beginning of the film, when journalist Gutch remarks that people believe two things: what they read in the newspapers, and what they want to. The discovery that Caraboo is a fraud is as much a shock to the audience as to the film's characters. Phoebe Cates creates such a marvelous persona that one wants to believe her story. This desire to believe her is based on the likability of the character, particularly compared to the unlikability of almost everyone else. From the Prince Regent on down, the English upper class is depicted as a bunch of dissolute snobs and toadying idiots, the Worralls included. As Mrs. Worrall admits in the end, as much to herself as to everyone else, they were as much at fault as the young woman. They accepted her as an Oriental princess because they wanted to—she to gain social standing and Mr. Worrall to curry business favors.

No one holds the Worralls more in contempt than their own Greek butler, Frixos, played to the hilt by an outstanding Kevin Kline—Phoebe Cates' real-life husband. From the outset, Frixos declares that "These Worralls, they are idiots," and adds that Mr. Worrall is an idiot and that Mrs. Worrall is too kind. Frixos scarcely deigns to wait on Caraboo, declaring her to be a mere gypsy. In a particularly amusing scene, Frixos, who suspects that Caraboo really does understand English, whispers in her ear as he serves her soup at the Worralls' dinner table, first that he has spit in her soup, then that he has urinated in it. Caraboo never bats an eyelash, as Frixos watches her sip her soup as calm and detached as always.

Frixos waits for a time when the Worralls are away to seek Caraboo out and examine her tattoo. This tattoo serves as a running joke throughout the film, as it is quite elaborate and located on her upper thigh. Frixos grabs her, tries to sneak a peek, and in their subsequent struggle, he breaks a priceless porcelain statue, and she bites him. Later, when Mr. Worrall sees the broken statue, he demands that Frixos fire the servant responsible. Caraboo then very nonchalantly pretends that she broke it, thus saving Frixos' position. This act wins Frixos' respect, and he ceases his efforts to oust her. He even goes so far as to join Mrs. Worrall in donning a turban.

This confrontation with Frixos points up one of the film's central themes: That Princess Caraboo can get away with things that the ordinary person cannot. The breaking of the statue would have gotten Frixos fired, but Caraboo goes on to break its mate while demonstrating her version of what happened, and the entire incident is dismissed with a laugh. Mary confesses to Gutch, from her prison cell after she has been discovered, that the whole thing started when she noticed how the English gentry were more sympathetic of a poor French girl she had seen than with one of "their own kind." From her life on the streets, she had heard many sailors' tales, hence the birth of Princess Caraboo. Ironically, while pretending to be the princess is when Mary Baker can truly be herself, when she can dare to do what she wants to do and live the life of which she has always dreamed.

The location filming in Wales and England complements the beautiful period interiors, designed by Michael Howells, and costumes, designed by Tom Rand. In fact, one of the most entertaining scenes occurs as Princess Caraboo is being outfitted by a local tailor. She stands amid bolts of beautiful cloth, as those around her examine books with illustrations of Oriental garb. From this cacophony of color Caraboo develops her unique look, which she maintains throughout the film—various fabrics of bright color and exotic design draped about her, topped with her ever-present turban. Also noteworthy are the period dances choreographed by Anthony van Laast for the Prince Regent's elaborate costume ball. Unfortunately, at least one reviewer complained that the costumes and sets were more substantial than the plot and characters.

All the performances are uniformly excellent, particularly those of Cates, Kline, Lithgow, and Rea. Cates's minimalistic acting in this role is quite effective, her face a blank slate. It is unfortunate that she lacks the star power of those who provided the stellar supporting roles. Kline is hilarious as the snobbish Greek butler, with an accent as tapestried as his waistcoats. His character has some of the best lines, as when Gutch inquires, "You are the butler, aren't you, Frixos?" and he replies, "Yes, regrettably." Lithgow has an amusing, if brief, role as the dry and dusty academic who

sheds his austere veneer as he is led down the proverbial garden path by the princess. Rea, too, is convincing as the cynical journalist who grows to appreciate the audacity and intelligence of this pretty young woman.

Although Gutch thwarts Caraboo's efforts at every turn, he is the one in the end who gallantly saves her from the gallows and escorts her to a new life in America. When Caraboo has been found out and sentenced to hang, Mrs. Worrall secretly hands over important documents to Gutch that implicate Worrall and his business partner, the local magistrate (Roger Lloyd Pack). Gutch agrees to suppress the documents on the condition that Worrall and the magistrate allow Caraboo to escape unpunished. In the dead of night, Gutch escorts Caraboo by horseback to a ship bound for America. Although Gutch initially returns to his printing office and resumes his work, he realizes how much he loves the woman and joins her on the ship.

The film ends on a fanciful note as Frixos and Mrs. Worrall—who has separated from her husband—read a news article about a mysterious Oriental princess named Caraboo, whose ship made an emergency landing in France, where she danced with Napoleon, before sailing on for the Americas. The final credits roll over a painting of Caraboo in Indian dress, with Gutch at her side, surrounded by Indian warriors.

Princess Caraboo is an entertaining family film, with a strong international cast, whimsical musical score, and detailed period costumes and settings. The story is very familiar, as it calls to mind aspects of such fairy-tale standards as "Cinderella" and "The Emperor's New Clothes." Despite good reviews, however, the film did not fare well at the box office and was quickly retired.

—*Cynthia K. Breckenridge*

REVIEWS

The Hollywood Reporter. August 29, 1994, p. 5.
Los Angeles Times. September 16, 1994, p. F4.
The New York Times. September 16, 1994, p. B9.
Variety. August 29, 1994, p. 9.

The Professional

"A perfect assassin. An innocent girl. They have nothing to lose except each other."—Movie tagline

"Four stars. A stunning, edgy, strangely romantic thriller."—Jamie Bernard, *The New York Daily News*

"One of the most intelligent and riveting thrillers to emerge in years."—Dolores Barclay, *Associated Press*

"Flying high on explosive action and sly wit."
—Peter Travers, *Rolling Stone*

 Box Office Gross: $18,053,054 (January 2, 1995)

The Professional, a far-fetched fable far from fabulous, might be considered one of the year's most interesting failures, which many viewers and fewer reviewers found oddly endearing. It is the first American feature directed by Luc Besson, highly regarded as an "action" filmmaker because of his hit French film *La Femme Nikita* (1990). Like *La Femme Nikita*, *The Professional* is an underworld yarn about a professional assassin. As with another 1994 release, Quentin Tarantino's internationally acclaimed *Pulp Fiction* (reviewed in this volume), *The Professional* attempts to humanize brutal killers. Yet *Pulp Fiction* was better able to make its hit men seem like ordinary people when they were not working. The hit man of *The Professional* never seems ordinary, despite his fondness for his houseplant and Gene Kelly musicals.

The Professional is an odd little fable, not about sex and violence but potentially about love and violence. At first

Jean Reno as Leon and Natalie Portman as Mathilda in *The Professional*. Copyright © 1994 Gaumont-les Films du Dauphin. All Rights Reserved. Courtesy of Columbia Pictures.

glance, it looks like a typical American action-adventure picture, but it feels like something out of the French New Wave. The story is bizarre, and the characters grotesque, except for an orphaned little waif of a girl named Mathilda (Nathalie Portman). She asks the neighbor who later becomes her protector, "Is life always this hard, or just when you're a kid?" Yet at this point, early in the film, although life may seem tough, the kid has not yet hit bottom.

No one is tougher than the neighbor the girl confides in, Leon (Jean Reno), a Mafia "cleaner," or hit man, imported from France, who is very good at his work, and quite brutal and ruthless. He is a loner and a paid killer, but he has a soft spot in his heart for that absurd houseplant and, later, for Mathilda. Until the girl comes into his life, his "best friend" is his houseplant, and that seems oddly appropriate. The only other human contact he has is with his Mafia "agent," Tony (Danny Aiello), who assigns him his contracts and also serves as his personal banker. Leon is very trusting, milk is his favorite beverage. He is illiterate, and he appears to be a little retarded, except in matters involving his survival. The details do not seem to mesh in any recognizable way. As Janet Maslin noted in *The New York Times*, the characters "speak like Americans, think like Frenchmen, and behave appallingly in any language."

The film begins with a demonstration of Leon's "professionalism," to establish his character as a cool, efficient, killing machine. What one sees is not very appealing. Leon would seem to be a man without a soul, without a life, without a bank account. The film tells nothing about his past, other than he is an immigrant who has come to the United States to practice his "profession." In the opening spasm of violence, Leon coolly dispatches a drug dealer and his band of bodyguards. The odds would seem to be against Leon, but no matter. It is all in a day's work.

Events come to a head when the girl's family is murdered by crooked cops from the Drug Enforcement Administration (DEA). The father had been holding a stash of cocaine, which DEA chief Gary Stansfield (Gary Oldman) knew was diluted. The bad cops stopped by to demand answers by noon the next day. When they returned, all they wanted was murderous vengeance. Stansfield is one of the creepiest sadists ever fabricated for the screen—evil writ large, as Oldman plays him. The whole family is to be exterminated. So why not simply whack the father on the street? Because the mass murder is more spectacularly repulsive and stylishly filmable in all instances, the spectacle drives the plot.

Mathilda escapes this gruesome bloodbath because she has gone to the market for groceries just before noon. When

CREDITS

Leon: Jean Reno
Stansfield: Gary Oldman
Mathilda: Natalie Portman
Tony: Danny Aiello
Malky: Peter Appel
Mathilda's father: Michael Badalucco
Mathilda's mother: Ellen Greene
No character identified: Elizabeth Regen
No character identified: Carl J. Matusovich
No character identified: Randolph Scott

Released: 1994
Production: Patrice Ledoux for Gaumont and Les Films Du Dauphin; released by Columbia Pictures
Direction: Luc Besson
Screenplay: Luc Besson
Cinematography: Thierry Arbogast
Editing: Sylvie Landra
Production design: Dan Weil
Art direction: Carol Nast and Gerard Drolon
Set decoration: Carolyn Cartwright and Francoise Benoit-Fresco
Casting: Todd Thaler and Nathalie Cheron
Special effects supervision: Nicky Allder
Sound: Pierre Excoffier, Gerard Lamps, Francois Groult and Bruno Tarriere
Costume design: Magali Guidasci
Music: Eric Serra
MPAA rating: R
Running time: 106 minutes

she returns to her building and senses what has happened, she goes to Leon's apartment and begs to be let in. He is aware of what has been going on down the hall and knows that the assassins will be looking for her, so he opens the door. She had offered to buy him milk before going to the store. She is the only person besides Tony, apparently, who has had any real human contact with him. He is a loner, however, and though he lets her spend the night, he is at a loss as to what to do with her. At one point while she sleeps, he takes a weapon and seems about to kill her, but he apparently decides to let her live.

Mathilda comes from a dysfunctional family. She has been abused by her father, so there is no love lost there; her mother seems to be a stepmother, and a self-indulgent one at that; and she does not get along with her older sister. Although Mathilda exhibits almost no grief for their passing, she is outraged by the death of her utterly innocent four-year-old brother and wants revenge. She asks Leon to train her as a

"Is life always this hard, or just when you're a kid?"—Mathilda in *The Professional*

AWARDS AND NOMINATIONS

Cesar Awards Nominations 1994: Best Film, Best Actor (Reno), Best Director (Besson)

"cleaner," so that she can avenge her brother's death. Although she has the best teacher in the world, she is only twelve years old, and when she goes after Stansfield, she gets caught. So Leon is faced with the challenge of rescuing her. To do so, he has to take on the entire New York Police Department Special Weapons and Tactics (SWAT) Unit. Though not physically imposing, he seems almost up to the challenge.

This brings about an incredibly violent conclusion. Leon manages to get both Mathilda and his houseplant out of harm's way but has to sacrifice himself. In the final show-down, he confronts the evil Stansfield one-on-one. He knows he cannot escape, but he has rigged himself with explosives and blows the two of them to kingdom come. Mathilda escapes with the plant down a ventilation chute and out through the basement. She later goes to Tony, who agrees to finance her from Leon's earnings, as Leon had instructed him to do. She then returns to her boarding school and tells the shocked headmistress what she has experienced. The film ends with Mathilda planting Leon's plant on the grounds outside her school. She does not seem to realize that it is sure to die when winter comes.

Jean Reno also worked with French director Luc Besson in *La Femme Nikita*, remade in the United States as *Point of No Return* (1993), in which a woman criminal was turned into a ruthless assassin. In that film, Reno played Victor the cleaner, so he is used to the kind of role created for him in *The Professional*. The roles of Besson's latest film are all stereotyped and cartoonish: The hit man, the street kid, the Mafia boss, and the dirty cop. Those inclined to praise Reno as a minimalist for his portrayal of an agonizingly private, laconic, murderous cipher could not ignore Gary Oldman's over-the-top performance. He plays an absolutely ruthless, pill-popping, sadistic villain who enjoys bloodletting and prepares himself for the murderous orgies he orchestrates by listening to Beethoven, like Alex in Stanley Kubrick's *A Clockwork Orange* (1971). In Kubrick's film, however, the violence was used to make a satiric point. The only point here seems to be sentiment and spectacle.

Besson has a perverse talent for mounting repulsive spectacles of murder and mayhem, but the universe he creates is extremely brittle and counterfeit. Stylistically, the film is impressive. Yet although the killings seem all too real, the world of this film is cartoonish and patently unreal. In *The Professional*, Besson has made an American film, with a borderline incoherent Frenchman as its antihero, that seems to be imitating Jean-Luc Godard's imitation of American noir crime films. While Godard's gangsters were enigmatic, however, the French setting made them seem somehow more believable and tolerable. Besson's Leon is in almost all respects inhuman, alien, and enigmatic, more thuggish than elegant, more empty than existential.

Reviews of the film were decidedly mixed. Hal Hinson of *The Washington Post* wrote reverentially of this "story of a doomed man redeemed by his love for a lost girl." Even though its hero is a killer, Hinson concluded weirdly that the film "pays tribute to the simple nobility of its craftsmanship." Richard Schickel of *Time* magazine found the film's violent mix of familiar yet disparate elements possibly distasteful and certainly odd but "undeniably arresting."

Other reviewers had other values to argue and refused to praise style over substance. Jack Kroll of *Newsweek* found an "emotional hollowness behind the film's flashy exterior. Mike Clark of *USA Today* remembered *La Femme Nikita* as being "woefully overrated" and described *The Professional* as a "cinematic equivalent of a *Nikita* head start program." Kroll trashed the director as a "vicious, sentimental counterfeit" and dismissed the film as a "pseudo-thinking man's *Pulp Fiction*."

In truth, *Pulp Fiction* was probably overrated too, but *Pulp Fiction* was far more interesting and subtle in its interweaving structure, and the characters seemed more closely to resemble human beings. Both films, along with Oliver Stone's *Natural Born Killers* (reviewed in this volume), were uncommonly violent and tended to reintroduce the argument against screen violence. At least Oliver Stone could argue that his intent was satiric, which would explain the way his film deviated from Quentin Tarentino's screenplay. No such case could be made for *The Professional*.

Reviewers objected to the film's sleaze factor—the way the child is disturbingly flirtatious with Leon and Leon's teaching her how to become an assassin. Stephen Hunter of the *Baltimore Sun* considered the plot development "despicably tasteless" and described the film as a "grotesque parody of a Charlie Chaplin movie," with the laconic Reno functioning as a cynical latter-day equivalent of Chaplin's Little Tramp. The costuming makes Mathilda look like a preteen Parisian hooker and, as one reviewer described her, "a pederast's delight." Her affair with Leon, however, is never more than sweetly platonic.

For many reviewers, Besson seemed to push all the wrong buttons. It is difficult to view the film too realistically because of its cultural remoteness, its absurd fabular plotting, and its stereotypical characters. It is equally wrong, however, to view the film as simply a triumph of style over substance. The film is profoundly strange and seems to suffer from terminal culture shock.

—*James M. Welsh*

REVIEWS

Baltimore Sun. Maryland Live, November 18-24, 1994, p. 10.
Entertainment Weekly. December 2, 1994, p. 46.
The Hollywood Reporter. November 14, 1994, p. 9.
Los Angeles Times. November 18, 1994, p. F10.
The New York Times. November 19, 1994, p. 11.
Newsweek. November 21, 1994, p. 96.
Time. December 5, 1994, p. 93.
USA Today. November 18, 1994, Sec. D, p. 4.
Variety. September 19-25, 1994, p. 77.
The Washington Post. November 18, 1994, Sec. F, p. 7.

Public Access

A mysterious stranger (Ron Marquette) provokes trouble in small town Brewster by starting a call-in complaint program called *Our Town* on a public-access cable channel, during which he encourages the locals to elaborate on the town's problems. Feature-film directorial debut of Bryan Singer.

CREDITS

Whiley Pritcher: Ron Marquette
Rachel: Dina Brooks
Bob Hodges: Burt Williams
Jeff Abernathy: Larry Maxwell
Mayor Breyer: Charles Kavanaugh
Kevin Havey: Brandon Boyce

Released: 1993
Production: Kenneth Kokin; released by Cinemabeam
Direction: Bryan Singer
Screenplay: Christopher McQuarrie, Michael Feit Dougan, and Bryan Singer
Cinematography: Bruce Douglas Johnson
Editing: John Ottman
Production design: Jan Sessler
Art direction: Bruce Sulzberg
Sound: Adam Joseph
Sound design: Mark A. Lanza
Costume design: Dean Jacobson
Music: John Ottman
MPAA rating: no listing
Running time: 87 minutes

REVIEWS

Variety. CCCL, February 8, 1993, p. 75.

AWARDS AND NOMINATIONS

Sundance Film Festival: Grand Jury Prize (tie)

The Puerto Rican Mambo (Not a Musical)

Stand-up comedian Luis Caballero plays off white America's prejudices concerning Puerto Ricans, in this low-budget comedy.

REVIEWS

Playboy. XXXIX, May 1992, p. 20.

CREDITS

No character identified: Luis Caballero
No character identified: Johnny Leggs
No character identified: Carolyn McDermott
No character identified: David Healy
No character identified: Ben Model
No character identified: Sandy McFadden
No character identified: Jeff Eyres
No character identified: Susan Gaspar
No character identified: Lucia Mendoza
No character identified: Mike Robles
No character identified: Carole M. Eckman
No character identified: John Fulweiler
No character identified: Howard Arnesson
No character identified: Mary Perez

Released: 1991
Production: Ben Model for Pinata Films; released by Cabriolet Films
Direction: Ben Model
Screenplay: Luis Caballero; adapted for the screen by Ben Model
Cinematography: Rosemary Tomosky-Franco, Vincent Manes and Paul Koestner
Editing: Ben Model
Sound: Alina Avila
Music: Eddie Palmieri
MPAA rating: no listing
Running time: 90 minutes

Pulp Fiction

"Wildly funny! Exhilarating! Daring and triumphant! A work of blazing originality. It places Quentin Tarantino in the front ranks of American filmmakers."—Janet Maslin, *The New York Times*

"The most entertaining film of the year." —Paul Wunder, *WBAI*

"Mesmerizing entertainment. Uma Thurman is marvelous!"—Desson Howe, *Washington Post*

"Electrifying!"—Howard Feinstein, *New York Post*

"A knockout!"—Mike Caccioppoli, *WABC Radio*

"It will leave audiences laughing, gasping and applauding."—Jack Matthews, *New York Newsday*

 Box Office Gross: $63,617,560 (January 2, 1995)

Because of Quentin Tarantino's brilliant debut as screenwriter-director with *Reservoir Dogs* (1992), the quality of his script for Tony Scott's *True Romance* (1993), the surreal energy of Oliver Stone's *Natural Born Killers* (reviewed in this volume), adapted from a Tarantino screenplay, and the Cannes Film Festival Palme d'Or won by his second film as writer-director, *Pulp Fiction* had been more eagerly awaited than any serious American film in the early 1990's. Sometimes films disappoint because of too much expectation by critics and audiences, but *Pulp Fiction* does not. It is brilliant, an instant American classic on the same level as *Bonnie and Clyde* (1967), *The Godfather* (1972), and *Chinatown* (1974).

Tarantino's film, as the title suggests, is a homage to the pulp fiction popular in such magazines of the 1930's and 1940's as *Black Mask*. The tough-guy, world-weary prose of writers like James M. Cain, Raymond Chandler, David Goodis, Dashiell Hammett, and Cornell Woolrich transported crime fiction to a violent, morally ambiguous, often existential universe. This hard-boiled literature was often the source material for some of the best films noirs of the 1940's and 1950's and their French nouvelle vague imitators of the 1960's.

Pulp Fiction was created on a modest budget of $8 million and earned eight times that much at the box office.

Tarantino's triumph is finding a way to pay tribute to this genre while redefining it. His innovation comes through presenting his material in three interrelated tales, offering such twists as presenting them out of chronological order so that a main character killed in the second episode reappears in the third. This character's narrow escape at the end of the film is heavily ironic since the audience knows what awaits him.

In the first episode, "Vincent Vega and Marsellus Wallace's Wife," Los Angeles hit men Jules Winnfield (Samuel L. Jackson) and Vincent Vega (John Travolta) shoot some college-age punks who have tried to double-cross their boss, Marsellus Wallace (Ving Rhames). Vincent is then assigned to escort Wallace's beautiful young wife, Mia (Uma Thurman), while her husband is out of town. Jules warns Vincent that a previous Mia-sitter was murdered just for massaging her feet. Their evening out ends with Mia overdosing on Vincent's heroin, his frantically driving the dying woman to the home of Lance (Eric Stoltz), his dealer, and Jody (Rosanna Arquette), Lance's nagging wife, and his plunging a harpoon-sized hyperdermic needle into her heart.

"The Gold Watch" deals another double-cross of Wallace as boxer Butch Coolidge (Bruce Willis) goes on the run after winning a fight Wallace has ordered him to lose. Just as Butch and his girlfriend, Fabienne (Maria de Medeiros) are about to make their getaway, he discovers she has left behind in their apartment his only important possession. His great-grandfather carried a wristwatch through World War I, his grandfather died wearing it during World War II, and his father had it when captured in the Vietnam War. In a prisoner-of-war camp, Butch's father hid the watch from his captors by carrying it in his rectum for five years. After he died, his fellow prisoner, Captain Koons (Christopher Walken), concealed it for two more years before being released and bringing the watch home to young Butch. In retrieving this badge of honor, Butch finds himself in a situation every bit as harrowing as those faced by his forebears.

"The Bonnie Situation" comprises a comic dessert following the horrors of the previous sections. After Vincent accidentally shoots someone inside Jules' car, the hit men go to Jules' friend Jimmie (Tarantino himself) for help. They must get rid of the corpse and clean the blood from the car and themselves before Jimmie's wife, Bonnie, comes home from working a late nursing shift. To the rescue, Wallace sends for the urbane hoodlum Winston Wolf (Harvey Keitel), who calmly takes control of the situation. With that problem resolved, Jules and Vincent go to a diner for breakfast only to find themselves in a holdup attempt by two sociopaths who call each other Pumpkin (Tim Roth) and Honey Bunny (Amanda Plummer).

CREDITS

Vincent Vega: John Travolta
Jules Winnfield: Samuel L. Jackson
Butch Coolidge: Bruce Willis
Mia Wallace: Uma Thurman
Winston Wolf: Harvey Keitel
Marsellus Wallace: Ving Rhames
Pumpkin: Tim Roth
Honey Bunny: Amanda Plummer
Captain Koons: Christopher Walken
Fabienne: Maria de Medeiros
Lance: Eric Stoltz
Jody: Rosanna Arquette
Jimmie: Quentin Tarantino
Esmerelda Villalobos: Angela Jones

Released: 1994
Production: Lawrence Bender for A Band Apart and Jersey Films; released by Miramax Films
Direction: Quentin Tarantino
Screenplay: Quentin Tarantino; based on stories by Tarantino and Roger Avary
Cinematography: Andrzej Sekula
Editing: Sally Menke
Executive producer: Danny DeVito, Michael Shamberg and Stacey Sher
Production design: David Wasco
Art direction: Charles Collum
Set decoration: Sandy Reynolds-Wasco
Casting: Ronnie Yeskel and Gary M. Zuckerbrod
Costume design: Betsy Heimann
Sound: Stephen H. Flick
Music supervision: Karyn Rachtman
MPAA rating: R
Running time: 154 minutes

AWARDS AND NOMINATIONS

Academy Awards 1994: Best Original Screenplay (Tarantino, Avary)
Nominations: Best Actor (Travolta), Best Supporting Actor (Jackson), Best Supporting Actress (Thurman), Best Director (Tarantino), Best Film Editing, Best Picture
British Academy Awards 1994: Best Original Screenplay, Best Supporting Actor (Jackson)
Cannes Film Festival Awards 1994: Palm d'Or
Chicago Film Critics Awards 1994: Best Director (Tarantino), Best Original Screenplay (Tarantino, Avary)
Directors Guild of America Awards Nomination 1994: Best Director (Tarantino)
Golden Globe Awards 1995: Best Screenplay (Tarantino, Avary)
Nominations: Best Film—Drama, Best Actor—Drama (Travolta), Best Supporting Actor—Drama (Jackson), Best Supporting Actress—Drama (Thurman), Best Director (Tarantino)
Independent Spirit Awards 1995: Best Film, Best Actor (Jackson), Best Director (Tarantino), Best Original Screenplay (Tarantino, Avary)
Nominatons: Best Supporting Actor (Stoltz)
Los Angeles Film Critics Association Awards 1994: Best Film, Best Actor (Travolta), Best Director (Tarantino), Best Original Screenplay (Tarantino, Avary)
MTV Movie Awards 1995: Best Film, Best Dance Sequence (Travolta/Thurman)
Nominations: Best Male Performance (Travolta), Best Female Performance (Thurman), Best On-Screen Duo (Travolta/Jackson), Best Song ("Girl, You'll Be a Woman Soon")
National Board of Review Awards 1994: Best Film, Best Director (Tarantino)
National Society of Film Critics Awards 1994: Best Film, Best Director (Tarantino), Best Original Screenplay (Tarantino, Avary)
New York Film Critics Awards 1994: Best Director (Tarantino), Best Original Screenplay (Tarantino, Avary)
Screen Actors Guild Awards Nominations 1994: Best Actor (Travolta)

Tarantino is adept at controlling his convoluted plots and making most of the characters appealing despite their brutality. These protagonists pride themselves on being street smart enough to survive and prosper in a hostile environment, but they are constantly being tormented by ingeniously conceived dilemmas. In the first tale, Vincent thinks his main problem will be restraining his lust for his boss's wife only to have a much more threatening situation develop. Jules and Vincent think they can relax over breakfast in the third only to find two lunatics pointing guns at them. The greatest complications occur in the second story: Butch thinks he is likely to be safe once he escapes from the boxing arena only to place himself directly in danger by going back for his watch. Pleased with himself when he recovers the watch in his apparently empty apartment, he pauses to toast some Pop-Tarts and sees an assassin coming out of his bathroom. After escaping, he confronts Marcellus unexpectedly, and when he escapes again after the two are taken prisoner, his honor compels him to go back to rescue his would-be killer.

"We gotta get this car off the road. Cops tend to notice s**t like you're drivin' a car drenched in f****n' blood."—Jules to Vincent in *Pulp Fiction*

While *Reservoir Dogs* has its comic moments, it is essentially a dark, graphically violent, even depressing film. With all three episodes of *Pulp Fiction*, Tarantino creates a wonderful balance between horror and comedy. The audience's disgust at the overdosing Mia turns to laughs as Vincent and Lance argue over who must ram the adrenaline solution into her heart with Jody kibitzing in the background. The comic inventiveness of the one-darn-thing-after-another problems facing Butch are worthy of comparison to P.G. Wodehouse at his best. Tarantino shows his awareness of the absurdly thin line between comedy and tragedy by having, in "The Bonnie Situation," seemingly the worse thing that could happen be a wife catching her husband helping his friends out of an awkward predicament.

Numerous other comic elements occur throughout *Pulp Fiction*: the unexplained adhesive strip on the back of Marcellus' broad, bald head; the calm, genuine solicitude Butch shows after his final ordeal when he must console Fabienne for not getting the blueberry pancakes she wanted for breakfast; Vincent's delight in explaining how European junk food differs from the American versions; the book Vincent carries with him to the toilet; Wolf's being summoned from a cocktail party at 8:30 A.M.; everyone's complimenting Jimmie on his gourmet coffee. The comic highlight, however, comes with Vincent and Mia's visit to Jackrabbit Slim's, a restaurant styled as a 1950's theme park complete with impersonators of such icons of the era as Ricky Nelson, Ed Sullivan, and Mamie van Doren.

Amid the laughs and gore, Tarantino comments on the necessity of honor and courage, even on the part of criminals. Wolf tells Jules and Vincent that there is a difference between being characters and having character, and each protagonist gets the opportunity to validate this belief. When a young hoodlum fires several shots point blank at Vincent and Jules and misses, Jules undergoes a highly unlikely religious experience. If he has been allowed to live because of some inexplicable miracle, he must change his life; therefore, he lets Pumpkin and Honey Bunny leave with their spoils. Far from imposing some moral message upon his material, Tarantino simply observes that good—albeit somewhat tainted—may emerge from unlikely quarters.

Compared with the visual pyrotechnics of *True Romance* and *Natural Born Killers*, the director of *Pulp Fiction* employs a surprisingly conservative style. The constantly moving camera of *Reservoir Dogs* is mostly gone. Except for distorting close-ups that make the characters appear almost cartoonish, Tarantino uses mostly static compositions reminiscent of the style of Jean-Luc Godard, one of his idols. The director knows that his stories, structure, and performances provide style enough.

Again as in *Reservoir Dogs*, Tarantino displays his skill at directing actors. He exploits the unsentimental side of Travolta's sensitivity often masked behind his blankly passive exterior. Willis, who too often retreats into smirks or stoicism, strikes the right balance between Butch's alternating world-weariness and fear, violence and tenderness. Also giving the best performance of his career is Jackson, too often saddled with undeveloped roles in bad films. He makes his philosophical hit man a convincing conscience for the film's gory milieu. Roth, Walken, and, especially, Keitel prove again that they are among the best character actors in films of this era. While Tarantino can be faulted for undervaluing his female characters, Thurman conveys, as film noir requires, the sexiness of Lauren Bacall and the cynicism of Barbara Stanwyck, while Plummer is delightful as her mousy Honey Bunny explodes into foul-mouthed aggression. These performers make the most of what is perhaps Tarantino's greatest talent: creating comic, profane, stylized, vibrantly original dialog, resembling a sublime blend of David Mamet and Elmore Leonard.

—Michael Adams

REVIEWS

ARTnews. XCIII, October, 1994, p. 434.
Cosmopolitan. CCXVII, October, 1994, p. 30.
Entertainment Weekly. October 14, 1994, p. 34.
Glamour. XCII, November, 1994, p. 138.
The Hollywood Reporter. May 23, 1994, p. 5.
Los Angeles. XXXIX, October, 1994, p. 180.
Los Angeles Times. October 14, 1994, p. F1.
Mademoiselle. C, October, 1994, p. 90.
The Nation. CCLIX, October 17, 1994, p. 433.
New York. XXVII, October 3, 1994, p. 96.
The New York Times. September 23, 1994, p. B1.
The New Yorker. LXX, October 10, 1994, p. 95.
Newsweek. CXXIV, October 10, 1994, p. 71.
People Weekly. XLII, October 17, 1994, p. 21.
Playboy. XLI, September, 1994, p. 24.
Rolling Stone. October 6, 1994, p. 79.
Sight and Sound. IV, November, 1994, p. 50.
Time. CXLIV, October 10, 1994, p. 76.
Variety. CCCLV, May 23, 1994, p. 52.
The Village Voice. XXXIX, October 11, 1994, p. 61.
Vogue. CLXXXIV, October, 1994, p. 204.
The Wall Street Journal. October 18, 1994, p. A16.
The Washington Post. October 14, 1994, p. F1.

The Puppet Masters

"Truly chilling"—*San Francisco Chronicle*
"Thrilling"—*WBAI Radio*

 Box Office Gross: $8,579,626 (December 18, 1994)

The basic body-snatching, alien-invasion design of *The Puppet Masters* will be familiar because it has been imitated several times over the last forty-five years since Robert A. Heinlein wrote the story, which first appeared in *Galaxy Science Fiction* magazine in 1951. A UFO lands in Ambrose, Iowa, to threaten the American heartland. Representing the Office of Scientific Intelligence, a covert branch of the CIA, Andrew Nivens (Donald Sutherland) and his son Sam (Eric Thal) are sent to Iowa to investigate, along with NASA exobiologist Mary Sefton (Julie Warner). By the time they arrive, the aliens have already taken over

CREDITS

Andrew Nivens: Donald Sutherland
Sam Nivens: Eric Thal
Mary Sefton: Julie Warner
Holland: Keith David
Graves: Will Patton
Jarvis: Richard Belzer
Ressler: Yaphet Kotto

Released: 1994
Production: Ralph Winter for Hollywood Pictures; released by Buena Vista Pictures
Direction: Stuart Orme
Screenplay: Ted Elliott, Terry Rossio, and David S. Goyer; based on the novel by Robert A. Heinlein
Cinematography: Clive Tickner
Editing: William Goldenberg
Production design: Daniel A. Lomino
Art direction: James C. Hegedus
Set design: Alan Manzer
Set decoration: Cloudia
Casting: Sharon Howard-Field
Visual effects supervision: Peter Montgomery
Sound: Robert Anderson, Jr.
Costume design: Tom Bronson
Stunt coordination: Jeffrey Dashnaw
Music: Colin Towns
MPAA rating: R
Running time: 108 minutes

most of the town. Before long these parasites (which can reproduce in twelve hours, hatching grapefruit-size eggs) have infiltrated the Iowa National Guard, and the problem seems to be getting out of hand.

The investigators are at first spared and manage to escape a creepy heartland population of body-snatched zombies, but, unbeknownst to them, their driver has been "snatched," taking the alien parasites with him to Washington, D.C. It begins to look as though even the President of the United States (Tom Mason) may be taken over before a solution can be found. The parasites consist mainly of brain tissue that is vulnerable to encephalitis, the investigators later discover, after many distracting plot complications. The investigators have to "mind-meld" with the parasites in order to learn their secrets. One advantage for the human types in this story is that the parasites can be removed, allowing the host to again become human. If the takeover were more permanent, as in later variations of this unfriendly alien motif, the situation would be much more frightening.

Hollywood Pictures wanted viewers to understand that Robert A. Heinlein's *The Puppet Masters* is a science-fiction classic, and for that reason put the author's name before the title. The film is a reworking of a now-familiar theme that was popularized by a B-movie directed by Don Siegel in 1956 based on a *Collier's* magazine story by Jack Finney in 1954, *The Invasion of the Body Snatchers*. That film became a classic and an icon for Red Scare paranoia during the McCarthy anti-Communist witch hunts of the early 1950's. It was remade by Philip Kaufman during the 1970's and again by Abel Ferrara in 1993, but after twenty or forty years, the political atmosphere had seriously changed, and the fable lost its allegorical resonance, since people no longer worried about their neighbors being secret illegal "alien" Communists. The Philip Kaufman version of 1978 also starred Donald Sutherland, whose body was "snatched" at the end, indicating that the alien takeover was complete.

It is therefore amusing to see Sutherland as the CIA UFO investigator Andrew Nivens in *The Puppet Masters*, which concerns yet another attempted alien takeover. In the Finney version the aliens sent absurd seed pods to planet earth bearing the body-snatching spores. In Heinlein's earlier, original version which predates Finney, the aliens are rather like space-glop jellyfish that attach themselves as parasites to the victim's back and neck, sending out nasty probes into the brain and spinal cord, while taking over the body. These monsters recall the parasites of Ridley Scott's *Alien* (1979) and the parasites of William Cameron Menzies' *Invaders from Mars* (1953) and the more campy Tobe Hooper remake of 1986. The idea has been reworked in several films with varying degrees of absurdity and attempts a new scary dimension in *The Puppet Masters*, released in time for Halloween as a reasonably effective creature feature.

With Donald Sutherland, a veteran of over seventy films, in the lead with relative newcomers Eric Thal and Julie Warner, the film is short of starpower; on the technical side, director Stuart Orme's experience has been mainly limited to British television and music videos. The screenplay was patched together by Ted Elliott and Terry Rossio, two of the four writers who created Disney's *Aladdin* (1992), and David S. Goyer, who has two Jean-Claude Van Damme pictures to his credit.

Science fiction is usually obsessed with technology, so the challenge of a good science-fiction movie is to infuse that technology with human interest. *The Puppet Masters* is better in its limited special effects than in its characterization. There is a father-son conflict between Sam Nivens and his workaholic father and a romantic attraction between Sam and his exobiologist sidekick, Mary. Julie Warner is a game trooper, but the chemistry with Eric Thal could be much more convincing. Sutherland is all business and seems like a zombie even before he is possessed by the aliens. He should be horrified by what he is witnessing, but he responds to the extraordinary as though it were all in a day's work. It's as though he has seen it all before in the last body-snatchers movie that featured him. If he is not frightened by these space-glop creatures, why should the viewer be? In fact, Sutherland has seen it all before, in better movies than this one.

—*James M. Welsh*

REVIEWS

Entertainment Weekly. No.247, November 4, 1994, p.49.
Films in Review. Vol. XLVI, Nos.1-2, January-February, 1995, pp. 59-60.
The New York Times. October 22, 1994, A18.
The Washington Post. October 22, 1994, C2.

The Puppetmaster (Hsimeng Jensheng)

The life and times of Taiwanese puppetmaster Li Tien-lu, set against the turbulent history of Taiwan during the Japanese occupation, is the focus of this drama. *The Puppetmaster* is the first part of a trilogy on Taiwan, and the award-winning *The City of Sadness* (1989) is the conclusion.

REVIEWS

Boston Globe. December 2, 1993, p. 71.
Chicago Tribune. December 3, 1993, p. 7C(43).
New Statesman & Society. VII, May 13, 1994, p. 34.
The New York Times. October 6, 1993, p. C19.

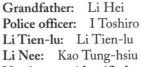

CREDITS

Li Tien-lu (as an adult):   Lin Chung
Li Tien-lu (as a teenager):   Cheng Kuei-chung
Li Tien-lu (as a child):   Cho Ju-wei
Father: Tsai Chen-nan
Stepmother: Yang Li-yin
Wife: Hwang Ching-ru
Grandfather: Li Hei
Police officer: I Toshiro
Li Tien-lu: Li Tien-lu
Li Nee: Kao Tung-hsiu
No character identified: Li Wen-chang
No character identified: Tsai Yi-hwa
No character identified: Chen Yi-shan

Origin: Taiwan
Released: 1993
Production: Chiu Fu-sheng for City Films; released by Era International
Direction: Hou Hsiao-hsien
Screenplay: Wu Nien-jen and Chu Tien-wen; based on the published memoirs by Li Tien-lu
Cinematography: Lee Pin-bing
Editing: Liao Ching-sung
Production design: Chang Hung and Lu Ming-jin
Sound: Du Du-jih and Meng Chi-liang
Costume design: Chang Kuang-hui and Juan Pei-yun
Music: Chen Ming-chang
MPAA rating: no listing
Running time: 142 minutes

Queen Margot (La Reine Margot)

"She was the wife of a king and the lover of a soldier. In a royal family, power, seduction and deception are all related."—Movie tagline.

"Romantic and wildly operatic!"—David Ansen, *Newsweek*

"One of the year's best films!"—Mike Clark, *USA Today*

"Grand entertainment. Glorious and visually stunning."—Paul Wunder, *WBAI*

 Box Office Gross: $836,162. (January 2, 1995)

France's official entry at the 1994 Cannes Film Festival lost the top prize but gained enough acclaim to make international audiences take notice. *Queen Margot* is a historical drama of grand proportions, which vividly dramatizes the 1572 St. Bartholomew's Day Massacre and its aftermath. Virna Lisi, who captured Cannes's Best Supporting Actress Award, plays the murderous Catherine of Médici, whose thirst for power is the catalyst of the bloody action.

Catherine is the mother of three sons: the present king, Charles IX (Jean-Hugues Anglade); Henri, the Duke of Anjou (Pascal Greggory); and François, the Duke of Alençon (Julien Rassam). Though Anjou is her special favorite, Catherine will be content as long as one of her sons is king. Catherine also has a daughter, Marguerite of Valois (Isabelle Adjani), known as Margot, whose gender renders her insignificant to Catherine. In a characteristic scene, Catherine announces that she loves devotedly all three of her children. After a beat, she adds dryly that she meant all four.

During the second half of the sixteenth century, the Wars of Religion threaten to tear apart the kingdom of France. French Protestants, known as Huguenots, campaign tirelessly against the Catholic French crown, seeking religious tolerance and political power. To effect peace between the warring religious factions, Catherine arranges the mar-

CREDITS

Margot: Isabelle Adjani
Henri of Navarre: Daniel Auteuil
Charles IX: Jean-Hugues Anglade
La Môle: Vincent Perez
Catherine of Médici: Virna Lisi
Henriette of Nevers: Dominique Blanc
Anjou: Pascal Greggory
Coconnas: Claudio Amendola
Guise: Miguel Bose
Charlote of Sauve: Asia Argento
Alençon: Julien Rassam
Nancay: Thomas Kretschmann
Coligny: Jean-Claude Brialy

Origin: France, Germany, and Italy
Released: 1994
Production: Claude Berri for Renn Productions, France 2 Cinema,/D. A. Films (Paris),-NEF Filmproduktion GmbH,/Degeto pour Ard,/Wmg (Munich),-R. C. S. Films and Television (Rome), with the participation of the Centre National de la Cinematographie and Canal Plus
Production: Released by Miramax Films
Direction: Patrice Chéreau
Screenplay: Daniéle Thompson and Patrice Chéreau; based on the novel by Alexandre Dumas
Cinematography: Philippe Rousselot
Editing: François Gédigier and Hélène Viard
Production design: Richard Peduzzi and Olivier Radot
Set decoration: Sophie Martel
Sound design: Guillaume Sciama and Dominique Hennequin
Makeup and special effects: Kuno Schlegelmilch
Costume design: Moidele Bickel
Music: Goran Bregovic
MPAA rating: R
Running time: 141 minutes

Jean-Hugues Anglade as Charles IX and Isabelle Adjani in *Queen Margot*. Copyright © Miramax Films.

AWARDS AND NOMINATIONS

Academy Awards Nomination 1994: Best Costume Design
Cannes Film Festival Awards 1994: Special Jury Prize, Best Supporting Actress (Lisi)
Cesar Awards 1995: Best Actress (Adjani), Best Supporting Actress (Lisi), Best Supporting Actor (Anglade), Best Cinematography, Best Costume Design *Nominations:* Best Film, Best Director (Chéreau), Best Supporting Actress (Blanc)
Golden Globe Awards Nomination 1995: Best Foreign Language Film

riage of her daughter, Margot, to Henri of Navarre (Daniel Auteuil), the leader of the Huguenots. Neither bride nor groom is pleased with the match. Margot has a lover she intends to keep and makes it clear she will not consummate her marriage. Henri fears his life is in danger from Catholics who would sooner murder him than acknowledge a Protestant as their possible future king.

To regain control over her vacillating son Charles, Catherine orders the assassination of his closest confidant and adviser, the Protestant Admiral Coligny (Jean-Claude Brialy). Coligny is not killed but critically wounded. There are rumblings of revenge among the Protestants, and Catherine insists that in order to avert an insurrection, they must kill the Protestant leaders. In a fit of grief over Coligny's attack, Charles sanctions the killing of all Protestants, so that none may survive to blame him. On August 23, 1572, six days after the wedding that attracted thousands of Protestants to Paris, a militia of Catholic courtiers slaughters thousands of Protestants, ferreting them out in alleyways, churches, hotel rooms, and even the Louvre.

One of the few survivors is La Môle (Vincent Perez), a young Protestant whom Margot encounters badly wounded. She recognizes him as the same man she picked up on her wedding night while roaming the streets in search of anonymous amorous encounters. Margot nurses, protects, and falls in love with La Môle. He soon disappears back into the streets, and Margot frantically searches for him. Once recovered, La Môle flees to Holland, where he amasses troops to return and fight the Catholics.

Due to Margot's intervention, Henri's life is spared, but only on the condition that he convert to Catholicism. Horrified by the butchery orchestrated by her family, Margot allies herself with Henri and the Protestants. She and Henri are placed under house arrest at the Louvre. Margot is briefly reunited with La Môle during his failed attempt to rescue the couple.

Still perceiving Henri as her adversary, Catherine twice attempts to poison him. One of these attempts is tragically misdirected, when Charles intercepts a poison-paged book that was intended for Henri. Charles befriends Henri after the latter saves his life on a hunting trip. Henri is freed, returns to Navarre, and renounces Catholicism. Margot is not allowed to go with him.

Catherine is remorseful at causing her son's slow, agonizingly painful demise, but ever-conniving, she convinces Charles to pin the blame on La Môle. Returning at Henri's behest to rescue Margot, La Mole is apprehended and sentenced to be executed. Margot's desperate pleas are too late to save her lover's life, and La Môle is beheaded. Sickened by her family's savagery, Margot flees to Navarre, to be with Henri and the Protestants.

When unleashed at the 1994 Cannes Film Festival, this big-budgeted epic ran two hours and forty-four minutes. *The Hollywood Reporter* called it "a lengthy, noisy reminder that the French can make movies every bit as elephantine, as overlong and as violent as their Hollywood counterparts." *Variety* also trounced the Cannes version, saying it "doesn't generate any fascination for its murderous characters, and is a mostly unpleasant chore to slog through." The production reportedly lost money, and its producers were eager to recoup their losses by exporting the film to the United States.

Miramax, the American distributor, insisted upon a complete re–edit, which was reluctantly agreed to by the producers. After 190 cuts, a total of twenty-three minutes was cut from the film. Director/co-screenwriter Patrice Chéreau, producer Claude Berri, and star Adjani all publicly praised the truncated version, as did the media. *USA Today* awarded the film four stars—out of four—declaring, "this rouser has the flesh-and-blood passion to match its staggering visual content." *Entertainment Weekly* observed, "history has rarely been so gorgeously, electrically, sensuously portrayed.

Adapted by Chéreau and Daniéle Thompson from Alexandre Dumas' 1845 novel, *Queen Margot* interweaves complex plots and subplots featuring dozens of significant historical characters. Data-packed opening titles and endnotes aid the viewer in sorting out the plot intricacies, but there is still much to absorb. The confusion engendered by the plot intricacies was cited as the film's only real drawback. *The Los Angeles Times*, which heralded the film as "rich and full of verve," also warned, "You may not be able to sort out all the players and the plotting—at least not without an encyclopedia and penlight handy." For those not already well-versed in French history, it may be enough to distinguish the good guys (Protestants) from the bad (Catholics).

Though a bit heavy on exposition, the film picks up speed about one-third of the way through, and from then on it is as frenzied and jolting as a roller-coaster ride. The cinematography by Philippe Rousselot favors tight close-ups over panoramic action shots. The camera zooms in on the blood and gore, and lovingly exploits Adjani's visage. This propensity for up-close, personal photography creates an intimacy for the viewer that is occasionally disturbing, as when the camera weaves among the bodies of the slaughtered masses.

The costumes, designed by Moidele Bickel, are magnificent, but pitiably it is only in the wedding sequence that the royals appear resplendent. Thenceforth, their lovely costumes are forever blood-soaked or ravaged. Despite the profusion of blood, there is little color in the production. The visuals are depressingly dark, in concert with the grisly nature of the subject matter.

Also drained of color is the cadaver-like face of Virna Lisi, whose chillingly sinister performance is the film's greatest revelation. Adjani's role is less flamboyant, as Margot acts mainly as a mirror of audience reaction. Margot is appalled by the events unfolding around her but is powerless to stop them, while the conniving Catherine is the propelling force behind all the intrigue. Both women are impressive in divergent roles. They are supported by powerful performances by the three leading men. Anglade's intensity, Auteuil's subtlety, and Perez's sensuality add spice to the proceedings.

A historical dramatization infused with a tragically doomed romance and a moral lesson that bears contemporary relevance, *Queen Margot* is a gripping film. The St. Bartholomew's Day Massacre was previously dramatized in D. W. Griffith's silent film *Intolerance* (1916) and has oft been recounted in print. Yet *Queen Margot* brings the players to life, presenting a fascinating first family for whom greed, deception, incest, debauchery, murder, and genocide were the order of the day.

—*Brenda Scott Royce*

REVIEWS

Daily Variety. May 23, 1994, p. 53.
Entertainment Weekly. January 27, 1995, p. 32.
The Hollywood Reporter. May 16, 1994, p. 6.
Los Angeles Times. December 14, 1994, p. F2.
The New Republic. December 19, 1994, p. 26.
The New York Times. December 9, 1994, p. C10.
Newsweek. December 12, 1994, p. 72.
People Weekly. December 19, 1994, p. 21.
Sight and Sound. January, 1995, p. 55.
USA Today. December 9, 1994, p. 8D.

Queen of Diamonds

A series of disconnected yet powerful images form the bulk of this experimental film by award-winning underground filmmaker Nina Menkes, which was filmed in Las Vegas and stars the filmmaker's sister, Tinka Menkes.

CREDITS

Las Vegas dealer: Tinka Menkes

Released: 1991
Production: Nina Menkes; released by Menkes Film
Direction: Nina Menkes
Screenplay: Nina Menkes
MPAA rating: no listing
Running time: 77 minutes

REVIEWS

Variety. CCCXLII, January 28, 1991, p. 71.

Quiz Show

"One of the year's ten best."—*Siskel & Ebert, People Magazine, USA Today*
"A must-see!"—*Entertainment Tonight*

Box Office Gross: $21,854,889 (January 2, 1995)

Nostalgia from the 1950's proved marketable in 1994, as witnessed by Tim Burton's *Ed Wood* (reviewed in this volume), starring Johnny Depp as the worst movie director of the decade, and Robert Redford's *Quiz Show*, starring Ralph Fiennes as Charlie Van Doren and concerning the scandal surrounding the television game show *Twenty-One*. These two films seemed to crest on a wave of nostalgia that started to surge with *Forrest Gump* (reviewed in this volume), the surprise hit of the 1994 summer market.

Quiz Show, however, is a standout effort. The screenplay by former *Washington Post* film critic Paul Attanasio dramatizes a story of quiz show people seduced by greed and celebrity into betraying the American public. The screenplay is based on a chapter from the book *Remembering America: a Voice from the Sixties*, by Richard N. Goodwin, published in 1988. Goodwin, who, according to the film version (which makes him a more important player than he was in actuality), was the young congressional attorney who sensed that *Twenty-One* was fixed and who exposed the scandal. In the film Goodwin is nicely played by Rob Morrow, the star of the popular 1990's television series *Northern Exposure*.

Twenty-One was created by television producer Dan Enright (played by David Paymer). Competing contestants placed in soundproof isolation booths were asked questions graded in difficulty from one to eleven points; the first to score twenty-one points won the game. The reigning champion was Herb Stempel (John Turturro in the film), who first met Charles Van Doren on November 28, 1956. In fact, these two contestants played tie games for three weeks before Van Doren emerged triumphant, but the film compresses the contest to a single dramatic encounter. Van Doren then reigned as champion until March 11, 1957, when he was beaten by a perky female attorney named Vivienne Nearing (Grace Phillips).

Herb Stempel had enjoyed being recognized as a know-it-all who was respected in his neighborhood and agonized over taking the dive, especially since the producers wanted him to miss an obvious question, to answer *On the Waterfront* when asked to name the film that won the Best Picture Oscar in 1955. Herb knows the answer is *Marty* and protests to his wife: "They have to blitz me with a question any child could answer!" He agreed to this only because Enright had apparently promised him a slot on another television show, a promise that was not kept.

Director Robert Redford was once a contestant on a quiz show called *Play Your Hunch* in 1959.

CREDITS

Herbie Stempel: John Turturro
Dick Goodwin: Rob Morrow
Charles Van Doren: Ralph Fiennes
Mark Van Doren: Paul Scofield
Dan Enright: David Paymer
Albert Freedman: Hank Azaria
Jack Barry: Christopher McDonald
Toby Stempel: Johann Carlo
Dorothy Van Doren: Elizabeth Wilson
Robert Kintner: Allan Rich
Sandra Goodwin: Mira Sorvino
Chairman: George Martin
Lishman: Paul Guilfoyle
Account guy: Griffin Dunne
Sponsor: Martin Scorsese
Dave Garroway: Barry Levinson
Vivienne Nearing: Grace Phillips
Judge Mitchell Schweitzer: Stephen Pearlman
Thomas Merton: Adam Kilgour
Bunny Wilson: Vince O'Brien
Snodgrass: Douglas McGrath

Released: 1994
Production: Robert Redford, Michael Jacobs, Julian Krainin, and Michael Nozik for Hollywood Pictures and Wildwood Enterprises/Baltimore Pictures; released by Buena Vista Pictures
Direction: Robert Redford
Screenplay: Paul Attanasio; based on the book *Remembering America: a Voice from The Sixties*, by Richard N. Goodwin
Cinematography: Michael Ballhaus
Editing: Stu Linder
Production design: Jon Hutman
Art direction: Tim Galvin
Set decoration: Samara Schaffer
Executive producer: Fred Zollo, Richard Dreyfuss and Judith James
Casting: Bonnie Timmermann
Sound: Tod A. Maitland
Sound design: Gary Rydstrom
Costume design: Kathy O'Rear
Music: Mark Isham
MPAA rating: PG-13
Running time: 124 minutes

Enraged by this, Stempel went to the District Attorney, who called a grand jury investigation in 1959, but the findings were sealed by Judge Mitchell Schweitzer (Stephen Pearlman), an apparent stooge for the network.

When Goodwin got wind of this, he began his own investigation for the Congressional Subcommittee on

AWARDS AND NOMINATIONS

Academy Awards Nominations 1994:   Best Supporting Actor (Scofield), Best Director (Redford), Best Picture, Best Adapted Screenplay
British Academy Awards 1994:   Best Adapted Screenplay
Directors Guild of America Awards Nomination 1994:   Best Director (Redford)
Golden Globe Awards Nominations 1994:   Best Film—Drama, Best Supporting Actor (Turturro), Best Director (Redford), Best Screenplay
New York Film Critics Awards 1994:   Best Film

Legislative Oversight. Stempel was the first witness to stand before this Subcommittee on October 6, 1959. Van Doren had by then a $50,000 contract for the *NBC Today Show* as a cultural reporter, the network's way of further exploiting the celebrity it had created. In 1959, when the scandal broke, NBC ordered Van Doren to send a telegram to the subcommittee requesting that his name be cleared, threatening to suspend his *Today Show* contract if he would not comply. In the film, he is asked to sign a statement denying that he had defrauded the public. The film's Goodwin seems to like Van Doren and advises him to lay low for a few weeks while the investigation is in progress, and in the film it is not apparent that the investigation came two years after the fact. Stempel's testimony indicates that all of the contestants were coached, however, making it impossible for his successor to avoid appearing before the subcommittee. Van Doren finally decides to tell the truth.

Paul Attanasio's screenplay effectively stresses the human drama of this expose. When he is first auditioned for the show and asked if he would like to know the answer to the winning question, Van Doren answers "I'd have to say no," adding, naively, "was that part of the test?" When the winning answer, however, proves to be one that he had already covered during the audition, it is surely clear to him that the game is crooked.

One of the film's best moments occurs not in the hearing room but in a classroom at Columbia University, when Van Doren confesses his wrongdoings to his father, who is stunned: "cheating on a quiz show is like plagiarizing a comic strip," the father protests, adding, "your name is mine!" His father's shame carries over to Van Doren's final, moving speech before the congressional hearing.

The film is a triumph of art direction (Jon Hutman), cinematography (Michael Ballhaus) and casting (Bonnie Timmermann), right down to cameos played by film directors Martin Scorsese (as the Geritol sponsor) and Barry Levinson (as Dave Garroway, the host of the *Today Show*). John Turturro plays Stempel—described by one cynical television producer as "an annoying Jewish guy with a sidewall haircut"—with high-level neurotic energy to perfection, and Johann Carlo is entirely believable as his wife, who is as surprised as the rest of the country when she discovers her husband's "performances" were rigged. That he has not confided in her is also in keeping with his character: he wants people to think he is smarter than he is. The man is crazy for attention and respect. After his fall, he believes that he has been discriminated against because he is Jewish: "They always follow a Jew with a Gentile," he tells Goodwin, "and the Gentile wins more money." Goodwin, a Harvard man who also happens to be Jewish, has more in common with Van Doren, whom he tries to protect, than Stempel, but when he checks the record, he discovers that what Stempel had said about Gentile winners is correct.

 "I have flown too high on borrowed wings. Everything came too easy. That's why I am here today."—Charles Van Doren from *Quiz Show*

Ralph Fiennes, who was outstanding in *Schindler's List* (1993) as the SS Commandant, is also memorable here in a more sympathetic role as the new champion, Charlie Van Doren, the son of the Pulitzer Prize-winning poet and critic Mark Van Doren (played by Paul Scofield). He is so far removed from the ordinary world by culture and class that he does not even own a television set. The film takes the viewer into Van Doren's literary circle, which includes Dorothy Van Doren (Elizabeth Wilson), a successful novelist who wrote *The Country Wife* and was once editor of *The Nation*; Thomas Merton (Adam Kilgour), whose book *The Seven-story Mountain* had popularized religion during the 1950's; and "Bunny" Wilson (Vince O'Brien), the most influential critic of American letters of his generation. The contrasts the film dramatizes involve not only the WASPish dominant majority to the Jewish champion but also the intellectual elite to the working class (Stempel moves on to a career with the New York Transit Authority), and high culture to popular culture.

Richard Goodwin is seeking justice through his investigation, but he learns that money and influence control the system. First, the network manages to get Judge Schweitzer to seal the findings of the New York Grand Jury investigation, an unusual measure that had not been enacted since 1869. Goodwin has hard proof that implicates NBC President Robert Kintner (Allan Rich). After talking with Stempel, whose testimony is suspect because Dan Enright had paid for psychiatric sessions for the former champion, Goodwin interviews a Greenwich Village artists named Snodgrass (Douglas McGrath). Snodgrass had written down the questions for which he had been coached and sent them by registered mail to himself, the postmark on the sealed letter proving that he knew ahead of time what he would be asked. When Goodwin confronts Kintner about this at NBC, Kintner reminds him that the congressman who heads the subcommittee is a personal friend of his.

The investigation, which seems to follow Van Doren's defeat on *Twenty-One* almost immediately in the film, establishes that a fraud had been perpetrated, but those most responsible, NBC President Kintner and the Geritol sponsor—both of whom were determined to manipulate the ratings—are exonerated. So, to a degree, is Van Doren, who confesses his guilt but is treated with sympathy by all of the congressmen except Representative Derounian of New York, who is not playing to the public. Herb Stempel is set up as the scapegoat, along with Dan Enright, but the point is made that the public memory is short: a few years later, Enright is back on television with yet another game show, *The Joker Is Wild*. Van Doren is merely a victim of circumstance, who is forced to testify after Stempel has blown the whistle so loudly. "A quiz show hearing without Van Doren is like *Hamlet* without Hamlet," Goodwin's wife (Mira Sorvino) remarks to her husband, once the hearings have started. Van Doren, too, is a loser after his confession, expelled from both Columbia University and the *Today Show*. "Why would a guy like that want to be on a quiz show?" Master of Ceremonies Jack Berry (Christopher McDonald) asks when he learns the background of the new champion. Van Doren shames his family and loses a promising academic career. The consequences are nearly tragic.

The film presents a powerful indictment of the media that is more effective in this regard than Oliver Stone's cartoonish *Natural Born Killers* (reviewed in this volume) because it is more subtle and believable. "We give the public what they want," Enright's associate Albert Freedman (Hank Azaria) tells the subcommittee. "It's like your business." So both politicians and the media are out to defraud the public. "I thought we were going to get television," Goodwin says, wistfully, at the end. "The truth is that television is going to get us." *Quiz Show* is a thesis film, then, and the message cannot be missed. It succeeds best, however, as a contemporary tragedy involving the fall from grace of an intellectual crown prince who makes a serious error in judgment in order to become, as one college student remarks, "as famous as Elvis Presley." After enjoying more than fifteen minutes of fame, he was to live the rest of his life as a recluse, avoiding the limelight.

Some critics objected to the way Attanasio's script manipulated the facts by making Goodwin responsible for uncovering the fraud. Judge Joseph Stone, who was himself involved in the investigation, told *The New York Times* (September 4, 1994) that the "mechanics of the fix were known to the public before Goodwin got into the act" and called the film "a tawdry hoax." Albert Freedman, himself characterized as one of the villains in the film, protested that "the film was fixed" and "even more rigged than the show it portrays." The real Richard Goodwin disagreed, claiming that historical accuracy was not the main issue. By and large the critical reception was favorable. For David Ansen of *Newsweek* it was Redford's best picture since *Ordinary People* (1980), for example, and for Hal Hinson of *The Washington Post* is was "not only the most accomplished film of Redford's directorial career, but one of the best to carry his name."

—*James M. Welsh*

REVIEWS

Entertainment Weekly. CCXLII, September 30, 1994, p. 22.
Interview. September, 1994, p. 108.
National Review. XLVI, No. 19, October 10, 1994, p. 76.
The New York Times. September 4, 1994, Sec. 2, p. 1.
The New York Times Magazine. August 21, 1994, p. 26.
The New Yorker. September 19, 1994, p. 102.
Newsweek. September 19, 1994, p. 62.
Rolling Stone. September 22, 1994, p. 103.
Rolling Stone. October 6, 1994, p. 72.
Time. September 19, 1994, p. 77.
Washington Post. September 16, 1994, p. F1.
Washington Post Weekend. September 16, 1994, p. 49.
Variety. September 12-18, 1994, p. 39.

Radioland Murders

"At station WBN, the hits just keep on coming."
—Movie tagline

"A great, funny film! It's a killer! What a cast! *Radioland Murders* is funny stuff!"—Bob Healy, *Satellite News Network*

 Box Office Gross: $1,234,065 (October 30, 1994)

Radioland Murders is a frenetic romantic comedy-mystery, with the emphasis on frenetic. The film is the brainchild of executive producer George Lucas, creator of the formidable *Star Wars* series and *Indiana Jones* series, as well as the Fantasy-adventure *Willow* (1988) and the Award-winning *American Graffiti* (1973). Lucas conceived the original story, and his Industrial Light and Magic provided the many special visual effects, most of which are not readily apparent to the average viewer, so well integrated are they into the film. Unfortunately, the technical innovations may have outshone the film itself.

The film is set in 1939 during the golden era of American radio and centers on the night that Chicago radio station WBN goes national, a night when anything that can go wrong will. Apparently, the normal scramblings of a small-time operation going big-time were not enough for the filmmakers, however, so they added a half dozen murders to enliven the plot. As further evidence of the film's excesses,

Radioland Murders is the first big-screen starring role for Brian Benben who is the star of the HBO series, *Dream On.*

this 112-minute motion picture boasts some 125 speaking parts. In order to accommodate them all, the characters are forced into rapid-fire dialogue such that they literally spit out their lines. Although it can be desirable to start with a bang, events never slow throughout the entire picture. The result is a confusing mess of period romantic comedy, slapstick comedy, and murder mystery.

Brian Benben stars as Roger Henderson, the station's head writer. He and his wife, Penny (Mary Stuart Masterson), who also works at the station, have recently separated. Apparently, Penny caught Roger in a compromising situation with sexy actress Claudette (Anita Morris). Roger, however, is innocent; he was set up. Over the course of the film, Roger and Penny's reconciliation is prolonged as Roger finds himself suspect number one in a string of murders. Thus Roger, who is simultaneously wooing his wife and doing frantic last-minute script rewrites, also evades the police and takes on the role of detective in order to clear his name.

WBN is run by the very militant General Whalen (Ned Beatty), and Penny is his girl Friday. She is not only extremely efficient but also multi-talented—she has filled in for almost everybody by the end of the evening. With Roger and Penny on the payroll, one wonders why the station hired anyone else. This particular night, everyone is in a panic. First, the station's sponsor is unhappy with the scripts and demands that they be rewritten—with the show due to begin momentarily. Also, multiple personal problems abound among the crew and cast, who

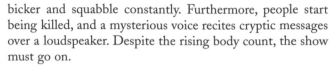

CREDITS

Penny: Mary Stuart Masterson
Roger: Brian Benben
General Whalen: Ned Beatty
Milt Lackey: George Burns
Billy: Scott Michael Campbell
Bernie King: Brion James
Lieutenant Cross: Michael Lerner
Rick Rochester: Michael McKean
Walt Whalen, Jr.:   Jeffrey Tambor
Max Applewhite: Stephen Tobolowsky
Zoltan: Christopher Lloyd
Katzenback: Larry Miller
Claudette: Anita Morris
Dexter Morris: Corbin Bernsen
Anna: Rosemary Clooney
Wild writer: Bobcat Goldthwaite
Jules Cogley: Harvey Korman
Tommy: Robert Walden
Jasper: Dylan Baker
Billy Barty: Billy Barty
Tracy Byrd: Tracy Byrd
Billy's mother: Candy Clark
Female writer: Anne De Salvo
Deirdre: Jennifer Dundas
Billy's father: Bo Hopkins
Father writer: Robert Klein
Frankie Marshall: Joey Lawrence
Son writer: Peter MacNicol

Released: 1994
Production: Rick McCallum, Fred Roos, and George Lucas (executive producer) for Lucasfilm Ltd.; released by Universal Pictures
Direction: Mel Smith
Screenplay: Willard Huyck, Gloria Katz, Jeff Reno, and Ron Osborn; based on a story by George Lucas
Cinematography: David Tattersall
Editing: Paul Trejo
Production design: Gavin Bocquet
Art direction: Peter Russell
Set decoration: Jim Ferrell
Casting: Linda Phillips-Palo, Rosalie Joseph and Mark Fincannon
Visual effects production: Tom Kennedy
Visual effects supervision: Scott Squires
Sound: Carl Rudisill
Costume design: Peggy Farrell
Stunt coordination: Leon Delaney
Music: Joel McNeely
MPAA rating: PG
Running time: 112 minutes

bicker and squabble constantly. Furthermore, people start being killed, and a mysterious voice recites cryptic messages over a loudspeaker. Despite the rising body count, the show must go on.

The production notes unintentionally point up one of the problems with the film: *Radioland Murders* features "a disgruntled sponsor, a tyrannical boss, an incompetent director, temperamental stars, unpaid writers on the verge of mutiny"—one cliche after another. There is nothing innovative here. Furthermore, the notes boast that "bits and pieces of at least two dozen radio shows move continuously through *Radioland Murders*." Sadly, the on stage action—inspired by such 1930's legends as the *Chase and Sanborn Hour* and the *Lux Radio Theater*—which is so highly touted in the film's production notes, is continually upstaged by the offstage antics. Although the filmmakers took the care to cast such veteran entertainers as comedian George Burns and singer Rosemary Clooney as performers for WBN, one rarely gets to see them. As soon as a number begins, the film cuts away to the action going on elsewhere. This film set during a 1930's evening radio show devotes almost no time to the actual radio show.

Furthermore, for a comedy, the murders themselves are rather gruesome. Herman Katzenback (Larry Miller), Claudette's jealous husband and WBN's uptight station manager, gets ground up in the clockwork-like gears beneath the rotating stage. Humorless sponsor Bernie King (Brion James) is killed with laughing gas—which may have looked funny on paper but is decidedly not on the big screen. General Whalen falls down an elevator shaft before Penny's very eyes. The very first murder was a bit vague: A musician takes a swig from a bottle hidden under his coat, which has been filled with rat poison. Although the murder is quick and painless, for the viewer anyway, one never does learn what the musician had to do with the plot. In fact, even at the film's end, the reason why the particular victims were chosen remains unclear.

Although the violence is admittedly cartoon violence, the film grows decidedly less funny as the murders mount. Many of the major characters one meets at the beginning are dead at the end. In fact, almost all the characters are so imbecilic that it is amazing not that there are so many deaths but that there are any survivors. None of the victims is sympathetic, and the discovery of the actual murderer is anticlimactic to all that has preceded it.

Radioland Murders is only the second feature film to be directed by celebrated British comic Mel Smith. His first feature, *The Tall Guy* (1989), was an underrated, quirky romantic comedy, which starred Jeff Goldblum and Emma Thompson. Smith attained fame in Great Britain starring on several top-rated television comedy shows, including *Alias Smith and Jones*. He also played the Albino in Rob Reiner's *The Princess Bride* (1987). Although *The Tall Guy* garnered renewed interest after its initial release, *Radioland Murders* will probably not be so fortunate.

Brian Benben, who starred in HBO's Emmy Award-winning television series *Dream On*, is an appealing lead—handsome with a comic bent. Over the course of the film, one gets to see him dressed both as a penguin and Carmen Miranda. Benben comes to *Radioland Murders* with an extensive comedy background, unlike co-star Mary Stuart Masterson, a dramatic actress attempting her first comic role. Masterson, however, is a motion-picture veteran, having starred in such films as *Fried Green Tomatoes* (1991), *Benny and Joon* (1993), and *Bad Girls* (reviewed in this volume). The two have an on-screen chemistry that rarely has a chance to work, so little time do they have together.

The film boasts an impressive ensemble cast that includes Michael Lerner as curmudgeonly Lieutenant Cross of the Homicide Bureau, Michael McKean as the loopy orchestra leader, Jeffrey Tambor as the station's incompetent director, Stephen Tobolowsky as Max the chief engineer, Christopher Lloyd as eccentric sound wizard Zoltan, Corbin Bernsen as suave announcer Dexter Morris, and offbeat comedian Bobcat Goldthwaite as one of the mutinous writers. Although none of these actors has a large part, perhaps the person who gets the shortest shrift is the very talented Harvey Korman, star of Mel Brooks's classics *Blazing Saddles* (1973) and *High Anxiety* (1977), and a major player in Carol Burnett's long-running hit television comedy show. He plays the alcoholic writer Jules Cogley, whose sole purpose in the film is that he can tell hooch from rat poison. Especially winning, however, is newcomer Scott Michael Campbell, who plays Billy the page, the enthusiastic station gofer.

Not to be overlooked are the exquisite sets and costumes, designed by production designer Gavin Bocquet and costumer Peggy Farrell, both Emmy Award winners. The sets are elaborate and one would liked to have had more time to examine them. Interestingly, according to the production notes, much of the design work was realized on computer. The visual effects team "filled in walls and ceilings where none existed, placed Benben atop an imaginary radio tower and called in a computer-generated airplane for a climactic scene." Thus the twenty or so rooms needed for the

Mary Stuart Masterson and Brian Benben in *Radioland Murders*. Copyright © by Universal City Studios, Inc. Courtesy of MCA Publishing Rights, a Division of MCA Inc. All rights reserved.

"Nobody comes into my dressing room uninvited. What the hell do you think that star means?" "You're Jewish?"—Claudette Cassenback and Roger Henderson from *Radioland Murders*

re-creation of radio station WBN were created more economically—only partial sets needed to be built and the parts could be reused on other sets. Also, the filmmakers were able, at times, to shoot the actors' parts separately and merge them seamlessly into a single scene.

Despite its technological innovations, all-star cast, and the imprint of motion-picture giant George Lucas, *Radioland Murders* flounders. The motives behind the various murders remain vague, the pace is too fast, there are too many characters, and the action is schizophrenic. In this instance, the whole is considerably less than its parts. Thus, *Radioland Murders* is merely functional rather than outstanding.

—*Cynthia K. Breckenridge*

REVIEWS

Daily Variety. October 17, 1994, p. 2.
The Hollywood Reporter. October 17, 1994, p. 16.
Los Angeles Times. October 21, 1994, p. F14.
The New York Times. October 21, 1994, p. B2.

Raining Stones

"Two thumbs up!"—*Siskel & Ebert*

"*Raining Stones* is brisk, richly characterized fiction that cuts deeply and truly as any documentary."—Vincent Canby, *The New York Times*

Annual income twenty pounds, annual expenditure nineteen six, result happiness. Annual income twenty pounds, annual expenditure twenty pounds ought and six, result misery." [Mr. Micawber, *David Copperfield*]

At first the plot of *Raining Stones* sounds as grim as a Charles Dickens novel. It is the story of life in a depressed area of northern England, where life on the dole is so inadequate

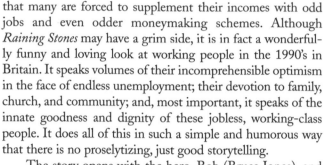

CREDITS

Bob: Bruce Jones
Anne: Julie Brown
Coleen: Gemma Phoenix
Tommy: Ricky Tomlinson
Father Barry: Tom Hickey
Tansey: Jonathan James
Jimmy: Mike Fallon
Butcher: Ronnie Ravey
Irishman: Lee Brennan
Young Mother: Karen Henthorn
May: Christine Abbott
Tracey: Geraldine Ward
Joe: William Ash
Sean: Matthew Clucas
Shop Assistant: Anna Jaskolka
Ted: Anthony Bodell

Origin: Great Britain
Released: 1993
Production: Sally Hibbin for Parallax Pictures, Channel Four, and Film Four International; released by Northern Arts Entertainment
Direction: Ken Loach
Screenplay: Jim Allen
Cinematography: Barry Ackroyd
Editing: Jonathan Morris
Production design: Martin Johnson
Art direction: Fergus Clegg
Production management: Lesley Stewart
Sound: Ray Beckett
Costume design: Anne Sinclair
Music: Stewart Copeland
MPAA rating: no listing
Running time: 90 minutes

that many are forced to supplement their incomes with odd jobs and even odder moneymaking schemes. Although *Raining Stones* may have a grim side, it is in fact a wonderfully funny and loving look at working people in the 1990's in Britain. It speaks volumes of their incomprehensible optimism in the face of endless unemployment; their devotion to family, church, and community; and, most important, it speaks of the innate goodness and dignity of these jobless, working-class people. It does all of this in such a simple and humorous way that there is no proselytizing, just good storytelling.

The story opens with the hero, Bob (Bruce Jones), and his best friend Tommy (Ricky Tomlinson) emerging from the fog in a pastoral scene of rolling green hills and grazing sheep. At first it appears that they are shepherding the sheep, but it soon becomes apparent that they are city folk trying to poach a sheep. They slip in the mud, they wrestle a frightened sheep into a van, and they are basically inept during the entire venture.

Back in the city, the two corral the sheep into a vacant backyard and prepare to butcher it. In a hilarious scene, the two men chase the sheep around the yard with a knife. This opening scene sets the funny yet tender mood that pervades the rest of the film. In the end, neither has the heart to kill the sheep, and they eventually pay a butcher to slaughter it. Going table to table in a local pub, they try to sell the mutton, with little or no success. When they exit the pub, they find that Bob's van has been stolen.

This is the beginning of Bob's bad luck—not that his life had been much better. Bob, his wife Anne (Julie Brown), and their little girl Coleen (Gemma Phoenix) live in government housing, and Bob is on the dole. Coleen is coming up for her first communion, and she needs an expensive communion dress; without his van, however, Bob's chances of finding day work are slim.

In order to get the dress, Bob seeks a series of jobs and scams that are as funny as they are heartrending. With each scene, however, one thing becomes more and more clear: Bob, a working-class man with working-class ethics, simply lacks one essential element in his life—work. Without work, he feels a failure, and getting his daughter a communion dress begins to symbolize his redemption.

He steals sod, cleans bogged drains, and works as a bouncer in generally aborted attempts to get money. Covered in feces, beaten to a pulp, and basically humiliated, he finally realizes that without a car, he can not make the money necessary to take care of his family. So, he takes half of the money he has earned and buys the dress, and with the other half, he makes a down payment on a used van.

When he falls behind on the payments, the debt is sold to loan sharks. One day while Bob is out, the loan shark,

Tansey (Jonathan James) goes to Bob's house and threatens his wife and daughter for the money. When he returns home and finds his family totally traumatized, he grabs a wrench and hunts for the loan shark. He stalks him at a pub, waiting until the drunken man is alone in a parking structure to confront him. Bob threatens Tansey with his wrench and tells him to give him the book with the names of the town's debtors. They fight, and, characteristically, Bob again loses.

As Tansey is speeding away, Bob, in frustration, takes his wrench and smashes the windshield. The already drunken Tansey loses control of the car and runs into a pillar, dying immediately. Bob tentatively reaches into the car and gets the book with his name in it.

Distraught, Bob goes to the church. He tells the priest, Father Barry (Tom Hickey), what has happened. Sobbing in his guilt and desperation, he says that he is going to surrender to the police. Father Barry advises him not to do so and, further, to tell no one what has happened. Father Barry takes the book from Bob and sets it on fire, telling Bob that he is a good man and that many will sleep better knowing Tansey is dead.

The next day at his daughter's first communion, bread and wine are being distributed. At the same time, the police pull in front of Bob's flat. At the alter, Father Barry gives Bob the sacrament, speaking of the body of Christ, which was given to wash away men's sins. Back at the flat, the police ask Bob's neighbors if he lives at that address. The priest gives the wine; the blood that was shed for man. The police ask Bob's neighbors if he owns a green van. Startled, they say yes, but it was stolen. The police have found the stolen van.

"For a working man, it rains stones seven days a week," says Bob's socialist father-in-law. Hence the name of the film; yet the audience senses that Bob's luck has just changed.

Director Ken Loach and writer Jim Allen have created a documentary-style film that chronicles the poverty and desperation of simple people who simply want to get on in life. They do not ask for wealth or fame, merely the dignity of a week's pay for a week's work. The filmmakers have successfully captured a realistic view of the working-class way of life with humor and with a love of the people they are filming. *Raining Stones* is a political statement about rampant unemployment and its ramifications of violence, drugs, and loss of dignity, as well as a testament to one man's tenacious hold on hope.

Jim Allen, who wrote the screenplay, has lived for many years on the estate where the film was shot and is familiar with the problems and joys of the people in the estate where he lives. Most of the people in the film are locals to the Middleton area, with little or no acting backgrounds, but the

> "When you're a worker, it rains stones seven days a week."—Bob's socialist father-in-law, in *Raining Stones*

AWARDS AND NOMINATIONS

Cannes Film Festival 1993:   Special Jury Prize

camera is so unobtrusive that most act in a quite natural way. Allen personally knows most of the cast as his own neighbors. His excellent screenplay is so attuned to the people he has cast, that he is able to introduce the viewer to a collage of characters that are mesmerizing. The dialogue, though at times difficult to understand through the thick northern accent, gives the viewer a feeling for the way these people interact on a daily basis, and, at times, one can almost forget that the film is fiction. Allen has worked with Loach on various television projects and also on the film *Hidden Agenda* (1990), which won the Cannes Jury Prize.

The director of photography Barry Ackroyd's use of a grainy documentary style coupled with the naturalness of the people filmed—whether they are talking in a pub or having an argument on the street—bring a level of realism to the film that is both convincing and touching. The audience almost feels like voyeurs in the townspeoples' lives.

Ackroyd's tight camera angles, especially in the council housing, are so claustrophobic, that the viewer becomes uncomfortably aware of the close quarters in which these people must live. When Ackroyd films the middle-class neighborhood, the expansiveness of large manicured front yards and elegant tree-lined streets effectively contrast with the littered and overcrowded working-class neighborhood.

Bruce Jones, who plays Bob, has had a few walk-on parts in films but currently works in a dairy. As Bob, he is instantly likeable. In one scene, where his daughter is modeling the communion dress for him, he projects Bob's great love and pride in his little "princess," and at the same time the viewer feels his deep sadness and ineptitude. Jones plays the part of the unlucky and sometimes not very wise Bob exceptionally well.

Ricky Tomlinson plays Tommy, Bob's friend and colleague in petty scams. He is hilarious in the role, cracking jokes even in the most dire of circumstances. He always has a scheme for getting money and always invites his friend Bob to share in the action. In one scene, where his teenage daughter gives him some money "to get a drink," he takes it and then, head in hands, is mortified. It is a powerful scene and Tomlinson—in a departure from his playful persona—is wonderful in it. He has worked with Loach before on the film *Riff Raff* (1991), which received the award for The European Film of the Year for 1991.

Director Ken Loach has dealt with the subject of unemployment in earlier films: *Poor Cow* (1968), *Kes* (1970), *Family Life* (1972), and *Looks and Smiles* (1981), which won the Cannes Prize for Contemporary Cinema in 1981. He was part of the movement in the 1960's that revitalized British cinema but has no illusions about the political effect his films have. "Politically, films have very little impact," says Loach. "I've made several television programmes on the plight of the miners, but they haven't had any effect." Although Loach may not be very effective in Parliament, he is most definitely effective in Cannes. *Raining Stones* won the Special Jury Prize for 1993, making it Loach's fourth award from Cannes.

In *Raining Stones*, Loach and Allen have created a real working-class hero. A man who—by simply never giving up the battle to survive against overwhelming obstacles—unwittingly has freed his whole community from their burden of debt. Bob has given himself and his neighbors a second chance, and the only ones who know this fact are the priest and (it is hinted) God.

—*Diane Hatch-Avis*

REVIEWS

Los Angeles Times. September 21, 1994, p. F1.
The New Republic. March 28, 1994, p. 30.
The New York Times. October 2, 1993, p. 11.
Variety. May 26, 1993, p.16.

Ramona

A young Mexican woman, Ramona (Heidi Von Palleske), has a brief affair with an American businessman, Henry Sinclair (Cain Devore), then enters the United States illegally in the trunk of his car.

REVIEWS

Variety. CCCXLIV, September 23, 1991, p. 77.

CREDITS

Ramona: Heidi von Palleske
Henry Sinclair: Cain Devore
Paco: Jason Scott
No character identified: Shannon Bradley
No character identified: Michael David Lally
No character identified: Beata Pozniak
No character identified: William Fitchner
No character identified: Steffen Foster
No character identified: Marilyn Adams
No character identified: Bruno Bossio

Released: 1991
Production: Jonathan Sarno; released by CNI Cinema
Direction: Jonathan Sarno
Screenplay: Jonathan Sarno
Cinematography: Russell Frazier
Editing: Jonathan Sarno
Production design: Evelyn Claude
Sound: Reinhart Sterger
Costume design: Stanka Preberg
MPAA rating: no listing
Running time: 89 minutes

Rapa Nui

"For the love of a woman, for the honor of their gods, they would destroy paradise."—Movie tagline

"300 years ago Easter Island was called *Rapa Nui*."—Movie tagline

"An amazing achievement of imagination and re-creation that dazzles the eye and challenges the mind. Quite simply one of the most haunting and provocative films I've ever seen."—Michael Medved, *Sneak Previews*

"A spectacular stretch of visceral filmmaking...undeniably thrilling."—Bob Strauss, *The L.A. Daily News*

"Director Reynolds, cinematographer Stephen F. Windon and editor Peter Boyle are at their best in the climactic Birdman event. Backed by a dashing, percussive score by Stewart Copeland, the footage here is good fun."—Kenneth Turan, *L.A. Times*

"The contest is excitingly staged, and there are ravishing images."—Owen Gleiberman, *Entertainment Weekly*

 Box Office Gross: $286,624 (October 9, 1994)

Director-writer Kevin Reynolds continues his professional relationship with Kevin Costner in this fictional tale about Easter Island. Costner, who co-produced and does not act in the film, and Reynolds first met working on Fandango (1985). Subsequent to that film, they continued their relationship on another tropical epic called Waterworld (1995), which has become known for its huge budget and for artistic differences between Costner and Reynolds.

Rapa Nui is Reynolds' paean to the mysterious South Pacific Easter Island, which was discovered by European explorers in the early 1700's. This film takes place in approximately 1680 and owes its story to a mixture of Reynolds' imagination, some historical accuracy, and to a host of other films from *Blue Lagoon* (1949, 1980) to *Conan the Barbarian* (1982) with a bit of *Bomba, the Jungle Boy* (1949) thrown in for good measure. It even borrows a bit from *Romeo and Juliet* and *West Side Story* (1961) with its subplot about a girl from one clan marrying into another clan.

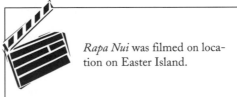

Rapa Nui was filmed on location on Easter Island.

Rapa Nui is the story of Noro (Jason Scott Lee) who reluctantly enters the "Birdman" competition to help maintain his family's place as the rulers of the "Long Ears." The Long Ears are the aristocrats of Easter Island, headed by Noro's dotty grandfather Ariki-Mau (Eru Potaka-Dewes). Noro's chief rival in the Birdman competition (which is sort of a seventeenth century version of the "Ironman Triathalon") is the brooding Make (Esai Morales), a leader of the worker-bee "Short Ears." Make is also Noro's rival for the affections of Short Ear beauty, Ramana (Sandrine Holt). Ramana is forced to enter "the Cave of the Virgins" for six months, at which time she will marry the winner of the Birdman competition. There is also a subplot (there are several) about the exploitation of workers on the giant statues of Easter Island. An early rebellion, much like union rebellions in *Norma Rae* (1979) or *F.I.S.T.* (1978), led by Make, rounds out the dramaturgical portion of the film. Needless to say, this is not the most original story ever devised.

It is difficult to take this film seriously, as a result of the often unintentionally humorous dialogue. When Noro decides to enter the contest, he turns to Make and asks, "so, will you help me train?" Combined with Jason Scott Lee's surfer-dude appearance, the anachronism is rather funny. "How much do you want to win?" growls trainer Haoa (Zac Wallace), echoing every fight film from *Golden Boy* (1939) to *The Karate Kid* (1984). And finally, one of the most unintentionally delightful moments comes when the aristocratic chieftain tells one of the monument's workers to "take rest of the day off."

However, *Rapa Nui* is liable to surprise audiences who stick with it long enough to witness the thrilling *Birdman* competition. Reynolds, together with cinematographer Stephen F. Windon and editor Peter Boyle, captures the action with precision, tension, and artistry. The Birdman sequence, and the training sequence preceding it, are emblematic of the schism existing nowadays between the artistry of storytelling and the artistry of film technique. Reynolds and company can captivate the eye with extraordinary images even while they provide dialogue and a story that are rudimentary at best. The training sequence, complete with panoramic shots of the athletes running on the tops of mountains are stunning. And the Birdman sequence is nothing short of extraordinary, with its close-ups of the competitors from in the water or over a cliff.

The actors, particularly Lee and Morales, deserve kudos for the extensive physical demands of their roles.

Morales rapells down the side of one of the "Maoi" (huge statues) as if climbing rope in a school gymnasium, and Lee dashes across enormous rocks as if running on a carpet. Both provide guileless readings of their simplistic good-guy/bad-guy roles sounding not unlike they stepped out of twentieth-century Southern California. Sandrine Holt is a radiant, sexy love interest. Eru Potaka-Dewes, a Maori actor from New Zealand, fares the best. He plays the grandfather as a fussy despot bewildered by his own aging process. A bizarre subplot where he lands on a glacier that appears out of nowhere is baffling, but Dewes manages to appear as if it all makes sense.

Finally, credit should be given to the stunning makeup by Peter Frampton and to the visceral and exciting music by the talented Stewart Copeland.

Faults aside, *Rapa Nui* is visually beautiful and politically correct (yet another subplot about the environment sends a nice message). Hopefully, Reynolds will not be too waterlogged after *Waterworld* to visit the South Pacific again—perhaps with another screenwriter to help navigate.

—Kirby Tepper

CREDITS

Noro: Jason Scott Lee
Make: Esai Morales
Ramana: Sandrine Holt
Ariki-mau: Eru Potaka-Dewes
Tupa: George Henare
Haoa: Zac Wallace
Heke: Faenza Reuben

Released: 1994
Production: Kevin Costner and Jim Wilson for Tig Productions and Majestic Films, in association with RCS; released by Warner Bros.
Direction: Kevin Reynolds
Screenplay: Kevin Reynolds and Tim Rose Price; based on a story by Reynolds
Cinematography: Stephen F. Windon
Editing: Peter Boyle
Production design: George Liddle
Art direction: Ian Allan
Set decoration: Brian Dusting
Casting: Elisabeth Leustig
Special effects: Steven Richard Courtley
Costume design: John Bloomfield
Stunt coordination: Glenn Boswell
MPAA rating: R
Running time: 107 minutes

REVIEWS

Chicago Tribune. September 30, 1994, p. 7L.
Daily Variety. April 13, 1994, p.2; April 18-24, 1994, p. 61.
Entertainment Weekly. September 23, 1994, p. 49.
Entertainment Weekly. February 3, 1995, p. 64.
The Hollywood Reporter. September 7, 1994, p.8.
Los Angeles Times. September 9, 1994, F4.
The New York Times. September 9, 1994, p. C3.
People Weekly. XLII, September 26, 1994, p. 20.
Variety. CCCLIV, April 18, 1994, p. 61.

"We just have this little space in time that we occupy the planet and, for as bad as we are, we're trying to open our eyes. And this film does that in the biggest and smallest of ways."—*Rapa Nui* co-producer, Kevin Costner

Ready to Wear (Pret-á-Porter)

"Sex. Greed. Murder. Some things never go out of style."—Movie tagline

"An exuberant comedy."—Peter Travers, *Rolling Stone*

"Four stars! Good fun."—*Playboy*

"A satisfyingly will-wrought film!"—Amy Fine Collins, *Harper's Bazaar*

Kim Basinger, Sally Kellerman, Danny Aiello, Tracey Ullman, and Linda Hunt in *Ready to Wear*. Copyright © Miramax Films.

The quality of the films directed by Robert Altman has varied widely during his up-and-down career of almost forty years. He has made two great films, *McCabe and Mrs. Miller* (1971) and *The Player* (1992); several very good films, including *The Long Goodbye* (1973), *Thieves Like Us* (1974), *Nashville* (1975), *Secret Honor* (1984), and *Vincent and Theo* (1990); flawed but interesting films, such as *Images* (1972) and *Three Women* (1977); only one film truly popular with the mass audience, *M*A*S*H* (1970); at least one film highly overrated by reviewers, *Short Cuts* (1993); and several embarrassingly bad films, such as *Brewster McCloud* (1970), *A Perfect Couple* (1979), *H.E.A.L.T.H.* (1979), and *Popeye* (1980). *Ready to Wear* belongs in the latter category.

As with many of his previous films, Altman takes a large, mostly talented cast and juggles their characters' interrelated stories. The setting this time is Paris during a week in which the world's most famous designers show their ready-to-wear lines. Altman brings together designers, models, buyers, journalists, photographers, and their relatives and hangers-on seemingly to satirize the fashion industry. Unfortunately, the cast, the director's visual style, and the film's satiric impulse all fall victim to a weak script by Altman and Barbara Shulgasser.

The subplots include the death, thought to be murder, of the head of the Fashion Council, Olivier de la Fontaine (Jean-Pierre Cassel); the indifference of his wife, Isabella (Sophia Loren); and her pursuit by a mysterious visitor from Russia, Sergio (Marcello Mastroianni), who turns out to be the husband who abandoned her for the Soviet Union years earlier. Olivier is mourned by his lover, Simone Lowenthal (Anouk Aimée), a designer. Her son, Jack (Rupert Everett), cheats on his model wife, Dane Simpson (Georgianna Robertson), with his sister-in-law, Kiki (Tara León). Arrogant Irish photographer Milo O'Brannigan (Stephen

In *Ready to Wear*, Loren and Mastroianni recreate the boudoir striptease scene from their 1964 film, *Yesterday, Today, and Tomorrow*.

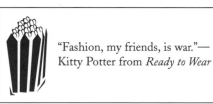

"Fashion, my friends, is war."—Kitty Potter from *Ready to Wear*

Rea) is being wooed by Regina Krumm (Linda Hunt), editor of *Elle*; Sissy Wanamaker (Sally Kellerman), editor of *Harper's Bazaar*; and Nina Scant (Tracey Ullman), editor of *British Vogue*. Designer Cort Romney (Richard E. Grant) is cheating on his wife, Violetta (Anne Canovas), with another designer, Cy Bianco (Forest Whitaker), whose assistant, Reggie (Tom Novembre), is having an affair with Violetta.

Circumstances force Anne Eisenhower (Julia Roberts), reporter for *The Houston Chronicle* and sportswriter Joe Flynn (Tim Robbins) to share the same hotel room, and they begin an affair. Then there are Slim Chrysler (Lauren Bacall), a former fashion editor; Clint Lammeraux (Lyle Lovett), a manufacturer of cowboy boots; Major Hamilton (Danny Aiello), a buyer for a department store; his wife (Teri Garr); and the police (Jean Rochefort and Michel Blanc) investigating Olivier's death. Working their way through these groups are Fiona Ulrich (Lili Taylor), a photojournalist for *The New York Times*, and Kitty Potter (Kim Basinger), a television reporter.

Adding flavor to this mix are appearances by real-life designers such as Gianfranco Ferré, Jean-Paul Gaultier, Christian Lacroix, and Sonia Rykiel; models such as Naomi Campbell and Christy Turlington; journalists such as CNN's Elsa Klensch; and celebrities such

CREDITS

Kitty Potter: Kim Basinger
Anne Eisenhower: Julia Roberts
Joe Flynn: Tim Robbins
Isabella de la Fontaine: Sophia Loren
Sergio: Marcello Mastroianni
Slim Chrysler: Lauren Bacall
Simone Lowenthal: Anouk Aimée
Jack Lowenthal: Rupert Everett
Milo O'Brannigan: Stephen Rea
Nina Scant: Tracey Ullman
Regina Krumm: Linda Hunt
Sissy Wanamaker: Sally Kellerman
Cort Romney: Richard E. Grant
Cy Bianco: Forest Whitaker
Fiona Ulrich: Lili Taylor
Clint Lammeraux: Lyle Lovett
Major Hamilton: Danny Aiello
Louise Hamilton: Teri Garr
Inspector Tantpis: Jean Rochefort
Inspector Forget: Michel Blanc
Olivier de la Fontaine: Jean-Pierre Cassel
Albertine: Ute Lemper
Dane Simpson: Georgianna Robertson
Kiki Simpson: Tara León
Violetta Romney: Anne Canovas
Reggie: Tom Novembre
Jean-Pierre: François Cluzet
Pilar: Rossy de Palma
Vivienne: Kasia Figura
Sophie: Chiara Mastroianni
Craig: Sam Robards

Released: 1994
Production: Robert Altman, Scott Bushnell, and Jon Kilik; released by Miramax Films
Direction: Robert Altman
Screenplay: Robert Altman and Barbara Shulgasser
Cinematography: Jean Lépine and Pierre Mignot
Editing: Geraldine Peroni
Production design: Stephen Altman
Art direction: William Amello
Set design: Jean Canovas
Set decoration: Françoise Dupertois
Sound: Alain Curvelier
Costume design: Catherine Leterrier
Music supervision: Allan Nicholls
Music: Michel Legrand
MPAA rating: R
Running time: 132 minutes

as Cher and Harry Belafonte. Shot during an actual ready-to-wear week, *Ready to Wear* has almost a documentary feel

AWARDS AND NOMINATIONS

Golden Globe Awards Nominations 1995:   Best Film—Musical/Comedy, Best Supporting Actress (Loren)

to it, much as Altman mixed real and fictional events in *Tanner '88*, his television satire of the 1988 presidential campaign.

The problem with this pseudo-documentary approach is that Altman seems to believe that by mixing the real and the fictional something interesting is bound to happen. Unfortunately, the fictional side is too weakly plotted and the characters too superficial. Almost everyone is a caricature, and most seem robotlike compared to the spontaneity of the real designers and others interviewed by Kitty Potter and Fiona Ulrich.

Altman's idea of farce is too heavy-handed, best exemplified by having several characters step into the dog excrement prevalent everywhere in his Paris. Making the Major-and-Mrs.-Hamilton subplot turn out to be nothing but the husband's preference for wearing chic women's fashions is especially trite. The sight of a large man dressed as a woman stopped being shockingly funny long ago—if it ever was funny. The clumsy way in which Altman maneuvers Cort and Cy and Violetta and Reggie into the same spot so that they can discover everyone is cheating on everyone else is extremely tired farce. Having Anne and Joe unable to leave their hotel room because their luggage has been stolen is weary since they could use their credit cards to buy new clothes.

Like many other satirists, Altman has a cruel, misanthropic, especially misogynistic streak that can be particularly disturbing when it displays itself without any wit or originality. Such is the case with the Milo O'Brannigan subplot, as the photographer not only humiliates the editors trying to convince him to sign an exclusive contract but photographs their embarrassment. Milo does this only out of impure maliciousness. These scenes are embarrassing both for the characters and the actors. Only Tracey Ullman, a skilled farceur, handles the situation with any aplomb, as her Nina Scant responds more with anger than humiliation.

Few of the performers have opportunities to display their skills. Julia Roberts coasts through her underwritten role with film-star charm. Similarly, Marcello Mastroianni turns Sergio's quest for his abandoned wife into subtle comedy until the couple is about to make love and he falls asleep, a situation indicative of the director's own ennui. Kim Basinger gives the liveliest performance, and the film always picks up energy when she is present. Kitty Potter is a caricature of a self-absorbed, mindless television journalist, but Basinger plays her as someone brighter and more humane than she appears. Her work gives some hint of the type of ironic satire Altman intended but rarely achieves.

Altman has said he has longed to make a film about this subject since attending his first Paris fashion show a decade ago because he fell in love with the pageantry of the runway spectacle. Ironically, the shows his fictional designers stage lack the flair of the footage of the real shows, partly because the fashions created by Cort and Cy emphasize the often silly excesses of real designers. It is pointless to make fun of something that already spoofs itself.

Altman fares better with the climactic show staged by Simone Lowenthal, who expresses her anger at having her son sell her business out from under her, and at the cutthroat nature of the fashion industry in general, by having her models parade down the runway completely nude. Despite the potential for yet more embarrassment and humiliation, this naked march has a strange, quiet dignity that contrasts sharply with the frantic events preceding it. This scene is also the only time Altman seems to be paying much attention to the visual impact of his story.

While *The Player* worked because it had a witty screenplay and a clear focus—the vindictive infighting at the top of the film studios—*Ready to Wear* fails because it lacks any focus. Altman is not really concerned with designers or the fashion industry at large but with the surrounding hoopla—a fuzzy premise for satire. *Ready to Wear* received considerable publicity for its distributor's last-minute decision to change its title. Miramax was concerned that the French name *Pret-á-Porter* would scare off potential viewers. It need not have worried. Altman's laziness and contempt ensured that the film would be a box-office flop.

—*Michael Adams*

REVIEWS

The Advocate. December 27, 1994, p. 50.
Atlanta Journal Constitution. December 23, 1994, p. P8.
Boston Globe. December 23, 1994, p. 48.
The Christian Science Monitor. LXXXVII, December 23, 1994, p. 11.
Daily Variety. CCCLVII, December 8, 1994, p. 2.
Entertainment Weekly. December 23, 1994, p. 44.
The Hollywood Reporter. December 9-11, 1994, p. 10.
Los Angeles Times. December 23, 1994, p. F1.
Maclean's. CVII, December 26, 1994, p. 36.
The Nation. CCLX, January 23, 1995, p. 106.
New York. XXVIII, January 2, 1995, p. 67.
The New York Times. December 23, 1994, p. B1.
The New Yorker. LXX, December 26, 1994, p. 144.
Newsweek. CXXV, January 9, 1995, p. 58.
People Weekly. XLIII, January 16, 1995, p. 20.
Playboy. XLII, February, 1995, p. 20.
Time. CXLIV, December 19, 1994, p. 79.
USA Today. December 23, 1994, p. D10.
The Village Voice. XXXIX, December 27, 1994, p. 61.
The Wall Street Journal. December 29, 1994, p. A8.
The Washington Post. December 23, 1994, p. WW37.

Reality Bites

"A comedy about love in the '90s."—Movie tagline

"*Reality Bites* scores the first comedy knockout of the year! It's pure entertainment."—Peter Travers, *Rolling Stone*

"A completely charming romance that manages to be warm and empathetic without losing its sharp comic edge."—Kenneth Turan, *Los Angeles Times*

"*The Graduate* for the '90s. Smart, romantic and enormously engaging."—Michael Medved, *Sneak Previews*

"Winona Ryder gives her first true star performance and Ethan Hawke is magnetic. Yearning and hilarious, *Reality Bites* gets an 'A.'"—Owen Gleiberman, *Entertainment Weekly*

Box Office Gross: $20,900,000 (February 1995)

F our friends celebrate their college graduation atop a downtown Houston office building. They drink, smoke dope, dance, talk, laugh, and hug. They talk about their dreams. Lelaina Pierce (Winona Ryder) records everything with her video camera. She says, sheepishly, "This may sound corny, but I'd like to somehow make a difference in people's lives." It does sound corny, but it is also sad. For all her urge to do good, Lelaina does not really know how she can make any difference in people's lives. *Reality Bites* is a film about people coming to adulthood in the 1990's made mostly by people coming to adulthood in the 1990's. Lelaina is at its center because she embodies the odd combination of vast sincerity, deep cynicism, good intentions, and continually dashed hopes of the self-titled "Generation X."

Valedictorian of her college class, Lelaina gives a speech indicting her parents' generation for betraying the values of their 1960's-based rebellion. Yet when she asks the big questions about how her generation will undo the mess their parents have left for them, she hesitates and then admits she does not know the answer.

The Baby Boomers who spawned her and her down-in-the-mouth comrades figured they knew everything, especially how to transform their parents tense, Cold War world into one big acid trip of peace, love and happiness. Yet the Generation X-ers are wise enough to know that they do not

"I'm a nonpracticing Jew."
"I'm a nonpracticing virgin."—
Michael and Lelaina from *Reality Bites*

know how to fix things. They have been forced by the reality that bites them—the reality of diminishing jobs, the reality of AIDS—to lapse into a premature cynicism. It is as if the rocket power of youthful rebellion fizzles on the launching pad.

Accurately depicting this aborted youthful dream, *Reality Bites* is a continual implosion. Like its main character, it wants to change something, it wants desperately to mean something, but when it creeps to the cliff of meaningfulness, it jumps back, afraid of failing, resigned to settling for less.

Lelaina longs to make a difference, but she has more artistic leanings than political sense. So she comes to believe that her contribution lies in making a self-conscious video documentary about her group of friends, whom she describes as "people trying to find their way without any role models or heroes." First-time director Ben Stiller's film has the same mission and suffers the same fate. "Reality Bites" is good anthropology—it has its ear finely tuned to the quirky attitude of youth culture—but it lacks any compelling vision or purpose, sliding distressingly easily into a trite love-triangle story.

The script by twenty-three-year-old first-timer Helen Childress and the direction by Stiller are knowing, bordering at times on being too smart, too cute, but saving themselves from those reefs with oceans of sincerity and self-abnegation. The dialogue is relentlessly authentic, capturing that quality of self-deprecating humor that is the essence of Generation X. The young characters are appealingly glib and funny. Yet the plot is hackneyed. One knows from the first tinkling of the triangle who will pair off at the end, and little else of interest occurs.

Lelaina is an assistant at a Houston television station, where she battles to maintain her pride while servicing a two-faced senior-citizen talk-show host (John Mahoney). The host, like all the older adults in the film, is morally bankrupt and ridiculous. When her irrepressible friend and roommate Vickie Miner (Janeane Garofalo), a manager at a clothing store, brings home Troy Dyer (Ethan Hawke), an aimless musician who needs a place to crash, the sparks start to fly. Enter Michael Grates (Stiller), a sincere but hopelessly materialistic music-video executive, and Lelaina gets all torn up between her desires, her ambitions, and her values.

The most irritating flaw of *Reality Bites* is not its failure of plot, but its failure of nerve. True to their generation, the filmmakers are wise beyond their years. They know that

CREDITS

Lelaina Pierce: Winona Ryder
Troy Dyer: Ethan Hawke
Michael Grates: Ben Stiller
Vickie Miner: Janeane Garofalo
Sammy Gray: Steve Zahn
Charlane McGregor: Swoosie Kurtz
Tom Pierce: Joe Don Baker
Wes McGregor: Harry O'Reilly
Helen Anne Pierce: Susan Norfleet
Grant Gubler: John Mahoney

Released: 1994
Production: Danny DeVito and Michael Shamberg for Jersey Films; released
by Universal Pictures
Direction: Ben Stiller
Screenplay: Helen Childress
Cinematography: Emmanuel Lubezki
Editing: Lisa Churgin
Production design: Sharon Seymour
Art direction: Jeff Knipp
Set design: Michael Armani
Set decoration: Maggie Martin
Casting: Francine Maisler
Sound: Stephen Halbert
Costume design: Eugenie Bafaloukos
Video sequences production: James Jones
Music supervision: Karyn Rachtman
Music: Karl Wallinger
MPAA rating: PG-13
Running time: 99 minutes

young and audacious people often overreach themselves, frequently landing in trouble. So, ultimately, they stay on safe ground, which is the path of those who know that they have been beaten, and it is a sad place to see promising, youthful energy and talent go.

Films of youthful rebellion tend to wallow in despair, attacks on elders, and cynicism, but the best are wildly unconventional, such as the low-budget but successful *Easy Rider* (1969). Unfortunately, in *Reality Bites*, the wildest scene is when the youthful comrades suddenly start dancing in a gas-station convenience store to a rock-and-roll song that was popular when they were toddlers. A moment that indicates how relatively tame the film is.

The four main characters—plus another hanger-on, Sammy Gray (Steve Zahn), whose character seems to have been edited most of the way out of the film—are all desperately lacking in self-esteem, hope, and prospects for the future. Lelaina shows flashes of wickedness when she plants verbal bombs among her happy-talk host's note cards, but she quickly crumbles in the face of adversity, sliding quick-

ly into a co-dependency with a phone psychic. Her girlfriend Vickie projects an air of sassy independence but is easily hurt and lives in fear of AIDS, although she takes no preventive measures. The egotistical Troy is—big surprise—revealed to be a lonely, doubting skunk. The smooth, successful Michael does not know how to escape his own shell.

The film becomes wearisome when the characters become too self-involved, getting ensnared in their tangled value systems, lashing out at one another, because their entire lives are so insular. None is making much of a difference in the world. Everyone is a know-it-all who feels utterly powerless to change anything.

Addiction to television could explain this strange set of feelings and attitudes. *Reality Bites* certainly depicts Generation X's immersion in television and how the tube shapes its young viewers' conception of themselves. Not only is the video project the soul of Lelaina's attempt to express her rebellion but also television is the continual reference point for all the characters. While Lelaina and Michael work in television, the others live in a world with little in common except the shared experiences of watching certain television shows. The set is always on and programs and characters are more familiar than family members. The young friends all seem mesmerized by their own lack of direction and initiative. Like in a situation comedy, they make fun of everything—including themselves and their prospects for happiness.

Reality Bites has oodles of sincerity and authenticity. Yet those very qualities seem to fence in an obviously very talented production crew. Stiller's direction is both wonderfully self-assured and astoundingly pedestrian; there is too much ice and too little fire. Childress' script is both brilliantly true-to-life and cloyingly trite. It is as if youth had grown old prematurely—perhaps a fitting description for the psyches of Generation X.

Ryder, one of the icons of her generation, is well-cast in the lead role. Hers is the most authentic portrayal, yet it is oddly distancing. She makes her character more pitiful than heartening. Hawke is wooden as the clueless, self-deceptive, mean-spirited "slacker" Troy. The name would better fit a character from a beach picture of the 1960's, and so would the performance. The film's big leap of credibility is that Lelaina should desire Troy, and Hawke does not help the viewer make the leap. Stiller does much better as Michael. In fact, his is the film's most believable

AWARDS AND NOMINATIONS

MTV Movie Awards Nomination 1994: Best Kiss (Hawke/Ryder)

portrayal. He deserves credit as director for keeping himself as actor from chewing up a bigger role. Making Michael's part in the film bigger would have been a mistake; Stiller is effective. Garofalo has an odd face and a great comic talent. Given little to do but bounce off Ryder, Garofalo takes over several scenes, including one where she talks about her fear of dying. Stiller's mother, comic Anne Meara, has a small role, as does Swoosie Kurtz.

Overall, it would be tough to justify the promotion of *Reality Bites* as some sort of anthem for a whole generation. Taken as something much less ambitious, it is a fine first film for Stiller and his young crew, and another giant rung on the star ladder for the undeniably appealing Ryder. Unfortunately, the film will probably not fare as well over the long term as did *Easy Rider*. That is the trouble with relying so heavily on contemporary cultural anthropology and so little on a good yarn.

—*Michael Betzold*

REVIEWS

Daily Variety. January 31, 1994, p. 4.
Entertainment Weekly. February 18-25, 1994, p. 92
The Hollywood Reporter. January 31, 1994, p. 8.
Los Angeles Times. February 18, 1994, p. F1.
The New York Times. February 18, 1994, p. B1.
New Yorker. March 7, 1994.
Newsweek. February 21, 1994, p. 68.
Premiere. February, 1992, p. 24.

Reckless Kelly

"The incredible untold story of the greatest outlaw of all time."—Movie tagline
"Irrepressible. A visual gagfest."—John Griffin, *Montreal Gazette*

 Box Office Gross: $59,115 (May 8, 1994)

Descendant of a legendary Australian outlaw, Ned Kelly (Yahoo Serious) lives a la Robin Hood, robbing banks to give money to the poor. When evil banker Sir John (Hugo Weaving) seeks revenge by putting Kelly's beloved island paradise up for sale, Kelly goes to Hollywood with aptly-named girlfriend Robin Banks (Melora Hardin) to strike it rich and save his home.

REVIEWS

Entertainment Weekly. September 23, 1994, p. 77.
Variety. CCCL, April 12, 1993, p. 76.

CREDITS

Ned Kelly: Yahoo Serious
Robin Banks: Melora Hardin
Major Wib: Alexei Sayle
Sir John: Hugo Weaving
Mrs. Delance: Kathleen Freeman
Sam Delance: John Pinette
Dan Kelly: Bob Maza
Ernie the Fan: Martin Ferrero
Joe Kelly: Anthony Ackroyd
Miss Twisty: Tracy Mann
Newsreader: Max Walker
Hank the Fan: Don Stallings
Movie director: J. Andrew Bilgore

Origin: Australia
Released: 1993
Production: Yahoo Serious and Warwick Ross for A Serious, with the assistance of the Australian Film Finance Corporation; released by Warner Bros.
Direction: Yahoo Serious
Screenplay: Yahoo Serious, David Roach, Warwick Ross, and Lulu Serious
Cinematography: Kevin Hayward
Editing: Yahoo Serious, David Roach, Robert Gibson and Antony Gray
Production design: Graham (Grace) Walker
Art direction: Ian Gracie
Casting: Judith Cruden
Special effects: Steve Courtley
Visual design concepts: Yahoo Serious
Sound: Tim Lloyd
Costume design: Margot Wilson
Choreography: Aku Kadogo
Stunt coordination: Douglas (Rocky) McDonald
Music design: Yahoo Serious
Music: Tommy Tycho
MPAA rating: no listing
Running time: 94 minutes

Red

"Passion. Obsession. Mystery. A beautiful woman is about to meet her destiny."—Movie tagline

"A stunning love story! An exhilarating experience."—David Ansen, *Newsweek*

"A masterpiece! An elegant, fascinating puzzle." —Roger Ebert, *Chicago Sun-Times*

"An indisputable masterwork!"—Dave Kehr, *New York Daily News*

"An unequivocal success! Iréne Jacob's performance is once again perfect..."—Janet Maslin, *The New York Times*

"Exhilarating!"—John Anderson, *New York Newsday*

Box Office Gross: $4,000,000 (May 19, 1995)

Not only is *Red* the final film in Krzysztof Kieslowski's trilogy *Three Colors*—with *Blue* (1993) and *White* (reviewed in this volume) having received much acclaim—but this absorbing motion picture is apparently to be Kieslowski's last. Predicated on the notion that there is a constant series of patterns in how people conduct their lives, and anchored upon the idea that a chain of coincidences nudge the individual toward a certain destiny, *Red* follows the trajectory of a young woman, Valentine (Iréne Jacob), as it crosses the ebbing arc of a retired man, Joseph Kern (Jean-Louis Trintignant).

Driving home at night from a photo shoot in the Swiss town of Geneva, Valentine, a young model, inadvertently

Iréne Jacob as Valentine in *Red*. Copyright © Miramax Films.

hits and wounds a dog with her car. Reading the address on the dog's collar, Valentine attempts to return the animal to its owner, Kern. He receives Valentine, as well as the news of his dog's injury, with surprising indifference, even telling the young woman to keep the animal. Valentine stalks out of his house, angry at Kern's nonchalance, and she returns to her car with the dog. Behind her back, Kern watches her leave.

As it turns out, Valentine lives alone and is glad of the dog's company. Close by lives a young man, Auguste (Jean-Pierre Lorit), who is studying law and drives a red Jeep that he parks on the street. Each day, Valentine buys her newspaper from the neighborhood cafe and puts a coin in its slot machine. One morning, she passes Auguste—he is in a public telephone booth talking to his girlfriend—and wins a torrent of coins when three red cherries appear in the machine. Auguste has finished his call when Valentine exits with her winnings. Always in proximity, the two young people miss even noticing each other.

Let loose in a park, Kern's dog runs from Valentine and gallops back to its owner's house. Pursuing the animal, a cautious Valentine encounters Kern again. The man shows Valentine his electronic equipment, which he uses to eavesdrop on his neighbors' conversations. Valentine's shock at Kern's illegal activity is compounded by his revelation that he is a retired judge.

Kern then broadcasts a private conversation between two young lovers: a young man (who is later identified as Auguste) and a young woman who runs a personalized weather forecasting service—one that Kern enjoys calling. After listening to the couple's conversation, Kern predicts the end of the relationship. When challenged by Valentine as to his electronic surveillance, he makes no apology for his occupation. Although Valentine is something of a moral innocent, the judge's brazen frankness serves to disarm her disapproval.

Auguste passes his bar exams to become a judge. As he enters chambers one morning, Kern is sitting silently in court, awaiting his own trial for his illicit surveillance. Later, Kern tells Valentine that he turned himself in to the authorities. Both lonely, Kern and Valentine are drawn to each other. One evening, by lamplight, they share a father-daughter intimacy, and the mood prevails despite the shattering of a window by a stone thrown by a disgruntled neighbor.

Valentine tells Kern that she is planning a trip to England to visit her boyfriend, and he advises her to cross the channel by ferry and enjoy the ride. Valentine agrees to do so. Meanwhile, Valentine's neighbor Auguste suspects that his girlfriend has found another man. Feverish to discover the truth, he does his own surreptitious surveillance and is shattered to witness his lover in bed with another man.

CREDITS

Valentine: Iréne Jacob
Judge Joseph Kern: Jean-Louis Trintignant
Karin: Frédérique Feder
Auguste: Jean-Pierre Lorit
Photographer: Samuel Lebihan

Origin: France
Released: 1994
Production: Marin Karmitz and Gérard Ruey for MK2
Productions; released by Miramax Films
Direction: Krzysztof Kieslowski
Screenplay: Krzysztof Piesiewicz and Krzysztof
Kieslowski
Cinematography: Piotr Sobocinski
Editing: Jacques Witta
Production design: Claude Lenoir
Costume design: Corinne Jorry
Music: Zbigniew Preisner
MPAA rating: R
Running time: 95 minutes

Valentine invites Kern to a fashion show in which she is appearing, but she is unable to spot him from the runway. Afterward, he reveals his presence in the now-deserted auditorium, which is flushed in the color red. Over coffee, Kern allows Valentine glimpses of the love affair that broke his heart many years ago. Like Auguste, Kern was betrayed by a woman and went after her, leaving France and crossing the English Channel—the very route Valentine and Auguste, who has also been seen with a ferry ticket in hand, are to take. A still-distraught Auguste has decided to leave his home and go abroad—echoing Kern's flight years past. His girlfriend, Kern discovers, is closing her weather forecasting business; she predicts that the weather over the English Channel will be favorable.

In fact, a huge storm capsizes the ship. In the final scene, Kern watches a news report that identifies only a handful of survivors from the ship. They include all the principals from Kieslowski's trilogy: Juliette Binoche from *Blue*, Julie Delpy from *White*, and Valentine and Auguste, finally about to meet—although under tragic circumstances. The screen darkens on a freeze-frame of Valentine's exquisite profile, her bearing serene and contemplative despite the turbulence of her rescue.

Krzysztof Kieslowski has long been a darling of American critics, and *Red* met with tribute after tribute. In *The New York Times*, Janet Maslin hailed the film as an

Though nominated for best screenplay, cinematography and director by the Academy, *Red* was ineligible to be named best foreign film because it failed to meet the Academy requirement that two out of three among director, producer and writer be natives of the nominating country. *Red* is the third in a trilogy, following *Blue* (1993) and *White* (1994), by filmmaker Krzysztof Kieslowski.

AWARDS AND NOMINATIONS

Academy Awards Nominations 1994: Best Director (Kieslowski), Best Original Screenplay, Best Cinematography
Cesar Awards 1994: Best Score
Nominations: Best Film, Best Director (Kieslowski) Best Actress (Jacob), Best Actor (Trintignant)
Golden Globe Awards Nomination 1995: Best Foreign Language Film
Independent Spirit Awards 1995: Best Foreign Film
Los Angeles Film Critics Association Awards 1994: Best Foreign Film
National Society of Film Critics Awards 1994: Best Foreign Film
New York Film Critics Awards 1994: Best Foreign Film

"unequivocal success," while Kenneth Turan in the *Los Angeles Times* enthused that director Kieslowski "is likely the world's most accomplished director." Accomplished is certainly a word one can apply to *Red*, although the film's ending has not won universal praise. It was claimed that the climax of *Red* twisted events in order to tie the trilogy. There is truth here, but the gamble surely pays off if one accepts Kieslowski's notion of coincidence and the patterning in people's lives. Audience members unfamiliar with *Blue* and *White*, however, will miss the significance of this confluence of the principals from Kieslowski's trilogy.

Director Kieslowski has been a champion of music to create mood and to comment emotionally on the action in his motion pictures, but in *Red*, the work of distinguished musician Zbigniew Preisner is used sparingly. In tandem with cinematographer Piotr Sobocinski, the film's look—as to be expected is suffused with shadings of red, which seem to appear in every frame. Sometimes the color is in the background in the form of a lamp shade; at other times, it is prominent: the backdrop of Valentine's modeling photograph is one example.

Kieslowski clearly has an affinity with beautiful young actresses, and the films in his *Three Colors* trilogy each feature a young woman faced with transitions in her life. Iréne Jacob, radiant in Kieslowski's *La Double vie de Veronique* (1991; *The Double Life of Veronique*), is no less striking here. Much of the pleasure offered by the film is simply the study of Jacob's wonderful face. In fact, Kieslowski perhaps depends too much on Jacob's loveliness. Still, the Swiss-born Jacob is a skillful actress, and she more than holds her own against veteran French actor Jean-Louis Trintignant.

Trintignant brings dignity to Kern's penchant for voyeurism. As Kern, Trintignant portrays a man who is afraid of intimacy because of his tragic love affair decades ago. Yet he is drawn to Valentine, a woman who craves companionship and love.

So central does the connection between Valentine and Kern grow that no other character in the film comes alive. Most notably, Valentine's neighbor Auguste remains a mystery throughout, which is probably how Kieslowski wants it. Auguste's enigma, however, is less than satisfying as one cannot care for him or his fate.

Another problem in *Red* is the lack of emotion. Although Kern's recounting of his love affair is poignant, there is not enough emotional resonance in the rest of the film. Despite the fact that Valentine is the center of the film, one never sees into her heart, the character who claims the audience's attention.

What Kieslowski has achieved in *Red*, however, is a compelling examination of the individual's singularity, and that individual's fragmented, sometimes unseen, connections to others. Taking the idea that red in the French flag signifies fraternity, or friendship, Kieslowski shows that relationships can spring forth when one is not prepared for them. The Polish director also delights in suggesting that Auguste is a younger version of Kern, complete with the broken heart. It is as if people live the same paradigms as others, usually unwittingly.

Visually stimulating and subtle in its unfolding, *Red* is never less than engaging. It is not a masterpiece; one should look to Kieslowski's television series *The Decalogue* for this director's best work. Yet it would be a loss indeed if this motion picture is to be, as Kieslowski has said, his last contribution to cinema.

—*Paul B. Cohen*

REVIEWS

Los Angeles Times. December 2, 1993, p. F1.
The New York Times. October 4, 1994, p. B1.

Red Rock West

"A cleverly plotted game of cat and mouse."
—*The Hollywood Reporter*

"A wry thriller with a keen edge."—*Variety*

"Two big thumbs up! A great film!"—*Siskel & Ebert*

"The best new American film of the year!"
—Gene Siskel, *Siskel & Ebert*

"Don't pass up this rotgut thriller. The mix of wanton sex and white-knuckle suspense proves undeniably riveting!"—Peter Travers, *Rolling Stone*

 Box Office Gross: $2,408,837 (October 9, 1994)

Red Rock West is a stylish film steeped in some of the finest elements of classic *film noir*: a mysterious femme fatale who is entrapped by an older benefactor/husband, a hapless younger male protagonist who becomes entangled in her web, murder, suspense, deception, greed, lust, and enough plot twists to make you wish you could hit the rewind button on your cable channel—because that's just where this 1993 gem first aired before it went directly to video. It was then snatched up by a San Francisco exhibitor who brought it to the big screen where it enjoyed a fairly wide release in 1994 to critical accolades.

Exhibited in theaters the same year as director John Dahl's other acclaimed first-seen-on-cable film, *The Last Seduction* (reviewed in this volume), *Red Rock West* was eclipsed by the attention surrounding this in-your-visage neo-*noir*. Nonetheless, these sister films are fine examples of the genre, both taking their cue from Billy Wilder's *Double Indemnity* (1944), with lusty shades of *The Postman Always Rings Twice* (1946).

From the moment good-guy drifter Michael (Nicolas Cage) pulls into a dusty, desolate Wyoming town in his vintage white Caddy after driving 1,200 miles from Texas with a bum leg, he seems to be in the wrong place at the wrong time. After he blows an oil rig job by admitting his disability, he wanders into the tiny town of Red Rock, where the local barkeep, Wayne Brown (J.T. Walsh), has mistaken him for the Texas hit man he has hired to kill his pretty, much younger wife, Suzanne (Lara Flynn Boyle). Michael takes the $5,000 advance Wayne hands him for the job then finds Suzanne and warns her of the murder. Suzanne responds by doubling Wayne's offer for Michael to "take care of Wayne." Michael mails a letter to the sheriff of Red Rock, warning of the murders planned by Wayne and Suzanne and flees town only to accidently hit a mysterious figure with his car. It isn't long

CREDITS

Michael: Nicolas Cage
Lyle: Dennis Hopper
Suzanne: Lara Flynn Boyle
Wayne: J. T. Walsh

Released: 1994
Production: Sigurjon Sighvatsson and Steve Golin for Propaganda Films; released by Polygram Filmed Entertainment
Direction: John Dahl
Screenplay: John Dahl and Rick Dahl
Cinematography: Mark Reshovsky
Editing: Scott Chestnut
Production design: Rob Pearson
Art direction: Don Diers
Sound: Mark Deren
Costume design: Terry Dresbach
Music: William Olvis
MPAA rating: no listing
Running time: 93 minutes

before Michael bounces back to Red Rock, where he begins to realize that things are not what they seem.

It turns out that barkeep Wayne's day job is sheriff of Red Rock (he bought every voter in the county a drink, Suzanne explains). We learn that "alias Wayne and Suzanne" are wanted for grand theft. It's also discovered that the mysterious man Michael accidently hit is a ranch hand who had already been shot twice by his lover, Suzanne, when he tried to blackmail her for her stolen money. Now the real killer, Lyle from Dallas (Dennis Hopper), has come striding into town and wants his share of the loot. Michael simply wants to get out of Red Rock alive.

Red Rock West has been compared to 1993's low-budget Mexican *noir*, *El Mariachi*, whose plot also revolves around an innocent man who has been mistaken for a killer and gets mixed up with a bad-luck broad. As *film noir* male protagonists go, Michael is certainly no "tough guy" Sam Spade, who gave as good as he got from any dame or mug and was not above some underhanded chicanery. Indeed, Michael seems to always be in situations where he's battling his conscience to "do the right thing": When, after Michael has been turned down for an oil rig job, his friend Jim asks him why he didn't wait until he was hired to tell a potential employer about his leg injury, Michael responds, "it wouldn't be right;" Michael walks away from a cash register drawer full of money at a desolate gas station; he risks interrogation by bringing a man to the hospital whom he had hit with his car as he was flee-

Red Rock West was first shown on cable television in 1993 and went direct to video until it was rescued by a San Francisco exhibitor who brought it to the big screen.

AWARDS AND NOMINATIONS

Independent Spirit Awards Nominations: Best Director (Dahl), Best Screenplay

ing town; and when Suzanne tries to seduce him, he resists, explaining, "I make a point of staying away from married women." Although Michael is desperate enough to take the money given to him by Wayne and Suzanne, he doesn't do the "jobs" he's been paid for and he tries to prevent their murders.

We learn that Michael is an ex-marine who injured his leg during a bombing while stationed in Lebanon, but it also appears that he may be either a fugitive or ex-convict, which might explain why he makes such a conscious effort to stay out of trouble. There are references in the film which imply that Michael has been involved in robbery. For example, when Michael is turned down for the job, Jim offers to lend him money, but Michael declines, joking (?), "Maybe I'll rob a bank." Later, when Michael is digging for Wayne's hidden money in the cemetery, Lyle says to Michael, "You're probably thinkin' to yourself, 'how'd I wind up with this bunch of losers?' Right? Well, I'll tell ya how. Cuz you're a thief, Mike. You wouldn't be here if you weren't." Maybe it's because Michael is a fellow marine, or perhaps Lyle is psychic, but we can't help but wonder if Lyle knows something about Michael's character that we don't. Whether Michael is simply morally upright, or is running from—or had a run-in with—the law, we can't be sure.

Nicolas Cage is perfectly cast as good-guy Michael, and his deadpan performance is engagingly simple and sympathetic. Cage, who has been in over twenty films since he starred in *Valley Girl* in 1983, has built a career playing the good guy/thief—most notably the diaper-stealing ex-convict/kidnapper and would-be adopted father, H.I. McDonnough in the Coen brothers' *Raising Arizona* (1987). Cage also played both good-guy and thief in two other films this year (both reviewed in this volume): *It Could Happen to You*, a Capra-esque semi-true story in which Cage plays a Jimmy Stewart-like cop who wins $4 million in the lottery and shares it with a waitress, according to his promise; and *Trapped in Paradise*, where he and his "dumb and dumber" bank robber brothers (Dana Carvey and Jon Lovitz) go soft after unsuccessfully trying to pull a heist in a big-hearted town.

Lara Flynn Boyle is known to *Twin Peaks* fans as Donna Hayward, the grief-stricken friend of Laura Palmer in the

1990 David Lynch TV series. Featured in nearly twenty films since her debut in *Poltergeist III* (1986)—including Wayne's klutzy ex-girlfriend Stacy in *Wayne's World* (1992) and starring roles in 1994's *Baby's Day Out* and *Threesome* (both reviewed in this volume)—Boyle does a nice turn as a cool and mysterious femme fatale in *Red Rock West*. Her Suzanne, although as greedy and conniving as any classic femme fatale, is not as ruthless as her over-the-top contemporaries of the year: the cruelly calculating Bridget Gregory (Linda Fiorentino, who won Independent Spirit and New York Film Critics Circle awards for her performance) in Dahl's other gem, *The Last Seduction*; or the animalistic cop-killer Mona Demarkov (Lena Olin) in *Romeo is Bleeding* (both reviewed in this volume). Although she shares their frank sexuality, Suzanne, as played by the delicately-featured Boyle, is femininely seductive—tough, yet entrapped. She is more akin to her *noir* sisters of the past—Bridgid O'Shaughnessy (Mary Astor) in *The Maltese Falcon* (1941), Phyllis (Barbara Stanwyk) in *Double Indemnity* (1944), Cora Smith (Lana Turner) in *The Postman Always Rings Twice* (1946), or Elsa Bannister (Rita Hayworth) in *The Lady from Shanghai* (1948)—than her more wicked, castrating nineties contemporaries.

Although Suzanne lies to and double-crosses Michael, tries to have her husband murdered, and, once he has been handcuffed, curses at, strikes, and kicks Wayne, she is demure compared to the beyond-feminist survivalists Bridget Gregory and Mona Demarkov, who are practically female "Terminators." What links these (and all) femme fatales, however, is that they are aware that the tools they need to gain power—or even survive—are sex and money—and they use them to their full advantage.

Despite on-target performances from Cage and Boyle, Dennis Hopper as "Lyle from Dallas" is a decidedly Nicholsonian scene-stealer in *Red Rock West*. Dressed in black from cowboy hat to boots and sporting a twisted Texas twang, Hopper looks like he's having as much fun in this film as he did with Jack in his *Easy Rider* (1969) days. From the minute Lyle blows into town after nearly running Michael over with his black Buick—"Folsom Prison Blues" jangling from the radio—to his ironic impalement on the musket of a veterans' memorial cemetery marker, Hopper chews the scenery with all the demented delight he's entitled

> "Marriage is just a state of mind."
> "Not in Texas."
> "We're not in Texas."—Suzanne and Michael in *Red Rock West*

to. Hopper also played the even more maniacal psycho-bomber Howard Payne in this year's high-action thriller, *Speed* (reviewed in this volume).

Veteran stage and screen character actor J.T. Walsh is tensely precise as the business-like seething pressure-cooker barkeep/sheriff Wayne Brown. Walsh also makes an appearance in Dahl's *The Last Seduction* as Frank Griffith, Bridget Gregory's seedy lawyer.

Critics raved about this "little *noir*." The *Los Angeles Times'* Kevin Thomas called it "a terrific *film noir*," comparing it to the Coen brothers' *Blood Simple (1985)*; Peter Travers, of *Rolling Stone*, called "this rotgut thriller" a "mix of wanton sex and white-knuckle suspense; "Caryn James of *The New York Times* called it "a terrifically acted, over-the-top thriller;" Gene Siskel called it "the best new American film of the year;" and *Siskel & Ebert* gave it "two big thumbs up." *Red Rock West* also received Independent Spirit award nominations for best director and best screenplay and earned over $2.4 million in 255 days shown at only 22 theaters. Not bad for a little film that almost didn't make to the theater.

—*Shawn Brennan*

REVIEWS

America. CLXX, June 4, 1994, p. 24.
The American Spectator. XXVII, July 1994, p. 63.
Atlanta Constitution. July 15, 1994, p. P8.
Boston Globe. May 20, 1994, p. 53.
Chicago Tribune. May 6, 1994, p. 7C.
Chicago Tribune. May 6, 1994, p. 7F.
Christian Science Monitor. September 2, 1994, p. 11.
Entertainment Weekly. June 17, 1994, p. 36.
Los Angeles Times. March 25, 1994, p. F8.
Maclean's. CVII, January 17, 1994, p. 61.
Mademoiselle. C, July 1994, p. 68.
New Statesman & Society. VI, July 2, 1993, p. 35.
New York. XXVII, May 30, 1994, p. 59.
The New York Times. April 8, 1994, p. C12.
Time. CXLIII, May 9, 1994, p. 74.
Variety. CCCLII, September 20, 1993, p. 28.
The Wall Street Journal. June 28, 1994, p. A16.
The Washington Post. April 15, 1994, p. D1.
The Washington Post. April 15, 1994, p. WW44.
DE Deception

Redwood Pigeon (Palombella Rossa)

When a man, Michele (Nanni Moretti), suffers partial amnesia following a car accident, his life is thrown into comic turmoil.

REVIEWS

Chicago Tribune. April 28, 1995, p. 7K.
The New Republic. CCII, April 23, 1990, p. 27.

CREDITS

Michele: Nanni Moretti
Coach: Silvio Orlando
Journalist: Mariella Valentini
Michele's daughter: Asia Argento
Michele (as a child): Gabriele Ceracchini
Priest: Raul Ruiz

Origin: Italy
Released: 1989
Production: Sachen Film and Nella Banfi-Talmyre Film
Direction: Nanni Moretti
Screenplay: Nanni Moretti
Cinematography: Giuseppe Lanci
Editing: Mirco Garrone
Music: Nicola Piovani
MPAA rating: no listing
Running time: 87 minutes

The Ref

"He's taken them hostage. They're driving him nuts."—Movie tagline

"Lose-your-breath, hurt-your-sides funny!"
—Joel Siegal, *Good Morning America*

"*The Ref* is a film to warm the hearts and touch the nerves of dysfunctional families everywhere."
—Caryn James, *The New York Times*

"Hysterically funny!"—*ABC-TV, Los Angeles*

 Box Office Gross: $11,310,953 (June 12, 1994)

Gus (Denis Leary) has established a lucrative practice as a cat burglar, lounging in Jamaica whenever he is not prowling somebody's mansion at midnight. Now he wants to make one big heist and retire. Gus chooses Christmas Eve and an estate in the seaside Connecticut village of Old Baybrook. The absent millionaire, however, has planted a few surprises for intruders. While attempting to cross-wire the alarm system, Gus is videotaped, sprayed with cat urine, and dumped via a trapdoor into the jowls of a watchdog. Gus's shaky getaway driver, Murray (Richard

Bright), flees when the bumbling but numerous Old Baybrook police swarm onto the scene. Gus' desperate hours—and the premise of *The Ref*—begin when Gus seeks to elude hot pursuit by kidnapping a local couple and holing up in their colonial home.

Caroline (Judy Davis) and Lloyd Chasseur (Kevin Spacey) personify every neurosis, every highly leveraged façade of affluence, and every dysfunction ever associated with a formerly urban life. Their marriage raises bickering to a lower plateau. Insults fly back and forth not like rapier thrusts so much as Freudian hand grenades and monogrammed pipe bombs. Gus, from the moment he slides into the back seat of the Chasseurs' car and tries to take control of their bitchy lives at gunpoint, becomes a cohostage. While Gus waves his automatic, the Chasseurs spit venom—mostly at each other, but in sufficient quantity and toxicity to numb anyone within thirty yards.

Such events and such a situation could be played for terror, as a sort of *Cape Fear* (1962 and 1991). *The Ref*, however, from beginning to end is played for laughs—of which there are many. The R rating stands strictly for risqué repartee. Gus points his gun, but it clearly functions only as glue to hold the situation together. The assaults are verbal, meaning the assaulters can repeat their crimes every minute on the minute.

CREDITS

Gus: Denis Leary
Caroline: Judy Davis
Lloyd: Kevin Spacey
Jesse: Robert J. Steinmiller, Jr.
Rose: Glynis Johns
Huff: Raymond J. Barry
Murray: Richard Bright
Connie: Christine Baranski
George: Bill Raymond

Released: 1994
Production: Ron Bozman, Richard LaGravenese, and Jeff Weiss for Touchstone Pictures; Released by Buena Vista Pictures
Direction: Ted Demme
Screenplay: Richard LaGravenese and Marie Weiss; based on a story by Weiss
Cinematography: Adam Kimmel
Editing: Jeffrey Wolf
Production design: Dan Davis
Art direction: Dennis Davenport
Set decoration: Jaro Dick
Casting: Howard Feuer
Sound: Bruce Carwardine
Costume design: Judianna Makovsky
Music: David A. Stewart
MPAA rating: R
Running time: 93 minutes

Just before their abduction, the Chasseurs are seen visiting a marriage counselor, which is much like eavesdropping on Quasimodo in a plastic surgery consultation. Their marriage has become sexless and bitter. Caroline recounts a dream in which Lloyd's head is served up on a plate with his penis protruding from an ear. Lloyd counters this with an obscene retort.

No wonder that Gus, who never had the idyllic upper-middle-class upbringing he envisions unfolding in all the homes he has burglarized, soon has no greater goal—including escape from the law—than making his hostages from hell shut up. "I hijacked my parents," Gus muses from the back seat just before Lloyd bickers his way into running a stop sign and missing a Cadillac by inches.

Christmas Eve hiding out at the Chasseurs becomes not as simple for Gus as one might envision. Caroline and Lloyd cannot be gagged, tied up, and stuffed in a broom closet. For one thing, son Jesse (Robert J. Steinmiller, Jr.) is on his way home from military school, where he earns good money by blackmailing the comman-

"Oh my God, I hijacked my parents."—burglar Gus, describing his hostages, Caroline and Lloyd, in *The Ref*

dant with some compromising photographs. Also, another entire carload of extended dysfunctional family is on the way for the traditional holiday gathering, loading up on junk food along the way to compensate for Caroline's traditionally inedible cuisine.

So with state police and Old Baybrook's finest scouring the town, Gus must find a way to keep up appearances amid a family tableau that is all about keeping up appearances. Meanwhile, he must reestablish contact with getaway driver Murray. He does this by asking the Chasseurs to name the sleaziest bar in the region, then dialing the bartender. The paging of Murray is, like many scenes in *The Ref* truly funny and borderline hilarious. Gus could be somewhat less diligent in his efforts to hide, however, if he only knew that the local cops mistakenly recorded *It's a Wonderful Life* (1946) on the surveillance camera videotape.

Jesse arrives first, just after a crotchety neighborhood Santa delivers a fruitcake and reminds Lloyd and Caroline to inquire whether their son happens to know where the town's baby Jesus is; it is still missing from last year. That Lloyd and Caroline's son has wreaked no greater havoc upon Old Baybrook than to filch the baby Jesus is a miracle in itself. Gus must hear this pair for only one night; Jesse has been listening to them since birth. Predictably, but believably, the screwed-up teenaged captive develops a certain admiration for his captor—especially the part about being on the beach in Jamaica. Why are you quitting now? he wonders. You have a great life.

Gus imprisons Jesse upstairs and, with that leverage in hand, establishes the evening's rules. Christmas Eve will go on as always, except that Jesse could not make it and the Chasseurs have a house guest. Donning a coat and tie, Gus becomes Dr. Wong, marriage counselor and dinner guest.

Up from the city come Lloyd's mother, Rose (Glynis Johns), brother George (Bill Raymond); sister-in-law Connie (Christine Baranski), and two children who mostly serve as props but who execute the jaw drop with skill uncommon for their age. Rose inspires fealty from Lloyd and Caroline not only through an intensely domineering personality but also through an old loan upon which she carefully adjusts the interest rate upward as the market requires.

The finest visual in a motion picture that is engagingly lighted and filmed is the dinner scene, a surreal piece of nonsense derived from Caroline's Scandinavian cooking class. Everyone, including Gus/Dr. Wong, is required to attend table wearing a crown of tall, blazing candles. A tribute to an obscure feminist saint, the fiery conclave is at once idiosyncratic and trendy. The real tribute is that scriptwriters Richard LaGravenese and Marie Weiss did not choose to wreck the sustained effect (the candles do burn low) by writing in a visit from the Old Baybrook Fire Department.

All the key resolutions of this suburban stew are predictable, but welcome and deftly drawn. Fittingly to the Scandinavian dinner theme, it is the Stockholm Syndrome rendered with Disney overtones. Mother Rose loses her matriarchal control over the lives of Lloyd and Caroline as the captor becomes catalyst for confrontational therapy. Lloyd and Caroline run short of venom as civility and reconciliation seep into their lives. Murray, seeking a boat for a getaway, finds one in the hands of a woman who happens to be an ex-con who is herself on the lam from probationers. Santa Claus gets tipsy on his house calls and becomes the only victim of physical assault (a well-placed uppercut from Gus). Son Jesse ultimately joins with his parents in aiding Gus's escape to the seashore.

The Ref is pure entertainment, revelatory of nothing—except to seekers of fresh dinner-party themes. The film's entertainment value, however, is substantial for anyone not offended by vitriolic scatology. Some viewers might see hints of an East Coast *Down and Out in Beverly Hills* (1986). Substitute Denis Leary's felon for Nick Nolte's homeless drifter and the parallels are numerous. An intruder from the other side of the class curtain descends upon a deep suburban domicile and forever changes those who live therein. A dysfunctional teenager finds some reference points in the scurvy guest, dysfunctional marriage partners are rejuvenated by the shock of it all. The Eastern version is more interior and more verbal, an expected spin.

However one responds to the story, it is difficult to quarrel with any of the cast. Leary, Spacey, and Davis remain believable even with candles on their heads. Leary had been known principally as a comedian, tweaking political correctness in MTV spots and starring in the one-man show *No Cure for Cancer*, where he also worked with *The Ref* director Ted Demme. Spacey—who played the office manager who bends to any prevailing wind's will in *Glengarry Glen Ross* (1992)—maintains Lloyd as a personality and not just a sarcastic mask. Davis—star of Woody Allen's *Husbands and Wives* (1992) and featured in a host of films since she came to prominence in *My Brilliant Career* (1979) from her native Australia—at times carries *The Ref* with mouth and eyes that pout, dart, conceal, and yearn. Demme and director of photography Adam Kimmel paint the cast in dense colors, framed in gilt lighting, as if to say, "Aren't they a piece of work?" Which they are.

The biggest mistake with this film might well have been the title. As referee, Gus holds only the most fragile control over the Chasseurs' mind game. Athletic references do not fit this household of Chagall prints and poached salmon. Such a title is more misleading than amusing and may repel the very viewers to whom such a film would appeal. 🎞

—Tom W. Ferguson

REVIEWS

Chicago Tribune. March 11, 1994, section 7A, p. k.
Entertainment Weekly. March 18, 1994, p. 75.
The Hollywood Reporter. March 7, 1994, p. 10.
Los Angeles Times. March 9, 1994, p. F1.
The New York Times. March 9, 1994, p. B1.
Newsweek. March 3, 1994, p. 72.
Variety. March 7, 1994, p. 4.

Renaissance Man

"A real summer treat."—Joy Browne, *WOR Radio Network*

"Danny DeVito is a definite delight."—*KCBS-TV, Los Angeles*

"*Renaissance Man* is a real crowd pleaser."—Jeff Craig, *Sixty Second Preview*

"Solid laughs!"—*People Weekly*

 Box Office Gross: $24,156,346 (October 30, 1994)

Danny DeVito has made a career of playing irascible losers. His Emmy-winning role on television's *Taxi* started the ball rolling, and from there he went to feature films, playing nasty characters in comedies such as *Ruthless People* (1986), *Throw Momma From the Train* (1987), *Twins* (1988), and others. In *Renaissance Man*, DeVito plays a role quite different from his usual irascible-loser character. Although he starts out playing this usual cantankerous self, his character quickly becomes sweet and endearing. This is one of the few times audiences have seen the gentle side of DeVito, and it is charming. Despite its hackneyed concept, *Renaissance Man* is a winning film because of DeVitos' charm, Penny Marshall's direction, some other fine performances, and Hans Zimmer's marvelous score.

Renaissance Man is a cross between *To Sir With Love* (1967) and *Private Benjamin* (1980). The opening scenes are very funny, as adman Bill Rago (DeVito) pitches an idea to a prospective advertising client by suggesting a commercial featuring actors dressed as "a melon, or a wedge of cheese." This tacky idea is the last straw for his employers. Rago loses his job and has to go on unemployment. Rago's choleric responses to a sharp-tongued unemployment-department worker are amusing: He responds to a question about what kind of work he would be willing to do by saying, "If you give me a check, I'd be willing to cash it."

One job does come through for him, and in desperation, he takes it. Rago discovers, to his horror, however, that he has accepted a job as a civilian teacher to a small group of low-achieving Army recruits, a group of misfits called the "Double-D's." He is to help them "learn how to learn" in order to improve their performance in boot camp. In Rago's words, "I've died and gone to Gomer Pyle's house!"

Renaissance Man is loosely based on the experiences of screenwriter Burnstein at an Army base in Michigan.

Just as in *Private Benjamin*, where Goldie Hawn's overindulged character became a better person in the Army, DeVito's character does the same—but not before he makes a few faux pas: Just like Private Benjamin, he challenges the system, wears the wrong clothes, and behaves in a completely unorthodox fashion, which in this case turns out to be just what his young students need.

There are a number of fun moments where the informal Rago clashes head-on with the rigid Army. The first is when he drives on to the Army base and asks directions. A guard answers, "Go past the AMPC, The PX, and Building four-three-one-oh. If you went to the RFPC you went too far." Another moment comes late in the film, when Rago's students walk out on him and he must win their respect. He follows them out to the Victory Tower, a huge structure that is best described as a vertical obstacle course. He scales the multistory tower and then must slide down to the ground on a rope, mountain-climber style. The sight of tiny, middle-aged DeVito clearly doing his own stunt work on the huge structure is a sight to behold.

The core of the film revolves around Rago's use of his favorite piece of literature, William Shakespeare's *Hamlet* (1600-1601) to teach the students a variety of things. They learn about literature, about writing—the literary technique of simile, for example, is the center of a fun scene—and they learn about themselves. The quote from Hamlet, "Above all, to thine own self be true" becomes a central theme. The importance of this quote is reminiscent of the importance of "Carpe Diem," or "Seize the day," in the Robin Williams film about a gifted teacher, *Dead Poet's Society* (1989).

Yet the best use of *Hamlet* is the parallel between *Hamlet*'s play-within-the-play and a rap interpretation of *Hamlet* that the students create for Rago. This could have been an embarrassing moment in the film, as often happens when Hollywood tries to get "hip" in the middle of a mainstream film. The "rap *Hamlet*" is a wonderful piece, however, written by Marky Mark and Mervy Warren and masterfully choreographed by Donovan Henry.

The music in the film is terrific. Hans Zimmer, Oscar nominee for *Rain Man* (1988) and composer of music for *Driving Miss Daisy* (1989), runs the gamut from contemporary sound to Sousa-like marches to lilting melodies, adding to the emotional life of the film.

Penny Marshall directs with subtlety and warmth. Her pacing in the classroom scenes is excellent in that she allows the characters to speak for themselves; the interaction flows, and the relationships develop in a realistic way. For example, when the recruits are first introduced, Rago asks all of them to say a little something about themselves. Marshall allows the discomfort of the classroom setting to come through: She is not afraid of silence, and she creates an improvisational quality that brings realism and humanity to the proceedings. With a predictable situation, she has made the most of the personalities of each character.

The Recruits are well played by some veteran and some newcomer performers. Kadeem Hardison, from television's *A Different World*, is a standout as a smooth smart aleck, without ever lapsing into a stereotype. Also notable is Lillo Brancato, Jr., as Benitez: He gets arguably the showiest of the roles, as a DeNiro impersonating charac-

"The choices we make dictate the life we lead. To thine own self be true."—Bill Rago from *Renaissance Man*

ter from New York. Brancato performs beautifully in a scene in which he delivers a perfect Shakespearean speech to dazed onlookers in the middle of a rainstorm. It is a highly improbable moment, given the circumstances, but he is wonderful doing it.

This also marks the feature debut of rap star and Calvin Klein underwear model Marky Mark, who appears in this film under his real name, Mark Wahlberg. He plays a kindhearted Southern bumpkin, a far cry from his bad-boy image. It was a shrewd move to give Wahlberg a simple and non-showy role his first time out, which seems to allow audiences to distinguish between actor Mark Wahlberg and rapper Marky Mark. Interestingly, when the students do the rap version of *Hamlet*, Marky Mark is nowhere to be seen: Appropriate to his character, Wahlberg does not participate.

The other standout among the recruits/students is Peter Simmons as Brian Davis. He is excellent as the perfectionistic but shy young man who lost his father to the Vietnam War. His final moments are definitely the most touching and uplifting of the film.

The cast is rounded out with some fine performances by some acting veterans: Cliff Robertson as the Colonel; James Remar as a thoughtful captain; and the excellent Gregory Hines as a tough drill sergeant who clashes with the casual Rago.

Renaissance Man was filmed on location at the U.S. Army's Fort Jackson in South Carolina. Fort Jackson is the world's largest and busiest basic training facility in operation. Par for the course for most films by the early 1990's the actors underwent rigorous training to bring authenticity to their roles. It is hard to imagine that they needed go through a mini-basic training in order to play their roles; but their realism in appearance, mannerisms, behavior, and the cohesion of the acting ensemble suggest that the training paid off. It is quite realistic, which makes the film more enjoyable for the viewer.

Unfortunately, aspects of the film are all too predictable: As the young recruits are introduced, audience members will find themselves guessing which one will get into trouble, which one will be hiding a secret from the past, which one will hold a special place in Rago's heart, and so on. Another problem lies in the rather syrupy secondary story of Bill's relationship with his estranged daughter. They are forced to say things like, "Do you want you a pennant [from the baseball game]?" "No," she replies, "I just want you to believe in me."

Also unfortunate are the number of false endings: DeVito's Victory Tower sequence feels like one ending and the discovery that the students passed their final exam feels like another. Since the film climaxes several times, by the time the real ending arrives it feels a bit overdue.

CREDITS

Bill Rago: Danny DeVito
Sergeant Cass: Gregory Hines
Captain Murdoch: James Remar
Colonel James: Cliff Robertson
Donnie Benitez: Lillo Brancato, Jr.
Miranda Myers: Stacey Dash
Jamaal Montgomery: Kadeem Hardison
Jackson Leroy: Richard T. Jones
Roosevelt Hobbs: Khalil Kain
Brian Davis: Peter Simmons
Mel Melvin: Greg Sporleder
Tommy Lee Haywood: Mark Wahlberg
Jack Markin: Ed Begley, Jr.

Released: 1994
Production: Sara Colleton, Elliot Abbott, and Robert Greenhut for Andrew G. Vajna, in association with Touchstone Pictures and Cinergi-Parkway; released by Buena Vista Pictures
Direction: Penny Marshall
Screenplay: Jim Burnstein
Cinematography: Adam Greenberg
Editing: George Bowers and Battle Davis
Production design: Geoffrey Kirkland
Art direction: Richard Johnson
Set design: Robert Fechtman
Set decoration: Jennifer Williams
Casting: Paula Herold
Sound: Les Lazarowitz
Costume design: Betsy Heimann
Music: Hans Zimmer
MPAA rating: PG-13
Running time: 129 minutes

Despite the clichéd, predictable plot, *Renaissance Man* is ultimately an inspirational film on the order of *To Sir With Love*, *Dead Poets Society*, or *Up the Down Staircase* (1967). Any film that inspires kids to learn can not be all bad.

—*Kirby Tepper*

REVIEWS

Entertainment Weekly. June 110, 1994, p. 47.
The Hollywood Reporter. May 27-30, 1994, p. 8.
Los Angeles Times. June 3, 1994, p. F4.
The New York Times. June 3, 1994, p. B1.
Variety. May 31, 1994, p. 4.

The Resurrected (Shatterbrain)

A detective, John March (John Terry), is called upon to investigate a man named Charles Dexter Ward (Chris Sarandon), the descendant of an eighteenth century sorcerer. March discovers that Ward, like his ancestor centuries earlier, has been conducting experiments to resurrect the dead.

REVIEWS

Variety. CCCXLVI, April 13, 1992, p. 65.

CREDITS

John March: John Terry
Claire Ward: Jane Sibbett
Charles Dexter Ward: Chris Sarandon
Lonnie Peck: Richard Romanus
Holly Tender: Laurie Briscoe
Captain Ben Szandor: Ken Cameroux
Raymond: Patrick Pon
Dr. Waite: Bernard Cuffling
Ezra Ward: Charles Kristian
Eliza: Megan Leitch
Main monster: Deep Roy
Joseph Curwen: Chris Sarandon

Released: 1992
Production: Mark Borde and Ken Raich; released by Scotti Bros. Pictures
Direction: Dan O'Bannon
Screenplay: Brent V. Friedman; based on the novel *The Case of Charles Dexter Ward*, by H. P. Lovecraft
Cinematography: Irv Goodnoff
Editing: Russell Livingstone
Production design: Brent Thomas
Art direction: Doug Byggdin
Production management: Don McLean
Casting: Fiona Jackson and Penny Ellers
Special visual effects: Todd Masters
Special physical effects coordination: Gary Paller
Sound: Robert Vollum
Costume design: Marcella Robertson
Stunt coordination: Scott Ateah
Music: Richard Band
MPAA rating: R
Running time: 106 minutes

Revolution!

Four Marxist friends—Ollie (Christopher Renstrom), Suzy (Kimberly Flynn), Steve (Johnny Kabalah), and Billie (George Osterman)—living in Manhattan's Lower East Side go to the Long Island home of Steve's wealthy aunt (Helen Schumaker) in order to steal her money to finance their half-baked revolution. Upon arriving, however, they cavort on her expansive estate, until the aunt and the group's Marxist theory professor (played by the film's producer, Travis Preston) unexpectedly arrive on the scene, in this comedy.

REVIEWS

Variety. CCCXLV, November 11, 1991, p. 54.

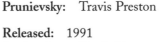

CREDITS

Suzy: Kimberly Flynn
Ollie: Christopher Renstrom
Steve: Johnny Kabalah
Billie: George Osterman
Kasha: Helen Schumaker
Prunievsky: Travis Preston

Released: 1991
Production: Travis Preston for Dream Bird Productions; released by Northern Arts Entertainment
Direction: Jeff Kahn
Screenplay: Jeff Kahn
Cinematography: Michael Stiller
Editing: Chris Tellefson
Production design: Kristen Ames
Sound: Steve Robinson, Chris Tellefson and Tom Foligno
Costume design: Eva Goodman
Music: Tom Judson
MPAA rating: no listing
Running time: 84 minutes

Richie Rich

"Five buddies, one butler, and a dog on an adventure so big...even the world's richest kid can't afford to miss it."—Movie tagline

"Comic fantasy destined to inspire plenty of giggles and gasps."—*Houston Chronicle*

"Wonderful, warm, and funny."—Roger Ebert, *Chicago Sun-Times*

"comedy adventure with heart."—Kevin Thomas, Los Angeles Times

 Box Office Gross: $23,350,385 (January 2, 1995)

Richie Rich, the Harvey Comics classic about the richest boy in the world, is given a sly, action-packed treatment in its first outing as a motion picture. It has wit and humor for the adults, and cartoon-like gadgets and gizmos (without excessive violence) for the kids. The film has a loopy, "Saturday-morning-cartoon" ality that is right "on the money" for its target audience of baby-boomer parents and their young children.

Ironically, one of *Richie Rich's* producers, Joel Silver, is arguably the most successful producer of adult action films in mainstream Hollywood, having produced the *Lethal Weapon* series (1987, 1989, 1992), *Demolition Man* (1993), the *Die Hard* series (1988, 1990), *Predator* (1987), and other tough action fare. Upon hearing that Silver is one of the masterminds of the film version of the naïve *Richie Rich*, audiences might expect that the comic book's sweetness will be forfeited in favor of overproduced action sequences appealing to a 1990's sensibility. On the contrary, Silver, coproducer John Davis, director Donald Petrie, and the rest of the filmmakers have provided *Richie Rich* fans a glossy and delightful version of the old comic that does not sacrifice sweetness in the name of "updating" the story for the present day.

Richie Rich was one of the most popular comics of the 1960's, outselling *Superman* and *Batman* in its heyday. It followed the adventures of Richie, the richest boy in the world, his valet, Cadbury, and his faithful dog, Dollar. The comic was known for its inventive gadgets that reflected Richie's extravagant wealth, and proved to be an ironic collective fantasy for American youth who, in the 1960's, were witness to the country's collective move away from materialism. It is not surprising that its loyal following, now grown up with children of their own, would want to revisit those fantasies—especially since American cultural fantasies of extravagant wealth had been replaced by the harsh fiscal realities of the 1990's.

Macaulay Culkin is perfectly typecast in the title role, after raking in millions for *Home Alone* (1990) and *Home Alone II: Lost in New York* (1992). He has a suaveness that undercuts his boyishness, and a wistful world-weariness perfectly suited to playing the richest boy in the world. He has been wisely surrounded by gifted character actors who dive into their roles with relish: Christine Ebersole as his mother, Edward Herrmann as his father, Jonathan Hyde as Cadbury the butler, Michael McShane as Professor Keenbean, and John Larroquette as the villain, Laurence Van Dough.

This film, scripted by Jim Jennewein and Tom S. Parker, who wrote the film version of *The Flintstones* (reviewed in this volume), centers on Laurence Van Dough's nefarious plot to kidnap Richie's parents and control the colossal Rich fortune. He is foiled by the clever Richie, who, along with Cadbury and Professor Keenbean, comes up with a high-tech plot to keep Van Dough from stealing the family fortune. There is a thread of a moral to this story, too, as Richie befriends a group of ragtag children who aid him in exposing the diabolic Van Dough. As he befriends these underprivileged children, Richie learns that money is not the most important thing in the world.

One humorous aside to the story is that the so-called underprivileged children have home computers—one of them even uses the Internet to help Richie. *Richie Rich* is a comic, after all, so reality is not really an issue.

In fact, reality is unwelcome here, and the film is all the better for it. Adults and children will enjoy all the fantastic gadgets and gags created for the film. There are a series of scenes at Richie's school, for example, which are comic-book fantasy of the type of schools attended by the richest of the rich. The classroom is in a beautiful mansion; Richie and his classmates sit at huge cherrywood executive desks; the students pass notes on fax machines; and the bad boys disrupt class by practicing their golf swing or reading *The Wall Street Journal*.

There are a multitude of other high-concept moments in the film: a Mount Rushmore-like sculpture of the Rich family on a nearby mountain; the "Dad locater," an elaborate contraption allowing Richie to locate his father anywhere in the world; and the numerous inventions of the offbeat Dr. Keenbean, such as the golden robot bee or the molecule changer.

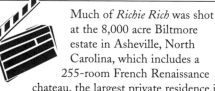 Much of *Richie Rich* was shot at the 8,000 acre Biltmore estate in Asheville, North Carolina, which includes a 255-room French Renaissance chateau, the largest private residence in the United States.

CREDITS

Richie Rich: Macaulay Culkin
Laurence Van Dough: John Larroquette
Richard Rich: Edward Herrmann
Cadbury: Jonathan Hyde
Regina Rich: Christine Ebersole
Gloria: Stephi Lineburg
Professor Keenbean: Michael McShane

Released: 1994
Production: Joel Silver and John Davis for Silver Pictures, in association with Davis Entertainment Company; released by Warner Bros.
Direction: Donald Petrie
Screenplay: Tom S. Parker and Jim Jennewein; based on a story by Neil Tolkin, and on characters appearing in Harvey Comics
Cinematography: Don Burgess
Editing: Malcolm Campbell
Production design: James Spencer
Art direction: William Matthews
Set decoration: John Anderson and Patricia Malone
Casting: Margery Simkin
Special effects coordination: Michael Wood
Sound: Scott Smith
Costume design: Lisa Jensen
Music: Alan Silvestri
MPAA rating: PG
Running time: 95 minutes

Furthermore, all these conceptual inventions and toys are pivotal to the plot. For example, "Mount Richmore" becomes the backdrop for the action-packed climax, as the Rich family hangs off their own giant ears and noses trying to escape Laurence Van Dough. The climax, in fact, is a wonderful send-up of the climactic scenes in *North by Northwest* (1959), in which the characters played by Cary Grant and Eva Marie Saint battle James Mason's character on Mount Rushmore; this satirical spirit is present throughout the film.

The performances underscore the satirical quality, with Christine Ebersole and Edward Herrmann achieving a wonderful blend of goofy charm and witty satire. One

"Welcome to your worst nightmare."—Herbert Cadbury from *Richie Rich*

of the film's first images is of the genial Herrmann as the proud father, Richard Rich, hovering over the cradle of his newborn Richie, cooing, "Can you say convertible debenture?" Ebersole is hilarious as she tries to keep looking beautiful when the couple is stranded at sea in a lifeboat: At one point, a piece of luggage (flotsam from a plane crash) floats to their raft, and she happily exclaims, "My Louie!" when she realizes it is her precious Louis Vuitton luggage. Ebersole is one of the best character actresses around, having proven herself in venues as diverse as Broadway's *Camelot* (as Guenevere) to television's *Saturday Night Live*. Her combination of wit and beauty are a wonderful contribution to this film.

John Larroquette, winner of numerous Emmy Awards from his years on *Night Court*, makes a fun comic villain. Constantly foiled by Richie and by his own henchmen's incompetence, Larroquette's Van Dough is hilarious as he tries to take over the Rich empire. He has a particularly fun series of scenes with his buxom secretary: One scene opens with her massaging his temples as he yells with exasperation, "I said clockwise!" Van Dough's snarling peevishness is great fun throughout.

Jonathan Hyde as Cadbury and Michael McShane as Keenbean, although lesser known, are delightful "finds" in this film. In particular, the enormous McShane brings good-natured fun to the eccentric Dr. Keenbean and his inventions. His frenetic demeanor and daffy warmth are assets that made him something of a celebrity in England, appearing on the improvisational television show *Whose Line is it Anyway?* The film's child actors, including Culkin, do not achieve the level of the more seasoned performers in the film, but their wholesome exuberance fits in nicely.

Donald Petrie, who directed *Grumpy Old Men* (1993) starring Jack Lemmon and Walter Matthau, does an excellent job here. In particular is his choice to keep things moving along at a brisk pace: The scenes never linger too long, nor are the numerous visual jokes heavy-handed. The pace contributes to the ditsy quality of the film: Quick cuts reveal the visual jokes with freshness. For example, when Richie's parents are kidnapped, he becomes the nominal head of Rich Industries, and a series of rapid scenes show him impressing the dour Board of Directors: In the first scene, they glumly sit at the conference table, and in subsequent scenes, they are all seen happily drinking chocolate milkshakes as Richie leads a board meeting.

Petrie deftly handles the film's climax with a style reminiscent of *The Perils of Pauline* (1947), as the Rich family narrowly escapes Van Dough. Another fun moment is Petrie's intercutting of Culkin's trademark wide-mouthed scream with Richie's parents' screams during a plane crash. Petrie utilizes much creativity in his camera shots. At one point, Cadbury is being stalked by some villains in a prison restroom. Cadbury starts out shaving in front of a mirror, and the camera stays on the mirror as a fight ensues, showing only the bits and pieces of the fight visible in the mirror.

All in all, Petrie and company are to be congratulated for creating a film for children which is entertaining for adults. In these days of cross remakes of 1960's and 1970's pop-culture icons such as *The Flintstones* and *The Beverly*

Hillbillies, Richie Rich provides nearly as much fun as did the original comic books. Only *The Brady Bunch Movie* (1995) exceeds this film in its ability to film a pop-culture phenomenon of the recent past without limply exploiting it. In fact, *Richie Rich* would be great fun regardless of whether audiences remembered the original comic.

—*Kirby Tepper*

REVIEWS

Daily Variety. December 21, 1994, p. 4.
The Hollywood Reporter. December 21, 1994, p. 10.
Los Angeles Times. December 21, 1994, p. F9.
The New York Times. December 21, 1994, p. B3.

Risk

"A love story of exceptional insight and reflection..."—Kevin Thomas, *Los Angeles Times*

A struggling young New York City artist, Maya (Karen Sillas), falls in love with a drifter, Joe (David Ilku), whom she meets on a bus. Unfortunately, Maya discovers that Joe suffers severe mental problems. Directorial debut of Deirdre Fishel.

CREDITS

Maya: Karen Sillas
Joe: David Ilku
Nikki: Molly Price
Karl: Jack Gwaltney
Alice: Christie MacFadyen

Released: 1994
Production: Gordon McLennan for Naked Eye Films, in association with Hank Blumenthal; released by Seventh Art Releasing
Direction: Deirdre Fishel
Screenplay: Deirdre Fishel
Cinematography: Peter Pearce
Editing: Deirdre Fishel
Editing: Gordon McLennan
Production design: Flavio Galuppo
Set decoration: Phillip Clarke
Music: John Paul Jones
MPAA rating: no listing
Running time: 85 minutes

REVIEWS

Chicago Tribune. June 2, 1994, Sec. 5 p. 11A.
Chicago Tribune. April 21, 1995, p. 7L.
Los Angeles Times. December 16, 1994, p. F8.
The New York Times. October 5, 1994, p. C18.

The River Wild

"The vacation is over."—Movie tagline

"A pulse-pounding thrill ride"—Peter Travers, *Rolling Stone*

"*The River Wild* takes your breath away, two times over."—Kenneth Turan, *Los Angeles Times*

Box Office Gross: $45,369,295 (January 2, 1995)

Fly-fishing aficionado Denis O'Neill wrote a nonfiction article for *Fly, Rod & Reel* about an unforgettable river experience, but he did not anticipate that a feature film would spring from that experience. Indeed, O'Neill traveled down Montana's Smith River for its beauty and for the commitment it forces from travelers: "[O]nce you get on that river, you can't get off.... You have to travel the length of it." O'Neill did travel it with the help of one of the country's premiere women fishing guides. From his adventure and his article arose the screenplay for *The River Wild*, O'Neill's first feature film to be produced.

Behind the opening credits of *The River Wild*, Gail (Meryl Streep) rows and rows, challenging herself with the water. Far from the white water and her

"I need your wife to get me down the river. I need your son to control her. You're expendable."— Wade from *The River Wild*

home in Montana, she nevertheless pushes herself to row the Charles River, sculling relentlessly, pushing for speed, relying on her strength. Agile, sure of herself on water, Gail is less surefooted in her marriage, less able to control the tricky domestic currents. For months, the marriage has floated adrift. Still, Gail cares for her two children, waits, and hopes. When her son Roarke (Joseph Mazzello) turns ten, Gail realizes that it is time to return to the wilds, where she is surefooted and believes she can reunite her family. Once joined in and with the wilds of Montana, mother, father (David Strathairn), and son begin a rafting trip. In order to survive the challenges ahead of them, they must become further lost to one another in order to be found once again.

One of the surprises of the film is Meryl Streep, who, well known for her complex, thoughtful characters, brings her character, Gail, believably to life. Two-time Oscar-winner Streep (*Sophie's Choice*, 1982; *Kramer vs. Kramer*, 1979) was drawn to the role for a variety of reasons, but she knew she had to make this film once she began to feel its pull. "I'd met Denis O'Neill socially a couple of times and he mentioned a project he'd written about a river

guide, a mother who takes her family on a spectacular Western river adventure," says Streep in the production notes. "I was intrigued, but when Curtis Hanson talked to me about it and how he wanted to develop it, my heart started pumping hard and I knew my adrenaline had already committed me to the project. You know, that feeling is addictive and it didn't stop until the day we wrapped."

Throughout her career, Streep has mastered complex accents and languages (*Sophie's Choice*) and in many ways, *The River Wild* required just as much of her, requiring that she learn the "language" of the river. For the two weeks before filming began, Streep (and the rest of the cast and crew) met in Oregon for rehearsals on land and water. Studying with two women rowers, Arlene Burns and Kelley Kalafatich (also Streep's stunt double), Streep mastered the art of rowing and of sculling, and the production notes report that she handled 90 percent of the rapids by herself. "She [Streep] was an exceptional student," remarks Burns, also in the production notes. "She was able to incorporate her new skills in "reading the river" and maneuvering the raft through rapids with such confidence and grace that she was still able to concentrate on acting. We were all amazed and impressed by Meryl's natural abilities and her affinity for the river environment. She is strong, intelligent and never lacking a sense of humor—all vital for success in river rafting. "Even Streep's look changed for this film. No longer a Victorian heroine (*The French Lieutenant's Woman*, 1981) or difficult artist/intellectual (*Out of Africa*, 1985), Streep in *The River Wild* shows new muscles and sun-bleached, wind-blown hair; she is quite believable.

While Streep is clearly the center of the film, appearing in all but a few scenes, she is surrounded by a strong supporting cast. By turns frustrating and appealing, Joseph Mazzello creates in Roarke the quintessential bratty, loveable kid. He expresses the boredom, the anger, and the winsomeness that serve as trademarks of childhood. For instance, he warms quickly to Wade (Kevin Bacon), the film's primary desperado, accepting in childlike fashion the friendly hand extended to him. With the same energy and blindness, he initially blames his often-absent father for the empty space in his family. Yet, perhaps most tellingly, Roarke learns that he has misread those around him, and in a split second, Mazzello captures pain, disappointment, anger, and little boy tears. It is a remarkable moment that makes clear Mazzello's

CREDITS

Gail: Meryl Streep
Wade: Kevin Bacon
Tom: David Strathairn
Roarke: Joseph Mazzello
Terry: John C. Reilly
Willa: Stephanie Sawyer
Maggie: Buffy
Gail's mother: Elizabeth Hoffman
Gail's father: Victor H. Galloway
Ranger: Diane Delano
Ranger: Thomas F. Duffy
Frank: William Lucking
Ranger Johnny: Benjamin Bratt
Violinist: Paul Cantelon
Policeman: Glenn Morshower

Released: 1994
Production: David Foster and Lawrence Turman for Turman-Foster Company; released by Universal Pictures
Direction: Curtis Hanson
Screenplay: Denis O'Neill
Cinematography: Robert Elswit
Editing: Joe Hutshing and David Brenner
Production design: Bill Kenney
Art direction: Mark Mansbridge
Set decoration: Rick T. Gentz
Set design: William Hiney
Casting: Nancy Klopper
Sound mixing: Ivan Sharrock, Kirk Francis
Costume design: Marlene Stewart
Stunt coordination: Max Kleven
Music: Jerry Goldsmith
MPAA rating: PG-13
Running time: 108 minutes

remarkable skill. Indeed, he has extraordinary credits, especially in light of his young age (he is eleven years old): *Presumed Innocent* (1990), *Shadowlands* (1993), and *Jurassic Park* (1993).

With a film like *The River Wild*, comparisons to John Boorman's *Deliverance* (1972) are inescapable. Certainly each explores the dangers of nature, including nature's arguably most dangerous creation, humans. Director Curtis Hanson, however, has already made a name for himself as a director who not only can handle suspense (*The Bedroom Window*, 1987), but also can believably take a family, place it in jeopardy, remove the father/husband, and let the strong women characters save the day (*The Hand that Rocks the Cradle*, 1992). Hanson sees *The River Wild* as a film about change and about strength, very much like the river itself. Hanson states in the production notes, "It's a story about a

AWARDS AND NOMINATIONS

Golden Globe Awards Nomination 1995: Best Actress—Drama (Streep), Best Supporting Actor (Bacon)
Screen Actors Guild Awards Nomination 1994: Best Actress (Streep)

couple who have to be separated in order to find each other. But then, it's also about a boy who chooses the wrong man to idolize and emulate. And, finally, it's about a conflict between a woman who respects and understands nature and a man who doesn't.... A family drama, a suspense picture, an action-adventure—I wanted it to be all of those things."

While it would be easy to do as one reviewer (Rita Kempley in *The Washington Post*) has done—capsulize this film as "suburban wife wrestles rapids and paddle-whips psychopaths to save her loved ones," including her workaholic husband—it would be wrong to do so. After all, *The River Wild* is an attractive, interesting film, in which characters defy such easy categories, such boundaries. Kevin Bacon's Wade, robber by trade, Romeo by choice, steals hearts and scenes in this film. For example, early in the film, he keeps up a lively, flirtatious banter with both Gail and Roarke, reeling each in for the catch. Coincidentally, in a later scene, Gail teaches Wade to fly cast, but the audience knows that Wade is an expert fisherman and an expert hunter. He is eerily engaging.

Despite all of its strengths, however, *The River Wild* is often too predictable and at times, not cohesive. The film includes several scenes of marital discord and the point is well established when Gail tells her mother (Elizabeth Hoffman) that the marriage is doomed in a gratuitous scene. The audience has recognized this fact long before it is stated, repeated, and made obvious. Additionally, within the first few minutes of water travel, "the Gauntlet" (the impossible, impassable white water) is mentioned many times. Therefore, it comes as little surprise that the bad guys want to run the rapids, to take the Gauntlet. While audience members can learn quickly by a glance or a mention, this film teaches viewers over and over again, finally taking on too much weight and capsizing.

For its often uneven pacing and its sometimes laborious storytelling, *The River Wild* is a fun outing with just the right amount of danger, intrigue, and muscle.

—Roberta F. Green

REVIEWS

Entertainment Weekly. October 14, 1994, p. 38.
Time Magazine. October 3, 1994, p. 74.
USA Today. September 30, 1994, p. 5D.
The Washington Post. September 30, 1994, p. F7.

The Road to Wellville

"Anthony Hopkins is Dr. John Harvey Kellogg, cereal inventor, health fanatic and head of America's flakiest family."—Movie tagline

"A madcap, marvelous bone-tickler."—Patrick Stoner, *WHYY-TV, Philadelphia*

"All health breaks out in this outrageous comedy romp."—*NBC News*

"Brilliant bold and outrageous...engagingly zany."—*Playboy*

"Cheerfully bawdy, lushly funny, richly detailed."—*Chicago Tribune*

 Box Office Gross: $6,487,257 (December 18, 1994)

Anthony Hopkins, as cereal magnate and health spa operator Dr. John Harvey Kellogg, Matthew Broderick, and Bridget Fonda in *The Road to Wellville*. Copyright © 1994 Beacon Communications Corporation. All Rights Reserved. Courtesy of Columbia Pictures.

Filmmaker Alan Parkers' *The Road to Wellville* is based on the 1993 best-selling book by T. Coraghessan Boyle about the messianic health faddist and cereal king, Dr. John Harvey Kellogg (1852-1943). Dr. Kellogg occupies a unique place in medical history. His patients anointed him a life-giving saint, while his equally numerous detractors branded him a charlatan.

The pioneering doctor studied medicine at Trall's Hygieo-Therapeutic College and earned his medical degree from New York's Bellevue Hospital. In 1876, Dr. Kellogg was appointed physician-in-chief of the Battle Creek Sanitarium, or "San" as it was affectionately known. For more than sixty-five years, Kellogg ran the institution, treating more than 300,000 patients, including such luminaries as President Taft, John D. Rockefeller, Alfred DuPont, J. C. Penney, and Montgomery Ward. At the peak of its popularity, the San could accommodate approximately one thousand guests.

The Road to Wellville is based on T. Coraghessan Boyle's fact-based historical novel.

Dr. Kellogg's medical treatments were highly unorthodox. He never prescribed drugs but did resort to frequent surgery and believed in natural therapy cures, employing water, air, sun, sleep, and a strict vegetarian diet: an approach he termed "biologic living." A prolific writer and health crusader, he authored more than fifty books, wrote dozens of articles, published a periodical, and gave countless lectures. In his work, he denounced alcoholism and sexual misconduct, including masturbation and marital cohabitation; he advocated high fiber meals and opposed the slaughter of animals as a food source. He vigorously championed daily enemas and the constant purging of the colon, which popularized America's obsession with bowel regularity. In his efforts to provide a dry bread product that his patients could chew easily, Kellogg experimented with the wheat flake. By 1899, his idea had grown into a cereal-based company, which earned him well over a million dollars.

Boyle's historical novel examined Battle Creek itself and Kellogg's sanitarium in the year 1907-1908 with its melange of health fads, crackpot cures, and rival medical hucksters. The film opens with two of the major characters—the young married couple Will and Eleanor Lightbody (Matthew Broderick and Bridget Fonda)—traveling by train to the Battle Creek Snaitarium. It is Eleanor's third trip to the San, whereas, a very sick Will is coming for the first time. During the journey. they meet Charles Ossining (John Cusack), a budding entrepreneur hoping to make a large fortune in the breakfast cereal business. Their paths part at the journey's end but will cross from time to time in the months ahead.

Will and Eleanor are introduced to Dr. Kellogg, who immediately separates the couple to different rooms. The rigidly controlled San does not permit conjugal relations during treatment, a stipulation that creates a hardship for the sexually overexcitable Will. Fortunately, he finds some measure of relief by being placed in the competent hand of nurse Irene Graves (Traci Lind), a pretty practioner of the

CREDITS

Dr. John Harvey Kellogg: Anthony Hopkins
Eleanor Lightbody: Bridget Fonda
Will Lightbody: Matthew Broderick
Charles Ossining: John Cusack
George Kellogg: Dana Carvey
Goodloe Bender: Michael Lerner
Dr. Lionel Badger: Colm Meaney
Endymion Hart-Jones: John Neville
Ida Muntz: Lara Flynn Boyle
Nurse Irene Graves: Traci Lind
Virginia Cranehill: Camryn Manheim
Poultney Dab: Roy Brocksmith
Dr. Spitzvogel: Norbert Weisser
Mrs. Hookstratten: Carole Shelley

Released: 1994
Production: Alan Parker, Armyan Bernstein, and Robert F. Colesberry for Beacon and Dirty Hands; released by Columbia Pictures
Direction: Alan Parker
Screenplay: Alan Parker; based on the novel by T. Coraghessan Boyle
Cinematography: Peter Biziou
Editing: Gerry Hambling
Executive producer: Tom Rosenberg and Marc Abraham
Production design: Brian Morris
Art direction: John Willett and Richard Earl
Set decoration: Claudette Didul
Casting: Howard Feuer and Juliet Taylor
Sound: Nelson Stoll
Costume design: Penny Rose
Music: Rachel Portman
MPAA rating: R
Running time: 120 minutes

five-a-day enema regime the patient must reluctantly endure. He also meets fellow sufferer Ida Muntz (Lara Flynn Boyle), convalescing from an unspecified illness, but one eager to discreetly satisfy Will's physical needs. In no time, Will is subjected to all of the San's unorthodox and terrorizing medical treatments, including colonic washes, electrically charged baths, hydreatic percussions, turbulent baths, vibrating belts, and an electric chastity belt.

Eleanor, still grieving from the death of her stillborn child, undergoes a less strenuous medical regimen than her husband. One of her fellow patients, Virginia Cranehill (Camryn Manheim) advises her to seek out more radical treatment. Soon, Eleanor is cavorting with two charlatans: Dr. Lionel Badger

"Sex is the sewer drain of a healthy body."—Dr. Kellogg from *The Road to Wellville*

(Colm Meaney), president of the American Vegetarian Society, whose specialty is the clitoris; and the German quack Dr. Spitzvogel (Norman Weisser), whose stock-in-trade is womb manipulation.

Viewers discover poor Charles Ossining with his Battle Creek partner, the charmingly crooked Goodloe Bender (Michael Lerner), who has already squandered Charles' $5,000 capital advance. Soon Charles and Goodloe begin churning out leaden breakfast flakes labeled Per-Fo ("Perfect Food") in cahoots with Dr. Kellogg's maladjusted adopted son, George (Dana Carvey), so they can cash in on the reputable Kellogg name. Charles eventually learns, to his regret, that there are no shortcuts to wealth, and he finds himself fleeing after his flim-flam partner and away from the police.

The fourth major character is Dr. Kellogg himself, the only historical personage in the film who loosely connects, in some way, with most of the other characters. Whether greeting arriving guests at the San, prescribing medical treatments, offering philosophical or healthy living advice, performing surgery, or simply protecting his institution and breakfast cereal's reputation, Dr. Kellogg comes across as a formidable figure. His Achilles' heel, however, is his adopted son, George. The dissolute wastrel, seeking love from his stern father since childhood, extorts money from him, terrorizes guests, and starts a fire that burns down the San. By film's end, all four characters endure much personal suffering and become hopefully, sadder but wiser people for their experiences.

Boyle's book makes it clear that Dr. John Harvey Kellogg was a figure ripe for satirical treatment and director Parker does not miss a trick from opening to closing sequences. Much of the main storyline and important characters of the original novel are kept. To his credit, Parker creates an elaborate comedy with some geniune insight and a few laughs on health fanaticism and faddism of another era. He also cleverly re-creates turn-of-the-century Americana with nice Edwardian touches in the costumes, sets, and unbelievable medical contraptions.

Much like the novel, however, *The Road to Wellville* is not well-realized as a work of art. Parker's major weakness is in trying to capture and enhance Boyle's deep pessimism, a major flaw that permeates both book and film. A fine filmmaker, Oscar-nominated Parker (*Mississippi Burning*, 1988) slips badly here and makes careless mistakes not evident in his other work. Unlike his award-winning picture, Parker (and Boyle) allows his audience to wander and forget about plot or characters to dwell on the historic plausibility of the events portrayed. Everything visualized at the San is much too preposterous, and the daily health activities are too ludicrous to be believed. Dr. Kellogg was a much-respected medical figure, and the San (a combination of lakeside health spa and grand hotel), an elegant place to vacation or recuperate.

Worse, Parker's sense of humor is certainly sour and decidedly morbid. He has a preoccupation with toilet and anal humor, bordering on adolescent obsession. There are so many bathroom and enema jokes that is is difficult to see a sophisticated audience eager to receive excremental instruction in what is essentially a gross-out comedy. A typical dialogue exchange: "With friends like you, who needs enemas?"

Further, both the characters and the storyline lead nowhere, certainly to no useful resolution. Four deaths occur at the San near the film's end, and they seem to have no meaning or dramatic shock. When Will's lover, Miss Muntz, dies suddenly and mysteriously, for example, the tragic event has no real impact on him. For that matter, all the characters are shallow, cartoonish, one-note creations despite energetic efforts from the cast.

Historical facts are ignored or treated cavalierly. Dr. Kellogg is wrongly attributed the famous statement by Dr. Horace Fletcher, the "Great Masticator," who once said, "My own stooks, Sir, are gigantic, and have no more odor than a hot biscuit." At film's end, the San burns down in 1908, but that event really occurred years earlier. Dr. Kellogg did not die in middle-age, as foolishly depicted on the screen, but lived a long and vigorous life until age ninety-one.

Parker alone is not to blame for the film's failure. Credit must also extend to the large ensemble cast, few of whom acquit themselves well here. In general, the acting

performances are broadly played, negating any seriocomic resonance the film attempts to achieve. Oscar-winner Anthony Hopkins is probably the biggest culprit. His portrayal of Dr. Kellogg is incomprehensible buffoonery and one of his worst screen appearances. Outfitted with "Bugs Bunny" prosthetic buck teeth, mustache and goatee, and sporting an awful American accept, Hopkins medical guru never comes to life and remains a caricaturish creation. The same can also be said for Matthew Broderick, Bridget Fonda, and John Cusack, wonderful young talent who never seemed so inept or lost in their roles. The minor characters fare somewhat better with Colm Meaney, John Neville, Traci Lind, Michael Lerner, and Dana Carvey bringing some spark to their roles, the latter unrecognizable in appearance. The best that can be said about Parker and the performers in The Road to Wellvilleis that the film will disappear quickly and their respective careers will survive.

—*Terry Theodore*

REVIEWS

Daily Variety. September 30, 1994, p. 2.
The Hollywood Reporter. September 30-October 2, 1994, p. 11.
Los Angeles Times. October 28, 1994, p. F1.
The New York Times, October 28, 1994, p. B4
Newsweek. October 31, 1994, p. 67.
People Weekly. November 14, 1994, p. 17.
Variety. October 3, 1994, p. 62.

Rock Hudson's Home Movies

Before Rock Hudson died of AIDS in 1985, he was the first major celebrity to admit to having the disease and the biggest film star ever to publicly admit to being gay. Up until that time, AIDS had been a disease which had become known virtually only to gay men, severe drug addicts, hemophiliacs, and their families. But with the publicity of Hudson's disease, Americans were able to witness nightly one of their great icons being slowly ravaged by the terrible affliction, and it was an important event in the history of AIDS in America. Hudson, fearful of discrimination, hid his condition until his final season on television's top-rated soap opera, *Dynasty*, where star Linda Evans was rumored to have been unwilling to kiss him because he was sick. His subsequent death helped promote a national discussion about AIDS.

After Hudson's death, his life was viewed through a truer lens than when he lived it. But the media accounts and

the by-the-numbers television films depicting Hudson's chronology and his homosexuality did not scratch the surface of the deeper issues raised by his coming-out and tragic death. Mark Rappaport's quirky and interesting Film, *Rock Hudson's Home Movies*, fills the void. It is a thoroughly unconventional look at Hudson's life and a refreshing, odd, yet intelligent discussion of the issues raised by his death.

The reference to "home movies" is misleading, though not unintentionally so. Rappaport takes clips from most of Hudson's films out of context so that he can show the "real" Rock Hudson behind the screen idol. Different than a traditional biography, this film uses the screen persona to show how important the facade was to both Hudson and his fans. Rappaport ultimately makes a larger statement about how Americans create idols and how they overlook truths that are right in front of their eyes. "Everyone" (the press, the

CREDITS

Rock Hudson: Eric Farr

Released: 1993
Production: Mark Rappaport; released by Couch Potato Productions
Direction: Mark Rappaport
Screenplay: Mark Rappaport
Editing: Mark Rappaport
MPAA rating: no listing
Running time: 63 minutes

entertainment industry) knew that Hudson was gay, and, Rappaport says, it was up there for anyone to see—if they wanted to admit they saw it.

Rappaport himself appears as a stand-in for Hudson, doing a videotaped running commentary as Rock Hudson talking about Rock Hudson. He shows out-of-context clips, which are arranged into informal segments intended to show how Hudson's homosexuality was thinly veiled on screen. A segment about his on-screen "significant others" is fascinating, with the clips overwhelmingly making the on-screen relationship between Hudson and Tony Randall appear to be a gay relationship. Rappaport also shows clips of the numerous "swishy and effeminate" characters inhabiting many of Hudson's films, particularly in the fifties and sixties, from characters played by everyone from Walter Slezak to Paul Lynde. Rappaport points out the cultural truth that these characters "can be gay, but as long as they're objects of ridicule, they're okay."

And Hudson, a big, strapping man's man, did not fit the cultural stereotype of a gay man—so it logically followed that he could not come-out in his real life. But from his sexually ambivalent ruse in *Pillow Talk* (1959) to his search for a husband for his soon-to-be "widow" in *Send Me No Flowers* (1964), Hudson's homosexuality is depicted as being inevitably visible through the thin veneer of his screen image.

AWARDS AND NOMINATIONS

National Society of Film Critics: Experimental Citation

A sequence showing Hudson "cruising" his male co-stars such as Kirk Douglas in *Winchester, 73* (1950) or in *Taza, Son of Cochise* (1954) are wryly done. Another sequence showing Paula Prentiss in *Man's Favorite Sport* (1964) saying, "I know that you're a phony...once you start lying to people it's too hard to stop" is quite compelling. It is at that point that the audience feels like they are watching home movies—where does Hudson stop and his character start? Rappaport provides a new way to view movies—assume that there is some truth behind the screen images, and the films of any major star become intensely personal.

The most impressive sequence shows a series of film clips of Hudson with various illnesses, as Rappaport eerily talks about "my death from AIDS." (He always speaks in the first person.) When Otto Kruger asks Hudson "did you get inoculated?" or when, in *Send Me No Flowers*, Hudson tells Doris Day that he has "a few weeks left" and "he'll just lie there and linger," the film rises above being charming and becomes chilling.

Rappaport has made an artistic and provocative piece which boldly explores the truth of a movie star's life without viewing his "real life." His "reel life" was true enough.

—Kirby Tepper

REVIEWS

Atlanta Constitution. May 31, 1993, p. B11.
Boston Globe. June 4, 1993, p. 54.
The New York Times. April 2, 1993, p. C20.

Romeo is Bleeding

"The story of a cop who wanted it bad and got it worse."—Movie tagline

"He's a cop. She's a cop-killer. This is not your average love affair."—Movie tagline

"A scorcher of a thriller...Stylish, sexy and fiendishly funny."—Peter Travers, *Rolling Stone*

"Lena Olin will go down in history as one of the greatest screen villains of all times. Oldman is just brilliant."—Dennis Dermody, *Paper Magazine*

"*Romeo* is the Olin sexual fireworks show. She is the demonic superwoman."—Joan Juliet Buck, *Vogue*

"A mind blowing, crazy, outrageous movie. Lena Olin gives a wild, all-stops-out performance!" —Pia Lindstrom, *WNBC-TV*

"One of the best movies of the year."—*WBBM*

Box Office Gross: $3,253,102 (March 27, 1994)

CREDITS

Jack Grimaldi: Gary Oldman
Mona Demarkov: Lena Olin
Natalie Grimaldi: Annabella Sciorra
Sheri: Juliette Lewis
Don Falcone: Roy Scheider
Nick Gazzara: Dennis Farina
Sal: Michael Wincott
Martie Cuchinski: Will Patton
Skouras: Paul Butler

Released: 1994
Production: Hilary Henkin and Paul Webster for Polygram Filmed Entertainment and Working Title; released by Gramercy Pictures
Direction: Peter Medak
Screenplay: Hilary Henkin
Cinematography: Dariusz Wolski
Editing: Walter Murch
Production design: Stuart Wurtzel
Art direction: W. Steven Graham
Set decoration: Beth A. Rubino
Casting: Bonnie Timmerman
Sound: Gary Alper
Costume design: Aude Bronson-Howard
Music: Mark Isham
MPAA rating: R
Running time: 108 minutes

A *film noir* with elements of black comedy is nothing new. John Huston's wickedly funny *Prizzi's Honor* (1985) is a masterpiece of the mixed genres, with Robert Altman's *The Long Goodbye* (1973) and Joel and Ethan Coen's *Blood Simple* (1985) near masterpieces. Even some of the *film noir* of the 1940's and 1950's have touches of dark or absurdist humor, as with Billy Wilder's *Double Indemnity* (1944) and Robert Aldrich's *Kiss Me Deadly* (1955). Combining comedy and the alienation, violence, and moral ambiguities associated with *film noir* offers the potential for insights into a host of subjects related to contemporary morality and sexuality. *Romeo is Bleeding*, however, is a confused failure with no such insights and only occasional spurts of style.

For $65,000 a tip, a Queens police detective on loan to the Organized Crime Task Force, Jack Grimaldi (Gary Oldman), tells local mob boss Don Falcone (Roy Scheider) where the Federal Bureau of Investigation (FBI) is holding witnesses about to testify against their former compatriots in crime. Falcone then sends a hit man (or woman) to kill the turncoats. Eagerly stuffing each payoff into a hole in his backyard, Jack is ruled entirely by his passions and impulses. Although he adores his wife, Natalie (Annabella Sciorra), he is unfaithful, primarily with waitress Sheri (Juliette Lewis). Why Natalie does not see what a creep he is and why Sheri is attracted to a man constantly bored and distracted when he is with her are only two of the film's many unanswered questions.

AWARDS AND NOMINATIONS

MTV Movie Awards Nomination 1994: Best Action Sequence

Jack's corrupt little world begins to unravel when Falcone's main assassin, Mona Demarkov (Lena Olin), murders several FBI agents along with her intended target and is arrested. Falcone now wants Mona killed, but she keeps eluding his grasp, taking the easily enthralled Jack with her. Mona's seduction and manipulation of Jack is an unsubtle variation on the smart-woman/dumb-man machinations of *Body Heat* (1981). Her gleefully bloody romp through Queens, including the grotesque lengths to which she goes to fake her own death, is the centerpiece to which the rest of *Romeo is Bleeding* merely builds.

Mona's exploits, including escaping from Jack after being shot and handcuffed, provide most of the film's black humor and are meant to be wildly excessive. The film fails to achieve most of its desired effects, however, because screenwriter Hilary Henkin and director Peter Medak cannot find a way of making all the diverse elements coalesce. *Romeo is Bleeding* comes across as a series of disconnected scenes desperately trying to find a common style.

This problem is aggravated by the carelessness of the storytelling. Mona is a larger-than-life figure whom the audience is supposed to admire perversely and who should triumph since she is more intelligent and dangerous than anyone else, yet clumsy Jack defeats her for no apparent purpose. Lust, avarice, and stupidity are not enough to justify Jack's behavior, leaving him neither a cartoon like Mona nor a believable character.

Despite these weaknesses, *Romeo is Bleeding* does have several effective moments: a gangster's boyish joy in recounting his crimes for his captors as if he were talking about his golf game or a fishing trip; Jack's being caught twice by his fellow officers as he begins to have sex with Mona, his prisoner; Mona shattering a wrecked car's windshield and kicking off her remaining shoe as she completes yet another escape; and Falcone's use of Robert Lowell's experiences as a conscientious objector during World War II to coerce Jack into killing Mona.

> "In the first three days of God's creation He made earth, sky, light and water. If He could do that in three days—I can make a million in a week easy."—Mona Demarkov from *Romeo is Bleeding*

A deft directorial touch is required for this kind of material to work consistently, and unfortunately, Medak lacks stylistic control. One film in Medak's uneven career stands out, and while *The Ruling Class* (1972) is one of the most effective black comedies in film history, even it shifts jarringly in tone from scene to scene. As with *The Krays* (1990), Medak's previous attempt to marry crime, violence, sex, and satire, *Romeo is Bleeding* seems uncertain of how it feels about its characters and themes, bouncing back and forth between compassion and cynicism.

The schizophrenic nature of the film is typified by Mark Isham's jazz combo score, with the composer on trumpet. While this music might have been effective in a straightforward *film noir*, it seems too serious for this material. Isham's intention may have been to provide an ironic counterpoint to the film's excesses, but the result is as if he has not been let in on the joke.

In contrast, the cinematography of Dariusz Wolski is perfect. Wolski provides more than the dark shadows, smoke, mist, and harsh light from the background or sides typical of *film noir*. He lights the actors to suggest a dark outline around them, emphasizing the cartoonish quality of the characters.

This material seems tailor-made for Gary Oldman. Along with Bruce Dern, Dennis Hopper, Tommy Lee Jones, Harvey Keitel, John Malkovich, Jack Nicholson, Tim Roth, and Christopher Walken, Oldman is one of the masters of scenery chewing, throwing himself fully into his characterizations, as seen especially in *Sid and Nancy* (1986), *Bram Stoker's Dracula* (1992), and *True Romance* (1993). The problem for Oldman in *Romeo is Bleeding* is that Jack is too weak and passive and his motivations alternately too obvious and too vague for the actor to have any scenery to chew. Mona's handcuffing Jack to a bed is a metaphor for Oldman's dilemma: Being the victim of a grandiose villain gives him little opportunity to seize command.

Mona, however, is a part Oldman could have taken off with, and that is just what Olin does. One of the rare performers who can easily convey intelligence and sexiness at the same time, Olin throws herself into the role of this calculating killer. While many other actresses might not have the courage to embody Mona's excesses and Olin is to be admired, the character's behavior is sometimes more genuinely disgusting than amusingly revolting and may make some viewers embarrassed for this talented actress.

The other members of the cast need sympathy for the opposite reason. Sciorra's and Lewis' roles are so underwritten that all they can do is pose and pout, and Jack's police colleagues are indistinguishable from one another. Two exceptions to this paucity are Dennis Farina, who shines in his one scene as a cocky mafioso, and Scheider, who makes the most of his suave don. Scheider's Falcone is equally debonair (in his smoking jacket) and dangerous, as when he orders gruesome punishment for Jack.

As she has stated in interviews, Henkin, whose credits include *Fatal Beauty* (1987) and *Road House* (1989), may intend an homage to *film noir* rather than a spoof, complete with voice-over narration and flashback structure, but *Romeo is Bleeding* is too goofy and sloppy to be taken seriously. An equally damaging failing is its attitude toward Mona: While the intention is to show that a woman can be as cold-blooded an assassin as a man, the film actually implies that a woman this intelligent is too dangerous to be allowed to survive in a male-dominated world.

—Michael Adams

REVIEWS

Atlanta Constitution. February 4, 1994, p. P3.
Boston Globe. February 4, 1994, p. 54.
Chicago Tribune. February 4, 1994, p. C7.
The Christian Science Monitor. LXXXVI, February 4, 1994, p. 12.
Entertainment Weekly. February 4, 1994, p. 39.
Glamour. XCII, March, 1994, p. 154.
The Hollywood Reporter. September 15, 1993, p. 5.
Interview. XXIV, February, 1994, p. 72.
Los Angeles. XXXIX, February, 1994, p. 110.
Los Angeles Times. February 4, 1994, p. F4.
Mademoiselle. C, February, 1994, p. 61.

The New Republic. CCX, March 7, 1994, p. 30.
New Woman. XXIV, February, 1994, p. 35.
New York. XXVII, February 14, 1994, p. 105.
The New York Times. February 4, 1994, p. B2.
People Weekly. XLI, February 14, 1994, p. 13.
Playboy. XL, December, 1993, p. 30.
Rolling Stone. February 10, 1994, p. 51.
San Francisco Chronicle. February 4, 1994, p. C3.
Time. CXLIII, February 14, 1994, p. 71.
USA Today. February 4, 1994, p. D7.
Variety. September 15, 1993, p. 11.
The Village Voice. XXXIX, February 8, 1994, p. 53.
Vogue. CLXXXIV, February, 1994, p. 116.
The Washington Post. February 4, 1994, p. WW43.

Roy Rogers: King of the Cowboys

Dutch filmmaker Thys Ockersen pays tribute to Hollywood's celebrated singing cowboy Roy Rogers, in this documentary.

CREDITS

Roy Rogers: Roy Rogers
Dale Evans: Dale Evans
Roy Rogers, Jr.: Roy Rogers, Jr.
William Witney: William Witney
Sons of the Pioneers: Sons of the Pioneers
Trigger: Trigger

Origin: The Netherlands
Released: 1992
Production: Kees Ryninks; released by Scorpio Film Productions
Direction: Thys Ockersen
Screenplay: Thys Ockersen
Cinematography: Peter Brugman
Editing: Stefan Kamp
Music: Sons of the Pioneers, Roy Rogers, Dale Evans, Roy Rogers, Jr. and Emma Smith
MPAA rating: no listing
Running time: 80 minutes

Safe Passage

"Life is a difficult journey. Family makes it worth the trip."—Movie tagline

"One of the year's very best films. Sarandon gives a performance of such gravity and depth that to not award her the Oscar would be a sin."—Rob Lurie, *Los Angeles Magazine*

"Another Academy Award caliber performance from Susan Sarandon in *Safe Passage*."—Luaine Lee, *Scripps Howard News Service/Knight Ridder*

Susan Sarandon brings her customary heart, soul and brains to *Safe Passage*, playing the frazzled mother of seven sons. It's a good thing she does, because the rest of the film is a half-baked stew of simmering pop psychology.

Sarandon is Mag Singer, who has been carried kicking and screaming all the way from a young hippie in love to a suburban mother whose kids are almost all grown up. She's recently booted out her husband, Patrick (Sam Shepard),

CREDITS

Mag Singer: Susan Sarandon
Patrick Singer: Sam Shepard
Alfred Singer: Robert Sean Leonard
Izzy Singer: Sean Astin
Cynthia: Marcia Gay Harden
Simon Singer: Nick Stahl
Gideon Singer: Jason London
Percival Singer: Matt Keeslar
Mort: Philip Bosco
Merle: Philip Arthur Ross
Darren: Steven Robert Ross

Released: 1994
Production: Gale Anne Hurd for Pacific Western; released by New Line Cinema
Direction: Robert Allan Ackerman
Screenplay: Deena Goldstone; based on the novel by Ellyn Bache
Cinematography: Ralf Bode
Editing: Rick Shaine
Production design: Dan Bishop
Art direction: Jefferson Sage
Set decoration: Dianna Freas
Casting: Pam Dixon Mickelson
Sound: Tod Maitland
Costume design: Renee Ehrlich Kalfus
Music: Mark Isham
MPAA rating: PG-13
Running time: 96 minutes

who is living at his office and having unexplained bouts of blindness. She's packed boxes to move her fourteen-year-old son to town, and she's ready to take a civil service exam and get her first full-time job, as a social worker.

Son Percival is a Marine stationed in the Middle East. From TV reports, Mag and Patrick learn there's been a bombing at his barracks. Percy may be dead or wounded, but the news of his fate is days in coming. That's plenty of time for the family to gather and pick over emotional scabs while monitoring TV reports and watching old home movies.

Early in her career, Sarandon played brainy, sexy oddballs. Reaching middle age, she turned to playing supermoms. Unlike *Little Women* (reviewed in this volume), where she has the patience and wisdom of a saint, Sarandon in *Safe Passage* is just one step ahead of a nervous breakdown. She is the harried heroine of everyday life struggling to pick up the pieces of her sons' emotional accidents and pick after her clueless husband.

Mag is always caring for everybody else and won't let anybody care for her. After all, she's surrounded by males. It's as if she's always in an enemy camp.

What spoils the character and makes this one of Sarandon's less appealing performances is that Mag is a self-pitying martyr. Why Mag is filled with such resentment about her lost chance at "her own life" is never explained. We're supposed to feel sorry for her because she's carried such a heavy burden. The joys she's had get short shrift.

Of course, that's the film's heavy-handed and unoriginal point: That only a crisis can make everybody wake up from the everyday struggles of existence and appreciate the life that's passing them by. Mag, her sons and her husband are healed in the cauldron of potential loss.

Why life has been such an unrelenting challenge for Mag and her family is a mystery. Though what Patrick does for a living isn't clear, he's apparently some sort of inventor. The Singers have a nice suburban home and the boys have turned out well, for the most part. Based on a novel by Ellyn Bache, Deena Goldstone's screenplay strains to wring pain out of every trifling remark or encounter.

As in most families, everybody has a set role. Izzy (Sean Astin) is the brainy one; Alfred (Robert Sean Leonard) the responsible one; Gideon (Jason London) the guilty one; Simon (Nick Stahl) the vulnerable one; and Percival (Matt Keeslar) the misfit. The two twins have little to say or do; they just add to the load Mag has to carry.

The performances of the actors playing the sons are uniformly good, despite their characters' narrowly defined personalities.

Shepard plays the father as the typical modern dad: distant, clueless, ineffectual and begging for Mag's attentions. The bouts of blindness are a transparent script device: it's easy to see they symbolize the fact that Patrick is so self-absorbed that he can't see or grasp what is going on around him. We know Mag has had to carry most of the burden because Patrick is always off in dreamland. Shepard stumbles through the part with disheveled indifference.

Sarandon's portrayal, as always, is close to the bone. She is no phony Hollywood mother; there is no glamour in her part. In fact, her lack of glamour is overplayed; it seems everyone's always telling Mag she needs a shower. But Sarandon overdoes the pain and the prickliness; it would be nice if we could see more often the qualities that make her family love her.

Instead, director Robert Allan Ackerman gives us plenty of wallowing. There is no unfolding of a plot, just a competition to see who can feel most guilty about Percival's fate, who can feel most victimized by family role-playing, who is most wounded by past or present slights, real or perceived. It's all done in a heartfelt fashion, but that's not enough to overcome the dead weight of so much angst. Rarely has family life and motherhood looked so unappealing.

—*Michael Betzold*

REVIEWS

Atlanta Constitution. January 6, 1995, p. P3.
Boston Globe. January 6, 1995, p. 54.
Chicago Tribune. January 6, 1995, p. 7H.
Christian Science Monitor. January 13, 1995, p. 11.
Entertainment Weekly. January 27, 1995, p. 34.
The Hollywood Reporter. January 19, 1994, p. 6.
Los Angeles Times. December 23, 1994, p. F6.
People Weekly. XLIII, January 23, 1995, p. 18.
Rolling Stone. January 26, 1995, p. 66.
The New York Times. January 6, 1995, p. C3.
USA Today. December 27, 1994, p. D5.
Variety. CCCLVII, December 19, 1994, p. 73.
The Wall Street Journal. January 19, 1995, p. A16.
The Washington Post. January 6, 1995, p. C7.
The Washington Post. January 6, 1995, p. WW37.
The Washington Post. January 12, 1995, p. C7.

Salmonberries

Box Office Gross: $31,274 (April 10, 1994)

This drama centers on a young Alaskan native woman, Kotzebue (k.d. lang), and her growing homosexual attraction to the town's librarian, a reclusive East German emigre, Roswitha (Rosel Zech).

REVIEWS

Los Angeles Times. April 7, 1994, p. F7.
The New York Times. September 2, 1994, p. C12.
The Washington Post. August 26, 1994, p. D7.

AWARDS AND NOMINATIONS

Montreal Film Festival 1991:   First prize

CREDITS

Kotzebue: k.d. lang
Roswitha: Rosel Zech
Noayak: Jane Lind
Bingo Chuck: Chuck Connors
Butch: Oscar Kawagley
Albert: Wolfgang Steinberg

Origin: Germany
Released: 1994
Production: Eleonore Adlon for Pelemele Film GmbH; released by Roxie
Direction: Percy Adlon
Screenplay: Percy Adlon
Cinematography: Tom Sigel
Editing: Conrad Gonzalez
Production design: Amadeus Capra
Sound: Jose Araujo
Costume design: Cynthia Flynt
Music: Bob Telson
Song: k.d. lang "Barefoot"
MPAA rating: no listing
Running time: 94 minutes

Samantha

"They had the perfect relationship...until they fell in love."—Movie tagline

"Lyrical, lovable, sensual—That's the only way to describe Martha Plimpton and Dermot Mulroney."—*The New York Times*

"A comedic look at an identity crisis of classical proportions."—*E! Entertainment*

"*Samantha* is kept aloft by the marvelous Martha Plimpton, an actress incapable of a false move."—*Movieline*

When a twenty-one-year-old violinist, Samantha (Martha Plimpton), discovers that she was adopted, she becomes angry with her loving adoptive parents, Walter (Hector Elizondo) and Marilyn (Mary Kay Place), and becomes obessed with finding her biological parents, in this drama.

CREDITS

Samantha: Martha Plimpton
Henry: Dermot Mulroney
Walter: Hector Elizondo
Marilyn: Mary Kay Place
Elaine: Ione Skye
Milos: Marvin Silbersher
Father O'Rourke: I. M. Hobson
Mrs. Schtumer: Bea Marcus

Released: 1992
Production: Donald P. Borchers; released by Planet Productions Corporation
Direction: Stephen La Rocque
Screenplay: John Golden and Stephen La Rocque
Cinematography: Joey Forsyte
Editing: Lisa Churgin
Production design: Dorian Vernacchio and Deborah Raymond
Casting: Linda Francis
Costume design: Stephen Chudej
Music: Joel McNeely
MPAA rating: PG
Running time: 100 minutes

REVIEWS

Entertainment Weekly. March 12, 1993, p. 70.
Variety. CCCXLIV, September 16, 1991, p. 88.

The Santa Clause

"Hysterical!"—Pam Thomson, *KABC-TV*

"This holiday's biggest comedy!"—Movie tagline

 Box Office Gross: $137,826,098 (January 2, 1995)

The Santa Clause is a goofy, uneven, yet surprisingly satisfying holiday offering from Disney. More than a star vehicle for television comic Tim Allen and much less than a new holiday classic, *The Santa Clause* resembles a typical Christmas morning. There are many packages under this cinematic tree: a boy-reconciles-with-dad heart-tugger, a special-effects dreamscape, a satire of "inner child" psychobabble, a cockeyed action-adventure, and plenty of skits and pratfalls, some stupid, others hilarious. Although not all the presents are memorable, there is plenty to enjoy.

The film starts slowly, lurches quickly into overdrive, drags to a near-stop, and then goes beserk near the end. There are so many changes of pace and mood that the film feels as if it was cobbled together by many different elves with many different ideas. In fact, that is exactly what happened. An original script by former stand-up comics Steve Rudnick and Leo Benvenuti met producers with new notions, who hired Allen, who in turn brought in his *Home Improvement* television series producer-director John Pasquin. The result is a film that goes in several directions at once. Nevertheless, it works on a number of levels for children, adolescents, and adults.

Allen, in his feature-film debut, plays Scott Calvin, a toy salesman with a zooming career and a crashing family life. He is bitter toward his former wife, Laura (Wendy Crewson), and distanced from his eight-year-old son, Charlie (Eric Lloyd). When Scott spends Christmas Eve with Charlie, neither suspects the night will transform them and their relationship permanently.

Before the magic, the pair stumble through some stale burn-the-turkey jokes and an awkward bedtime. Then, in the middle of the night, Charlie hears a clatter on the roof and awakens his dad. They find an old man in a red suit stumbling atop the house and then watch in horror as he slides off and lands motionless in the snow. By taking a business card from the man's hand, Scott finds himself drafted as a replacement.

In one of the film's screwiest jokes, a ladder appears. It is made by the Rose Suchak Ladder Co.—which is Charlie's misinterpretation of the line "there arose such a clatter" from Clement C. Moore's classic poem "The Night Before

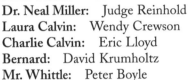

CREDITS

Scott Calvin: Tim Allen
Dr. Neal Miller: Judge Reinhold
Laura Calvin: Wendy Crewson
Charlie Calvin: Eric Lloyd
Bernard: David Krumholtz
Mr. Whittle: Peter Boyle
Detective Nunzio: Larry Brandenburg
Ms. Daniels: Mary Gross
Judy: Paige Tamada

Released: 1994
Production: Brian Reilly, Jeffrey Silver, and Robert Newmyer for Walt Disney Pictures, in association with Hollywood Pictures and Outlaw; released by Buena Vista Pictures
Direction: John Pasquin
Screenplay: Leo Benvenuti and Steve Rudnick
Cinematography: Walt Lloyd
Editing: Larry Bock
Production design: Carol Spier
Art direction: James McAteer
Set decoration: Elinor Galbraith
Casting: Renee Rousselot
Visual effects supervision: John E. Sullivan
Sound: David Lee
Special makeup/animatronic effects: Alec Gillis and Tom Woodruff, Jr.
Costume design: Carol Ramsey
Santa fat suit: Linda Benavente-Notaro
Elf wrangling: Christy Garland
Music: Michael Convertino
MPAA rating: PG
Running time: 97 minutes

Christmas." When father and son mount the ladder, they enter a dream world of the collective imagination.

Suddenly, the sleigh carrying Scott and Charlie takes off, and so does the film, into a dizzying realm where the Santa legend gets literal comic illustration. Guided by grunting reindeer, the flabbergasted new Santa and his awestruck son make the rounds. Along the way, they answer the skeptics' silly rational questions. How does Santa squeeze down narrow chimneys? He deflates. How does he get back up? His bag of toys lifts him. What about houses with no fireplaces? They magically appear.

To Scott's consternation, the sleigh returns to the North Pole—and a fantastic underground workshop. The elves, played by scores of children, are slaving under the command of head elf Bernard (David Krumholtz). Bernard has a Brooklyn accent and bad news for Scott. The fine print on Santa's calling card contains the "Santa clause": Scott must remain Santa or disappoint millions of children.

This segment of the film, in which Scott is initiated into the Santa business, is very appealing. Young children can be in awe of the wonders unfolding on the screen; older children can marvel at the special effects; and adults can cue into the wisecracking.

Also appealing is the inventive notion that ordinary mortals—particularly morally challenged types such as Scott Calvin—might be drafted to become Santa. Many modern parents tell their children that Santa Claus is the embodiment of the spirit of generosity. If so, he makes more sense as a sort of spiritual challenge for humans than an other-worldly apparition in a red suit.

Makeup artists went through thirty sets of prosthetics to add about one hundred pounds to Tim Allen's appearance in *The Santa Clause.*

Unfortunately, Scott's adventures in Santa's world soon end, and he wakes up at home wearing the red pajamas Elf Judy (Paige Tamada) gave him. He must decide whether what he experienced was a dream or reality, but Charlie has no doubts.

The Santa Clause now drags into a torpid middle section that revolves around Scott's attempts to come to grips with his new mission in life. Charlie's belief in his dad and his dad's new job infuriates his mother and her boyfriend, a psychiatrist named Neal (Judge Reinhold). As in the original *Miracle on 34th Street* (1947), Santa's nemesis is a psychiatrist, who preaches that belief in the St. Nick legend is dangerous to a child's emotional health. Charlie and his dad labor to prove otherwise. The two parents long have battled for Charlie's affections, with Scott the loser, but the adventures on Christmas Eve have won the boy's heart. There ensues a tedious family struggle that is needlessly heavy baggage in this otherwise zippy comedy.

There is diversion in Allen's transformation. Scott first battles against, and then literally grows into, his new role.

Makeup artists went through thirty sets of prosthetics to add about one hundred pounds to Allen's appearance as he turns from a trim businessman to a fat, bearded old man. This is fertile ground for comic skits, many lame.

As the next Christmas approaches, the film's disparate moods—the dour battle over Charlie's favors and the wondrous flights of fancy of the Santa improvisation—collide with many bangs and several thuds. There are ugly scenes of Santa pursued as a criminal and the high camp of "elves with an attitude" on a rescue mission to spring him from jail.

The film jolts from scene to scene with a noticeable lack of aplomb, and cannot seem to decide on a finale, so there are several of them. As befitting the Disney tradition, everyone is redeemed at the end.

Many aspects of the film, however, stretch the Disney envelope. The filmmakers have the courage to be whimsical, preposterous and audacious. The loony features of *The Santa Clause* rescue it from the dismal attempts at finding deep meaning in the father-son reconciliation.

Allen is no comic genius, but he is funny enough in his plum part. He is more appealing once he sheds the sarcastic regular-guy persona that is part of his television schtick. As Charlie, the young but veteran Lloyd is fine though occasionally cloying, and Reinhold is suitably annoying. The Laura role is underwritten—the familiar mother-in-the-background. The elves and their workshop steal the show, as do the special effects of Santa's journeys, which indulge a modern high-tech sensibility yet keep a traditional look.

Allen said he wanted kids to be wowed and adults to laugh at *The Santa Clause*, and he gets his wish. There is something for almost anyone, making the film a holiday crowd-pleaser. There are sufficient but not overly generous doses of sentiment, gusto, and wackiness to compensate for a sometimes strained story line and several missteps in execution.

—*Michael Betzold*

AWARDS AND NOMINATIONS

Blockbuster Entertainment Awards 1995: Best Male Newcomer, Theatrical (Allen)
MTV Movie Awards Nominations 1995: Best Comedic Performance (Allen), Breakthrough Performance (Allen)

REVIEWS

The Hollywood Reporter. November 11-13, 1994, p. 9.
Los Angeles Times. November 11, 1994, p. F10.
The New York Times. November 11, 1994, p. B3.
The New Yorker. December 12, 1994, p. 39.
Time. November 28, 1994, p. 80.
Variety. November 11, 1994, p. 2.

Sara

ased on Henrik Ibsen's *A Doll's House*, this drama centers on a submissive and dedicated Iranian wife, Sara (Niki Karimi), who is cruelly abused by her banker husband, Hessam (Amin Tarokh), for a selfless act she committed to save his life. Yet just like the protagonist of Ibsen's play, Sara finds the strength to leave Hessam and begin life anew.

REVIEWS

Boston Globe. October 7, 1994, p. 56.

CREDITS

Sara: Niki Karimi
Hessam: Amin Tarokh
Goshtasb: Khosro Shakibai
Sima: Yassaman Malek-Nasr

Origin: Iran
Released: 1994
Production: Hashem Sayfi and Dariush Mehrjui; released by Dena Films
Direction: Dariush Mehrjui
Screenplay: Dariush Mehrjui; adapted from *A Doll's House*, by Henrik Ibsen
Cinematography: Mahmud Kalari
Editing: Hassan Hassandust
Production design: Faryar Javaherian
Sound: Asghar Shahverdi and Sasan Nakhad
MPAA rating: no listing
Running time: 102 minutes

Satan

ne'er-do-well man, Vitaly (Sergei Kuprianov), kidnaps and murders the young daughter (Zhanna Schipkova) of his former lover, Alyona (Svetlana Bragarnik), as revenge for her breaking up with him, in this grim indictment of the Soviet social system.

CREDITS

Vitali: Sergei Kuprianov
Alyona: Svetlana Bragarnik
Alyona's husband: Veniamin Malotschevski
Armen: Armen Nasikyan
Vera: Mariya Averbach
Vitaly's grandfather: Anatoly Aristov
Alyona's daughter: Zhanna Schipkova
Braut: Anna Sagalovitsch

Inna: Margarita Alekseyeva
Heinrich: Mikhail Starodubov

Origin: USSR
Released: 1991
Production: Sergei Avrutin and Valentina Goroschnikova; released by Lenfilm Studios
Direction: Viktor Aristov
Screenplay: Viktor Aristov
Cinematography: Yuri Voronzov
Editing: J. Vigdorshik
Production design: Vladimir Bannykh
Sound: Nikolai Astachov
Music: Arkady Gagulaschvili
MPAA rating: no listing
Running time: 106 minutes

Saturday Night, Sunday Morning: The Travels of Gatemouth Moore

This documentary centers on the Reverend A.D. (Gatemouth) Moore, who was an up-and-coming blues singer in the 1930's and 1940's, until he underwent a religious conversion.

REVIEWS

Variety. CCCXLVIII, August 3, 1992, p. 41.

CREDITS

The Reverend A.D. (Gatemouth) Moore: The Reverend A. D. (Gatemouth) Moore
B.B. King: B.B. King
Al Green: Al Green
Rufus Thomas: Rufus Thomas
Benjamin Hooks: Benjamin Hooks

Released: 1992
Production: Louis Guida; released by Co-Media
Direction: Louis Guida
Cinematography: Richard Gordon
Editing: David Carnochan
Sound: Tim Callahan
MPAA rating: no listing
Running time: 65 minutes

Savage Nights (Les Nuits Fauves)

"A landmark film."—Caryn James, *The New York Times*
"Outspoken, unsentimental, defiantly sexual and relentlessly in-your-face. Bohringer, a stunning new actress, gives her role a blazing intensity."—Peter Travers, *Rolling Stone*

Box Office Gross: $565,924 (April 17, 1994)

Three days before his film won a series of Césars (the French equivalent of the American Academy Awards), Cyril Collard, director, screenwriter, and star of *Savage Nights*, died of AIDS. He leaves behind him an autobiographical novel and this film made from it.

As the film begins, Jean (Collard) has traveled to Morocco, filming location shots for a motion-picture that becomes lost in this picture shortly afterward. Upon his return to Paris, Jean notices a spot on his arm and goes in for an AIDS test. Found HIV positive, Jean rails against the disease, his impending death, and any change in his lifestyle it will necessitate. *Savage Nights* tracks Jean's life from the moment he learns of his dis-

ease, showing the toll such information takes on him and those around him, in particular, the effect on his lovers, Laura (Romane Bohringer) and Samy (Carlos Lopez).

While *Savage Nights* earned strictly rave reviews in France, American reviews were more cautious. Most applauded the film for painting a more realistic picture of AIDS than that found in Jonathan Demme's film *Philadelphia* (1993), for example. For many reviewers, however, Jean's narcissism took center stage and finally became quite boring; several reviewers became mired in their dislike for the character Jean, and by extension, the director Collard. Others found the film raw, a larger version of the one car-crash scene it presents, an accident without antecedent or explanation.

Despite Jean's nights of "anonymous group passion under bridges by the Seine," it seems pretty clear that this is not a film in praise of passion. No one's life is improved by physical proximity to anyone else. In fact, such activity has resulted in Jean's illness and impending death. Further, the varieties of sexual acts in the film are largely intended to humiliate the participants or are of an autoerotic nature—masochism, masturbation, urination. They are neither intimate nor comforting. Further, Samy soon evolves past intimate contact all together, replacing sex with skinhead vio-

CREDITS

Jean: Cyril Collard
Laura: Romane Bohringer
Samy: Carlos López
Laura's mother: Corine Blue
Jean's mother: Claude Winter
Marc: Rene-Marc Bini
Noria: Maria Schneider

Origin: France
Released: 1993
Production: Nella Banfi for Banfilm Ter, La Septcinema S.N.C., Erre Productions, Canal Plus, Sofinergie 2, and C.N.C.; released by Gramercy Pictures
Direction: Cyril Collard
Screenplay: Cyril Collard; based on his novel
Cinematography: Manuel Teran
Editing: Lise Beaulieu
Art direction: Jacky Macchi and Katja Kosenina
Sound: Michel Brethez: Dominique Hennequin
Costume design: Regine Arniaud
MPAA rating: no listing
Running time: 126 minutes

lence. While Laura and Jean seem to have a passionate, pleasurable relationship, Jean's illness, his bisexuality, and his inability to care for anyone soon drives Laura mad, as he purportedly had his previous girlfriend. Physical human relationships are incredibly costly in this film.

Yet the film offers few alternatives. Jean's parents, for example, are completely passive, restrained past anything that approaches life. Laura's mother (Corine Blue), divorced now, lives life as a functionary, sleeping alone, eschewing life with others. Samy's mother worked as a cafe girl, only rarely leaving with customers: sex without love. On a larger scale, the film showcases Paris—the view from Jean's balcony, the view from his bright red sports car as he speeds through the night—yet it is a Paris devoid of people. The panoramic view shows little beyond buildings, and the drives show other Parisians in their cars, heading to unnamed places, largely alone. The only real contact Jean has with other Parisians is the previously mentioned car wreck. At one point, the film focuses on a boatload of elderly people floating down the Seine. They are like wax figures, emotionless, nearly motionless (even those dancing)—while in the distance Jean and Laura couple, huddled under the bridges, in the same location where Jean comes for his late-night encounters. The choices are difficult, the options, unappealing.

Savage Nights writer-director-star Cyril Collard died from AIDS less than a week before the film won four French César Awards, including Best Film. The film won both Best First Film and Best French Film Césars—a first in César history.

AWARDS AND NOMINATIONS

César Awards: Best Film, Best Debut Film, Best French Film, Best New Actress (Bohringer)

Clearly this world offers few actual pleasures. Sex is plentiful, but ungratifying. People eat and drink to excess, yet are not satiated. None of the characters is presented as poor, unemployed, uneducated—yet each is anchorless, directionless, peevish. Everyone talks—actually, they usually yell—yet little gets said. Communication has ground to a halt. What is missing from this world? Arguably Collard might say love and forgiveness. At one point, Samy professes love for Jean, but when Jean asks him to repeat it, Samy refuses. Laura professes love nonstop for Jean, but he deflects her love, even as he rejects her. Late in the film, Jean travels, perhaps thinking, feeling, coming to terms with his life and his death. Upon his return, he is able to profess his love for Laura, and the film ends. An argument could be made that only in accepting and coming to terms with his mortality is Jean able to care about anyone else, that it is only the recognition of one's brief tenure on earth that allows one to drop one's guard and hold others dear. The film's structure would support such a finding, yet that may prove too provincial and pat an answer for Collard.

Savage Nights is in many ways a typically French film, as the French film tradition is understood in this country. For example, when Jean tells Laura that he is HIV positive, Laura initially berates him, then insists on unprotected sex with him. At least one reviewer, Anthony Lane, writing in *The New Yorker*, has identified this as "that old French refrain, the dark poetry of the death wish." More concretely, however, the film is not unlike Jean-Luc Godard's *Breathless* (1959), in which good and evil become indistinguishable and stylized, and in which Paris becomes merely a backdrop for the "play" and misadventures of young, beautiful, arguably lost people. In *Savage Nights*, when Jean drives his little red sports car impossibly quickly through tunnels, across bridges, and through the night, he runs from life and death in much the same manner as do the characters in *Breathless*—and with equally unsuccessful results.

While both Samy and Laura are interesting characters, it is perhaps Romane Bohringer's Laura that warms the screen most palpably. *Savage Nights* is Bohringer's screen debut, yet she ably portrays her character's complexities. Childlike, yet voluptuous and ardent in her passion, Laura fights for recognition, for the heat of emotion that she feels should—or that for her does—accompany physical sex. Her passion and her dismay are visible, persuasive. If the fault of everyone else in the film is that they give too little of themselves, hers is that she gives too much—and her scenes of confusion and loss may be the most tragic scenes of the film. Beyond her acting ability, Bohringer is lovely in the way of youth and thereby serves as a reminder of better things in this often relentlessly dark film. Since receiving the Best New Actress César for *Savage Nights*, she has appeared in the much-acclaimed film *The Accompanist* (1994).

The film is largely unremarkable to look at. Once again, the most visually interesting scenes may be the shots from the sports car. Otherwise, much of what appears is stereotypical: time-lapse photography of sunrise/sunset and panoramic pans of Paris. Some of the footage of men groping and coupling under the bridges in the dark is interesting for its chiaroscuro quality.

Savage Nights is a film about life without "life"—without joy, without hope, without love. Many of its characters are unlikable. Much of its footage is trite and static. Yet, finally, it is an interesting film, vaguely disturbing, lingering. As our lives become more and more impacted by AIDS, the world of cinema is developing a body of films—perhaps a new genre—about AIDS. *Savage Nights* does not romanticize the disease. It does not cushion the end. It tries to reflect one variety of life, and in that way, it is an honest and valuable film.

—*Roberta F. Green*

REVIEWS

Entertainment Weekly. March 18, 1994, p. 76.
The Hollywood Reporter. March 2, 1994, p. 12.
Los Angeles Times. March 4, 1994, p. F18.
The New York Times. March 20, 1993, p. 13.
The New Yorker. March 7, 1994, p. 30.

Scanners III: The Takeover

When Helena (Liliana Komorowska)—a scanner (one who can scan and control or destroy others' minds)—takes a certain drug to relieve her migraine headaches, she turns evil and seeks to dominate the world. The film is the sequel to *Scanners* (1981) and *Scanners II: The New Order* (1991).

CREDITS

Helena Monet: Liliana Komorowska
Joyce Stone: Valerie Valois
Alex Monet: Steve Parrish
Dr. Elton Monet: Collin Fox
Michael (the lawyer): Daniel Pilon
Charlie: Michel Perron
Doctor Baumann: Harry Hill
George: Christopher Macabe
Mitch: Michael Copeman
Suzy: Claire Cellucci
Sam: Charles Landry
Thomas Drake: Chip Chuipka
Max: Jean Frenette
Monk: Sith Sekae

Origin: Canada
Released: 1992
Production: Rene Malo for Malofilm Group; released by Republic Pictures
Direction: Christian Duguay
Screenplay: B. J. Nelson, Julie Richard, David Preston, and Rene Malo; based on the original characters created by David Cronenberg
Cinematography: Hughes De Haeck
Editing: Yves Langlois
Production design: Michael Joy
Art direction: Lynn Trout
Set decoration: Andre Chamberland
Sound: Gabor Vadnay
Special makeup: Mike Maddi
Costume design: Laurie Drew
Stunt coordination: Peter Cox
Music: Marty Simon
MPAA rating: no listing
Running time: 101 minutes

The Scent of Green Papaya (Mui du du Xanh)

"One of the year's best films."—Roger Ebert, *Chicago Sun-Times*

"Remarkable. Elegantly beautiful."—Kenneth Turan, *Los Angeles Times*

"A luxuriant, beautiful film about a lost Vietnam."—Janet Maslin, *The New York Times*

"Enchanting. A precious jewel."—Joan Juliet Buck, *Vogue*

 Box Office Gross: $1,725,124 (June 5, 1994)

Director-screenwriter Tran Anh Hung has said that he took the title of his first feature film, *The Scent of Green Papaya*, from a childhood memory. Tran, who moved to Paris in the early 1970's when he emigrated with his family from Vietnam, recalls that the sound and smell of green papaya being prepared permeated the environment of his childhood, becoming intimately associated with women's work.

Papaya, which is regarded in Vietnam as a vegetable when green and a fruit when ripe, also serves as an evocative metaphor for the film's theme and structure. *The Scent of Green Papaya* is divided into two parts, the first set in Saigon in 1951, the second taking place in the same location ten years later. When the film's main character, Mui, is first introduced as a shy ten-year-old peasant girl, she is played by Lu Man San. In the second half of the film, the twenty-year-old Mui has grown into a beauty played by Tran Nu Yên-Khê.

The first half of *The Scent of Green Papaya* contains little by way of drama or plotting. Mui has come from a distant village to act as a domestic servant to a bourgeois Vietnamese family. She performs her duties—food preparation and serving, floor scrubbing—with grace and quiet good humor, the peace of her world disturbed only occasionally by the two young sons of the household, who like to tease her.

In contrast, the family Mui serves is racked with problems. They are still mourning the death some years

> *The Scent of Green Papaya* is the feature-film debut of director Tran Anh Hung. Hung wanted to shoot the film in Vietnam, but was unable to find a village or house that suited him. Therefore, he built a soundstage in his native France and re-created the beautiful scenes of Saigon. The film was the first Academy submission by Vietnam.

> "It was born from the images I have of my mother, the freshness and the beauty of my mother's gestures."—director Tran Anh Hung on the meaning of the title *The Scent of Green Papaya.*

Lu Man San as Mui and Nguyen Anh Hoa as Thi in *The Scent of Green Papaya.* Courtesy of First Look Pictures.

earlier of a beloved daughter—who would have been Mui's age—and they are haunted by the frequent disappearances of the father (Tran Ngoc Trung), during which he squanders the family's wealth. This money seems to consist, at least in part, of the earnings of his wife (Truong Thi Lôc) from her garment business. The household also includes his mother (Vo Thi Hai), who adds to her daughter-in-law's sorrows by telling her that it is her own fault that her husband wanders.

None of this drama impinges on Mui, whose life is shaped by the rhythms of the menial work which—as Tran portrays it—is informed with graciousness and dignity. Mui's existence is also marked by her communion with the natural world. Despite the narrowness of her sphere, because of the openness of Vietnamese architecture of that era—which organized domestic life around an open-air central courtyard—Mui is able to commune with the frogs, birds, insects, and lush vegetation that are as common there as furniture.

Virtually all the action of the first half of *The Scent of Green Papaya* takes place in this setting. After weeks spent scouting locations in Ho Chi Minh City, Tran realized that the large, airy, multilevel houses

CREDITS

Mui (twenty years old): Tran Nu Yên-Khê
Mui (ten years old): Lu Man San
Mother: Truong Thi Lôc
Old Thi: Nguyen Anh Hoa
Khuyen: Vuong Hoa Hôi
Father: Tran Ngoc Trung
Grandmother: Vo Thi Hai
Trung: Souvannavong Kéo

Origin: Vietnam and France
Released: 1993
Production: Christophe Rossignon for Les Productions Lazennec, with La SFP Cinema and La SEPT Cinema, in association with Canal Plus, Centre National de la Cinematographie, Fondation GAN pour le Cinema, and Procirep; Released by First Look Pictures
Direction: Tran Anh Hung
Screenplay: Tran Anh Hung
Cinematography: Benoît Delhomme
Editing: Nicole DeDieu and Jean-Pierre Roques
Production design: Alain Negre
Casting: Nicolas Cambios
Sound: Michel Guiffan
Sound mixing: Joël Faure
Costume design: Jean-Philippe Abril
Music: Ton-That Tiêt
MPAA rating: no listing
Running time: 104 minutes

AWARDS AND NOMINATIONS

Academy Awards Nomination: Best Foreign Language Film
Cannes Film Festival: Camera d'Or

he remembered from Vietnam no longer existed, having been destroyed by war and its aftermath. This environment is integral to Tran's attempt to evoke the lost world of his childhood, a time so far removed from the realities of present-day Vietnam that the director was forced to construct his set in France, where he could also access the technical personnel and processes unavailable in his original home.

For the most part, however, Tran spurned expatriate professional actors who, he discovered, either do not speak Vietnamese or speak it with a French accent. All the actors hired were amateurs, with the exception of Tran Nu

Yên-Khê and Nguyen Anh Hoa, who plays Thi, the old servant woman who acts as Mui's mentor. Nguyen Anh Hoa was in fact brought to France from Vietnam to school the other actors—all of them born in France—in Vietnamese traditions and body language.

The difficulties Tran encountered in trying to reconstruct his past, a past characterized by tranquillity rather than warfare, underscore the poignant nostalgia of his film, which dwells lovingly on the minute particulars of a humble, everyday existence. The haunting beauty Tran's camera conveys remains in the second part of *The Scent of Green Papaya*, despite the film's change of pace. After ten years, the balance of power in the family Mui serves has shifted, and the mother, who has come to regard Mui as a surrogate daughter, is forced by her jealous new daughter-in-law to get rid of Mui, who has grown into a beautiful young woman.

Mui then goes to work for a wealthy young musician, Khuyen (Vuong Hoa Hôi), a friend of the family for whom she originally worked. As it happens, Mui has been in love with Khuyen since she was a child. Mui's new home, filled with the sounds of Debussy and Chopin, contrasts markedly with that she previously occupied, but Mui herself remains much the same, going about her duties with silent grace and living in utter simplicity.

Tran is at some pains to show all strata of the Vietnamese society of his youth, illustrating along the way the manner in which it changes. To that end, he gives Mui's new employer, Khuyen, European tastes and a thoroughly Westernized girlfriend, whose demonstrativeness falls far short of the feminine ideal which, in the film's terms, Mui embodies. The girlfriend, clothed in the height of French fashion, soon grows jealous of Mui, whose finest raiment is the traditional Vietnamese garb the Mother had given her upon her departure from her previous employment.

Khuyen soon reciprocates Mui's heartfelt, but unexpressed, affection for him. Some viewers might object to the paternalistic way Khuyen effects his servant girl's redemption, first teaching her to read, then impregnating her. This resolution of Mui's story is, however, in keeping with the nostalgic, backward-looking perspective Tran adopts throughout *The Scent of Green Papaya*. Mui is less a personage than a force of nature, an embodiment of the feminine principle. Her simple work is made ritualistic and thereby exalted, her pregnancy portrayed as the fulfillment of her destiny. Mui's life unfolds outside the sound of guns and before the advent of anything resembling women's liberation in Vietnam, and its conclusion is appropriate both to the time in which the film is set and to its values.

The film was a critical success, not only winning the Camera d'Or at the 1993 Cannes Film Festival but also garnering an Academy Award nomination for Best

Foreign-Language Film. *The Scent of Green Papaya* was the first-ever submission by Vietnam to the Academy.

—Lisa Paddock

REVIEWS

The Christian Science Monitor. January 26, 1994, p. 16.
The Hollywood Reporter. May 18, 1993, p. 10.
Interview. XXIV, January, 1994, p. 28.

Los Angeles Times. February 2, 1994, p. F1.
The New Republic. February 28, 1994, p. 30.
The New York Times. October 13, 1993, p. B3.
The New York Times. January 28, 1994, p. C15.
Playboy. XLI, February, 1994, p. 22.
Variety. May 26, 1993, p. 16.
Variety. CCCLI, June 7, 1993, p. 42.
The Village Voice. XXXVIII, October 12, 1993, p. 49.
The Wall Street Journal. February 10, 1994, p. A16.

Schtonk

Two men, Hermann Willie (Gotz George) and Fritz Knobel (Uwe Ochsenknecht), forge Adolf Hitler's diaries and pass them off as the genuine article to a major German magazine, in this satire based on a real-life scandal.

REVIEWS

Chicago Tribune. September 10, 1993, p. 7F(28).
New Statesman & Society. VI, Jan 22, 1993, p. 33.

CREDITS

Hermann Willie: Gotz George
Fritz Knobel: Uwe Ochsenknecht
Freya von Hepp: Christiane Horbiger
Karl Lentz: Rolf Hoppe
Biggi: Dagmar Manzel
Martha: Veronica Ferres
Frau Lentz: Rosemarie Fendel
Professor Strasser: Karl Schonbock
Managing editor: Harald Juhnke
Dr. Wieland: Ulrich Muhe
Uwe Esser: Martin Benrath
Kurt Gluck: Hermann Lause
Von Klantz: Georg Marischka
SS officer: Peter Roggisch
Knopp: Andreas Lukoschik
Cornelius: Thomas Holtzmann
Priest: Hark Bohm

Origin: Germany
Released: 1992
Production: Gunter Rohrbach and Helmut Dietl; released by Bavaria Film
Direction: Helmut Dietl
Screenplay: Helmut Dietl and Ulrich Limmer
Cinematography: Xaver Schwarzenberger
Editing: Tanja Schmidbauer
Production design: Gotz Weidner and Benedikt Herforth
Casting: An Dorthe Braker
Sound: Chris Price
Costume design: Bernd Stockinger and Barbara Ehret
Music: Konstantin Wecker
MPAA rating: no listing
Running time: 110 minutes

Scorchers

"One knows all the secrets...One wants to learn...One is afraid to find out."—Movie tagline

This comedy-drama set in the Louisiana bayou centers on three women: newly-married bride Splendid (Emily Lloyd), scorned wife Talbot (Jennifer Tilly), and town tramp Thais (Faye Dunaway). As Splendid stalls consummating her marriage to her over-eager new husband, Dolan (James Wilder), Talbot confronts Thais about her husband's affair.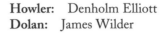

CREDITS

Splendid: Emily Lloyd
Talbot: Jennifer Tilly
Jumper: Leland Crooke
Thais: Faye Dunaway
Bear: James Earl Jones
Howler: Denholm Elliott
Dolan: James Wilder

Released: 1991
Production: Morrie Eisenman and Richard Hellman for Goldcrest; released by Nova Entertainment
Direction: David Beaird
Screenplay: David Beaird
Cinematography: Peter Deming
Editing: David Garfield
Production design: Bill Eigenbrodt
Casting: David Cohn
Sound: Walt Martin
Costume design: Heidi Kaczenski
Music: Carter Burwell
MPAA rating: no listing
Running time: 88 minutes

La Scorta (The Escort)

"Smart. Fresh. Absorbing. Unlike any other film on screen."—Caryn James, *The New York Times*

This political thriller, based on the true story of the experiences of Italian judge Francesco Taurisano, met with wide acclaim and box-office success because of its taut direction, excellent acting, and accurate depiction of the frightening battle between good and evil being waged in Italian government. Following in the tradition of such politically charged Italian films as *Indagine Su Un Cittadino Al DiSopra Di Ogni Sospetto* (1970; *Investigation of a Citizen above Suspicion*), *Ladri Di Biciclette* (1948; *The Bicycle Thief*, and *Porte Aperte* (1989; *Open Doors*), *La Scorta* takes a hard look at the way government power is shared with the Mafia.

An interesting aspect of this film, especially for an American audience, is the lack of common Mafia archetypes: This film is not *The Godfather* (1972). The true villains in this film are instead the Italian political system and its entrenched, corrupt bureaucrats. In the past, films such as this—*The Bicycle Thief*, for example—were excoriated by Italian government officials. Indeed, director Ricky Tognazzi was accused in the Italian press of exploiting this topical subject for personal gain. So it is easy to understand why Tognazzi has stated in interviews that "the real enemy of the Italian cinema is not the Mafia, it is the Italian State."

Even American audiences unfamiliar with the political drama in Italy will have no trouble identifying with the themes of political cover-up, backroom dealings, media sensationalism, and ever-widening scandals. Americans need look no further than the Watergate scandal and *All the President's Men* (1976) for a similarly well-directed and performed account of the discovery of the abuses of political power.

Sadly, in the late twentieth century, the Italian politicians and judges who tried to stand firm against corruption were systematically threatened and murdered. Magistrates such as the real-life Francesco Taurisano had to have twenty-four-hour escorts. It is from the point of view of these dedicated escorts that Tognazzi and writers Graziano Diana and Simona Izzo have built their story. Four young men, all Carabinieri (state police officers), are assigned to protect a new judge in the city of Trapani, Sicily. Judge De Francesco (Carlo Cecchi) comes from Northern Italy into the politically sensitive job of investigating a corrupt alliance between local water officials and the Mafia. The young escorts—Angelo Mandolesi (Claudio Amendola), Andrea Corsale (Enrico Lo Verso), Raffaele Frasca (Tony Sperandeo), and

CREDITS

Angelo Mandolesi: Claudio Amendola
Andrea Corsale: Enrico Lo Verso
Judge De Francesco: Carlo Cecchi
Fabio Muzzi: Ricky Memphis
Polizzi: Leo Gullotta
Raffaele Frasca: Tony Sperandeo

Origin: Italy
Released: 1994
Production: Claudio Bonivento; released by First Look Pictures
Direction: Ricky Tognazzi
Screenplay: Graziano Diana and Simona Izzo
Cinematography: Alessandro Gelsini
Editing: Carla Simoncelli
Production design: Mariangela Capuano
Sound: Remo Ugolinelli
Costume design: Catia Dottori
Music: Ennio Morricone
MPAA rating: no listing
Running time: 92 minutes

Fabio Muzzi (Ricky Memphis)—quickly bond together as they see the importance of their mission. The alliance is strengthened by their personal devotion to the judge. They become like sons to him, and the male bonding becomes as much a part of the story as do the dramatic plot points.

The story unfolds in a direct and simple way. The action begins with a brief, quiet scene of an older man preparing a meal. Close-ups of the dishes and the food, combined with the lack of underscore, lull the audience into a sense of calm. Then a bomb is heard outside the man's home and he runs outside to discover that his son, a police escort, has been killed. The man's sobs reverberate as the initial credits begin to roll.

Then the audience is introduced to Angelo as he visits his mother, to whom he stoically proclaims that he got himself transferred home to Trapani to replace his friend—the escort killed in scene one. He says that his dead friend "taught me everything. It's my way to thank him." This character is reminiscent of the archetypal American motion-picture hero, especially in classic Westerns, who rolls into town to clean things up. Furthermore Angelo has apparently had a previous relationship with a beautiful woman, in this case an attorney working in the magistrate's office. On his first day on the job he encounters her in the judge's office; they exchange a long glance and she says, "Hi Angelo. You're back." This scene recalls the stereotypical Western schoolmarm who reencounters the traveling cowboy whom she has always loved. It

"The real enemy of the Italian cinema is not the Mafia, it is the Italian State."—Ricky Tognazzi, director of *La Scorta*

is straight out of a John Ford Western, such as *She Wore a Yellow Ribbon* (1949) or *The Searchers* (1956).

Without apology, these men are too good to be true, and their subsequent male bonding is, paradoxically, idealized and realistic. The stress of the constant threat of death brings these men together in such a way as to appear too perfect. For example, Angelo and Corsale initially dislike each other and get into a fistfight, but their differences are resolved when Corsale explains to another escort that he got his black eye from "a friend." By Corsale showing this respect to Angelo, their friendship is sealed. Another example of the idealization of the male camaraderie is when Fabio finally receives the transfer he has been requesting—and realizes he wants to stay with his friends, even though their lives are in danger.

None of these rather idealized relationships seem cliché, however, in the hands of Tognazzi and his fine cast. Tognazzi, the son of legendary film star Ugo Tognazzi of *La Cage Aux Folles* (1978), has chosen a straightforward style similar to Sidney Lumet's *Prince of The City* (1981) or *Serpico* (1973). Both of these films told the story of the discovery of corruption in the same restrained manner as *La Scorta*. The restraint, revealed in its cinematography, stunts, and plot, allows the audience to experience the same constant stress as the escorts: The story moves along at a clip, having no time for overly indulgent histrionics or cinematic pyrotechnics.

Yet Tognazzi achieves an electrifying and exciting feel precisely because he is restrained. As the escorts begin their duty, the procedure seems very detailed and rather dull: They arrive in two vehicles to pick up the magistrate in the morning and wait for him outside his office all day. Tognazzi's camera follows them as they arrive at the judge's door, escort him to one of the two cars, ride to his office, and use the electronic gate opener to enter the parking lot. Tognazzi exposes the audience to this procedure several times, so that when something goes wrong and the judge's life is endangered, the audience empathizes completely with the tension felt by the escorts. The tension builds before the audience is even aware of what happened: This subtlety is what makes this a wonderful film.

Tognazzi and cinematographer Alessandro Gelsini use light to maximum effect. The film has much interplay between shadow and light: When Angelo is talking to an informer, their faces are silhouetted, conveying the dangerous nature of their interaction. Similarly, when Angelo and Corsale are listening in on a telephone conversation between corrupt government officials, they are seen in a cubicle that looks like a radio engineer's booth. With darkness surrounding them, they are lit by a dim source of light—a metaphor for the fragile glimmer of hope sparked by these dedicated officers.

Performances are uniformly excellent. It is consistent with the no-nonsense style of this film that none of the actors overplays his role, creating a tight and believable ensemble. Besides the bodyguards, Leo Gullotta is particularly good as the sniveling bureaucrat, Polizzi. His portrayal of a two-faced office worker is not a large role, but he is a perfect example of what is ailing the Italian political system.

Ennio Morricone provides one of his trademark excellent musical scores. Like the rest of the film, it is quite subtle, with pulsating rhythms underscoring the tense drives through the streets of the town, and touching music punctuating the warmth and understanding between the judge and his bodyguards. Morricone is the composer of numerous excellent scores, most notably for *Cinema Paradiso* (1989), the Oscar-nominated *Days of Heaven* (1978), and the immortal score for *The Good, the Bad, and the Ugly* (1967).

Clearly, Ricky Tognazzi is an assured and dedicated filmmaker, whose passion is evident in his attention to the story and the mood. He stays on course to the final credits of the film: The ending, however, comes rather abruptly; there is no huge climactic gun battle or any of the visual overdramatization that could easily accompany a political thriller. Instead, he ends his film with a long, uninterrupted shot that winds through the halls of the justice building, capturing glimpses of the apparently ordinary lives of the people involved in the politically corrupt government. It is clear that Tognazzi is making a point about how the ordinary and the respectable are not always what they seem. It is a profound statement.

—*Kirby Tepper*

REVIEWS

Los Angeles Times. July 8, 1994, p. F11.
The New York Times. May 9, 1994, p. B3.

The Scout

"He was praying for a miracle. What he got was Steve Nebraska."—Movie tagline

"Won't Strike. Will Play"—Movie tagline

Who needs the World Series. We have *The Scout*. It's a laugh riot!"—Barry ZeVan, *Channel America*

"Funny, funny, funny!"—Neil Rosen, *New York News*

"The best comedy-fantasy about baseball ever made."—*Time*

"Delightfully batty...genuine and immensely enjoyable. "—*The Washington Post*

"Albert Brooks is hilarious!"—*USA Today*

"A sunny and warm tale...that touches all the bases."—*Fort Lauderdale Sun Sentinel*

 Box Office Gross: $2,631,391 (October 16, 1994)

Al Percolo (Albert Brooks) is a baseball scout for the New York Yankees who desperately needs a break and gets one after he has been banished to Mexico. He was banished to what is called "the really Deep South" because his boss, Ron Wilson (Lane Smith) wanted to punish and humiliate him. Al had signed a pitcher from the sticks, Tommy Lacy (Michael Rapaport) for big money. Tommy, a sweetly religious country boy, believed he should finish college before considering the Major Leagues, but Al talked him into signing. In his first game, Tommy was so panicked that he threw up

Brendon Fraser trained with USC Trojans coach Frank Sanchez for his role as pitcher Steve Nebraska in *The Scout*.

on the pitcher's mound, then ran out of Yankee Stadium in his uniform and was last seen headed towards the turnpike.

In Mexico, Al finds no talent until a hotel clerk tells him about Steve Nebraska (Brendan Fraser), "the greatest baseball player that ever lived." Al discovers that Steve is a scout's dream. He has a fastball that is so fast it knocks catchers off their feet. At bat he hits home runs off of every pitch. Steve is too good to

"I would have sent you to the leper colony except I think that's against the law."—Ron Wilson from *The Scout*

be true, but there is a catch. Steve is dysfunctional in most other respects, a misfit with a repressed memory who gets angry when asked personal questions.

When Al calls Ron in New York to say "I've found the most outstanding pitcher that ever lived: I'll stake my repu-

tation on it," Ron tells him that he is fired, and Steve becomes a free agent, with Al as his manager. Al brings Steve to New York and arranges an exhibition at Yankee Stadium. After watching Steve pitch and hit, all the teams want him. The Yankees make the best offer, $55 million, but Ron wants to make sure Steve won't freeze up on the mound the way Tommy Lacy did and demands a letter from a psychiatrist that will vouch for Steve's stability.

Al takes Steve to Dr. Harriet Aaron (Dianne Wiest) and tries to con her into writing the letter, but she will only agree to write the letter if Al will put Steve under her care. "He's disconnected in some way," she says after testing him. His responses to pictures she shows him are confused. She suspects a blocked memory. "If he remembers, he could get violent," she warns, adding: "I think you should know that Steve will look to you as a father figure." If he gets angry enough, "he might want to put a bullet through you." So Al, desperate for Steve's psychological clearance, promises to bring Steve to see Dr. Aaron every day. If Dr. Aaron is successful in treating him, Steve might lose his spontaneous skills.

According to his contract, Steve won't play until the next season unless the Yankees make it to the World Series, in which case Steve will pitch the first game. To make a tidy conclusion, the screenplay puts the Yankees in the World Series. Will this goofy, dysfunctional kid be able to meet the challenge of pitching in front of all those fans? He is more screwed up than Tommy Lacy, and Al knows it. As the first game of the series is about to start, Steve is found on the roof of the stadium. Al has to go up and literally talk him down.

That's the story, such as it is. The screenplay comes up with complications but does not resolve the mystery of Steve Nebraska, other than to disclose the fact that Steve had an "abusive father." The script makes a potentially promising turn when it brings in Dr. Aaron, but it doesn't know how to use her to full comic effect. For the most part, Dianne Wiest is wasted in this role.

As comedy, this flawed baseball fantasy has its moments, as Al plays the role of the protective father. Ultimately the audience learns nothing about Steve, why he was in Mexico, where he is from, who his parents were, or how he learned baseball. All viewers know is that "Steve had an abusive father and he's blocked a lot of memories." That's not enough.

CREDITS

Al Percolo: Albert Brooks
Steve Nebraska: Brendan Fraser
Dr. Aaron: Dianne Wiest
Ron Wilson: Lane Smith
Jennifer: Anne Twomey
Tommy Lacy: Michael Rapaport

Released: 1994
Production: Albert S. Ruddy and André E. Morgan; released by Twentieth Century- Fox
Direction: Michael Ritchie
Screenplay: Andrew Bergman, Albert Brooks, and Monica Johnson; based on *The New Yorker* article by Roger Angell
Cinematography: Laszlo Kovacs
Editing: Don Zimmerman and Pembroke Herring
Production design: Stephen Hendrickson
Art direction: Okowita
Set decoration: Merideth Boswell
Set design: Thomas Betts and Gina B. Cranham
Casting: Richard Pagano, Sharon Bialy and Debi Manwiller
Sound: Kim Ornitz
Costume design: Luke Reichle
Music: Bill Conti
MPAA rating: PG-13
Running time: 101 minutes

A cast packed with baseball celebrities and two appearances by the singer Tony Bennett cannot compensate for a weakly developed plot. Moreover, the timing for the release of this film, on the heels of a protracted baseball strike that made both owners and players look greedy and foolish, was not especially good. The film succeeds merely as a farce.

Albert Brooks is pretty good as Al, but too much of the comedy depends on him, and the film needs more variety.

The screenplay was based upon a *New Yorker* piece by Roger Angell and developed by Andrew Bergman, who has written better and funnier scripts, such as *Honeymoon in Vegas* (1992) and *The Freshman* (1990). Michael Ritchie, who also directed *The Bad News Bears* (1976) and *Semi-Tough* (1977), was a logical choice to direct, but the screenplay needed more doctoring than the writing team of Andrew Bergman, Albert Brooks, and Monica Johnson could provide. *The Scout* resembles a confused television sitcom. Just when it begins to hit its comic stride, it turns serious by focusing on Steve's generally unexplained "abusive" background. Like Steve Nebraska, the film suffers from an identity crisis. There is too much Albert Brooks here, and not enough ensemble comedy.

—James M. Welsh and Alexandra M. Mather

REVIEWS

Atlanta Constitution. September 30, 1994, p. P6.
Boston Globe. September 30, 1994, p. 65.
Chicago Tribune. September 30, 1994, p. 7I.
Christian Science Monitor. November 18, 1994, p. 14.
Entertainment Weekly. October 14, 1994, p. 39.
Entertainment Weekly. February 10, 1995, p. 78.
Los Angeles Times. September 30, 1994, p. F6.
The New York Times. September 30, 1994, p. C23.
Time. CXLIV, October 10, 1994, p. 84.
TV Guide. XLIII, February 18, 1995, p. 34.
USA Today. September 30, 1994, p. D5.
Variety. CCCLVI, September 26, 1994, p. 61.
The Washington Post. September 30, 1994, p. F1.
The Washington Post. October 6, 1994, p. B7.
The Washington Times. September 30, 1994, Metropolitan Times, C17.

Scream of Stone

Two champion mountain climbers (Vittorio Mezzogiorno and Stefan Glowacz) compete to scale the most treacherous mountain in the world, in this weak drama.

CREDITS

Martin: Vittorio Mezzogiorno
Katrina: Mathilda May
Roger: Stefan Glowacz
Fingerless: Brad Dourif
Ivan: Donald Sutherland
No character identified: Al Waxman
No character identified: Gunilla Karlzen
No character identified: Chavela Vargas
No character identified: Georg Marischka
No character identified: Volker Prechtl
No character identified: Hans Kammerlander
No character identified: Lautaro Murua

Origin: Germany, France, and Canada
Released: 1991

Production: Walter Saxer, Henry Lange, and Richard Sadler for SERA Filmproduktions GmbH (Munich)/Molecule Films A2 (Paris)/Les Films Stock International (Montreal), in association with ZDF/Canal Plus/Telefilm Canada/Lucky Red-Raidue
Production: Released by Cine International
Direction: Werner Herzog
Screenplay: Hans-Ulrich Klenner and Walter Saxer; based on an original idea by Reinhold Messner
Cinematography: Rainer Klausmann and Herbert Raditschnig
Editing: Suzanne Baron
Production design: Juan Santiago
Set design: Kristine Steinhilber, Cornelius Siegel and Wolfgang Siegel
Sound: Christopher Price
Costume design: Ann Poppel
Music: Ingram Marshall, Alan Lamb, Sarah Hopkins and Atahualpa Yupanqui
MPAA rating: no listing
Running time: 105 minutes

Seasons

Narrated by William Shatner and set to Vivaldi's music *The Four Seasons*, this IMAX offering celebrates the four seasons of the year and examines the Earth and its relationship to the Sun and the solar system.

REVIEWS

Los Angeles Times. February 25, 1994, p. F12.

CREDITS

Narrator: William Shatner

Released: 1994
Production: Ben Shedd for the Minnesota Office of Tourism and the Science Museum of Minnesota; released by the Museum Film Network
Direction: Ben Shedd
Screenplay: George Casey
Cinematography: David Douglas
Computer animation: Vibeke Sorenson
Soundtrack production: Michael Stearns
Digital film recording: Richard A. Weinberg, Richard Y. Ostiguy and Richard A. Harrington
Music direction: Pinchas Zukerman
Music: Vivaldi
MPAA rating: no listing
Running time: 40 minutes

Second Best

"Fascinating. Engrossing. Emotionally Packed. William Hurt gives an Oscar-caliber performance."—Jules Peimer, *WNWK Radio*

"Deeply absorbing. William Hurt gives one of the best performances of his career."—Jeffrey Lyons, *Sneak Previews/Lyons Den Radio*

"Beautifully directed and sensitively acted. Real, hypnotic and profoundly touching."—Rex Reed, *New York Observer*

 Box Office Gross: $66,467 (October 16, 1994)

 illiam Hurt stars as a lonely middle-aged postmaster living in a small Welsh village who decides to adopt a troubled young boy (Chris Cleary Miles in his film debut). Adapted from screenwriter Cook's novel *Second Best*

REVIEWS

Boston Globe. October 14, 1994, p. 59.
Chicago Tribune. October 14, 1994, p. 7P.
Entertainment Weekly. October 14, 1994, p. 40.
Entertainment Weekly. March 17, 1995, p. 99.
Los Angeles Times. September 30, 1994, p. F8.
The New York Times. September 30, 1994, p. C10.
The New York Times. CXLIV, March 24, 1995, p. B11.
People Weekly. XLII, October 17, 1994, p. 23.
USA Today. October 5, 1994, p. D4.
Variety. CCCLVI, September 19, 1994, p. 79.

CREDITS

Graham Holt: William Hurt
James: Chris Cleary Miles
John: Keith Allen
Margery: Prunella Scales
Debbie: Jane Horrocks
Bernard: Alan Cumming
Uncle Turpin: John Hurt
Jimmy: Nathan Yapp

Origin: USA and Great Britain
Released: 1994
Production: Sarah Radclyffe for Regency Enterprises, Alcor Films, and Fron Film; released by Warner Bros.
Direction: Chris Menges
Screenplay: David Cook; based on his novel
Cinematography: Ashley Rowe
Editing: George Akers
Production design: Michael Howells
Art direction: Roger Thomas
Set decoration: Sam Riley
Casting: Susie Figgis
Sound: Peter Glossop
Costume design: Nic Ede
Music: Simon Boswell
MPAA rating: PG-13
Running time: 105 minutes

"I need to know what happened to send you scuttlin' inside yourself."—Debbie from *Second Best*

The Secret of Roan Inish

"It thrills you! *Roan Inish* may firmly establish Sayles as one of the greatest contemporary filmmakers"—Michael Wilmington, *Chicago Tribune*

"Wonderous!"—Stephen Holden, *The New York Times*

"Pure magic!...This heartfelt and haunting folktale is more that a masterwork; it's a gift." —Peter Travers, *Rolling Stone*

"Glorious. Ravishingly beautiful."—Manohla Dargis, *L.A. Weekly*

This wonderful, evocative film is further proof of the artistry of writer-director John Sayles. Sayles has taken an Irish novella by Rosalie K. Fry called *Secret of the Ron Mor Skerry*, and has fleshed out the characters and dialogue to create a film which can best be described as "lyrically realistic." Ultimately, *The Secret of Roan Inish* informs its audience about the deep-rooted spirituality present in the people of Ireland, and sends the message that one man's myth is another man's reality.

The film takes place in the 1940's, and tells the story of ten-year-old Fiona (Jeni Courtney), who is sent to live with her grandparents, Hugh (Mick Lally) and Tess (Eileen Colgan) on Ireland's West Coast after the death of her mother. The first image sets the scene perfectly, as the camera rests its eye on Fiona as she stands on the deck of a small boat, wearing a tag on her coat as if she were a parcel being sent from one place to another. As her boat arrives at the shore of her grandparents' fishing village, she notices a seal who appears to stare at her as the ship passes, foreshadowing the adventures that follow.

Once at her grandparents' home, Hugh rather quickly tells Fiona the story of how her little brother, Jamie, was lost at sea. Over Tess's protestations, Hugh spins the tale of how Jamie was whisked away by the ocean, as if the ocean had a mind of its own, saying "what the sea gives, the sea takes away..." Fiona, entranced by the tale, wants to hear more, but Tess insists that the myth that Jamie is still alive and living somewhere in the nearby island of Roan Inish is false. She warns Hugh that Fiona is just like him in her fascination with the mythology of the sea, and of Roan Inish: "the love of the sea is a sickness, and you two'll find your death in it," she warns.

But Fiona is undaunted, and becomes obsessed with learning the true story of Jamie's disappearance, and of the possibility that he is actually still alive and living on Roan Inish, floating on the sea by day, protected by seals and living in Tess and Hugh's former cottage on Roan Inish by night. Her curiosity leads her to her cousin, Tadhg (John Lynch), who is thought of as crazy by the

The Secret of Roan Inish. Copyright © 1994 Overseas Filmgroup/First Look Pictures Releasing. All rights reserved. Courtesy of First Look Pictures.

rest of the family, but who tells her the full story of Roan Inish. He tells her about their ancestor Liam, who married a sea-creature who was half woman and half seal, and who made the cradle that generations later would carry Fiona's brother Jamie to sea.

Believing Liam's story, Fiona convinces another cousin, Eamon (Richard Sheridan) to take her to Roan Inish. Together they uncover Jamie's secret and reclaim him and the island of Roan Inish for the Connelly family.

It appears that Sayles wishes to underscore the importance of mythology to the daily life of these people. To that end, he films the story as if it were a simple family drama, using no fancy special effects, but instead relying on the natural light and pastoral scenery to create the necessary atmosphere. The extraordinary west coast of Ireland is a majestic and mysterious backdrop for the tale, with its somber light and its rustic beauty. Sayles and cinematographer Haskell Wexler make the most of the foggy Irish coast to help create a sense that the these people share their workaday world with a host of mythological creatures. For example, when Tadgh tells Fiona about the Connelly family legend, he is presented in the most mundane of settings, a fish market. The simplicity of Tadgh's job is juxtaposed with the fantastic elements of the Connelly family story to help the audience sense that the mundane and the fantastic are inextricably woven together. It further underscores one of the film's themes, that the tales found in regional folklore have an important place in a person's spiritual development: In other words, folklore springs from real life situations, and helps people make sense out of their world.

Another extraordinary aspect of the work of Sayles and Wexler is the use of animals as characters. In the film's first sequence, as Fiona arrives, the seal that she notices becomes almost human in his "performance." Careful attention to "point of view," i.e., matching the angles from which Fiona looks (in closeup) to the angle at which the seal is filmed, gives the appearance that Fiona and the seal make eye contact. And perhaps because Sayles has edited this film himself, he makes the seal appear to react to the movement of the boat and to Fiona. This scene foreshadows the remarkable climax of the film, in which numerous seals appear to nudge Jamie away from the sea to the arms of his waiting family.

"I'm interested in not so much what I think about something, but in seeing things through someone else's perspective and that's part of the reason my stories are so different."—John Sayles on *The Secret of Roan Inish*

Not only are the seals and seagulls used as characters in the film, but allusions to the sea, such as Mick's admonishment that "the sea is angry for us leaving Roan Inish," and the loving photography of the scenery emphasize the theme that humanity shares the earth with nature—and nature demands respect.

Sayles appears to love a good fable, especially one that can be made relevant for today's world. He has provided a fable-like quality to many of his other films, such as *Brother from Another Planet* (1984), *Matewan* (1987), *Passion Fish* (1992), and *Eight Men Out* (1988). Sayles always directs his own screenplays, which makes him one of the few "auteurs," such as Woody Allen, who have found success in American cinema.

Like Allen, Sayles continues to work with a team of producers (Maggie Renzi and Sarah Green) a composer (Mason Daring), and others who have worked on many other of Sayles's films. Daring provides a haunting score, evoking the Irish folk atmosphere particularly well in the climactic scene with the use of Gaelic folk songs.

Cinematographer Wexler has also worked with Sayles before, being nominated for an Oscar for *Matewan*. Wexler is something of a legend himself, having won Academy Awards for *Who's Afraid of Virginia Woolf* (1966) and *Bound for Glory* (1976). In addition, he has been the cinematographer on many of American cinema's great films, including *In the Heat of the Night* (1967), *Coming Home* (1978), and *One Flew Over the Cuckoo's Nest* (1975). From lush views of the hillsides of Roan Inish, to the shimmering views of the ocean at night, lit (apparently) only from the moon and from hand-held lamps, Wexler's contributions help make this film a visual feast.

As Fiona, Jeni Courtney is a plucky and tenacious young heroine. She is reminiscent of young Anna Paquin in *The Piano* (1993)—a pretty little blond girl who has strength which exceeds her age. Courtney was chosen for the role after her mother inadvertently heard about the casting call on a television commercial. Courtney had not acted before, yet proves to be comfortable and assured in front of the camera. Sayles wisely ensures a good performance with his artful editing, but Courtney's soulful pleas for the seals to "come ashore with me," or her ecstatic discovery of Jamie on the Roan Inish countryside prove her natural acting ability.

As her grandparents, Mick Lally and Eileen Colgan are perfectly cast, looking and sounding every bit the rustic Irish grandparents. Both are highly respected actors in their country, having roots in the classical theater, and playing husband and wife on a popular Irish television series. Their background is evident here, and is helpful in bringing a reality to the fanciful dialogue which Sayles has

CREDITS

Hugh: Mick Lally
Tess: Eileen Colgan
Tadhg: John Lynch
Fiona: Jeni Courtney
Eamon: Richard Sheridan
Jamie: Cillian Byrne
No character identified: Pat Slowey
No character identified: Dave Duffy
No character identified: Declan Hannigan
No character identified: Fergal McElherron
No character identified: Frankie McCafferty
No character identified: Gerald Rooney
No character identified: Susan Lynch
No character identified: Linda Greer

Released: 1994
Production: Sarah Green and Maggie Renzi for Jones Entertainment Group Ltd., in association with Peter Newman Productions; released by First Look Pictures Releasing
Direction: John Sayles
Screenplay: John Sayles; based on the novel *Secret of the Ron Mor Skerry*, by Rosalie K. Fry
Cinematography: Haskell Wexler
Production design: Adrian Smith
Art direction: Henry Harris, Dennis Boscher and Lucy Richardson
Set decoration: Tom Conroy
Casting: John Hubbard and Ros Hubbard
Sound: Clive Winter
Costume design: Consolata Boyle
Music: Mason Daring
MPAA rating: PG
Running time: 103 minutes

written for them. A typical line of dialogue for both characters is Hugh's response to the possibility that Jamie is still alive: "and cows could have wings, dear, and cows could have wings." Without Colgan's ability, her character's motivations might appear a bit unclear, for even though Tess insists that no one discuss the possibility of Jamie being alive, it is she that decides the family should go to Roan Inish to reclaim Jamie from the sea. It is unclear why Sayles chooses to have Tess drop her reluctance when she does; however, Colgan appears to justify this lack of clarity through her resolve, and the film does not suffer for it.

One of the film's pivotal roles is Tadhg, played by John Lynch. He embodies the struggle between reality and legend in which the Connelly family has been caught since its self-exile from Roan Inish. Reaching into the water and catching a fish bare-handed, Lynch perfectly captures the essence of the Irish black-sheep cousin whose oddness allows him to tell the family truths. Without overplaying, Lynch's performance bridges the mystical and the real, and exemplifies the theme of an individual's struggle to overcome his skepticism in order to achieve a truly spiritual nature.

The Secret of Roan Inish works on several levels. As a fable, it teaches us the moral lesson that we must look into and embrace our ancestry in order to better understand the present.

As a visual portrait of the beautiful Irish coast, it is a hypnotic view into a simple world fast becoming obsolete. And as a story, it is simply entertaining and enchanting.

—*Kirby Tepper*

REVIEWS

Atlanta Constitution. March 3, 1995, p. P1.
Atlanta Journal and Atlanta Constitution. March 5, 1995, p. M1.
Boston Globe. February 24, 1995, p. 67.
Chicago Tribune. March 3, 1995, p. 7C.
Christian Science Monitor. February 3, 1995, p. 13.
Los Angeles Times. July 30, 1993, p. F12.
Los Angeles Times. February 3, 1995, p. F1.
National Catholic Reporter. XXXI, April 7, 1995, p. 15.
The New York Times. February 3, 1995, p. C12.
People Weekly. XLIII, February 27, 1995, p. 18.
Playboy. XLII, February 1995, p. 20.
Rolling Stone. February 23, 1995, p. 81.
Variety. CCCXLIII, June 3, 1991, p. 53.
The Wall Street Journal. March 2, 1995, p. A12.
The Wall Street Journal. April 4, 1995, p. A18.
The Washington Post. March 17, 1995, p. B7.
The Washington Post. March 17, 1995, p. WW38.
The Washington Post. March 23, 1995, p. C7.

Serial Mom

"*Serial Mom* is a killer comedy"—Bruce Williamson, *Playboy*

"Uproarious...killingly funny...Kathleen Turner is dynamite in a performance that keeps springing surprises!"—Peter Travers, *Rolling Stone*

"I couldn't stop laughing"—Guy Fatley, *Cosmopolitan*

 Box Office Gross: $7,811,335 (July 31, 1994)

Critics as well as the general public demonstrated great surprise and enthusiasm for the no-holds-barred performance of Kathleen Turner in this offbeat comedy about a suburban housewife who goes psychotic. Leave it to John Waters, the king of the "gross-out" films, to turn a Donna Reed-type mom into a serial killer. Waters' past films, *Pink Flamingos* (1974), *Female Trouble* (1975), *Cry-Baby* (1990), and *Polyester* (1981), among others, have been cult favorites for years among filmgoers who enjoy campy, raunchy come-

dy mixed with acerbic social commentary and satire. Waters is at his best, however, in this deliciously sick film, aided and abetted by Turner and several Waters regulars, including Mink Stole and Ricki Lake.

Beverly Sutphin (Kathleen Turner) is supposedly a typical housewife living on a beautiful, tree-lined block in a serene suburb of Baltimore. Her family consists of her dentist husband (Sam Waterston), her boy-crazy daughter, Misty (Ricki Lake), and her son, Chip (Matthew Lillard), who is obsessed with gory films. At first, everything seems to be just fine in the Sutphin household, except that Misty has some troubles with her boyfriend, Carl (Lonnie Horsey), and that Beverly is overly concerned about Chip's being driven to school by his best friend (Justin Whalin), who does not wear a seat belt.

The morning's apparent calm is broken, however, when the busybody neighbor, Mrs. Ackerman (Mary Jo Catlett), comes over to discuss the obscene phone calls received by Dottie Hinkle (Mink Stole) and discovers that Beverly is the one who has been making them. Then a teacher calls Beverly in to talk about Chip's school problems, and she

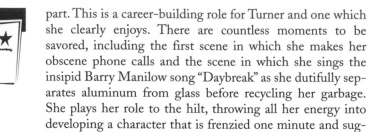

CREDITS

Beverly Sutphin: Kathleen Turner
Eugene Sutphin: Sam Waterston
Misty Sutphin: Ricki Lake
Chip Sutphin: Matthew Lillard
Rosemary Ackerman: Mary Jo Catlett
Scott: Justin Whalin
Birdie: Patricia Dunnock
Dottie Hinkle: Mink Stole
Carl: Lonnie Horsey
Carl's date: Traci Lords
Suzanne Somers: Suzanne Somers
Pike: Scott Wesley Morgan
Gracey: Walt MacPherson

Released: 1994
Production: John Fiedler and Mark Tarlov for Polar Entertainment; released by Savoy Pictures
Direction: John Waters
Screenplay: John Waters
Cinematography: Robert M. Stevens
Editing: Janice Hampton and Erica Huggins
Production design: Vincent Peranio
Art direction: David J. Bomba
Set decoration: Susan Kessel
Casting: Paula Herold and Pat Moran
Sound: Rick Angelella
Costume design: Van Smith
Music: Basil Poledouris
MPAA rating: R
Running time: 93 minutes

goes overboard in her response, to say the least. The body count begins to rise, and Beverly becomes crazier with every passing frame of film.

Waters has always had a fancy for twisting innocent archetypes into bizarre comments on American life. In *Cry-Baby*, Ricki Lake's loving mom was played by 300-pound drag queen Divine. In fact, Divine's loony and grotesque presence is felt here: If he were still alive, Divine might have played the "Serial Mom" of the title, for Waters, as usual, skewers the image of the adored suburban mom who always has a smile, a kind word, and a batch of cookies. He slyly reminds the audience that appearances can be deceiving.

In the past, Waters had the obvious presence of the enormous Divine to underscore his point. In *Serial Mom*, he has the beautiful and sunny Kathleen Turner, who is all the more frightening and hilarious because she truly looks the

"I don't like to read about movies, they're too violent"—Beverly from *Serial Mom*

part. This is a career-building role for Turner and one which she clearly enjoys. There are countless moments to be savored, including the first scene in which she makes her obscene phone calls and the scene in which she sings the insipid Barry Manilow song "Daybreak" as she dutifully separates aluminum from glass before recycling her garbage. She plays her role to the hilt, throwing all her energy into developing a character that is frenzied one minute and sugary sweet the next.

Just like a stage farce, the highs and lows of the action define the comedy: One moment Beverly is dashing all over town, trying to kill Chip's best friend for not wearing his seat belt, and the next minute she is offering a chipper "It's been quite a day, hasn't it?" to her bewildered family. Turner has displayed her comic sensibilities before in such films as *Romancing the Stone* (1984) and another dark comedy called *The War of the Roses* (1989). In *Serial Mom*, however, she is given the kind of role that actors dream of: a leading role that steals all the scenes. She rarely misses a chance to be laugh-out-loud funny. A scene in which she makes lewd gestures to a witness for the prosecution at her trial is worth the price of admission.

The brains behind the operation is Waters. He is a curious blend of Ed Wood—the mysterious C-film director of the 1950's who created such dreadful cult classics as *Plan 9 from Outer Space* (1959) and *Glen or Glenda?* (1953)—and Walt Disney. Waters has a way of making the most disgusting cinematic moments seem as if they were part of a television situation comedy. Obviously, it is his intent to juxtapose the horrific and the prosaic in order to suggest that these elements are not really so different from each other.

Beverly's murders are truly grotesque, and not without blood and gore. The opening shot is a close-up of a fly being smashed to bits by a flyswatter. In a curious and rather perverse way, under the direction of Waters the swatting of the fly becomes humorous: This scene establishes the tone of the rest of the film. Other visual images will evoke varying responses from filmgoers: For the most part, audiences have enjoyed a scene in which Beverly discovers that the fire poker she used to kill someone has an internal organ stuck to the end of it, like a piece of tissue on the bottom of a shoe. It is over-the-top and disgusting, and clearly the audiences that love it are of the die-hard variety. In these moments, Waters' humor is reminiscent of the less savory parts of the Monty Python films. There has always been, and always will be, an audience for humor that uses shock value as a comic weapon.

Yet the shock value serves a satirical purpose as well. Waters created *Serial Mom* in an age where the dominant media images were of murders and arrests on such real-life television programs as *Cops* or *Rescue 911*; where gossip was equivalent to news on such programs as *Hard Copy* or *A Current Affair*; and where daytime television was dominated by ridiculous intrafamily squabbles and salacious stories of murder and mayhem. He does a wonderful job satirizing American "family values," which tout a pretty house and two sweet children, but which also tolerate a fascination with violence and sleaze.

As Beverly's violence comes to a crashing finale, she becomes a hero to her town, and her trial turns her into a celebrity, complete with a television motion-picture deal. In an inspired moment, Suzanne Somers appears as herself to "research" Beverly in order to portray her on television. Somers' good nature is evident, but what it truly hilarious is that, even though she is lampooning herself as an actress of questionable ability, she is barely adequate at portraying herself with any reality or true comic flair, making the situation that much more ludicrous.

Waters' regular Mink Stole turns in another daffy portrayal as Dottie Hinkle, the overdressed neighbor who is the recipient of Beverly's obscene phone calls. Stole creates a prudish, uptight character who loses her cool for one brief moment on the witness stand when she releases a pent-up torrent of obscenity. Similarly funny is Mary Jo Catlett, recognizable from countless television appearances and commercials, as the dippy lady next door who is thoroughly appalled at Beverly's behavior.

Ricki Lake and Matthew Lillard acquit themselves well in the rather simple roles of the shocked-yet-supportive children. Lillard's maturation from goofy kid to high-powered show-business tycoon—he becomes Beverly's agent during the trial, complete with cellular telephone—is entertaining. Finally, Sam Waterston is an unexpected and delightful choice as Beverly's husband. Waterston is one the most highly respected serious actors in the entertainment business, and his appearance adds weight to the proceedings. His wide-eyed, rather dim character is appropriately silly.

Waters does go too far at one point when a young man is visibly burned to death in front of a large crowd. It is one of those revolting moments on film in which an audience member can recoil and dismiss the entire film or can try to understand why the filmmaker included such a vile image. In Waters' case, he is clearly an individual who knows how to utilize crassness to make a point.

It is not coincidental that Beverly recycles her trash and develops a special relationship with the garbagemen. "Trash" was recycled daily on television, film, and over the back fence in every neighborhood in the country in the 1990's. In *Serial Mom*, Waters depicts a fascination with trash as well as a revulsion for those who are fascinated by it. Audiences can enjoy the film for its baseness or its satire, but there is a good chance they will enjoy it either way.

—*Kirby Tepper*

REVIEWS

Entertainment Weekly. April 22, 1994, p. 36.
The Hollywood Reporter. March 31, 1994, p. 6.
Los Angeles Times. April 13, 1994, p. F1.
The New York Times. April 13, 1994, p. B1.
Variety. March 3, 1994, p. 2.

The Servants of Twilight

A mother, Christine Scavello (Belinda Bauer), and son, Joey (Jarrett Lennon), take flight when a religious zealot, Grace Spivey (Grace Zabriskie), and her minions target Joey as the anti-Christ. Spivey's followers trail the pair, while a detective (Bruce Greenwood) tries to help them in this horror thriller.

CREDITS

Charlie: Bruce Greenwood
Christine Scavello: Belinda Bauer
Grace Spivey: Grace Zabriskie
Henry Rankin: Richard Bradford
Joey Scavello: Jarrett Lennon
Kyle: Carel Struycken
Dr. Denton Boothe: Jack Kehoe
Sherri: Kelli Maroney
Wilford: Dale Dye
No character identified: James Haner
No character identified: Bruce Locke
No character identified: Al White
No character identified: Dante D'Andre

Released: 1991
Production: Jeffrey Obrow and Venetia Stevenson; released by Trimark Pictures
Direction: Jeffrey Obrow
Screenplay: Jeffrey Obrow and Stephen Carpenter; based on the novel *Twilight*, by Dean R. Koontz
Cinematography: Antonio Soriano
Editing: Doug Ibold and Eric Ghaffari
Production management: David Witz
Casting: Michelle Guillermin
Sound: George Alch
Bat effects: Michael McCraken
Stunt coordination: Bud Davis
Music: Jim Manzie
MPAA rating: no listing
Running time: 95 minutes

Sex, Drugs, and Democracy

 Box Office Gross: $172,255 (October 9, 1994)

Employing contemporary and archival footage as well as interviews, this documentary presents a no-holds-barred look at the drug and sexual excesses in the Netherlands of the 1990's.

REVIEWS

Atlanta Constitution. May 5, 1995, p. P4.
Chicago Tribune. March 10, 1995, p. 7J.
Los Angeles Times. November 7, 1994, p. F4.
The New York Times. February 17, 1995, p. C6
Playboy. XLII, March 1995, p. 18.
The Washington Post. April 1, 1995, p. C5.

CREDITS

Origin: The Netherlands
Released: 1994
Production: Barclay Powers and Jonathan Blank; released by Red Hat Productions
Direction: Jonathan Blank
Screenplay: Jonathan Blank
Cinematography: Jonathan Blank
Editing: Jonathan Blank
MPAA rating: no listing
Running time: 87 minutes

Shades of Doubt (L'Ombre du Doute)

A young girl, Alexandrine (Sandrine Blancke), accuses her father (Alain Bashung) of incest.

REVIEWS

The New York Times. October 2, 1993, p. A16.

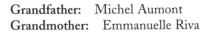

CREDITS

Alexandrine: Sandrine Blancke
Jean: Alain Bashung
Marie: Mireille Perrier
Sophia: Josiane Balasko
Pierre: Luis Issermann
Grandfather: Michel Aumont
Grandmother: Emmanuelle Riva

Origin: France
Released: 1993
Production: Ciby 2000/TF1 Films, in association with Cofimage 4 and Investimage 4; released by Ciby 2000
Direction: Aline Issermann
Screenplay: Aline Issermann
Cinematography: Darius Khondji
Editing: Herve Schneid
Production design: Cyr Boitard
Costume design: Maritza Gligo
Music: Reno Isaac
MPAA rating: no listing
Running time: 107 minutes

The Shadow

"Who knows what evil lurks in the hearts of men?"—Movie tagline

"The wittiest action-adventure since *Indiana Jones*! *The Shadow* is a spellbinding, runaway entertainment ride."—*NBC News*

"If ever a film looked exactly the way you hoped it would, *The Shadow* is it."—Kenneth Turan, *Los Angeles Times*

 Box Office Gross: $31,951,990 (September 18, 1994)

Among the pulp comic-book adventure heroes to reach the big screen, several combine good and evil, an inner turmoil and outer strength. Just as Batman, or Bruce Wayne (Michael Keaton), in *Batman Returns* (1992) laments his inability to quell his dark side, so too in *The Shadow* the hero, Lamont Cranston (Alec Baldwin), battles his dark background even as he battles crime.

The Shadow begins in Tibet, where Cranston, known as Ying Ko, the "Butcher of Lhasa," reigns as a murderous drug lord over an opium kingdom. Taken captive by a mystic named The Tulku, Cranston is forced to reform, in the process learning the secret powers of the mind. He emerges from the experience as the Shadow and returns to his home in Depression-era New York, where he battles everyday crime. The Shadow's first big challenge comes with the arrival of Shiwan Khan (John Lone), the last living descendant of Genghis Khan. Like Cranston, Khan is trained in the arts of mind control, and the two battle for control of each other, the world, and the first atom bomb.

Some of the problems with *The Shadow* are evident from the first scene. For example, as a Tibetan drug lord, Baldwin is outfitted in a ridiculous shoulder-length wig and claw-like fingernails. While clearly Baldwin is an appropriate choice to play the charming, handsome millionaire recluse/playboy (always an intriguing paradox), it seems lunacy then to put him in a mop of a wig and have him tumble through battles with such special-effect monsters as a knife handle outfitted with razor-sharp teeth. It is distracting to the audience, it is an against-type move for Baldwin, and it weighs down the film, as audience members try to determine whether this is a joke. Certainly it would seem that Baldwin could portray evil even with his original haircut, but then this does seem to be a film plagued by bad hair decisions. For example, Penelope Ann Miller plays Margo Lane, a Depression-era vamp, com-

Penelope Ann Miller as Margo Lane and Alec Baldwin as Lamont Cranston, also known as *The Shadow*. Copyright © by Universal City Studios, Inc. Courtesy of MCA Publishing Rights, a Division of MCA Inc. All rights reserved.

plete with a variety of period costumes in rich fabrics, accented with jewels. Yet perhaps her most eye-catching feature is her hair—how it defies the finger waves into which she would force it. It is a battle of wills to rival that between Khan and Cranston, and most regrettably, it is unnecessary.

Nevertheless, *The Shadow*, which originated from a vintage radio program, is in many ways a wonderful film visually. According to the film's production notes, the filmmakers tried to create a world on film commensurate with a radio listener's imagination. Production designer Joseph Nemec made living rooms out of ballrooms and used huge living rooms to make bedrooms. Cranston's living room is equipped with an enormous fireplace, which, located as it is in a large sparsely furnished room, is reminiscent of the fireplace in the classic *Citzen Kane* (1941)—large, beautiful, yet incapable of emitting much

The Shadow's budget was $45 million; close to $35 million was spent on advertising and marketing.

"I do what I do to fight back the evil inside me, but some part of it is still there, waiting."—Lamont Cranston from *The Shadow*

heat or light. Also attractive are The Cobalt Club (reminiscent of Golden Age Busby Berkeley sets) and dreamy, stylized versions of such New York landmarks as the Brooklyn Bridge and the Empire State Building.

Among its special effects is a high-power mail tube, actually a creative version of the everyday pneumatic tube. Through it, the Shadow's messages cross the city from a variety of lookout points, and the audience follows along as the camera scurries down buildings, into walls, through living rooms, and into the Shadow's inner sanctum. Also, Baldwin's profile was altered slightly in scenes in which he played the Shadow, as the Shadow has a trademark profile: with hawk-nosed, deep-set eyes.

Oddly enough, for all its glamour and action, *The Shadow* is a bit dull. Written by David Koepp, who had collaborated on the megahit *Jurassic Park* (1993), the film is rather tame. For example, the attraction between Cranston and Lane generates some smoke but no real fire, while Lane's relationship with her father, Reinhardt Lane (Ian McKellen), rings more true. Master comedian Jonathan Winters is mired in his role of police commissioner Barth—a straight role from which it appears he longs to escape. Even the usually irrepressible Tim Curry is repressed in his role as a demented lab assistant. For all its beauty, *The Shadow* seems weighed down by its style. Perhaps that is where the radio show had its advantage.

The 1930's weekly radio show *Detective Story Hour* spawned one great success: "The Shadow." The program was announced each week by an anonymous deep-voiced announcer (Frank Readick) dubbed the Shadow. When listeners began asking for more information about the Shadow, a character who did not exist beyond the announcer's voice, the radio show's sponsors hired Walter B. Gibson, one of the most prolific pulp-fiction writers, to create adventures for the Shadow. Gibson, writing under the pseudonym of Maxwell Grant (taken from the names of two magician-supply dealers), created a "weird creature of the night...a tall, black clad figure...like a specter from the world beyond...like a messenger of vengeance," who was an instant success.

While the original Shadow had no special powers, years later Gibson gave him supernormal mental abilities, including the ability to hypnotically "cloud men's minds so they cannot see him." Additionally, while the original pulp Shadow was an aviator named Kent Allard, who borrowed the identity of reclusive playboy Lamont Cranston, more recent versions of the character made the two synonymous: Cranston

CREDITS

Lamont Cranston (The Shadow):   Alec Baldwin
Shiwan Khan: John Lone
Margo Lane: Penelope Ann Miller
Moe Shrevnitz: Peter Boyle
Reinhardt Lane: Ian McKellen
Barth: Jonathan Winters
Farley Claymore: Tim Curry
Burbank: Andre Gregory

Released: 1994
Production: Martin Bregman, Willi Baer, and Michael S. Bregman; released by Universal Pictures
Direction: Russell Mulcahy
Screenplay: David Koepp
Cinematography: Stephen H. Burum
Editing: Peter Honess
Production design: Joseph Nemec III
Art direction: Dan Olexiewicz, Steve Wolff and Jack Johnson
Set decoration: Garrett Lewis
Casting: Mary Colquhoun
Special effects coordination: Kenneth D. Pepiot
Sound: Keith Wester
Costume design: Bob Ringwood
Music supervision: Jellybean Benitez
Music: Jerry Goldsmith
MPAA rating: PG-13
Running time: 112 minutes

and the Shadow are one. Gibson wrote 283 of the Shadow's 325 adventures before dying in 1985 at the age of eighty-five. Among the many actors who played the Shadow, perhaps the most famous is Orson Welles, who never was able to master the Shadow's trademark laugh. Therefore, Readick's version of the laugh continued to be used. Margo Lane, the Shadow's love interest, was first played by Agnes Moorehead—who played Kane's mother in Welles's *Citzen Kane*.

During its opening weekend, *The Shadow* averaged $7,330 per screen on more than 1,600 screens, for an opening weekend total of $12.3 million. More successful and entertaining than *Dick Tracy* (1990), less engaging than *Batman* (1989), *The Shadow* nevertheless offers an escape worthy of the investment of a summer afternoon.

—*Roberta F. Green*

REVIEWS

Chicago Tribune. July 1, 1994, Tempo section, p. 5.
Entertainment Weekly. July 8, 1994, p. 37.
The Hollywood Reporter. July 1-3, 1994, p. 5.
Los Angeles Times. July 1, 1994, p. F1.
The New York Times. July 1, 1994, p. B1.
USA Today. July 1, 1994, p. 7D.
Variety. July 1, 1994, p. 2.
The Washington Post. July 1, 1994, p. D1.

The Shawshank Redemption

"Fear can hold you prisoner. Hope can set you free"—Movie tagline

"...undeniably powerful and moving...a riveting guessing game."—*Rolling Stone*

"A mighty movie...superbly written and directed...you're likely to remember *The Shawshank Redemption* for a long, long time, and with pleasure."—*The Today Show*

"Two thumbs up!"—*Siskel & Ebert*

"Marvelous entertainment...one of the year's best films."—*Chicago Tribune*

 Box office: $16,461,051 (January 2, 1995)

The *Shawshank Redemption*, based on Stephen King's novella *Rita Hayworth and the Shawshank Redemption*, is a story of friendship between two men incarcerated at Shawshank State Prison in Maine from 1947 through the late 1960's. Andy Dufresne (Tim Robbins) is a young, mild-mannered banker incarcerated at Shawshank in 1947 for two consecutive life sentences for the murder of his wife and her lover. Andy maintains his innocence at his trial, but the evidence suggests that he is guilty. When Andy arrives at Shawshank, Red (Morgan Freeman), who narrates parts of this story, has already been there for twenty-five years.

Andy copes with his incarceration by keeping to himself. Red is the man who can get items from outside the prison, and when Andy finally finds his way to Red to ask for a small rock hammer, their friendship begins. Red later secures a week-long job for his gang and Andy, resurfacing one of the prison roofs. Red picks Andy because he feels sorry for him. For two years, Andy has been regularly victimized by another gang. Andy always fights back, but he is outnumbered, and he endures this abuse and torment because he believes he is on his own and because no one does anything to help him. Red is the first person to intervene.

One afternoon on the roof, Andy offers Captain Hadley (Clancy Brown) financial advice and assistance. Andy is rewarded by being reassigned from laundry service to the prison library, where he is made available to the prison staff—for financial consultation. Before too long, Andy is doing tax returns for the staff and laundering money for the warden. Andy is also freed from his abusers by Captain Hadley and the guards, who cripple the gang's leader (Mark Rolston) and move him to another facility.

Both Andy and Red gain something from their friend-

CREDITS

Andy Dufresne: Tim Robbins
Ellis Boyd "Red" Redding: Morgan Freeman
Warden Norton: Bob Gunton
Captain Byron Hadley: Clancy Brown
Brooks Hatlen: James Whitmore
Heywood: William Sadler
Tommy Williams: Gil Bellows
Bogs Diamond: Mark Rolston
1946 D.A: Jeffrey DeMunn
Skeet: Larry Brandenburg
Jigger: Neil Giuntoli
Floyd: Brian Libby
Snooze: David Proval
Ernie: Joseph Ragno
GuaMert: JuCiccolella
Guart Trout: Paul McCrane
Andy Dufresne's wife: Renee Blaine
Glenn Quentin: Scott Mann

Released: 1994
Production: USA Niki Marvin for Castle Rock Entertainment; released by Columbia Pictures
Direction: Frank Darabont
Screenplay: Frank Darabont; based on the novella *Rita Hayworth and the Shawshank Redemption* by Stephen King
Cinematography: Roger Deakins
Editing: RichaFrancis-Bruce
Production design: Terence Marsh
Art direction: Peter Smith
Set decoration: Michael Sierton
Casting: Deborah Aquila
Costume design: Elizabeth McBride
Music: Thomas Newman
MPAA rating: R
Running time: 142 minutes

ship. Andy gradually opens up to Red, and Andy brings strength and hope to Red and to others. Unfortunately, the scenes establishing Andy's strength of will and vision are either highly improbable or sentimental. When Andy offers to help Captain Hadley, he also asks for cold beer for the men working on the roof. This is a daring request. When the beer comes, Andy does not drink any—he has procured it for the others. Several years later, Andy broadcasts throughout the prison an aria sung by a woman in Italian. It is not hard to imagine Andy sneaking into an office upon seeing a phonograph, or to imagine Andy locking himself in the office and broadcasting the music prison-wide. It is hard, however, to imagine an entire prison population rapt at an unexpected and scratchy Mozart aria. Darabont establishes Andy's daring and humanity with these gestures. Yet he fails to convince the viewer of the beauty and power of music. For this stunt, Andy is given two weeks in the solitary confinement, "the hole."

Critics agree that Darabont exercises good restraint in this film, with the exception of a few scenes and the development of one particular character: a long-timer, the old librarian Brooks Hatlen (James Whitmore). This character is barely mentioned in King's story, but Darabont builds him up to show the devastating effect prison has on some convicts, especially those who spend a long time inside. Brooks receives his release when he is seventy-five years old and has been inside for fifty years. He panics and almost kills a man (a friend) so he can stay inside. The film follows Brooks outside, through the busy city streets, to a small apartment, a job as grocery clerk and, though it is indeed terrible to imagine, into a loneliness and fear worse than that which he suffered at Shawshank. He is weary, too arthritic to do his job without pain, and hangs himself after a short time.

 "Prison time is slow time so you do what you can to keep going. Some fellows collect stamps, others build match stick houses. Andy built a library. Now he needed a new project. Tommy was it."—Ellis Boyd "Red" Redding from *The Shawshank Redemption*

Brooks exemplifies the convicts' fear: loss of freedom and dignity. He is a broken man and the opposite of Andy, who is independent, tough, resourceful, resilient, patient, and always hopeful. Brooks also serves to add conflict to the friendship between Andy and Red. Red is growing old, and though warm and fatherly, he is beginning to resign himself to the idea of living the rest of his life in prison. Red summarizes this experience: men begin by hating prison, then they get used to it, and ultimately they come to depend on it.

Darabont otherwise illustrates well the boredom and despair of life inside without lingering on the toilsome work and solitude of any of the characters. There are scenes of Andy and Red in their cells and other parts of the prison, and of men working, talking, eating, smuggling contraband, and relaxing in the yard, but they are never too long.

Andy is entrusted with the library after Brooks' departure. He lobbies with the state to improve it and makes it something to do. After almost twenty years, a young man (Gil Bellows) arrives who has heard a confession from a convict in another prison for the double murder for which Andy is in jail. Andy makes the mistake, perhaps in desperation and enthusiasm, of telling the warden. Andy, however, is dangerous to the warden (responsible for laundering money into phantom accounts). The warden kills the young man and provokes Andy to seek his freedom and revenge.

Andy's escape is his greatest triumph of will. He escapes on a stormy night through a tunnel he has dug from his cell and through sewage pipes extending beyond the prison. The next day, he withdraws hundreds of thousands of dollars from the phantom accounts he established in various banks around town and tips the police and media to the warden's corruption. Andy escapes with the warden's money to the western coast of Mexico, and the warden shoots himself in his office as the police close in on him.

Red too learns, after the escape, that Andy had been digging for several years with his tiny rock hammer, and that he kept the tunnel in his cell covered with posters of glamorous women. Rita Hayworth was the first, and presumably she symbolizes the idea for the tunnel and when Andy started digging it. It may seem ironic for Andy to hide this symbol of freedom with images of women, for he was betrayed by his wife and is in prison for her murder. Yet he is not bitter, and he tells Red he loved his wife and feels responsible for her death, for failing to love her. These images may then symbolize Andy's hope and desire.

The film concludes with Red's release a year or so after Andy's escape and his own struggle for freedom. He takes Brooks' old apartment and job before he decides to join Andy. Andy hides a note (hinting at his whereabouts) and money for Red outside a small town in rural Maine, in the event of his release. Red must learn to dream again before he is curious enough to discover what Andy has left him. The film ends with a sweeping overhead shot of these two friends—Andy looking considerably younger—embracing on a sunny beach in Mexico.

Deborah Aquila, Darabont, and Niki Marvin collaborated in casting *The Shawshank Redemption*. They got Robbins and Freeman but had to hold auditions to fill many of the supporting roles. The film benefits from excellent performances by the entire cast. Two of the many excellent secondary players deserve special mention. New York stage actor Bob Gunton shines as the pious and corrupt warden and young stage actor Gil Bellows brings naivete, cockiness, and nervous energy to petty thief Tommy Williams.

AWARDS AND NOMINATIONS

Academy Awards Nominations 1994: Best Actor (Freeman), Best Cinematography, Best Film Editing, Best Original Score, Best Picture, Best Sound, Best Adapted Screenplay
Directors Guild of Ameria Awards Nominations 1994: Best Director (Darabont)
Golden Globe Awards Nominations 1995: Best Actor—Drama (Freeman), Best Screenplay
Screen Actors Guild Awards Nominations 1994: Best Actor (Freeman, Robbins)

Shawshank State Prison is a maximum security penitentiary in Maine. The film, however, was shot at the Ohio State Reformatory in Mansfield, Ohio, a century old facility vacant for more than three years prior to the film; demolition of the reformatory, scheduled for 1993, had to be postponed. The prison, old stone and brick and an intimidating and depressing force, was selected for its gothic appearance and the geographic likeness between the surrounding area and Maine. Production designer Terence Marsh was responsible for preparing the old facility, making repairs and designing new sets, including a cellblock and the library.

The film is rather slow-moving compared to many contemporary dramas, mostly due to its prison context and a lot of voice-over narrative. It also drags toward the end and is periodically dialogue-heavy—specifically when Andy tries to share his thoughts about the spirit with his friends, and when Red tries to summarize the more depressing realities of prison life—fantastic in plot, and sentimental in feeling. It is well acted, however, and meaningful by dealing with powerful and traumatic experiences: violence, cruelty, deprivation, suffering of different kinds, desire for freedom and dignity, strength of will and perseverance, liberation, and the complicity between convicts and prison staff. Darabont has achieved a fairly fluid and exciting film from the King novella.

—*Michael Forstrom*

REVIEWS

Chicago Tribune. September 23, 1994, II, p. 4.
Daily Variety. Spetember 9, 1994, p. 6.
Entertainment Weekly. September 23, 1994, p. 44.
The Hollywood Reporter. September 9-11, 1994, p. 10.
Los Angeles Times. September 23, 1994, p. F1.
The New York Times. September 23, 1994, p. B3.
The New Yorker. September 26, 1994, pp. 108-110.
Newsweek. September 26, 1994, p. 64.
Time. September 26, 1994, p. 78.

Shelf Life

Three siblings (O-Lan Jones, Andrea Stein, and Jim Turner) grow up alone in a bomb shelter, with television as their sole contact with the outside world for some three decades, in this comedy-drama. Director Paul Bartel also directed *Eating Raoul* (1982). According to Bartel, the Sundance Film Festival "rejected (the film), saying that 'it wasn't a Paul Bartel film.' " *Shelf Life* creators Olan Jones, Andrea Stein, and Jim Turner originally performed the tale as a stage play in Los Angeles.

REVIEWS

Boston Globe. September 13, 1993, p. 33.
Variety. CCCL, February 15, 1993, p. 83.

 "This film is unlike other films in that it does not have three distinct acts. Rather, it is comprised of a series of vignettes in which the three characters act out some of their fantasies."—*Shelf Life* director Paul Bartel.

CREDITS

Tina: O-Lan Jones
Pam: Andrea Stein
Scotty: Jim Turner
Various apparitions: Paul Bartel
Young Scotty: Justin Houchin
Young Pam: Shelby Lindley
Young Tina: Jazz Britany
Mrs. St. Cloud: Andrea Stein
Mr. St. Cloud: Jim Turner

Released: 1993
Production: Bradley Laven and Anne Kimmel; released by Shelf Life, Inc.
Direction: Paul Bartel
Screenplay: Based on materials created by O-Lan Jones, Andrea Stein, and Jim Turner
Cinematography: Phillip Holahan
Editing: Judd Maslansky
Production design: Alex Tavoularis
Art direction: Devon Meadows
Set decoration: Dawn Ferry
Sound: Pat Toma
Music: Andy Paley
MPAA rating: no listing
Running time: 83 minutes

The Silencer

A retired professional hit woman, Angelica (Lynette Walden), returns to the streets when she is hired to kill a group of criminals.

REVIEWS

Chicago Tribune. June 3, 1993, Sec. 5 p. 6.
Variety. CCCXLVII, June 8, 1992, p. 55.

CREDITS

Angelica: Lynette Walden
George: Chris Mulkey
Tony: Paul Ganus
Didi: Brook Parker

Released: 1992
Production: Brian J. Smith for Marimark; released by Crown International Pictures
Direction: Amy Goldstein
Screenplay: Scott Kraft and Amy Goldstein
Cinematography: Daniel Berkowitz
Editing: Rick Blue
Production design: John Myhre
Casting: Carol Lefko
Sound: Tony Cannella
Costume design: Pilar Limosner
Stunt coordination: Cole McKay
Music: Carole Pope and Ron Sures
MPAA rating: no listing
Running time: 84 minutes

Silent Fall

"Absorbing, intriguing, spine-chilling."—Jules Peimer, *WNWK Radio*

"A thinking person's murder mystery. Richard Dreyfuss is superb."—Scott & Barbara Siegel, *Siegel Entertainment Syndicate*

 Box Office Gross: $3,148,946 (November 27, 1994)

Richard Dreyfuss plays a psychiatrist who is called in on a double murder case when the only witness is an autistic boy (Ben Faulkner), who can mimic the voices he heard while the murders took place. Film debut for Faulkner and Tyler.

REVIEWS

Atlanta Constitution. October 28, 1994, p. P4.
Boston Globe. October 28, 1994, p. 49.
Chicago Tribune. October 28, 1994, p. 7L.
Christian Science Monitor. December 9, 1994, p. 13.
Entertainment Weekly. March 31, 1995, p. 71.
Los Angeles Times. October 28, 1994, p. F2.
The New York Times. November 5, 1993, p. C3.
The New York Times, October 28, 1994, p. C10.
USA Today. October 28, 1994, p. D4.
Variety. CCCLVII, October 31, 1994, p. 90.
The Washington Post. October 28, 1994, p. F7.
The Washington Post. October 28, 1994, p. WW44.
The Washington Post. November 3, 1994, p. D7.

CREDITS

Jake Rainer: Richard Dreyfuss
Karen Rainer: Linda Hamilton
Dr. Harlinger: John Lithgow
Sheriff Mitch Rivers: J. T. Walsh
Tim Warden: Ben Faulkner
Sylvie Warden: Liv Tyler

Released: 1994
Production: James G. Robinson for Morgan Creek; released by Warner Bros.
Direction: Bruce Beresford
Screenplay: Akiva Goldsman
Cinematography: Peter James
Editing: Ian Crafford
Production design: John Stoddart
Art direction: David Bomba
Set decoration: Patty Malone
Casting: Shari Rhodes and Joseph Middleton
Sound: Chris Newman
Costume design: Colleen Kelsall
Music: Stewart Copeland
MPAA rating: R
Running time: 100 minutes

Silent Tongue

"Some words are never spoken. Some spirits are never silenced."—Movie tagline

"Phoenix rewards Sam Shepard with a performance of unbearable poignancy...a fitting capper to an extraordinary career."—Peter Travers, *Rolling Stone*

"There's a strange, lyrical beauty to this western." —Giselle Benatar, *Mademoiselle*

*S*ilent Tongue reached New York and Los Angeles theaters in February 1994 after more than a year on the shelf awaiting distribution. Then the film was quickly pulled from the market and consigned to videotape, on which it emerged in late summer. Blockbuster's blurb on the tape sleeve spoke volumes: "Weird Western."

Looking at *Silent Tongue* in the most crass marketing light possible, one might have expected it to generate box-

CREDITS

Eamon McCree: Alan Bates
Prescott Roe: Richard Harris
Reeves McCree: Dermot Mulroney
Talbot Roe: River Phoenix
Awbonnie: Sheila Tousey
Ghost: Sheila Tousey
Velada McCree: Jeri Arredondo
Comic: Bill Irwin
Straight Man: David Shiner
Lone Man: Tim Scott
Silent Tongue: Tantoo Cardinal

Released: 1994
Production: Carolyn Pfeiffer and Ludi Boeken for Belbo Films, Alive Films, and Le Studio Canal Plus; released by Trimark Pictures
Direction: Sam Shepard
Screenplay: Sam Shepard
Cinematography: Jack Conroy
Editing: Bill Yahraus
Production design: Cary White
Art direction: John Frick and Michael Sullivan
Set decoration: Barbara Haberecht
Casting: Jennifer Shull
Sound: Susumu Tokunow
Costume design: Van Ramsey
Music: Patrick O'Hearn
MPAA rating: R
Running time: 106 minutes

office interest as River Phoenix's final motion picture. Here was the immensely talented young actor, six months after he died of a cocaine and heroin overdose at a Los Angeles nightclub, filling the screen with a haunting image—a real-life ghost playing the role of a troubled young frontiersman confronting the ghost of his dead wife. Yet despite the tabloid media frenzy surrounding Phoenix's death, no such market push emerged.

This is unfortunate, because not only is Phoenix's final completed effort well worth seeing, it is secondary to the outstanding work of Alan Bates and Richard Harris. Furthermore, the acting, fine as it is, is secondary to Shepard's reworking of the seemingly bottomless well that is the Western tableau. This is Federico Fellini drenched in trail dust. Or perhaps it is John Ford drenched in metaphor. It is certainly many things.

Prescott Roe (Harris) is a father grieving for the immeasurable sorrow of his unstable son, Talbot Roe (Phoenix). Playing his lonely craft as trader somewhere in the high plains of the 1870's, Prescott Roe is a single parent who thought he had solved his son's melancholia by trading three horses for a daughter-in-law. As the film begins, however, the half-breed bartered bride Awbonnie (Sheila Tousey) has been dead for some days or weeks. Young Talbot Roe clings to the corpse, wrapping it in blankets and surrounding it with talismans.

Awbonnie's soul needs release, by fire, coyote, or vulture, but Talbot refuses to surrender her body. One half of her face withers and one eye clouds with decay while the other half remains vital and—when Awbonnie's ghost swoops about the scrub and dust—vengeful against the irrational will of the young man who loves her so much, who took her against her will, and who now refuses her final freedom. While the ghost of Awbonnie and her maddened captor joust, Talbot's father departs to save his son's dilapidated mind the only way he knows.

Prescott Roe sits on a bluff astride a horse. Below him a traveling medicine show has found a sagebrush amphitheater in which to park its wagons and play out its minstrelsy. Clowns, comics, fire eaters, dwarfs, musicians, and a camel have assembled for the purpose of selling a tonic consisting principally of alcohol, the lubrication that allows the moving parts of proprietor Eamon McCree (Bates) to stay adrift through the West. Perhaps a dozen Indians and white settlers have materialized from nowhere to witness the spectacle. Roe has seen it before. As before, he has brought three horses, this time to purchase McCree's other daughter, Velada (Jeri Arredondo).

Two old Irishmen, then, are about to do business in his so foreign land. While the medicine-show comics do a skit and a song about ghosts, Prescott rides down the ravine in a desperate quest to exorcise a malevolent spirit who was born of the same unrightful commerce. The richly layered metaphors of native versus intruder will be taken in as many lights as there are viewers. All are substantial fare.

The alcohol-sodden and voluble huckster McCree and the laconic and lean Prescott Roe mesh like cheap satin and worn leather. Roe explains his son's desperate need, the true tonic that Awbonnie had been for young Talbot until she died, the logic of an identical trade—three horses, straight up, for Velada. McCree explains that his second daughter is essential to the show, that her horseback riding draws the crowds. He also casts a nervous eye toward his son, Reeves McCree (Dermot Mulroney), who wants no part of losing his other half sister to the trader Roe. Reeves, in fact charges at Roe and—in a curiously startling moment—is knocked to the ground. The instant stands alone to define the dangerous skill of the plainsman, hardly even a piece of action as Westerns go, but the only violence—other than that visited by the ghost of Awbonnie—by the main protagonists of this "weird" Western.

Silent Tongue is the last film appearance of River Phoenix, who died in 1993 of a cocaine and heroin overdose. The film was completed in 1992 but was not released until 1994.

Inside McCree's wagon, where the bargaining takes place, one sees artifacts of the coupling that produced Awbonnie and Velada. The grainy photos themselves are important minor characters, because only by their presence does one come to understand that Silent Tongue—the girls' Native American mother—has been anything to McCree but a target of opportunity. One learns through a flashback that McCree found her picking bones from the desert, her tongue removed as punishment for affronting a tribal chief. One sees that he raped her in the presence of his young son, and later took her as a wife. Eventually, one discerns that somehow Silent Tongue made her way back to the Kiowas, leaving McCree with their offspring.

The desperate Roe has no patience with McCree's unwillingness to barter on the spot. Roe kidnaps Velada in the dead of night and heads hell-bent into the wilderness to replace the corpse and ghost of Awbonnie with yet another elixir bride from McCree's private stock. When Velada is found missing at dawn, Reeves and Eamon McCree give chase. The son seeks to rescue a half sister; the father, with far less resolution, seeks to right a business wrong. The son's disgust for his father is strong enough to leave the old man in harm's way when their quest is interdicted by a band of Kiowa warriors.

Bates's blathering brogue as McCree recognizes the futility of their quest and, more important, as he runs out of alcohol, is itself worth the price of admission. His lines are spoken so broadly, for so big a stage, that it almost matters not that some of the dialect escapes the average ear.

Tied up and marched toward his death by the Kiowas, he prattles on bravely about Ireland and his stature as a medicine man. From a distance, on horseback, Silent Tongue watches.

Things are not so tidily resolved with the Roe family. Awbonnie finds her release, finally, at the strong hands of Prescott Roe, who overcomes his sentry son and tosses her body to the flames. The ghost Awbonnie, however, has done her work. There will be no second life for Talbot Roe with Awbonnie's sister.

As these characters move about Shepard's vast Western canvas, one twice meets a nameless character bathed in the authentic trappings that consistently add so much life to such a surreal tale. Credited as the Lone Man (Tim Scott), he is an angular soul bearing a backpack that must weigh 100 pounds and pushing a wheelbarrow that contains all his other possessions. He heads from left to right on the screen, yet he is westward ho, and the doubt and fear on his face are exceeded only by his sense of purpose and manifest destiny.

The first time the Lone Man is seen, a leaderless medicine show is passing him headed east. One of the minstrels yells across the prairie: "Where to?" The Lone Man yells back: "Land!" The minstrel replies: "You can have it! We've lost out leader!" The second time it is he who yells at the two creatures approaching him, many yards to the side, headed east. One man is older. The other is young enough to be his son, walking behind dazed, one hand on the old man's back. "Where to?" the lone man yells. The Roes, seeing probably the only human they will see that day, march dolefully onward without responding. The Lone Man picks up his wheelbarrow and continues.

This is a Western of unusual strength. The photography by Jack Conroy is superb, and even on the square video screen the sideset framing of individuals and animals against the Western panorama is compelling. One can only wonder what it looked like on the theatrical screen. Shepard may have accomplished the unenviable achievement of creating one of the finest films ever to be released into video-store limbo.

—*Tom W. Ferguson*

REVIEWS

Entertainment Weekly. August 8, 1994, p. 62.
The Hollywood Reporter. February 25-27, 1994, p. 16.
Los Angeles Times. February 25, 11994, p. F10.
The New York Times. February 25, 1994, p. B1.
Rolling Stone. February 24, 1994, p. 62.
Variety. February 4, 1993, p. 8.

The Silent Touch

A celebrated but unpleasant composer, Henry Kesdi (Max Von Sydow), lives in quiet retirement with his long-suffering wife, Helena (Sarah Miles), until a mystical young man, Stefan (Lothaire Bluteau), arrives and persuades him to complete one more work.

CREDITS

Henry Kesdi: Max Von Sydow
Stefan Bugajski: Lothaire Bluteau
Helena Kesdi: Sarah Miles
Annette Berg: Sofie Grabol
Professor Jerzy Kern: Aleksander Bardini
Joseph Kesdi: Peter Hesse Overgaard

Origin: Great Britain, Poland, and Denmark
Released: 1993
Production: Mark Forstater; released by Castle Hill Productions, Inc.
Direction: Krzysztof Zanussi
Screenplay: Peter Morgan and Mark Wadlow
Cinematography: Jaroslaw Zamojda
Editing: Marek Denys
Production design: Ewa Braun
Music: Wojciech Kilar
MPAA rating: PG-13
Running time: 92 minutes

Silent Victim

A husband (Kyle Secor) sues his wife (Michelle Greene) for murder when her attempted suicide results in the abortion of her fetus, in this drama.

REVIEWS

Variety. CCCL, March 22, 1993, p. 53.

CREDITS

Bonnie Jackson: Michelle Greene
Lauren McKinley: Ely Pouget
Jed Jackson: Kyle Secor
Carter Evans: Alex Hyde-White
C. Ray Thompson: Ralph Wilcox
Chrissy Lee: Leann Hunley
Emily: Rosemary Newcott
Hilda Pollack: Dori Brenner
Judge Tucker: Dan Biggers

Released: 1993
Production: Menahem Golan for Wells Company; released by 21st Century Film Corporation
Direction: Menahem Golan
Screenplay: Nelly Adnil and Jonathan Platnick; based on a story by Bob Spitz
Cinematography: David Max Steinberg
Editing: Bob Ducsay
Production design: Cecilia Vettraino
Casting: Kathy Smith, Dan Bernstein and Shay Griffin
Sound: David K. Neesley
Music: William T. Stromberg
MPAA rating: no listing
Running time: 104 minutes

A Simple Twist of Fate

"A twist of fate brought them something wonderful...each other."—Movie tagline

"Steve Martin is excellent as always"—*ABC-TV*

"Warm and comic"—*New York Times*

 Box Office Gross: $3,396,898 (December 4, 1994)

The life of Michael McCann (Steve Martin) seems to be inordinately subject to the whims of fate. He starts like everyman, a well-adjusted music teacher in Washington, D.C., who is excited about his pending parenthood. Suddenly, however, his life is turned upside down when his pregnant wife reveals that the baby she is carrying is not his.

It is a blow with which McCann seems unable to cope, so he runs away. He rents a small house in rural Virginia, where he abandons humans in favor of the solitary occupation of making furniture. He becomes the town recluse, whose only friend is the local antique store owner, Mrs. Simon (Catherine O'Hara), who sells him the one thing he takes any joy in—gold coins.

Hidden in a secret drawer with a false bottom, the coins are pulled out, counted, examined, and lovingly replaced each night by McCann. Unlike the wife and the child he thought were his forever, McCann believes the gold will always be there for him. He has not, however, reckoned with Tanny (Stephen Baldwin), the sleazy younger brother of the local landed gentry, John Newland (Gabriel Byrne). Tanny is tired of being controlled by his brother, who has political aspirations and does everything possible to keep the family name as pristine as possible.

Tanny is a drinker and a womanizer, and the family name would seem prone to a bit of dirtying. Then, after an automobile accident kills Tanny's current girlfriend and puts the Newland family in a compromising position, the younger brother remembers rumors about McCann's gold. To escape from his guilt and his brother, Tanny steals McCann's precious collection and runs away.

Once again McCann has been "robbed" of the focus of his life. Not long afterward, however, the distraught loner finds that a young woman (Amelia Campbell) has frozen to death in his front yard and her little girl (Victoria and Elizabeth Evans) has wandered into his house. No one seems to know who the woman is or who the father of the girl is. Yet someone does. John Newland is the father, but since his political career is just starting to ascend, he can not afford to associate himself with the drug-addicted mother or her baby, whom the doctor declares to be "damaged goods."

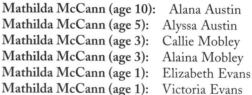

CREDITS

Michael McCann: Steve Martin
John Newland: Gabriel Byrne
Nancy Newland: Laura Linney
Mrs. Simon: Catherine O'Hara
Mathilda McCann (age 10): Alana Austin
Mathilda McCann (age 5): Alyssa Austin
Mathilda McCann (age 3): Callie Mobley
Mathilda McCann (age 3): Alaina Mobley
Mathilda McCann (age 1): Elizabeth Evans
Mathilda McCann (age 1): Victoria Evans
Tanny Newland: Stephen Baldwin
Keating: Byron Jennings
Bryce: Michael des Barres
Rob: Tim Ware
Joe the bartender: David Dwyer
Dad the cop: Tom Even
Judge Marcus: Ed Grady
Marsha Swanson: Amelia Campbell
Dr. Roberts: Danny Nelson

Released: 1994
Production: Ric Kidney for Touchstone Pictures; released by Buena Vista Pictures
Direction: Gillies MacKinnon
Screenplay: Steve Martin; suggested by the novel *Silas Marner*, by George Eliot
Cinematography: Andrew Dunn
Editing: Humphrey Dixon
Production design: Andy Harris
Art direction: Tim Galvin
Set decoration: Maria Nay
Executive producer: Steve Martin
Costume design: Hope Hanafin
Music: Cliff Eidelman
Casting: Dianne Crittenden
MPAA rating: PG-13
Running time: 106 minutes

McCann, who in a way is also "damaged goods," however, feels an immediate kinship with the baby. Grasping at anything to give his life meaning, he believes she has come into his life to replace the gold he has lost. Against all odds (and probably with a little behind the scenes string-pulling by Newland), McCann manages to adopt the baby whom he names Mathilda. With a few practical pointers from Mrs. Simon, McCann becomes a loving and doting father as Mathilda grows under his creative parenting.

In the meantime, Newland has been elected to the

House of Representatives, has gotten married, and his wife (Laura Linney) has lost several babies during pregnancy. It would appear that they are destined to be childless, but every time Newland sees Mathilda, he is reminded of what he could have had. Eventually, Newland and his wife take Mathilda under their wing by offering to give her riding lessons and even buying a horse for her. As Mathilda grows accustomed to the life of the rich and famous, the Newlands grow accustomed to having a child around. When John confesses to his wife the secret of his paternity, they decide to take the matter to court. Because of the Newland's standing in the community, their family connections, and their wealth, they feel assured that their claim will take legal precedence over the years of fathering Michael has given Mathilda.

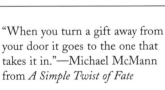

Several sets of twins played the role of Mathilda in *A Simple Twist of Fate*. It is the first film to be shot in America for director Gillies MacKinnon.

During the trial, emotions run in Michael's favor, but the legal system, as expected, sees the child's welfare just in terms of what money can buy (that is an exclusive education). As the judge is about to deliver his opinion in the Newland's favor, Mrs. Simon's son runs into the courtroom with news. The judge adjourns the court and everyone travels to the quarry, which is being drained for an exclusive Newland housing subdivision. There they find Tanny's skeleton and next to it are all Michael's stolen gold coins. Now, because Michael has money just as the Newlands' do, the judge can tip the scales in McCann's favor.

Steve Martin borrowed the story's premise from George Eliot's *Silas Marner* (1861). The story of an eighteenth century recluse, miser, and weaver who adopts a little girl, Eppie, who is really the local squire's daughter. It is a moving and believable story—in the eighteenth century (even Eliot set the story prior to her own nineteenth century birth). Trying to modernize this pre-Victorian English tale of the redemptive power of love into twentieth century America proves to be a difficult reach.

Adapting classic stories to modern settings is not new to *A Simple Twist of Fate*'s writer, executive producer, and leading man, Steve Martin. In 1987's *Roxanne* he did a superb job of updating *Cyrano de Bergerac* (1897). That story, however, and especially the character that resulted from adapting it spotlighted Martin's acting strengths: his comic timing, his onscreen energy, his ability to convey emotion, his intellectual acuteness—all of which worked to create a believable and updated Cyrano. His adaptation of Silas Marner as a character, however, seems to revel more in self-pity and maudlin sentiment than in high-spiritedness and modern relevance.

This is not to say that the film is bad. Its wistful, old-fashioned feeling does evoke a longing for times gone by, and even though its plot creaks along, there is still enough of the moral power of Eliot's book to provide appealing characters, although they do not always react in a twentieth century manner.

A large part of the attraction of the characters in this gentle story is the result of the main actors. When Martin wants to, he can bring the potency of intelligence to any character he plays—even when he is acting the "wild and crazy guy" who can make us laugh at his physical comedy or writing about his all-too-human characters. In this film, he is at his best when interacting with Alaina and Alyssa Austin, who do an excellent job of playing Mathilda at the ages of five and ten.

Gabriel Byrne's John Newland is solemn and brooding but still human, even if he puts his own interests above everyone else's. He presents a seductive and charming exterior to the world, but inside he is less attractive. Byrne is good at communicating all these facets of his character, even if his Irish tongue does have trouble wrapping itself around Southern vowels.

Helping to keep the story afloat both in believability and spirit is Catherine O'Hara's Mrs. Simon. She is both funny and sympathetic. She can tell McCann the secrets of rearing a baby, sell him a weather balloon as a toy, and find anything she wants on her computer. O'Hara, one of the stand-out talents from the classic "SCTV" television show, is often the hidden gem of any film in which she appears and is much too underused by the entertainment industry.

A Simple Twist of Fate is also helped by its looks. Visually, it has the patina of a favorite old fairy tale. From the rolling Virginia countryside (the picture was really filmed in Georgia) to the dark and overgrown greenhouse that brightens and blossoms just as McCann does with Mathilda's love, the film is rich in physical details and lush colors.

"When you turn a gift away from your door it goes to the one that takes it in."—Michael McMann from *A Simple Twist of Fate*

There are, however, two real problems with *A Simple Twist of Fate*. One is that it cannot decide if it is a gentle comedy or a heart-tugging drama and consequently does both, neither of them very well. Each time the humor really gets rolling, the dramatic plot stops it mid-laugh. On the other hand, the dramatic tension of the story often finds itself upstaged by the humor. So, the viewer is left to somehow reconcile suspenseful or emotional moments with those of out-and-out slapstick.

The other major complaint is that the resolution involving a courtroom drama seems contrived. It offers too neat a resolution to a problem that may have been simple in the time of the original story but is much more complicated in light of America's twentieth century legal system. This scene further misfires when yet one more not-so-simple "twist of fate" prevents the judge from delivering his verdict.

The film is obviously a labor of love for Martin, who was given a special tribute at the 1994 Montreal Film Festival, where the film premiered. While it may have problems, *A Simple Twist of Fate* does succeed in providing something unusual: a family film with heart, intelligence, and virtually no animals. It may seem to be archaic, contrived, and burdened with a split personality, but it still manages to be sensitive and compelling in its own quiet way. At

the very least, it could prove to be a painless way to expose another generation to Eliot's sturdy story.

—*Beverley Bare Buehrer*

REVIEWS

Chicago Tribune. September 2, 1994, p. 7C.
Entertainment Weekly. September 16, 1994, p. 92.
Hollywood Reporter. August 29, 1994, p. 5.
Los Angeles Times. September 2, 1994, p. F1.
The New York Times. September 2, 1994, p. B1.
USA Today. September 2, 1994, p. 4D.
Variety. September 5-11, 1994, p. 53.
Village Voice. September 13, 1994, p. 66.

Sioux City

"The truth was buried with his mother. Revenge was his only choice."—Movie tagline

A Lakota Indian who was reared by a Jewish couple in Beverly Hills, Jesse Rainfeather Goldman (Lou Diamond Phillips), travels to a Sioux City reservation to locate his estranged mother who gave him up for adoption at a young age. Upon arrival, Jesse discovers that his mother has been murdered, and he decides to investigate—at his own peril. The film's budget was under $2 million; it was shot in less than 20 days.

REVIEWS

Boston Globe. September 13, 1994, p. 65.
Entertainment Weekly. December 2, 1994, p. 88.
Los Angeles Times. September 16, 1994, p. F12.

CREDITS

Jesse Rainfeather Goldman: Lou Diamond Phillips
Chief Drew McDermott: Ralph Waite
Leah Goldman: Melinda Dillon
Jolene: Salli Richardson
Blake Goldman: Adam Roarke
Dan Larkin: Bill Allen
Russell Baker: Gary Farmer
Clifford: Apesanahkwat
Allison: Lise Cutter

Released: 1994
Production: Brian Rix and Jane Ubell for Cabin Fever Films, in association with Facet Films, Inc.; released by I.R.S. Releasing
Direction: Lou Diamond Phillips
Screenplay: L. Virginia Browne
Cinematography: James W. Wrenn
Editing: Christopher Rouse and Mark Fitzgerald
Production design: Rando Schmook
Casting: Melissa Skoff
Sound: Geoffrey Lucius Patterson
Music: Christopher Lindsey
MPAA rating: PG-13
Running time: 100 minutes

Sirens

"In a magical place, a controversial artist and his models will show a young couple that they have nothing to lose but their inhibitions."—Movie tagline

"Two Thumbs Up!"—*Siskel & Ebert*

"Four stars! One of the most erotic movies of the year."—Bruce Williamson, *Playboy*

 Box Office Gross: $7,766,473 (August 21, 1994)

I n Greek mythology, the Sirens were seductive nymphs whose sweet songs led sailors to shipwreck on rocky shoals. In John Duigan's *Sirens*, an Australian artists' naughty models sing ditties to an uptight British cleric and his prim wife.

Trouble is, their song is as thin and silly as Musak. *Sirens* is a transparent set-up to get Hugh Grant a star vehicle and model Elle MacPherson a lot of undraped camera time. Dressed up as a light comedy with artistic and philosophical pretensions, this film is really very soft, insipid pornography—unthreatening, unsubstantial and not really very seductive despite all its flesh.

Grant diffidently plays Anglican priest Anthony Campion, sent to the Australian outback to confront libertine painter Norman Lindsay. Lindsay was a real-life artist who stirred up controversy in the 1930's with his paintings of nudes. But this is not a biography; it's mostly frothy and overwrought fiction.

Campion is supposedly sent to persuade Lindsay (Sam Neill) to drop his most offensive works from an upcoming exhibition in London. It's a hopeless task, as Lindsay has nothing but contempt for the religious scruples of Campion.

All the two male leads get out of this thin plot are a few hurried verbal battles. The device evaporates completely when the exhibit's organizers vote to include all of Lindsay's paintings. You might miss that resolution; Grant mentions it almost as an aside. By the time he does, the ostensible reason for the Campions' visit has been smothered in fleshy mush. It is clear Duigan has prurient purposes that overshadow the plot.

The Campions' overnight stay is prolonged a few days by the flimsiest of script devices—a train derailment. That allows plenty of time for the Campions to wilt in the hothouse atmosphere of the Lindsay commune. There reside, in

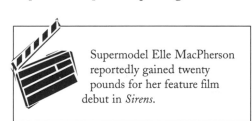 Supermodel Elle MacPherson reportedly gained twenty pounds for her feature film debut in *Sirens*.

Sam Neil as Norman Lindsay and Hugh Grant as Anthony Campion in *Sirens*. Copyright © Miramax Films.

accommodations not clearly delineated, Lindsay's wife Rose (Pamela Rabe), two tykes, three buxom models (MacPherson, Kate Fischer and Portia de Rossi), and a half-blind hunk (Mark Gerber) who does odd jobs and nude modeling.

What transpires is a tamer version of a *Playboy* layout. The reverend and wife constantly stumble on nude modeling sessions, skinnydipping at the swimming hole, or the handyman hunk doing some nude sunbathing. When she's not bare-bosomed, MacPherson is always eating something and licking her fingers. There are ridiculous scenes of the models tickling and caressing one another, such dalliance with hints of lesbianism being a standard staple of the strained male imagination. We even get a glimpse of a strip-poker game. It's the sort of stuff you might find on late-night pay-for-view TV.

This fare might excite the adolescent male viewer, but there is little of the genuinely erotic or dangerous that would hold the interest of a mature adult. Grant's cleric is never implicated, just continually shocked, allowing Grant to do his customary schtick as the repressed Brit on the edge of a sexual meltdown.

The focus is on the sexual awakening of his wife, Estella (Tara Fitzgerald). As in many such soft-core fantasies, it is the repressed wife who is gradually unbuttoned and turned into the filmmakers' image of women as naturalistic sex kittens. Fitzgerald, the most accomplished and provocative of the actresses, does the best she can with this jaded material.

CREDITS

Reverend Anthony Campion: Hugh Grant
Estella Campion: Tara Fitzgerald
Norman Lindsay: Sam Neill
Sheela: Elle MacPherson
Giddy: Portia de Rossi
Prue: Kate Fischer
Rose Lindsay: Pamela Rabe
Lewis: Ben Mendelsohn
Tom: John Polson
Devlin: Mark Gerber
Jane: Julia Stone
Honey: Ellie MacCarthy
Bishop of Sydney: Vincent Ball

Origin: Australia and Great Britain
Released: 1994
Production: Sue Milliken for WMG, with the participation of British Screen; released by Miramax Films
Direction: John Duigan
Screenplay: John Duigan
Cinematography: Geoff Burton
Editing: Humphrey Dixon
Production design: Roger Ford
Art direction: Laurie Faen
Set decoration: Kerrie Brown
Casting: Liz Mullinar
Sound: David Lee
Costume design: Terry Ryan
Music: Rachel Portman
MPAA rating: R
Running time: 94 minutes

She strains mightily to give some shadings to a character that could have been a caricature, as most of the others in the film are.

Duigan is a master of the leering style of filmmaking, but *Sirens* is more boring than titillating. Duigan doesn't understand that nudity doesn't equal eroticism, that more sexual tension can emanate from a raised eyebrow amidst a heated plot than an undraped bosom in a lifeless tableau.

Sirens is a startlingly old-fashioned film. It could have been made in the 1960s. Its pitched battle between sexual repression and artistic freedom long ago was resolved, yet Duigan is still carrying the torch, a sort of Hugh Hefner of the cinema whom time has passed by.

Duigan's previous *Wide Sargasso Sea* (1992) indulged in the same mix of pseudo-mysticism and egregious nudity. In *Sirens*, repeated shots of slithering snakes and primitive Australian wildlife are supposed to evoke a Garden of Eden mentality, and the models are frequently clothed in angelic garb. This is all so much art film pretense, designed to give a window dressing of weightiness to Duigan's glorified peep show.

Apart from the intriguing Fitzgerald, the acting is perfunctory. Neill is underused, conveying only Lindsay's sanctimoniousness and little of his reputation for danger. Grant appears to be sleepwalking through a performance that he has down pat—the stuffed shirt constantly on the verge of a nervous breakdown. MacPherson, who reportedly put on 20 pounds for her feature film debut, is as voluptuous as she is supposed to be and more wry than you might expect. The others are merely adequate.

The cinematography by Geoff Burton is lush but largely wasted. *Sirens* is a come-on that is only a little more entrancing and revealing than a magazine swimsuit layout.

—*Michael Betzold*

REVIEWS

Atlanta Constitution. March 11, 1994, p. P3.
Boston Globe. March 11, 1994, p. 68.
Chicago Tribune. March 11, 1994, p. 7C.
Christian Science Monitor. April 8, 1994, p. 17.
Entertainment Weekly. April 22, 1994, p. 39.
Entertainment Weekly. October 14, 1994, p. 71.
The Hollywood Reporter. March 9, 1994, p. 14.
Los Angeles Magazine. XXXIX, March 1994, p. 114.
Los Angeles Times. March 9, 1994, p. F7.
Maclean's. CVII, March 21, 1994, p. 60.
National Review. XLVI, May 16, 1994, p. 71.
The New Republic. CCX, April 4, 1994, p. 25.
The New York Times. March 4, 1994, p. C16.
People Weekly XLI, April 11, 1994, p. 19.
Playboy. XLI, May 1994, p. 20.
Variety. CCCLIII, January 24, 1994, p. 64.
Variety. March 8, 1994, p. 40.
The Washington Post. March 11, 1994, p. G1.

Sleep With Me

"Very sexy, very realistic...funny, poignant and slick."—*WOR Radio Network*

"A captivating sexual and psychological roundelay"—*The Hollywood Reporter*

 Box Office Gross: $137,912 (September 9, 1994)

When Sarah (Meg Tilly) and Joseph (Eric Stoltz) decide to get married, their best friend Frank (Craig Sheffer) realizes that he also is in love with Sarah and actively pursues her over the course of six social gatherings. Made for $3 million dollars, the film was written by six screenwriters who were assigned to write a separate segment. Feature-film directorial debut of Rory Kelly. Cameo by Quentin Tarantino as a guest at a party giving a speech about homoeroticism in *Top Gun*.

REVIEWS

Atlanta Constitution. February 10, 1995, p. P3.
Boston Globe. September 12, 1994, p. 40.
Boston Globe. September 30, 1994, p. 65.
Chicago Tribune. September 30, 1994, p. 7J.
Cosmopolitan. CCXVII, October 1994, p. 30.
Entertainment Weekly. October 7, 1994, p. 55.
Los Angeles Times. September 23, 1994, p. F2.
Maclean's. CVII, October 3, 1994, p. 56.
Variety. CCCLV, May 30, 1994, p. 44.

 "I'm trying to tell your wife I'm in love with her."—Frank from *Sleep With Me*

CREDITS

Joseph:	Eric Stoltz
Sarah:	Meg Tilly
Frank:	Craig Sheffer
Duane:	Todd Field
Deborah:	Susan Traylor
Leo:	Dean Cameron
Nigel:	Thomas Gibson
Rory:	Tegan West
Amy:	Amaryllis Borrego
Athena:	Parker Posey
Lauren:	Joey Lauren Adams
Marianne:	Vanessa Angel
Pamela:	Adrienne Shelly
Sid:	Quentin Tarantino
Caroline:	June Lockhart
Josh:	David Kriegel
Minister:	Lewis Arquette

Released: 1994
Production: Michael Steinberg, Roger Hedden, and Eric Stoltz for August Entertainment, in association with Paribas Film Corporation, Revolution Films, and Joel Castleberg
Production: Released by Metro-Goldwyn-Mayer/United Artists
Direction: Rory Kelly
Screenplay: Duane Dell'Amico, Roger Hedden, Neal Jimenez, Joe Keenan, Rory Kelly, and Michael Steinberg
Cinematography: Andrzej Sekula
Editing: David Moritz
Production design: Randy Eriksen
Art direction: J. Michael Gorman
Set decoration: Adam Mead Faletti
Casting: Ellie Kanner
Sound: Giovanni Di Simone
Costume design: Isis Mussenden
Music: David Lawrence
MPAA rating: R
Running time: 86 minutes

The Slingshot (Kadisbellan)

"A gem."—Jack Mathews, *New York Newsday*

"Mesmerizing and deeply absorbing."—Jeffrey Lyons, *Sneak Previews/Lyons Den Radio*

"Reminiscent of *My Life as a Dog* and *Europa, Europa*. A spellbinding 10. It's an incredible, life-affirming film about courage and the power of the human spirit."—Susan Granger, *CRN & AMC*

"Refreshingly tart."—Julie Salamon, *Wall Street Journal*

"Funny and touching. *The Slingshot* hits the bull's-eye dead on."—*The San Francisco Examiner*

 Box Office Gross: $249,262 (August 21, 1994)

 This autobiographical tale centers on a ten-year-old boy, Roland Schutt (Jesper Salen), growing up among a loving family in 1920's Sweden. 🎞️

REVIEWS

Atlanta Constitution. August 12, 1994, p. P3.
Boston Globe. June 10, 1994, p. 55.
Chicago Tribune. July 22, 1994, p. 7J.
Los Angeles Times. July 8, 1994, p. F18.
The New York Times. June 3, 1994, p. C19.
Playboy. XLI, July 1994, p. 22.
The Wall Street Journal. June 2, 1994, p. A12.
The Washington Post. July 15, 1994, p. B6.

CREDITS

Roland Schutt: Jesper Salen
Fritlof Schutt: Stellan Skarsgard
Zipa Schutt: Basia Frydman
Bertil Schutt: Niclas Olund

Origin: Sweden
Released: 1993
Production: Waldemar Bergendahl for Svensk Filmindustri, Svt Kanal 1 Drama, Nordisk Film A/S, and Svenska Film Institute; released by Sony Pictures Classics
Direction: Ake Sandgren
Screenplay: Ake Sandgren; based on the novel by Roland Schutt
Cinematography: Goran Nilsson
Editing: Grete Moldrup
Production design: Lasse Westfelt
Art direction: Lasse Westfelt
Costume design: Inger Pehrsson
Music: Bjorn Isfalt
MPAA rating: R
Running time: 102 minutes

AWARDS AND NOMINATIONS

Swedish Academy Awards: Best Picture

Smoke

This episodic drama centers on a lonely and isolated middle-aged homosexual man, Michael (Mark D'Auria), who is repeatedly rebuffed in his sexual pursuits.

CREDITS

Michael: Mark D'Auria
No character identified: Nick Discenza
No character identified: Tom Dorsey
No character identified: Maryjane Chalaire
No character identified: Barbara Andrews
No character identified: David Philips
No character identified: Jeffrey D'Auria
No character identified: Joe Colaccio
No character identified: Tom Lee Sinclaire
No character identified: David Interrante
No character identified: Agostin Szabo

Released: 1993
Production: Mark D'Auria
Direction: Mark D'Auria
Screenplay: Mark D'Auria
Cinematography: Teodoro Maniaci
Editing: Mark D'Auria
Music: Arnie Bieber
MPAA rating: no listing
Running time: 90 minutes

Something to Do with the Wall

Married documentary filmmakers Ross McElwee and Marilyn Levine traveled to Berlin in 1986 to document the twenty-fifth anniversary of the Berlin wall and later returned in 1989 to capture its historic dismantling.

REVIEWS

Variety. CCCXLII, March 11, 1991, p. 63.

CREDITS

Ross McElwee: Ross McElwee
John Runnings: John Runnings

Released: 1991
Production: Marilyn Levine and Ross McElwee; released by First Run Features
Direction: Marilyn Levine and Ross McElwee
Screenplay: Marilyn Levine and Ross McElwee
Cinematography: Marilyn Levine and Ross McElwee
Editing: Marilyn Levine and Ross McElwee
MPAA rating: no listing
Running time: 88 minutes

Something Within Me

This award-winning documentary sings the praises of a pioneering arts school located in the South Bronx.

REVIEWS

Los Angeles Times. January 9, 1995, p. F5.
The New York Times. May 28, 1993, p. C15.
Variety. CCCL, March 1, 1993, p. 57.

AWARDS AND NOMINATIONS

Sundance Film Festival: Audience Award, Filmmakers Trophy, Special Jury Award

CREDITS

Released: 1993
Production: Jerret Engle; released by Panorama Entertainment Corporation
Direction: Emma Joan Morris
Cinematography: Juan Cristobal Cobo
Editing: Jean Tsien
MPAA rating: no listing
Running time: 54 minutes

Son of Darkness: To Die For II

Vampire Vlad Tepish returns in this sequel, now going by the name of Dr. Max Schreck (Michael Praed). Schreck examines an adopted baby only to discover not only that the child is a half-vampire but also that he himself is the father. Sequel to *To Die For* (1989).

REVIEWS

Variety. CCCXLIII, May 6, 1991, p. 336.

CREDITS

Nina: Rosalind Allen
Tom: Steve Bond
Martin: Scott Jacoby
Max Schreck (Vlad Tepish): Michael Praed
Danny: Jay Underwood
Celia: Amanda Wyss
Jane: Remy O'Neill

Released: 1991
Production: Richard Weinman for Greg H. Sims and Arrowhead Entertainment/Lee Caplin; released by Trimark Pictures
Direction: David F. Price
Screenplay: Leslie King
Cinematography: Gerry Lively
Editing: Barry Zetlin
Special effects: John Buechler
Sound: Rick Waddel
Music: Mark McKenzie and Cliff Eidelman
MPAA rating: no listing
Running time: 96 minutes

Spanking the Monkey

"Very funny...an unexpected crowd-pleaser! The sort of astonishingly fresh and self-assuring work that can make a reputation. *Spanking the Monkey* is ultimately a triumph of freedom."—Caryn James, *The New York Times*

"Outrageous...Russell's accomplishment is to mesmerize us and make us laugh..."—David Ansen, *Newsweek*

"Shockingly funny!"—Peter Travers, *Rolling Stone*

 Box Office Gross: $1,225,250 (September 9, 1994)

Part *Portnoy's Complaint* (1972), part *Oedipus Rex*, *Spanking the Monkey* could be described as a black comedy with melodramatic overtones. A highly successful entrant into the 1994 Sundance Film Festival, this independent film by first-time director/writer David O. Russell achieved great critical acclaim. Without being particularly humorous, this tale of a young man's painful relationship with his parents is darkly funny at times simply because of the extremity of its characters' behavior. Some will find

CREDITS

Raymond Aibelli: Jeremy Davies
Susan Aibelli: Alberta Watson
Tom Aibelli: Benjamin Hendrickson
Toni Peck: Carla Gallo
Nicky: Matthew Puckett
Aunt Helen: Judette Jones

Released: 1994
Production: Dean Silvers for Buckeye Communications; released by Fine Line Features
Direction: David O. Russell
Screenplay: David O. Russell
Cinematography: Michael Mayers
Editing: Pamela Martin
Production design: Susan Block
Casting: Ellen Parks
Sound: William Tzouris
Costume design: Carolyn Greco
Music: Mark Sandman
MPAA rating: no listing
Running time: 98 minutes

humor in the protagonist's quest to extricate himself from his despicable parents; some will squirm at the very realistic portrayal of incest; and virtually everyone will identify with a young man's frustration and confusion. Though the film is billed as a comedy, audiences should be aware that it is a comedy in the same vain as much of the work of playwright Anton Chekhov: it deals with characters in extreme situations who are powerless to change their situation, and finds absurdity in the simplest of human quests. The comedy is not the kind where audiences laugh out loud; it is the kind where they nod and chuckle, a bit embarrassed that they are laughing at the foibles of the main characters.

The simple human quest at the center of this film is the desire of nineteen-year-old Ray (Jeremy Davies) to escape the lunacy of his parents' home. Specifically, one of the ways Ray initially tries to escape is through masturbation (called "spanking the monkey" in the vernacular), and the film's few lightly humorous situations come when Ray closes the door to the bathroom, begins to masturbate, and is interrupted by his dog, Frank.

In fact, the film is actually about interruptions of all kinds. First Ray is interrupted in his attempt to accept an internship at the prestigious Surgeon General's office in Washington, D.C. when he has to come home to take care of his clinically depressed mother who has broken her leg. Then he discovers that his father (Benjamin Hendrickson) won't pay for next year's college tuition, nearly dashing Ray's hopes of becoming a physician. Another interruption comes when the girl he starts seeing, Toni (Carla Gallo) stops his sexual advances and nearly accuses him of date rape. Sexual encounters with his sexy mother (Alberta Watson) are similarly interrupted, as are his attempts at suicide.

Interruptions are part of his mother's life, too. She informs Ray that she stopped medical school in order to give birth to him, because it was "part of the deal" between her and Ray's tyrannical father. In addition, Ray's parents' relationship is constantly interrupted by his father's business trips, which prove to be more than just business.

Nothing much has any real follow-through for Ray; not his job, family, or love life, not even his attempts at masturbation. His friendships seem half-hearted as well: In one scene he spends time with his former buddies from high-school only to discover that they haven't changed, so that evening gets aborted, too. The only thing that seems to actually happen is the first sexual encounter with his lonely and disturbed mother. Perhaps there is symbolism in the sad fact that the only thing that actually "works" (albeit briefly) is something as destructive as incest with his mother.

Writer-Director David O. Russell maintains a quiet and leisurely pace which belies the inexorable tragic climax to which the characters are headed. Using a minimal musical score (mostly dulcimer and other string music by David Carbonara) and virtually no underscoring under the tense scenes between Ray and his mother, Russell creates an edgy, moody, almost eerie silence between and around the characters

Russell's screenplay and direction are evocative of Sophocles' *Oedipus* plays in more than just passing ways. As the film opens, Ray is taking his father to the airport, and when they arrive, his father begins an absurd tirade about how Ray should walk the dog but not tell the mother he is walking the dog. The absurdity of the father's speech, happening as it does while they are traveling, is reminiscent of Oedipus' solving of the Sphinx' riddle, which happens on a road where he meets some "travelers", and which leads him back to his birthplace and into a sexual relationship with his mother. Another image evocative of the *Oedipus* plays is in Toni's eye injury, which (for those who want to stretch the *Oedipus* metaphor) is a twist on Oedipus' blinding himself. Finally, Ray's abdication of his future at the end, and the fact that he hides in the forest after trying to kill himself, seem more than coincidentally similar to Oedipus' self-exile into the forest.

That aside, this film does not need to be evocative of the *Oedipus* plays to have depth and resonance. Russell and his fine company of actors create a sense of isolation and alienation that is palpable and painful. Ray's relationship with his uncaring parents and his lack of connection with virtually everyone is a very real evocation of the kind of alienation felt by many people (and not just young people) today. Purveyors of "family values" might say that it is the lack of parental attachment and attention that would cause Ray's pain. But this film shows estrangement at every level: When Ray's mom goes to the doctor's office, she and another patient never connect eyes as they speak to each other while reading; when Aunt Helen comes to take care of Ray's mom, there is absolutely no form of affection or connection between them, just as there is no connection between Ray's parents. For her part, Aunt Helen says that she is taking care of Ray's mom because "it's a matter of family," but she has no idea who her sister-in-law really is.

Simplicity seems fundamental to Russell and his actors, and it pays off handsomely. Russell creates shots that are interesting but never overly fancy: his continuous return to Ray's hands making yet another vodka tonic for his mother have a cumulative effect on the audience—without special effects or elaborate technique. His willingness to allow the action to take place without an overabundance of close-ups and intercutting underscores the tension between the characters and builds anxiety in an audience most likely used to shorter camera shots.

The villains of the piece are clearly the parents, but somehow their attempts at control over Ray, while horrible, seem to come from their powerlessness—which tends to make them look like unwitting villains rather than people bent on their son's destruction. They are just as unhappy as Ray is: the mother is on Prozac and has just broken her leg. Lying around with the television constantly turned to medical programming, she is clearly a miserable creature who selfishly wants her needs met, without regard to the potentially disastrous consequences. Watson plays her with a mixture of sexuality and childishness; at times her motivations seem to be purely manipulative and at times she seems to be the victim of her own decision to long ago let someone else run her life.

As her husband, Hendrickson is pushy and despotic, about to explode any moment into rage, and certain that he is the only person who knows how to do things right. When he tells Ray that "you only think of yourself" his self-righteousness fills the screen. The monstrousness of these two parents is in the reality of both actors' performances.

As Ray, Davies starts out to be a befuddled young man clearly uncomfortable about being around his mother, and turns into a desperately unhappy soul. When Ray makes his final escape, dirty from a night in the forest and desperate for some sort of understanding, Davies makes a credible case for why children from apparently "normal" homes become runaways. The scenes in which Davies and Watson have their sexual encounters are quiet and still, and Davies' disbelief that he is touching his mother in this way is perfect. Davies takes Ray into his descent incrementally, never trying too hard to show the pain just underneath Rays surface, and always working at a level of frustration and anxiety that contributes to the edginess of the film.

In the nineties, it seems sadly appropriate that a contemporary version of *The Summer of '42* (1971) is about frustration and incest instead of romance. For those who are squeamish about the concept of incest (even though there is virtually nothing graphically depicted) this film will be hard to take. But for others, it is a rewarding exercise in independent filmmaking, an exceptionally well-acted and directed piece about coming-of-age in an era where noth-

AWARDS AND NOMINATIONS

Independent Spirit Awards 1995: Best First Feature *Nominations:* Best Debut Performance (Davies), Best Supporting Actress (Gallo) **Sundance Film Festival Awards 1994:** Audience Award

ing is easy. Where *Portnoy's Complaint* caused quite a furor when released because of its masturbation scene, this film's allusions to masturbation are actually the easiest spots to take in a story that is sadly evocative of the current sense of alienation felt by everyone. Times have changed. Portnoy didn't know how good he had it.

—*Kirby Tepper*

The Specialist

"The government taught him to kill. Now, he's using his skills to help one woman seek revenge against the Miami underworld."—Movie tagline

"a high explosive picture that delivers...is loaded with star power"—Jeff Craig, *Sixty Second Preview*

"James Woods blasts through the screen with his trademark intensity"—*Cincinnati Post*

"Enormously Entertaining"*The New York Post*

 Box Office Gross: $57.8 million (February 9, 1995)

The *Specialist* packages a big budget, a resourceful special-effects crew, the talents of three popular stars, and a script that offers some surprises. Action-adventure films can sometimes blunder by relying too much on special effects and too little on dramatic elements. *The Specialist* features some exciting special-effects sequences; however, it conforms to the formula of the adventure film most shrewdly by not taking itself too seriously.

A pre-credit sequence explains the background of a feud between demolition experts Ray Quick (Sylvester Stallone) and Ned Trent (James Woods). In Bogota in 1984, Ray and Ned worked as CIA operatives assigned to kill a drug lord. Ray places a bomb on a bridge over which their target's car will soon pass and then yields to Ned, the triggerman. When Ray spots a child in the approaching car, however, he insists that Ned abort their plan. Ned angrily refuses. Ray runs to the bridge to defuse the charge at the last minute and is barely able to leap from the bridge before the explosion destroys the passengers in the car. The action then switches to present-day Miami, after Ray and Ned have both been dismissed from government service. Ned now works for the León crime family, whose operations he has modernized. Ray has been recently contacted by May Munro (Sharon Stone), whose parents were killed years earlier by the León family. May insists that Ray's technical

CREDITS

Ray Quick: Sylvester Stallone
May Munro: Sharon Stone
Ned Trent: James Woods
Joe León: Rod Steiger
Tomás León: Eric Roberts

Released: 1994
Production: Jerry Weintraub; released by Warner Bros.
Direction: Luis Llosa
Screenplay: Alexandra Seros; suggested by *The Specialist* novels by John Shirley
Cinematography: Jeffrey L. Kimball
Editing: Jack Hofstra
Production design: Walter P. Martishius
Art direction: Alan Muraoka
Set decoration: Scott Jacobson
Casting: Jackie Burch
Special effects: Clay Pinney
Sound: Andy Wiskes
Costume design: Judianna Makovsky
Stunt coordination: Allan Graf
Music: John Barry
MPAA rating: R
Running time: 109 minutes

skills make him the only person able to penetrate the family's security and fulfill her plans for revenge.

The subsequent exposition is presented economically through voice-over narration and dialogue. Ray Quick and May Munro communicate only by telephone in conversations that Ray has recorded on microcassettes. In the opening scenes, he follows May to a cemetery and observes her decorating her parents' grave. While watching her arrange flowers at the graveside, Ray replays a tape of their conversations and listens on a concealed earpiece. Ray and the audience hear May describing her parents' violent murder at the hands of three members of the León mob. She also says that, lacking Ray's help, she will use the name Adrian Hastings and ingratiate herself into the León family circle.

Against Ray's objections, May attends a late-night party and attracts the attentions of Tomás (Eric Roberts), the son of León patriarch Joe (Rod Steiger). She permits Tomás to begin a flirtation, and while she later dances with him in a bar, Ray sits at a background table listening to another tape of their telephone exchanges. May's recorded voice-over describes her repulsion at being touched by one of her parents' murderers, while on screen she dances alluringly with Tomás. This use of conflicting dialogue and images not only communicates background information concisely but also dramatizes well May's dissembling personality.

Following these scenes of exposition, the film organizes itself around a series of memorable set pieces. The striking nature of these nearly self-contained scenes accounts for much of the motion picture's overall effectiveness. Screenwriter Alexandra Seros and director Luis Llosa manage to create an action film that is a gallery of special effects-driven, one-act plays. One of the first of these depicts Ray's execution of the first of the León hit men while in a bar. Ray has set an explosive charge near the door of the bar manager's inner office. The filmmakers add tension to the scene when the target's pocket telephone rings at the moment he begins to open the booby-trapped door. After a few seconds of conversation, he pulls the door and detonates the blast. This first act of revenge alerts the León family to be more cautious and makes Ned begin to suspect Ray's involvement; the killing also raises curiosity in the audience as to how Ray will breach the family's tightened security to make his second hit. Like the next intended target, the audience warily watches for traps.

The next execution adds some wit to the suspense of the anticipated killing. The target warily approaches his car in an underground parking garage. He gropes under the fender and finds a dynamite charge and connecting wires. Still not satisfied that he has made the car safe, he orders the garage attendant out of his kiosk and forces him to start the car and to race the engine while the intended target waits behind a concrete pillar. When everything finally appears normal, the mark gets behind the wheel and tosses the decoy bomb to the attendant. He unexpectedly meets with Ray's real trap at the turnstile leading out of the garage. Ray looks down with satisfaction from an upper level as the target punches the exit code into the keypad by the turnstile. Instead of raising the barrier, however, the keypad flashes in its viewfinder a quick countdown that ends with the words "bye-bye." The victim's eyes widen just before the explosion propels the driver's seat out of the car, his burning body still secured by the seat belt. Ned arrives at the scene and again suspects Ray's involvement.

These two revenges prepare for Ray's attempt on May's chief target, Tomás. With each new set piece, the filmmak-

ers attempt to top themselves more in cleverness than in special effects. The surprise concerning the third killing involves May's unexpected entrance into Tomás' poolside cabana. Ray has wired a charge to the coffee cup that a waiter has wheeled into Tomás' private room. Having already activated the countdown by radio remote, Ray notices May enter the room right before the explosion. He thumbs the remote too late to deactivate the blast. Though Tomás dies, an insert shows a newspaper notice of a funeral service for Adrian Hastings. It develops, however, that May's injuries were not fatal. By dropping her false identification into the purse of a dying trauma victim at the hospital, May created the diversion of the funeral for Adrian Hastings. She attends this funeral and meets Ray for the first time. When Ned eventually realizes her ruse and begins pursuing the couple, they are sharing a hotel room many stories high that extends out over the ocean.

The film's most memorable set piece excels at both cleverness and special effects. May is confronted in the hotel lobby by Ned and threatened into revealing the location of Ray's room. As she is escorted away by Ned's henchmen, May wants to warn Ray of the men rushing upstairs. She sees a woman with a pocket telephone walk into a restroom, and, making a hurried excuse, she follows her. May grabs the woman's phone and calls Ray's room minutes before Ned and the other hit men arrive. In the empty room, the thugs find an array of surprises courtesy of Ray. A sequence of timed charges starts to explode, and Ned escapes from the room into the hallway just as the blasts dislodge the supports of the cantilevered hotel room and send the entire suite plummeting into the ocean. The remainder of the film continues the cat-and-mouse game between Ray and Ned with a final set piece occurring at Ray's warehouse hideaway.

The performers revel in the larger-than-life roles of this adventure story. In a script that calls for some overacting, Rod Steiger at times thickens his Spanish accent to cartoon proportions. He growls like a bulldog in the scene in which Joe grieves over the death of Tomás.

James Woods in particular makes the most of his many scenes that lend themselves to colorful exaggeration. One good example appears when Ned takes control of the police's bomb squad. Joe León had instructed the captain of the squad to cooperate with Ned's efforts to tighten the family's security, but Ned scowls at the indifference of the captain. At the bomb squad's workroom, the captain's repeated rebuffs make Ned lose control. He coolly assembles a bomb

AWARDS AND NOMINATIONS

MTV Movie Awards Nomination 1995: Most Desirable Female (Stone)

by piecing together the random objects on a desktop—a pinch of plastic explosive, detonator, timer, ballpoint pen— all the while pointing out the captain's incompetence and his own need to be in charge. He engages the timer by pressing the top of the pen and forcing a test of wills. As his homemade device ticks down, the captain finally yields. Woods also adds energy to the scene in which Ned and Ray speak for the first time since their fight in Bogota. Ned has traced Ray's involvement in the killings of the mob henchmen, and he finally contacts him on the telephone, while the police secretly try to trace Ray's line. Ned and Ray bait each other and rehash their feud in a dramatic confrontation. Woods' performance is enjoyably theatrical, and he conveys well the many registers—ironic, coy, irate—of Ned's wild lunacy.

The Specialist has fun with the genre of the action-adventure film. Without a trace of subtlety, the film relies on brashness of design for its appeal. Its plotting, performances, and touches of tongue-in-cheek humor enhance its attraction.

—*Glenn Hopp*

REVIEWS

Daily Variety. October 7, 1994, p.2.
Entertainment Weekly. October 14, 1994, p. 18.
Entertainment Weekly. October 21, 1994, p. 46.
The Hollywood Reporter. October 10, 1994, p.5.
Los Angeles Times, October 8, 1994, p. F1.
The New York Times. October 8, 1994, p. B14.
The New Yorker. October 24, 1994, p. 32.
People Weekly. October 24, 1994, p. 19.
USA Today. October 10, 1994, p. 1D.

Speechless

"Once in a lifetime you find that perfect, unexpected, irresistible enemy."—Movie tagline
"Michael Keaton and Geena Davis are a winning ticket!"—Joel Siegel, *Good Morning America*
"Smart, sexy, side-splitting funny!"—*CBS-TV*
"A movie dream date."—*Newhouse News Service*

 Box Office Gross: $15,186,825 (January 2, 1995)

W hile promoting *Speechless*, a romantic comedy about two competing political speechwriters who fall in love despite all odds, the filmmakers insisted that the film was not based on the real-life romance between Bill Clinton's 1992 Democratic presidential campaign consultant, James Carville, and his George Bush/Republican counterpart, Mary Matalin. It was in 1989 that screenwriter Robert King, whose only other major studio release was the Dana Carvey comedy *Clean Slate* (reviewed in this volume), says he first pitched the idea of warring "spindoctors" to studio heads. It is too bad that those involved with the project never looked beyond fiction to fact, that they did not give serious thought to stealing from what real life had served up to them on a proverbial golden platter; they might have produced an interesting, hot-blooded, no-holds-barred romance. Instead, they created *Speechless*, a film that plays

CREDITS

Kevin: Michael Keaton
Julia: Geena Davis
Freed: Christopher Reeve
Annette: Bonnie Bedelia
Ventura: Ernie Hudson
Kratz: Charles Martin Smith
Cutler: Gailard Sartain
Garvin: Ray Baker
Wannamaker: Mitchell Ryan

Released: 1994
Production: Renny Harlin and Geena Davis for Forge; released by Metro-Goldwyn-Mayer
Direction: Ron Underwood
Screenplay: Robert King
Cinematography: Don Peterman
Editing: Richard Francis-Bruce
Production design: Dennis Washington
Art direction: Tom Targownik
Set decoration: Marvin March
Casting: Howard Feuer
Sound: Richard Bryce Goodman
Costume design: Jane Robinson
Music: Marc Shaiman
MPAA rating: PG-13
Running time: 99 minutes

everything so safe, so "politically correct," so eager to please that it ultimately ends up being so predictable.

Kevin Vallick (Michael Keaton) is a television situation-comedy writer whose former wife, Annette (Bonnie Bedelia), an aggressive campaign manager, persuades him to help her on the campaign trail. She wants him to work on the Senate race in New Mexico as speechwriter for the cold and seemingly insensitive Republican candidate, Garvin (Ray Baker). Unaware that the woman of his dreams, Julia Mann (Geena Davis), is also a political speechwriter, but for the other side, Kevin pursues Julia relentlessly after the two insomniacs meet at an all-night convenience store, reaching for the last bottle of Nytol on the shelf. Fate seems determined to throw these two full-lipped, grinning romantics together.

After meeting again in a diner later that same night, the two take a drive into the New Mexico night, where they, of course, run out of gas. Several clichés later, the two discover the awful truth about each other's true identity—in an obscenity-strewn scene played out in front of schoolchildren that degenerates from sparring to juvenile insults—and the film slides into a mire of predictability from which it fails to escape. Endlessly, the two meet, fall in love, part, reunite, part again, only to reunite again finally under the dropping of celebratory balloons. Through it all, one longs for a sense of urgency, for a reason to believe that these two people need to be together for all eternity, that each would die without the other. Unfortunately, *Speechless* never affords the opportunity to really care.

Michael Keaton's natural cynicism and razor-sharp comic timing serve him well in his part as the television sitcom writer-turned-political speechwriter. He is charming, cocky, yet vulnerable. Perhaps best known for his controversial casting as the Caped Crusader in Tim Burton's *Batman* (1989) and *Batman Returns* (1992), Keaton earned critical acclaim for his portrayal as the recovering chemical addict in the drama *Clean and Sober* (1988). This role, along with his work in the outrageous title role in Burton's *Beetlejuice* (1988), won for him the Best Actor award by the National Society of Film Critics. Keaton's other credits include his feature-film debut in Ron Howard's *Night Shift* (1982), *Gung Ho* (1986), *One Good Cop* (1991), and *The Paper* (1994), as well as a turn as the antagonist in the John Schlesinger thriller *Pacific Heights* (1990).

The role of Julia, and Geena Davis' interpretation of the character, is most problematic and proves ultimately to be the film's weakest link. As Davis is a self-proclaimed member of the Mensa Society (an organization whose members must all have I.Q.'s of genius caliber), her decision to play the experienced political speechwriter more as quirky and

insecure than as strong-willed, decisive, and fiercely incisive is even more perplexing. Julia's distractingly inappropriate attire throughout the film further undercuts her professionalism. It is no wonder that Julia believes that no one on the campaign takes her seriously: She is dressed more like a schoolgirl than a hard-hitting, intelligent ten-year veteran of politics. One is presented with an image of a professional, experienced woman who needs to be advised by a television writer on the merits of simply raising one's voice in order to be regarded as an equal. Unbelieving in the role of an aggressive careerist, Davis instead offers up a one-dimensional character, all toothy grin and fetchingly geeky sexuality. Her character makes it difficult to believe that her male counterpart would view her as anything more than an insomnia-driven one-night stand, let alone a serious political candidate.

It is puzzling why certain actresses in Hollywood, who finally find themselves in the enviable position of being able to produce their own films, resort to such light fare after years of complaining about the dearth of meaty, substantial women's roles. Demi Moore, as well as Geena Davis, spring to mind. Finally presented with the opportunity to make an impact by offering audiences alternatives to the submissive, insecure child-woman so perfected by Julia Roberts and the contrasting hard-edged, obsessive, single, career woman favored by Glenn Close, successful actress/producers seem terrified to grasp the power and effect change in role models. Davis made her feature-film debut in a small part opposite Dustin Hoffman in Sydney Pollack's gender-bending comedy *Tootsie* (1982), and her quirky role in Lawrence Kasdan's *The Accidental Tourist* (1988) won for her the Academy Award for Best Supporting Actress. Davis would later receive another Academy Award nomination, this time in the Best Actress category, for Ridley Scott's *Thelma and Louise* (1991). She starred opposite Michael Keaton once before as one half of the yuppie ghost couple in *Beetlejuice*.

Offering a potential gold mine of witticisms, quips, and scathing social observations, the 1990's political scene nevertheless takes a backseat to the cute interplay between the two leads. Their lack of chemistry, however, only serves to point up all the clichés of the romantic-comedy genre inherent in the material and fails to inspire the audience to root for these two people to end up together by film's end. *Speechless* has serious difficulties achieving its goals. One assumes that the filmmakers were hoping for the kind of rapport established by Meg Ryan and Tom Hanks in the highly commercially successful *Sleepless in Seattle* (1993). Unfortunately, the dialogue never catches fire as in those sparring Katharine Hepburn/Spencer Tracy films such as *Adam's Rib* (1949) and *Woman of the Year* (1942), or the Cary Grant/Rosalind Russell pairing in *His Girl Friday*

"Shall we speak the unspoken language of love?"
"You mean the kind only dogs can hear?"—Julia and Kevin from *Speechless*

Golden Globe Awards Nomination 1995: Best Actress—Musical/Comedy (Davis)

(1940). While both Keaton and Davis are adept at rapid-fire delivery, the scripted dialogue lacks naturalness. It sounds merely like dialogue that was written for someone else to say. There is no intensity, no drive, no urgency behind the words. They remain little more than words cleverly strung together. In an arena like politics—and love—that lack of respect for the power of words can prove fatal.

The filmmakers are quick to point out that this is not a film about politics. It is first and foremost a film about love. Yet what the filmmakers have failed to grasp is that, like it or not, love is often quite political. While the film makes some amusing observations about the behind-the-scenes workings of a political campaign, these are few and far between. Ron Underwood's stodgy direction fails to ignite any flames, never helping the film to transcend its inherent limitations.

Romantic comedy is one of the most difficult of all film genres to master. The director seems most uncomfortable trying to fathom the rough waters of the romantic part of *Speechless*, feeling at ease more with the comedy demands. This is not surprising considering Underwood's other directing credits, which include the hit comedy *City Slickers* (1991), starring Billy Crystal and Academy Award winner Jack Palance, along with his feature-film directorial debut, *Tremors* (1990), a science-fiction comedy, and the Robert Downey, Jr. vehicle, *Heart and Souls* (1993), often described as a fantasy-comedy.

Speechless does have its funny moments, but ultimately the filmmakers have missed what appeared to be a golden opportunity to make an intelligent, sexy, adult comedy that could revel in the power of the spoken word. Instead, they chose to remain speechless. Critics were less than gracious to the film, and it was by most standards a box-office failure.

—*Patricia Kowal*

REVIEWS

Daily Variety. December 12, 1994, p. 13.
Entertainment Weekly. December 23, 1994, p. 46.
The Hollywood Reporter. December 12, 1994, p. 13.
Los Angeles Times. December 16, 1994, p. F1.
The New York Times. December 16, 1994, p. B13.
San Francisco Chronicle. December 16, 1994, p. C3.
The Village Voice. December 27, 1994, p. 61.
The Washington Post. December 16, 1994, p. F1.

Speed

"Get ready for rush hour."—Movie tagline

"A crackling blend of suspense and fun that gives you the rush of a runaway roller coaster...the thrill ride of the summer."—Peter Travers, *Rolling Stone*

 Box Office Gross: $121,000,000 (February 3, 1995)

The huge and somewhat unexpected success of 1988's *Die Hard* starring Bruce Willis spawned a slew of imitators: *Under Siege* (1992) has been described as *Die Hard* on a ship; *Passenger 57* (1992) was known as *Die Hard* on a plane. Even though these films are not actual sequels, they fell prey to the typical sequel problems: a lack of inventiveness, originality, and interest. Yet both of the aforementioned films raked in huge box office receipts. This is probably why Twentieth Century-Fox, the same studio that Released *Die Hard*, has tried to strike gold again with *Speed*, or *Die Hard* on a bus. The surprise is that for the first time since it was released, *Die Hard* has been outdone.

Within a few moments of the opening credits, *Speed* kicks into high gear and never stops until the lights come on in the theater. This film is virtually two solid hours of non-stop heart-pounding action, thrills, and excitement. Keanu Reeves takes a huge leap to the foreground of action-adventure films playing Jack Traven, a loose cannon on the Los Angeles Police Department Special Weapons and Tactics (SWAT) Team. At the film's opening, there are thirteen people trapped in an elevator rigged with explosives thirty stories up. Enter Jack and his partner, Harry, played by Jeff Daniels—and what an entrance it is. Their arrival seems a bit overdone at first, but in hindsight it sets the tone for the entire film.

What follows is an incredibly tense sequence in which Jack and Harry try to save the people in the elevator. It is here that the first glimpse is seen of Howard Payne (Dennis Hopper), the gleeful madman who asks for several million dollars in exchange for the lives of those trapped. It is impossible to describe these scenes without giving too much away, but suffice it to say it left the audience cheering and applauding at the end of it. In fact, the first twenty minutes almost stand apart as a separate film—*Die Hard* in an elevator shaft, perhaps?

Bent on vengeance, Howard decides to pursue Jack and sets him up as a witness to an explosion that rips a vacant Santa Monica city bus to pieces. A phone call lets Jack know that a similar bomb is rigged to a bus full of people and that once the bus attains a speed of fifty miles per hour the device is activat-

CREDITS

Jack Traven: Keanu Reeves
Howard Payne: Dennis Hopper
Annie: Sandra Bullock
Captain McMahon: Joe Morton
Harry: Jeff Daniels
Stephens: Alan Ruck
Jaguar owner: Glenn Plummer
Norwood: Richard Lineback
Helen: Beth Grant
Sam: Hawthorne James
Ortiz: Carlos Carrasco
Terry: David Kriegel
Mrs. Kamino: Natsuko Ohama
Ray: Daniel Villarreal

Released: 1994
Production: Mark Gordon; released by Twentieth Century-Fox
Direction: Jan De Bont
Screenplay: Graham Yost
Cinematography: Andrzej Bartkowiak
Editing: John Wright
Production design: Jackson De Govia
Art direction: John R. Jensen
Set design: Louis Mann, Peter Romero and Stan Tropp
Set decoration: K. C. Fox
Casting: Risa Bramon Garcia and Billy Hopkins
Special visual effects: Sony Pictures Imageworks
Sound: David R. B. MacMillan
Costume design: Ellen Mirojnick
Stunt coordination: Gary Hymes
Music: Mark Mancina
MPAA rating: R
Running time: 115 minutes

ed. If the bus then falls below this speed, the bomb will explode.

With the reluctant aid of the owner of an expensive Jaguar, played wonderfully by Glenn Plummer, Jack manages to board the moving bus and the action gets cranked up even higher. When the bus driver is injured, a sarcastic and resilient passenger named Annie (Sandra Bullock) is recruited to take over the wheel. Bullock could not have been more perfectly cast. The rest of the film is a race to find a way to get the people off the bus without getting blown up.

It is amazing how the filmmakers and screenwriters have set up such tension in what amounts to a fairly silly premise. The concept, from the onset, stretches believability, and each successive plot twist pushes into territories bordering on ludicrous. Yet they work. For example, as the bus is careening down an unopened freeway, it is mentioned that there is a gap in the road three miles ahead. In hindsight, it is hard not to wonder why they did not simply exit and go around the incomplete section. Such logic is unnecessary here, however, since it is almost impossible not to get caught up in the tension focusing on the question of whether they will make it. Every obstacle put in their way is set up beautifully and the payoffs are enormously satisfying.

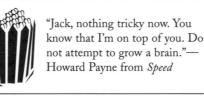

"Jack, nothing tricky now. You know that I'm on top of you. Do not attempt to grow a brain."— Howard Payne from *Speed*

Reeves plays the tough-as-nails hero of the film with a great Clint Eastwood sneer, quite different from his role in *Bill and Ted's Excellent Adventure* (1989). In films such as *My Own Private Idaho* (1991), Reeves stretched his acting muscles and showed remarkable versatility. Nevertheless, this is his watershed role—one that will open him up to a whole new audience.

Equally enjoyable is Sandra Bullock, the reluctant heroine. Last seen in *Demolition Man* (1993) with two other action stars, Sylvester Stallone and Wesley Snipes, Bullock takes over the bus and the film with great humor and marvelously underplayed fear. Her character is written for some much-needed comic relief, and the actress uses that to her advantage. The result is a rich screen portrayal that, like Reeves, could boost her to the head of the A-list of Hollywood actors, as evidenced by her appearance in 1995's *While You Were Sleeping*.

The $30 million-budgeted *Speed* was the seventh top-grossing and the fifth most profitable movie of 1994.

Solid support is lent by Jeff Daniels and Dennis Hopper. Daniels is great as the put-upon partner of Reeves's character. Yet once the action shifts to the bus, his role becomes little more than a cameo. It was a minor disappointment that more was not done with this talented actor. The elevator shaft sequence, for instance, shows Daniels keeping pace with Reeves step by step—no easy feat.

Hopper, meanwhile, anchors the film with his quietly crazy performance as the mad bomber Howard. Although the character's motivation is a little murky, Hopper effectively portrays a man who controls every situation like a demented puppeteer. The villain is a crucial role in these types of films. Without a believable bad guy, the film can not work up any suspense. Alan Rickman did it perfectly in *Die Hard*, and while Hopper does not reach those levels, this failure is mostly due to some minor script holes and not his acting ability.

Even the smaller roles are cast and performed with style: the aforementioned Glenn Plummer; Alan Ruck, as a nervous and naïve tourist visiting Los Angeles for the first time; and Joe Morton and the always enjoyable Richard Lineback as fellow SWAT team members.

Two first-timers scored big with *Speed*: Director Jan De Bont and screenwriter Graham Yost are new to their respective titles yet fared better than many seasoned veterans. De Bont cut his teeth on the action-adventure genre as a cinematographer for films such as *Basic Instinct* (1992), *Lethal Weapon III* (1992), and yes, even the original *Die Hard*. In fact, De Bont took all of their best elements and wrapped them up into a neat and suspenseful little package. He knows how to milk every last bit of tension, humor, and excitement out of every scene in *Speed* and does it with great style.

Yost, meanwhile, has hit the proverbial home run his first time at bat with this terrific screenplay. The concept, as mentioned, is not grounded in everyday reality but instead creates its own crazy logic. At turns breath-taking and laugh-out-loud Funny, *Speed* is the perfect summer film. Special mention should also be made of the special-effects team and stuntpersons who helped make *Speed* the thrill ride that it is.

All in all, *Speed* does what it was designed to do: provide nonstop excitement for the thrill-seeking summer film crowd. It strikes a perfect balance between fun and drama and never takes itself too seriously.

—*Rick Garman*

AWARDS AND NOMINATIONS

Academy Awards 1994: Best Sound
Nomination: Best Film Editing
Blockbuster Entertainment Awards 1995: Best Movie—Video, Best Action Actress—Video (Bullock), Best Action Actress—Theatrical (Bullock)
MTV Movie Awards 1995: Best Female Performance (Bullock), Most Desirable Female (Bullock), Best On-Screen Duo (Reeves/Bullock), Best Villain (Hopper), Best Action Sequence
Nominations: Best Film, Best Male Performance (Reeves), Most Desirable Male (Reeves), Best Kiss (Reeves/Bullock)

REVIEWS

Entertainment Weekly. June 17, 1994, p. 32.
The Hollywood Reporter. June 6, 1994, p. 6.
Los Angeles Times. June 10, 1994, p. F1.
The New York Times. June 10, 1994, p. B1.
Variety. June 6, 1994, p. 4

Squanto: A Warrior's Tale

"Action-filled!"—*Los Angeles Times*

"A remarkable adventure."—*Orange County Register*

Box Office Gross: $3,319,344 (December 26, 1994)

Squanto: A Warrior's Tale begins with ceremony, a prayer within a prayer circle and a wedding. In many ways, it continues to be a story of ceremonies, of cultural clashes over competing ceremonies, and of the changes the warring cultures must make in their ceremonies in order to coexist. *Squanto* tells the true story of the American Indian, Squanto (Adam Beach), who is credited with teaching the Pilgrims survival techniques that made the first Thanksgiving possible. His adventures in England and in New England in the early 1600's have been read by generations of school children, and his story was brought to the big screen by Walt Disney Pictures for the 1994 holiday season.

When English explorers came to the New World, they discovered friendly tribes of Americans Indians, among them the Patuxets, Squanto's tribe. In addition to trading for furs, the English captured the Americans to take back to the Continent as curiosities. One of those captured was Squanto, a young leader in his tribe and a newlywed. Another American from a neighboring tribe, named Epenow (Eric Schweig), was also taken. Once in England, the young men were put on display and forced to perform for the jaded audiences who came to see the marvels from the New World. Fearful of this unknown land and eager to return home, Squanto escaped his captors and began a long, perilous and educational journey home. Before returning to his homeland, he would learn of and participate in the ceremonies of a variety of cultures; he would grow up.

Some of Squanto's history is known. "It is true there was a young Eastern Massachusetts warrior named Squanto, or Squantum, who was kidnapped by English slave traders," explains producer Kathryn F. Galan in the production notes. "We know that after learning their language and customs, he found passage back to North America. However, by the time he returned to his village, he found his family had died of a virus brought by the Europeans." Based on this thumbnail-sketch of a story and on historical accounts of life in the seventeenth century in North America and in Europe, screenwriter Darlene Craviotto developed the details of Squanto's

life that became *Squanto: A Warrior's Tale*. What was not provided by the actual records of Squanto, the historical person, arose from other persons and characters in literature and history, both of which are filled with stories of persons who travel from their homes and fight to return.

Perhaps the two most famous such travelers are Odysseus and Gulliver, from the classic literary works by Homer (*The Odyssey*, ninth century B.C.) and Jonathan Swift (*Gulliver's Travels*, 1726-1727). Each character undergoes a variety of tests and encounters a variety of different civilizations, before returning home. For example, Gulliver travels to a place called Country of the Houyhnhnms that is ruled by wise horses who oversee their idiot charges, men. He also encounters a race of persons whose culture is defined by a continuing disagreement over which end of the egg is to be opened first. Odysseus, on the other hand, tests his strength against wily and dangerous foes such as Cyclops, and Scylla and Charybdis (the whirlpool and the clashing rocks), and indeed stays with persons in places that tempt him to stay, to give up his dreams of returning home. Through their travels, these two characters gain perspective, grow sophisticated in their responses to oppression and danger, and learn the value of their homes. Their stories are episodic—in some ways, in fact, the adventures are picaresque, showcasing the travels of hero-adventurers.

In much the same manner, Squanto travels to unknown lands, initially learning what he must of the culture to stay alive, subsequently learning all he can of the cultures out of curiosity. For example, when Squanto escapes from his captors, he finds shelter and solace with a group of monks (who are not unlike Snow White's Seven Dwarfs in appearance and demeanor). Not all of the monks are happy to shelter Squanto—the Seven Dwarfs have Grumpy, Squanto has Brother Paul (Donal Donnelly). Soon, however, Squanto has won over even the most skeptical. Squanto initially sees the monks as a tribe as he tries to adapt to life in the rural "monastery," which he views as a small farm with a library filled with illuminated texts. Brother Daniel (Mandy Patinkin) is quick to befriend Squanto and teaches him English. One of Squanto's first observations in his new language is that a tribe without women will soon die. While most of the assembled monks find his statement humorous, it also serves as a lesson in point of view for the characters and for the viewing audience. Indeed, the religious order functions like a tribe, gathers together to meet and to dine like a tribe, and yet, due to its very specialized goal, is very unlike the extended family that

Squanto: A Warrior's Tale, the first American film from Swiss filmmaker Xavier Koller, was shot on location in Nova Scotia and Cape Breton island, featuring Eskasoni tribal members.

is an American Indian tribe. Squanto's other observations regarding God, prayer, and books also highlight the differences between cultures and will allow audience members to see their worlds through new eyes. For instance, Squanto has not seen a horse before, and through his amazement, audience members will also appreciate anew the size and strength of the animal.

Further, when a search party comes to look for him, Squanto listens to the monks' wisdom as they advise him to hide from his would-be captors rather than to follow his inclination and try to fight—one warrior and a handful of monks against a group of trained, armed soldiers. Squanto also has much to give and to teach these learned monks. He makes moccasins to comfort their tired feet. He coaxes a half-dead, forgotten tropical plant into bloom. He roasts popping corn for the monks' entertainment and nourishment. These details appear to be added

"There have been small books written about Squanto but I think this is a version that has never been told, in that it is from the point of view of a Native American."—*Squanto*'s screenwriter Darlene Craviotto

to the narrow historical frame as part of the storytelling, embroidery to enhance the development of Squanto's character. In adding the details, the filmmakers have drawn on the classical concept of hero-adventurer.

The comparisons between cultures continue throughout the film. When Squanto returns to his homeland and, after a time, helps the Pilgrims, audiences are shown the power of prayer and medicine in each culture. Epenow's son Pequod (Leroy Peltier) becomes ill after receiving a gunshot wound during the initial altercations between the Pilgrims and the Americans. The Pilgrim's doctor works on the young man, as does the tribe's medicine man. After each practitioner has ministered to the sick boy, the two groups adjourn to their prayers. The result is almost a "battle of the bands" approach to prayer, as each group prays to its god in its own fashion. The filmmakers use crosscut shots of the American Indian ceremony and prayer with the Pilgrim prayer and medical attentions. When Pequod recovers, the groups are united; adversity, dissolved through joint (albeit different) prayer and medical care, turns into understanding and the beginnings of friendship.

While *Squanto* is indeed a film that contrasts cultures and conveys the wisdom and beauty of American Indian philosophy and life, it also is a film that conveys a sense of wonder. For instance, when Squanto and Epenow are captive, they are placed in a pit to battle wild animals in order to show their warriorly skills. (The scenes of such manly arts are reminiscent of similar scenes in *Spartacus* 1960, in which Kirk Douglas, a Roman slave named Spartacus, battles his peers for the edification of a bored patrician class.) In *Squanto*, the warrior outsmarts his captors, lulling to sleep his grizzly bear opponent with a variety of chants. The bear is remarkable to behold, both in his size and his ardor. He is particularly engaging as he makes his slow descent into sleep, and audience members of all ages are charmed.

Director Xavier Koller is perhaps best known to audiences as the 1991 Academy Award winner for Best Foreign Language Film for *Journey of Hope*, which Koller wrote, directed, and produced. In bringing *Squanto* to the screen, Koller stressed the details of the story, ensuring that every part of the story was told accurately. For example, Olga Dimitrov did extensive research into each of the sets of costumes she needed to design: working sailors, Pilgrims, monks, English aristocracy, and commoners, and American Indians of various tribes. In all, she designed more than six hundred different costumes for the film. Every effort went to making each costume authentic, except for one detail. "We were supposed to have real eagle feathers but we could not use them because they are sacred.

CREDITS

Squanto: Adam Beach
Brother Daniel: Mandy Patinkin
Sir George: Michael Gambon
Thomas Dermer: Nathaniel Parker
Epenow: Eric Schweig
Brother Paul: Donal Donnelly
Brother Timothy: Stuart Pankin
Harding: Alex Norton
Nakooma: Irene Bedard
Mooshawset: Sheldon Peters Wolfchild
Pequod: Leroy Peltier

Released: 1994
Production: Kathryn F. Galan and Don Carmody (executive producer) for Walt Disney Pictures; released by Buena Vista Pictures
Direction: Xavier Koller
Screenplay: Darlene Craviotto
Cinematography: Robbie Greenberg
Editing: Lisa Day
Production design: Gemma Jackson
Art direction: Claude Pare
Set decoration: Anthony Greco
Casting: Lynn Stalmaster
Animal training: Joe Camp
Sound: Patrick Rousseau
Costume design: Olga Dimitrov
Song: Arvo Pärt ("Sarah Was Ninety Years Old")
Music: Joel McNeely
MPAA rating: PG
Running time: 102 minutes

So we took turkey feathers and had to paint and dye them to match the real thing," explained Dimitrov in the production notes.

Even the ship on which the warriors traveled was authentic. The filmmakers searched the Eastern seaboard and discovered *The Half Moon* (*De Halve Maen*), a replica of the Dutch East India Company's 1609 trading and exploration ship that Henry Hudson later used to voyage to America. Ultimately, finding the ship was easy; using it was much more difficult. "This particular ship sits so high that any wind over fifteen m.p.h. blows it sideways, so it required a 2,000 pound block just to anchor it..." explained executive producer Don Carmody.

While in places *Squanto: A Warrior's Tale* lags, it is an educational and enjoyable film for family, or student, viewing. It broadens the Thanksgiving story into a story of the history of the many different peoples whose heroism and wisdom, and whose fear and inexperience, helped form the America of today.

—*Roberta F. Green*

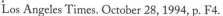

Star Trek Generations

"Two Captains. One Destiny."—Movie tagline

"a smashingly entertaining mix of outer-space adventure"—Richard Zoglin, *Time*

"A supernova of unpredictable sci-fi thrills!"
—Michael Marriott, *Newsweek*

"A cosmic hit that all generations will love."
—Pat Collins, *WWOR-TV*

 Box Office Gross: $71,293,610 (January 2, 1995)

"I take it the odds are against us and the situation is grim?" asks Captain James T. Kirk (William Shatner) of Captain Jean-Luc Picard (Patrick Stewart) midway through this seventh film in the popular *Star Trek* motion-picture series. Indeed, yet again, millions of lives are at stake, and it is up to the crew of the starship Enterprise—both the crew of the original 1960's television series and that of its spin-off, *Star Trek: The Next Generation*—to save the day. Although this film is independent of the first six in the series, *Star Trek Generations* will only be intelligible to fans of the two television series, on whose characters it is based. The first film based on *Star Trek: The Next Generation*, this sequel is a strong debut effort of the "new" crew of the Enterprise.

The film opens on a whimsical note as a Champagne bottle—Dom Perignon, vintage 2265—floats slowly through outer space while the opening credits roll. It strikes the bow of a starship—the newly remodeled Enterprise. Who should be aboard but the original crew members Kirk, Scotty (James

Patrick Stewart as Capt. Jean-Luc Picard, Jonathan Frakes as Cmdr. William Riker, Michael Dorn as Lt. Cmdr. Worf, and Marina Sirtis as Counselor Deanna Troi. Copyright © 1994 Paramount Pictures. All rights reserved.

Doohan), and Chekov (Walter Koenig), now retired from Starfleet, who are special guests along for the first shakedown cruise of the Enterprise B. It is a media event, with hordes of reporters making themselves a nuisance.

Unfortunately, something goes terribly wrong. The Enterprise B receives a distress call from two transport ships caught in some sort of energy ribbon. Although the Enterprise B is not yet fully operational, it is the only ship that can reach them in time. Despite the Enterprise crew's best efforts, including the collaboration of Kirk with the ship's new commander, Captain Harriman (Alan Ruck), both of the endangered ships are destroyed and only forty-some are rescued of the hundreds that were aboard. Among the survivors are an alien scientist, Dr. Soran (Malcolm McDowell), of the long-lived El Aurian race, and Guinan (Whoopi Goldberg), the sage bartender from *Star Trek: The Next Generation*. Kirk dies in a desperate attempt to jerry-rig a device that enables the Enterprise B to escape from the ribbon.

Cut to seventy-eight years later and, incongruously, an eighteenth century-style sailing vessel on the high seas. The *Next Generation* crew, dressed in period costume, are celebrating the recent promotion of Lieutenant Commander Worf (Michael Dorn). The scene is actually taking place on the Enterprise's holodeck—an invention that originated with the

CREDITS

Captain Jean-Luc Picard: Patrick Stewart
Captain James T. Kirk: William Shatner
Dr. Soran: Malcolm McDowell
Commander William Riker: Jonathan Frakes
Lieutenant Commander Data: Brent Spiner
Lieutenant Commander Geordi La Forge: LeVar Burton
Lieutenant Commander Worf: Michael Dorn
Dr. Beverly Crusher: Gates McFadden
Counselor Deanna Troi: Marina Sirtis
Montgomery Scott: James Doohan
Commander Pavel Chekov: Walter Koenig
Guinan: Whoopi Goldberg
Lursa: Barbara March
B'Etor: Gwynyth Walsh
Captain Harriman: Alan Ruck

Released: 1994
Production: Rick Berman and Bernie Williams (executive producer); released by Paramount Pictures
Direction: David Carson
Screenplay: Ronald D. Moore and Brannon Braga; based on a story by Rick Berman, Moore, and Braga, and on *Star Trek*, created by Gene Roddenberry
Cinematography: John A. Alonzo
Editing: Peter E. Berger
Production design: Herman Zimmerman
Art direction: Sandy Veneziano
Casting: Junie Lowry-Johnson and Ron Surma
Special visual effects: Industrial Light and Magic
Special visual effects supervision: Ronald B. Moore and John Knoll
Sound: Thomas Causey
Special makeup effects: Michael Westmore
Hair Styling: Jay Zapata
Costume design: Robert Blackman
Music: Dennis McCarthy
MPAA rating: PG
Running time: 118 minutes

Next Generation series. It is in essence a virtual reality corridor aboard the Enterprise, in which the participants can program themselves into any setting of their choosing. During the festivities, Picard receives a personal message, which causes him to exit abruptly.

The rest of the crew are forced to exit shortly after when another message is received that the Amargosa Observatory has been attacked. When members of the Enterprise crew go aboard to investigate, they find Dr. Soran, the sole survivor, who is then taken against his will to the Enterprise. While Lieutenant Commander Geordi La Forge (LeVar Burton) and Lieutenant Commander Data (Brent Spiner) examine the devastated science vessel, Soran returns, attacks them, and is whisked away by a Klingon "Bird of Prey" starship, with Geordi as his prisoner.

Apparently, Soran has enlisted the aid of the Klingons in his efforts to return to the Nexus, the energy ribbon seen earlier in the film. As Guinan informs Picard, the Nexus is a version of Paradise, where time has no meaning and one is blissfully content. Soran had found the Nexus, then was torn away, as was Guinan, and now seeks desperately to return. It is never explained, however, how Soran discovered the Nexus. Yet the fact remains that he has become a madman in his single-minded determination to return to the Nexus, whatever the cost.

Picard offers himself in a prisoner exchange with the Klingons, both to retrieve Geordi and to be able to try to talk Soran out of his dastardly plan, which will kill millions of people. The Klingons have escorted Soran to a planet in the Veridian system, where he has constructed a missile that will destroy the system's sun; the resulting explosion will alter the path of the Nexus to pass over the planet's surface, sweeping Soran back into the Nexus. All the planets in the system will be destroyed in the explosion, including the millions of inhabitants. In a last-ditch effort, Picard hopes to prevent Soran from completing this monstrous act of destruction and arranges with the Klingons to be beamed to the planet's surface.

Meanwhile, the Klingons—devious as ever—return Geordi but with a transmitter hidden in his visor. They gain information that enables them to find a way to penetrate the Enterprise's shields and launch a full-scale attack. The Enterprise manages to rally and destroys the Klingon ship. Nevertheless, the ship has suffered serious damage, as well as a "core breach" in engineering, and everyone aboard must be evacuated to the "saucer" section of the ship, which can separate from the engineering decks. The resulting blast causes them to crash-land on the planet's surface, in a breath-taking action sequence devised by George Lucas' special-effects company Industrial Light and Magic. The sight of the indomitable Enterprise striking the planet's surface and mowing down trees at high speed before it finally settles to a stop is one of the best sequences in the film.

Unfortunately, Picard fails to dissuade Soran, and the

Nexus sweeps up both men as it passes on its way. As the sun explodes, the downed Enterprise and its crew perish along with the planet. When Picard "awakens," he finds himself in a Victorian Christmas scene, complete with decorated Christmas tree, children squealing with delight while opening presents, and a wife asking him if he would like a cup of Earl Grey tea. As he begins to realize that it is not "real," that he has no wife and children, he is joined by Guinan, or rather a visible "echo" of Guinan, who informs him that he is in the Nexus, where this world has been created from his own inner desires. Not only can he leave if he wants but he can also go backward or forward to any point in time. It turns out that Kirk was also swept up in the Nexus. Picard then seeks Kirk's help to go back in time, to the moment before the missile was launched in order to stop Soran.

Star Trek Generations is the seventh film in the *Star Trek* movie franchise, which has grossed more than $475 million domestically.

Thus, it is because of the Nexus that twenty-third century captain Kirk and twenty-fourth century captain Picard are given the opportunity to work together. In the Nexus, Picard finds Kirk at a remote Southern California-style cabin, chopping wood and frying eggs for his ladylove upstairs. Unlike Picard who found himself in a fictional place, Kirk is reliving events in his past. Picard's attempts to convince Kirk that he is really only inside the Nexus culminate in the two men riding horses through the wilderness. Such nostalgic and scenic moments are part of what make the *Star Trek* series so appealing. For all their otherworldly travels, the characters inevitably yearn to return to Earth, to home.

Ultimately, the two captains succeed in stopping Soran, and Kirk dies yet again, this time with a protracted death scene more appropriate for a legend such as Kirk. Although the Enterprise is not salvageable, rescue ships pick up the crew, and Picard ends with the hint of a sequel when he says, "I doubt that this will be the last ship to carry the name Enterprise." Judging from the box-office results, viewers, too, will doubt that this will be the last voyage of the Enterprise. *Star Trek Generations* not only had the best box-office debut of any of the *Star Trek* films, but it also was the number one film its opening weekend, earning an estimated $23.2 million in its first three days of release.

As producer Rick Berman stated in the film's production notes, the "film made it possible to involve *Star Trek: The Next Generation* characters in a story larger in scope and more epic in design [than the television series allowed], offering action-adventure and the thought-provoking elements that have distinguished the *Star Trek* films." Besides the expected adventure and action sequences, *Star Trek Generations* explores "universal facets of the human condi-

"This isn't a buddy movie. It's not the Kirk-Picard *Lethal Weapon* experience."—*Star Trek Generations* screenwriter Brannon Braga

tion while illuminating new aspects of well-known and revered *Star Trek* characters."

Indeed, both Kirk and Picard lament their total devotion to duty at the expense of having a family. While aboard the Enterprise B, Kirk is introduced to the daughter of his former helmsman Sulu (George Takei). She now serves as helmsman on the Enterprise B. This meeting prompts Kirk to query, "When did he find time for a family?" Picard, too, has an experience wherein he recognizes his own mortality. Early in the film, he is devastated by the news of the deaths of his brother and beloved nephew, Rene, in a fire. As he confides to Counselor Deanna Troi (Marina Sirtis), he had counted on his brother, through Rene, to carry on the family name. With their deaths, there will be an end to the Picard name: "Rene was as close as I would get to having a child of my own," laments Picard. Hence, Picard's own personal slice of heaven in the Nexus: a loving wife and a bevy of adorable children, and—perhaps a reference to Stewart's critically acclaimed one-man stage interpretation of Charles Dickens' classic, *A Christmas Carol*—a nostalgic Victorian Christmas scene.

Some much-needed levity is supplied by Data, an artificial life form and the counterpart of the half human, half Vulcan Mr. Spock (Leonard Nimoy) of the original series. Unlike Spock, Data aspires to become as human as possible and decides to have an "emotion" chip implanted in his positronic brain. Thus, throughout the film, Data attempts to deal with feelings, which he has never before experienced. Some of the best scenes are those in which he discovers a sense of humor. For example, he approaches a locked door, waves his arm, and says, "Open, Sesame." Later, Data does a hilarious calypso number when asked to conduct the otherwise mundane task of searching for life forms. When the Enterprise succeeds in blowing the nasty Klingons sky-high, Data turns toward the camera, clenches his fist, and says with obvious relish, "Yes!" Ironically, android Data has always been the most emotive and "human" of all the *Next Generation* characters. In this film, he gets to laugh, cry, and show fear, unlike most of his human—and sometimes almost superhuman—colleagues. He is the Everyman, with whom viewers will most identify.

Many of the television series sets, redressed and embellished, were used in the filming of *Star Trek Generations*. Two new sets, a solar observatory and Stellar Cartography, had to be constructed. In Stellar Cartography, Picard and Data are surrounded by star charts on a cantilevered computer platform—a scene that is both beautiful and dizzying. It gives the effect that the two are standing in the center of the universe. For the holodeck scene, the film's cast and crew set sail on a replica of a famous eighteenth century sailing vessel, the *Lady Washington*, off the coast of Santa Monica, California. Various Southwestern locales were used in the film. For example, Kirk's rustic cabin in the Nexus was actually filmed in California's Owens Valley. The site of Soran's outpost in the Veridian system was filmed in Nevada's Valley of Fire, an hour's drive northeast of Las Vegas.

Star Trek Generations certainly met fans' expectations as a bigger and better version of the *Star Trek: The Next Generation* television series, with a larger budget, state-of-the-art special effects, and extensive location shooting. What other film could incorporate an eighteenth century sailing ship at sea, a twenty-fourth century starship cruising the galaxy, intergalactic warfare, a state-of-the-art crash sequence, fisticuffs, two legendary starship captains scrambling eggs together in a kitchen, horseback riding, a Victorian Christmas, and Southern California chic all in a single, logical narrative?

—*Cynthia K. Breckenridge*

REVIEWS

Entertainment Weekly. November 25, 1994, p. 44.
The Hollywood Reporter. November 14, 1994, p. 5.
Los Angeles Times. November 17, 1994, p. F1.
The New York Times. November 18, 1994, p. B1.
Variety. November 14, 1994, p. 2.

Stargate

"It will take you a million light years from home. But will it bring you back?"—Movie tagline

"The most amazing film of the year!"—Howard Benjamin, *Entertainment Network*

"A visually stunning, exciting and eye-popping trip!"—Paul Wunder, *WBAI Radio*

"I loved it so much I hope they start the sequel tomorrow!"—Jeff Craig, *Sixty Second Preview*

"A terrific epic action adventure!"—Bob Healy, *Satellite News Network*

"Part *Star Wars*, part *Close Encounters*, part *Indiana Jones* and all fun!"—Scott Siegel, *Siegel Entertainment Syndicate*

 Box Office Gross: $68,644,252 (January 2, 1995)

Dr. Daniel Jackson (James Spader) is an undoubtedly brilliant archeologist with some unpopular—if not laughable—ideas about ancient Egypt. He believes that the Egyptians of the IV Dynasty could not have possibly built the pyramids. For one thing, there was no writing inside the structures, even though it was invented during the first two dynasties. For him, that is enough to believe someone or something else built them. His colleagues, however, laugh him off the podium.

He does find one ally: Catherine Langford (Viveca Lindfors). She is the daughter of the archeologist who, in 1928, discovered a coverstone that was believed to be of great significance. Unfortunately, all attempts to translate the hieroglyphics on it have been unsuccessful—until Catherine hires Daniel to do the job. He does in thirteen days what her previous scholars had not been able to do in two years.

With Daniel's insight, the coverstone, now housed in a Colorado military installation, is determined to be a portal that charts a path into space—from Earth to the planet Abydos. All the scientists have to do is set the rings of the portal correctly and immediately and mysteriously the door is open.

Ready to step through the door is a group of military men headed by Colonel Jack O'Neil (Kurt Russell) and Daniel, who promises that he can get them back as soon as he reads the hieroglyphs on the portal at the other end of the journey. They enter the portal and, after a trip through time and space, find themselves at the other end of their journey inside a pyramid at Abydos that is a replica of the Great Pyramid at Giza. When they step outside, however, there is nothing but desert. The planet appears uninhabited.

Unfortunately, there is also no sign of the opposite portal stone. Daniel cannot get the men home without it, and they are very angry. Soon, however, they discover that the planet is inhabited. They stumble on people who look like Earth bedouins of old, who seem to be virtual slaves working in the mines at the mercy of some unseen power. Daniel's linguistic expertise, and a relationship with the native woman Sha'uri (Mili Avital), finally allow him to interpret their language. His excitement grows when their language turns out to be a spoken derivative of the ancient Egyptian hieroglyphs from Earth.

At the same time, he also discovers who their master

is: Ra (Jaye Davidson). On Earth, Ra was the mythological Egyptian sun god, but on Abydos he is a living, breathing, and vengeful ruler who occasionally stops by, landing his spaceship pyramid and terrorizing his slave population.

Daniel now has his answer as to who really built the pyramids. Ra was the last member of a dying race. He searched the galaxy for a way to save his life. When he stumbled upon the primitive people of Egypt on Earth,

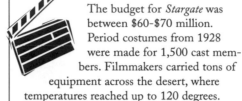

The budget for *Stargate* was between $60-$70 million. Period costumes from 1928 were made for 1,500 cast members. Filmmakers carried tons of equipment across the desert, where temperatures reached up to 120 degrees.

he found how easy it was to repair human bodies and decided to inhabit one. Immediately, he began to change Egyptian civilization until, one day, his Earthlings rebelled against his rule. So, Ra moved on, through the space portal, to a new location, Abydos, where he also took along enough Earthlings to work his mines.

Since Daniel is still unable to find the way back to Earth, O'Neil reveals his secret mission: if he finds the situation to be dangerous on the other side of the portal, he is to blow it up. Since he is depressed and suicidal anyway because of the accidental shooting death of his son, he seems the perfect candidate for the job. When O'Neil realizes how much power Ra has, he sets the nuclear weapon to go off. Ra, however, discovers the bomb and plans on using the gate to send it back to Earth—along with the metal he mines on Abydos, which will increase its power.

By this time, Daniel has taught the transplanted slaves about their history, and O'Neil has taught them about rebellion. As Ra's pyramidical spaceship lifts off, the natives are restless and the bomb is transported not to Earth but aboard Ra's ship at the last minute. Daniel finds the other portal stone and is able to translate it to return the remnants of the troop back to earth again. He, however, will remain behind to study (and probably lead) the remnants of the ancient civilization he has given his intellectual life to.

The premise for *Stargate* is a great one. It takes on one of modern society's popular myths (that men from outer space built the pyramids—both in Egypt and in South and Central America) and fleshes it out into a science fiction motion picture complete with impressive special effects, stirring music, spectacular cinematography, and solid acting. What could possibly go wrong? According to critics, a lot. According to moviegoers, nothing.

On its opening weekend, *Stargate* was first at the box office, with receipts of $16.8 million—the biggest October opening as of 1994. It was also the biggest box office return for shaky MGM since *Rocky IV* did $19 million in 1984. *Stargate*'s numbers prove that there is a market for spectacular cinematic science fiction, even if it is panned by the critics. Unlike the oppressive and unsuccessful *Dune* (1984) with which it invites obvious comparison, *Stargate* has enough going for it to elevate it above its ponderous counterpart. It has the grandeur and spectacle of a *Star Wars* (1977), the history, action, and adventure of a *Raiders of the Lost Ark* (1981), and the special effects of a *Star Trek* (1979). What this also shows, is that *Stargate* is also a bit derivative.

Even if one concedes that virtually all science fiction films are derivative of one another, there is still another

CREDITS

Colonel Jonathan "Jack" O'Neil: Kurt Russell
Dr. Daniel Jackson: James Spader
Ra: Jaye Davidson
Catherine: Viveca Lindfors
Skaara: Alexis Cruz
Sha'uri: Mili Avital
General W. O. West: Leon Rippy
Lieutenant Kawalsky: John Diehl
Anubis: Carlos Lauchu
Horus: Djimon
Kasuf: Erick Avari
Lieutenant Feretti: French Stewart
Nabeh: Gianin Loffler
Lieutenant Freeman: Christopher John Fields
Lieutenant Brown: Derek Webster
Lieutenant Rielly: Jack Moore
Lieutenant Porro: Steve Giannelli

Released: 1994
Production: Joel B. Michaels, Oliver Eberle, and Dean Devlin for Mario Kassar (executive producer) and Le Studio Canal Plus/Centropolis Film, in association with Carolco Pictures; released by Metro-Goldwyn-Mayer
Direction: Roland Emmerich
Screenplay: Dean Devlin and Roland Emmerich
Cinematography: Karl Walter Lindenlaub
Editing: Michael J. Duthie and Derek Brechin
Production design: Holger Gross
Art direction: Peter Murton and Frank Bollinger
Set decoration: Jim Erickson
Casting: April Webster
Visual effects supervision: Jeffrey A. Okun
Sound: David Ronne
Stunt coordination: Andy Armstrong
Costume design: Joseph Porro
Special creature effects: Patrick Tatopoulos
Music: David Arnold
MPAA rating: PG-13
Running time: 119 minutes

problem with this film, and it is the one that caused rejection by critics. The film takes a great central idea and buries it in a story that ranges from complex to hokey to ludicrous to absent. There are many very obvious, logical questions left unanswered by this film, and each one of them puts a bigger hole in its believability—and suspension of disbelief is absolutely essential to a science fiction film. First, where has the portal stone been since 1928 and why? Why was only one scientist sent through the portal—and an archeologist at that? Why would the army chose soldiers who were psychologically so negative and hostile to go into uncharted territory? Why did the writers have to rely on so many convenient plot ploys? (O'Neil's dead child providing his suicidal tendency that would jeopardize and destroy such an important mission, and also prevent him from wanting to arm the rebelling children; Jackson's loss of income and homelessness causing him to have no reason to return to Earth.) Furthermore, why would slave children who are frightened by a cigarette lighter take so easily to rebellion and modern weapons? What was Ra mining metal for anyway?

"....there was a wave of theories about aliens visiting earth thousands of years ago and being responsible for the pyramids and such. It wasn't so much that I believed in the theories, but I always thought the idea could be the basis for a fantastic adventure movie."—Roland Emmerich on *Stargate*

If one is willing, however, to put one's sense of logic on hold, *Stargate* can be an appealing afternoon's entertainment. The plot may have holes, and the actors may be a bit one-dimensional and archetypical (Russell's macho colonel, Spader's befuddled scholar, Davidson's exotic evilness), but all the other positive elements (its looks, action, basic premise, music, and special effects) can be more than enough for some filmgoers to plunk down the price of a ticket.

—*Beverley Bare Buehrer*

REVIEWS

Chicago Tribune. October 28, 1994, p. 7D.
Daily Variety. October 24, 1994, p. 2.
Entertainment Weekly. November 11, 1994, p. 50.
The Hollywood Reporter. October 24, 1994, p. 5.
Los Angeles Times. October 28, 1994, p. F15.
The New York Times. October 28, 1994, p. B1.
Time. November 21, 1994, p. 116.
USA Today. October 28, 1994, p. 4D.

Street Fighter

"Adventure is the name of the game."—Movie tagline

 Box Office Gross: $21,290,680 (January 2, 1995)

Allied Nations commander Colonel Guile (Jean-Claude Van Damme) heads a rescue mission into a fictional Southeast Asian country to retrieve hostages held by demented dictator General Bison (Raul Julia), in this action/adventure based on a popular video game. *Street Fighter* marks the last film performance of Raul Julia, who died in 1994. The film was shot in Bangkok, Thailand (where the Thai government reportedly allowed the filmmakers to use important military equipment) and Queensland, Australia, using more than 3,000 extras. Feature film directorial debut of Steven E. de Souza

Jean-Claude Van Damme as Colonel Guile and Raul Julia as General M. Bison in *Street Fighter*. Copyright © by Universal City Studios, Inc. Courtesy of MCA Publishing Rights, a Division of MCA Inc. All rights reserved.

REVIEWS

Atlanta Constitution. December 27, 1994, p. E8.
Boston Globe. December 24, 1994, p. 23.
Chicago Tribune. December 25, 1994, Sec. 5 p. 4.
Entertainment Weekly. January 13, 1995, p. 40.
Los Angeles Times. December 24, 1994, p. F1.
The New York Times. December 24, 1994, p. A11.
The New York Times. January 8, 1995, Sec. 2 p. 23.
USA Today. December 27, 1994, p. D5.
Variety. CCCLVII, Jan 2, 1995, p. 72.
The Washington Post. December 24, 1994, p. B3.
The Washington Post. January 5, 1995, p. C7.

CREDITS

Colonel Guile: Jean-Claude Van Damme
Bison: Raul Julia
Chun-Li: Ming-Na Wen
Ken: Damian Chapa
Cammy: Kylie Minogue
A. N. official: Simon Callow
Dhalsim: Roshan Seth
Sagat: Wes Studi
Ryu: Byron Mann
Balrog: Grand L. Bush
Honda: Peter Tuiasosopo
Vega: Jay Tavare
Carlos: Robert Mammone

Released: 1994
Production: Edward R. Pressman and Kenzo Tsujimoto for Capcom; released by Universal Pictures

Direction: Steven E. de Souza
Screenplay: Steven E. de Souza; based on the Capcom video game *Street Fighter II*
Cinematography: William A. Fraker
Editing: Anthony Redman, Robert F. Shugrue, Ed Abroms, Donn Aron and Dov Hoenig
Production design: William Creber
Art direction: Ian Gracie
Set design: Michael Chorney
Set decoration: Lesley Crawford
Casting: Mary Jo Slater and Steven Brooksbank
Special effects supervision: Brian Cox
Sound: Gary Wilkins
Costume design: Deborah La Gorce Kramer
"Bison" costume design: Marilyn Vance
Stunt coordination: Charles Picerni
Music: Graeme Revell
MPAA rating: PG-13
Running time: 95 minutes

 "In *Street Fighter*, there's adventure, stunts, thrills, spills, futuristic technology, a secret subterranean base and damsels in distress—except that this is the nineties and our damsels can take care of themselves"—*Street Fighter* director Steven E. de Souza

Street Wars

When older brother Frank (Bryan O'Dell), a gangster and drug dealer, is murdered, younger brother Sugarpop (Alan Joseph Howe) vows revenge: An aviation cadet at a military academy, Sugarpop mounts an all-out attack on rival gang members.

REVIEWS

Entertainment Weekly. August 5, 1994, p. 58.
Variety. CCCXLVII, June 29, 1992, p. 67.

CREDITS

Sugarpop: Alan Joseph Howe
Frank: Bryan O'Dell
Humunus: Cliff Shegog
No character identified: Jean Pace
No character identified: Brigid Coulter

Released: 1992
Production: Jamaa Fanaka, Bryan O'Dell, Ben Caldwell, and Ayanna DuLaney; released by Bea, Bob and Bea Honey
Direction: Jamaa Fanaka
Screenplay: Jamaa Fanaka
Cinematography: John Demps
Editing: Alain Jacubowicz and Taesung Yim
Production design: Keeda
Music: Michael Dunlop and Yves Chicha
MPAA rating: no listing
Running time: 94 minutes

Strictly Propaganda

A compilation of educational and instructional films made in East Germany from the 1940's to 1989, this amusing documentary points up the extent to which the Communist government tried to shape popular opinion.

REVIEWS

Los Angeles Times. March 4, 1994, p. F10.
The Nation. CCLVII, November 8, 1993, p. 541.

CREDITS

Origin: Germany
Released: 1994
Production: C. Cay Wesnigk; released by First Run Features
Direction: Wolfgang Kissel
Screenplay: Wolfgang Kissel
Editing: Peter Vatter
MPAA rating: no listing
Running time: 94 minutes

Strip Jack Naked (Nighthawks II)

Filmmaker Ron Peck focuses on his growing up gay in the repressed social climate of 1960's and 1970's England, in this autobiographical drama.

Origin: Great Britain
Released: 1991
Production: The British Film Institute
Direction: Ron Peck
Screenplay: Ron Peck and Paul Hallam
Cinematography: Ron Peck and Christopher Hughes
Editing: Ron Peck and Adrian James Carbutt
Music: Adrian James Carbutt
MPAA rating: no listing
Running time: 91 minutes

REVIEWS

Christopher Street. XIV, July 1991, p. 13.

CREDITS

No character identified: Ken Robertson
No character identified: John Brown
No character identified: Nick Bolton
No character identified: Derek Jarman
No character identified: John Daimon

Sugar Hill

"Between dreams and reality...Trust and deception...The rules have changed"—Movie tagline

 Box Office Gross: $18,212,683 (May 30, 1994)

Dear Momma: Sugar Hill is now a memory ... the boy you loved has grown up to be the man you feared." This narration, by Wesley Snipes as drug lord Roemello Skuggs, sets up the drama of the stylish and well-performed *Sugar Hill*. A variation on a familiar theme—the gangster who has grown tired of his life of crime—it is a classic story of a young man who wants out, only to discover that anyone leaving the underworld will pay a weighty price.

Roemello and his brother, Raynathan (Michael Wright), are well-to-do, beautifully dressed gangsters who live in Sugar Hill, Harlem. Roemello does not touch the drugs his people sell for him; he is cultured and well-educated and constantly struggling with his family's violent past. His volatile older brother is even more troubled by their past: An early flashback shows young Raynathan being forced to help his mother inject herself with heroin. Their mother died, but their father (Clarence Williams III) is still alive and still a junkie. The brothers are involved in an arrangement with Gus Molino (Abe Vigoda), an old-style mobster who runs a grocery store as a front for his Harlem "branch office" of his family's operation.

The action is propelled by the introduction of two new characters: Melissa (Theresa Randle)—a beautiful actress with whom Roemello sees a future and a way out—and Lolly (Ernie Hudson)—a dangerous gangster who is a newcomer to Harlem and a threat to the stability of the arrangement between Gus and the two brothers. Lolly's arrival, which starts a dangerous turf war, coupled with Roemello's romantic interest in Melissa, makes Roemello realize that he "wants out." In his opening narration, Roemello says, "I am consumed by chaos, consumed by guilt, consumed by grief." Roemello is representative, according to the screenwriter, Barry Michael Cooper, of an emerging generation of young African American men who prosper because of street crime, but are alienated from true street life.

Sugar Hill is one in a series of films that were released in the early 1990's dealing honestly with the treachery of inner-city life. *Boyz N the Hood* (1991), *New Jack City* (1991; also written by Barry Michael Cooper), and the chilling *Menace II Society* (1993) are excellent examples of the genre. They are all thoughtful films that deal realistically with the problems facing African American men in the inner city. Yet

Sugar Hill also follows in the footsteps of *Carlito's Way* (1993), in which Al Pacino plays a gangster who wants to go straight. Thus *Sugar Hill* is a hybrid of gritty urban street drama and gangster film.

True to form, Cooper and director Leon Ichaso have included several obligatory items: There is the turf war over who is master of the territory; the violence, which escalates after the brutal murder of a trusted friend; the beautiful woman who is torn between her love of the man and her hatred of his profession; and the burnt-out victims of this way of life. Furthermore, there is even a scene that has become a film cliché, in which Melissa asks Roemello, "Do you dream?"

"...the boy you loved became the man you feared."—Roemello Skuggs in *Sugar Hill*

Having taken all that into account, however, there is one thing *Sugar Hill* has that many others before it did not: style. Any discussion of this film will inevitably turn to its wonderful design and photography: production designer Michael Helmy, art director J. Jergensen, costume

CREDITS

Roemello Skuggs: Wesley Snipes
Raynathan Skuggs: Michael Wright
Melissa: Theresa Randle
A. R. Skuggs: Clarence Williams III
Gus Molino: Abe Vigoda
Harry Molino: Larry Joshua
Lolly Jonas: Ernie Hudson
Doris Holly: Leslie Uggams
Ella Skuggs: Khandi Alexander
Sal Marconi: Raymond Serra
Tony Adamo: Joe D'Allesandro
Mark Doby: Vondie Curtis-Hall

Released: 1994
Production: Rudy Langlais and Gregory Brown for Beacon and South Street Entertainment Group; released by Twentieth Century-Fox
Direction: Leon Ichaso
Screenplay: Barry Michael Cooper
Cinematography: Bojan Bazelli
Editing: Gary Karr
Production design: Michael Helmy
Art direction: J. Jergensen
Set decoration: Kathryn Peters and Elaine O'Donnell
Casting: Mary Gail Artz and Barbara Cohen
Sound: Malcolm Morris and Rolf Pardula
Costume design: Eduardo Castro
Music: Terence Blanchard
MPAA rating: R
Running time: 123 minutes

designer Eduardo Castro, and set decorators Kathryn Peters and Elaine O'Donnell have created a lush, rich, textured world that reflects the grit of the streets and the lavishness of the apartments in which the well-to-do characters live. Roemello is dressed in beautiful, deep purples and oranges, with elegant cashmere overcoats that contrast with the earthy interiors against which the story is played. Raynathan contrasts him by wearing much more black—his clothes are hipper, but messier. His style reflects the increasing desperateness of his own situation.

Somehow, even the tough urban backgrounds look beautiful with the wonderful use of light and interesting choices of camera composition by director Ichaso and cinematographer Bojan Bazelli. For example, an important scene between Melissa and Roemello takes place at night in front of the gate to Melissa's apartment. The gate is actually an entrance to a huge courtyard, and several of the windows in the vast building surrounding the courtyard have lights on. The lights from the buildings and the courtyard itself provide a depth that shows that Ichaso and Bazelli know their craft. In addition, the camera uses the gate's grating to great effect, shooting Melissa through a pattern on the grate as she desperately asks Roemello, "Why did you have to pick me?" The emotion of the scene and the fine performances of the actors are enhanced by such fine craft.

Another most important element of this film is its complex and moody jazz score by Terence Blanchard, who provided music for *Do the Right Thing* (1989) and *Malcolm X* (1992). The edgy music helps to set in context the complex lives of these people. The film aims to illuminate the psychological lives of these characters, and their feelings are beautifully underscored by Blanchard's trumpet: When there is danger, the music is jumbled and complicated.

The performances are uniformly excellent. Wesley Snipes is a somber Roemello. He is economical and thoughtful, but lights up when he needs to, such as in a funny scene where he brings Raynathan to their father's house and blesses the "fast food" that the Lord has provided. His strength is the fulcrum of the film.

Michael Wright has the showy part and makes the most of it. Raynathan is a lost soul who has not the least idea how to run the family business. He is ashamed of himself and spirals deeper into despair, masked by drugs. "You're my little brother, and I've always looked up to you, and how do you think that feels?" he asks Roemello. It is a fine tragic performance because Wright knows that the tragedy lies in his character's denial and fear.

Theresa Randle is notable as Melissa. She is not merely a beautiful appendage, as so many female characters tend to be in such films. The filmmakers wisely include a scene in which she decides to go out with someone else because she wants nothing to do with Roemello's life. Seeing this woman take care of herself by going out with someone new, and then taking care of herself when her date turns dangerous, is refreshing. Randle is tough and vulnerable, innocent and sexy, and an excellent foil for Snipes.

Several film and television veterans round out the cast: Abe Vigoda as the jaded Gus, innocuous on the surface but dangerous underneath; Leslie Uggams in the very small role (which does not utilize her exceptional talents) of Melissa's suspicious mother; and Clarence Williams III, formerly of television's *The Mod Squad*, in a stunning performance as the burnt-out father. Williams' is such a fully realized performance that the director wisely chooses to leave the camera in close-up during an extraordinary scene in which his character shoots up, eyes rolling back in his head, delivering a powerful speech that not only describes his own downfall but serves as metaphor for the downward spiral of much of American youth. Tragically, he quotes Matthew 13:49, saying, "And so it shall be at the end of the world, the angels shall come forth and sever the wicked from the just." His performance suggests that he sees himself as both the wicked and the just, deserving deliverance and damnation at the same time.

Yet the filmmakers have chosen to end not on a tragic note but on a hopeful one: the filmmakers offer the hope that the devastation and tragedy that engulf so much of urban black America may one day be turned around. As such, *Sugar Hill* may serve as inspiration for positive change.

—*Kirby Tepper*

REVIEWS

Entertainment Weekly. March 11, 1994, p. 38.
The Hollywood Reporter. September 2, 1993, p. 5.
Los Angeles Times. February 25, 1994, p. F1.
The New York Times. February 25, 1994, p. B4.
Variety. September 2, 1993, p. 2.

Sunday's Children

"Two thumbs up"—*Siskel & Ebert*

"A spectacular coup de cinema! Gorgeous. Mysterious. Exciting."—Vincent Canby, *The New York Times*

Film legend Ingmar Bergman may have retired from directing his own scripts, but his presence in world cinema is still vital. In the screenplay of *Sunday's Children*, Bergman has written a painful yet lyrical work propelled by two of his obsessions: his childhood and his relationship with his father. Now, one of his sons, Daniel, has directed it as a first feature, and this dual Bergman project is little short of a triumph.

A chorus of bird song, and the lush, heavy green trees form an enticing playground for the vacationing Bergman family. It is a summer in the late 1920's. Young Pu (Henrik Linnros) walks alone along a railway track toward the station at Dufnas to welcome his father, Erik (Thommy Berggren), back from his post in the royal court at Stockholm. The boy is very excited by the prospect.

Although in *The Best Intentions* (1991)—Ingmar Bergman's recent autobiographical screenplay that concentrates on the early years of his parents' tempestuous marriage—much fuss was made of Erik's appointment to the Swedish court, Pastor Bergman's arrival at Dufnas is greeted quietly by the family and neighbors. Pu's reception for his father is far more abundant. Although he wishes to avoid it, Erik is soon sucked into the family turbulence at Dufnas, and Pu spends less time with his father than he would want.

Erik and his wife Karin (Lena Endre) have an uneasy relationship, and Pu—the middle child—becomes acutely aware of the fact. Pu is in any case an unusually reflective child; indeed, he is self-consciously a "Sunday's child." In a fleeting and precocious explanation, the young boy indicates that this means he is a "seer": he can see into the future. This ability is later demonstrated, and subsequently forms part of the fabric of the action.

Ingmar's script and Daniel's direction proceed at a summer's leisure pace. The mood is generally cheerful, if reserved, and only references to the suicide of a village watchmaker (Carl Magnus Dellow) at a nearby stream threaten to cloud the setting. Pu and his brother Dag (Jakob Leygraf), however, are fascinated by the story of the watchmaker, and they implore the elderly Märta (Malin Ed) to tell them what she knows. After several refusals, she relents, and in grainy gray images, the watchmaker's descent into madness is revealed. Insanity and death—concerns of Ingmar Bergman throughout his career—cast a shadow on a golden summer.

Tensions increase between Erik and Karin. An eavesdropping Pu learns of his mother's wish to spend more time with her well-to-do family in Upsala. Erik is distraught at

CREDITS

Henrik Bergman: Thommy Berggren
Karen Bergman: Lena Endre
Pu: Henrik Linnros
Dag: Jakob Leygraf
Märta: Malin Ek
Marianne: Marie Richardson
Aunt Emma: Irma Christensson
Grandmother: Birgitta Valberg
Maj: Maria Bolme
Uncle Carl: Börje Ahlstedt
Lalla: Majlis Granlund
Lalla: Birgitta Ulfsson
Watchmaker: Carl Magnus Dellow
Ingmar: Per Myrberg
Nurse Edit: Helena Brodin
Girl: Melinda Kinnaman

Origin: Sweden
Released: 1993
Production: Katinka Faragó for Sandrew Film and Theatre AB; released by First Run Features/Castle Hill
Direction: Daniel Bergman
Screenplay: Ingmar Bergman
Cinematography: Tony Forsberg
Editing: Darek Hodor
Art direction: Sven Wichmann
Costume design: Mona Theresia Forsén
MPAA rating: no listing
Running time: 118 minutes

Karin's idea, claiming that he is being humiliated by such plans, and stalks off for a predawn walk. He is joined by Pu, and father and son sit on a bench watching the sun rise.

Here the film takes an unexpected twist: the time sequence jumps to 1968. A now silver-haired Ingmar (Per Myrberg) is visiting his ailing father, and the mood is grim.

The juxtaposition of time sequences is intentionally jarring, and it serves to act as a glimpse of the man young Pu will become more than forty years into the future. By 1968, Karin has died, and nurse Edit (Helena Brodin) fears that the elderly Erik has lost his faith; unfortunately, Ingmar is not the person to restore it.

All at once, with tension strong between father and son, the viewer is transported back to summery Dufnas: this flash to the future was only an interlude. A close-up of a brooding Pu makes clear that he has seen his (and his father's) discomforting future.

Still seated on the bench, Pu falls asleep and dreams of

Sunday's Children is the directorial debut of Daniel Bergman, Ingmar Bergman's son. Loosely based on Ingmar's childhood, it is also intended as a sequel to the elder Bergman's *Fanny and Alexander* (1982) and *Best Intentions (1993)*.

the hanging watchmaker. It is a terrifying sequence. The boy asks about his own death, and the watchmaker answers, even though the hanging man's mouth is horrifyingly aghast and no lips move.

As summer continues, and Pu suffers at the hands of his bullying brother Dag, a Sunday morning trip to another village with Erik is proposed to Pu. The boy vacillates on deciding: his uncertainty stems from his love and fear of his stern father.

Pu decides at last to go, and at this point *Sunday's Children* becomes gripping. It focuses on the emotional core of the project: the relationship between Pu and Erik. The trip begins in bright sunshine and in good spirits, although Erik's condescending attitude to Pu's naturally childish questions makes its mark on the boy. Later, the two encounter a mourning party by a river, and as Pu paddles his bare feet on a ferry crossing, a frightened Erik brutally slaps him as a rebuke and a warning; Erik is terrified that his son might fall underneath the barge and be drowned. Once more, the specter of death for young and old is unnaturally present in the mind of Pu.

With red marks unpleasantly visible on the young boy's face, another jump to 1968 finds the frail Erik reviewing his fifty-year marriage through Karin's diary. An unemotional, aloof Ingmar listens impassively. It is clear that Ingmar is still blaming his father for her disciplinarian manner, yet also ignoring the love Erik manifestly demonstrated.

After a time transition back to the 1920's, the two Bergmans are seen to reach their destination, and Pu is told to play outside while his father prepares for the church service. Pu stumbles upon a body laid in a coffin. He is fascinated; once again, death is all around, despite the golden sunshine. In church, the boy imagines he is Jesus being resurrected and proclaims to another child of his age that he does not believe in God. Anyone who does, Pu says, must be crazy.

Clearly the boy is angry with his father. In the final jump to 1968, as Erik lays feebly on the bed, the adult Ingmar somewhat cruelly removes his father's solace-seeking hand from off of him. Yet the film concludes with father and son back in a Dufnas rainstorm, as close as they surely ever came. Equally drenched by the storm, they walk home together, happy.

Having enjoyed a brilliant career primarily as a director of his own scripts, one might suppose that Ingmar Bergman's triumphs lie in the past. The critical reception for *Sunday's Children*, however, affirm Ingmar's vital genius. Credit, of course, must be shared with his son Daniel for the latter's sensitive handling of material very close to his own heart. Caryn James of *The New York Times* praised

Sunday's Children as "an exquisite autobiographical film"; Gene Siskel and Roger Ebert enthusiastically recommended the work, and *The New Yorker* singled out Daniel Bergman for giving "this rambling memoir a shimmering, lyrical clarity."

Behind the camera, Tony Forsberg's photography captures the summer glories of the Swedish countryside and its capricious moods. Mona Theresia's costumes highlight the comfortable material standing of the Bergman family, and despite several lapses in visual continuity, the film is technically well-executed.

Thanks to the foundation of Ingmar's illuminating yet ambiguous script, and under the careful hand of director Daniel, performances throughout are pleasing. Of the principals, Thommy Berggren's Erik is subtle and also stern; Lena Endre's Karin is a wounded woman who bewilders her husband, and Henrik Linnros as Pu delivers a sometimes haunting yet natural performance. Wide-eyed, but not so innocent, Linnros shows Pu to be both vulnerable and resourceful. He is impressionistic but at the same time strangely prescient.

Pu's ability as the seer takes *Sunday's Children* beyond a remembrance of things past. Because of Ingmar Bergman's unnerving talent—and willingness—to cast a cold eye not

> "My father's screenplay *Sunday's Children* (*Sondagsbarn*) is about his father and his son, my father. It describes loving memories of summer, 1926 in the heart of Sweden, the province of Dalarna."—*Sunday's Children* director Daniel Bergman

only on the father he came to deeply dislike but also on himself, the film is involving and occasionally deeply disturbing.

If anyone appears the most blameworthy for the schism between father and son, it is ultimately the distant adult Ingmar: it is astonishing how honest Ingmar is able to be as he revisits his past for all the world to know.

During filming, director Daniel Bergman insisted that his father not set foot on the set, and one can understand why. For Daniel, the challenge was surely tremendous: Not only would he be working in the shadow of his celebrated father, but he also would be revivifying lives from which he had ultimately sprung. Spurred on by both tasks, Daniel—and Ingmar—have memorably succeeded in *Sunday's Children*.

—*Paul B. Cohen*

REVIEWS

Entertainment Weekly. May 27, 1994, p. 68.
The Hollywood Reporter. April 1, 1993, p. 8.
Los Angeles Times. August 26, 1994, p. F8.
The New York Times. April 3, 1993, p. 11.

Surviving the Game

"The ultimate manhunt...the thrill to kill."—
Movie tagline

"The rules are simple: Kill or be killed."—Movie tagline

"...fast and furious...a winner."—Betsy Sherman, *The Boston Globe*

Box Office Gross: $7,638,351 (June 26, 1994)

Inspired by the oft-filmed Richard Connell short story *The Most Dangerous Game,* this action film stars Ice-T as a homeless man who is hired to lead a group of hunters on an expedition in the Pacific Northwest only to discover that he is to be their prey. Shades of Van Damme's *Hard Target.* Second film directed by Ernest Dickerson.

REVIEWS

Atlanta Constitution. April 19, 1994, p. D6.
Boston Globe. April 16, 1994, p. 31.
Entertainment Weekly. April 29, 1994, p. 54.
Entertainment Weekly. September 30, 1994, p. 70.
Los Angeles Times. April 18, 1994, p. F3.
The New York Times. April 16, 1994, p. A11.
People Weekly. XLI, May 2, 1994, p. 18.
USA Today. April 18, 1994, p. D3.
Variety. CCCLIV, April 25, 1994, p. 30.
The Washington Post. April 16, 1994, p. C2.

"Allow yourself to feel the purity of your primal essence!"—Burns from *Surviving the Game*

Mason: Ice-T
Burns: Rutger Hauer
Cole: Charles S. Dutton
Hawkins: Gary Busey
Wolfe, Sr.: F. Murray Abraham
Griffin: John C. McGinley
Wolfe, Jr.: William McNamara
Hank: Jeff Corey

Released: 1994
Production: David Permut; released by New Line Cinema
Direction: Ernest Dickerson
Screenplay: Eric Bernt
Cinematography: Bojan Bazelli
Editing: Sam Pollard
Production design: Christiaan Wagener
Art direction: Madelyne Marcom
Set decoration: George Toomer, Jr.
Casting: Jodi Rothfield and Katie Ryan
Sound: Felipe Borrero
Costume design: Ruth Carter
Stunt coordination: Bob Minor
Music: Stewart Copeland
MPAA rating: R
Running time: 96 minutes

Suture

"A thriller where nothing is black and white"
—Movie tagline

"Riveting with a smart-assed style! A hard-boiled thriller with a subversive heart"—Lawrence Chua, *The Village Voice*

"A taut shocker that would have made Hitchcock proud!"—*Details Magazine*

"Stunning! Sleek, cool utterly original."—*Paper Magazine*

Sometimes good art is only as good as its interpretations. Some people hate Picasso's paintings because they think they are nothing more than ugly representations of beautiful things. But others see them as beautiful deconstructions of familiar images; the deconstructions are meant to deliver the essence of the image rather than to merely represent the exterior of that image.

Similarly, an artistic film which leaves room for interpretation can be fascinating, because different people will see different things in it based on their own experience. *Suture* is such a film. It has that slow, deliberate "art house" quality which immediately renders it an "important" film. There are numerous clues that it is an art house film: it is filmed in black and white; one of its lead characters is named after an important philosopher; it has seemingly "color blind" casting (a black actor and a white actor play identical brothers); and it has a ponderous voice-over about the nature of our "knowledge of ourselves". Whatever one can interpret about its meaning, it clearly concerns itself with big themes.

Suture can be seen as a heavy-handed art-film, an eerie, noir-ish murder mystery, or a quasi surrealistic nightmare about the identity of black people in a white world. Maybe it is about all three, who knows? But the certainty is that producer-director-authors Scott McGehee and David Siegel have created an unquestionably stylish and intelligent film.

The film seems to be about two brothers, Clay (Dennis Haysbert) and Vincent (Michael Harris), who only learned of each other's existence at the recent funeral of their wealthy father. The film opens with Clay's arrival in Phoenix, where Vincent resides. It is important to note that Clay is a blue-collar worker, a "regular guy", while Vincent is wealthy and spoiled. Vincent retrieves Clay in a white Rolls Royce. They have apparently arranged this visit simply to find out about each other (Clay says, "I'm not here for the money... at the funeral, I saw how much we look alike, and I

"Our physical similarity is disarming, isn't it?"—Vincent from *Suture*

just wanted to get to know you"); yet before Clay has a chance to get settled, Vincent says he is leaving for a business trip. He insists that Clay wear his clothes and drive his Rolls Royce until his return. But Vincent doesn't return; he is actually staging his own "death." Since no one knows of Clay and Vincent's relationship, Clay becomes a perfect stand-in for Vincent's body, and is nearly killed by a car bomb. Vincent, it turns out later, is the suspect in his father's murder, and has staged his death to escape the dogged pursuit of Lieutenant Weismann (David Graf).

But Vincent hasn't bargained for one thing: Clay is not killed by the bomb. With the help of plastic surgeon Renee Descartes (Mel Harris, from TV's *thirtysomething*) and psychiatrist Max Shinoda (Sab Shimono), Clay begins to reconstruct his life. Suffering physical disfigurement and complete amnesia, Clay slowly and painfully thinks he is returning to his former self. But unwittingly, the people around him, having retrieved the fake identification in his wallet, and seeing the general physical resemblance, help restore the wrong identity.

For much of this slowly-paced film, it is hard to discern just what statement McGehee and Siegel are making; the audience's impatience to understand what this film is about will not serve them well. But if the audience can wait it out, the final frames and the final voice-over summation by Shinoda will clarify the author's intent. The mystery of this film is twofold: there is the mystery of whether Clay will discover his true identity and whether he will (wrongly) be held as the murderer of his father; and there is also the mystery of the film's meaning and intent. One of the clues lies in Shinoda's dialogue: "Freud said that nothing is insignificant." If the audience uses that as a guide, and sums up the film's odd characteristics, its meaning can become clearer.

First of all, the bi-racial casting: what at first seems to be a visual conceit can actually be seen as a comment on the assimilation of African-Americans into traditional white culture. Shinoda says, "he may dress in Vincent's clothes, he may play golf at his club, take his box at the opera, but nothing can change this... If he achieves happiness, he will not be happy; he has buried his soul, of this we can completely be certain." If the audience is to take nothing for granted, then it is not coincidental that the psychiatrist is an Asian man who is providing a cautionary note about the assimilation of another minority—specifically African-Americans—into American culture.

Another clue to this theme comes from the character and nature of some of the people Clay encounters on his

CREDITS

Clay Arlington: Dennis Haysbert
Dr. Renee Descartes: Mel Harris
Dr. Max Shinoda: Sab Shimono
Alice Jameson: Dina Merrill
Vincent Towers: Michael Harris
Lieutenant Weismann: David Graf
Mrs. Lucerne: Fran Ryan
Sidney Callahan: John Ingle

Released: 1994
Production: Scott McGehee and David Siegel; released by the Samuel Goldwyn Company
Direction: Scott McGehee and David Siegel
Screenplay: Scott McGehee and David Siegel
Cinematography: Greg Gardiner
Editing: Lauren Zuckerman
Production design: Kelly McGehee
Art direction: Steven James Rice
Casting: Sally Dennison and Patrick Rush
Sound: David Chernow
Sound design: Mark Magini
Costume design: Mette Hansen
Music: Cary Berger
MPAA rating: no listing
Running time: 96 minutes

journey to becoming Vincent. For example, Dina Merrill is outstanding in an appearance as Alice Jameson, a wealthy family friend who seems particularly blind to the truth about Vincent. She continually says that he is "misunderstood", and tries to convince him that he is a wonderful person who can put his troubled past behind him. Merrill perfectly plays the society woman oblivious to the truth of the world around her. That the lovely Merrill herself comes from the most privileged American socioeconomic class underscores the authors' intent to show Clay's blind drive to become Vincent. The metaphors are clear: Blue-collar, black Clay is indoctrinated into the world of white-collar, white Vincent, irrespective of the truth of his prior culture and ethnicity. The metaphor is extended when Clay is blinded in one eye, symbolizing the need for someone to blind themselves to the truth in order to become something they are not.

The casting of African-American Dennis Haysbert as Clay, then, is not an example of color-blind casting. It is, in fact, essential that a black man play the role. A scene with Dr. Descartes makes this clear. As they begin to discover their mutual attraction, she talks about Clay's "Greco-Roman nose", his "fine, straight hair, and thin, smooth lips", saying these are "not the features of a killer." When seen in the context of racial discrimination, these statements become a sharp commentary on the duality of justice in American society.

Descartes is saying that a white man can't commit a crime, which unwittingly means that a black man can. Harris, like Merrill, plays a character who lives only in the highest strata of society, skeet-shooting or going to the opera for pleasure, and dressing in the finest clothes. She brings a sense of privilege and goodness to her role, and her innate goodness makes the subtle racist messages all the more unsettling. She has no idea of the inherent racism in her comments about Clay's features.

In his Los Angeles Times review of the film, Peter Rainer talked about the naming of Harris' character as a joke that outlasts its initial humor. But it doesn't seem to be a joke at all: Renee Descartes was a nineteenth century philosopher who said, "I think, therefore I am." If one views *Suture* as a film about the discovery of identity in general, and the assimilation of African-Americans in particular, then the name is a clever (if obvious) clue to the thematic content. Clay feels that he can decide to remember who he is; the invention of his past in order to improve his future is an unmistakable perversion of Descartes' idea, and it is why Shinoda says "he has buried his soul."

Haysbert, Shimono, Harris, and Merrill are all excellent in their roles. One cannot say that any of the roles are exciting or fascinating roles to act. Each seems to be a cog in the thematic machinery, and each fits perfectly. Haysbert, remembered from the wonderful *Love Field* (1992) with Michelle Pfeiffer, has a vivid presence and a soothing gentility essential to his role.

McGehee and Siegel prove themselves to be highly inventive and thoughtful writer/directors. The intermittent images of Clay's past, done on grainy film stock, contrast well with the crisp images of the present-day. The slow-moving camera is probably slow for the MTV generation audiences. Sometimes they linger on images when the point could be made in a shorter span of time. The cerebral nature of the plot and theme may also render this film a bit too arty, even for audiences who like challenging films. But cineastes will appreciate the gorgeous camerawork of Greg Gardiner, and the clever symbolism of Kelly McGehee's production design.

Like a piece of art on a museum wall, everyone who sees and discusses this film will find something different. Visually reminiscent of *Wings of Desire* (1988), and thematically related to Ralph Ellison's book *The Invisible Man*, this film will give dedicated viewers much to chew on after the show. It may be difficult to wade through, but it's worth it.

—*Kirby Tepper*

REVIEWS

Daily Variety. September 16, 1994. p. 12
Los Angeles Times. March 25, 1994. p. F14
New York Times. March 21, 1994. p. B5
Hollywood Reporter. September 21, 1994.

The Swan Princess

"Absolutely enchanting. Parents and children will adore it!"—Jeffrey Lyons, *Sneak Previews/ABC World News Now*

 Box Office Gross: $8,976,104 (January 2, 1995)

The *Swan Princess* comes from the animation studios of director Richard Rich and Nest Entertainment, but it borrows a formula that the Disney studios have capitalized on with their string of successes. *Beauty and the Beast*

CREDITS

Rothbart: Jack Palance (voice)
Prince Derek: Howard McGillin (voice)
Princess Odette: Michelle Nicastro (speaking voice)
Jean-Bob: John Cleese (voice)
Speed: Steven Wright (voice)
Puffin: Steve Vinovich (voice)
Bromley: Joel McKinnon Miller (voice)
King William: Dakin Matthews (voice)
Lord Rogers: Mark Harelik (voice)
Chamberlain: James Arrington (voice)
Queen Uberta: Sandy Duncan (voice)
Princess Odette: Liz Callaway (singing voice)
Narrator: Brian Nissen

Released: 1994
Production: Richard Rich and Jared F. Brown for Nest Entertainment and Rich Animation Studios; released by New Line Cinema
Direction: Richard Rich
Screenplay: Brian Nissen; based on a story by Richard Rich and Nissen
Cinematography: Tom Priestley, Jr.
Editing: James Koford and Armetta Jackson-Hamlett
Animation direction: Steven E. Gordon
Supervising effects animation: Michael Gagne
Production design: Mike Hodgson and James Coleman
Post animation production supervision: Colene Riffo
Casting: Geoffrey Johnson, Vincent G. Liff and Tara Jayne Rubin
Costume design: Karen Perry
Character design: Steven E. Gordon
Music: Lex de Azevedo
Songs: David Zippel and Lex de Azevedo
MPAA rating: G
Running time: 90 minutes

(1991) is the most obvious Disney influence on *The Swan Princess*. Like its acclaimed forerunner, *The Swan Princess* uses a fairy tale—in this case, a fairy-tale turned-ballet—and songs to tell a charming story of true love overcoming obstacles.

The best of the eight songs that David Zippel and Lex de Azevedo wrote for the film is the first one, "My Idea of Fun." After the opening narration spoken by co-writer Brian Nissen sets the scene in the days of myth and fairy tale, this song shows the frustrated attempts of two royal houses to unite young Prince Derek (voice of Howard McGillin) and Princess Odette (speaking voice of Michelle Nicastro; singing voice of Liz Callaway) in a dynastic marriage. The song both introduces the characters of the royal couple and musically compresses their childhood and youth into a series of melodic rebuffs of Odette by Derek. At the end of this song, however, the couple have matured beyond their childhood disdain of each other and are truly in love.

The first obstacle to their union comes when young Derek, showing the ill effects of his sheltered and pampered life, disappoints Odette by failing to recognize qualities in her beyond her comely appearance. When asked by Odette if beauty is all that matters to him, Derek replies innocently, "What else is there?" Odette sends him away.

Derek's frustration and loneliness quickly mature him, but before he can reunite with Odette, he learns that she has disappeared. In fact, she has been kidnapped by the evil Rothbart (voice of Jack Palance), a malcontent who vowed revenge on the royal household after being exiled following a failed attempt to take over the kingdom. He turns Odette into a swan that changes back to human form only during the light of the full moon. Naturally, Odette refuses to marry Rothbart and make him the ruler of her father's kingdom. The only way to break the spell is for someone to make a vow of everlasting love to Odette and prove it to the world.

While Odette pines away, Derek hones his archery skills. The song "Practice, Practice, Practice" shows a playful contest between Derek and another courtier, which Derek wins by plucking his opponent's arrow out of mid-air and firing it back at him. "Longer Than Forever" is the young couple's love ballad, somewhat reminiscent of the lovely title song from *Beauty and the Beast*. This sequence shows Derek and Odette in different settings and alternating verses, he in his lonely castle and she on her silvery lake.

Also in the manner of *Beauty and the Beast*, the animators give Odette some colorful supporting characters for comic relief. She has befriended a turtle named Lorenzo Trudgealong, nicknamed Speed, whose lugubrious voice characterizations by Steven Wright match his character perfectly. A pompous but likable frog named Jean-Bob (voice of John Cleese) and a bird named Puffin (voice of Steve Vinovich) complete the trio of Odette's protector/helpers. The animators also use these talking animals as reactive characters. A quick shot of their reactions or a short line of dialogue from them guides the audience's responses to the unfolding story. The song "No Fear" is their attempt to encourage Odette by searching for a map of their location.

With the help of this map, Puffin guides Odette toward Derek's castle. Derek knows only that Odette's kidnapping involved some change of form, and he mistakes this strange bird and swan to be the evil forces that took her away. Puffin and Odette barely make it back to their lake ahead of Derek's arrows. When Derek arrives at night and sees the swan transform into Odette, however, he finally vows his love for her. He then invites her to a ball at the castle at which they will announce their engagement.

Rothbart, however, plots to thwart the lover's plan by locking Odette in his dungeon and crafting a false Odette to send to Derek's ball—to the tune of "No More Mr. Nice Guy." Back at the palace, the playful song "Princesses on Parade" shows the desperate attempts of Queen Uberta (voice of Sandy Duncan) to find a suitable match for Derek. On the night of the ball, Odette's trio of helpers distracts the hungry crocodiles in Rothbart's castle moat so that Odette can escape. Still a swan, she hurries to Derek's castle, where the false Odette has already made her appearance. Flying from one castle turret to another in search of an open window, Odette desperately tries to catch Derek's eye. When Derek realizes he has been taken in, he proves his love for Odette to the world by fighting Rothbart. The final battle climaxes with Derek catching Rothbart's arrow in flight just as he had earlier practiced and returning it in a winning shot. Odette and Derek sing a reprise of "Longer Than Forever."

The Swan Princess shows careful work by the animators, especially in the background landscapes. These settings are consistently rich in detail and atmosphere, including the key locations of Odette's pond, the dungeon, and the woods where Derek first pursues the swan. The character animation also evokes the personalities of the figures effectively. Derek's court adviser Lord Rogers (voice of Mark Harelik) is drawn with the supercilious leer of a Basil Rathbone. The royal chamberlain (voice of James Arrington), rendered as a Lou Costello type, adds some touches of physical comedy. Queen Uberta is given a spinsterish disdain that recalls the character actress Edna May Oliver. Unlike some of Disney's animated vehicles, however, none of the characters resembles the actor who voices the role, but such evocative character drawings more than serve as compensation.

The songs, however, fail to maintain the same level of inspiration and execution. Though the musical numbers appear in the narrative at apt moments, only the first really advances the plot at the same time that it creates a pleasant mood and defines characters. The other songs fall flat musically and dramatically, a shortcoming that may be more noticeable since many of them, like "No Fear" and "Princesses on Parade," aim for the show-stopping zest of "Be Our Guest" from *Beauty and the Beast*.

In spite of its musical lapses and its limited theatrical release, *The Swan Princess* does not embarrass itself in taking on the genre that the Disney company has all but perfected. In its story and animation, *The Swan Princess* makes for a pleasant and diverting animated musical.

—*Glenn Hopp*

REVIEWS

Daily Variety. November 14, 1994, p. 10.
Entertainment Weekly. November 18, 1994, p. 118.
The Hollywood Reporter. Nobember 14, 1994, p. 5.
Los Angeles Times. November 18, 1994, p. F4.
The New York Times. November 18, 1994, p. B2.
The New Yorker. November 21, 1994, p. 40.
The Wall Street Journal. November 17, 1994, p. A18.

Sweet Emma, Dear Bobe: Sketches, Nudes (Edes Emma, Draga Bobe: Vazlatok, Aktok)

Two young women teachers, Emma (Johanna Ter Steege) and Bobe (Eniko Borcsok), share a room in Budapest and struggle to make ends meet in post-Communist Hungary.

REVIEWS

New Statesman & Society. VI, January 22, 1993, p. 33.

AWARDS AND NOMINATIONS

Berlinale Film Festival: Special Jury Prize

CREDITS

Emma: Johanna Ter Steege
Bobe: Eniko Borcsok
Headmaster: Peter Andorai
Sleepy: Eva Kerekes

Origin: Hungary
Released: 1992
Production: Objektiv Filmstudio, with the cooperation of Manfred Dornick Filmproduktion
Direction: Istvan Szabo
Screenplay: Istvan Szabo; based on an idea by Szabo and Andrea Veszits
Cinematography: Lajos Koltai
Editing: Eszter Kovacs
Production design: Attila Kovacs
Sound: Gyorgy Kovacs
Costume design: Zsuzsa Stenger
Music: Robert Schumann, Tibor Bornai, Mihaly Moricz, Ferenc Nagy and Beatrice
MPAA rating: no listing
Running time: 78 minutes

A Tale of Winter (Conte d'Hiver)

"Four stars. One of Rohmer's most romantic movies."—John Hart, *Seattle Times*

 Box Office Gross: $184,764 (July 10, 1994)

The four seasons of the year certainly symbolize a continuing cycle of change in the overall sequence of life. Each season symbolizes not only the passage of time but also a transition from one set of emotional experiences to another. Summer evokes lightheartedness and play a time for frolic. Fall begins the slide into a more serious state of mind. Then comes winter a time of enclosure from the elements, but also a time of reflective thinking and hibernation from activity. Spring connotes a new beginning, a chance at rebirth. All four seasons present their own set of challenges and their own personal impact on the human psyche.

Those four mysteries of Mother Nature are the focus of Eric Rohmer's latest cycle of films, appropriately titled *Tales*

CREDITS

Félicié: Charlotte Véry
Charles: Frédéric Van Dren Driessche
Maxence: Michel Voletti
Loïc: Hervé Furic
Elise: Ava Loraschi
Mother: Christiane Desbois
Sister: Rosette
Brother-in-law: Jean-Luc Revol
Edwige: Haydée Caillot
Quentin: Jean-Claude Biette
Dora: Marie Riviere

Origin: France
Released: 1992
Production: Margaret Menegoz for Les Films du Losange, with the participation of Soficas-Investimage et Sofiarp and the cooperation of Canal Plus; released by MK2 Productions USA
Direction: Eric Rohmer
Screenplay: Eric Rohmer
Cinematography: Luc Pagès
Editing: Mary Stephens
Sound: Pascal Ribier
Costume design: Pierre-Jean Larroque
Music: Sébastien Erms
MPAA rating: no listing
Running time: 114 minutes

of the Four Seasons. Rohmer directed the first of this series, *A Tale of Springtime*, in 1989. It was chosen as the closing film of the 1990 Berlin Film Festival and was also shown as part of the 1990 New York Film Festival.

A Tale of Winter, the second installment, focuses on the romantic life of an attractive young woman, Félicié (Charlotte Véry), and her two suitors, Maxence (Michel Voletti) and Loïc (Hervé Furic). Maxenceis a handsome hairdresser who owns the salon where Félicié is employed. Although physically attracted to each other, they find they are not very compatible. Then there is Loïc, the librarian and intellectual, who challenges and expands the mind of this some what confused heroine.

Matters are further complicated by the fact that Félicié happens to still be in love with Charles (Frédéric Van Dren Driessche), a man with whom she had an affair five years earlier. Félicié lives with her mother (Christiane Desbois) and her daughter Elise (Ava Loraschi). Her undying love for the father of her child prevents her from committing to either one of her current beaus. Her dilemma is real, as is the frustration of Maxence and Loïc, who both love her very much.

The premise of this intricate love triangle certainly presents an interesting plot line. Initially, it whets the appetite and curiosity of the filmgoer and offers a vast array of intrigue and conflict. Holding a multitude of possibilities for human drama and conflict,the film unfortunately never lives up to these high expectations.

Writer/director Eric Rohmer has been making some noteworthy films about "charismatic" women for more than thirty years. His earlier work, such as *Six Moral Tales* and *Comedies and Proverbs*, also focuses on attractive, intelligent, and self-absorbed women. They all deal with difficult decisions concerning affairs of the heart. These are not women grappling with tough decisions about their careers or family. Love is the central theme and their romantic lives are the priority.

Rohmer has always attempted to depict these women without sentimentality but with clarity and straightforwardness. He chooses to allow them to reveal themselves through dialogue, detailed conversations, gestures and movements. He has been quoted as saying, "I learned from television not to use too many effects, to leave the camera immobile in front of the speakers.... What interests me is to show people who have feelings, and feelings are expressed by gestures and by the spoken word. In real life, people speak a lot....to show people who don't talk is false."

It is clear upon viewing *A Tale of Winter* that the main characters do, indeed, talk. They talk incessantly for nearly two hours about love, sex, commitment to one another, immortality, spirituality, fate, philosophical problems, and the size of their noses. It is like watching an exceedingly verbose episode of *thirtysomething* on television without the relief of a commercial break. This film is directed by Rohmer with such a tight hand of constraint that it stifles the creativity and spontaneity of the piece.

The characters appear flat and uninteresting, making it difficult for an audience to care about their problems or their lives. Their seemingly endless, cerebral discussions about Félicié's confused state of mind become tiresome and boring. They offer no new insights about these people after the first twenty minutes of the film. Their verbal self-indulgence seems insignificant and frivolous and eventually alienates the viewer.

The filmmaker's style has been called observational with a strict sense of realism. He eschews the use of heavy background music and unnatural light in his films. The opening sequence depicts a montage of two people in love, on a holiday romp. They are shown together swimming, boating, clowning on the beach, making love, and taking snapshots. It is as if the viewer were watching home movies of the couple in their living room and sets up a sense of intimacy about them.

Abruptly, it is five years later and obviously winter. Everything appears cold, gray, and gloomy. There is a depressing sense of steely bleakness to the surroundings and a sharp contrast in mood to the earlier shot. It does provide an effective transition in the telling of the upcoming story. The facts of what has taken place are revealed through a series of conversations that Félicié has with her mother, her boyfriend, and her lover.

It seems that she gave Charles, whom she met on vacation, the wrong address five years earlier, making it impossible for him to contact her. She has never seen him since that time and longs for the day when she can be reunited with him. As the story unfolds, it becomes apparent that Félicié is involved with two men and cannot decide on what to do. She is seen taking a train to work and back again, "thinking things over."

She hops a train to a small town outside Paris to visit her sexy boyfriend, Maxence, and back home again. She takes another train to move in with him and when that does not work out, she is back on the train one more time. These "travel-time" shots are supposedly meant to show this perplexed heroine "mulling things over" about what to do next. Should she marry Maxence in Nevers or return to Loïc in Paris? Should she hold out for Charles and continue to live with her mother?

This continual introspection on the train becomes repetitive, annoying, and downright boring. When she is not contemplating what to do, she is discussing it with her sister or her mother or Maxence or Loïc or anyone who will listen.

Since Eric Rohmer is a respected filmmaker, it would be somewhat unfair to dismiss his work totally. Afterall, there

> "I love you. Not enough to live with, only to ruin your life."
> —Félicié to Loïc in *A Tale of Winter*.

is an abundance of good dialogue. In one scene, Félicié is breaking up (once again) with Loïc. She looks at him and says, "I love you. Not enough to live with you, only to ruin your life." These little gems are scattered throughout the film and do offer a penetrating insight into the sometimes searing dynamics of intimate relationships.

Yet the action and the actors lack passion. These players all seem to be removed from their problems, reciting their feelings rather than experiencing them. It is as if there were nothing at stake they do not really care. If the characters do not care, how can an audience?

There is one scene in particular where Félicié is supposed to have a revelation about her life. It occurs in a church where she has taken her daughter to view a Nativity scene. The camera cuts to her face as she looks up at the large crucifix above the altar, as she takes in her surroundings. She furrows her brow and then the camera cuts to a mundane scene in her apartment. Later on, she describes this moment as a pivotal, life-altering experience. There is certainly power in subtlety, but in this shot it looked as if the only thing running through her mind was what she was going to have for supper.

Eric Rohmer was born in Nancy, France in 1920, and was, for a time, a schoolteacher. Later, he became deeply interested in film and formed many friendships with such luminaries as François Truffaut, Jean-Luc Godard, and Jacques Rivette. As previously mentioned, he has a fascination with the spoken word, with dialogue. At one point in this film, Félicié says to Loïc, "To you, only what's written is true. It's a gulf between us." Perhaps, this is the filmmaker revealing himself that only the written word is what is important to him.

Writing is the best vehicle for Rohmer to express his ideas. In fact, in *A Tale of Winter*, Rohmer seems to have concentrated his attention on the screenplay, neglecting other elements of filmmaking. Cinema should illuminate the feelings and emotions in a script, not just recite the words. *A Tale of Winter*'s detachment only serves to further alienate the viewer. Criticized by reviewers for being talky and slow-moving, the film fails to evoke the magical quality it strives for.

—*Jarred Cooper*

REVIEWS

The Hollywood Reporter. February 24, 1992, p. 49.
The Hollywood Reporter. October 1, 1992, p. 9.
The Hollywood Reporter. April 13, 1994, p. 5.
Los Angeles Times. April 13, 1994, p. F4.
The New York Times. October 3, 1992, p. 13.
Variety. February 6, 1992, p. 16.

Talons of the Eagle

American Drug Enforcement Agency operative Tyler Wilson (Billy Blanks) teams with Canadian agent Michael Reed (Jalal Merhi) to combat a drug kingpin, Mr. Li (James Hong), in this action/adventure.

CREDITS

Tyler Wilson: Billy Blanks
Michael Reed: Jalal Merhi
Mr. Li: James Hong
Cassandra: Priscilla Barnes
Khan: Matthias Hues
Master Pan: Pan Qing Fu
Bodyguard: Eric Lee
Niko: Harry Mok
Tara: Kelly Gallant

Origin: Canada
Released: 1992
Production: Jalal Merhi for Film One; released by Shapiro Glickenhaus Entertainment
Direction: Michael Kennedy
Screenplay: J. Stephen Maunder
Cinematography: Curtis Petersen
Editing: Reid Dennison
Production design: Jasna Stefanovich
Sound: Jack Buchanan
Fight choreography: Jalal Merhi and Billy Blanks
Music: VaRouje
MPAA rating: R
Running time: 96 minutes

Terminal Velocity

"It's not the fall that kills you..."—Movie tagline

Box Office Gross: $16,455,799 (December 26, 1994)

Terminal Velocity is a visceral film, complete with thrilling stunts and amazing pyrotechnics. Unfortunately, the plot is not as well choreographed as many of the film's aerial maneuvers.

Charlie Sheen plays Ditch Brodie, a disillusioned world-class gymnast, who missed his opportunity to compete in the Olympics because of the U.S. boycott of the Moscow Games. Instead of fighting his fate, he has decided to tempt it. His forte is low-altitude skydiving, and the film is sprinkled with them.

When a giddy but gorgeous young woman (Nastassja Kinski) comes into the paracenter where Brodie teaches skydiving, the cocky womanizer gladly accepts her as a student. On her first jump, she apparently falls out of the plane while Brodie is in the cockpit. Brodie, in an attempt to catch her, hurtles through the air, head down and body stretched into a human arrow. In this breathtaking scene, director of photography Oliver Wood captures the sky divers' tremendous

speed. Unfortunately, Brodie is not as successful in capturing his student, and she falls to her death.

After the tragedy, Brodie is questioned by the FAA, who ultimately close the paracenter, citing them for negligence. Certain that her death was no accident, Brodie decides to investigate.

Using the dead woman's keys, he enters her apartment and unwittingly also enters her drama. Attacked by the KGB, buzzed by airplanes, chased off rooftops, and finally reunited with the not-so-dead woman, Brodie finally discovers the truth.

The woman, using the pseudonym "Chris Morrow," actually is a former KGB agent who, together with her roommate, was trying to locate a hijacked plane loaded with $600 million in gold bullion from the Russian treasury. They are trying to stop former KGB agents turned Russian mafia from succeeding in a coup d'etat that would return the country to communism. When her roommate locates the plane, however, she is murdered. This is when Chris uses her roommate's body to feign her own death, having her dropped from another plane as she jumped in another direction.

Brodie needs her to clear him of any suspicions of manslaughter and she needs him to locate the gold. Now working together, Brodie and Chris find the flight plans for the movement of the gold. After along chase, however, Chris is captured and thrown into the trunk of a car, which is loaded onto the cargo plane carrying the gold.

In an attempt to save her, Brodie leaps from the wing of a biplane onto the cargo plane. He climbs into the car just as it is jettisonedout of the plane. There follows one of the most exciting aerial stunts in the film.

Although the plot may not sound like a formula for comedy, the filmmakers never take the story too seriously. The basic premise is timely but not entirely credible. It begins like a Hitchcockian thriller, with the body

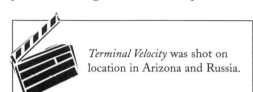

Terminal Velocity was shot on location in Arizona and Russia.

switch reminiscent of *Vertigo* (1958), then turns into an action/comedy in the style of old James Bond films.

The plot is weak in many areas. The viewer is never told how a Russian plane could be hijacked and brought to the Arizona desert without everyone from the National Guard to Interpol knowing about it. There is also little real motivation for Chris to fake her own death if she already knows exactly where the flight plans are. Further more, why does she let Brodie know she is alive? As an ace skydiver, she certainly does not need him to get the flight plans.

There is also the unbelievable romantic subplot. Chris, a beautiful secret agent, adept at hand-to-hand combat, a crack shot, a first-rate sky diver, and a skilled strategist, is attracted to a goofy womanizer with a puerile sense of humor. Chris moves from one scene, where she convincingly threatens to blow Brodie's head off, to the next, in which after drinking some mescal, she passionately kisses him and confides how she misses her three-legged dog, Tripod, back in Russia. It would take more than a bottle of mescal for anyone to make that leap in personality, even a sky diver.

Despite the fact that the writer gives little reason to consider these two romantically, they marry in the end and head to Russia for medals Russian gold medals.

David Twohy wrote *Terminal Velocity*. He is best known for his excellent work on *The Fugitive* (1993). It is therefore surprising that in *Terminal Velocity* Twohy has ignored some major weaknesses in the narrative. The interrelationships among the characters are never developed and, therefore, never become realistic. It also appears that Twohy is not concerned about resolving any of the plot in congruities.

The film received mixed reviews from critics. Wade Major in *Entertainment Today* conceded that "Credibility...is not what brings audiences into action films, and with a more-than-adequate collection of dynamic stunts and set pieces, Twohy and Sarafian appear to have easily compensated for the material's inherent weaknesses."

In contrast, Stephen Holden from *The New York Times* wrote "There is a thin line between an action-adventure movie that has a human touch and one that doesn't, and *Terminal Velocity* falls on the inhuman side.... After all its rollercoaster thrills, the movie provides no romantic payoff."

Sheen plays well the part of a wiseguy skydiving instructor who comes to realize his own courage and heroism. He is best known for his critically acclaimed dramatic roles in *Platoon* (1986) and *Wall Street* (1987). More recently he has been seen in comedy films, such as *Major League* (1989) and *Hot Shots* (1991), and their subsequent sequels.

His role in *Terminal Velocity* is more comedy than drama. Sheen embodies the ordinary man reluctantly thrown into an overwhemingly dangerous situation. The

CREDITS

Ditch Brodie: Charlie Sheen
Chris Morrow: Nastassja Kinski
Ben Pinkwater: James Gandolfini
Kerr: Christopher McDonald
Lex: Gary Bullock
Sam: Hans R. Howes
Noble: Melvin Van Peebles
Karen: Cathryn de Prume
Dominic: Richard Sarafian, Jr.
Robocam: Suli McCullough
Helicopter newscaster: Lori Lynn Dickerson
Birthday mother: Terry Finn
Newscaster: Martha Vazquez

Released: 1994
Production: Scott Kroopf and Tom Engelman for Hollywood Pictures, Interscope Communications, and Polygram Filmed Entertainment, in association with Nomura Babcock and Brown; released by Buena Vista Pictures
Direction: Deran Sarafian
Screenplay: David Twohy
Cinematography: Oliver Wood
Editing: Frank J. Urioste and Peck Prior
Production design: David L. Snyder
Art direction: Sarah Knowles
Set decoration: Beth A. Rubino
Set design: John O. Warnke
Casting: Terry Liebling
Special Visual effects: Christopher F. Woods
Sound: Stephan Von Hase Mihalik
Costume design: Poppy Cannon-Reese
Stunt coordination: Buddy Joe Hooker
Aerial coordination: Kevin Donnelly
Aerial stunt coordination: Jerry Meyers
Music: Joel McNeely
MPAA rating: PG-13
Running time: 100 minutes

character, however, is limited. Moving from cocky to confused to courageous and back again to cocky seems to be the spectrum of Ditch Brodie's emotional range.

Nastassja Kinski plays Chris Morrow, a top undercover agent who, when pitted against her own colleagues, chooses the good of her country over her past loyalties. The German-born star of *Tess* (1980) and *Paris, Texas* (1984) does fairly well with the material in *Terminal Velocity*, but her part is too schizophrenic forcing her to switch from tough, smart, ruthless spy to vulnerable beauty with no transition.

James Gandolfini is convincing as the ineffectual district attorney Ben Pinkwater, who later turns out to be the mastermind of the gold theft. Gandolfini effectively portrays the ruthless yet brilliant KGB agent and is the most powerful presence in the film.

Playing Kerr, the KGB hit man, is Christopher McDonald, seen recently in *Grumpy Old Men* (1993) and earlier as Geena Davis' husband in *Thelma and Louise* (1991). Perhaps in an effort to disguise his well-known features, the hair stylists bleached McDonald's hair, giving him a cartoonish bad-guy look.

Director Deran Sarafian is a veteran of action films; his most well-known is the prison thriller *Death Warrrant* (1990), starring Jean-Claude Van Damme.

Frank Urioste and Peck Prior have done professional work in the editing of *Terminal Velocity*, giving the film a fast pace that moves smoothly from scene to scene without dropping the pace. Urioste is best known for his Oscar nominated work on *Robocop* (1987), *Die Hard* (1988), and *Basic Instinct* (1992).

The visual effects are significant. Out of many, there are two that really stand out. The first is a high-speed ride in a homemade rocket-powered dragster on rails, with a last-minute ejector-seatescape from a firey explosion. The other is a startling scene in which Brodie is in a car falling out of a plane in midflight. Getting out of the car, he opens a sticky trunk to free Chris; they fly with one parachute and land amid moving windmills. Christopher Woods, the visual effects supervisor, successfully combines digital imaging, miniatures, and live-action photography to create these unique visual images.

With the beauty of Arizona and the Mojave Desert as a backdrop, cinematographer Oliver Woods and stunt coordinator Buddy Joe Hookerare to be applauded for some of the most amazing aerial stunts ever filmed in a major motion picture.

Terminal Velocity is, in the end, exciting yet shallow. Perhaps some films are not meant to be believed simply to be experienced and then forgotten.

—*Diane Hatch-Avis*

REVIEWS

Entertainment Today. September 23, 1994.
Entertainment Weekly. September 7, 1994, p. 53.
Hollywood Reporter. September 23-25, 1994, p. 10.
Los Angeles Times. September 23, 1994, F4.
The New York Times. September 23, 1994, p. B4.
Variety. September 23, 1994, p. 2.

Texas Tenor: The Illinois Jacquet Story

The life and art of jazz saxophonist Illinois Jacquet is the subject of this documentary.

REVIEWS

Chicago Tribune. October 3, 1993, Sec. 13 p. 10.
Los Angeles Times. December 19, 1993,
p. CAL64.
Variety. CCCXLVII, July 20, 1992, p. 65.

CREDITS

Illinois Jacquet: Illinois Jacquet
Lionel Hampton: Lionel Hampton
Dizzy Gillespie: Dizzy Gillespie
Sonny Rollins: Sonny Rollins
Buddy Tate: Buddy Tate
Milt Hinton: Milt Hinton
Cecil Payne: Cecil Payne
Carol Scherick: Carol Scherick
Clark Terry: Clark Terry

Released: 1992
Production: Ronit Avneri for Arthur Elgort Ltd.
Direction: Arthur Elgort
Cinematography: Morten Sandtroen
Editing: Paula Heredia
Sound: Ronit Anveri
Music: Illinois Jacquet
MPAA rating: no listing
Running time: 81 minutes

That's Entertainment! III

"From a time when dreams really did come true"
—Movie tagline

"An exuberant eruption of showbiz energy, an intoxicating song-and-dance phantasmagoria. Judy Garland, Lena Horne and Astaire & Rogers raise the roof in scenes never before publicly shown."—Bob Campbell, *Newhouse News Service*

"*That's Entertainment III* is a total 10!"—Susan Granger, *CRN Radio Network & American Movie Classics*

"The greatest stars from Hollywood's greatest era as you've never seen them before!"—Steve Kmetko, *E! Entertainment Television*

Box Office Gross: $171,242 (June 19, 1994)

This sequel to *That's Entertainment!* (1974) and *That's Entertainment! Part II* (1976) not only shows more clips from classic musicals and interviews with the likes of Lena Horne, Ann Miller, and Gene Kelly but also includes behind-the-scenes footage and outtakes. Drawn from over 100 films to the present, and including 62 musical numbers, the film was released to coincide with MGM's 70th anniversary.

REVIEWS

The Advocate. May 17, 1994, p. 75.
Boston Globe. July 22, 1994, p. 69.
Chicago Tribune. July 22, 1994, p. 7C.
Entertainment Weekly. May 6, 1994, p. 48.
Los Angeles Magazine. XXXIX, May 1994, p. 167.
Los Angeles Times. April 29, 1993, p. F1.
Los Angeles Times. May 6, 1994, p. F1.
The New York Times. May 6, 1994, p. C17.
People Weekly. XLI, May 23, 1994, p. 18.
Playboy. XLI, June 1994, p. 26.
USA Today. July 13, 1993, p. D6.
USA Today. May 6, 1994, p. D1.
Variety. CCCLIV, April 25, 1994, p. 29.

CREDITS

June Allyson: June Allyson
Cyd Charisse: Cyd Charisse
Lena Horne: Lena Horne
Howard Keel: Howard Keel
Gene Kelly: Gene Kelly
Ann Miller: Ann Miller
Debbie Reynolds: Debbie Reynolds
Mickey Rooney: Mickey Rooney
Esther Williams: Esther Williams

Released: 1994
Production: Bud Friedgen and Michael J. Sheridan, in association with Turner Entertainment Co.; released by Metro-Goldwyn-Mayer
Direction: Bud Friedgen and Michael J. Sheridan
Screenplay: Bud Friedgen and Michael J. Sheridan
Cinematography: Howard A. Anderson III
Editing: Bud Friedgen and Michael J. Sheridan
Sound: Dave Kelson and Bill Teague
Music supervision: Marilee Bradford
Additional music: Marc Shaiman
MPAA rating: G
Running time: 113 minutes

"We spent years and years literally crawling around in the film vaults. There's a tremendous amount of research here."—Bud Friedgen, director and screenwriter of *That's Entertainment! III*

There Goes My Baby

"It was the summer of '65 and rock 'n' roll was alive."—Movie tagline

Box Office Gross: $84,137 (September 5, 1994)

Eight recent high school graduates contemplate their future, in this drama set in 1965. Compared to George Lucas' *American Graffiti* (1973), the film was shelved for a couple of years due to Orion Pictures' bankruptcy.

REVIEWS

Atlanta Constitution. September 6, 1994, p. B7.
Christian Science Monitor. September 6, 1994, p. 13.
Los Angeles Times. September 12, 1993, p. BR9.
Los Angeles Times. December 16, 1994, p. F10.
TV Guide. XLIII, March 4, 1995, p. 51.

CREDITS

Pirate: Dermot Mulroney
Stick: Rick Schroder
Sunshine: Kelli Williams
Finnegan: Noah Wyle
Babette: Jill Schoelen
Tracy: Kristin Minter
Mary Beth: Lucy Deakins
Calvin: Kenny Ransom
Pop: Seymour Cassel
Burton: Paul Gleason

Maran: Frederick Coffin
Frank: Andrew Robinson
The Beard: Humble Harve Miller
Morrisey: Shon Greenblatt
George: J. E. Freeman

Released: 1994
Production: Robert Shapiro for Nelson Entertainment; released by Orion Pictures
Direction: Floyd Mutrux
Screenplay: Floyd Mutrux
Cinematography: William A. Fraker
Editing: Danford B. Greene and Maysie Hoy
Production design: Richard Sawyer
Art direction: Louis Mann
Set decoration: Peg Cummings
Casting: Lynn Stalmaster, Janet Hirshenson and Jane Jenkins
Sound: William J. Randall
Costume design: Molly Maginnis
Music production: Budd Carr
MPAA rating: R
Running time: 99 minutes

"It's my last night on AM. I'll be movin' on to a new thing called...FM."—local deejay from *There Goes My Baby*

There Goes the Neighborhood

A prison psychiatrist (Jeff Daniels), tipped off by a dying inmate (Harris Yulin), goes on a treasure hunt in the basement of a New Jersey home belonging to an attractive divorcee (Catherine O'Hara) with whom he teams. Two other prisoners escape from jail in order to beat him to the fortune, but get the address wrong, in this screwball comedy.

REVIEWS

Variety. CCCXLIX, November 9, 1992, p. 63.

CREDITS

Willis Embris: Jeff Daniels
Jessie: Catherine O'Hara
Norman: Hector Elizondo
Peedi: Judith Ivey
Jeffrey: Dabney Coleman
Lydia: Rhea Perlman
Convict: Harris Yulin

Released: 1992
Production: Stephen Friedman for Kings Road; released by Paramount Pictures
Direction: Bill Phillips
Screenplay: Bill Phillips
Cinematography: Walt Lloyd
Editing: Sharyn L. Ross
Production design: Dean Tschetter
Casting: Mary Jo Slater
Music: David Bell
MPAA rating: PG-13
Running time: 88 minutes

The Thing Called Love

"Stand by your dream"—Movie tagline

An aspiring singer-songwriter, Miranda (Samantha Mathis), forsakes New York for Nashville, where she hopes to find success. Instead, she falls in love with a fellow songwriter, James (River Phoenix), while yet another songwriter, Kyle (Dermot Mulroney), falls in love with her.

REVIEWS

Atlanta Constitution. August 27, 1993, p. D1.
Chicago Tribune. January 21, 1994, p. 7C.
Variety. CCCLII, September 6, 1993, p. 27.

CREDITS

James Wright: River Phoenix
Miranda Presley: Samantha Mathis
Kyle Davidson: Dermot Mulroney
Linda Lue Linden: Sandra Bullock
Lucy: K. T. Oslin
Billy: Anthony Clark
Ned: Webb Wilder
Floyd: Earl Poole Ball
Jimmy Dale Gilmore: Jimmy Dale Gilmore
Pam Tillis: Pam Tillis
Trisha Yearwood: Trisha Yearwood

Released: 1993
Production: John Davis; released by Paramount Pictures
Direction: Peter Bogdanovich
Screenplay: Carol Heikkinen
Cinematography: Peter James
Editing: Terry Stokes
Production design: Michael Seymour
Art direction: Thomas D. Wilkins
Set decoration: Cloudia
Casting: Dianne Crittenden
Sound: James Edward Webb, Jr.
Costume design: Rita Riggs
Music supervision: G. Marq Roswell
Executive music consultant: J. Steven Soles
MPAA rating: PG-13
Running time: 116 minutes

Thirty-Two Short Films About Glenn Gould

"A most unconventional motion picture about a most unusual man."—Movie tagline

"...brilliant and transfixing."—*The New York Times*

"Distinctive and irresistible"—*The Los Angeles Times*

"A fascinating guy and a fascinating film. Two thumbs up."—*Siskel & Ebert*

"Intelligence, eccentricity, and a sharp vision."
—Richard Corliss, *Time*

"A masterpiece! Remarkable, eye-opening and fabulously inventive."—*Toronto Globe and Mail*

Canada's thriving film community is once again masterfully represented with this riveting impressionistic documentary about the eccentric pianist Glenn Gould. With films such as *Jesus of Montreal* (1989), *Léolo* (1992), and this one, the Canadian cinema has presented a wonderful and exciting challenge to Hollywood in terms of thoughtful and insightful filmmaking.

Glenn Gould was a highly idiosyncratic pianist who was arguably best known for his unique and definitive interpretations of Bach's Goldberg Variations (of which there are thirty-two, hence the title of this film). His interpretations of various pieces by Bach, Beethoven, and other masters form the sound track to this film.

Perhaps the most idiosyncratic event in Gould's career was his abrupt retirement at an early age, after playing to overwhelmingly successful concert audiences and developing a large and devoted following. Gould was loved with nearly the same ardor as many rockstars, and his fans were shocked and disappointed when, in the1960's, he stopped performing

entirely to follow various other pursuits. He died at a rather young age, with very little of the grandeur promised by his early years. In fact, he died something of a pauper, after many years of addiction to pain pills and numerous other drugs.

This documentary is nonlinear and nonnarrative. It informs about its subject without ever having narration describe the events of Gould's life in the third person and without following him through concert footage and the usual family pictures that are present in other documentaries. An audience might expect to see footage of Gould in concert, similar to *From Mao to Mozart: Isaac Stern in China* (1980) or, for that matter, *Truth or Dare* (1991), about pop phenomenon Madonna. Here director Francois Girard opts to offer a series of impressionistic vignettes that are nondidactic and offer glimpses of more than just biographical material.

Each of the thirty-two vignettes has a different title and a distinct point of view. For example, "CD 318" is merely a series of visual images of the inner workings of a piano as it is being played. Close-ups of the hammers and strings, the pegs, and the golden inner frame of the piano are hypnotically edited in such a way as to share with the audience Gould's love of a Steinway (serial number CD 318). This impression touches the audience on a visceral level, helping them to enter the complex and abstract world of Gould from within. So often a documentary tries to describe its subject's passion; here director Girard has chosen to illustrate that passion rather than describe it.

Another way in which Girard is able to depict his subject is to create a few vignettes in which events in Gould's life are dramatized. Gould is played by actor Colm Feore in an excellent performance. In one vignette entitled "Passion," Feore enters a green room (waiting room) underneath a stage prior to a concert and he narrates, in voice-over: "Some of the pianos were so bad, I just decided to ignore them. It required a sort of mystical transcendence; I have no idea what the audience resorted to. I would not have listened. I just don't like piano music that much." Following this, one sees Gould's version of practicing: He listens to a recording of himself playing, conducting, moving, becoming engrossed in the rhythms and melodies. The camera circles around him, following him in his trance-like behavior. No didactic description of Gould's connection to the music inside him could ever describe it as well as this brief dramatization.

CREDITS

Glenn Gould: Colm Feore

Origin: Canada
Released: 1993
Production: Niv Fichman for Rhombus Media; released by the Samuel Goldwyn Company
Direction: François Girard
Screenplay: François Girard and Don McKellar
Cinematography: Alain Dostie
Editing: Gaétan Huot
Sound: Jane Tattersall: John D. Smith and Stuart French
Costume design: Linda Muir
Music: Glenn Gould
MPAA rating: no listing
Running time: 94 minutes

AWARDS AND NOMINATIONS

Genie Awards: Best Film, Best Director (Girard), Best Cinematography, Best Film Editing
Independent Spirit Awards Nomination: Best Foreign Language Film

Some other interesting vignettes or "short films" are "Variations in C Minor," in which animated lines vibrate to the music; "Gould Meets MacLaren," another animated vignette in which circles multiply and converge and move around the screen, representing the multiplication and division of ideas in an interesting voice-over conversation; and "The Tip," a depiction of Gould's interest in the stock market, with Gould telling a waiter a fake stock tip, who in turn tells someone else, who tells someone else, driving up the price of the stock.

"In the end, the great thing about *Thirty-Two Short Films About Glenn Gould* is that rather than creating a desire to meet this formidable individual, it makes you feel as if in some way you actually had."—Kenneth Turan, *The Los Angeles Times*

Some of the films are quite serious; some are great fun. One extremely witty vignette deals with the questions and answers that various newspaper and television reporters asked of Gould. The interviews are edited so that they form a jumbled mass of questions that build to a crescendo of frustration for each of the interviewers, since Gould's off-camera responses are either nonexistent or completely absurd. One of the funniest moments comes when a little girl no more than seven years old asks Gould to teach her to play the piano. The last question in this segment is a young woman asking, "Why didn't you return my calls?" indicating that not all difficult questions for Gould were journalistic ones. Girard consistently weaves in new information in this way, focusing on the important information from Gould's life without being hamstrung by convention to present information chronologically.

Girard also retains a wonderful thread of symbolism throughout the film. The film opens with a long, static shot of a barren plain of ice and snow, with the tiny figure of a man way off in the distance. The man slowly walks toward the camera, a small dot on the landscape looming larger and larger as music plays. The image seems to say that Gould came out of the frozen wasteland of cold and rigid musical performance to "heat things up" with his passion. The image of ice and cold recurs at various times throughout the film.

One vignette shows Gould standing alone on the midst of a similar (perhaps the same) plain of ice and snow as in the first shot. His answers to questions about his life while in the middle of nowhere underscore the desolation and alienation which led Gould to his premature and tragic end. The images of ice and snow return in another vignette entitled "The Idea of North," taken from a radio broadcast Gould made that was actually a cleverly edited series of voices all talking about going north or living in the north. From these images audiences can gather that Gould was entranced by the northern climates—he was, after all, born in Canada—and by the ideas and images of cold and desolation which the north symbolized and which resonated so deeply with him.

Even when he was in the middle of the glow of audience adulation or the warmth of friends—who talk about him in interviews in this film—or making his music, Gould was alone and desolate. He is quoted as saying, "For x number of hours you spend with human beings, you require x number of hours alone." His desolation, combined with chronic bronchitis, led him to bizarre behavior and to a pill addiction, which is strikingly chronicled here in the form of a series of pictures of all the pills he took daily, combined with shots of his written daily record of his pill intake.

Production values on the film are excellent. In particular, director of photography Alain Dostie makes the most of the various forms the film takes. From the rich and earthy colors of light in the initial sequences in Gould's birthplace, to the dark shadows of the backstage areas, to the eerie desolation of the "northern" scenes, Dostie provides a beautiful and elegant photographic atmosphere. In addition, the musical score, utilizing the best of Glenn Gould's recordings, is a wonderful reminder of Gould's artistry. Sometimes the music is allowed to speak for itself, as in the animated vignette illustrating the vibrations made by the music, and sometimes Gould's recordings are used to underscore the drama of a sequence; a wonderful example is the use of Bach's "Well-Tempered Clavier," the first piece learned by Gould as a young pianist, as the last piece inthe film. Gould's interpretation is simple and delicate, belying his inner struggles and underscoring the dramatic progression of the film perfectly.

This film has received numerous accolades and well-deserved praise for its interesting investigation into the life of quirky Glenn Gould. Girard has directed a film of dignity and drama and of humor and tragedy. Somehow he has managed to capture the humanity of this enigmatic man without becoming maudlin or stagy. It is certainly adaring choice to use dramatization in documentary, because the director and actors run the risk of appearing disrespectful at best and defamatory at worst about their subject. The limited use of actor Feore as Gould is most appropriate; any more would have taken the film out the realm of documentary and into the nether world of docudrama, which is best left to television.

The balance achieved by Girard and company between a conventional documentary, a dramatic depiction of a person's life, and a unique art-house film has made *Thirty-Two Short Films About Glenn Gould* one of the most interesting films of the year.

—*Kirby Tepper*

REVIEWS

The Hollywood Reporter. September 21, 1993, p. 72.
Los Angeles Times. April 14, 1994, p. F4.
The New Times. April 14, 1994, p. B3.

3 Ninjas Kick Back

"Colt, Rocky and Tum Tum are back in an all new adventure"—Movie tagline

"As lively and engaging as the original. This smart-looking movie is actually more inventive and better paced than many a comedy for adults. The film shows a genuine concern for values."
—*Los Angeles Time*

"The kids will crack up over the ninja-style variations on Three Stooges slapstick, while adults will appreciate the equal opportunity message."
—*Atlanta Journal Constitution*

"Gags galore"—*Washington Post*

Three young brothers (Max Elliott Slade, Sean Fox, and Evan Bonifant) travel to Japan with their grandpa (Victor Wong), where he is to present a ceremonial dagger to the winner of a ninja tournament. Once there, the boys' martial-arts expertise is called upon to fight Grandpa's old nemesis, Koga (Sab Shimono), and a trio of heavy-metal-rockers who are trying to steal the dagger, which is also a key to hidden treasure. Sequel to *3 Ninjas* (1992). Filmed mainly on location in Japan.

REVIEWS

Atlanta Constitution. May 6, 1994, p. P4.
Boston Globe. May 6, 1994, p. 90.
Chicago Tribune. May 6, 1994, Sec. 5 p. 8.
Entertainment Weekly. May 13, 1994, p. 44.
Los Angeles Times. May 6, 1994, p. F18.
The New York Times. May 7, 1994, p. A18.
USA Today. May 6, 1994, p. D5.
Variety. CCCLV, May 9, 1994, p. 72.
The Washington Post. May 12, 1994, p. C7.
The Washington Post. May 6, 1994, p. B7.

CREDITS

Grandpa: Victor Wong
Colt: Max Elliott Slade
Rocky: Sean Fox
Tum Tum: Evan Bonifant
Miyo: Caroline Junko King
Koga: Sab Shimono
Glam: Dustin Nguyen
Vinnie: Jason Schombing
Slam: Angelo Tiffe

Released: 1994
Production: James Kang, Martha Chang, and Arthur Leeds for Sheen, in association with Ben-Ami/Leeds Productions; released by TriStar Pictures
Direction: Charles T. Kanganis
Screenplay: Mark Saltzman; based on a screenplay by Simon Sheen
Cinematography: Christopher Faloona
Editing: David Rennie and Jeffrey Reiner
Production design: Hiroyuki Takatsu and Gregory Martin
Art direction: Scott Meehan
Set decoration: Karin McGaughey
Casting: Lucy Boulting
Sound: Clifford Gynn
Costume design: Takeshi Yamazaki and Miye Matsumoto
Music: Richard Marvin
MPAA rating: PG
Running time: 99 minutes

Threesome

"One girl. Two guys. Three possibilities."—Movie tagline

"A romantic lark."—*Cosmopolitan*

"It is accurate and honest about the sexuality of young people."—*Chicago Sun-Times*

"Unique. A daringly explorative nature in dealing with anxiety toward sexual orientation."
—*Daily Trojan*

"a sweet funny tale."—*Out Magazine*

 Box Office Gross: $14,722,491 (June 26, 1994)

Threesome takes place on a college campus, and its three principal characters are college students—two males and one female—sharing the same dormitory room. This setting and premise are traditionally the realm of teen exploitation films along the lines of *National Lampoon's Animal House* (1978) and its legion of imitators—*T & A*

CREDITS

Alex: Lara Flynn Boyle
Stuart: Stephen Baldwin
Eddy: Josh Charles
Dick: Alexis Arquette
Renay: Martha Gehman
Larry: Mark Arnold
Kristen: Michele Matheson

Released: 1994
Production: Brad Krevoy and Steve Stabler for Motion Picture Corporation of America; released by TriStar Pictures
Direction: Andrew Fleming
Screenplay: Andrew Fleming
Cinematography: Alexander Gruszynski
Editing: William C. Carruth
Production design: Ivo Cristante
Art direction: Ken Larson
Set decoration: Tim Colohan
Casting: Ed Mitchell and Robyn Ray
Sound: Giovanni Di Simone
Costume design: Deborah Everton
Music: Thomas Newman
MPAA rating: R
Running time: 93 minutes

Academy, (1979), *Toga Party* (1979), and *Fraternity Vacation* (1985), to name a few. The film even contains such obligatory college hijinks as food fights, drunken binges, nude romps, explicit sex, and extremely frank language.

Despite all these potentially exploitative ingredients, however, *Threesome* avoids dissolving into a simpleminded teen sex romp. In fact, it has much more in common with a highly respected film also dealing with a man/woman/man relationship, to which it pays homage in its final moments—François Truffaut's *Jules et Jim* (1962; *Jules and Jim*). In a voice-over narration, Eddy (Josh Charles) defines the word "deviant," saying that it originally meant a person who strays from the main road, but that now it refers to someone who is considered a sexual pervert. He then says that the story he is about to tell explores both meanings of the word.

Eddy is a film major at a prestigious Southern California university. When the film opens, he is just arriving and checks into his on-campus dorm. He shares his room with a business major, Stuart (Stephen Baldwin), whom Eddy quickly realizes is his exact opposite. While Eddy is reserved, fastidiously neat, and devoted to his studies, Stuart is a loudmouth slob whose main concerns are partying and womanizing. Nevertheless, as Eddy explains during a brief but effective montage, the two quickly develop a friendly tolerance for each other's disparate likes and dislikes. Soon, the roommates are friends and engaging in shared activities.

Their friendly bond is challenged with the arrival of Alex (Lara Flynn Boyle). Because of a computer mix-up, Alex has been classified as a male and assigned to room with Stuart and Eddy. When she tries to straighten out the mess with university officials, Alex is told that she will have to wait several months before she can be reassigned to another room. Alex is resigned to her fate, but then lays down some hard rules to Eddy and Stuart about respecting her privacy. Eddy agrees to her demands, but Stuart is not so quick to embrace them. Soon, he is plotting ways to seduce her.

Alex remains unmoved by Stuart's unsubtle advances. When the three bump into one another at a local pizza parlor, Stuart once again tries to impress her by feigning interest in the book she is reading, *The Catcher in the Rye* (1945). When Eddy joins in on the conversation, however, Alex begins to warm up to him, much to Stuart's chagrin.

Later, Alex runs into Eddy at the library and tries to seduce him while he reads from a book by Nathaniel Hawthorne. When he remains indifferent to her advances, she sprawls out on the desk in front of him and asks him to read out loud while she writhes in sexual ecstasy. When Eddy later tells Stuart about the library scene, Stuart is happy for him and gives him pointers on effective sexual-techniques. While he goes into graphic detail, Eddy becomes aroused and realizes that he is much more attracted to Stuart than he is to Alex.

Alex is now determined to have sex with Eddy. When she makes another play for him, he ends up confessing his sexual preferences to her, saying that he has had brief affairs with women in the past but is more attracted to men. At first, she is confused, but then accepts him as a friend, promising to honor his request to keep his revelation from Stuart. Stuart soon figures out Eddy's gay tendencies, however, and bluntly confronts him with his suspicions. With the truth of the matter now revealed, Alex insists the three of them make a sacred vow not to ruin their friendly threesome with sex.

Although the roommates try to honor their new agreement, the sexual tension between them grows. When Alex brings home a male friend, Larry (Mark Arnold), Eddy and Stuart provoke Alex until the three of them engage in a rowdy food and pillow fight, much to Larry's horror. A variation of this scene occurs when Stuart invites a woman friend, Kristen (Michele Matheson) over for dinner. Then, after Alex and Stuart try to fix up Eddy with the dormitory's gay desk clerk, Dick (Alexis Arquette), which also ends in disaster, the roommates realize they are intentionally sabotaging one another's outside friendships in order to keep the special bond between them strong.

The sexual tension comes to a head when the threesome goes for a nature outing. They end up skinny-dipping together, then nearly having sex. A passing troupe of young hikers interrupts their activities, but Eddy intones that things were never the same afterward. Back in the dormitory, Alex and Eddy quarrel, he accusing her of purposely getting involved with men who she knows will frustrate her, and she accusing him of being a "closet heterosexual." After Eddy storms out, Stuart appears and takes advantage of Alex's emotional state. Soon, the two are having sex on a regular basis, although it is obvious that Alex still longs for Eddy.

Eddy finally agrees to give heterosexuality another try and lets Alex seduce him. Afterward, however, he confesses that he felt like a fraud. He also tells her that, because Stuart is so brazen about his preference for women, he must be a latent homosexual. When the two young men get drunk together one evening, Eddy makes a move on Stuart, but Stuart strongly rebukes him.

The following day in one of his film classes, Eddy sees *Jules et Jim* and realizes that his situation parallels that of the characters in the film. Because two of the film characters end up destroying each other, Eddy decides to avoid a similar fate by moving out. Yet when he tries to leave, the trio finally become lovers, engaging in a sexual threesome, each one pleasuring the other two.

Afterward, the three avoid one another, all of them confused by the intimate turn of events their friendship has taken. Alex later shocks the others when she announces that she is pregnant. When they force her to take a home pregnancy test and it comes up negative, the threesome becomes even more disoriented and distant.

During a final montage, Eddy tells how the trio fell apart after the pregnancy scare, with first Alex moving out, followed by Eddy. By graduation time, they are hardly associating with one another. In the film's final moments, Eddy compares the affair to a well-planned vacation that goes awry, one in which the vacationers take a wrong turn and end up engaging in activities they never would have conceived of doing, but upon returning home, realize that the unplanned detour was the best part of the trip.

The strengths of *Threesome* are many, the most obvious being its unpretentious, lighthearted treatment of such traditionally somber subjects as the bonds of friendship, love, and sexual attraction. The film makes no claims to be the definitive statement on these matters. It is much more concerned with capturing the unrestrained exuberance that comes with being out on one's own for the first time surrounded by companions who value freedom of expression if such forms of expression are sincere attempts to define one's true identity.

"I'll mold you into a heterosexual with my bare hands!"—Alex from *Threesome*

For example, after the scene in the library where Alex becomes sexually aroused while Eddy reads "big words" from his Hawthorne book, Stuart tries the same technique on her, this time reading from Dostoyevsky. Alex is at first receptive to his advances until he begins quoting from the book, at which point, she admonishes him, saying, "You tap into something savage and emotional but then ruin it by being something you're not." This is the film's emotional crux—all actions are permitted if they are sincere expressions of the person's search for his or her true identity.

This theme is emphasized by the way in which the characters are portrayed. Stuart may be a shameless, sex-obsessed slob, but because these traits truly define his character, he is accepted by the others and the audience as well. The same applies to Eddy and his homosexuality, and to Alex and her problems with becoming involved with men who can never satisfy her emotional needs. This total acceptance of one another's true character and the importance the threesome grant to testing the boundaries of their feelings give the film a zestful honesty even when the actions on screen are bluntly provocative. For example, the sex scenes are extremely explicit, yet they have an innocence about them because the characters themselves are portrayed as innocents.

Director/writer Andrew Fleming keeps the film's momentum lively by concentrating exclusively on the trio's emotional entanglements. Although it is set on a college campus, there are few scenes of the characters actually attending classes or studying. The focus is finely and effectively narrowed so the real world of emotional angst, sexually transmitted diseases, and failing grades does not intrude on the film's free-spirited tone. Fleming has also coaxed some fine performances out of his talented young cast. All three principals remain true to the spirit of their well-defined characters, capturing the heart and soul of each in a straightforward, unpretentious manner.

The film's critical reception was mixed, many critics condemning it for failing to capture the troubled, dispirited angst of its "Generation X" characters and for treating such volatile subjects as homosexuality and sexual experimentation in a brazenly guilt-free manner. Also, many disliked the film's refusal to delve deeper into the college milieu, and its trivializing of such artistic giants as Hawthorne, Dostoyevsky, Salinger, and Truffaut. Yet some critics appreciated its refreshingly lighthearted approach to such tradi-

tionally heavy themes and references, applauding the film's sincerity, exuberant spirit, and small-scale intimacy.

Overall, *Threesome* accomplishes what its narrator sets up in the film's opening scene. It broadens the definition of "deviant," giving it a much more universal appeal so that it applies not only to "sexual perverts" but to all of those who stray from the traditional path as they seek to find themselves.

—Jim Kline

REVIEWS

Entertainment Weekly. April 15, 1994, p. 40.
The Hollywood Reporter. January 31, 1994, p. 17.
Los Angeles Times. April 8, 1994, p. F1.
The New Times. April 8, 1994, p. B8.
Newsweek. April 18, 1994, p. 60.
Variety. January 31, 1994, p. 10.

Time Indefinite

Filmmaker Ross McElwee chronicles his own life, engagement, and marriage, and the deaths of his father and grandmother and his wife's miscarriage, in this autobiographical documentary. Sequel to *Sherman's March* (1986).

REVIEWS

Atlanta Journal and Atlanta Constitution, July 2, 1993, p. D3.
Boston Globe. May 21, 1993, p. 25.
Chicago Tribune. October 29, 1993, p. 7K(31).
Christian Science Monitor. May 14, 1993, p. 14.
Los Angeles Times. January 8, 1994, p. F7.
The New York Times. May 12, 1993, p. C13.
Variety. CCCLI, June 28, 1993, p. 23.
The Washington Post. May 7, 1993, p. B7.
The Washington Post. May 7, 1993, p. WW50.

CREDITS

Ross McElwee: Ross McElwee
Marilyn Levine: Marilyn Levine

Released: 1994
Production: Ross McElwee; released by First Run Features
Direction: Ross McElwee
Screenplay: Ross McElwee
Editing: Ross McElwee
Sound: Ross McElwee
MPAA rating: no listing
Running time: 117 minutes

Timecop

"Murder is forever...until now."—Movie tagline

 Box Office Gross: $44,327,925 (December 11, 1994)

Timecop is another in a long tradition of films involving time travel. Perhaps the most successful version of this theme to appear in contemporary cinema was *The Terminator* (1984), which amazed audiences with its intricate plot involving a chase through time to save the world from apocalypse. This film secured Arnold Schwarzenegger a position as one of the leading stars in the action/adventure genre, and led to a sequel. Critics have implied that *Timecop* is a film in pursuit of a similar success for leading man Jean-Claude Van Damme, who for the past several years has been trying to surpass his status as a second-string action star.

Timecop focuses primarily on two different time periods: 1994 and 2004. In 1994, the government

A major intersection in Vancouver was transformed into old New York's Wall Street of 1929 for the filming of *Timecop*.

learns of the development of a new technology which makes possible time travel. It is demonstrated that this technology could lead to a rearrangement of current global economies, which might prove disastrous to the United States. At a congressional meeting, it is agreed that a government agency called the Time Enforcement Commission (TEC) will be created to police time—to make sure that no one goes back and to pursue and punish those who do. Senator McComb (Ron Silver) volunteers to over see the new agency.

Later, viewers are introduced to a young TEC officer, Max Walker (Jean-Claude Van Damme). One evening as his wife Melissa (Mia Sara) prepares to tell him that she is expecting a child, he receives a call from work and rushes out the door, giving her no time to reveal her good news. He is met outside his home by a group of thugs who attack and shoot him. As he lay beaten on the lawn, having survived the shooting thanks to a bullet-proof vest, he sees through the window that his wife is being attacked inside the house. Before he can drag himself to her aid, the entire house explodes, killing everyone inside.

In the year 2004, Max Walker has still not recovered from the loss of his wife. In a scene which illustrates well the anguish of time and lost opportunity, Walker sits alone in his apartment watching a home video of his wife in which they discuss plans to remodel their victorian home. He speaks along with his former voice repeating every word of the

"Smart kid, he read my mind."
"With your English, he doesn't have much choice."—Walker and Melissa from *Timecop*

video verbatim, engaging in a time-split conversation of sorts with his lost wife.

The TEC agency is in crisis at this point. Walker has followed his partner back in time only to discover that he is cashing in on the stock market in the early part of the century. Upon being caught, his partner confesses that he and half the agency are working for Senator McComb to make money for his bid for the presidency, either because they have been bought out or threatened with the complete extinction of themselves and their families through the use of time travel.

McComb has been lobbying to abolish the TEC on the platform that it is vulnerable to corruption, while in fact his actual motive is to establish a monopoly on the technology for his own gain. Walker becomes obsessed with stopping McComb—if he cannot break the law to go back and save his wife, McComb should not be allowed to do so for money and power.

Walker's struggle to stop McComb takes him back to 1994, where McComb is trying to remedy a previous bad business decision by murdering his former partner and giving some valuable information to his former self. Things do not go well for Walker, and upon his return to 2004, he finds the TEC being dismantled and McComb in power. McComb has in fact so altered the future that Walker's former allies no longer know him or understand the dynamics of what has happened.

Walker gains the trust of his boss, Matuzak (Bruce McGill), who believes him and helps him make one final trip into the past. In this last attempt to save the future, he decides to rescue his wife, and in doing so, discovers that her fate was not accidental but the result of McComb's attempt, through the use of time travel, to eliminate him before he could prove dangerous. After some high-action combat Walker prevails and returns to the future uncertain of the results. At the end of this hard day's work he returns home and, to his surprise, is greeted by his ten-year-old son and his wife at the door of their renovated victorian house.

Like other films that illustrate the human desire to transgress time, *Timecop* deals with the pursuit of power, justice, and the redemption of love, the three things that suffer most at the hands of life's contingency. By achieving the ability to travel in time, one becomes capable of remaking one's life by fixing old wrongs, repossessing what was lost, and carrying knowledge into the past. These abilities are ultimately threatening to those

CREDITS

Max Walker: Jean-Claude Van Damme
Melissa Walker: Mia Sara
Senator McComb: Ron Silver
Matuzak: Bruce McGill
Fielding: Gloria Reuben
Ricky: Scott Bellis
Atwood: Jason Schombing
Spota: Scott Lawrence
Utley: Kenneth Welsh
Shotgun: Brent Woolsey
Reyes: Brad Loree
Rollerblades: Shane Kelly
Cole: Richard Faraci
Lansing: Steve Lambert
Parker: Kevin McNulty

Released: 1994
Production: Moshe Diamant, Sam Raimi, and Robert Tapert for Signature/Renaissance/Dark Horse Production and Largo Entertainment, in association with JVC Entertainment; released by Universal Pictures
Direction: Peter Hyams
Screenplay: Mark Verheiden; based on the story and comic series by Verheiden and Mike Richardson
Cinematography: Peter Hyams
Editing: Steven Kemper
Production design: Philip Harrison
Art direction: Richard Hudolin
Set decoration: Rose Marie McSherry and Ann Marie Corbett
Executive producer: Mike Richardson
Visual effects supervision: Gregory L. McMurry
Stunt coordination: Glenn Randall
Casting: Penny Perry
Music: Mark Isham
MPAA rating: R
Running time: 95 minutes

in power because of the possibility of undoing reality and putting their privileged position at risk. Limitations are established and enforced by the time police, a group of individuals hired to maintain the hegemony of the government. Max Walker is portrayed as a man of duty, upholding the law on principle; Senator McComb as an opportunistic politician, eager to remake the world to his advantage. Therefore neither character is capable of establishing any truly interesting moral conflict. The revolutionary potential of time travel expressed in *Terminator* is lacking in this film, making the outcome less critical. The film's tension therefore relies heavily on the love story between Walker and his wife Melissa.

The story is based on a comic series created by Mike Richardson and Mark Verheiden, and the screenplay written by Verheiden, who wrote *The Mask* (reviewed in this volume). The success of a time-travel film is strongly determined by the ability of the screenwriter to sort through the tangle of logical problems and establish enough credible sequences to overshadow the many loose ends and paradoxes which will never completely make sense. Verheiden does an adequate job of tying together the many strands in this plot and, in moments, pulls off the logic of time travel with ease and cleverness: Senator McComb quickly develops a scar on his face when his younger double is assaulted; characters, whose deaths are erased by the new sets of circumstances, pop back into existence in the new 2004; and the problem of doubles is handled by allowing them to coexist but never touch—if they touch they melt and are both destroyed.

Problems do remain in the script with the issues of memory and clear, logical scenarios, resulting from traveling through and changing time continuums. Beyond the problems of the logic of time travel, however, the script manages to entwine several different genres—action/adventure, romance, and science fiction drama—into one coherent script.

Director Peter Hyams, whose credits include *2010* (1984), establishes a subtle and believable version of a future, which is only ten years away from the film's release date. Computer technology is more advanced—people have a more passive relationship with cars, which resemble space ships and respond to vocal commands; interiors are remodeled versions of the old; and the exterior world remains basically the same.

One aspect that distinguishes Van Damme among American action/adventure stars is his training in martial arts and ballet. These skills, among others, made him the perfect leading man for the Hollywood debut film of critically acclaimed Chinese director John Woo (*Hard Target*, 1993). Van Damme's films are defined by their hands-on contact fights, involving physical prowess, technical skill, and split-second cunning; *Timecop* is no exception. Van Damme engages in intricate knife fights, karate and fist fights, and even leaps into splits on the kitchen counter to escape electrocution. In this particular film, there is a greater emphasis on dramatic sequences in an effort to improve his acting reputation—an effort which backfires.

Timecop is a film which closely mirrors Van Damme's fate of being quite good but remaining second-string to the greater versions of this theme. 🎞

—*Reni Celeste*

REVIEWS

Chicago Tribune. September 16, 1994, II, p. 5.
Daily Variety. September 12, 1994, p. 12.
The Hollywood Reporter. September 12, 1994, p. 10.
Los Angeles Times. September 16, 1994, p. F10.
The New York Times. September 16, 1994, p. B1.

To Die Standing (Crackdown)

An American Drug Enforcement Administration (DEA) agent, Shaun Broderick (Cliff De Young), teams with a South American agent, Lieutenant Delgado (Robert Beltran), to extradite a Latin American drug kingpin, Don Castillo (Orlando Sacha), to the United States.

REVIEWS

Variety. CCCXLI, Jan 7, 1991, p. 22.

CREDITS

Shaun Broderick: Cliff De Young
Lieutenant Delgado: Robert Beltran
Constance Bigelow: Jamie Rose
Castillo: Orlando Sacha
Cowley: Kevin Reidy

Thurmond: Gerald Anthony
Menendez: Ramon Garcia

Released: 1991
Production: Luis Llosa; released by Concorde
Direction: Louis Morneau
Screenplay: Ross Bell and Daryl Haney
Cinematography: Pili Flores Guerra
Editing: Eric L. Beason
Production design: Jaime Gonzales
Casting: Kevin Reidy and Steve Rabiner
Sound: Edgard Lostaunau
Costume design: Greg LaVoi
Music: Terry Plumeri
MPAA rating: R
Running time: 88 minutes

To Live

"A Chinese *Gone With The Wind*."—Andrew Sarris, *New York Observer*

"Two magnificent performances by Ge You and Gong Li."—Caryn James, *The New York Times*

"One of the best films of the year."—*Siskel & Ebert*

 Box Office Gross: $742,651 (January 2, 1995)

Director Zhang Yimou and his stars, Ge You and Gong Li, have created a lyrical and emotional epic depicting the tumultuous lives of a Chinese family, set against the sweeping changes that overtook China from the 1940's to the 1970's. *To Live* won the coveted Cannes Film Festival Grand Jury Prize, as well as the Best Actor award for GeYou, in 1994. The film is an adaptation of the novel *Lifetimes* by Yu Hua, who adapted his novel with Lu Wei. There is no doubt that *To Live* will be considered a classic: It is emotionally powerful, visually beautiful, and historically resonant.

Reminiscent of the splendid film *The Blue Kite* (reveiwed

in this volume), *To Live* is the story of the hardships endured by a family during the turbulent times of the Communist takeover and Cultural Revolution in China. The two films are quite similar in their focus on the effects of the cultural turbulence on ordinary families. Their settings are similar, in that they both focus on the simple courtyard home of their central families, and on the pain of every day existence under a mercurial and controlling government. Nevertheless, whereas *The Blue Kite* was told through the eyes of a child, *To Live* retains an epic quality as it focuses on an entire family.

To Live begins in the 1940's. Fugui (Ge You) is a young man who lives with his young wife, Jiazhen (Gong Li), and his parents in a vast andopulent home. He spends most of his time in a gambling den, running up a huge debt with the unsavory owner, Long Er (Ni Dahong). His gambling passion ruins him early in the film: He loses his family's home and possessions to the clever Long Er. Jiazhen, three months pregnant and devastated by Fugui's behavior, returns to her family. The humiliated and now penniless Fugui begs Long Er for a loan. Instead, Long Er gives him a box of shadow puppets, telling him to earn a living with them. By this time, Jiazhen has returned to Fuguiwith their baby daughter, Fengxia (Xiao Cong).

CREDITS

Fugui: Ge You
Jiazhen: Gong Li
Town chief: Niu Ben
Chunsheng: Guo Tao
Erxi: Jiang Wu
Long Er: Ni Dahong
Fengxia (as an adult): Liu Tianchi
Youqing: Dong Fei
Fengxia (as an adolescent): Zhang Lu
Fengxia (as a child): Xiao Cong

Origin: China
Released: 1994
Production: Chiu Fusheng for ERA International, in association with Shanghai Film Studios; released by the Samuel Goldwyn Company
Direction: Zhang Yimou
Screenplay: Yu Hua and Lu Wei; based on the novel *Lifetimes*, by Yu
Cinematography: Lu Yue
Editing: Du Yuan
Production design: Cao Jiuping
Production management: Hu Shaofeng and Zhang Zhengyan
Sound: Tao Jian
Costume design: Dong Huamiao
Music: Zhao Jiping
MPAA rating: no listing
Running time: 125 minutes

Fugui creates a small traveling troupe of puppeteers, including his good friend Chunsheng (Guo Tao). He leaves his home to earn money for his young family, and during his travels he learns the life lessons that will help him through the rest of his life. In particular, he is captured by Chiang Kai-shek's army and is witness to starvation and death. A simple and beautiful scene illustrates the lessons learned by Fugui: He and Chunsheng dream of what it would be like to return home; Chunsheng says, "I'd be happy if I could drive," and Fugui simply says, "I want to live." This desire "to live" will help Fugui through the agonizing years ahead.

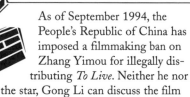

As of September 1994, the People's Republic of China has imposed a filmmaking ban on Zhang Yimou for illegally distributing *To Live*. Neither he nor the star, Gong Li can discuss the film in any form.

Eventually, Fugui returns home, in a tearful and beautiful reunion with Jiazhen. The simplicity of this moment belies its emotional power. Battered and exhausted, Fugui returns to his village at night and accidentally sees his wife and daughter hard at work filling water cans. Upon seeing him, Jiazhen walks toward him, begins to cry, and falls to her knees. It is a powerful moment.

AWARDS AND NOMINATIONS

British Academy Awards 1994: Best Foreign Film
Cannes Film Festival Awards 1994: Grand Jury Prize, Best Actor (Ge You)
Golden Globe Awards Nomination 1995: Best Foreign Language Film

The political landscape changes. During the 1950's, they have a son, Youqing (Dong Fei). Tragedy strikes the family during the Great Leap Forward, as Youqing is killed in an accident directly related to the modernization effort. During the 1960's, tragedy strikes again. Nevertheless, Fugui and Jiazhen's resolve comes from deep within, and they find the emotional means to continue their lives in the wake of one setback or tragedy after another.

To Live echoes the classic story of *Candide* (1759) by Voltaire. In *Candide*, the hero and heroine continue to live their lives assuming that unexpected tragedies happen for a benevolent reason and that life will improve. *To Live* and *Candide* share a thematic similarity in their endings: Where *Candide* ends with its protagonists baking bread and gardening—discovering the richness of simply existing, *To Live* ends with its main characters eating a meal, sharing the simple pleasure of living a simple life. The director has stated in interviews that this is his statement that "life continues," and that the departure from his usual dramatic endings is a conscious change in style to serve the simplicity and theme of this film.

Yimou is the acclaimed director of many of China's most notable films. In particular, his films have won for him great attention and acclaim in the United States. They include: *Hong Gaoliang* (1987; *Red Sorghum*); *Ju Dou* (1990) and *Raise the Red Lantern* (1991), both of which were nominated for Best Foreign-Language Film Oscars; and *QiuJu Da Guansi* (1992; *The Story of Qiu Ju*).

Yimou creates a rich combination of intimate and epic moments in this film. From the delicate light and playful tone of the shadow puppets, to the extraordinary scene where Fugui and Chunsheng are captured by scores of Nationalist Army soldiers who appear out of nowhere, Yimou displays his mastery of the visual image. A strikingly evocative image comes during a depiction of the steel melting that took place during the Great Leap Forward. As the families happily engage in melting "nonessential" items for the modernization effort, they turn their work into a celebration of sorts—Fugui entertains with his puppets as they work; there is music, drink, and laughter. Then, there is the aftermath, with people sleeping in the street, exhausted after their never-ending efforts. The dark street with pockets of light looks like a painting, at the hand of Yimou. With a few images, he makes the audience feel the townspeople's exhaustion and exhilaration, and he underscores his theme of the irony of how simple lives are intruded upon by monumental cultural forces.

Yimou's sense of the absurd is also present in this film. In a scene prior to their capture by the army, Chungsheng and Fugui, hiding in a foxhole, decide they must surrender. They come out with their hands up, only to discover there is no one alive in the vicinity. They look on in disbelief, keeping their hands in the air, sure that someone must be alive. Another similar moment occurs when, during the Civil War, the townspeople must decide which economic class they fit into, in order to avoid trouble from Revolutionary forces. "What are we?" someone exclaims. "Poor townspeople," says another person, to which Fugui responds, "Sounds good to me; nothing like being poor."

Their insistence on their powerlessness may seem ironic to a Western audience. It may be difficult for Americans to understand the forces that kept one billion people with their hands metaphorically raised above their heads during a time when they might have asserted their power. Clearly, Yimou sees the absurdity in such a thing as well, and as a result, his political views were not welcome in China.

Yimou is joined in this film by long time collaborator Gong Li as Jiazhen. Gong Li is recognized as one of China's preeminent actresses. She is as beautiful as she is talented, in this film portraying a woman who endures more hardships than any person should face in a lifetime. She does so with the same earthy stoicism and resolve that characterized her wonderful performance in *The Story of Qiu Ju*. She is also the star of *Farewell My Concubine* (1993), for which she won the New York Film Critics Circle Award and a Golden Globe nomination.

Gong Li is particularly wrenching in scenes leading up to the death of her children: Her screams are frightening and are filled with the panic of a woman who cannot believe

> "That wasn't my family's timber, that was counter revolutionary timber."—Fugui from *To Live*

that tragedy is striking her family once again. In each successive scene, Gong Li appears to be wearier, as if each tragedy weighs heavier on her character's soul. When blaming Chunsheng for the death of her child, Jiazhen says, "You owe us a life," with a realistic ache and anger that cuts to the bone.

Ge You received the Cannes Film Festival award for Best Actor for his portrayal of Fugui. He had been best known, however, as a comic actor in China. His complex portrayal of a man who shifts from lazy gambler to devoted family man to tireless worker is marvelous. He utilizes his humor in ways that underscore the humanity of the film. For example, when Chunsheng gives a picture of Mao Tse-tung to their daughter at her wedding, Jiazhen insists Fugui return it. "But it's Chairman Mao!" he replies, with an innocence and disbelief that are very funny. Ge You infuses his character, who has suffered great tragedy in the name of Mao, with reverence—and the satirical edge with which he delivers his line is funny and biting.

This film provides so much to its audience. It is at once a history lesson, a family drama, and a visually beautiful addition to world cinema. Perhaps its universality is ultimately the contribution for which it should be cherished. Its final scene, in which Fugui hopefully states that "life will get better all the time," is a beautiful reminder that one of the great ironies of life is that there is beauty and dignity in merely surviving.

—*Kirby Tepper*

REVIEWS

Daily Variety. May 18, 1994, p. 2.
Entertainment Weekly. December 16, 1994, p. 47.
Los Angeles Times. December 14, 1994, p. F1.
The New York Times. September 30, 1994, p. B3.

To Render a Life

The difficult life of a poor, rural American family is the focus of this engrossing documentary.

REVIEWS

Boston Globe. April 23, 1993, p. 48.
The Nation. CCLV, December 7, 1992, p. 713.
Variety. CCCXLIX, November 23, 1992, p. 50.

CREDITS

Alice Glass: Alice Glass
Obea Glass: Obea Glass
Robert Coles: Robert Coles
Frederick Wiseman: Frederick Wiseman
Howell Raines: Howell Raines
Jonathan Yardley: Jonathan Yardley

Released: 1992
Production: Ross Spears and Silvia Kersusan; released by the James Agee Film Project
Direction: Ross Spears
Screenplay: Silvia Kersusan
Cinematography: Ross Spears
MPAA rating: no listing
Running time: 88 minutes

Tom & Viv

"The story of passion...and the unspeakable secret that divides two lovers."—Movie tagline

"He was the most gifted poet of his time. She was his inspiration, his love and his greatest secret."—Movie tagline

"Superb!"—Gene Siskel, *Siskel & Ebert*

"Exquisitely passionate!"—*CBS-TV, Los Angeles*

"Fascinating!"—*The New York Times*

"Unforgettable!"—*The Dallas Morning News*

 Box Office Gross: $48,644 (December 11, 1994)

Nobel Prize-winning poet T.S. Eliot said he believed that "poetry should not be a turning loose of emotion, but an escape from emotion, and personality itself should not be expressed." Eliot, whose major works include *The Waste Land* and *Old Possum's Book of Practical Cats* (which was made into the Broadway musical *Cats*) was one of the most influential poets of this century, and *Tom & Viv* sheds light on the emotional subtext of his work. The film is a first-rate romantic tragedy, its historical relevance made all the more interesting due to its superb performances, writing, and direction.

Eliot, who was known as Tom (Willem DaFoe) and Vivienne Haigh-Wood (Miranda Richardson) meet at Oxford in 1914. Tom is a brilliant American student studying in England with the legendary Bertrand Russell (Nickolas Grace). (Russell was a renowned philosopher who, as is pointed out in this film, was "the most hated man in London" for his pacifist views about World War I.) After a very brief courtship, dignified Tom and flamboyant Viv elope, without the knowledge of her parents Rose (Rosemary Harris) and Charles (Philip Locke).

The impetuousness of their elopement has a price, however. Ominously foreshadowing problems to come, Viv's brother Maurice (Tim Dutton) warns Tom to "be kind" to Viv, hinting that she has some problems that the family doesn't talk about. On their honeymoon, Viv's

CREDITS

Tom Eliot: Willem Dafoe
Vivienne Haigh-Wood: Miranda Richardson
Rose Haigh-Wood: Rosemary Harris
Maurice Haigh-Wood: Tim Dutton
Bertrand Russell: Nickolas Grace
Charles Haigh-Wood: Philip Locke
Harwent: Geoffrey Bayldon
Louise Purdon: Clare Holman

Origin: Great Britain and USA
Released: 1994
Production: Marc Samuelson, Harvey Kass, and Peter Samuelson for Samuelson Productions, Harvey Kass, and IRS Media, Inc., with the participation of British Screen; released by Miramax Films
Direction: Brian Gilbert
Screenplay: Michael Hastings and Adrian Hodges; based on the play by Hastings
Cinematography: Martin Fuhrer
Editing: Tony Lawson
Production design: Jamie Leonard
Art direction: Mark Raggett
Set decoration: Jill Quertier
Casting: Michelle Guish
Sound: Peter Glossop
Makeup: Morag Ross
Costume design: Phoebe De Gaye
Music: Debbie Wiseman
MPAA rating: no listing
Running time: 125 minutes

Willem Dafoe as T.S. Eliot and Miranda Richardson as Vivienne Haigh-Wood in *Tom & Viv*. Copyright © Miramax Films.

problems are revealed: she suffers from a rare hormonal imbalance which causes her to undergo a menstrual cycle two or more times per month. She is under the treatment of a stuffy physician (James Greene) who says first that she has "what I call intestinal catarrah," and then "what I call a fibrule disease of the mind...defined as 'moral insanity.'" Under a dangerous mixture of expensive medicines, Viv's mental condition worsens. She continually shows what the doctor calls "a reckless disregard for propriety"; her inappropriate responses to situations, her outlandish outbursts in public, and her manic temperament cause a rift in her relationship with Tom. Eventually, Tom decides to commit Viv to an asylum.

The tragedy is twofold: not only does their marriage

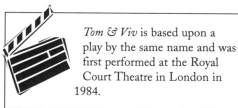

Tom & Viv is based upon a play by the same name and was first performed at the Royal Court Theatre in London in 1984.

disintegrate, but at the end of the film it is discovered that Viv's condition was treatable, and that with menopause and the reduction in her medicines, Viv was perfectly sane for many years while living in the asylum. Their physical and emotional estrangement magnifies the themes explored by Eliot in his poetry: In private, Eliot cries that "I crave companionship, but I am completely alone." A scene where Tom and Viv introduce *The Waste Land* to her parents illustrates the poetry of his loneliness: "I think we are in a rat's alley, where the dead men lost their bones," reads Tom as he catches Viv's mother's eye.

Michael Hastings and Adrian Hodges have adapted the screenplay from Hastings' play of the same title. The screenplay depicts Eliot as an American who desperately wishes to become British, practically erasing all trace of his past and further confirming Eliot's own comments about how "personality should not be expressed" in poetry.

Hastings and Hodges do an exemplary job of juxtaposing Eliot's own writings with their dialogue. For instance, Viv's mother delivers a powerful speech toward the film's close about Tom's obsession with subsuming his American personality in order to become British. Alluding to Tom's association with author Virginia Woolf, Rose tells him, "You mustn't think that riff-raff [the Bloomsbury group] is the heart of English life," saying that the real British are "quite unexceptional" and that "now you're famous on a bookshelf; what do we have left to give you." Harris powerfully delivers this eloquent and understated

AWARDS AND NOMINATIONS

Academy Awards Nominations 1994: Best Actress (Richardson), Best Supporting Actress (Harris)
British Academy Awards Nominations: Best Film, Best Actress (Richardson)
Golden Globe Awards Nominations 1995: Best Actress—Drama (Richardson), Best Supporting Actress (Harris)
National Board of Review Awards 1994: Best Actress (Richardson), Best Supporting Actress (Harris)

reproach. The writers use Eliot's real words to show his regret for Viv's incarceration: in a radio speech, Eliot refers to "the shame of motives late revealed."

Hastings and Hodges also powerfully portray the contribution Viv made to Eliot's early work. Eliot is depicted as a highly conservative and pragmatic man who takes a job in a bank in order to pay the bills—against Viv's wishes. "What my husband wants is to be boring...to have a boring conventional life." She becomes furious at Eliot's laborious attempt to be baptized in the Church of England, dismissing it as if he were a child wishing to be accepted into a club. And Eliot's steady progress toward replacing his American past do seem odd. He affects an English accent rather early on, and is apparently patient with Viv's strange behavior, but clearly uncomfortable with what it will do to his reputation. A scene in which Viv is locked out of his office is quietly indicative of Eliot's discomfort, and when Viv tells him "you always wanted to be a perfect Englishman," DaFoe, as Tom, reveals a bit of embarrassment, as if the truth is too hard to bear.

Like *Shadowlands* (1993), the filmmakers have done more than to tell the tragic love story of a great writer. This film illuminates the story of Tom and Viv by exploring the underlying theme of the consequences of suppressing true personality. Viv, for all her lunacy, is quite truthful, cutting through the British-aristocratic tradition of avoiding the truth. Like *Equus* (1977), this film calls attention to the fact that the "crazy" may be living a richer and truer life than the "sane."

Director Brian Gilbert shows elegance and grace in telling his story. Beautiful visual images such as Tom's walk by the seaside during his disastrous honeymoon, or the arrival of a train winding its way through the verdant countryside, show Gilbert's aesthetic eye. The brief scene in which Viv is "carted off to the lunatic asylum" is a restrained, intense scene which shows that Gilbert can allow the inherent drama of the situation to carry the

"Poetry is not an expression of emotion but an escape from emotion."—T.S. Eliot from *Tom & Viv*

scene. Gilbert and his actors sometimes walk a fine line between tragedy and comedy, as in a scene where the reading of Viv's father's will prompts her to ask "how much do I get?" and then escalates into a tirade that is only stopped by her mother's gentle hug. Apologizing, Viv leaves the room like a tornado that brushed over a small town and left extensive damage. The stunned looks of her family's faces would be humorous if not for the gravity of the situation, and Gilbert is to be commended for not ignoring the humor of Viv's inappropriate and sudden outburst.

The acting is, of course, excellent. DaFoe at times seems a bit too carefully rehearsed in his overly calm behavior, but that may be Dafoe's own interpretation of Eliot's overly rehearsed attempts at becoming British. DaFoe's final scene, in which he stares out from the door of an elevator, metaphorically descending into the depths of his own personality, is well done. DaFoe's vacant stare and monotone voice throughout the film underscore Eliot's intense need to "put away" his own personality. He underplays the monstrousness of Eliot's climb toward being British, which results in the incarceration of his wife. It is only at the end of the film, after the revelations about her illness, that his actions seem unjustifiable. At one point, he leaves a letter of his intention to spend a year at Harvard on the desk, hoping that Viv will find it. Dafoe seems to be able to find a way to nonverbally defend Tom's callous behavior, and it is commendable. Without discovering Eliot's own motivations, Tom would merely seem cruel.

Miranda Richardson received an Oscar nomination for her portrayal. She is the center of the film. Without Richardson's performance, it is possible that the film could have lapsed into being maudlin. Richardson finds the humor in Viv's outrageous actions; "You have to fight tooth and nail to get a cab at this time of day," she says after threatening Virginia Woolf with a knife in the rear of a cab. She also mines the tragedy for all it is worth, looking like *Hamlet's* Ophelia in her "mad" scenes with hair askew, eyes darting about, skin mottled with anxiety. Richardson moves in and out of the massive mood swings with ease, providing a depth to her character that makes sense of the madness. This performance is one that should not be missed.

The production values are splendid, lending authenticity to the story while providing striking visual images. In particular, the costume designs by Phoebe De Gaye are wonderful. From Viv's plaid stockings,to the authentic top hats of the banker's assistants, De Gaye brings texture to the film with her wonderful eye.

Though first-rate in its detail, its performances, and its

writing, the film itself did not receive unequivocally good reviews. Perhaps its literary nature or its discomforting lead characters might be the cause. There is a bit of a sense of melodrama in the acting, directing, and musical score, but it seems appropriate. This story is a true-to-life melodrama, played for all it is worth in this fine film adaptation.

—Kirby Tepper

REVIEWS

America. CLXXII, April 15, 1995, p. 32.
Atlanta Constitution. February 17, 1995, p. P4.
Boston Globe. February 17, 1995, p. 40.
Christian Science Monitor. December 2, 1994, p. 14.

Christopher Street. February 1995, p. 4.
Commonweal. CXXII, January 27, 1995, p. 24.
Daily Variety. February 15, 1994. p. 2
Entertainment Weekly. February 17, 1995, p. 42.
Harper's Bazaar. January 1995, p. 53.
Los Angeles Magazine. XXXIX, December 1994, p. 170.
Los Angeles Times. December 2, 1994. p. F4
The New Republic. CCXII, January 23, 1995, p. 30.
New Statesman & Society. March 18, 1994, p. 50.
The New York Times. October 24, 1993, Sec. 2 p. 15.
The New York Times. December 2, 1994, p. C3.
The New Yorker. LXX, December 12, 1994, p. 125.
Playboy. XLII, February 1995, p. 24.
USA Today. December 2, 1994, p. D4.
Variety. CCCLIV, April 18, 1994, p. 61.
The Washington Post. February 17, 1995, p. F1.
The Washington Post. March 2, 1995, p. D7.

Totally F***ed Up

Box Office Gross: $13,908 (August 21, 1994)

This drama from independent filmmaker Gregg Araki centers on six homosexual teenagers living in Los Angeles and their feelings of confusion and alienation.

REVIEWS

The Advocate. December 28, 1993, p. 72.(1)
Atlanta Constitution. January 6, 1995, p. P7.
Los Angeles Times. November 2, 1994, p. F4.
The New York Times. October 9, 1993, p. A16.

CREDITS

Andy: James Duval
Tommy: Roko Belic
Michele: Susan Behshid
Patricia: Jenee Gill
Steven: Gilbert Luna

Deric: Lance May
Ian: Alan Boyce
Brendan: Craig Gilmore

Released: 1994
Production: Andrea Sperling and Gregg Araki for Desperate Pictures and Blurco/Muscle and Hate Studios; released by Strand Releasing
Direction: Gregg Araki
Screenplay: Gregg Araki
Cinematography: Gregg Araki
Editing: Gregg Araki
Sound: Marianne Dissard
Postproduction sound design: Alberto Garcia
MPAA rating: no listing
Running time: 79 minutes

Touki-Bouki

A young Senegalese couple, Mory (Magaye Niang) and Anta (Marame Niang), dream of escaping their poverty-ridden lives in West Africa and going to Paris.

CREDITS

Mory: Magaye Niang
Anta: Marame Niang

Origin: Senegal
Released: 1973

Production: Released by International Film Circuit
Direction: Djibril Diop Mambety
Screenplay: Djibril Diop Mambety
Cinematography: Pap Samba Sow
Editing: Siro Asteni and Emma Mennenti
Sound: El Hadj M'Bow
MPAA rating: no listing
Running time: 95 minutes

Toward the Within

This concert film combines footage of the Dead Can Dance Santa Monica concert with interviews with the band's members.

REVIEWS

Los Angeles Times. November 18, 1994, p. F15.

CREDITS

Lisa Gerrard: Lisa Gerrard
Brendan Perry: Brendan Perry
Lance Hogan: Lance Hogan
Andrew Claxton: Andrew Claxton
John Bonnar: John Bonnar

Ronan O'Snodalsh: Ronan O'Snodalsh
Robert Perry: Robert Perry

Released: 1994
Production: Mark Magidson and Alton Walpole for Magidson Films and 4AD
Direction: Mark Magidson
Cinematography: David Aubrey
Editing: Mark Magidson and David Aubrey
Music: Dead Can Dance
MPAA rating: no listing
Running time: 78 minutes

Trading Mom

"No more vegetables. No more homework. No more cleaning your room..."—Movie tagline

"Delightful! Entertaining!"—Duane Byrge, *The Hollywood Reporter*

"Thoroughly enchanting!"—Joanna Langfield, *The Movie Minute*

"An enjoyable film for the whole family!"—Susan Granger, *CRN Radio Network & American Movie Classics*, Jeff Craig, *Sixty Second Preview*, Emanuel Levy, *Daily Variety*

 Box Office Gross: $243,816 (May 15, 1994)

Sissy Spacek gets a chance to strut her stuff in four distinctly different roles in this unremarkable (though well-intended) children's film. Tia Brelis has adapted her mother's children's book, *The Mommy Market*, for the big

CREDITS

Mommy: Sissy Spacek
Elizabeth: Anna Chlumsky
Jeremy: Aaron Michael Metchik
Harry: Asher Metchik
Mrs. Cavour: Maureen Stapleton
Mr. Leeby: Merritt Yohnka
Giant: Andre the Giant
Edward: Sean MacLaughlin
Mama: Sissy Spacek
Mom: Sissy Spacek
Natasha: Sissy Spacek

Released: 1994
Production: Raffaella De Laurentiis for First Look Pictures; released by Trimark Pictures
Direction: Tia Brelis
Screenplay: Tia Brelis; based on the novel *The Mommy Market*, by Nancy Brelis
Cinematography: Buzz Feitshans IV
Editing: Isaac Sehayek
Production design: Cynthia Charette
Set decoration: Lisa Caperton
Makeup: Jennifer Bell
Costume design: Terry Dresbach
Music: David Kitay
MPAA rating: PG
Running time: 83 minutes

screen. It is a film that has good production values, some charming moments, and a fine message for its young audience. However, sophisticated film goers may be disinterested by its simple plot; it is meant to be a family film, and it succeeds in its attempt to be a broad, funny, and very sweet cautionary tale about children's expectations.

Elizabeth (Anna Chlumsky) who also starred in *My Girl II* (reviewed in volume), Jeremy (Aaron Michael Metchik), and Harry (Asher Metchik) are three siblings who are dissatisfied with their mom (Sissy Spacek). As a single mom, Spacek's character is overworked and underappreciated, but is also a bit of a drag for the three children who wish that they could "zap mom, and she'd be history." The children ask the kindly sorceress Mrs. Cavour (Maureen Stapleton) how they can get "one of those mom's that did everything for us." Mrs. Cavour suggests an ancient spell that will erase any trace of their mom (even from their memories) so that the children are free to go to "the Mommy Market" downtown and pick up a new one.

This is a simply wonderful idea (not just for the children: who in the audience wasn't once a child who wanted a new mommy?) The children use up their "three chances" at getting a new mommy and each new mom is played to the hilt by Spacek. The first is "Maman," a selfish rich lady picked by Elizabeth. The next mom is an enthusiastic rustic type who loves all sports, picked by Jeremy. The last is a circus performer who brings her odd assortment of circus friends to the house.

Obviously, the children discover that even though they don't remember her, they want their real mom back. The film's message is admirably clear, with the children realizing that their own selfish ideas of what a mom is are not worth replacing the practical, realistic, and loving mom they already have.

To quibble with such a nice idea seems nasty, but there are a few things about the film that keep it from being the thoroughly charming film it aims to be. First, Spacek's "real" mom character is not given a chance to be anything more than just a harried single mom. The initial sequence in which her character is introduced lasts for only a few moments, and the worst thing that she does is to admonish Elizabeth that she be a bit more responsible because "you're in the eighth grade now." She does not seem particularly strict or mean, and this makes the kids seem like they are over-reacting when they wish to entirely wipe out their memories of this woman.

The children, though very cute, are not magnetic enough to completely endear themselves to the audience the way that Shirley Temple or even Macauley Culkin (in *Home Alone*, 1990) might have done. The scene where they wake up and discover that their mom is no longer there is particularly strained: "Do you remember her?" they ask each other, affecting wide-eyed, overdramatic responses that try and telegraph to the audience that this is an important moment in the film. Brelis' script falls a bit short here, having difficulty making it clear for the audience just what the children remember of their mother.

Trading Mom is based on the book *The Mommy Market* by Nancy Brelis. It is the directorial debut for her daughter Tia Brelis.

But enough quibbling. Spacek has fun with the three oddball "mom" characters. Her French and Russian accents are surprisingly unpolished for such an accomplished actress, but she is nonetheless a riot as the sexy, coiffed "maman," who, when she makes a hasty exit, says "I am sorry children, I must go, but there is cold octopus in the refrigerator." Her outdoorsy mom is the funniest. She affects a great Katherine Hepburn-style accent and blusters around hilariously. She is a camp counselor gone haywire, and it is fun to watch.

The film is reminiscent of Shirley MacLaine's *Woman Times Seven* (1967) and *What a Way to Go* (1964) in that its star portrays multiple characters. It also has some of the magic of *Big* (1988), though it lacks the sophistication and polish of that more adult film.

From Brelis delightful staging of the circus-like "Mommy market," to David Kitay's lovely musical underscore, *Trading Mom* is a perfect film for young children and their moms.

—Kirby Tepper

REVIEWS

Christian Science Monitor. May 13, 1994, p. 10.
Daily Variety. March 15, 1994. p. 15
Entertainment Weekly. May 27, 1994, p. 98.
Hollywood Reporter. March 11-13, 1994. p. 8
Los Angeles Times. May 13, 1994, p. F4.
The New York Times. May 13, 1994, p. C10.
The New York Times. May 29, 1994, Sec. 2 p. 19.
People Weekly. XLI, May 23, 1994, p. 17.

Trapped in Paradise

"The Firpo brothers can get away with anything. They just can't get away."—Movie tagline
"The story of a town that gave so much...even these guys couldn't take anymore."—Movie tagline
"A warm-hearted blend of sentiment and silliness."—*Sneak Previews/New York Post*

Box Office Gross: $5,821,500 (January 2, 1995)

Writer-director George Gallo is responsible for this engaging comedy about three dim-witted brothers who can't seem to make a life of crime pay. It is sweet and funny, and though it cannot be considered a perfect comedy, it is quirky, entertaining, and filled with richly funny performances and situations.

Jon Lovitz, Dana Carvey, and Nicolas Cage play, respectively, Dave, Alvin, and Bill Firpo—three inept criminals with hearts of gold. Bill (Cage) has recently tried to retire from the family business of petty

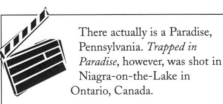

There actually is a Paradise, Pennsylvania. *Trapped in Paradise*, however, was shot in Niagra-on-the-Lake in Ontario, Canada.

thievery, but Dave (Lovitz) and Alvin (Carvey) have just finished a stint in the state penitentiary. Bill is working as a manager of an upscale New York restaurant when his brothers get out of prison. Through a series of events, propelled by Alvin's kleptomania (he even manages to steal the tie tack from the head of the parole board), the brothers end up on the lam in idyllic Paradise, Pennsylvania. Coincidentally, this beautiful town of Paradise has a bank run by genial Clifford Anderson (Donald Moffat) which begs to be robbed. The bank has minimal security and the townspeople have minimal suspicion, so even Bill agrees to participate in stealing the $275,000 in the vault. The bulk of the film involves their failed efforts to get out of town with the loot. First their getaway car, driven by brainless Alvin, goes in circles and ends up back in Paradise. Then an accident leaves them stranded and at the mercy of the magically kind townsfolk.

Their Christmas Eve encounters with the warm-hearted townspeople make Bill and Alvin decide to return the money, and they are so inept that their attempts to do that go awry as well. Eventually, a subplot about a mafia boss (Vic Manni) and his beautiful daughter

(Madchen Amick) merges with the boys' attempts to return the money and give up their life of crime, and there is a happy ending.

George Gallo directed the well-regarded *29th Street* (1991) and wrote the funny *Midnight Run* (1988), starring Robert De Niro and Charles Grodin. Gallo has a wonderful ability to create situations which are ridiculous but plausible, and his gentility and warmth area welcome diversion from the witlessness of recent screen comedies such as *In the Army Now* or *Ace Ventura: Pet Detective* (both reviewed in this volume). *Trapped in Paradise* is not only about three brothers too inept to successfully rob a bank, but it is about the generosity of small-town people and a little bit about personal redemption at Christmastime. In that sense, it borrows from Frank Capra, reminiscent of *It's a Wonderful Life* (1941) and *Pocketful of Miracles* (1961).

"Hey Ma, don't hold back! That's creamed corn!"—Alvin Firpo in *Trapped in Paradise*

Carvey, Lovitz, and Cage make an excellent trio of not-so-wise men. Lovitz plays a variation on his pathological liar character, Tommy Flanagan, from *Saturday Night Live*, and is very funny. He is at his best during the bank holdup, keeping the bank patrons calm with yoga exercises he learned in prison, saying "and breathe in, and let it out" without a trace of irony. Lovitz is simply a master at what he does.

Carvey is a bit more extravagant with his crazy character than Lovitz. He plays Alvin as if he were Harpo to the others' Chico and Groucho. Gallo wisely chooses to have him subtly try to steal something in virtually every shot. Carvey is particularly funny stealing all the candy cane pens at the bank, and being diverted by Bill from stealing everything in the home of a kindly Paradise family.

Cage provides a wonderful foil to Carvey and Lovitz. His exasperation at (and awareness of) their ineptitude is especially funny: When they reach a highway and try to hitchhike out of Paradise he says, "let's put our thumbs out and look pathetic; that ought to be easy."

The film is filled with witty performances from a host of wonderful character actors. Angela Paton is plain hilarious as the dotty Mrs. Anderson. And gravel-voiced Florence Stanley is a riot as Ma Firpo, telling two kidnappers they should be ashamed of themselves for "putting a gun to my head and going through three states on the night Baby Jesus was born."

The film looks absolutely beautiful, thanks to production designer Bob Ziembicki and cinematographer Jack N. Green. Picture-postcard views of the quaint town, dotted by constantly falling snow, were inspired by director Gallo's own award-winning paintings of small-town life. This film received surprisingly mixed reviews when released, but should not be overlooked by fans of comedy or fans of any of its three able stars.

—*Kirby Tepper*

CREDITS

Bill Firpo: Nicolas Cage
Dave Firpo: Jon Lovitz
Alvin Firpo: Dana Carvey
Ed Dawson: John Ashton
Sarah Collins: Madchen Amick
Clifford Anderson: Donald Moffat
Shaddus Peyser: Richard Jenkins
Ma Firpo: Florence Stanley
Hattie Anderson: Angela Paton
Vic Mazzucci: Vic Manni
Caesar Spinoza: Frank Pesce
Chief Burnell: Sean McCann
Deputy Timmy Burnell: Paul Lazar
Clovis Minor: John Bergantine
Dick Anderson: Sean O'Bryan
Father Ritter: Richard B. Shull

Released: 1994
Production: Jon Davison and George Gallo; released by Twentieth Century-Fox
Direction: George Gallo
Screenplay: George Gallo
Cinematography: Jack N. Green
Editing: Terry Rawlings
Production design: Bob Ziembicki
Art direction: Gregory P. Keen
Set decoration: Gord Sim
Casting: Donna Isaacson
Sound: Bruce Carwardine
Costume design: Mary E. McLeod
Stunt coordination: Glenn R. Wilder and Branko Racki
Music: Robert Folk
MPAA rating: PG-13
Running time: 111 minutes

REVIEWS

The Hollywood Reporter. December 2-4, 1994, p. 13.
Los Angeles Times. December 2, 1994, p. F6.
The New York Times. December 2, 1994, p. B3.
Variety. December 2, 1994, p.2.

The Trial

"Outstanding performances...a powerful story."
—John Anderson, *New York Newsday*

"Mesmerizing"—Jeffrey Lyons, *Sneak Previews/The Lyons Den*

"Go see this movie!"—Casper Citron, *WOR Radio*

Based on the novel by Franz Kafka, this drama stars Kyle MacLachlan as Josef K, a Prague bank clerk who finds himself arrested and on trial although he is never informed of his crime. The film features a screenplay by Harold Pinter and supporting performances by Anthony Hopkins as the Priest and Jason Robards as K's attorney.

REVIEWS

Atlanta Constitution. June 10, 1994, p. P3.
Boston Globe. March 25, 1994, p. 51.
Chicago Tribune. April 8, 1994, p. 7I.
Christian Science Monitor. November 22, 1993, p. 17.
Entertainment Weekly. September 25, 1992, p. 35.
Los Angeles Times. April 22, 1994, p. F8.
Maclean's. CVII, April 25, 1994, p. 63.
The New Republic. CCIX, December 20, 1993, p. 36.
The New York Times. November 24, 1993, p. C16.
Playboy. XLI, January 1994, p. 32.
USA Today. December 3, 1993, p. D7.
Variety. CCCL, February 1, 1993, p. 99.

CREDITS

Josef K: Kyle MacLachlan
Priest: Anthony Hopkins
Huld: Jason Robards
Landlady: Jean Stapleton
Leni: Polly Walker
Titorelli: Alfred Molina
Fraulein Burstner: Juliet Stevenson
Block: Michael Kitchen
Washerwoman: Catherine Neilson
Court usher: Patrick Godfrey
Franz: David Thewlis

Origin: Great Britain
Released: 1993
Production: Louis Marks for BBC Films and Europanda Entertainment; released by Angelika Films
Direction: David Jones
Screenplay: Harold Pinter; based on the novel by Franz Kafka
Cinematography: Phil Meheux
Editing: John Stothart
Production design: Don Taylor
Art direction: Jim Holloway
Casting: Leo Davis and John Lyons
Sound: Jim Greenhorn
Costume design: Anushia Nieradzik
Music: Carl Davis
MPAA rating: no listing
Running time: 120 minutes

Trial by Jury

"A first-class thriller! Entertaining, suspenseful and provocative. Wonderful performances."
—Paul Wunder, *WBAI Radio*

"An absorbing and ingenious lady-in-distress thriller."—*Los Angeles Times*

Box Office Gross: $6,965,009 (October 23, 1994)

Part courtroom drama, part *film noir*, part suspense thriller, *Trial by Jury* is a respectable, though uneven, film about a woman intimidated into a not-guilty verdict to save a cruel Mafia kingpin. Some stock characters and uninspired directing choices take the luster off fine performances by Armand Assante and William Hurt. But those performances, together with a well-developed theme

about the erosion of morality in the pursuit of justice, ultimately make this a worthwhile film.

Valerie Alston (Joanne Whalley-Kilmer) is a single mother in New York City who sees it as her civic duty to serve on a jury. She is chosen to serve in the trial of immoral mafioso Rusty Pirone (Armand Assante). Tommy Vesey (William Hurt), a former cop who now does dirty work for Pirone, threatens the lives of Valerie and her son, Robbie (Bryan Shilowich), in order to intimidate her into a not-guilty verdict. Vesey's nemesis is the district attorney, Daniel Graham (Gabriel Byrne), who uses unorthodox tactics of his own in order to win a conviction. After having been exposed to the political and criminal underside of justice, Valerie tells Vesey, "you've changed me" and she herself becomes willing to manipulate others to achieve her own ends.

Courtroom drama in general, and jury dramas in particular, are a staple of modern cinema. The great *Witness for the Prosecution* (1957) set the standard for excellent courtroom drama; *Twelve Angry Men* (1957), directed by Sidney Lumet, examined the jury as an excellent source of drama. And Lumet later examined morality within the justice system in *Serpico* (1973) and *Prince of the City* (1981).

The themes in *Trial by Jury* have some of the resonance of Lumet's themes, without some of the artistic skill that Lumet brought to his work. Director and co-writer (with Jordan Katz) Heywood Gould examines the erosion of morality from many angles. Perhaps where he is less effective is in being too conscious of the seriousness of the thematic content. In other words, the film could have been more of an entertaining suspense story than the somewhat heavy-handed morality story it is.

Whalley-Kilmer is credible as the moderately naïve Valerie, and her subtle transition from willing civil servant to cynical survivor is a good one. The scene in which she is kidnapped by Vesey and informed that she will vote not guilty is excellent. When she emerges from Vesey's van, her huge eyes register a new perspective on the world. As the film progresses, Whalley-Kilmer uses more of the seductive qualities which earned her fame in *Scandal* (1989) as she tries to manipulate the other jurors. In one scene, she sits quietly in a chair sipping coffee after manipulating arguments between factions within the jury. The change within her becomes less subtle in a climactic scene with Assante that is straight out of a 1940's mystery: she dons a silver gown and long gloves, drives to his mansion, and mixes violence with seduction. That this single mom knows how to be this seductive is a bit hard to believe, but Whalley-Kilmer is sultry and sexy enough to make it work.

The other actors are excellent. Hurt's boozy character is the kind that actors love to play: he's a down-and-out loser

CREDITS

Valerie Alston: Joanne Whalley-Kilmer
Rusty Pirone: Armand Assante
Daniel Graham: Gabriel Byrne
Tommy Vesey: William Hurt
Wanda: Kathleen Quinlan
Jane Lyle: Margaret Whitton
John Boyle: Ed Lauter
Leo Greco: Richard Portnow
Johnny Verona: Joe Santos
Emmett: Stuart Whitman

Released: 1994
Production: James G. Robinson, Chris Meledandri, and Mark Gordon for Morgan Creek; released by Warner Bros.
Direction: Heywood Gould
Screenplay: Jordan Katz and Heywood Gould
Cinematography: Frederick Elmes
Editing: Joel Goodman
Production design: David Chapman
Art direction: Barbra Matis
Set decoration: Steve Shewchuk
Casting: Heidi Levitt
Costume design: Mary Malin
Costume supervision: Arthur Rowsell
Sound: Bill Daly
Music: Terence Blanchard
MPAA rating: R
Running time: 106 minutes

who was once a wonder-boy homicide detective. His scenes in Pirone's bar with his henchmen are a bit over the top, especially a scene with Kathleen Quinlan as a sleazy gun moll-type. But Hurt's ability to find specific behavior (such as rolling up a newspaper or finding something in his teeth while he talks) helps to fill out the humanity of the character, and he is a pleasure to watch.

"I'm the guy that falls into a sewer and comes out with his pants pressed."—Rusty Pirone from *Trial by Jury*

Armand Assante as Rusty and Gabriel Byrne as the overzealous prosecutor are similarly excellent in stock roles. In particular, Assante's role as the tough-guy mafioso appears to be straight out of *The Godfather* (1972), especially when he rants about the government's conspiracy against him.

Gould appears to misstep in his inability to work against the cliché nature of the characters and plot. The scenes in which Assante sexually threatens Whalley-Kilmer and when she seduces him have a vaguely familiar feel. The

music by Terence Blanchard tries to have the grand drama of scores by Bernard Herrman, but a good deal of ominous music appears to manipulate the audience's response rather than enhance the action.

The evocation of memories of Hitchcock, Douglas Sirk, suspense, filmnoir, and old-fashioned courtroom drama seems to be the raison d'etre of *Trial by Jury*. It is a credible film which may not be incredibly inspired but is enjoyable nonetheless.

—*Kirby Tepper*

REVIEWS

The Hollywood Reporter. September 9-11, 1994, p. 38.
Los Angeles Times. September 10, 1994. p. F2
Variety. September 9, 1994. p. 27

Trouble Bound

An ex-convict, Harry Talbot (Michael Madsen), and a woman from a large crime family, Kit Califano (Patricia Arquette), head to Las Vegas with a dead body in the trunk of their car and pursued by various gangsters.

REVIEWS

Variety. CCCXLIX, January 18, 1993, p. 78.

CREDITS

Harry Talbot: Michael Madsen
Kit Califano: Patricia Arquette
Granny: Florence Stanley
Santino: Seymour Cassel
Danny: Sal Jenco
Zand: Paul Ben-Victor
Raphael: Darren Epton
Coldface: Billy Bob Thornton
Ratman: Rustam Branaman

Released: 1993
Production: Tom Kuhn and Fred Weintraub; released by ITC Entertainment Group
Direction: Jeff Reiner
Screenplay: Darrell Fetty and Francis Delia
Cinematography: Janusz Kaminski
Editing: Neil Grieve
Production design: Richard Sherman
Set decoration: Michael Warga
Casting: Mike Fenton and Jory Weitz
Special effects coordination: Steve Galich
Sound: Giovanni Di Simone and Stephan Halbert
Costume design: Merrie Lawson
Stunt coordination: Rawn Hutchinson
Music: Vinnie Golia
MPAA rating: R
Running time: 89 minutes

True Lies

"a gargantuan thrill machine"—David Ansen, *Newsweek*

"fast, flashy, furious and funny..."—Ralph Novak, *People*

Box Office Gross: $146,000,000 (February 3, 1995)

Arnold Schwarzenegger and Jamie Lee Curtis star as Harry and Helen Tasker in this action comedy. As the film opens, Helen and Harry have been married for fifteen dull years. She is a legal secretary and he is a workaholic

CREDITS

Harry Tasker: Arnold Schwarzenegger
Helen Tasker: Jamie Lee Curtis
Gib: Tom Arnold
Simon: Bill Paxton
Juno: Tia Carrere
Aziz: Art Malik
Dana: Eliza Dushku
Faisil: Grant Heslov
Spencer Trilby: Charlton Heston
Khaled: Marshall Manesh

Released: 1994
Production: James Cameron and Stephanie Austin for Lightstorm Entertainment; released by Twentieth Century-Fox
Direction: James Cameron
Screenplay: James Cameron; based on a screenplay by Claude Zidi, Simon Michael, and Didier Kaminka
Cinematography: Russell Carpenter
Editing: Mark Goldblatt, Conrad Buff and Richard A. Harris
Production design: Peter Lamont
Art direction: Robert Laing and Michael Novotny
Set design: Joseph Hodges
Set decoration: Cindy Carr
Casting: Mali Finn
Digital Domain visual effects supervision: John Bruno
Special effects coordination: Thomas L. Fisher
Sound: Lee Orloff
Costume design: Marlene Stewart
Stunt coordination: Joel Kramer
Music: Brad Fiedel
MPAA rating: R
Running time: 141 minutes

AWARDS AND NOMINATIONS

Academy Awards Nomination 1994: Best Visual Effects
Golden Globe Awards 1995: Best Actress—Musical/Comedy (Curtis)
MTV Movie Awards Nominations 1995: Best Action Sequence, Best Comedic Performance (Arnold), Best Female Performance (Curtis), Best Kiss (Schwarzenegger/Curtis), Best Dance Sequence (Schwarzenegger/Carrere)

computer salesman. He is so caught up in his work that he often comes home late and tired. Helen feels neglected and is starting to wonder if life is passing her by. All Helen wants is a little excitement.

Then into her life one day comes the mysterious Simon (Bill Paxton). He says he is a secret agent and needs her help. Intrigued, Helen now has a chance to feel useful and to enjoy a little excitement on the side. Unfortunately, he lied. Simon is nothing more than a used-car salesman who uses this ploy to "get the babes."

When Harry finds out about Helen's secret meetings with Simon, however, he suspects her of cheating on him. So Harry has a few "boys from his office" catch Helen and Simon together and kidnap them. It does not take long for Helen to find out that Simon was not the only person lying to her. It seems Harry is not just a colorless computer salesman. Incredibly, he has been leading a double life, and it is really he who is the secret agent.

Currently, Harry is working on finding four nuclear warheads that have disappeared from a former Soviet republic. They have turned up in the hands of a terrorist organization, the Crimson Jihad, which is run by Aziz (Art Malik) with the help of the amoral antiquities dealer Juno (Tia Carrere). Before Harry and his Omega Sector organization can stop Aziz, however, the terrorist captures both Taskers and sets a warhead to explode in the Florida Keys. Helen now has more excitement than she bargained for.

True Lies, which borrows from the small French comedy entitled *La Totale*, really revolves around two stories. The mundane story of the Taskers' marital problems is interwoven with a fantastical cloak-and-dagger subplot. When the two plots overlap, the result is some new kind of marriage counseling.

Arnold Schwarzenegger plays both the loving-if-neglectful husband as well as an American James Bond convincingly—despite the director's reliance on a few too many close-ups of the actor's famous menacing scowl. Schwarzenegger is proving himself to be adept at both action and light comedy, at playing James Bond for laughs or

Ward Cleaver in danger. There should be no question that he has recovered from the disastrous failure of *The Last Action Hero* (1993).

Another *True Lies* actor facing a possible turning point in his career is Tom Arnold. Often said to be riding the coat tails of his famous wife, Roseanne, Tom's marital problems and failed television sitcoms reinforced this notion. Luckily, it is the humor in his character that provides the laughter needed to release the tension or to keep the film from taking itself too seriously.

True Lies was the third top-grossing movie of 1994. The budget was reportedly nearly $120 million.

As for Jamie Lee Curtis, while her character would appear to be one-half the story, she is given much less leeway. She seems to be more awkward than able, more inattentive than alert. One wonders if she is in the film just to do the striptease number—a scene that causes one to wonder whether dowdy Helen really would

"Have you ever killed anyone?" "Yeah, but they were all bad."— Harry Tasker responding to his wife Helen Tasker in *True Lies*

have "that" kind of underwear in her wardrobe. The scene is not only insulting and demeaning but also unnecessary. By the time Helen realizes it is Harry she has been stripping for and not some nemesis, her much-anticipated angry retaliation is suspended as the other plot picks up again and the couple is kidnapped by terrorists.

Besides Curtis' humiliating scene, there was another bone of contention. When *True Lies* was initially released, a few theaters found themselves picketed by protesters who objected to the fact that the villain in the film was an Arab. In reality, while Aziz was portrayed as Islamic, his Arab nationality can only be inferred. The actor who played Aziz, Art Malik, is an English-reared Pakistani better known for his roles in *A Passage to India* (1984) and the PBS television adaptation of *The Jewel in the Crown*. With initial box-office receipts indicating that audiences do not care who their terrorists are as long as the film is good, the protest quietly died

down. Producer, director, and screenwriter James Cameron has indicated that any group that participates in terrorism in reality is fair game in films.

Terrorists and protesters aside, *True Lies*, with its spies and lovers, is an engrossing, nail-biting, and funny film. The true stars of *True Lies* are the incredibly imaginative action sequences, which are a hallmark of director Cameron. Here he has allegedly spent more than $120 million on the film, and virtually every dime of it is on the screen. Every action scene is more immense and more outrageous than anything Cameron has done before. The scene in which Harry flies a Harrier jet to save his daughter and capture Aziz is enough to justify the price of admission.

Once again, Cameron—whose films include *The Terminator* (1984), *Terminator II: Judgment Day* (1991), and *Aliens* (1986)—has pushed the envelope for excitingly precarious and awesome stunts. *True Lies* is a cinematic oxymoron: it is both amusing and exciting, gory and romantic; and somehow, with but a few slow spots in the middle, it works.

—*Beverley Bare Buehrer*

REVIEWS

Chicago Tribune. July 15, 1994, p. 7C.
Entertainment Weekly. July 22, 1994, p. 30.
The Hollywood Reporter. July 11, 1994, p. 6.
Los Angeles Times. July 14, 1994, p. F1.
The New York Times. July 15, 1994, p. B1.
Time. July 18, 1994, p. 55.
USA Today. July 15, 1994, p. D1.
Variety. July 11, 1994, p. 2.

Turtle Beach (The Killing Beach)

An Australian journalist and mother, Judith Wilkes (Greta Scacchi), is sent to Malaysia to write about the plight of the Vietnamese boatpeople.

REVIEWS

Entertainment Weekly. September 24, 1993, p. 101.

CREDITS

Judith: Greta Scacchi
Lady Minou Hobday: Joan Chen
Ralph Hamilton: Jack Thompson
Kanan: Art Malik
Sir Adrian Hobday: Norman Kaye
Sancha Hamilton: Victoria Longley
Richard: Martin Jacobs

Origin: Australia
Released: 1992
Production: Matt Carroll, Graham Burke (executive producer), and Greg Coote (exective producer) for Village Roadshow Pictures-Regency International and with the support of the Australian Film Finance Corporation
Direction: Stephen Wallace
Screenplay: Ann Turner; based on the novel by Blanche d'Alpuget
Cinematography: Russell Boyd
Editing: William Russell, Lee Smith and Louise Innes
Production design: Brian Thomson
Casting: Alison Barrett
Sound: Ben Osmo
Costume design: Roger Kirk
Music: Chris Neal
MPAA rating: no listing
Running time: 85 minutes

Two Small Bodies

"Ward and Amis are endlessly fascinating. Sexual and unsettling."—Caryn James, *The New York Times*

"Extraordinary! Incredibly hot!"—Amy Taubin, *Village Voice*

"A plunge into the murky depth of eroticism."
—*Premiere*

This two-character drama stars Suzy Amis as a divorced mother whose two young children are missing, and Fred Ward, a police detective who suspects her of murdering them.

REVIEWS

Chicago Tribune. July 15, 1994, p. 7J.
Christian Science Monitor. June 17, 1994, p. 12.
Los Angeles Times. May 27, 1994, p. F11.
The New York Times. April 15, 1994, p. C10.
Playboy. XLI, May 1994, p. 24.

CREDITS

Eileen Maloney: Suzy Amis
Lieutenant Brann: Fred Ward

Released: 1994
Production: Daniel Zuta and Beth B; released by Castle Hill
Direction: Beth B
Screenplay: Neal Bell and Beth B; based on Bell's play
Cinematography: Phil Parmet
Editing: Melody London and Andrea Feige
Art direction: Agnette Schlosser
Costume design: Bea Gossman
Music: Swans
MPAA rating: no listing
Running time: 85 minutes

"I read them bedtime stories from the Kama Sutra."—Eileen sarcastically referring to her children in *Two Small Bodies*

Twogether

Two California singles, John (Nick Cassavetes)—a struggling artist—and Allison (Brenda Bakke), meet at a social gathering and, after sleeping together, marry on an impulse. Equally impulsive is their decision to divorce, which becomes complicated by Allison's unexpected pregnancy.

REVIEWS

Los Angeles Times. February 11, 1994, p. F10.
Playboy. XLI, February 1994, p. 24.
Variety. CCCXLVII, June 15, 1992, p. 58.

CREDITS

John Madler: Nick Cassavetes
Allison McKenzie: Brenda Bakke
Arnie: Jeremy Piven
Oscar: Jim Beaver
Paul: Tom Dugan
Mark Saffron: Damian London

Released: 1994
Production: Emmett Alston and Andrew Chiaramonte for Dream Catcher Entertainment Group; released by Borde Film
Direction: Andrew Chiaramonte
Screenplay: Andrew Chiaramonte
Cinematography: Eugene Shlugleit
Editing: Todd Fisher and Andrew Chiaramonte
Production design: Philip M. Brandes
Art direction: Phil Zarling
Casting: Lori Cobe
Sound: Kip Gynn
Costume design: Jacqueline Johnson
Music: Nigel Holton
MPAA rating: no listing
Running time: 122 minutes

Undertow

An ex-convict (Burtt Harris) agrees to help the FBI entrap an alleged gay congressman (Greg Mullavey) in order to stay out of jail. He then enlists his heterosexual son (Peter Dobson) to seduce the congressman while the FBI videotapes them. Directorial debut of Thomas Mazziotti.

REVIEWS

Los Angeles Magazine. XXXVI, September 1991, p. 149.
Variety. CCCXLIV, September 16, 1991, p. 86.

CREDITS

Sam: Peter Dobson
Mel: Burtt Harris
Nina: Erica Gimpel
Marlene: Anita Gillette
William Gary: Greg Mullavey
Hustler: Tom Mazziotti

Released: 1991
Production: Burtt Harris and Thomas Mazziotti for Edmond D. Cruea and CapstoneFilms; released by Capstone Films
Direction: Thomas Mazziotti
Screenplay: Thomas Mazziotti; based on the play *Raw Youth*, by Neal Bell
Cinematography: Kevin Lombard
Editing: John Carter
Production design: Michael Moran
Casting: Joy Todd
Sound: Buzz Turner
Costume design: Ticia Blackburn
Music: Paata
MPAA rating: no listing
Running time: 95 minutes

Vanya on 42nd Street

"Astonishingly beautiful! A splendid demonstration of how great art seduces us, has its way with us. Everything in *Vanya on 42nd Street* works."
—Terrence Rafferty, *The New Yorker*

"*Vanya* is magic! This live-wire *Vanya* is fiercely funny, touching and vital!"—Peter Travers, *Rolling Stone*

"Call it *My Dinner With Uncle Vanya*"—Thelma Adams, *New York Post*

"Extraordinary! Breathtaking!"—James Kaplan, *New York Magazine*

"Wonderful!"—Stanley Kauffmann, *The New Republic*

 Box Office Gross: $771,321 (January 2, 1995)

The actors in *Vanya on 42nd Street* rehearsed Anton Checkhov's play *Uncle Vanya* (1902) in workshop for four years. They endured endless rehearsals and improvisations; they ate together, partied together—all in an attempt to get to know one another, their characters, and the essence of Chekhov's written word. Although they knew the play would never go to the stage, the director, André Gregory, started inviting people to watch (after the second year of rehearsal). Soon, twenty to thirty people were coming to watch in the old Victory Theatre off Times Square. People like Jerome Robbins, Richard Avedon, Susan Sontag, Mike Nichols, Robert Altman, and Louis Malle carted their chairs around from set to set under Gregory's direction.

After four years, the actors knew their roles so well that their characters grew. Each rehearsal brought about new nuances in the roles, nuances evolving out of the very nature of the four-year relationship. Thus, the characters have become complex, multifaceted individuals, yet remain faithful interpretations of the characters who peopled the creative world of the master of human complexity—Chekhov.

André Gregory, Louis Malle, and Wallace Shawn, collaborators on *My Dinner with André* (1981), then filmed the rehearsal of this ongoing work-in-progress performed in street clothes, with only a few tables, the odd bench, and paper "I Love NY" coffee cups as props. The film begins with a street scene on Times Square, as, from all corners, the ensem-

CREDITS

Vanya: Wallace Shawn
Yelena: Julianne Moore
Sonya: Brooke Smith
Dr. Astrov: Larry Pine
Serybryakov: George Gaynes
Maman: Lynn Cohen
Marina: Phoebe Brand
Waffles: Jerry Mayer
Mrs. Chao: Madhur Jaffrey
André Gregory: André Gregory

Released: 1994
Production: Fred Berner for Laura Pels Productions and New Media Finance; released by Sony Pictures Classics
Direction: Louis Malle and André Gregory
Screenplay: David Mamet; adapted from *Uncle Vanya*, by Anton Chekhov
Cinematography: Declan Quinn
Editing: Nancy Baker
Production design: Eugene Lee
Sound: Tod A. Maitland
Costume design: Gary Jones
Music: Joshua Redman
MPAA rating: PG
Running time: 119 minutes

ble heads toward the decaying tomb of a theater—the New Amsterdam. Inside, nets are strung over what was the orchestra to catch any falling plaster from the myriad cracks of the ten-story-high ceiling in the ornate theater that once housed the Ziegfeld Follies. Gregory, charming as always, welcomes visitors to the rehearsal. The actors have formed informal groups, chatting among themselves. Shawn lounges on a bench as two actors can be overheard at a nearby table. One actor asks an older woman if he has changed in the last ten years. Knitting, she looks up casually and tells him he drinks more than he used to. Yet something is different. They are not getting ready for rehearsal—they are in the play.

Together, Louis Malle, the film's director, and André Gregory, the stage director, have taken what began as an experiment in theater and-turned it into cinematic magic. Originally, Gregory had his audience follow the characters around, sometimes even sitting at the same table during the performance. "From the beginning the audience became the camera in close-up. The intimacy of the production always made it feel more like a movie than a play," said Gregory. Malle took it a step further by having the camera react like the audience. Cinematographer Declan Quinn rocks the hand held cam-

Vanya on 42nd Street was shot in two weeks.

AWARDS AND NOMINATIONS

Independent Spirit Awards Nominations 1995:
Best Supporting Actress (Smith), Best Supporting Actor (Pine)

era slightly as each actor speaks, much like one's attention would focus on the speaker without excluding the other actors from one's vision. At times, the camera angle even includes the director and his small audience in the scene. The effect is mesmerizing.

Wallace Shawn's interpretation of Uncle Vanya colors the character's despair over his wasted life with an unintentional clownishness that speaks of the foolishness of all lives. Chekhov's deep compassion for human suffering is often fused with this sense of irony, and Shawn's Vanya is a magnificent expression of that incongruity.

Vanya runs the family estate for his dead sister's husband, Serybryakov (George Gaynes), who lives in town on the estate's proceeds. Serybryakov's daughter, Sonya (Brooke Smith), helps Vanya with the estate, and Vanya's mother, Maman (Lynn Cohen), also lives there. The three have virtually devoted their lives to keeping the small estate going so that Serybryakov could dedicate himself to his books.

As the play opens, Vanya has begun to regret his sacrifice and to doubt his brother-in-law's genius. Part of his change of heart has to do with Serybryakov's return to the estate. He has brought with him his new wife, the young and beautiful Yelena (Julianne Moore), with whom Vanya has fallen madly in love.

Yelena at first seems irritatingly vapid, yet later the viewer is also is seduced by her. She was very naïve and young when she married the famous professor. It was simply a young girl's mistake, but Yelena has chosen to live with this mistake, fighting off admirers and watching her beauty fade as she remains in a sterile marriage to the selfish old professor.

The family waits on the professor hand and foot as he endlessly bemoans his age and failing health. Yet, even though everyone on the estate loses sleep trying to mollify the aging prima donna, Serybryakov never notices. He is in fact so self-absorbed that he does not even realize that both Vanya and the local physician, Dr. Astrov (Larry Pine), are in love with his young wife, nor that his daughter, Sonya, is in love with Dr. Astrov.

Sonya is perhaps the most poignant character in the story. Her nun-like sacrifice is so endearing, her love and trust so close to the surface that when she laments not being beautiful like Yelena, her inner beauty becomes all the more apparent. Her unrequited love for the doctor is so deeply touching and fragile that one finds oneself hoping against hope that her love will be returned.

The object of her affections, the doctor is a contradiction untohimself: a confirmed cynic who plants trees in an effort to give life to future generations; a worldly man who stubbornly remains in a small provincial town. His inconsistencies redouble after he meets and falls in love with Yelena. His practice suffers, his drinking increases, and finally he even asks Yelena to run away with him.

"It was difficult to film such an ambitious project in two weeks. I don't think it's ever been done before. It was an enormous amount of work. I was obsessed with not leaving anything behind."—director Louis Malle, on *Vanya on 42nd Street*

Vanya, also changed by his love for Yelena, professes his love to her whenever they are alone. Yelena seems amused and often a trifle tired of Vanya's attentions. He speaks the truth to her, scolding her for her laziness and indifference to her own fate. Yet her affection for Vanya begins and ends with ennui. She is bored with everything, yet faithful to the professor and stoic in her martyrdom.

The story comes to a head when the unthinking professor holds a family meeting to discuss his plans to sell the estate so that he and his wife can live elsewhere in more financial comfort. The soon-to-be-homeless Sonya, Maman, Waffles the caretaker (Jerry Mayer), and Marina the old nanny (Phoebe Brand) are speechless, horrified at the insensitivity of the man for whom they have sacrificed their own futures. Vanya's disillusionment has been simmering since Serybryakov's return, and this puts him into crisis. Vanya suddenly realizes all he has lost, all he might have been, have done, have achieved—if not for this man.

Vanya grabs a gun and tries to shoot the professor. Instead, he finds that he is incapable of murder and turns the gun on himself. His friends and family stop him, and he is bereft of his one chance to execute his free will. The professor recants his decision to sell the estate, and he and his wife leave to go to another provincial town where they can still live off the efforts of Vanya and Sonya.

When the professor and Yelena are gone, Sonya and Vanya are left alone to face all they have lost and the miserable lives they must continue to lead. Sonya, in a wonderful speech, gives Vanya hope, not because she believes there is any, but because she and he cannot go on without that illusion.

David Mamet has adapted Chekhov's *Uncle Vanya* with changes in the dialogue that modernize without losing the Russian flavor. His efforts infuse the play with meanings that are applicable to the late twentieth century as well as the fin de siècle when it was written. The device of the "play within the film" and the modern dress on hundred-year-old characters pulls one back and forth so often that "then and now" become merged and unimportant to the content of the story. Old truths are still true.

Julianne Moore who plays Yelena is marvelous in this play. She has a vivid stage presence and a face that interacts with the camera. She is timeless—even in slacks and a sweater, she is convincing as a woman from the turn of the century. The same effect comes from Brooke Smith, who has a beauty that is absolutely of that period. Shawn as Vanya, however, is most definitely of the present. When he speaks of giving up everything to duty, his lament is a modern one, although his reaction is from a more dramatic time.

All of the actors are exquisite in their roles and work truly as an ensemble. Larry Pine is at once weary and dashing as the doctor. George Gaynes as the professor brings unconscious selfishness to a new height. Jerry Mayer as Waffles is a master of self-effacement and placation. The four years of study and hard work have created characters who are fluid in their roles, comfortable with one another, and—above all else—indisputably real.

Vanya on 42nd Street was filmed in two weeks in the unheated and dilapidated old theater. The ambience of the fading beauty of the New Amsterdam gives the added sense of loss and abandonment that a real stage set could never achieve. In fact, the stage is never even used. Production designer Eugene Lee tore out seats in the orchestra and set up old tables and benches on a platform there. The result is that the theater itself becomes the set, and this neglected monument to the past is a fitting environment for Chekhov.

Although Chekhov purists may have a problem with the changes in the play, it is undeniably successful in its characterizations. All the actors bring such an understanding of their characters to the screen that, when they break to have coffee, it is difficult to see the actors for who they are as opposed to whom they play.

Gregory's experiment in theater and Malle's experiment in cinema are both successful and yet remain true to the essence of Chekhov. They have brought to life that part of Chekhov that deals with the frailties and the greatness of the human soul. As we move into the new millennium, it is somehow reassuring to remember that the human soul remains and will forever remain unchanged.

—*Diane Hatch-Avis*

REVIEWS

Entertainment Weekly. November 25, 1994, p. 47.
The Hollywood Reporter. September 14, 1994, p. 9.
Los Angeles Times. November 4, 1994, p. F10.
The New York Times. October 19, 1994, p. B1.
Variety. September 8, 1994, p. 4.

Vermont is for Lovers

In this quaint romantic comedy, a pair of New York yuppies, George (George Thrush) and Marya (Marya Cohn), go to a Vermont farm to get married. To offset the prenuptial jitters, George visits with the locals—all nonactors and actual residents—conducting informal interviews on love and marriage.

REVIEWS

Atlanta Constitution. January 14, 1994, p. P3.
Boston Globe. April 11, 1993, p. B8.
Los Angeles Times. January 8, 1994, p. F6.
The New York Times. March 26, 1993, p. C6.
Variety. CCCXLIX, November 9, 1992, p. 64.
The Washington Post. June 25, 1993, p. C7.

CREDITS

George: George Thrush
Marya: Marya Cohn
Ann: Ann O'Brien
Euclid Farnham: Euclid Farnham
Jeramiah Mullen: Jeramiah Mullen
Dan Mullen: Dan Mullen
Ann Milliman: Ann Milliman
Edgar Dodge: Edgar Dodge
George Lyford: George Lyford
Alan Lyford: Alan Lyford
Robert Button: Robert Button
Joe Tuttle: Joe Tuttle
Fred Tuttle: Fred Tuttle
Gladys Noyes: Gladys Noyes

Released: 1992
Production: John O'Brien for Bellwether Films; released by Zeitgeist Film
Direction: John O'Brien
Screenplay: John O'Brien
Cinematography: John O'Brien
Editing: John O'Brien
Sound: Gordon Eriksen
Music: Tony Silbert
MPAA rating: no listing
Running time: 88 minutes

La Vie de Boheme

Three struggling artistes—painter Rodolfo (Matti Pellonpaa), playwright Marcel (Andre Wilms), and composer Schaunard (Kari Vaananen)—meet periodically over drinks and cigarettes at a Parisian neighborhood cafe to commiserate on life.

REVIEWS

Boston Globe. October 1, 1993, p. 53.
Christian Science Monitor. July 21, 1993, p. 13.
Los Angeles Times. March 18, 1994, p. F4.
The Nation. CCLVII, August 9, 1993, p. 186.
The New Republic. CCIX, August 16, 1993, p. 24.
The New Yorker. LXIX, August 9, 1993, p. 93.
Playboy. XL, August 1993, p. 18.
Vogue. CLXXXIII, August 1993, p. 146.
The Washington Post. November 6, 1993, p. D1.
The Washington Post. November 5, 1993, p. WW52.

CREDITS

Mimi: Evelyne Didi
Marcel: Andre Wilms
Schaunard: Kari Vaananen
Musette: Christine Murillo
Blancheron: Jean-Pierre Leaud

Baudelaire: Laika
Barman: Carlos Salgado
Henri Bernard: Alexis Nitzer
Madame Bernard: Sylvie van den Elsen
Hugo: Gilles Charmant
Lady at shop: Dominique Marcas
Gassot: Samuel Fuller
Francis: Jean-Paul Wenzel
Gentleman: Louis Malle

Origin: Finland
Released: 1992
Production: Aki Kaurismaki for Sputnik Oy, in association with Pyramide Productions S.A. and Films A2, the Swedish Film Institute, and Pandora Film GmbH, supported by the Finnish Film Foundation and the Nordic Film and Television Fund
Production: Released by Kino International
Direction: Aki Kaurismaki
Screenplay: Aki Kaurismaki; based on the novel *Scenes de la Vie de Boheme*, by Henri Murger
Cinematography: Timo Salminen
Editing: Veikko Aaltonen
Production design: John Ebden
Sound: Jouko Lumme and Timo Linnasalo
MPAA rating: no listing
Running time: 100 minutes

Voyeur

A thirty-something, voyeuristic young man, Abel (Alex Van Warmerdam), who is still tied to the apron strings of his doting mother (Olga Zuiderhoek), has not left his parents' home in a decade. When his father (Henri Garcin) finally throws him out, Abel is taken in by his father's mistress (Annet Malherbe) in this Dutch comedy. *Voyeur* won a Dutch film critics' prize as best Dutch film of the 1980's.

CREDITS

Abel: Alex Van Warmerdam
Victor: Henri Garcin
Dove: Olga Zuiderhoek
Sis: Annet Malherbe

Christine: Loes Luca

Origin: The Netherlands
Released: 1986
Production: Laurens Geels, Dick Maas, and Robert Swaab; released by Prestige Films
Direction: Alex Van Warmerdam
Screenplay: Alex Van Warmerdam
Cinematography: Marc Felperlaan
Editing: Hans Van Dongen
Production design: Harry Ammerlaan
Music: Vincent Van Warmerdam
MPAA rating: no listing
Running time: 100 minutes

Wagons East!

"They came. They saw. They changed their minds."—Movie tagline

 Box Office Gross: $4,289,963 (October 2, 1994)

A cinematic failure is often heartbreaking because of all the work that goes into writing, acting, producing, and marketing a film. It is doubly heartbreaking in the case of *Wagons East!* because this substandard film is the final one made by brilliant comedian John Candy.

Candy died during the shooting of the film and sarcastic critics might say that this film was the reason. Candy had not finished all of his scenes before he passed away, but it is hard to tell what more he could have done to make *Wagons East!* palatable. Happily, Candy's own performance in the film is dignified, and he does not diminish the wonderful memories his fans have of him.

The usually jovial Candy plays a more serious character here than his usual happy-go-lucky goon. He is James Harlow, a Wagonmaster in the old west who is hired by a group of pioneers to take them back east. The group consists of former doctor Phil (Richard Lewis), fey bookseller Julian (John C. McGinley), hooker-with-a-heart-of-gold Belle (Ellen Greene), fussy Ben (Robert Picardo) and assorted other characters. What the unwitting group doesn't know (until halfway through the film) is that the drunken Harlow (Candy) was one of the leaders of the ill-fated Donner party. This fact is the basis for much of the attempts at humor, given that Donner party travelers resorted to cannibalism upon getting lost in the mountains. The bulk of the story concerns the wagon train's struggles against a series of unscrupulous villains set on them by a greedy railroad tycoon (Gaylord Sartain).

 "This country was *founded* by quitters. English quitters, French quitters..."—Phil Tayor from *Wagons East!*

Though the premise is actually a good one, writer Matthew Carlson and director Peter Markle avoid the inherent humor of the situation and reach for an off-the-wall sensibility that simply doesn't work. Perhaps Carlson and Markle were trying to capture some of the feel of Mel

 "I had this feeling that it was a tough shoot for John....He called me, he was as happy as he could be as an actor, he was proud of his work. I wrote a note to him: 'This [scene] confirmed to me that you are a one-of-a-kind talent. P.S. Can I borrow a quarter of a million dollars?' I brought that note to the set only to find out that John had died."—Richard Lewis on working with John Candy during his last scene in *Wagon's East!* (*Premiere*, June 1994)

Brooks' classic western spoof *Blazing Saddles* (1973), but the result here is witless rather than witty. Much of the film's humor comes in the form of scatological ("potty") humor. The jokes about bestiality, bodily functions, sexual organs, and homosexuality never rise above the level of locker room humor. (But it is highly doubtful that even the most thick-skulled viewer would actually find humor in these jokes).

To be fair, there are a few genuinely funny moments. One of them comes when Phil's children halt the entire wagon train because they have to go to the bathroom, as if they are a nineties family taking a vacation by car. Lewis is funny when he threatens his fidgety children with, "If you don't stop I will have your mother turn this wagon around right now!" Another funny moment comes when one of the settlers, speaking to an Indian, refers to the east as "land of the rising sun" (or something like that) and the hip Indian, Little Feather (Rodney E. Grant), says, "Skip the euphemisms, I know which way east is."

Candy plays his character seriously and it actually works to his advantage. In spite of the material, he manages to be funny in a scene where his drunken character tries to show the settlers the route they will take by using pots, pans, muffin tins, and kitchen utensils to make a three-dimensional map.

The only other actor to emerge unscathed is the winsome and fascinating Ellen Greene who manages to find warmth and grace in her hooker role. Greene is an accomplished stage actress who is best known for playing Audrey in the musical version of *Little Shop of Horrors* (1986).

Richard Lewis seems to have had trouble finding his place in motion pictures. His other major screen credit is in Mel Brooks' *Robin Hood: Men in Tights* (1993). In both films, Lewis plays his uptight New York character as if he were in a Woody Allen film. Somehow his character seems too much of an anomaly to create a foundation of believability necessary for humor that relies on anachronisms. The anachronisms in general, and Lewis' anachronistic performance inparticular, seem to serve themselves rather than serve character or plot.

It is hard to say anything more positive than "they tried," when referring to Markle's direction or Carlson's

CREDITS

James Harlow: John Candy
Phil Taylor: Richard Lewis
Julian: John C. McGinley
Belle: Ellen Greene
Ben Wheeler: Robert Picardo
John Slade: Ed Lauter
Little Feather: Rodney A. Grant
Zeke: William Sanderson
Constance Taylor: Melinda Culea
Lindsey Thurlow: Robin McKee
The Chief: Russell Means
General Larchmont: Charles Rocket

Released: 1994
Production: Gary Goodman, Barry Rosen, Robert Newmyer, and Jeffrey Silver for Carolco and Outlaw, in association with Goodman-Rosen Productions; released by TriStar Pictures
Direction: Peter Markle
Screenplay: Matthew Carlson; based on a story by Jerry Abrahamson
Cinematography: Frank Tidy
Editing: Scott Conrad
Production design: Vince J. Cresciman
Art direction: Hector Romero C.

Set design: Miguel Angel Gonzalez B.
Set decoration: Enrique Estevez L.
Casting: Richard Pagano, Sharon Bialy, Debi Manwiller and Tory Herald
Sound: Pud Cusak
Costume design: Adolfo "Fito" Ramirez
Music: Michael Small
MPAA rating: PG-13
Running time: 106 minutes

screenplay. Nastier words than "they tried" may be appropriate, but there is no point in being mean. Candy's fans should avoid this film and see *Planes, Trains, and Automobiles* (1987) or *Who's Harry Crumb?* (1989) or try to find re-runs of his astonishing performances in the *SCTV* comedy series of the 1980's. Perhaps the filmmakers of *Wagons East!* would do well to study those shows as well.

—*Kirby Tepper*

REVIEWS

Daily Variety. August 24, 1994. p. 2
Los Angeles Times. August 26, 1994. P. F6
The Hollywood Reporter. August 24, 1994. p. 10
The New York Times. August 26, 1994. p. B6.

The War

"What's worth fighting for?"—Movie tagline
"*The War* touches the heart. A must-see movie."
—Bonnie Churchill, *National News Syndicate*
"One of the best films of the year."—Jeffrey Lyons, *Sneak Previews*

Box Office Gross: $16,480,770 (December 18, 1994)

T*he War* has a perfect pedigree. Jon Avnet directed, who also directed the superb *Fried Green Tomatoes* (1991). It starred Kevin Costner, the Oscar-winning director and actor of *Dances With Wolves* (1990), and Elijah Wood, a splendid young actor who made his first big impression opposite Macaulay Culkin in *The Good Son* (1993). Geoffrey Simpson, the director of photography who provided the lush

photography of *Fried Green Tomatoes*, and Kristi Zea, the production designer of *Philadelphia* (1993) and *The Silence of the Lambs* (1991), created the look of this film. Finally, it was produced by Jon Avnet and Jordan Kerner, who produced *Fried Green Tomatoes* as well. Yet a great pedigree does not ensure a great film.

The script, by newcomer Kathy McWorter, explores the theme of war and its impact on individuals, families, and, in particular, children. The script and the direction aim high, tackling the painful subject of the Vietnam War combined with the current American thematic fascination with family values.

This is a "baby boomer" film: it brings the audience down memory lane to the 1970's, with the music of the period as a backdrop; it presents the horrors of the first "baby boomer" war and its terrible emotional aftermath; it shows its social conscience in its obvious disgust with racism; and it slickly wraps its characters and conflicts up in a resolution worthy of a television drama. While the film clearly extols the virtues of moral restraint even in the face of grave danger, it does so in such a cliche way that it ultimately undermines its own credibility.

The film centers on one summer in the life of Lidia Simmons (Lexi Randall) and her brother Stu (Elijah Wood). They and their parents, Stephen (Kevin Costner) and Lois (Mare Winningham), have lost their home. They are barely making ends meet as Stephen searches for a job and struggles with post-traumatic stress syndrome caused by his service in the Vietnam War. Just as Stephen finds a job and regains his self-respect, his children begin to learn some self-respect, too, as they fight a "war" with the dreaded Lipnickis, a family of scruffy children.

The Lipnickis fight with Lidia and Stu over the right to a tree fort that Stu and Lidia built with parts of their old family home. As the fighting among the children escalates, the symbolism becomes more apparent: these children and their skirmishes represent the childish-turf wars that led to the Vietnam War. The film puts forth the idea that war is something that creeps up on its participants, causing them to fight gratuitous, deadly fights even when the original conflicts have long faded from memory.

An auxiliary theme regarding the duty of friends to help friends illustrates the film's formulaic tendencies. Stephen has been suffering from guilt over having to leave behind his closest buddy during a skirmish in Vietnam. The

The tree that supports the tree-house in *The War* is estimated to be between 700 and 800 years old, and was found in Beaufort, South Carolina.

"I can't tell you never to fight. But if you want to know what I think...I think the only thing that truly keeps people safe and happy is love. And in the absence of love, there's nothing in this world worth fighting for."—Stephen Simmons from *The War*

pain of Stephen's guilt is eased when he saves his new friend while working in a mine. Unfortunately, it is obvious as soon as they enter the mine that Stephen will have an opportunity to save his friend because so much has been made of his guilt about not saving his Vietnam buddy. Pathos and emotion dominate the film by this time to the point that redemption is inevitable, and its inevitability makes the redemptive quality seem unearned and therefore less compelling.

Another area of difficulty was the use of so many children who are making their acting debuts. All the actors playing the Lipnicki children are newcomers, and it is evident. They are made up to look like unkempt hoodlums of the rural South, but their inexperience combined with the blond wholesomeness underneath their makeup make them look like a group of kids auditioning for the Beverly Hills Community Theatre production of *Lil' Abner*. Now clearly, it is unfair to expect these children to deliver anything but the committed performances that they deliver. Yet, since the film's central conflict and theme revolve around the danger of these children, it is disappointing to see that they are more naughty than threatening.

Elijah Wood, however, received wonderful notices for his naturalistic and charismatic performance as the devoted Stu. Wood is an exceptionally compelling young actor, who renders Stu's breakdown toward the end of the film both wrenching and believable. Lexi Randall is similarly believable and poignant as the gawky but loving Lidia. Her two best friends, Elvadine and Amber, are portrayed with heart and style by LaToya Chisholm and Charlette Julius.

Kevin Costner delivers one of his more laconic performances, which, though likable, is not particularly believable. He assays a fine Southern accent and attacks the scene where he discloses his guilt about the loss of his Vietnam buddy with great relish, although his emotionality in that scene appears heavy-handed. He is at his best in a desperate moment when he protects his young son from the father of the Lipnicki children, threatening that "you can say what you want to me, but you pick on my son and you push a button in me." At that moment, it is evident that Costner is best emoting with another character on the screen, reacting to real external events rather than relying on his internal emotional life to guide his portrayal.

One additional aspect of Costner's performance that diminishes his credibility perhaps lies with the costume designer: He does not appear at all to be a rural man down on his luck. In one scene, when the family barely has enough

Lexi Randall, Elijah Wood, and Latoya Chisholm play three young children growing up in the rural South in the 1970's in *The War*. Copyright © by Universal City Studios, Inc. Courtesy of MCA Publishing Rights, a Division of MCA Inc. All rights reserved.

to eat, he is wearing a crisp white shirt and clean chinos, in contrast to the rest of his family. In addition, he wears a nice watch in several scenes.

Mention should be made of always excellent Mare Winningham. She appeared with Costner in Lawrence Kasdan's *Wyatt Earp* (reviewed in this volume). Here, as usual, she provides a vividly drawn character. Winningham is capable of capturing the essence of many types of

CREDITS

Stu: Elijah Wood
Stephen: Kevin Costner
Lois: Mare Winningham
Lidia: Lexi Randall
Miss Strapford: Christine Baranski
Mr. Lipnicki: Raynor Scheine
Moe: Bruce A. Young
Elvadine: LaToya Chisholm
Amber: Charlette Julius
Billy: Christopher Fennell

Released: 1994
Production: Jon Avnet and Jordan Kerner for Island World; released by Universal Pictures
Direction: Jon Avnet
Screenplay: Kathy McWorter
Cinematography: Geoffrey Simpson
Editing: Debra Neil
Production design: Kristi Zea
Art direction: Jeremy Conway
Set decoration: Karen O'Hara
Casting: David Rubin and Debra Zane
Sound: Mary H. Ellis
Costume design: Molly Maginnis
Music: Thomas Newman
MPAA rating: PG-13
Running time: 125 minutes

American women and has done so in films from Andrei Konchalovsky's *Shy People* (1987) to her Emmy-winning performance in *Amber Waves* (1980). Though she is underused here, she shines.

Avnet, much as he did in *Fried Green Tomatoes*, shows an affinity for the rural South. He provides fine direction on the wide range of this film, from Vietnam footage, to a suspenseful fight on an antique water tower, to a tender moment where Lidia curls her father's hair. Yet, there are inconsistencies in the quality of the storytelling that diminish its impact. For example, one scene opens with Stephen and Stu in a donut shop. Then Stephen takes Stu outside the shop to tell him something important. They sit on a bench, talk briefly, and then Stephen brings Stu back inside for a donut, satisfied that he has conveyed his message to Stu. One questions the logic in having the two exit the shop, then reenter it, especially when the scene is not particularly important. Another example is the rather mysterious resolution, where in the family is saved with a bit of magic involving an auction and a kindly bureaucrat.

Perhaps Avnet sensed he had another touching, bittersweet tale that audiences would be unable to resist. From the lush music by Thomas Newman, to the evocative locations, to the Southern accents, Avnet was in territory too close to his previous success. Inevitably, audiences will compare *The War* to *Fried Green Tomatoes*. It is clear ,however, that while it sends a loving and important message, *The War* will lose the battle. It is simply too preachy and self-important to become the classic that it aspires to be.

—*Kirby Tepper*

REVIEWS

Entertainment Weekly. November 4, 1994, p. 48.
The Hollywood Reporter. October 26, 1994, p. 10.
Los Angeles Times. November 4, 1994, p. F1.
The New York Times. November 4, 1994, p. B8.
Variety. October 26, 1994, p. 2.

The War Against the Indians

This ambitious documentary covers some five hundred years of American history from a Native American point of view.

REVIEWS

The New York Times. April 16, 1993, p. C15.

CREDITS

Narrator: Harry Rasky
Graham Greene: Graham Greene

Origin: Canada
Released: 1992
Production: Harry Rasky; released by the Canadian Broadcasting Corporation and the Societe Radio-Canada
Direction: Harry Rasky
Screenplay: Harry Rasky
Cinematography: Milan Klepl and Kenneth W. Cregg
Editing: Ken Mullally
MPAA rating: no listing
Running time: 145 minutes

The Wedding Gift

"Endearing and Uplifting!"—*Los Angeles Times*
"Witty! Spirited!"—*Cleveland Plain Dealer*
"Extraordinarily Rich."—*Cosmopolitan*
"Real Brilliance!"—*Kansas City Star*
"Sexy irony."—*Chicago Tribune*

 Box Office Gross: $187,027 (August 21, 1994)

Andrew Lancel as Nick Longden, Julie Walters as Diana Longden, Anastasia Mulrooney as Sally Longden, and Jim Broadbent as Deric Longden in *The Wedding Gift*. Copyright © Miramax Films.

As a nation, the British have taken pride in their humor during adversity. In *The Wedding Gift*, based on the true story of Diana and Deric Longden, one finds an admirable tale of fortitude in extremity (helped along with liberal doses of grim wit) and the triumph of unselfish love.

The first sight of Diana (Julie Walters) is during a blackout while she is taking a bath. She is rescued by Deric (Jim Broadbent), and his saving action is symbolic of his efforts throughout the story. Despite her reserves of strength, Diana needs Deric and—infatuated husband that he is—Deric neglects all else, including his factory, to look after Diana. An early scene finds the couple singing merrily on another trip to the hospital; their jolly mood is soon dispatched when confronted by the crawling bureaucracy of Britain's overstretched National Health Service.

The doctors are unable to put a name to, and even less, to suggest a treatment for Diana's increasingly severe affliction. Meanwhile, Diana has recently been confined to a wheelchair, and she finds that her fingers are painfully curling in on themselves. The couple's habitual joking dissipates in the face of one consultant's inept question about Diana's menstrual cycle, and a furious Diana wheels herself out of the hospital.

Deric's mother (Thora Hird) lives partially in a world of make-believe, and she is a comforting voice on the other end of the telephone for the couple. She facilitates some relief for Deric as he increasingly centers his world on his wife's predicament. The couple's children, Sally (Anastasia Mulrooney) and Nick (Andre Lancel) return home for Christmas just as their mother worsens. Nick, however, has

 The Wedding Gift was originally titled "Wide Eyed and Legless."

 "Blind? She'd have to be if she took a shine to you!"—Diana Logden to her husband, Deric, on Aileen Armitage from *The Wedding Gift*

good news: he is to be married in March, and Diana makes a resolution to walk down the church aisle at the wedding.

In another meeting with a consultant, it is suggested that Diana's illness is in fact hysteria. This is a conclusion both Longdens reject, although there are indications that, as the consultant suggests, Deric inadvertently boosts Diana's condition with his constant and tender ministrations.

While Deric's factory continues to lose money, and he discovers that Diana has hidden pills around the house in the event of her decision to resort to suicide, Deric finds some social relief at a literary luncheon. It is there that he meets and befriends Aileen (Sian Thomas), a virtually blind novelist. After Diana has a seizure in London, Deric visits Aileen in the spa town of Harrogate, but the relationship remains platonic.

At Diana's insistence, she is taken to Harrogate and rapidly makes friends with the Aileen. On the day of Nick's wedding, Diana manages to walk down the aisle as she promised, and then makes Deric find Aileen at a writers' conference in Blackpool. He bears a gift to Aileen from Diana. It is a bikini Diana has never been able to wear, and a note with it asks Aileen to take it as her wedding gift.

In a twist of irony, Diana drowns in the bath. After her funeral, Deric and Aileen view the Yorkshire moors, and once again, Deric is the caretaker.

Shot in the mundane colors of the English everyday, with domestic interiors solidly in the middle-class, *The Wedding Gift* is a small gem. There are a few minor flaws, including the fact that Deric's attempts at writing are mentioned several times, but left unexplored to be satisfying or even truly relevant to the story.

In sum, however, director Richard Loneraine and screenwriter Jack Rosenthal (the latter working from Deric's book about Diana), together with the empathetic cast, work effectively and with subtlety. Yet not all the critics were

impressed. Caryn James in *The New York Times* found the Longdens' dialogue to be "grating" and she concluded that the film was something akin to "a Monty Python routine." Her conclusion was not explained. Kevin Thomas, however, writing in the *Los Angeles Times*, was more taken with the motion picture. He appreciated Rosenthal's "sharp commentary on the inefficiency and inadequacy of Britain's socialized medicine system," and he called the acting "stellar."

Indeed, gutsy but finessed performances transform a story of courage into a celebration of unselfish love. Julie Walters combines her trademark wit with vulnerability, while Jim Broadbent shows himself to be an actor of nuance and compassion. Essentially carrying the film, Broadbent's Deric is both self-effacing yet needy. His needs are met by Sian Thomas' nicely played Aileen; her near-blindness is always there but never overstated.

The Wedding Gift is most English in its understatement of a small tragedy, and therein lies its virtues. As a tale of ordinary folk in trying circumstances, it is a fine tribute to Diana Longden, her husband Deric, and an engaging human story to all who will listen.

—Paul B. Cohen

CREDITS

Diana Longden: Julie Walters
Deric Longden: Jim Broadbent
Deric's mother: Thora Hird
Aileen Armitage: Sian Thomas
Nick Longden: Andrew Lancel
Sally Longden: Anastasia Mulrooney

Origin: Great Britain
Released: 1994
Production: David Lascelles for BBC Films, in association with Island World; released by Miramax Films
Direction: Richard Loncraine
Screenplay: Jack Rosenthal; based on the books *Diana's Story* and *Lost for Words*, by Deric Longden
Cinematography: Remi Adefarasin
Editing: Ken Pearce
Production design: Tony Burrough
Costume design: James Keast
Music: Colin Towns
MPAA rating: PG-13
Running time: 87 minutes

REVIEWS

Boston Globe. August 5, 1994, p. 46.
Chicago Tribune. July 22, 1994, p. 7F.
Entertainment Weekly. December 16, 1994, p. 84.
Harper's Bazaar. August 1994, p. 85.
The New Republic. CCXI, August 22, 1994, p. 34.
The New York Times. July 20, 1994, p. C18.
People Weekly. XLII, July 18, 1994, p. 13.
Playboy. XLI, August 1994, p. 17.
USA Today. July 15, 1994, p. D5.
The Washington Post. August 5, 1994, p. C2.
The Washington Post. August 5, 1994, p. WW38.

A Weekend with Barbara und Ingrid

A depressed Los Angeles man (Jim Metzler) finds his home invaded by two German performance artists, Barbara (Anna Katarina) and Ingrid (Michelle Holmes), who claim to be friends of a former girlfriend.

REVIEWS

Los Angeles Times. January 15, 1994, p. F4.
Variety. CCCXLIX, January 11, 1993, p. 66.

CREDITS

Danny: Jim Metzler
Barbara: Anna Katarina
Ingrid: Michelle Holmes
Jack: Bob Cady
Jerzy Louis: John Fleck

Released: 1994
Production: Gregory Neri; released by Rabbit in the Moon
Direction: Gregory Neri
Screenplay: Gregory Neri
Cinematography: Stephen Timberlake
Editing: David Notowitz
Production design: Robert Lovy
Music: Stephen Lovy and Tim Kelly
MPAA rating: no listing
Running time: 91 minutes

Weininger's Last Night

This drama centers on the crazed delusions of genius and philosopher Otto Weininger (Paulus Manker) on the night he committed suicide.

CREDITS

Otto Weininger: Paulus Manker
Adelaide Weininger: Hilde Sochor
Double: Josefin Platt
Leopold Weininger: Sieghardt Rupp
Clara: Andrea Eckert
Berger: Peter Faerber
Adele: Hilde Sochor
Sigmund Freud: Sieghardt Rupp

Origin: Austria
Released: 1991
Production: Released by WEGA Film Vienna
Direction: Paulus Manker
Screenplay: Paulus Manker; based on the play *Weininger's Last Night: The Soul of A Jew*, by Joshua Sobol
Cinematography: Walter Kindler
Editing: Ingrid Koller and Marie Homolkova
Music: Hansgeorg Koch
MPAA rating: no listing
Running time: 100 minutes

Wes Craven's New Nightmare

"Wes Craven returns to his now classic horror premise and takes it to a new dimension"
—Janet Maslin, *The New York Times*

"It's the cleverest, wittiest, most twisted scarefest in ages"—Peter Travers, *Rolling Stone*

"It's smart, it's scary and it's curiously thought-provoking"—Roger Ebert, *Chicago-Sun Times*

 Box Office Gross: $17,377,375 (December 4, 1994)

Freddy Krueger, the maniac with five sharp knives on his hand inplace of fingers, is one of the most popular villains ever to appear on the screen. Like the Frankenstein monster, he has been broiled and mangled in many previous incarnations, but he has always managed to pull himself together in time for the next sequel. Now his creator has resurrected Freddy again and has affixed the name "Wes Craven" to the title to assure viewers that this is the genuine article and not another of the exploitative sequels that followed his horror classic *A Nightmare on Elm Street* (1984).

The plot of *Wes Craven's New Nightmare* is convoluted. One reviewer described it as "post-modernist," evidently because of its spotlighting of the "ropes and pulleys" to remind the viewer that the film is not to be mistaken for reality because the makers are only playing a sophisticated game. The production seems aimed at filmmakers and critics. Instead of being scared to death, the viewer is expected to appreciate the craftsmanship that went into this expensive state-of-the-art

Matt Winston as Chuck, Rob LaBelle as Terry, David Newsom as Chase, Miko Hughes as Dylan, and Heather Langenkamp in *Wes Craven's New Nightmare*. Photo: Joseph Viles © 1994 New Line Productions, Inc. All rights reserved.

production. It was praised by the trade but received no word-of-mouth acclaim from theater-going teenagers.

Several of the major characters in this seventh Freddy Krueger story play themselves, including Wes Craven, a screenwriter working on a script for a film about Freddy Krueger. Craven's imagination is somehow bringing Freddy back to life and making gruesome events in the script take place in reality, even while the script is still in the process of being written. It becomes apparent that Craven—at least the Craven in the film—is not in control of his own story but that it is really Freddy who is dictating the script through his control of Craven's dreams.

Robert Englund, who has played Freddy in all seven films, appears as Robert Englund. He is scheduled to play Freddy again when the script is finished—but he is not the "real" Freddy; there is another Freddy, also played by Englund, who is not Englund. This sort of cinematic double talk makes the story hard to follow. The viewer does not know who is "real" and who is not, who is getting murdered and who is dreaming. At least Freddy does not murder Wes Craven; otherwise the script would never be finished and not even Craven would find out what happened.

Most of the gruesome events center around Heather Langenkamp, playing herself, who starred in the original *A Nightmare on Elm Street* as a teenager. In that earlier film, she had managed to defeat the maniacal Freddy—but he is still not dead, not even after all his setbacks in *A Nightmare on Elm Street 2: Freddy's Revenge* (1985), *A Nightmare on Elm Street 3: Dream Warriors* (1987), *A Nightmare on Elm Street 4: The Dream Master* (1988), *A Nightmare onElm Street 5: The Dream Child* (1989), *Freddy's Dead: The Final Nightmare* (1991).

Craven had no hand in any of the five sequels to his original creation. He has made such horror films as *The Last House on the Left* (1972), *The Hills Have Eyes* (1977), *The Serpent and the Rainbow* (1988), and *The People Under the Stairs* (1991) and came to be stereotyped as the "Sultan of Slash" and the "Guru of Gore." He has, however, continued to be identified with Freddy Krueger and has had to take the blame for the grossness of the sequels, without sharing in the profits.

After making *A Nightmare on Elm Street*, Craven sold all rights to his creation. The original film and its five sequels have since made more than $500 million worldwide, but Craven collected a total of only $400,000. None of the sequels measured up to the prototype. His *New Nightmare* cost considerably more than the original—a total of eleven-million dollars, much of which went into special effects.

After killing Heather's husband, Chase (David Newsom), early in the film, Freddy predictably goes after

CREDITS

Freddy Krueger: Robert Englund
Heather Langenkamp: Heather Langenkamp
Dylan: Miko Hughes
Chase Porter: David Newsom
Julie: Tracy Middendorf
Dr. Heffner: Fran Bennett
John Saxon: John Saxon
Wes Craven: Wes Craven
Robert Shaye: Robert Shaye
Sara Risher: Sara Risher
Marianne Maddalena: Marianne Maddalena
Robert Englund: Robert Englund

Released: 1994
Production: Marianne Maddalena; released by New Line Cinema
Direction: Wes Craven
Screenplay: Wes Craven; based on characters created by Craven
Cinematography: Mark Irwin
Editing: Patrick Lussier
Executive producer: Wes Craven and Robert Shaye
Production design: Cynthia Charette
Art direction: Troy Sizemore and Diane McKinnon
Set design: Stephen Alesch
Set decoration: Ruby Guidara
Casting: Gary Zuckerbrod
Visual effects supervision: William Mesa
Special visual effects: Flash Film Works
Sound: Jim Steube
Sound supervision: Paul B. Clay
Costume design: Mary Jane Fort
Music: J. Peter Robinson
MPAA rating: R
Running time: 112 minutes

AWARDS AND NOMINATIONS

Independent Spirit Awards Nomination 1995:
Best Film

honest-to-goodness horror for the sake of making money; instead, it is a socially responsible horror film, trying to find excuses for making money by showing people slashed to pieces by a sadistic maniac. Craven seems to be distancing himself by blaming everything on Freddy, who is a product of his own imagination. The main theme running throughout the film is that the script is not dictating the behavior of the characters but the characters are dictating the development of the script. No one, including the author, knows how the story will end. Craven cannot help himself; he cannot be blamed for all these killings. The characters must come to life and take charge of their own destinies, as in Luigi Pirandello's modernist play *Sei Personaggi In Cerca D'Autore* (*Six Characters in Search of an Author*, 1921).

Is this a way of saying that violent films do not beget violent social behavior but, to the contrary, that violent social behavior begets violent films? Craven at age fifty-five may have gotten too old to be making horror films; he seems to feel guilty about making another one but has become so "type cast" that he has no viable alternative. Like the aging Peter Lorre and Vincent Price, he has only one direction in which to develop, and like Shakespeare's Macbeth he might say, "I am in blood/Stepped in so far, that, should I wade no more,/Returning were as tedious as go o'er."

Dylan begins to act as if he is totally possessed by an evil spirit and might even be capable of murdering his own mother. He ends up in a private hospital room guarded by his faithful nanny Julie (Tracy Middendorf). Julie does not stand much of a chance against Freddy, who has the power to materialize through people's minds once they are asleep. He leaves the dead nanny stuck to the blood-spattered ceiling with his trademark of parallel slashes all over her body.

Meanwhile Dylan, under Freddy's hypnotic spell, has slipped out of the hospital and is attempting to cross one of Los Angeles' eight-lane freeways at night, with Heather right behind him dodging trucks and cars in a situation that combines several of a parent's worst nightmares. Freddy again proves himself to be the kind of sadist who gets more pleasure out of evoking terror than out of inflicting violence. This gleeful sadism is what has endeared him to his young fans. The authorities cooperated with the filmmakers by closing down a major freeway for the shooting of this single scene, which took almost a week's work and employed more than one hundred vehicles.

The final scenes are shot in a simulated corner of hell, which took more than two months to construct. These state-

her son. Young Miko Hughes does an excellent job of portraying little Dylan, whose mind is being taken over by the vengeful monster. The contrast between Dylan's angelic face and the satanic consciousness ripening inside him is one of the most effective concepts in the film. It recalls such films as *The Bad Seed* (1956), *The Exorcist* (1973), *The Omen* (1976), and *Poltergeist* (1982).

Ironically, Heather is unable to stay home to protect her little boy because she is at the studio making a film about the fictitious Freddy. She was reluctant to accept the role but was persuaded to do so by Craven, who convinced her that the only way to exorcise her recurring nightmares about Freddy—which have always turned out to be authentic precognitions—is to confront him and defeat him for the last time.

Heather's reluctance to appear in another Freddy Krueger film reflects the spirit of this production. It is not

of-the-art effects are impressive but fail to frighten as much as the elementary slash-and-chase scenes in the original. This may be partly because Heather is no longer a hysterical teenager but a grown woman who has better self-control and more experience in handling Freddy.

Remakes and sequels are seldom if ever as effective as the originals, even though the remakes and sequels usually cost more money. None of the many films about the Frankenstein monster, including the most recent version, *Mary Shelley's Frankenstein* (reviewed in this volume), has the same uncanny dreadfulness as the original version of 1931 starring Boris Karloff. Billy Wilder, who directed such classic films as *Double Indemnity* (1944), *The Lost Weekend* (1945), and *Sunset Boulevard* (1950), stated in a televised interview that Hollywood is producing more and more remakes and sequels because the success of the originals gives investors a sense of security. The number of remakes and sequels that have come out in recent years is so great that it seems to represent almost a new stage in cinematic evolution.

Wes Craven was quoted as saying that he wanted to make a movie about twenty-five to thirty-year-olds and how they, as parents, see Freddy. "Since the audience that saw the first *Nightmare* is now that age," he explained, "I wanted to make a movie for them." He seems to have been expecting people who were fifteen to twenty years old in 1984 to want to attend a sequel for nostalgic reasons and perhaps even to bring their own children to share the experience. Their children, however, would not be much older than cute little eight-year-old Miko Hughes, and it is highly questionable

> "The fans, God bless 'em, they're clammering for more. I guess evil never dies, right?"—Robert Shaye from *Wes Craven's New Nightmare*

whether they would want to bring them to an R-rated film about a maniac who can leap from nightmares into reality. It is also questionable whether these adults would have the same tastes they had as teenagers. Teenagers may be troubled by their bad dreams, but young adults have more realistic fears, such as burglars, kidnappers, gang violence, unemployment, and bankruptcy.

Young adults with small children tend to stay at home watching television. When the whole family goes to the movies together they usually patronize the G, PG, and PG-13 films such as *The Lion King* (reviewed in this volume) and the phenomenally successful *Jurassic Park* (1993). People who take small children to R-rated features hardly qualify as model parents. Craven might have been more successful trying to appeal directly to the teenagers of 1994. *Wes Craven's New Nightmare* failed to please either teenagers or young adults, as was quickly evidenced by the fact that only a few weeks after its release it was being billed in many multiplexes as a double-feature with *The Puppetmasters* (reviewed in this volume), another box office disappointment of 1994.

—*Bill Delaney*

REVIEWS

Daily Variety. September 12, 1994, p. 20.
Entertainment Weekly. October 28, 1994, p. 72.
The Hollywood Reporter. September 12, 1994, p. 14.
Los Angeles Times. October 14, 1994, p. F4.
The New York Times. October 14, 1994, p. B1.

What Happened Was...

"Comedy. Romance. Terror. The perfect first date."—Movie tagline

"One of my favorite films of the year!"—Gene Siskel, *Chicago Tribune*

Box Office Gross: $324,222 (December 18, 1994)

Tom Noonan and Karen Sillas star as Michael and Jackie, co-workers in a New York City law firm whose first date is the focus of this drama. Jackie invites Michael to her apartment for dinner, and over the course of a very awkward evening the two get to know each other and reveal their mutual loneliness and isolation.

REVIEWS

Entertainment Weekly. September 23, 1994, p. 46.
Harper's Bazaar. September 1994, p. 256.
Newsweek. CXXIV, September 12, 1994, p. 59A.
People Weekly. XLII, September 12, 1994, p. 19.
Playboy. XLI, October 1994, p. 21.
Rolling Stone. September 22, 1994, p. 106.
Variety. CCCLIV, February 7, 1994, p. 37.

"You finally grow up, you figure out who you are, and just when you've got something interesting to say, they're not interested anymore!"—Jackie from *What Happened Was...*

CREDITS

Jackie: Karen Sillas
Michael: Tom Noonan

Released: 1994
Production: Robin O'Hara and Scott Macaulay for Good Machine and Genre Film; released by the Samuel Goldwyn Company
Direction: Tom Noonan
Screenplay: Tom Noonan
Cinematography: Joe DeSalvo
Editing: Richmond Arrley
Production design: Dan Ouelette
Set decoration: Andras Kanegson
Sound: Rick Stevenson
Costume design: Kathy Nixon
Music: Ludovico Sorret
MPAA rating: no listing
Running time: 91 minutes

AWARDS AND NOMINATIONS

Independent Spirit Awards Nominations 1995: Best Actress (Sillas), First Screenplay
Sundance Film Festival Awards 1994: Grand Jury Prize, Best Screenplay

When a Man Loves a Woman

"Two thumbs up!"—*Siskel & Ebert*

"An unforgettable celebration of the human spirit."—*ABC Radio Network*

"Garcia and Ryan deliver Oscar-caliber performances."—*ABC-TV*

"Powerful, poignant, exceptional."—Jeffrey Lyons, *Sneak Previews/Lyons Den Radio*

"One of the richest, most thought-provoking adult movies this year."—Susan Granger, *CRN/American Movie Classics*

 Box Office Gross: $50,000,813 (October 9, 1994)

Meg Ryan and Andy Garcia are excellent in this sentimental film about a passionate relationship nearly destroyed by alcoholism. *When a Man Loves a Woman* brings a unique perspective to the genre of films about alcoholism: It examines the behavior and the character of the "co-addict" in addition to depicting the ravages of alcoholism on the family. This film reflects the clinical and popular understanding of alcoholism that emerged in the early 1990's and is a sentimental and touching portrait of the struggle to redefine family relationships during recovery.

When a Man Loves a Woman succeeds on several levels. First, the performances are excellent. Particularly outstanding are Ryan, Garcia, and two wonderful children, Tina Majorino and Mae Whitman. Second, director Luis Mandoki deftly guides his cast through intense material; he creates a modern film that feels like a classic Hollywood tearjerker. Finally, the film is educational. It is an astonishingly accurate case study of the struggles of a family stricken by alcoholism. The film does have its pathetic moments, such as two wrenching good-bye scenes between Garcia's character and the two children, and may be a bit sentimental for many film goers. Nevertheless, its sincerity more than makes up for its melodramatic inclinations.

This material has, of course, been touched on before in film, most notably in *Days of Wine and Roses* (1962) with Lee Remick and Jack Lemmon and the Academy Award-winning *The Lost Weekend* (1945) with Ray Milland and Jane Wyman. More recently, Michael Keaton established himself as a serious actor in *Clean and Sober* (1988). *Clean and Sober* and *When a Man Loves a Woman* have something else in common: both films examine alcoholism and addiction from the Twelve Step perspective of Alcoholics Anonymous. *When a Man Loves a Woman* goes one step further: it addresses issues of "Al-Anon" (the group for significant others of alcoholics) as much as the issues of Alcoholics Anonymous, showing both protagonists in their respective "Twelve Step" meetings.

As the film opens, Michael Green (Garcia), an airline pilot, is married to Alice (Ryan), a school counselor. They have two children, Jess (Majorino), Alice's nine-year-old daughter from a previous marriage, and Casey (Whitman), a precocious four-year-old. The film begins in a bar, depicting the playful attitude of Alice and Michael, who pretend not to know each other as they put on a steamy show for the other bar patrons. The audience comes to know Alice and Michael as a passionate and fun-loving pair who deeply love each other and their daughters. It is also evident, however, that Alice has a problem: she rarely is without a drink in her hand; Michael has to save her from nearly drowning after she falls—drunk—into the ocean during a vacation; and she neglects her children. Finally, a disastrous accident convinces Alice that she needs help, and she checks into a rehabilitation clinic to begin her recovery.

The start of Alice's recovery is hardly the end of the film, however. It is Alice's struggle to recover that causes stress and pain in her relationship with Michael, forming the second half of the film. When she returns from the clinic, she is a changed person. Because Michael has become used to his role as the protector and enabler, he has a difficult time coping with the ineffable changes in his wife. She is no longer helpless, needing him to pick her up and carry her home; she is no longer incapable of dealing with the children and the house; and she is no longer available to be weak so that he can be strong. The experience forces Alice and Michael to reexamine their marriage learning painful lessons in the process.

 "I know we have pressures, and we need to have fun, but wringing you out at the end of an evening is less fun than it used to be."—Michael from *When a Man Loves a Woman*

Screenwriters/executive producers Ronald Bass and Al Franken know this territory well and do a fine job of creating a script that is emotional, educational, and engrossing. It is particularly good to see Franken putting his wonderful talent to work on a serious film: He is one of the original writers of television's venerable comedy show, *Saturday Night Live*. Particularly well-crafted is a scene where Michael and Alice see a marriage counselor, perfectly depicting the uncomfortable interaction of such encounters, especially when both parties are engaged in a volley of blame and counter-blame. When Michael frowns at Alice's description of her feelings, the therapist asks Michael about the face he made in

CREDITS

Michael Green: Andy Garcia
Alice Green: Meg Ryan
Amy: Lauren Tom
Gary: Philip Seymour Hoffman
Jess Green: Tina Majorino
Casey Green: Mae Whitman
Emily: Ellen Burstyn
Walter: Eugene Roche
Dr. Gina Mendez: Latanya Richardson

Released: 1994
Production: Jordan Kerner and Jon Avnet for Touchstone Pictures; released by Buena Vista Pictures
Direction: Luis Mandoki
Screenplay: Ronald Bass and Al Franken
Cinematography: Lajos Koltai
Editing: Garth Craven
Production design: Stuart Wurtzel
Art direction: Steven A. Saklad
Set design: Stan Tropp
Set decoration: Kara Lindstrom
Casting: Amanda Mackey and Cathy Sandrich
Sound: Thomas D. Causey
Costume design: Linda Bass
Music: Zbigniew Preisner
MPAA rating: R
Running time: 124 minutes

response to Alice, and he replies, "It's the only face I've got, doctor."

Bass and Franken do extremely well at verbalizing the themes of the script and the feelings of the characters. After Alice returns from rehab, Michael, unable to accept her new seriousness, suggests a vacation; Alice replies, "Maybe I should learn to live in reality before I try to escape from it again." When Michael continues to pressure her to feel better, seemingly unable to understand why the problem cannot simply go away, she yells, "I am not your problem to solve!"

Another aspect of the writing that serves the theme beautifully is the insidious way that Michael appears to take care of everything, from one daughter's hairstyle to check-in at the rehabilitation center. When a woman comes to the lobby to check Alice into the center, Michael steps in front of Alice, saying, "Hi, we're Alice Green." "We're Alice" is a wonderful symbol for the problems of this and millions of other alcoholic relationships: the lack of boundaries. This clear understanding of these boundary issues makes this an important film for dysfunctional families to see.

As weepy as the film becomes in its second half, it is a rather extraordinary accomplishment that it examines dysfunctional relationships without resorting to cliché. "Dysfunctional relationships" is a key phrase in the lexicon

AWARDS AND NOMINATIONS

Blockbuster Entertainment Awards 1995: Best Drama Actress—Video (Ryan)
MTV Movie Awards Nominations 1995: Best Female Performance (Ryan), Most Desirable Male (Garcia)
Screen Actors Guild Awards Nomination 1994: Best Actress (Ryan)

of popular culture. Though this film is clearly didactic in nature, educating about boundaries, the process of recovery, how to talk to children (and how not to talk to them) about separation and divorce, and codependency, it remains fresh considering its roots in popular cliché.

This freshness is due in large part to the performances of its four lead actors. Meg Ryan is as bubbly and adorable as she was in *When Harry Met Sally* (1989) and *Sleepless in Seattle* (1993), but this time she adds an undercurrent of sadness and fear. Her drunk scenes, of which there are many, are as good as any on film. For an actress who in interviews has said that she does not consider herself to be a great actress, she is great in this film. Portraying a drunk character has to be one of the most difficult challenges an actor faces, and she pulls it off beautifully. Her transformation from drunk to victim to responsible mother is subtle and believable. This heartfelt and nuanced performance should bring her new respect within the Hollywood community, having been seen as Oscar-caliber by many critics.

Andy Garcia delivers a similarly multi leveled and graceful performance as the perfectionistic Michael. It is no accident that Michael is an airline pilot; he tries to pilot and control everything from breakfast to his wife's drunken sprees. It is interesting to note that most of Garcia's scenes with Ryan and the children are shot so that he is nose-to-nose with them, looking them squarely in the eye. The effect is that he is always "in their faces," that he is practically smothering them with his love. Garcia's intensity is perfectly suited to the role. He is appropriately melodramatic in the second half of the film, when he feels abandoned and rejected by Alice as she begins to separate from the codependency of the relationship. Occasionally, however, Garcia's character appears to be headed for self-righteous nobility, particularly when he is required to say good-bye to his daughters or to express his anger by turning over a coffee table.

Director Mandoki has a sensitive way with his actors; he clearly respects them and the material. His loving close-ups of Ryan and Garcia allow the audience to empathize with the painful story as it unfolds. He clearly respects the children as well. For example, he follows the agonizing response of Jess as she is slapped by her mother, then discovers her unconscious on the bathroom floor; his camera stays with her as she goes for the telephone. By continuing to include the children's responses, Mandoki maintains the focus on the entire family. The emotional stakes are raised as a result of the wonderful performances of the girls, and the audience is rewarded with a truly cathartic experience.

Mandoki creates a sumptuous atmosphere. With the aid of cinematographer Lajos Koltai, he underscores the diffuse family boundaries and intense interaction with dark light and shadow. Production designer Stuart Wurtzel provides a beautiful home interior that reveals the family's closeness even as it appears to hide the family's secrecy and despair.

When a Man Loves a Woman is important for its even-handed representation of what has commonly become known as co-dependency. The fact that it occasionally descends into weepy Hollywood romance should not detract from its fine direction, excellent performances, and admirable sincerity.

—*Kirby Tepper*

REVIEWS

Entertainment Weekly. April 29, 1994, p. 52.
The Hollywood Reporter. April 27, 1994, p. 24.
Los Angeles Times. April 29, 1994, p. F1.
The New York Times. April 29, 1994, p. B1.
Variety. April 25, 1994, p. 7.

Where The Rivers Flow North

"A Vermont frontier film...an American love story."—Movie tagline

"Tantoo Cardinal nails her part with such astonishing grace that Oscars should come pouring from the heavens."—*Interview*

"Stunning."—*Philadelphia Inquirer*

"Fantastic. A must-see."—*Vermont Sunday Magazine*

"Magnificent."—*New York Daily News*

"Rip Torn is brilliant!"—*Vancouver Sun*

 Box Office Gross: $497,295 (July 31, 1994)

A cantankerous Vermont backwoodsman, Noel Lord (Rip Torn), fights a losing battle with developers who are building a dam that will force Lord to relocate, in this low-budget drama set in the 1920's. Directorial debut of Jay Craven.

REVIEWS

Boston Globe. September 13, 1993, p. 33.
Boston Globe. March 25, 1994, p. 52.
Chicago Tribune. September 16, 1994, p. 7H.
Entertainment Weekly. October 7, 1994, p. 85.
Los Angeles Times. December 7, 1994, p. F4.
The New York Times. March 4, 1994, p. C15.
TV Guide. XLII, October 15, 1994, p. 46.
Variety. CCCLI, June 14, 1993, p. 57.
The Washington Post. May 6, 1994, p. B7.
The Washington Post. May 6, 1994, p. WW47.

CREDITS

Noel Lord: Rip Torn
Bangor: Tantoo Cardinal
Wayne Quinn: Bill Raymond
New York Money: Mark Margolis
Clayton Farnsworth: Michael J. Fox
Mitchell: George Woodard
Champ's manager: Treat Williams
Loose woman: Amy Wright
Rollins: David Bailey

Released: 1994
Production: Bess O'Brien and Jay Craven; released by Caledonia Pictures
Direction: Jay Craven
Screenplay: Don Bredes and Jay Craven; based on the novel by Howard Frank Mosher
Cinematography: Paul Ryan
Editing: Barbara Tulliver
Production design: David Wasco
Art direction: Charles Collum
Set decoration: Sandy Reynolds-Wasco
Casting: Bess O'Brien and Jay Craven
Costume design: Stephanie Kerley
Music: The Horse Flies and Ben Wittman
MPAA rating: PG-13
Running time: 104 minutes

White

"The story of a husband who would do anything to get his wife back...or anything to get back at her."—Movie tagline

"An intoxicating, erotic treat! A dazzling, witty film packed with breathtaking surprises!"
—Guy Flatley, *Cosmopolitan*

"Marvelously funny!"—*The Village Voice*

"Devilishly clever!"—*Time*

"An original tale of heartbreak, revenge and devastating irony."—*Cincinnati Enquirer*

"Brilliant satire."—*Detroit News*

"Extraordinary."—*Baltimore Sun*

Box Office Gross: $1,192,897 (September 11, 1994)

White is the second in director Krzysztof Kieslowski's trilogy *Three Colors*. Like his other two films, *Blue* and *Red* (reviewed in this volume), this film is loosely based on the concepts associated with the French flag: Liberty, Equality, and Fraternity. *White* explores "equality" in the very personal sense of equality of the sexes, and also

CREDITS

Karol: Zbigniew Zamachowski
Dominique: Julie Delpy
Mikolaj: Janusz Gajos
Jurek: Jerzy Stuhr

Origin: France, Switzerland, and Poland
Released: 1993
Production: Marin Karmitz for MK2 Productions; released by Miramax Films
Direction: Krzysztof Kieslowski
Screenplay: Krzysztof Piesiewicz and Krzysztof Kieslowski
Cinematography: Edward Klosinski
Editing: Urszula Lesiak
Production design: Halina Dobrowolska and Claude Lenoir
Set decoration: Magdalena Dipont
Casting: Margot Capelier and Teresa Violetta Buhl
Sound: Jean-Claude Laureux
Music: Zbigniew Preisner
MPAA rating: R
Running time: 90 minutes

AWARDS AND NOMINATIONS

Berlin Film Festival: Best Direction (Kieslowski)

extends its exploration to include Poland's desire to be an equal member of the European community. Director and co-writer Kieslowski, a Pole working in France, has created a humorous yet touching portrait of a changing Poland.

The film opens as its unprepossessing Polish hero, Karol, hesitates on the steps of an imposing French courthouse. A pigeon unceremoniously defecates on his shoulder, eloquently setting the mood for Karol's plight. In the courtroom with the aid of an interpreter, Karol is promptly divested of his marriage, his hairdressing business, his credit cards—in fact everything except his suitcase, a comb, and a two franc piece. His wife Dominique (Julie Delpy) has divorced him, claiming that Karol never consummated their marriage, which Karol admits is true. Karol's pleas that the condition was only temporary are refuted when he and his ex-wife once more try to make love, only to again find Karol impotent.

This is the last straw for his wife, Dominique, who out of utter contempt, reacts with cruelty, setting her own business on fire in order to get the police after Karol. Her cruelty reaches such depths that when Karol calls to beg for her return, she leaves the phone beside the bed while making love with someone else.

Down on his luck, Karol manages to fall even further. Playing his comb in the Metro for spare change, he meets another expatriate, Mikolaj (Janusz Gajos) who takes pity on him and makes him two offers: one, to take Karol back to Poland with him, and two, to get him a job killing a suicidal man who can't take his own life. Karol accepts the first, but refuses the second.

Karol, without a passport and avoiding the police, has to find another way to get back to Poland. In a wonderfully funny scene that owes much of its ironic humor to Kieslowski's tribute to Chaplin in the film, Karol (Polish for Charles) decides to travel in his own suitcase as checked luggage. The suitcase, with Karol inside, travels from a moving belt to teeter precariously on the top of a luggage wagon and finally to come to rest in the bowels of an airplane. Of course nothing in Karol's life goes without a hitch and the flight back to his homeland is no exception. His suitcase is stolen at the airport, and when the thieves open it in a deserted field by a garbage dump, they are outraged to find

Karol as their booty. They beat him up, then leave him bleeding in the snow. Karol, humiliated, impoverished, and bloodied, sentimentally gazes about the garbage strewn countryside and cries, "Home at last!"

He somehow makes it, limping and bleeding, to the door of the family hairdressing salon that his brother, Jurek (Jerzy Stuhr), has kept going in his absence. Their humble shop in a tiny old village is illuminated by—of all things—a bright neon sign. "This is Europe now," Jurek explains, giving Karol his first hint of the changes taking place in Karol's homeland as desperate capitalism sweeps through the land.

Karol has changed as well and is no longer happy working in the family beauty salon. So, this innocuous hairdresser becomes a bodyguard for a gangster who runs an illegal money-changing operation. When Karol inadvertently overhears their plan to buy cheap land from peasants that will soon become an important industrial park, Karol plots his move. Feeling the opportunity of the changes happening around him, he decides to become a venture capitalist. But he needs capital to begin, and so Karol embarks on his plan, a plan that is mysteriously incomprehensible until the very end of the film.

Desparate for cash, Karol looks up his old friend from the Parisian Metro, Mikolaj, and finally agrees to kill the suicidal man. The man turns out to be none other than Mikolaj himself. In one of the best scenes of the film, they meet for the murder in a deserted subway station. A trembling Karol holds a gun to Mikolaj's chest and asks, "Are you sure?" "Yes" Mikolaj tells him and the gun goes off. A moment of slow motion graphically illustrates the enormity of Karol's action, when suddenly it becomes apparent that Mikolaj is very much alive. Karol explains that the first was a blank, but the second is real. Then asking him again, "Are you sure?" Mikolaj smiles and says, "No." But Karol gets his money anyway, because, as he says, "I earned it." And he most definitely did, for he has given his friend more than his life back, he has given him a whole new life, and in a romp on a frozen lake, the two celebrate that life in a raucous, drunken escapade that cements their friendship.

Through buying parcels of land in the center of the tracts his gangster boss planned to buy, and selling them to him at top dollar, Karol takes his money and reinvests it so shrewdly that by the time he's finished he has built a conglomeration of businesses and made his fortune. But he has also under-

> *White* is the second film in Kieslowski's trilogy, *Three Colors*. Each film in the trilogy is named for one of the three colors and concepts associated with the French flag: *Blue* (Liberty), *White* (Equality), and *Red* (Fraternity).

gone a metamorphosis. Sporting a cashmere coat, slicked back hair, a Volvo and a chauffeur, Karol is every inch the successful entrepreneur. Yet he is still so likable that even this new guise sits lightly on him.

The first step in his plan finished, Karol makes his friend Mikolaj his business partner as well as a partner in his master plan. The elaborate plan includes the procurement of a body, but in a statement indicative of the state of post-communist Poland, one of the characters says, "In these times you can buy anything." He buys the corpse of a Russian whose face was smashed beyond recognition while leaning too far out of a train window. Mikolaj then buys Karol a house in Hong Kong and gets him a new passport and an entirely new identity. Karol makes out his will, leaves everything to his ex-wife, and then plans his own death.

He watches his own funeral from a distance, and sees his ex-wife grieving at his graveside. Convinced that she loves him, Karol surprises Dominique in her hotel room and they have a night of sexual ecstasy. He then steals out of the hotel room in the morning to begin the last phase of his plan—her arrest for his murder.

White is a touching black comedy that explores equality in the sense of "getting even," and looks at how, for this gentle man, revenge is a double-edged sword. In the end, our hero has his ex-wife committed for his own murder, and at the same time condemns himself to a life-sentence of his own making, where he has no life, no love, nothing but his "equality."

In the final touching scene, he bribes his way into the prison grounds and sadly looks up at her window. Her regretful stare confirms what we already know—that she is not the only prisoner. Exiled from home, friends, and their love, they have at last found true equality.

> "We looked very closely at the three ideas, how they functioned in everyday life, but from an individual's point of view, when you deal with [the ideas] practically, you do not know how to live with them. Do people really want liberty, equality, fraternity?"—*White* director Krzysztof Kieslowski explaining the relationship between the three films in his trilogy, *Three Colors*

In explaining the relationship between the three films in his trilogy, director Kieslowski said, "We looked very closely at the three ideas, how they functioned in everyday life, but from an individual's point of view...When you deal with [the ideas] practically, you do not know how to live with them. Do people really want liberty, equality, fraternity?" Kieslowski uses many symbols to reinforce his white (equality) theme, from his snowy Polish landscapes to pigeon droppings, Dominique's white car and sequences fading to white, and yet the symbolism enhances, never intruding or distracting from the movement of the film.

The first film in the trilogy, *Blue*, deals with a grieving widow whose husband and daughter are killed in a car wreck, and whose subsequent "liberty" is more of a death for her. She must come to terms with her new found liberty in much the same way Karol has to come to terms with his "equality." Liberty, equality, fraternity, but at what price?

White, winner of the Best Director award at the Berlin Film Festival in 1994, is more than an analogy about an individual's search for equality. The different moods that Kieslowski evokes from France and Poland simulate the characters they represent: Dominique, cold, imposing, beautiful, and Karol, homespun, ingeniuous, and lovable. In a much larger sense, Kieslowski is equating Karol to a Poland that is bumbling toward an equal position in the European community, just as Dominique represents the glamourously decadent and intimidating power France has over the Polish imagination.

A noticeable change occurs when the location shifts from France, where the mood is stiff and lacking warmth, to Poland, where the film takes on power and reality. The characters are also suddenly more interesting, more intense, and definitely more real. Kieslowski's images of Poland and of Karol are captivating, funny, and lovable in contrast to the coldness of his French urban landscapes, and the coldness of Dominique herself. Poland forms a perfect backdrop for the Eastern European wit and sense of the absurd that is unmistakable in *White*.

Kieslowski, the director of the *Double Life of Veronique*, which was released in the United States, and *Decalogue*, which has yet to be released here, announced at the screening of *Red* at the Cannes Film Festival that the last film in his trilogy would also be the last film in his career.

Kieslowski's subtle chronicling of a changing Poland, his eloquent visual style, and his vivid sense of characterization all combine in *White*, making it a film not to be missed. But *White* also confirms that Kieslowski is a talent that will be sorely missed.

—*Diane Hatch-Avis*

REVIEWS

Atlanta Constitution. June 24, 1994, p. P5.
Boston Globe. June 24, 1994, p. 49.
Chicago Tribune. June 17, 1994, p. 7L.
The Christian Century. CXI, March 16, 1994, p. 267.
Christian Science Monitor. June 10, 1994, p. 12.
Cosmopolitan. CCXVI, June 1994, p. 20.
Entertainment Weekly. July 15, 1994, p. 46.
Entertainment Weekly. December 9, 1994, p. 94.
Hollywood Reporter. June 17-19, 1994, p.6.
Los Angeles Weekly. June 17, 1994, p. 39.
The Los Angeles Times. June 17, 1994, p. F15.
The Nation. CCLIX, July 25, 1994, p. 137.
National Review. XLVI. July 11, 1994, p. 62.
The New Republic. CCX, June 13, 1994, p. 32.
The New York Times. June 10, 1994, p. C23.
The New Yorker. LXX, June 20, 1994, p. 88.
People Weekly. XLII, July 11, 1994, p. 14.
Playboy. XLI, July 1994, p. 22.
TV Guide. XLIII, January 14, 1995, p. 39.
Variety. January 28, 1994, p. 22.
Village Voice. June 14, 1994, p. 52.
Vogue. CLXXXIV, July 1994, p. 68.
The Washington Post. June 24, 1994, p. B7.
The Washington Post. June 24, 1994, p. WW42.

White Badge

This award-winning drama centers on South Korea's role in the Vietnam War.

REVIEWS

Los Angeles Times. November 11, 1994, p. F4.

AWARDS AND NOMINATIONS

Tokyo International Film Festival: Grand Prix, Best Direction.

CREDITS

Han Kiju: Ahn Sung-Ki
Pyon Chinsoo: Lee Kyung-Young
Kim Yongok: Shim Hae-Jin
Kim Munki: Tokko Youngjae
Chon Hisik: Kim Sejun
Hong Bangjang: Huh Junho

Origin: Korea
Released: 1994
Production: Cook Chong-Nam for Deil Film; released by Morning Calm Cinema
Direction: Chung Ji-Young
Screenplay: Gong Su-Young, Jo Young-Chel, Shim Seung-Bo, and Chung Ji-Young; based on the novel by Ahn Jung-Hyo
Cinematography: Yu Young-Gil
Editing: Bark Soon-Duck
Music: Sin Byung-Ha
MPAA rating: no listing
Running time: 125 minutes

White Dog

When a young woman (Kristy McNichol) adopts a stray German shepherd, she discovers that her otherwise friendly pet viciously attacks black people. She takes it to an animal training center where a patient black man (Paul Winfield) attempts to reprogram it.

CREDITS

Julie Sawyer: Kristy McNichol
Keys: Paul Winfield
Carruthers: Burl Ives
Roland Gray: Jameson Parker

Released: 1991
Production: Jon Davison; released by Paramount Pictures
Direction: Samuel Fuller
Screenplay: Samuel Fuller and Curtis Hanson; based on a story by Romain Gary
Cinematography: Bruce Surtees
Editing: Bernard Gribble
Production design: Brian Eatwell
Dog training: Karl Lewis Miller
Music: Ennio Morricone
MPAA rating: PG
Running time: 90 minutes

White Fang II: Myth of the White Wolf

"An Ancient Myth. A Land of Mystery. An Extraordinary Adventure."—Movie tagline

"Beautifully mounted and well-acted."—David Hunter, Q: *The Hollywood Reporter*

"Great outdoor action!"—*KCOP-TV, Los Angeles*

"Heroic."—*Entertainment Weekly*

"Rousing adventure."—Roger Ebert, *Chicago Sun Times*

Box Office Gross: $8,733,565 (July 4, 1994)

This sequel to Disney's hit film *White Fang* (1991) did not receive the critical or box-office success of the original. Though it is not without merits, it is an action-adventure film for those who are not too discriminating about their action or their adventure. This sequel, like many sequels, apparently was created to capitalize on a prior success, and is thus lacking the originality and the depth of its predecessor. It is an acceptable film, but is not up to the standards of films such as *Old Yeller* (1957) or *Black Stallion* (1979).

Five trained dogs played the role of White Fang.

Ethan Hawke reprises his role from the original long enough to set up the story of this film. Jack Conroy (Hawke) has left his Alaskan gold mining claim to young Henry Casey (Scott Bairstow). He has also left him the half-dog, half-wolf White Fang saying, "please take care of White Fang, or is White Fang taking care of you?"

And White Fang is taking care of Henry, demonstrating for the audience very quickly his lightning speed and near-human intelligence while outfoxing a prospective thief. Screenwriter David Fallon deserves credit here, as the episode is actually quite a good introduction to the characters and the relationship of Henry and White Fang, and also serves as a catalyst for the ensuing adventure. Having decided that he should protect his gold by sending it back to his native San Francisco, Henry and White Fang embark on a raft to head for the nearest town down river.

"Please take care of White Fang, or is White Fang taking care of you?"—Jack Conroy from *White Fang II*

But on the way, they encounter the obligatory whitewater rapids, are nearly killed and separated from each other and from their gold. (The themes of separation and reconciliation have been a staple of films from *Old Yeller*, 1957 to *Pinocchio*, 1940, and Disney is not about to break the mold.)

Somehow, this film does not achieve the level of "will they be reunited?" or "will they be separated?" found in other more classic films, or even in the *Lassie* television series of the 1960's. But White Fang's separation from his master does provide the basis for the rest of the film: A young Indian princess, Lily (Charmaine Craig), rescues Henry from the river thinking that he is the human incarnation of "the white wolf" (White Fang) that she saw fighting the rapids. The White Wolf is thought to be a leader who can help the friendly Haida tribe find the Caribou necessary for their survival.

Tribal chief Moses (Al Harrington), Lily's uncle, becomes a mentor to Henry who becomes a savior to the tribe. Henry learns the Haida "ways," falls in love with Lily, and sets out to find the Caribou. Along the way, he is nearly foiled by evil Leland Drury (Alfred Molina). As to whether or not Henry prevails, and is reunited with White Fang, and saves the tribe—well, let's just say that this is a Disney film.

Fallon, the writer responsible for the first *White Fang* screenplay, provides a script that ultimately succumbs to its clichés. There is a plethora of new-age type dialogue about the wisdom of the Indians ("The wolf is a great hunter with a warrior's heart; but you are like every other white man.") Like another recent film, *The Air Up There* (reviewed in this volume), the callow, white youth single-handedly saves a tribe of people that have lived off the land for centuries. It seems a bit arrogant.

The performances are perfunctory with Bairstow and Craig, though committed to their roles, looking like a Calvin Klein ad and sounding more like an episode of *Little House on the Prairie* than an epic film. Harrington and Molina fare a bit better with Harrington being particularly likable as the wise Moses.

This is the first feature film of director Ken Olin, best known to audiences as Michael on TV's *thirtysomething*. (One critic said that Olin's presence explains why the wolves whine.) Olin handles the action sequences with confidence and creates a well-defined character for White Fang with the help of editor Elba Sanchez-Short and animal trainers Joe Camp and Tammy Maples. This smaller-budget film is a good start for Olin who is sure to have better material to direct in the future.

CREDITS

Henry Casey: Scott Bairstow
Lily Joseph: Charmaine Craig
Moses Joseph: Al Harrington
Peter: Anthony Michael Ruivivar
Katrin: Victoria Racimo
Reverend Leland Drury: Alfred Molina
Adam John Hale: Paul Coeur
Heath: Geoffrey Lewis
Halverson: Matthew Cowles
Bad Dog: Woodrow W. Morrison
Leon: Reynold Russ
Jack Conroy: Ethan Hawke

Released: 1994
Production: Preston Fischer for Walt Disney Pictures;
released by Buena Vista Pictures
Direction: Ken Olin
Screenplay: David Fallon
Cinematography: Hiro Narita
Editing: Elba Sanchez-Short
Production design: Cary White
Art direction: Glen W. Pearson
Set decoration: Tedd Kuchera
Casting: Gail Levin

Sound: Rob Young
Costume design: Trish Keating
Animal training: Joe Camp and Tammy Maples
Music: John Debney
MPAA rating: PG
Running time: 106 minutes

One curious aspect of the film is that those who see it after Disney's 1995 release of *Pocahontas* may see more than a passing resemblance between the Indian Princess played by Craig, the numerous canoeing sequences, the form-fitting bucksin costumes, and the "I am not of your world" storyline. A cynic would say that this film was used as a prototype for *Pocahontas*. Lily says to Henry Casey, "all you believe in is your gold." She could say the same to the Disney company.

—*Kirby Tepper*

REVIEWS

Daily Variety. April 15, 1994. p. 23.
Los Angeles Times. April 15, 1994. p. F6
The Hollywood Reporter. April 15-17, 1994. p. 13
The New York Times. April 15, 1994, p. B2

Why Has Bodhi-Dharma Left for the East?

Set in a remote South Korean monastery, this slow-moving but beautifully photographed drama centers on an aging Zen Buddhist monk (Yi Pan Yong), his disciple (Sin Won Sop), and an orphaned child (Huang Hae Jin), who seek the path to enlightenment.

REVIEWS

Boston Globe. January 28, 1994, p. 47.
Film Quarterly. XLVIII, Fall 1994, p. 27.
The New York Times. September 25, 1993, p. A13.
The Washington Post. October 4, 1993, p. B7.

CREDITS

Hye Gok: Yi Pan Yong
Ki Bong: Sin Won Sop
Hae Jin: Huang Hae Jin
Superior: Ko Su Yong
Fellow disciple: Kim Hae Yong

Origin: Korea
Released: 1993
Production: Bae Yong Kyun; released by Milestone
Direction: Bae Yong Kyun
Screenplay: Bae Yong Kyun
Cinematography: Bae Yong Kyun
Editing: Bae Yong Kyun
Music: Chin Kyu Yong
MPAA rating: no listing
Running time: 135 minutes

Widows' Peak

"Passion. Secrets. Scandal. It's just another day in the country, in a place called *Widows' Peak*"
—Movie tagline

"Very funny...This movie is entertaining every step of the way..."—Gene Siskel, *Siskel & Ebert*

"All the performances are impeccable, a superb ensemble cast...it deserves to become a sleeper hit like *Enchanted April* or *Four Weddings and a Funeral*"—*New York Post*

 Box Office Gross: $6,188,676 (September 25, 1994)

Jim Broadbent as Clancy, Joan Plowright as Mrs. Doyle Counihan, and Mia Farrow as Miss O'Hare in *Widows' Peak*. Photo: Jonathan Hassion © 1994 Fine Line Features. All rights reserved.

Widows' Peak is a smug little contrivance that fancies itself an intricate and masterful tale of deceit. It is the tepid yarn of a gingerly showdown between two women in the matriarchal Irish town of Kilshannon in the 1920's. The archrivals in pettiness are a poor middle-aged spinster, Miss O'Hare (Mia Farrow), and a flashy young new arrival, Edwina Broome (Natasha Richardson). The film's thin, uninteresting plot is nothing but a setup for a surprise ending.

Broome, an Americanized English woman and war widow of a British officer, is the latest widow to join Kilshannon's exclusive ruling clique. The wealthy Mrs. Doyle Counihan (Joan Plowright) lords over the matriarchy, composed almost entirely of well-to-do widows except for O'Hare whose poverty remains a mystery to everyone else in town. Broome's arrival seems to send O'Hare around the bend, and the two women start a bizarre feud.

If one has tired of violent action adventures, *Widows' Peak* provides a change of diet—to weak tea. The film's most gripping confrontation comes when the giddy Broome, who has just accepted an offer of marriage from Mrs. Doyle Counihan's son, sails her boat too close to O'Hare's skiff, sending it on a shoal. If this seems unbearably tame, it is almost breathtaking compared to an earlier sequence in which Broome and O'Hare squabble for a door prize at a dance and another in which Broome throws two of O'Hare's prize roses on the ground.

There is little more that can be said about the plot of *Widows' Peak*, because little else goes on until its trick resolution, which cannot be revealed without spoiling the film's little game. The ending is supposed to be a bomb shell but is closer to a tiny firecracker. Those in the audience who have not fallen asleep by the point in the film where O'Hare's secret is revealed will not be hard pressed to guesswhat the film's larger secret is. The denouement is clever but hardly clever enough to sustain an entire film

that is so devoid of sustaining moments, characters, or mystery.

Like a good magician, a trick film such as *Widows' Peak* needs something to divert the audience's interest until the rabbit comes out of the hat. Saddled with a pedestrian script by Irish playwright Hugh Leonard, director John Irvin can not find a formula to work any magic, though he toys with many. For much of the film, characters ask questions about why O'Hare is allowed to be in the rich widows' club when she is so poor—as if the viewer must be reminded what the nub of the mystery is.

Irvin dawdles with a number of tactics to sustain some measure of interest, none successful. *Widows' Peak* starts out being narrated bya drunken dentist named Clancy (Jim Broadbent), but he disappears as a narrator a few minutes into the film, never to return until the very end. The film could use a lot more of his drollery. There are some lame attempts at wry Irish humor, but they lack zing.

Since the film was shot in Ireland, there is the possibility of making the landscape into a starring character, as in many films witha Gaelic background. The cinematography by Ashley Rowe is uninspiring, however, and the shores of the River Shannon look like a faded postcard. With neither plot, humor, nor scenery to carry it,

Widows' Peak must sink or swim with its female ensemble, since the male lead—Adrian Dunbar as the matriarch's son, Godfrey—is merescenery, and Broadbent's role is slight.

Unfortunately, Plowright fails to make her spying, petty matriarch into a character of any great impact. It would help the film mightily if Mrs. Doyle Counihan were amusing, but she is rarely so. It would help the ending mightily if she were treacherous, but she is more venial in her sins than venal. Plowright, playing it safe, is a major disappointment.

Natasha Richardson brings much-needed spunk to the dismal proceedings. Hers is by far the most fetching and fascinating portrayal. In costume and ravishing good looks, her Broome stands out from the rest of the widows like a harlot in a church. Yet even that is a bit of a problem: It is a little too obvious that she is not what she appears to be.

Widows' Peak marks the first film released for Farrow since her much-publicized and extremely nasty legal battle with renowned filmmaker Woody Allen, for whom she made the previous thirteen of her more than two dozen films. Unfortunately, the war with her former romantic and professional partner appears to have taken its toll. The

Farrow of *Widows' Peak* is wan and subdued, showing none of the spark or wit of most of her Allen films.

Farrow seems to be sleepwalking through the film, occasionally turning on a brogue, then turning it off. The mere effort of acting appears wearisome to her, and she can muster little heart for the points where she is supposed to be full of rage or sorrow. For *Widows' Peak* to work at all, O'Hare needed to be as intriguing as a half-glimpsed rainbow in an Irish mist, but Farrow is monochromatic in the role. Her failure is at the heart of the the film's dullness.

Interestingly, Farrow's role was originally written by Leonard for Farrow's mother, actress Maureen O'Sullivan, whom Leonard met at a dinner party in the early 1980's. Originally, Farrow was supposed to have played Edwina Broome. It took more than a decade for the *Widows' Peak* script to make it to the screen and by then the original casting scheme did not work.

The revised casting does not succeed either. Farrow and Richardson do not connect on screen; the sparks do not fly. Then again, nothing much happens in *Widows' Peak*. Even in Ireland there are bad days, and *Widows' Peak* is one of them. It is a day when the rain does not stop, and the green fields look dull and brown, and the conversation in a dank and dreary pub is uninspired.

Widows' Peak can not be properly classified, because it does not work in any meaningful way. As a period piece, it is diffident. As a mystery, it is slight. As a comedy, it is parched. As a character study, it is sadly lacking in interesting characters. Hence, it is a clever sort of trifle without any sort of magic at all.

—Michael Betzold

CREDITS

Miss O'Hare: Mia Farrow
Mrs. Doyle Counihan: Joan Plowright
Edwina Broome: Natasha Richardson
Godfrey: Adrian Dunbar
Clancy: Jim Broadbent
Maddie: Ryhagh O'Grady

Origin: Great Britain
Released: 1994
Production: Jo Manuel for British Screen and Rank Film Distributors; released by Fine Line Features
Direction: John Irvin
Screenplay: Hugh Leonard; based on his story
Cinematography: Ashley Rowe
Editing: Peter Tanner
Production design: Leo Austin
Casting: Nuala Moiselle
Sound: Peter Lindsay
Costume design: Consolata Boyle
Music: Carl Davis
MPAA rating: PG
Running time: 101 minutes

REVIEWS

Entertainment Weekly. May 20, 1994, p. 44.
The Hollywood Reporter. May 13-15, 1994, p. 8.
Los Angeles Times. May 13, 1994, p. F8.
The New York Times. May 13, 1994, p. B8.
People. May 30, 1994, p. 17.
Variety. April 18, 1994, p. 13.

Window Shopping

This romantic comedy, set in an underground shopping mall, centers on two love triangles. A beauty salon employee, Mado (Lio), loves a young man, Robert (Nicolas Tronc), who works with his parents, Jeanne (Delphine Seyrig) and Monsieur Schwartz (Charles Denner), in a men's boutique. Robert, however, prefers Mado's boss, Lili (Fanny Cottencon). When an American businessman, Eli (John Berry), comes to the mall, he discovers that Jeanne was his lover decades ago when he was a soldier stationed in France.

CREDITS

Sylvie: Miriam Boyer
Eli: John Berry
Jeanne: Delphine Seyrig
Robert: Nicolas Tronc
Mado: Lio
Pascale: Pascale Salkin
Lili: Fanny Cottencon
Monsieur Schwartz: Charles Denner
Monsieur Jean: Jean-Francois Balmer

Origin: Belgium and France
Released: 1986
Production: Martine Marignac; released by World Artists
Direction: Chantal Akerman
Screenplay: Chantal Akerman, Jean Gruault, Leora Barish, Henry Bean, and Pascal Bonitzer
Cinematography: Gilberto Azevedo and Luc Benhamou
Editing: Francine Sandberg
Production design: Serge Marzolff
Music: Marc Herouet
MPAA rating: no listing
Running time: 96 minutes

Wiping the Tears of Seven Generations

The hardships suffered by generations of Native Americans following the violent 1890 massacre at Wounded Knee is the subject of this consciousness raising documentary.

REVIEWS

Variety. CCCXLVII, July 20, 1992, p. 65.

CREDITS

Narrator: Hanna Left Hand Bull Fixico

Released: 1992
Production: Gary Rhine; released by Kifaru Productions
Direction: Gary Rhine and Fidel Moreno
Screenplay: Gary Rhine and Phil Cousineau
Cinematography: Gary Rhine and Fidel Moreno
Editing: Laurie Schmidt
Music: Robert La Batte
MPAA rating: no listing
Running time: 60 minutes

With Honors

"You will love every moment. Magnificently acted, magnificently written, and magnificently directed."—Jules Peimer, *WNWK Radio*

"wonderful and funny"—Bill Diehl, *ABC Radio*

"Inspiring and deeply moving."—Jeffrey Lyons, *Sneak Previews/Lyons Den*

 Box office: $19,946,834 (August 21, 1994)

Set at Harvard University, Alek Keshishian's *With Honors* tells the tale of the unique relationship that develops among several college seniors and a sickly, homeless man. As the film begins, Monty Kessler (Brendan Fraser) has almost completed his senior thesis on government for the demanding Professor Pitkannan (Gore Vidal) when his computer's hard drive dies. En route to photocopy his original, he loses it in Widener Library's basement heating plant. A bearded vagabond, Simon Wilder (Joe Pesci), who takes shelter there, hoards

CREDITS

Simon: Joe Pesci
Monty: Brendan Fraser
Courtney: Moira Kelly
Everett: Patrick Dempsey
Jeff: Josh Hamilton
Pitkannan: Gore Vidal

Released: 1994
Production: Paula Weinstein and Amy Robinson for Spring Creek; released by Warner Bros.
Direction: Alek Keshishian
Screenplay: William Mastrosimone
Cinematography: Sven Nykvist
Editing: Michael R. Miller
Production design: Barbara Ling
Art direction: Bill Arnold
Set design: Suzan Wexler
Set decoration: Cricket Rowland
Casting: Marion Dougherty: Nessa Hyams
Sound: Curt Frisk
Costume design: Renee Ehrlich Kalfus
Music: Patrick Leonard
MPAA rating: PG-13
Running time: 100 minutes

the eighty-eight-page thesis, agreeing to return it—one page per favor rendered.

Thus a curious rapport develops between Simon and Monty, much to the chagrin of the latter's housemates, Courtney (Moira Kelly), Everett (Patrick Dempsey), and Jeff (Josh Hamilton). Despite Simon's lack of formal education, he manages to teach Monty a few things and gradually develops into a surrogate father figure. As Simon develops serious health complications from his earlier work with asbestos, the Harvard students accept him into their lives and provide a final touching tribute to him. Although Monty does not end up graduating with honors from Harvard—thanks to Simon's philosophy of life, which he has adopted—he is now prepared to face the world much more honorably and realistically.

Coming to the production from his provocative work on the Madonna documentary *Truth or Dare* (1991), Harvard alumnus Keshishian relied heavily on his own experiences of university life. He interpreted playwright William Mastrosimone's script through his own eyes, as a 1986 Harvard graduate who was considerably involved in his studies, with a keen interest in drama.

At the core of the film is the gradual awakening of Monty, an ambitious and insensitive student majoring in government. As far as he is concerned, the world revolves around him and his thesis. When Simon disrupts the logical progression of his studies, Monty's life, however, takes a turn for the better. His final thesis on government, although submitted too late for honors, reflects his personal growth and independence of thought.

In light of the chance hostile meeting of Monty and Simon, each character evolves in a unique way. Incredibly driven and socially awkward, Monty is forced to face the harshness of life outside the ivory-tower existence he leads. For him, appearances mean everything: People like Simon are mere parasites on society. Brendan Fraser, who also starred in *School Ties* (1992), set at a snooty prep school, is believable in his role as a Harvard student.

The rough-edged and homeless Simon as played by Joe Pesci becomes the father that Monty never had and the professor who makes an indelible imprint on his soul. Pesci had become very popular by the early 1990's, appearing in a number of films, most notably *Goodfellas* (1990), for which he won an Oscar, and *My Cousin Vinny* (1992). Ironically, the demanding professor with the most potential influence, Philip Hayes Pitkannan, as portrayed by novelist Gore Vidal, finally understands Monty's need for creative independence on his thesis project after reading the revised work.

The behavior and philosophy of each roommate also

evolve because of Simon's presence. Radio host Everett with his pet rooster "Gorky" offers comic relief. As played by Patrick Dempsey, who had previously starred in such films as *Mobsters* (1991) and *Run* (1991), Everett becomes increasingly sensitive to the ailing Simon. Courtney, for whom love equals sex, develops more responsibly as her relationship with Monty grows. Moira Kelly, who had also starred in *The Cutting Edge* (1992) and *Chaplin* (1992), brings out Courtney's spirit as well as her immaturity. Studious Jeff, on the periphery of the group, sees the light and becomes involved with caring for Simon in his last hours. Josh Hamilton, who also starred in *Alive* (1993), plays Jeff as a whining, immature young man who suddenly awakens to reality.

These personality changes occur primarily because the witty, nonconformist Simon challenges the students to think independently, to reexamine their stereotypes about the homeless, and to face the unsettling realities of life. As a Socratic gadfly, this unlikely character provokes them to distinguish the real world from the shadow world of academia.

"When it comes to relationships everybody is a used car salesman."—Simon B. Wilder in *With Honors*

In keeping with its academic setting, the film is layered with literary metaphor. Homeless Simon reads Émile Zola's *Germinal*, about the unfortunate lot of French miners struggling for human rights. Equally appropriate is Walt Whitman's *Leaves of Grass*: As the Whitman lookalike Simon is dying, the four students in this quasi-Greek chorus read lyrical and philosophical excerpts from the work. A la Marcel Proust's *Rememberance of Things Past*, Simon carries a pouch filled with small stones, each of which causes him to recall some important aspect of his earlier life.

The subdued and aesthetically composed scenes captured by Ingmar Bergman's former cinematographer Sven Nykvist, render Harvard and the other academic communities in which the film was shot most stimulating. Widener Library's towering columns, Radcliffe Yard's serenity, as well as Harvard Square, visually draw the eye into each composition. The low-key music by Patrick Leonard adds to the sober atmosphere of the film. Keshishian's connection with

Madonna from his earlier work *Truth or Dare* has yielded the film's theme song "I'll Remember," performed by the pop music star.

With Honors was filmed not only at Harvard and Radcliffe, but also in Chicago, at the University of Illinois Champaign-Urbana campus, the University of Illinois Medical School, the Chicago Theological Seminary, the University of Minnesota, and Northwestern University. The interior sets were primarily constructed in a warehouse in the Chicago suburb of Cicero, while the students' house was shot in a small complex of clapboard and brick structures in the old suburb of Hyde Park.

Despite some powerfully tense scenes between Monty and Simon, the film in general suffers from multiple weaknesses. Hardly credible is the central premise of a vagabond existing comfortably in the heating plant at Harvard University, not to mention his parlaying favors from a college senior. Also unrealistic is the staged and didactic government class on the Constitution taught by Professor Pitkannan. One could hardly expect such a prominent lecturer to debate the outspoken vagabond in front of the class and then offer him a handout. Also unrealistic is the death scene, as the students refuse to get medical help for the dying Simon.

In the end, Monty and his friends learn that there is more to life than delivering a senior thesis in time to graduate with honors. Unfortunately, the film handles its moral lessons rather too simplistically, for which it was duly criticized by many reviewers. Composed of one contrived scene after the next, *With Honors* is saved only by the on-screen chemistry of Fraser and Pesci, who play well off each other.

—*John J. Michalczyk*

AWARDS AND NOMINATIONS

Golden Globe Awards Nomination 1995: Best Song ("I'll Remember")
MTV Movie Awards Nomination 1995: Best Song ("I'll Remember")

REVIEWS

Boston Globe. April 29, 1994, p. 48.
Chicago Tribune. May 12, 1994, 90.
Entertainment Weekly. May 13, 1994, p. 42.
The Hollywood Reporter. April 18, 1994, p. 8.
The Houston Chronicle. April 29, 1994, p. 1 (Weekend Ed.).
Los Angeles Times. April 29, 1994, F6.
The New York Times. April 29, 1994, p. B2.
Variety. April 18, 1994, p. 4.

Wittgenstein

The life and philosophy of Austrian-born Ludwig Wittgenstein (Karl Johnson)—including his friendship with fellow philosopher Bertrand Russell (Michael Gough) and economist John Maynard Keynes (John Quentin), and his repressed homosexuality—is the focus of this avant-garde drama.

REVIEWS

The Advocate. August 24, 1993, p. 71.
Atlanta Constitution. May 27, 1994, p. P6.
Boston Globe. December 3, 1993, p. 57.
Chicago Tribune. May 20, 1994, Sec. 5 p. 3.
The Nation. October 4, 1993, p. 364.
The New Republic. CCIX, October 11, 1993, p. 38.
New Statesman & Society. VI, March 26, 1993, p. 33.
The New York Times. September 17, 1993, p. C15.
Variety. CCCL, February 15, 1993, p. 86.
The Washington Post. October 23, 1993, p. D4.

CREDITS

Ludwig Wittgenstein: Karl Johnson
Bertrand Russell: Michael Gough
Lady Ottoline Morrell: Tilda Swinton
John Maynard Keynes: John Quentin
Johnny: Kevin Collins
Wittgenstein (as a child): Clancy Chassay
Martian: Nabil Shaban
Hermine Wittgenstein: Sally Dexter
Lydia Lopokova: Lynn Seymour

Origin: Great Britain
Released: 1993
Production: Tariq Ali for Channel 4 and the British Film Institute, in association with Uplink and Bandung; released by Zeitgeist Films Ltd.
Direction: Derek Jarman
Screenplay: Derek Jarman, Terry Eagleton, and Ken Butler
Cinematography: James Welland
Editing: Budge Tremlett
Production design: Annie Lapaz
Sound: George Richards, Toby Calder and Paul Carr
Costume design: Sandy Powell
Music: Jan Latham-Koenig
MPAA rating: no listing
Running time: 75 minutes

Wolf

"Two thumbs up for *Wolf*! An all-pro production with Jack Nicholson at the top of his game."
—*Siskel & Ebert*

"Four stars. Nicholson's *Wolf* has style and bite..."—*USA Today*

"Nicholson is amazing, finding humor and poignancy in a role that could have slid into caricature."—*Rolling Stone*

 Box Office Gross: $65,002,597 (October 23, 1994)

Jack Nicholson and Michelle Pfeiffer star in *Wolf*. Copyright © 1994 Columbia Pictures Industries Inc. All rights reserved. Courtesy of Columbia Pictures.

While descriptions of lycanthropy appear in writings as early as A.D.161, the first medical dictionary published in English—Stephen Blancard's *A Physical Dictionary* (1684)—defines it as "a Madness proceeding from a Mad wolf, where in Men imitate the howling of Wolves." Stephen Kaplan, founder of the Werewolf Research Center in Elmhurst, N.Y., is quoted in *Entertainment Weekly* as reporting that, as of the early 1990's the werewolf population in America alone was 200 to 300. Alice Hoffman's novel *Second Nature*, a story about a child raised by wolves who returns to society as an adult who is more wolf than man, rose to the best-seller's list in the spring of 1994. About the same time, a *Smithsonian* magazine feature article chronicled America's romance and fascination with wolves, telling of the dangers of adopting the wild, never-to-be-tamed wolves as pets. Thus, fascination with werewolves was alive and well at the time of this film's release. It is little wonder that such a high-concept, big-budget film as *Wolf* was made—and made such a splashy arrival in theaters across the country. Indeed, according to the film's production notes, screenwriter Jim Harrison said, "Lycanthropy tended to arise as a phenomenon during historical periods of extreme suppression of natural instincts. Like right now."

Wolf begins at night, with Will Randall (Jack Nicholson), a timid, put-upon book editor, driving his ancient Volvo along a country road in New England. As he maneuvers timidly across the snow and ice, a dark figure appears before him in the road. He hits the brakes but cannot avoid striking the figure, which then lies immobilized in the road before him. Randall leaves his car and approaches the fallen figure, only to discover it is a large gray wolf that appears to be dead. When Randall attempts to move the wolf from the road, however, it springs to life, biting Randall and sealing his fate. Initially, the bite is one more worry for the timid Randall, another change that can bring only ill. To

his surprise, however, Randall soon feels energized. He can see better and hear extremely well. He has a purpose; he knows what he must do, and he does it.

Wolf has effectively evaded categorization by those who have studied it, reviewed it, tried to classify it by genre. The filmmakers have labeled it a "romantic thriller and contemporary tale of the supernatural." Yet, while it is clearly "a horror film about office politics," *Wolf* is not the typical, traditional transformation film such as *The Wolf Man* (1941), starring Lon Chaney, nor is it a slick, satiric shiver of a send-up, such as *An American Werewolf in London* (1981), nor is it a love-will-conquer-all story à la *Beauty and the Beast*. Some might say it is a film about building character, about the costs of achieving success, about finally putting people in their places. Others might claim that it is nothing more than sheer entertainment.

Director Mike Nichols sees *Wolf* as a "poetic expression of an innerstate. It's a metaphor for the experience of becoming different from everyone else and leaving humanity behind, which is a kind of nightmare that happens to people in the middle of their lives. There's also the idea that, on the other side of such a horror, there is something that isn't necessarily only dark, that endings aren't necessarily endings, and metamorphoses and changes aren't necessarily only bad." Perhaps most accurately, in traditional horror terms, *Wolf* is itself a shape-shifter, allowing each viewer to look into its depths and to see reflected there his or her special concerns. That would seem to be its magic.

Wolf is a film driven by a series of fine performances. Nicholson is his usual screen-commanding self, even when at his meekest. Early in the film, his demeanor, his stance,

CREDITS

Will Randall: Jack Nicholson
Laura Alden: Michelle Pfeiffer
Stewart Swinton: James Spader
Charlotte Randall: Kate Nelligan
Detective Bridger: Richard Jenkins
Raymond Alden: Christopher Plummer
Mary: Eileen Atkins
Roy: David Hyde Pierce

Released: 1994
Production: Douglas Wick; released by Columbia Pictures
Direction: Mike Nichols
Screenplay: Jim Harrison and Wesley Strick
Cinematography: Giuseppe Rotunno
Editing: Sam O'Steen
Production design: Bo Welch
Art direction: Tom Duffield
Set decoration: Linda DeScenna
Casting: Juliet Taylor
Sound: Arthur Rochester
Costume design: Ann Roth
Special makeup effects: Rick Baker
Music: Ennio Morricone
MPAA rating: R
Running time: 121 minutes

all signal submission. His character is actively failing, even as he is a failure. For example, when the new publisher, Raymond Alden (Christopher Plummer), sacks Randall, he accepts the blow, accepts the humiliation of a demotion, accepts the fact of another colossal failure. Nicholson's face is slack; ever so slightly his shoulders slump. Yet when playing a wolf, Nicholson is more himself. Randall redresses each of the slights he has received and plots the best way to do so. Marshaling his few faithful friends around him, Randall changes his world—and the worlds around him. Interestingly, when the film begins by showing Nicholson alone on a snowy country road, many viewers will recall *The Shining* (1980), another Nicholson transformation, although of a slightly different ilk.

In the production notes, Nicholson encourages viewers to try to "eliminate ... value judgments as to whether Will is better off as a wolf. You know, there are good wolves and bad wolves. Mike [Nichols] and I discussed that point at great length. Neither of us wanted to make a film that says we're better off being wolves. That's not what it's about. In fact, Will resists becoming a wolf, and it's only the events of the story that make him unable to." *Wolf* marks

"What're you, the last civilized man?"—Laura Alden to Will Randall in *Wolf*

a reunion for Nicholson and director Mike Nichols, who together have made *Carnal Knowledge* (1971), *The Fortune* (1975), and *Heartburn* (1986).

Also fine is James Spader, who plays Stewart Swinton, a ruthlessly ambitious young editor and "friend" to Will Randall. While Spader rose to fame as a misunderstood misfit in *sex, lies, and videotape* (1989), he has made his name playing dislikable characters in such films as *Less than Zero* (1987), *Wall Street* (1987), *Bad Influence* (1990), and *True Colors* (1991). Yet *Wolf* is perhaps his finest hour. For example, Swinton commiserates with Randall on the day the decisions are announced concerning who will stay or who will go. Swinton even appears to be willing to go with Randall, to threaten to leave if Randall's job is threatened. Unfortunately, Randall not only loses his job but also his friend, realizing in the process Swinton's true colors. Spader's Swinton is delightfully hateful throughout.

If it is true that werewolves eventually kill the ones they love—or are killed by them—then Laura Alden (Michelle Pfeiffer) is arguably the most in danger in the film. Although Pfeiffer plays another one of her beautiful but confused characters, the chemistry between Nicholson and Pfeiffer is quite strong. One particularly fine scene occurs when Randall comes to see Laura's father, Raymond Alden—the man who fired him—and is summarily dismissed. As Laura does whatever will ensure her father's ire, she invites Randall to stay for lunch at her place, a guest house adjoining the Alden estate's main house. During that stay, Randall and Laura stroll to a lake, and sit and talk as the afternoon ends.

Amid the amber-colored world around them—day ending, autumn upon them—the two talk about their lives, hopes, failures. Randall tells her of the wolf bite, of the changes in him. She listens, understands, believes him, and believes in him. It is a finely drawn, carefully played scene; it plays well and is memorable. "Laura has always been the outcast, the black sheep within her family," Pfeiffer says in the production notes. "And I think that the wildness within her is attracted to the new found wildness in Will. She's used to caring for wounded animals in her life, metaphorically speaking, and I think that Will is another wounded animal. That's how she cares for him, and it comes as a complete surprise to her."

Also particularly fine are Eileen Atkins, who plays Mary, Will Randall's dedicated secretary, and David Hyde Pierce, who plays his loyal assistant Roy. As the new Will Randall evolves, Mary and Roy watch in amazement; when the new Will Randall springs into action, Mary and Roy are by his side. For example, it is Roy who draws to the audience's attention the fact that Randall no longer needs his glasses for reading, and it is Roy who declares the new ruthless Randall his hero. Not unlike Miss Moneypenny, the loyal secretary in the James Bond films, Mary is exceedingly supportive of her boss, even when he is meek. When Randall finally starts to turn the tables on his enemies, it is Mary who announces, "It's about time."

Beyond its remarkable performances, *Wolf* is also wonderful just to look at. For example, Randall walks to work through a New York that is falling to pieces around him, construction ongoing, yet nothing ever completed. His office at MacLeish House, the publishing company, is overwhelmed by books and papers: chaos. The building that houses the publishing company is actually the Bradbury Building, a light-filled, glass, iron, and marble building that had just been restored to celebrate its hundredth birthday. Production designer Bo Welch selected the building because to him it resembled a zoo: "The ironwork suggests a zoo or prison to me. For all the Bradbury Building's beauty, it is depicted in the film as a fancy jail." Also lovely is Alden Manor, which is actually the Old Westbury Gardens in Westbury, Long Island. Built in 1906 and listed on the National Register of Historic Places, the estate was the home of railroad magnate John S. Phipps. The Charles II-style house is surrounded by 88 acres of tree-lined walks, formal gardens, ponds, and playful architectural follies. Laura Alden's cottage was actually

constructed on Stage 27 at Sony Pictures Studios in Culver City, California.

Screenwriter Jim Harrison found the roots for the *Wolf* story in a variety of places: "The idea for *Wolf* springs from Native American stories about men turning into animals, and also from children's stories with similar themes. [French philosopher Michel] Foucault, too, inspired it—the fact that modern man feels nervous, because we all live in a zoo. Sometimes to get out of this zoo, one needs to go to any lengths. For obvious reasons, this idea appeals to Alpha-type males under serious pressure." Even with its flaws, *Wolf* has great doses of all the wonderful stuff of which successful summer films are made. ⊕

—*Roberta F. Green*

REVIEWS

Boston Globe. June 17, 1994, p. 73.
Chicago Tribune. June 17, 1994, Tempo, p. 5.
Entertainment Weekly. June 24-July 1, 1994, p. 80.
The Hollywood Reporter. June 13, 1994, p. 12.
Los Angeles Times. June 17, 1994, p. F1.
The New York Times. June 17, 1994, p. B1.
Variety. June 13, 1994, p. 4.
The Washington Post. June 17, 1994, p. B1.

The Wonderful, Horrible Life of Leni Riefenstahl (Die Macht der Bilder)

"A vital Artistic Event! One of the Year's Ten Best. Riefenstahl deserves to be classed with D.W. Griffith, Sergei Eisenstein and Orson Welles."—Richard Corliss, *Time*

"Two thumbs up!"—*Siskel & Ebert*

"Riefenstahl takes the breath away!"—Vincent Canby, *The New York Times*

"Absolutely mesmerizing!"—Georgia Brown, *The Village Voice*

Box Office Gross: $243,973 (July 4, 1994)

CREDITS

Leni Riefenstahl: Leni Riefenstahl
Ray Muller: Ray Muller
Luis Trenker: Luis Trenker
Walter Frentz: Walter Frentz
Guzzi Lantscheer: Guzzi Lantscheer

Origin: Germany
Released: 1993
Production: Hans-Jurgen Panitz, Jacques Clerq, Dimitri Clerq, Waldemar Janusczak, and Hans-Peter Kochenrath for Omega Film, Nomad Films, Channel 4, and Zweites Deutsches Fernsehen; released by Kino International
Direction: Ray Muller
Screenplay: Ray Muller
Cinematography: Walter A. Franke, Michael Baudour, Ulrich Jaenchen, and Jurgen Martin
Editing: Beate Koster, and Vera Dubsikova
Music: Ulrich Bassenge, and Wolfgang Newmann
MPAA rating: no listing
Running time: 187 minutes

Ray Müller's documentary *The Wonderful Horrible Life of Leni Riefenstahl*, though made in 1993, did not enter American markets until 1994, whereupon it was hailed as one of the year's ten best pictures by *Entertainment Weekly*, *Time*, *The Philadelphia Inquirer*, *New York Newsday*, and *The Seattle Post-Intelligencer*. Even though the film was too specialized for wide distribution, it was highly regarded by American reviewers from coast to coast and it is now available on videocassette from Kino on Video, as well it should be, since it consists of an extended interview with Riefenstahl herself, clear-headed and still feisty at the age of ninety.

Helene Berta Amalie Riefenstahl was born in Berlin in 1902. She was incontestably the most gifted woman filmmaker the world has seen, but, unfortunately, also the most controversial. Müller's documentary, better described by its German title *Die Macht der Bilder* (*The Power of Images*) presents a remarkable survey of her career utilizing a representative sampling of those images, and a primary account by Riefenstahl herself.

Müller briefly summarizes her early career as a dancer and allows Riefenstahl herself to explain how she first became involved with the Bergfilms ("mountain films") of Arnold Franck, who invented this genre and whom she credits as her mentor. The documentary includes extended clips from her first mountain picture, *Der Heilige Berg* (*The Sacred Mountain*, 1926) but not from all of the six films directed by Franck in which she appeared, the last of which was *S.O.S. Eisberg* (1933).

After this introduction the documentary rightly concentrates on the films Riefenstahl directed, starting with *Das Blaue Licht* (*The Blue Light*, 1932, in collaboration with Béla Balázs), in which she also starred as Diotima, and *Sieg des Glaubens* (*Victory of Faith*, 1933), her first attempt to film a Party Congress rally, and a film once believed lost. There is also footage from her last film, *Tiefland* (*Lowland*, made in 1944 in collaboration with G.W. Pabst, but not released until 1954), in which Riefenstahl played the Spanish dancer Marta.

"I was never anti-Semitic and I never joined the Nazi Party. What am I guilty of? I didn't drop any atom bombs. I didn't denounce anyone. So where does my guilt lie?"—Leni Riefenstahl in *The Wonderful, Horrible Life of Leni Riefenstahl*

But most of the attention of this three-hour documentary is focused on the Riefenstahl masterworks subsidized by the Nazi Party, *Triumph des Willens* (*The Triumph of the Will*, 1935) and *Olympische Spiele*, (*Olympia*, 1938). These two films respresent her best work but it is also work done in the service of the state and the Minister of Propaganda and hence reprehensible for many viewers.

When she first saw Hitler speak, Riefenstahl was impressed: "He radiated something very powerful," she explains, "but as a man he didn't interest me," the latter statement no doubt intended to counteract rumors that had persisted that she became Hitler's mistress. At any rate, she wrote to Hitler, who remembered having seen her dance in *Der Heilige Berg* (a clip of this dance is included); and he wrote her back, inviting her to film the Party Congress of 1933, not a successful effort, in her opinion: "It was not a proper film," she remarks, dismissively, "merely some shots."

Riefenstahl claims Hitler ordered her to make *The Triumph of the Will*, the documentary of the 1934 Party Congress at Nuremberg. She agreed on the condition that Hitler would never again force her to make another film about him, the Party, or the Reich. After the war, German courts ruled in 1948 that Riefenstahl had not been active in the Nazi Party but had merely been a sympathizer, and in 1952 she was exonerated of war crimes. She is constantly on the defensive all the way through this documentary. "I was never anti-Semitic and I never joined the Nazi Party," she asserts at the end. "What am I guilty of? I didn't drop any atom bombs. I didn't denounce anyone. So where does my guilt lie?" To others, however, the answer to that question may be obvious. This is not simply a matter of guilt by association. As Ray Müller remarked to Robert Sklar, "Her talent was her tragedy. It depends to what use you put your talent, and that's her guilt."

German courts ruled in 1948 that Leni Riefenstahl had not been active in the Nazi Party but had merely been a sympathizer, and in 1952 she was exonerated of war crimes.

The documentary gives visual evidence of how this genius filmmaker worked, as she discusses in detail, for example, her technique for editing *Olympia*. It is also amusing to watch the interplay between Riefenstahl and Müller early in the film as she attempts to advise and direct the director. Among the credited advisors for the film are Kevin Brownlow and David Culbert, the editor of *The Historical Journal of Film, Radio, and Television*. Though interesting in its own right, this film also has obvious importance for scholars and anyone especially interested in German cinema.

—*James M. Welsh*

REVIEWS

Cinéaste. Vol.XX, No.3 (1994), pp.18-23.
Entertainment Weekly. April 1, 1994, p.36.
Film Comment. Vol.29, No.6 (November-December 1993), pp. 70-76.
The Hollywood Reporter. April 14, 1994, p.8.
Los Angeles Times. April 14, 1994, F6.
The New York Times. October 14, 1993, B1

Woodstock

"Experience the event that named a generation."
—Movie tagline

Box Office Gross: $20,813 (June 4, 1994)

No one has been able to define accurately the Woodstock phenomenon. It has been called everything from the premier symbol of the 1960's counterculture movement to a disaster area responsible for the biggest traffic jam in New York history. Some have said it defined a generation while others pronounced it the ultimate example of hippie-excess. Somewhere in between these extreme points of view might lie the truth, but even this is doubtful. For, as stated before, Woodstock was a phenomenon, one that quickly took on mythic proportions even while it was occurring, and one whose legendary status has grown ever since. Every extravagant music festival held after Woodstock has been compared to it, but no other concert has come close to matching its mythic aura.

One of the key factors contributing to the Woodstock legend is Michael Wadleigh's extraordinary documentary of the event. When it first premiered in 1970, it was praised for its innovative approach to documentary filmmaking and went on to win the Academy Award for Best Documentary. Since its original release, however, its reputation has diminished, primarily because of the Woodstock legend itself, which has received much criticism from new generations of rock-and-roll enthusiasts. These newer generations are rightfully incensed over being reminded by the "Woodstock Generation" that their musical tastes are inferior to the legendary music of the 1960's. The constant repetition of this classic music, along with frequent showings of the documentary on television, has also served to demean the film's reputation.

Although it seemed that Wadleigh's timing of the documentary's re-release to coincide with Woodstock '94 was a blatantly commercial move, the fact that the film did play briefly in theaters—with a vastly improved digital sound track and forty minutes of additional footage—gave the public a fleeting chance to see this landmark film as it was originally intended to be seen.

The film quickly establishes its playfully rebellious counter culture attitude even before it begins: To the tune of Jimi Hendrix's electrifying rendition of "The Star-Spangled Banner"—a version he first played at Woodstock—the Motion Picture Association of America's rating rode of R catches fire, then explodes. This is Wadleigh's not-so-subtle attack on the MPAA for restricting the audience he feels would most appreciate the film.

The first image to appear is, ironically, an elderly man with decaying teeth who stands awkwardly in front of the camera and gives his impressions of the three-day festival, which was held practically in his backyard near the town of Bethel, New York. "This thing was too big," the man says, "too big for the world." Then, the film pans across a gorgeous pastoral landscape while the song "Long Time Coming" by Crosby, Stills and Nash plays on the sound track. Scenes of other aged Bethel townsfolk tending to vegetable gardens are intercut with scenes of youthful, long-haired construction workers putting together a massive wooden stage where the musicians will perform.

> This release of *Woodstock* marks the 25th anniversary of the event. The budget for *Woodstock* was about $1 million.

These opening images suggest an unusual yet hopeful coexistence between generations, both young and old performing labors of love amid rural splendor. Things quickly become stranger when the song "Going Up the Country" by Canned Heat begins playing while youths dressed in flowing gowns, embroidered jeans, flowers, and other colorful adornments begin arriving in an endless stream of humanity. Again, the sight of these multitudes of young people milling about, setting up tepees, and cavorting in open fields is both strange and beguiling. It is as if the audience is watching a peculiar yet vaguely familiar tribe of youthful vagabonds preparing for an elaborately bizarre ritual. A slight air of pretension surrounds these tribe members; their movements, their dress, their smugly serene attitude are all slightly off-putting. Yet, this feeling quickly vanishes when the camera pans over the area again. This time, instead of open fields and rolling hills there is an endless sea of these scraggly, uninhibited young people gathered in front of the huge stage. The sight of these hundreds of thousands of hippie revelers cheering, waving, and dancing together is truly an awe-inspiring, epic spectacle.

When the first performer hits the stage, folk singer Richie Havens, the true significance of this massive ritualistic gathering becomes apparent. Although Havens at first seems totally out of place singing and playing by himself in front of such a massive audience, Wadleigh and his battalion of cameramen quickly set the mood for the rest of the concert by creating an intimate bond between viewer and performer. By having the camera literally become part of each act, weaving in and around the musicians as they thrash their instruments and sing expressively to the sea of adoring fans, Wadleigh makes the film audience a participant in the festival.

Wadleigh also uses multiple-screen images to pull the viewer even more intimately into the action. Up to three separate images of a performer flash upon the screen at one time; other times two identical images bracket a contrasting central image; still other split-screen images of performer and audience complement one another while the music acts as a force that bonds the images together. Although Wadleigh uses the multiple-image technique extensively throughout the film, the viewer never gets the sense of it being overused. This is because Wadleigh customizes the technique to fit the mood and style of each performer. For example, when Santana performs a driving, upbeat number, Wadleigh has an image of the band's wildly kinetic drummer bracketed by scenes of audience members gyrating to the high-voltage beat. For Joan Baez, Wadleigh dispenses with the multiscreen technique altogether, choosing to film her intimate, acappella performance in a long take from one stationary camera. This respect for each performer's unique style is in radical contrast to the way in which early 1990's music videos were filmed, most of them consisting of incongruous and uncomplimentary quick-cutting images that have more to do with commercial advertising and sur-

CREDITS

Released: 1994 (original release 1970)
Production: Bob Maurice; released by Warner Bros.
Direction: Michael Wadleigh
Editing: Jere Huggins, Hubert De La Bouillerie and Steven C. Brown
Sound: Larry Johnson
MPAA rating: R
Running time: 228 minutes

AWARDS AND NOMINATIONS

Academy Awards 1970: Best Documentary
Nominations: Best Editing (Thelma Schoonmacher), Sound (Larry Johnson)

face glamour than with capturing the essence of the performer or the music.

If *Woodstock* were merely a "filmed concert," it most assuredly would not have been the landmark documentary that it is. Instead, Wadleigh had the foresight to let this cameramen and crew wander into the audience and into the surrounding community to cover the event from every imaginable point of view. Wadleigh includes several unflattering aspects about the event. Many of those interviewed are openly hostile, lashing out at the hordes of attendees for disrupting the community, for destroying private property, and for creating a borderline disaster area requiring military troops to helicopter in food and provisions. One young woman becomes hysterical over the fact that she cannot leave the area because of the massive traffic snarl. For the most part, however, those interviewed speak in rapturous tones of the peaceful nature of the event, everyone from the good-natured sanitation man servicing the portable toilets to the chief of police of Bethel.

"The Woodstock Generation: 1967-20?? R.I.P. It Up. Tear It Up. Have A Ball."—closing credits from *Woodstock*

Wadleigh also includes involved scenes of counter culture life: a young man leading a Kundalini yoga session; a young couple talking about living together in a commune; hordes of youths skinny-dipping in a muddy lake; and a multitude of men and women smoking marijuana from a wide range of drug paraphernalia.

These disparate moments, all filmed in a roving, down-to-earth style, ultimately combine to give the festival an extraordinary sense of fleeting wholeness, as if this were indeed a documentary about a unique, Brigadoon-like phenomenon in the making. Adding to the sense of a complete yet temporary community are the stage announcements heard throughout the film, some of which call for a doctor to assist in a birth, a clergy man to perform a marriage, and much general advice about where to find lost friends and relatives, where to lineup for a free breakfast, and which drugs to avoid ingesting.

Most of the additional forty minutes of footage is devoted to performers who were cut from the original version due to time constraints: Jefferson Airplane, Janis Joplin, Canned Heat, and an addition number by Jimi Hendrix. By far, the most effective additional scene is the performance by Canned Heat. During this segment, the essence of the Woodstock phenomenon is expressed. While the band plays a raucously upbeat number, a young man from the audience suddenly jumps on stage and begins dancing around, then approaches the beefy, bearded lead singer and hands him a marijuana cigarette. Without missing a beat, the singer accepts the cigarette, then wraps his arm around the man and gives him an affectionate hug while still belting out the lyrics to the song. Meanwhile, the cameraman continues to weave and dart among the band members, at one point moving in for an extremely tight close-up of the guitarist, so close in fact that a collision seems imminent. In this one brilliantly exuberant segment, the performer, the audience, the filmmakers and the film viewers come together as one to celebrate the phenomenon known as Woodstock.

Near the end of the film's closing credits, while Crosby, Stills, Nash, and Young sing "The Cost of Freedom," a list of names scrolls across the screen—the names of performers, counter culture heroes, and causes that have died since Woodstock was held. The final name is "The Woodstock Generation: 1967-20??" followed by the phrase, "R.I.P. It Up. Tear It Up. Have a Ball." For many—Wadleigh and his film crew included—the Woodstock nation did not fold up and disappear after Jimi Hendrix closed the concert and the technical crew dismantled the stage. For many, Woodstock is still a vibrant entity, still touching and influencing millions of lives each day. This documentary is vivid proof of the Woodstock phenomenon's timeless potency, a fact with which the attendees of Woodstock '94 would most assuredly agree.

—*Jim Kline*

REVIEWS

Entertainment Weekly. July 15, 1994, p. 45.
The Hollywood Reporter. June 27, 1994, p. 16.
Los Angeles Times. June 29, 1994, p. F6.
The New York Times. June 29, 1994, p. C1.

The Wrong Man

"Accused of a crime he didn't commit. Obsessed by a woman he can't possess."—Movie tagline

"A hell of a ride!"—*Time*

"Old style thriller with up-to-date nudity."—*The New York Times*

American sailor Alex Walker (Kevin Anderson) is on shore leave in Mexico when he meets a fellow American named Felix in a bar. Felix, a self-professed smuggler, befriends Alex and sets him up with a woman for the night—a favor which turns out to be a distraction while Felix steals his wallet.

When Alex goes to Felix's place to confront him, Felix is sitting behind a desk. On the desk is a gun. Alex picks up the gun and threatens Felix. Felix falls over dead; someone else has shot him. Alex hears police sirens and, gun in hand, escapes out the front door as police arrive.

Chased by cops, Alex dives into the backseat of a convertible. The owners of the car are two very strange Americans. Phillip Mills (John Lithgow) is in "the importing and exporting business" and says he is on the verge of striking it rich; he seems more on the verge of exploding.

CREDITS

Missy Mills: Rosanna Arquette
Alex Walker: Kevin Anderson
Phillip Mills: John Lithgow
Captain Diaz: Jorge Cervera, Jr.
Detective Ortega: Ernesto Laguardia
Felix Crawley: Robert Harper

Released: 1993
Production: Alan Beattie and Chris Chesser for Viacom Pictures; released by Polygram Filmed Entertainment
Direction: Jim McBride
Screenplay: Michael Thoma; based on a story by Roy Carlson
Cinematography: Affonso Beato
Editing: Lisa Churgin
Production design: Jeannine Oppewall
Art direction: Hector Romero
Costume design: Tracy Tynan and Rudy Dillon
Music: Los Lobos
MPAA rating: no listing
Running time: 110 minutes

Missy (Rosanna Arquette), his traveling companion, is a bored, sultry temptress who puts Alex into a dither.

That's some of what happens in the first fifteen minutes of *The Wrong Man*. It's a promising start to what seems to be a taut, quirky thriller. Unfortunately, *The Wrong Man* turns into a faltering road movie featuring one of the most bizarre and overplayed lust triangles ever filmed.

The original version of *The Wrong Man* was a meticulous 1957 Hitchcock *film noir* in which police mistake a New York City musician, played by Henry Fonda, for a dangerous thief. This remake, written by Michael Thoma and based on a story by Roy Carlson, keeps the basic premise of police pursuing an innocent man for a crime, but not much else.

Director Jim McBride deflates the tension by making the police languid and stupid, almost as if to justify Mills' racist epithets about Mexicans. As Mills, Lithgow is wonderfully despicable playing a misanthrope on the verge of a psychotic breakdown. He is a mean, pathetic pig stuck in the mud of his own miserable life, enraged that he can't find a way out. Lithgow's performance is the only thing to sustain the film.

Arquette, a talented actress who seems doomed to being cast as a bimbo, strains to create a deliciously wicked tease. For most of the film, she has the task of keeping Lithgow and Anderson on edge. But although her physical attributes are appropriate, she fails to ignite lethal flames. She plays Missy so bored that she ultimately becomes boring despite all her posing and stripping.

The performances of Arquette and Lithgow are fine as caricatures and would work if McBride stuck with a campy tone. But McBride spends too much time letting the luckless trio simmer in their own stale juices. And the central character, as played by Anderson, lacks any emotional appeal. Alex is almost a cipher, and Anderson portrays him as a wooden, stupefied dolt.

When McBride gets serious, he seems to be begging us to care about what happens to Alex and Missy. And beg he must, because these are characters who have been little more than cartoon figures for much of the film. It's easy to feel pity for Alex, who seems a rather luckless slob with enormously bad judgment, but it's ridiculous to suppose audiences will feel sympathy with a character who has no depth, motivation, purpose or redeeming qualities.

The film comes to a grinding and embarrassing halt when the trio ends up in a seedy, half-abandoned hotel on the Guatemalan border. They booze, Missy flirts and everyone betrays one another. What this long, pointless psychological drama is doing in the middle of what began as a tense crimer is anyone's guess. Not only that, but it takes no imagination to figure out the secret of who really is Felix's killer. By the time McBride gears up for what is supposed to be a boffo surprise ending, all the life has long since gone out of *The Wrong Man*.

—*Michael Betzold*

REVIEWS

Variety. CCCLI, May 24, 1993, p. 46.
The Wall Street Journal. August 30, 1993, p. A7.

Wyatt Earp

"The epic story of love and adventure in a lawless land."—Movie tagline

"A great, classic American performance. It ranks with John Wayne in *The Searchers* and Henry Fonda in *The Grapes of Wrath*."—Bob Campbell, *Newhouse Newspapers*

"*Wyatt Earp* sets the standard for modern westerns."—Bruce Forer

Box Office Gross: $25,032,746 (October 2, 1994)

Most Westerns of the 1930's, 1940's, and 1950's look rather mundane with the notable exception of those in which the filmmakers achieved the poetic by exploring the mythic side of the West, as with King Vidor's *Duel in the Sun* (1946), Howard Hawks' *Red River* (1948), and John Ford's *The Searchers* (1956). The fading form was revitalized in the 1960's by Sam Peckinpah's graphic realism and Sergio Leone's operatic splendors only to die in the 1970's of the cynicism inherent in the realism. In the 1990's, the genre was again revived, inspired by the commercial success of *Dances with Wolves* (1990)—Kevin Costner's New Age ode to political correctness—and *Unforgiven* (1992)—Clint Eastwood's psychological revenge tale. Reminiscent of the truly success-

CREDITS

Wyatt Earp: Kevin Costner
Doc Holliday: Dennis Quaid
Nicholas Earp: Gene Hackman
Virgil Earp: Michael Madsen

Morgan Earp: Linden Ashby
James Earp: David Andrews
Josie Marcus: Joanna Going
Johnny Behan: Mark Harmon
Big Nose Kate: Isabella Rossellini
Ed Masterson: Bill Pullman
Bat Masterson: Tom Sizemore
Bessie Earp: JoBeth Williams
Allie Earp: Catherine O'Hara
Lou Earp: Alison Elliott
Mattie Blaylock: Mare Winningham
Urilla Sutherland Earp: Annabeth Gish
Warren Earp: James Caviezel
Ike Clanton: Jeff Fahey
John Clum: Randle Mell
Curly Bill Brocius: Lewis Smith

Released: 1994
Production: Jim Wilson, Kevin Costner, and Lawrence Kasdan for Tig Productions and Kasdan Pictures; released by Warner Bros.
Direction: Lawrence Kasdan
Screenplay: Dan Gordon and Lawrence Kasdan
Cinematography: Owen Roizman
Editing: Carol Littleton
Production design: Ida Random
Art direction: Gary Wissner
Set design: Charles Daboub, Jr., Tom Reta and Barry Chusid
Set decoration: Cheryl Carasik
Casting: Jennifer Shull
Sound: John Pritchett
Costume design: Colleen Atwood
Music: James Newton Howard
MPAA rating: PG-13
Running time: 189 minutes

AWARDS AND NOMINATIONS

Academy Awards Nomination 1994: Best
Cinematography

ful epic Western *Little Big Man* (1970), director Lawrence Kasdan has attempted to create an epic vision of a psychologically complex historical figure in *Wyatt Earp*.

The screenplay by Dan Gordon and Kasdan attempts to cover most of the significant events in the first half of the long life of Wyatt Earp (Kevin Costner), who lived from 1848 to 1929. These events include his attempt, as an Iowa farm boy, the Iowa farm boy who attempts to run away to join the Union army during the War Between the States; young Wyatt's study of the law; his courtship of and marriage to Urilla Sutherland (Annabeth Gish) only to see her die of typhoid fever shortly thereafter; his self-pitying decline into drunkenness and crime until rescued by his stern father, Nicholas (Gene Hackman); his time as a buffalo hunter and friendship with Ed (Bill Pullman) and Bat Masterson (Tom Sizemore); and his days as a marshal in Dodge City, Kansas.

All this builds to Earp's period in Tombstone, Arizona, where he and brothers Virgil (Michael Madsen) and Morgan (Linden Ashby), with the aid of consumptive gambler/gunslinger Doc Holliday (Dennis Quaid), try to maintain the law despite the corruption of fellow lawman Johnny Behan (Mark Harmon) and the unruliness of a gang led by Ike Clanton (Jeff Fahey). After Morgan is murdered and Virgil severely-wounded, Wyatt slowly tracks down and kills his adversaries.

Kasdan takes as his model not another Western but David Lean's epic *Lawrence of Arabia* (1962). As in Lean's masterpiece, Kasdan combines sweeping vistas, leisurely pacing, and a protagonist who progresses from naïve innocence to uncontrolled violence. Like the T. E. Lawrence of Lean and Peter O'Toole, the Earp created by Gordon, Kasdan, and Costner is an intelligent, peaceful man who grows to love killing despite himself. Costner correctly eschews the folksiness of Henry Fonda's Earp in John Ford's *My Darling Clementine* (1946), easily the best film about this subject, and the righteousness of Burt Lancaster's characterization in John Sturges' *Gunfight at the O.K. Corral* (1957), but he fails, in part because of the general weakness of the screenplay, to replace these qualities with anything of much interest.

Costner is a good actor in certain roles, as with the swashbuckling baseball player of *Bull Durham* (1988), but too often he is as stolid and humorless as Gregory Peck and Charlton Heston at their most wooden. His Earp is supposed to be a compelling portrait of ambiguous motivations, but the marshal is primarily a dyspeptic bully. Costner's

Earp is a selfish, weak, impulsive man. He allows the drug-addicted prostitute Mattie Blaylock (Mare Winningham) to attach herself to him only to discard her casually and cruelly when he falls for the vibrant actress Josie Marcus (Joanna Going). Costner did a much better job of depicting a man torn between the good and bad sides of his nature with his self-righteous Jim Garrison in *JFK* (1991).

As for the other performers, Gene Hackman dominates, with old-fashioned film-star presence, his too few scenes as the patriarch who rules the Earps with Old Testament authority. Dennis Quaid, having lost forty-three pounds to suggest the effects of tuberculosis, is physically impressive as Doc Holliday. Unfortunately, he merely adds a phlegmy growl to his usual smirk and swagger. Both Hackman and Quaid suffer from underwritten parts, as do such talented actors as David Andrews as James, the weak Earp brother, and Michael Madsen as Virgil. The women's parts are apparently underdeveloped because of the characters' primary functions as appendages to their men. Nevertheless, Catherine O'Hara stands out as the angriest of the Earp wives and lovers, fighting to preserve the family despite her brother-in-law's excesses. The only bad performance is given by Mare Winningham as Earp's laudanum-soaked, self-pitying common-law wife, whose self-indulgent overacting becomes tedious.

A major drawback in *Wyatt Earp* is that while its 189 minutes are crammed with incident, not much happens. Earp arrives in a town, becomes angry at its disorder, and kills people, creating more disorder. The repetition of this pattern makes the film monotonous. For a film of this length, characters and situations are surprisingly underdeveloped. Earp and Holliday, seemingly opposites, meet in one scene and arc bosom pals in the next for no apparent reason. The screenplay fails to explore the contradiction at its center: The Earp brothers stay together because, as their father has taught them, blood is the only meaningful connection among people in this violent universe, yet their closeness creates endless turmoil in their private lives and, finally, death, with Morgan a martyr to his older brother's stubbornness.

Kasdan is a talented director with no distinctive style or vision. His early films, the thoroughly entertaining *film noir, Body Heat* (1981) and *The Big Chill* (1983), a popular treatment of baby-boomer self-absorption, are slick, but beginning with the surprisingly conventional Western *Silverado* (1985), Kasdan's efforts had become increasingly awkward, with the unwatchable black comedy *I Love You to Death* (1990) and the smug, pompous *Grand Canyon* (1991). His *Wyatt Earp* seems made by someone considerably less experienced: Many scenes are poorly paced, go on too long, or seem pointless. The film cries out for additional editing, not to shorten it, but to release it from its inertia. The prevailing tone is too bleak to create concern for the characters, and Kasdan provides few clues about how he expects the audience to respond to certain episodes, as with a depressingly graphic buffalo hunt.

While Kasdan and such contemporaries as Brian De Palma and Steven Spielberg deeply love the films of Hollywood's Golden Age, they do not seem to have learned much from these models about coherent storytelling. Instead of clearly establishing the Clanton gang as antagonists for the Earp brothers and Holliday, Kasdan makes all but two of them, an Indian and an outlaw who stands out for being short and clean-shaven, indistinguishable from one another. As Earp carries out his revenge, it is almost impossible to determine who is being killed. Their anonymity negates the cathartic intentions of the film's final half hour. An ironic coda suggesting that the myths of the old West are more vital than their reality is, however, fairly effective.

Seven months before the release of *Wyatt Earp*, George P. Cosmatos' comparably modest version of the Earp-Holliday saga, *Tombstone* (1993), appeared and was a surprise box-office success. Many reviews of Kasdan's film compared it unfavorably to the crude B-movie gusto of *Tombstone*. At least Cosmatos' version is memorable for

the composition of shots of men on horseback, William A. Fraker's cinematography—especially the ghostly images during a lightning storm—and Val Kilmer's flamboyant portrayal of Holliday. Style that succeeds most of the time is better than sluggish pretensions.

—*Michael Adams*

REVIEWS

Atlanta Constitution. June 24, 1994, p. P3.
The Christian Science Monitor. June 24, 1994, p. 12.
Entertainment Weekly. July 8, 1994, p. 34.
The Hollywood Reporter. June 20, 1994, p. 10.
Los Angeles Times. June 24, 1994, p. F1.
Maclean's. July 1, 1994, p. 61.
The New York Times. June 24, 1994, p. B1.
Newsweek. CXXIV, July 4, 1994, p. 71.
People Weekly. XLII, July 4, 1994, p. 13.
Time. CXLIV, July 4, 1994, p. 73.
USA Today. June 24, 1994, p. D1.
Variety. CCCLV, June 20, 1994, p. 4.

You So Crazy

"Uncut. Unrated. Unbelievably funny"—Movie tagline

"a film for people who think Beavis and Butthead are genteel wimps."—Caryn James, *The New York Times*

 Box Office Gross: $10,144,569 (July 24, 1994)

Martin Lawrence's bawdy humor is showcased in this one-man stand-up comedy show.

REVIEWS

Atlanta Constitution. April 27, 1994, p. C11.
Chicago Tribune. April 27, 1994, Sec. 5 p. 7.
Entertainment Weekly. April 29, 1994, p. 56.
Los Angeles Times. April 27, 1994, p. F1.
The New York Times. April 27, 1994, p. C18.
Newsweek. CXXIII, May 9, 1994, p. 69.
People Weekly. XLI, February 14, 1994, p. 15.
Rolling Stone. March 10, 1994, p. 60.
USA Today. April 27, 1994, p. D7.
Variety. CCCLIV, February 14, 1994, p. 38.
The Washington Post. April 27, 1994, p. B1.

CREDITS

Martin Lawrence: Martin Lawrence

Released: 1994
Production: Timothy Marx and David Knoller for HBO Independent Productions, in association with You So Crazy Productions; released by the Samuel Goldwyn Company
Direction: Thomas Schlamme
Cinematography: Arthur Albert
Editing: John Neal and Stephen Semel
Production design: Richard Hoover
Art direction: John Gisondi
Lighting design: Allen Branton
MPAA rating: no listing
Running time: 89 minutes

 *You So Crazy* was given an X-rating and was dropped by its previous distributor Miramax, but Samuel Goldwyn released it with an NC-17 rating.

Zero Patience

"Audacious. Stimulating. A ribald musical comedy. A bouncy stylistic hybrid crammed with ideas."—Stephen Holden, *The New York Times*

This absurdist musical centers on the subject of AIDS. A modern-day Sir Richard Burton (John Robinson) blames Patient Zero (Normand Fauteux), an airline attendant who was supposedly responsible for the introduction of the disease to North America, only to encounter Zero's ghost, who tells a different story.

REVIEWS

The Advocate. March 22, 1994, p. 72.
Atlanta Constitution. August 19, 1994, p. P7.
Boston Globe. June 17, 1994, p. 77.
Chicago Tribune. June 10, 1994, Sec. 5 p. 5.
Christian Science Monitor. June 17, 1994, p. 12.
Los Angeles Times. May 13, 1994, p. F14.
The New York Times. March 26, 1994, p. A14.
The Washington Post. June 10, 1994, p. D6.

CREDITS

Sir Richard Burton: John Robinson
Zero: Normand Fauteux
Mary: Dianne Heatherington
George: Richardo Keens-Douglas
Dr. Placebo: Bernard Behrens
African Green Monkey: Maria Lukofsky
Miss HIV: Michael Callen
Maman: Charlotte Boisjoli
Dr. Cheng: Brenda Kamino

Origin: Canada
Released: 1993
Production: Louise Garfield and Anna Stratton for Zero Patience Productions; released by Cinevista
Direction: John Greyson
Screenplay: John Greyson
Cinematography: Miroslaw Baszak
Editing: Miume Jan
Production design: Sandra Kybartas
Set decoration: Armando Sgignuoli
Casting: Dorothy Gardner
Costume design: Joyce Schure
Choreography: Susan McKenzie
Music: Glenn Schellenberg
MPAA rating: no listing
Running time: 100 minutes

Zombie and the Ghost Train

The bleak life of a perennially unemployed alcoholic named Zombie (Silu Seppala) is the focus of this Finnish drama.

REVIEWS

The New York Times. August 7, 1994, Sec. 2 p. 19.
The New York Times. January 27, 1995, p. D17.
The Washington Post. May 12, 1995, p. B7.

CREDITS

Zombie: Silu Seppala
Marjo: Marjo Leinonen
Harri: Matti Pellonpaa
Mother: Vieno Saaristo
Father: Juhani Niemela

Origin: Finland
Released: 1991
Production: Mika Kaurismaki for Villealfa Film productions Oy
Direction: Mika Kaurismaki
Screenplay: Pauli Pentti and Sakke Jarvenpaa; based on a story by Mika Kaurismaki
Cinematography: Olli Varja
Editing: Mika Kaurismaki
Music: Mauri Sumen
MPAA rating: no listing
Running time: 88 minutes

List of Awards

Academy Awards

Best Picture: *Forrest Gump*

Direction: Robert Zemeckis (*Forrest Gump*)

Actor: Tom Hanks (*Forrest Gump*)

Actress: Jessica Lange (*Blue Sky*)

Supporting Actor: Martin Landau (*Ed Wood*)

Supporting Actress: Dianne Wiest (*Bullets Over Broadway*)

Original Screenplay: Quentin Tarantino and Roger Avary (*Pulp Fiction*)

Adapted Screenplay: Eric Roth (*Forrest Gump*)

Cinematography: John Toll (*Legends of the Fall*)

Editing: Arthur Schmidt (*Forrest Gump*)

Art Direction: Ken Adam, Allen Hall, George Murphy, and Stephen Rosenbaum (*The Madness of King George*)

Visual Effects: Ken Ralston (*Forrest Gump*)

Sound Effects Editing: Stephen Hunter Flick (*Speed*)

Sound: David R.B. MacMillan (*Speed*)

Makeup: Rick Baker, Ve Neill, and Yolanda Toussieng (*Ed Wood*)

Costume Design: Lizzy Gardiner and Tim Chappel (*The Adventures of Priscilla, Queen of the Desert*)

Original Score: Hans Zimmer (*The Lion King*)

Original Song: "Can You Feel the Love Tonight?" (*The Lion King*: music by Elton John, lyrics by Tim Rice)

Foreign-Language Film: *Burnt By the Sun* (Russia)

Short Film, Animated: *Bob's Birthday* (Alison Snowden and David Fine)

Short Film, Live Action: *Franz Kafka's It's a Wonderful Life* (Peter Capaldi and Ruth Kenley-Letts) and *Trevor* (Peggy Rajski and Randy Stone), tie

Documentary, Feature: *Maya Lin: A Strong Clear Vision* (Freida Lee Mock and Terry Sanders)

Documentary, Short Subject: *A Time For Justice* (Charles Guggenheim)

Honorary Oscar: Michelangelo Antonioni

Jean Hersholt Humanitarian Award: Quincy Jones

Directors Guild of America Award

Director: Robert Zemeckis (*Forrest Gump*)

Writers Guild Awards

Original Screenplay: Richard Curtis (*Four Weddings and a Funeral*)

Adapted Screenplay: Eric Roth (*Forrest Gump*)

New York Film Critics Awards

Best Picture: *Quiz Show* (Robert Redford)

Direction: Quentin Tarantino (*Pulp Fiction*)

Actor: Paul Newman (*Nobody's Fool*)

Actress: Linda Fiorentino (*The Last Seduction*)

Supporting Actor: Martin Landau (*Ed Wood*)

Supporting Actress: Dianne Wiest (*Bullets Over Broadway*)

Screenplay: Quentin Tarantino and Roger Avary (*Pulp Fiction*)

Cinematography: Stefan Czapsky (*Ed Wood*)

Foreign-Language Film: *Red* (France)

Los Angeles Film Critics Awards

Best Picture: *Pulp Fiction*

Direction: Quentin Tarantino (*Pulp Fiction*)

Actor: John Travolta (*Pulp Fiction*)

Actress: Jessica Lange (*Blue Sky*)

Supporting Actor: Martin Landau (*Ed Wood*)

Supporting Actress: Dianne Wiest (*Bullets Over Broadway*)

Screenplay: Quentin Tarantino and Roger Avary (*Pulp Fiction*)

Cinematography: Stefan Czapsky (*Ed Wood*)

Original Score: Howard Shore (*Ed Wood*)

Foreign Film: *Red* (France)

Outstanding Documentary: *Hoop Dreams* (Steve James, Frederick Marx, and Peter Gilbert)

National Society of Film Critics Awards

Best Picture: *Pulp Fiction*

Direction: Quentin Tarantino (*Pulp Fiction*)

Actor: Paul Newman (*Nobody's Fool*)

Actress: Jennifer Jason Leigh (*Mrs. Parker and the Vicious Circle*)

Supporting Actor: Martin Landau (*Ed Wood*)

Supporting Actress: Dianne Wiest (*Bullets Over Broadway*)

Screenplay: Quentin Tarantino and Roger Avary (*Pulp Fiction*)

Cinematography: Stefan Czapsky (*Ed Wood*)

Documentary: *Hoop Dreams* (Steve James, Frederick Marx, and Peter Gilbert)

Foreign-Language Film: *Red* (France)

Experimental Citation: *Satantango* and *The Pharaoh's Belt*, tie

National Board of Review Awards

Best English-Language Film: *Forrest Gump* and *Pulp Fiction*, tie

Direction: Quentin Tarantino (*Pulp Fiction*)

Actor: Tom Hanks (*Forrest Gump*)

Actress: Miranda Richardson (*Tom & Viv*)

Supporting Actor: Gary Sinise (*Forrest Gump*)

Supporting Actress: Rosemary Harris (*Tom & Viv*)

Foreign-Language Film: *Eat Drink Man Woman* (Taiwan)

Documentary: *Hoop Dreams* (Steve James, Frederick Marx, and Peter Gilbert)

The D.W. Griffith Career Achievement Award: Sidney Poitier

Golden Globe Awards

Best Picture, Drama: *Forrest Gump*

Best Picture, Comedy or Musical: *The Lion King*

Direction: Robert Zemeckis (*Forrest Gump*)

Actor, Drama: Tom Hanks (*Forrest Gump*)

Actress, Drama: Jessica Lange (*Blue Sky*)

Actor, Comedy or Musical: Hugh Grant (*Four Weddings and a Funeral*)

Actress, Comedy or Musical: Jamie Lee Curtis (*True Lies*)

Supporting Actor: Martin Landau (*Ed Wood*)

Supporting Actress: Dianne Wiest (*Bullets Over Broadway*)

Screenplay: Quentin Tarantino and Roger Avary (*Pulp Fiction*)

Original Score: Hans Zimmer (*The Lion King*)

Original Song: "Can You Feel the Love Tonight?" (*The Lion King*: music by Elton John, lyrics by Tim Rice)

Foreign-Language Film: *Farinelli* (Italy)

Cannes International Film Festival Awards

Palme d'Or: *Pulp Fiction* (Quentin Tarantino)

Grand Jury Prize: *Burnt By the Sun* (Nikita Mikhalkov) and *To Live* (Zhang Yimou), tie

Actor: Ge You (*To Live*)

Actress: Verna Lisi (*Queen Margot*)

Direction: Nanni Moretti (*Caro Diario*)

Jury Prize: *Queen Margot* (Patrice Chereau)

Grand Technical Prize: Pitof (*Dead Tired*)

Camera d'Or: *Coming to Terms With the Dead*

Palme d'Or, Short Film: *El Heroe*

British Academy Awards

Best Picture: *Four Weddings and a Funeral*

Direction: Mike Newell (*Four Weddings and a Funeral*)

Actor: Hugh Grant (*Four Weddings and a Funeral*)

Actress: Susan Sarandon (*The Client*)

Supporting Actor: Samuel L. Jackson *Pulp Fiction*

Supporting Actress: Kristen Scott Thomas (*Four Weddings and a Funeral*)

Original Screenplay: Quentin Tarantino and Roger Avary (*Pulp Fiction*)

Adapted Screenplay: Paul Attanasio (*Quiz Show*)

Original Score: Don Was (*Backbeat*)

Best Foreign-Language Film: *To Live* (Zhang Yimou)

Short Film, Live Action: *Zinky Boys Go Underground* (Paul Tickell)

Short Film, Animated: *The Big Story* (Tim Watts and David Stoten)

Alexander Korda Award for Best British Film: *Shallow Grave* (Danny Boyle)

Michael Balcon Award for Outstanding Contribution to Cinema: Ridley Scott and Tony Scott

Life Achievement Award

Jack Nicholson

The American Film Institute's 1994 Life Achievement Award was bestowed upon an award-winning actor known as much for his rebellious charisma and star bankability as for having paid his dues. John Joseph "Jack" Nicholson was born in New York City on April 22, 1937 and grew up in Neptune, New Jersey, without knowing the facts of his parentage. He was raised by his grandparents, Ethel May and John Joseph Nicholson, under the belief that June Nicholson (actually his mother) was his elder sister; the identity of his father is a mystery. He attended Roosevelt Grammar School and Manasquan High School, graduating in 1954. He passed up a chance to attend the University of Delaware, choosing instead to go to California.

When Jack arrived in California he lived for a while with June, who had married, divorced and moved to Inglewood, about ten miles from Hollywood. He eventually found work as an office boy in the animation department of MGM Studios in Culver City, where he was befriended by famous animators Bill Hanna and Joe Barbera.

During the 1950's Nicholson affected a bohemian lifestyle and was known to hang out with "Beat Generation" types. His friends helped place him as an apprentice at the Player's Ring Theatre, where he met Roger Corman, who specialized in low-budget pictures and gave Nicholson his first starring role in *The Cry Baby Killers* (1957). He again worked for Corman two years later in *The Little Shop of Horrors* (1960), playing a masochistic dental patient. He acted in three other Corman features and made connections with other low-budget directors. Richard Rush used him in *Too Soon to Love* (1960), *Hell's Angels on Wheels* (1967), and *Psych-Out* (1968). Monte Hellman gave him work in *Back Door to Hell* (1964) and in three pictures in 1966, *Flight to Fury* and the two existentialist Westerns, *The Shooting* and *Ride in the Whirlwind*.

After fifteen years on the Hollywood fringe, finding bit roles in low-budget pictures and TV soap operas, and working as a "jack-of-all-trades," Nicholson was ready to give up acting and concentrate on writing and directing, having not yet been "discovered" as an actor. However, in 1969 his luck changed when producer Bert Schneider offered him a supporting role in a biker movie—a role turned down by Rip Torn. Nicholson had worked previously with Schneider and director Bob Rafelson, who had taken a chance on the movie

by agreeing to let Dennis Hopper direct it. Not only, to everyone's surprise, did the movie become immensely popular, it became a symbol of the counterculture generation of the sixties.

That film, *Easy Rider*, was named Best Film at the Cannes Film Festival in 1969 and struck a responsive chord with what Stanley Kauffmann later called the "Film Generation" of young Americans who were fed up with the "Establishment" values reflected by most Hollywood pictures and ready to embrace movie images of the counterculture.

Nicholson was nominated for an Academy Award for his performance in *Easy Rider*, in which he played an alcoholic attorney attempting to drop out of the mainstream and turn on to the counterculture. Although the Oscar went to Gig Young for *They Shoot Horses, Don't They?*, Jack

Nicholson had finally arrived, not only as an actor, but as a player.

The following year, Nicholson's portayal of the existentially troubled classical pianist-turned-drifter, Bobby Dupea, in Rafelson's *Five Easy Pieces* established Nicholson as a star talent. This film is famous for its classic restaurant scene in which the rebellious Bobby rudely orders toast via a chicken salad sandwich from a snide, procedure-bound, unimaginative waitress.

Since his breakthrough with *Easy Rider*, Nicholson's development as an actor can be charted through a series of dramatic, as well as manic, almost comical roles: Bobby Dupea in *Five Easy Pieces* (1970), Jonathan, in *Carnal Knowledge* (1971), David Staebler in *The King of Marvin Gardens* (1972), Billy Buddusky in *The Last Detail* (1973), Jake Gittes in *Chinatown* (1974), Randal Patrick McMurphy in *One Flew Over the Cuckoo's Nest* (1975), Jack Torrence in *The Shining* (1980), Frank Chambers in *The Postman Always Rings Twice* (1981), Garrett Breedlove in *Terms of Endearment* (1983), Charley Partanna in *Prizzi's Honor* (1985), Francis Phelan in *Ironweed* (1987), the Joker in *Batman* (1989), and Colonel Nathan R. Jessep in *A Few Good Men* (1992).

These are some of Nicholson's most colorful roles, developed in collaboration with some of the world's finest directors: Bob Rafelson, Mike Nichols, Hal Ashby, Roman Polanski, Milos Forman, Stanley Kubrick, John Huston, James L. Brooks, Tim Burton, Hector Babenco, and Rob Reiner.

Nicholson also worked with such talents as Michelangelo Antonioni (*The Passenger*, 1975), Tony Richardson (*The Border*, 1981), and George Miller (*The Witches of Eastwick*, 1987) and with other well-regarded American directors such as Arthur Penn (*The Missouri Breaks*, 1976), and Elia Kazan (*The Last Tycoon*, 1976).

During his forty-year career, Jack Nicholson won a New York Film Critics Award for Best Supporting Actor in *Easy Rider*; British Academy, Cannes Film Festival, National Society of Film Critics, and New York Film Critics Awards for Best Actor in *The Last Detail*; British Academy, Golden Globe, and New York Film Critics Awards for Best Actor in *Chinatown*; Academy, British Academy, Golden Globe, National Board of Review, National Society of Film Critics, and New York Film Critics Awards for Best Actor in *One Flew Over the Cuckoo's Nest*; Academy and Golden Globe Awards for Best Supporting Actor in *Terms of Endearment*; a Golden Globe Award for Best Actor in *Prizzi's Honor*; Los Angeles Film Critics Association and New York Film Critics Awards for Best Actor in *The Witches of Eastwick*; and the Chicago Film Critics Award for Best Supporting Actor in *A Few Good Men*. He's also received dozens of nominations over the years.

Nicholson also picked up credits as co-producer with Monte Hellman and Bob Rafelson, as well as writer on several minor films such as *Thunder Island* (1963), *Flight to Fury* (1966), *Ride in the Whirlwind* (1966), *The Trip* (1967), *Head* (1968), and *Drive, He Said* (1970), which he also directed. Later Nicholson directed the Western romantic comedy *Goin' South* (1978) and *The Two Jakes* (1990), writer Robert Towne's sequel to *Chinatown*. These pictures represent respectable achievements, but pale in comparison to what Nicholson has achieved as an actor.

Nicholson's personal life and off-screen antics—his reputation as a partier and a carouser; his long relationship with actress Angelica Huston, daughter of film legend John Huston; his bachelor lifestyle (he was married from 1961-1966 to Sandra Knight, and has two daughters, one from this marriage, another out of wedlock with actress Rebecca Broussard); and his frequent attendance at NBA games (he's a die-hard Lakers fan)—all contribute to Jack's nonconformist intrigue.

Jack Torrence's mad mantra in *The Shining* was "All work and no play makes Jack a dull boy." And whatever one may say about the colorful joker who played him, Jack Nicholson has never been dull. No actor of his generation has a stronger presence in front of the camera than Nicholson, and his exuberance dominates nearly all of the films he has performed in. The Institute—and the industry—should honor his achievements, with gratitude.

—James M. Welsh

Obituaries

Claude Akins (May 25, 1918–January 27, 1994). Akins was an actor best known for his character roles. In films, he specialized in Westerns, usually playing the heavy. Late in his career, he starred in lighter roles in two popular television series. His film credits include *From Here to Eternity* (1953), *The Caine Mutiny* (1954), *Johnny Concho* (1956), *Rio Bravo* (1959), *How the West Was Won* (1962), *The Killers* (1966), *Battle For the Planet of the Apes* (1973), and *Falling From Grace* (1992).

Claude Akins

Lindsay Anderson (April 17, 1923–August 30, 1994). Anderson was a British director who began his career in the documentary field and eventually went on to make feature films. He was a major figure in England's Free Cinema movement in the 1950's; his documentary *Thursday's Children* (1954; co-directed with Guy Brenton) won an Academy Award as Best Short Subject. His first feature film was *This Sporting Life* (1963), a gritty examination of the life of a rugby player that made a star of lead Richard Harris. Malcolm McDowell's career was similarly launched by Anderson's *If...* (1968), a scathing critique of England's private school system. Anderson and McDowell paired up again in *O Lucky Man!* (1973), a musical satire that was a critical success but a commercial failure. Anderson spent much of the 1970's and 1980's working in theater and television; his most successful film of the period was *The Whales of August* (1987), starring Bette Davis and Lillian Gish. Anderson acted occasionally, appearing in his own *O Lucky Man!* (1973) as well as in *Inadmissable Evidence* (1968) and *Chariots of Fire* (1981). His additional directing credits include *Meeting the Pioneers* (1948), *O Dreamland* (1953), *Green and Pleasant Land* (1955), *Every Day Except Christmas* (1957), *The White Bus* (1967), *The Singing Lesson* (1967), *In Celebration* (1975), and *Britannia Hospital* (1982).

Noah Beery, Jr. (August 10, 1913–November 1, 1994). Beery was an actor who made his film debut at the age of seven in *The Mark of Zorro* (1920). He appeared primarily in supporting roles throughout his long career, specializing in Westerns featuring stars such as Tom Mix and Johnny Mack Brown. He is best known to modern audiences for his role as James Garner's father in the television series

Noah Beery, Jr.

The Rockford Files. He was the son of actor Noah Beery, and the nephew of actor Wallace Beery. His screen credits include *Penrod* (1922), *Rustler's Roundup* (1933), *Sergeant York* (1941), *Red River* (1948), *The Texas Rangers* (1951), *The Spirit of St. Louis* (1957), *Inherit the Wind* (1960), *Little Fauss and Big Halsy* (1970), *Walking Tall* (1973), and *The Best Little Whorehouse in Texas* (1982).

Robert Bloch (April 5, 1917–September 23, 1994). Bloch was a novelist and screenwriter best known for *Psycho* (1960), the Alfred Hitchcock film which was adapted from his 1959 novel. The success of Hitchcock's film led Bloch into screenwriting, where he specialized in the horror genre. His film credits include *The Couch* (1962), *The Cabinet of Dr. Caligari* (1962), *The Night Walker* (1965), *The Torture Garden* (1968), *The House That Dripped Blood* (1971), and *Asylum* (1972).

Sergei Bondarchuk (September 25, 1920–October 20, 1994). Bondarchuk was a Ukranian who first became an actor and later one of the most respected directors in the Soviet Union during the 1960's and 1970's. Unlike most Soviet films of that era, which were primarily vehicles for propaganda, Bondarchuk's work was known for its realism. His epic version of *War and Peace* (1968), in which he also starred, won the Academy Award for Best Foreign Language Film. As an actor, Bondarchuk appeared in *Taras Schevchenko*

(1951), *Admiral Ushakov* (1953), and *The Grasshopper* (1955). His directing credits include *Destiny of a Man* (1959), *Waterloo* (1970), *They Fought for Their Country* (1975), *The Steppe* (1978), and *Boris Godunov* (1986).

Sorrell Booke (1926–February 11, 1994). Booke was an actor who specialized in character roles. He also worked in television, where he is best remembered as Boss Hogg in *The Dukes of Hazzard*. Booke's film credits include *Gone Are the Days* (1963), *Black Like Me* (1964), *Fail-Safe* (1964), *Up the Down Staircase* (1967), *Bye Bye Braverman* (1968), *What's Up Doc?* (1972), *The Iceman Cometh* (1973), and *The Other Side of Midnight* (1977).

Rossano Brazzi (September 18, 1916–December 24, 1994). Brazzi was an Italian actor who played romantic leads in his native country for a decade before moving to Hollywood in 1949. His performance in *The Barefoot Contessa* (1954), opposite Ava Gardner and Humphrey Bogart, brought him stardom in the United States, where he specialized in playing suave Europeans. His best remembered role is probably that of Emile de Becque in *South Pacific* (1958). Brazzi's additional film credits include *Ritorno* (1939), *The King's Jester* (1941), *The Great Dawn* (1946), *Little Women* (1949), *Three Coins in the Fountain* (1953), *Summertime* (1955), *The Story of Esther Costello* (1957), *Count Your Blessings* (1959), *Light in the Piazza* (1962), *Dark Purpose* (1964), *The Bobo* (1967), *Krakatoa East of Java* (1969), *The Italian Job* (1969), *The Great Waltz* (1972), *The Final Conflict* (1981), and *Michelangelo and Me* (1989).

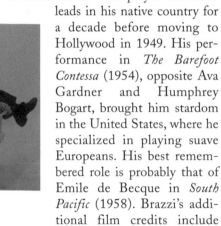

Rossano Brazzi

Pat Buttram

Pat Buttram (1915–January 8, 1994). Buttram was a comic actor best known for his long-standing role as Gene Autry's sidekick in seventeen B Westerns made between 1948 and 1952, and also in Autry's radio and television series. In the 1960's, Buttram played Mr. Haney in the popular television series *Green Acres*. His film credits include *The Strawberry Roan* (1948),

Riders in the Sky (1949), *Mule Train* (1950), *Texans Never Cry* (1951), *Hills of Utah* (1951), *The Old West* (1952), and *Blue Canadian Rockies* (1952).

Cab Calloway (1907–November 18, 1994). Calloway was a bandleader and singer who was known as the "Hi De Ho Man," from a line in his signature song, "Minnie the Moocher." Though predominantly a musician, Calloway appeared in several films, including *The Big Broadcast* (1932), *The Singing Kid* (1936), *Stormy Weather* (1943), and *The Blues Brothers* (1980).

Cab Calloway

John Candy (October 31, 1950–March 4, 1994). Born in Canada, Candy was a heavyset actor known for his comic roles. Candy acted in several minor films in the early 1970's, but first attained prominence in the 1980's as a member of television's satiric SCTV ensemble. He appeared in over twenty films thereafter, most notably in *Splash* (1984) and *Uncle Buck* (1989). He was often featured with alumni of SCTV and/or Saturday Night Live. Candy died of a heart attack while filming *Wagons East!* (reviewed in this volume) in Mexico. His additional screen credits include *Face-Off* (1971), *Class of '44* (1973), *The Blues Brothers* (1980), *Stripes* (1981), *National Lampoon's Vacation* (1983), *Volunteers* (1985), *Planes, Trains and Automobiles* (1987), *Who's Harry Crumb?* (1989), *Home Alone* (1990), *JFK* (1991), and *Cool Runnings* (1993).

John Candy

MacDonald Carey (March 15, 1913–March 21, 1994). Carey was an actor who appeared in over fifty films, in both leads and supporting roles. His most notable film role was probably in Alfred Hitchcock's *Shadow of a Doubt* (1943), but he will be best remembered as Dr. Horton, in the long running television soap opera *The Days of Our Lives*. Carey's additional film credits include *Take a Letter Darling* (1942), *Suddenly It's Spring* (1947), *The Great Gatsby* (1949), *Let's Make It Legal* (1951), *Stranger at My Door* (1956), *Blue Denim* (1959), *Tammy and the Doctor* (1963), and *American Gigolo* (1980).

Timothy Carey (1925–May 11, 1994). Carey was an actor who specialized in character roles, often as the bad guy. His resume included both critically acclaimed films such as *The Killing* (1956), *Paths of Glory* (1957), and *One-Eyed Jacks* (1961), as well as exploitation films such as *Bikini Beach* (1964). His additional film credits include *White Witch Doctor* (1953), *East of Eden* (1955), *Waterhole 3* (1967), *Head* (1968), *Minnie and Moskowitz* (1971), and *The Killing of a Chinese Bookie* (1976).

Christian-Jaque (September 4, 1904–July 8, 1994). Born Christian Maudet, Christian-Jaque was a director who was one of France's most popular filmmakers of the 1930's and, following World War II, of the 1950's as well. He worked in a wide variety of genres and had critical as well as popular success. He was named best director at the Cannes Film Festival for *Fanfan la Tulipe* (1952). His additional film credits include *Le Bidon d'Or* (1932), *Francois Ier* (1947), *Les Disparus de Saint-Agil* (1938), *Barbe-Bleue* (1951), *Madame du Barry* (1954), *La Loi c'est la Loi* (1958), *Babette Goes to War* (1959), and *La Tulipe Noir* (1964).

James Clavell (October 10, 1924–September 7, 1994). Born in Australia, Clavell was a director, producer, screenwriter, and novelist who moved to the United States in 1953. He worked on the screenplays of *The Fly* (1958), *Watusi* (1959), and *The Great Escape* (1963). He wrote, produced, and directed a handful of films, the most successful of which was *To Sir With Love* (1967). He was also a best selling novelist, writing books such as *Tai Pan* and *Shogun*. Clavell's additional screen credits, as writer, producer, and director, include *Five Gates to Hell* (1959), *Walk Like a Dragon* (1960), *The Sweet and the Bitter* (1962), and *The Last Valley* (1971). He also directed *Where's Jack?* (1968).

William Conrad (September 27, 1920–February 11, 1994). Conrad was a heavyset actor best known for his deep, mellifluous voice as the star of the television series *Cannon* and *Jake and the Fatman*, as well as the narrator of *The Rocky and Bullwinkle Show* in the 1960's. He was the radio voice of Marshall Dillon on *Gunsmoke* for eleven years, but his girth prevented him from being cast in the role for television. In films, he specialized in character roles, playing detectives and villains with equal facility. In the 1960's, he also produced and/or directed several films, including *The Man From Galveston* (1964), *My Blood Runs Cold* (1965), *An American Dream* (1966), *The Cool Ones* (1967), and *Assignment to Kill* (1969). His film acting credits include *The Killers* (1946), *Body and Soul* (1947), *Sorry Wrong Number* (1948), *The Naked Jungle* (1954), *Five Against the House* (1955), and *Johnny Concho* (1956).

Joseph Cotten (May 15, 1905–February 6, 1994). Cotten was an actor best known for his work with Orson Welles, including *Citizen Kane* (1941), *The Magnificent Ambersons* (1942), and *The Third Man* (1949). Cotten began acting on Broadway, working in several of Welles' Mercury Theater productions. When Welles began making films, he cast Cotten in important support-

Joseph Cotten

ing roles. He was signed by David O. Selznick, who loaned him to Alfred Hitchcock for *Shadow of a Doubt* (1943), and appeared memorably in *Gaslight* (1944), *Duel in the Sun* (1946), and *Portrait of Jennie* (1948). For some reason, however, Cotten established a reputation as an actor who was only as good as his material. He never transcended mediocre scripts but became a star, and by the 1950's, his forgettable roles began to outnumber his memorable ones. He continued making films into the 1980's, and also made numerous television appearances. His additional screen credits include *Lydia* (1941), *Journey Into Fear* (1942, which he also co-wrote), *Since You Went Away* (1944), *The Farmer's Daughter* (1947), *Othello* (1952), *Niagra* (1953), *Hush Hush...Sweet Charlotte* (1965), *The Oscar* (1966), *Petulia* (1968), *The Abominable Dr. Phibes* (1971), *F for Fake* (1974), *Airport '77* (1977), and *Heaven's Gate* (1981).

Nick Cravat (1911–January 29, 1994). Cravat was a diminutive actor best known for his work with Burt Lancaster. He and Lancaster worked as acrobats in vaudeville and circuses and later teamed up in two films which featured acrobatic stunts, *The Flame and the Arrow* (1950) and *The Crimson Pirate* (1952). Cravat's additional film credits include *My Friend Irma* (1949), *Veils of Bagdad* (1953), *Davy Crockett: King of the Wild Frontier* (1955), *Run Silent Run Deep* (1958), *The Way West* (1967), *Ulzana's Raid* (1972), and *The Island of Dr. Moreau* (1977).

Peter Cushing (May 26, 1913–August 11, 1994). Cushing was a British actor who starred in numerous horror films for Hammer Films from the late 1950's through the 1970's. He had appeared in several films before his performance as Baron Frankenstein in *The Curse of Frankenstein* (1957) made him famous. Cushing had a gaunt face and sharp features, and was often cast as a mad scientist. He complained about typecasting but was unable to establish a significant identity apart from his roles in horror films. He was often featured with fellow Hammer star Christopher Lee. His

Peter Cushing

film credits include *Hamlet* (1948), *Moulin Rouge* (1953), *Horror of Dracula* (1958), *The Revenge of Frankenstein* (1958), *The Hound of the Baskervilles* (1959), *The Brides of Dracula* (1960), *Frankenstein Created Woman* (1967), *The House That Dripped Blood* (1971), *The Beast Must Die* (1974), and *Star Wars* (1977).

Virginia Dale (1919–October 3, 1994). Dale was an actress who played second leads for several studios in the 1940's. Her best work was done at Paramount, where she was featured opposite Fred Astaire in *Holiday Inn* (1942). Her additional film credits include *Start Cheering* (1938), *Buck Benny Rides Again* (1940), *The Quarterback* (1940), *Kiss the Boys Goodbye* (1941), *Dragnet* (1947), and *Danger Zone* (1951).

Lili Damita (July 19, 1901–March 21, 1994). Born Liliane-Marie-Madeleine Carre, Damita was a French actress who was featured in numerous European films before moving to Hollywood in the late 1920's. She retired from films when she married Errol Flynn in 1935; the pair were divorced in 1942. Damita's film credits include *Fille sauvage* (1922), *Das Spielzeug von Paris* (1925), *Der Goldene Schmetterling* (1926), *The Bridge of San Luis Rey* (1929), *The Woman Between* (1931), *Brewster's Millions* (1935), and *The Devil on Horseback* (1936).

Royal Dano (November 16, 1922–May 15, 1994). Dano was a character actor who appeared in over forty films between 1950 and 1990, most often in "bad guy" roles. His film credits include *Undercover Girl* (1950), *The Red Badge of Courage* (1952), *Johnny Guitar* (1954), *Moby Dick* (1956), *King of Kings* (1960), *Welcome to Hard Times* (1967), *Electra Glide in Blue* (1973), *The Outlaw Josey Wales* (1976), *The Right Stuff* (1983), *Ghoulies II* (1989), and *Spaced Invaders* (1990).

Royal Dano

Johnny Downs (October 10, 1913–June 6, 1994). Downs was an actor who was best known for his work in the "Our Gang" comedy shorts as a child. He was a singer and a dancer, and as he grew older he often landed prominent roles in musicals and romantic comedies, many of which were set on college campuses. His film credits include *Outlaws of Red River* (1927), *Babes in Toyland* (1934), *College Scandal* (1935), *Pigskin Parade* (1936), *College Holiday* (1936), *Hold That Co-Ed* (1938), *Melody and Moonlight* (1940), *Campus Rhythm* (1943), *The Kid from Brooklyn* (1946), and *Cruisin' Down the River* (1953).

Tom Ewell (April 29, 1909–September 12, 1994). Born Yewell Tompkins, Ewell was an actor known for his "everyman" looks and his flair for comedy. He appeared in two films in the early 1940's before embarking upon a Broadway career. In 1949, he was cast in a major role in *Adam's Rib* (1949), and his film career resumed in earnest. He also starred in *Up Front* (1951), a film version of car-

Tom Ewell

toonist Bill Mauldin's popular army comic strip. He continued working on Broadway, and in 1952 had a successful run in a play called *The Seven Year Itch,* a role which was to define his career. When *The Seven Year Itch* (1955) was made into a film starring Marilyn Monroe, Ewell repeated his stage performance, winning accolades for his comic portrayal of a middle-aged man bewitched by a young woman. The following year, he starred opposite Jayne Mansfield in one of the finest rock 'n' roll films, *The Girl Can't Help It* (1956). In the early 1960's, he had his own television series, starring for two years in *The Tom Ewell Show.* His additional film credits include *They Knew What They Wanted* (1940), *A Life of Her Own* (1950), *An American Guerrilla in the Philippines* (1950), *Finders Keepers* (1952), *The Lieutenant Wore Skirts* (1956), *Tender Is the Night* (1962), *State Fair* (1962), *The Great Gatsby* (1974), and *Easy Money* (1983).

Zoltan Fabri (1917–August 23, 1994). Fabri was a Hungarian director whose film *The Boys of Paul Street* (1968, which he also co-wrote) was nominated for an Academy Award as Best Foreign Film. Fabri was one of the prime exponents of the Hungarian New Cinema movement, and his work was much honored at European film festivals. His additional films include *Underground Colony* (1951), *Merry-go-round* (1955), *Professor Hanibal* (1956), *Twenty Hours* (1964), *141 Minutes from the Unfinished Sentence* (1975), and *The Fifth Seal* (1976).

Lynne Frederick (1953–April 27, 1994). Frederick was a British actress who was married to Peter Sellers at the time of his death in 1980. They appeared together in *The*

Prisoner of Zenda (1979). Her additional film credits include *No Blade of Grass* (1970), *Vampire Circus* (1971), *Henry VII and His Six Wives* (1973), and *Voyage of the Damned* (1976).

Frances Gifford (December 7, 1920–January 22, 1994). Gifford was an actress who played leads and second leads in numerous films of the 1940's. She broke into film as a teenager, and her first prominent part was the title role in the serial *Jungle Girl* (1941). A serious injury in an automobile accident in 1948 shortened her acting career. Gifford's additional film credits include *Stage Door* (1937), *Mr. Smith Goes to Washington* (1939), *Louisiana Purchase* (1941), *Beyond the Blue Horizon* (1942), *Tarzan Triumphs* (1943), *She Went to the Races* (1945), *Luxury Liner* (1948), and *Sky Commando* (1953).

Sidney Gilliat (February 15, 1908–May 31, 1994). Gilliat was a British director and screenwriter best known for his work with collaborator Frank Launder on a series of film comedies set in the fictional girls' boarding school of St. Trinian's. Gilliat also wrote the script for Alfred Hitchcock's *The Lady Vanishes* (1938). His additional screenwriting credits include *Rome Express* (1932), *Alias Bulldog Drummond* (1935), *A Yank at Oxford* (1938), *I See a Dark Stranger* (1946), *The Blue Lagoon* (1948), *The Belles of St. Trinian's* (1954), and *The Pure Hell of St. Trinian's* (1960). As a director, Gilliat's credits include *The Rake's Progress* (1945), *Gilbert and Sullivan* (1953), *Left Right and Centre* (1959), *The Great St. Trinian's Train Robbery* (1966), and *Endless Night* (1972).

Joan Harrison (1911–August 14, 1994). Harrison was a British screenwriter best known for her work with Alfred Hitchcock, both in England and the United States. These collaborations included *Rebecca* (1940), *Foreign Correspondent* (1940), and *Suspicion* (1941). She also produced the television series *Alfred Hitchcock Presents* from 1955 to 1962, as well as such films as *Phantom Lady* (1944), *Uncle Harry* (1945), *Eye Witness* (1950), and *Circle of Danger* (1951). Her additional screenwriting credits include *Jamaica Inn* (1939), *Saboteur* (1942), and *Dark Waters* (1944).

Harry Horner (July 24, 1910–December 5, 1994). Born in Czechoslovakia, Horner was a production designer and art director who won Academy Awards for his work on *The Heiress* (1949) and *The Hustler* (1961). In addition, Horner also directed films, including *Red Planet Mars* (1952), *Beware My Lovely* (1952), *Vicki* (1953), and *The Wild Party* (1956). His additional art direction credits include *Our Town* (1940), *Stage Door Canteen* (1943), *Winged Victory* (1944), *Born Yesterday* (1950), *Separate Tables* (1958), *They Shoot Horses, Don't They?* (1969), *Audrey Rose* (1973), and *The Jazz Singer* (1980).

Rudolf Hrusinsky (October 17, 1920–April 13, 1994). Born in Czechoslovakia, Hrusinsky was an actor whose film career spanned over five decades. His most memorable performance was in the title role of *The Good Soldier Schweik* (1957). In addition to his acting, Hrusinsky also directed two films, *Jarni Pisen* (1944) and *Pancho Takes a Wife* (1946). His additional acting credits include *Humoresque* (1939), *Night Moth* (1941), *Jan Zizka* (1956), *A Compact With Death* (1960), *How to Steal a Million* (1966), *Short Cuts* (1980), *My Sweet Little Village* (1985), and *It's All Right, Dear Comrade* (1990).

Robert Hutton (June 11, 1920–August 7, 1994). Born Robert Bruce Winne, Hutton was an actor who had leading roles in numerous B movies in the 1940's and 1950's. Later in his career, he appeared in numerous low budget British productions. His film credits include *Destination Tokyo* (1944), *Janie Gets Married* (1946), *And Baby Makes Three* (1949), *Casanova's Big Night* (1954), *Cinderfella* (1960), *Finders Keepers* (1966), *You Only Live Twice* (1967), *Torture Garden* (1967), *Trog* (1970), and *Tales from the Crypt* (1971).

Derek Jarman (1942–February 19, 1994). Jarman was a British director known for his use of homosexual themes in his work. He also directed music videos for prominent rock artists in the 1980's. His film credits include *Sebastiane* (1976), *Jubilee* (1978), *The Tempest* (1979), *Caravaggio* (1986), *The Last of England* (1987), *Edward II* (1991), *Wittgenstein* (1993), and *Blue* (reviewed in this volume),

Derek Jarman

which featured a solid blue screen and soundtrack commentary by Jarman about AIDS, from which he was dying.

Raul Julia (March 9, 1940–October 24, 1994). Julia was a Puerto Rican born actor who was a leading man in both theater and film. Julia left Puerto Rico for the United States at the age of twenty-four to further his acting career. He worked on the New York stage during the 1960's, often in Joseph Papp productions. His first major film roles were in *One From the Heart* (1982) and *The Tempest* (1982). Three

Raul Julia

years later he vaulted into prominence with his starring role opposite William Hurt in *Kiss of the Spider Woman* (1985).

He continued to work in both theater (where he earned four Tony nominations) and in film. In the 1990's, he appeared as Gomez in *The Addams Family* (1991) and its sequel, *Addams Family Values* (1993). Julia's additional film credits include *Panic in Needle Park* (1971), *Been Down So Long It Looks Like Up to Me* (1971), *The Eyes of Laura Mars* (1978), *Compromising Positions* (1985), *Moon Over Parador* (1988), *Tequila Sunrise* (1988), *Mack the Knife* (1989), *Presumed Innocent* (1990), *Frankenstein Unbound* (1990), *The Plague* (1992), and *Street Fighter* (reviewed in this volume).

Martin Kosleck (March 24, 1907–January 16, 1994). Born Nicolai Yoshkin, Kosleck was a German actor who moved to Hollywood in the 1930's and quickly specialized in playing Nazi war criminals. He portrayed Nazi propaganda minister Joseph Goebbels in *Confessions of a Nazi Spy* (1939), *The Hitler Gang* (1944), and *Hitler* (1962). Kosleck's additional screen credits include Nick Carter: *Master Detective* (1939), *Foreign Correspondent* (1940), *Berlin Correspondent* (1942), *The Mummy's Curse* (1945), *Half Past Midnight* (1948), *Morituri* (1965), *Which Way to the Front?* (1970), and *The Man With Bogart's Face* (1980).

Irwin Kostal (1915–November 30, 1994). Kostal was a conductor who won two Academy Awards for his work on *West Side Story* (1961) and *The Sound of Music* (1965). He was nominated for three additional Academy Awards for his work on three Disney films, *Mary Poppins* (1964), *Bedknobs and Broomsticks* (1971), and *Pete's Dragon* (1977). His additional film credits include *A Funny Thing Happened on the Way to the Forum* (1966), *Half a Sixpence* (1967), *Chitty Chitty Bang Bang* (1968), and *Charlotte's Web* (1973).

Burt Lancaster

Burt Lancaster (November 2, 1913–October 20, 1994). Lancaster was an actor whose career as a leading man lasted for four decades. He broke into show business as an acrobat, and his athleticism was a part of his appeal as an actor. After serving in World War II, Lancaster began acting, and his first film role, in *The Killers* (1946), followed shortly thereafter. His vivid portrayal of a boxer seduced by a mobster's girlfriend catapulted him to stardom. Lancaster was equally at home in adventure films such as *Brute Force* (1947) and *Jim Thorpe: All American* (1951), which emphasized his physicality, and in dramatic roles in films such as *Come Back Little Sheba* (1952) and *The Rose Tattoo* (1955), which displayed his sensitive side. He won an Academy Award as Best Actor for his portrayal of a cynical preacher in *Elmer Gantry* (1960), and was nominated for Academy Awards for his work in *From Here to Eternity* (1952) and *Birdman of Alcatraz* (1962). He continued to work productively well into his seventies; as an older man, he recaptured audiences' attention with notable performances in *Atlantic City* (1981) and *Local Hero* (1983); the former film earned him his final Academy Award nomination.

Lancaster was one of the first actors to function as an independent producer, forming a production company with his agent, Harold Hecht in 1948; later producer James Hill became a partner. Lancaster also directed one film, *The Kentuckian* (1955), in which he also starred; he described the experience as the most difficult job of his life. He also co-directed and co-wrote (with Roland Kibbee) *The Midnight Man* (1974).

Lancaster's additional acting credits include *Sorry Wrong Number* (1948), *The Crimson Pirate* (1952), *Trapeze* (1956), *Gunfight at the O.K. Corral* (1957), *Sweet Smell of Success* (1957), *Separate Tables* (1958), *The Unforgiven* (1960), *Judgment at Nuremberg* (1961), *Seven Days in May* (1964), *The Professionals* (1966), *The Swimmer* (1968), *Ulzana's Raid* (1972), *Moses* (1976), *Go Tell the Spartans* (1978), *Zulu Dawn* (1979), *The Osterman Weekend* (1983), *Tough Guys* (1986), *Field of Dreams* (1989), and *The Jeweller's Shop* (1990).

Robert Lansing (June 5, 1928–October 23, 1994). Born Robert Brown, Lansing was an actor who played leading roles in several Hollywood films. He also starred in three television series in the 1960's, most notably *Twelve O'Clock High*. His screen credits include *The 4-D Man* (1959), *A Gathering of Eagles* (1963), *Under the Yum Yum Tree* (1963), *Namu the Killer Whale* (1966), *Empire of the Ants* (1977), *Private Tutor* (1988), and *Blind Vengeance* (1990).

Walter Lantz

Walter Lantz (April 27, 1900–March 22, 1994). Lantz was an animator best known for creating the character "Woody Woodpecker," the subject of numerous cartoon shorts in the 1940's and 1950's. Other Lantz characters included "Chilly Willy," "Andy Panda," and "Oswald the Rabbit." Lantz's cartoon shorts were nominated for eight Academy Awards, including *The Merry Old Soul* (1933), *Boogie Woogie Bugle Boy of Company B* (1941), *Juke Box Jamboree* (1942), *The Dizzy Acrobat* (1943), *Poet and Peasant* (1945), *Chopin's Musical Moments* (1946), *Crazy Mixed Up Pup* (1954), and *The Legend of Rock-A-Bye Point* (1955). In 1978, Lantz was given an honorary Academy Award "for bringing joy and laughter to every part of the world through his unique animated motion pictures."

Henry Mancini

Henry Mancini (April 16, 1924–June 14, 1994). Mancini was a composer, songwriter, and recording artist who became one of the most prolific composers of film scores of the 1960's and 1970's. He was a staff composer for Universal in the early 1950's, working on such films as *The Glenn Miller Story* (1954), the score which earned him an Academy Award nomination; *Six Bridges to Cross* (1956), and *The Benny Goodman Story* (1956). But it was his work in television, with theme songs for the series *Peter Gunn* and *Mr. Lucky*, that first brought him fame. Those series marked the beginning of an association with director Blake Edwards that was to be very productive for both men.

Mancini's work on Edwards' *Breakfast at Tiffany's* (1961), earned Mancini his first two Academy Awards, one for the score and one for Best Song, "Moon River," with lyrics by Johnny Mercer. Mercer and Mancini teamed up the following year for another Academy Award-winning song, the title tune from Edwards' *Days of Wine and Roses* (1962). Mancini also scored *The Pink Panther* (1964) and its sequels, including *A Shot in the Dark* (1964) and *The Return of the Pink Panther* (1975). His fourth Academy Award came for the score of Edwards' *Victor/Victoria* (1982).

Mancini's additional film credits include *Touch of Evil* (1958), *The Great Imposter* (1961), *The Second Time Around* (1961), *Hatari!* (1962), *Charade* (1963), *Arabesque* (1966), *Wait Until Dark* (1967), *The Party* (1970), *Darling Lili* (1970), *Silver Streak* (1976), *Revenge of the Pink Panther* (1978), *10* (1979), *Mommie Dearest* (1981), *The Man Who Loved Women* (1983), *Blind Date* (1987), *Sunset* (1988), *Physical Evidence* (1989), *Ghost Dad* (1990), and *Switch* (1991).

Giulietta Masina

Giulietta Masina (February 22, 1920–March 23, 1994). Masina was an Italian actress best known for her work with her husband, director Federico Fellini. Masina met Fellini when she acted in one of his radio plays in 1942, and they were married a year later. She began acting in film in Roberto Rossellini's *Paisan* (1946), and won critical acclaim for her supporting role in *Without Pity* (1948). She appeared in Fellini's first film, *Variety Lights* (1951), and thereafter became closely associated with his work. Her Chaplinesque role in *La Strada* (1954) won accolades and brought her international attention when the film won an Academy Award as Best Foreign Film. Her portrayal of a prostitute in *The Nights of Cabiria* (1956) was also memorable, and earned her the award as best actress at the Cannes Film Festival. Masina was also featured in Fellini's first color film, *Juliet of the Spirits* (1965). Her additional screen credits include *The White Sheik* (1952), *Il Bidone* (1955), *Bluebeard* (1972), *The Madwoman of Chaillot* (1969), *Ginger and Fred* (1986), and *A Day to Remember* (1991).

Melina Mercouri (October 14, 1923–March 6, 1994). Mercouri was a Greek actress known for the passion she brought to her work as well as to her life. Mercouri came from a politically active family, and was an ardent nationalist and socialist who mixed politics with art over long periods of her life. Her first film, *Stella* (1955), made her a star in Europe, and she became internationally famous with her portrayal of an exuberant prostitute in *Never on Sunday* (1960). Thereafter she worked in American as well as European productions. She was exiled from Greece from 1967 to 1974 for her opposition to the military junta that ruled her nation, but later won a seat in the Greek parliament. She also served as Greece's Minister of Culture. She retired from politics when she lost the election for mayor of Athens. Her additional film credits include *The Gypsy and the Gentleman* (1958), *Phaedra* (1962), *The Victors* (1963), *Topkapi* (1964), *A Man Could Get Killed* (1966), *Gaily Gaily* (1969), *Nasty Habits* (1976), and *A Dream of Passion* (1978).

Anita Morris (1943–March 3, 1994). Morris was an actress who specialized in roles that emphasized her sultry looks and sexuality. She first won acclaim on Broadway, earning a Tony Award nomination for her work in *Nine* in 1982. Her film credits include *The Broad Coalition* (1972), *The Happy Hooker* (1975), *The Hotel New Hampshire* (1984), *Absolute Beginners* (1986), *Ruthless People* (1986), *Bloodhounds of Broadway* (1989), and *Martians Go Home* (1990).

Mildred Natwick (June 19, 1908–October 25, 1994). Natwick was an actress who earned an Academy Award nomination as Best Supporting Actress for her portrayal of Jane Fonda's mother in *Barefoot in the Park* (1967). She also worked extensively on Broadway, and co-starred in the television series *The Snoop Sisters* in 1973 and 1974. Her additional film credits include *The Long Voyage Home* (1940), *The Late George Apley* (1947), *She Wore a Yellow Ribbon* (1949), *Cheaper by the Dozen* (1950), *The Quiet Man* (1952), *The Trouble With Harry* (1955), *Tammy*

Mildred Natwick

and the Bachelor (1957), *The Maltese Bippy* (1969), *Daisy Miller* (1974), *At Long Last Love* (1975), and *Dangerous Liaisons* (1988).

Harriet Nelson (July 18, 1914–October 2, 1994). Nelson was an actress best known for playing herself on the long running radio and television series *The Adventures of Ozzie and Harriet.* One film, *Here Come the Nelsons* (1952), was based on that series. Prior to her marriage to Ozzie Nelson, she was a singer and film actress. Under her maiden name, Harriet Hilliard, her film credits include *Follow the Fleet* (1936), *Cocoanut Grove* (1938), *Confessions of Boston Blackie* (1941), *Honeymoon Lodge* (1943), and *Swingtime Johnny* (1944).

George Peppard

George Peppard (October 1, 1928–May 8, 1994). Peppard was an actor who worked extensively in television as well as film. A starring role opposite Audrey Hepburn in *Breakfast at Tiffany's* (1961) was his first big break, but plum roles in subsequent films eluded him. He was often cast in action films, including *The Blue Max* (1966) and *Tobruk* (1967), and it was these films which led to a successful television career. He played a detective in the series *Banacek* from 1972-1974, and was cast as the leader of a colorful band of mercenaries in *The A-Team*, one of the most popular series of the mid-1980's. Peppard directed one film, *Five Days From Home* (1978). His additional film credits include *Pork Chop Hill* (1959), *The Subterraneans* (1960), *How the West Was Won* (1962), *The Carpetbaggers* (1964), *Rough Night in Jericho* (1967), *What's So Bad About Feeling Good?* (1968), *Damnation Alley* (1977), *Battle Beyond the Stars* (1980), *Your Ticket Is No Longer Valid* (1982), *Night of the Fox* (1990), and *The Tigress* (1992).

Esther Ralston (September 17, 1902–January 14, 1994). Ralston was a leading lady of the silent and early sound eras. Her beauty earned her the nickname "American Venus," and she specialized in playing nice girls. She made her first film, *Phantom Fortunes* (1916), at the age of fourteen, and appeared in over fifty films by the time she ended her screen career in 1941 to concentrate on radio. Her screen credits include *Huckleberry Finn* (1920), *Pals of the West* (1922), *Peter Pan* (1925), *The American Venus* (1926), *Children of Divorce* (1927), *Betrayal* (1929), *Black Beauty* (1933), *Hollywood Boulevard* (1936), and *Tin Pan Alley* (1940).

Martha Raye (August 27, 1916–October 19, 1994). Born Margaret O'Reed, Raye was an actress known for her comic

roles. She had a mobile face, a large mouth, and an exuberance which led to a successful career in live entertainment. She worked in vaudeville, on Broadway, and in radio and television; and she is also remembered for her devotion to entertaining military personnel, often under risky conditions. She was given the Jean Hersholt Humanitarian Award at the 1968 Academy Award ceremonies for these efforts. Her film credits include *Rhythm on the Range* (1936), *The Big Broadcast of 1937* (1936), *Artists and Models* (1937), *College Swing* (1938), *The Farmer's Daughter* (1940), *Hellzapoppin* (1941), *Monsieur Verdoux* (1947), *Jumbo* (1962), and *The Concorde: Airport '79* (1979).

Gottfried Reinhardt (1911–July 18, 1994). Reinhardt was a German-born screenwriter, producer, and director. He was the son of Max Reinhardt, a major figure in German theater in the early twentieth century, and he came to the United States as an assistant to filmmaker Ernst Lubitsch. His best known work was *Town Without Pity* (1960), which he produced and directed. As a writer, Reinhardt contributed screenplays to *I Live My Life* (1935), *The Great Waltz* (1938), and *Bridal Suite* (1939). He was a contract producer for MGM for two decades, where his films included *Comrade X* (1940), *Rage in Heaven* (1941), *Two-Faced Woman* (1941), *Command Decision* (1948), and *The Red Badge of Courage* (1951). He also directed several films, including *Invitation* (1952), *Betrayed* (1954), and *Situation Hopeless—But Not Serious* (1965).

Fernando Rey (September 20, 1915–March 9, 1994). Born Fernando Casado Arambillet Vega, Rey was a Spanish actor who was an international film star, appearing in over one hundred films produced both in Europe and the United States. His goatee was his trademark, and he specialized in suave leading and supporting roles. He is best remembered for his work with Spanish director Luis Buñuel in *Viridiana* (1961), and as the

Fernando Rey

villain in *The French Connection* (1971). His additional screen credits include *Los Cuatro Robinsones* (1940), *Don Quijote de la Mancha* (1947), *The Last Days of Pompeii* (1959), *The Ceremony* (1963), *Chimes at Midnight* (1966), *Guns of the Magnificent Seven* (1969), *Tristana* (1970), *The Discreet Charm of the Bourgeoise* (1972), *French Connection II* (1975), *Seven Beauties* (1976), *Voyage of the Damned* (1976), *That Obscure Object of Desire* (1977), *The Hit* (1984), *Moon Over Parador* (1988), and *1492* (1992).

Gilbert Roland

Gilbert Roland (December 11, 1905–May 15, 1994). Born Luis Antonio Damaso de Alonso in Mexico, Roland was an actor whose film career spanned nearly sixty years. He began working in the silent era, during which his most prominent role was that of Armand, opposite Norma Talmadge in *Camille* (1927). He continued to prosper in the sound era, often appearing in Westerns and adventure films such as *The Sea Hawk* (1940), *Captain Kidd* (1945), and *Apache War Smoke* (1952). He starred as the Cisco Kid in eleven B Westerns, including *The Gay Cavalier* (1946) and *Robin Hood of Monterey* (1947). Roland's additional film credits include *The Plastic Age* (1925), *Rose of the Golden West* (1927), *She Done Him Wrong* (1931), *Thunder Trail* (1937), *Juarez* (1939), *Beauty and the Bandit* (1946), *King of the Bandits* (1947), *The Bullfighter and the Lady* (1951), *Thunder Bay* (1953), *The Big Circus* (1959), *Cheyenne Autumn* (1964), *Islands in the Stream* (1977), and *Barbarosa* (1982).

Cesar Romero

Cesar Romero (February 15, 1907–January 1, 1994). Romero was an actor known for his suave Latin looks and manner. Born in New York City of Cuban parents, he called himself "the Latin from Manhattan." He was featured in romantic lead roles in such films as *Weekend in Havana* (1941) and *Carnival in Costa Rica* (1947). He took over the role of the Cisco Kid for a few years in the popular Western adventure series. He continued to appear in films and television through the 1980's; two of his more memorable roles were that of the Joker in television's *Batman*, and Peter Stavros in *Falcon Crest*. Romero's film credits include *The Thin Man* (1934), *Wee Willie Winkie* (1937), *The Cisco Kid and the Lady* (1939), *The Gay Caballero* (1940), *Springtime in the Rockies* (1942), *Vera Cruz* (1954), *Around the World in 80 Days* (1956), *Ocean's Eleven* (1960), *Donovan's Reef* (1963), *Midas Run* (1969), *Lust in the Dust* (1985), and *Simple Justice* (1989).

Heinz Ruehmann (March 6, 1912–October 4, 1994). Ruehmann was a German actor who was one of his country's most popular film personalities in the 1950's and 1960's. A small man, he specialized in comedy. His film credits include *Das Deutsche Mutterherz* (1926), *You Don't Need Any Money* (1933), *The Grand Duke's Finances* (1934), *Charley's Aunt* (1956), *The Captain from Koepenick* (1956), *It Happened in Broad Daylight* (1958), *The Good Soldier Schweik* (1959), and *Ship of Fools* (1960).

Harry Saltzman (October 27, 1915–September 28, 1994). Born in Canada and raised in the United States, Saltzman was a producer who made his mark in England, where, with co-producer Albert Broccoli, he brought Ian Fleming's James Bond novels to the screen. His first film productions were quite different from the flashy Bond films. *Look Back in Anger* (1959), *The Entertainer* (1960), and *Saturday Night and Sunday Morning* (1960) were stark examples of the "angry young man" genre of the day. His first Bond film was *Dr. No* (1962), featuring Sean Connery as 007; the third film in the series, *Goldfinger* (1964) was enormously popular, and set the stage for a series that would endure for decades despite multiple changes in the lead role. Saltzman left the Bond series after *The Man with the Golden Gun* (1974), and retired from film after suffering a stroke in 1980. His additional film credits include *From Russia with Love* (1963), *The Ipcress File* (1965), *Thunderball* (1965), *Funeral in Berlin* (1966), *You Only Live Twice* (1967), *On Her Majesty's Secret Service* (1969), *Diamonds Are Forever* (1971), *Live and Let Die* (1973), *The Man With the Golden Gun* (1974), and *Nijinsky* (1980).

Telly Savalas (January 21, 1924–January 22, 1994). Born Aristotle Savalas, Savalas was an actor best known for his bald head and his starring role in the television series *Kojak* in the 1970's. In films, Savalas was usually cast as the heavy. These roles included that of Pontius Pilate in *The Greatest Story Ever Told* (1965) and a psychotic soldier in *The Dirty Dozen* (1967). He was nominated for an Academy Award

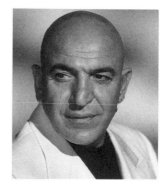

Telly Savalas

as Best Supporting Actor for his role opposite Burt Lancaster in *The Birdman of Alcatraz* (1962). His additional film credits include *The Young Savages* (1961), *Cape Fear* (1962), *Johnny Cool* (1963), *Genghis Khan* (1966), *On Her Majesty's Secret Service* (1969), *Kelly's Heroes* (1970), *Beyond Reason* (1977, which he also directed), *Beyond the Poseidon Adventure* (1979), and *Cannonball Run II* (1984).

Ferdinando Scarfiotti (1941–April 30, 1994). Scarfiotti was an Italian production designer who won an Academy Award for his work on *The Last Emperor* (1987). He worked with major directors in Europe and Hollywood, and *Toys* (1992) also earned him an Academy Award nomination.

His additional film credits include *Death in Venice* (1971), *The Conformist* (1971), *Avanti!* (1972), *Last Tango in Paris* (1973), *Daisy Miller* (1974), *American Gigolo* (1980), *Cat People* (1982), *Scarface* (1983), and *Bring on the Night* (1985).

Dinah Shore (March 1, 1917–February 24, 1994). Born Frances Rose Shore, Shore was a popular singer in the 1940's and early 1950's. She appeared in several films during that period, but she was more successful in television, where she had her own variety show in the 1950's as well as several talk shows in the 1970's and 1980's. Shore's film credits include *Thank Your Lucky Stars* (1942), *Follow the Boys* (1944), *Belle of the Yukon* (1944), *Till the Clouds Roll By* (1946), *Aaron Slick From Punkin Crick* (1952), *Oh God!* (1977), and *Health* (1979).

Ginny Simms (1916–April 4, 1994). Simms was a singer and actress who was featured in several musicals and light romantic comedies during the Big Band era. She was a vocalist with the Kay Kyser band, and her first film appearance was with that group in *That's Right, You're Wrong* (1939). Her additional film credits include *You'll Find Out* (1940), *Playmates* (1941), *Seven Days' Leave* (1942), *Hit the Ice* (1943), and *Shady Lady* (1945).

Lilia Skala (1901–December 18, 1994). Skala was an Austrian actress who emigrated to the United States in 1939. She worked in television and on Broadway as well as in film, where her best remembered role was that of the Mother Superior in *Lilies of the Field* (1963), which earned her an Academy Award nomination as Best Supporting Actress. Her additional screen credits include *Call Me Madam* (1953), *Ship of Fools* (1965), *Roseland* (1977), *Heartland* (1979), *Flashdance* (1983), and *House of Games* (1989).

Murray Spivak (1903–May 8, 1994). Spivak was a sound mixer who won an Academy Award for his work on *Hello, Dolly!* (1969). He was also nominated for an Academy Award for *Tora! Tora! Tora!* (1970). His additional film credits include *King Kong* (1933), *Flying Down to Rio* (1933), *Fantasia* (1940), *The Robe* (1953), *Oklahoma!* (1955), *West Side Story* (1961), *My Fair Lady* (1964), and *The Sound of Music* (1965).

Lionel Stander (January 11, 1908–November 30, 1994). Stander was an actor who specialized in character roles. Often cast as a heavy, Stander's thriving career was interrupted when he refused to cooperate with the House Un-American Activities Committee's investigations of communist influence in Hollywood and was blacklisted for over a decade. He returned to films in *The Loved One* (1965), and

Lionel Stander

made several movies in Europe. He also had a featured role in the 1980's television series *Hart to Hart*. Stander's additional film credits include *The Scoundrel* (1935), *Mr. Deeds Goes to Town* (1936), *A Star Is Born* (1937), *Guadalcanal Diary* (1943), *The Kid From Brooklyn* (1946), *Call Northside 777* (1948), *St. Benny the Dip* (1951), *A Dandy in Aspic* (1968), *Once Upon a Time in the West* (1968), *The Gang That Couldn't Shoot Straight* (1971), *New York New York* (1977), *Wicked Stepmother* (1989), and *Joey Takes a Cab* (1990).

Jule Styne (December 31, 1905–September 20, 1994). Born in England, Styne was a songwriter who moved to the United States as a child. He worked extensively in Hollywood from the late 1930's through the 1950's, often collaborating with Frank Loesser and Sammy Cahn. Styne and Cahn won an Academy Award for their title song from *Three Coins in the Fountain* (1954). His additional film credits include *Hold That Co-Ed* (1938), *Sweater Girl* (1942), *Youth on Parade* (1942), *Follow the Boys* (1944), *Anchors Aweigh* (1945), *The Sweetheart of Sigma Chi* (1946), *It Happened in Brooklyn* (1947), *Romance on the High Seas* (1948), *Gentlemen Prefer Blondes* (1953), *My Sister Eileen* (1955), *Bells Are Ringing* (1960), *Gypsy* (1963), *Funny Girl* (1968), and *Thieves* (1977).

Barry Sullivan (August 29, 1912–June 6, 1994). Born Barry Patrick, Sullivan was an actor who appeared in leading roles in numerous films of the 1940's and 1950's. Perhaps his most memorable role was that of Tom Buchanan in *The Great Gatsby* (1949). He also worked extensively in television and on stage. Sullivan's film credits include *Lady in the Dark* (1944), *Framed* (1947), *The Gangster* (1947), *The Outriders* (1950), *The Bad and the Beautiful* (1952), *Jeopardy* (1953), *Wolf Larsen* (1959), *The Light in the Piazza* (1962), *Harlow* (1965), *Tell Them Willie Boy Is Here* (1970), *Earthquake* (1974), and *Oh God!* (1977).

Barry Sullivan

Jessica Tandy (June 7, 1907–September 11, 1994). Born in England, Tandy was an actress who was much honored

Jessica Tandy

for her work on stage and in film. Best known for most of her career as a stage actress, Tandy won four Tony Awards for her work on Broadway, the first coming in 1954 when she originated the role of Blanche DuBois in *A Streetcar Named Desire*. Her American film career was undoubtedly set back when Vivien Leigh was awarded the plum DuBois role in the film. Indeed, although her film career spanned six decades, it was not until her performance in *Cocoon* (1985) at the age of 78 that Tandy became a film star. That performance led to the lead role in *Driving Miss Daisy* (1989), for which she won an Academy Award as Best Actress. She was nominated for an Academy Award as Best Supporting Actress for her performance in *Fried Green Tomatoes* (1991). Tandy was married to actor Hume Cronyn, and the two often appeared together on stage; Cronyn was also in *Cocoon*. Her additional film credits include *The Indiscretions of Eve* (1932), *Murder in the Family* (1938), *Dragonwyck* (1946), *Forever Amber* (1947), *The Desert Fox* (1951), *The Light in the Forest* (1958), *The Birds* (1963), *Butley* (1974), *The World According to Garp* (1982), *The Bostonians* (1984), *Batteries Not Included* (1986), *The House on Carroll Street* (1988), *Cocoon: The Return* (1988), *Used People* (1992), *Camilla*, and *Nobody's Fool* (both reviewed in this volume).

Dub Taylor   (February 26, 1907–October 3, 1994). Born Walter Clarence Taylor, Jr., Taylor was an actor who played supporting and character roles in a career that lasted over half a century. Later in his career, he specialized in playing grizzled southerners and westerners in films such as *Bonnie and Clyde* (1967) and *Maverick* (reviewed in this volume). He also worked extensively in television. His additional film credits include *You Can't Take It With You* (1938), *Mr. Smith Goes to Washington* (1939), *Riding High* (1950), *No Time for Sergeants* (1958), *A Hole in the Head* (1962), *Sweet Bird of Youth* (1962), *How the West Was Won* (1962), *Major Dundee* (1965), *The Wild Bunch* (1969), *Thunderbolt and Lightfoot* (1974), *Gator* (1976), *Back to the Future Part III* (1990), and *My Heroes Have Always Been Cowboys* (1991).

Gian Maria Volante   (April 9, 1933–December 6, 1994). Volante was an Italian actor and political activist. He worked often with directors Elio Petri and Francesco Rosi on films which exposed the darker sides of Italian society in the 1960's and 1970's, such as terrorism and crime. His screen credits include *Girl with a Suitcase* (1961), *Il Terrorista* (1963), *A Fistful of Dollars* (1964), *For a Few Dollars More* (1966), *Investigation of a Citizen Above Suspicion* (1970), *Re: Lucky Luciano* (1973), *Todo Modo* (1976), *For Your Eyes Only* (1981), *Greystoke: The Legend of Tarzan, Lord of the Apes* (1984), *Chronicle of a Death Foretold* (1987), and *A Simple Story* (1991).

Terence Young   (June 20, 1915–September 7, 1994). Young was a British director best known for his work on the James Bond films. Of the Bond series, Young directed three of the first four, *Dr. No* (1962), *From Russia With Love* (1963), and *Thunderball* (1965). He introduced British singing idol Cliff Richard to the screen in *Serious Charge* (1959). His additional screen credits include *Corridor of Mirrors* (1948), *Valley of the Eagles* (1951), *The Red Beret* (1953), *Safari* (1956), *Too Hot to Handle* (1960), *The Amorous Adventures of Moll Flanders* (1965), *The Poppy Is Also a Flower* (1966), *Mayerling* (1968), *The Valachi Papers* (1972), *Sidney Sheldon's Bloodline* (1979), *Inchon* (1982), and *The Jigsaw Man* (1984).

Mai Zetterling   (May 24, 1925–March 17, 1994). Zetterling was a Swedish actress who also directed. Her blonde good looks won her roles in British and American productions as well as films in her native country. In the 1960's, she began making her own films. Her first effort, the documentary *War Games* (1963), which she made with her husband David Hughes, won a prize at the Venice Film Festival. Her second feature film was *Night Games* (1966), which she adapted from her own novel. Zetterling's additional acting credits include *Sunshine Follows Rain* (1946), *Frieda* (1947), *The Girl in the Painting* (1948), *The Truth About Women* (1958), *Only Two Can Play* (1961), *The Main Attraction* (1963), and *The Witches* (1990). Among the films she directed were *Loving Couples* (1964), *Vincent the Dutchman* (1972), *Love* (1981), *Scrubbers* (1982), and *Amarosa* (1986).

Selected Film Books of 1994

Abel, Richard. *The Cine Goes to Town: French Cinema 1896-1914.*
Berkeley, California: University of California Press, 1994.

Abel charts the Pathe-Freres company and its influence on the film industry worldwide at the turn of the century, when cinema first began to move from novelty shorts to longer films tied to narratives.

Alexander, Paul. *Boulevard of Broken Dreams.*
New York: Viking, 1994.

This biography of actor/legend James Dean is aimed at the popular audience, and is profusely illustrated.

Armes, Roy. *Action and Image: Dramatic Structure in Cinema.*
New York: Manchester University Press, 1994.

Examining eight films, Armes argues that film criticism's emphasis on the visual has resulted in a neglect of the role of the film's dramatic structure.

Bacall, Lauren. *Now.*
New York: Alfred A. Knopf, 1994.

This is not a sequel to the actress's autobiography *By Myself;* rather, it is a collection of observations and opinions on such topics as children, acting, and friendship.

Barbera, Joseph, with Alan Axelrod. *My Life in 'Toons: From Flatbush to Bedrock in Under a Century.*
Atlanta, Georgia: Turner Publishing, 1994.

This is the autobiography of the animator, who, with partner William Hanna, created the Academy Award winning characters Tom and Jerry, as well as a host of animated television series such as *The Flintstones.*

Baxter, John. *Fellini.*
New York: St. Martin's Press, 1994.

Baxter admires the Italian filmmaker's genius, but does not ignore his personal and professional faults in this biography.

Beaver, Frank. *Oliver Stone: Wakeup Cinema.*
New York: Twayne, 1994.

Beaver examines Stone's career through 1993, paying particular attention to the ways in which film critics have influenced the shape of the filmmaker's work.

Beeman, Marsha Lynn. *Joan Fontaine: A Bio-Bibliography.*
Westport, Connecticut: Greenwood Press, 1994.

A biography of the American leading lady, including a filmography and an annotated bibliography.

Bernstein, Matthew. *Walter Wanger: Hollywood Independent.*
Berkeley, California: University of California Press, 1994.

Wanger was a Hollywood producer from 1920 through his disastrous involvement with *Cleopatra* in 1962. Bernstein's biography is the first detailed study of his career.

Bikel, Theodore. *Theo.*
New York: HarperCollins, 1994.

This is the autobiography of the musician, political activist, and Academy Award nominated actor.

Bingham, Dennis. *Acting Male: Masculinities in the Films of James Stewart, Jack Nicholson, and Clint Eastwood.*
New Brunswick, New Jersey: Rutgers University Press, 1994.

Bingham traces the development of Hollywood's portrayal of masculinity through the careers of three prominent actors in this scholarly work.

Black, Gregory D. *Hollywood Censored: Morality Codes, Catholics, and the Movies.*
New York: Cambridge University Press, 1994.

Black outlines the interrelationship between Hollywood, politics, and the Roman Catholic church in institutionalizing film censorship in the 1930's.

Bowles, Stephen. *The Film Anthologies Index.*
Metuchen, New Jersey: Scarecrow Press, 1994.

Indexed by film name, key word, and author, this reference work covers essays printed in 716 monographic works on film.

Brady, Ben. *Principles of Adaptation for Film and Television.*
Austin, Texas: University Press of Texas, 1994.

Brady, a writer, professor, and former producer, offers insights into the process of adapting works of fiction into screenplays.

Brady, Kathleen. *Lucille: The Life of Lucille Ball.*
New York: Little, Brown, 1994.

This biography of the comic actress puts more stress than previous efforts on the film career she established before becoming one of the stars of early television.

Brando, Marlon. *Brando: Songs My Mother Taught Me.*
New York: Random House, 1994.

The emotional center of Brando's autobiography focuses on his tangled childhood relationships with his parents and a female housekeeper; he blames these relationships for his manipulative behavior as an adult.

Browne, Nick, Paul G. Pickowicz, Vivian Sobchack, and Esther Yau, editors. *New Chinese Cinemas: Forms, Identities, Politics.*
New York: Cambridge University Press, 1994.

This collection of nine scholarly essays analyzes the effects of social changes on the cinema in China, Taiwan, and Hong Kong since the late 1970's.

Burt, George. *The Art of Film Music.*
Boston: Northeastern University Press, 1994.

Burt examines the practical and aesthetic aspects of scoring a film, paying particular attention to the work of Hugo Friedhofer, Alex North, David Raskin, and Leonard Rosenman.

Callan, Michael Feeney. *Anthony Hopkins: The Unauthorized Biography.*
New York: Scribner's, 1994.

This work supplements the actor's 1989 authorized biography, offering additional information about Hopkins' first marriage and his problems with alcohol, and adding information about his recent career.

Cameron, Kenneth M. *Africa on Film: Beyond Black and White.*
New York: Continuum, 1994.

Cameron examines the image of Africa and Africans in British and American films, from the silent era to the present day, noting the changes in the portrayal of black-white relations as the continent progressed from colonialism to independence.

Cancalon, Elaine D., and Antoine Spacagna, editors. *Intertextuality in Literature and Film.*
Gainesville, Florida: University Press of Florida, 1994.

This is a collection of twelve scholarly papers on literature and film, from a conference held in 1988.

Card, James. *Seductive Cinema: The Art of Silent Film.*
New York: Alfred A. Knopf, 1994.

Collector and film historian James Card is perhaps the foremost authority on silent film. He draws upon his knowledge of the period and its major players to offer a fresh look at a neglected era.

Carney, Ray. *The Films of John Cassavetes.*
New York: Cambridge University Press, 1994.

Carney argues that Cassavetes was one of the most important artists of the century in this scholarly survey of the American filmmaker's career.

Carriere, Jean-Claude. *The Secret Language of Film.*
New York: Pantheon Films, 1994.

Carriere is a prominent French screenwriter. In this book, he analyzes the language of films—the use of camera angles, settings, and lighting—and how this language has been used by major filmmakers.

Caute, David. *Joseph Losey: A Revenge on Life.*
New York: Oxford University Press, 1994.

Best known for his collaborations with playwright Harold Pinter, the American-born director moved to Britain as a result of the McCarthy era blacklist. This is a scholarly account of his life and work.

Chion, Michel. *Audio-Vision: Sound on Screen.*
New York: Columbia University Press, 1994.

In this scholarly study of the function of sound in cinema, Chion notes the symbiotic relationship between sound and image, which the audience perceives in largely visual terms.

Chutkow, Paul. *Depardieu: A Biography.*
New York: Alfred A. Knopf, 1994.

Chutkow had the cooperation of his subject, and thus this biography of Depardieu contains very personal insights into the French actor's life and work.

Coates, Paul. *Film at the Intersection of High and Mass Culture.*
New York: Cambridge University Press, 1994.

Coates analyzes the relationship of film to high and low culture in the United States and Europe.

Cooper, Stephen, editor. *Perspectives on John Huston.*
New York: G.K. Hall, 1994.

This collection of fifteen essays on various aspects of Huston's career as a filmmaker includes a lengthy interview as well as a filmography and brief bibliography.

Darin, Dodd. *Dream Lovers.*
New York: Warner Books, 1994.

The author is the son of singer Bobby Darin and actress Sandra Dee; in this book, he examines his parents' troubled marriage.

Davies, Anthony, and Stanley Wells, editors. *Shakespeare and the Moving Image.*
New York: Cambridge University Press, 1994.

This is a collection of fourteen scholarly essays on film and television versions of Shakespeare's plays, focusing on the work of Olivier, Kurosawa, and Zeffirelli, as well as the BBC Television productions.

Dissanayake, Wimal, editor. *Colonialism and Nationalism in Asian Cinema.*
Bloomington, Indiana: Indiana University Press, 1994.

This work consists of a dozen scholarly essays on films from nine Asian countries and Australia, emphasizing the themes of colonialism and nationalism.

Edelman, Rob. *The Great Baseball Films: From Silent Days to the Present.*
Secaucus, New Jersey: Citadel, 1994.

Edelman examines 185 films on the national pastime, offering a critique of each film as well as a summary of its plot.

Erlich, Linda C., and David Desser, editors. *Cinematic Landscapes: Observations on the Visual Arts and Cinema of China and Japan.*
Austin, Texas: University of Texas Press, 1994.

This work contains fourteen scholarly essays on the influence of traditional Asian art forms such as scroll painting and printmaking on Chinese and Japanese cinema.

Falsetto, Mario. *Stanley Kubrick: A Narrative and Stylistic Analysis.*
Westport, Connecticut: Greenwood Press, 1994.

Falsetto analyzes the narrative, stylistic, and thematic concerns in nine of Kubrick's major films, from *The Killing* through *Full Metal Jacket.*

Faris, Jocelyn. *Ginger Rogers: A Bio-Bibliography.*
Westport, Connecticut: Greenwood Press, 1994.

This is a biography of the American actress, including a filmography and an annotated bibliography.

Fetrow, Alan G. *Feature Films, 1940-1949.*
Jefferson, North Carolina: McFarland, 1994.

This reference work provides filmographies for 4,296 American films released in the 1940's. Each entry contains a brief plot summary, and the book is indexed by personal name.

Flamini, Roland. *Thalberg: The Last Tycoon and the World of M-G-M.*
New York: Crown, 1994.

This is a useful biography of M-G-M's Boy Wonder, the influential producer of the 1920's and 1930's who inspired F. Scott Fitzgerald's *The Last Tycoon.*

Forman, Milos, and Jan Novak. *Turnaround: A Memoir.*
New York: Villard Books, 1994.

This is the autobiography of the Czech filmmaker who defected to the United States and won acclaim for films such as *One Flew Over the Cuckoo's Nest* and *Amadeus.*

Funicello, Annette, with Patricia Romanowski. *A Dream Is a Wish Your Heart Makes: My Story.*
New York: Hyperion, 1994.

The former Mouseketeer and actress has nothing but kind words for everyone with whom she has worked in this autobiography.

Galbraith, Stuart, IV. *Japanese Science Fiction, Fantasy, and Horror Films.*
Jefferson, North Carolina: McFarland, 1994.

This is a critical analysis of 103 Japanese films, in the science fiction or related genres, released in the United States between 1950 and 1992.

George, Nelson. *Blackface: Reflections on African-Americans and the Movies.*
New York: HarperCollins, 1994.

George is a critic, screenwriter, and producer; this is a highly personal survey of the changing film images of African-Americans over the past three decades.

Grandinetti, Fred M. *Popeye.*
Jefferson, North Carolina: McFarland, 1994.

This is a history of E.C. Segar's cartoon character, covering Popeye's first appearance in print in 1929 and including print, film, radio, recordings, and television appearances through 1993.

Grindon, Leger. *Shadows on the Past.*
Philadelphia: Temple University Press, 1994.

Grindon offers a collection of scholarly essays analyzing the historical fiction film through such examples as *Reds, The Birth of a Nation,* and several films on the French Revolution.

Harris, Warren G. *Audrey Hepburn: A Biography.*
New York: Simon & Schuster, 1994.

In this first biography published since Hepburn's death, Harris offers a flattering portrayal of the actress' life and career.

Haupt, Clyde V. *Huckleberry Finn on Film.*
Jefferson, North Carolina: McFarland, 1994.

This is a detailed analysis of the eleven film and television adaptations, released between 1920 and 1993, of Mark Twain's famous novel.

Higashi, Sumiko. *Cecil B. DeMille and American Culture: The Silent Era.*
Berkeley, California: University of California Press, 1994.

In this scholarly study of DeMille's early features, Higashi examines DeMille's role as a disseminator of middle class values in early twentieth century America.

Hill, Ona L. *Raymond Burr: A Film, Radio and Television Biography.*
Jefferson, North Carolina: McFarland, 1994.

This study of the life and career of the late actor includes lists of his films, radio shows, and television credits, with a detailed guide to each episode of Perry Mason.

Jameson, Richard T. *They Went Thataway: Redefining Film Genres.*
San Francisco: Mercury House, 1994.

This collection of essays on recent trends in genre films includes the work of many prominent film critics.

Jeffords, Susan. *Hard Bodies: Hollywood Masculinity in the Reagan Era.*
New Brunswick, New Jersey: Rutgers University Press, 1994.

Jeffords argues that the popularity of the muscular Rambo-type hero during the 1980's was no coincidence, but rather a reflection of the nation's desire for get-tough politics at home and abroad, as exemplified by Reagan conservatism.

Kael, Pauline. *For Keeps: Thirty Years at the Movies.*
New York: Dutton, 1994.

This is an anthology of writings from over thirty years of work by Kael, perhaps the most influential American film critic of the postwar era.

Karlin, Fred. *Listening to Movies.*
New York: Schirmer Books, 1994.

Karlin examines the way in which music is written and performed for film, and the interplay between composers and filmmakers.

Karnick, Kristine Brunovska, and Henry Jenkins, editors. *Classical Hollywood Comedy.*
New York: Routledge, 1994.

This is a collection of sixteen scholarly essays on the conventions of film comedy from the silent era through the 1950's.

Kashner, Sam, and Nancy Schoenberger. *A Talent For Genius.*
New York: Villard Books, 1994.

This is a biography of Oscar Levant, a musician and actor of the 1940's who was known as much for his eccentric habits as for his undeniable talent.

Katz, Ephraim. *The Film Encyclopedia.*
New York: HarperPerennial, 1994.

In 1979, the first edition of this encyclopedia became the definitive single volume English language reference work on cinema. Katz (who died in 1992) and his collaborators have enhanced its usefulness by updating it fifteen years later.

Kauffmann, Stanley. *Distinguishing Features.*
Baltimore, Maryland: The Johns Hopkins University Press, 1994.

Kauffmann is a respected film critic for *The New Republic*. This book collects his reviews for that magazine from 1985 through 1992.

Lacey, Robert. *Grace.*
New York: G.P. Putnam's Sons, 1994.

Lacey is a veteran biographer of political dynasties; this biography of Grace Kelly portrays the actress/princess as driven by a need to win the approval of her distant father.

Lang, Robert, editor. *The Birth of a Nation: D.W. Griffith, Director.*
New Brunswick, New Jersey: Rutgers University Press, 1994.

This history of one of the most important films in American cinema includes the continuity script, as well as contemporary reviews and scholarly analysis.

Langman, Larry, and Daniel Finn. *A Guide to American Silent Crime Films.*
Westport, Connecticut: Greenwood Press, 1994.

This is a filmography of over 2,000 crime films released before the advent of sound. Each entry contains information on cast and credits, and many offer plot summaries as well.

Lanning, Michael Lee. *Vietnam at the Movies.*
New York: Fawcett Columbine, 1994.

Lanning is a former Army officer and Vietnam veteran; he brings his unique perspective to this study of Vietam war films.

Levy, Emanuel. *George Cukor: Master of Elegance.*
New York: William Morrow, 1994.

This biography of the filmmaker known as a "women's director" is based on extensive interviews with many actors, both male and female, who worked with Cukor.

Lupack, Barbara Tepa. *Take Two: Adapting the Contemporary American Novel to Film.*
Bowling Green, Ohio: Bowling Green State University Popular Press, 1994.

A collection of eleven scholarly essays on ten American novels of the past three decades and the films made from them, analyzing the ways in which the director's vision complements and/or alters the vision of the author.

McCarty, John. *The Fearmakers.*
New York: St. Martin's Press, 1994.

McCarty offers twenty short essays, by himself and others, on directors from the silent era to the 1990's who specialized in horror films. Each essay features a filmography, and is illustrated with production stills.

McCreadie, Marsha. *The Women Who Write the Movies.*
New York: Birch Lane Press, 1994.

In analyzing the work of dozens of female screenwriters from the silent era to the present day, McCreadie ties Hollywood's portrayal of women to the number of screenplays written by women at any given point in time.

McGilligan, Patrick. *Jack's Life: A Biography of Jack Nicholson.*
New York: W.W. Norton, 1994.

This is a well researched analysis of the life and career of the talented American leading man. The book includes a filmography.

McMurtry, Jo. *Shakespeare Films in the Classroom.*
Hamden, Connecticut: Archon, 1994.

McMurtry offers a Shakespeare filmography, annotated with an eye toward their use by high school and college students. Annotations include notes on how each film differs from the play, and advantages and disadvantages for classroom use.

Madsen, Axel. *Stanwyck.*
New York: HarperCollins, 1994.

Madsen's biography of Barbara Stanwyck is a welcome addition to the rather sparse literature on one of Hollywood's most important actresses.

Maltin, Leonard, editor. *Leonard Maltin's Movie Encyclopedia.*
New York: Dutton, 1994.

Maltin supplements his popular annual film guides with this biographical directory of over 2,000 actors and filmmakers, with an emphasis on mainstream American films.

Mank, Gregory William. *Hollywood Cauldron.*
Jefferson, North Carolina: McFarland, 1994.

Mank offers a detailed examination of thirteen influential horror films of the 1930's and 1940's, covering the styles of the various studios which specialized in the genre.

Manso, Peter. *Brando: The Biography.*
New York: Hyperion, 1994.

Manso offers the most detailed biography of the acclaimed and controversial actor yet, but this popular treatment emphasizes the complexities of Brando's personal life over his achievements as an artist.

Mathews, Tom Dewe. *Censored.*
London: Chatto & Windus, 1994.

Great Britain takes the most rigorous approach to film censorship in Western Europe. This is a scholarly history of the work of the British Board of Film Censors from its inception in 1912 up through the present day.

Miller, Frank. *Censored Hollywood: Sex, Sin, & Violence on Screen.*
Atlanta, Georgia: Turner Publishing, 1994.

Miller surveys the history of film censorship, from the silent era to the present day, outlining the philosophy of various groups involved in the process, and offering a detailed look at specific examples of the way films have been altered to appease censors.

Miracle, Berniece Baker, and Mona Rae Miracle. *My Sister Marilyn.*
Chapel Hill, North Carolina: Algonquin Books of North Carolina, 1994.

Marilyn Monroe's half-sister shares her insights on the complicated relationship they had with their mother.

Monder, Eric. *George Sidney: A Bio-Bibliography.*
Westport, Connecticut: Greenwood Press, 1994.

This is a biography of the director best known for his musicals. Includes a filmography and an annotated bibliography.

Mowrey, Peter C. *Award Winning Films: A Viewer's Reference to 2700 Acclaimed Motion Pictures.*
Jefferson, North Carolina: McFarland, 1994.

This reference work lists the winners of twenty-nine international film awards, including the Academy Awards, the Cannes Film Festival awards, and the winners of the New York Film Critics awards.

Norden, Martin F. *The Cinema of Isolation: A History of Physical Disability in the Movies.*
New Brunswick, New Jersey: Rutgers University Press, 1994.

Norden argues that films from the silent era to the present day have reinforced stereotypes about persons with physical disabilities, not only via their narratives but also from the point of view of framing, editing, and other technical perspectives.

Oderman, Stuart. *Roscoe "Fatty" Arbuckle.*
Jefferson, North Carolina: McFarland, 1994.

This is a biography of the silent era comic actor whose career was ruined by a sex murder scandal, for which he was ultimately exonerated.

Paietta, Ann C., and Jean L. Kauppila. *Animals on Screen and Radio: An Annotated Sourcebook.*
Metuchen, New Jersey: Scarecrow Press, 1994.

This reference work contains 1,515 entries, most of which are devoted to theatrical and television films, in which animals are featured prominently; entries include information on cast and credits, as well as a plot synopsis which emphasizes the role of the animal(s) in the film.

Palmer, R. Barton. *Hollywood's Dark Cinema: The American Film Noir.*
New York: Twayne, 1994.

This relatively brief analysis of American *film noir* focuses on several major examples of the genre, and concludes with a chapter on recent noir films.

Parish, James Robert. *Ghosts and Angels in Hollywood Films.*
Jefferson, North Carolina: McFarland, 1994.

This reference work provides cast and credit information, plot summaries, and critiques for 264 American films and television movies which feature angels or ghosts.

Paul, William. *Laughing Screaming: Modern Hollywood Horror and Comedy.*
New York: Columbia University Press, 1994.

In this scholarly study of lowbrow horror and comedy films of the 1970's and 1980's, Paul links such films as *Animal House* and *The Exorcist,* arguing that the primary focus of "gross out" films in both genres is the human body's sexual and excretory functions.

Peterson, James. *Dreams of Chaos, Visions of Order.*
Detroit: Wayne State University Press, 1994.

This analysis of post-World War II American avant-garde cinema serves as a useful introduction to the conventions of the genre.

Queenan, Joe. *If You're Talking To Me, Your Career Must Be In Trouble.*
New York: Hyperion, 1994.

This collection of previously published essays attempts to deflate its subjects with a hip, sarcastic attitude.

Rapping, Elayne. *Media-tions: Forays Into the Culture and Gender Wars.*
Boston: South End Press, 1994.

Rapping offers a leftist and feminist analysis of the films of the 1980's and early 1990's.

Rich, Sharon. *Sweethearts.*
New York: Donald I. Fine, 1994.

Rich tells the story of the on and offscreen romance between singer-actors Nelson Eddy and Jeanette MacDonald, stars of the 1930's and 1940's.

Saunders, Thomas J. *Hollywood in Berlin.*
Berkeley, California: University of California Press, 1994.

When American films were first introduced in Germany in the 1920's, they induced strong and often conflicting reactions among the critics and the filmgoing public. This scholarly study explores the impact of these films not only on German filmmaking, but also on German culture as a whole.

Seger, Linda, and Edward Jay Whetmore. *From Script to Screen: The Collaborative Art of Filmmaking.*
New York: Henry Holt, 1994.

This work emphasizes the work of all creative participants, from director to makeup artist, in bringing a film to the screen.

Server, Lee. *Sam Fuller: Film Is a Battleground.*
Jefferson, North Carolina: McFarland, 1994.

This study of the films of Sam Fuller includes interviews with Fuller's major collaborators as well as with the director himself; and appendices on his unrealized projects and novels.

Siegel, Scott, and Barbara Siegel. *American Film Comedy.*
New York: Prentice-Hall, 1994.

This reference work contains over 300 entries on the personalities, terminology, and major films in the history of film comedy in the United States.

Sikov, Ed. *Laughing Hysterically: American Screen Comedy of the 1950s.*
New York: Columbia University Press, 1994.

Focusing on the comic works of Hawks, Wilder, Hitchcock, and Tashlin in the 1950's, Sikov analyzes their films as critiques of that decade's social mores.

Slide, Anthony. *Early American Cinema.*
Metuchen, New Jersey: Scarecrow Press, 1994.

This is a thorough revision of Slide's seminal 1970 work on American film prior to 1920. Like its predecessor, this is an excellent one volume introduction to the early silent era in American film.

Smith, Paul Julian. *Desire Unlimited: The Cinema of Pedro Almodovar.*
New York: Verso, 1994.

This is the first widely available book-length study of the works of the controversial Spanish filmmaker.

Smoodin, Eric, editor. *Disney Discourse: Producing the Magic Kingdom.*
New York: Routledge, 1994.

A collection of fourteen scholarly essays which analyze the impact of Walt Disney's works on American and international culture, from art to commerce.

Snead, James. *White Screens Black Images.*
New York: Routledge, 1994.

This is a collection of essays by the late film scholar on the subject of the representation of African Americans in Hollywood films.

Stewart, John. *Italian Film: A Who's Who.*
Jefferson, North Carolina: McFarland, 1994.

This reference work lists 5,000 filmmakers and actors who have worked in Italian film; entries include biographical information and a list of film credits.

Ukadike, Nwachukwu Frank. *Black African Cinema.*
Berkeley, California: University of California Press, 1994.

This is a scholarly analysis of the cinema of black Africa, focusing both on independent filmmakers and national film industries, and their efforts to portray Africa from an African perspective.

Vaughn, Stephen. *Ronald Reagan in Hollywood: Movies and Politics.*
New York: Cambridge University Press, 1994.

Vaughn's biography examines Reagan's fifteen year career at Warner Bros., and how events of the period from 1937-1952 changed Reagan from a New Deal liberal to a militant anti-communist whose conservative views led him into politics and eventually the presidency.

Vickers, Hugo. *Loving Garbo.*
New York: Random House, 1994.

This is an account of Garbo's personal life after her retirement, offering an inside account of her affairs with Cecil Beaton and Mercedes de Acosta.

Wapshott, Nicholas. *Carol Reed: A Biography.*
New York: Alfred A. Knopf, 1994.

This biography of the British filmmaker is a welcome addition to the literature on a director who was once considered to be the equal of Alfred Hitchcock.

Wasko, Janet. *Hollywood in the Information Age: Beyond the Silver Screen.*
Cambridge, England: Polity Press, 1994.

Wasko offers an analysis of how new electronic technologies such as cable television and videocassette recorders have affected the American film industry.

Weaver, Tom. *Attack of the Monster Movie Makers.*
Jefferson, North Carolina: McFarland, 1994.

This is a collection of twenty interviews with directors, actors, writers, and producers of science fiction and horror films, most dating from the 1940's and 1950's.

Weddle, David. *"If They Move...Kill 'Em!"*
New York: Grove Press, 1994.

Weddle combines biography with critical analysis in this study of the works of filmmaker Sam Peckinpah, best known for his innovations in screen violence in films such as *The Wild Bunch.*

Willemen, Paul. *Looks and Frictions: Essays in Cultural Studies and Film Theory.*
Bloomington, Indiana: Indiana University Press, 1994.

This is a collection of scholarly essays on the variety of influences of ethnocentrism on cinema throughout the world.

Williamson, J.W. *Southern Mountaineers in Silent Films.*
Jefferson, North Carolina: McFarland, 1994.

Williamson offers plot synopses of 476 films released between 1904 and 1929 on the subject of hillbillies, moonshiners, and related topics.

Wollstein, Hans J. *Strangers in Hollywood.*
Metuchen, New Jersey: Scarecrow Press, 1994.

This volume offers biographical information on sixty Scandanavian actors who worked in Hollywood films between 1910 and the World War II era.

Wyatt, Justin. *High Concept: Movies and Marketing in Hollywood.*
Austin, Texas: University of Texas Press, 1994.

Wyatt analyzes the influence of "high concept"—simple, easily marketable movies with a clear target audience—on the films produced in contemporary Hollywood.

Magill's Cinema Annual 1995
Indexes

Title Index

This cumulative index is an alphabetical list of all films covered in the fourteen volumes of the *Magill's Cinema Annual*. Film titles are indexed on a word-by-word basis, including articles and prepositions. English and foreign leading articles are ignored. Films reviewed in this volume are cited in bold with an arabic number indicating the page number on which the review begins; films reviewed in past volumes are cited with a roman numeral indicating the volume number in which the film was originally reviewed (consult the index of the cited volume for the page number on which the film review begins). Film sequels are indicated with a roman numeral following the film title. Original and alternate titles are cross-referenced to the American release title. Titles of retrospective films, as well as those cited in the Life Achievement Award section are followed by the year, in brackets, of their original release. Films cited in the Life Achievement Award section are indexed with the page number of the section in bold.

A corps perdu. *See* Straight for
   the Heart.
A la Mode (Fausto) (In Fashion)
   1
A nos amour   IV
Abgeschminkt! *See* **Making Up!.**
About Last Night...   VI
Above the Law   VIII
Above the Rim   3
Absence of Malice   I
Absolute Beginners   VI
Absolution   VIII
Abyss, The   IX
Accidental Tourist, The   VIII
Accompanist, The   XIII
Accused, The   VIII
Ace in the Hole [1951]   XI, VI
Ace Ventura: Pet Detective   4
Aces: Iron Eagle III   XII
Acqua e sapone. *See* Water and
   Soap.
Across the Tracks   XI
Acting on Impulse   6
Action Jackson   VIII
Actress   VIII
Adam's Rib   XII
Addams Family, The   XI
Addams Family Values   XIII
Addition, L'. *See* Patsy, The.
Adjo, Solidaritet. *See* Farewell
   Illusion.
Adjuster, The   XII
Adolescente, L'   II
Adventure of Huck Finn, The
   XIII
Adventures in Babysitting   VII
Adventures of Baron
   Munchausen, The   IX
Adventures of Buckaroo Banzai,
   The IV
Adventures of Ford Fairlane, The
   X
Adventures of Mark Twain, The
   VI
Adventures of Milo and Otis,
   The   IX
Adventures of Priscilla, Queen
   of the Desert, The   7
Adventures of the American
   Rabbit, The   VI
Advocate   10
Aelita   11
Affaire de Femmes, Une. *See*
   Story of Women.
Affengeil   XII

Afraid of the Dark   XII
Africa the Serengeti   11
After Dark, My Sweet   X
After Hours   V
After Midnight   IX
After the Rehearsal   IV
Against All Odds   III
Age Isn't Everything (Life in the
   Food Chain)   12
Age of Innocence, The   XIII
Agent on Ice   VI
Agnes of God   V
Aid   VIII
Aileen Wuornos: The Selling of
   a Serial Killer   12
Air America   X
Air Up There, The   13
Airborne   XIII
Airheads   14
Airplane II: The Sequel   II
Akira Kurosawa's Dreams   X
Aladdin (Corbucci)   VII
Aladdin (Musker & Clements)
   XII
Alamo Bay   V
Alan and Naomi   XII
Alberto Express   XII
Alchemist, The   VI
Alfred Hitchcock's Bon Voyage
   & Aventure Malgache. *See*
   Aventure Malgache.
Alice (Allen)   X
Alice (Svankmajer)   VIII
Alien Nation   VIII
Alien Predator   VII
Alien3   XII
Aliens   VI
Alive   XIII
All Dogs Go to Heaven   IX
All I Desire [1953]   VII
All I Want for Christmas   XI
All of Me   IV
All Quiet on the Western Front
   [1930]   V
All the Right Moves   III
All the Vermeers in New York
   XII
All's Fair   IX
All-American High   VII
Allan Quatermain and the Lost
   City of Gold   VII
Alley Cat   IV
Alligator Eyes   X
Allnighter, The   VII
Almost an Angel   X

Almost You   V
Aloha Summer   VIII
Alphabet City   III
Alpine Fire   VII
Altars of the World [1976]   V
Always (Jaglom)   V
Always (Spielberg)   IX
Amadeus   IV, V
Amanda   IX
Amantes. *See* Lovers.
Amants du Pont Neuf, Les   16
Amateur, The   II
Amazing Grace and Chuck
   VII
Amazon Women on the Moon
   VII
Ambition   XI
Amelia Lopes O'Neill   17
America   VI
American Anthem   VI
American Blue Note   XI
American Cyborg: Steel Warrior
   18
American Dream   XII
American Dreamer   IV
American Fabulous   XII
American Flyers   V
American Friends   XIII
American Gothic   VIII
American Heart   XIII
American in Paris, An [1951]
   V
American Justice   VI
American Me   XII
American Ninja   V
American Ninja II   VII
American Ninja III   IX
American Ninja IV   XI
American Pop   I
American Stories   IX
American Summer, An   XI
American Taboo   IV, XI
American Tail, An   VI
American Tail: Fievel Goes
   West, An   XI
American Werewolf in London,
   An   I
Ami de mon amie, L'. *See*
   Boyfriends and Girlfriends.
Amin-The Rise and Fall   III
Amityville II: The Possession   I
Amityville 3-D   III
Among People   VIII
Amongst Friends   XIII
Amor brujo, El   VI

Amos and Andrew   XIII
Amour de Swann, Un. *See*
   Swann in Love.
Anchors Aweigh [1945]   V
And God Created Woman
   VIII
...And God Spoke   19
And Life Goes On (Zebdegi
   Edame Darad)   20
And Nothing but the Truth   IV
And the Ship Sails On   IV
And You Thought Your Parents
   Were Weird   XI
Andre   20
Android   IV
Ane qui a bu la lune, L'. *See*
   Donkey Who Drank the
   Moon,   The.
Angel   IV
Angel III   VIII
Angel at My Table, An   XI
Angel Dust   VII
Angel Heart   VII
Angel Town   X
Angelo My Love   III
Angels in the Outfield   22
Angie   24
Angry Harvest   VI
Anguish   VII
Angustia. *See* Anguish.
Anima Mundi   26
Animal Behavior   IX
Animal Kingdom, The [1932]
   V
Anna   VII
Anna Karamazova   27
Année des meduses, L'   VII
Années sandwiches, Les. *See*
   Sandwich Years, The.
Annie   II
Annihilators, The   VI
Another 48 Hrs.   X
Another Stakeout   XIII
Another State of Mind   IV
Another Time, Another Place
   IV
Another Woman   VIII
Another You   XI
Anslag, De. *See* Assault, The.
Antarctica (Kurahara)   IV
Antarctica (Weiley)   XII
Antigone/Rites of Passion   XI
Antonia and Jane   XI
Any Man's Death   X
Apache [1954]   I

Wombling Free [1979]   IV
Women on the Verge of a
    Nervous Breakdown   VIII
Women's Affair   VIII
**Wonderful, Horrible Life of
    Leni Riefenstahl, The (Die
    Macht der Bilder)   666**
Wonderland   IX
Woodstock   667
Working Girl   VIII
Working Girls   VII
World According to Garp, The
    II
World Apart, A   VIII
World Gone Wild   VIII
World of Henry Orient, The
    [1964]   III
Worth Winning   IX
Wraith, The   VI
Wrestling Ernest Hemingway
    XIII

Wrong Couples, The   VII
Wrong Guys, The   VIII
Wrong Is Right   II
Wrong Man, The   670
Wyatt Earp   671

X. *See* Malcolm X.
Xero. *See* Home Remedy.
Xica [1976]   II
Xica da Silva. *See* Xica.

Yaaba   X
Yari No Gonza Kasane Katabira.
    See Gonza the Spearman.
Year My Voice Broke, The   VII,
    VIII
Year of Living Dangerously, The
    III
Year of the Comet   XII

Year of the Dragon   V
Year of the Gun   XI
Year of the Quiet Sun, A
    VI
Yearling, The [1946]   IX
Yellowbeard   III
Yen Family   VIII, X
Yentl   III
Yes, Giorgio   II
Yol   II
Yor: The Hunter from the Future
    III
You Can't Hurry Love   VIII
You So Crazy   673
You Talkin' to Me?   VII
You Toscanini   VIII
Young Dr. Kildare [1938]   V
Young Doctors in Love   II
Young Einstein   VIII
Young Guns   VIII
Young Guns II   X

Young Sherlock Holmes   V
Young Soul Rebels   XI
Youngblood   VI

Zappa   IV
Zapped!   II
Zebdegi Edame Darad. *See* **And
    Life Goes On.**
Zebrahead   XII
Zegen. *See* z Pimp, The.
Zelig   III
Zelly and Me   VIII
Zentropa   XII
Zero Patience   674
Zjoek   VII
**Zombie and the Ghost Train
    675**
Zombie High   VII
Zoot Suit   I

Directors

Screenwriters

Cinematographers

Editors

Editors

Editors

Art Directors

Music Directors

Music Directors

Performers

Performers

Performers

Performers

Performers

Performers

Performers

MEWES, JASON
Clerks 117

MEZZOGIORNO,
  VITTORIO
Scream of Stone 537

MIDDENDORF, TRACY
Wes Craven's New Nightmare
  644

MIGUEL, NIGEL
The Air Up There 13

MIHAILOVITCH, SMILJA
Bitter Moon 51

MIHUT, MARIANA
The Oak 437

MIKHALKOV, NADIA
Burnt by the Sun 85

MIKHALKOV, NIKITA
Burnt by the Sun 85

MIKUNI, RENTARO
My Sons (Musuko) 413

MILANO, ALYSSA
Double Dragon 164

MILES, CHRIS CLEARY
Second Best 538

MILES, SARAH
The Silent Touch 555

MILLER, ANN
That's Entertainment! III
  601

MILLER, BARRY
Love Affair 364

MILLER, BETTY
Angie 24

MILLER, CHARLES
Being Human 41

MILLER, DENNIS
Disclosure 159

MILLER, HELEN
Being Human 41

MILLER, HUMBLE HARVE
There Goes My Baby 602

MILLER, JENNIFER
Hit the Dutchman 260

MILLER, JOEL MCKINNON
The Swan Princess 592

MILLER, LARRY
Corrina, Corrina 138
Dream Lover 165
The Favor 198
Radioland Murders 481

MILLER, PENELOPE ANN
The Shadow 545

MILLIMAN, ANN
Vermont is for Lovers 634

MILLS, JOHNNY
The Garden 224

MILLS, KIRI
Desperate Remedies 158

MILO, JEAN-ROGER
L.627 326

MING, FAN XIAO
Dream of Light (El Sol del
  Membrillo) 167

MINNS, BYRON
Above the Rim 3

MINOGUE, KYLIE
Street Fighter 582

MINTER, KRISTIN
There Goes My Baby 602

MIRREN, HELEN
Dr. Bethune 163
The Hawk 251
The Madness of King George
  372

MISCHON, HERMINE
Passages 452

MISHIMA, YUKIO
Black Lizard 58

MITCHELL, COLIN
Combination Platter 134

MITCHELL, DARRYL
  (CHILL)
Fly by Night 210

MITCHELL, HERB
The Last Seduction 333

MITCHELL, JOHN
  CAMERON
Misplaced 397

MITCHELL, RED
8 Seconds 183

MITCHELL, SHARON
Kamikaze Hearts 320

MOBLEY, ALAINA
A Simple Twist of Fate 556

MOBLEY, CALLIE
A Simple Twist of Fate 556

MOCHRIE, PETER
Frauds 219

MODEL, BEN
The Puerto Rican Mambo
  (Not a Musical) 469

MODINE, MATTHEW
The Browning Version 81

MOFFAT, DONALD
Clear and Present Danger
  114
Trapped in Paradise 621

MOFOKENG, JACKIE
A Good Man in Africa 233

MOK, HARRY
Talons of the Eagle 597

MOKAE, ZAKES
Dust Devil: The Final Cut
  177

MOLINA, ALFRED
Maverick 386
The Trial 623
White Fang II: Myth of the
  White Wolf 655

MOLL, RICHARD
The Flintstones 207

MONGERMONT,
  MARTINE
Docteur Petiot (Dr. Petiot)
  162

MONROE, BILL
High Lonesome: The Story
  of Bluegrass Music 258

MONROE, DREW
Lost Prophet 363

MOOR, ANDREA
Over the Hill 444

MOORE, BURLEIGH
Jason's Lyric 309

MOORE, DEMI
Disclosure 159

MOORE, JACK
Stargate 579

MOORE, JULIANNE
Vanya on 42nd Street 631

MOORE, MICHAEL
Paper Hearts 452

MOORE, R. J.
Hard Hunted 249

MOORE, THE REVEREND
  A. D. (GATEMOUTH)
Saturday Night, Sunday
  Morning: The Travels of
  Gatemouth Moore 526

MOORE, TYRIA
Aileen Wuornos: The Selling
  of a Serial Killer 12

MORALES, ESAI
In the Army Now 289
Rapa Nui 487

MORAN, JOHNNY
Night of the Demons II
  428

MORANIS, RICK
The Flintstones 207
Little Giants 354

MOREAU, JEANNE
Anna Karamazova 27

MOREAU, MARGUERITE
D2: The Mighty Ducks
  172

MORENO, MARIA
Dream of Light (El Sol del
  Membrillo) 167

MORENO, RITA
Age Isn't Everything (Life in
  the Food Chain) 12
I Like It Like That 274

MORETTI, NANNI
Caro Diario (Dear Diary)
  98
Redwood Pigeon (Palombella
  Rossa) 501

MORGAN, SCOTT
  WESLEY
Serial Mom 541

MORGENSTERN, MAIA
The Oak 437

MORIARTY, CATHY
Pontiac Moon 459

MORITA, PAT
Do or Die 162
Even Cowgirls Get the Blues
  188
The Next Karate Kid 427

MORK, ERIK
Europa 187

MORRA, GIGIO
Ciao, Professore! 106

MORRIS, ANITA
Radioland Murders 481
Obituaries 687

MORRIS, AUBREY
My Girl II 410

MORRIS, DEAN
The Last Seduction 333

MORRIS, ROBB EDWARD
China Moon 105

MORRISON, JENNY
Intersection 294

MORRISON, WOODROW
  W.
White Fang II: Myth of the
  White Wolf 655

MORROW, ROB
Quiz Show *478*

MORSE, DAVID
The Getaway *225*

MORSHOWER, GLENN
The River Wild *511*

MORTENSEN, VIGGO
Floundering *209*

MORTON, JOE
The Inkwell *291*
Speed *572*

MOSES, BOB
Freedom On My Mind *220*

MOSS, ELISABETH
Imaginary Crimes *282*

MOST, DON
Acting on Impulse *6*

MOSTEL, JOSH
The Chase *102*
City Slickers II: The Legend of Curly's Gold *108*

MOTLEY, KAREN
Lillian *347*

MOUNT, PEGGY
The Princess and the Goblin *461*

MTUKUDZI, OLIVER
Jit *313*

MUELLER, MAUREEN
The New Age *423*
Over Her Dead Body (Enid Is Sleeping) *444*

MUELLER-STAHL, ARMIN
The House of the Spirits *265*

MUHE, ULRICH
Schtonk *531*

MULGREW, KATE
Camp Nowhere *94*

MULKEY, CHRIS
The Silencer *551*

MULL, MARTIN
Mr. Write *400*

MULLAVEY, GREG
Undertow *631*

MULLEN, DAN
Vermont is for Lovers *634*

MULLEN, JERAMIAH
Vermont is for Lovers *634*

MULLER, RAY
The Wonderful, Horrible Life of Leni Riefenstahl (Die Macht der Bilder) *666*

MULLINS, ROBIN
Nell *420*

MULRONEY, DERMOT
Angels in the Outfield *22*
Bad Girls *35*
Samantha *522*
Silent Tongue *553*
There Goes My Baby *602*
The Thing Called Love *603*

MULROONEY, ANASTASIA
The Wedding Gift *641*

MUNNE, PEP
Barcelona *37*

MUNOZ, LUCIO
Dream of Light (El Sol del Membrillo) *167*

MURAVYOVA, IRINA
Bread and Salt *79*

MURDOCCO, VINCE
Flesh Gordon Meets the Cosmic Cheerleaders *206*

MURILLO, CHRISTINE
La Vie de Boheme *635*

MURNIK, PETER
Golden Gate *232*

MURPHY, EDDIE
Beverly Hills Cop III *47*

MURPHY, MICHAEL
Clean Slate *111*

MURPHY, REILLY
Body Snatchers *77*
Dangerous Game *152*

MURRAY, BILL
Ed Wood *181*

MURRAY, JILLIAN
Body Melt *76*

MURRAY, PETER
The Princess and the Goblin *461*

MURUA, LAUTARO
The Plague *458*
Scream of Stone *537*

MUSKUNA, ARIE
Over the Ocean *445*

MUTOMOBO, ILO
The Air Up There *13*

MYERS, LOU
Cobb *125*

MYRBERG, PER
Sunday's Children *586*

NAGASE, MASATOSHI
My Sons (Musuko) *413*

NAJIMY, KATHY
It's Pat *307*

NANCE, JACK
Love and a .45 *367*

NAPLES, TONI
Munchie *406*

NASIKYAN, ARMEN
Satan *525*

NASRULLAH, HAMZAH
Hors la Vie (Out of Life) *264*

NATWICK, MILDRED
Obituaries *687*

NAVARRETE, ROBERTO
Amelia Lopes O'Neill *17*

NAYAR, NISHA
Bhaji on the Beach *49*

NAZAROV, PAVEL
Freeze-Die-Come to Life *221*

NDABA, THEMBA
A Good Man in Africa *233*

NDEMERA, WINNIE
Jit *313*

NDIAYE, THIERNO
Guelwaar *245*

NEEDHAM, TRACEY
Lush Life *371*

NEELY, CAM
Dumb and Dumber *174*

NEESON, LIAM
Nell *420*

NEGRET, FRANCOIS
Night and Day *428*

NEGRON, TAYLOR
Angels in the Outfield *22*

NEILL, SAM
The Jungle Book *315*
Sirens *559*

NEILSON, CATHERINE
The Trial *623*

NEIWILLER, ANTONIO
Caro Diario (Dear Diary) *98*

NELLIGAN, KATE
Wolf *663*

NELSON, DANNY
A Simple Twist of Fate *556*

NELSON, HARRIET
Obituaries *688*

NELSON, JUDD
Airheads *14*
Every Breath *191*
Primary Motive *460*

NELSON, PATRIECE
Crooklyn *145*

NELSON, SEAN
Fresh *222*

NEMEC, CORIN
Drop Zone *169*

NENE, SIBONGILE
Jit *313*

NERO, FRANCO
Amelia Lopes O'Neill *17*

NEUMEIER, MARCO
Passages *452*

NEUWIRTH, BEBE
The Paint Job *448*

NEVILLE, JOHN
Baby's Day Out *30*
Little Women *359*
The Road to Wellville *513*

NEVILLE, SARAH
Archangel *28*

NEWCOTT, ROSEMARY
Silent Victim *555*

NEWMAN, PAUL
The Hudsucker Proxy *268*
Nobody's Fool *431*

NEWMAN, PHYLLIS
Only You *442*

NEWMAN-PHILLIPS, AMANDA
Exchange Lifeguards (Wet and Wild Summer) *192*

NEWSOM, DAVID
Wes Craven's New Nightmare *644*

NEWTON, THANDIE
Interview with the Vampire *296*

NGHIEU, TIEU QUAN
China, My Sorrow *106*

NGUYEN, DUSTIN
Three Ninjas Kick Back *606*

Performers

Performers

Performers

Performers

Performers

Performers

Performers

Subjects